The Butterflies of Hispaniola

Heraclides machaonides, male, from Los Cerezos, Prov. de Dajabón, República Dominicana, taken 4 August 1981.

The Butterflies of Hispaniola

Albert Schwartz

UNIVERSITY OF FLORIDA PRESS
Gainesville

Printed in the U.S.A. on acid-free paper

❧

Library of Congress Cataloging-in-Publication Data

Schwartz, Albert, 1923–
The Butterflies of Hispaniola / Albert Schwartz.
p. cm.
Bibliography: p.
Includes index.
ISBN 0-8130-0902-2 (alk. paper)
1. Butterflies—Hispaniola—Identification. 2. Butterflies—Hispaniola—Geographical distribution. 3. Insects—Hispaniola—Identification. 4. Insects—Hispaniola—Geographical distribution. I. Title.
QL553.H57S38 1988
595.78′9097293—dc19 88-17035
CIP

❧

UNIVERSITY PRESSES OF FLORIDA is the central agency for book publishing services of the State of Florida's university system. It produces books selected for publication by the faculty editorial boards of Florida's nine university presses: Florida A&M University Press (Tallahassee), Florida Atlantic University Press (Boca Raton), Florida International University Press (Miami), Florida State University Press (Tallahassee), University of Central Florida Press (Orlando), University of Florida Press (Gainesville), University of North Florida Press (Jacksonville), University of South Florida Press (Tampa), University of West Florida Press (Pensacola).

ORDERS for books published by all member presses should be addressed to University Presses of Florida, 15 NW 15th Street, Gainesville, FL 32603.

Contents

Papilionidae

Pieridae

Lycaenidae

Libytheidae

Heliconiidae

Nymphalidae

Apaturidae

Satyridae

Ithomiidae

Danaidae

List of Plates

Acknowledgments

MY WORK ON HISPANIOLA was originally stimulated by comments from the late Harry K. Clench, then at the Carnegie Museum of Natural History. He had an early interest in *Calisto* and encouraged me to make general rhopaloceran collections in 1974 in both Haiti and the República Dominicana.

I have examined some specimens in the collections of the American Museum of Natural History (AMNH), New York, and the Museum of Comparative Zoology (MCZ), Harvard University, Cambridge, and wish to thank Frederick H. Rindge, Kurt Johnson, and Scott E. Miller for loans from these institutions.

The essence of any undertaking such as this is the cooperation and enthusiasm offered to me by my field companions over the years. I wish to thank the following for their companionship and interest in our work: Porfirio E. Amador, Brian I. Crother, Jose Escobio, Frank Gali, Alvis A. Gineika, Fernando L. Gonzalez, Eugene D. Graham, Jr., Robert W. Henderson, Kurt M. Iketani, Carlos J. Jimenez, David C. Leber, John C. Lucio, Joel W. Raburn, S. Craig Rhodes, Luis Rivera, Barton L. Smith, Donald E. Smith, Jean R. Sommer and William W. Sommer, T. Mark Thurmond, Richard Thomas, and Randolph W. Wisor. Of them, Gonzalez, Gali, Raburn, Lucio, Graham, and William W. Sommer each spent more than 10 weeks in the field.

Gali also made the original maps of the species' distributions for the present publication. These have been modified by Rose M. Henderson. I am grateful to both for their work.

Photographs of habitats have been contributed by Gali, N.E. Kraucunas, Leber, Raburn, and William W. Sommer. The frontispiece of *Heraclides machaonides*, a papilionid that is endemic to Hispaniola, was executed by Dr. Leber with the usual attention to detail that makes his work so outstanding.

Donald J. Harvey, Jacqueline Y. Miller and Lee D. Miller (Allyn Museum of Entomology, Florida State Museum), Clarence J. McCoy, Susan Borkin (Milwaukee Public Museum), Donald W. Buden, Robert W. Henderson, and Scott E. Miller have answered literature requests with unfailing kindness and dispatch. Alfredo Lebrón and Victor García have been our hosts at the Cabo Rojo headquarters of the Alcoa Exploration Company (now Ideal Dominicana) on several occasions. David K. Wetherbee has made significant collections along the Dominico-Haitian frontier near Restauración. At the Museo Nacional de Historia Natural in Santo Domingo, Carlos José Peña, Blas Reinoso, and Andrés Zaglul of the Departamento de Entomología have been enthusiastic colleagues. Sixto J. Incháustegui at the same institution has likewise served in many capacities during our work in the República Dominicana. Finally, at the Museo Nacional de Historia Natural in Santo Domingo, the former directors Eugenio de J. Marcano and Francisco X. Geraldes, have been both helpful and interested in the completion of the present publication. Dr. Marcano has generously identified many plant specimens for me, but any errors are mine, not his. Ralph M. Adams and Daniel F. Austin, both of Florida Atlantic University, have generously answered my botanical questions as the work progressed.

The Spanish *clave* to the butterflies of Hispaniola is the work of Juan C. Correa, updated by Fernando Gonzalez and Fernando Luis Gonzalez; they have rendered the English key into felicitous Spanish. I hope that the presence of a *clave* will aid Latin American lepidopterists in the identification of Hispaniolan *mariposas diurnas*.

Frank Gali has read the entire manuscript and has made corrections and pertinent comments. For this unrewarding task I can do no more than render him my respect, homage, and gratitude.

Finally, Thomas C. Emmel and Lee D. Miller have offered suggestions and made corrections in the final proof; to them I am also grateful.

To all of the above, in their various capacities as field workers, friends, or logistic and moral supporters, I am indebted.

Introduction

STUDY OF THE RHOPALOCERAN FAUNA of the Greater Antilles has been erratic. The butterflies of Cuba (Bates, 1935a), Puerto Rico (Comstock, 1944), and Jamaica (Brown and Heineman, 1972) are reasonably well known; those of the Lesser Antilles have been ably summarized by Pinchon and Enrico (1969), although there are still many details of Lesser Antillean distributions to be clarified and refined (Schwartz and Jimenez, 1982; Schwartz, Gonzalez, and Henderson, 1987). The butterflies of Hispaniola, on the other hand, have been generally overlooked; Hall's (1925) summary is the only one covering that island. This is all the more surprising since Hispaniola, composed of the Republic of Haiti and the República Dominicana, has a central position within the Greater Antilles and is paleogeographically the most interesting of the islands. Its topography, basically a series of east-west mountain ranges with interposed valleys, lends itself ideally to speciation. At least one genus (*Calisto* Lathy; Satyridae) is renowned for its explosive radiation on Hispaniola in contrast to other Antillean islands. Yet examination of Riley's field guide (1975) quickly shows that most of the records of Hispaniolan butterflies published therein are taken from Hall's antiquated list. Other than Hall's paper, very little (other than various papers on *Calisto*) has been done prior to the 1970s. Hall's comments on Hispaniolan butterflies are based on 2 collections made by himself and Kaempffer for 4 months (May, June, November, December) in 1921 and 1924; the nomenclature used in that paper is outdated, and Hall's ideas of abundance and seasonality are often misleading or erroneous.

This situation has been partly remedied by 2 major papers on Antillean butterflies (Scott, 1972, and Brown, 1978). Yet both these summaries of West Indian butterflies suffer from a paucity of data on the Hispaniolan fauna. With the publication of the Riley field guide, there has been an increased interest in the butterflies of the Antillean region. The publication of a lengthy paper by Schwartz (1983a) on a collection of Haitian butterflies tends to fill in the gap in our knowledge of the butterflies of the western one-third of Hispaniola. But little detailed information on the butterflies of the República Dominicana has been published. A series of short notes by Marcano (1976) and Marión Heredia (1978a-d, 1979, 1980a-e) and 2 lists (Cucurullo, 1959; Marión Heredia, 1974) are contributions to the information on the Lepidoptera of that country. Schwartz and Gali, as well as Gonzalez, and Johnson, Quinter, and Matusik, have named new species of *Calisto* and *Choranthus* (Hesperiidae) from the Dominican portion of Hispaniola. Schwartz and Miller (1985) named a new species of hairstreak. Revisionary studies on *Urbanus* (Steinhauser, 1981), *Hamadryas* (Jenkins, 1983), *Myscelia* (Jenkins, 1984), and *Asterocampa* (Friedlander, 1988) have inevitably had to deal with species that occur on Hispaniola. Biological data on Hispaniolan butterflies are likewise very limited; 3 recent papers (Gali and Schwartz, 1983a-c) deal with rare or poorly known species from Hispaniola (*Myscelia aracynthia* —Nymphalidae; *Battus zetides*—Papilionidae; *Epargyreus spanna*—Hesperiidae). Johnson and Matusik (1986) gave some data on the latter species. Coutsis (1983) published notes on the occurrence of several species of butterflies in Haiti and (1986) on the differentiation and determination of *Phoebis editha* from *Phoebis sennae*. Data on life histories of Hispaniolan butterflies are even more limited; one has merely to peruse Riley's field guide and note the "Not known" after "Early stages" of many species to realize in what a deplorable state our knowledge of that aspect of lepidopterology is at present. But intensive research on the caterpillars is not for visiting biologists; such work must be carried out by resident scientists. Wetherbee (1987) has contributed to our knowledge of the life histories of *Hamadryas amphitoe diasia*, *Dynamine egaea*, and *Archimestra teleboas* (Nymphalidae). Entomologists at the Museo Nacional de Historia Natural in Santo Domingo are in an enviable position to fill the abundant blanks concerning the life histories of Hispaniolan butterflies.

The Island

The island of Hispaniola lies in a central position in the Greater Antilles, between Cuba to the west, Puerto Rico to the east, and Jamaica to the southwest. The channels separating Hispaniola from Cuba (Windward Passage—77 km) and Puerto Rico (Mona Passage—102 km) are of about equal width, but that between Hispaniola and Jamaica is wider (200 km). Hispaniola lies between 17°40′ and 19°56′ N latitude, and 74°26′ and 68°30′ W longitude (basic geographic data from Núñez Molina, 1968). The area of Hispaniola is about 77,250 km^2, of which about one-third forms the Republic of Haiti and two-thirds the República Dominicana. The climate consists of a "rainy" season between May and November, with the balance of the year "dry." In the northeast República Dominicana, rainfall may be 2400 mm/year, but elsewhere the land may receive as little as 700 mm/year. Those stations with little rainfall (Azua, Monte Cristi, Neiba, Jimaní, Pedernales) are located in deserts or highly xeric areas.

Lora Salcedo, Czerwenka, and Bolay (1983) presented data on several meteorological characteristics at 69 stations in the República Dominicana, these data gathered at each station for 20 or more years. The sites vary from Pedernales and Enriquillo on the Península de Barahona in the southwest, to Samaná on the Península de Samaná in the northeast, and from Monte Cristi and Pepillo Salcedo in the northwest, to Cabo Engaño and San Rafael del Yuma in the southeast. Elevations vary from many sea-level (or nearly so) localities to a high of 1164 m (Constanza). Pertinent data in the present context include: (1) temperatures (in °C), varying from a mean annual low of 18.2°C (Constanza) to a mean annual high of 28.3°C (La Descubierta); the former is in the Cordillera Central, the latter in the Valle de Neiba near the Dominico-Haitian border; (2) average annual rainfall, varying from a low of 126.7 mm (Monción, on the northern lower slopes of the Cordillera Central and between that montane mass and the xeric Valle de Cibao) to a high of 2291.1 mm (Samaná, on the mesic Península de Samaná).

In addition, these authors have a series of climatological diagrams that graphically show rainfall and its seasonality for each of the 69 stations. At 4 localities (Duvergé, Neiba, Pepillo Salcedo, Villa Vásquez—the first 2 in the Valle de Neiba, the last 2 in the Valle de Cibao), rainfall in excess of 100 mm/yr has not been reported. At 7 localities (Bonao, Cabrera, Gaspar Hernández, Nagua, Sabana de la Mar, Samaná, Villa Riva), there is rain reported in every month of the year, with maximum rainfall in May (Bonao, Villa Riva) or November (Cabrera, Gaspar Hernández, Nagua, Samaná, Sabana de la Mar). Average annual rainfall amounts at these localities vary between 1998.2 mm (Nagua) and 2291.1 mm (Samaná).

Lora Salcedo et al. (1983) showed serial climatographs for Santo Domingo for the years 1973–78 (fig. 3). This graph simultaneously demonstrates 2 facts. (1) In the years 1973–76, the rainfall pattern was "normal" in that there were 2 annual peaks, 1 varying between January and May and of brief duration, and a second, longer summer-fall rainy period between July and November-December. This

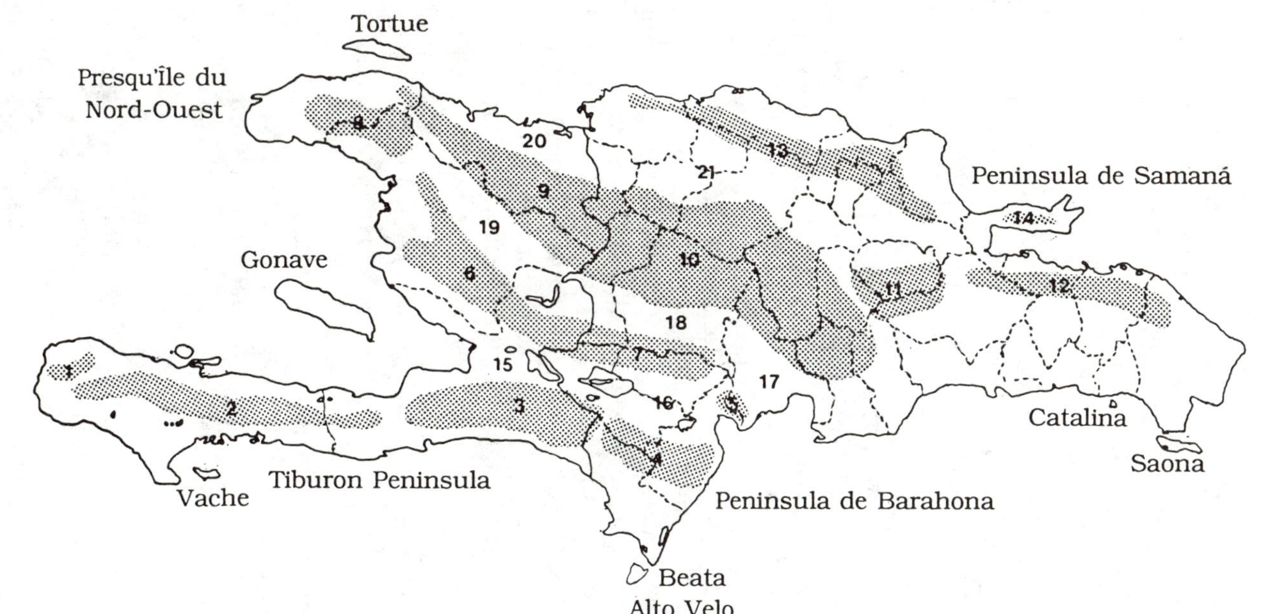

Figure 1. Map of Hispaniola, showing satellite islands and peninsulae, as well as mountain ranges (1–14) and lowland areas (15–21), as follows:

1. Monts Cartaches
2. Massif de la Hotte
3. Massif de la Selle
4. Sierra de Baoruco
5. Sierra Martín García
6. Chaîne de Matheux
7. Sierra de Neiba
8. Montagnes du Nord-Ouest
9. Massif du Nord
10. Cordillera Central
11. Sierra de Yamasá
12. Cordillera Oriental
13. Cordillera Septentrional
14. Sierra de Samaná
15. Plaine de Cul de Sac
16. Valle de Neiba
17. Llanos de Azua
18. Valle de San Juan
19. Plateau Central
20. Plaine de Nord
21. Valle de Cibao

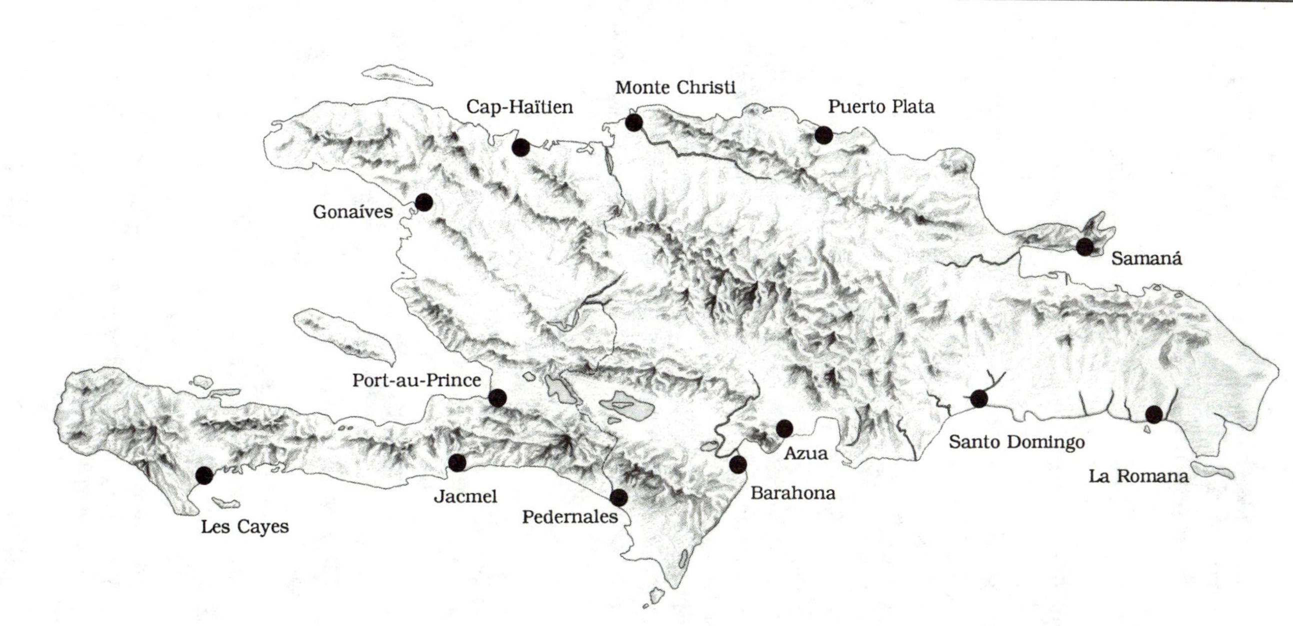

Figure 2. Map of Hispaniola showing cities and town.

bimodal rainfall pattern is typical of Hispaniola in general. (2) But at Santo Domingo in 1977 and 1978, there was almost continual rain between spring (April-May) and fall-winter (November-January), with only occasional and minor periods below 100 mm. This pattern is not only unusual for Santo Domingo but for the island in general.

Finally, Lora Salcedo et al. presented a north-south profile across the Dominican portion of Hispaniola, from Pedernales in the south to Puerto Plata in the north, and crossing the Sierra de Baoruco, the Valle de Neiba, the Sierra de Neiba (no recording station), the Valle de Neiba, the Llanos de Azua, the southern slopes (San José de Ocoa), a central upland valley (Constanza), and the north-central slopes (Jarabacoa) of the Cordillera Central, the Valle de Cibao, and the Cordillera Septentrional (Yásica), as well as the northern littoral (Puerto Plata). The climatographs for this transect show about what is expected: lowland stations (Pedernales, Azua, Santiago) have little or no rainfall in excess of 100 mm/yr, whereas upland stations (Polo in the Sierra de Baoruco), the Cordillera Septentrional (Yásica), and Puerto Plata have several months of rainfall above 100 mm.

Tropical hurricanes pass with frequency across Hispaniola; there have been 8 serious hurricanes since 1855. Hurricane Inez in 1966 crossed the Dominican Península de Barahona and then proceeded along the south coast of, and crossed, the Haitian Tiburon Peninsula, virtually destroying the high-canopy forests on the former area. In 1979 and 1980, 2 hurricanes (David and Allen) either considerably damaged the República Dominicana or caused heavy rainfall in both countries, even though Allen's eye was about 300 km south of the island.

Recorded temperatures in the República Dominicana vary from a high of 40°C (Bonao, Samaná, Sánchez), with many other stations recording highs of 37–39°C. The lowest recorded temperature is 0°C at Constanza, in the Cordillera Central. Average annual temperatures at 2 Dominican stations are 25.6°C at Santo Domingo on the south coast and 18°C at Constanza. Theoretically, the average annual temperature on Pico Duarte, the highest Antillean mountain, should be 10°C, but there is no station to record meteorological data there. There is at least 1 record (Wetmore and Swales, 1931:19) of a ground covering of frost in late February near the headwaters of the Río Yaque del Sur in the region of Pico Duarte.

At first glance, Hispaniola is relatively simple physiographically.

Basically, it is a series of east-west mountain ranges of varying heights, alternating with a series of lowland (and usually xeric) valleys. This statement is indeed simplistic, since the situation is made more complex by the fact that present Hispaniola is in actuality a fusion of 2 paleoislands. These 2 islands, now usually called the "north" and "south" islands by biologists, join at the Cul de Sac–Valle de Neiba plain that cuts across both countries in the south. This low-lying plain, at places below sea level, is extremely xeric, despite the presence of 2 saline lakes (Etang Saumâtre, Lago Enriquillo), 2 freshwater lakes (Trou Caïman, Laguna de Rincón), and 1 fugitive lake (Laguna Limón, whose appearance varies with the amount of rainfall). Although this Enriquillo Basin (= the Cul de Sac–Valle de Neiba plain) is hot and dry, there are several local areas (usually with settlements or towns) that are "mesic" due to the presence of springs whose waters come from the abundant rainfall in the adjacent mountain ranges (Massif de la Selle–Sierra de Baoruco in the south: Montagnes du Trou d'Eau–Sierra de Neiba in the north; de León, 1983:18–22).

After this primary division into north and south islands, details of the geography and physiography of the 2 sections of Hispaniola are more simple. The south island, most of which is in Haiti, comprises about 9550 km^2 (Schwartz, 1980a) and is a series of west-east–arranged mountain masses—the Massif de la Hotte, the Massif de la Selle, and the Sierra de Baoruco; in addition, to the south of the latter range and in its rain shadow is the xeric Península de Barahona. Of these 3 ranges, the La Hotte lies in Haiti and the Baoruco in the República Dominicana. The La Selle is primarily Haitian, but it extends into the República Dominicana along the border, between Pedernales and El Aguacate. The highest peak of the La Hotte is Pic Macaya (2347 m), that of the Baoruco 1601 m. The La Selle has its culminating peak in Pic la Selle (2574 m) near the Dominico-Haitian border. Associated with the south island are several satellite islands: Îles Grande and Petite Cayemite, Île-à-Vache in Haiti, and Isla Beata and Isla Alto Velo in the República Dominicana.

The north island is larger (67700 km^2) and somewhat more complex than the south island. In the República Dominicana centers the major mountain mass of the island, the Cordillera Central, with its highest mountain, Pico Duarte (3087 m); this range extends to the Haitian coast near Port-de-Paix as the Massif du Nord. South of the Cordillera Central lies the Montagnes du Trou-d'Eau–Sierra de Neiba massif; this range is separated from the

Cordillera Central on the north by the Plateau Central in Haiti and the Valle de San Juan in the República Dominicana. The highest peak in this complex is Monte Neiba (2279 m). Exclusively in the República are the Cordillera Septentrional (Pico Diego de Ocampo, 1250 m), between Monte Cristi in the west and Arenoso and Villa Riva in the east. This range is separated from the Cordillera Central by the Valle de Cibao, whose western extreme is xeric (in the rain shadow of the Septentrional) and whose eastern extreme is mesic. The western Cibao extends into northern Haiti as the Plaine du Nord, whose eastern region is xeric but which becomes mesic as it approaches Cap-Haïtien. Minor Dominican ranges include: the Sierra de Samaná, the backbone of the Península de Samaná (606 m); the Sierra de Yamasá (853 m), an east-central affiliate of the Cordillera Central; and the Cordillera Oriental (681 m), which borders the southern shore of the Bahía de Samaná. Associated with the latter is a region of karst topography, the *haitises;* another section of *haitises* lies north of the Cordillera Septentrional from the vicinity of Puerto Plata eastward. Of special interest is the Sierra Martín García. This range is ideally an isolated semimesic range (1343 m) completely surrounded by either the ocean or extremely xeric regions. In Haiti, the Montagnes du Nord-Ouest lie on the Presqu'île de Nord-Ouest. Associated with the north island is another group of satellites (Île de la Tortue in Haiti, Isla Catalina, Isla Saona, and the Cayos Siete Hermanos in the República Dominicana).

One other satellite merits special attention. This is the Haitian Île de la Gonâve (area = 658 km^2), which lies in the Baie de Port-au-Prince, between the south island Tiburon Peninsula and the western coast of the north island and approximately equidistant between the 2. Gonâve's herpetofauna has more north-island than south-island species. Its highest point is 778 m; it is basically an interior range of high hills or low mountains surrounded by a more or less xeric coastal plain.

From this brief description of the physiography and climate, it should be obvious that Hispaniola is an excellent foundation upon which animals, including butterflies, have had an ample opportunity to diversify. Although there are lepidopteran species that are widespread in a variety of habitats and at a wide variety of elevations, others are geographically and altitudinally restricted. The picture is not a simple one in many cases. In addition, as I (1980b) pointed out, some butterflies are either absent from or extremely rare in Haiti, whereas these same species are common and widespread in the República Dominicana. One factor is the extreme deforestation in Haiti, since often it is forest-dwelling butterfly species that are most profoundly affected.

Current Collections

In 1977, I oversaw the making of a collection of butterflies by one of my students, T. Mark Thurmond, who wrote a report on the collection. Material was identified by Harry K. Clench, who was enthusiastic in his praise. Further collections were made in Haiti by myself and parties in 1978–79, resulting in the assemblage of 3003 specimens from that country. An additional brief spring visit to Haiti by Gali and myself in 1982 yielded data for several important species, and a winter visit in 1985–86 allowed observtions on the abundance of some species at that time. Dates for Haitian visits are: 3.vii–19.viii.1977, 19.vi–14.viii.1978, 21.vi–13.viii.1979, 23.iv–1.v.1982, and 20.xii.1984–5.i.1985. Collecting in the República Dominicana has occupied the time between 1980 and 1986, with visits on the following dates: 18.vi–17.viii.1980, 20.xii.1980–3.i.1981, 20.vi–17.viii.1981, 19.vi–19.viii.1982, 19.vi–13.viii.1983, 29.ix–2.xi.1983, 3.iii–29.iv.1984, 16–17.ii.1985, 25.vi–21.viii.1985, and 15.v–17.viii.1986. The total number of man-months is 52.1, with 15.7 in Haiti and 36.4 in the República Dominicana.

Specimens from 1977 are in the collection of the Carnegie Museum, except for voucher specimens in Thurmond's and my collections. Most other specimens from 1978–84 are in the collections of myself and Frank Gali, except for those in the collections of William W. Sommer and Randolph W. Wisor, both of whom were in the field with me during parts of the collecting in Haiti and the República Dominicana. Material from 1985–86 is in the collections of myself and Fernando L. Gonzalez. In addition, Robert W. Henderson of the Milwaukee Public Museum has very generously donated material, collected by him when he was otherwise involved with herpetological research on the Tiburon Peninsula in Haiti and the Peninsula de Barahona in the República Dominicana, and more importantly, from 4 of the Hispaniolan satellite islands: Isla Catalina, Isla Saona, Isla Beata, and Île de la Gonâve. Very significant collections were made on my behalf by Sixto J. Incháustegui on Isla Beata and Isla Alto Velo. S.R. Yocom made a small collection on the Tiburon Peninsula (Morne Formond, Pic Macaya) in the Massif de la Hotte and in the Massif de la Selle (Morne la Visite) for the Allyn Museum of Entomology, Florida State Museum (FSM), in

January-February 1984. Frank Gali visited these same 2 areas in September 1984. I have examined these collections; they contain very interesting material. I have also had access to the collections in the Museo Nacional de Historia Natural in Santo Domingo (MNHNSD) and have donated specimens to that institution.

Much of the Haitian collection was reported upon by me (Schwartz 1983a), although additional material is now available from that country. The present treatment does indeed deal again with that Haitian material, but the Haitian butterflies are discussed here in the context of Hispaniolan (rather than purely Haitian) distribution, and comparisons are often made between abundance and distributions in the 2 countries that divide Hispaniola.

Localities, Place-names, Times

Localities for all specimens in our collections are listed under each species, and range maps of all species are presented; on these maps, our material and that in other collections examined by me are represented by solid symbols, whereas published literature records are hollow symbols. Our own sight records of many species are indicated by semisolid symbols.

The matter of type-localities on Hispaniola is bothersome. The name "Hispaniola" has only recently come into general use for the island as a geographical unit. Previously, due to both the French and Spanish influences on the island, the entire island was often referred to as "Haiti," "Hayti," "St.-Domingue," "San Domingo," or "Santo Domingo." Many Hispaniolan residents still use the names St.-Domingue or Santo Domingo for the entire island. Since much of the basic work on Hispaniolan Lepidoptera was done long before the names of the countries themselves were stabilized (or indeed before the boundary between them was stabilized in 1844), the old type-localities using the designations of "Haiti" or "Santo Domingo" do not refer to either the (former) country or the (latter) city as the terms are properly used today. Thus a type-locality designated as "Haiti" should in no way be interpreted as being within that country; the site could have been anywhere on Hispaniola.

I may seem overly precise in my recording of locality data and elevations. I (1983a) have already inveighed against the imprecision of Riley's (1975) field guide in such matters. But the fault in no way is Riley's; entomologists in general seem guilty of using a populational center only as a locality, with at times an appended (and often nonsensical) elevation. On Hispaniola, differences of a very few kilometers may mean radical differences in ecology; anyone who has traveled from La Descubierta in the Valle de Neiba to Puesto Pirámide 204 in the high uplands of the Sierra de Neiba can readily testify to the almost amazing differences between the very xeric area at La Descubierta and the hardwood forested uplands of the Sierra de Neiba. The same may be said about the road between Fond Parisien and Forêt des Pins (in pine forest) in the Haitian Massif de la Selle, or between Pedernales and El Aguacate in the Dominican portion of that same range. The examples could be multiplied. But in each of these cases one begins in desert or xeric areas, proceeds through bands of broadleaf forest, and ends in the high uplands in pines or mixed pine-hardwoods. Even differences of as little as 5 kilometers may mean very different ecologies. To use merely the populational centers (La Descubierta, Puesto Pirámide 204, Fond Parisien, Forêt des Pins, etc.) as the source of specimens is not only misleading, it is almost venal.

I also am adamant in decrying the use of only local place-names on specimens. Many such names are used by locals in both countries (one has only to look at the 1:100,000 map of Haiti to see the amazing proliferation of local names); but sole usage of such local names leads to confusion and uncertainty on the part of later workers. An instance of this is Hall's (1925) use of the Dominican place-name "La Cumbre"; were it not for his brief qualification that *this* La Cumbre is in the "Monte Cristi mountains," one would have extreme uncertainty as to which "pass" and in which mountain range the locality lies, since "La Cumbre" is a common name for passes (not always in high mountains) in the República Dominicana. I urge other workers, if they feel secure only in using local place-names for localities, to qualify these by a label notation of "La Cumbre, 15 km NE Santiago," for instance.

In much of our Hispaniolan work, at the urging of Harry K. Clench, I have recorded times (on the 24 h system) of collection at each site, the local weather conditions at the time of collection, and the temperature (in degrees Celsius). As our collecting on Hispaniola proceeded, it became obvious that the "best" times for securing Lepidoptera are between 1000 and 1400 h. Maximum activity in the mountains is delayed by about 1 hr. Very early collecting (0600 h) shortly after dawn yields nothing, but as the temperature increases with the passage of time, activity becomes greater, so that by about 0930 h a wide spectrum of butterflies (albeit at first few individuals) begins to appear, with an obvious increase until about 1400 h. Thereafter there is a decline in numbers of individuals, although some butterflies are still active just before sunset. In some localities that we have repeatedly visited, there is a steady increase in numbers of butterflies (especially pierids —*Phoebis* and *Anteos*) into the afternoon, with a sudden decline in the late afternoon, by which time representatives of most other families have disappeared for the day.

Collecting Specimens

Although they are obvious facts to anyone who has collected butterflies, I emphasize the importance of 3 factors in making good collections. Most important is the amount of sunlight. Two examples will suffice. At a locality in the Cordillera Central in 1980, a fallow cabbage field at 1373 m, on a day with rapid alternation of sunlight and overcast, during the sunlit periods the field was a whirling mass of butterflies with many pierids but with other families well represented. When the sky was overcast, the pierids disappeared almost instantly (thereby reducing the number of volant butterflies strikingly), only to reappear once the sun was again shining.

Secondly, when attempting to secure specimens of forest-dwelling species (and this automatically includes those species that now occur principally in *caféières* and *cafetales-cacaotales* [= pseudoforest]), one must select days or periods when there is maximum insolation outside the forest or pseudoforest. Even on hot but overcast days, such interior collecting is an exercise in futility; nothing or very little is flying. There have been occasions in both Haiti and the República Dominicana when an hour's walk through a *cafetal* or *caféière* has yielded nothing, or at best an occasional *Heliconius* or *Siproeta*. Even on sunlit days, forest or pseudoforest collecting may be disappointing, except for collecting in openings or clearings within woods or at the edges thereof. There are very few Hispaniolan butterflies that are confirmedly forest dwellers, and ecotonal situations (i.e., forest edges or openings) are far more rewarding than the deep shade of *caféières* or *cafetales*.

A third factor is the presence of flowers. It is of course a dictum that there are terrestrial angiosperms everywhere, in all habitats, as indeed there are. But the flowers therein may be small and inconspicuous. This is especially true in forest or pseudoforest. Even xeric situations have some flowers; one can hardly imagine a more harsh and rigorous habitat than that occupied by *Oarisma stillmani* and members of the *Calisto lyceia* complex. Yet these small and delicate butterflies survive there, feeding on the flowering plants present.

But the question of flowers in Haiti, in contrast to that in the República Dominicana, is instructive. In highly cultivated and vegetationally disturbed Haiti, so much of the original broadleaf forest has been cut that many butterflies use ornamental plants or weeds as a major nectar source. Primary among these are *Hibiscus* and *Ixora*, 2 plants that are rather rarely utilized by Dominican butterflies. At Carrefour la Mort in northern Haiti, I found that the old ornamental *Hibiscus* hedges at a French colonial *habitation* were an excellent source of such species as *Heraclides androgeus* and *Phoebis sennae;* yet one very rarely encounters these or other species on *Hibiscus* in the República Dominicana. There is no question that the nectar sources utilized by butterflies in the 2 countries differ markedly, with Haitian butterflies using introduced and ornamental species and Dominican butterflies using native species. Even with the presence of many kinds of flowering plants in the República Dominicana, relatively few of these are used by butterflies for nectar. Repeatedly, my notes indicate the collection of butterflies from such plants as *Lantana ovatifolia*, *Bauhinia divaricata*, *Palicourea barbinervia*, *Stachytarpheta jamaicensis*, *Bidens pilosa*, *Tournefortia hirsutissima*, and various species of *Heliotropium* and *Cordia*. These seem to be "favorite" plants for nectar, regardless of the diversity of flowering plants in any particular area. One quickly learns what flowers are productive of butterflies and concentrates his attentions on them. Some obvious families of plants (i.e., Apocynaceae) are rarely used by Hispaniolan butterflies, whereas others (Verbenaceae, Asclepiadaceae, Boraginaceae) are readily and eagerly used. In the text, all references to plants used by butterflies are to those used as nectar sources by imagines, not as food for caterpillars.

We have collected specimens in all 5 of the Haitian *départements* (84 localities) and all but 2 (Salcedo, El Seibo) of the Dominican *provincias* (402 localities). We have collected only on Île de la Gonâve of the satellite islands but have material from Isla Saona, Isla Catalina, Isla Beata, and Isla Alto Velo. Of the mountain ranges, we have made collections at high elevations of all but the Massif de la Hotte in Haiti, but we have made collections on both its northern and southern slopes. I have not myself been on the Montagnes du Nord-Ouest in Haiti, but I have studied a small collection from the coastal lowlands of the Presqu'île du Nord-Ouest made by Sommer and Lucio. I feel that our coverage of Hispaniola has been reasonably complete and that we are now in a position to discuss the rhopaloceran fauna of the island. This is not to imply that there is not much more alpha-level work needed on the island, and especially on its satellites. But to withhold the mass of information longer will result in its not being available to other workers. The fact that we have visited Hispaniola in all 4 seasons of the year (although our major collecting period has been summer) improves our conclusions on seasonality and abundance.

Classification Schemata

I am aware of the evidence for recognition of only 4 families (Papilionidae, Pieridae, Nymphalidae, Lycaenidae) of butterflies (Murphy and Ehrlich, 1984), and that the subordinal name Rhopalocera is apparently no longer "tenable." But I have continued to use those family names employed by Riley (1975) and others and to refer to butterflies and skippers by the outmoded name "rhopalocerans" as a matter of convenience to the readers of the present work. On the other hand, and despite much argument in progress, I have adopted the generic classification proposed by Miller and Brown (1981). Since generic boundaries in the diurnal Lepidoptera appear to be poorly drawn in nature, and since the generic concept is for the convenience of biologists, it seems to me a matter of little import whether the name of a particular butterfly is *Papilio aristor* or *Heraclides aristor*, as long as biologists (especially lepidopterists) are in agreement that the entity known as *aristor* is distinct from other entities of papilionids.

In the following species accounts, I have followed the sequence of families and genera in the Miller and Brown (1981) checklist. Within the genus *Calisto*, the phylogenetic schema proposed by Munroe (1950) and Gonzalez and Schwartz (in press) is reasonable, and I have followed it rather than that of Riley (1975).

I have followed the Comstock-Needham system of naming wing veins and spaces (Miller, 1970).

The use of the pronoun "we" may be disquieting to many readers. The word is used not in an editorial sense but rather as an open acknowledgment that collecting and amassing such a large number of butterflies must be a joint cooperative project. No single individual can collect by himself and secure such a large number of specimens. Additionally, the citation of sight records herein bespeaks the cooperation and implicit trust the field worker must have in his associates. Thus, use of "we" is not a hedge but is rather a high compliment to all my field companions who have contributed so much in the 10 years this study has been in progress.

In the species accounts, I have abbreviated localities when referring to observations of reproduction, feeding, or temperatures by citing only the populational centers; thus, "Constanza" in the text may refer to a locality "12 km SW Constanza" in the list of specimens.

Hesperioidea Latreille, 1809

Family Hesperiidae Latreille, 1809

Subfamily Pyrginae Burmeister, 1878

1. *Phocides pigmalion bicolor* Boddaert, 1783

TL (type-locality) Haiti.

FW (forewing length) 29–32 mm.

Schwartz (1983a:58–59) noted the capture of 3 individuals in Haiti, and we have taken 4 more in the República Dominicana. There is also a specimen in the Allyn Museum of Entomology taken by Mark J. Simon at La Romana, a coastal locality, from the wall of a building.

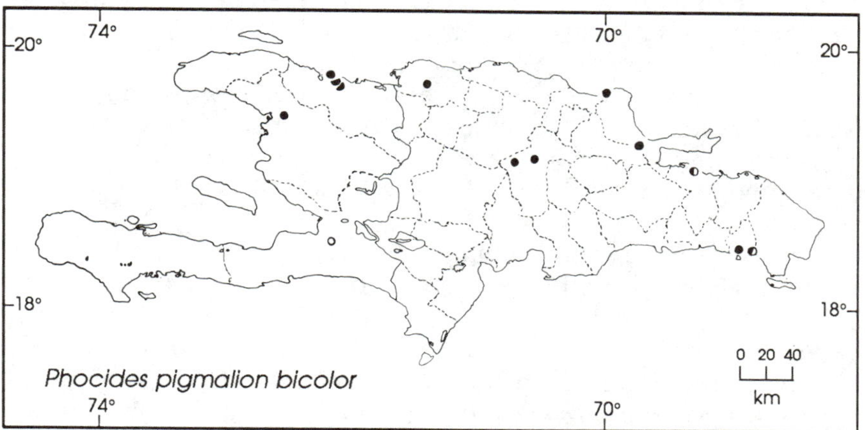

The Haitian specimens were collected on a shaded xeric hillside near the ocean (Cormier Plage), at the edge of a large clearing in a dense *caféière* (Carrefour la Mort), and on an open road through semidesert (Les Poteaux). Comstock (1944:pl. 11, fig. 11) figured a specimen from Pétionville, Haiti. Our long series from Jarabacoa was collected by locals, and the specimen from Manabao is from the edge of a mature *cafetal.* The common occurrence of this species far from the coast (70 km) in the mountains is surprising, since the larval food plant is known to be Red Mangrove (*Rhizophora mangle*). It seems probable that *Ph. p. bicolor* uses another food plant (in addition to Red Mangrove?) that allows it to invade montane areas. The Haitian specimens were collected as far away from known mangrove stands as 7 km, and the Pétionville individual was secured about 8 km (airline) from the coast. The Les Poteaux locality is 24 km from the coast.

We did not encounter *Ph. p. bicolor* in the República Dominicana until 1984. During March and April of that year, we collected 3 specimens: in an oasis (Villa Vásquez), in a hotel garden (Río San Juan), and in a *cacaotal* (Cruce de Rincón). Another skipper was seen with wings open on a leaf of a mango tree (*Mangifera indica*) in a weedy *Cocos* grove (Sabana de la Mar). The Villa Vásquez site is minimally 18 km from the ocean and across the xeric western end of the Cordillera Septentrional; all other localities (except Jarabacoa and Manabao) are virtually coastal or within 3 km of the shore.

Combining the data from all specimens and sight records, July ranks first with 12, June is represented by 6, March by 3, and April, May, and August by 1 each. It is puzzling why we have not previously encountered *Ph. p. bicolor* more commonly and more often in the República Dominicana, since on Hispaniola the species is not restricted to mangroves or coastal situations (in fact we have never seen individuals close to or in *Rhizophora* stands despite repeated visits to such localities in the República Dominicana). In southern Florida, *Ph. p. okeechobee* Worthington flies virtually throughout the year (MacNeill, 1975:575) and is often extremely abundant.

The elevational distribution is between sea level and 530 m. Times of activity were between 1030 and 1645 h, at temperatures between 29°C (Manabao) and 37°C (Río San Juan). *Phocides p. bicolor* has been seen or taken feeding on *Bauhinia divaricata* (Fabaceae) at Les Poteaux, on *Bougainvillea glabra* (Nyctaginaceae) at Río San Juan, and on *Geoffroea inermis* (Fabaceae) at Río Chavón. Although Schwartz (1983a:58) reported that *Ph. p. bicolor* pitches up to land on the underside of a leaf, this is not always the case, since 3 of these skippers landed on the upper sides of leaves (Cruce de Rincón, Sabana de la Mar, Manabao). At the latter locality, the skipper was on a *Coffea* leaf about 2 m above the ground with the wings spread. The individual feeding at Río San Juan likewise had the wings spread, and that from Sabana de la Mar was on a mango leaf about 3 m above the ground with the wings spread. As Schwartz also pointed out, *Ph. p. bicolor* literally glitters in bright sunlight, the iridescent blue flashing as the skipper flies into and out from sunlight into shade.

Specimens: Haiti: Nord: Cormier Plage, s.l., 1; Cap-Haïtien, s.l., 1 (MPM [Milwaukee Public Museum]); Carrefour la Mort, s.l., 1; *l'Artibonite:* 4.5 km E Les Poteaux, 183 m, 1; *República Dominicana: Monte Cristi:* 4 km NW Villa Vásquez, 61 m, 1; *María T. Sánchez:* Río San Juan, s.l., 1; 1 km S Cruce de Rincón, s.l., 1; *La Romana:* La Romana, s.l., 1; *La Vega:* Jarabacoa, 530 m, 17; 1 km W Manabao, 793 m, 1.

Sight records: República Dominicana: Hato Mayor: 7 km E Sabana de la Mar—1 seen, 19.iv; *La Romana:* Río Chavón, 8 km SE La Romana, s.l.—1 seen, 9.vii.

2. *Proteides mercurius sanchesi* Bell and Comstock, 1948

TL Pétionville, Dépt. de l'Ouest, Haiti.

FW males 23–32 mm, females 28–36 mm.

Proteides m. sanchesi appears to be much more abundant in the República Dominicana than in Haiti; Schwartz (1983a:59) listed only 2 specimens with an additional sight record from Haiti, but we have a short series from the República Dominicana. Females are larger than males, and males have the fw hyaline markings more reduced than females, most especially that in Cu2–2A, which is tiny or absent.

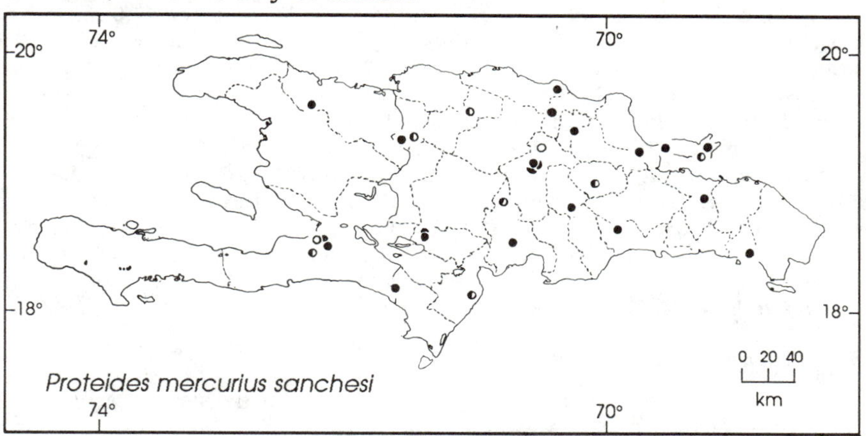

Habitats of this skipper are invariably mesic, usually broadleaf forest, including pseudoforest. *Proteides p. sanchesi* flies on both sunny and overcast days. At Sánchez, an individual was collected as it drank from the mud adjacent to a small stream at the edge of a *cafetal-cacaotal*, and the same behavior was observed at Los Quemados, Monte Bonito, and 11 and 14 km N Neiba. These skippers are often encountered at or near small streams, especially if these streams are adjacent to, or within, woods. The flight is very rapid and direct, with brief stops; the insect is easily alarmed but, once disturbed, tends to return to the same resting or drinking site from which it departs repeatedly. This behavior at times facilitates capture.

Most specimens and sightings are from August (15), with 13 in July, 7 in June, 3 in April, 2 in December, and 1 in March. Times of activity were between 0915 and 1730 h, except for a specimen taken at 2145 h at a porch light (Pétionville). Temperatures varied between 26°C (Neiba) and 37°C (Los Quemados). The elevational distribution is from sea level (Cruce de Rincón) to 915 m (Boutilliers Road).

Proteides m. sanchesi has been taken while feeding on *Lantana ovatifolia* and *L. reticulata* (Verbenaceae) at Santo Domingo and Sosúa, *Tournefortia hirsutissima* (Boraginaceae) at Peralta, and *Geoffroea inermis* (Fabaceae) at Río Chavón.

Specimens: Haiti: Nord: 3.5 km S Plaisance, 336 m, 1; *l'Ouest:* Pétionville, 458 m, 1; *República Dominicana: Dajabón:* Restauración, 400–800 m, 1; *Espaillat:* 14 km SW Jamao al Norte, 534 m, 1; *Puerto Plata:* 9 km SE Sosúa, 15 m, 6; *Duarte:* 10 km SE Tenares, 183 m, 2; *María T. Sánchez:* Cruce de Rincón, s.l., 1; *La Vega:* Jarabacoa, 530 m, 4; 6 km S Jarabacoa, *ca.* 610 m, 1; 1.7 km S Jarabacoa, 488 m, 1; *Samaná:* 6.9 km NE Sánchez, 336 m, 1; 2.8 km S Las Galeras, 61 m, 1; *Hato Mayor:* 18 km NE Hato Mayor, 198 m, 1; *Monseñor Nouel:* 14 km SW Piedra Blanca, 427 m, 2; *La Romana:* Río Chavón, 8 km SE La Romana, s.l., 6; *Dist. Nac.:* 30 km NW Santo Domingo, 122 m, 5; *Azua:* 5 km S Peralta, 305 m, 1; *Baoruco:* 11 km N Neiba, 519 m, 1; 14 km N Neiba, 671 m, 1; *Pedernales:* 1 km SE Banano, 2.

Sight records: Haiti: l'Ouest: Boutilliers Road, 854–915 m—1 seen; *República Dominicana: Dajabón:* Los Cerezos, 12 km NW Río Limpio, 580 m—1 seen, 14.vii; *Valverde:* 3 km W Los Quemados, 122 m—1 seen, 13.vii; *Samaná:* 4.5 km E Samaná—1 seen, 25.xii; *Sánchez Ramírez:* 1 km NE Las Lagunas, 183 m, 14.iv; *Azua:* 5 km SW Monte Bonito, 702 m—1 seen, 4.viii; *Barahona:* 8 km NW Paraíso, 153 m—1 seen, 6.iv.

3. *Epargyreus zestos zestos* Geyer, 1832

TL "Suriname"; probably in error (Miller and Brown, 1981).

The status of this species on Hispaniola is equivocal. We have not collected it. Riley (1975:157) stated that *E. zestos* does not occur on any of the Greater Antilles, whereas Brown and Heineman (1972:65) included both Hispaniola and Puerto Rico in their chart as harboring *E. zestos*. Riley's statement is all the more puzzling in the light of Comstock's (1944:544) listing of 7 localities for the species on Puerto Rico. Clench and Bjorndal (1980:25) stated that it is still questionable whether or not *E. zestos* occurs on Hispaniola. They (p. 26) examined 1 specimen from Puerto Rico. It remains for someone to secure *E. zestos* on Hispaniola.

4. *Epargyreus spanna* Evans, 1952

TL Santo Domingo.

FW males 27–32 mm, females 30–35 mm.

Gali and Schwartz (1983a) discussed the second recorded specimen of *E. spanna*. It, like the holotype, is a female and was taken in mesic streamside broadleaf forest at an elevation of 915 m in August. A third specimen, also secured in August, is from the Sierra Martín García at an elevation of 534–610 m. The locality is in xeric forest; the Martín García, at the time of the taking of the specimen, had not had any appreciable rainfall for 2 months. The skipper was secured by Porfirio E. Amador as it flew across a path and landed on the underside of a leaf of a pathside shrub. It is a male, with a fw length of 32 mm.

Gali and Schwartz (1983b) noted that the female reported by them differed in some minor details from the figure in Riley (1975:pl. 21, fig. 7). The first male agrees very well with the Riley plate, especially in the arrangement and placement of the hyaline fw markings. The costal groove is basal and measures 9 mm. On the unhw (underside of hindwing), the more distal white costal bar is almost completely separated from the remainder of the white figure in Rs, and the pale crescent in 2A-3A is relatively bold and more barlike (rather than comma-shaped) than in the Riley figure. Obviously, *E. spanna* is not sexually dichromatic.

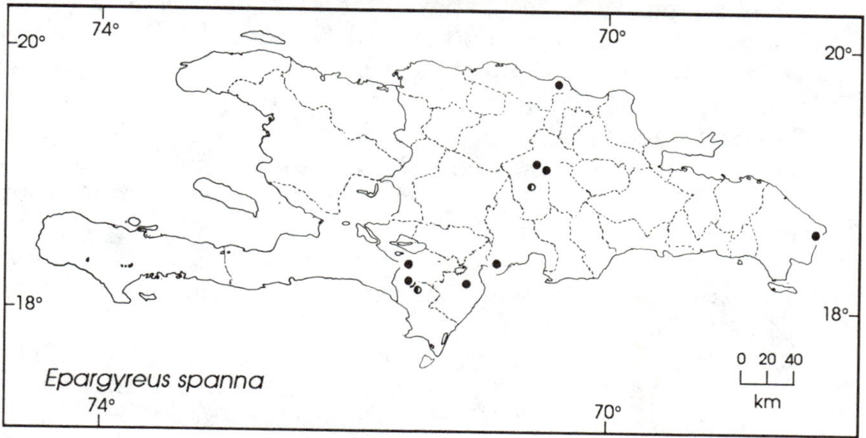

Johnson and Matusik (1986) reported 4 specimens (including the first reported male) from the Las Abejas–Aceitillar area, Prov. de Pedernales, República Dominicana, in mesic broadleaf deciduous forest in vi–vii.1985 at elevations of 1250–1350 m. They also gave information on flight pattern and behavior.

Our long series shows that *E. spanna* is broadly distributed geographically in the República Dominicana (no Haitian records) from sea level (Punta Cana) to 1403 m (Constanza) in the Cordillera Central. The skipper is almost exclusively an inhabitant of broadleaf forest (2 exceptions), usually mesic, rarely xeric (Punta Cana; Sierra Martín García). We have never seen or taken *E. spanna* more than 7 m away from this habitat, and then only when feeding; 1 exception is an individual seen on 27.xii.1986 feeding on *Ageratum conyzoides* (Asteraceae) 1 km N Aceitillar, 1281 m, in pine forest. At Constanza, a single *E. spanna* was observed in pinewoods adjacent to mixed pine-hardwoods.

Epargyreus spanna inhabits dense deciduous forests. Two examples are illustrative. At Jarabacoa, Gonzalez and I observed an individual patrolling a regular beat in a narrow, dark, and steep-sided ravine with a tiny stream. The skipper flew erratically and rapidly, stopping occasionally to feed (on a small white-flowered unidentified composite) or to rest, very briefly, on leaves 2 m above the ground. The Sosúa locality is at the edge of karst topography, where the dolines have uncut hardwoods and the interdoline valleys are pasture with fence rows with much *Tournefortia hirsutissima.* Here, *E. spanna* was common on these flowers. But the skippers were visiting the flowers briefly; once disturbed or satiated, they returned quickly to the sanctuary of the doline forests. I observed the same behavior at El Aguacate. *Epargyreus spanna* is easily identifiable on the wing because of its bright silver unhw bar. This marking must also serve for species recognition within its dense forest habitat.

Most specimens and records are from July (19), with 12 from August, 5 from December, and 3 from June. Times of activity varied from 0915 to 1530 h, at temperatures between 25°C (1 km N Aceitillar) and 37°C (Sosúa).

We have taken *E. spanna* on *Tournefortia hirsutissima* (Sosúa, 18.vii, 21.vii, 20.viii) and on *Ageratum conyzoides* (Las Abejas, 14.vi; El Aguacate, 28.xii).

Hall (1925) listed *Epargyreus antaeus* Hewitson as occurring on Hispaniola above La Vega in the República Dominicana. *Epargyreus antaeus* is endemic to Jamaica and resembles *E. spanna* in having a white bar on the unhw (not unfw—underside forewing—as stated by Brown and Heineman), although the details of this band differ in the 2 taxa. Brown and Heineman (1972:357) stated that Hall's specimen is not Evan's holotype of *E. spanna;* it seems hardly likely that *E. antaeus* occurs on Hispaniola. Brown and Heineman also suggested that *E. antaeus* and *E. spanna* may be subspecifically related; Johnson and Matusik (1986) showed conclusively that these 2 taxa are separate species.

Specimens: República Dominicana: Puerto Plata: 9 km SE Sosúa, 15 m, 14; *La Vega:* 5 km SE Jarabacoa, 595 m, 1; 10 km W Jayaco, 915 m, 1; *La Altagracia:* Punta Cana, s.l., 1; *Independencia:* 4–7 km NE El Aguacate, 519–732 m, 1; *Barahona:* west slope, Sierra Martín García, 305–610 m, 8; 1.8 km W Monteada Nueva, 1007 m, 1; *Pedernales:* Las Abejas, 11 km NW Aceitillar, 1220 m, 1; Las Abejas, 12 km NW Aceitillar, 1129 m, 2.

Sight records: La Altagracia: Punta Cana—1 seen, 10.vii; *La Vega:* 6 km SSE Constanza, 1403 m—1 seen, 23.vii; *Independencia:* 4–7 km NE El Aguacate, 519–732 m—3 seen, 29.xii; *Pedernales:* 1 km N Aceitillar, 1281 m—1 seen, 27.xii.

5. *Polygonus leo lividus* Hübner, 1819

TL America; restricted by Comstock (1944:541–542) to Hispaniola.

FW 23–28 mm.

As far as Haitian specimens, Schwartz (1983a:59) stated that only 2 had been taken by him in that country; the situation was a beach with flowers near Grand-Goâve on the north shore of the Tiburon Peninsula in July. Only 1 more individual has been taken in Haiti (Paillant). *Polygonus l. lividus* is much more common in the República Dominicana, where it occurs on both the north and south islands (although it appears to be much less common on the latter). The skipper is almost exclusively an inhabitant of wooded situations, most usually mesic (but also xeric) broadleaf forest. On 1 occasion (Restauración) a specimen was secured in pine-broadleaf forest, another (Las Galeras) among scattered trees, a third (Las Terrenas) along a mangrove border, and a fourth in an overgrown palm grove (Estero Hondo). The long series from Río Chavón is from a riverside open palm grove with much *Morinda citrifolia* (Rubiaceae), on the white flowers of which *P. l. lividus* was not taken feeding but which was much utilized by other rhopalocerans. These 5 examples are the major exceptions to the forest-dwelling habits of this species. When alarmed, *P. l. lividus*, like related subspecies, darts across a path and lands on the underside of a leaf with the head downward.

Polygonus l. lividus occurs from sea level to 915 m. The latter record (Jayaco) is exceptional, since most records are below 640 m, with most specimens from near sea level. Temperatures of activity varied between 24°C (El Aguacate) and 42°C (La Romana). Times varied between 0900 and 1730 h. Although this skipper is most active during bright and sunny days, we have secured specimens during periods of overcast, even just preceding rain. Specimens have been collected in January, March, April, May, June-August, October, and December, with the highest number (53 of 85) in July. Pseudoforests (*cafetales, cacaotales*) often serve as suitable habitats (Sánchez, Piedra Blanca), and arid woods with *Acacia* (Vallejuelo) are likewise occupied. But certainly *P. leo* is most frequently encountered in mesic broadleaf forest.

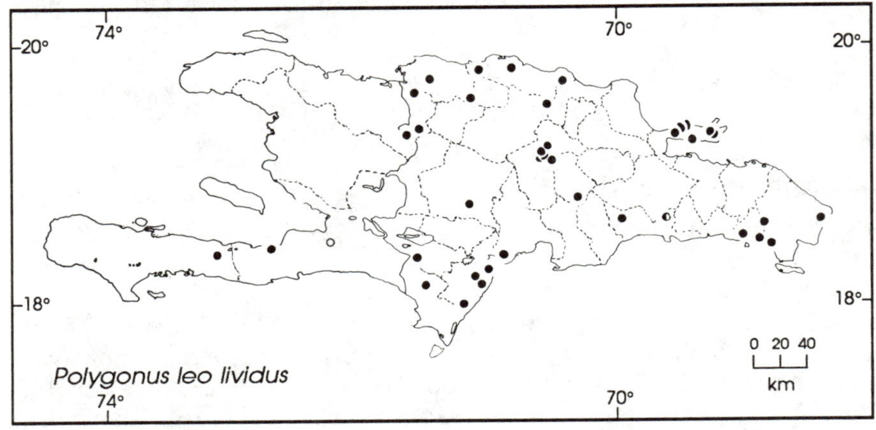

We have taken *P. l. lividus* feeding on *Geoffroea inermis* (Río Chavón) and *Ageratum conyzoides* (Paillant, Cabo Rojo).

Brown and Heineman (1972:359), while discussing the Jamaican *P. l. hagar* Evans, noted that there are 2 other species of this genus in the West Indies: *P. manueli* and *P. ishmael.* The latter name was used by Riley (1975:158) for the Hispaniolan subspecies of *P. leo.* Brown and Heineman (1972:158) stated that *ishmael* Evans is based on a Haitian series of relatively large insects on which the underside is not purplish but has a peculiar greenish gray gloss and on which the upper side is darker than that of any subspecies of *Polygonus leo.* They also quoted extensively an E. L. Bell manuscript concerning the subspecies of *P. leo,* in which Bell diagnosed *lividus* as "very dark brown on the upper side and on the under side the glazing is greenish-grey." Brown and Heineman (1972:65), in their summary table of Antillean hesperiid distributions, unaccountably did not mention *P. ishmael.* Our specimens agree in coloration with Evans's definition of *P. ishmael:* the unhw is distinctly greenish gray, certainly not purplish. The up (upper side) is dark brown. There is no obvious way of differentiating our series into 2—*P. l. lividus* and *P. ishmael.* Thus we are faced with the problem of Comstock's (1944:541) restriction of the type-locality of *lividus* to Hispaniola; Comstock also stated that only Hispaniolan *Polygonus* corresponds with Hübner's figures. Our specimens do, however, agree with Evans's description of *P. ishmael*; if Riley had similar material before him, it is no surprise that he used *ishmael* as the name for this population but relegated it to subspecies status under *P. leo*.

Satellite to this problem is the peculiar distribution of *P. l. savigny* Latreille 1824 (TL "Antilles"). This subspecies is known from Florida, Cuba, the Bahamas, Puerto Rico and the Virgin Islands, and the Lesser Antilles as far south as Montserrat. Thus, *P. l. lividus* is interposed within the distribution of *P. l. savigny*. Brown and Heineman (1972:359) noted that this split distribution of *P. l. savigny* suggests that there may be 2 subspecies involved under that taxon, rather than 1. The situation would be perhaps less anomalous if the Hispaniolan population were to be regarded as a species (*P. ishmael*) distinct from *P. leo*. Note that all other subspecies of *P. leo* (*leo, savigny, hagar*) have the un (underside) purple, not green. The situation requires resolution.

Specimens: Haiti: l'Ouest: just W Grand-Goâve, s.l., 2; *Sud:* 3 km SW Paillant, 793 m, 1; *República Dominicana: Monte Cristi:* 4 km NW Villa Vásquez, 61 m, 1; *Dajabón:* 0.5 km N Cañongo, 31 m, 1; Los Cerezos, 12 km NW Río Limpio, 550 m, 2; 4 km S Restauración, 590 m, 1; *Valverde:* 3 km W Los Quemados, 122 m, 1; *Puerto Plata:* 13 km SE Luperón, 214 m, 5; 0.6 km NE Estero Hondo, 1; 9 km SE Sosúa, 15 m, 2; *Santiago:* 2 km E Pedro García, 427 m, 1; *La Vega:* Buena Vista, 11 km NE Jarabacoa, 641 m, 1; Jarabacoa, 530 m, 1; 5 km SE Jarabacoa, 595 m, 5; 6 km S Jarabacoa, *ca.* 610 m, 1; 10 km W Jayaco, 915 m, 1; *Monseñor Nouel:* 14 km SW Piedra Blanca, 427 m, 3; *Samaná:* 6.9 km NE Sánchez, 336 m, 1; 8.9 km NE Sánchez, 336 m, 2; 13.2 km NE Sánchez, 92 m, 1; 3.1 km E Las Terrenas, s.l., 1; 10.2 km W Samaná, 61 m, 1; 14.1 km E and N Samaná, 31 m, 1; 2.8 km S Las Galeras, 61 m, 1; *La Altagracia:* 2 km W Punta Cana, s.l., 1; 16 km NE La Romana, 61 m, 9: 1 km N Playa Bayahibe, s.l., 4; *La Romana:* Río Chavón, 8 km SE La Romana, s.l., 16; Río Cumayasa, 13.5 km W La Romana, 31 m, 14; *Dist. Nac.:* 30 km NW Santo Domingo, 122 m, 1; *San Juan:* 9 km E Vallejuelo, 610 m, 1; *Independencia:* 4–7 km NE El Aguacate, 519–824 m, 4: *Barahona:* west slope, Sierra Martín García, 610 m, 1; Barahona, 1 (MPM); 12 km SW Barahona, 427 m, 1; 5 km SE, 3 km W Barahona, 183 m, 1; 3 km NW Enriquillo, 244 m, 2: *Pedernales:* 26 km NE Cabo Rojo, 732 m, 1.

Sight record: República Dominicana: Dist. Nac.: 9 km NE Guerra—1 seen, 7.iii.

6. *Chioides ixion* Plötz, 1881

TL Haiti.

FW 22–27 mm.

In Haiti, this skipper is widespread geographically, occurring on both the north and south islands. In the República Dominicana, it is much more common in the western two-thirds of the country than it is in Haiti but appears to be absent from the eastern one-third, as well as from the Península de Samaná. Most of our specimens have been taken in July (40), but there are 1 each from April and May, 2 each from March and October, 5 from December, 6 each from January and June, and 35 from August. Times of activity varied between 0930 and 1715 h, and temperatures between 23°C (Puesto Pirámide 204) and 39°C (Los Quemados).

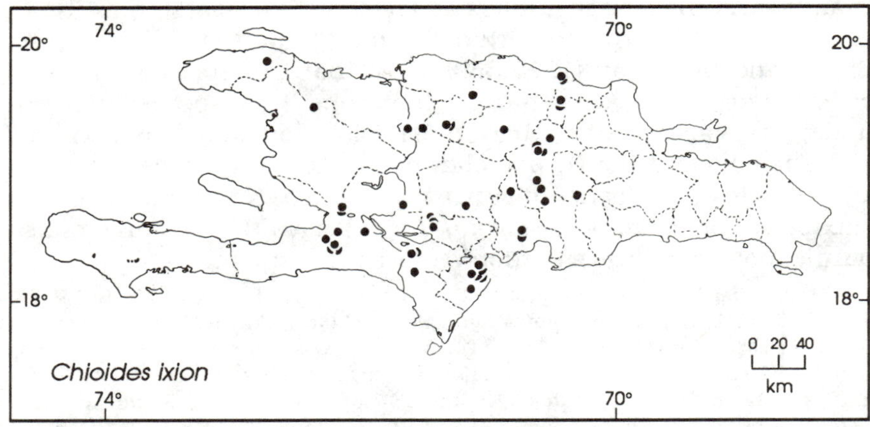

Chioides ixion is primarily an inhabitant of mesic broadleaf forest at elevations from sea level (Fond Parisien) to 1678 m (Kenscoff), both in Haiti. But in Haiti, individuals are most often encountered in uplands (Carrefour Marmelade, Pétionville, Boutilliers Road, Kenscoff), where vegetation is very often pines; Fond Parisien is unique not only in its low elevation but also in that the locality lies in the xeric Cul de Sac plain. In the República Dominicana, the most frequent captures of *Ch. ixion* occur in mesic forest or pseudoforest, again at high elevations, most frequently above about 500 m. However, specimens have been taken in mixed pine-hardwoods (Monción), fields (Constanza), mixed *Acacia*—xeric woods (Vallejuelo), semixeric open woods (Barahona), and transitional xeric-mesic forest (El Aguacate). The lowest record is from 15 m (Sosúa). On occasion (Puesto Pirámide 204), the insects have been taken while foraging in the open along the edges of roads or in fields, but these situations are uncommon, and these open areas are adjacent to primarily mesic forest.

In flight, *Ch. ixion* resembles members of the genus *Urbanus* since all are tailed. Once these skippers have landed, which they do often, the bold white or silvery patch on the unhw is obvious and there can be little mistake in the identification. *Urbanus* and *Ch. ixion* fly in different manners. The flight of both species of *Urbanus* is rapid and erratic, usually close to the ground, with much "indecision" as to a landing site; landing is often (but not always) on the underside of a leaf. *Chioides ixion*, on the other hand, does not fly erratically; its flight is direct, and landing is "deliberate." Both species of *Urbanus* are much less confirmedly inhabitants of wooded situations but occur most frequently in fallow fields, along roadsides, and in other open areas; *Ch. ixion* prefers shaded areas associated with forest and has only rarely been seen removed from this habitat.

Flowers utilized as nectar sources include *Cordia* sp. (Boraginaceae), *Ixora* sp. (Rubiaceae), *Stachytarpheta jamaicensis* (Verbenaceae), *Hibiscus rosasinensis* (Malvaceae), *Tournefortia hirsutissima* (Boraginaceae), *Bougainvillea glabra* (Nyctaginaceae), *Antigonon leptopus* (Fabaceae), *Lantana ovatifolia* (Verbenaceae), *Croton barahonensis* (Euphorbiaceae), and *Parthenium hysterophorus* (Asteraceae). The last, with its tiny white inflorescences, along with *Croton barahonensis*, would seem unlikely choices for such a large skipper, but at Vallejuelo, these were the preferred plants of *Ch. ixion*.

Specimens: Haiti: Nord-Ouest: 1.3 km S Balladé, 31 m, 1; *l'Artibonite:* 1.6 km E Carrefour Marmelade, 854 m, 1; *l'Ouest:* 2.9 km S Terre Rouge, 549 m, 1; 1.1 km N Terre Rouge, 549 m, 1; 2 km SE Fond Parisien, s.l., 2; Boutilliers Road, 732–854 m, 7; Pétionville, 2; 3.7 km S Kenscoff, 1647 m, 1; 5.8 km SW Kenscoff, 1678 m, 1; 0.3 km NE Obléon, 1617 m, 1; *República Dominicana: Dajabón:* Restauración, 400–800 m, 1; Los Cerezos, 12 km NW Río Limpio, 580 m, 1; *Valverde:* 3 km W Los Quemados, 122 m, 1; *Puerto Plata:* 9 km SE Sosúa, 15 m, 6; 11 km SE Sosúa, 46 m, 1; *Santiago Rodríguez:* Loma Leonor, 18 km SW Monción, 534 m, 2; Loma Leonor, 19 km SW Monción, 610 m, 1; *Espaillat:* 14 km SW Jamao al Norte, 534 m, 1; 20 km SW Jamao al Norte, 610 m, 1; *La Vega:* 3.5 km E Paso Bajito, 732 m, 1; Jarabacoa, 530 m, 2; 1.7 km S Jarabacoa, 488 m, 1; Buena Vista, 11 km NE Jarabacoa, 641 m, 1; 10 km S Constanza, 1373 m, 3; 18 km SE Constanza, 1586 m, 1; 10 km NW La Horma, 1496 m, 2; *Santiago:* Río Bao, 8 km SE Montones Abajo, 488 m, 1; *Monseñor Nouel:* 14 km SW Piedra Blanca, 427 m, 1; *Azua:* 5 km SE Monte Bonito, 702 m, 1; 5 km S Peralta, 305 m, 2; 2.5 km W, 6.6 km N Azua, 183 m, 2; *San Juan:* 9 km E Vallejuelo, 610 m, 13; *Elías Piña:* 2 km NE Puesto Pirámide 204, 1586 m, 7; *Independencia:* 1 km NE El Aguacate, 976 m, 8; 4–7 km NE El Aguacate, 519–824 m, 3; *Baoruco:* 11 km N Neiba, 519 m, 10; 14 km N Neiba, 671 m, 2; 1 km NW El Veinte, 1230 m, 1; *Barahona:* 8 km SW Barahona, 366 m, 1; Polo, 702 m, 1; 2 km SW Barahona, 122 m, 2; 3 km SW Barahona, 2; 5 km SE, 3 km W Barahona, 183–397 m, 4; 1.3 km W Monteada Nueva, 1037 m, 6; 8–10 km NW Paraíso, 2 (MPM); *Pedernales:* Las Abejas, 12 km NW Aceitlllar, 1129 m, 1.

7. *Aguna asander haitensis* Mabille and Boullet, 1912

TL Haiti.

FW 25–28 mm.

Aguna a. haitensis is widely distributed in Haiti but seems to be strangely rare in most of the República Dominicana, notably that portion north of the Valle de Neiba; there is only 1 specimen from the far north (Santiago). Rarity of records from this very large area can hardly be an artifact of collecting, since we have often collected in the proper months and proper habitats, when and where this skipper is abundant in the south. Records from northern Haiti (= north of the Cul de Sac plain) are only 2 (Les Poteaux, Délugé), suggesting that in northern Haiti *A. a. haitensis* is also not abundant. The skipper is primarily an inhabitant of broadleaf woods —usually mesic but at times xeric (3 km NW Enriquillo, Oviedo). In such situations, its flight is rapid and darting, and it lands with regularity on the underside of leaves, often of small (0.5 m) shrubs or even herbs (if the weight of the skipper can be supported by the plant), with the head down. Elsewhere, *A. a. haitensis* has been taken in palm forest with shrubby undergrowth near Etang Saumâtre (Fond Parisien), in pine forest (Furcy), on a semidesert roadside (Les Poteaux), and in xeric forest (Oviedo) on *Bauhinia divaricata.* On Boutilliers Road in Haiti and at Monteada Nueva in the República Dominicana, individuals were taken while feeding on roadside *Stachytarpheta jamaicensis*, and at Peralta several were feeding on *Tournefortia hirsutissima.* A specimen from Banano was taken on *Bauhinia divaricata.* Many individuals were taken in December and January on *Ageratum conyzoides* (El Aguacate, Cabo Rojo, El Naranjo). Other plants used as nectar sources include *Solanum* sp. (Solanaceae), *Ixora* sp. (Rubiaceae), and *Cynoglossum amabile* (Boraginaceae) at Las Abejas, *Antigonon leptopus* at Santiago, and *Acacia vogeliana* (Fabaceae) at Vallejuelo.

Elevations in Haiti range from sea level (Délugé, Fond Parisien) to 1464 m (Furcy), and in the República Dominicana from 153 m (Paraíso) to 1617 m (Los Arroyos); at the latter locality the skippers were in mesic broadleaf forest. Temperatures varied between 21°C (Los Arroyos) and 37°C (Peralta); most specimens were collected on bright and sunny days, but others were taken on days that were alternately sunny and overcast. Times of activity varied between 0900 and 1600 h.

Most specimens were collected in July (27), with 11 in January, 14 in April, 2 in May, 21 in June, 25 in August, 6 in October, and 18 in December. Those taken at Fond Parisien in April-May are worn, as are those from Enriquillo in October, suggesting that they are remnants of earlier broods (spring and winter). But April material from elsewhere (Paraíso, Banano, 3 km NW Enriquillo, Peralta) includes both fresh and worn individuals.

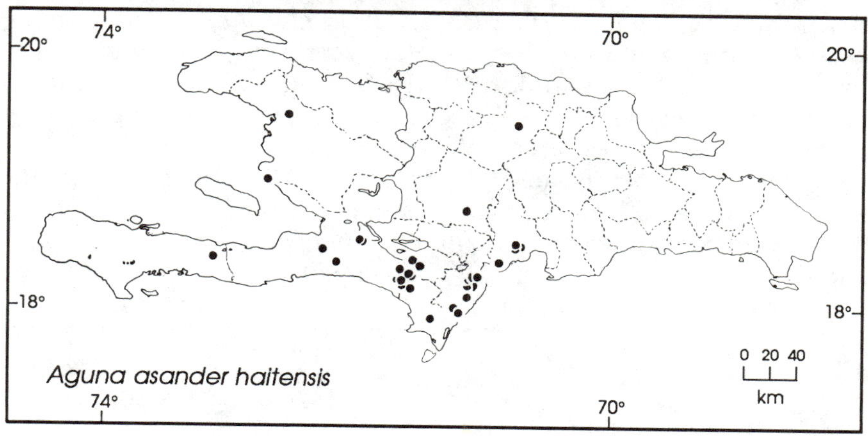

Specimens: Haiti: l'Artibonite: 4.6 km E Les Poteaux, 183 m, 1; Délugé, s.l., 1; *Sud:* 6.7 km SW Paillant, 763–854 m, 3; *l'Ouest:* Boutilliers Road, 915 m, 1; Peneau, 1.6 km SW Furcy, 1464 m, 1; 2 km SE Fond Parisien, s.l., 3; 4 km SE Fond Parisien, s.l., 1; *República Dominicana: Santiago:* 7 km SW Santiago, 214 m, 1; *Azua:* 5 km S Peralta, 305 m, 3; 4 km S Peralta, 366 m, 3; 2.5 km W, 6.6 km N Azua, 183 m, 1; *San Juan:* 9 km E Vallejuelo, 610 m, 1; *Independencia:* 4–7 km NE El Aguacate, 519–824 m, 30; 7 km NE El Aguacate, 519 m, 10; 6 km SW El Naranjo, 519 m, 2; *Barahona:* El Limón, summit, Sierra Martín García, 1037 m, 1; west slope, Sierra Martín García, 305–915 m, 18; 5 km SE, 6.4 km W Barahona, 488 m, 10; 3 km SW Barahona, 1; 12 km SW Barahona, 427 m, 2; 13 km SW Barahona, 732 m, 1; 22 km SW Barahona, 1098 m, 1; 1.8 km W Monteada Nueva, 976 m, 1; 8 km NW Paraíso, 153 m, 9 (3 MPM); 3 km NW Enriquillo, 244 m, 18; 9 km NW Enriquillo, 671 m, 4; *Pedernales:* 17 km NW Oviedo, 183 m, 5; Mencía, 397 m, 3; 1 km SE Banano, 183 m, 1; 5 km NE Los Arroyos, 1617 m, 2; 26 km NE Cabo Rojo, 732 m, 14; Las Abejas, 11 km NW Aceitillar, 1220 m, 1; Las Abejas, 12 km NW Aceitillar, 1129 m, 15.

8. *Urbanus proteus domingo* Scudder, 1872

TL Haiti.

FW 22–25 mm.

Urbanus p. domingo is one of the most widely distributed skippers on Hispaniola. It occurs throughout Haiti (but appears to be uncommon on the distal half of the Tiburon Peninsula) and throughout the República Dominicana. Its altitudinal distribution is from sea level to 1464 m (Peneau) in Haiti, and from sea-level to 1281 m (Aceitillar) in the República Dominicana. Habitats vary from sea-level oases and *Acacia* scrub through *cacaotales* and deciduous forest to pinewoods. Perhaps the most favored habitat of *U. p. domingo* is along roads, paths, or clearings, through and in *caféières* and *cafetales*, where its erratic flight is often seen. Food plants include *Bauhinia divaricata, Zinnia elegans, Lantana ovatifolia, Stachytarpheta jamaicensis, S. cayennensis, Ageratum conyzoides, Daucus* sp., an unidentified white-flowered tree in *Acacia* scrub, and *Urena lobata* (Malvaceae), the latter a mallow found in fallow fields, roadsides, and disturbed and/or cultivated areas. Although this skipper is associated with wooded areas, its habit, contrary to that of *Ch. ixion*, for instance, of regularly foraging in open areas at the woods' margins or in open areas is very distinctive. As previously noted, *U. p. domingo* can be separated from *Ch. ixion* in the field by the differences in their flight patterns.

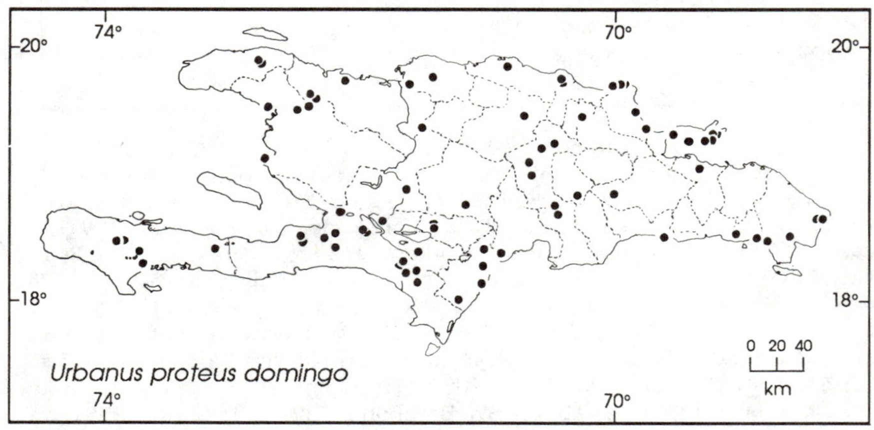

Temperatures of activity varied between 23°C (Los Arroyos) and 39°C (Samaná, San José de Ocoa), and times between 0900 and 1730 h. Specimens have been collected in March, April, May, June, July, August, September, October, December, January, and February, with the highest frequency in July. The dates suggest that *U. p. domingo* is present throughout the year, as Comstock (1944:545) suggested for Puerto Rico. However, we saw few individuals between late September and late March in the República Dominicana. In southern Florida, *U. p. proteus* Linnaeus shows great seasonality, and the same seems to be true of *U. p. domingo* on Hispaniola.

Steinhauser (1981) recently revised the *proteus* group of *Urbanus*. He, in contrast to Comstock (1944) and Brown and Heineman (1972), recognized *U. p. domingo* as a valid subspecies, restricted to the Antilles, of *U. proteus*, which occurs on the mainland from North America to Argentina and Brasil in South America. He examined only 31 specimens of *U. p. domingo*, of which 2 males and 2 females were from Hispaniola (= Haiti). He characterized *U. p. domingo* by a series of traits, as follows: male fw frequently lacks subapical hyaline spots, small size of hyaline spots (in both sexes), hw fringe usually pale brown (rather than white), fw fringe checkering usually not reaching apex, and females with body and basal hair-scales blue-green (rather than green). A series of 27 males and 26 females from Hispaniola agrees with the above definition. The color trait of green versus blue-green is difficult to assess, unless one has many completely fresh specimens, but my material seems to bear this out. The hyaline spots in the fw are indeed larger in females than in males. Of 27 males, 41% (in contrast to Steinhauser's 43%) have spots in M1-M2 and/or M2-M3; the percentages are very close indeed. I have 1 of 26 females that lacks hyaline spots in these spaces, whereas Steinhauser reported that 100% of his females had spots. Nonoverlap of hyaline spots in the fw cell and Cu2-Cu3 occurs in all (27) males and 18 (of 26) females: Steinhauser gave 100% for males and 86% for females. My percentage for females (69%) is lower than his. Finally, nonoverlap of the hyaline spots in fw Cu2-Cu3 and Cu3–1A occurs in all my specimens of both sexes, whereas Steinhauser found this condition in 100% of the males and 86% of the females (2 of my females have the spots very closely juxtaposed).

Certainly my long series from Hispaniola bears out Steinhauser's characters for *U. p. domingo;* differences in percentages between his and my data do not weaken those differences but rather reinforce them. The variation between his and my figures on the nonoverlap of spots in fw Cu2-Cu3 and Cu3–1A perhaps reflects the fact that he examined less material than I and that his material was from throughout the Antilles, whereas mine is from 1 island.

On 29.vi.1982, at a locality 1 km S Constanza, 1098 m, in a grassy field, weather bright and sunny, there was little butterfly activity at 0900 h; starting at 0930 h, skippers began to become active, with *Urbanus* the earliest, followed by *Wallengrenia druryi, Pyrrhocalles antiqua, Atalopedes mesogramma*, and finally *Panoquina sylvicola* at about 1100 h. The temperature at 1100 h was 34°C. *Urbanus p. domingo* is the first of the hesperiids to become active in the morning.

Specimens: Haiti: Nord-Ouest: 7.5 km SE Port-de-Paix, 1; 1.3 km S Balladé, 31 m, 1; *Nord:* Carrefour la Mort, s.l., 1; 3.5 km W Plaisance, 305 m, 1; 3.5 km S Plaisance, 336 m, 4; *l'Artibonite:* 1.6 km E Carrefour Marmelade,

854 m, 4; 12.2 km W Ça Soleil, 2; 7.4 km E Les Poteaux, 2; Les Bains des Amani-y, s.l., 1; *l'Ouest:* 2 km SE Fond Parisien, s.l., 1; 5 km SE Fond Parisien, s.l., 1; Pétionville, 366–458 m, 4; 2.9–8.5 km S Terre Rouge, 1; Boutilliers Road, 1.8–2.1 km W Kenscoff rd., 5; Peneau, 1.1–1.6 km SW Furcy, 1464 m, 1; 1.3 km N Béloc, 702 m, 2; 8.6 km N Béloc, 549 m, 1; *Sud:* 5.4 km W Miragoâne, s.l., 1; 6.7 km SW Paillant, 763 m, 2; 7 km SW Cavaillon, 122 m, 1; 6.4 km NW Marceline, 671 m, 1; Formond, 900 m, 1 (FSM); ravine between Pic Formond and Macaya, 1050 m, 1 (FSM); *República Dominicana: Monte Cristi:* 6 km W Copey, s.l., 1; 4 km NW Villa Vásquez, 61 m, 2; *Dajabón:* Los Cerezos, 12 km NW Río Limpio, 580 m, 2; *Elías Piña:* 15 km S Comendador, 976 m, 1; *Puerto Plata:* 10 km W Luperón, 1; 9 km SE Sosúa, 15 m, 1; 11 km SE Sosúa, 46 m, 1; *Duarte:* 10 km SE Tenares, 183 m, 1; *Santiago:* 7 km SW Santiago, 214 m, 1; *María T. Sánchez:* Río San Juan, s.l., 1; 11 km NE Río San Juan, 1; 9 km NE Río San Juan, s.l., 3; 14 km S La Entrada, s.l., 1; 9 km SE Nagua, s.l., 1; *Samaná:* 6.9 km NE Sánchez, 336 m, 5; 18 km N and E Samaná, s.l., 6; 4.5 km E Samaná, 2; 10.2 km W Samaná, 6l m, 1; 10.5 km S Las Galeras, 16 m, 1; 2.8 km S Las Galeras, 61 m, 2; *Hato Mayor:* 6 km N El Valle, 1; *La Altagracia:* Punta Cana, s.l., 1; 3 km W Punta Cana, s.l., l; 0.5–3.5 km W Boca de Yuma, 4; 1 km N Playa Bayahibe, 1; *La Romana:* Río Chavón, 8 km SE La Romana, s.l., 1; Río Cumayasa, 13.5 km W La Romana, 1; *Dist. Nac.:* Punta Caucedo, 2 km W, 2 km S Andrés, s.l., 2; *Monte Plata:* 2 km W Esperalvillo, 92 m, 2; *Peravia:* 6 km W La Horma, 1159 m, 1; 5 km N San José de Ocoa, 580 m, 1; *La Vega:* La Palma, 19 km W Jayaco, 1007 m, 1; Jarabacoa, 530 m, 3; 12 km NE Constanza, 1220 m, 1; 1 km S Constanza, 1098 m, 5; *Monseñor Nouel:* 14 km SW Piedra Blanca, 427 m, 1; *San Juan:* 9 km E Vallejuelo, 610 m, 1; *Baoruco:* 9 km N Neiba, 366 m, 1; 11 km N Neiba, 519 m, 1; *Independencia:* 5 km NW Tierra Nueva, s.l., 1; 6 km SW El Naranjo, 519 m, 2; *Barahona:* El Limón, summit, Sierra Martín García, 1037 m, 1; west slope, Sierra Martín García, 458–610 m, 1; 8 km ESE Canoa, 1; Barahona, s.l., 1; 3.3 km NE La Ciénaga, 2; 9 km NW Enriquillo, 671 m, 2; *Pedernales:* Mencía, 397 m, 3; 3 km SE Los Arroyos, 976 m, 1; 0.6 km SE Los Arroyos, 1098 m, 1; 26 km NE Cabo Rojo, 732 m, 3; 1 km N Aceitillar, 1281 m, 2.

9. *Urbanus dorantes cramptoni* Comstock, 1944

TL Mayagüez, Puerto Rico.

FW 13–22 mm.

Like its congener *U. p. domingo, U. d. cramptoni* is widely distributed throughout much of Hispaniola. This subspecies occurs as well on Puerto Rico and the Virgin Islands, whereas *U. d. santiago* Lucas occurs on Cuba and the Isla de la Juventud. In the Bahamas, *U. d. santiago* occurs on Andros Island (Rindge, 1952:15; Clench, 1977a:281; Clench, 1977b:190) as well as on Grand Bahama Island. The nominate subspecies, *U. d. dorantes* Stoll, is apparently a recent adventive to south Florida, where it was first collected in 1969 (Clench, 1970:242).

Urbanus d. cramptoni occurs most frequently in open areas: roadsides, edges of and clearings within *caféières* and *cafetales*, and open fields, usually with flowers. But *U. d. cramptoni* has also been taken in *Acacia* woods (Fond Parisien, Oviedo), pinewoods (Kenscoff, Peneau, 18 km SE Constanza), mixed pine-hardwoods (Restauración, Buena Vista), oases (Croix des Bouquets), adjacent to mangroves (Miragoâne), and behind beaches (Grand-Goâve). The species also may be encountered along paths or in clearings in mesic forest (Jayaco, Las Abejas, Puesto Pirámide 204, Los Arroyos), xeric forest (Boca de Yuma, Punta Cana, La Romana, Río Cumayasa), *Cocos* groves (Río San Juan), and transitional woods (El Aguacate). In general, *U. d. cramptoni* seems less common than *U. p. domingo*, but many more individuals of both species were seen but not collected. Unless one sees the iridescent green on the body and wing bases of *U. p. domingo* in contrast to the noniridescent body and wings of *U. d. cramptoni*, the 2 species are not readily distinguishable in the field. Their habits are similar (see account of *U. p. domingo*).

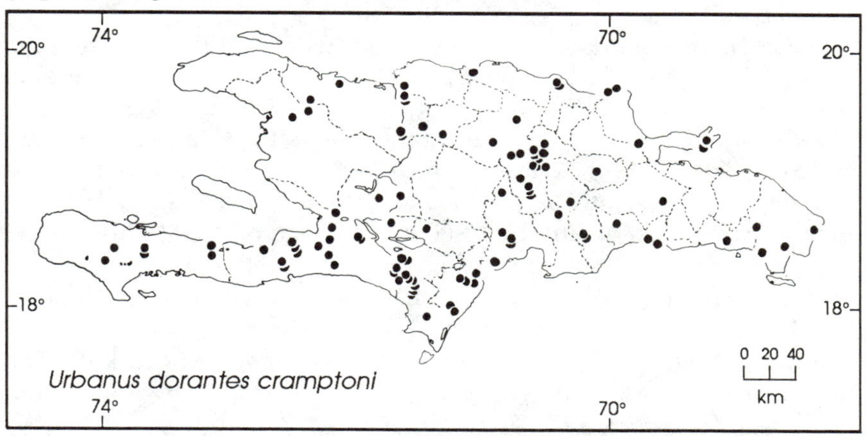

The elevational distribution is from sea level (Carrefour la Mort, Fond Parisien, Croix des Bouquets, Grand-Goâve, Miragoâne, Río San Juan, Punta Cana, Andrés, Tres Ojos, Barahona) to 1922 m (14 km SE Constanza) in the Cordillera Central, 1617 m (5 km NE Los Arroyos) in the Massif de la Selle, and 1586 m (Puesto Pirámide 204) in the Sierra de Neiba. These high elevations are not exceptional, however, and *U. d. cramptoni* is well distributed up to them.

Urbanus d. cramptoni and *U. p. domingo* are syntopic at 25 localities. At 4 of these (3.5 km S Plaisance, Pétionville, Boca de Yuma, Mencía) *U. p. domingo* outnumbers *U. d. cramptoni* (about 4:1); at 6 (Fond Parisien, Boutilliers Road, 6.7 km SW Paillant, Formond, 4.5 km E Samaná, 1 km S Constanza), *U. d. cramptoni* outnumbers *U. p. domingo* (about 3:1). The ratio of *U. d. cramptoni* to *U. p. domingo* is well shown at Boutilliers Road (15 specimens: 5 specimens) and 1 km S Constanza (11 specimens: 5 specimens). Both localities have been visited many times, and the samples are unbiased. At the remaining 11 localities, both species are represented by about equal numbers of specimens.

Times of collection were between 0900 and 1715 h, at temperatures between 20°C (18 km SE Constanza) and 38°C (Barahona).

Most specimens have been taken in July (90), with 33 in June and 20 in August. December is represented by 19, and January, February, March, April, May, and October each by 14 (May) to 3 (February, March) individuals. Although *U. d. cramptoni* is on the wing throughout the year, observations in the spring and fall indicate that the skippers are much less common at those times than in the summer and midwinter, suggesting that *U. d. cramptoni* is bivoltine.

Like *U. p. domingo, U. d. cramptoni* feeds avidly on *Stachytarpheta jamaicensis* (many localities); we have also seen these skippers feeding on the flowers of *Tournefortia hirsutissima* (Sosúa), *Zinnia elegans* (La Ciénaga), *Antigonon leptopus* (El Cruce del Quince), *Bidens pilosa* (Mao), *Lantana ovatifolia* (Río Bao), *Cynoglossum amabile* (Las Abejas), *Ageratum conyzoides* (Peralta, Cabo Rojo, Aceitillar), and on an unidentified white-flowered tree (5 km NE Los Arroyos). On 1 occasion (La Palma), we observed a great many *U. d. cramptoni* flying over a meadow with many *Emilia javanica* (Asteraceae) in flower, but the skippers did not take nectar from this red composite. We have observed a few *U. d. cramptoni* drinking from mud in a dirt road (1 km NE El Aguacate).

Specimens: Haiti: Nord: Carrefour la Mort, s.l., 1; 3.5 km S Plaisance, 336 m, 1; *l'Artibonite:* 1.6 km E Carrefour Marmelade, 854 m, 3; 16 km E Gonaïves, 1; *l'Ouest:* 6.2 km E Lascahobas, 275 m, 1; 2.9 km N Terre Rouge, 534 m, 1; 2 km SE Fond Parisien, s.l., 3; 4 km SE Fond Parisien, s.l., 1; 13.1 km E Croix des Bouquets, s.l., 1; Pétionville, 458 m, 1; Boutilliers Road, 1.8–2.1 km W Kenscoff rd., 793–885 m, 1; Boutilliers Road, 734–915 m, 15; 5.8 km S Kenscoff, 1586 m, 1; Peneau, 1.1 km S Furcy, 1464 m, 1; 8.6 km N Béloc, 534 m, 1; 1.3 km N Béloc, 702 m, 1; 0.8 km S Découzé, 702 m, 2; 6 km NW Jacmel, 244 m, 1; 9.3 km NW Jacmel, 183 m, 1; nr. Péredo, 570 m, 2 (FSM); just W Grand-Goâve, s.l., 1; *Sud:* 5.4 km W Miragoâne, s.l., 1; 6.6 km SW Paillant, 793 m, 1; 6.7 km SW Paillant, 763 m, 5; 16.3 km N Cavaillon, 488 m, 1; 26.1 km N Cavaillon, 610 m, 1; Formond, 900 m, 2 (FSM); Les Platons, 650 m, 1 (FSM); *República Dominicana: Monte Cristi:* 6 km W Copey, s.l., 1; *Dajabón:* 0.5 km N Cañongo, 31 m, 1; 2 km NW El Pino, s.l., 1; Restauración, 400–800 m, 1; 4 km S Restauración, 580 m, 1; 8 km S Restauración, 625 m, 1; *Elías Piña:* 2 km NE Puesto Pirámide 204, 1586 m, 1; *Valverde:* 12 km SW Mao, 244 m, 6; Río Guarabo, 3 km W Los Quemados, 122 m, 2; *Puerto Plata:* 9 km

SE Sosúa, 15 m, 4; 10 km SE Sosúa, 1; 0.6 km NE Estero Hondo, 1; *Santiago:* Río Bao, 8 km SE Montones Abajo, 488 m, 3; 7 km SW Santiago, 214 m, 2; *La Vega:* 3.5 km E Paso Bajito, 732 m, 1; 13 km E Manabao, 610 m, 1; 1 km W Manabao, 793 m, 1; La Ciénaga, 915 m, 4; 10 km W Jayaco, 9l5 m, 5; La Palma, 19 km W Jayaco, 1007 m, 5; Buena Vista, 11 km NE Jarabacoa, 640 m, 5; Jarabacoa, 530 m, 5; 5 km SE Jarabacoa, 595 m, 4; 6 km S Jarabacoa, *ca.* 610 m, 1; 1 km S Constanza, 1098 m, 11; 10 km SE Constanza, 1647 m, 1; 14 km SE Constanza, 1922 m, 1; 18 km SE Constanza, 1586 m, 5; *María T. Sánchez:* Río San Juan, s.l., 1; 9 km NE Río San Juan, s.l., 1; 1 km S Cruce de Rincón, s.l., 1; *Samaná:* 4.5 km E Samaná, 5; 2.8 km S Las Galeras, 61 m, 1; *La Altagracia:* Punta Cana, s.l., 2; 0.5–3.5 km W Boca de Yuma, 1; l6 km NE La Romana, 61 m, 9; 2.5 km SE Playa Bayahibe, 1; *La Romana:* Río Cumayasa, 13.5 km W La Romana, 2; *Dist. Nac.:* 8 km NE Bayaguana, 1; Punta Caucedo, 2 km W, 2 km S Andrés, s.l., 2; Tres Ojos, s.l., 1; 30 km NW Santo Domingo, 122 m, 4; *Monseñor Nouel:* 17 km SW Piedra Blanca, 854 m, 1; *Sánchez Ramírez:* 1 km NE Las Lagunas, 183 m, 1; *San Cristóbal:* 6 km NW Cambita Garabitos, 488–519 m, 2; 11 km NW Cambita Garabitos, 671 m, 3; *Peravia:* 2 km SW Rancho Arriba, 671 m, 1; *Azua:* 4 km S Peralta, 366 m, 1; 5 km S Peralta, 305 m, 3; 5 km SW Monte Bonito, 702 m, 1; 13 km NW El Cruce del Quince, 1; *Independencia:* 5 km S Angel Feliz, 1; 4–7 km NE El Aguacate, 519–732 m, 5; 1 km NE El Aguacate, 976 m, 1; *Baoruco:* 14 km N Neiba, 671 m, 3; *Barahona:* west slope, Sierra Martín García, 610 m, 1; Barahona, s.l., 3; 5 km SE, 3 km W Barahona, 183 m, 2; 8 km NNE Polo, 793 m, 1; 12 km SW Barahona, 427 m, 1; 9 km NW Enriquillo, 671 m, 1; 3 km NW Enriquillo, 244 m, 1; *Pedernales:* 18 km NE Cabo Rojo, 366 m, 1; 23 km NE Cabo Rojo, 488 m, 1; 26 km NE Cabo Rojo, 732 m, 2; Las Abejas, 11 km NW Aceitillar, 1220 m, 1; Las Abejas, 12 km NW Aceitillar, 1129 m, 3; 1 km N Aceitillar, 1281 m, 2; 0.6 km SE Los Arroyos, 1098 m, 1; 5 km NE Los Arroyos, 1617 m, 1; Mencía, 397 m, 2; 17 km NW Oviedo, 183 m, 2.

10. *Polythrix octomaculata decussata* Ménétriés, 1855

TL Haiti.

We have never collected *P. o. decussata.* Riley (1975:164) noted that the species occurs "only in Haiti," which is very unlikely. Hall (1925:189) did not collect specimens. Neither Cucurullo (1959) nor Marión Heredia (1974) listed the species, and Schwartz (1983a) did not collect Haitian specimens. There seem to be 2 possibilities: (1) *P. o. decussata* may be extremely rare on Hispaniola, or (2) the species may be incorrectly attributed to Hispaniola. Considering the time of description (1855) of *P. o. decussata,* it is possible that the original material was improperly labeled as to provenance.

11. *Astraptes talus* Cramer, 1777

TL Suriname.

FW 23–28 mm.

I have no specimens of this species from Haiti and only 39 from the República Dominicana. These were collected or observed in January (6), March (5), April (3), June (9), July (3), August (6), September (1), October (6), November (1), and December (1), at 18 localities. The elevational range is from sea level (Cabrera) to 1007 m (La Palma). All *A. talus* were taken in or near mesic forest or *cafetales-cacaotales*, in 2 cases (Loma Leonor, Neiba) associated with rivers (Río Toma, Río Danza). Temperatures were between 26°C and 38°C, and times between 0915 and 1600 h.

Riley (1975:165) considered *A. talus* "Not common" throughout its Antillean range of Cuba, Hispaniola, Jamaica, Puerto Rico, and St. Vincent. Hall (1925:189) listed only La Vega as a locality and considered the species "scarce." Bates (1935a:209) examined only 1 specimen from Cuba and noted the existence of other Cuban specimens in the National Museum of Natural History (USNM). Comstock (1944:550) studied only 2 Puerto Rican specimens. Pinchon and Enrico (1969:132–133) noted the occurrence of *A. talus* on Martinique and St. Vincent: they had captured only 1 specimen on Martinique (although both of them lived on that island and had collected butterflies extensively and in "toutes les époques de l'année"). Brown and Heineman (1972:368) knew of only 1 record from Jamaica and apparently were dubious that the species was resident there.

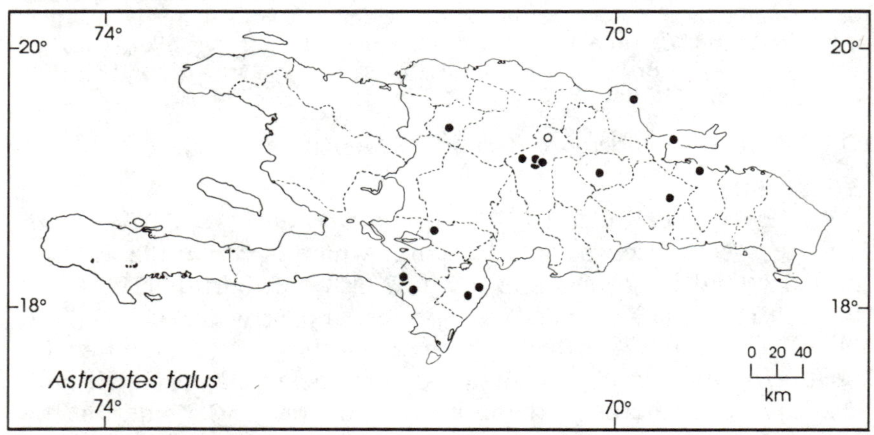

All of the above suggests strongly that *A. talus* is uncommon on the Antilles. Note also that our 6 August specimens are the result of 9 years of field work in that month—hardly a reassuring number of skippers. But on a brief visit to Puerto Rico in ix.1982, Wisor and I secured 3 specimens 4.8 km S Florida, 244 m, in mesic forest on karst topography (38°C, 1215–1500 h). This late date suggested that *A. talus* emerges later in the year (= August-

September) than most other skippers, and in fact late emergence seems also to be the case with *A. a. anausis* and *A. h. heriul* (see beyond). The short series collected by Raburn and me in September-November 1983 reinforces the above scenario as far as *A. talus* is concerned. The species appears to be univoltine, the time of eclosion is summer and fall (June-October). The March-April specimens suggest a spring brood as well, but it may be a partial brood. The March specimens are very worn, the April specimens fresh.

Unlike other *Astraptes*, *A. talus* lands most often on the upper (in contrast to lower) surfaces of leaves, although it lands in the latter position occasionally (always so in the Puerto Rican individuals). At Cabrera, we took 6 *A. talus* (along with 1 *A. a. anausis*) on 28.x.1983 in a karst region. There was a large sinkhole, well wooded in its depths and along its periphery, surrounded by pasture, with a few scattered trees about 3 m from the sinkhole-associated forest. The edge of the sinkhole forest was draped with luxuriant vines, and the *A. talus* were flying between this drapery and a single, isolated *Citrus* tree. The tree had an epiphytic vine with huge, elongate yellow flowers, which seemed to interest the skippers since they landed on the leaves of this pendant vine; there were no attempts to feed on the yellow flowers. During the hour that we collected at this precise locality, the skippers were seen flying above (6 m) the vines at the edge of the sinkhole forest, often 2 or more at once, indulging in territorial whirling. The skippers might land high in the vines or fly rapidly to the isolated *Citrus* tree with its vine and land on the leaves of the latter. The behavior was so ritualistic that, once an individual skipper was noted, it was merely a matter of patience to secure it, since individuals returned repeatedly to the same landing site. A visit to this same locality on 22.iii.1984 yielded 1 more specimen as well as sightings of a few others behaving in the same manner.

At Sánchez, the series of 3 *A. talus* was taken (11.viii.1981) in a *cafetal;* 2 other individuals were seen at this same locality, deep in the pseudoforest, on 25.x.1983. At La Palma, we have seen or taken only 2 individuals (29.ix.1983) after 13 visits there in 1980–86; the skippers were flying along the edge of a well-shaded *cafetal* and landed repeatedly on the upper surfaces of *Coffea* leaves 3 m above the ground. It seems likely that *A. talus* is not truly uncommon.

Astraptes talus has been taken feeding on *Bougainvillea glabra* (1.7 km S Jarabacoa, twice) and *Ageratum conyzoides* (Cabo Rojo, twice).

Specimens: República Dominicana: Santiago Rodríguez: Loma Leonor, 18 km SW Monción, 534 m, 1: *María T. Sánchez:* 6 km S Cabrera, s.l., 7; *Samaná:* 6.9 km NE Sánchez, 336 m, 3; *La Vega:* La Palma, 19 km W Jayaco, 1007 m, 1; Jarabacoa, 530 m, 3; 1.7 km S Jarabacoa, 488 m, 2; 1 km W Manabao, 793 m, 5; *Hato Mayor:* 7 km E Sabana de la Mar, 1; 4 km E Sabana de la Mar, 1; *Monte Plata:* 8 km NE Bayaguana, 1; *Sánchez Ramírez:* 1 km NE Las Lagunas, 183 m, 1; *Baoruco:* 11 km N Neiba, 519 m, 4; *Barahona:* 5 km SE, 6.4 km W Barahona, 488 m, 1; 10 km NW Paraíso, 2; 8–10 km NW Paraíso, 2 (MPM); *Pedernales:* 1 km SE Banano, 488 m, 1; Mencía, 397 m, 1; 26 km NE Cabo Rojo, 732 m, 2.

Sight record: República Dominicana: La Vega: La Palma, 19 km W Jayaco, 1007 m—1 seen, 17.vii.

12. *Astraptes anaphus anausis* Godman and Salvin, 1896

TL St. Vincent.

FW 25–30 mm.

Like *A. talus, A. a. anausis* is uncommon on Hispaniola in summer. My 24 specimens are from both countries and from both north and south islands, with the elevational range between sea level (Terrier Rouge, Cabrera) and 488 m (Río Bao). Temperatures varied between 27°C (Samaná, Las Lagunas) and 37°C (Río Bao), and times between 0915 and 1530 h.

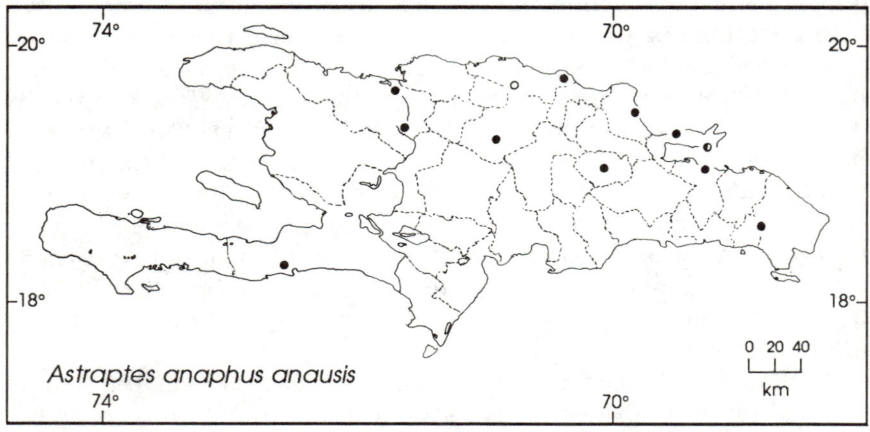

This skipper is an inhabitant of mesic forest (Las Lagunas, Sabana de la Mar, Cabrera), mesic oases (Terrier Rouge), xeric forest (La Romana), or *cafetales-cacaotales* (Río Bao); 1 specimen was taken (Lavaneau) in the artificial "woods" surrounding a restored and occupied French colonial *habitation*. Seven specimens were taken in August, 11 in November, 3 in March, and 1 each in April, May, July, and October. There is a sight record from December. The April specimen is in pristine condition, and most of the others are fresh except for 2 from March, 1 from November, and 1 from October. The peak months for *A. a. anausis* are in late summer to fall (August-November). Brown and Heineman (1972:371) considered *A. a. anausis* rare in Jamaica, where the records are peculiarly clustered at the eastern end of the island except for 2 further west in St. Catherine Parish. Their dates center around February (6), with 2 from March and 1 from August. There may well be 2 broods of *A. a. anausis*, 1 in March-April, another in August-November.

At Las Lagunas, in a fine stand of hardwood forest at the edge of karst topography, *A. a. anausis* was abundant on 1–2.xi.1983. On the first date, the weather was both overcast and raining; still, *A. a. anausis* were observed during the heavy rain, resting on the upper sides of exposed leaves of low (1 m) shrubs. On the following day, these skippers were observed flying along roads, paths, and in clearings in the forest, usually landing on the upper sides of leaves, but occasionally on the underside, much as in the fashion of *A. talus* but not as in *A. h. heriul.* The specimens from Cabrera were associated with *A. talus* (see account of that species).

Astraptes a. anausis has been taken feeding on *Bidens pilosa* in an open field adjacent to xeric forest (La Romana), on *Tournefortia hirsutissima* (Sosúa), and on *Lantana ovatifolia* (Sabana de la Mar).

Specimens: Haiti: Nord: 12.3 km E Terrier Rouge, s.l., 2; *l'Ouest:* Lavaneau, 229 m, 1; *República Dominicana: Dajabón:* Restauración, 400– 800 m, 2; *Puerto Plata:* 9 km SE Sosúa, 15 m, 2; *Santiago:* Río Bao, 8 km SE Montones Abajo, 488 m, 4; *María T. Sánchez:* 6 km S Cabrera, s.l., 2; *Samaná:* 13.2 km NE Sánchez, 92 m, 1; *Hato Mayor:* 7 km E Sabana de la Mar, 1; *La Altagracia:* 16 km NE La Romana, 61 m, 1; *Sánchez Ramírez:* 1 km NE Las Lagunas, 183 m, 11.

Sight record: República Dominicana: Samaná: 4.5 km E Samaná—1 seen, 23.xii.

13. *Astraptes christyi* Sharpe, 1899

TL La Vega, Prov. de la Vega, República Dominicana.

FW males 24–30 mm, females 26–31 mm.

I have no specimens from Haiti and 28 from the República Dominicana, almost all of which were native-collected. The exceptions are from Tenares and La Palma. The first was taken on 9.vii.1981 in a *cafetal-cacaotal;* the day was very hot and humid, but no temperature or collecting time was taken. The skipper was 1 of many *Astraptes* taken; all others are *A. h. heriul*, which is very abundant at this site. The habit of alighting on the upper side of a leaf, typical of some other *Astraptes*, occurs in this species as well. The La Palma individual was taken on 21.xii.1986 at 1100–1400 h, on a bright and sunny day, at 30°C, in a high-canopied *cafetal.*

One of the Jarabacoa specimens was taken at 1000–1200 h (no temperature).

All the Jarabacoa specimens were collected by locals, and there are no data on temperatures, times, or habitats. The Jarabacoa region is predominantly pinewoods with many mesic, deciduously forested ravines, creeks, and a river valley.

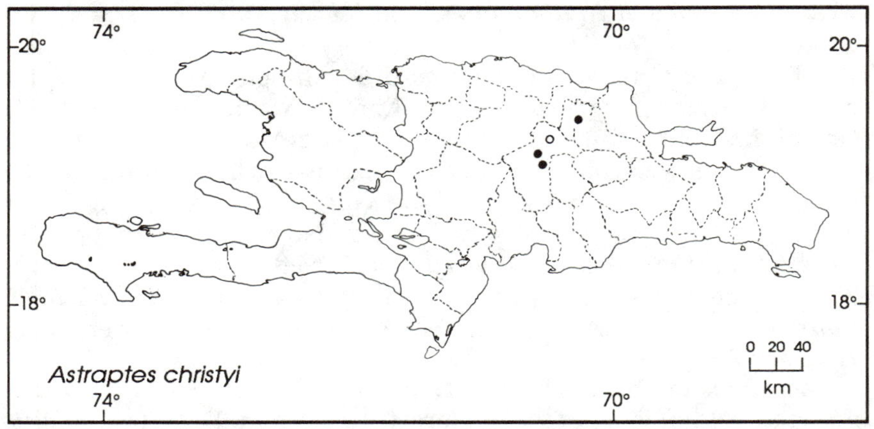

Most specimens (17) are from July, with 8 from June and 1 each from August and December.

Astraptes christyi appears to be uncommon on Hispaniola. Bates (1935a:211) reported only 3 Cuban specimens of the related *A. xagua* in the MCZ, and Riley (1975:165) noted 3 Oriente localities for the species on that island.

Specimens: República Dominicana: Duarte: 10 km SE Tenares, 183 m, 1; *La Vega:* La Palma, 19 km W Jayaco, 1007 m, 1; Jarabacoa, 530 m, 26.

14. *Astraptes habana heriul* Mabille and Boullet, 1912

TL "Brazil"; restricted to "San Domingo" by Evans (1952:112).

FW 23–30 mm.

In contrast to other Hispaniolan *Astraptes*, *A. h. heriul* is often locally very common. Its habitat is regularly mesic forest or pseudoforest, and my notes repeatedly refer to this sort of situation. Occasionally, these skippers are found in mixed pine-deciduous woods (Comendador, Buena Vista) or transitional forest (Sierra Martín García). At other localities specimens have been netted at a clearing in broadleaf forest (Jayaco) and in an open area adjacent to a *cafetal* (Cambita Garabitos). All these situations are exceptional, and the skippers are closely associated with mesic stands of deciduous trees, including *Coffea* and *Theobroma*. The long series from Tenares and San Francisco de Macorís are from just such situations. *Astraptes h. heriul* is known from sea level (Cruce de Rincón), but the species is not common at such low elevations. *Astraptes h. heriul* is more common at and above elevations of about 122 m. The highest localities are Las Abejas and El Veinte (1220 m), where these skippers were abundant in and adjacent to mesic broadleaf forest. Temperatures of activity varied between 27°C (Cambita Garabitos, La Palma, Las Abejas, Las Lagunas) and 40°C (Tenares), and times between 0900 and 1620 h. Most specimens and sightings have been in July (51) and August (57), with fewer in April (12), June (21), March (10), October (6), and November and December (2 each). This suggests a late-summer peak in eclosion.

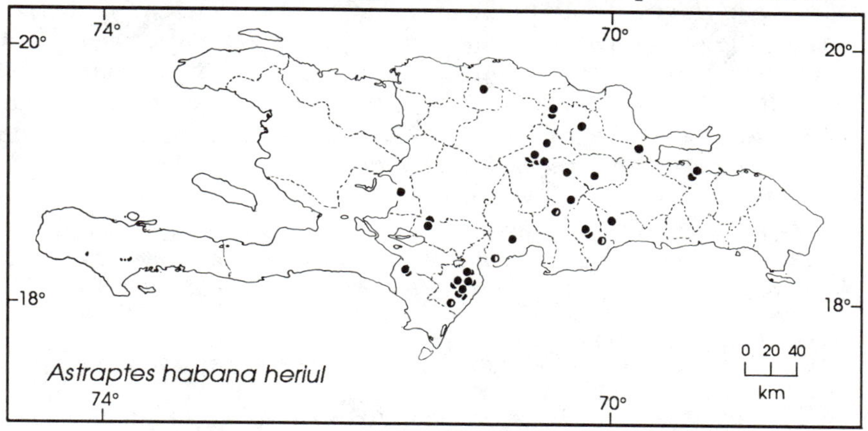

Astraptes h. heriul, like *A. christyi* but unlike *A. talus* and *A. a. anausis*, regularly lands on the underside of leaves with the head pointing downward; these skippers rarely land on the upper sides of leaves, and then especially on *Musa*. At Las Abejas, 1 *A. h. heriul* was taken as it sunned with wings open on a leaf (1 m above the ground) along the road through mesic canopy forest. At Cambita Garabitos, we observed 2 copulating pairs on 19.vi; in the same area the skippers were avidly feeding on *Inga vera* (Fabaceae). Elsewhere, *A. h. heriul* was seen feeding on *Tournefortia hirsutissima* (Peralta, El Veinte), *Bougainvillea glabra* (Jarabacoa, 1.7 km S Jarabacoa), *Leonurus sibericus* (Lamiaceae) at Monteada Nueva, and *Palicourea barbinervia* (Rubiaceae) at Jamao al Norte. Although bright and sunny days are favored for activity, *A. h. heriul* is often active under overcast or alternately sunny and overcast conditions. Two *A. h. heriul* were seen "cartwheeling" about each other in an open grassy field adjacent to mesic woods (Rancho Arriba, 17.viii,

36°C, 1145–1330 h).

An unusual record of predation on *A. h. heriul* is that of a domestic chicken (*Gallus gallus*) taking a skipper that was perched on a leaf 0.3 m above the ground.

The lack of records for *A. h. heriul* in Haiti is indeed very puzzling. In the 15.7 man-months spent collecting in Haiti, we often collected in *caféières* and moderate-elevation pseudoforest but never saw an individual. Although Haiti has suffered immense deforestation (Schwartz, 1980b), and this may well have played a role in the rarity of *A. h. heriul* in that country, I cannot visualize any reason for this species to be absent, for instance, from the regions about Plaisance and Carrefour la Mort in the north, or Béloc-Découzé in the south, to name only 3 of several apparently suitable places. The presumed larval food plant (*Erythrina;* Fabaceae) is not a common plant in either country (although it is often used in the República Dominicana as a "living fence" within *cafetales-cacaotales*), so invoking the absence of this plant as a reason for the Haitian rarity or absence of *A. h. heriul* is not a completely satisfactory solution.

Specimens: República Dominicana: Elías Piña: La Laguna, 10 km S Comendador, 732 m, 2; *Puerto Plata:* 11 km N Cruce de Guayacanes, 275 m, 1; *Espaillat:* 14 km SE Jamao al Norte, 549 m, 3; 20 km SW Jamao al Norte, 793 m, 9; *La Vega:* Buena Vista, 11 km NE Jarabacoa, 630 m, 1; La Palma, 19 km Jayaco, 1007 m, 1; 10 km W Jayaco, 915 m, 4; Jarabacoa, 530 m, 6; 1.7 km S Jarabacoa, 530 m, 2; 5 km SE Jarabacoa, 595 m, 1; *Monseñor Nouel:* Bonao, 153 m, 1; 14 km SW Piedra Blanca, 427 m, 6; *Duarte:* 10 km SE Tenares, 183 m, 30; 12 km SE San Francisco de Macorís, 19: *María T. Sánchez:* 1 km S Cruce de Rincón, s.l., 5; *Sánchez Ramírez;* 1 km NE Las Lagunas, 183 m, 12; *Hato Mayor:* 7 km E Sabana de la Mar, 1; 6 km N El Valle, 2; *Dist. Nac.:* 30 km NW Santo Domingo, 122 m, 11; *San Cristóbal:* 11 km NW Cambita Garabitos, 671 m, 3; 6 km NW Cambita Garabitos, 488 m, 6; *Azua:* 5 km S Peralta. 305 m, 2; *Baoruco:* 14 km N Neiba, 671 m, 3; 1 km NW El Veinte, 1220 m, 1; *Barahona:* Polo, 702 m, 5; 3 km NNE Polo, 854 m, 5; 12 km SW Barahona, 427 m, 1; 22 km SW Barahona, 1098 m, 1; 5 km SE, 6.4 km W Barahona, 488 m, 3; 1.8 km W Monteada Nueva, 1007 m, 20; 1.3 km W Monteada Nueva, 1007 m, 1; 8 km NW Paraíso, 153 m, 26 (19 MPM); 8–10 km NW Paraíso, 1 (MPM); 10 km NW Paraíso, 244 m, 1; *Pedernales:* Las Abejas, 11 km NW Aceitillar, 1220 m, 1; Las Abejas, 12 km NW Aceitillar, 1129 m, 3.

Sight records: República Dominicana: Puerto Plata: 11 km N Cruce de Guayacanes, 290 m—1 seen, 19.vii; *Espaillat:* 20 km SW Jamao al Norte, 793 m—1 seen, 24.vii; *María T. Sánchez:* Cruce de Rincón, s.l.—1 seen, 28.x; *Sánchez Ramírez:* 1 km NE Las Lagunas, 183 m—1 seen, 14.iv; *Monseñor Nouel:* Bonao, 153 m—2 seen, 14.iv; *San Cristóbal:* 3 km S Hato Damas, 92 m—1 seen, 18.iv; *Peravia:* 2 km SW Rancho Arriba, 686 m—2 seen, 17.viii; *Barahona:* west slope, Sierra Martín García, 488 m—1 seen, 13.viii; Polo, 702 m—2 seen, 23.vi; 9 km NW Enriquillo, 671 m—1 seen, 5.vii.

15. *Burca stillmani* Bell and Comstock, 1948

TL Río Yaque, 10 mi. (16 km) S Monte Cristi, Prov. de Monte Cristi, República Dominicana.

FW males 13–16 mm, females 16–17 mm.

Riley (1975:168) listed 2 Dominican localities (Monte Cristi, Monserrate) for this small skipper, and 1 (Port-au-Prince) in Haiti. Dates are February-July. Schwartz (1983a: 61) noted 2 Haitian specimens, 1 from Les Poteaux and the other from Boutilliers Road. Since that time we have taken many more specimens. Months are January (1), March (8), April (8), May (12), June (7), July (4), August (9), October (1), and December (2). Elevations are from sea level (Fond Parisien, Source Matelas, Playa Bayahibe) to 915 m (Boutilliers Road). All specimens except those from Boutilliers Road and Polo are from xeric situations —*Acacia* desert and *Acacia* forest, along the edges of a xeric forest (Playa Bayahibe), transitional forest (El Aguacate), and an oasis (Villa Vásquez). Temperatures varied from 27°C (Fond Parisien) to 38°C (Peralta). Times of activity were between 0900 and 1530 h.

The records for Boutilliers Road and Polo are anomalous, since most other specimens are from between sea level and 183 m. *Burca stillmani* is almost exclusively an inhabitant of desert or arid regions. Its known distribution is the Cul de Sac plain and the western portion of the valley of the Rivière d'Ennery in Haiti. In the República Dominicana, *B. stillmani* is known from the western portion of the Valle de Cibao, the Valle de Neiba and the Llanos de Azua, the Valle de San Juan, the northern mesic slopes of the Sierra de Baoruco, the Península de Barahona, the extreme eastern end of the island (Playa Bayahibe), and a single locality in the east-central region (Maimón).

Bell and Comstock (1948:13) noted the occurrence, in female *B. stillmani*, on the unhw of "an overscaling which varies from red brown to dark red which sharply contrast with the color of the rest of the wing, but in some individuals this overscaling may be entirely absent." In most females, the unhw has an incomplete raspberry or purplish red, broad postdiscal crescent that follows the curvature of the hw margin, as well as a pair of similarly colored costal blotches and a single basal truncate curved bar. This pattern is quite striking and much more complex than simple overscaling.

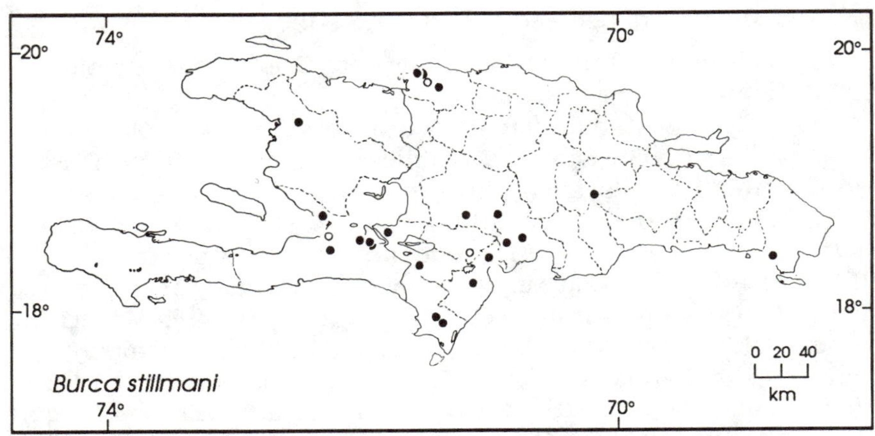

We have taken *B. stillmani* feeding on the flowers of *Croton linearis* (Euphorbiaceae) at Monte Cristi (3 occasions), *C. barahonensis* at Vallejuelo, *Tournefortia hirsutissima* at Peralta (several observations), *Bidens pilosa* at Tábara Abajo and Peralta (many observations), and *Melochia tomentosa* (Sterculiaceae) at La Canoa and Tábara Abajo.

Specimens: Haiti: l'Artibonite: 4.6 km E Les Poteaux, 183 m, 2; *l'Ouest:* 5 km SE Source Matelas, s.l., 2; Boutilliers Road, 915 m, 1; 2 km W Fond Parisien, s.l., 1; 2 km SE Fond Parisien, s.l., 3; 4 km SE Fond Parisien, s.l., 1; *República Dominicana: Monte Cristi:* 1 km SE Monte Cristi, 7; 4 km SE Monte Cristi, 13; 4 km NW Villa Vásquez, 61 m, 3; *La Altagracia:* 2.5 km SE Playa Bayahibe, s.l., 1; *Monseñor Nouel:* 6 km SE Maimón, 122 m, 1; *Azua:* Tábara Abajo, 1; 5 km S Peralta, 305 m, 9; 2 km SE La Canoa, 397 m, 1; *San Juan:* 9 km E Vallejuelo, 610 m, 2; *Independencia:* 4 km NW Tierra Nueva, s.l., 1; 4–7 km NE El Aguacate, 519–824 m, 1; *Barahona:* 8 km ESE Canoa, s.l., 1; 8 km NNE Polo, 793 m, 1; *Pedernales:* 17 km NW Oviedo, 183 m, 1; 4 km NW Tres Charcos, 4.

16. *Burca hispaniolae* Bell and Comstock, 1948

TL Frères, Dépt. de l'Ouest, Haiti.

FW males 16–17 mm, females 17–20 mm.

Of the 2 species of Hispaniolan *Burca*, *B. hispaniolae* is more abundant and more widely distributed than *B. stillmani.* Like its congener, *B. hispaniolae* is primarily an inhabitant of arid situations, but it is more tolerant of less harsh environments. One female was taken adjacent to a *caféière* during a light rain (Dondon), others were secured along the edge of a mesic oasis in the Cul de Sac plain (Croix des Bouquets), 4 were taken in mesic woods along the Río Toma (Monción), and 1 was secured in mixed pine-deciduous woods (Loma Leonor). The most surprising specimens are those from El Aguacate, 2 of which were taken on a road through forest at 793 m. Even more intriguing is a specimen from Canote Mine at 1495 m in open pine forest; the record stands alone geographically and altitudinally. The lowest elevation is sea level. Most field notes associate this species with *Acacia*. On 1 occasion, several individuals were taken while they fed on an unidentified white-flowering shrub, about 2 m high; this area (Copey) had abundant *Cordia* sp. and *Lantana ovatifolia*, but the skippers were not observed on these plants. *Burca hispaniolae* has been taken on *Bidens pilosa* (Tábara Abajo, Los Quemados, Peralta), *Lantana involucrata* (Puerto Escondido), *Antigonon leptopus* (Azua, 2 occasions), *Pithecellobium circinale* (Fabaceae) (Canoa), *Ageratum conyzoides* (Peralta, Vallejuelo), *Croton linearis* (Copey, Monte Cristi), *Croton barahonensis* (2 km NE and 2 km N Cabo Rojo, Vallejuelo [2 occasions]), and *Tournefortia hirsutissima* (Peralta). One *B. hispaniolae* was taken drinking from mud (Loma Leonor, Río Toma). Temperatures of activity varied between 26°C (Peralta) and 38°C (Copey, Loma Leonor, Vallejuelo, Peralta), and times of activity between 0840 and 1725 h. Although *B. hispaniolae* seems most abundant in bright and sunny weather, it has been taken twice under overcast conditions (Vallejuelo, Peralta).

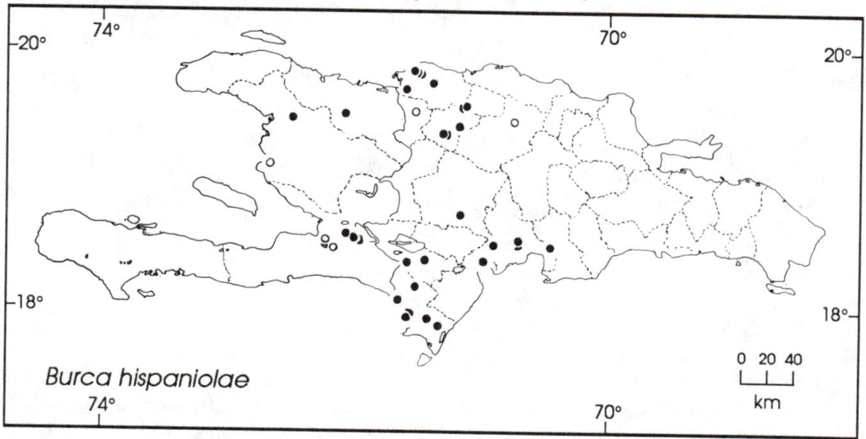

Riley (1975:170) gave 4 Haitian and 2 Dominican localities for this skipper; the Haitian ones are (with the exception of Pétionville) all in lowland arid regions (including the Cul de Sac plain), and the Dominican sites are associated with the western Valle de Cibao. *B. hispaniolae* also also occurs in Haiti in the arid western portion of the valley of the Rivière d'Ennery and on the Massif du Nord and in the República Dominicana on the northern front of the Cordillera Central (Moncíón), in the dry eastern part of the valley between the 2 ranges of the Sierra de Neiba, in the arid Llanos de Azua, and on the Península de Barahona (and into the Sierra de Baoruco uplands near Aceitillar). One surprising record is from mesic forest (Santo Domingo). *Burca hispaniolae* and *B. stillmani* have been taken syntopically at Fond Parisien, 1 km and 4 km SE Monte Cristi, Tábara Abajo, 5 km S Peralta, Vallejuelo, El Aguacate, 17 km NW Oviedo, and Tres Charcos. Most of these xeric localities are open *Acacia* forest, but at Oviedo, 3 specimens were taken in a ravine with dense xeric hardwood forest, and at El Aguacate, these skippers were abundant in openings in transitional xeric-mesic forest.

One of these localities of syntopy (5 km S Peralta) is quite interesting. The road from Azua to Peralta passes at first through xeric lowland *Acacia* scrub and woods as it gradually ascends. About 6 km S Peralta, the road crosses the Río Jura and one suddenly parallels that river in a deciduous-wooded river valley along which the road proceeds to Peralta. At the 5 km S Peralta locality, the collector is at a point of transition between xeric and mesic habitats, with well-forested hillslopes on the east side of the road and overgrown and irrigated fields on the left. The roadsides have many *Bidens pilosa* and *Lantana reticulata*, along with some *Lantana ovatifolia* and *Ixora* sp. and several large clumps of *Tournefortia hirsutissima*. The butterfly fauna at this locality is extremely diverse, with large numbers of most species, due in part to the transitional nature of the locality as far as habitat is concerned and the abundance of those plants that often serve as nectar sources. The occurrence of xerophilic *B. stillmani* (9) and more tolerant *B. hispaniolae* (27) results from the xeric-mesic interface at this locality.

Specimens: Haiti: Nord: 1.8 km S Dondon, 366 m, 1; *l'Artibonite:* 7.4 km E Les Poteaux, 1; *l'Ouest:* 2 km W Fond Parisien, s.l., 1; 2 km SE Fond Parisien, s.l., 1; 13 km E Croix des Bouquets, s.l., 3; *República Dominicana: Monte Cristi:* 6 km W Copey, s.l., 17; 1 km SE Monte Cristi, 8; 2 km SE Monte Cristi, 1; 4 km SE Monte Cristi, 2; 4 km NW Villa Vásquez, 61 m, 1; *Valverde:* Río Guarabo, 3 km W Los Quemados, 122 m, 3; *Santiago Rodríguez:* 3 km W Los Quemados, 183 m, 1; Loma Leonor, 18 km SW Moncíón, 534 m, 4; Loma Leonor, 19 km SW Moncíón, 610 m, 1; 15 km SW Moncíón, 320 m, 1; *Azua:* 25 km NE Azua, 92 m, 2; 2.5 km W, 6.6 km N Azua, 183 m, 6; Tábara Abajo, 1; 5 km S Peralta, 305 m, 27; *San Juan:* 9 km E Vallejuelo, 610 m, 40; *Independencia:* 5 km N Puerto Escondido, 427 m, 3; 4–7 km NE El Aguacate, 519–824 m, 10; *Barahona:* 11.5 km ESE Canoa, s.l., 1; *Pedernales:* Pedernales, 1; Cabo Rojo, s.l., 2; 2 km NE Cabo Rojo, s.l., 12; 17 km NW Oviedo, 183 m, 4; 4 km NW Tres Charcos, 3; Canote Mine, 6 km NW Aceitillar, 1495 m, 1.

17. *Cabares potrillo potrillo* Lucas, 1857

TL Cuba.

FW 16–20 mm.

Cabares p. potrillo is widely distributed on Hispaniola but appears to be absent from large areas. This skipper is primarily an inhabitant of mesic situations of low and moderate elevation, such as the grassy edges of forests and pseudoforests. Schwartz (1983a:61–62) considered its Haitian range to be mainly lowland mesic situations and noted its occurrence in local springside woods (Balladé). In the República Dominicana, *C. p. potrillo* has been taken in similar situations but has also been secured in xeric woods (18 km S Peralta, Playa Bayahibe, Punta Cana), and once (Cruce de Guayacanes) in roadside grasses and shrubby growth with no adjacent forest. Brown and Heineman (1972:372) noted that this species occurs on Jamaica in coastal coconut groves and that it flies low in the underbrush; they also stated that it is a slow flyer. I agree with the latter assessment, since individuals, once seen, are easily taken.

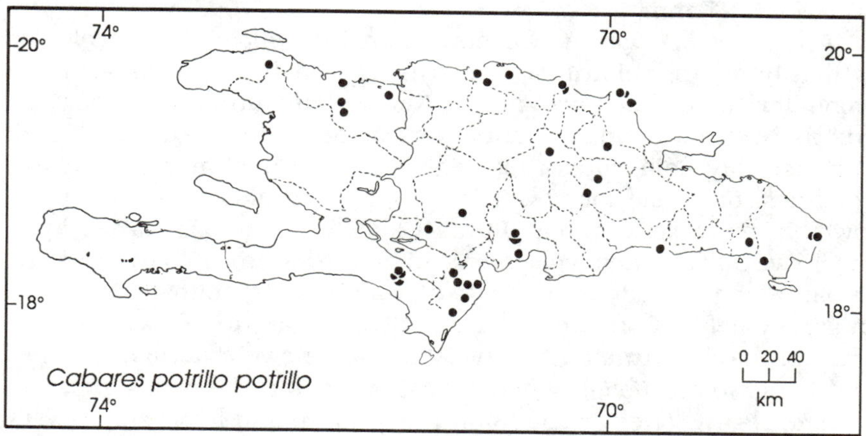

Elevations range from sea level (Terrier Rouge, Punta Cana, Río San Juan, Cabrera, Playa Bayahibe) to 671 m (Neiba). Temperatures varied from 25°C (5 km SE, 3 km W Barahona) to 38°C (Río Cumayasa), and times of activity from 0845 to 1545 h. Most specimens are from August (26), with July (14) and October (10) next in abundance. There are 9 from April, 7 each from June and November, 5 from March, 4 from January, and 2 each from May and December. The species is on the wing during the entire year, with a peak in July-October.

Specimens: Haiti: Nord-Ouest: 0.6 km NW Balladé, 1; *Nord:* Carrefour la

Mort, s.l., 2; 16.5 km E Terrier Rouge, 1; 2.9 km N Dondon, 366 m, 1; 5.6 km SE Dondon, 336 m, 2; *República Dominicana: Puerto Plata:* 12 km N Cruce de Guayacanes, 214 m, 1; 0.6 km NE Estero Hondo, 2; 13 km SE Luperón, 214 m, 1; 9 km SE Sosúa, 15 m, 5; 11 km SE Sosúa, 46 m, 1; *Duarte:* 12 km SE San Francisco de Macorís, 6; *La Vega:* Buena Vista, 11 km NE Jarabacoa, 640 m, 1; *María T. Sánchez:* 9 km NE Río San Juan, s.l., 1; 11 km NE Río San Juan, 2; 6 km S Cabrera, s.l., 4; *La Altagracia:* Punta Cana, s.l., 1; 2 km W Punta Cana, s.l., 1; 1 km N Playa Bayahibe, s.l., 4; *Dist. Nac.:* Punta Caucedo, 2 km W, 2 km S Andrés, s.l., 1; *Sánchez Ramírez:* 1 km NE Las Lagunas, 198 m, 9; *Monseñor Nouel:* 6 km SE Maimón, 122 m, 1; *La Altagracia:* Río Chavón, 10 km NE La Romana, 1; *Azua:* 2.5 km W, 6.6 km N Azua, 183 m, 3; 18 km S Peralta, 122 m, 2; 5 km S Peralta, 305 m, 2; *San Juan:* 9 km E Vallejuelo, 610 m, 1; *Baoruco:* 14 km N Neiba, 671 m, 1; *Barahona:* 10 km W Cabral, s.l., 1; 10 km SSW Cabral, 427 m, 1; 12 km SW Barahona, 427 m, 7; 5 km SE, 3 km W Barahona, 183–397 m, 13; 8 km NW Paraíso, 153 m, 1; 3 km NW Enriquillo, 244 m, 1; *Pedernales:* Mencía, 397 m, 1; El Mulito, 21 km N Pedernales, 214 m, 8; 1 km N Cabeza de Agua, 275 m, 2; 3 km N Cabeza de Agua, 305 m, 1.

18. *Achlyodes papinianus sagra* Evans, 1952

TL Haiti.

FW 21–27 mm.

Achlyodes p. sagra is widespread on Hispaniola. The species is primarily an inhabitant of mesic areas and thus shuns arid regions like the Cul de Sac–Valle de Neiba plain, although it does occur there in more shaded situations or oases in the desert (Fond Parisien). My field notes repeatedly note the habitat as *caféières, cafetales,* or mesic forests. The skipper may also be common in lowland, more xeric woods (Punta Cana, La Romana, Playa Bayahibe); we have taken specimens in a *Citrus* grove (San José de Ocoa), along the edges of a *cafetal* (Cambita Garabitos), and even in grassy fields (Constanza, 11 km NE Río San Juan), where they were probably attracted by the abundant flowers (*Zinnia elegans* and *Lantana ovatifolia*). When at rest or feeding, the wings are held spread; resting sites are often on the ground, and if the soil is wet, the dark purplish coloration blends with the color of the moist soil. The flight is rapid and deliberate and not especially erratic; the skippers are easily taken when resting on the ground or feeding. Forage plants include *Zinnia elegans* (Asteraceae), *Urena lobata* (Malvaceae), *Tournefortia hirsutissima, Cordia globosa* and *C. exarata* (Boraginaceae), *Lantana ovatifolia* (both orange- and white-flowered varieties) and *L. reticulata, Asclepias nivea* (Asclepiadaceae), *Croton barahonensis* (Euphorbiaceae), and an unidentified white-flowered tree at 2.5 km SE Playa Bayahibe.

Elevational distribution is from sea level (Fond Parisien, Playa

Bayahibe, and many other localities) to 1098 m (22 km SW Barahona) in the Sierra de Baoruco and Constanza (Cordillera Central). The latter elevation is exceptional, and there are only a few records from above 610 m; *Achlyodes p. sagra* occurs primarily at low to moderate elevations. Temperatures of collection varied between 24°C (El Aguacate) and 40°C (Tenares, Río San Juan, 1 km N Playa Bayahibe), and times of activity between 0830 and 1700 h. The skippers are about equally abundant in July (61) and August (63); we have also taken specimens in January (6), February (2), March (11), April (6), May (8), June (32), October (6), and December (14). There are imagines present throughout the year; the large numbers from June-August suggest that *A. p. sagra* is univoltine.

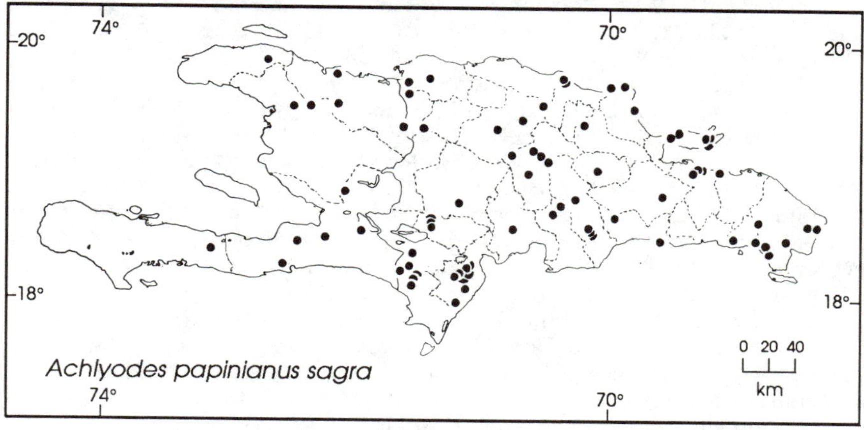

Achlyodes papinianus sagra

I have once more considered the status of *A. p. minor* Comstock, 1944. This subspecies occurs on the Lesser Antilles, the Virgin Islands, and Puerto Rico (although Riley, 1975:171, attributed *A. p. sagra* to Puerto Rico). Schwartz and Jimenez (1982) considered *minor* a very weakly differentiated subspecies. In addition to the 2 Montserrat specimens, I now have 4 specimens from Puerto Rico. In suite, these 6 specimens are indeed small, but the supposed pattern differences between them and *A. p. sagra* are not distinctive when even this short series is compared with my long series from Hispaniola. I am still not certain of the validity of *A. p. minor*, but the material at hand suggests strongly that these eastern *A. papinianus* do not differ in any trenchant ways (including fw length) from more western *A. p. sagra*.

Specimens: Haiti: Nord-Ouest: 1.3 km S Balladé, 31 m, 2; *Nord:* Cap-Haïtien, 1 (MPM); 1.8 km S Dondon, 366 m, 1; *l'Artibonite:* 1.6 km E Carrefour Marmelade, 854 m, 1; 7.4 km E Les Poteaux, 183 m, 1; *l'Ouest:* 1.6 km N Saut d'Eau, 183 m, 2; Boutilliers Road, 732–854 m, 2; Boutilliers Road, 1.9

km W Kenscoff rd., 763 m, 1; 2 km SE Fond Parisien, s.l., 1; Lavaneau, 229 m, 2; 5.0 km S Béloc, 732 m, 1; *Sud:* 6.7 km SW Paillant, 763 m, 1; *República Dominicana: Monte Cristi:* 6 km W Copey, s.l., 5; 4 km NW Villa Vásquez, 61 m, 1; *Dajabón:* 2 km NW El Pino, 183 m, 1; Los Cerezos, 12 km NW Río Limpio, 580 m, 1; Restauración, 400–800 m, 1; *Santiago:* Río Bao, 8 km SE Montones Abajo, 488 m, 5; 7 km SW Santiago, 214 m, 1; 2 km E Pedro García, 417 m, 1; *Puerto Plata:* 9 km SE Sosúa, 15 m, 18; 11 km SE Sosúa, 47–183 m, 2; *Duarte:* 10 km SE Tenares, 183 m, 2; *La Vega:* 1 km S Constanza, 1098 m, 6; 3.5 km E Paso Bajito, 732 m, 2; Jarabacoa, 530 m, 4; La Ciénaga, 915 m, 2; 10 km W Jayaco, 915 m, 1; *Monseñor Nouel:* 14 km SW Piedra Blanca, 427 m, 2; *María T. Sánchez:* Río San Juan, s.l., 2; 11 km NE Río San Juan, s.l., 2; 6 km S Cabrera, s.l., 1; *Samaná:* 6.9 km NE Sánchez, 336 m, 1; 13.2 km NE Sánchez, 92 m, 3; 4.5 km E Samaná, 1; 14.1 km E and N Samaná, 31 m, 1; 2.8 km S Las Galeras, 61 m, 4; *Hato Mayor:* 4 km E Sabana de la Mar, 1; 7 km E Sabana de la Mar, 1; 25 km E Sabana de la Mar, 1; 6 km N El Valle, 1; *La Altagracia:* Punta Cana, s.l., 4; 6 km W Punta Cana, s.l., 1; 0.5–3.5 km W Boca de Yuma, 4; 16 km NE La Romana, 61 m, 9; 2.5 km SE Playa Bayahibe, s.l., 20; 1 km N Playa Bayahibe, s.l., 15; *La Romana:* Río Chavón, 8 km SE La Romana, s.l., 2; Río Cumayasa, 13.5 km W La Romana, 5; *Dist. Nac.:* Punta Caucedo, 2 km W, 2 km S Andrés, s.l., 5; 30 km NW Santo Domingo, 122 m, 2; *Sánchez Ramírez:* 1 km NE Las Lagunas, 183 m, 1; *Monte Plata:* 8 km NE Bayaguana, 2; *San Cristóbal:* 11 km NW Cambita Garabitos, 671 m, 3; 8 km NW Cambita Garabitos, 580 m, 1; 6 km NW Cambita Garabitos, 488 m, 1; *Peravia:* 5 km N San José de Ocoa, 580 m, 2; 2 km SW Rancho Arriba, 671 m, 1; *Azua:* 5 km S Peralta, 305 m, 5; *San Juan:* 9 km E Vallejuelo, 610 m, 2; *Baoruco:* 9 km N Neiba, 366 m, 1; 11 km N Neiba, 519 m, 3; 14 km N Neiba, 671 m, 1; *Independencia:* 4–7 km NE El Aguacate, 519–824 m, 11; *Barahona:* 2 km NW Las Auyamas, 1; 12 km SW Barahona, 427 m, 3; 22 km SW Barahona, 1098 m, 1; 8 km NNE Polo, 793 m, 1; 1.8 km W Monteada Nueva, 1007 m, 6; 1.3 km NW Monteada Nueva, 1037 m, 5; 8 km NW Paraíso, 153 m, 3 (1 MPM): 8–10 km NW Paraíso, 2 (MPM); 3 km NW Enriquillo, 244 m, 1; *Pedernales:* 18 km NE Cabo Rojo, 366 m, 1; 23 km NE Cabo Rojo, 488 m, 1; 26 km NE Cabo Rojo, 732 m, 3; Las Abejas, 12 km NW Aceitillar, 1129 m, 1; Mencía, 397 m, 15.

19. *Anastrus sempiternus dilloni* Bell and Comstock, 1948

TL Pétionville, Dépt. de l'Ouest, Haiti.

FW 20–24 mm.

Brown and Heineman (1972:381) stated that *A. s. dilloni* is "another skipper that one does not see too often" in Jamaica, and the same statement applies almost equally to Hispaniola. My specimens, often 1 per locality, suggest a wide tolerance of habitats, from xeric open areas in the Cul de Sac–Valle de Neiba plain (Fond Parisien, La Furnia) to mixed pine-deciduous woods (Loma Leonor) to upland (Las Abejas, La Laguna, 5 km SE, 6.4 km W Barahona)

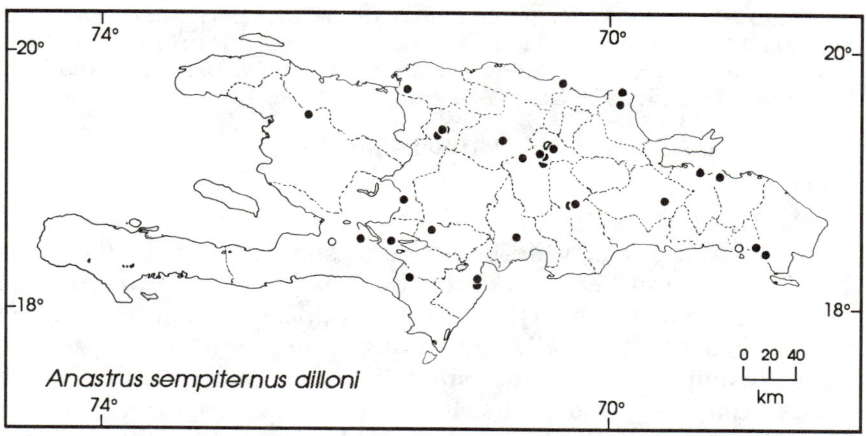

or lowland (Bayaguana) deciduous forest. We have also taken specimens in xeric forest (Playa Bayahibe) and in roadside grasses (Piedra Blanca). The long series (38) from Río Chavón is from an open riverside palm grove with an abundance of flowers. Times of collection varied between 0930 and 1630 h. Temperatures were between 29°C (Sosúa) and 40°C (Playa Bayahibe). Elevation ranges from sea level (Fond Parisien, La Furnia, Río Chavón, Playa Bayahibe) to 1129 m (Las Abejas). Most specimens were collected in July (57), with 9 in June, 7 in April, 4 in March, 6 in August, 2 in May, and 1 each in October and December. Brown and Heineman (1972:381–83) gave Jamaican dates throughout the year. These skippers are most common on Hispaniola in July-August.

Anastrus s. dilloni feeds on the white flowers of *Tournefortia hirsutissima* (Peralta, Playa Bayahibe, Sosúa, Río Bao) and on those of *Morinda citrifolia* (Río Chavón, whence the long series was taken).

Specimens: Haiti: l'Artibonite: 1.6 km E Carrefour Marmelade, 854 m, 1; *l'Ouest:* 2 km SE Fond Parisien, s.l., 1; *República Dominicana: Monte Cristi:* 6 km W Copey, s.l., 1; *Elías Piña:* La Laguna, 10 km S Comendador, 732 m, 1; *Santiago Rodríguez:* Loma Leonor, 19 km SW Monción, 610 m, 1; Loma Leonor, 18 km SW Monción, 534 m, 1; 4.7 km SW Loma Leonor, 732 m, 1; *Puerto Plata:* 9 km SE Sosúa, 15 m, 13; *María T. Sánchez:* 11 km NE Río San Juan, s.l., 1; 14 km SE Río San Juan, 1; *Hato Mayor:* 7 km E Sabana de la Mar, 2; 25 km E Sabana de la Mar, 1; *La Vega:* La Palma, 19 km W Jayaco, 1007 m, 1; Buena Vista, 11 km NE Jarabacoa, 640 m, 1; Jarabacoa, 530 m, 6; 1 km W Manabao, 793 m, 1; 3.5 km E Paso Bajito, 732 m, 6; *Monseñor Nouel:* 17 km SW Piedra Blanca, 854 m, 1; 14 km SW Piedra Blanca, 427 m, 1; *La Altagracia:* 1 km N Playa Bayahibe, s.l., 2; *La Romana:* Río Chavón, 8 km SE La Romana, s.l., 38; *Monte Plata:* 8 km NE Bayaguana, 1; *Azua:* 5 km

S Peralta, 305 m, 8; *Santiago:* Río Bao, 8 km SE Montones Abajo, 488 m, 1; *Baoruco:* 14 km N Neiba, 671 m, 1; *Independencia:* La Furnia, s.l., 1; *Barahona:* 2 km SW Barahona, 122 m, 1; 5 km SE, 6.4 km W Barahona, 488 m, 1; *Pedernales:* Las Abejas, 12 km NW Aceitillar, 1129 m, 1.

20. *Gesta gesta gesta* Herrich-Schäffer, 1863

TL Cuba.

FW 14–16 mm.

Gesta g. gesta is widespread on Hispaniola, where it occurs from the Tiburon Peninsula and the Presqu'île du Nord-Ouest to the eastern tip of the island. This skipper is an inhabitant of wooded situations, usually mesic but at times xeric, and is secured most readily in ecotonal and disturbed areas adjacent to woods—roadsides and paths. It is rather uncommon at sea level (Môle St.-Nicholas, Punta Cana, Boca de Yuma, Río Chavón, Tres Ojos, Río San Juan, Sombrero, La Descubierta, Barahona, Canoa) and occurs as high as 1220 m (Constanza); the latter elevation stands almost alone except for other Cordillera Central localities. Most records are between 305 and 854 m, at moderate elevations. Temperatures varied between 21°C (4 km SSE Constanza) and 42°C (Mencía), and times between 0830 and 1600 h. Most specimens (50) are from July; but *G. g. gesta* has been taken (in smaller numbers) in June (26), March (8), and April (1) and may be locally common in May (19), August (29), October (12), December (7), January (6), and February (2).

Riley (1975:172) stated that *G. g. gesta* is "A butterfly of open country, where it flies low and often settles on the ground with its wings spread flat." This habit distinguishes this species from other small dark skippers; in fact, *G. g. gesta* is one of the few small hesperiids that are attracted to mud puddles. On 4 occasions (El Aguacate, Santiago, Barahona, 11 km N Neiba) we collected individuals in this situation. The flight is low; when disturbed on the ground, *G. g. gesta* circles and returns repeatedly to the same spot.

At 2 localities (Sombrero, La Descubierta) we have taken *G. g. gesta* on *Antigonon leptopus*. At La Ciénaga, these skippers were feeding on *Urena lobata* (Malvaceae) and *Zinnia elegans;* at Río San Juan, *G. g. gesta* foraged on *Wedelia trilobata* (Asteraceae), *Lantana reticulata*, and *Jatropha gossypiifolia* (Euphorbiaceae); at 11 km N Neiba, these skippers were feeding on *Tournefortia hirsutissima*, at Guananico on *Lantana reticulata*, and at Río Bao on *L. ovatifolia*. Habitats were an open but weedy coastal *Cocos* grove, a large grassy and weedy field with scattered clumps of low (3 m) fanpalms, and roadsides through mesic forest.

This is the first record of *G. g. gesta* from Isla Beata.

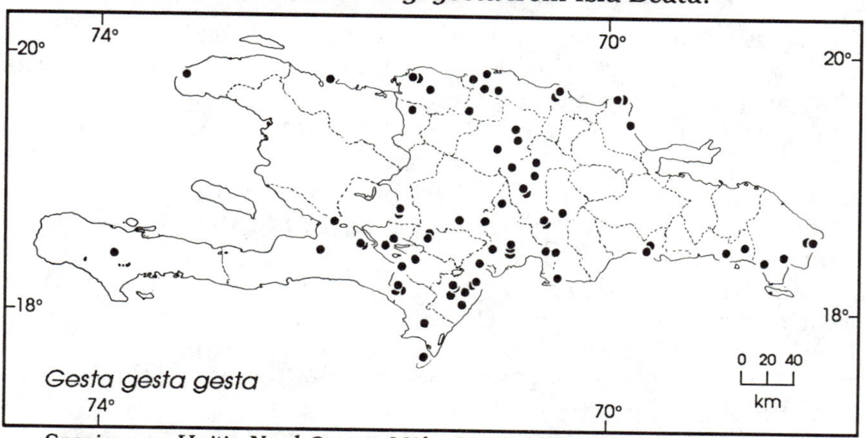

Specimens: Haiti: Nord-Ouest: Môle St.-Nicolas, 1; *Nord:* Cormier Plage, s.l., 2; *l'Ouest:* 5.6 km S Terre Rouge, 366 m, 2; 5 km SE Fond Parisien, s.l., 1; 4 km SE Fond Parisien, s.l., 6; Boutilliers Road, 732–854 m, 3; Boutilliers Road, 854 m, 2; *Sud:* 4.5 km E Cavaillon, 31 m, 1; 4.8 km N Camp Perrin, 244 m, 1; *República Dominicana: Monte Cristi:* 1 km SE Monte Cristi, 6; 4 km SE Monte Cristi, 1; 4 km NW Villa Vásquez, 61 m, 1; *Dajabón:* 2 km NW El Pino, 183 m, 1; *Valverde:* 12 km SW Mao, 244 m, 4; *Elías Piña:* 14 km S Comendador, 976 m, 1; 15 km S Comendador, 976 m, 1; *Puerto Plata:* 11 km N Cruce de Guayacanes, 275 m, 1; 0.6 km NE Estero Hondo, 1; 8 km W Luperón, 1; 10 km W Luperón, 1; 10 km W Guananico, 529 m, 2; 9 km SE Sosúa, 15 m, 1; 5 km NE El Choco, 503 m, 1; *Santiago:* Río Bao, 8 km SE Montones Abajo, 488 m, 1; 8 km E Jánico, 4; 7 km SW Santiago, 17: *La Vega:* Jarabacoa, 530 m, 1; La Ciénaga, 915 m, 3; 1 km S Constanza, 1098 m, 12; 12 km NE Constanza, 1220 m, 1; 4 km SSE Constanza, 1159 m, 1; *Monseñor Nouel:* 17 km SW Piedra Blanca, 854 m, 4; *María T. Sánchez:* 8 km NE Río San Juan, s.l., 1; 9 km NE Río San Juan, s.l., 2; 6 km S Cabrera, s.l., 1; *La Altagracia:* Punta Cana, s.l., 1; 2 km W Punta Cana, s.l., 1; 0.5 km W Boca de Yuma, 3; 2.5 km SE Playa Bayahibe, s.l., 2; Río Chavón, 10 km NE La Romana, 1; *La Romana:* Río Chavón, 8 km SE La Romana, s.l., 1; Río Cumayasa, 13.5 km W La Romana, 1; *Dist. Nac.:* 5 km S San Isidro, 2; Tres Ojos, s.l., 1; *Peravia:* 4 km S Carreras, 1; Sombrero, s.l., 2; 5 km SW Monte Bonito, 702 m, 2; 10 km NW San José de Ocoa, 946 m, 1; 2 km W La Horma, 2; *Azua:* 25 km NE Azua, 92 m, 7; 4 km S Peralta, 366 m, 1; 5 km S Peralta, 305 m, 1; 2.5 km W, 6.6 km N Azua, 183 m, 2; Tábara Abajo, 3; 2 km SE La Canoa, 397 m, 3; *San Juan:* 9 km E Vallejuelo, 610 m, 6; *Baoruco:* 11 km N Neiba, 519 m, 5; 14 km N Neiba, 671 m, 3; *Independencia:* 1 km S La Descubierta, 5; La Furnia, s.l., 3; 8 km W Duvergé, 2; 1 km NE El Aguacate, 976 m, 2; *Barahona:* 11.5 km ESE Canoa, s.l., 1; Polo, 702 m, 7; 8 km NNE Polo, 793 m, 1; 7 km SSW Cabral, 214 m, 1; 9 km SW Cabral, 305 m, 1; Barahona, s.l., 1; 3 km SW Barahona, 3; 2 km SW Barahona, 122 m, 4; 12 km SW Barahona, 427 m, 1; 8 km NW Paraíso, 153 m, 1; *Pedernales:* Mencía, 397 m, 17; 2 km SW Mencía, 275–336 m, 2; 3 km W Aguas Negras, 519 m, 1; 17 km NW Oviedo, 183 m, 1; *Isla Beata:* 1.

The *Ephyriades* and *Erynnis* Problem

There are 3 species of *Ephyriades* (*zephodes* Hübner, *arcas* Drury, and *brunneus* Herrich-Schäffer) and 1 of *Erynnis* (*zarucco* Lucas) that occur on Hispaniola or on islands or the mainland near it. These 4 species present problems of identification, using only the coloration, pattern, or external morphology (i.e., not genitalia). Some of them have puzzled others as well, and the way to begin a discussion of the situation on Hispaniola is to outline what has gone before.

The distributions, as now accepted, and type-localities of the 4 taxa are *zephodes*—Cuba, Hispaniola, Virgin Islands, St.-Barthélémy: apparently accidental on, or incorrectly attributed to, Puerto Rico (Ramos, 1977 and 1982:67), Jamaica (Brown and Heineman, 1972:386), and the Bahamas (Clench and Bjorndal, 1980:67), TL not designated; *arcas*—St. Christopher, Antigua, St. Eustatius (subsp. *arcas;* TL = St. Christopher), Jamaica, Cuba, Puerto Rico, St. Thomas (subsp. *philemon* Fabricius, TL "In America,"; *brunneus*—Bahamas, Cuba (subsp. *brunneus;* TL = Cuba); Jamaica (*jamaicensis*, TL = Jamaica); Florida (*floridensis* Bell and Comstock, TL = Key Largo, Monroe Co., Florida); *zarucco*—Cuba, Hispaniola, eastern North America (TL = Cuba). In addition, but of no concern now, is a Lesser Antillean "subspecies" of *brunneus* (*dominicensis* Bell and Comstock) on Dominica; Brown and Heineman (1972:386) considered *dominicensis* a distinct species. In western North America also occurs *funeralis* Scudder and Burgess, which is at times considered a subspecies of *zarucco* (Riley, 1975:175) and at times a distinct species (Burns, 1964; MacNeill, 1975:529). Clench (1977a:281–82) reported *E. brunneus brunneus* from throughout the Bahamas, but later he and Bjorndal (1980:27) apparently felt that the Little and Great Inagua islands populations were not identical with those from Cuba, and they did not use a trinomen. Finally, Schwartz (1983a:63) recorded *brunneus* (no subspecies) from Haiti, based on 9 specimens from 2 localities. It is from this base, then, that I proceed.

Males. Male *zephodes* and *arcas* (at least *a. philemon*) are inseparable from one another (Riley, 1975:174); both are silky jet black above, with a massive costal groove that extends two-thirds of the way to the apex. Male *brunneus* are very similar to *Ephyriades zephodes* but are not so black, and the forewing has *a circle of very small hyaline spots in the apical third*, and the costal fold reaches little more than halfway along the costa (paraphrased from Riley, 1975:175; italics his). Male *zarucco* are rather shiny dark brown on the up, and the costal fold extends to "just beyond the mid-point" of the costa. Males have very little definite pattern except that the fw has 4 small subapical hyaline spots and a fifth in M3-Cu1. There is a "dark diagonal postdiscal shadow followed by faint submarginal gray sagittate marks and a marginal series of very small pale dots."

Females. Female *zephodes* are dull brown above, with a series of 3 ("narrow subbasal, broad discal, and less well-defined macular postdiscal") bands and a "curved series of small hyaline spots" in spaces R2-R5 to M3-Cu1, and 2 *large spots, in cell and space* Cu1-Cu2, *with their inner edges in line.* Female *arcas* differ in that the spot in Cu1-Cu2 on the fw extends farther toward the wing base than does the spot above it in the cell, i.e., they are *not strictly in line* as they are in *zephodes.* Female *brunneus* are more lilac than *zephodes,* the dark bands are better defined, the hyaline spots in the cell and Cu1-Cu2 are narrow and not markedly larger than the others, and the spot in M3-Cu1 is equidistant between those in M2-M3 and Cu1-Cu2, not nearer that in Cu1-Cu2 as in *zephodes.* Riley (1975:175) stated "nearer 3 [= M3-Cu1]" as in *zephodes,* a contradiction; see his fig. 21. Brown and Heineman (1972:386) noted that female *brunneus* have many hyaline spots in the fw, the spot in Cu2–2A being diagnostic for *brunneus* females, since it is lacking on the females of *E. arcas* and *E. zephodes.* Female *zarucco* are patterned like males, except that the markings are better defined in the females.

It is obvious that, in this quartet of species, females reveal more than males; at least in theory, the females of *zephodes, arcas,* and *brunneus* should be easily distinguishable by the arrangement of hyaline dots in the fw. Female *zarucco* should likewise be identifiable by the up pattern with its submarginal gray sagittate marks and marginal row of very small pale dots. Males of the 4 taxa are somewhat less easily defined, but the up patterns of *zarucco* and *brunneus* are distinctive; male *zephodes* and male *arcas* are apparently not distinguishable on the basis of pattern or morphology.

First, let me dismiss Schwartz's (1983a) records of *brunneus* from Haiti; these specimens, upon reexamination, prove to be 1 male and 8 female *zarucco.* As far as I am aware, *Ephyriades brunneus* does not occur on Hispaniola. A series of 2 male and 15 female *Erynnis zarucco* indicates that this taxon may most easily be distinguished in the following ways, as far as hyaline spot arrangement is concerned: male—a subapical *row* of 4 dots (3 in a row in *brunneus*), the fourth displaced apically, the last at times tiny and obsolescent, and another tiny submarginal dot in M3-

Cu1; occasionally a tiny postdiscal dot in the distal end of the cell. Both females have a complete complement of fw dots (= 6), including the cell-end dot. The net effect of these fw dots in *E. zarucco* is a circlet, usually used to identify *brunneus;* the ground color and markings of *E. zarucco* (especially the pale band of submarginal pale spots on the un) aid greatly in differentiating the 2 species.

Brown and Heineman, as noted above, stated that in female *brunneus* there is a hyaline dot in fw Cu2–2A and that this dot is diagnostic. In a series of 26 female *brunneus floridensis*, this dot is present in 7 (27%) and absent in the remainder (73%). Thus, this character cannot be used without error in diagnosing *all brunneus*. The significance of this will be shown shortly.

The situation with *arcas* and *zephodes* is not so straightforward as with *brunneus* and *zarucco*. Only *zephodes* has been attributed to Hispaniola by recent authors; however, *arcas* occurs to the east on Puerto Rico, and there is a possibility that *arcas* also occurs with *zephodes* in at least the eastern portion of Hispaniola. This contention was reinforced by the fact that in my long series of specimens, not all (females) agreed with the distinguishing characteristics of *zephodes*. In 2 copulating pairs, 1 from eastern República Dominicana and the other from the Cul de Sac in Haiti, the females differ quite strongly from descriptions; in the former case, the hyaline spot in Cu1-Cu2 does not even reach the cell spot (and thus the mesial edges of these spots are not strictly in line as they should be in *zephodes*), and in the Dominican female, the inner edge of this spot projects more basally than that in the cell (the condition in *arcas*). The 2 males from these pairs are undistinguished. Thus, the extent of the basal extension of the spot in Cu1-Cu2 is not a satisfactory diagnostic tool for distinguishing *zephodes*. These 2 females show the 2 extremes; of 51 females, very few show the alignment of the edges of these 2 spots. I refrain from giving actual figures, because in many cases interpretation of this condition is subjective; in others it is not. But the fact remains that strict alignment of the basal edges of these 2 dots is not constant in *zephodes*. In a short series of 4 female *arcas* from Puerto Rico, 3 have the lower spots projecting more basally than the cell spot—but this condition can be matched exactly by many specimens from Hispaniola (= *zephodes*). In some (9) *zephodes* the hyaline spot in Cu1-Cu2 is very reduced (not dumbbell-shaped and constricted as is usually the case), even to only an inconspicuous vertical bar.

Finally, and perhaps most confusingly, 3 Hispaniolan females (*zephodes*) and 1 Puerto Rican female (*arcas*) have a clearly defined round spot in Cu3–2A, a character that is supposedly diagnostic of female *brunneus* (see discussion above).

My conclusions concerning these 3 taxa, then, are that *Ephyriades zephodes* and *Erynnis zarucco* are the only members represented on Hispaniola. This is precisely the situation currently, with the exception of my listing *E. brunneus* from the island. However, the amount of variation in those specimens (females) that I call *E. zephodes* is so great and involves the *diagnostic characteristics* of that taxon and *E. arcas and E. brunneus* as well, that I may well be overlooking specimens of *E. arcas* from Hispaniola. Variation in all 3 taxa is far greater than previously noted.

21. *Ephyriades zephodes* Hübner, 1825

TL not stated.

FW males 17–21, females 19–21 mm.

Ephyriades zephodes is widely distributed on Hispaniola. However, I have many more specimens from the República Dominicana than from Haiti. I also have specimens from Île de la Gonâve and Isla Saona, the first records for these satellite islands. Distribution is from sea level (Ça Soleil, Punta Caucedo, etc.) to 1921 m (Constanza), but the skipper is much more abundant at low to moderate (610 m) elevations. As far as habitats are concerned, *E. zephodes* occurs in a wide spectrum: xeric and mesic woods, *caféières* and *cafetales*, oases, shaded ravines, along roadsides backed by deciduous woods, pine forests, behind beaches in woods and open areas, open scrubby or weedy fields, stands of *Cocos* with scrubby undergrowth along the ocean, open weedy woods, *Citrus* groves, and *Acacia* scrub. We have observed *E. zephodes* feeding on *Antigonon leptopus* (Fabaceae), *Cordia globosa* and *C. integrifolia* (Boraginaceae), *Lantana ovatifolia* and *L. reticulata* (Verbenaceae), *Croton linearis* and *C. barahonensis* (Euphorbiaceae), *Tournefortia hirsutissima* (Boraginaceae), *Bidens pilosa* (Asteraceae), *Morinda citrifolia* (Rubiaceae), *Melochia tomentosa* (Sterculiaceae), *Ageratum conyzoides* (Asteraceae), and an unidentified white-flowered tree (Azua). At Río San Juan, *E. zephodes*, along with other skippers, found the white flowers of a horticultural variety of *L. ovatifolia* especially attractive. On 2 occasions we have seen individuals drinking from the edges of mud puddles in the road (Barahona, Manabao), on another drinking from the sandy bank of a slowly flowing river (Loma Leonor), and 3 times drinking from road surfaces wetted by small creeks (6 km SW Barahona, 5 km SE, 3 km W Barahona, Banano).

Copulating pairs have been taken on 30.iv (Fond Parisien, s.l., 1015–1530 h, 30—34°C), 25.vi (2.5 km SE Playa Bayahibe, s.l., 1230–1330 h, 36°C), 11.vii (Río Chavón, s.l., 1255 h, 33°C, overcast), and 24.xii (Vallejuelo, 610 m, 1030–1415 h, 28°C). Times of activity varied between 0830 and 1700 h, at temperatures between 21°C (Los Arroyos) and 40°C (Río San Juan, 1 km N Playa Bayahibe).

Most specimens are from July (85), with 84 from August and 58 from June. May is represented by 19 specimens, March by 17, and April by 14. There are 12 specimens from October, 15 from December, 5 from January, and 2 from February. *Ephyriades zephodes* is active throughout the year, with a lesser abundance in March-May and a strong peak in summer (June-August). Schwartz's (1983a: 63) assumption that the species is uncommon during the summer is unfounded.

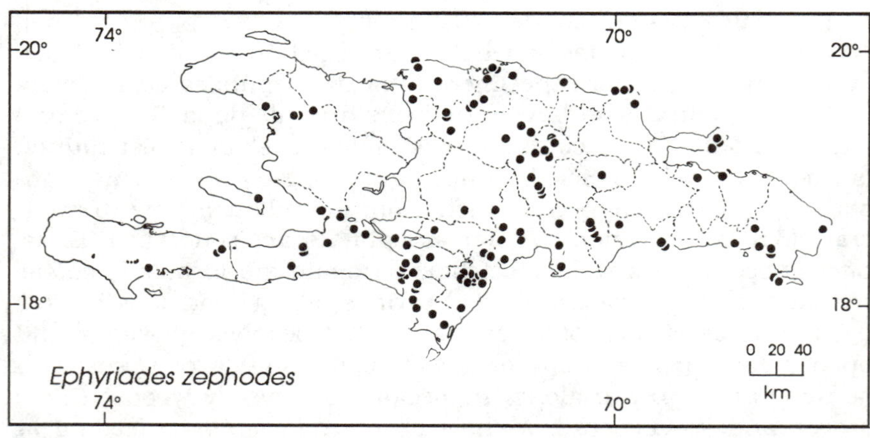

Specimens: Haiti: l'Artibonite: 4.6 km E Les Poteaux, 183 m, 1; 2 km E Les Poteaux, 1; *l'Artibonite:* 12.2 km W Ça Soleil, s.l., 2; 1.6 km E Carrefour Marmelade, 854 m, 1; *l'Ouest:* 2.9–8.5 km S Terre Rouge, 122–1488 m, 1; 5 km SE Source Matelas, s.l., 1; 13 km E Croix des Bouquets, s.l., 1; 2 km SE Fond Parisien, s.l., 6; Boutilliers Road, 1.9 km W Kenscoff rd., 763 m, 1; Boutilliers Road, 732–854 m, 2; 5.4 km S Découzé, 397 m, 2; 0.8 km S Découzé, 702 m, 2; 1.3 km N Béloc, 702 m, 1; *Sud:* 6.7 km SW Paillant, 763 m, 2; 3 km SW Paillant, 793 m, 1; 6 km NW Jacmel, 244 m, 2; 7 km SW Cavaillon, 122 m, 1; *Île de la Gonâve:* Anse-à-Galets, 1; *República Dominicana: Monte Cristi:* 1 km SE Monte Cristi, 2; 6 km W Copey, s.l., 3; 4 km NW Villa Vásquez, 61 m, 2; 4 km N Monte Cristi, s.l., 1; *Dajabón:* 0.5 km N Cañongo, 31 m, 1; *Santiago Rodríguez:* 4.8 km S Zamba, 183 m, 2; 3 km S Zamba, 214 m, 2; Loma Leonor, 18 km SW Monción, 534 m, 3; 3 km W Los Quemados, 183 m, 1; *Valverde:* 3 km W Los Quemados, 122 m, 2; 4 km N Cruce de Guayacanes, 198 m, 1; *Puerto Plata:* 8 km W Luperón, 1; 10 km W Luperón, 1; 13 km SE Luperón, 214 m, 2; 9 km SE Sosúa, 15 m, 14; 11 km N Cruce de Guayacanes,

275 m, 1; *Santiago:* Río Bao, 8 km SE Montones Abajo, 488 m, 1; 8 km E Jánico, 610 m, 5; 7 km SW Santiago, 183 m, 6; *María T. Sánchez:* Río San Juan, s.l., 1; 9 km NE Río San Juan, s.l., 2; 11 km NE Río San Juan, 1; 6 km S Cabrera, s.l., 1; *Samaná:* 2.8 km S Las Galeras, 61 m, 2; 10.5 km S Las Galeras, 15 m, 1; 18.0 km E and N Samaná, s.l., 1; *Hato Mayor:* 25 km E Sabana de la Mar, 1; 6 km N El Valle, 1; *La Altagracia:* Punta Cana, s.l., 2; 1 km N Playa Bayahibe, s.l., 6; 2.5 km SE Playa Bayahibe, s.l., 16; 16 km NE La Romana, 61 m, 2; *La Romana:* Río Chavón, 8 km SE La Romana, s.l., 17; Río Cumayasa, 13.5 km W La Romana, 14; *La Vega:* 1 km S Constanza, 1098 m, 2; 10 km SE Constanza, 1647 m, 2; 13 km SE Constanza, 1403 m, 1; 14 km SE Constanza, 1921 m, 1; 3.5 km E Paso Bajito, 732 m, 1; Jarabacoa, 530 m, 6; Manabao, 825 m, 1; 17 km E Manabao, 1; Buena Vista, 11 km NE Jarabacoa, 641 m, 1; *Dist. Nac.:* 5 km S Aeropuerto Internacional de las Américas, Punta Caucedo, s.l., 1; Punta Caucedo, 2 km W, 2 km S Andrés, s.l., 10; 30 km NW Santo Domingo, 122 m, 1; *Sánchez Ramírez:* 1 km NE Las Lagunas, 183 m, 2; *San Cristóbal:* 3 km W Cambita Garabitos, 366 m, 2; 6 km NW Cambita Garabitos, 519 m, 1; 8 km NW Cambita Garabitos, 580 m, 2; 11 km NW Cambita Garabitos, 671 m, 2; *Peravia:* 5 km N San José de Ocoa, 593 m, 1; 1 km N Fundación de Sabana Buey, 1; *Azua:* 25 km NE Azua, 92 m, 1; 2 km N Yayas de Viajama, 366 m, 2; 2 km SE La Canoa, 397 m, 1; 5 km S Peralta, 305 m, 11; 2.5 km W, 6.6 km N Azua, 183 m, 2; Tábara Abajo, 1; *San Juan:* 9 km E Vallejuelo, 610 m, 31; *Baoruco:* 11 km N Neiba, 519 m, 2; *Independencia:* La Furnia, s.l., 4; 4 km E El Limón, s.l., 1; 2 km S Duvergé, 1; 4–7 km NE El Aguacate, 529–732 m, 2; *Barahona:* west slope, Sierra Martín García, 576 m, 1; 8 km ESE Canoa, 12; 11.5 km ESE Canoa, s.l., 1; Barahona, s.l., 2; 10 km SSW Cabral, 427 m, 1; 7 km SSW Cabral, 214 m, 3; 8 km NNE Polo, 793 m, 1; 2 km SW Barahona, 122 m, 4; 6 km SW Barahona, 122 m, 3; 12 km SW Barahona, 427 m, 1; 5 km SE, 3 km W Barahona, 732 m, 5; 2 km S La Lanza, 1; 5 km SE, 3 km W Barahona, 183–397 m, 11; 3 km NW Enriquillo, 244 m, 2; *Pedernales:* 2 km NE Cabo Rojo, s.l., 1; 23 km NE Cabo Rojo, 488 m, 1; 26 km NE Cabo Rojo, 732 m, 5; Las Abejas, 12 km NW Aceitillar, 1129 m, 1; 1 km SE Banano, 183 m, 4; Mencía, 397 m, 6; 3 km N Cabeza de Agua, 305 m, l: 0.6 km SE Los Arroyos, 1098 m, 4; 5 km NE Los Arroyos, 1617 m, 3; 9 km SE Pedernales, s.l., 1; 17 km NW Oviedo, 183 m, 5; 1.3 km S Tres Charcos, 2; *Isla Saona:* 1.5 km N Mano Juan, 1; 2 km W Mano Juan, 1.

22. *Erynnis zarucco* Lucas, 1857

TL Cuba.

FW males 17–21 mm, females 20–21 mm.

Burns (1964:170) reported *E. zarucco* from Cabaret, Fond Parisien, Manneville, Pétionville, and Port-au-Prince, all in the Dépt. de l'Ouest, Haiti; he examined no Dominican material.

Erynnis zarucco is widely distributed but apparently rather uncommon. With exception of the short series from Découzé and Villa Anacaona, most other localities are represented by single specimens. Elevations range from sea level (Grand-Goâve, Andrés) to *ca.* 1990 m (Loma Nalga de Maco). Habitats are extremely variable, from a mangrove border (Grand-Goâve) to open fields (Constanza), open pinewoods (Hondo Valle) and open, weedy, and bare roadsides (Découzé, ESE Villa Anacaona). One specimen taken (Hondo Valle) was attracted to a puddle in a dirt road. Temperatures of activity varied between 28°C and 42°C, and times between 0900 and 1745 h, the latter along the coast as the sun was setting (Grand-Goâve). Most specimens are from July (22), with 16 in May, 7 in August, and 1 each in June and September. At Hondo Valle, a specimen was taken in an open montane field as it fed on the blue flowers of *Cynoglossum amabile* (Boraginaceae), and another was on *Bidens pilosa* at Villa Anacaona. At the latter locality, several of these skippers were landing briefly on the mud on the bridge over the Río Libón, and others were drinking from a trickle (3 km ESE Villa Anacaona, along the Carretera International).

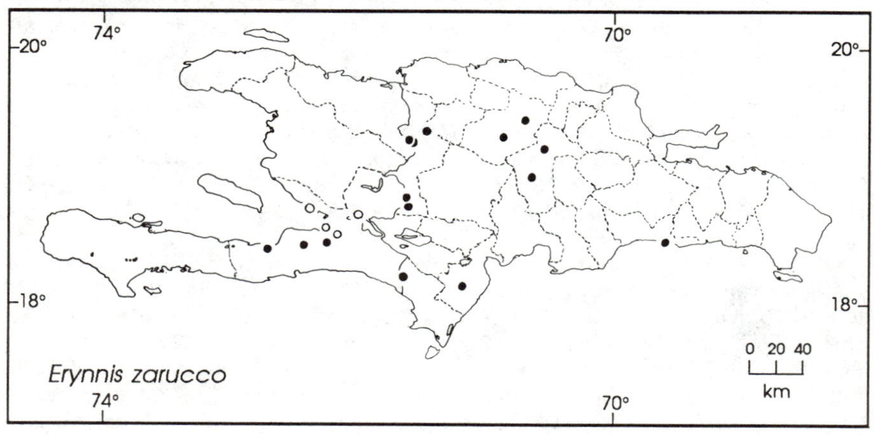

Specimens: Haiti: l'Ouest: 5.4 km S Découzé, 397 m, 8; Boutilliers Road, 732–854 m, 1; 5.6 km E Grand-Goâve, s.l., 1; *República Dominicana: Dajabón:* Los Cerezos, 12 km NW Río Limpio, 580 m, 1; Cañada Tirolís, just S Villa Anacaona, 418 m, 3; 3 km ESE Villa Anacaona, 458 m, 9; *Elías Piña:* 16 km E Hondo Valle, 702 m, 1; 21 km S Comendador, 1464 m, 1; 16 km SW Hondo Valle, 1617 m, 1; summit, Loma Nalga de Maco, *ca.* 1990 m, 1; *Santiago:* Río Bao, 8 km SE Montones Abajo, 488 m, 1; 7 km SW Santiago, 214 m, 3; *La Vega:* Jarabacoa, 530 m, 11; 1 km S Constanza, 1098 m, 2; *Dist. Nac.:* Punta Caucedo, 2 km W, 2 km S Andrés, s.l., 1; *Barahona:* Polo, 702 m, 1; *Pedernales:* 2 km SW Mencía, 275–336 m, 3.

23. *Pyrgus oileus* Linnaeus, 1767

TL "Algeria"; see Miller and Brown, 1981:23.

FW 13–15 mm.

Pyrgus oileus is one of the most common and widely distributed skippers on Hispaniola. These are also the first records of *P. oileus* from Île de la Gonâve, Isla Catalina, and Isla Saona. The skipper is regularly associated with weed-grown roadsides, open fields, and other exposed situations, and only rarely is it encountered within forests or pseudoforests; in such situations, it can be found along paths or in clearings. We have also taken this skipper in an open *Citrus* grove and in tall grasses. The species is much more common than the specimens reported, and in many cases individuals were simply not collected because of their abundance. We have, remarkably, few records from truly xeric regions such as the Cul de Sac–Valle de Neiba or the western Valle de Cibao (exception: Cabo Rojo on the Peninsula de Barahona); *P. oileus* tends to avoid such rigorous habitats, although it may be found in xeric forests that offer some shade.

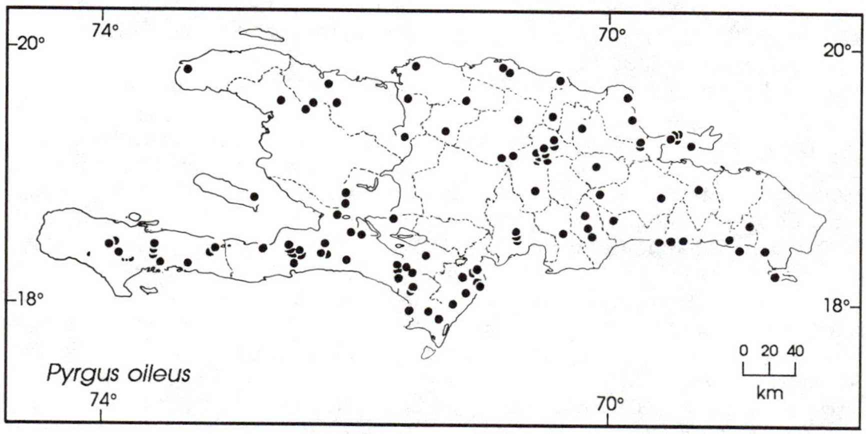

Temperatures of activity range from 23°C to 40°C, and times between 0835 and 1635 h. Elevations are between sea level (Môle St.-Nicholas, Cabo Rojo, Playa Bayahibe, Fond Parisien) and 1373 m (Aceitillar) on the Sierra de Baoruco. The period of greatest abundance is June and July, with smaller numbers in January, February, March, April, May, August, October, and December. The species apparently flies throughout the year. Comstock (1944:551) stated that *P. oileus* is on the wing during the entire year in Puerto Rico, and Brown and Heineman (1972:389) noted its abundance on Jamaica. They considered it "perhaps most abundant in the lowlands and especially so in the hot semiarid grasslands."

We have taken *P. oileus* feeding on *Blechum pyramidatum* (Acanthaceae) and *Bidens pilosa* at Las Lagunas. Copulating pairs have been taken on 8.vi (Peralta, 305 m, 1250 h, 36°C), 27.vii (Bayaguana, 1100–1150 h, 34°C) and 28.vii (Vallejuelo, 610 m,

1430–1630 h).

Riley (1975:178) used the trinomen *P. o. oileus* for these skippers in much of the Antilles, but Brown and Heineman, following Bell, used only a binomen. Bell has shown that the more southern *P. orcus* Stoll, 1780, is distinct and overlaps *P. oileus* in the southern Lesser Antilles.

Specimens: Haiti: Nord-Ouest; Môle St.-Nicholas, s.l., 1; *Nord:* Carrefour la Mort, s.l., 3; 3.5 km W Plaisance, 305 m, 1; 2.9 km N Dondon, 366 m, 1; *l'Artibonite:* 1.6 km Carrefour Marmelade, 854 m, 3; 3.4 km N Carrefour Joffre, 114 m, 1; *l'Ouest:* 1.6 km N Saut d'Eau, 183 m, 1; 19.7 km SE Mirebalais, 183 m, 2; 5.6 km S Terre Rouge, 366 m, 1; 3.0 km SE Fond Parisien, s.l., 1; 13.3 km E Croix des Bouquets, s.l., 1; Boutilliers Road, 1.8–3.7 km W Kenscoff rd., 793 m, 7 (5 MPM); Boutilliers Road, 732–915 m, 2; 0.3 km SE Obléon, 1678 m, 1; Peneau, 1.1–1.6 km SW Furcy, 1474 m, 1; 8.6 km N Béloc, 534 m, 1; 1.3 km N Béloc, 702 m, 2; 1.6 km N Béloc, 702 m, 1; 1.3 km S Découzé, 702 m, 1; 0.6 km S Découzé, 761 m, 1; 2.1 km S Découzé, 640 m, 2; 7.7 km N Jacmel, 92 m, 1; nr. Péredo, 570–600 m, 3 (FSM); just W Grand-Goâve, s.l., 1; *Sud:* 3 km SW Paillant, 678 m, 1; 6.7 km SW Paillant, 793–854 m, 1; Vieux Bourg d'Aquin, s.l., 7; 6.2 km N Cavaillon, 580 m, 2; 14.1 km N Cavaillon, 366 m, 1; 19.7 km N Cavaillon, 580 m, 4; 4.5 km E Cavaillon, 31 m, 4; 5.6 km N Camp Perrin, 275 m, 1; Trou Carfineyes, 0.5 km SSE Soi Bois, 950 m, 3 (FSM); Formond Base Camp #1, 975 m, 8 (FSM); *Île de la Gonâve:* Anse-à-Galets, 2; *República Dominicana: Monte Cristi:* 4 km SE Monte Cristi, 2; *Dajabón:* 0.5 km Cañongo, 31 m, 2; 9 km S Restauración, 519 m, 1; *Valverde:* Río Guarabo, 3 km W Los Quemados, 122 m, 1: *Santiago Rodríguez:* Loma Leonor, 19 km SW Monción, 610 m, 1; *Puerto Plata:* 8 km W Luperón, 1; 13 km SE Luperón, 214 m, 1; 9 km SE Sosúa, 15 m, 2; *Espaillat:* 20 km SW Jamao al Norte, 793 m, 1; *Duarte:* 10 km SE Tenares, 183 m, 3; *María T. Sánchez:* 14 km SE La Entrada, s.l., 1; 6 km S Cabrera, s.l., 1; Cruce de Rincón, s.l., 2; 1 km S Cruce de Rincón, s.l., 3; *La Vega: ca.* 3 km SW Boca del Rio, 976 m, 1; La Ciénaga, 915 m, 1; 2 km S La Vega, 366 m, 2; Güaigüí, S of La Vega, 336 m, 1; 10 km W Jayaco, 915 m, 1; La Palma, 19 km W Jayaco, 1007 m, 1; Buena Vista, 11 km NE Jarabacoa, 640 m, 1; Jarabacoa, 530 m, 1; 5 km SE Jarabacoa, 595 m, 1; 3.5 km E Paso Bajito, 732 m, 1; 18 km SE Constanza, 1586 m, 1; *Santiago:* 7 km SW Santiago, 214 m, 1; *Samaná:* 6.9 km NE Sánchez, 336 m, 3; 8.9 km NE Sánchez, 336 m, 1; 12.3 km NE Sánchez, 244 m, 1; 13.2 km NE Sánchez, 92 m, 1; 4.8 km W Samaná, s.l., 2; *Hato Mayor:* 11 km NW Hato Mayor, 122 m, 1; *La Altagracia:* 16 km NE La Romana, 61 m, l; 1 km N Playa Bayahibe, s.l., 2; *La Romana:* Río Cumayasa, 13.5 km W La Romana, 1; *San Pedro de Macorís:* 13 km SE Boca Chica, 1; *Dist. Nac.:* 33 km W San Pedro de Macoris, 1 (MPM); Punta Caucedo, 2 km W, 2 km S Andrés, s.l., 1; 30 km NW Santo Domingo, 122 m, 1; *Sánchez Ramírez:* 1 km NE Las Lagunas, 183 m, 6; *Monte Plata:* 8 km NE Bayaguana, 2; 11 km W Esperalvillo, 92 m, 1; *San Cristóbal:* 6 km NW Cambita Garabitos, 488 m, 4; 11 km NW Cambita Garabitos, 671 m, 1; *Azua:* 4 km S Peralta, 336 m, 1; 5 km S Peralta, 305 m, 2; 2.5 km W, 6.6 km N Azua, 183 m, 1; *Peravia:* 22 km NW Cruce de Ocoa, 61 m, 1; 5 km N San José de Ocoa, 580 m, 1; *Independencia:* 2 km S Duvergé, 1; 21 km N Los Pinos, 1708 m, 1; *Barahona:* 8 km NNE Polo, 793 m, 1; 2 km SW Barahona, 122 m, 1; 7 km SW Barahona, 2; 5

km SE, 6.6 km W Barahona, 488 m, 1; 3.3 km NE La Ciénaga, 1; 9 km NW Enriquillo, 671 m, 1; 8 m NW Paraíso, 153 m, 6 (4 MPM); 8–10 km NW Paraíso, 3 (MPM); *Pedernales:* Cabo Rojo, s.l., 1; 21 km NE Cabo Rojo, 488 m, 1; 23 km NE Cabo Rojo, 488 m, 2; Las Abejas, 12 km NW Aceitillar, 1129 m, 1; 4.5 km NE Aceitillar, 1373 m, 1; 1 km N Cabeza de Agua, 275 m, 2; 1 km SE Banano, 183 m, 1; 0.6 km SE Los Arroyos, 1098 m, 1; 17 km NW Oviedo, 183 m, 1; 4 km NW Tres Charcos, 1; *Isla Saona;* 0.25–2 km N Mano Juan, 3; *Isla Catalina:* 2.

24. *Pyrgus crisia odilia* Oberthür, 1912

TL Port-au-Prince, Dépt. de l'Ouest, Haiti.

FW males 9–13 mm, females 10–14 mm.

Pyrgus crisia Herrich-Schäffer occurs in the Antilles as 2 subspecies: *P. c. crisia* on Cuba, where it is said to be rare (Bates, 1935a:220), and *P. c. odilia* on Hispaniola. Its occurrence on Hispaniola is extremely peculiar. Schwartz (1983a:64) listed 7 specimens from 3 Haitian localities and stated that this skipper "is restricted to moderate and high elevations." Since only 7 specimens had been collected in 3 years, it is a logical assumption that the species is rare. In the República Dominicana, on the other hand, *P. c. odilia* is widely distributed and occurs from sea level (Canoa, Playa Bayahibe) to 1922 m (Valle de Tetero), in contrast to 672 m (Paillant) to 1678 m (Obléon) in Haiti.

Impressions were that *P. c. odilia* was a montane species, usually found in or near open areas in pinewoods, and this is generally the situation for the skippers in Haiti. But in the República Dominicana, on the other hand, not only does *P. c. odilia* occur at low elevations, but it occupies a diversity of habitats, from xeric woods to *cafetales*. In the latter country, the species is most often encountered along roadsides or paths and in open and unshaded fields; it is never so locally abundant as *P. oileus*. Perhaps the most rigorous (and most contrasting with the Haitian sites) place where we have taken *P. c. odilia* is Canoa; this sea-level locality is extremely harsh, with high temperatures and humidity and a flora of *Acacia*, arborescent as well as low cacti, and tussocks of a 0.5 m tall stiff grass (*Uniola virgata*)—altogether a striking contrast to the montane pinewoods where we encountered *P. c. odilia* in Haiti. To say that *P. c. odilia* is ecologically tolerant is to understate the facts. Schwartz (1983a:64) also noted that in Haiti the species was sporadic, being present in 2 years and then absent at the same locality the next. The same seems to be true in the República Dominicana; the only locality where we have taken specimens repeatedly is La Palma, in a mesic *cafetal*. On 1 occasion, we collected *P. c. odilia* drinking from a mud puddle in a dirt road (El Aguacate), along with *P. oileus*, which regularly drinks in this fashion.

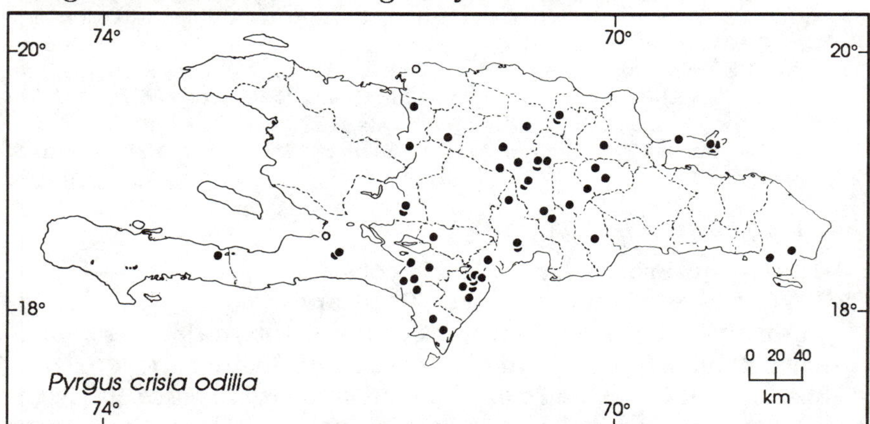

Times of activity varied between 0845 and 1545 h, and temperatures between 24°C (Comendador, La Palma) and 36°C (La Ciénaga). We have taken more specimens (30) in August than in March, April, June, July, October, November, and December (from 8 to 24), which suggests that August may be the primary time of eclosion; still, the skippers are on the wing during the entire year. Comstock (1944:617) has a photograph of a male from Monte Cristi, taken 2.iii.

Pyrgus c. odilia feeds on the flowers of *Blechum pyramidatum*, *Bidens pilosa* (Las Lagunas), and *Tournefortia hirsutissima* (Constanza).

Specimens: Haiti: l'Ouest: Obléon, 1678 m, 1; Peneau, 1.1–1.6 km SW Furcy, 1464 m, 4; *Sud:* 2.9 km SW Paillant, 672 m, 1; *República Dominicana: Dajabón:* 2 km NW El Pino, 183 m, 1; Cañada Tirolís, just S Villa Anacaona, 576 m, 1; *Elías Piña:* 14 km S Comendador, 976 m, 1; 21 km S Comendador, 1464 m, 1; *Santiago Rodríguez:* Loma Leonor, 18 km SW Monción, 534 m, 1; *Santiago:* Río Bao, 8 km SE Montones Abajo, 488 m, 4; entrance of Valle de Tetero to Valle de Tetero, 1342–1922 m, 1; 7 km SW Santiago, 214 m, 1; *Espaillat:* 3 km N Puesto Grande, 580 m, 1; 20 km SW Jamao al Norte, 793 m, 1; *Sánchez Ramírez:* 1 km SE La Mata, 1; 1 km NE Las Lagunas, 183 m, 4; *Duarte:* 12 km SE San Francisco de Macorís, 1; *Samaná:* 12.3 km NE Sánchez, 244 m, 1; 14.1 km E and N Samaná, 31 m, 1; 2 km S Las Galeras, 1; 2.8 km S Las Galeras, 61 m, 3; *La Vega:* La Palma, 19 km W Jayaco, 1007 m, 16; La Ciénaga, 915 m, 6; 3.5 km E Paso Bajito, 732 m, 2; 1.7 km S Jarabacoa, 488 m, 1; 1 km S Constanza, 1098 m, 3; 6 km SSE Constanza, 1403 m, 2; 10 km NW La Horma, 1496 m, 1; *Monseñor Nouel:* 17 km SW Piedra Blanca, 854 m, 2; 6 km SE Maimón, 122 m, 1; *La Altagracia:* 1 km N Playa Bayahibe, s.l., 4; 2–3 km W Boca de Yuma, 2; *San Cristóbal:* 11 km NW Cambita Garabitos, 671 m, 1; *Peravia:* 6 km W La Horma, 1159 m, 1; *Azua:* 4 km S Peralta, 366 m, 1; 5 km S Peralta, 305 m, 1; 5 km SW Monte Bonito, 702 m,

3; *Baoruco:* 9 km N Neiba, 366 m, 1; *Independencia:* 1 km NE El Aguacate, 976 m, 2; 4–7 km NE El Aguacate, 519–732 m, 2; 0.6 km NW Puerto Escondido, 519 m, 1; *Barahona:* 12 km ESE Canoa, s.l., 1; 12 km SW Barahona, 427 m, 1; 5 km SE, 3 km W Barahona, 183 m, 1; 8 km NW Paraíso, 153 m, 1; 1.8 km W Monteada Nueva, 1007 m, 1; 1.3 km W Montada Nueva, 1037 m, 1; 5 km NW Las Auyamas, 1; 20 km SE Cabral, 946 m, 1; *Pedernales:* 23 km N Cabo Rojo, 488 m, 1; Las Abejas, 12 km NW Aceitillar, 1129 m, 1; Mencía, 397 m, 2; 17 km NW Oviedo, 183 m, 3; 1.3 km S Tres Charcos, 1.

Subfamily Hesperiinae Latreille, 1809

25. *Pyrrhocalles antiqua antiqua* Herrich-Schäffer, 1863

TL "Cuba"; restricted to "Haiti" by Skinner (1920:151).

FW 21–29 mm.

Pyrrhocalles a. antiqua is primarily an inhabitant of mesic and shaded situations, such as the edges of and within *caféières* and *cafetales* and overgrown *Cocos* groves. Its flight is rapid and direct, and it is often seen as a large orange blur that alights on the upper side of a leaf with wings folded above the back, resting briefly before darting off once more, only to return to the same site repeatedly. The species is also not uncommon in lowland xeric forest, provided there is sufficient shade; a long series from 1 locality (Samaná) is from a weedy roadside and a mesic ravine, a mesic lowland situation. The species is widely distributed geographically; the specimens recorded here are the first from Isla Saona. The species occurs there in low beach vegetation, and a specimen from Haiti (Grand-Goâve) was taken in a similar exposed oceanfront site.

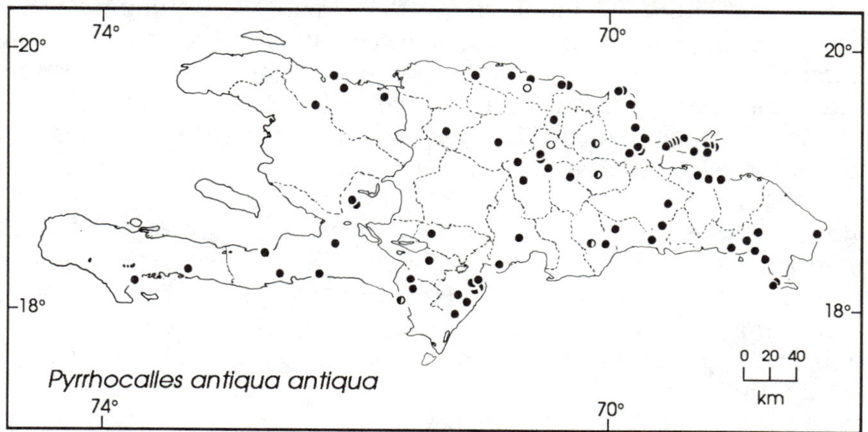

Pyrrhocalles antiqua antiqua

Elevations range from sea level (Grand-Goâve, Cormier Plage, Nagua, Punta Cana, Río Chavón, Playa Bayahibe, Las Terrenas) to 1129 m (Las Abejas); the latter is an area of high-canopied upland forest. Temperatures varied between 26°C (Peralta, Neiba) and 39°C (Samaná), and times between 0900 and 1710 h. Most specimens and observations are from July (63) and June (58), with 28 in August, 34 in December, 33 in October, 19 in March, 16 in May, and 7–1 in January, September, and November. The species appears to be on the wing during the entire year, with 2 peaks (June-August and December).

At Jayaco, *P. a. antiqua* was attracted to the small yellow flowers of *Palicourea barbinervia* (Rubiaceae) in an opening in the forest, and at Enriquillo, *P. a. antiqua* was feeding on the small white flowers of *Morinda citrifolia* (Rubiaceae) in a large clearing in xeric forest. We have taken *P. a. antiqua* on *Lantana ovatifolia* (7 km E Sabana de la Mar), on *Geoffroea inermis* (Río Chavón), *Tournefortia hirsutissima* (Sosúa), *Bougainvillea glabra* (1.7 km S Jarabacoa), *Ageratum conyzoides* (Cabo Rojo), and *Catharanthus roseus* (Apocynaceae), a plant rarely used by Hispaniolan butterflies (Les Cayes). At Grand-Goâve, a *P. a. antiqua* was taken from an ornamental white-flowered tree, very attractive to large black bees.

The most abundantly we have encountered *P. a. antiqua* was in a coastal *Cocos* grove on 27.xi.1983 (Nagua). (The long series from Jarabacoa was native-collected over several days.) The site included an open but flowery (*Wedelia trilobata*) beach with *Yucca* sp. and *Coccoloba uvifera*, as well as the coconut grove which had been apparently untended and had a dense understory of weeds (*Urena lobata*) and ferns. On the beach and in the grove, *P. a. antiqua* was abundant, more so in the grove. The skippers were behaving in their usual darting manner, alighting on the surfaces of leaves (from 15 cm to 2 m above the ground). There was some interaction between individuals; it was not unusual to see 2 or 3 in the air, swirling about each other, at a time. On several occasions, 2 *P. a. antiqua* were seen to land near each other on the same leaf surface. Raburn and I collected 21 specimens, most from the grove, between 1415 and 1500 h, at a temperature of 36°C, and many more were seen. It is indeed rare to see so many *P. a. antiqua* at 1, quite circumscribed, locality; during October 1983, *P. a. antiqua* was generally common in the northeastern portion of the República Dominicana. Wisor and I returned to this same locality on 20.iii.1984. The *Cocos* grove had been cleared; only 2 *P. a. antiqua* were seen.

At Constanza, on 29.vi, in a sequence of skipper activity between 0930 and 1100 h, this species became active at about 1000 h, after *U. p. domingo* and *W. druryi* had already been flying.

Specimens: Haiti: Nord: Cormier Plage, s.l., 1; Carrefour la Mort, s.l., 1; 12.3 km E Terrier Rouge, s.l., 2; 3.5 km S Plaisance, 336 m, 1; 6.2 km W Plaisance, 259 m, 1; *l'Ouest:* 1.6 km N Saut d'Eau, 183 m, 2; 12.0 km SE Mirebalais, 305 m, 1; Pétionville, 366–458 m, 2; 13.6 km E Jacmel, s.l., 1; Lavaneau, 229 m, 2; just W Grand-Goâve, s.l., 2; *Sud:* Vieux Bourg d'Aquin, s.l., 1; Les Cayes, s.l., 1; *República Dominicana: Santiago Rodríguez:* Loma Leonor, 18 km SW Monción, 534 m, 1; *Puerto Plata:* 13 km SE Luperón, 214 m, 2; 0.6 km NE Estero Hondo, 1; 8 km E Puerto Plata, *ca.* 15 m, 1; 9 km SE Sosúa, 15 m, 2; 1 km NW Sabaneta de Yásica, 1; *Espaillat:* 20 km SW Jamao al Norte, 793 m, 1; *Santiago:* Río Bao, 8 km SE Montones Abajo, 488 m, 1; *Duarte;* 1 km N El Abanico, 1; *La Vega:* 10 km W Jayaco, 915 m, 14; Jarabacoa, 530 m, 61; 1.7 km S Jarabacoa, 488 m, 4; 1 km W Manabao, 793 m, 1; 1 km S Constanza, 1098 m, 1; *María T. Sánchez:* 8 km NE Río San Juan, s.l., 3; 9 km NE Río San Juan, s.l., 7; 6 km S Cabrera, s.l., 1; 9 km SE Nagua, s.l., 25; 14 km S La Entrada, s.l., 2; Cruce de Rincón, s.l., 1; 1 km S Cruce de Rincón, s.l., 2; *Samaná:* 6.9 km NE Sánchez, 336 m, 2; 2.3 km NE Sánchez, 92 m, 2; 13.2 km NE Sánchez, 92 m, 4; 3.1 km E Las Terrenas, s.l., 1; 4.5 km E Samaná, 9; 10.2 km W Samaná, 61 m, 1; 14.1 km E and N Samaná, 31 m, 7; El Francés, 14 km N and E Samaná, s.l., 2; 10.5 km S Las Galeras, 15 m, 2; *Hato Mayor:* 7 km E Sabana de la Mar, 13; 17 km E Sabana de la Mar, 1; 25 km E Sabana de la Mar, 1; *Monte Plata:* 8 km NE Bayaguana, 1; *La Altagracia:* Punta Cana, s.l., 1; 1 km N Playa Bayahibe, s.l., 8: 16 km NE La Romana, 61 m, 2; Río Chavón, 10 km NE La Romana, 4; *La Romana:* Río Chavón, 8 km SE La Romana, s.l., 14; Río Cumayasa, 13.5 km W La Romana, 31 m, 12; *Dist. Nac.:* 9 km NE Guerra, 4; 5 km S San Isidro, 1; 30 km NW Santo Domingo, 122 m, 2; *Monseñor Nouel:* Bonao, 153 m, 1; *San Cristóbal:* 3 km S Hato Damas, 92 m, 1; *Azua:* 5 km S Peralta, 305 m, 1; *Baoruco:* 11 km N Neiba, 519 m, 1; *Independencia:* 0.5 km E Duvergé, 1; *Barahona:* west slope, Sierra Martín García, 458–610 m, 1; Polo, 702 m, 1; 2 km SW Barahona, 122 m, 1; 12 km SW Barahona, 427 m, 5; 5 km SE, 3 km W Barahona, 183 m, 4; 5 km SE, 6.4 km W Barahona, 488 m, 2; 8 km NW Paraíso, 1653 m, 6 (2 MPM); 8–10 km NW Paraíso, 1 (MPM); 3 km NW Enriquillo, 244 m, 7; *Pedernales:* 26 km NE Cabo Rojo, 732 m, 1; Las Abejas, 12 km NW Aceitillar, 1129 m, 1; *Isla Saona:* Mano Juan, 2; 2 km W Mano Juan, 2.

Sight records: República Dominicana: Puerto Plata: 0.6 km NE Estero Hondo—2 seen, 30.v; *Duarte:* 12 km SE San Francisco de Macorís—1 seen, 6.viii; *Monseñor Nouel:* Bonao, 153 m—2 seen, 22.vii; *Sánchez Ramírez:* 1 km NE Las Lagunas, 183 m—4 seen, 2.xi; *San Cristóbal:* 6 km NW Cambita Garabitos, 488 m—1 seen, 20.vi; *Pedernales:* Pedernales, s.l.—2 seen, 12.vi.

26. *Argon* sp.

FW males 18–19, female 18 mm.

The genus *Argon* has been previously unknown from the West Indies. The discovery of a species, as yet undetermined, of *Argon* in the Las Abejas area by K. Johnson and D. Matusik in 1986–87 is an outstanding feat. The population is known from 3 males and 1 female, all from the vicinity of Lower Abejas, Prov. de Pedernales, República Dominicana; all were taken in 8–17.vii in 2 years.

Argon sp. is easily differentiated from other Hispaniolan skippers by the presence, on the unhw, of 5 distinct black spots ringed with white; these spots are smaller in the female than in the male but nonetheless present.

Johnson (*in litt.*, 1987) summarized the behavior of this skipper as follows: it "has a quick, rapid, wing-fanning flight. It darts in a rather straight line, below 1 m from the ground, alighting on nectar sources for brief periods. All specimens have been taken while nectaring on treetop vine blossoms abutting of ravine ledges. Captures have occurred where the steepness of the ravine slopes allows a collector to stand on broad ledges abutting the tops of trees growing out of the ravine bottoms." The elevational datum for "Lower Abejas" is 3800 ft. (1159 m).

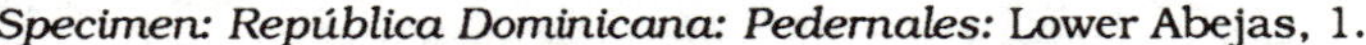

Specimen: República Dominicana: Pedernales: Lower Abejas, 1.

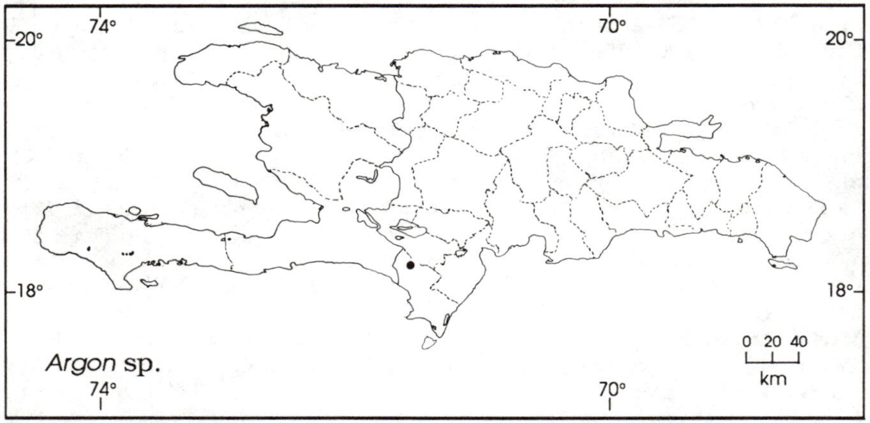

27. *Perichares philetes philetes* Gmelin, 1790

TL Jamaica.

FW males 22–25 mm, females 22–27 mm.

Despite its apparent abundance on Cuba (Bates, 1935a:234), Puerto Rico (Comstock, 1944:572–73), and Jamaica (Brown and Heineman, 1972:405–6), *P. ph. philetes* appears less common in general on Hispaniola. The Haitian specimens are from only 2 *départements*, both on the south island; the Dominican skippers are from widely scattered localities. All but 5 (Canapé Vert, Paillant, Copey, Imbert, Santiago) localities are very mesic and are *caféières*, *cafetales*, *cafetales-cacaotales*, mesic forest, oases (Villa Vásquez), and rice field edges (Cruce de Rincón). The exceptions are an open field with *Hibiscus rosasinensis* (Paillant; even this site is near mesic *caféières*), hotel corridors (Canapé Vert, Santiago), *Acacia* woods (Copey), and a sugarcane field (Imbert).

Elevations range from sea level (Copey, Cruce de Rincón) to 1617 m (Los Arroyos) in the Massif de la Selle and to 1647 m (Constanza) and 2105 m (Valle Nuevo) in the Cordillera Central. Despite this broad elevational range, *P. ph. philetes* is more abundant at low to moderate elevations. Times of collection were between 0915 and 1800 h, and temperatures between 24°C (La Palma) and 40°C (Tenares).

Perichares ph. philetes has been taken on 6 occasions (La Palma, El Abanico, Cruce de Rincón and 1 km S Cruce de Rincón, Sabana de la Mar, 30 km NW Santo Domingo) in deep (0.3–0.6 m), dense grass during the day; in such situations, the skippers fly erratically upward and then downward, almost deliberately, with little attempt to escape or fly away from a precise spot. Examination of these places shows nothing to keep the skipper at that site —neither flowers nor (often) other *P. ph. philetes*. At Boca del Río, 1 specimen was taken (1500–1555 h) in a dense and dark bamboo (*Bambusa vulgaris;* Poaceae) "forest."

Riley (1975:181), as well as Brown and Heineman (1972: 403–5), emphasized the crepuscular habits of this species; not only are adults crepuscular, but oviposition takes place in low light intensity and eclosion occurs at night. Our specimens have been taken throughout much of the day, with no clumping of times in the late afternoon. It is possible that the peculiar "bouncing" behavior noted above may be correlated with a need for reduced light during the time of maximum insolation.

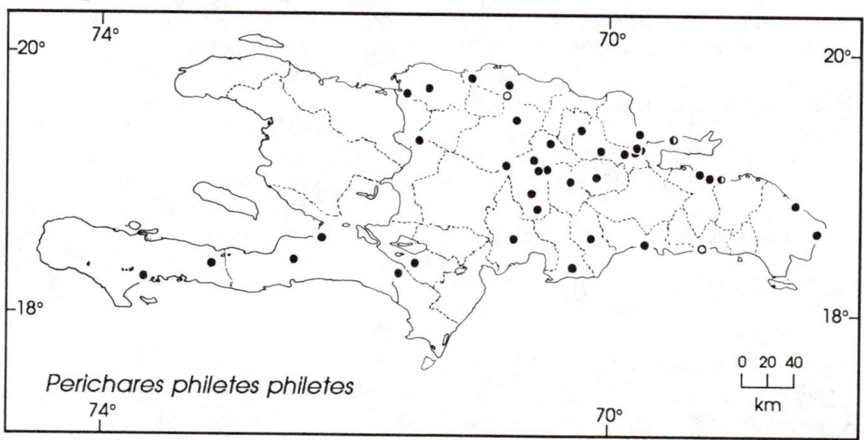

At Bonao, we collected 1 *P. ph. philetes* and saw 1 other (14.iv) in a *cafetal-cacaotal.* The weather was overcast but hot (35°C). One individual was resting on the underside of a leaf of a low (1 m)

shrub, and the other was on the exposed upper side of a large *Theobroma* leaf, 1.5 m above the ground. These observations differ strongly from the grass-inhabiting proclivities of *P. ph. philetes*.

At Imbert, we took a *P. ph. philetes* feeding on the purple flowers of *Jacquemontia* sp. (Convolvulaceae) along a dirt road in an open sugarcane field (1030–1130 h, 37°C).

I have collected *P. ph. philetes* or have sight records or have examined specimens in the MNHNSD taken in January (1), March (30), April (2), May (3), June (39), July (53), August (8), September (1), October (6), November (2), and December (3). From these dates, it is apparent that *P. ph. philetes* is on the wing during the entire year, with March and June-July the periods of greatest abundance. Brown and Heineman (1972:405–6) recorded this skipper during almost every month of the year.

Specimens: Haiti: l'Ouest: 2.1 km S Découzé, 641 m, 1; Canapé Vert, Port-au-Prince, 1; *Sud:* 6.7 km SW Paillant, 763 m, 2; *Sud:* 7 km SW Cavaillon, 122 m, 1; *República Dominicana: Monte Cristi:* 6 km W Copey, s.l., 1; 4 km NW Villa Vásquez, 61 m, 1; *Dajabón:* Los Cerezos, 12 km NW Río Limpio, 580 m, 1; *Puerto Plata:* 0.6 km NE Estero Hondo, 1; 2 km S Imbert, 92 m, 1; *La Vega: ca.* 3 km SW Boca del Río, 976 m, 1; 10 km W Jayaco, 915 m, 1; La Palma, 19 km W Jayaco, 1007 m, 2; Jarabacoa, 530 m, 76; 10 km SE Constanza, 1647 m, 1; Valle Nuevo, 1 (MNHNSD); La Vega, 1 (MNHNSD): *Santiago:* Santiago, 1; *Duarte:* 10 km SE Tenares, 183 m, 2: 1 km E El Abanico, 1; 2 km SW Pimentel, 1; *María T. Sánchez: ca.* 18 km W, 1.2 km S Sánchez, rd. to Rincón Molinillos, 31 m, 1; 9 km SE Nagua, s.l., 1; Cruce de Rincón, s.l., 2; 1 km S Cruce de Rincón, s.l., 6: *Sánchez Ramírez;* 1 km NE Las Lagunas, 183 m, 3; *Hato Mayor:* 7 km E Sabana de la Mar, 1; 17 km E Sabana de la Mar, 1; *La Altagracia:* El Macao, 1 (MHNHSD); Punta Cana, s.l., 1; *Monseñor Nouel:* Bonao, 153 m, 2; *Dist. Nac.* Santo Domingo, 2 (MNHNSD); 30 km NW Santo Domingo, 122 m, 2; *San Cristóbal:* 11 km NW Cambita Garabitos, 671 m, 1; *Peravia:* La Angostura, Baní, 1 (MNHNSD); *Azua:* 5 km S Peralta, 305 m, 1; *Independencia:* 7 km NE El Aguacate, path to El Limón, 519–580 m, 1; *Pedernales:* 5 km NE Los Arroyos, 1617 m, 1.

Sight records: República Dominicana: María T. Sánchez: 1 km S Cruce de Rincón, s.l.—10 seen, 20.iii; *Samaná:* 13.2 km NE Sánchez, 92 m—1 seen, 24.xii; *Hato Mayor:* 25 km E Sabana de la Mar—1 seen, 8.iii.

28. *Pheraeus unia* Butler, 1870

TL San Domingo.

We have never collected *Ph. unia* on Hispaniola. Riley (1975: 180) stated that this skipper is known only from the República Dominicana and is "apparently very rare." Hall (1925) did not list the species, nor did Cucurullo (1959). Marión Heredia (1975:15) listed *Ph. u. unia* but had never collected specimens. Schwartz (1983a) did not encounter the species in Haiti.

29. *Synapte malitiosa adoceta* Schwartz and Sommer, 1986

TL 16 km NE La Romana, 61 m, Prov. de la Altagracia, República Dominicana.

FW males 13–16 mm, females 14–16 mm.

Schwartz et al. (1985) first reported *Synapte malitiosa* from Hispaniola, although there are 3 specimens in the AMNH collected in 1922 and 1932. The species occurs on the continental mainland from Texas to Brasil. In the West Indies, *Synapte malitiosa* is known from Cuba, Jamaica, and Hispaniola; the first 2 islands are inhabited by the nominate subspecies. *Synapte malitiosa* was recorded from 3 localities in the República Dominicana, whence it was represented by 7 specimens. Since 1982 (the year to which the above paper summarized the data), we have taken many more *S. m. adoceta* at a total of 17 localities. The species is much more widely distributed than has been reported; some of these additional records are in the original description of the Hispaniolan subspecies (Schwartz and Sommer, 1986).

Synapte m. adoceta is an inhabitant of wooded areas, usually mesic (Monteada Nueva, Las Lagunas) but occasionally xeric (La Romana). Mesic wooded areas include pseudoforest (*cafetales*), as at Polo. These skippers are exceptionally abundant at Paraíso in a small patch of mesic lowland forest and in transitional woods at El Aguacate. At the latter locality, most specimens have been taken along a path at the lower end of the slope, where the forest is more xeric than mesic.

The elevational distribution is between 61 m (La Romana) and 1037 m (El Limón, 1.3 km W Monteada Nueva). The localities for *S. m. adoceta* center about the Sierra de Baoruco, the Sierra Martín García, the northern and eastern slopes of the Cordillera Central, with isolated occurrences in the extreme eastern lowlands (La Romana) and the north face of the Sierra de Yamasá. The Haitian record for "Pivert" is presumably from the north face of the Chaîne des Matheux. Times of collection were between 0905 and 1620 h, at temperatures between 25°C (El Aguacate, 5 km SE, 3 km W Barahona) and 38°C (Río Bao). These skippers are much less abundant during the heat of the day than in the morning.

At 3 localities (El Aguacate, Paraíso, 5.4 km SE, 6.4 km W Barahona), *S. malitiosa* displayed the same behavior patterns. Areas occupied were primarily small openings in the woods or forests, where sunlight reached the floor and where there were low herbaceous plants. The skippers land on the upper sides of leaves of herbs, up to about 1.5 m above the ground but usually much lower. The skippers can be recognized as *S. malitiosa* by their flight pattern when disturbed or when alarmed: they fly in tight spirals, perhaps 0.3 m in diameter and about 0.3 m above the ground, then dash off to disappear only to return to the same sunning spot from which they had departed. Often, 2 *S. malitiosa* will perform this spiral flight with each other; the flight is usually so rapid that the skippers are visible only as a blur. I have never seen other skippers perform this spiral flight so consistently as *S. malitiosa*.

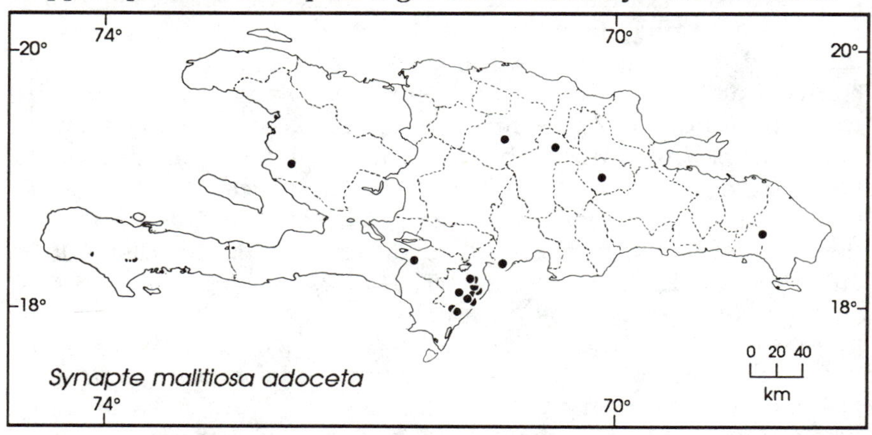

Most specimens are from July (30) and August (29), with 16 from April, 14 from October, 2 from March, and 1 each from January and December. The species appears to be univoltine.

Specimens: Haiti: l'Artibonite: Pivert, east of St.-Marc, 1 (AMNH); *República Dominica: Santiago:* Río Bao, 8 km SE Montones Abajo, 488 m, 1; *La Vega:* Buena Vista, 11 km NE Jarabacoa, 640 m, 1; *La Altagracia:* 16 km NE La Romana, 61 m, 2; *Sánchez Ramírez:* 1 km NE Las Lagunas, 183 m, 9; *Independencia:* 4–7 km NE El Aguacate, 519–824 m, 46; *Barahona:* El Limón, summit, Sierra Martín García, 976–1037 m, 1; west slope, Sierra Martín García, 640 m, 1; west slope, Sierra Martín García, 488–534 m, 1; Polo, 702 m, 2; 1.3 km W Monteada Nueva, 1037 m, 1; 1.8 km W Monteada Nueva, 1007 m, 1; 12 km SW Barahona, 427 m, 2; 5 km SE, 3 km W Barahona, 183 m, 1; 5 km SE, 6.4 km W Barahona, 488 m, 7; Paraíso, "549 m," 2 (AMNH); 8 km NW Paraíso, 153 m, 38; 3 km NW Enriquillo, 244 m, 1; 9 km NW Enriquillo, 671 m, 1.

30. *Cymaenes tripunctus tripunctus* Herrich-Schäffer, 1865

TL Cuba.

FW 11–15 mm.

Cymaenes t. tripunctus is an abundant skipper, preferring grassy and weedy areas. Occasional specimens have been taken in xeric or mesic forest, but even there these skippers are encountered along paths or in clearings, very rarely within the forests themselves. In xeric areas, *C. t. tripunctus* occurs in more or less shaded oases (Villa Vásquez, Tábara Abajo, Canoa) and around their margins; grassy areas on exposed xeric and rocky mountainsides are inhabited (Terre Rouge). Although these skippers are most abundant on bright and hot days, they can be taken (often in moderate abundance) on days that are overcast (Pedro García) or rainy (Samaná, Las Lagunas). *Cymaenes t. tripunctus* occurs from sea level (Fond Parisien, Vieux Bourg d'Aquin, Río San Juan, Cabrera, Cruce de Rincón, Las Terrenas, Punta Cana) to 1098 m (Constanza, 22 km SW Barahona, Los Arroyos), but certainly these insects are most common at low to moderate elevations (576 m), and higher records are in a distinct minority. The specimen reported from Isla Beata is the first record for that island.

At Constanza, where various species of skippers are common in an open grassy field, only 1 *C. t. tripunctus* has been taken (1984); the elevation is 1098 m. In fact, the lack of records from most of the interior uplands of the Cordillera Central is noteworthy (exceptions: La Ciénaga, 915 m; Jarabacoa, 488 m); most records from this range are from its periphery (Río Bao, Jayaco, La Palma). In the Sierra de Neiba, *C. t. tripunctus* reaches an elevation of 976 m (Comendador), in the Cordillera Septentrional 793 m, in the Massif de la Selle 488 m, and in the Sierra de Baoruco 1098 m. In the isolated Sierra Martín García, it occurs in a clearing at the summit (El Limón) at 1037 m.

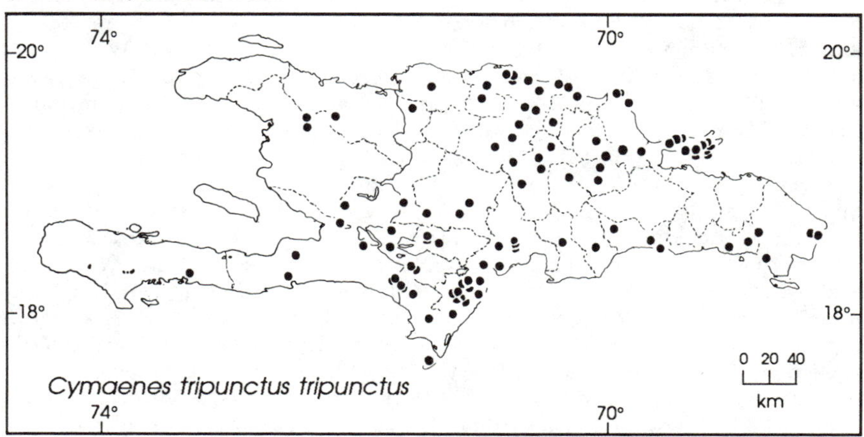

Cymaenes tripunctus tripunctus

Cymaenes t. tripunctus is unusual in that it has a wide temperature tolerance, being active from 20°C (Jayaco) to 42°C (Mencía); times of activity varied between 0830 and 1600 h.

I have specimens from January (10), March (11), April (5), May

(2), June (7), July (56), August (25), October (24), November (4), and December (40), with 2 peaks, July-August and October-December, suggesting 2 broods. Comstock (1944:566) and Brown and Heineman (1972:400–401) recorded *C. t. tripunctus* flying throughout the year.

We have taken *C. t. tripunctus* feeding on *Antigonon leptopus* (Cruce de Guayacanes), *Jacquemontia* sp. (Imbert), *Zinnia elegans* (Constanza), and *Ageratum conyzoides* (El Naranjo).

Specimens: Haiti: Nord: 1.8 km S Dondon, 366 m, 1; *l'Artibonite:* 1.6 km E Carrefour Marmelade, 854 m, 2; 2.9 km E Ennery, 305 m, 1; *l'Ouest:* 1.6 km N Saut d'Eau, 183–275 m, 1; 2.9–8.5 km S Terre Rouge, 122–488 m, 1; 4 km SE Fond Parisien, s.l., 1; 0.6 km S Découzé, 671–702 m, 1; 2.1 km S Découzé, 641 m, 2; 3.0 km S Découzé, 488 m, 1; 6 km NW Jacmel, 244 m, 2; *Sud:* Vieux Boug d'Aquin, s.l., 1; *República Dominicana: Monte Cristi:* 4 km NW Villa Vásquez, 61 m, 5; *Dajabón:* 2 km NE El Pino, 183 m, 1; *Elías Piña:* 15 km S Comendador, 976 m, 1; *Valverde:* 4 km N Cruce de Guayacanes, 198 m, 1; *Puerto Plata:* 11 km N Cruce de Guayacanes, 275 m, 2; 2 km S Imbert, 92 m, 6; 10 km W Luperón, 1; 13 km SE Luperón, 214 m, 3; 8 km E Puerto Plata, *ca.* 15 m, 1; Yásica, 22 km SE Puerto Plata, 122 m, 2; 9 km SE Sosúa, 16 m, 1; 1 km NW Sabaneta de Yásica, 1; *Espaillat:* 3 km N Puesto Grande, 580 m, 3; 2 km NW Gaspar Hernández, 15 m, 2; *Santiago:* 7 km SW Santiago, 1; La Cumbre, 610 m, 1; 2 km E Pedro García, 427 m, 2; Río Bao, 8 km SE Montones Abajo, 488 m, 1; 8 km E Jánico, 1; *La Vega:* La Palma, 19 km W Jayaco, 1007 m, 4; 2 km S La Vega, 366 m, 1; 1.7 km S Jarabacoa, 488 m, 1; La Ciénaga, 915 m, 4; 1 km S Constanza, 1: *Monseñor Nouel:* Bonao, 153 m, 3; *Duarte:* 12 km SE San Francisco de Macorís, 1; 2 km SW Pimentel, 1; 1 km N El Abanico, 1; *María T. Sánchez:* 8 km NE Río San Juan, s.l., 3; 9 km NE Río San Juan, s.l., 1; 6 km S Cabrera, s.l., 1; 1 km S Cruce de Rincón, s.l., 5; *Samaná:* 10.2 km W Samaná, 61 m, 3; 6.9 km NE Sánchez, 336 m, 1; 13.2 km NE Sánchez, 92 m, 4; 3.1 km E Las Terrenas, s.l., 1; 4.8 km W Samaná, s.l., 1; 4.5 km E Samaná, 7; *cayo* in Samaná harbor, 1; 18.0 km E and N Samaná, s.l., 3; El Francês, 14 km E and N Samaná, s.l., 4; 10.5 km S Las Galeras, 15 m, 2; 2.8 km S Las Galeras, 61 m, 8; 3.8 km S Las Galeras, s.l., 1; *Sánchez Ramírez:* 1 km SE La Mata, 1; 1 km NE Las Lagunas, 183 m, 4; *La Altagracia:* Punta Cana, s.l., 1; 6 km W Punta Cana, 1; 1 km N Playa Bayahibe, s.l., 1; 16 km NE La Romana, 61 m, 2; Río Chavón, 10 km NE La Romana, 2; *La Romana:* Río Chavón, 8 km SE La Romana, s.l., 2; Río Cumayasa, 13.5 km W La Romana, 31 m, 4; *Dist. Nac.:* Punta Caucedo, 2 km W, 2 km S Andrés, s.l., 2; 5 km S San Isidro, 1; 30 km NW Santo Domingo, 122 m, 6; *San Cristóbal:* 3 km NW Cambita Garabitos, 702 m, 1; *San Juan:* 4 km E El Cercado, 702 m, 1; 9 km E Vallejuelo, 610 m, 4; 14 km E San Juan, 427 m, 1; *Peravia:* 22 km NW Cruce de Ocoa, 61 m, 1; *Azua:* 4 km S Peralta, 366 m, 2; 5 km S Peralta, 305 m, 2; 2.5 km W, 6.6 km N Azua, 183 m, 1; Tábara Abajo, 4; *Independencia:* 5 km S Angel Feliz, 1; La Furnia, s.l., 1; 4–7 km NW El Aguacate, 519–732 m, 2; 6 km SW El Naranjo, 519 m, 1; *Baoruco:* 14 km N Neiba, 671 m, 3; 11 km N Neiba, 519 m, 1; 2 km SE Galván, 1; *Barahona:* El Limón, summit, Sierra Martín García, 976–1037 m, 3; west slope, Sierra Martín García, 305–458 m, 1; 11.5 km ESE Canoa, s.l., 1; 9 km SW Cabral, 305 m, 1; 8 km NW Paraíso, 153 m, 3 (1 MPM); 1.3 km W Monteada Nueva,

1037 m, 1; 5 km SE, 7 km W Barahona, 183 m, 1; 5 km SE, 6.4 km W Barahona, 488 m, 1; 15 km S Cabral, 1; 20 km SE Cabral, 946 m, 1; 8 km NNE Polo, 793 m, 2; Polo, 702 m, 1; 2 km SW Barahona, 122 m, 1; 22 km SW Barahona, 1098 m, 1; 9 km NW Enriquillo, 671 m, 1; *Pedernales:* 23 km NE Cabo Rojo, 275 m, 1; 1 km N Cabeza de Agua, 244 m, 1; Mencía, 397 m, 5; 2 km SW Mencía, 366 m, 1; 0.6 km SE Los Arroyos, 1098 m, 1; 17 km NW Oviedo, 183 m, 1; *Isla Beata:* 1.

31. *Rhinthon bushi* Watson, 1937

TL Paraíso, Prov. de Barahona, República Dominicana.

FW males 19–20 mm, females 20–22 mm.

These skippers are unquestionably *Rhinthon*, and presumably *Rh. bushi*; that species has been known only from the male holotype. Of our 7 specimens, 2 are males, the remaining 5 females; it was upon 1 of the latter sex that Schwartz's (1983a:65) record of *Rh. cubana* Herrich-Schäffer from Haiti is based. Females have not been previously described, and they differ from males in details of hyaline spot placement, and coloration; this caused me to consider the Haitian specimens *Rh. cubana*. Even with added material, however, the situation with Hispaniolan *Rhinthon* is not clear.

Riley (1975:182) described *Rh. bushi* (based on the holotypic male) as (paraphrased) having the head and palpi above bright green, the palpi orange beneath, and the thorax and base of the abdomen bright green. The fw apical spots are semihyaline and yellowish white in Cu2–2A, on vein 2A, in Cu1-Cu2 (subquadrate and larger than the others), in M3-Cu1 (the smallest), and in the cell. The unfw markings are as on the up with the addition of *greenish yellow streaks above the cell* (all italics his) and beyond the fourth subapical spot; the *hindwing with 2 large silvery white spots below the cell;* there is an irregular white spot in the cell, more or less ringed with orange, and an orange spot beyond it and another in Sc-Rs.

Our 2 males agree in general with the description above. But in some ways they do not agree: there is no greenish tinge above the cell and on the apex of the fw (although these areas are vaguely pale); on the unhw, there is a single large silvery white spot (rather than 2) in the cell end and basally in Rs-M1 and M1-M2, and there are 2 pale orange dots marginal to the white spot in Rs-M1 and M1-M2; there is an additional very pale orange spot in Sc-R1 basally. Thus the male specimens in general resemble the description of the holotype but differ in details.

The females are alike and quite distinct from the males. The up ground color is rich dark brown; all hyaline spots in the fw are clear white and not tinged with yellow as in the male specimens and as described for the holotype male. The spots are arranged as in the males, *except* that the subapical fw dots are not aligned in a row; the most posterior of them, in R5-M1, is displaced apically and is thus out of line with the remaining 2. Additionally, the hyaline spot present in the males in Cu2–2A is absent in females; thus there is a total of 6 spots in the females, and 7 spots in the males. The un in females is matte brown, paler than the dark brown of the up, and without pattern.

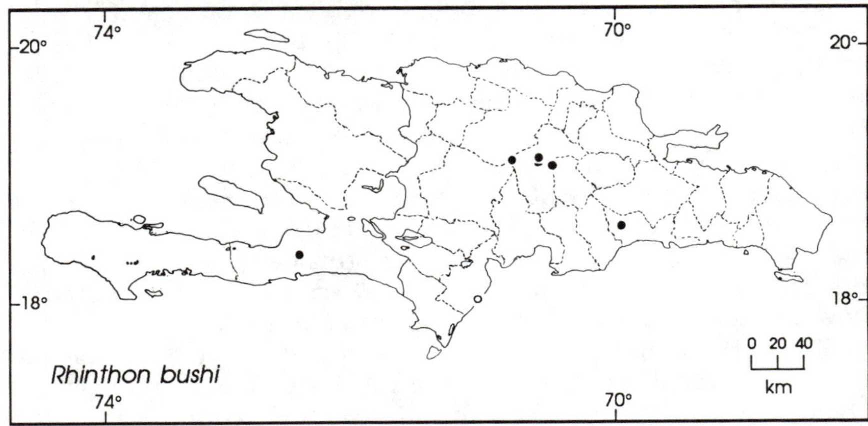

Two males (Jayaco, Los Tablones) and 4 females (Santo Domingo, Jayaco, Jarabacoa, 1 km S Jarabacoa) are from the north island. The female from Découzé in Haiti is from the south island, on which the type-locality lies. Until more specimens of *Rhinthon* are taken, I cannot be certain as to the affinities of these specimens: we may be dealing with individual variation or with geographic variation. It is sure that there is strong sexual dichromatism in these skippers.

Two of these skippers were taken on 21 and 22.vi, in 1980 and 1981. One was taken on 6.vii.1979, and the fourth on 17.viii.1981. The remaining 3 were taken on 28.vi–3.vii.1986. Elevations vary between 122 m (Santo Domingo) and 1678 m (Los Tablones). Temperatures were 27°C (Los Tablones) and 31°C (1 km S Jarabacoa); times varied between 1015 h (Jayaco) and 1750 h (1 km S Jarabacoa). All localities are either mesic broadleaf forest or (Haiti) a cutover *caféière*. Four specimens (Jayaco, Santo Domingo, 1 km S Jarabacoa) are from woods associated with creeks. One specimen from Jayaco was secured as it fed on the pink blossoms of *Fuchsia triphylla* (Oenanthaceae). That from 1 km S Jarabacoa was perched on the leaf of a shrub, 0.75 m above the ground adjacent to a deciduous-wooded creek through pines, and that from Los

Tablones was in hardwood forest on a leaf of a tree, 3 m above the trail.

Specimens: Haiti: l'Ouest: 2.1 km S Découzé, 640 m, 1; *República Dominicana: La Vega:* 10 km W Jayaco, 915 m, 2; 1 km SW Los Tablones, 1678 m, 1; Jarabacoa, 530 m, 1; 1 km S Jarabacoa, 519 m, 1; *Dist. Nac.:* 30 km NW Santo Domingo, 122 m, 1.

32. *Oarisma stillmani* Bell and Comstock, 1948

TL Monte Cristi, Prov. de Monte Cristi, República Dominicana.

FW males 10–11 mm, females 10–11 mm.

Oarisma stillmani is 1 species of the genus in the West Indies; the others are *O. nana* Herrich-Schäffer and *O. bruneri* from Cuba. The species was named from 6 males and 3 females, all collected in March in the extreme northwest of the República Dominicana in the vicinity of Monte Cristi (Bell and Comstock, 1948:18–19). Riley (1975:183) added no new locality records. Through a *lapsus*, Bell and Comstock gave the "length of 1 primary wing" as 20–22 mm in males and 24 in females. Riley, on the other hand, gave the fw length in both sexes as 10 mm, much closer to reality.

In January 1982, Henderson took a male on Isla Catalina, at the southeastern end of Hispaniola. In July of the same year, Gali and I collected 3 specimens near Canoa, near the southwestern extreme of the República Dominicana, again far removed from all other records. Since that time, specimens of *O. stillmani* have been taken near Duvergé (including Puerto Escondido), Tábara Abajo, El Limón, Monte Cristi and vicinity, and near Cabo Rojo. There is a specimen in the MNHNSD from Los Cuatro Vientos, between Azua and Barahona (locality not determinable). Thus, *O. stillmani* is now known from 4 general regions: Monte Cristi and environs, the Valle de Neiba (El Limón, Duvergé, Puerto Escondido, Canoa) east in the Llanos de Azua (Sabana Buey), the Península de Barahona, and Isla Catalina.

Oarisma stillmani is 1 member of a trio of lepidopterans that occur together in xeric habitats of a particular sort; *Hesperia nabokovi* and various members of the *Calisto lyceia* complex are the other members of the trio. The habitat occupied by these rhopalocerans is extreme xeric scrub forest, with *Acacia* and cacti, coupled with a xerophytic grass (*Uniola virgata*). This grass is pale gray and appears inert; it grows in spaced tussocks up to 0.5 m in diameter, the fine leaves up to 1 m in height. There are dense stands of this grass near Canoa, near Monte Cristi, and near Cabo Rojo. It occurs randomly on the road between Barahona and Azua (the

Llanos de Azua) and in the Valle de Neiba (I have not seen it in the Cul de Sac plain in Haiti). Since both hesperiids and *Calisto* regularly use the Poaceae as larval food, I presume that the intimate association between the 2 skippers and satyrids (*Calisto*) and this grass is not fortuitous. At least the *Calisto* use the grass in their behavioral routines (see accounts of *C. crypta*, *C. franciscoi*, and *C. hendersoni*); *O. stillmani* perches on the leaves of the grass, up to 0.75 m above the ground. We have never taken these species away from stands of *U. virgata*: the reverse is also almost true, in that stands of *U. virgata* almost always harbor all 3 species of rhopalocerans. The absence of more than 1 species may be accounted for by the season.

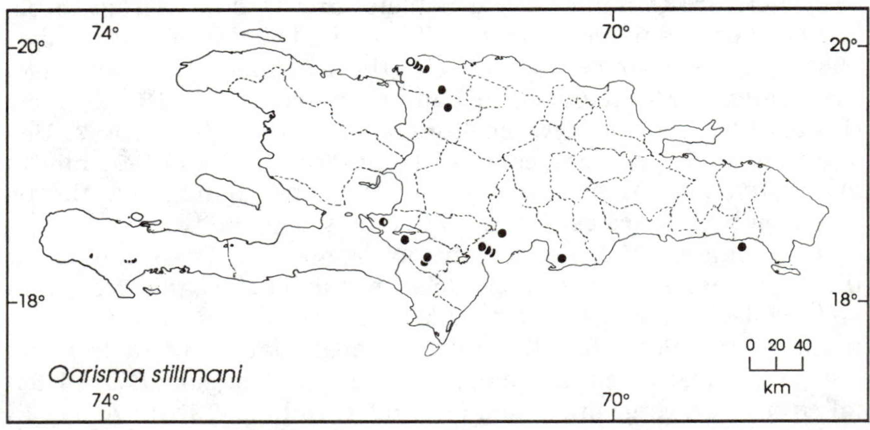

At Monte Cristi, *O. stillmani* was taken in a very large "field" of *U. virgata*, unshaded and without a large number of flowers. At Canoa, the grass stands were somewhat shaded by *Acacia*, and a few more flowers were present; the skippers buzzed (we likened them to an "orange blur") about and over the grass tussocks. On 1 occasion (22.vi.1982) they seemed to favor the more shaded areas, but on 26.vi.1982, they distinctly favored the more open spots. Temperatures were about the same on the 2 days, and collecting times comparable.

The area at El Limón is open *Acacia* scrub with *U. virgata*. The situation at Duvergé is somewhat different, in that there, the single *O. stillmani* was taken in a locally "mesic" area, a hillside adjacent to an irrigation ditch. The grass with which the skipper was immediately associated was not that at Canoa and El Limón, but further down the slope, I found small patches of *U. virgata*. Since *U. virgata* occurs throughout the Llanos de Azua, albeit patchily, I expect that *O. stillmani* will be found throughout this region.

Certainly the habitat of *O. stillmani* is locally 1 of the least appealing for butterfly collecting; it is regularly hot and dry, and often very humid (Canoa) near the ocean. The site on Isla Catalina where *O. stillmani* was collected is a stand of open xeric woods; there are large "meadows" of grass (not *U. virgata*) nearby.

The occurrence of *O. stillmani* on Isla Catalina, far to the east of all other localities and isolated from them by many kilometers of mesic areas (see map), is interesting. The distribution of the lizard *Ameiva lineolata* Duméril and Bibron is comparable to that of *O. stillmani*. This lizard, in the República Dominicana, has a disjunct distribution, occurring in the extreme western portion of the Valle de Cibao in the Monte Cristi region, the Valle de Neiba and the Llanos de Azua as far east as Baní, Prov. de Peravia (and including the Valle de San Juan, whence *O. stillmani* is not known), the Península de Barahona, and Isla Catalina. Schwartz (1966:56–57) suggested that the large hiatus between the Catalina population and that to the west at Baní may be the result of changing ecologies. It seems likely that this xerophilic lizard at one time occurred along a more or less xeric coastal strip as far east as Isla Catalina. With changing ecology, this xeric strip has become mesic, whereas Isla Catalina has remained virtually unchanged. Thus Isla Catalina is an isolated outpost for *A. lineolata;* the same scenario applies equally well to *O. stillmani*. *Calisto lyceia* also occurs on Catalina but is unknown from the mainland, although there is another species of the *lyceia* complex (*Calisto franciscoi*) that occurs as far east as Sabana Buey. *Hesperia nabokovi* is still unknown from Isla Catalina.

Specimens of *O. stillmani* have been taken in March (68, including the type-series), April (27), May (31), June (26), July (14), August (7), October (7), December (6), and January and February (1 each). *Oarisma stillmani* is on the wing during the entire year but is much more common in March-June. Temperatures were between 26°C (overcast) and 39°C (both 4 km SE Monte Cristi), and times between 0820 and 1645 h. Elevations are usually at or near sea level to 427 m (Puerto Escondido). A copulating pair was taken on 16.iii (1 km SE Monte Cristi, 1230–1400 h, 28°C).

Oarisma stillmani uses a variety of flowers as nectar sources. At Canoa, we collected these skippers on *Lantana ovatifolia* and *Hibiscus brasiliensis* (Malvaceae), the latter a mallow of xeric areas that has bright purple-red flowers. At Monte Cristi (both localities) these skippers used *Croton linearis*, *Lantana pauciflora* (an endemic orange-flowered member of the genus, limited in its distribution to the northwestern República Dominicana), and *Lippia micromera*

(Verbenaceae), a short (less than 0.3 m) herbaceous plant with yellow flowers. Both *L. pauciflora* and *L. micromera* were extremely abundant at 4 km SE Monte Cristi in a burned-over area; they both appear to be pioneer plants, the former growing from the bases of grass tussocks with the inflorescences almost hidden. At 1 km SE Monte Cristi, *O. stillmani* was taken on *Urechites lutea* (Apocynaceae), whose large yellow flowers allowed *O. stillmani* to enter the corolla; as many as 3 of these skippers were seen to be within a single flower simultaneously! Both Monte Cristi localities, in iii.1984, literally teemed with *O. stillmani*, and it was not unusual to collect 2 or 3 specimens with 1 stroke of the net. At Tábara Abajo, we took *O. stillmani* on *Melochia tomentosa*, and at Zamba on *Lantana reticulata*.

At El Limón, *O. stillmani* was taken feeding on *Lantana ovatifolia* in x.1983; in iv.1984, at the same locality, these skippers were less common than previously and were feeding (2 specimens) on the small white flowers of *Pithecellobium circinale* (Fabaceae) and *Melochia nodiflora* (Sterculiaceae); both plants are rather tall (2.5 m) and the skippers, in contrast to *Calisto hendersoni*, used only those blooms close to the ground.

The situation at Tábara Abajo was quite different. Although this region is typical of the *U. virgata*—cacti habitat favored by *O. stillmani*, the skippers were very uncommon in that habitat. But Henderson and I found a small (10 m X 2 m) patch of very scrubby and open *Acacia* adjacent to a rail fence which enclosed an irrigated field. In the open patch of *Acacia* were many *Bidens pilosa*, all in very poor condition and almost withered. These flowers were immensely attractive to *O. stillmani*, and the numbers of this skipper seemed almost inexhaustible. We observed them crossing the unpaved road from less flowery *Acacia* scrub and woods, heading for the patch of *Bidens pilosa*; once there, they were easily secured because of their concentration on the flowers.

Specimens: República Dominicana: Monte Cristi: 1 km SE Monte Cristi, 23; 2 km SE Monte Cristi, 1; 4 km SE Monte Cristi, 65; 3.9 km SE Martín García, 92 m, 4; *Santiago Rodríguez:* 3.0 km S Zamba, 214 m, 1; *Peravia:* 4 km E Sabana Buey, 61 m, 5; *Azua:* Tábara Abajo, 20; *Independencia:* 2 km S Duvergé, 1; 5 km N Puerto Escondido, 427 m, 2; 4 km E El Limón, s.l., 12; *Barahona:* Los Cuatro Vientos, 1 (MNHNSD); 8 km ESE Canoa, 32; 11.5 km ESE Canoa, s.l., 5; 12 km ESE Canoa, 3; *Pedernales:* 2 km N Cabo Rojo, s.l., 3; 2 km NE Cabo Rojo, s.l., 4; *Isla Catalina:* 1.

Sight record: República Dominicana: Independencia: 4 km NW Tierra Nueva, s.l.—5 seen, 30.xii.

33. *Polites baracoa loma* Evans, 1955

TL Haiti.

FW males 10–11 mm, females 11–13 mm.

I have few specimens of *P. b. loma* and most generalizations are not possible. The species appears to be uncommon, especially during June-August. The elevational range is between sea level (Río San Juan) and 1403 m (13 km SE Constanza). Temperatures were between 26°C (Loma Leonor) and 37°C (Río San Juan, Vallejuelo); times varied between 0940 and 1710 h. Two specimens were taken in January, 18 in May, 8 in June, 8 in July, 3 in August, 5 in December, 2 each in March and April, and 1 in October. May appears to be the time of major eclosion.

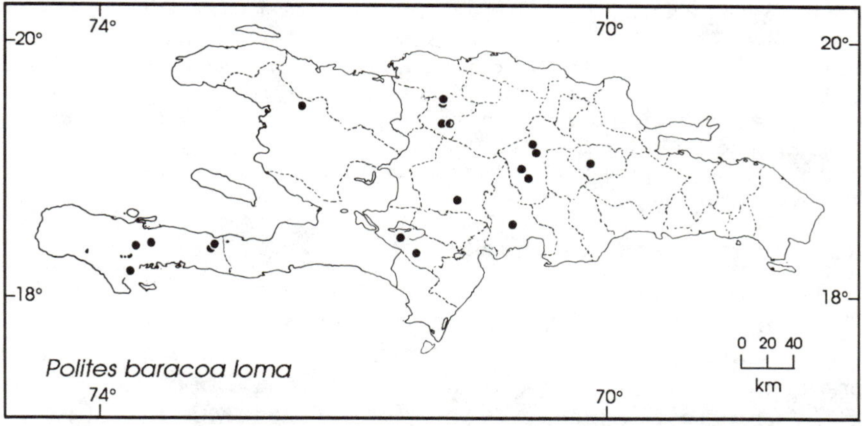

At Las Lagunas, *P. b. loma* was taken foraging on *Bidens pilosa* along the roadside through and adjacent to mesic forest. The Loma Leonor specimens are from mixed pine-hardwoods; those from Zamba (both localities), Vallejuelo, and Puerto Escondido are from *Acacia* scrub; and that from Río San Juan was taken in a hotel garden, where it was foraging on the white-flowered horticultural variety of *Lantana ovatifolia*. The Paillant specimens were taken in a mesic *caféière* within deciduous forest and in an open field of *Ageratum conyzoides* (on which the skipper was not feeding). The 2 specimens from Carrefour Marmelade were perched on *Sida* sp. (Malvaceae). The specimens from Constanza were taken in a semishaded ravine and in an open grassy field, both with *Cynoglossum amabile* (Boraginaceae); 1 was feeding on *Melanthera* sp. (Asteraceae). Other plants used for nectar include *Wedelia trilobata* at Peralta, *Croton barahonensis* at Vallejuelo, and *Croton linearis* at 3.0 km S Zamba.

The El Limón skipper was netted on a gravel road in *Acacia* scrub. In fact, the habit of these small skippers of resting briefly on bare earth or small stones or rocks was observed at Loma Leonor, Peralta, and La Palma (2 different dates). The specimens from Les Cayes were taken from the mowed grass of a hotel lawn.

The apparent rarity of *P. b. loma* is unaccountable. Bates (1935a:224) noted 52 specimens of *P. b. baracoa* Lucas from central and eastern Cuba; thus the species does not appear to be uncommon there.

Specimens: Haiti: l'Artibonite: 1.6 km E Carrefour Marmelade, 854 m, 2; *Sud:* 3 km SW Paillant, 793 m, 1; 6.6 km SW Paillant, 793 m, 1; Les Cayes, s.l., 2; 6.4 km NW Marceline, 610 m, 1; 19.7 km N Cavaillon, 580 m, 2; *República Dominicana: Santiago Rodríguez:* 4.8 km S Zamba, 183 m, 3; 3.0 km S Zamba, 214 m, 13; Loma Leonor, 19 km SW Monción, 610 m, 3; *María T. Sánchez:* Río San Juan, s.l.,1; *La Vega:* La Palma, 11 km W Jayaco, 1007 m, 2; Jarabacoa, 530 m, 6; 1 km S Constanza, 1098 m, 3; 13 km SE Constanza, 1403 m, 1; *Sánchez Ramírez:* 1 km NE Las Lagunas, 183 m, 2; *Azua:* 5 km S Peralta, 305 m, 2; *San Juan:* 9 km E Vallejuelo, 610 m, 1; *Independencia:* 4 km E El Limón, s.l., 1; 0.6 km NW Puerto Escondido, 519 m, 1.

Sight record: República Dominicana: Santiago Rodríguez: Loma Leonor, 18 km SW Monción, 549 m—3 seen, 20.v.

34. *Wallengrenia druryi* Latreille, 1824

TL Haiti.

FW males 11–12 mm, females 12–15 mm.

Although Riley (1975:184–85) considered all Antillean *Wallengrenia* as subspecies of North American *W. otho* Abbot and Smith, the research of Jacqueline Y. Miller of the Allyn Museum of Entomology indicates that this arrangement is incorrect. Rather, the West Indian taxa are best regarded (at least temporarily) as species distinct from both *W. otho* and from each other. Accordingly, I use the name *W. druryi*.

Wallengrenia druryi is widespread on Hispaniola. Hall (1925: 190) considered the species "very common," and Schwartz (1983a: 66) reported 31 specimens from 17 Haitian localities. These skippers occur primarily in grassy or weedy areas, where their low and buzzing flight is quite obvious. The skippers occur from sea level (Carrefour la Mort, Punta Cana, Playa Bayahibe, El Limón, Barahona, Mano Juan) to 1810 m (Scierie) on the Massif de la Selle. The upper extreme is not unique, since the species occurs in other mountain ranges to elevations of 1586 m (10 km SE Constanza) on the Cordillera Central, 1485 m (Macaya) on the Massif de la Hotte, 1220 m (1 km SE Los Arroyos) on the Dominican portion of the Massif de la Selle, and only 976 m (Comendador) on the Sierra de

Neiba.

Considering the broad elevational range of *W. druryi*, it is not surprising that the ecological tolerances of this skipper are broad as well. *Wallengrenia druryi* occurs in pines (Obléon, Scierie), *caféières* (Carrefour la Mort, Découzé, Paillant, La Palma, Tenares, Piedra Blanca), *Syzygium jambos* woods (Loma Leonor), mesic forest (Jayaco, Paraíso), mixed pine-hardwoods (Güaigüí), and roadsides and clearings associated with these habitats. *Wallengrenia druryi* shuns xeric situations; there are very few records from the Cul de Sac–Valle de Neiba, even in oases there. In the western xeric Valle de Cibao, these skippers occur only in an oasis (Villa Vásquez). *Wallengrenia druryi* is often very abundant; the most commonly we have encountered these skippers was at Peralta on 21–29.iv.1984, where they were very abundant on roadside flowers in mesic forest. These are the first records of *W. druryi* from Isla Saona, where the species seems to be rather uncommon.

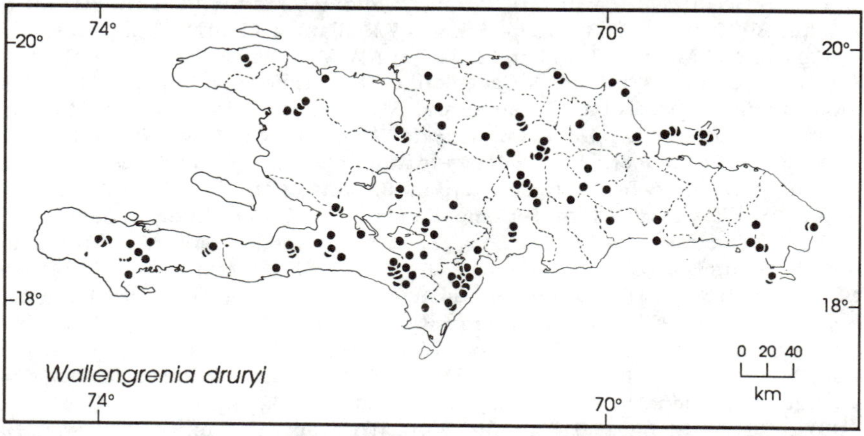

Specimens have been collected between 0830 and 1710 h, at temperatures between 19°C (Scierie) and 39°C (Jánico). Months from which we have material include: January (7), February (2), March (10), April (20), May (20), June (40), July (158), August (100), September (4), October (29), November (20), and December (29). *Wallengrenia druryi* is most common during the late summer (July-August) but appears to be multivoltine.

In a sequence of skipper activity at Constanza, between 0930 and 1100 h, *W. druryi* was second (after only *Urbanus proteus*) to become active in the morning (at about 0945 h).

We have taken *W. druryi* feeding on a variety of flowers: *Daucus* sp. (Carrefour Marmelade), *Bauhinia divaricata* (Les Poteaux), *Cynoglossum amabile* (1 km S Constanza), *Tournefortia hirsutissima* (9 km and 11 km SE Sosúa, Río Bao, 11 km N Neiba, 8 km SE Constanza, Paso Bajito, Peralta), *Emilia javanica* (La Palma), *Urena lobata* (La Cienega, 4.5 km E Samaná), *Lantana ovatifolia* (Las Mercedes), *Zinnia elegans* (La Ciénaga), *Antigonon leptopus* (Santiago), *Stachytarpheta jamaicensis* (Playa Bayahibe), *Stachytarpheta cayennensis* (3 km SE Los Arroyos), *Bougainvillea glabra* (1.7 km S Jarabacoa), *Turnera ulmifolia* (Turneraceae) (9.1 km S Restauración), and *Mormodica charantia* (Cucurbitaceae) (Peralta).

Specimens: Haiti: Nord-Ouest: 7.5 km SE Port-de-Paix, 31 m, 1; 1.3 km S Balladé, 31 m, 1; *Nord:* Carrefour la Mort, s.l., 1; *l'Artibonite:* 1.6 km E Carrefour Marmelade, 854 m, 2; 1.1 km N Carrefour Marmelade, 793 m, 1; 2.9 km E Ennery, 305 m, 1; 4.6 km E Les Poteaux, 183 m, 2; *l'Ouest:* 3.8 km N Terre Rouge, 534 m, 1; 1.3 km N Terre Rouge, 580 m,1; 1.1 km N Terre Rouge, 519 m, 1; 4 km SE Fond Parisien, s.l., 3; Pétionville, 458 m, 2; Boutilliers Road, 732–915 m, 5 (1 FSM); Peneau, 1.6 km SW Furcy, 1464 m, 4; 0.3 km N Obléon, 1617 m, 4; 2 km NW Scierie, 1785–1810 m, 1 (FSM); 1.6 km N Découzé, 702 m, 2; 0.6 km S Découzé, 671 m, 1; 2.1 km S Découzé, 640 m, 7; 5.0 km S Découzé, 1; Lavaneau, 229 m, 2; *Sud:* 6.6 km SW Paillant, 793 m, 1; 6.7 km SW Paillant, 763 m, 1; 4.8 km SW Paillant, 671 m, 2; Les Cayes, s.l., 1; 6.4 km NW Marceline, 671 m, 2; 14 km NW Marceline, 671 m, 1; 6.2 km N Cavaillon, 61 m, 1; 25.6 km N Cavaillon, 640 m, 1; Formond, 900 m, 1 (FSM); along ravine between Pic Formond and Macaya, 1050 m, 1 (FSM); Macaya, 1485 m, 1 (FSM); *República Dominicana: Monte Cristi:* 4 km NW Villa Vásquez, 61 m, 2; *Dajabón:* 4 km S Restauración, 580 m, 1; 8 km S Restauración, 640 m, 1; 9.1 km S Restauración, 519 m, 6; Cañada Tirolís, S Villa Anacaona, 458 m, 1; *Elías Piña:* 14 km S Comendador, 876 m, 4; 15 km S Comendador, 336 m, 1; *Santiago Rodríguez:* Loma Leonor, 19 km SW Monción, 610 m, 2; 4.8 km S Zamba, 183 m, 1; *Puerto Plata:* 13 km SE Luperón, 214 m, 1; 9 km SE Sosúa, 16 m, 18; 11 km SE Sosúa, 47–183 m, 5; *Duarte:* 10 km SE Tenares, 183 m, 2; 12 km SE San Francisco de Macorís, 1; *Santiago:* 7 km SW Santiago, 214 m, 2; 8 km E Jánico, 625 m, 2; 7 km NE Jánico, 488 m, 2; Río Bao, 8 km SE Montones Abajo, 488 m, 7; *La Vega:* 10 km S La Vega (= Güaigüí), 1; Buena Vista, 11 km NE Jarabacoa, 641 m, 1; 1 km E El Río, 1037 m, 1; La Ciénaga, 915 m, 3; 10 km W Jayaco, 915 m, 3; La Palma, 19 km W Jayaco, 1007 m, 33; Jarabacoa, 520 m, 21; 1.7 km S Jarabacoa, 488 m, 8; 5 km SE Jarabacoa, 595 m, 1; 3.5 km E Paso Bajito, 732 m, 3; 1 km S Constanza, 1098 m, 31; 6 km SSE Constanza, 1403 m, 2; 7 km SE Constanza, *ca.* 1312 m, 1; 8 km SE Constanza, 1495 m, 2; 18 km SE Constanza, 1586 m, 1; 19 km NW La Horma, 1496 m, 3; *María T. Sánchez:* 8 km NE Río San Juan, s.l., 2; 6 km S Cabrera, s.l., 1; Cruce de Rincón, s.l., 2; 1 km S Cruce de Rincón, s.l., 2; *Samaná:* 6.9 km NE Sánchez, 336 m, 4; 13 km NE Sánchez, 92 m, 1; 3 km SW Las Terrenas, s.l., 1; 4.5 km E Samaná, 6; El Francés, 14 km E and N Samaná, s.l., 2; 14.1 km E and N Samaná, 31 m, 1; 18.0 km E and N Samaná, s.l., 4; 10.5 km S Las Galeras, 61 m, 2; 2.8 km S Las Galeras, 61 m, 2; 2 km S Las Galeras, 1; *La Altagracia:* Punta Cana, s.l., 3; 2 km W Punta Cana, s.l., 1; 16 km NE La Romana, 61 m, 1; 1 km N Playa Bayahibe, 1; 2.5 km SE Playa Bayahibe, s.l., 4; *La Romana:* Río Chavón, 8 km SE La Romana, s.l., 3; *Dist. Nac.:* 9 km NE Guerra, 2; Punta Caucedo, 2 km W, 2 km S Andrés, s.l., 1; 30 km NW Santo Domingo, 4; *Sánchez Ramírez:* 1

km NE Las Lagunas, 183 m, 1; *Monseñor Nouel:* 14 km SW Piedra Blanca, 427 m, 5; 6 km SE Maimón, 122 m, 1; *Monte Plata:* 8 km W Esperalvillo, 92 m, 1; *Azua:* 2.5 km W, 6.6 km N Azua, 183 m, 2; 18 km S Peralta, 122 m, 2; 5 km S Peralta, 305 m, 22; *San Juan:* 9 km E Vallejuelo, 610 m, 8; *Baoruco:* 9 km N Neiba, 366 m, 1; 11 km N Neiba, 519 m, 4; 2 km SE Galván, 1; *Independencia:* 7 km NE El Aguacate, 519–580 m, 2; 4 km E El Limón, s.l., 1; 0.5 km E Duvergé, 1; *Barahona:* 11.5 km ESE Canoa, s.l., 2; Polo, 702 m, 5; 2 km SW Las Auyamas, 2; 3 km NNE Polo, 854 m, 2; 8 km NNE Polo, 793 m, 2; 20 km SE Cabral, 946 m, 6; 1.3 km W Monteada Nueva, 1037 m, 30; 1.8 km W Monteada Nueva, 1007 m, 5; Barahona, s.l., 2; 12 km SW Barahona, 427 m, 1; 22 km SW Barahona, 1098 m, 1; 8–10 km NW Paraíso, 153 m, 3 (2 MPM); 9 km NW Enriquillo, 671 m, 2; 3 km NW Enriquillo, 244 m, 1; *Pedernales:* 1 km SW Las Mercedes, 397 m, 1; 1 km S La Altagracia, *ca.* 534 m, 1; Mencía, 336 m, 1; 2 km SW Mencía, 336 m, 1; 3 km N Cabeza de Agua, 305 m, 1; 6 km N Cabeza de Agua, 580 m, 1; 1 km NE Los Arroyos, 1220 m, 1; 0.6 km NE Los Arroyos, 1098 m, 3; 3 km SE Los Arroyos, 976 m, 1; 1 km N Aceitillar, 1281 m, 1; Las Abejas, 12 km NW Aceitillar, 1129 m, 2; 17 km NW Oviedo, 183 m, 5; *Isla Saona:* 1.2 km N Mano Juan, s.l., 1; 1.5 km N Mano Juan, s.l., 1.

35. *Hylephila phylea phylea* Drury, 1773

TL Antigua, St. Christopher, Nevis; restricted to Antigua by Evans (Miller and Brown, 1981:33).

FW males 14–16, females 14–18.

Hylephila ph. phylea is widespread on Hispaniola, but it is rare above 1098 m (Constanza), and most records are from sea level (Grand-Goâve, Punta Cana, Playa Bayahibe, Barahona) to about 671 m (exception: Puesto Pirámide 204, 1586 m). Its habitat preferences are primarily grassy fields, where it may be modestly common, the bright orange males flying conspicuously just above the grass tops. However, these skippers are occasionally found along paths and in open areas in *caféières* and *cafetales*. They do not shun exposed areas behind beaches (Playa Bayahibe), where there is open forest with *Acacia*. Likewise, 1 was taken along a mangrove border (Grand-Goâve). Certainly the region about Carrefour Joffre in northern Haiti is one of the bleakest areas seen by me, and *Hylephila ph. phylea* was taken there, as well as others in *Acacia* scrub at El Limón and Canoa. At Villa Riva, several were seen and 2 collected in the rank weedy growth around an abandoned basketball court at the southern edge of town.

Food plants include *Zinnia elegans*, *Cynoglossum amabile* and *Melanthera* sp. (Constanza), *Sida* sp. (Rancho Arriba, Villa Riva), *Lantana ovatifolia* (Santiago, El Limón), *L. reticulata* (Barahona, Playa Bayahibe), the white-flowered climbing milkweed, *Funastrum clausum* (Palmar de Ocoa), *Antigonon leptopus* (Santiago, twice; Azua), *Jacaranda acutifolia* (Bignoniaceae) (Santiago), *Bidens pilosa*

(Los Quemados), *Croton barahonensis* (Vallejuelo), *Stachytarpheta jamaicensis* (1.3 km W Monteada Nueva), and *Ageratum conyzoides* (Barahona, twice). Temperatures of activity were between 23°C (Puesto Pirámide 204) and 39°C (Playa Bayahibe), and times between 0900 and 1800 h. At Constanza, *H. ph. phylea* was common in the morning (3.vii; 0900–1130 h) but was much less common in the afternoon (1400–1600 h). The morning temperature was 28°C, the afternoon 30°C. One individual was taken in the late afternoon when the sun was setting (Grand-Goâve).

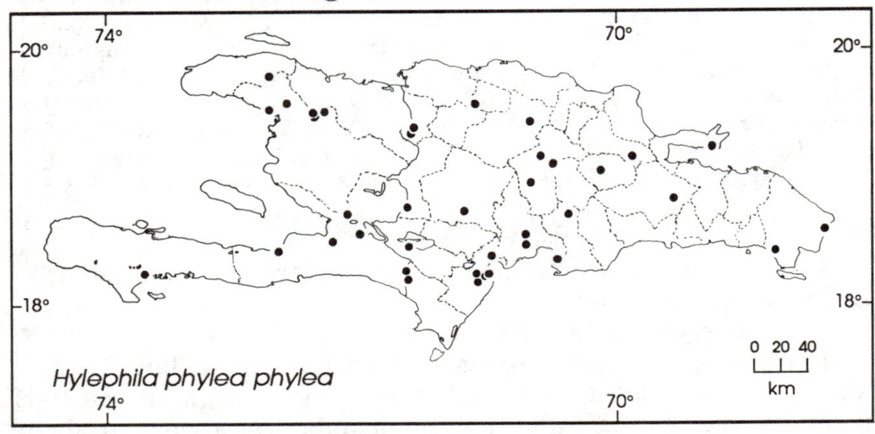

One striking fact is that most of our specimens are from July (36), with only 3 from April, 17 from May, 15 from June, 16 from August, 9 from January, 8 from October, and 4 from December. We have several times commented among ourselves on the virtual absence of these skippers in June; it is not until late July that they begin to appear in some numbers. Comstock (1944:358) considered that *H. ph. phylea* "probably flies throughout the year" on Puerto Rico. The data presented by Brown and Heineman (1972: 410–11) likewise suggested that the species flies during the entire year on Jamaica. The same is true on Hispaniola, considering the spread of our records; but the species is uncommon during some months.

A copulating pair was taken on 16.viii (Playa Bayahibe) and another on 17.viii (Rancho Arriba); in the latter case, the male was flying, and the time was between 1145 and 1330 h.

Specimens: Haiti: Nord-Ouest; between Bassin Bleu and Gros Morne, 1; *l'Artibonite:* 1.6 km E Carrefour Marmelade, 854 m, 1; Platon, 6 km E Carrefour Marmelade, 793 m, 1; 6.4 km W Ennery, 336 m, 2; 3.4 km N Carrefour Joffre, 114 m, 1; 8.5 km W Ça Soleil, s.l., 2; *l'Ouest:* 3.8 km N Terre Rouge, 519 m, 1; 2 km NW Fond Parisien, 1; Boutilliers Road, 266–915 m, 1; 6.7 km

E Grand-Goâve, s.l., 1; *Sud:* 7 km SW Cavaillon, 122 m, 1; *República Dominicana: Elías Piña:* 2 km NE Puesto Pirámide 204, 1586 m, 1; *Dajabón:* Restauración, 400–800 m, 1; 7 km N Restauración, 671 m, 1; *Santiago Rodríguez:* 3 km W Los Quemados, 183 m, 4; *Santiago:* 7 km SW Santiago, 214 m, 13; *La Vega:* La Palma, 19 km W Jayaco, 1007 m, 1; Jarabacoa, 530 m, 4; 1 km S Constanza, 1098 m, 16; *Duarte:* Villa Riva, 2; *Sánchez Ramírez:* 1 km NE Las Lagunas, 183 m, 2; *Samaná:* 4.5 km E Samaná, 1; *La Altagracia:* Punta Cana, s.l., 3; 2.5 km S Playa Bayahibe, s.l., 2; *Monte Plata:* 8 km NE Bayaguana, 1; *Peravia:* 2 km SW Rancho Arriba, 10; *Azua:* 5 km S Peralta, 305 m, 1; 2.6 km N, 6.6 km W Azua, 183 m, 1; 1 km E Palmar de Ocoa, s.l., 1; *San Juan:* 9 km E Vallejuelo, 610 m, 2; *Independencia:* 4 km E El Limón, 183 m, 1; *Barahona:* 11.5 km ESE Canoa, s.l., 1; Barahona, s.l., 14; 2 km SW Barahona, 122 m, 2; 12 km SW Barahona, 427 m, 1; 1.3 km W Monteada Nueva, 1037 m, 2; *Pedernales:* Mencia, 397 m, 1; 6 km N Cabeza de Agua, 580 m, 1; 26 km NE Cabo Rojo, 732 m, 2.

36. *Atalopedes mesogramma apa* Comstock, 1944

TL Aibonito, Puerto Rico.

FW males 16–18 mm, females 17–19 mm.

Abundant locally, *Atalopedes m. apa* seems generally uncommon. I have only 3 specimens from Haiti, and the Dominican localities yielded only 13, with a long series from only 1 of them. Usually, single specimens are taken. Geographically, *A. m. apa* has been collected more often on the north island than on the south (2 localities, 2 specimens, from Haiti; 4 localities, 8 specimens from the República Dominicana). Elevational distribution is between sea level (Santo Domingo, Barahona) and 1891 m (Puesto Pirámide 204).

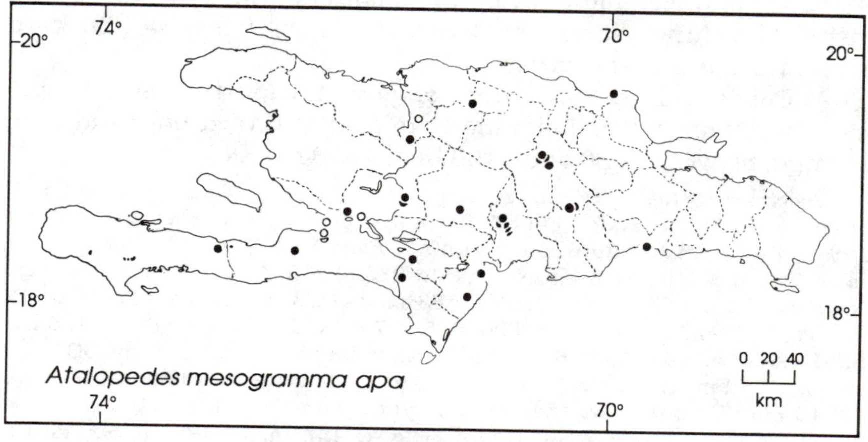

Atalopedes mesogramma apa

Atalopedes m. apa is a skipper of mesic and semimesic situations. Open areas are more often occupied: *cafetales*, fields, lawns, fallow fields, roadsides, and road cuts. We have taken *A. m. apa* feeding on *Zinnia elegans* (Asteraceae) and *Cynoglossum amabile* (Boraginaceae) at Constanza, on the introduced *Leonurus sibericus* (Lamiaceae) southeast of that town, and on *Lantana ovatifolia* (Río San Juan) and *Lantana reticulata* (Barahona). The plants at Río San Juan were of the white-flowered horticultural variety. At Barahona, these skippers were feeding on *Ageratum conyzoides*, on *Bidens pilosa* at Los Quemados, and on *Bougainvillea glabra* at 1.7 km S Jarabcoa.

Temperatures varied between 23°C (Puesto Pirámide 204, La Laguna) and 40°C (Río San Juan), and times between 0830 and 1630 h; more individuals are encountered before midday than in the afternoon.

Comstock (1944:561) recorded, for the Hispaniolan paratypes of *A. m. apa*, December-March and June, suggesting a winter brood. My material is peculiarly grouped, with most specimens in July (43), and only 8 in June, 3 each in January and April, 2 in March, and 1 each in May, August, and December. Even in the summer, our material has been taken only between 26.vi and 6.viii, a relatively limited period of abundance. There are many localities that we have revisited over the years without seeing *A. m. apa*, and I have little doubt that it is absent from such localities as La Romana, Playa Bayahibe, 10 km W Jayaco, Samaná, and Boutilliers Road, to note only a few. It is intriguing that Hall (1925:190) mentioned having taken only 1 specimen near La Vega; we have not seen the species there and from Hall's statement assume that *A. m. apa* was uncommon during the months of his and Kaempffer's visits (May-June, November-December), times when we too have found the species uncommon.

At Constanza, on 29.vii, *A. m. apa* was the fourth hesperiid species to become active (following *U. p. domingo*, *W. druryi*, and *P. a. antiqua*, between 0930 and 1100 h) at 1030 h.

Specimens: Haiti: l'Ouest: 20 km S Mirebalais, 580 m, 1; 5.4 km S Découzé, 397 m, 1; *Sud:* 3 km SW Paillant, 793 m, 1; *República Dominicana: Dajabón:* 4 km S Restauración, 580 m, 1; *Elías Piña:* 1 km SW Puesto Pirámide 204, 1891 m, 1; 2 km NE Puesto Pirámide 204, 1586 m, 1; *Santiago Rodríguez:* 3 km W Los Quemados, 183 m, 1; *La Vega:* La Palma, 19 km W Jayaco, 1007 m, 1; Jarabacoa, 530 m, 5; 1.7 km S Jarabacoa, 488 m, 1; 5 km SE Jarabacoa, 595 m, 1; 6 km SSE Constanza, 1403 m, 1; 7 km SE Constanza, 1312 m, 1; 8 km SE Constanza, 495 m, 1; 1 km S Constanza, 1098 m, 33; 10 km SE Constanza, 1647 m, 1; *María T. Sánchez:* Río San Juan, s.l., 1; *Monseñor Nouel:* 14 km SW Piedra Blanca, 427 m, 3; 17 km SW Piedra Blanca, 854 m, 1; *Dist. Nac.:* Santo Domingo, 1 (MNHNSD); *Santiago:* 0.3 km NE La Laguna, 1723 m, 1; *San Juan:* 9 km E Vallejuelo, 610 m, 2; *Independencia:* 4–7 km NE El Aguacate, 519–824 m, 1; *Barahona:* Barahona, s.l., 5; 8 km NW Paraiso, 1 (MPM); *Pedernales:* Mencía, 397 m, 1.

37. *Hesperia nabokovi* Bell and Comstock, 1948

TL Thomazeau, Dépt. de l'Ouest, Haiti.

FW males 18–22, females 19–21 mm.

This skipper was described as a species of *Atalopedes*, but recently Burns (1987) has shown that *nabokovi* is to be referred to *Hesperia*. *Hesperia nabokovi* is the only member of its genus that occurs outside the Holarctic.

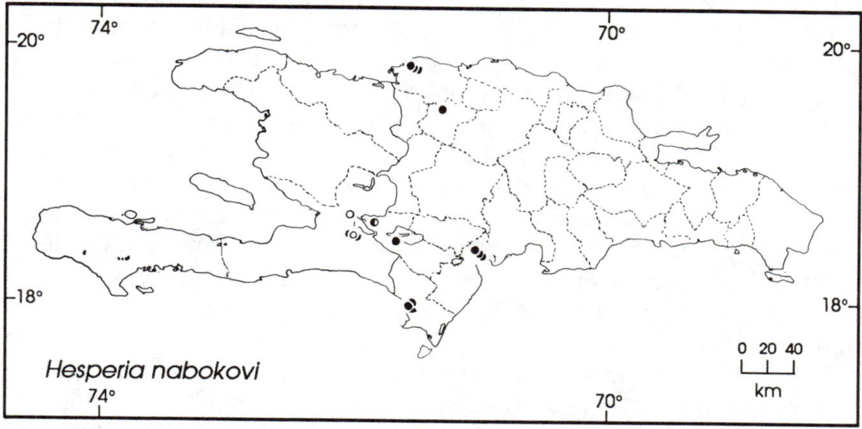

Hesperia nabokovi was described on the basis of a male (the holotype) and a female from Fond Parisien, Dépt. de l'Ouest, Haiti. The 2 localities are on the north and south sides of Etang Saumâtre in the Cul de Sac plain. Since this plain continues into the República Dominicana as the Valle de Neiba, without appreciable floral changes, it seemed only likely that *H. nabokovi* should occur in the latter country.

On 24.iv.1982, Gali took a male *H. nabokovi* near Fond Parisien as it perched on an *Acacia* bush; this is the only specimen I have from Haiti. On 31.iv.1982, Gali saw another at the same place as it landed on the gravel road. On 31.vii.1982, Gali took a second male near Canoa in the República Dominicana, the first Dominican record. (*Hesperia nabokovi* was not listed by Cucurullo, 1959; Marión Heredia, 1974, listed the species but had not taken specimens.) But both these specimens do not add appreciably to the known distribution of *H. nabokovi*, since they are in the Cul de Sac–Valle de Neiba plain and in the extreme western Llanos de Azua. At least they give some hints as to the ecological situation where *H. nabokovi* occurs, namely arid *Acacia* scrub, near sea level.

In the summer of 1983, Raburn and I secured no further *H. nabokovi*, despite 2 visits to the Canoa area. But observations there suggested that *H. nabokovi*, like *O. stillmani* and the local member of the *Calisto lyceia* complex (*Calisto franciscoi*), is associated with large stands of tussocky grass (*Uniola virgata*) that are common near Canoa (see account of *O. stillmani*). This grass occurs not only in the Cul de Sac–Valle de Neiba but at least as far east as Azua in the Llanos de Azua and also on the Península de Barahona to the south and the Valle de Cibao in the north—both areas that we had visited in preceding years. But this habitat is bleak and sere and is not conducive to butterfly collecting; it simply looks too uninviting and unproductive.

On 8.x.1983, Raburn and I looked for *Calisto* near Cabo Rojo, in a large area of the tussocky grass with very scattered trees. Within a minute of leaving the car, I saw a moderately sized orange butterfly cross the paved road, land for a moment on the low yellow flower of a *Urechites lutea* (Apocynaceae), and then dash away. During the brief time the skipper was on the flower, I was able to identify it as a male *H. nabokovi*. With this incentive, we spent 1 h at this locality and secured 2 males and saw 1 female. On a return visit on 10.x.1983, 6 more males were seen, of which 4 were netted. All individuals on the latter date were taken feeding on the flowers of *Urechites lutea*. These flowers are themselves of interest: they open in the very early morning, and, despite the robustness of the plant and the flower, they are shriveled and inaccessible to Lepidoptera by about 1200 h. At Cabo Rojo, these flowers were the only ones used by *H. nabokovi;* the earliest skipper was seen at 0815 h, and, after a brief flurry of activity, none was seen after 0945 h, even though the flowers were still open.

We attempted to collect *H. nabokovi* at a locality 9 km SE Pedernales on 9.x.1983 between 0945 and 1030 h, with no success. *Urechites lutea* was abundant and open, but we may simply have been too late in the morning to secure the skippers.

On 12.x.1983, we searched for *H. nabokovi* near Canoa; 1 skipper was taken at 1130 h as it landed on the tip of a stick about 3 cm in diameter, 1 m above the ground. We saw no others, and once again the time may have been too late.

In an attempt to secure *Calisto* near Monte Cristi in the northwest República Dominicana, Raburn, Amador, and I collected on 31.vii.1983 at 1 km SE and 4 km SE Monte Cristi; both sites are large expanses of *U. virgata*. We did not secure the satyrids but did collect *O. stillmani;* it seemed likely that *H. nabokovi* also occurred there, although this Valle de Cibao area is many kilometers and at least 2 mountain ranges removed from the Cul de Sac–Valle de Neiba plain. Raburn and I revisited both localities on 18.x.1983 and secured a series of 5 *H. nabokovi.* These skippers were flying above the tussocky grass, landing on low shrubs and very stunted trees, 1 m or less above the ground. Although *U. lutea* was present, we did not see the skippers feeding on it or any other flower. One female was taken by Raburn as it "skipped" short distances (1–2 m) from place to place on the ground and did not land on any foliage. The last skipper was taken at 1145 h; collecting had begun at 1000 h.

At El Limón in the Valle de Neiba, Raburn and I took a series of 6 *H. nabokovi* on 15–16.x.1983 as they fed on large shrubby roadside *Lantana ovatifolia.* Here they were accompanied by *O. stillmani, H. ph. phylea,* as well as various nymphalids, and *Calisto hendersoni.* Although we collected (on 16.x) between 0940 and 1130 h, no *H. nabokovi* were seen after 1115 h. On 2.iv, I saw a male and a female *H. nabokovi* as they fed briefly on *Pithecellobium circinale* and *Melochia nodiflora.* Henderson also saw 2 *H. nabokovi* 5 km NW Tierra Nueva on 8.iv in *Acacia* scrub.

Since the above detailed experiences, Gonzalez and I have taken *H. nabokovi* in all the above areas, at times in modest abundance. We have reconfirmed the predilection of *H. nabokovi* for *Urechites lutea* as a nectar source (2 km NE and 4 km NE Cabo Rojo); these large skippers also fed on *Croton linearis* (4 km SE Monte Cristi, Zamba) and on *Melochia nodiflora* (4 km NE Monte Cristi). At 11.5 km ESE Canoa, *H. nabokovi* was feeding on *Lippia micromera.*

Thus, *H. nabokovi* is now known from 3 general regions: the Cul de Sac–Valle de Neiba plain and the extreme western edge of the Llanos de Azua, from Thomazeau and Fond Parisien in Haiti in the west to Canoa in the east; the Península de Barahona; and the western Valle de Cibao. Although these 3 areas are widely separated and divided from each other by high mountain ranges, the samples from the 3 regions are very similar. The series from Cabo Rojo, however, may represent a different taxon. *Hesperia nabokovi* should be looked for in Haiti in the xeric scrub along the shore of the Golfe de la Gonâve as far north as Gonaïves, and thence onto the southern shore of the Presqu'île du Nord-Ouest; this entire region is not only confluent with the Cul de Sac plain but also is sufficiently arid to offer suitable habitat for this skipper. We have never taken *H. nabokovi* away from *Uniola virgata,* and there likely is an intimate association between them. Wherever the grass occurs, one should look not only for *H. nabokovi* but also for *O. stillmani* and a member of the *Calisto lyceia* complex.

Most specimens and observations are from August (18) and October (18) with 11 in May, 7 in June, 5 in April, and 2 in July. The type-material was taken in February and September. Times of collection and observation were between 0820 and 1400 h, with temperatures between 30°C (Cabo Rojo, 11.5 km ESE Canoa) and 38°C (Cabo Rojo, El Limón, Tierra Nueva). Elevations were from sea level to 214 m (Zamba).

Specimens: Haiti: l'Ouest: 2 km W Fond Parisien, s.l., 1; *República Dominicana: Monte Cristi:* 1 km SE Monte Cristi, 4; 2 km SE Monte Cristi, 1; 4 km SE Monte Cristi, 11; *Santiago Rodríguez:* 3.0 km S Zamba, 214 m, 1; *Barahona:* 8 km ESE Canoa, s.l., 1; 11.5 km ESE Canoa, s.l., 4; 12 km ESE Canoa, s.l., 1; *Independencia:* 4 km E El Limón, s.l., 6; *Pedernales:* 2 km N Cabo Rojo, s.l., 2; 2 km NE Cabo Rojo, s.l., 7; 4 km NE Cabo Rojo, s.l., 13.

Sight records: Haiti: l'Ouest: 2 km W Fond Parisien, s.l.—1 seen, 31.iv; *República Dominicana: Independencia:* 5 km NW Tierra Nueva, s.l.—2 seen, 8.iv; *Pedernales:* 2 km N Cabo Rojo, s.l.—4 seen, 15.vi.

38. *Choranthus haitensis* Skinner, 1920

TL Haiti, Santo Domingo; restricted to Port-de-Paix, Dépt. du Nord-Ouest, Haiti, by Gillham and Ehrlich (Miller and Brown, 1981:44).

FW males 13–15 mm, females 14–16 mm.

Of the 3 species of *Choranthus* on Hispaniola, *Ch. haitensis* is the most widely distributed geographically. It inhabits weedy or grassy areas, often associated with mesic *caféières* and *cafetales*, either along their margins or enclosed within them. On 1 occasion (Yamasá) we took a specimen at the edge of a cane field, and elsewhere on roadsides adjacent to a cornfield (Découzé) and in weedy areas in the karst *haitises* (9 and 11 km SE Sosúa). *Choranthus haitensis* also occurs in xeric woods (La Romana) and along roads through mesic upland broadleaf forest (Las Abejas), but even in such situations, these skippers are along paths or roads, not in the forest proper. Additionally, the species shuns truly xeric areas and is unknown from oases in the Cul de Sac–Valle de Neiba plain or in the western Valle de Cibao. The species has also been taken in grassy areas immediately adjacent to the ocean (Jacmel, 8 km NE Río San Juan).

The elevational distribution is from sea level (Jacmel, Carrefour la Mort, Río San Juan, Cruce de Rincón, Río Chavón) to 1129 m (Las Abejas); despite this broad distribution, *Ch. haitensis* is uncommon at elevations above about 610 m. The highest elevations on the north island are in the Cordillera Central (La Palma), where the species reaches 1007 m; but all Central localities are peripheral to the main mass of these mountains. We have not seen *Ch. haitensis* within the mountains at Constanza or La Ciénaga, for instance, or between Constanza and La Horma. In the Sierra de

Neiba it reaches an elevation of 732 m, in the Cordillera Septentrional 610 m, and in the Sierra de Baoruco, 1129 m (Las Abejas), at which elevation it is far outnumbered by *Ch. melissa* in these mountains. Times of flight were between 0900 and 1750 h, and temperatures varied between 22°C (La Palma) and 42°C (La Romana). We have collected *Ch. haitensis* most commonly in March–April, July-August, and October-November; I have only 29 June, 5 May, 2 September, and 5 December specimens. This skipper flies during the entire year, but there may be 3 broods (spring-late summer-fall) and scattered individuals at other times of the year.

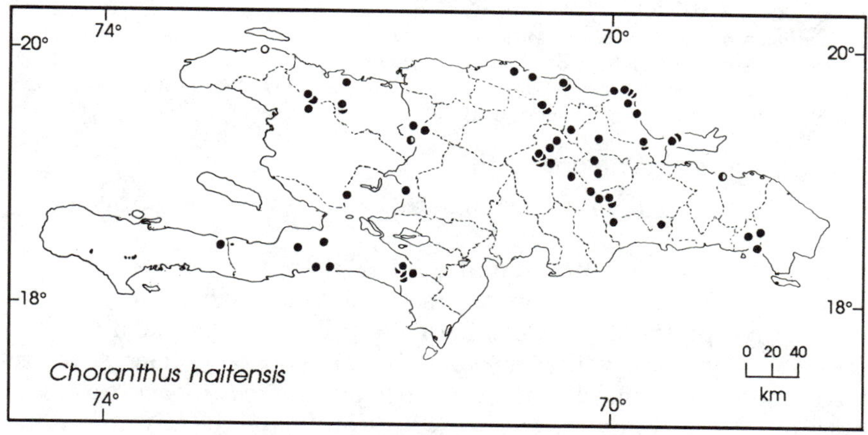

We have taken *Ch. haitensis* on *Blechum pyramidatum* (Las Lagunas), on the white-flowered horticultural variety of *Lantana ovatifolia* (La Vega, Río San Juan), on *Morinda citrifolia* (Río Chavón), *Bidens pilosa* (9 km NE Río San Juan), and on *Tournefortia hirsutissima* (9 km SE Sosúa).

Specimens: Haiti: Nord: Carrefour la Mort, s.l., 2; 5.6 km SE Dondon, 366 m, 1; 1.8 km S Dondon, 366 m, 1; 3.5 km W Plaisance, 305 m, 1; 3.5 km S Plaisance, 336 m, 1; *l'Artibonite:* 1.6 km E Carrefour Marmelade, 854 m, 2; *l'Ouest:* 1.6 km N Saut d'Eau, 183–275 m, 1; Boutilliers Road, *ca.* 266–915 m, 4; 13.6 km E Jacmel, s.l., 1; 21.3 km E Jacmel, s.l., 1; 1.6 km N Découzé, 702 m, 1; 0.8 km S Découzé, 702 m, 1; 2.1 km S Découzé, 641 m, 1; *Sud:* 2.9 km SW Paillant, 681 m, 1; *República Dominicana: Dajabón:* Los Cerezos, 12 km NW Río Limpio, 580 m, 2; 10 km NE Restauración, 610 m, 1; *Elías Piña:* La Laguna, 10 km S Comendador, 1; *Puerto Plata:* 13 km SE Luperón, 214 m, 2; 8 km E Puerto Plata, *ca.* 15 m, 3; 9 km SE Sosúa, 15 m, 3; 11 km SE Sosúa, 47 m, 1; *Santiago:* La Cumbre, 610 m, 1; 2 km E Pedro García, 427 m, 1; *Espaillat:* 3 km N Puesto Grande, 580 m, 5; *María T. Sánchez:* Río San Juan, s.l., 2; 19 km SE Río San Juan, 92 m, 1; 8 km NE Río San Juan, s.l., 4; 9 km NE Río San Juan, s.l., 5; 11 km NE Río San Juan, 1; 14 km S La Entrada, s.l., 8; Cruce de Rincón, s.l., 1; 1 km S Cruce de Rincón, 10; *Sánchez Ramírez:* 1

km NE Las Lagunas, 183 m, 28; 1 km SE La Mata, 1; *Duarte:* 12 km SE San Francisco de Macorís, 1; *La Vega:* 5 km NW La Vega, 122 m, 1; 10 km W Jayaco, 915 m, 3; La Palma, 19 km W Jayaco, 1007 m, 33; Buena Vista, 11 km NE Jarabacoa, 640 m, 4; Jarabacoa, 530 m, 17; 1 km S Jarabacoa, 519 m, 1; 1.7 km S Jarabacoa, 488 m, 5; 2 km S Jarabacoa, 488 m, 1; *Monseñor Nouel:* Bonao, 153 m, 3; 6 km SE Maimón, 122 m, 2; *Samaná:* 6.9 km NE Sánchez, 336 m, 6; 13.2 km NE Sánchez, 92 m, 5; *La Altagracia:* 16 km NE La Romana, 61 m, 6; Río Chavón, 10 km NE La Romana, 4; *La Romana:* Río Chavón, 8 km SE La Romana, s.l., 7; *Monte Plata:* 7 km SE Yamasá, 31 m, 1; 2 km W Esperalvillo, 92 m, 1; 11 km W Esperalvillo, 153 m, 1; *Dist. Nac.:* 9 km NE Guerra, 4; 5 km S San Isidro, 2; 30 km NW Santo Domingo, 122 m, 7; *Pedernales:* Las Abejas, 12 km NW Aceitillar, 1129 m, 3; 1 km SE Banano, 183 m, 2; 6 km N Cabeza de Agua, 580 m, 1; 1 km N Cabeza de Agua, 275 m, 1; Mencía, 197 m, 1.

Sight records: República Dominicana: Dajabón: 3 km ESE Villa Anacaona, 478 m—1 seen, 27.v; *Puerto Plata:* 13 km SE Luperón, 214 m—1 seen, 17.v; *La Vega:* La Palma, 19 km W Jayaco, 1007 m—1 seen, 27.vi. *Hato Mayor:* 25 km E Sabana de la Mar—2 seen, 8.iii.

39. *Choranthus schwartzi* Gali, 1983

TL 10 km W Jayaco, 915 m, Prov. de la Vega, República Dominicana.

FW males 14–15 mm, females 16–17 mm.

Choranthus schwartzi was described from 3 localities on the eastern periphery of the Cordillera Central. At these localities, the species is syntopic with *Ch. haitensis*, and the 2 species seem to have similar ecologies: both are most often encountered in clearings or along roads in mesic forest and *cafetales*. *Choranthus schwartzi* has not been taken at higher elevations (Constanza), and

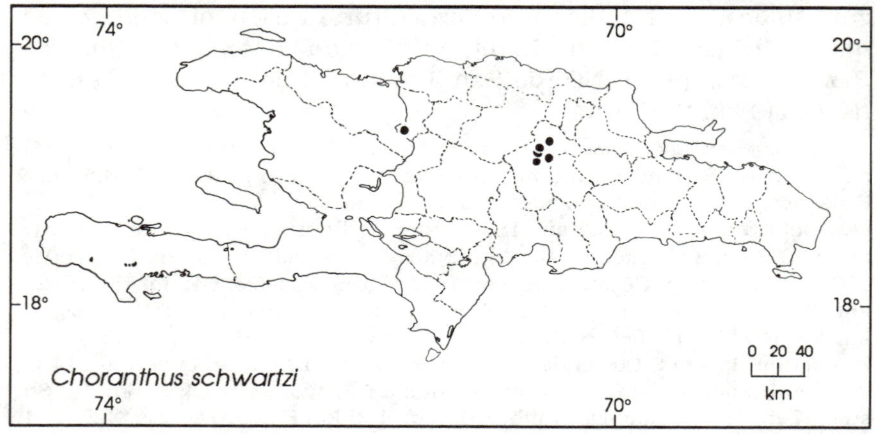

its elevational distribution is between 488 m (1.7 km S Jarabacoa) and 1007 m (La Palma). Gali (1983) and Gali and Schwartz

(1983b) discussed the ecology of the 10 km W Jayaco locality; that site had changed (1983) in that there has been cutting of timber and obliteration of the small grassy meadow where *Ch. schwartzi* had been collected. By 1986, the meadow had "reappeared," and *Ch. schwartzi* were once more present. Likewise, the site of collection (pinewoods) at Buena Vista has been modified or destroyed. La Palma remains unchanged, and *Ch. schwartzi* is still (1986) abundant there. Times of collection varied between 0915 and 1745 h, although the skippers were most active in the morning. Temperatures varied beteen 20°C and 36°C. Most specimens (20) have been collected in July, with 11 in August, 2 in June, and 1 in December.

I have examined a specimen of *Ch. schwartzi* from the vicinity of Restauración, far to the west of the known range. *Choranthus schwartzi* should be looked for at appropriate elevations along the northern slopes of the Cordillera Central, and possibly even onto the northern slopes of the Massif du Nord near the Dominico-Haitian border.

Specimens: República Dominicana: La Vega: 10 km W Jayaco, 915 m, 4; La Palma, 19 km W Jayaco, 1007 m, 25; Buena Vista, 11 km NE Jarabacoa, 640 m, 1; Jarabacoa, 530 m, 9; 1.7 km S Jarabacoa, 488 m, 2.

40. *Choranthus melissa* Gali, 1983

TL Las Abejas, 11 km NW Aceitillar, 1220 m, Prov. de Pedernales, República Dominicana.

FW males 13–15 mm, females 14–15 mm.

The known distribution of this skipper is in the uplands of the Sierra de Baoruco–Massif de la Selle, at elevations between 732 m (El Aguacate, 26 km NE Cabo Rojo) and 1281 m (Aceitillar). The 7 localities whence it is known are (1) deciduous forest, slightly drier at El Aguacate and at the type-locality than at Las Abejas (12 km NW Aceitillar), where there is an excellent stand of rich hardwood forest, virtually untouched (until 1983), and (2) pine forest and mixed pine-hardwoods (1 km N Aceitillar, both Cabo Rojo localities). All specimens have been taken along roads through forest or in clearings in these situations (type-locality). *Choranthus melissa* is syntopic with *Ch. haitensis* at 12 km NW Aceitillar. Such syntopy is exceptional between these 2 species; this locality likewise is the highest from which *Ch. haitensis* has been recorded in these southern mountains. Although the situation at Las Abejas proper is very specialized—broadleaf forest surrounded by pinewoods—I suspect that *Ch. melissa* will be found elsewhere in these mountains (as it has at 12 km NW Aceitillar and

El Aguacate) and in Haiti as well. We did not succeed in finding it in the vicinity of Forêt des Pins in the latter country; the area there lacks extensive stands of hardwoods and is predominantly pine.

Until 1986, *Ch. melissa* was considered an endemic of the Sierra de Baoruco–Massif de la Selle. But in that year, Gonzalez took a single fresh individual between 458 and 610 m on the isolated Sierra Martín García. This mountain range is on the north island, some 100 km to the west of the nearest locality (El Aguacate) on the south island. The taking of this skipper there is completely unexpected. It is very difficult to regard it as a vagrant, since the distance of the Sierra Martín García from the eastern extreme of the La Selle, as well as the interposed arid and low-lying Valle de Neiba, preclude a vagrant making this journey. What seems likely is that *Ch. melissa* occurs on the north island Sierra de Neiba, where it remains uncollected; the Sierra Martín García is an isolated remnant of that range and *Ch. melissa* occurs there as an upland relict.

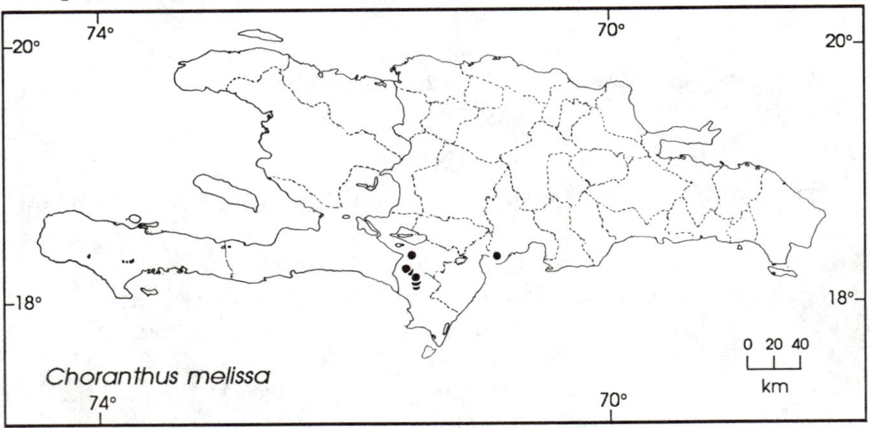

Temperatures of collection varied between 25°C and 33°C, and times between 0900 and 1435 h. Most specimens, however, were collected in early to midmorning (0900–1030 h), when these jewellike skippers are seen perched on shrubs, usually less than 1 m above the ground. At El Aguacate, *Ch. melissa* was taken only at higher elevations (732 m), resting in the morning sun on *Bryophyllum pinnatum* (Crassulaceae).

Almost all specimens have been taken in June (27) and July (49), with smaller numbers in August (3), October (14), and December (1). Males are very common, but females have remained unknown. I have 2 females taken in October; these are colored and patterned like males, except that the black fw margin is broader in females than in males.

At Las Abejas, in October, *Ch. melissa* were feeding on the small white flowers of *Chamissoa altissima* (Amaranthaceae). The inflorescences are elongate, lax, and somewhat pendant, and the *Ch. melissa* flew up to 1.3 m above the ground to forage on these flowers. When not feeding, the skippers fly and perch no more than 0.6 m above the ground. At 27 km NE Cabo Rojo, *Ch. melissa* was taken feeding on roadside *Ambrosia artemisiifolia* (Asteraceae).

Although Las Abejas and El Aguacate seem close to each other on a map, they are in actuality on the south and north slopes of the Sierra de Baoruco–Massif de la Selle ranges. There is no evidence that *Ch. melissa* occurs in the pine forests between these 2 localities, and the north- and south-slope populations are almost certainly not in genetic contact.

Specimens: República Dominicana: Barahona: west slope, Sierra Martín García, 458–610 m, 1; *Independencia:* 4–7 km NE El Aguacate, 732 m, 7; *Pedernales:* 26 km NE Cabo Rojo, 732 m, 1; 27 km NE Cabo Rojo, 793 m, 2; 1 km N Aceitillar, 1281 m, 1; Las Abejas, 11 km NW Aceitillar, 1220 m, 10: Las Abejas, 12 km NW Aceitillar, 1129 m, 73.

41. *Paratrytone batesi* Bell, 1935

TL Massif de la Selle, 5000–7000 ft., Dépt. de l'Ouest, Haiti.

FW 15–17 mm.

Paratrytone batesi has been known only from the region of the type-locality on the south island in Haiti. Gali and I visited the high ridge of the Massif de la Selle at Forêt des Pins in search of this skipper without success. On the Dominican side of the border in these same moutains (Los Arroyos) we have taken 1 example, and I have 2 specimens from the Sierra de Baoruco. Elsewhere in the República Dominicana, I have specimens from the Sierra de Neiba and the Cordillera Central, and from the isolated Sierra Martín García, a range affiliated with the Sierra de Neiba but reaching only a relatively low elevation. Thus *P. batesi* is widespread on the north island in the República Dominicana and doubtless occurs in Haiti at least in the Montagnes du Trou-d'Eau where these mountains reach the border and become the Sierra de Neiba.

Yocom, in ii.1984, took 1 *P. batesi* in the Massif de la Hotte (Morne Formond), the first record for that range. Gali, in ix.1984, secured a long series in the Massif de la Selle (nr. Scierie) and presumably close to the type-locality. The skippers were extremely abundant in this region, in open pine forest, often with a fern understory. At Pic Formond and Pic Macaya in the Massif de la Hotte, Gali found *P. batesi* less common in the same habitat.

Miller (1966:26), quoting from Bell's original description, stated that *P. batesi* occurs in "the pine forests and the edge of the cloud forest." Neither of these ecologies appears to be occupied in the República Dominicana. We have spent many man-hours in the pine forests of the Cordillera Central and the Dominican portion of the Massif de la Selle as well as in the pinewoods of the Sierra de Neiba; despite the abundance in these forests of *Cynoglossum amabile* (Boraginaceae), whose blue flowers are immensely attractive to *P. batesi*, we have never encountered these skippers in this habitat. As far as cloud forest is concerned, there are fine stands of mesic broadleaf forest in the Massif de la Selle (between El Aguacate and Los Arroyos); but once more, we have seen only 1 *P. batesi* there. In mesic forest in the Sierra de Neiba we have collected 5 specimens; 4 of these, however, were along a road through the forest and were perched to sun on the lower leaves of trees or bushes, about 1.5 m above the ground. The El Veinte specimen is from a small clearing in hardwoods. At Jayaco, on the east face of the Cordillera Central, 1 *P. batesi* was taken in a clearing adjacent to a mountain torrent; the clearing was surrounded by broadleaf forest.

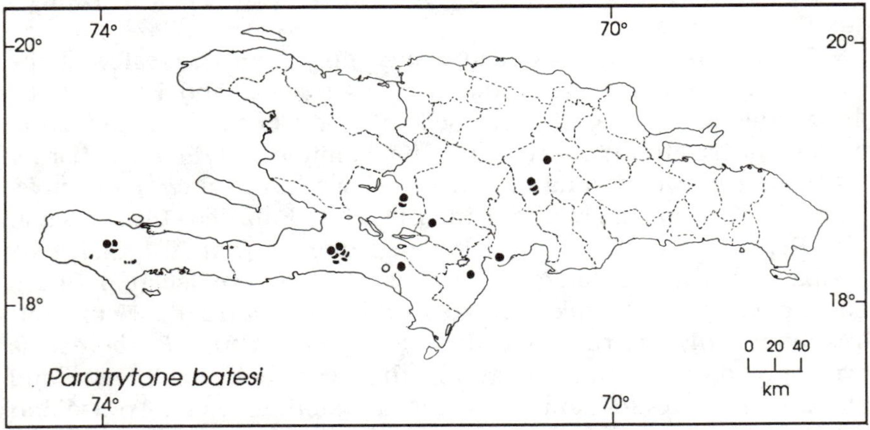

But these examples are exceptional. Most Dominican specimens have come from open areas: a fallow cabbage field with *Leonurus sibericus* (Lamiaceae), upon which the skippers were feeding, on a row of tall roadside *Melilotus alba* (Fabaceae), upon whose leaves the skippers were resting, in scrubby growth between 2 small creeks, where *P. batesi* was feeding on *C. amabile*, and at

El Limón, where the skippers were on leaves of low (0.6 m) plants adjacent to a large cutover area in semimesic deciduous woods. The Monteada Nueva specimens were from a roadside with abundant *Stachytarpheta jamaicensis* (on which the skippers were not feeding) through a *cafetal*. The Morne Formond specimen was taken on *Ageratum* sp. (Asteraceae). At Los Arroyos, a specimen was taken in cutover deciduous forest, perched on a grass leaf in the sun.

The elevational distribution of *P. batesi* is between 915 m (Jayaco) and 2300 m (Scierie, Pic Macaya). Temperatures of activity were low—between 19°C and 31°C—and flying times were 0930–1445 h; more so than many other upland butterflies, *P. batesi* is affected by overcast or rainy weather—a virtually daily occurrence at the altitudes where this skipper occurs. This, coupled with its seeming rarity, makes collecting one of these skippers a rewarding experience. Most of our specimens were taken in September (50), with 7 in July, 1 in February, 3 in June, and 8 in August. *Paratrytone batesi* is obviously more abundant in the fall (September); note the low number in June, with slight increases in July and August.

Gali took a copulating pair on 4.ix (5 km WNW Scierie, 1891 m, 0930–1030 h, 21°C) in an open meadow in pine forest.

Specimens: Haiti: l'Ouest: 200 m N Scierie, 2300 m, 2 (FSM); 1.2 km S Scierie, 1950 m, 1 (FSM); 1 km SE Scierie, 1891 m, 1 (FSM); 4.8 km NW Scierie, 2187 m, 1 (FSM); 2 km NW Scierie, 1785–1810 m, 8 (FSM); 1–4 km WNW Scierie, 1830–1891 m, 2 (FSM); 5 km WNW Scierie, 1891 m, 24 (FSM); 1 km W Roche Cabrit, 2000 m, 1 (FSM); east side, Pic Cabaïo, 2.4 km from Scierie, 2100 m, 2 (FSM); *Sud:* Morne Formond, 1750 m, 1 (FSM); Pic Formond, near top, 1900–1910 m, 5 (FSM); Pic Macaya, near top, 2300 m (FSM); *República Dominicana: Elías Piña:* summit, Loma Nalga de Maco, *ca.* 1990 m, 1; 2 km NE Puesto Pirámide 204, 1586 m, 3; 1 km SW Puesto Pirámide 204, 1891 m, 1; *Baoruco: ca.* 8 km SW El Veinte, 1617 m, 1; *Barahona:* El Limón, summit, Sierra Martín García, 976–1037 m, 2; 1.3 km W Monteada Nueva, 1037 m, 2; *La Vega:* 10 km SE Constanza, 1647 m, 4; 14 km SE Constanza, 1921 m, 3; 18 km SE Constanza, 1586 m, 2; 10 km W Jayaco, 915 m, 1; *Pedernales:* 5 km NE Los Arroyos, 1617 m, 1.

42. *Euphyes singularis insolata* Butler, 1878

TL Jamaica.

FW males 16–19, females 18–21 mm.

Euphyes s. insolata is widely distributed in the República Dominicana but apparently is quite rare in Haiti, whence I have only 1 specimen. This skipper is an inhabitant of roadside weedy and shrubby areas, but these are almost always associated with mesic areas—*cafetales*, deciduous forest, palm forest, or mixed pine-hardwood forests. The skippers are often associated with creeks and streams (Barahona), and 1 was taken from a small rock adjacent to a montane creek (Constanza). At La Palma, *E. s. insolata* is relatively common; there, these skippers are regularly encountered in a large meadow with *Emilia javanica* and along a wet road adjacent to a river with forest and *Coffea*.

The precise situation at Duvergé, which is within the xeric Valle de Neiba, is of especial interest; it seems an unlikely place to encounter a mesophilic skipper. On 22.vii.1982, Gali and I collected near the Cabral-Duvergé main road, just to the east of Duvergé. The temperature was 37°C at 1000–1045 h, and the weather was sunny to slightly overcast. At this locality, there was an overgrown drainage ditch paralleling the road, the ditch backed up by palm forest. Duvergé lies in the xeric Valle de Neiba, but because of its spring, the local area is very mesic. Eight *E. s. insolata* were secured between the ditch and the fence enclosing the palm forest, a distance of perhaps 2 m. This ditch-fence strip was heavily overgrown with shrubs and bushes, and the skippers were landing on the leaves of these plants; none was seen feeding. They were the most conspicuous and common skippers at this site. In the afternoon we returned (temperature 34°C, 1515–1545 h) and secured 4 more skippers in addition to the 4 taken in the morning.

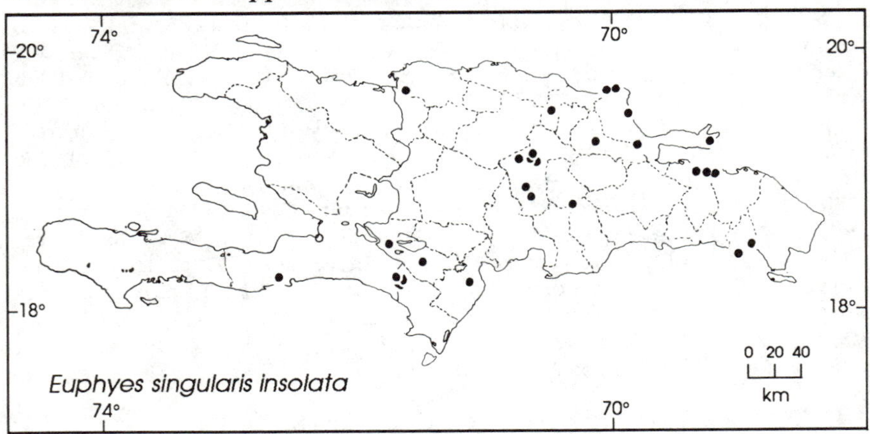

At another locality (La Furnia) in the Valle de Neiba, *E. s. insolata* was taken feeding on *Cordia* sp. in a very local mesic strip along an irrigation ditch; away from the ditch, the area is *Acacia* scrub. The skippers were feeding on the white flowers up to 3 m above the ground and generally out of the reach of the collectors. At Constanza, 1 *E. s. insolata* was taken feeding on the white flowers of *Tournefortia hirsutissima.*

At La Entrada, we encountered *E. s. insolata* rather commonly. There these skippers were in a large, grassy (0.5 m high) area within a *cafetal-cacaotal*, accompanied by other hesperiids; no *E. s. insolata* was seen feeding at this site. There, as elsewhere, males far outnumbered females. At Punta Cana and Copey, *E. s. insolata* was abundant at the roadside through and adjacent to xeric forest. In a mesic *Cocos* grove (7 km E Sabana de la Mar), *E. s. insolata* was taken feeding on the orange flowers of *Lantana ovatifolia*, and at Banano, 1 specimen was taken feeding on *Sida* sp. At Copey, these skippers were feeding on *Croton linearis*, *Lantana ovatifolia*, and *L. reticulata.*

But the most abundantly I have taken *E. s. insolata* is in Río San Juan. In the hotel garden there, these skippers were very common, feeding on the nectar from the white-flowered horticultural variety of *Lantana ovatifolia*. Twenty-four specimens were taken by me between 1030–1300 h and 1430–1530 h on 24.iii.1984 (temperature 37°C in the morning, 40°C in the afternoon).

The elevational distribution is from sea level (Duvergé, La Furnia, Copey, Cruce de Rincón, Río San Juan, La Entrada, Samaná, Punta Cana) to 1586 m (18 km SE Constanza), with temperatures between 24°C (La Palma) and 40°C (Río San Juan). Times of collection varied from 0830 to 1545 h. Most specimens were from March (37) and October (20), with 14 in June, 12 in August, 9 in July, 5 in May, 3 each in April and December, and 1 each in September and November. These data suggest that *E. s. insolata* is bivoltine (March, October) on Hispaniola.

This is the first record of *E. s. insolata* on Isla Catalina.

Specimens: Haiti: l'Ouest: Lavaneau, 229 m, 1; *República Dominicana: Monte Cristi:* 6 km W Copey, s.l., 5; *Duarte:* 12 km SE San Francisco de Macorís, 2; *Espaillat:* 14 km SW Jamao al Norte, 534 m, 1; *La Vega:* La Palma, 19 km W Jayaco, 1007 m, 10; 1 km W Manabao, 793 m, 7; Jarabacoa, 530 m, 2; 6 km S Jarabacoa, 610 m, 1; 6 km SSE Constanza, 1403 m, 3; 18 km SE Constanza, 1586 m, 1; *Monseñor Nouel:* 14 km SW Piedra Blanca, 427 m, 1; *María T. Sánchez:* Río San Juan, 26; 9 km NE Río San Juan, s.l., 1; 14 km S La Entrada, s.l., 6; 1 km S Cruce de Rincón, s.l., 3; *Samaná:* El Francés, 14 km E and N Samaná, s.l., 1; *Hato Mayor:* 7 km E Sabana de la Mar, 6; 17 km E Sabana de la Mar, 1; 25 km E Sabana de la Mar, 1; *La Romana:* Río Chavón, 8 km SE La Romana, s.l., 3; *Independencia:* 0.5 km E Duvergé, s.l., 8; La Furnia, s.l., 1; *Barahona:* 12 km SW Barahona, 427 m, 1; *Pedernales:* 1 km SE Banano, 183 m, 1; El Mulito, 21 km N Pedernales, 214 m, 1; Mencía, 397 m, 2.

Sight record: República Dominicana: Isla Catalina—1 seen, 14.viii.

43. *Calpodes ethlius* Stoll, 1784

TL "Suriname."

FW 25–26 mm.

Although *C. ethlius* occurs on Hispaniola, it must be very rare there; we have taken only 3 specimens from the República Dominicana and have examined 2 others (MNHNSD). We have never seen *C. ethlius* in Haiti. The larval food plants (*Canna, Marantia*) are not common except the former as a garden plant. Our specimens were taken on 21.vii at an elevation of 702 m (Polo) and on 2.vii at 488 m (Jarabacoa), those in the MHNHSD on 14.viii and 22.vi. The temperature was 30°C (Polo), and the skipper was taken between 1115 and 1430 h as it rested upon a leaf 0.3 m above the ground on an open path through a *cafetal.* The 2 skippers from Jarabacoa were taken as they fed on *Bougainvillea glabra* at 1400–1600 h.

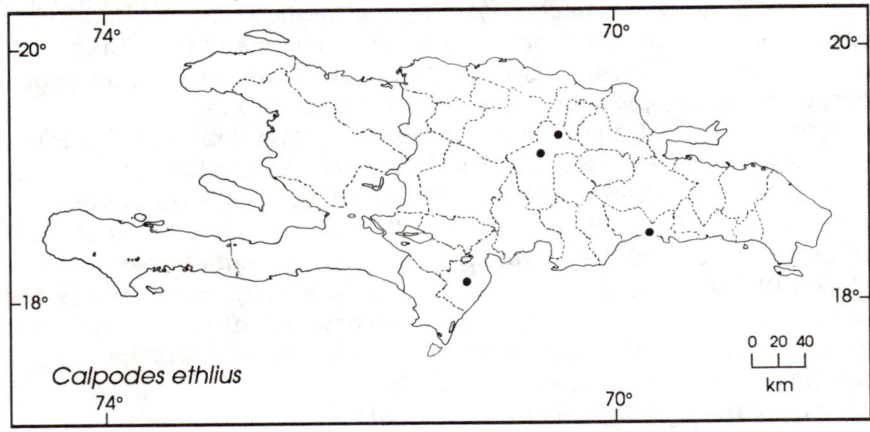

Hall (1925:224) did not record *C. ethlius* in his collections. Cucurullo (1959:13) listed the species but with a symbol showing that he had no specimens, and Marión Heredia (1974:15) listed *C. ethlius* but there were still no recent specimens. Bates (1935a:224) noted the crepuscular habits of this species and reported only 2 specimens from "Provincia de Oriente" in Cuba (others had been seen at Soledad, Prov. de Cienfuegos, but not collected). Comstock (1944:567) stated that the species was common on Puerto Rico. Brown and Heineman (1972:420) reported *C. ethlius* from only 6 Jamaican localities, with occurrences in January-March and August-September. Pinchon and Enrico (1969:143–44) noted the occurrence of this skipper on 8 Lesser Antillean islands; they stated that it was common on Martinique, but that imagines were seldom seen until late afternoon or even until nightfall—another reference to the crepuscular habits of *C. ethlius*. Their late habits may well account for the paucity of Hispaniolan specimens.

Specimens: República Dominicana: La Vega: La Vega, 1 (MNHNSD); 1.7 km S Jarabacoa, 488 m, 2; *Dist. Nac.:* Santo Domingo, 1 (MNHNSD); *Barahona:* Polo, 702 m, 1.

44. *Panoquina sylvicola woodruffi* Watson, 1937

TL Puerto Rico.

FW 16–20 mm.

Panoquina s. woodruffi is widely distributed in both Haiti and the República Dominicana. It is a skipper of open and primarily mesic (but at times xeric) areas, generally shunning those which are xeric or completely shaded; in the latter situation these skippers may be found within *caféières* or *cafetales*, but only in clearings or along roads and paths that have some sun. *Panoquina s. woodruffi* has a broad elevational distribution, from sea level (Fond Parisien, Las Terrenas, Punta Cana, Barahona) to 1891 m (Puesto Pirámide 204), but it is uncommon at both these extremes and is primarily a skipper of moderate elevations (610–1098 m). In this broad altitudinal band, it occupies a variety of habitats, from mangrove borders (Las Terrenas) to open pine and mixed pine-deciduous forest (Puesto Pirámide 204, Gũaigũí, Jarabacoa, Forêt des Pins), and from mesic oases (Ça Soleil, Villa Vásquez) to xeric lowland woods (La Romana, Oviedo). It is encountered in greatest abundance in open grassy fields (Carrefour Marmelade, Constanza) but has also been taken on ferns (Puesto Pirámide 204), on grasses and shrubs within *caféières* and *cafetales* (Paillant, Découzé), and in an exposed *Cajanus cajan* field (Terre Rouge).

Panoquina s. woodruffi uses the following plants as nectar sources: *Bauhinia divaricata* (Fabaceae) in semidesert (Les Poteaux), *Tournefortia hirsutissima* (Boraginaceae) in karst (Sosúa) and in the Cordillera Central (Paso Bajito), *Cynoglossum amabile* (Boraginaceae) near an open bushy creek (Constanza), *Cordia globosa* (Boraginaceae) in open xeric woods (Punta Caucedo), *Ixora* sp. (Rubiaceae) in a town (Boca de Yuma), *Daucus* sp. (Apiaceae) in the uplands of the Massif du Nord (Carrefour Marmelade), *Funastrum clausum* (Asclepiadaceae) in xeric areas (Villa Vásquez, Palmar de Ocoa), *Antigonon leptopus* (Fabaceae) and *Jacaranda acutifolia* (Bignoniaceae) in *Acacia* scrub (Santiago), *Melochia tomentosa* (Sterculiaceae) in grassy *Acacia* woods (La Canoa), *Ageratum conyzoides* (Asteraceae) (Peralta, Barahona, and 1 km N Aceitillar), *Bidens pilosa* in a xeric roadcut (Los Quemados), and *Stachytarpheta cay-*

ennensis (Verbenaceae) in the Massif de la Selle (Los Arroyos). These skippers were extremely abundant at Carrefour Marmelade, and 1 pair was taken while copulating (22.vii). Another copulating pair was taken 3.vii (Constanza).

Times of activity varied between 0900 and 1715 h. In the sequence of skippers at Constanza. *P. s. woodruffi* was the last (of 5) species to become active at about 1100 h at 34°C. But this species remained active later than other hesperiids; individuals were still flying at 1545 h and even later (1715 h), when the day was cool and after it had rained in the afternoon; at this time they were accompanied only by *Calisto obscura* and *C. confusa.* Temperatures of activity cover a broad range, from 19°C (Scierie) to 39°C (Jánico, Playa Bayahibe). The species is most common in July and August. I have 32 specimens from May, 15 each from June and December, 5 each from January and April, 2 from September, and 1 each from March and November. Comstock (1944:570) mentioned only that *P. s. woodruffi* was "common" on Puerto Rico, and Brown and Heineman (1972:425–26) listed dates from throughout the year on Jamaica.

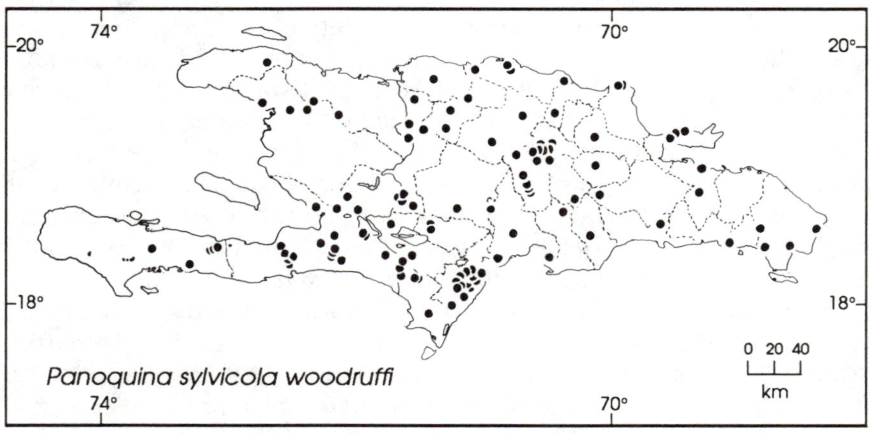

The status of the populations called *P. s. woodruffi* has been questioned (Comstock, 1944:569; Riley, 1975:194; Schwartz, 1983a:68), but Brown and Heineman (1972:424) accepted the subspecific designation. Certainly, my long series from Hispaniola agrees with a short series from Puerto Rico and from St.-Martin and Montserrat in the Lesser Antilles. None of these specimens agrees with Riley's (1975) color plate of a Cuban topotype of *P. s. sylvicola* Herrich-Schäffer. The nominate subspecies is characterized primarily by the presence of a blue to blue-green unhw band; this band in *P. s. woodruffi* is always white, very narrow, and often obsolete. *Panoquina s. woodruffi* seems distinct from the Cuban subspecies. However, fresh material from eastern Cuba is like Hispaniolan specimens and lacks the bold unhw blue line. The situation is anomalous.

Specimens: Haiti: Nord-Ouest: 1.3 km S Balladé, 1; *Nord:* 3.5 km W Plaisance, 793 m, 1; 1.1 km N Carrefour Marmelade, 794 m, 3; *l'Artibonite:* 1.6 km E Carrefour Marmelade, 854 m, 14; 7.4 km E Les Poteaux, 1; 12.2 km W Ça Soleil, s.l., 2; *l'Ouest:* 20.3 km SW Thomonde, 2; 5 km E Source Matelas, s.l., 1; 1.6 km N Saut d'Eau, 183 m, 1; 3.8 km N Terre Rouge, 519 m, 4; 2 km SE Fond Parisien, s.l., 1; 4 km SE Fond Parisien, s.l., 1; Forêt des Pins, 1525 m, 1; Pétionville, 366–458 m, 1; Boutilliers Road, 266–915 m, 5; 3.7 km S Kenscoff, 1547 m, 1; Peneau, 1.1–1.6 km SW Furcy, 1464 m, 9: 0.3 km N Obléon, 1617 m, 1; 2 km NW Scierie, 1785–1810 m, 1 (FSM); 1.1 km S Dufort, 1; 1.6 km N Découzé, 702 m, 6; 2.1 km S Découzé, 640 m, 1; 0.6 km S Découzé, 671–702 m, 1; 1.3 km N Béloc, 702 m, 2; *Sud:* 2.9 km SW Paillant, 671 m, 3; 3 km SW Paillant, 793 m, 1; 6.7 km SW Paillant, 793–854 m, 5; Vieux Bourg d'Aquin, s.l., 2; 16.2 km N Cavaillon, 488 m, 2; *República Dominicana: Monte Cristi:* 4 km NW Villa Vásquez, 61 m, 2; *Dajabón:* 2 km NW El Pino, 183 m, 1; Los Cerezos, 12 km NW Río Limpio, 580 m, 1; 7 km N Restauración, 671 m, 1; 3 km ESE Villa Anacaona, 437 m, 1; *Elías Piña:* 16 km E Hondo Valle, 702 m, 1; 14 km S Comendador, 976 m, 1; 21 km S Comendador, 1646 m, 3; 1 km SW Puesto Pirámide 204, 1891 m, 5; 2 km NE Puesto Pirámide 204, 1586 m, 2; *Santiago Rodríguez:* 4.8 km S Zamba, 183 m, 1; Loma Leonor, 18 km SW Monción, 534 m, 1; 3 km W Los Quemados, 183 m, 7; 7 km SW Santiago, 214 m, 19; *Santiago:* 8 km E Jánico, 610 m, 1; Río Bao, 8 km SE Montones Abajo, 488 m, 3; *Puerto Plata:* 8 km W Luperón, 1; 12 km SE Luperón, 264 m, 1; 0.6 km NE Estero Hondo, 1; 11 km SE Sosúa, 47 m, 1; *Espaillat:* 3 km N Puesto Grande, 580 m, 1; *Duarte:* 12 km SE San Francisco de Macorís, 1; *La Vega:* 1 km S Constanza, 1098 m, 20; 10 km SE Constanza, 1648 m, 5; 13 km SE Constanza, 1403 m, 2; 18 km SE Constanza, 1586 m, 6; 3.5 km E Paso Bajito, 732 m, 1; 10 km S La Vega (= Güaigüí), 5; Buena Vista, 11 km NE Jarabacoa, 640 m, 1; Jarabacoa, 530 m, 2; 2 km S Jarabacoa, 488 m, 1; 5 km SE Jarabacoa, 595 m, 2; La Ciénaga, 1098 m, 2; 10 km W Jayaco, 915 m, 4; La Palma, 19 km W Jayaco, 1007 m, 48; *Monseñor Nouel:* 14 km SW Piedra Blanca, 417 m, 1; *María T. Sánchez:* 8 km NE Río San Juan, s.l., 2; 9 km NE Río San Juan, s.l., 1; *Samaná:* 6.9 km NE Sánchez, 336 m, 1; 13.2 km NE Sánchez, 92 m, 1; 3.1 km E Las Terrenas, s.l., 1; *Hato Mayor:* 7 km E Sabana de la Mar, 2; 17 km E Sabana de la Mar, 1; 12 km S El Valle, 3; *La Altagracia:* Punta Cana, s.l., 4; 3 km W Punta Cana, s.l., 1; 0.5 km W Boca de Yuma, 1; 16 km NE La Romana, 61 m, 1; 2.5 km SE Playa Bayahibe, 1; *La Romana:* Río Cumayasa, 13.5 km W La Romana, 61 m, 1; *Sánchez Ramírez:* 1 km NE Las Lagunas, 183 m, 2; *Dist. Nac.:* 9 km NE Guerra, 1; Punta Caucedo, 2 km W, 2 km S Andrés, s.l., 1; *San Cristóbal:* 11 km NW Cambita Garabitos, 671 m, 1; *Monte Plata:* 11 km W Esperalvillo, 153 m, 1; *Peravia:* 2 km SW Rancho Arriba, 671 m, 1; *Azua:* 1 km E Palmar de Ocoa, s.l., 2; 5 km S Peralta, 305 m, 5; 2 km SE La Canoa, 397 m, 1; *San Juan:* 9 km E Vallejuelo, 610 m, 4; *Baoruco:* 9 km N Neiba, 366 m, 1; 11 km N Neiba, 519 m, 1; 14 km N Neiba, 671 m, 3; *Independencia:* 1 km S Boca de Cachón, s.l., 1; 4–7 km NE

El Aguacate, 519–824 m, 6; *Barahona:* west slope, Sierra Martín García, 458–610 m, 1; 9 km SW Cabral, 305 m, 1; 10 km SSW Cabral, 427 m, 1; 2 km S La Lanza, 1; Polo, 702 m, 1; 3 km NNE Polo, 854 m, 1; 1.3 km W Monteada Nueva, 1037 m, 2; 1.8 km W Monteada Nueva, 1007 m, 2; Barahona, s.l., 2; 5 km SE, 3 km W Barahona, 183 m, 1; 8 km SW Barahona, 366 m, 1; 12 km SW Barahona, 427 m, 6; 20 km SW Barahona, 1098 m, 1; 22 km SW Barahona, 1098 m, 2; 8 km NW Paraíso, 1 (MPM); 9 km NW Enriquillo, 671 m, 3; 3 km NW Enriquillo, 244 m, 3; *Pedernales:* Aceitillar, 36 km NNE Cabo Rojo, 1281 m, 2; 1 km N Aceitillar, 1281 m, 1; Mencía, 397 m, 2; 0.6 km SE Los Arroyos, 1098 m, 4; 3 km SE Los Arroyos, 976 m, 4; 5 km NE Los Arroyos, 1617 m, 2; 17 km NW Oviedo, 183 m, 1.

45. *Panoquina nero* Fabricius, 1798

TL Haiti.

FW males 19–23 mm, female 25 mm.

Panoquina nero is less common than the other, moderately sized Hispaniolan *Panoquina.* Riley (1975:194) stated the situation accurately when he noted that this species is "Widespread but not common," although, judging from Comstock's (1944:369) Puerto Rican records, it is more abundant on that island than on Hispaniola.

My 11 specimens are from 5 localities. The single individual from Piedra Blanca was taken on 12.vii on a day that was first overcast and then sunny, between 1115 and 1530 h, in a mesic

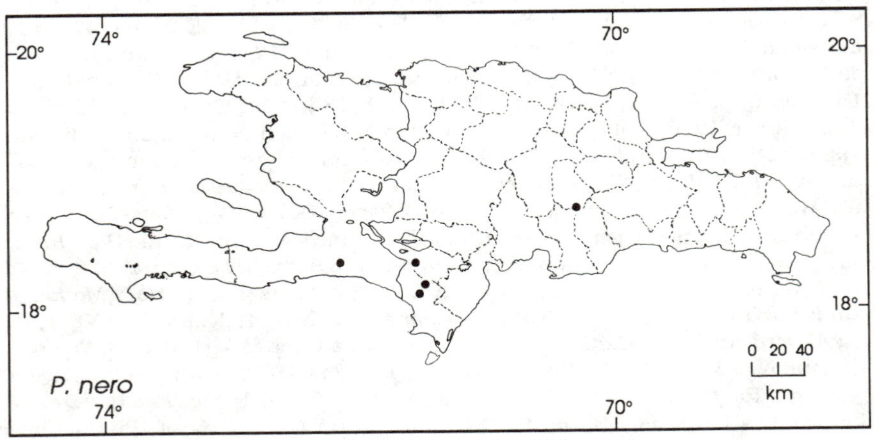

cafetal; the temperature was 34°C. The specimen from Scierie was taken in semiopen pinewoods with shrubs and tall grasses on 4.ix, between 0930–1030 h at 21°C. Of the 6 specimens from El Aguacate, 4 were taken on 30.vii on an overcast day between 0945 and 1245 h, with a temperature of 28°C. The 2 others were secured on

29.xii on a bright day, between 1015 and 1400 h, at a temperature of 24°C. On the former date, these skippers were on the leaves of shrubs and sunning on the gravel road surface in mesic hardwoods. The flight is very rapid and darting, and the skippers rested only briefly before once more flying. They did not return to the same site, as many hesperiids often do. On the latter date, they were feeding on *Ageratum conyzoides*. The same plant was used by *P. nero* at Aceitillar (25°C, 1130–1300 h, 2.i) and at Cabo Rojo (29°C, 1300–1500 h, 2.i). Both localities were bright and sunny, the first in open pinewoods, the second in mesic hardwoods.

Riley (1975:194) did not accept *P. n. belli* Watson, although this taxon was considered distinct by Comstock (1944:569) and by Brown and Heineman (1972:73). I have compared my short series (6 males, 1 female) from Hispaniola with 9 specimens (9 males, no females) from Puerto Rico (*P. n. belli*). The Hispaniolan material differs only in its smaller size (fw 19–23 mm in males), in contrast to 22–25 mm (Puerto Rican males). The supposed difference in the width of the unhw white band does not differentiate the 2 subspecies. Accordingly, I follow Riley in not recognizing subspecies in *P. nero*.

Specimens: Haiti: l'Ouest: 5 km WNW Scierie, 1891 m, 1 (FSM); *República Dominicana: Monseñor Nouel:* 14 km SW Piedra Blanca, 427 m, 1; *Independencia:* 4–7 km NE El Aguacate, 732–824 m, 6; *Pedernales:* 1 km N Aceitillar, 1281 m, 2; 26 km NE Cabo Rojo, 1.

46A. *Panoquina ocola ocola* Edwards, 1863

TL Georgia, Florida, Texas; restricted to Ocala, Marion Co., Florida (Brown and Miller, 1987:61).

FW 16–19 mm.

Panoquina o. ocola seems to have a peculiar Hispaniolan distribution. I have only 2 specimens from Haiti, and the records from the República Dominicana are widely scattered. There are only 4 Dominican specimens from the south island. Elevational distribution is from sea level (Copey, Cruce de Rincón, Samaná) to 1891 m (Puesto Pirámide 204), but most records are from sea level to moderate elevations. Habitats are variable, from xeric woods (Copey, Monte Bonito) to *cafetales-cacaotales* (Tenares, Rincón Molinillos, El Valle, Bayaguana, Monteada Nueva) or to clearings in mesic forest (Jayaco). As with its congener, *P. s. woodruffi*, *P. o. ocola* is a skipper of marginal situations, edges, and open grassy fields (Constanza, Cruce de Guayacanes, Samaná, Los Arroyos), but it may occur in open mixed pine-deciduous forest (Loma Leonor) or in open and weedy *Cocos* groves (Samaná, 9 km NE Río San Juan).

We have taken *P. o. ocola* feeding on *Antigonon leptopus* (Cruce de Guayacanes) in thorn scrub, on *Wedelia trilobata* (El Abanico), on white-flowered *Lantana ovatifolia* (Río San Juan), and on *Funastrum clausum* (Villa Vásquez). A copulating pair was secured on 5.vii (Villa Vásquez), where the skippers were very abundant in sunlit clearings in an oasis. Another pair was taken on 26.x (Río San Juan) in a weedy *Cocos* grove (0900–1100 h; 32°C), and a third on 13.viii (Monteada Nueva) at the edge of a *cafetal* (1403 h; 30°C). Temperatures of activity varied between 23°C (Puesto Pirámide 204) and 40°C (Tenares), and times between 0900 and 1530 h, although this species tends to be active earlier than *P. s. woodruffi*.

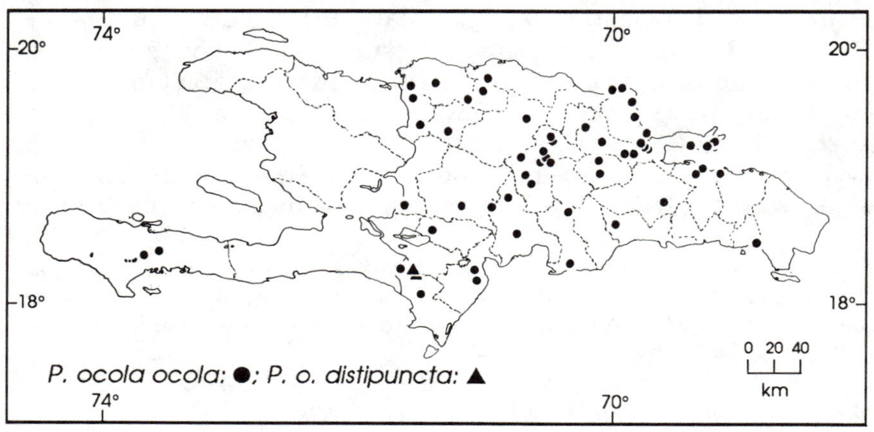

P. ocola ocola: ●; P. o. distipuncta: ▲

Most specimens are from July (37), with 34 in October, 30 in June, 20 in March, 13 in August, 9 in December, 4 in November, 2 in April, and 1 in January; *P. o. ocola* is on the wing during the entire year, with 2 peaks (June-July, October). We have taken *P. o. ocola* feeding on *Bidens pilosa* (Cañongo), *Ageratum conyzoides* (Vallejuelo), and *Bougainvillea glabra* (1.7 km S Jarabacoa). On 1.vii Gonzalez saw a perched dragonfly with a *Panoquina* in its mandibles at Buena Vista. Neither *P. o. ocola* nor *P. s. woodruffi* is known from that locality; thus the identity of the species involved is uncertain.

The rarity of *P. o. ocola* in Haiti is peculiar. However, Bates (1935a:231) had only 1 specimen from Cuba. Holland (1916:509) recorded 4 *P. ocola* from the Isla de la Juventud, but this represented the total catch of this species in over a year. Comstock (1944:570) merely mentioned that *P. ocola* had a general distribution on Puerto Rico. Brown and Heineman (1972:423) listed only 5 localities for this species on Jamaica, so it is apparently not common there. Riley (1975:195) noted under the distribution that *P. ocola* is "always rather sporadic." It seems hardly likely that we have missed this skipper in Haiti during the 15.7 man-months spent collecting in that country.

Panoquina o. ocola and *P. s. woodruffi* have generally complementary distributions. But they have been taken syntopically at 22 localities. At 6 of these, *P. s. woodruffi* is more common than *P. o. ocola* (Puesto Pirámide 204, 5:1; 1 km S Constanza, 20:3; Peralta, 3:1; La Palma, 48:3; Santiago, 19:1; Los Arroyos, 4:1). At 6 others, *P. o. ocola* outnumbers *P. s. woodruffi* (Jayaco, 7:4; Jarabacoa, 22:2; Villa Vásquez, 13:1; Las Lagunas, 4:1; Sabana de la Mar, 6:2; San Francisco de Macorís, 5:1). At the remainder (Loma Leonor, 1.8 km W Monteada Nueva, 5 km S Jarabacoa, La Canoa, 11 km N Neiba, Vallejuelo, La Ciénaga, 9 km NE Río San Juan, Rancho Arriba), the 2 species occur in about equal numbers. It is interesting that 10 of the 22 localities are at or above 530 m.

Specimens: Haiti: Sud: 6.4 km NW Marceline, 671 m, 1; 19 km N Cavaillon, 580 m, 1; *República Dominicana: Monte Cristi:* 4 km NW Villa Vásquez, 61 m, 21; 6 km W Copey, s.l., 4; *Dajabón:* 0.5 km N Cañongo, 31 m, 1; Pico Gallo, *ca.* 10 km E El Carrizal, 1302 m, 1; *Elías Piña:* 1 km SW Pirámide 204, 1891 m, 1; *Valverde:* Río Guarabo, 3 km W Los Quemados, 122 m, 1; 4 km N Cruce de Guayacanes, 198 m, 2; *Santiago:* 7 km SW Santiago, 1; *Santiago Rodríguez:* Loma Leonor, 19 km SW Monción, 514 m, 1; *Puerto Plata;* 11 km N Cruce de Guayacanes, 275 m, 2; *La Vega:* 1 km S Constanza, 1098 m, 3; 10 km SE Constanza, 1648 m, 3; 10 km W Jayaco, 915 m, 8; La Palma, 19 km W Jayaco, 1007 m, 3; 2 km S La Vega, 366 m, 1; 5 km NW La Vega, 122 m, 2; Jarabacoa, 530 m, 22; 1.7 km S Jarabacoa, 488 m, 1; 5 km SE Jarabacoa, 595 m, 1; La Ciénaga, 915 m, 1; *Sánchez Ramírez:* 1 km SE La Mata, 4; 1 km NE Las Lagunas, 183 m, 4; *Samaná:* 10.2 km W Samaná, 61 m, 1; 4.5 km E Samaná, 2; 18.0 km E and N Samaná, s.l., 1; *María T. Sánchez:* Río San Juan, s.l., 2; 9 km NE Río San Juan, s.l., 5; 6 km S Cabrera, s.l., 1; 14 km S La Entrada, s.l., 4; 9 km SE Nagua, s.l., 5; Cruce de Rincón, s.l., 2; 1 km S Cruce de Rincón, s.l., 12; *ca.* 18 km W, 1.2 km S Sánchez, rd. to Rincón Molinillos, 31 m, 1; *Duarte:* 10 km SE Tenares, 183 m, 2; 12 km SE San Francisco de Macorís, 5; 1 km N El Abanico, 6; Villa Riva, 7; *Hato Mayor:* 7 km E Sabana de la Mar, 8; 25 km E Sabana de la Mar, 2; 6 km N El Valle, 1; *La Romana:* Río Chavón, 8 km SE La Romana, s.l., 1; *Monte Plata:* 8 km NE Bayaguana, 1; *Dist. Nac.:* 30 km NW Santo Domingo, 153 m, 1; *Peravia:* 2 km SW Rancho Arriba, 671 m, 1; 5 km SW Sombrero, 1; *Azua:* 5 km S Peralta, 305 m, 1; 5 km SW Monte Bonito, 702 m, 1; 2 km SE La Canoa, 397 m, 1; *San Juan:* 9 km E Vallejuelo, 610 m, 1; *Baoruco:* 11 km N Neiba, 2; *Barahona:* 12 km SW Barahona, 427 m, 1; 1.8 km W Monteada Nueva, 1007 m, 1; *Pedernales:* 0.6 km SE Los Arroyos, 1098 m, 1; 19 km NE Cabo Rojo, 427 m, 1.

46B. *Panoquina ocola distipuncta* Johnson and Matusik, 1988

TL "1987 CMNH Expedition Base Camp, 18°10′ N, 71°37′ W, 1600 m., ca. 4 km. from upper Abejas," Prov. de Pedernales, República Dominicana.

FW males 16–18 mm, females 18 mm.

Panoquina o. distipuncta has been recently named from a suite of 9 males and 6 females from the Las Abejas region in the Sierra de Baoruco. The subspecies differs from *P. o. ocola* in consistently having a yellow-white spot or dot in the upfw cell, a feature absent in the nominate subspecies. *Panoquina o. distipuncta* appears to be endemic to the Las Abejas region, where it is restricted to pine forest at elevations between about 1520 and 1600 m. These skippers are rapid flyers, appearing quickly and alighting for only a few seconds unless taking nectar. Most specimens were taken while feeding on *Rubus* sp. and other flowers in xeric grasslands in pine forest.

The relationships of *P. o. distipuncta* are not clear (Johnson and Matusik, 1988). In effect, the presence of the cell pale marking seems to ally this form to *P. sylvicola*, but the male genitalia are more similar to those of *P. ocola*. It seems remarkable that *P. ocola* would have given rise to a distinctive subspecies in the Baorucan uplands. The occurrence of *P. o. ocola* at Los Arroyos, only 22 km to the NW of the type-locality, suggests that *P. o. distipuncta* is a species distinct from *P. ocola*.

Specimens: República Dominicana: Pedernales: ca. 4 km from upper Abejas, 3.

[*Panoquina hecebolus* Scudder, 1871]

This species has been reported from Hispaniola (Johnson and Matusik, 1988) on the basis of 1 male and 3 females from Port-au-Prince, Dépt. de l'Ouest, Haiti, 1–6.ii.1922 (AMNH). Johnson and Matusik (1988) stated that like other members of the genus, *P. hecebolus* is often associated with domestic monocots. "It is possible that the Port-au-Prince occurrence is a transplantation, or that additional *P. hecebolus* have been collected from Hispaniola but not properly identified." I have rechecked all my *P. ocola* and *P. s. woodruffi* and found no material assignable to this taxon (note also the peculiar lack of records of *P. o. ocola* from Haiti). I therefore do not formally include *P. hecebolus* in the present work, pending its confirmation as an established resident species.]

47. *Panoquina panoquinoides panoquinoides* Skinner, 1892

TL Key West, Monroe Co., Florida.

FW 14 mm; Riley (1975:195) gave 13–14 mm for both sexes.

The status of this skipper in the West Indies has been equivocal. Riley (1975:207), in his table of Antillean distributions, showed its occurrence only on Jamaica of the Greater Antilles. Brown and Heineman (1972:42) considered that the species had been introduced (both on Jamaica and the Cayman Islands) with sugar cane, a larval food plant. These authors also reported the species (p. 73) from Cuba, Hispaniola, and Puerto Rico. Klots (1951:pl. 39) has an up black-and-white photograph of an individual from Puerto Plata, República Dominicana. As far as I am aware, this is the only published locality for the species on Hispaniola.

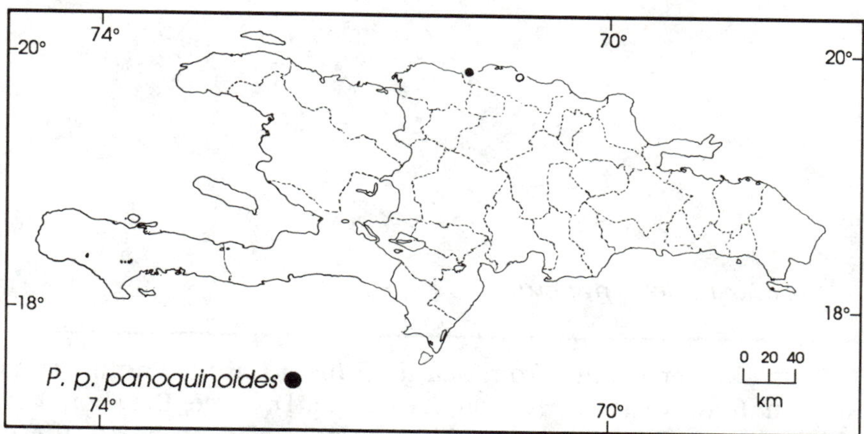

Until 1986, we had not taken *P. p. panoquinoides*. But in that year we unwittingly took 2 specimens in Puerto Plata Province on 30.v. They (and others) were in deep (0.5 m) grass in an open salt flat with stands of *Batis maritima* and scattered trees—an altogether hostile situation. The time was 1015–1100 h and the temperature 32°C. The species is probably widely distributed (in more or less coastal situations?) but rarely collected due to the inhospitality of the ecology.

Specimens: República Dominicana: Puerto Plata: 0.4 km E Punta Rucia, s.l., 2.

48. *Nyctelius nyctelius nyctelius* Latreille, 1823

TL Brasil or Suriname.

FW 16–21 mm.

Riley (1975:196) considered *N. n. nyctelius* "generally common" in the West Indies, and Comstock (1944:569) and Brown and Heineman (1972:426) so considered it on Puerto Rico and Jamaica. The species seems to be much less common on Cuba (Bates, 1935a:232) and on Hispaniola as well. *Nyctelius n. nyctelius* is uncommon in Haiti, whence I have 6 specimens, and is somewhat more abundant in the República Dominicana, but it does not approach the abundance of some other hesperiines.

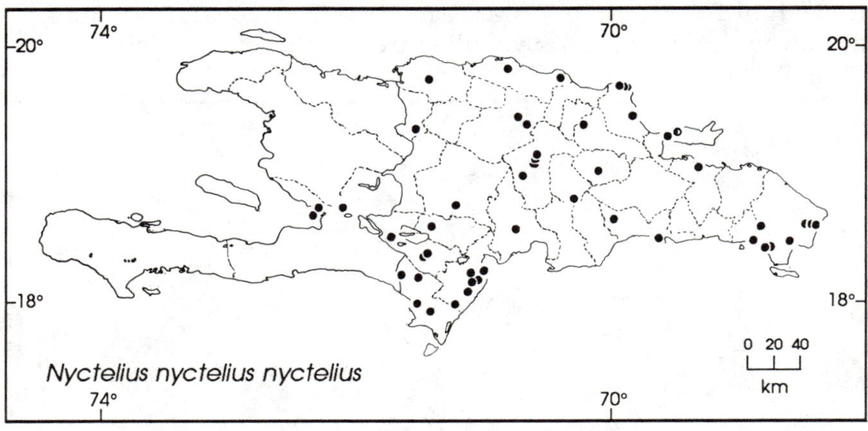

This skipper occurs from sea level (Île à Cabrit, Punta Cana, Río San Juan, Cruce de Rincón, La Furnia, Duvergé, Barahona) to 1281 m (Aceitillar). It is primarily a skipper of open areas; these may be mesic (Piedra Blanca, Río San Juan, Las Lagunas) or xeric (Vallejuelo). Although *N. n. nyctelius* occurs in the Valle de Neiba at Duvergé, the precise site where it was taken there is mesic (see account of *E. s. insolata*). At La Furnia, in the same xeric lowlands, we took 4 specimens feeding on *Cordia* sp., and on *Lantana reticulata* at Jánico. We have collected specimens also feeding on *Zinnia elegans* and *Cordia globosa;* the former plant was used both at Constanza and Punta Cana, at the 2 extremes of the elevational range. At Boca de Yuma and Cabo Rojo, *N. n. nyctelius* was visiting the large flowers of *Urechites lutea* (Apocynaceae); the skippers entered the corollas of these flowers so that only the ends of the elongate fw were visible; at times they even entered the flowers totally. This behavior was observed on 4 occasions at this locality and is quite different from the orthodox manner that, for example, *H. na-*

bokovi uses to gather nectar from these same flowers. Elsewhere, *N. n. nyctelius* has been taken feeding on *Antigonon leptopus* and *Jacaranda acutifolia* (Santiago), on *Paullina pinnata* (Sapindaceae) and *Geoffroea inermis* at Río Chavón, on *Tournefortia hirsutissima* at Sosúa, on *Ageratum conyzoides* at Aceitillar (twice), Barahona, Peralta, and Vallejuelo (twice), and on *Stachytarpheta jamaicensis*, *Cordia exarata*, and an unidentified white-flowered tree at 2.5 km SE Playa Bayahibe.

The record for Île à Cabrit is almost unique in that this island (and La Furnia, as noted above) is hot and xeric, with some dry woods but primarily exposed and with grasses (see Schwartz, 1979, for description of islet).

Times of activity were between 0800 and 1700 h. Temperatures of activity varied between 25°C (Aceitillar) and 37°C (Duvergé). At Enriquillo, on a heavily overcast and rainy day, these skippers were inactive at 23°C; they sat motionless, with the wings closed, on the upper surfaces of large aroid leaves near an abandoned homestead adjacent to a *cafetal*, and a series of 6 was collected. At Las Lagunas, on an overcast and rainy day, *N. n. nyctelius* rested in a similarly exposed manner on the upper surfaces of large leaves; the temperature was 27°C. On other visits to Enriquillo, the skippers were active at 31°C and were not uncommon on an open path through the *cafetal* with many weeds and bushes. Apparently the critical temperature of activity of this species is between 23°C and 27°C.

Most specimens are from July (63), with 29 from August, 25 from June, 19 from March, 11 from October, 10 from November, 6 from December, 4 from May, and 3 each from January and April.

Specimens: Haiti: l'Ouest; 3.8 km N Terre Rouge, 519–534 m, 2; 5 km SE Source Matelas, s.l., 3; Île à Cabrit, 1; *República Dominicana: Monte Cristi:* 4 km NW Villa Vásquez, 61 m, 1; *Dajabón:* 16 km NW Río Limpio, 702 m, 1; *Puerto Plata:* 13 km SE Luperón, 214 m, 2; 9 km SE Sosúa, 15 m, 2; *Santiago:* 7 km NE Jánico, 488 m, 1; 7 km SW Santiago, 214 m, 7; *La Vega:* La Palma, 19 km W Jayaco, 1007 m, 3; Jarabacoa, 530 m, 5; 1.7 km S Jarabacoa, 488 m, 1; 2 km S Jarabacoa, 488 m, 1; 1 km S Constanza, 1098 m, 4; *Duarte:* 10 km SE Tenares, 183 m, 1; *María T. Sánchez:* 8 km NE Río San Juan, s.l., 8: 9 km NE Río San Juan, s.l., 7; 11 km NE Río San Juan, s.l., 1; 14 km S La Entrada, s.l., 3; 1 km S Cruce de Rincón, s.l., 3; *Samaná:* 6.9 km NE Sánchez, 336 m, 4; *Hato Mayor:* 7 km E Sabana de la Mar, 2; *La Altagracia:* Punta Cana, s.l., 4; 3 km W Punta Cana, s.l., 1; 6 km W Punta Cana, s.l., 3; 0.5 km W Boca de Yuma, 3; 1 km N Playa Bayahibe, s.l., 1; 2.5 km SE Playa Bayahibe, s.l., 21; 16 km NE La Romana, 61 m, 1; *La Romana:* Río Chavón, 8 km SE La Romana, s.l., 19; *Dist. Nac.:* Punta Caucedo, 2 km W, 2 km S Andrés, s.l., 5; 30 km NW Santo Domingo, 122 m, 1; *Sánchez Ramírez:* 1 km NE Las Lagunas, 183 m, 10; *Monseñor Nouel:* 14 km SW Piedra Blanca,

427 m, 1; *Azua:* 5 km S Peralta, 305 m, 1; *San Juan:* 9 km E Vallejuelo, 610 m, 5; *Baoruco:* 11 km N Neiba, 519 m, 2; *Independencia:* 0.5 km E Duvergé, 2; 2 km S Duvergé, 1; La Furnia, s.l., 4; *Barahona:* 1.8 km W Monteada Nueva, 1007 m, 2; Barahona, s.l., 1; 5 km SE, 6.4 km W Barahona, 488 m, 2; 22 km SW Barahona, 1098 m, 3; 8–10 km NW Paraíso, 1 (MPM); 9 km NW Enriquillo, 671 m, 13; *Pedernales:* Mencía, 397 m, 1; 4 km NE Cabo Rojo, s.l., 1; 1 km N Aceitillar, 1281 m, 3; 17 km NW Oviedo, 183 m, 1.

Sight record: República Dominicana: Samaná: 3 km SW Las Terrenas, s.l.—1 seen, 11.viii.

Papilionoidea Latreille, 1809

Family Papilionidae Latreille, 1809
Subfamily Papilioninae Latreille, 1809

1. *Battus zetides* Munroe, 1971

TL "St. Domingo," *fide* Munroe, 1971a.

FW males 35–40 mm, females 39–44 mm.

Battus zetides is endemic to Hispaniola. Hall (1925:162) considered the species "apparently very rare" and reported a single specimen from La Vega, Prov. de la Vega, República Dominicana. Riley (1975:140) cited the same record (but carelessly placed La Vega in Haiti!). Lewis (1973:23, fig. 5) figured a tailed (male) specimen and clarified Riley's (1975:pl. 18, fig. 2) painting of a tailless male. Gali and Schwartz (1983c) discussed a series of 6 males and 4 females from Las Abejas, Prov. de Pedernales, República Dominicana. Coutsis (1983) reported the capture of 1 male in Haiti ("at a considerable altitude and patrolling a specific area"; no locality given).

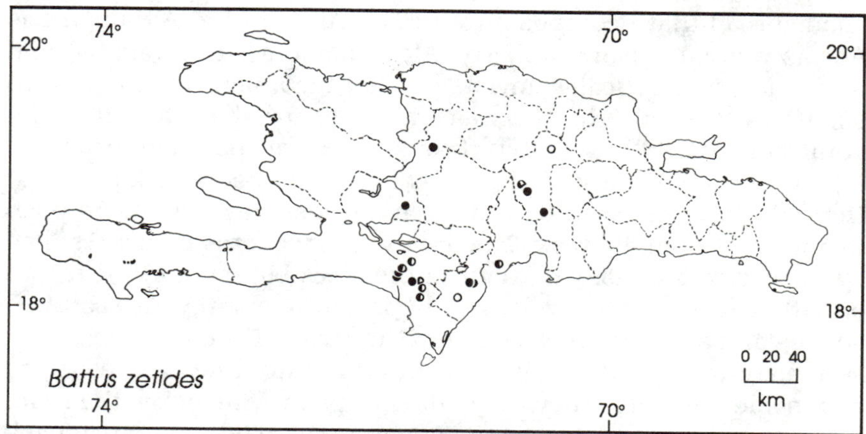

Battus zetides

As with many other presumably rare rhopalocerans, *B. zetides* is common but very local. I know of only 3 places where one can be certain of at least seeing, and almost sure of netting, specimens of this swallowtail. We have seen or taken specimens in the Sierra de Baoruco, Massif de la Selle (Los Arroyos), Cordillera Central (Loma Nalga de Maco, Constanza), Sierra Martín García, and the Sierra de Neiba. We have never seen or collected the species in Haiti. However, the prime habitat for *B. zetides* (mesic upland hardwood forest) is of such uncommon occurrence in Haiti, that Haitian "colonies" may be very local. Since the Sierra de Neiba harbors this butterfly, and the Neiban hardwood forests continue across the border into the Montagnes du Trou-d'Eau (between the Dominico-Haitian border and Savanette), this region, extremely difficult of access from the Haitian side, surely has a population of *B. zetides*. Since *B. zetides* occurs very rarely in pine forest (but has been seen twice in mixed pine-hardwoods at 6 km SSE Constanza), I do not expect this species to be found at Forêt des Pins or Peneau in Haiti, localities that are relatively easy of access.

The 3 localities where *B. zetides* is common are Las Abejas, Prov. de Pedernales; La Horma, Prov. de la Vega; and Puesto Pirámide 204, Prov. de Elías Piña.

Gali and Schwartz (1983c) discussed the ecology at Las Abejas. Since that time (1981) we have visited Las Abejas 11 times, never failing at least to see *B. zetides*, often abundantly. Although the area locally has been massively disturbed (1983), the cutting of many hectares of virgin forest there has not seriously affected the abundance of *B. zetides*. The population remains unchanged, primarily because the butterflies are only rarely encountered along forest paths and are much more common along the open but shaded road that descends into the Las Abejas area. Although Las Abejas was on private property (Alcoa Exploration Company) and was thus theoretically inviolate, the incursion of Dominican squatters who cut the magnificent forest for the planting of legumes indicates the potential risks involved for these butterflies.

The second locality where *B. zetides* is abundant is La Horma. Here, the road between La Horma and Constanza crosses an open ravine with a small creek. The area was once forested (as testified by the vegetation along portions of the creek bottom and the slopes on either side of the ravine) but is presently open, with scattered shrubs and arborescent vegetation. Numerous *B. zetides* have been seen here on 5 visits (1982–83). But the butterflies are collected with some difficulty. They frequent the open ravine below the road, fly up the steep roadside verge and cross the road, and circle back to their haunts, only occasionally crossing the road to descend once more into the continuation of the ravine on its lower side. A small, roadside patch of sugarcane, inhabited by *Calisto p. darlingtoni*, serves as a haven for *B. zetides* as well. The ravine is used by local Dominicans for bathing and washing clothes, as well as a water source for a few houses nearby. It is thus often a busy place, with children and young adults attentive to the arrival of strangers (especially with nets!). Once learning the object of the attentions of the visitors, the Dominicans attempt to swat down *B. zetides* as they come onto the road, using branches of varying (and often lethal and destructive) diameters. Many of our series from La Horma were secured by Dominicans in this fashion, and the condition of the butterflies is less than fine. But the ability of *B. zetides*, despite its slow and deliberate flight, to dodge into and among shrubs and low trees, as well as its "panic" when alarmed, make the butterflies difficult to net.

The third locality where *B. zetides* is abundant is Puesto Pirámide 204. We have visited the site 5 times (1982–83), once more never failing to see *B. zetides* in some numbers. Here, the gravel road descends from Puesto Pirámide 204 toward Puesto Aniceto Martínez along the Dominico-Haitian border. The slope is well forested. The lower side of the road is insolated in the morning, but as the day progresses, shadow covers the lower side; only the treetops on the upper side are in sun in the afternoon. In the mornings, *B. zetides* flies on the lower side of the road, especially about trees (*Gyrotaenia myriocarpa;* Urticaceae) to which they are definitely attracted, even though we have never been there when the trees were in flower. Eugenio de J. Marcano of the Universidad Autónoma de Santo Domingo told me that the flowers of this tree, which is known vernacularly as *azucarero*, are rich in nectar; they may be, at the proper time of year, a major souce of food for *B. zetides*. (*Gyrotaenia myriocarpa* also occurs at La Horma.) As the day progresses and the lower side of the road comes into shade, the *B. zetides* move to the treetops on the upper side of the road and are inaccessible. Thus, taking specimens is a task for the morning (up to about 1130 h); after that time, only an occasional individual comes low enough to be netted. At the bottom of the slope, there is a large and locally marshy meadow. Some large *Lantana ovatifolia* are there, and the *B. zetides* use them as a nectar souce; while feeding, with their wings vibrating rapidly, the butterflies are secured with relative ease, although they seem more alert to intruders and less prone to remain on a single *Lantana* inflorescence than other papilionids.

All the above localities are (or were) forested with hardwoods. Elsewhere, we have taken or seen 1 to 3 individual *B. zetides* in a hardwood ravine in pine forest (Las Abejas), in transitional forest (4–7 km NE El Aguacate), in an open *cafetal* (0.6 km SE Los Arroyos, Monteada Nueva—both localities), in mesic forest (5 km NE Los Arroyos, 5 km SE El Aguacate), in mixed pine-hardwoods (6 km SSE Constanza), and in cutover pine forest (Aceitillar). A single individual was seen crossing the road 26 km NE Cabo Rojo.

Marión Heredia (1980c) reported *B. zetides* from Las Auyamas in the Valle de Polo, Sierra de Baoruco, collected in x.1976. We have not seen these swallowtails in that area, although it is present at Monteada Nueva. The occurrence of *B. zetides* on the Sierra Martín García rests on the sightings of several individuals there (at an elevation of 915 m) by Gali on 25.vii.1982, and the collection of 1 specimen that cannot now be located. Ascents of this range by Raburn, Amador, and Gonzalez yielded no other sight records or specimens; whether there is an aggregation there or merely transient individuals remains to be determined. The former seems much more likely; this range is far from any obvious source for *B. zetides*.

The month of greatest abundance is July (69), with lesser numbers in August (24), June (7), October (6), December (4), and September (2). Specimens from the latter portion of the year are often very worn, suggesting that the species is univoltine and emerges in midsummer.

Gali and Schwartz (1983c) pointed out the slight sexual dimorphism in size and the sexual dichromatism in *B. zetides*. The parameters given by them are reinforced by a much longer series. The chromatic differences are also reaffirmed; in both sexes, the upfw submarginal band is always less bright than the uphw band (seen clearly in their photograph of a male from Las Abejas). Also, the up submarginal bands of yellows and oranges are less bright in females than in males. As the butterflies become worn, however, the dark chocolate up surface becomes paler, and the submarginal bands fade to a very pale yellow in both sexes. Thus, worn individuals are best distinguished (as to sex) by their abdomens.

The elevational distribution is between 732 m (El Aguacate, Cabo Rojo) and *ca.* 1990 m (Loma Nalga de Maco). Collecting times were between 0900 and 1630 h, at temperatures between 21°C (Constanza) and 33°C (Las Abejas, Monteada Nueva). In general, at the high elevations where *B. zetides* occurs, mornings are sunny and bright, but by noon overcast conditions, usually ending in rain, occur almost daily. Although *B. zetides* flies most often in sunny conditions, we have seen and taken specimens during overcast conditions but never during even light rain.

Flowers used by *B. zetides* include: *Lantana ovatifolia* (Puesto Pirámide 204—2 times, Constanza, Las Abejas, Monteada Nueva),

Cynoglossum amabile (La Horma, Las Abejas), *Leonurus sibericus* (La Horma), *Palicourea barbinervia* (Las Abejas—2 times), *Ixora* sp. (Las Abejas—2 times), *Chamissoa altissima* (Las Abejas), *Stachytarpheta jamaicensis* (Monteada Nueva), *Ageratum conyzoides* (El Aguacate, Las Abejas), and *Tournefortia hirsutissima* (Constanza). At 5 km NE Los Arroyos, a *B. zetides* fed briefly on the white flowers of an unidentified tree; another *B. zetides* was seen to feed on another unidentified white-flowered tree at Constanza. In addition, at Las Abejas *B. zetides* frequently flies about the crowns of a woody member of the Solanaceae when they bear white flowers. We have never seen these swallowtails take nectar from these flowers, but they seem attracted to them.

Other than their attraction to *Gyrotaenia myriocarpa*, we have not seen *B. zetides* engaged in any sort of reproductive or ovipositional activity. There is of course no assurance that *Gyrotaenia myriocarpa* serves in any capacity other than a possible nectar source.

Specimens: República Dominicana: Elías Piña: Loma Nalga de Maco, summit, *ca.* 1990 m, 1; 2 km NE Puesto Pirámide 204, 1586 m, 14; *La Vega:* 8 km SE Constanza, 1496 m, 1; 10 km NW La Horma, 1496 m, 28; *Barahona:* 1.3 km W Monteada Nueva, 1037 m, 1; 1.8 km W Monteada Nueva, 1007 m, 1; *Pedernales:* Las Abejas, 12 km NW Aceitillar, 1129 m, 53.

Sight records: República Dominicana: La Vega: 6 km SSE Constanza, 1403 m,—2 seen, 29.ix; 1 seen, 23.vii; *Barahona:* 1.8 km W Monteada Nueva, 1007 m—2 seen, 13.viii; *Independencia:* 4–7 km NE El Aguacate, 732 m—1 seen, 27.vii; 4–7 km NE El Aguacate, 519–732 m—3 seen, 28.xii; *Pedernales:* 0.6 km SE Los Arroyos, 1098 m—1 seen, 30.vi; 5 km NE Los Arroyos, 1617 m—1 seen, 2.vii; 5 km SE El Aguacate, 1463 m—1 seen, 14.vii; 26 km NE Cabo Rojo, 732 m—1 seen, 1.viii; 1 km N Aceitillar, 1281 m—1 seen, 27.xii; Las Abejas, 11 km NW Aceitillar, 1220 m—1 seen, 18.vii.

2. *Battus polydamas polycrates* Hopffer, 1866

TL "Para"; correctly "Haiti."

FW males 41–43 mm, females 44–51 mm.

Battus polydamas Linnaeus, 1758, is widely distributed on the continental mainland from the southern United States to Argentina; throughout this broad range, there is only 1 subspecies recognized (*B. p. polydamas*). But in the West Indies and Bahamas, there are 13 subspecies—1 on each of the Greater Antilles, 1 in the Bahamas, and the balance from Antigua to Grenada in the Lesser Antilles. *Battus p. polycrates*, the Hispaniolan subspecies, is widely distributed geographically and occurs in moderate to great abundance over the entire island. Noteworthy is the absence of specimens or records from the distal portion of the Tiburon Peninsula in Haiti; our only visit there was in June, a time when most papilionids are not overly abundant. Still, we have taken *B. p. polycrates* elsewhere in June, and the species may be truly uncommon in that area. Hall (1925:162) considered *B. p. polycrates* "generally distributed and not scarce; Puerto Plata, La Vega, and San Pedro de Macorís in June." Riley (1975:141) quoted these localities and month but unaccountably added Puerto Rico to the range of *B. p. polycrates*. The subspecies on Puerto Rico and the Virgin Islands is *B. p. thyamus* Rothschild and Jordan (Comstock, 1944:533).

Marión Heredia (1980b) reported *B. p. polycrates* from El Número-Azua, and Schwartz (1983a:55) listed 43 specimens from 22 localities in Haiti. Although one often sees *B. p. polycrates* in areas modified by human habitation (gardens; edges of fields, towns, and villages), these swallowtails are at times very abundant in "natural" situations. These include mesic forest and pseudoforest, xeric woods and forests, *Acacia* scrub, open xeric mountainsides, oases, edges of mangroves, pine forest, and *Cocos* groves. In fact, *B. p. polycrates* seems to have no predilection as far as habitat is concerned and may be encountered in a broad spectrum of ecologies.

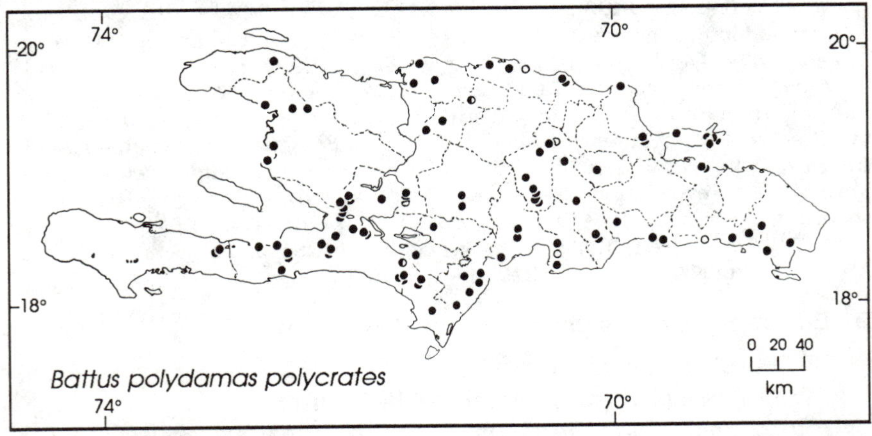

This wide ecological tolerance is a reflection of the elevational distribution of *B. p. polycrates*. I have specimens from sea level (Ça Soleil, Colmini, Grand-Goâve, Croix des Bouquets, Les Bains des Amani-y, Fond Parisien, Copey, Río San Juan, Cruce de Rincón, Samaná, Playa Bayahibe, Punta Caucedo) to 2288 m (18 km SE Constanza, 5 km NW Valle Nuevo) on the Cordillera Central, 1647 m (Kenscoff) on the Massif de la Selle front ranges, 1891 m (Puesto Pirámide 204) on the Sierra de Neiba, 1098 m (El Charco) on the Sierra Martín García, and 732 m (Cabo Rojo, El Aguacate)

on the Sierra de Baoruco. The rarity of *B. p. polycrates* in the higher uplands of the Sierra de Neiba is peculiar, since the appropriate habitats are there. The absence of this species from the higher areas in the Sierra de Baoruco is likewise strange: a locality such as Las Abejas seems very suitable for *B. p. polycrates*. It is perhaps significant that in these 2 ranges, *B. zetides* is the dominant upland swallowtail. We have seen only 1 *B. p. polycrates* in the areas where *B. zetides* occurs in the Sierra de Neiba, and 2 on the Massif de la Selle (Los Arroyos) feeding on the same unidentified tree as 1 *B. zetides*.

Times of collection were between 0900 and 1800 h, at temperatures between 20°C (18 km SE Constanza, 2288 m) and 42°C (La Romana).

Battus p. polycrates is on the wing during the entire year but is most abundant in summer—July (105), June (45), and August (24). I also have 15 specimens from December, 7 from March, 3 from April, 4 from October, 2 from January, and 1 each from February and May. In the fall-winter-spring, *B. p. polycrates* is obviously less abundant—one simply sees far fewer of them during that period.

Food plants of adult *B. p. polycrates* include: *Cordia* sp. (1.1 km N Terre Rouge, Pétionville), *Hibiscus rosasinensis* (Thomonde), *Tournefortia hirsutissima* (Sosúa), *Zinnia elegans* (1 km S Constanza), *Ixora* sp. (Río Cumayasa, Boca de Yuma), *Lantana ovatifolia* (Cabral, Cabo Rojo, Mencía), *Ageratum conyzoides* (16 km NE La Romana, Cabo Rojo), *Poinsettia pulcherrima* (Neiba), *Ipomoea indica* (= *I. acuminata*) (Convolvulaceae) (4 km SE Fond Parisien), and an unidentified white-flowered tree (Los Arroyos). At Les Bains des Amani-y, where there is an entrance road with ornamental rows of *Poinciana regia* (Fabaceae), specimens of *B. p. polycrates* had the abdomens and unhw smeared with the bright orange pollen of the flowers of these trees. Of the flowers used for nectar, *P. pulcherrima* and *I. indica* are remarkable, since few species use these blossoms; at Neiba, *P. pulcherrima* was the flower of choice upon which many *B. p. polycrates* were feeding. *Battus p. polycrates* drinks from muddy puddles in dirt roads (Saut d'Eau, 8.8 km W Grand-Goâve, 2 km SW Mencía).

A copulating pair was taken on 16.iv (7 km E Sabana de la Mar): they were in an overgrown *Cocos* grove at 1315 h (temperature 32°C), 0.3 m above the ground on a low herb. On 28.vi, 2 were seen "cartwheeling" above a paved road (14.8 km N Terre Rouge).

Specimens: Haiti: Nord-Ouest: 1.3 km S Balladé, 31 m, 2; *l'Artibonite:* 1.6 km E Carrefour Marmelade, 854 m, 8; 4.6 km E Les Poteaux, 183 m, 1; 12.2

km W Ça Soleil, s.l., 2; Les Bains des Amani-y, s.l., 3; Colmini, 6.4 km W Terre Noire, s.l., 1; 4.0 km N Thomonde, 1; *l'Ouest:* 1.6 km N Saut d'Eau, 183 m, 6; 20.2 km SE Mirebalais, 366 m, 1; 20.0 km S Mirebalais, 580 m, 2; 14.8 km N Terre Rouge, 122 m, 1; 1.1 km N Terre Rouge, 534 m, 2; 1.3 km S Terre Rouge, 458 m, 1; 2.9–8.5 km S Terre Rouge, 122–488 m, 3; 13.1 km E Croix des Bouquets. s.l., 3; 2 km SE Fond Parisien, s.l., 2; 4 km SE Fond Parisien, s.l., 2; Pétionville, 458 m, 3; Boutilliers Road, 732–854 m, 4; 3.7 km S Kenscoff, 1647 m, 1; Peneau, 1.6 km SW Furcy, 1464 m, 1; 0.6 km S Découzé, 671 m, 1; 8.6 km N Béloc, 534 m, 1; Lavaneau, 229 m, 2; 6.7 km E Grand-Goâve, s.l., 1; 8.8 km W Grand-Goâve, s.l., 1; *Sud:* 2.9 km SW Paillant, 672 m, 1; 6.7 km SW Paillant, 763 m, 1; *República Dominicana; Monte Cristi:* 1 km SE Monte Cristi, 1; 6 km W Copey, s.l., 6; 4 km NW Villa Vásquez, 61 m, 5; *Dajabón:* Los Cerezos, 12 km NW Río Limpio, 580 m, 1; *Elías Piña:* 14 km S Comendador, 976 m, 1; 15 km S Comendador, 976 m, 2; *Santiago Rodríguez:* 6 km NE Los Almácigos, 1; *Puerto Plata:* 13 km SE Luperón, 214 m, 1; 10 km W Luperón, 1; 9 km SE Sosúa, 16 m, 4; 11 km SE Sosúa, 183 m, 2; *La Vega:* Buena Vista, 11 km NE Jarabacoa, 640 m, 1; Jarabacoa, 530 m, 4; 1 km S Constanza, 1098 m, 18; 14 km SE Constanza, 1921 m, 1; 18 km SE Constanza, 1586 m, 1; 18 km SE Constanza, 2227–2288 m, 2; 5 km NW Valle Nuevo, 2288 m, 1; Valle Nuevo, 25 km SE Constanza, 2105 m, 1; *María T. Sánchez: ca.* 18 km W, 1.2 km S Sánchez, rd. to Rincón Molinillos, 31 m, 1; 1 km S Cruce de Rincón, s.l., 2; 9 km NE Río San Juan, s.l., 1; *Samaná:* 13.2 km NE Sánchez, 92 m, 2; 4.5 km E Samaná, 2; El Francés, 14 km E and N Samaná, s.l., 1; 18.0 km E and N Samaná, s.l., 1; 2 km S Las Galeras, 2; *Sánchez Ramírez:* 1 km NE Las Lagunas, 1; *Hato Mayor:* 4 km E Sabana de la Mar, 2; 7 km E Sabana de la Mar, 4; *La Altagracia:* 0.5–3.5 km W Boca de Yuma, 3; 1 km N Playa Bayahibe, s.l., 4; 16 km NE La Romana, 61 m, 5; *La Romana:* Río Chavón, 10 km NE La Romana, 1; Río Cumayasa, 13.5 km W La Romana, 31 m, 17; *Dist. Nac.:* Punta Caucedo, 5 km S Aeropuerto Internacional de las Américas, s.l., 1; Tres Ojos, s.l., 1; 30 km NW Santo Domingo, 122 m, 2; *Monseñor Nouel:* 7 km W Jayaco, 671 m, 1; 14 km SW Piedra Blanca, 427 m, 1; *San Cristóbal:* 2 km NW Cambita Garabitos, 305 m, 1; 3 km NW Cambita Garabitos, 366 m, 2; *Peravia:* 3 km W Sabana Buey, s.l., 1; *Azua:* 25 km NE Azua, 92 m, 2; 5 km S Peralta, 305 m, 2; 2.5 km W, 6.6 km N Azua, 183 m, 1; *San Juan:* 9 km E Vallejuelo, 610 m, 6; 7 km NE Vallejuelo, 671 m, 1 *Baoruco:* 11 km N Neiba, 519 m, 2; ; *Independencia:* 4–7 km NE El Aguacate, 519–824 m, 4; *Barahona:* west slope, Sierra Martín García, 915 m, 1; 10 km SSW Cabral, 427 m, 2; 2 km SW Barahona, 122 m, 1; 5 km SE, 3 km W Barahona, 183 m, 3; 8 km NW Paraíso, 153 m, 3 (2 MPM); 9 km NW Enriquillo, 671 m, 1; *Pedernales:* 23 km NE Cabo Rojo, 488 m, 2; 26 km NE Cabo Rojo, 732 m, 2; Mencía, 397 m, 6; 2 km SW Mencía, 275–336 m, 3; 2 km N Banano, 244 m, 1; 17 km NW Oviedo, 183 m, 1.

Sight records: República Dominicana: Valverde: Río Guarabo, 3 km W Los Quemados, 122 m—3 seen, 13.vii; *Elías Piña:* 1 km SW Puesto Pirámide 204, 1891 m—1 seen, 5.viii; *Samaná:* 13.2 km NE Sánchez, 92 m—several seen, 25.xii; *Barahona:* El Charco, summit, Sierra Martín García, 1098 m—1 seen, 13.viii; *Pedernales:* 5 km NE Los Arroyos, 1617 m,—2 seen, 2.vii.

3. *Eurytides zonarius* Butler, 1869

TL "San Domingo."

FW males 26–35 mm, females 28–38 mm.

Eurytides zonarius is 1 of a trio of related species on the Greater Antilles (*celadon* Lucas on Cuba and *marcellinus* Doubleday on Jamaica). All 3 are related in turn to *marcellus* Cramer from North America and *philolaus* Boisduval from México (Brown and Heineman, 1972:340).

Hall (1925:163) saw "one or two on Mt. Isabella and several . . . at La Vega, flying very high. Apparently not rare, but as in most species of this group there is only a single brood, and this on the wing only for a short time." Schwartz (1983a:58) reported 1 specimen from Haiti and saw (but did not capture) 3 additional individuals at the same locality in the following year. Marión Heredia (1980b) listed *E. zonarius* from El Número-Azua. From the above, one can logically assume that *E. zonarius* is indeed an uncommon species on Hispaniola.

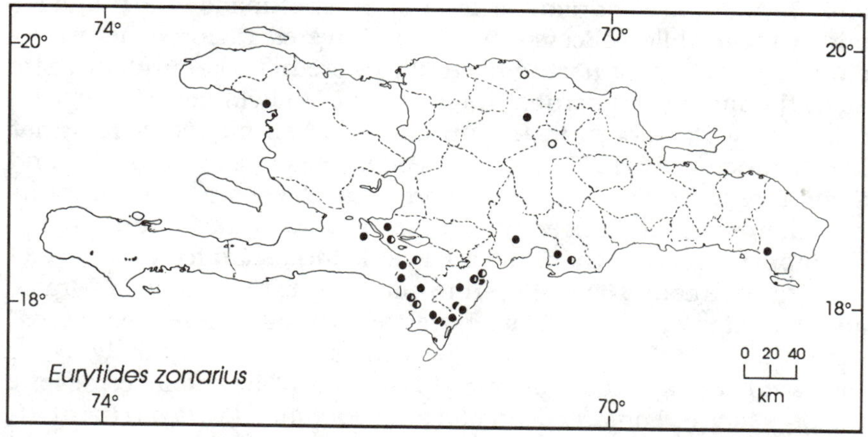

Like many other supposedly rare species, *E. zonarius* is locally common; Brown and Heineman (1972:340) made the same comment concerning *E. marcellinus* on Jamaica. Some of our specimens have been taken singly or from very small numbers at a particular locality. But to demonstrate the abundance of *E. zonarius*, the following anecdote serves well.

On 27.vi.1983, Raburn and I drove from the city of Barahona across the arid lowlands of the Península de Barahona to the Alcoa Exploration Company headquarters at Cabo Rojo. After leaving the town of Oviedo, as we began to ascend the limestone ridge that bisects the Península de Barahona from north to south, we observed *E. zonarius* flying across and along the road. Between that point and the intersection of the Oviedo-Pedernales road with that to Cabo Rojo, there was hardly a moment when there were no *E. zonarius* in our sight. The day was breezy but bright and sunny, and the butterflies were being wafted along the road, often flying erratically and with some "desperation." Obviously, *E. zonarius* was quite abundant. On 28.vi, Raburn and I returned to the locality near Oviedo (see account of *H. aristor* for details), which seemed a likely spot to try for *E. zonarius*, which were just as abundant that day as the one previous. The wind was blowing rather stiffly. At Oviedo, there were many *E. zonarius*, once more buffetted by the wind. Raburn positioned himself on an old dirt road, about 8 m from the main paved road, in *Acacia* scrub. Between 1115 and 1200 h, he collected 11 *E. zonarius;* the butterflies were flying along the paved road and were being blown, or were flying, into the shelter of the *Acacia* along the dirt road, where Raburn was standing. Between 1230 and 1330 h (temperature 34°C), Raburn took 39 more *E. zonarius* —a total of 50 specimens in 1 h and 45 min. I meanwhile collected in a xeric forested ravine, where I secured a few *E. zonarius;* the butterflies were not so abundant there as in the more open scrub. The number of individuals at this 1 locality must have been in the hundreds; when one considers that the distance between Oviedo and Pedernales is about 45 km, and along most of this distance we had seen *E. zonarius* the previous day, there must have been thousands of *E. zonarius* on the wing!

Raburn observed that only a few individuals landed in the lee of the *Acacia.* About 10 were seen to come to rest on the short grass, and 1 landed on a tree 3 m above the ground. These "rest stops" were brief, and the butterflies flew away almost immediately. None was seen taking nectar during this period of abundance, despite the presence of *Lantana ovatifolia* and *Bauhinia divaricata* (both attractive to papilionids and other butterflies). On the dirt road where Raburn had taken his stance, he observed that when 2 individuals met, flying from opposite directions, 1 "always" turned to follow the other. He also observed 4 "pairs" of *E. zonarius* "cartwheeling" above the dirt road in the scrub and collected 2 of these "pairs." The fight is rapid and very erratic, even under the best of weather conditions, and with the added presence of a stiff breeze, collecting *E. zonarius* was not easy. Of the series collected on 28.vi, almost all are fresh and unworn (except for damage resulting from the act of collection); only a very few are faded or have missing tails or ragged wings. This suggests that this was a major time of at least a very local (Península de Barahona) eclosion.

But perhaps even more amazing is that on 4.vii.1983, a return visit to Oviedo yielded not even the sighting of 1 *E. zonarius*, nor were any seen between the Cabo Rojo–Pedernales intersection. What had been, 6 days earlier, teeming with *E. zonarius* was now unexciting *Acacia* scrub! I suspect that most individuals had scattered to other localities, so that now the huge concentrations present in late June were no longer localized. Amador, Raburn, and I visited the Oviedo locality again on 10.viii.1983 and saw no *E. zonarius*. Still another visit on 5.x.1983 by Raburn and me yielded no specimens or sight records of this swallowtail. But in the latter month, scattered or small (2–3 individuals) groups of *E. zonarius* were seen elsewhere in the Península de Barahona lowlands. An interesting observation is the repeated sighting of an individual 7 km N Cabo Rojo, at the intersection of the Cabo Rojo–Pedernales roads; this (presumably) single individual was seen daily, between 4–10.x.1983, patrolling the immediate area of the intersection.

Gali's and my observations at Fond Parisien in Haiti are perhaps more orthodox as far as the behavior of *E. zonarius* is concerned. There, on 30.iv.1982, we encountered relatively large numbers of *E. zonarius* between 1015 and 1530 h, at temperatures of 30–34°C. Most individuals were seen in *Acacia* forest; but even here the butterflies were seen flying most commonly within the sun-dappled open areas abandoned by charcoal makers. As Schwartz (1983a:58) observed for the *E. zonarius* at Ça Soleil, here the butterflies were each flying an oval "beat," about 3.5 m above the ground, the "beat" taking them into and out of shade and sunlight. When the sky became overcast (it rained lightly between 1230 and 1300 h), *E. zonarius* seemed to frequent more open (less sheltered) situations. When disturbed by the collector, the *E. zonarius* abandoned the areas of their "beats" but returned thereto very shortly (within 5–10 min) and resumed flying the "beat" once more. About 20 more individuals were seen than were collected. Along this same road and on the same day, on a hillslope with some hardwoods, Gali saw 3 *E. zonarius* and collected 1. On the following day (0945–1400 h, temperature 30–35°C), the weather hot and humid but not breezy or windy, far fewer butterflies in general were seen, among them only 5 more *E. zonarius* seen than those taken. Gali netted 1 *E. zonarius* on this second day in an open grove of *Mangifera indica*.

Other specimens of *E. zonarius* have been taken or individuals seen in an oasis (Ça Soleil), *Acacia* scrub (Santiago, Barahona, La Furnia), semixeric woods (Playa Bayahibe, 2 km SW Barahona), xeric forest (3 km NW Enriquillo), *cafetales* (Polo, 9 km NW Enriquillo), and in mesic forest (Los Arroyos). One *E. zonarius* was seen flying in downtown Baní! Most localities are xeric or at least tending toward the xeric end of the hydrologic spectrum. Most specimens have been collected (or individuals observed) in June (61), with 23 in October, 11 in May, 21 in April, 11 in July, 7 in August, and 1 in March. The very high June number is due to the Oviedo incident recounted above. The relatively large number for October is due almost exclusively to specimens collected on or near the Península de Barahona, that area where the species had been so abundant in midsummer. Times of collection or observation varied between 0930 and 1530 h, at temperatures between 21°C (Los Arroyos) and 39°C (Playa Bayahibe).

The elevational distribution of *E. zonarius* is between sea level (Ça Soleil, Fond Parisien, Barahona, Tierra Nueva, 7 km N Cabo Rojo, Pedernales) and 1617 m (Los Arroyos). At the latter locality, an *E. zonarius* was seen foraging on the white flowers of an unidentified tree at the edge of forest. At Peralta, *E. zonarius* fed commonly on *Tournefortia hirsutissima.* Occurrences of *E. zonarius* above about 488 m are extremely few. The butterfly is primarily an inhabitant of lowland xeric situations within a few hundred meters of sea level.

Eurytides zonarius is a confirmed drinker; the small (5–10) aggregations are unique among Hispaniolan papilionids in that the butterflies hold the wings closed and motionless over the back and do not flutter them as do most papilionids. This habit, along with their cryptic un coloration and pattern, makes small, compact drinking groups of *E. zonarius* relatively invisible. Drinking aggregations or single individuals have been seen 4 times: 2 km SW Barahona, 6 km SW Barahona, Banano, 6 km NE Oviedo (Nuevo). The occurrence at 6 km SW Barahona was from a paved road with the water from a spring flowing across it; 2 incidents (2 km SW Barahona, Banano) involved drinking from mud adjacent to small creeks, and that at Oviedo involved drinking from the moist earth at the edge of a very large mudhole in the gravel highway.

Specimens: Haiti: l'Artibonite: 12.2 km W Ça Soleil, s.l., 1; *l'Ouest:* 2 km SE Fond Parisien, s.l., 18; *República Dominicana: Santiago:* 7 km SW Santiago, 214 m, 1; *La Altagracia:* 2.5 km SE Playa Bayahibe, 5; *Azua:* El Número, 2 (MNHNS); 5 km S Peralta, 305 m, 12; *Independencia:* 5 km NW Tierra Nueva, s.l., 1; *Barahona:* Polo, 702 m, 1; 9 km NW Enriquillo, 671 m, 1; 3 km NW Enriquillo, 244 m, 1; *Pedernales:* 23 km NE Cabo Rojo, 488 m, 1; 1 km SE Banano, 183 m, 8; 5 km NE Los Arroyos, 1617 m, 1; 17 km NW Oviedo, 183 m, 54; 13 km NW Oviedo, 1; 0.5 km S Tres Charcos, s.l., 1; 6 km NE Oviedo (Nuevo), 1.

Sight records: República Dominicana: Peravia: Baní—1 seen, 12.iv; *Independencia:* La Furnia, s.l.—8 seen, 31.iii; 4 km NE El Aguacate, 824 m—1 seen, 14.vii; *Barahona:* Barahona, s.l.—1 seen, 10.iv; 6 km SW Barahona, 122 m—1 seen, 12.x; *Pedernales:* 7 km N Cabo Rojo, s.l.—1 seen, 4–10.x; 9 km SE Pedernales, s.l.—2 seen, 9.x.

4. *Heraclides aristodemus aristodemus* Esper, 1794

TL "Hispaniola"; not "Cuba" as stated by Miller and Brown (1981:85).

FW males 41–52 mm, females 47–57 mm.

Heraclides aristodemus Esper is endemic to the West Indies, although 1 subspecies, *H. a. ponceanus* Schaus, occurs on some of the Bahama Islands and peripherally in south Florida and on some of the Florida Keys. The nominate subspecies is found on Hispaniola (and questionably on Puerto Rico; see Miller, 1987, and Collins and Morris, 1985:301, for conflicting opinions), with *H. a. temenes* Godart on Cuba and Little Cayman (Askew, 1980:129), *H. a. bjorndalae* Clench on Great Inagua Island in the Bahama Islands and in the Turks and Caicos Islands (Simon and Miller, 1986:11, 13), and *H. a. majasi* Miller on Crooked Island in the Bahamas.

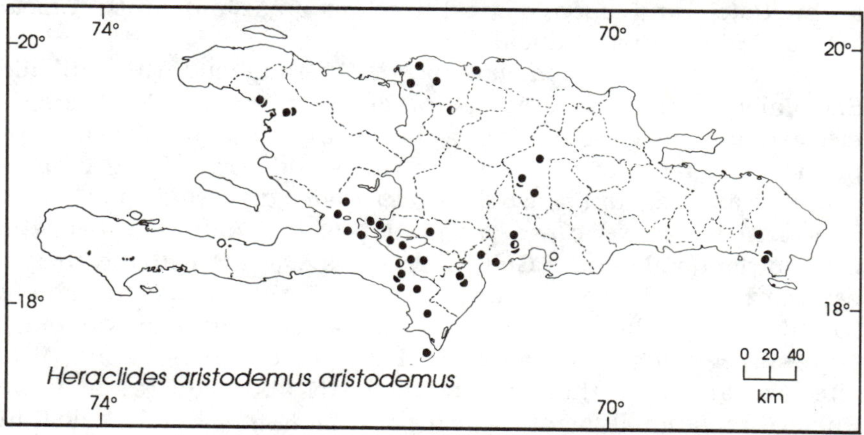

Heraclides aristodemus aristodemus

Hall (1924:162) stated that *H. a. aristodemus* occurs only at low elevations and is rather scarce. Marión Heredia (1980b) recorded the species from El Número-Azua. Schwartz (1983a:55) noted 22 specimens from 8 Haitian localities, with an elevational distribution from sea level to 366 m. Bates (1935a:111) noted that *H. a. temenes* was known from few specimens from Oriente and Matanzas provinces in Cuba. Clench (1977b:190) noted only 2 localities for *H. a. ponceanus* on Andros in the Bahamas, and *H. a. bjorndalae* was named from only 2 specimens from Great Inagua

(Clench, 1978:275), where the species appears to be quite rare (Clench and Bjorndal, 1980:24; but see Simon and Miller, 1986). Clench (1978:274) recorded 4 specimens of *H. a ponceanus* from Cat Island, and 6 from Andros, and *H. a. majasi* was named on a series of 6 males (Miller, 1987).

Heraclides a. aristodemus is a butterfly of arid areas, most commonly encountered in *Acacia* woods, forest, or scrub. Thus, *H. a. aristodemus* and *H. aristor* form a pair of xerophilic swallowtails, just as *H. a. epidaurus* and *H. machaonides* form a mesophilic pair. Interestingly, there is a third member in each group: *E. zonarius* with the former, and *P. p. imerius* with the latter.

Just as with the other Hispaniolan papilionids, *H. a. aristodemus* occurs in habitats other than lowland deserts (although it is most common there). We have collected specimens in oases (Ça Soleil, Croix des Bouquets, Villa Vásquez, 1 km SE Tierra Nueva), bare open hillsides (Polo, Terre Rouge), mesic hardwood forests (Mirebalais, Neiba, Sierra Martín García, Los Arroyos, Banano), open fields (1 km S Constanza), mixed pine-hardwoods (6 km SSE Constanza), pinewoods (21 km SE Constanza), transitional woods (Cabo Rojo), and open, almost treeless grasslands with *Uniola virgata* (Monte Cristi, Canoa).

Heraclides a. aristodemus occurs throughout the Cul de Sac–Valle de Neiba, where it is the dominant papilionid. The species extends thence to the east as far as about Baní and then reappears in the far eastern portion of the island (Prov. de la Altagracia), just as *E. zonarius* also does. *Heraclides a. aristodemus* is also abundant in the xeric western portion of the Valle de Cibao, the xeric lowlands along the Golfe de la Gonâve (Ça Soleil) and thence eastward (Les Poteaux), and on the Península de Barahona (Oviedo). From these lowland xeric areas, individuals "wash up" onto surrounding mountainsides (Los Arroyos, El Aguacate, Peralta, Neiba), where they may be modestly abundant, as at Cabo Rojo in transitional forest. Specimens from Estero Hondo (taken in a mesic palm grove) are less easily explained; there are, however, arid areas to the north and west which may support a population of *H. aristodemus*. The situation at Banano will be discussed below. This is the first report of *H. a. aristodemus* from Isla Beata.

There remain 2 areas where *H. a. aristodemus* has been taken that are indeed puzzling. The specimen from Mirebalais was captured in mesic high-canopied forest adjacent to a stream. The locality is, however, only 20 km to the west of the rather xeric, open, and grassy plains between Lascahobas and Belladère, whence *H. a. aristodemus* is unknown, but where it is expected. More puzzling are the specimens from high elevations (1098–1952 m) in the Cordillera Central. Two of the 5 specimens from there are fresh and unflown and must have originated in that area. These were taken in 1981 (1), 1982 (3), and 1985 (1). The conclusion is inescapable that there is a locally breeding population of *H. a. aristodemus* in the Cordillera Central.

One's impression is that during April-August *H. a. aristodemus* is widespread throughout the xeric lowland areas of Hispaniola; it is nowhere common, but nonetheless it is far from rare during those months. During 6–9.x.1983, Raburn and I were amazed at seeing hundreds of these butterflies on the Península de Barahona and on the southern slopes of the Massif de la Selle (Banano) and the Sierra de Baoruco (Cabo Rojo). At the latter locality, on 6.x, *H. a. aristodemus* were flying abundantly in transitional woods along the Alcoa Exploration Company road. The flight is rather slow and deliberate and 1 m or less above the ground. Between 0930 and 1145 h, we collected 13 specimens and could have had many more. We returned to the same site between 1400 and 1430 h and saw not even a straggler *H. a. aristodemus*. The temperature in the morning had been 28°C; that in the afternoon was not taken but was considerably higher than in the morning.

On 8.x, Raburn and I drove from Pedernales to above Los Arroyos. Near Banano, at the spring run with much mud and horse manure as well as along the small creek itself, *H. a. aristodemus* was extremely abundant, more so than at Cabo Rojo. The Banano locality was literally aswarm with these swallowtails, most of which were drinking. Thirty-six specimens were collected, and once more this represents but a small fraction of the numbers present there. A return visit to this same site on 4.ix.1984 yielded sight records of 3 *H. a. aristodemus*.

On 8.x, the day of the above-mentioned abundance of *H. a. aristodemus* at Banano, Raburn and I saw several other isolated drinking clubs between Pedernales and the turnoff to Don Juan below Mencía. One of these aggregations was in a low spot, perhaps 1×1.5 m, in the road with broken pavement. This small area was literally covered with living *H. a. aristodemus*, and the immediate area about the hole was littered with the dead and broken remains of many individuals that had not avoided the few trucks and cars that travel this road.

This unaccountable abundance of *H. a. aristodemus* in October (1983) made me reassess the abundance of *H. a. aristodemus*. Certainly, it was among the most common of the moderate- to large-sized butterflies in an area where, during 9 previous and subsequent visits, *H. a. aristodemus* was uncommon. In the ravine at Oviedo (discussed in detail under *H. aristor*), *H. a. aristodemus* was moderately abundant (most specimens somewhat to well flown) on 28.vi and 1.vii.1983, yet on 5.x, only 2 individuals were observed there. There is little doubt that the modest numbers of *H. a. aristodemus* at this locality in June and July were remnants of a previous brood, and the huge number present at Banano in October was a relatively local phenomenon, more or less limited to the Pedernales-Mencía area and not affecting the Oviedo region, just 45 km to the southeast. Once more I was impressed with the fortuitous nature of butterfly collecting and observation.

What is even more puzzling is that life-history data on *H. aristodemus* elsewhere suggests the spring as the time of eclosion. Pyle (1981:339), writing of *H. a. ponceanus*, stated that that subspecies is univoltine, in April-early June, and that there is a partial second brood in late summer in some years. Clench (1977b:190), writing about *H. a. ponceanus* on Andros, felt that "the principal flight is probably late May and early June." A single individual from September he attributed perhaps to being abnormal or being a member of a partial second brood.

Finally, the principal known larval food plant of *H. aristodemus* (at least *H. a. ponceanus*) is *Amyris elemifera;* Pyle (1981:339) also mentioned *Zanthoxylum fagara*. In southern Florida, where both species of plants occur, they are components of the tropical hammock flora, living in dense stands of mesophilic hardwoods. Likewise, in southern Florida, *H. a. ponceanus* inhabits such hardwood enclaves. Although *Amyris elemifera* occurs on Hispaniola, it is neither a xerophyte nor does it occur at high elevations. There are several Hispaniolan *Zanthoxylum*, at least 1 of which occurs in *Acacia* forest in the lowlands. It is obvious that the life cycle of *H. a. aristodemus* differs in many ways from at least that of *H. a. ponceanus*.

Most specimens and observations are from October (57), with 33 in July. There are 20 from April, 20 from June, 24 from August, 9 from May, and 1 each from March and November.

The elevational distribution is from sea level (Ça Soleil, Fond Parisien, Croix des Bouquets, Playa Bayahibe, Las Lajas, La Furnia, El Limón, Canoa, Pedernales, Isla Beata) to 1952 m (21 km SE Constanza) on the Cordillera Central and 1617 m (Los Arroyos) on the Massif de la Selle. High elevational records (793 m) in the Sierra de Baoruco and elsewhere do not approch these.

Times of collection were from 0930 to 1630 h, at temperatures between 28°C (21 km SE Constanza, Cabo Rojo) and 39°C (2.5 km

SE Playa Bayahibe).

Heraclides a. aristodemus takes nectar from *Bauhinia divaricata*, a white-flowered xerophytic member of the Fabaceae (Les Poteaux, Gonaïves), *Lantana ovatifolia* (Copey, Neiba, El Limón, Cabral), *L. reticulata* (Copey), *Tournefortia hirsutissima* (5 km S Peralta), *Cordia exarata* (1 km N Playa Bayahibe), and the white flowers of an unidentified tree (Los Arroyos). The butterfly has also been observed (Peralta) coursing along a narrow lane whose fences on both sides were abloom with *Antigonon leptopus;* the lepidopteran was not feeding. *Heraclides a. aristodemus* forms drinking aggregations. Aside from those at Banano noted above, I have also observed this behavior at Ça Soleil (a few on moist mud in dirt road through oasis) and 9 km N Pedernales (many on mud in cattle pen). Two individuals were seen at Neiba on 3.viii (35°C) "cartwheeling." Both were captured in a single net-sweep, but the sexes were unfortunately not determined.

Specimens: Haiti: l'Artibonite: 4.6 km E Les Poteaux, 183 m, 7; 16 km E Gonaïves, 1; 12.2 km W Ça Soleil, s.l., 12; 16.8 km W Ça Soleil, 3; *l'Ouest:* 20 km SE Mirebalais, 366 m, 1; 8 km S Terre Rouge, 440 m, 1; 2 km SE Fond Parisien, s.l., 7; 13 km E Croix des Bouquets, s.l., 2; 17.6 km E Croix des Bouquets, s.l., 1; *República Dominicana: Monte Cristi:* 4 km SE Monte Cristi, 1; 6 km W Copey, s.l., 3; 4 km NW Villa Vásquez, 61 m, 8; *Puerto Plata:* 0.6 km NE Estero Hondo, 3; *La Vega:* 6 km S Jarabacoa, *ca.* 610 m, 1; 1 km S Constanza, 1098 m, 2; 6 km SSE Constanza, 403 m, 1; 21 km SE Constanza, 1952 m, 1; *La Altagracia:* 1 km N Playa Bayahibe, s.l., 2; 2.5 km SE Playa Bayahibe, 10; 16 km NE La Romana, 61 m, 2; *Azua:* 5 km S Peralta, 305 m, 6; *Baoruco:* 9 km N Neiba, 366 m, 3; *Independencia:* Las Lajas, s.l., 1; 1 km SE Tierra Nueva, s.l., 1; 5 km NW Tierra Nueva, s.l., 1; La Furnia, s.l., 1; 4 km NE El Limón, s.l., 1; 2 km S Duvergé, 1; 4–7 km NE El Aguacate, 519–732 m, 2; *Barahona:* west slope, Sierra Martín García, 458 m, 1; 8 km ESE Canoa, s.l., 3; 8 km NNE Polo, 793 m, 1; 7 km SSW Cabral, 214 m, 2; *Pedernales:* 23 km NE Cabo Rojo, 488 m, 16; 1 km SE Banano, 183 m, 36; Mencía, 397 m, 2; 9 km N Pedernales, 244 m, 5; 9 km SE Pedernales, s.l., 1; 17 km NW Oviedo, 183 m, 6; *Isla Beata:* 1.

Sight records: República Dominicana: Santiago Rodríguez: 4.8 km S Zamba, 183 m—1 seen, 28.v; *Azua:* 14 km S Peralta—1 seen, 21.iv; 2.5 km W, 6.6 km N Azua, 183 m—1 seen, 13.viii; *Independencia:* La Furnia, s.l.—3 seen, 31.iii; *Pedernales:* 1 km SE Banano, 183 m—3 seen, 4.iv; Mencía, 397 m—1 seen, 2.vii; 5 km NE Los Arroyos, 1617 m—1 seen, 2.vii; 17 km NW Oviedo, 183 m—1 seen, 5.x.

5. *Heraclides machaonides* Esper, 1796 (*frontispiece*)

TL Port-au-Prince, Dépt. de l'Ouest, Haiti.

FW males 51–57 mm, females 55–61 mm; dwarf female 41 mm.

Heraclides machaonides is endemic to Hispaniola; the species has been reported from Puerto Rico (Riley, 1975:148), but Ramos (1977:216) was unaware of any Puerto Rican records and later (1982:63) did not list it from that island. There is also a record of *H. machaonides* from the Cayman Islands; Schwartz, Gonzalez, and Henderson (1987) gave justification for dismissal of this record.

Despite Riley's (1975:148) statement that *H. machaonides* is "uncommon" but "widespread above 1000 ft," this species is the most common and widespread of the Hispaniolan papilionids. Riley's statement is from Hall (1925:162), who took specimens at 3 localities and who reported Kaempffer's capture of "several" in December, suggesting that there are 2 broods. Cucurullo (1959:11) did not list *H. machaonides* from the República Dominicana; Marión Heredia (1974:1) reported *H. machaonides* from the country and later (1980b) reported it from El Número-Azua. Schwartz (1983a:55–56) reported 21 specimens from 9 Haitian localities.

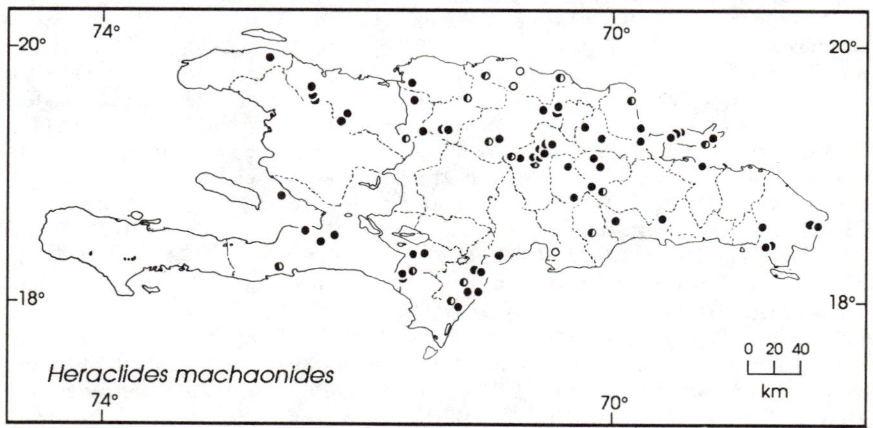

Heraclides machaonides prefers wooded habitats, much like *H. a. epidaurus;* in fact, the 2 species are often found together. The flight of *H. machaonides*, however, is much slower and "floppier" than the strong and direct flight of *H. a. epidaurus*. The former species also customarily flies lower than *H. a. epidaurus*, which may often be seen near or at treetop level.

Heraclides machaonides prefers mesic wooded situations: *caféières* and their margins (Gaubert, Dondon), *cafetales-cacaotales* (Jamao al Norte, Tenares, San Francisco de Macorís, Sánchez, Cruce de Rincón, Bonao, Las Terrenas, Piedra Blanca, Manabao, Mencía), mesic hardwood forest (Plaisance, Los Cerezos, Guerra, Maimón, Santo Domingo, Sierra Martín García, La Ciénaga,

Paraíso, Las Abejas, Río Bao), transitional forest (El Aguacate), xeric woods and forest (Punta Cana, Playa Bayahibe, La Romana, Enriquillo), mixed pine-hardwoods (Loma Leonor, Buena Vista, Jarabacoa), and even, but rarely, in *Acacia* forest (Copey). Outside of wooded situations, *H. machaonides* has been taken or observed on exposed mountain roadsides (Boutilliers Road), hotel gardens (Pétionville), behind a beach (Grand-Goâve), riverine woods (Güaigüí, El Río), and open fields (Sabana de la Mar).

The elevational distribution is from sea level (Grand-Goâve, Copey, Cruce de Rincón, Las Terrenas, Punta Cana, Playa Bayahibe, Cabrera) to 1129 m (Las Abejas) on the Sierra de Baoruco, 1037 m (El Río) on the Cordillera Central, 885 m (Boutilliers Road) on the Massif de la Selle front ranges, 793 m (20 km SW Jamao al Norte) on the Cordillera Septentrional, and 854 m on the Sierra Martín García. *Heraclides machaonides* apparently is absent from moderate elevations (above 1096 m) within the Cordillera Central (Constanza); the absence of records from the mesic forests of the Sierra de Neiba is peculiar, although the species is not expected in the pine forests of that range nor of the Cordillera Central.

Most specimens have been taken in July and August (104 and 76), with 11 in April, 28 in June, 12 in March, 6 in October, 4 each in May and December, 3 in November, and 2 in January. There is no evidence for a midwinter brood; indeed, *H. machaonides* is much less often seen in the fall-winter-spring than in the late summer.

Times of collection were between 0830 and 1730 h, at temperatures between 27°C (El Aguacate, 4.5 km E Samaná, Las Abejas) and 42°C (La Romana). Contrary to many other Hispaniolan papilionids, *H. machaonides* often flies in very overcast to rainy weather. This has been observed at Dondon, 14 km SW Jamao al Norte, San Francisco de Macorís, Buena Vista, Playa Bayahibe, Santo Domingo, El Aguacate, and 4.5 km E Samaná. *Heraclides machaonides* has been observed taking nectar from *Cordia haitiensis* (Pétionville), *Ixora* sp. (1 km N Playa Bayahibe), *Citrus* sp. (Güaigüí), *Asclepias curassavica* (13.2 km NE Sánchez), *Bauhinia divaricata* (5 km SE, 3 km W Barahona), *Lantana ovatifolia* (Copey), and *Psychotria brachiata* (Rubiaceae) at Guerra. We have never observed drinking aggregations of *H. machaonides*, yet single individuals have been observed to drink from a puddle in a road (Barahona) and from moist mud (Banano). On 1 occasion (20 km SW Jamao al Norte), in a narrow, humid ravine, several *H. machaonides* were seen to be "interested" in the small yellow flowers of *Palicourea barbinervia* (Rubiaceae), but none landed to take nectar.

A pair of *H. machaonides in copula* was observed by Wisor on 21.iii (Cruce de Rincón, s.l., 1130 h, 30°C). The pair was resting on a leaf of a shrub in an open field, about 0.3 m above the ground.

Specimens: Haiti: Nord-Ouest: 0.6 km NW Balladé, 1; *Nord:* Gaubert, 1; 3.5 km W Plaisance, 305 m, 1; 3.5 km S Plaisance, 336 m, 1; 5.6 km SE Dondon, 336 m, 3; 6.1 km S Dondon, 366 m, 1; *l'Ouest:* Pétionville, 458 m, 2; Boutilliers Road, 854 m, 3; Boutilliers Road, 1.8–1.9 km W Kenscoff rd., 763–885 m, 5; just W Grand-Goâve, s.l., 1; *República Dominicana: Monte Cristi:* 6 km W Copey, s.l., 1; *Dajabón:* 2 km NW El Pino, 183 m, 1; Los Cerezos, 12 km NW Río Limpio, 580 m, 3; *Santiago Rodríguez:* Loma Leonor, 18 km SW Monción, 534 m, 1; *Santiago:* 2 km E Pedro García, 427 m, 1; Río Bao, 8 km SE Montones Abajo, 488 m, 1; *Espaillat:* 14 km SW Jamao al Norte, 427 m, 2; 20 km SW Jamao al Norte, 793 m, 1; *Duarte:* 10 km SE Tenares, 183 m, 7; 12 km SE San Francisco de Macorís, 2; *La Vega:* La Palma, 19 km W Jayaco, 1007 m, 1; Güaigüí, S La Vega, 336 m, 2; Buena Vista, 11 km NE Jarabacoa, 640 m, 2; 1 km W Manabao, 793 m, 1; Jarabacoa, 530 m, 31; 5 km SE Jarabacoa, 595 m, 3; 9 km S Jarabacoa, *ca.* 610 m, 1; *María T. Sánchez:* 1 km S Cruce de Rincón, s.l., 3; 9 km SE Nagua, s.l., 1; *Samaná:* 6.9 km NE Sánchez, 336 m, 1; 13.2 km NE Sánchez, 92 m, 3; 3 km SW Las Terrenas, s.l., 1; 14.4 km E and N Samaná, 31 m, 1; *Hato Mayor:* 7 km E Sabana de la Mar, 1; *La Altagracia:* Punta Cana, s.l., 1; 6 km W Punta Cana, s.l., 2; 1 km N Playa Bayahibe, s.l., 25; 2.5 km SE Playa Bayahibe, 2; 16 km NE La Romana, 61 m, 16; *Dist. Nac.:* 9 km NE Guerra, 1; 30 km NW Santo Domingo, 122 m, 4; *Monseñor Nouel:* Bonao, 153 m, 2; 14 km SW Piedra Blanca, 442 m, 2; 6 km SE Maimón, 122 m, 1; *Sánchez Ramírez:* La Piedra, 7 km SW Pimentel, 2; 1 km NE Las Lagunas, 183 m, 1; *Independencia:* 0.6 km NW Puerto Escondido, 519 m, 1; 4–7 km NE El Aguacate, 519–824 m, 9; *Barahona:* west slope, Sierra Martín García, 458–534 m, 5; Polo, 702 m, 1; 1.8 km SW Monteada Nueva, 1007 m, 1; 2 km SW Barahona, 122 m, 1; 10 km SW La Ciénaga, 61 m, 1; 8 km NW Paraíso, 153 m, 12 (4 MPM); 3 km NW Enriquillo, 244 m, 4; *Pedernales:* Mencía, 397 m, 2; 1 km SE Banano, 183 m, 1.

Sight records: Haiti: l'Ouest: Lavaneau, 229 m—6 seen, 25.iv; *República Dominicana: Monte Cristi:* 6 km W Copey, s.l.—2 seen, 16.v; *Dajabón:* Cañada Tirolís, just S Villa Anacaona, 458 m—1 seen, 3.vii; *Valverde:* Río Guarabo, 3 km W Los Quemados, 122 m—2 seen, 13.vii; *Santiago:* Río Bao, 4 km SW Mata Grande, 702 m—2 seen, 15.vii; Río Bao, 8 km SE Montones Abajo, 488 m—3 seen, 1.viii; *Santiago Rodríguez:* Loma Leonor, 19 km SW Monción, 610 m—1 seen, 13.viii; *Puerto Plata:* 11 km N Cruce de Guayacanes, 275 m—2 seen, 18.vii; 9 km SE Sosúa, 15 m—1 seen, 17.v; *Espaillat:* 14 km SW Jamao al Norte, 534 m— 2 seen, 26.vii: 20 km SW Jamao al Norte, 793 m—10 seen, 16.vii; *La Vega:* 1 km E El Río, 1037 m—1 seen, 6.vii; La Ciénaga, 915 m—1 seen, 8.viii; *María T. Sánchez:* 6 km S Cabrera, s.l.—2 seen, 22.iii; Cruce de Rincón, s.l.— 2 seen, 21.iii; *Samaná:* 4.5 km E Samaná—4 seen, 23.xii; *Hato Mayor:* 7 km E Sabana de la Mar—1 seen, 6.iii; *Dist. Nac.:* 9 km NE Guerra—1 seen, 6.iii; *Monte Plata:* 8 km W Esperalvillo, 915 m—3 seen, 29.vii; *Monseñor Nouel:* Bonao, 153 m—1 seen, 11.viii; 6 km SE Maimón, 122 m—1 seen, 1.xi; *Sánchez Ramírez:* 1 km NE Las Lagunas, 183 m—2 seen, 2.xi; *San Cristóbal:* 11 km NW Cambita Garabitos, 671 m—1 seen, 14.viii; *Barahona:* west slope, Sierra Martín García, 793–854 m—13.viii; 3 km NNE Polo, 854 m—1 seen, 4.viii; 9 km NW Enriquillo, 671 m—1 seen, 5.vii; *Pedernales:* Las Abejas, 12 km NW Aceitillar, 1129 m—1 seen, 20.vii.

6. *Heraclides androgeus epidaurus* Godman and Salvin, 1890

TL not stated.

FW males 55–63 mm, females 56–68 mm; dwarf male 41 mm.

Heraclides a. epidaurus was not seen by Hall (1925:163), but Schwartz (1983a:56) recorded 29 specimens from 7 Haitian localities. Cucurullo (1959:11) and Marión Heredia (1974:1, 1980b) also reported *H. a. epidaurus* (or at least *H. androgeus*) from the República Dominicana but only from El Número-Azua. *Heraclides a. epidaurus* also occurs on Cuba (Bates, 1935a: 112–13), where it appears to be rare, and Puerto Rico (Comstock, 1944:537; Ramos, 1982:63).

Of the Hispaniolan papilionids, *H. a. epidaurus* is the second most abundant. This may at least in part be due to the use by this species of members of the Rutaceae (*Citrus* sp., among others) as the larval food plant. Not only are there many native rutaceans on Hispaniola, but the widespread cultivation of oranges, limes, and grapefruit has surely aided the distribution of *H. a. epidaurus*. This butterfly occurs primarily in mesic situations, including pseudoforests (Carrefour la Mort, Dondon, La Entrada, Tenares, Mencía) and hardwood forests and woods (Saut d'Eau, Mirebalais, Plaisance, Los Cerezos, Villa Anacaona, 8 km SE Montones Abajo, Guerra, Paraíso, Banano). But the species is also encountered in xeric forests and woods (Boca de Yuma, Playa Bayahibe, La Romana, Enriquillo), open fields, especially where there are appropriate flowers as nectar sources (Jarabacoa, Constanza), transitional forests (El Aguacate), and oases (Villa Vásquez) or roadsides (3 km W Aguas Negras). There are no records from the Cul de Sac–Valle de Neiba, and records are only from Villa Vásquez in the extreme western Valle de Cibao.

The elevational distribution is between sea level (Cormier Plage, Carrefour la Mort, Playa Bayahibe, Barahona, La Entrada, Cruce de Rincón, Punta Cana) and 2166 m (32 km SE Constanza). There are no records or sightings from the Sierra de Neiba and few from the Sierra de Baoruco. Likewise, specimens or records from the Massif de la Selle are lacking. Only on the Cordillera Central does *H. a. epidaurus* reach high elevations (2166 m); this is not an isolated elevational record for that range, since there are specimens or sightings from Manabao (824 m), La Ciénaga (915 m), and La Palma (1007 m). *Heraclides a. epidaurus* occurs rarely (1 specimen) in the pine forests to the southeast of Constanza but not in the pinewoods on the Morne l'Hôpital (Kenscoff, Furcy, Peneau).

Times of collection were between 0900 and 1740 h, at temperatures of 26°C (Loma Leonor) to 38°C (Cruce de Guayacanes, Bonao).

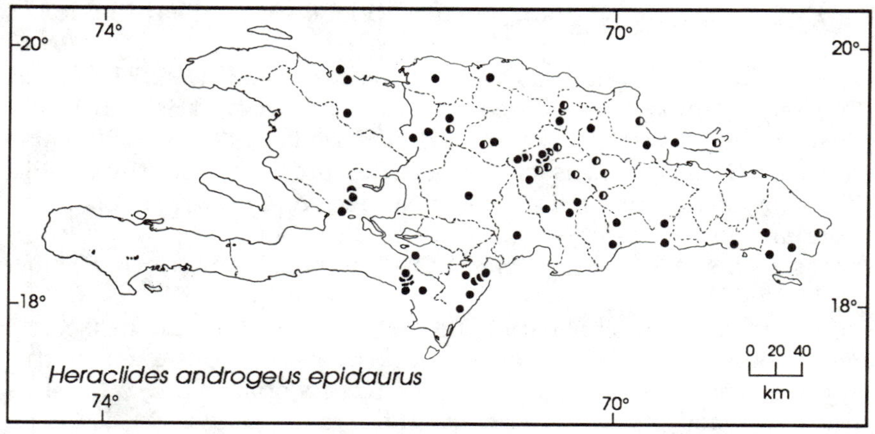

Most specimens and sight records are from July (116), with 48 from August and 76 from June. There are 8 specimens and records from October, 6 from March, 5 from April, 2 from December, and 1 each from January and May. *Heraclides a. epidaurus* is much more abundant beginning in June than it is at other times of the year. One simply sees fewer individuals in the fall-winter-spring than during the late summer.

Heraclides a. epidaurus has been seen feeding on a variety of flowers: *Hibiscus rosasinensis* (Carrefour la Mort, Las Lagunas), *Cordia haitiensis* (Terre Rouge), *Lantana ovatifolia* (Monción, Cabral), *Zinnia elegans*, a favorite flower (Constanza—many observations; San Juan), *Solanum* sp. (Solanaceae; a white-flowered, 1.5-m-tall species; Constanza), an unidentified white-flowered tree (Playa Bayahibe), and *Ixora* sp. (La Romana). Drinking, either by single individuals or small groups, has been observed at El Aguacate (small group of about 10 individuals drinking with a few pierids from a small, rain-filled depression in the gravel road), 2 km S Aguas Negras (male drinking alone from a mud puddle in the gravel road), Banano (single individuals drinking from moist mud made by water from a spring seepage), 0.5 km W Manabao (single male drinking from creek ford in dirt road), and Los Cerezos (single individuals drinking from mud at the edge of a small stream in the village). At Pedernales, a few *H. a. epidaurus* were drinking from the mud of a cattle pen with many *H. a. aristodemus*.

We have observed female *H. a. epidaurus* ovipositing on *Citrus* sp. on the following occasions: 15.vii (Mata Grande, 702 m, 1230 –1330 h, 35°C), 5.viii (La Piedra, 1145–1245 h, 34°C), 9.viii (Tenares, 183 m), 15.viii (Piedra Blanca, 427 m, 1030–1300 h, 30°C), and 1.i (Güaigüí, 336 m, 1045–1400 h, 29°C). Female specimens are regularly less perfect than males; a badly damaged and bedraggled female was taken on 30.vii at El Aguacate as it struggled on the ground to cross the dirt road.

Copulating pairs have been taken or seen on 17.iv (La Romana, 61 m, 1127 h, 34°C) and on 3.vii (Constanza, 1098 m, 1000–1130 h, 28°C).

Schwartz (1983a:56) noted the capture of *H. a. epidaurus* by the spider *Nephila* sp. at Carrefour la Mort; there these spiders had spun their webs adjacent to tall *Hibiscus* hedges about the ruins of a French colonial *habitation.* I also saw a female *H. a. epidaurus*, at the same locality, trailing about 2 m of sticky silk as it flew; the spiders are not always successful in trapping such big and powerful butterflies as *H. a. epidaurus*.

Specimens: Haiti: Nord: Cormier Plage, s.l., 1; Carrefour la Mort, s.l., 18; 3.5 km SE Dondon, 336 m, 1; *l'Ouest:* 20.2 km SE Mirbalais, 366 m, 1; 20 km SE Mirebalais, 366 m, 1; 1.6 km N Saut d'Eau, 183 m, 5; 1.3 km N Terre Rouge, 595 m, 1; *República Dominicana: Monte Cristi:* 4 km NW Villa Vásquez, 61 m, 2; *Dajabón:* Los Cerezos, 12 km NW Río Limpio, 580 m, 1; 1 km S Villa Anacaona, 397 m, 1; *Santiago Rodríguez:* 17 km SW Monción, 458 m, 1; *Puerto Plata:* 11 km N Cruce de Guayacanes, 275 m, 1; *Espaillat:* 3 km N Puesto Grande, 580 m, 1; *Santiago:* Río Bao, 8 km SE Montones Abajo, 488 m, 4; *María T. Sánchez:* 1 km S Cruce de Rincón, s.l., 3; *Samaná:* 6.9 km NE Sánchez, 336 m, 1; *La Vega:* Manabao, 824 m, 1; 0.5 km W Manabao, 793 m, 1; Jarabacoa, 530 m, 93; 5 km SE Jarabacoa, 595 m, 1; 6 km S Jarabacoa, *ca.* 610 m, 2; La Ciénaga, 915 m, 1; 1 km S Constanza, 1098 m, 21; 32 km SE Constanza, 2166 m, 1; *Duarte:* 10 km SE Tenares, 183 m, 5; *La Altagracia:* 0.5–3.5 km W Boca de Yuma, 2; 1 km N Playa Bayahibe, s.l., 9; 16 km NE La Romana, 61 m, 5; *La Romana:* Río Cumayasa, 13.5 km W La Romana, 6; *Dist. Nac.:* 9 km NE Guerra, 1; Punta Caucedo, 2 km W, 2 km S Andrés, s.l., 1; 30 km NW Santo Domingo, 122 m, 1; *Monseñor Nouel:* 14 km SW Piedra Blanca, 427 m, 1; *San Cristóbal:* 2 km N Hato Damas, 1; *Peravia:* 9 km ENE Rancho Arriba, 1; *Azua:* 5 km S Peralta, 305 m, 1; *San Juan:* San Juan, 1; *Independencia:* 4–7 km NE El Aguacate, 519–824 m, 16; *Barahona:* 7 km SSW Cabral, 214 m, 1; Barahona, s.l., 1; 4 km SW Barahona, 305 m, 1; 12 km SW Barahona, 427 m, 1; 8 km NW Paraíso, 153 m, 3; 3 km NW Enriquillo, 244 m, 2; *Pedernales:* 23 km NE Cabo Rojo, 488 m, 1; 9 km N Pedernales, 244 m, 1; 2 km S Aguas Negras, 610 m, 1; 3 km W Aguas Negras, 519 m, 1; 1 km SE Banano, 183 m, 3; Mencía, 397 m, 1; 2 km SW Mencía, 336 m, 1.

Sight records: República Dominicana: Dajabón: Los Cerezos, 12 km NW Río Limpio, 580 m—2 seen, 4.viii; *Santiago Rodríguez:* Loma Leonor, 19 km SW Monción, 610 m—2 seen, 17.iii; *Santiago:* Río Bao, 4 km SW Mata Grande, 702 m—1 seen, 15.vii; *Espaillat:* 20 km SW Jamao al Norte, 793 m—1 seen,

16.vii; 14 km SW Jamao al Norte, 534 m—2 seen, 26.vii; *La Vega:* 1 km E El Río, 1037 m—3 seen, 15.vii; Güaigüí, S La Vega, 336 m—1 seen, 1.i; La Palma, 19 km W Jayaco, 1007 m—1 seen, 13.viii; Buena Vista, 11 km NE Jarabacoa, 640 m—1 seen, 31.xii; *María T. Sánchez:* 14 km S La Entrada, s.l.—24.x; *Samaná:* 6.9 km NE Sánchez, 336 m—1 seen, 25.x; 14.4 km E and N Samaná, 31 m—1 seen, 26.xii; *La Altagracia:* Punta Cana, s.l.—1 seen, 30.x; *Monte Plata:* 8 km W Esperalvillo, 92 m—1 seen, 29.vii: *Monseñor Nouel:* Bonao, 153 m—11.viii; *Sánchez Ramírez:* La Piedra, 7 km SW Pimentel—5.viii; 1 km NE Las Lagunas, 183 m—1 seen, 3.iii; *Peravia:* 2 km SW Rancho Arriba, 671 m—2 seen, 17.viii; *Barahona:* 12 km SW Barahona, 427 m—1 seen, 29.iii.

7. *Heraclides aristor* Godart, 1819

TL Port-au-Prince, Dépt. de l'Ouest, Haiti.

FW males 44–55 mm, females 45–55 mm.

Heraclides aristor is an endemic Hispaniolan species, apparently most closely related to (or at least resembling) Cuban *H. caiguanabus* Poey. Hall (1925:162) noted only the unique holotype from near Port-au-Prince, Haiti. Riley (1975:151) rerecorded the type-locality and noted the existence of 1 female from Haut Turgeau, near sea level, in the city of Port-au-Prince. Marión Heredia (1980b) did not record the species from El Número-Azua, but Schwartz (1983a:57) reported 2 specimens (and the sighting of 2 additional individuals) from 2 Haitian localities. Without question, *H. aristor* is 1 of the great prizes among Hispaniolan papilionids. One assumes automatically from the above meager data that it is a rare species.

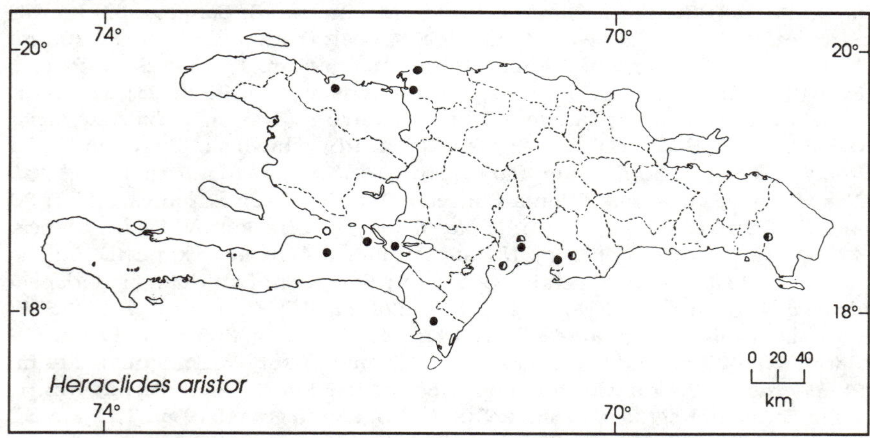

Heraclides aristor

But like so many supposedly rare species, *H. aristor* is at times locally common. Although I have sight records of single individuals and isolated specimens (as those noted for Haiti above), we have on 2 occasions stumbled on localities where *H. aristor* is abundant and at a third locality collected only 1 but saw 2 others.

Schwartz (1983a:57) reported the taking of 1 specimen by S. C. Rhodes in a mesic *caféière* at Carrefour la Mort on 6.viii at 1000 h. The butterfly was at the margin of the *caféière* (within 10 m of the main road between Cap-Haïtien and Limonade) and flying leisurely along a grassy road in the well-shaded *caféière*. A second specimen was taken at Boutilliers Road, on an open mountainside on 10.viii, again by Rhodes. At the same time another large (female?) and a smaller (male?) individual were seen flying in the same general area. On 30.iv, Gali and I saw 3 individuals (of which Gali collected 1) at Fond Parisien. The habitat was *Acacia* forest with an herbaceous understory along with cacti and many flowers, including *Lantana ovatifolia* and *Bauhinia divaricata*. The times were between 1015 and 1530 h, temperatures 30–34°C; the weather was generally bright and sunny to overcast, with a brief but heavy downpour between 1230–1300 h.

In the República Dominicana I saw at close range (1 m) a *H. aristor* at Cruce de Ocoa as it fed briefly on a roadside patch of prostrate *Antigonon leptopus* with many other butterflies (primarily *J. g. zonalis*, *E. h. hegesia*, and *D. g. cleothera*). The habitat was *Acacia*—arborescent cactus forest; the day was bright and sunny between 1140 and 1230 h. Gineika reported seeing an *H. aristor* at La Romana on 29.vi in xeric forest; the time was between 1030 and 1140 h, temperature 37°C. These reports encompass all our individual sightings and captures between 1977 and 1982—a total of 9 butterflies, of which 3 were collected. Again, the conclusion that *H. aristor* is rare is inescapable.

The first of 2 localities where *H. aristor* is abundant is Copey. The area (in viii.1982) was xeric *Acacia* forest and scrub, with some abandoned homesteads and many flowers (*Lantana ovatifolia* and 2 species of *Cordia*) both in abandoned fields and along paths and roads. *Heraclides aristor* was abundant there, feeding avidly on the 3 above flowers, fluttering in the customary manner of most papilionids, on 11.viii between 1130 and 1430 h, temperature 38°C. On 12.viii, Gali and I revisited the same site at 1530 h and took 1 *H. aristor;* no others were seen. On 14.viii, a third visit (0940–1430 h, temperature 34°C) yielded more *H. aristor*. The first individual on 14.viii was seen at 0950 h; Gali saw about 7 and I saw 12 more than were collected on that date. The butterflies are not easily alarmed while feeding, and even while patrolling, the flight is leisurely. But once alarmed, like most papilionids, *H. aristor* dodges and flies rapidly away from the collector. Return visits to this precise site on 31.vii.1983 by Amador, Raburn, and me not only yielded no *H. aristor*, but very little else was even seen. The area was extremely dry and there were no flowers. *Anaea troglodyta* and *Ph. s. sennae* were present, along with a few *Eurema*. Raburn and I visited the site once again on 23.viii.1983; the area was then very hot and dry, and there were no flowers. The only papilionids seen were 2 *H. a. aristodemus*. Finally, Wisor and I visited the same place on 13.iii.1984; the situation was even more desperate on that date. Only about 3 *A. troglodyta* were seen, and the area was dust-dry. By 1985, the area had been to a large extent cleared for pasture, but in 1986, 5 *H. aristor* were seen by Gonzalez and myself.

A second locality where *H. aristor* is common is Oviedo. Here, there is a xeric forested ravine to the north of the Oviedo-Pedernales road on the eastern slope of the limestone ridge that bisects the Peninsula de Barahona from north to south. The ravine lies in otherwise undistinguished *Acacia* scrub. On 28.vi.1983, Raburn and I visited this area; I collected in the ravine while Raburn collected in the scrub. *Heraclides aristor* was common in the ravine, patrolling the single path through the forest there (1030–1330 h, temperature 34°C). Many individuals (along with *H. a. aristodemus*) were seen; all those collected were badly flown or were missing wings (some specimens looked like "flying abdomens" in that they had only the barest remnants of the hw). Several more were taken on 1.vii.1983. There were some flowers present (including *Bauhinia divaricata* and *L. ovatifolia*), but these were not in the ravine but rather in the scrub, into which the *H. aristor* did not venture. Amador, Raburn, and I visited this locality on 10.viii.1983; the time was late in the day (1545–1630 h, temperature 33°C) and "cool" for this desert region. We saw 2 *H. aristor* and 1 *H. a. aristodemus* (in the ravine) but secured none. Raburn and I returned to the locality again on 5.viii.1983, and the area was drier than usual with little butterfly action. The only papilionid seen was 1 *H. a. aristodemus*.

The above anecdotes show, first of all, the very chancy nature of butterfly collecting in lowland xeric areas in the tropics. Although both Copey and Oviedo are in arid regions, in both cases prior to our first encounters with *H. aristor* there, there must have been sufficient rainfall to spur flower development and the eclosion of large numbers of *H. aristor*. Without this stimulus, the emergence of the butterflies would have been futile—there simply are not large enough numbers of xerophytic angiosperms of large enough size to accommodate a large population of *H. aristor*. Anyone visiting

Copey in 1983–84 would find it very difficult to believe that this site in 1982 was teeming not only with *H. aristor* but also with a broad variety of other butterflies. The last visits to Oviedo in viii.1983 likewise would make a newcomer incredulous that *H. aristor*, along with *E. zonarius* and other species, were abundant there earlier that year (see account of the latter species).

It seems likely that there are local aggregations of *H. aristor* in particularly suitable localities, all in the arid lowlands, and that the butterflies mate and deposit eggs at these sites, finally pupating there. There must be a long diapause, depending upon the external conditions (primarily moisture), and the butterflies emerge under the proper conditions. Delays between these "broods" may be more than 1 year, as has been suggested for *H. a. ponceanus* on the Florida Keys. The bedraggled specimens from Oviedo in June were doubtless remnants of a much earlier "brood," perhaps even from 1982. As the summer-fall period of 1983 progressed, numbers of *H. aristor* became less and less and finally "disappeared" completely. I suspect that isolated individuals (Carrefour la Mort, Cruce de Ocoa, etc.) are literally that—butterflies that are wandering from their places of emergence, perhaps in search of another area where a "colony" may eventually become established, or merely in search of flowers upon which to feed when population pressures or conditions at the place of emergence become too stringent to support a large number of individuals. It is perhaps noteworthy that of the *H. aristor* localities, all but 3 (Carrefour la Mort, Peralta, Boutilliers Road) are xeric; the latter locality is also the high elevation record for the species. But Boutilliers Road is such an "abnormal" locality that one cannot place too much emphasis on the occurrence of a xerophile in that rather mesic upland site. Carrefour la Mort is mesic pseudoforest; but only a very few kilometers to the east lies the arid eastern portion of the Plaine du Nord. *Heraclides aristor* has not been taken there, but, since this arid lowland plain is contiguous with the western Valle de Cibao where Copey lies, there is little doubt that *H. aristor* occurs in northeastern Haiti in some sheltered and as yet unknown sites. Peralta lies in a xeric-mesic transitional zone (see account of *Burca hispaniolae*).

Most specimens and sight records (35) are from August, with 12 in June, 9 in May, 6 in July, 2 in April, and 1 in March. The elevational distribution is from sea level (Carrefour la Mort, Copey, La Furnia) to 854 m (Boutilliers Road); other than the latter elevation, the next highest elevation is 183 m (Oviedo). Times of collection were between 0930 and 1530 h, at temperatures between 32°C

(Oviedo) and 38°C (Copey, Peralta, La Furnia).

Food plants include *Latana ovatifolia*, *Cordia globosa*, and *Cordia haitiensis* (all Copey), and *Antigonon leptopus* (Cruce de Ocoa, Azua). I have also seen *H. aristor* feed very briefly once on *Ixora* sp. (Peralta).

On 14.viii, 2 male *H. aristor* were seen (individually) flying closely about young saplings (1.5 m high) of *Zanthoxylum* (Rutaceae) at Copey and landing on the leaves; the sex is certain since the individuals were collected. Since members of the Rutaceae are the larval food plants of several Hispaniolan (and other) papilionids, it may be that *Zanthoxylum* serves that purpose for *H. aristor* also. On the same day, 2 *H. aristor* were seen "cartwheeling" at about 1400 h in *Acacia* scrub; they were not taken and the sexes are unknown. These observations suggest that copulation and oviposition may have occurred in mid-August in that year at that locality. Presumably *H. aristor* is univoltine.

Riley (1975:151) suggested that there is some sexual dichromatism and dimorphism in *H. aristor*, namely, that the up pale (yellow) spots were paler in females than in males and that the pale discal band upfw spots in M1-M2 and M2-M3 were smaller in females than in males. The long series at hand shows that both these suppositions (based upon 1 male and 1 female) are not true; in both sexes the upfw pale color is the same shade (and in fact shows very little variation) and, although there is variation in the size of the 2 pale spots in the upfw discal band, these spots vary in the same manner and degree in both sexes.

Specimens: Haiti: Nord: Carrefour la Mort, s.l., 1; *l'Ouest:* 2 km SE Fond Parisien, s.l., 1; Boutilliers Road, 854 m, 1; *República Dominicana: Monte Cristi:* 1 km SE Monte Cristi, 4; 6 km W Copey, s.l., 32; *Azua:* El Numero, 3 (MNHNSD); 2.5 km W, 6.6 km N Azua, 183 m, 1; *Independencia:* La Furnia, 1; *Pedernales:* 17 km NW Oviedo, 183 m, 12.

Sight records: República Dominicana: Monte Cristi: 6 km W Copey, s.l.—5 seen, 16.v; *La Altagracia:* 16 km NE La Romana, 61 m,—1 seen, 29.vi; *Azua:* 15 km NW Cruce de Ocoa, 76 m—1 seen, 22.vii; 5 km S Peralta, 305 m—1 seen, 28.iv; *Barahona:* west slope, Sierra Martín García, below 305 m—2 seen, 9.viii.

8. *Priamides pelaus imerius* Godart, 1824

TL "Ind. Or." = Haiti.

FW males 47–52 mm, females 48–51 mm; dwarf female 44 mm.

Priamides pelaus Fabricius occurs on all the Greater Antilles: *P. p. pelaus* on Jamaica, *P. p. atkinsi* on Cuba, and *P. p. imerius* on Hispaniola and Puerto Rico. Riley (1975:151–52) attempted to differentiate *P. p. imerius* from the 2 other subspecies; the subspecies are diagnosed on the basis of 2 characters: (1) the width of the upfw band, and (2) the *number* of uphw submarginal red spots, along with their general *size* (large or small). Bates (1935a:113) stated that *pelaus* and *imerius* resemble each other in the reduced number of uphw red spots, and that *pelaus* and *atkinsi* resemble each other in the width of the upfw diagonal pale band. Comstock (1944:538), studying Puerto Rican specimens, considered them *P. p. imerius* and stated that Puerto Rican *P. p. imerius* had the upfw band about 2 mm wide in males, twice as wide in females. Examination of 5 Puerto Rican specimens and comparisons of them with my series from Hispaniola show that the width of the upfw pale band is *rarely* only 2 mm wide in both sexes and is never so wide as 4 mm in females. Part of the problem is that previous authors have not specified just where they have measured the width of the band. My measurements were taken at the (usually) widest part of the band, in M1-M2. Measurements for 3 Hispaniolan males are always 3 mm, whereas in 11 Hispaniolan females, the band width is 2–3 mm ($\bar{x}$ = 2.7 mm). The number of uphw red spots (*not* including the red-centered white crescent in Cu1-Cu2) is 2 in 2 males and varies between 2 and 4 ($\bar{x}$ = 3.0) in 10 females. In Jamaican *P. p. pelaus* the most anterior of the uphw red spots is usually yellow (Bates, 1935a). Brown and Heineman (1972:pl. 8, fig. 6), however, showed a male *P. p. pelaus* with only 3 uphw red spots, with the most anterior not yellow. The width of the upfw band in their illustration is relatively greater than that of Hispaniolan male *P. p. imerius*. The problem (if there is one) cannot now be resolved. Perhaps some of the confusion results from 2 facts: Bates's naming *P. p. atkinsi* on the basis of only 1 specimen, and Comstock's measurement of the width of the upfw band in Puerto Rican *P. p. imerius*. At this point, there is no agreement between descriptions and specimens. I suspect that the 3 populations are separable, but not on the basis of the limited information now given. The female from La Hermita is a dwarf.

Priamides p. imerius is the least commonly encountered of the Hispaniolan papilionids. Typically, these butterflies inhabit forested situations, *caféières*, and *cafetales;* 1 was taken in a hotel garden (Pétionville), an unusually open situation for the species. At Constanza, *P. p. imerius* occurs with some frequency along the borders of a large grassy field; but even here, the species is not common. Most specimens have been taken by chance inasmuch as one cannot be certain, even in the appropriate habitat, of even seeing an individual. Despite 14 visits to La Romana in 1980–86, and the abundance of butterflies, I have only 1 specimen of *P. p. imerius* from there; the habitat is xeric forest. On 3 occasions we have seen or taken *P. p. imerius* in transitional forest (El Aguacate).

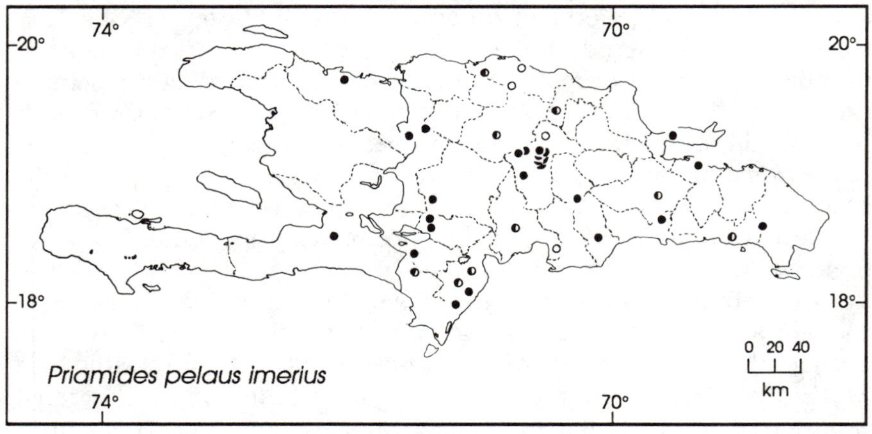

Most *P. p. imerius* records and specimens are from July (39), with 10 from March, 36 from June, 11 from August, 3 from April, and 1 each from December and from January. These data suggest that the species is univoltine, with the time of maximum abundance in June-July. Most specimens are slightly to well flown; the tails are especially fragile.

The elevational distribution is between sea level (Carrefour la Mort) and 1220 m (El Veinte), with about even distribution between these 2 extremes. *Priamides p. imerius* is absent from the forests to the southeast of Constanza, despite occurrence in the Valle de Constanza itself. Times of collection or observation were between 0900 and 1830 h, the latter as the sun was setting (Constanza). Temperatures were between 24°C (El Aguacate) and 37°C (Cambita Garabitos, Sabana de la Mar). We have seen *P. p. imerius* feeding only 5 times, on *Tournefortia hirsutissima* (Peralta), on *Lantana ovatifolia* (Guerra, Río Bao, Paso Bajito), and *Ageratum conyzoides* (El Aguacate).

Specimens: Haiti: Nord: Carrefour la Mort, s.l., 1; *l'Ouest:* Pétionville, 458 m, 1; *República Dominicana: Dajabón:* Los Cerezos, 12 km NW Río Limpio, 580 m, 3; Cañada Tirolís, just S Villa Anacaona, 458 m, 1; *La Vega:* 1 km W Manabao, 793 m, 3; Jarabacoa, 530 m, 42; 1.7 km S Jarabacoa, 488 m, 2; 2 km S Jarabacoa, 488 m, 1; 5 km SE Jarabacoa, 595 m, 9; La Ciénaga, 915 m, 1; 3.5 km E Paso Bajito, 732 m, 2; 1 km S Constanza, 1098 m, 3; *Samaná:* 6.9 km NE Sánchez, 336 m, 1; *Hato Mayor:* 7 km E Sabana de la Mar, 1; *La Altagracia:* 16 km NE La Romana, 61 m, 1; *Monseñor Nouel:* 14 km SW Piedra Blanca, 427 m, 1; *Dist. Nac.:* 9 km NE Guerra, 3; *San Cristóbal:* 6 km NW Cambita Garabitos, 488 m, 1; *San Juan:* La Hermita, El Cercado, 1

(MHNHSD); *Baoruco:* 9 km N Neiba, 2; 1 km NW El Veinte, 1220 m, 1; *Independencia:* 4–7 km NE El Aguacate, 519–824 m, 2; *Barahona:* 8 km NW Paraíso, 153 m, 3; 9 km NW Enriquillo, 671 m, 1.

Sight records: República Dominicana: Dajabón: Cañada Tirolís, just S Villa Anacaona, 458 m—1 seen, 3.vii; *Puerto Plata:* 11 km N Cruce de Guayacanes, 275 m—1 seen, 18.vii; 20 km SW Jamao al Norte, 1007 m—1 seen, 21.vi; *Santiago:* Río Bao, 8 km SE Montones Abajo, 488 m—1 seen, 23.v; *La Vega:* La Palma, 19 km W Jayaco, 1007 m—4 seen, 17.vii; *Samaná:* 6.9 km NE Sánchez, 336 m—1 seen, 20.iii; *Hato Mayor:* 7 km E Sabana de la Mar—4 seen, 6.iii; 1 seen, 16.iv; *La Romana:* Río Cumayasa, 13.5 km W La Romana—1 seen, 25.vi; *Monte Plata:* 8 km NE Bayaguana—1 seen, 7.iii; *Azua:* 5 km S Peralta, 305 m—1 seen, 21.iv; *Independencia:* 4–7 km NE El Aguacate, 763 m—1 seen, 2.vi; *Barahona:* Polo, 702 m— 1 seen, 21.vii; 1.8 km W Monteada Nueva, 1007 m— 1 seen, 13.viii; 1 seen, 15.viii; *Pedernales:* Las Abejas, 12 km NW Aceitillar, 1129 m—1 seen, 27.vii.

Family Pieridae Duponchel, 1832

Subfamily Pierinae Duponchel, 1832

1. *Ganyra josephina josephina* Godart, 1819

TL "Hispaniola" = probably Port-au-Prince, Dépt. de l'Ouest, Haiti (Miller and Brown, 1981:73).

FW males 35–43 mm, females 34–44 mm.

Ganyra josephina Godart is represented by 3 Antillean subspecies: *paramaryllis* Comstock on Jamaica, *krugi* Dewitz on Puerto Rico, and the nominate subspecies on Hispaniola. At least *G. j. krugi* is uncommon, occurring only in southwestern Puerto Rico (Comstock, 1944:532). *Ganyra j. paramaryllis* is widely distributed on Jamaica; Riley (1975:116) incorrectly assigned that subspecies only to the Blue Mountains between 500 and 800 ft. Brown and Heineman (1972:266) listed localities from throughout much of the island and from sea level (Portland Ridge lighthouse) to 7000 ft. (Blue Mountain Peak).

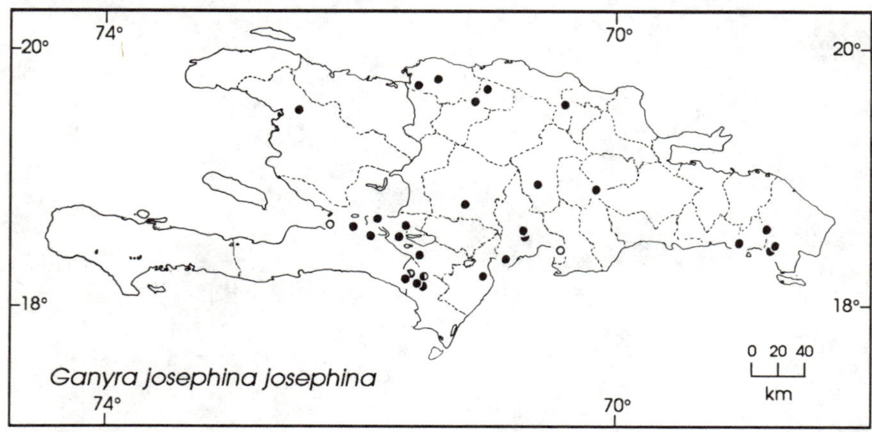

Ganyra josephina josephina

On Hispaniola, Hall (1925:163) considered *G. j. josephina* "rather scarce" and reported 1 seen near Port-au-Prince, Haiti. Marión Heredia (1980d) reported the species from El Número-Azua. Schwartz (1983a:42) listed 8 specimens from only 2 Haitian localities and considered the species "uncommon."

Although *G. j. josephina* is apparently rare in Haiti, it is locally common in the República Dominicana and is almost always encountered in xeric forests or woods, where its lazy flight among trees and saplings, rarely high above the ground, is characteristic. Outside of xeric forests, *G. j. josephina* is most often encountered in open arid areas (Les Poteaux, Croix des Bouquets, Fond Parisien, Azua) and oases (Villa Vásquez). The elevational distribution is from sea level (Croix des Bouquets, Fond Parisien, Copey, Playa Bayahibe, Las Lajas, La Furnia) to 1496 m (Constanza). The latter elevation is completely unexpected and higher than high elevations elsewhere (1251 m, Aceitillar, Sierra de Baoruco; 625 m, Vallejuelo, Sierra de Neiba), elevations that are themselves unusual. At Constanza, the single *G. j. josephina* was taken feeding on a large (3-m-tall) roadside *Lantana ovatifolia* with a *Battus zetides*—an altogether unusual juxtaposition of species. The area was cutover pine forest and cultivation, and in no obvious way similar to xeric lowland habitats. The Aceitillar record is from open pine forest. The Vallejuelo records are from the high but arid intermontane valley between the 2 ranges of the Sierra de Neiba, presenting an ecology that is commensurate with our experiences with *G. j. josephina* elsewhere. On the Sierra Martín García, *G. j. josephina* occurs to 458 m. But it is much more appropriate to consider *G. j. josephina* a butterfly of low to moderate elevations (about 214 m). We have taken *G. j. josephina* only once in a mesic area (Jamao al Norte) in a *cafetal*.

Most specimens and sightings are from July (61), with 46 in August and 27 in June; there is 1 specimen each from March and April, 2 each from May and October, 4 from February, and 6 from December. *Ganyra j. josephina* is univoltine, with major eclosion during midsummer.

Times of collection were between 0915 and 1700 h at temperatures between 21°C (Constanza) and 42°C (La Romana).

Ganyra j. josephina feeds on the flowers of *Bauhinia divaricata* (Les Poteaux), *Antigonon leptopus* (Villa Vásquez—2 occasions, Cruce de Guayacanes), *Lantana ovatifolia* (Constanza, Vallejuelo, Las Mercedes), *Cordia* sp. (La Furnia), *Plumbago scandens* (Plumbaginaceae) at Playa Bayahibe, *Ixora* sp. (Peralta, 26 km NE Cabo Rojo), *Croton barahonensis* (Vallejuelo), *Ageratum conyzoides* (26 km NE Cabo Rojo, El Aguacate, La Descubierta, Vallejuelo, La Romana), and an unidentified white-flowered tree (2.5 km SE Playa Bayahibe).

Another observation is extremely unusual. On 29.vi.1980, I saw on 2 occasions at La Romana *G. j. josephina* land on the white flowers of the epiphytic orchid *Oncidium variegatum* Swartz. Since the flowers of this orchid species lack nectar, as do all members of the genus, the reason for this attraction must not be food but is perhaps a reaction to the white flower's color (although the flowers are much smaller than these large butterflies). In contrast to all other Hispaniolan pierids, *G. j. josephina* flutters its wings in the fashion of most papilionids, rather than appressing the wings above the back like other pierids, while feeding. Thus, in the cases of the orchid visitations, wing motion could not be used as a clue for the purpose of the visit. The incidents are outstanding, since this behavior was observed only on this particular day (despite 14 visits to the locality), and it is also the only occasion we have seen a rhopaloceran show any interest in any orchid flowers. At Villa Vásquez, several *G. j. josephina* had the abdomens and unhw covered with the pollen of *Poinciana regia* (Fabaceae), but we did not observe the butterflies feeding on the flowers of this tree.

A copulating pair was taken on 25.vi (Playa Bayahibe, s.l., 1030–1220 h, 35°C). On 12.viii, at 1 km N Playa Bayahibe, Gonzalez and I observed a female *G. j. josephina* perform rejection behavior to an attendant male. The female, on a bush about 1 m above the ground, deeply depressed her wings and raised her abdomen vertically at a right angle, while the male attempted repeated copulations with her thorax and, when she lowered her abdomen somewhat, with the most anterior portion thereof. The female finally left her perch, after this behavior had been observed by us for about 4 minutes.

Specimens: Haiti: l'Artibonite: 4.6 km E Les Poteaux, 183 m, 6; *l'Ouest:* 13.1 km E Croix des Bouquets, s.l., 1; 2 km SE Fond Parisien, s.l., 1; *República Dominicana: Monte Cristi:* 6 km W Copey, s.l., 3; 4 km NW Villa Vásquez, 61 m, 10; *Valverde:* Río Guarabo, 3 km W Los Quemados, 122 m, 1; 4 km N Cruce de Guayacanes, 198 m, 1; *Espaillat:* 14 km SW Jamao al Norte, 534 m, 1; *La Vega:* 8 km SE Constanza, 1496 m, 1; *La Altagracia:* 1 km N Playa Bayahibe, 41; 2.5 km SE Playa Bayahibe, 5; 16 km NE La Romana, 621 m, 23; *La Romana:* Río Cumayasa, 13.5 km W La Romana, 31 m, 9; *Monseñor Nouel:* 6 km SE Maimón, 122 m, 1; *Azua:* 25 km NE Azua, 92 m, 1; 5 km S Peralta, 305 m, 1; 2.5 km W, 6.6 km N Azua, 183 m, 1; *San Juan:* 9 km E Vallejuelo, 610 m, 12; *Independencia:* Las Lajas, s.l., 1; La Furnia, s.l., 4; 1 km S La Descubierta, 1; 4–7 km NE El Aguacate, 519–824 m, 12; *Barahona:* west slope, Sierra Martín García, 305–458 m, 1; 3 km SW Barahona, 1; *Pedernales:* 1 km SW Las Mercedes, 397 m, 1; El Mulito, 21 km N Pedernales, 214 m, 1; Cabo Rojo, s.l., 1; 26 km NE Cabo Rojo, 732 m, 2.

Sight records: República Dominicana; Pedernales: Mencía, 397 m—1 seen, 2.vii; 2 km SW Aceitillar, 1251 m—1 seen, 1.viii.

2. *Ascia monuste eubotea* Latreille, 1819

TL unstated; restricted to the Antilles (Comstock, 1943:3).

FW males 28–32 mm, females 26–32 mm; dwarf male 20 mm.

Ascia monuste Linnaeus is widely distributed throughout the West Indies. The nominate subspecies occurs in the extreme southern Lesser Antilles as far north as the Grenadines and Barbados; the islands between the Virgin Islands and St. Vincent are occupied by *A. m. virginia* Godart, and the Bahamas, Cayman Islands, and the Greater Antilles have *A. m. eubotea*. The North American subspecies, *A. m. phileta* Fabricius, is presumed to migrate into the islands (Riley, 1975:116).

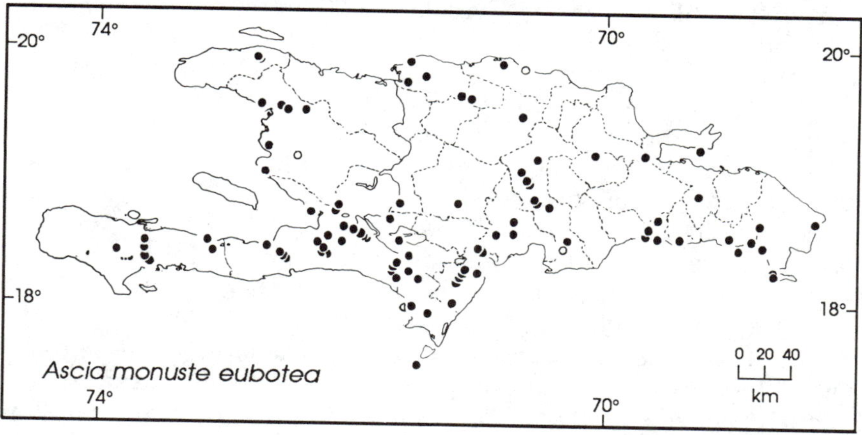

Ascia monuste eubotea

Schwartz (1983a:42–43) examined 9 females that were dull gray or translucent from wear; he was uncertain whether these might be *A. m. phileta* on Hispaniola. Comparison of these, as well as other dusky females from Hispaniola, with dark phase *A. m. phileta* shows that the 2 samples are distinct. In *A. m. phileta*, the unhw dark gray striate markings are virtually invisible, since they blend with the gray ground color. In dark female *A. m. eubotea*, even in the darkest specimens, the unhw dark gray striae are clearly visible against the gray ground color. In addition, there is a strong tendency in female *A. m. eubotea* to have the dark discocellular spot in the upfw tied by a dark, rather broad line to the dark upfw costal edge, forming a generally comma-shaped mark; this is not the case in gray female *A. m. phileta*, and the dark discocellular spot is discrete and distinct from the dark costal margin. Accordingly, I do not regard any of these specimens as *A. m. phileta*.

There is, however, a nongray female from Isla Saona, taken 19.i.1982, that merits attention. The fw length is 28 mm. The distal halves of both hw are missing, and the specimen is somewhat torn. On the upfw, the entire dark border is reduced to a series of gray wedges at the ends of the veins. The unhw is pale yellow and nonstriate. There is a very small discocellular spot in the upfw. The specimen is very like *A. m. virginia*. The other Saona specimen is a male, typical *A. m. eubotea*. Comstock (1944:531) commented on these 2 subspecies on the Greater Antilles. On Puerto Rico, *eubotea* is predominant; on Jamaica, there were a few female *virginia*, and among 85 specimens of *eubotea* from Hispaniola, there are no *virginia* nor any suggestive intergrades. Both Cucurullo (1959) and Marión Heredia (1974) listed *A. m. eubotea* and *A. m. monuste* from Hispaniola, but not *A. m. virginia*. I regard this individual as an extremely aberrant *A. m. eubotea* primarily because of the presence of the upfw discocellular spot, which is always absent in both sexes of *A. m. virginia*.

Ascia m. eubotea has a broad distribution on Hispaniola and also occurs on the satellite islands of Beata, Alto Velo, Catalina, Saona, and Île à Cabrit. It is primarily a butterfly of open areas—grassy fields and roadsides—but has also been taken in *caféières* (Port-de-Paix), mesic hardwood forest (Puesto Pirámide 204), pine forest (Obléon), xeric woods and forests (Playa Bayahibe, Boca Chica), *Acacia* scrub and woods (Colmini, Fond Parisien, Oviedo), oases (Croix des Bouquets, Ça Soleil, Villa Vásquez), gardens (Pétionville, Délugé), pine forest (Aceitillar), and mangrove borders (Miragoâne, Cabo Rojo). Most habitats, however, are xeric rather than mesic, although mesic habitats are not completely shunned.

The elevational distribution is from sea level (Cormier Plage, Colmini, Délugé, Croix des Bouquets, Samaná, Punta Cana, Boca Chica, and many others) to 2227 m (37 km SE Constanza) in the Cordillera Central. The species reaches 1891 m in the Sierra de Neiba (Puesto Pirámide 204), 1647 m in the Massif de la Selle's front ranges (3.7 km S Kenscoff), and 1373 m in the Sierra de Baoruco (Aceitillar). Most specimens are from July (87), with 40 in June, 28 in November, and 13 in May. August, January, March, April, September, October, and December are represented by 1–10 specimens. Although these data suggest a bivoltine life cycle, the large number of specimens from November is from Isla Alto Velo, where *A. m. eubotea* was 1 of only 3 species of butterflies encountered by Incháustegui. *Ascia m. eubotea* is uncommon during the fall-winter-spring throughout the Hispaniolan mainland; it seems likely that the situation on Isla Alto Velo is somehow special and that *A. m. eubotea* is univoltine, although there are individuals on the wing during the entire year.

Times of collection were between 0900 and 1700 h, at temperatures of 18°C (La Nevera) to 38°C (Río Cumayasa, Cruce de Ocoa, Vallejuelo). A copulating pair was taken on 20.vii (Délugé, s.l.) behind the beach in a *Cocos* grove.

We have once taken *A. m. eubotea* feeding on the small white flowers of *Heliotropium curassavicum* (Boca Chica), and these butterflies were feeding avidly on the flowers of *Conocarpus erecta* (Combretaceae) at Cabo Rojo. Other plants used as nectar sources include *Lantana ovatifolia* (Mao), *L. reticulata* (Copey), *Ageratum conyzoides* (Vallejuelo), *Jacaranda acutifolia* and *Antigonon leptopus* (Santiago), *Palicourerea barbinevia* (Las Abejas), and *Tournefortia hirsutissima* (Neiba). Drinking aggregations have been at a mud puddle (Carrefour Joffre), on the muddy banks of a canal (Cruce de Ocoa), and around mud in a road (2 km SW Barahona).

Specimens: Haiti: Nord-Ouest: 1.3 km S Balladé, 31 m, 1; 7.5 km SE Port-de-Paix, 1; *Nord:* Cormier Plage, s.l., 2; *l'Artibonite:* 1.6 km E Carrefour Marmelade, 854 m, 4; 2.7 km W Carrefour Joffre, 11; 16 km E Gonaïves, 1; 12.2 km W Ça Soleil, s.l., 1; Colmini, 5.4 km W Terre Noire, s.l., 4; Délugé, s.l., 4; *l'Ouest:* 5.6 km S Terre Rouge, 366 m, 1; 3.8 km N Terre Rouge, 519 m, 1; 13 km E Croix des Bouquets, s.l., 1; 18.1 km SE Croix des Bouquets, s.l., 1; 2 km NW Fond Parisien, s.l., 1; 3.0 km SE Fond Parisien, s.l., 1; 2 km SE Fond Parisien, s.l., 1; 4 km SE Fond Parisien, 1; Pétionville, 458 m, 2; Boutilliers Road, 732–854 m, 6; 5.8 km S Kenscoff, 1586 m, 1; 3.7 km S Kenscoff, 1647 m, 8; 0.3 km N Obléon, 1617 m, 1; 0.8 km S Découzé, 702 m, 2; 5.4 km S Découzé, 397 m, 5; 6.6 km S Découzé, 397 m, 1; 1.3 km N Béloc, 702 m, 1; just W Grand-Goâve, s.l., 1; *Sud:* 8 km SW Paillant, 824 m, 2; 10.7 km W Miragoâne, s.l., 1; 6.2 km N Cavaillon, 61 m, 1; 7.8 km N Cavaillon, 31 m, 4; 19.7 km N Cavaillon, 580 m, 1; 25.6 km N Cavaillon, 610 m, 1; 4.5 km E Cavaillon, 31 m, 2; 4.8 km N Camp Perrin, 244 m, 1; *Île à Cabrit:* 3; *República Dominicana: Monte Cristi:* 6 km W Copey, s.l., 4; 1 km SE Monte Cristi, 1; 4 km NW Villa Vásquez, 61 m, 2; *Elías Piña:* 1 km SW Puesto Pirámide 204, 1891 m, 1; *Valverde:* 12 km SW Mao, 244 m, 2; *Santiago Rodríguez:* 3 km W Los Quemados, 183 m, 2; *Puerto Plata:* 10 km W Luperón, 1; *Santiago:* 7 km SW Santiago, 214 m, 6; *La Vega:* La Palma, 19 km W Jayaco, 1007 m, 1; Jarabacoa, 530 m, 6; 1 km S Constanza, 1098 m, 5; 13 km SE Constanza, 1403 m, 1; 18 km SE Constanza, 2288 m, 1; Valle Nuevo, 25 km SE Constanza, 2105 m, 2; La Nevera, 37 km SE Constanza, 2227 m, 1; *María T. Sánchez:* 1 km S Cruce de Rincón, s.l., 1; *Samaná: cayo* in Samaná harbor, s.l., 1; *La Altagracia:* Punta Cana, 1; 1 km N Playa Bayahibe, s.l., 2; 16 km NE La Romana, 61 m, 2; *La Romana:* Río Chavón, 8 km SE La Romana, s.l., 1; Río Cumayasa, 13.5 km W La Romana, 4; *San Pedro de Macorís:* 13 km SE Boca Chica, s.l., 1; *Hato Mayor:* 4 km S Hato Mayor, 1; *Dist. Nac.:* 9 km NE Guerra, 1; Punta Caucedo, 2 km W, 2 km S Andrés, s.l., 2; 5 km S San Isidro, 1; Tres Ojos, s.l., 1; *Sánchez Ramírez;* La Piedra, 7 km SW Pimentel, 1; *Peravia:* 22 km NW

Cruce de Ocoa, 61 m, 2; 2.7 km W La Horma, 3; *Azua:* 25 km NE Azua, 92 m, 2; 5 km S Peralta, 305 m, 1; Tábara Abajo, 1; *San Juan:* 9 km E Vallejuelo, 610 m, 5; *Independencia:* 21 km N Los Pinos, 1708 m, 1; 4 km E El Limón, s.l., 1; 4–7 km NE El Aguacate, 519–824 m, 1; *Barahona:* 8 km ESE Canoa, 1; 11.5 km ESE Canoa, s.l., 1; Polo, 702 m, 1; 3 km NNE Polo, 854 m, 1; 8 km NNE Polo, 793 m, 1; 12 km NNE Polo, 534 m, 1; 2 km SW Barahona, 122 m, 1; 9 km NW Enriquillo, 671 m, 1; *Pedernales:* 2 km N Cabo Rojo, s.l., 1; Las Abejas, 12 km NW Aceitillar, 1129 m, 1; 4.5 km NW Aceitillar, 1373 m, 3; 5 km NE Los Arroyos, 1617 m, 2; 0.6 km SE Los Arroyos, 1098 m, 1; 1 km N Cabeza de Agua, 275 m, 1; 1 km SE Banano, 183 m, 1; 17 km NW Oviedo, 183 m, 2; *Isla Beata,* 3; *Isla Alto Velo:* 28 (18 MNHNSD); *Isla Catalina:* nr. naval base, 3; *Isla Saona:* Mano Juan, s.l., 1; 2 km W Mano Juan, s.l., 1.

Sight record: República Dominicana: Pedernales: Cabo Rojo, s.l.—many seen, 2.viii.

3. *Appias drusilla boydi* Comstock, 1943

TL Barahona, Prov. de Barahona, República Dominicana.

FW males 25–34 mm, females 24–32 mm.

Appias drusilla Cramer is represented by 5 subspecies in the West Indies: *poeyi* Butler on Cuba (including the Isla de la Juventud) and the Cayman Islands; *castalia* Fabricius on Jamaica; *comstocki* Dillon from Saba to St. Lucia; *monomorpha* Hall on Grenada; and *boydi* on Hispaniola, Puerto Rico, and the Virgin Islands. Differentiation of the subspecies involves primarily the dark pigmentation of the female wet season forms; this is especially true in the case of *A. d. poeyi* and *A. d. boydi.* In the latter subspecies, wet season females have the fw cell entirely gray to black, whereas in *A. d. poeyi* only three-quarters of the fw cell is black (males are indistinguishable). Additionally, in these 2 subspecies at least, female "white" forms can be told from males by the presence of a yellow to orange wash at the base of the unfw.

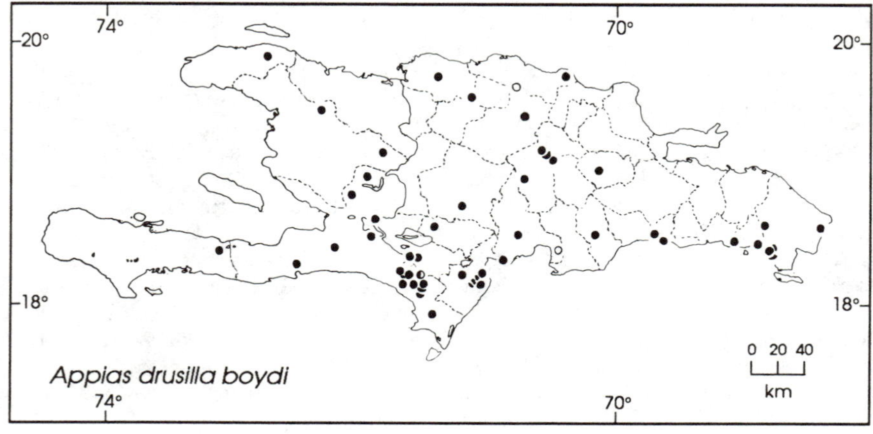

Of my material, 45 females are dark and represent the wet season form. Dates for these specimens are between 23.vi and 20.viii, with 1 from 28.iii, 1 from 20.xii, and 3 from 2–3.i. Most wet season females are from July (19), with June and August represented by 10 and 11 respectively. The March and December females were 1 of many white individuals. Most wet season females agree with the diagnosis of the subspecies (cell wholly black to very dark gray) and have a broad blackish to gray fw border, widest at the fw apex and with a more or less broad regular "tooth" of dark scales extending basally in M3-Cu1, this dark "tooth" extending almost to meet the dark scales in the cell in a few individuals. The uphw is pale yellow, with a scalloped grayish margin, at times complete and at others reduced to dark smudges at the marginal ends of the hw veins. The basal portion of the fw is black or dark gray, slightly paler than the fw cell, and often connected to the dark fw margin by a fine "line" along the inner margin. The un is white, with, on the unfw, a yellow to orange wash basally and black to dark gray submarginal blotches in M3-Cu1 and Cu1-Cu2. The fw cell is more or less outlined by dark gray along its anterior and posterior veins, the dark scales at times filling into the cell but never so extensively as on the upfw.

There are some variants that are modifications of the above wet season pattern. A worn female (2.i) has only a pale gray edge to the upfw cell, and the gray outer margin and apical areas are much reduced. Another female (21.vi), also somewhat flown, has the cell dark gray, and the dark gray fw outer margin is less bold than usual. A very worn female (3.i) is almost unidentifiable since most of the scales are missing except for a dark gray ring within the cell on both fw. The most peculiar females are fresh (25.vii, and 13.viii—2 specimens) and from the Sierra Martín García. In these specimens, the cell is dark gray only along its anterior edge, and there is a black discocellular spot connected to the dark anterior cell margin. This black spot is vividly distinct on the unfw, set in a deep yellow area; there are no other unfw markings. Some of the above "variants" are undoubtedly due to wear, but others (notably the last discussed) are peculiar wet season females.

Bates (1935a:119) examined 24 *A. d. poeyi* from west-central and eastern Cuba. Brown and Heineman (1972:269–70) listed specimens of *A. d. castalia* from throughout Jamaica. Comstock (1944:527) listed 6 Puerto Rican localities for *A. d. boydi* (and Isla Mona as well). Hall (1925:163) recorded taking a few specimens at

La Cumbre, República Dominicana, and "diagnosed" the subspecies well by the pigmentation of the upfw cell, comparing the Hispaniolan population with *A. d. poeyi.* Schwartz (1983a:43) reported 18 specimens from 8 Haitian localities. He regarded *A. d. boydi* as an inhabitant of wooded situations, from xeric to *Pinus* forest, and gave the elevational distribution between sea level and 1647 m (Kenscoff). However, most records are from 300 m or less.

Much additional material of *A. d. boydi* from the República Dominicana does not greatly alter the above assessments. *Appias d. boydi* is widespread geographically and is almost invariably associated with forests or woods—either xeric (Cormier Plage, Punta Cana, La Romana, Playa Bayahibe, Cabral, Oviedo) or mesic (Thomonde, Sosúa, Sierra Martín García, Cabeza de Agua). Only rarely does *A. d. boydi* venture into open areas (Kenscoff, Jacmel, Punta Caucedo, San Isidro, 2 km SW Mencía). These butterflies occur occasionally in *caféières* and *cafetales* (Paillant, Cambita Garabitos).

The elevational distribution is from sea level (Cormier Plage, Playa Bayahibe, Punta Caucedo) to 1647 m (Kenscoff); however, there are only 5 records (Jayaco, El Aguacate, Constanza, Sierra Martín García—2 elevations) at or above 915 m. *Appias d. boydi* is primarily a butterfly of low to moderate elevations, occasionally ascending higher. The species is absent from all high mountain ranges on Hispaniola; Hall's record from La Cumbre in the Cordillera Septentrional is the only record for that range, and the elevation is only about 640 m.

Most specimens are from July (67), with 38 from June and 31 from August. There are 17 from January, 11 from December, 3 from March, 2 each from February and October, and 1 each from April and May; some from January are much tattered. *Appias d. boydi* is apparently univoltine, with a summer peak of abundance.

Collection times were between 0830 and 1645 h, at temperatures between 26°C (Neiba) and 42°C (2 km SW Mencía).

We have taken *A. d. boydi* feeding once on *Hibiscus rosasinensis* (4 km N Thomonde), 3 times on *Lantana ovatifolia* (Cabral, Cabo Rojo, Las Mercedes), 4 times on *Tournefortia hirsutissima* (Sosúa [twice], 1 km N Playa Bayahibe, 5 km SE, 3 km W Barahona), on *Cordia curassavica* (Santiago), on *Morinda citrifolia* (Río Chavón), *Ageratum conyzoides* (26 km N Cabo Rojo), *Croton barahonensis* (Vallejuelo, twice), and *Ixora* sp. (26 km N Cabo Rojo, Las Abejas). Drinking clubs on mud in dirt roads after rain or at the edges of creeks or rivers have been observed 9 times (SW Thomonde, Playa Bayahibe, La Romana, Río Cumayasa, Vallejuelo, Neiba, 1 km NE El Aguacate, 2 km and 12 km SW Barahona, and Banano). *Appias d. boydi* is attracted in large numbers to fresh cow and horse manure; in such situations, the butterflies are often pressed so closely to each other that they completely cover the surface of the fecal pile, forming a shimmering white dome. While thus occupied, the butterflies are exceedingly tame.

Specimens: Haiti: Nord-Ouest: 1.3 km S Balladé, 31 m, 4; *Nord:* Cormier Plage, s.l., 4; *l'Artibonite:* Platon, 6 km E Carrefour Marmelade, 793 m, 1; 24.0 km N Thomonde, 1; *l'Ouest:* 20.3 km SW Thomonde, 1; 1.6 km N Saut d'Eau, 183 m, 1; 4 km SE Fond Parisien, s.l., 1; 3.7 km S Kenscoff, 1647 m, 1; 7.7 km N Jacmel, 92 m, 1; *Sud:* 6.7 km SW Paillant, 763 m, 2; *República Dominicana: Monte Cristi:* 4 km NW Villa Vásquez, 61 m, 1; *Valverde:* Río Guarabo, 3 km W Los Quemados, 122 m, 1; *Puerto Plata:* 9 km SE Sosúa, 16 m, 15; *Santiago:* 7 km SW Santiago, 214 m, 1; *La Vega:* 10 km W Jayaco, 915 m, 1; Jarabacoa, 530 m, 1; 3.5 km E Paso Bajito, 732 m, 1; 6 km SSE Constanza, 1403 m, 1; *La Altagracia:* Punta Cana, s.l., 1; 2 km N Playa Bayahibe, s.l., 1; 1 km N Playa Bayahibe, s.l., 15; 2.5 km SE Playa Bayahibe, s.l., 1; 16 km NE La Romana, 61 m, 11; *La Romana:* Río Chavón, 8 km SE La Romana, s.l., 3; Río Cumayasa, 13.5 km W La Romana, 19; *Sánchez Ramírez:* 1 km NE Las Lagunas, 183 m, 1; *Dist. Nac.:* Punta Caucedo, 2 km W, 2 km S Andrés, 2; 5 km S San Isidro, 7; *San Cristóbal:* 11 km NW Cambita Garabitos, 610 m, 1; *Azua:* 2.5 km W, 6.6 km N Azua, 183 m, 1; *San Juan:* 9 km E Vallejuelo, 610 m, 8; *Baoruco:* 11 km N Neiba, 519 m, 2; *Independencia:* Las Lajas, s.l., 1; 1 km NE El Aguacate, 976 m, 1; 7 km NE El Aguacate, 519 m, 2; 4–7 km NE El Aguacate, 519– 824 m, 20; *Barahona:* west slope, Sierra Martín García, 458 m, 1; west slope, Sierra Martín García, 763–915 m, 4; west slope, Sierra Martín García, 610–640 m, 2; 10 km SSW Cabral, 427 m, 1; 2 km SW Barahona, 122 m, 2; 7 km SW Barahona, 2; 11 km SW Barahona, 1; 12 km SW Barahona, 427 m, 2; 5 km SE, 3 km W Barahona, 183–397 m, 1; *Pedernales:* 18 km NNE Cabo Rojo, 305 m, 1; 23 km NE Cabo Rojo, 488 m, 1; 26 km NE Cabo Rojo, 732 m, 4; 1 km SW Las Mercedes, 397 m, 2; 2 km SW Mencía, 336 m, 1; Mencía, 397 m, 2; 1 km SE Banano, 183 m, 2; 1 km N Cabeza de Agua, 275 m, 2; 17 km NW Oviedo, 183 m, 2.

Sight record: República Dominicana: Pedernales: 12 km NW Aceitillar, 1129 m—1 seen, 26.viii.

4. *Melete salacia salacia* Godart, 1819

TL not stated; restricted to Hispaniola by Bates (1935a:120).

FW males 22–29 mm, females 23–26 mm.

Although Brown (1978:20) stated that *M. salacia* is endemic to Hispaniola, Bates (1935a:119–21) reported the species from Cuba in some abundance, and Riley (1975:119) noted the existence of 2 subspecies, 1 of which is Cuban (*M. s. cubana* Fruhstorfer). Brown's remark is surely a *lapsus*.

Hall (1925:163) stated that Kaempffer took a "short series at La Vega," where Hall also took a single individual. Schwartz (1983a: 43) reported only 1 specimen from Haiti. From these meager data, one could assume that *M. s. salacia* is distinctly uncommon. Such is not the case in the República Dominicana, at least; but the butterflies are indeed very local. There is, for example, a long series of 47 *M. s. salacia* in the MNHNSD from a single locality, taken on 9.iv.1983 by Reinoso in less than 0.5 h. Gonzalez and I collected 82 specimens in a *Roystonea hispaniolana* (Arecaceae) grove at Estero Hondo. Likewise, I have a series from El Cercado and could have secured many more there. At La Vega, a series of 19 was collected. On most occasions, however, one secures only 1 or a very few specimens at a particular locality; these may be strays from centers of abundance.

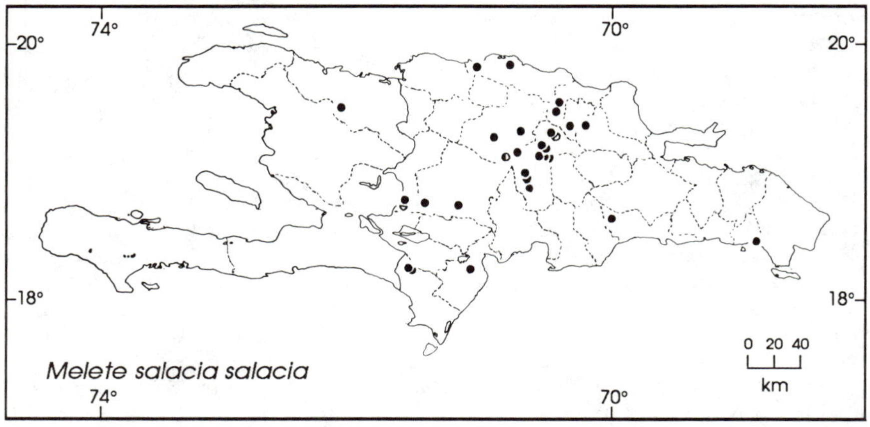

Elevational distribution is from sea level (Río Chavón) to 1891 m (Puesto Pirámide 204); however, *M. s. salacia* is much more abundant at moderate to high elevations (above 450 m) than at lower ones. In the lower elevational range, localities below 305 m are only 4: Santo Domingo, Estero Hondo, La Vega, and Tenares. In fact, the first capture of *M. s. salacia* at Santo Domingo (122 m) was so surprising that the butterflies (2 taken, 19.vi.1982) were considered elevational vagrants; however, another was taken at the same locality on 19.vi.1983, showing that *M. s. salacia* does occur there as a resident. The long series from Estero Hondo and La Vega indicate that this species may be locally very abundant in the lowlands.

The lack of Haitian material is inexplicable. Between 1977–79, only 1 individual was seen and collected. The habitat was a mesic *caféière* at 336 m. Much of northern Haiti is to human eyes the same sort of pseudoforest, and similar situations occur in the Massif de la Selle (Découzé, Béloc) without *M. s. salacia.* There are also many Dominican localities where one might expect to find *M. s.*

salacia but does not. Noteworthy is the apparent rarity of *M. s. salacia* on the south island in general (records only from Las Abejas and Monteada Nueva) and its absence from the Península de Samaná or (near sea level) along the southern mesic forested shore of the Bahía de Samaná.

Typically, *M. s. salacia* occupies mesic hardwood forests, where it usually flies too high (3 m or more) for ready capture; it may be netted with ease as it forages on flowers of trees and shrubs. Occasionally *M. s. salacia* leaves forests or flies peripherally to them (Jánico, 9 km W Jayaco). On 1 occasion we took 2 specimens in a mesic forested ravine surrounded by pine forest (11 km NW Aceitillar), the latter a habitat in which *M. s. salacia* does not occur. *Cafetales* and *cacaotales* are occupied (Tenares, La Palma). Perhaps the most unusual situation was at an upland (1647 m) fallow cabbage field (10 km SE Constanza); hundreds of butterflies (including several species of pierids) crowded the field, most (but not *M. s. salacia*) feeding on *Leonurus sibericus* (see accounts of *Anetia b. briarea* and *A. p. pantherata*, for example). *Melete s. salacia* did not fly out into the open field but rather flew only along its bushy and shrubby border.

Most specimens are from May (85), July (63), and April (47), with 19 from August and 20 from June. The lack of fall and winter specimens suggests that *M. s. salacia* has a relatively brief flight period (April-August) and then is reduced to very small populations or local individuals. Riley (1975:120) gave January-June for *M. s. cubana*, however. Times of collection were between 0900 and 1530 h, at temperatures between 23°C (Las Abejas, La Vega) and 39°C (Jánico).

Melete s. salacia has been taken feeding on a variety of flowers: *Asclepias nivea* (9 km W Jayaco, Monteada Nueva), *Palicourea barbinervia* (Jayaco, Las Abejas), *Cordia globosa* (Santo Domingo), *Lantana ovatifolia* (El Cercado, Vallejuelo, Luperón, Estero Hondo), the white-flowered horticultural variety of *L. ovatifolia* (La Vega), *Morinda citrifolia* (Río Chavón), *Tournefortia hirsutissima* (Río Bao, Paso Bajito), *Ageratum conyzoides* (Vallejuelo), *Coffea arabica* (La Palma), and *Croton barahonensis* (Vallejuelo). At La Palma, I saw a *M. s. salacia* completely enter the corolla of *Zantedeschia aethiopica*, a large white-flowered aroid, wherein the butterfly was easily captured.

A pair *in copula* was taken at Estero Hondo (1240 h, 31°C, 30.v) in a shaded palm (*Roystonea hispaniolana*) grove; the female was feeding on *Lantana ovatifolia* during the act.

Specimens: Haiti: Nord: 5.6 km SE Dondon, 336 m, 1; *República Domini-*

cana: Elías Piña: 21 km S Comendador, 1464 m, 1; *Puerto Plata:* 13 km SE Luperón, 214 m, 1; 0.6 km NE Estero Hondo, 82; *Espaillat:* 14 km SW Jamao al Norte, 534 m, 8; 20 km SW Jamao al Norte, 793 m, 1; *Duarte:* 10 km SE Tenares, 183 m, 1; *Salcedo:* Las Cuevas, 47 (MNHNSD); *Santiago:* Río Bao, 8 km SE Montones Abajo, 488 m, 2; 8 km SE Jánico, 61 m, 1; *La Vega:* 5 km NW La Vega, 122 m, 19; 9 km W Jayaco, 915 m, 1; 10 km W Jayaco, 915 m, 5; La Palma, 19 km W Jayaco, 1007 m, 11; La Ciénaga, 915 m, 1; Jarabacoa, 530 m, 9; 3.5 km E Paso Bajito, 732 m, 3; 10 km SE Constanza, 1647 m, 3; 18 km SE Constanza, 1586 m, 1; *La Romana:* Rio Chavón, 8 km SE La Romana, s.l., 1; *Dist. Nac.:* 30 km NW Santo Domingo, 122 m, 3; *San Juan:* 9 km E Vallejuelo, 610 m, 1; 4 km E El Cercado, 702 m, 12; *Barahona:* 0.6 km W Monteada Nueva, 1098 m, 1; *Pedernales:* Las Abejas, 11 km NW Aceitillar, 1220 m, 4; Las Abejas, 12 km NW Aceitillar, 1129 m, 17.

Sight records: República Dominicana: Elías Piña: 1 km SW Puesto Pirámide 204, 1891 m—several seen, 5.viii; *La Vega:* 1 km SW Los Tablones, 1159 m—1 seen, 20.vii.

Subfamily Coliadinae Swainson, 1827

5. *Eurema lisa euterpe* Ménétriés, 1832

TL Antilles; probably Hispaniola (Comstock, 1944:523).

FW males 11–18 mm, females 12–18 mm.

Eurema lisa Boisduval and Leconte is widely distributed on the continental mainland from North America to southern Central America. One subspecies, *E. l. euterpe*, is usually attributed to the entire Antillean region. However, Clench (1977b:188) and Elliott, Riley, and Clench (1980:124) used *E. l. sulphurina* Poey (TL Cuba) for the populations on Andros and San Salvador islands in the Bahama Islands.

Certainly 1 of the most common of the small pierids on Hispaniola, *E. l. euterpe* occurs in both mesic and xeric situations. At Carrefour Joffre, *E. l. euterpe* was the most abundant small butterfly in the most bleak arid region in Haiti; the butterflies were on fresh cow dung. Other xeric localities include Croix des Bouquets, Fond Parisien, Anse-à-Galets, Monte Cristi, Copey, Cruce de Guayacanes, Las Calderas, La Furnia, Cabo Rojo, Isla Catalina, and Isla Beata. But in these xeric areas, *E. l. euterpe* often occupies locally more mesic and shaded enclaves or is found most commonly where there are flowers as a nectar source. Although *E. l. euterpe* at times occurs along paths and roads through *caféières* and *cafetales* and along their margins, these butterflies form a conspicuous element of the roadside rhopaloceran fauna. Their weak flight makes them an easy mark, and they are not expert in dodging among bushes and shrubs as other species may be.

The elevational distribution is between sea level (Môle St.-Nicholas, Croix des Bouquets, Picmi, Grand-Goâve, Copey, Nagua, Samaná, Playa Bayahibe, Las Calderas, Cabo Rojo) to 1678 m (Obléon) on the front range of the Massif de la Selle. In the Cordillera Central, *E. l. euterpe* reaches 1586 m (18 km SE Constanza), and in the Sierra de Neiba it ascends to 1464 m (Comendador). However, *E. l. euterpe* is more common at low to moderate elevations (below about 915 m) than in the high uplands. These are the first reports of *E. l. euterpe* from Île de la Gonâve, Isla Catalina, and Isla Beata; the butterflies seem common on all three islands.

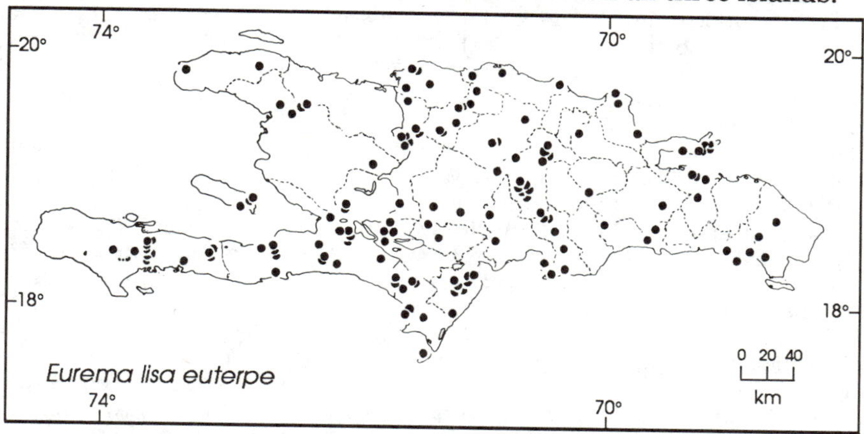

Times of collection were between 0815 and 1700 h, at temperatures between 23°C (4.8 km W Samaná) and 40°C (Tenares). *Eurema l. euterpe* flies throughout the year. Most specimens are from July (158), with 103 in June. Other months from which we have material are January (10), February (5), March (11), April (16), May (2), August (31), September (1), October (19), November (3), and December (17). There is apparently a lesser midwinter (December-January) peak, when *E. l. euterpe* is less common than in midsummer.

Eurema l. euterpe customarily drinks at mud puddles in dirt roads (Los Cerezos, Villa Anacaona, Río Cumayasa, 2 km and 12 km SW Barahona, Polo) and also from a small sandbar in a creek (Mirebalais). Plants that are used for nectar are *Antigonon leptopus* (Croix des Bouquets, Cruce de Guayacanes, La Descubierta), *Daucus* sp. (Carrefour Marmelade), *Tephrosia purpurea* (Sombrero, Cabo Rojo), *Bidens pilosa* (Los Quemados), *Melochia tomentosa* (La Canoa), *Croton barahonensis* (Vallejuelo), *Ageratum conyzoides* (Vallejuelo, twice), and *Lantana ovatifolia* (Las Mercedes). *Eurema l.*

euterpe uses fresh horse manure as a moisture source (Río Bao).

Copulating pairs of *E. l. euterpe* have been taken on 29.vi (La Romana, 1030–1145 h, 37°C) and 27.x (Nagua, 1330–1500 h, 36°C).

Specimens: Haiti: Nord-Ouest: Môle St.-Nicholas, s.l., 3; 1.3 km S Balladé, 31 m, 1; *Nord:* 1.2 km N Carrefour Marmelade, 793 m, 1; *l'Artibonite:* 1.6 km E Carrefour Marmelade, 854 m, 6; 6.4 km W Ennery, 336 m, 1; 16 km N Carrefour Joffre, 183 m, 23; *l'Ouest:* 4 km N Thomonde, 1; 20 km SE Mirebalais, 366 m, 2; 19.7 km SE Mirebalais, 6; 1.3 km S Terre Rouge, 458 m, 3; 13 km E Croix des Bouquets, s.l., 1; 18.1 km SE Croix des Bouquets, s.l., 1; Forêt des Pins, 1586 m, 2; 2 km W Fond Parisien, s.l., 2; 2 km NW Fond Parisien, s.l., 2; Boutilliers Road, 1.8–3.7 km W Kenscoff rd., 793–885 m, 4 (2 MPM); Boutilliers Road, 854–946 m, 3 (1 FSM); 0.3 km NE Obléon, 1678 m, 1; Peneau, 1.1 km S Furcy, 1464 m, 6; 8.7 km N Béloc, 534 m, 1; 1.3 km N Béloc, 702 m, 2; Lavaneau, 229 m, 2; nr. Péredo, 600 m, 1 (FSM); just W Grand-Goâve, s.l., 3; 6.7 km E Grand-Goâve, s.l., 2; *Sud:* 3 km SW Paillant, 681 m, 5; 6.6 km SW Paillant, 793 m, 3; 6.7 km SW Paillant, 763 m, 1; Vieux Bourg d'Aquin, s.l., 5; 6.2 km N Cavaillon, 61 m, 11; 7.8 km N Cavaillon, 31 m, 3; 1.4 km N Cavaillon, 366 m, 1; 16.3 km N Cavaillon, 488 m, 2; 19.7 km N Cavaillon, 580 m, 1; 25.6 km N Cavaillon, 610 m, 6; 7 km SW Cavaillon, 122 m, 1; 5.6 km N Camp Perrin, 275 m, 2; 4.8 km N Camp Perrin, 244 m, 6; 14 km NW Marceline, 671 m, 1; *Île de la Gonâve:* hills behind Anse-à-Galets, 3; Anse-à-Galets, 2; Picmi, 1; *República Dominicana: Monte Cristi:* 1 km SE Monte Cristi, 9; 4 km SE Monte Cristi, 1; 6 km W Copey, s.l., 2; 4 km NW Villa Vásquez, 61 m, 2; *Dajabón:* 0.5 km N Cañongo, 31 m, 3; Los Cerezos, 12 km NW Río Limpio, 580 m, 8; 16 km NW Río Limpio, 702 m, 1; 4 km S Restauración, 580 m, 3; 7 km N Restauración, 671 m, 1; 8.4 km S Restauración, 580 m, 1; Cañada Tirolís, just S Villa Anacaona, 458 m, 2; 3 km ESE Villa Anacaona, 458 m, 3; *Elías Piña:* 21 km S Comendador, 1464 m, 1; *Valverde:* 12 km SW Mao, 244 m, 2; 3 km W Los Quemados, 122 m, 2; 4 km N Cruce de Guayacanes, 198 m, 4; *Santiago Rodríguez:* Loma Leonor, 18 km SW Monción, 534 m, 1; Loma Leonor, 19 km SW Monción, 610 m, 2; 15 km SW Monción, 320 m, 14; 3 km W Los Quemados, 183 m, 1; *Santiago:* Río Bao, 4 km SW Mata Grande, 702 m, 3; Río Bao, 8 km SE Montones Abajo, 488 m, 2; 7 km SW Santiago, 214 m, 7; entrance of Valle de Tetero to Valle de Tetero, 1342–1922 m, 1; *Puerto Plata:* 10 km W Luperón, 1; 0.6 km NE Estero Hondo, 1; 9 km SE Sosúa, 15 m, 2; *Duarte:* l0 km SE Tenares, 183 m, 2; *La Vega:* 2 km S La Vega, 366 m, 1; Güaigüí, S La Vega, 336 m, 6; Buena Vista, 11 km NE Jarabacoa, 641 m, 7; La Palma, 19 km W Jayaco, 1007 m, 4; La Ciénaga, 915 m, 1; Jarabacoa, 530 m, 4; 3.5 km E Paso Bajito, 732 m, 2; 12 km NE Constanza, 1220 m, 1; 1 km S Constanza, 1098 m, 26; 6 km SSE Constanza, 1403 m, 5; 7 km SE Constanza, *ca.* 1312 m, 1; 7.4 km SE Constanza, 1388 m, 2; 18 km SE Constanza, 1586 m, 5; 10 km NW La Horma, 1496 m, 1; *María T. Sánchez:* 14 km SE Río San Juan, 3; 9 km NE Río San Juan, s.l., 4; 9 km SE Nagua, s.l., 3; *Samaná:* 10.2 km W Samaná, 61 m, 1; 4.5 km E Samaná, 6; 4.8 km W Samaná, 3; El Francés, 14 km E and N Samaná, s.l., 1; 18.0 km E and N Samaná, s.l., 1; 2.8 km S Las Galeras, 61 m, 2; *Hato Mayor:* 4 km E Sabana de la Mar, 1; 7 km E Sabana de la Mar, 2; 17 km E Sabana de la Mar, 2; 11 km NW Hato Mayor, 122 m, 1; *La Altagracia:* 5 km S Higüey, 2; 2.5 km SE Playa Bayahibe, s.l., 3; 16 km NE La Romana, 61 m, 11; *La Romana:* Río Chavón, 8 km SE La Romana, s.l., 1; Río Cumayasa, 13.5 km W La Romana, 31 m, 1; *Dist. Nac.:* 9 km NE Guerra, 1; 5 km S San Isidro, 1; 30 km NW Santo Domingo, 122 m, 8; *Monte Plata:* 8 km NE Bayaguana, 3; *Monseñor Nouel:* 6 km SE Maimón, 122 m, 1; *Peravia:* Las Calderas, s.l., 3; 5 km SW Sombrero, 2; 5 km N San José de Ocoa, 580 m, 5; 2.7 km W La Horma, 2; 6 km W La Horma, 1159 m, 2; *Azua:* Tábara Abajo, 1; 5 km S Peralta, 305 m, 10; 2.5 km W, 6.6 km N Azua, 183 m, 1; 1 km E Palmar de Ocoa, s.l., 1; 22 km NW Cruce de Ocoa, 61 m, 1; 2 km S La Canoa, 397 m, 1; *San Juan:* 7 km E El Cercado, 854 m, 2; 9 km E Vallejuelo, 610 m, 5; *Independencia:* 1 km S La Descubierta, 1; 1 km S Boca de Cachón, 1; La Furnia, s.l., 1; 14 km N Los Pinos, 1159 m, 2; *Baoruco:* 1 km NW El Veinte, 1220 m, 2; 2 km SE Galván, 1; *Barahona:* 14 km SSW Cabral, 854 m, 1; Polo, 702 m, 6; 8 km NNE Polo, 793 m, 1; 1.8 km W Monteada Nueva, 1007 m, 1; 2 km SW Barahona, 122 m, 3; 8 km SW Barahona, 366 m, 1; 12 km SW Barahona, 427 m, 5; 20 km SW Barahona, 1098 m, 2; 3 km NW Enriquillo, 244 m, 3; *Pedernales:* Cabo Rojo, s.l., 3; 5 km NE Cabo Rojo, 1; 26 km NE Cabo Rojo, 732 m, 1; 1 km N Aceitillar, 1281 m, 1; 1 km SW Las Mercedes, 397 m, 1; Mencía, 397 m, 1; 1 km SE Banano, 183 m, 2; 17 km NW Oviedo, 183 m, 2; *Isla Beata:* 7; *Isla Catalina:* 2.

6. *Eurema euterpiformis* Munroe, 1947

TL Kenscoff, 4826 ft., Dépt. de l'Ouest, Haiti.

FW males 13–16 mm, females 13–16 mm.

Eurema euterpiformis was named on the basis of 3 specimens from Kenscoff and Furcy, on the Haitian portion of the south island on the Morne l'Hôpital (a La Selle northern front range), and from Ennery in northern Haiti. The latter locality's given elevation (2500 ft.) makes it certain that the Ennery material is from the adjacent Massif du Nord rather than from the valley in which the town of Ennery lies. In the República Dominicana, the species was reported from La Vega (Hall, 1925:163, as *T. euterpe*). This city is in the lowlands at about 153 m. Thus, although *E. euterpiformis* appears on first glance to have an upland distribution in the Massif de la Selle, Massif du Nord, and the Cordillera Central, the La Vega locality, taken at face value, suggests that the butterfly occurs in the lowlands as well. The elevational range given by Munroe's material (2500–5500 ft; 762–1678 m), exclusive of La Vega, also suggests occurrence of *E. euterpiformis* in the highlands.

Schwartz (1983a:43–44) reported 27 specimens of *E. euterpiformis* from 14 Haitian localities. Some of these sites are at sea level. When Clench identified the 1977 material, he considered many of the specimens *E. euterpiformis* but cautioned (*in litt.):* "I am not certain about the identity of these. They match Munroe's original description reasonably well. . . . Two things worry me: (1) most of the present specimens are from sea level or near it ([this species] is described as montane); and (2) females seem to be from different localities than ... males." I have reexamined some of these Haitian specimens and compared them with high-elevation and unquestioned *E. euterpiformis* and agree with Clench's identification. Female *E. euterpiformis* have been unknown, but fresh Hispaniolan material includes many of them; a description is given below.

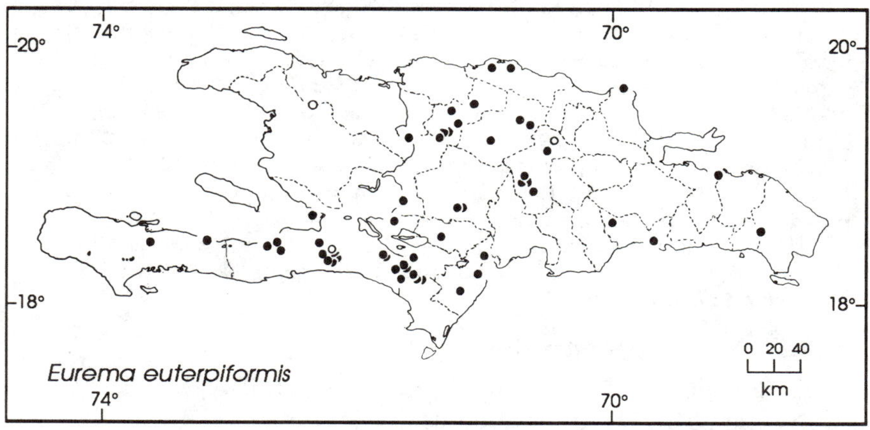

Male *E. euterpiformis* and the closely related *E. l. euterpe* can be differentiated by, in the former, (1) the absence of an upfw cell end black dot, (2) the continuation of the upfw black marginal band to meet the inner margin squarely, not tapering toward the anal angle as in *E. l. euterpe*, and (3) the absence of the unhw round orange marginal spot in Rs-M1, almost always present in *E. l. euterpe*. Two more subjective characters differentiate the males of the 2 species: (1) the up yellow is brighter and clearer in *E. euterpiformis* than the greenish yellow in *E. l. euterpe*; (2) the inner edge of the black fw marginal band is less scalloped (black does not extend basally along the veins into the yellow disc) in *E. euterpiformis* than in *E. l. euterpe*. Riley's illustrations (1975;pl. 14, figs. 7a-b) of *E. l. euterpe* and his line drawing of *E. euterpiformis* (p. 120) show this trait excellently.

Female *E. euterpiformis* are at once distinguished from female *E. l. euterpe* in that, in the former, the up ground color is yellow (pl. 9L1) to yellow-orange (pl. 9L6; all colors coded using Maerz and Paul, 1950) rather than the very pale yellow (pl. 9G1) in *E. l. euterpe*. Un coloration is likewise deeper and richer in *E. euterpiformis*, with the more orange females having the un deep ochraceous due to overlying brown scales; un coloration in *E. l. euterpe* is as pale as the up color. The unhw pattern in *E. l. euterpe* consists of a pinkish to brownish round marginal spot in Rs-M1, and some scattered grayish to tan postdiscal markings, as well as a horizontally oriented discal W between the costa and M1. On the unfw, a discocellular grayish spot is present. In female *E. euterpiformis*, the unhw pattern is bold, brown, and contrasting with the yellow unhw ground color. There is a round to transversely oblong marginal orange spot, followed in M1-M2 and M2-M3 by 2 dark brown blotches in transverse sequence. In M3-Cu1 and Cu1-Cu2, there is also a pair of round brown blotches, but these are displaced marginally and thus not in line with the blotches in the more anterior spaces. Another brown blotch lies in Cu2–2A, this blotch displaced basally and in transverse line with the orange marginal spot. The horizontally oriented discal brown W between the costa and M1 is well developed and resembles an irregularly edged dark bar. On the unfw a discocellular dot is present. The unhw pattern of female *E. euterpiformis* is much like that of female *E. l. euterpe;* however, that of the former is much more intense, definite, and better expressed than in *E. l. euterpe*. Not only are the dark markings brown rather than gray, but the bright yellow to orange ground color of *E. euterpiformis* offers more contrast than the pale yellow of *E. l. euterpe*. Both sexes of *E. l. euterpe* reach larger sizes (18 mm) than both sexes of *E. euterpiformis* (16 mm).

Most specimens of *E. euterpiformis* have been taken in June (42) and July (39), with 22 in August, 13 each in March and May, and 3–9 in April, October, and December. These data suggest a summer (June-July) peak in abundance. Elevational distribution is from sea level (Grand-Goâve, Miragoâne, Île à Cabrit, Tres Ojos, Playa Bayahibe, Canoa) to 1708 m (Los Pinos) in the Sierra de Neiba, 1678 m (Kenscoff) on the Montagne Noire, 1586 m (18 km SE Constanza) in the Cordillera Central, and 1495 m (Canote Mine) in the Sierra de Baoruco.

Times of collection were between 0900 and 1800 h, at temperatures between 21°C (Los Arroyos) and 38°C (Loma Leonor).

Habitats of *E. euterpiformis* are variable. In the uplands, *E. euterpiformis* occurs in pine forest (Forêt des Pins, Kenscoff, Peneau, Aceitillar, 11 km NW Aceitillar, Los Arroyos) and less commonly in hardwood forest (Los Pinos, 12 km NW Aceitillar). Mixed pine-hardwoods are also favored (Loma Leonor—all sites, Buena Vista, 6 km SSE Constanza). In the lowlands, the habitats of *E. euterpiformis* are extremely variable, including beach and mangrove border (Grand-Goâve), margins of mesic or xeric woods and forests (Tres Ojos, Santo Domingo, La Romana, Playa Bayahibe), a very arid islet (Île à Cabrit), and *Acacia* scrub (Santiago, 9 km E Vallejuelo,

Zamba). Occasionally, *E. euterpiformis* is encountered on the weedy and bushy shoulders of roads (Boutilliers Road, Béloc, Comendador, Luperón, 18 km SE Constanza, Jánico, Galván) or in open grassy fields (1 km S Constanza, Sabana de la Mar).

The elevational ranges of *E. euterpiformis* and *E. l. euterpe* overlap almost completely (the latter reaches only an elevation of 1678 m at Obléon and has not been taken in the high uplands of the Sierra de Neiba). Yet I have the strong feeling that *E. euterpiformis* is basically an upland butterfly and *E. l. euterpe* a butterfly of low to moderate elevations. The 2 species are syntopic at 22 localities (Forêt des Pins, Boutilliers Road, Obléon, Peneau, Béloc, just W Grand-Goâve, 25.6 km N Cavaillon, Mao, Loma Leonor, Mata Grande, Santiago, Buena Vista, 1 km S, 6 km SSE, and 18 km SE Constanza, La Romana, Santo Domingo, Galván, Vallejuelo, Polo, Aceitillar, Banano). At most of these, the 2 species are represented by about equal numbers of specimens. However, at 7 (Peneau, Cavaillon, 1 km and 18 km S Constanza, La Romana, Santo Domingo, Polo), *E. l. euterpe* is more abundant than *E. euterpiformis*, and at only 2 (Aceitillar, 19 km SW Monción) is the relationship reversed.

We have never taken *E. euterpiformis* at flowers but have 1 record of the species on fresh horse manure (Río Bao). At Banano, 1 individual was taken from a manure-earth-water mixture, the water (from a spring) crossing the paved road. This site is a favorite drinking place for many species of butterflies. Elsewhere, *E. euterpiformis* has been taken drinking from a puddle in a paved road (Polo) with other pierids.

Specimens: Haiti: l'Ouest: Forêt des Pins, 1586 m, 4; 1 km NW Forêt des Pins, 1556 m, 1; Boutilliers Road, 854–946 m, 3; 5.8 km SW Kenscoff, 1678 m, 2; 1.6 km SW Furcy, 1464 m, 2; Peneau, 1.1 km S Furcy, 1464 m, 2; 0.3 km NE Obléon, 1617 m, 1; 1.3 km N Béloc, 702 m, 1; 6.7 km E Grand-Goâve, s.l., 1; just W Grand-Goâve, s.l., 4; *Sud:* 10.7 km W Miragoâne, s.l., 1; 25.6 km N Cavaillon, 610 m, 1; *Ile à Cabrit:*, s.l., 2; *República Dominicana: Dajabón:* 9 km S Restauración, 519 m, 1; *Valverde:* 12 km SW Mao, 244 m, 1; *Elías Piña:* 15 km S Comendador, 976 m, 1; *Santiago Rodríguez:* Loma Leonor, 18 km SW Monción, 534 m, 4; Loma Leonor, 19 km SW Monción, 610 m, 32; 4.7 km SW Loma Leonor, 732 m, 1; 15 km SW Monción, 320 m, 5; 3 km S Zamba, 214 m, 1; *Puerto Plata:* 13 km SE Luperón, 214 m, 2; 8 km W Luperón, 1; *Santiago:* Río Bao, 4 km SW Mata Grande, 686 m, 1; 8 km E Jánico, 610 m, 1; 7 km SW Santiago, 214 m, 5; *La Vega:* Buena Vista, 11 km NE Jarabacoa, 640 m, 9; 1 km S Constanza, 1098 m, 3; 6 km SSE Constanza, 1403 m, 4; 7 km SE Constanza, *ca.* 1312 m, 1; 18 km SE Constanza, 1586 m, 1; *María T. Sánchez:* 11 km NE Río San Juan, 1; *Hato Mayor:* 25 km E Sabana de la Mar, 1; *La Altagracia:* 16 km NE La Romana, 61 m, 1; 2.5 km SE Playa Bayahibe, s.l., 1; *Dist. Nac.:* Tres Ojos, s.l., 1; 30 km NW Santo Domingo, 122 m, 1; *San Juan:* 7 km NE Vallejuelo, 671 m, 1; 9 km E Vallejuelo, 610 m, 1; *Independencia:* 21 km N Los Pinos, 1708 m, 2; 4–7 km NE El Aguacate, 579–732 m, 4; *Baoruco:* 2 km SE Galván, 2; *Barahona:* 11.5 km ESE Canoa, s.l., 1; Polo, 702 m, 1; 2 km SW Barahona, 122 m 1; *Pedernales:* 1 km SE Banano, 183 m, 1; 1 km NE Aceitillar, 1281 m, 18; 4.5 km NE Aceitillar, 1373 m, 1; Las Abejas, 11 km NW Aceitillar, 1220 m, 5; Las Abejas, 12 km NW Aceitillar, 1229 m, 4; Canote Mine, 6 km NW Aceitillar, 1495 m, 1; 5 km NE Los Arroyos, 1617 m, 1.

7. *Eurema dina mayobanex* Bates, 1939

TL Ennery, 2500 ft., Dépt. de l'Artibonite, Haiti.

FW males 16–22 mm, females 21–23 mm.

Eurema dina Poey is known from Cuba (*E. d. dina*), Jamaica (*E. d. parvumbra* Kaye), and Hispaniola (*E. d. mayobanex*). The Hispaniolan subspecies was described (Bates, 1939a:45) from 3 males and 1 female from Ennery, Dépt. de l'Artibonite, in Haiti. Riley (1975:126) considered the Hispaniolan subspecies "very rare." *Eurema d. mayobanex* is very like *Eurema l. memula;* the 2 species have been taken (sympatrically if not syntopically) at Ennery.

Eurema d. mayobanex is apparently very uncommon in Haiti, whence I have 3 specimens, all from the same locality, taken in 2 separate years (1978, 1979), despite 6 visits to that locality. We have visited the Ennery region (and the Carrefour Marmelade region from which the type-material of *E. d. mayobanex* presumably originated, judging from the elevation) 6 times (1977–79) without finding *E. d. mayobanex* there. In the República Dominicana, on the other hand, *E. d. mayobanex* is locally common on the northern slopes of the Sierra de Baoruco and the adjacent portion of the Massif de la Selle and on the southern slopes of the Sierra de Neiba. On that range, 1 specimen was taken (Los Pinos) at the very edge of the mesic hardwood forest (just beyond which that habitat has been destroyed) and not further on the Neiban plateaulike uplands, nor at the area near and below Puesto Pirámide 204. But *E. d. mayobanex* is common north of Neiba.

In the Sierra de Baoruco–Massif de la Selle, *E. d. mayobanex* is abundant on the transitional-wooded slope 4–7 km NE El Aguacate. Here, the butterflies are often confused with *E. pyro;* both species (especially male *E. pyro*) are deep orange above, and the flights are comparable—both low (0.5 m) to the ground and favoring open areas such as roads and paths. But once alarmed, a particular individual reveals its identity. *Eurema pyro* simply speed their flights and proceed down the road or path; *E. d. mayobanex,* on the other hand, dash into the forest, dodging expertly among bushes and saplings.

All our specimens have been taken in June, July, August, and December, with most in June, fewer in July, and many fewer in August and December. Visits to El Aguacate in October and April yielded no specimens or sight records. This suggests that *E. d. mayobanex* is univoltine with a brief flight period in summer with a few individuals on the wing in midwinter; such a scenario may account for the supposed "rarity" of the species. Note that Bates's type-material was taken in August.

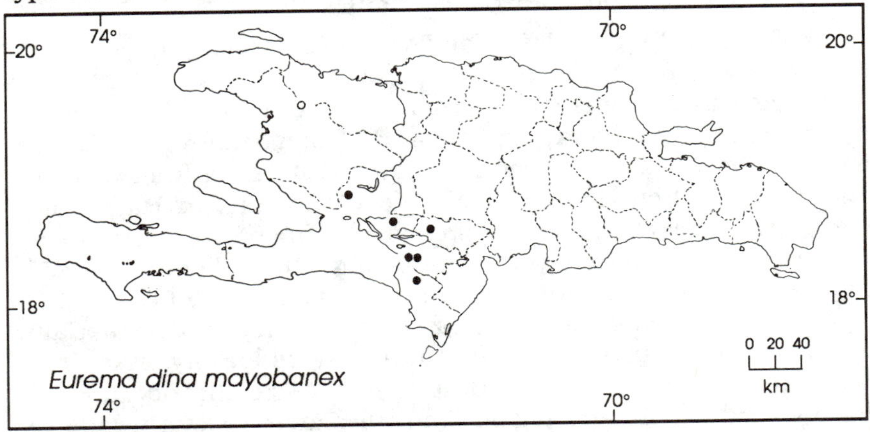

Eurema dina mayobanex

The elevational distribution is between 183 m (Saut d'Eau) and 1678 m (Los Pinos). The Saut d'Eau elevation is exceptional, since all other elevations are at or above 519 m. The locality at Saut d'Eau is unusual; 1 or more springs open at the top of a hillslope with little gradient, and the runoffs from these springs cause the hillside to be soggy, supporting a lush, open but shaded woods. Since the hillside is not suitable for cultivation, the woods there have been little disturbed; because of the extreme wetness of the soil, there is little shrubby undergrowth. All other localities are either transitional forests (4–7 km NE El Aguacate), mesic hardwoods (Los Pinos, Neiba, 4 km NE El Aguacate), or open pine forest (Aceitillar).

Times of activity were between 0905 and 1500 h, at temperatures between 24°C and 36°C (both 4–7 km NE El Aguacate).

At 4–7 km NE El Aguacate, we several times observed *E. d. mayobanex* feeding on the yellow flowers of a tall (0.5 m) composite. This feeding activity was invariably carried on *within* the forest, not along the roadside. Like most pierids, *E. d. mayobanex* feeds with the wings closed; the bright yellow and virtually unmarked (in males) un is boldly visible in the shadow of the forest. At Aceitillar,

1 individual was taken feeding on the white flowers of *Cordia curassavica* in pines. We have taken *E. d. mayobanex* drinking with *Anteos c. clorinde* and *Appias d. boydi* from a small puddle in a gravel road (El Aguacate).

Specimens: Haiti: l'Ouest: 1.6 km N Saut d'Eau, 183 m, 3; *República Dominicana: Baoruco:* 11 km N Neiba, 519 m, 27; *Independencia:* 21 km N Los Pinos, 1708 m, 1; 4 km NE El Aguacate, 976 m, 1; 7 km NE El Aguacate, 519 m, 1; 4–7 km NE El Aguacate, 519–824 m, 44; *Pedernales:* 1 km N Aceitillar, 1281 m, 1.

8. *Eurema leuce memula* Butler, 1871

TL Haiti.

FW males 17–21 mm, females 17–21 mm.

Eurema leuce Boisduval occurs in 3 subspecies in the West Indies: *antillarum* Hall occurs in the Lesser Antilles on St.-Martin, St. Christopher, Montserrat, Dominica, St. Lucia, and Guadeloupe; *sanjuanensis* Watson is on Puerto Rico; and *memula* occurs on Hispaniola.

Eurema l. memula differs from the related *E. larae* and *E. d. mayobanex* on Hispaniola in that it is yellow above, in contrast to orange in the other 2 species.

On Hispaniola, *E. l. memula* is widely distributed geographically but only locally common; it is especially abundant in the xeric forested lowlands in Prov. de la Altagracia. *Eurema l. memula* is strictly a woodland and forest (including occasionally pseudoforest) butterfly; there it flies lazily, usually 1 m or less above the ground, down narrow roads or paths. When alarmed, it quickly seeks refuge within the woods themselves, dodging expertly and erratically among vegetation and often flying 3 or more m high, beyond the reach of the collector. This pierid is most often encountered in xeric forest but has also been taken, in lesser numbers, in or adjacent to mesic forest (Comendador, Luperón, Sosúa, Los Pinos, Las Lagunas, Peralta, 5 km SW El Aguacate, 12 km SW Barahona, Las Abejas), *cafetales* (Polo, 13 km SW Barahona, 9 km NW Enriquillo, 3 km N Cabeza de Agua), oases (Terrier Rouge), pine forest (Kenscoff), and transitional forest (4–7 km NE El Aguacate). Although the Punta Caucedo record is from a more open area (scrubby forest), this area supported, prior to the passage of Hurricane David in 1979, a fine stand of mesic lowland forest, and the butterflies still persist in that area. The individual from Monte Bonito was taken in a formerly wooded ravine, now almost completely cut over and exposed. Only the Boutilliers Road specimen came from a presently unforested locality; it is pertinent that between 1977 and

1984, with 18 visits there, only 1 *E. l. memula* has been taken.

The elevational distribution of *E. l. memula* is between sea level (Terrier Rouge, Copey, Punta Cana, Playa Bayahibe, Punta Caucedo) and 1739 m (Los Pinos). The high elevation is from the Sierra de Neiba. There are no high elevation records for the Cordillera Central (Monte Bonito, 702 m, the highest). But *E. l. memula* seems most abundant on the south island ranges, primarily the Sierra de Baoruco (4–7 km NE El Aguacate) and the adjacent portion of the Massif de la Selle. *Eurema l. memula* is very uncommon in pine forest. Most records are from lowlands rather than high uplands.

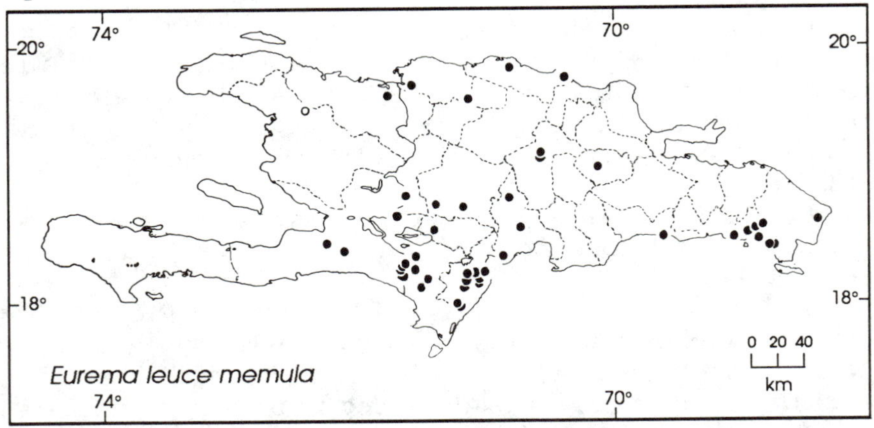

Times of collection were between 0900 and 1630 h, at temperatures between 23°C (9 km NW Enriquillo) and 42°C (La Romana). Contrary to most pierids, *E. l. memula* flies on days that are overcast. This is doubtless due to the fact that *E. l. memula* lives in habitats that are customarily shaded and is thus more tolerant of much less sunny conditions than are many other pierids.

Most specimens have been taken in July (83), with 54 in June and 39 in August. From 8 (April), 4 (October), to 3 (March) and 1 (January, February, May, November) specimens have been taken in the fall to spring months. *Eurema l. memula* appears to be univoltine, the major emergence between June and August, with a few individuals on the wing at other times of the year.

We have seen *E. l. memula* feeding on roadside *Bidens pilosa* (Las Lagunas), on *Tournefortia hirsutissima* (Sosúa, 2 occasions), on *Ixora* sp. (1 km N Playa Bayahibe), and on *Croton barahonensis* (Vallejuelo).

Specimens: Haiti: Nord: 12.3 km E Terrier Rouge, s.l., 1; *l'Ouest:* Boutilliers Road, 854 m, 1; 5.8 km S Kenscoff, 1586 m, 1; *República Dominicana: Monte Cristi:* 6 km W Copey, s.l., 1; *Valverde:* Río Guarabo, 3 km W Los Quemados, 122 m, 1; *Elías Piña:* 15 km S Comendador, 976 m, 1; *Puerto Plata:* 13 km SE Luperón, 214 m, 2; 9 km SE Sosúa, 16 m, 10; *La Altagracia:* 3 km W Punta Cana, s.l., 1; Río Chavón, 10 km NE La Romana, 1; 1 km N Playa Bayahibe, s.l., 38; 2.5 km SE Playa Bayahibe, s.l., 8; 16 km NE La Romana, 61 m, 24; *La Romana:* Río Chavón, 8 km SE La Romana, s.l., 2; 3 km N Altos de Chavon, 1 (MPM); Río Cumayasa, 13.5 km W La Romana, 31 m, 1; *Sánchez Ramírez:* 1 km NE Las Lagunas, 183 m, 4; *La Vega:* Jarabacoa, 530 m, 2; 1.7 km S Jarabacoa, 488 m, 1; *Dist. Nac.:* Punta Caucedo, 2 km W, 2 km S Andrés, s.l., 1; *Azua:* 5 km S Peralta, 305 m, 18; 5 km SW Monte Bonito, 702 m, 2; *San Juan:* 4 km E El Cercado, 702 m, 1; 9 km E Vallejuelo, 610 m, 1; *Baoruco:* 9 km N Neiba, 366 m, 1; *Independencia:* 23 km N Los Pinos, 1739 m, 2; 4–7 km NE El Aguacate, 519–824 m, 26; *Barahona:* west slope, Sierra Martín García, 610 m, 1; west slope, Sierra Martín García, 458–610 m, 1; west slope, Sierra Martín García, 305–458 m, 2; Polo, 702 m, 1; 3 km NNE Polo, 854 m, 1; 14 km SSW Cabral, 854 m, 1; 2 km SW Barahona, 122 m, 3; 12 km SW Barahona, 427 m, 4; 13 km SW Barahona, 732 m, 1; 1.8 km W Monteada Nueva, 1007 m, 2; 3 km NW Enriquillo, 244 m, 1; 9 km NW Enriquillo, 671 m, 4; *Pedernales:* 5 km SW El Aguacate, 1464 m, 1; 26 km NE Cabo Rojo, 732 m, 5; Las Abejas, 12 km NW Aceitillar, 1129 m, 8; 4.5 km NE Aceitillar, 1373 m, 1; El Mulito, 21 km N Pedernales, 214 m, 1; 1 km SE Banano, 183 m, 1; 3 km N Cabeza de Agua, 305 m, 2;

Sight record: República Dominicana: Sánchez Ramírez: 1 km NE Las Lagunas, 183 m—1 seen, 2.xi.

9. *Eurema larae* Herrich-Schäffer, 1862

TL Cuba.

FW males 16–20 mm, females 20–23.

Eurema larae occurs on Cuba (Bates, 1935a:130), on Andros Island in the Bahama Islands (Clench, 1977a:274; 1977b:188), and on Hispaniola. On Andros, Clench (1977b:188) considered *E. larae* "not rare, in scrub, usually in or near pine forest." Riley (1975: 121) noted only the occurrence of this pierid on Hispaniola in the "district of the Rio Yuma," in the extreme southeastern República Dominicana in Prov. de la Altagracia. Schwartz (1983a:44) reported 1 specimen from Haiti; that specimen, however, was misidentified and is *E. l. memula*.

I do have 1 Haitian specimen from the south island at an elevation of 397 m on the western extreme of the Massif de la Selle. The butterfly was collected on 4.vii in an area of *caféières* and upland deciduous forest. A second specimen (female) from El Mulito, taken 4.iv, is from mesic forest along an affluent of the Río Pedernales, on the south slope of the Massif de la Selle, near the Haitian border. The time was 1350–1415 h, at a temperature of 33°C. The specimen is slightly flown. Three specimens (El Aguacate) were collected on 27.vi in transitional forest between 1130 and 1445 h at temperatures of 28°C and 32°C. Two individuals (Neiba) were secured on 18.vi at 1130–1415 h and 33°C.

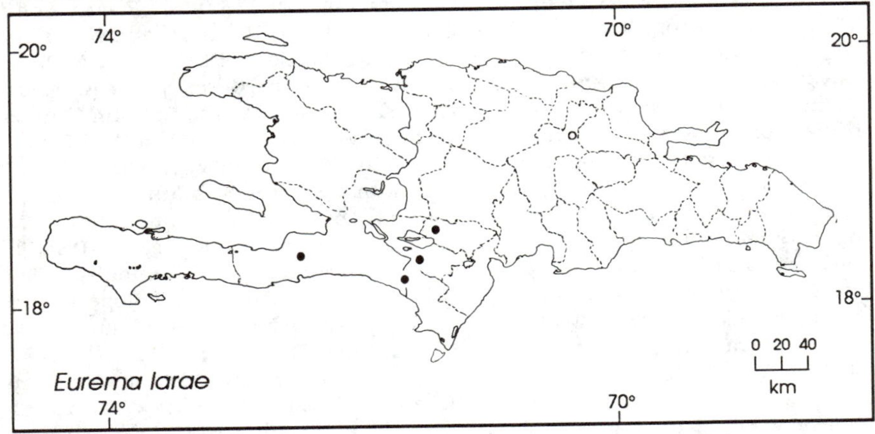

Eurema larae is unaccountably rare in both the República Dominicana and Haiti, at least during the summer months. There is nothing unusual about the regions where our *E. larae* were taken.

Specimens: Haiti: l'Ouest: 5.4 km S Découzé, 397 m, 1; *República Dominicana: Baoruco:* 11 km N Neiba, 519 m, 2; *Independencia:* 4–7 km NE El Aguacate, 519–732 m, 3; *Pedernales:* El Mulito, 21 km N Pedernales, 214 m, 1.

10. *Eurema proterpia proterpia* Fabricius, 1775

TL Jamaica.

FW males 17–24 mm, females 17–25 mm.

Eurema p. proterpia occurs on Cuba (Bates, 1935a:128–29), where it is moderately common and known from central and eastern Cuba, Jamaica (Brown and Heineman, 1972:287), where it is "uncommon and local," and Hispaniola. On the latter island, Hall (1925:163) considered *E. p. proterpia* common at Puerto Plata and near Santo Domingo and included records of f. *gundlachia* from Puerto Plata. Marión Heredia (1980d) reported *E. p. proterpia* (including f. *gundlachia*) from El Número-Azua. Schwartz (1983a: 47) reported 72 specimens from 28 Haitian localities and commented on Riley's (1975:127) statement that *E. p. proterpia* is an upland butterfly. Riley also did not use a trinominal for the Antillean populations, but Brown and Heineman (1972:286) used *E. p. watsonia* Klots for an Ecuadorian subspecies.

Of 31 winter specimens (December-February), 4 males and 3 females show the f. *gundlachia* condition, in which the unhw has a "dead-leaf" pattern and the hw are distinctly pointed and tailed. Many members of both sexes from throughout the year and with f.

proterpia hw shape have the unhw with scattered brownish markings; other specimens, collected with these, have the unhw a completely immaculate orange to yellow.

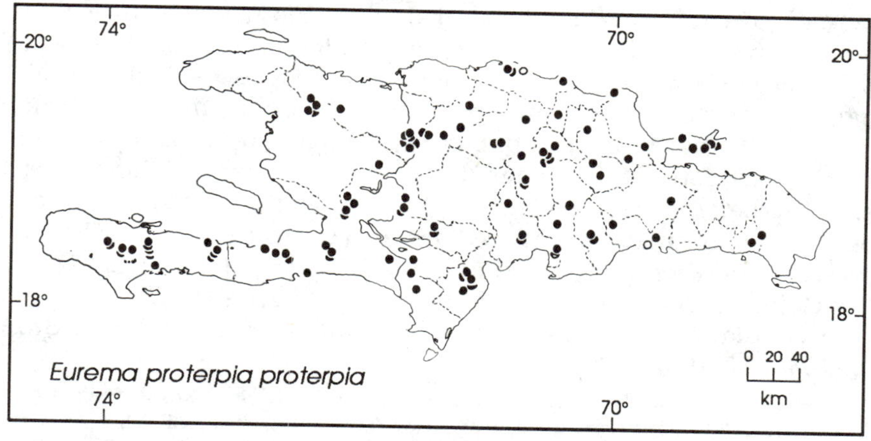

Eurema p. proterpia is an inhabitant of mesic wooded (forest and pseudoforest) situations, both within the wooded areas themselves or along paths and roads paralleling them or coursing along their edges. Exceptions include a xeric open mountainside (Terre Rouge), xeric forest (7 km SSW Cabral), beach (Grand-Goâve), and open fields (above Cavaillon, Carrefour Marmelade, Sosúa, Río San Juan, Constanza, Piedra Blanca).

Elevational distribution is from sea level (Jacmel, Grand-Goâve, Miragoâne, Río San Juan, Cruce de Rincón, Las Terrenas, Samaná) to 1891 m (1 km SW Puesto Pirámide 204) on the Sierra de Neiba, 1617 (Obléon) on the Montagne Noire, a northern La Selle front range, 1220 m (Las Abejas) in the Sierra de Baoruco, and 1403 m (6 km SSE Constanza) in the Cordillera Central. *Eurema p. proterpia* does not occur in the high pine forests of the Cordillera Central. Of the 94 localities for *E. p. proterpia*, 85% (80) are below 915 m and only 15% are at or above 915 m. Riley's (1975:127) statement that *E. p. proterpia* is an "upland" species is not confirmed by these data; rather, *E. p. proterpia* is primarily a butterfly of low to moderate elevations (to 915 m).

Most specimens have been taken in July (83), with 62 in June and 23 in August; December is represented by 13, and March, April, January, September, October, and February by 8–1 each. Times of collection were between 0830 and 1730 h, at temperatures beween 20°C (La Palma) and 40°C (Tenares).

Schwartz (1983a:46) noted a drinking club of *E. p. proterpia*

(Carrefour Marmelade) along a spring run and another (Saut d'Eau) where a small congregation was drinking from a mud puddle. Other instances of *E. p. proterpia* drinking from mud puddles in roads are at Terre Rouge (twice), Jacmel, Río Limpio (where *E. p. proterpia* were drinking within an aggregation of *Rh. t. watsoni* and *A. c. clorinde*), and Luperón (on moist mud in a roadside ditch). We have once seen *E. p. proterpia* on fresh horse manure (Mata Grande). We have taken *E. p. proterpia* foraging on *Daucus* sp. (1.1 km N Carrefour Marmelade), *Hibiscus rosasinensis* (Thomonde), and *Tournefortia hirsutissima* (Sosúa). *Eurema p. proterpia* flies on bright and sunny days, and we have also taken these butterflies in overcast and even rainy weather (4.8 km W and 4.5 km E Samaná, Las Galeras, Las Lagunas, Polo, 14 km SSW Cabral).

A copulating pair was taken on 20.vi (Cambita Garabitos, 871 m, 1045–1230 h).

Specimens: Haiti: Nord: 1.8 km S Dondon, 366 m, 1; 6.2 km W Plaisance, 259 m, 1; 1.1 km N Carrefour Marmelade, 793 m, 1; 3 km ESE Villa Anacaona, 458 m, 1; *l'Artibonite:* 1.6 km E Carrefour Marmelade, 854 m, 16; Platon, 6 km E Carrefour Marmelade, 793 m, 1; 4 km N Thomonde, 1; *l'Ouest:* 1.6 km N Saut d'Eau, 193 m, 2; 19.7 km SE Mirebalais, 183 m, 2; 3.8 km N Terre Rouge, 397 m, 1; 1.1 km N Terre Rouge, 519 m, 1; 2.9–8.5 km S Terre Rouge, 122–488 m, 3; Forêt des Pins, 1525 m, 1; Boutilliers Road, 732–915 m, 7 (2 FSM); Boutilliers Road, 1.8–2.1 km W Kenscoff road, 793–885 m, 2; 0.3 km N Obléon, 1617 m, 2; Peneau, 1.1 km S Furcy, 1464 m, 1; Ravine Roseau, 4 km SW Dufort, 1; 1.4 km N Béloc, 702 m, 2; 0.6 km S Découzé, 671 m, 2; 9.9 km E Jacmel, s.l., 1; just W Grand-Goâve, s.l., 1; *Sud:* 10.7 km W Miragoâne, s.l., 1; 2.9 km SW Paillant, 671 m, 1; 3 km SW Paillant, 671–793 m, 3; 6.7 km SW Paillant, 854 m, 2; 4.5 km E Cavaillon, 31 m, 1; 14.4 km N Cavaillon, 366 m, 3; 16.3 km N Cavaillon, 488 m, 3; 19.7 km N Cavaillon, 580 m, 1; 25.6 km N Cavaillon, 610 m, 5; 4.8 km N Camp Perrin, 244 m, 2; 5.6 km N Camp Perrin, 275 m, 3; 14 km NW Marceline, 671 m, 1; Formond, 800 m, 1 (FSM); Formond Base Camp #1, 975 m, 4 (FSM); *República Dominicana: Dajabón:* 16 km NW Río Limpio, 702 m, 1; Los Cerezos, 12 km NW Río Limpio, 580 m, 7; 7 km N Restauración, 671 m, 1; 4 km S Restauración, 580 m, 1; 8 km S Restauración, 625 m, 1; 8.4 km S Restauración, 580 m, 1; Cañada Tirolís, just S Villa Anacaona, 458 m, 2; 3 km ESE Villa Anacaona, 458 m, 3; *Elías Piña:* 15 km S Comendador, 976 m, 1; 2 km NE Puesto Pirámide 204, 1586 m, 2; 1 km SW Puesto Pirámide 204, 1891 m, 1; *Santiago Rodríguez:* 15 km SW Monción, 320 m, 5; 4.7 km SW Loma Leonor, 732 m, 1; 3 km W Los Quemados, 183 m, 1; *Espaillat:* 20 km SW Jamao al Norte, 793 m, 2; *Puerto Plata:* 8 km W Luperón, 1; 13 km SE Luperón, 214 m, 1; 9 km SE Sosúa, 16 m, 3; *Santiago:* Río Bao, 4 km SW Mata Grande, 702 m, 1; Río Bao, 8 km SE Montones Abajo, 488 m, 4; 7 km SW Santiago, 214 m, 1; *Duarte:* 10 km SE Tenares, 183 m, 2: Villa Riva, 1: *María T. Sánchez:* Río San Juan, s.l., 1; 11 km NE Río San Juan, 1; Cruce de Rincón, s.l., 1; *La Vega:* Güaigüí, S La Vega, 336 m, 1; La Palma, 19 km W Jayaco, 1007 m, 3; Jarabacoa, 530 m, 4; 5 km SE Jarabacoa, 595 m, 2; La Ciénaga, 915 m, 5; 3.5 km E Paso Bajito, 732 m, 1; 1 km S Constanza, 1098 m, 7; 6 km SSE Constanza, 1403 m, 1; *Samaná:* 3.1 km E Las

Terrenas, s.l., 3; 4.8 km W Samaná, s.l., 2; 4.5 km E Samaná, 3; El Francés, 14 km E and N Samaná, s.l., 1; 2.8 km S Las Galeras, 61 m, 4; *La Romana:* Río Chavón, 10 km NE La Romana, 1; *La Altagracia:* 16 km NE La Romana, 61 m, 1; *Dist. Nac.:* 30 km NW Santo Domingo, 122 m, 2; 5 km S San Isidro, 1; *Sánchez Ramírez:* 1 km SE La Mata, 1; 1 km NE Las Lagunas, 183 m, 1; *Monseñor Nouel:* 17 km SW Piedra Blanca, 854 m, 3; *Monte Plata:* 8 km NE Bayaguana, 1; *San Cristóbal:* 6 km NW Cambita Garabitos, 488 m, 1; 11 km NW Cambita Garabitos, 671 m, 9; *Peravia:* 5 km N San José de Ocoa, 580 m, 1; *Azua:* 25 km NE Azua, 92 m, 2; 4 km S Peralta, 366 m, 3; 5 km S Peralta, 305 m, 9; 5 km SW Monte Bonito, 702 m, 1; *Baoruco:* 11 km N Neiba, 519 m, 3; 14 km N Neiba, 366 m, 2; *Independencia:* 4–7 km NE El Aguacate, 519–824 m, 4; *Barahona:* Polo, 702 m, 8; 1.8 km W Monteada Nueva, 1007 m, 3; 14 km SSW Cabral, 854 m, 1; 7 km SSW Cabral, 214 m, 1; 20 km SW Barahona, 1098 m, 1; *Pedernales:* 23 km NE Cabo Rojo, 488 m, 1; Las Abejas, 11 km NW Aceitillar, 1220 m, 1.

11. *Eurema daira palmira* Poey, 1819

TL Cuba.

FW males 13–16 mm, females 14–17 mm.

Eurema d. palmira is widely distributed throughout the West Indies, occurring on all the Greater Antillean islands, the Cayman Islands (Cayman Brac, Little Cayman: Askew, 1980:124; Grand Cayman: Schwartz, Gonzalez, and Henderson, 1987), the Virgin Islands, and the Lesser Antilles as far south as Grenada. The mainland subspecies (*E. d. daira* Godart) occurs on the Bahama Islands (Rindge, 1955:5, Exuma Cays; Clench, 1977b:188, Andros). Smith et al. (1982) discussed the (erroneously reported) sympatry of *daira* and *palmira* in southern Florida.

Two small, similarly patterned (in males) *Eurema* occur on Hispaniola and elsewhere in the Antilles: *E. daira* and *E. elathea* Cramer. Males of these 2 species have a bold, very dark (black to very dark gray) bar along the inner margin of the fw. In male *E. daira*, this bar is arched or bowed, and its end toward the fw anal angle is near to the inner margin. In male *E. elathea*, the fw dark bar is straight and parallels the inner margin. On the other hand, females of the 2 species are much less easily differentiated. Various authors (Comstock, 1944:522–23; Brown and Heineman, 1972: 278; Riley, 1975:122–23) have given criteria to distinguish between them, with varying degrees of success. When Clench identified the first of our Haitian material in 1978, he wrote that he was reasonably sure that he had determined females of the 2 species correctly but was not absolutely certain. Combining the data from the above 3 sources, one can differentiate most female *E. elathea* on the basis of having the upfw some shade of yellow, or yellow scales at least present somewhere on the upfw (often only basally or along the costal margin). Often the presence of yellow on the fw is best determined by stepping back from the specimens —the overall yellowish effect is more apparent at half a meter than upon very minute examination. Although this may seem subjective, using the yellow on the fw is more satisfactory than uphw characters that have been suggested. In *E. d. palmira* females, the up is white, without yellow tones (see Smith *et al.*, 1982).

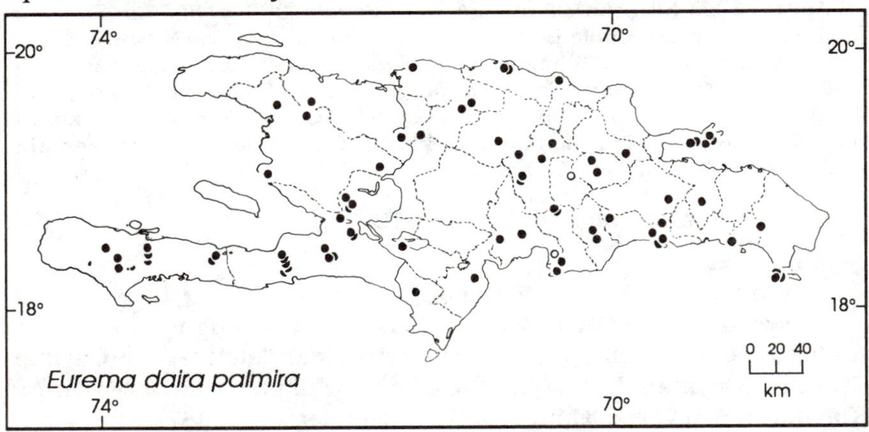

In most cases of comparison of the distributions of *E. daira* and *E. elathea* on Hispaniola made below, males of both species are available, and there is no doubt that the species occur together. Brown and Heineman (1972:278), quoting Avinoff's notes, stated that these 2 species do not occur together on Jamaica. However, the authors themselves noted that "at times" they have been taken syntopically.

On Hispaniola, *E. d. palmira* is the more distinctly mesophilic of the pair. Although *E. d. palmira* occurs in grassy areas, along roadsides, in grassy fields, and in and along the margins of cornfields, it is also found associated with *caféières* (Paillant, 1.6 km N Béloc), *cafetales* (La Palma), mesic forest (Las Lagunas), and open mesic meadows (12 km SW Barahona). On Punta Caucedo, which prior to Hurricane David in 1979 supported a fine stand of little-disturbed mesic forest that is now reduced to scrubby woods, *E. d. palmira* still occurs. *Eurema d. palmira* is rare in the fine xeric forests of eastern República Dominicana (La Romana) but occurs in disturbed mesic woods at Río Cumayasa. This species occurs without *E. elathea* on the mesic Península de Samaná and is apparently very uncommon on the xeric Península de Barahona and the southern and upper slopes of the Sierra de Baoruco. I have 3 specimens from Isla Saona, where *E. elathea* is abundant; Isla Saona is basically xeric and has vegetation like that of eastern Hispaniola. There are only 3 records of *E. d. palmira* from the Cul de Sac–Valle de Neiba plain (El Limón, 5 km and 2 km NW Fond Parisien) and none from the xeric western Valle de Cibao and the xeric Valle de San Juan, all areas represented by *E. elathea*. It is interesting that in these arid regions, *E. d. palmira* has not even invaded (or at least persisted in) oases, which are shaded and usually mesic. But on the other hand, occasionally *E. d. palmira* does occur in extremely xeric areas (Las Calderas, Fundación de Sabana Buey, Tábara Abajo, El Limón). Such occurrences are distinctly in the minority.

Eurema d. palmira occurs from sea level (Délugé, Las Galeras, Punta Caucedo, El Limón, Cabo Rojo) to 1647 m (10 km SE Constanza) in the Cordillera Central and to 1617 m (Obléon) on the Montagne Noire to the north of the main mass of the Massif de la Selle. These high elevations are in contradistinction to the elevational range of *E. elathea*, which is known no higher than 1098 m (see account of *E. elathea* for details). Of the localities for *E. d. palmira*, 39% (of 61) are at or above 610 m, whereas of the 52 *E. elathea* localities, only 17% are at or above 610 m. Aside from pine forests, which are essentially xeric and which are not occupied by either species, there are no truly (as opposed to physiologically) arid upland habitats. Mountains are mesic, and the occurrence of *E. d. palmira* reflects this. Even so, *E. d. palmira* is not common at elevations above 915 m (6 localities).

Remarkably, *E. d. palmira*, along with *E. elathea*, are both unknown from the Sierra de Neiba and the uplands of the Sierra de Baoruco and of the Dominican portion of the Massif de la Selle (Los Arroyos to El Aguacate). The absence of *E. d. palmira* at least from these ranges is inexplicable.

Most specimens have been taken in July (27), with 23 in June, 12 in August, and 9 in March. December, October, January, February, April, and May are represented by 8–1 specimens. *Eurema d. palmira* appears to be on the wing throughout the year, perhaps with a peak in late summer. Of *E. d. palmira* and *E. elathea*, the latter is the more common.

Times of collection were between 0925 and 1730 h, at temperatures from 23°C (4.8 km W Samaná) to 39°C (10.2 km W Samaná). The butterflies fly on overcast or even rainy days.

In contrast to *E. elathea*, we have seen *E. d. palmira* feeding only 3 times (Tábara Abajo, Las Lagunas, Los Quemados) on *Bidens pilosa*, but *E. d. palmira* drinks (usually in the company of other pierids, such as *Phoebis* sp., or by itself in very large numbers). Such drinking sites may be a moist sandbar in a creek (20.2 km SE Mirebalais), mud in dirt roads (Los Cerezos, Río Cumayasa), or moist mud in a ditch (8 km W Luperón).

Copulating pairs have been taken on 7.vi (Las Lagunas, 1110–1250 h, 37°C), 5.viii (La Mata, 1015–1130 h, 34°C), and 27.ix (Villa Riva, 1145–1300 h, 37°C).

Specimens: Haiti: Nord: 3.5 km W Plaisance, 305 m, 2; *l'Artibonite:* 1.6 km E Carrefour Marmelade, 854 m, 1; 16 km N Carrefour Joffre, 183 m, 1; Délugé, s.l., 1; 4 km N Thomonde, 2; *l'Ouest:* 1.6 km N Saut d'Eau, 275 m, 1; 19.7 km SE Mirebalais, 183 m, 1; 20.2 km SE Mirebalais, 366 m, 1; 1.3 km S Terre Rouge, 458 m, 1; 5 km NW Fond Parisien, 2; 2 km NW Fond Parisien, 1; Boutilliers Road, 3.7 km W Kenscoff road, 2 (MPM); 0.3 km N Obléon, 1617 m, 2; Peneau, 1464 m, 1; 8.6 km N Béloc, 534 m, 1; 1.6 km N Béloc, 702 m, 1; 0.6 km S Découzé, 802 m, 1; 2.1 km S Découzé, 640 m, 1; 9.3 km NW Jacmel, 183 m, 1; *Sud:* 3 km SW Paillant, 2; 6.6 km SW Paillant, 793 m, 3; 16.3 km N Cavaillon, 488 m, 1; 19.7 km N Cavaillon, 580 m, 2; 25.6 km N Cavaillon, 610 m, 2; 5.6 km N Camp Perrin, 244 m, 1; Formond Base Camp #1, 975 m, 1 (FSM); Lévy, 1; *República Dominicana: Monte Cristi:* 1 km SE Monte Cristi, 1; *Dajabón:* Los Cerezos, 12 km NW Río Limpio, 580 m, 2; 4 km S Restauración, 580 m, 1; *Valverde:* 12 km SW Mao, 244 m, 3; *Santiago Rodríguez:* 3 km W Los Quemados, 183 m, 1; *Puerto Plata:* 8 km W Luperón, 4; 10 km W Luperón, 1; 9 km SE Sosúa, 16 m, 1; *Santiago:* Río Bao, 8 km SE Montones Abajo, 488 m, 1; *La Vega:* 10 km S La Vega (= Güaigüi), 1; La Palma, 19 km W Jayaco, 1007 m, 1; La Ciénaga, 915 m, 2; 1 km S Constanza, 1098 m, 2; 6 km SSE Constanza, 1043 m, 1; *Duarte:* Villa Riva, 3; *Samaná:* 10.2 km W Samaná, 61 m, 1; 4.8 km W Samaná, s.l., 1; 4.5 km E Samaná, 2; 2.8 km S Las Galeras, 61 m, 2; 3.8 km S Las Galeras, s.l., 1; *La Altagracia:* 16 km NE La Romana, 61 m, 4; *La Romana:* Río Cumayasa, 13.5 km W La Romana, 31 m, 2; *Hato Mayor:* 4 km S Hato Mayor, 1; *Dist. Nac.:* 9 km NE Guerra, 1; 33 km W San Pedro de Macorís, 3 (MPM); Punta Caucedo, 5 km S Aeropuerto Internacional de las Américas, s.l., 1; 5 km S San Isidro, 1; 30 km NW Santo Domingo, 122 m, 1; *Sánchez Ramírez:* 1 km SE La Mata, 3; 1 km NE Las Lagunas, 183 m, 6; *Monte Plata:* 8 km NE Bayaguana, 1; *San Cristóbal:* 3 km NW Cambita Garabitos, 366 m, 1; 11 km NW Cambita Garabitos, 671 m, 1; *Peravia:* Las Calderas, s.l., 1; 1 km N Fundación de Sabana Buey, 1; 2.7 km W La Horma, 1; 1.6 km SE La Horma, 2; *Azua:* Tábara Abajo, 2; 5 km S Peralta, 305 m, 2; *Independencia:* 4 km E El Limón, s.l., 1; *Barahona:* 12 km SW Barahona, 427 m, 1; *Pedernales:* Cabo Rojo, s.l., 1; 23 km NE Cabo Rojo, 488 m, 1; *Isla Saona:* 2 km N Mano Juan, 1; 1.5 km N Mano Juan, 1; 0.5 km N Mano Juan, 1.

12. *Eurema elathea* Cramer, 1775

TL North and Central America.

FW males 13–17 mm, females 14–18 mm.

Eurema elathea occurs in the West Indies on Cuba, Jamaica, Puerto Rico, the Cayman Islands, and the Bahama Islands (Great Exuma, Long, Great Inagua, San Salvador; Clench, 1977a:273; Clench and Bjorndal, 1980:22; Elliott, Riley, and Clench, 1980:

124), and the Lesser Antilles (St. Christopher, Antigua, Montserrat, Guadeloupe, St.-Martin, St.-Barthélémy, and St. Lucia; Riley, 1975:123; Schwartz and Jimenez, 1982:10). *Eurema elathea* is also widely distributed on the continental mainland of Central and South America. Clench and Bjorndal (1980:22) and Elliott, Riley, and Clench (1980:124) used a trinominal (*E. e. elathea*) for material from the southern Bahamas, but Riley (1975:123) did not use a trinomen, and I follow him here.

Differentiation of male *E. elathea* from male *E. d. palmira*, as well as differentiation of the females of the 2 species, has already been discussed (see account of *E. d. palmira*). These 2 species are generally allopatric on Hispaniola, but on occasion they have been taken together. Such sites of syntopy will be discussed beyond.

Eurema elathea on Hispaniola is primarily an inhabitant of xeric areas; Schwartz (1983a:45) at that time held the reverse view —that *E. elathea* inhabited mesic regions. But additional material from less ecologically disturbed República Dominicana and reassessment of the Haitian localities suggest strongly that *E. elathea* is more xerophilic than mesophilic. For example, many Haitian localities (Môle St.-Nicholas, Colmini, Terre Rouge, Carrefour Joffre, Etang Saumâtre, Anse-à-Galets, Picmi) as well as Dominican localities (Cruce de Guayacanes, Mao, Santiago, La Canoa, Playa Bayahibe, Las Calderas, Cruce de Ocoa, Hatillo, Vallejuelo, La Descubierta, Duvergé, Cabo Rojo, Oviedo, Mano Juan) are arid, often very bleak and rigorous (Carrefour Joffre) or are thorn scrub. In the Cul de Sac–Valle de Neiba plain, *E. elathea* occurs in open areas (Croix des Bouquets) and in local shaded enclaves (Fond Parisien). In the Valle de Cibao, these butterflies occur in oases (Villa Vásquez). But there are some localities that are unqualifiedly mesic (Béloc, Cavaillon, Lévy, 20.2 km SE Mirebalais) or at least transitional mesic-xeric (23 km NE Cabo Rojo, Barahona, Angel Feliz, Peralta). From the above lists, it is obvious that *E. elathea* favors xeric over mesic habitats.

Because of the lack of high-elevation arid areas (other than the Valle de San Juan, where *E. elathea* does occur), *E. elathea* does not reach so high an elevation as *E. d. palmira*. The species occurs from sea level (Môle St.-Nicholas, Grand-Goâve, Colmini, Playa Bayahibe, Punta Caucedo, Las Calderas, Cabo Rojo, Mano Juan) to 1830 m (La Laguna). Only 17% (9 of 52) of the *E. elathea* localities are at or above 610 m, whereas 39% (24 of 61) of the *E. d. palmira* localities are at or above 610 m.

Specimens of *E. elathea* have been taken in July (59), June (47), January (37), May (13), August and December (7 each), October

(5), February and March (4 each), and April (1). Schwartz and Jimenez (1982:10) suggested that on Montserrat *E. elathea* is bivoltine (August and December); the same may be true on Hispaniola, with peaks in June-July and December-January.

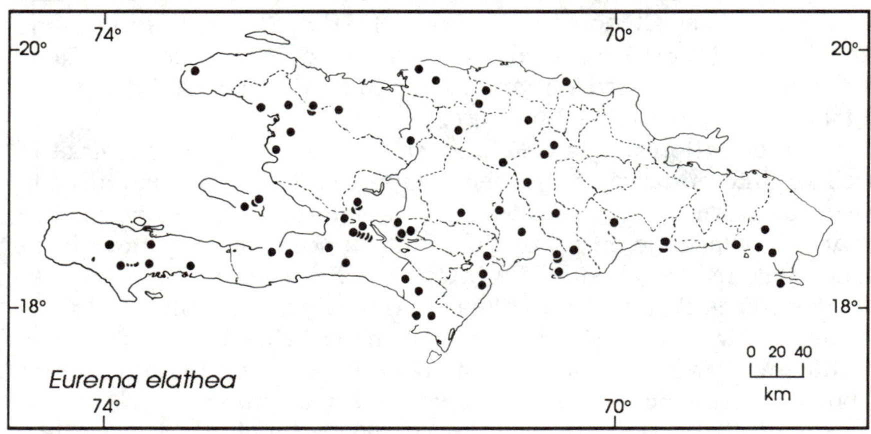

Times of collection were between 0900 and 1630 h, at temperatures between 26°C (Boutilliers Road, La Laguna) and 38°C (Río Cumayasa, Las Calderas, Hatillo, Cabo Rojo).

Eurema elathea feeds on the flowers of *Bidens pilosa* (Fond Parisien, Mao), *Antigonon leptopus* (Cruce de Guayacanes, Cruce de Ocoa, La Descubierta), *Tephrosia purpurea* (Cabo Rojo), *Parthenium hysterophorus* (Vallejuelo), *Melochia tomentosa* (La Canoa), and *Daucus* sp. (Carrefour Marmelade). Schwartz (1983a:45) noted the retreat of *E. elathea* in large numbers to the bases of grass culms during inclement weather. At Playa Bayahibe, a large area that had been xeric forest-thorn scrub near the beach has been cleared and burned (1983) for development. Collecting in the burn in 1983 revealed that *E. elathea* was the only small butterfly to have invaded this extremely hostile area; the only flowers still remaining were those of *Stachytarpheta jamaicensis;* apparently *E. elathea* is a pioneer species among the small butterflies, rather rapidly entering newly created ecological situations.

We have observed *E. elathea* drinking from mud in dirt roads at Barahona (2 different years, June and July, high numbers in the latter month) and Río Cumayasa.

Pairs *in copula* have been taken on 20.v, 1510 h, 33°C, and 26.v, 1445–1530 h, 30°C (Mao), and 28.vi, 1116 h, 33°C (Santiago); all matings were in *Acacia* woods. In the 26.v instance, the male was feeding on *Bidens pilosa* during the act.

Eurema elathea occurs on Île de la Gonâve and Isla Saona; these are the first reports of the species from the latter island, where it is very common. On Saona, *E. elathea* far outnumbers *E. d. palmira*, and the latter is not known from Gonâve; all stations for Île de la Gonâve thus far sampled have been more or less coastal and extremely arid, a habitat much more suitable for *E. elathea* than *E. d. palmira*. *Eurema d. palmira* may occur on Gonâve on the higher interior and more mesic hills.

Other than on Isla Saona, *E. elathea* and *E. d. palmira* are syntopic at 7 Haitian and 9 Dominican localities (1.6 km E Carrefour Marmelade, 16 km N Carrefour Joffre, 20.2 km SE Mirebalais, 19.7 km SE Mirebalais, Fond Parisien, 25.6 km N Cavaillon, Lévy, Formond Base Camp #1, Monte Cristi, Mao, Sosúa, Güaigüí, 1 km S Constanza, La Romana, Río Cumayasa, Punta Caucedo, La Horma). Only at La Romana is there is preponderance of 1 species (*E. elathea*) over the other. La Romana is xeric forest, a preferred habitat of *E. elathea*. Elsewhere the species occur in about equal numbers. Except for Carrefour Joffre and Fond Parisien, all other lowland Haitian localities are much disturbed and cultivated. Of the Dominican localities, Punta Caucedo has been mentioned previously as a locality where *E. d. palmira* has persisted despite the destruction of mesic forest; *E. elathea* also occurs there. Constanza is near the upper elevational extreme of *E. elathea;* the area is essentially a highly modified xeric-mesic interface. Güaigüí is mixed pine-hardwoods, and Río Cumayasa has both mesic and xeric forests and woods within a few meters of each other (woods on hillsides, mesic forest in the river valley itself). Sosúa lies in karst topography with dolines and transitional forest. Mao and Monte Cristi are *Acacia* forest; at both localities, the expected *E. elathea* outnumbers *E. d. palmarum* slightly (4:1, 7:3). Both localities are in areas disturbed by man (road building; modified by construction). Thus, in most cases of Dominican syntopy, there are factors that have allowed *E. elathea* and *E. d. palmira* to coexist in what should be (but is not) strongly preferred habitat for 1 or the other species.

Specimens: Haiti: Nord-Ouest: Môle St.-Nicholas, s.l., 2; *Nord:* 1.8 km S Dondon, 366 m, 1; 1.1 km N Carrefour Marmelade, 793 m, 1; *l'Artibonite:* 1.6 km E Carrefour Marmelade, 854 m, 1; 16 km N Carrefour Joffre, 183 m, 1; 16.8 km W Ça Soleil, 1; 13 km ESE Pont Gaugin, s.l., 1; Colmini, 6.4 km W Terre Noire, 3; *l'Ouest:* 19.7 km SE Mirebalais, 183 m, 3; 20.0 km S Mirebalais, 580 m, 1; 20.2 km SE Mirebalais, 366 m, 1; 5.6 km S Terre Rouge 366 m, 8; 18.1 km SE Croix des Bouquets, s.l., 1; Etang Saumâtre, 1 (FSM); 2 km SE Fond Parisien, s.l., 1; 3.0 km SE Fond Parisien, s.l., 6; 2 km NW Fond Parisien, 1; 5 km NW Fond Parisien, 3; Boutilliers Road, 843–915 m, 2; 8.6 km N Béloc, 534 m, 1; nr. Péredo, at river, 2 (FSM); just W Grand-Goâve, s.l.,

1; *Sud:* Vieux Bourg d'Aquin, s.l., 1; 7.8 km N Cavaillon, 31 m, 1; 25.6 km N Cavaillon, 610 m, 1; 26.1 km N Cavaillon, 610 m, 1; Lévy, 3; Formond Base Camp #1, 975 m, 1 (FSM); *Île de la Gonâve:* hills behind Anse-à-Galets, 1; Anse-à-Galets, 1; Picmi, 1; *República Dominicana: Monte Cristi:* 1 km SE Monte Cristi, 4; 4 km NW Villa Vásquez, 61 m, 1; *Dajabón:* Cañada Tirolís, just S Villa Anacaona, 458 m, 2; *Valverde:* 4 km N Cruce de Guayacanes, 198 m, 4; 12 km SW Mao, 244 m, 7; *Santiago Rodríguez:* 15 km SW Monción, 320 m, 17; *Puerto Plata:* 9 km SE Sosúa, 16 m, 2; *Santiago:* La Laguna, 1830 m, 1; 7 km SW Santiago, 214 m, 6; *La Vega:* Güaigüí, S La Vega, 336 m, 1; Jarabacoa, 530 m, 1; 1 km S Constanza, 1098 m, 4; *La Altagracia:* 2.5 km SE Playa Bayahibe, 2; 16 km NE La Romana, 61 m, 7; *La Romana:* Río Chavón, 8 km SE La Romana, s.l., 1; Río Cumayasa, 13.5 km W La Romana, 31 m, 1; *Dist. Nac.:* 33 km W San Pedro de Macorís, 2 (MPM); Punta Caucedo, 5 km S Aeropuerto Internacional de las Américas, s.l., 1: Punta Caucedo, 2 km W, 2 km S Andrés, s.l., 3; 30 km NW Santo Domingo, 122 m, 1; *Peravia:* Las Calderas, s.l., 3; 2.7 km W La Horma, 2; *Azua:* 15 km NW Cruce de Ocoa, 76 m, 1; 2 km NW Hatillo, 183 m, 1; 5 km S Peralta, 305 m, 3; 2 km SE La Canoa, 397 m, 5; *San Juan:* 9 km E Vallejuelo, 610 m, 2; *Independencia:* 5 km S Angel Feliz, 2; 1 km S La Descubierta, 1; 3.3 km E La Descubierta, 5; 2 km S Duvergé, 1; *Barahona:* 12 km ESE Canoa, s.l., 2; 2 km SW Barahona, 122 m, 13; 5 km SE, 3 km W Barahona, 183 m, 1; *Pedernales:* Cabo Rojo, s.l., 3; 23 km NE Cabo Rojo, 488 m, 2; Mencía, 397 m, 1; 17 km NW Oviedo, 183 m, 5; *Isla Saona:* 0.5 km N Mano Juan, 3; 1 km N Mano Juan, 3; 1.5–1.75 km N Mano Juan, 6; Mano Juan, 6; 3 km N Mano Juan, 10.

13. *Eurema lucina priddyi* Lathy, 1898

TL Haiti.

FW males 13–14 mm, female 13 mm.

Although Riley (1975:124) considered *priddyi* a species distinct from Cuban *E. lucina* Poey, Clench (*in litt.*, 1978) used the combination *E. l. priddyi* and I follow that course here. The 2 taxa are very similar, but *E. l. lucina* has the up white (yellow in *E. l. priddyi*), is larger, and in both sexes has a large black apical patch on the uphw.

Bates (1935a:125) did not give numbers of specimens examined from Cuba (except for 18 from Santa Clara, Habana, and the Isla de la Juventud), but the widespread distribution of *E. l. lucina* as given by him suggests that the species is not uncommon there and ranges widely. Hall (1925:164) did not collect *E. l. priddyi* on Hispaniola. Schwartz (1983a:46) reported 5 specimens from 5 Haitian localities; of these specimens, 3 (those from 54A, 55A, and 55B) were incorrectly identified.

I now have 6 specimens from 5 localities; 4 of these are in Haiti and 1 is in the República Dominicana. The "longest series" is the 2 specimens from Lévy near the distal portion of the Tiburon Peninsula. *Eurema l. priddyi* is very uncommon on Hispaniola; the taking of the 2 Lévy specimens in January and the single Fond Parisien specimen in December suggests that midsummer is not the time of maximum abundance of the species. The elevational distribution is from sea level (Fond Parisien) to 946 m (Boutilliers Road). Times of collection were between 1015 and 1500 h; the only recorded temperatures are 29°C (Fond Parisien) and 36°C (El Aguacate). Habitats include: an open *Cajanus cajan* field (Terre Rouge), an open mountainside road (Boutilliers Road), a road through xeric woods (El Aguacate), roadside *Acacia* scrub (Fond Parisien), and brushy and weedy growth along the edges of a dry creekbed (Lévy). None of these habitats in unusual. At El Aguacate, *E. l. priddyi* was taken in the company of *Nathalis iole;* the 2 species fly close (0.5 m) to the ground and have a weak flight.

Specimens: Haiti: l'Ouest: 3.8 km N Terre Rouge, 534 m, 1; 5 km NW Fond Parisien, s.l., 1; Boutilliers Road, 854–946 m, 1; *Sud:* Lévy, 200 m, 2; *República Dominicana: Independencia:* 7 km NE El Aguacate, 534 m, 1.

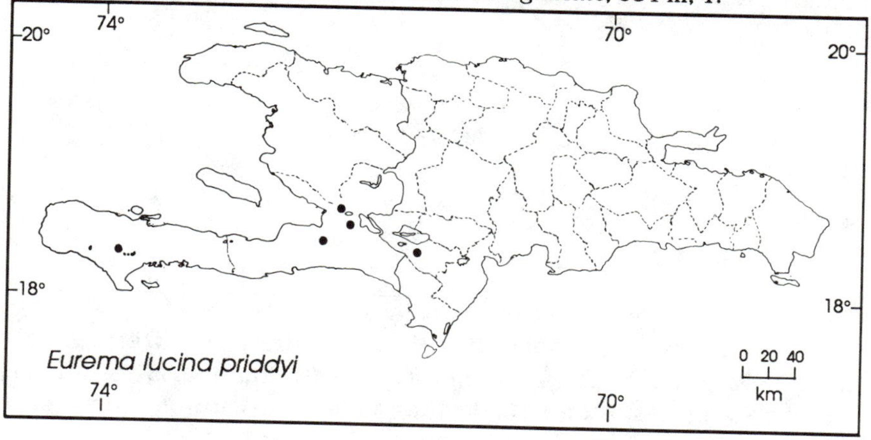

14. *Eurema pyro* Godart, 1819

TL not stated; restricted to Haiti by Riley (1975:125).

FW males 12–19 mm, females 15–20 mm.

Eurema pyro is restricted to Hispaniola, where it has been reported from Pico Isabela de Torres (at 1000 ft.) and La Vega, as well as Santo Domingo, República Dominicana (Hall, 1925:163–64). Riley (1975:125) added Port-au-Prince in Haiti and gave an elevational range of 700–900 m. Riley also noted the occurrence of *E. pyro* in April, June, and October-December. The male f. *hyona* Ménétriés has been noted by Hall, and there are specimens of this form in my material.

Eurema pyro is much more widely distributed altitudinally than noted above. Schwartz (1983a:46–47) reported 29 specimens from 13 Haitian localities; all localities were above about 300 m. However, in the República Dominicana, *E. pyro* occurs at sea level (Cabrera, Río San Juan, Cruce de Rincón) and many other localities far less than 300 m (Cruce de Guayacanes, Gaspar Hernández, Sánchez, Bonao, Maimón, Santo Domingo, Cruce de Ocoa, 14 km S Peralta, Oviedo). On the other hand, *E. pyro* occurs in the uplands to 1922 m (Valle de Tetero, Constanza) on the Cordillera Central, 1708 m (Los Pinos) on the Sierra de Neiba, and 1617 m (Obléon, 5 km NE Los Arroyos) on the Massif de la Selle and its affiliates. The altitudinal records are fairly evenly spread between the 2 extremes.

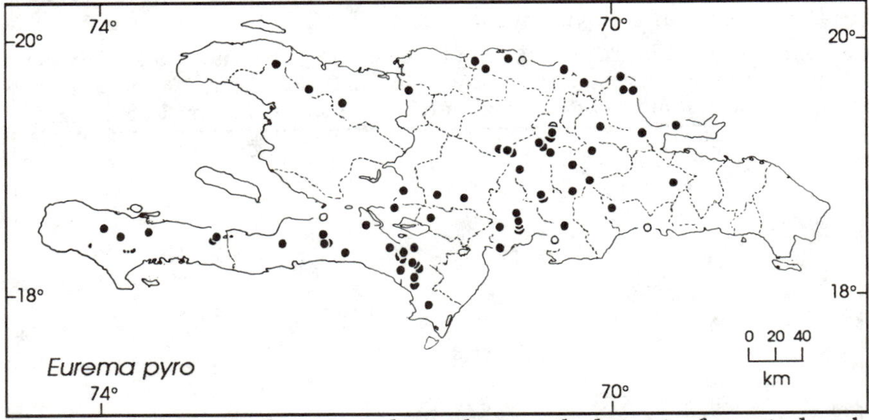

Eurema pyro is almost exclusively an inhabitant of mesic hardwood forests and pseudoforests. It is 1 of the few butterflies that one regularly encounters *within* these vegetational associations, as well as along paths and roads that penetrate through them. The few exceptions to the above habitats are Forêt des Pins (open pine forest), Gros Morne (open dry river valley), Boutilliers Road (open mountainside road), Obléon and Aceitillar (pine forest), Cruce de Ocoa (*Musa* grove), El Aguacate (transitional forest), Sierra Martín García, 305–458 m (xeric forest), 5 km NE Los Arroyos (pine forest), 0.6 km SE Los Arroyos (hilltop pasture), and Oviedo (xeric wooded ravine). The most unusual site for *E. pyro* is Piedra Blanca. This locality in 1980 was devoid of trees, and the *E. pyro* was taken in open roadside grasses. But prior to the passage of Hurricane David in 1979, there had been a fine mesic hardwood forest following a tumbling stream down the mountainside. In 1980, the stream was literally covered from bank to bank with huge boulders (the result of flooding during David), and the ravine forest had been totally destroyed. Even under these circumstances, *E. pyro* had persisted there, at least temporarily.

The months of greatest abundance are June (73) and July (77), with a sharp decline in August (20). December is represented by 11 specimens, October by 5, February by 7, May by 4, and January, March, April, September, and November each by 2. *Eurema pyro* apparently flies during the entire year but is univoltine in June-July. Times of collection were between 0830 and 1715 h, at temperatures between 21°C (5 km NE Los Arroyos) and 39°C (Gaspar Hernández).

Eurema pyro feeds on the flowers of *Melilotus alba* (Constanza), *Parthenium hysterophorus* (Vallejuelo), and *Ageratum conyzoides* (18 km NE Cabo Rojo).

Specimens: Haiti: Nord: 5.6 km SE Dondon, 336 m, 1; 3.5 km W Plaisance, 305 m, 1; *l'Artibonite:* 15.0 km N Gros Morne, Rivière Pendu, 1; *l'Ouest:* 5 km SE Fond Parisien, s.l., 1; Forêt des Pins, 1525 m, 1; 4 km NW Forêt des Pins, 1496 m, 1; Boutilliers Road, 732–915 m, 11; Boutilliers Road, 1.8–3.7 km W Kenscoff road, 793–885 m, 5 (1 MPM); 0.3 km N Obléon, 1586 m, 3; Peneau, 1.1 km S Furcy, 1464 m, 6; 0.6 km S Découzé, 671 m, 1; nr. Péredo, at river—570 m, 3 (FSM); *Sud:* 6.6 km SW Paillant, 793 m, 2; 6.7 km SW Paillant, 854 m, 7; 26.1 km N Cavaillon, 610 m, 5; 5.6 km N Camp Perrin, 275 m, 3; ravine bet. Pic Formon and Macaya, 1050 m, 1 (FSM); *República Dominicana: Dajabón:* 1.4 km SE El Pino, 183 m, 2; *Elías Piña:* 2 km NE Puesto Pirámide 204, 1586 m, 2; *Santiago Rodríguez:* 1 km SE La Mata, 2; *Puerto Plata:* 13 km SE Luperón, 214 m, 1; 0.6 km NE Estero Hondo, 1; 11 km N Cruce de Guayacanes, 275 m, 5; 9 km SE Sosúa, 15 m, 1; *La Vega:* Güaigüi, S La Vega, 336 m, 1; 10 km W Jayaco, 915 m, 6; Buena Vista, 11 km NE Jarabacoa, 640 m, 2; Jarabacoa, 530 m, 2; 5 km SE Jarabacoa, 595 m, 2; 6 km SSW Boca del Río, 1220 m, 1; *ca.* 3 km SW Boca del Río, 976 m, 2; 6 km SSE Constanza, 1403 m, 6; 44 km SE Constanza, 1922 m, 1; 10 km NW La Horma, 1496 m, 1; *Espaillat:* 2 km NW Gaspar Hernández, 16 m, 1; *Duarte:* 12 km SE San Francisco de Macorís, 2; *Santiago:* entrance of Valle de Tetero to Valle de Tetero, 1922–1342 m, 4; *María T. Sánchez:* 11 km NE Río San Juan, s.l., 2; 19 km SE Río San Juan, 92 m, 2; 6 km S Cabrera, s.l., 1; Cruce de Rincón, s.l., 1; *Samaná:* 13.2 km NE Sánchez, 92 m, 2; *Monte Plata:* 8 km NE Bayaguana, 3; *Monseñor Nouel:* Bonao, 153 m, 1; 6 km SE Maimón, 122 m, 2; 15 km SW Piedra Blanca, 534 m, 1; *Dist. Nac.:* 30 km NW Santo Domingo, 122 m, 9; *Azua:* 22 km NW Cruce de Ocoa, 61 m, 4; Tábara Abajo, 3; 2.5 km W, 6.6 km N Azua, 183 m, 1; 5 km S Peralta, 305 m, 4; 14 km S Peralta, 1; 18 km S Peralta, 122 m, 1; *San Juan:* 4 km E El Cercado, 702 m, 1; 9 km E Vallejuelo, 610 m, 1; *Baoruco:* 14 km N Neiba, 671 m, 1; *Independencia:* 21 km N Los Pinos, 1708 m, 2; 4–7 km NE El Aguacate, 519–824 m, 26; *Barahona:* west slope, Sierra Martín García, 305–610 m, 3; *Pedernales:* 18 km NE Cabo Rojo, 366 m, 1; 26 km NNE Cabo Rojo, 702 m, 1; 5 km SW El Aguacate, 1474 m, 1; 5 km NE Los Arroyos, 1617 m, 2; 0.6 km SE Los Arroyos, 1098 m, 1; Las Abejas, 11 km NW Aceitillar, 1220 m, 4; Las Abejas, 12 km NW Aceitillar, 1129 m, 21; 1 km N Aceitillar, 1281 m, 1; 1 km SE Banano, 43 m, 2; 17 km NW Oviedo, 183 m, 2.

15. *Eurema nicippe* Cramer, 1779

TL "Virginia."

FW males 20–27 mm, females 22–27 mm.

Eurema nicippe is widely distributed from North to Central America (Costa Rica) and in the Antilles occurs on: Cuba and the Isla de la Juventud (Bates, 1935a:127; Holland, 1916:498), where it is common; Puerto Rico (Comstock, 1944:525), whence there were only 2 records, but at least in the southwest *E. nicippe* is not uncommon (pers. observation); Jamaica (Brown and Heineman, 1972:283), where the butterflies are not uncommon but are local in distribution; the Bahama Islands (New Providence, Eleuthera, Great Inagua, Grand Bahama, Cat, Long, Acklin's, Andros [Rindge, 1952:5; Rindge, 1955:4; Clench, 1977a:273; Clench, 1977b:189]), where *E. nicippe* seems to be rather rare; and Hispaniola. On the latter island, Hall (1925:163) considered *E. nicippe* "not uncommon at low elevations" and noted its occurrence at Puerto Plata, Santo Domingo, and Port-au-Prince. Schwartz (1983a:47–48) reported 35 specimens from 22 Haitian localities and considered the species "common." Marión Heredia (1980d) reported *E. nicippe* from El Número-Azua.

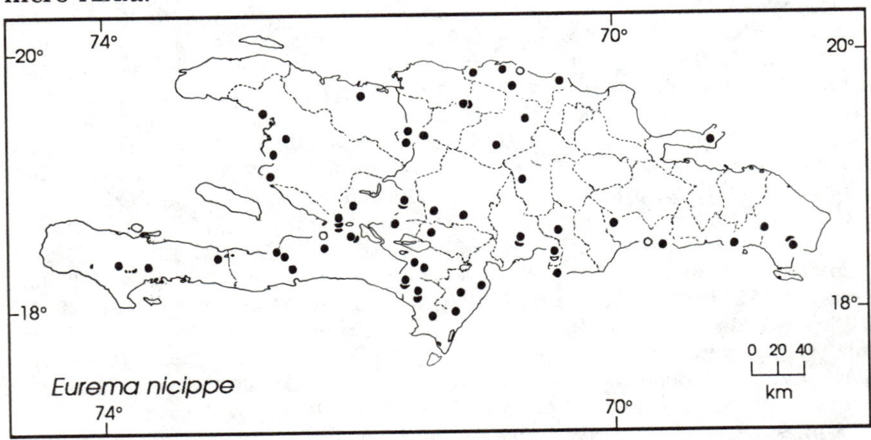

Eurema nicippe occurs throughout Hispaniola and is moderately abundant in both Haiti and the República Dominicana. The butterfly occurs in both xeric and mesic areas and seems to favor the former. We have taken *E. nicippe* in *Acacia* scrub and woods (Limonade, Colmini, Las Calderas, Azua, Vallejuelo, Oviedo), but we have also netted specimens in mesic wooded situations and pseudoforest (Camp Perrin, Paillant, Restauración, Las Galeras, Peralta, Los Pinos, Enriquillo). *Eurema nicippe* also frequents roadsides, especially those with flowers (Terre Rouge, Cavaillon, Béloc, La Romana, Mencía), and I have specimens from palm groves (Délugé, Estero Hondo), along a mangrove border (Grand-Goâve), springside woods in the Cul de Sac plain (Fond Parisien), an oasis (Ça Soleil), a *Musa* grove (Cruce de Ocoa), and mixed pine-hardwoods (8 km S Restauración). Open fields are likewise visited by *E. nicippe* (Jacmel, Croix des Bouquets, Luperón, Santiago, Constanza, 0.5 km W Boca de Yuma). There seems to be no preference for any of the above habitats; likewise, in none of them does the collector find an abundance of *E. nicippe*. One usually sees 1 or 2 of these butterflies, rarely more, at a locality.

The elevational distribution is from sea level (Colmini, Délugé, Fond Parisien, Grand-Goâve, Croix des Bouquets, Punta Caucedo, Las Calderas) to 1708 m (Los Pinos) in the Sierra de Neiba, 1098 m (Constanza) in the Cordillera Central, and 854 m (Boutilliers Road) on the Massif de la Selle front ranges (Morne l'Hôpital). The high record from Los Pinos is exceptional; the specimen from there is the only individual from above 1220 m. In fact, most (78%) of the localities for *E. nicippe* are from elevations below 610 m, suggesting that this species is a butterfly of low to moderate elevations.

Most *E. nicippe* were collected in July (48), June (39), and August (31). There are 16 specimens from May, 6 each from April and December, and single specimens from March, September, and October. Collection times were between 0830 and 1800 h, at temperatures between 24°C (Comendador) and 42°C (Mencía).

We have encountered *E. nicippe* foraging on *Bidens pilosa* (Los Quemados, 19 km NE Cabo Rojo), *Lantana reticulata* (Guananico), *Antigonon leptopus* (Azua, twice), *Ageratum conyzoides* (Vallejuelo, twice), *Croton barahonensis* (Vallejuelo), and *Cordia exarata* (La Romana). Along with other small pierids, a few *E. nicippe* were drinking from moist mud in a ditch (Luperón).

Copulating pairs were taken on 16.viii (Punta Caucedo, s.l., 1030–1300 h) and 5.viii (Vallejuelo, 610 m, 1400 h, 35°C).

Specimens: Haiti: Nord: 3.5 km E Limonade, s.l., 1; *l'Artibonite:* 12.2 km W Ça Soleil, 1; 13 km ESE Pont Gaugin, s.l., 1; Colmini, 6.4 km W Terre Noire, s.l., 2; Délugé, s.l., 2; *l'Ouest:* 19.7 km SE Mirebalais, 183 m, 2; 1.1 km N Terre Rouge, 244 m, 1; 1.3 km S Terre Rouge, 458 m, 1; 2.9–8.5 km S Terre Rouge, 122–488 m, 1; 18.1 km SE Croix des Bouquets, s.l., 1; 5 km NW Fond Parisien, 1; 3.0 km SE Fond Parisien, s.l., 1; Boutilliers Road, 732–854 m, 3 (1 FSM); 1.3 km N Béloc, 702 m, 3; 7.7 km N Jacmel, 92 m, 2; 6.7 km E Grand-Goâve, s.l., 2; *Sud:* 6.7 km SW Paillant, 763 m, 2; 7.8 km N Cavaillon, 31 m, 2; 4.8 km N Camp Perrin, 244 m, 2; 5.6 km N Camp Perrin, 275 m, 1; *República Dominicana: Dajabón:* Los Cerezos, 12 km NW Río Limpio, 580 m, 1; 7 km N Restauración, 671 m, 1; 8 km S Restauración, 610 m, 1; *Elías Piña:*

14 km S Comendador, 976 m, 1; 15 km S Comendador, 976 m, 1; *Valverde:* Río Guarabo, 3 km W Los Quemados, 122 m, 1; *Santiago Rodríguez:* 3 km W Los Quemados, 183 m, 4; *Puerto Plata:* 8 km W Luperón, 1; 0.6 km NE Estero Hondo, 2; 10 km W Guananico, 259 m, 1; 9 km SE Sosúa, 15 m, 1; *Santiago:* 7 km SW Santiago, 12; Río Bao, 8 km SE Montones Abajo, 488 m, 1; *La Vega:* 1 km S Constanza, 1098 m, 1; *Samaná:* 2.8 km S Las Galeras, 61 m, 1; *La Altagracia:* 0.5 km W Boca de Yuma, 3; 2–3 km W Boca de Yuma, 1; 16 km NE La Romana, 61 m, 3; *La Romana:* Río Cumayasa, 13.5 km W La Romana, 31 m, 1; *Dist. Nac.:* Punta Caucedo, 2 km W, 2 km S Andrés, s.l., 10; 30 km NW Santo Domingo, 122 m, 1; *Peravia:* Las Calderas, s.l., 1; *Azua:* 22 km NW Cruce de Ocoa, 61 m, 3; 25 km NE Azua, 92 m, 3; 5 km S Peralta, 305 m, 10; 2.4 km W, 6.6 km N Azua, 183 m, 4; *San Juan:* 4 km E El Cercado, 702 m, 1; 9 km E Vallejuelo, 610 m, 24; *Baoruco:* 11 km N Neiba, 519 m, 4; *Independencia:* 21 km N Los Pinos, 1708 m, 1; 4–7 km NE El Aguacate, 519–824 m, 5; 0.6 km NW Puerto Escondido, 3; *Barahona:* Polo, 702 m, 1; 5 km SE, 3 km W Barahona, 183–397 m, 1; 9 km NW Enriquillo, 671 m, 1; *Pedernales:* Mencía, 397 m, 3; 2 km SW Mencía, 336 m, 1; 19 km NE Cabo Rojo, 427 m, 1; 24.5 km NE Cabo Rojo, 656 m, 1; 17 km NW Oviedo, 183 m, 3.

16. *Eurema nicippiformis* Munroe, 1947

TL ravine of Pétionville, *ca.* 1600 ft., Dépt. de l'Ouest, Haiti.

FW males 20–22 mm, females 20–26 mm.

Eurema nicippiformis was named from a series of 11 individuals from scattered localities in Haiti and Prov. de Monte Cristi in the República Dominicana. Brown and Heineman (1972:282), in their discussion of *E. nicippe,* stated that, if one accepts the genus *Abacis* Hübner (as distinct from *Eurema* Hübner), then *nicippe* is the "lone occupant" of *Abacis.* Also, in their table of Antillean generic distributions (p. 62), they did not mention *E. nicippiformis.* These comments and actions suggest that they were not convinced that *E. nicippiformis* was a recognizable entity. Riley (1975:130) recognized *E. nicippiformis* (as did Clench, since he identified some of our 1977 collection as this species).

Eurema nicippiformis is distinguished (in males) from *E. nicippe* in that the former has the dark marginal hw edge narrow and lacking a dark "tooth" from that band into hw M2-M3. Females are much less easily determined; Riley (1975:130) noted that female *E. nicippiformis* have the upfw veins scaled with yellow (not orange) and lack black scales intruding into the fw orange discal area along Cu1 and Cu2. The result of the latter character is that the upfw black margin is more smooth along its discal edge in *E. nicippiformis* than in *E. nicippe.*

Most of these differentiating characters are extremely difficult to interpret when one has a long series of both sexes of both species. Most reliable is the width of the hw margin, which is distinctly narrower in *E. nicippiformis* (3 mm) than in *E. nicippe* (5 mm). In females, the lack of black scales along the 2 fw veins is the best trait for distinguishing members of that sex. But inevitably one faces those problem specimens that do not fall clearly into one or the other category. Most unreliable is the hw black marginal tooth in males; some *E. nicippe* have the tooth well-developed and obvious, and some *E. nicippiformis* lack the tooth almost completely. But there are some intermediates that must be judged on other characters. Still, despite all these problems, there do seem to be 2 distinct biological entities (species) involved.

Like *E. nicippe, E. nicippiformis* has a broad ecological tolerance; I have specimens from deciduous woods (Port-de-Paix), *caféières* (Mirebalais, Paillant), *Acacia* scrub (Colmini, Croix des Bouquets, Monte Cristi, Santiago, Vallejuelo, Azua, Las Calderas, Oviedo), a beachside area with flowers (Délugé), and an open mountainside (Boutilliers Road). The specimen from Île à Cabrit is from a tiny offshore islet in the Golfe de la Gonâve.

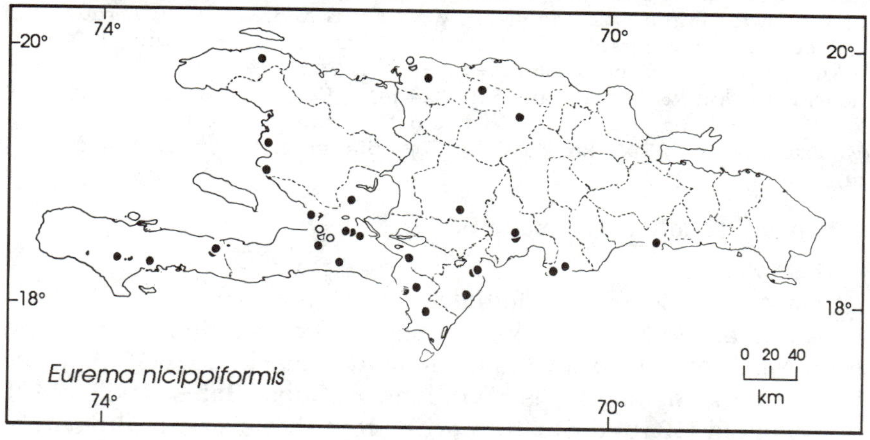

Most specimens were taken in July (15), with between 7 and 1 specimens in February, March, April, May, June, August, October, December, and January. Times of collection were between 0930 and 1500 h, at temperatures between 28°C and 38°C (both Vallejuelo).

Elevations are between sea level (Délugé, Croix des Bouquets, Fond Parisien, Las Calderas, Sombrero, Île à Cabrit) and 854 m (Boutilliers Road). Like *E. nicippe*, most localities (77%) for *E. nicippiformis* are from elevations at or below 610 m, with only 4 (23%) above 610 m. *Eurema nicippe* and *E. nicippiformis* have been taken syntopically at 15 localities: Colmini, Délugé, Croix de Bouquets, Fond Parisien, 6.7 km SW Paillant, Santiago, Punta Caucedo, Las Calderas, Peralta, Vallejuelo, Oviedo, El Aguacate, 24.5 km N Cabo Rojo, Mencía). At all of these, *E. nicippiformis* is represented by fewer or only about as many specimens as *E. nicippe.*

We have taken *E. nicippiformis* feeding on *Antigonon leptopus* on 4 occasions (Croix des Bouquets, Cruce de Guayacanes, Sombrero, Azua) and at 2 localities have taken specimens drinking from mud on unpaved roads (Barahona, Mencía). At Villa Vásquez, we took 1 *E. nicippiformis* feeding on a tall (1 m), vivid yellow introduced composite being grown in *Acacia* scrub.

Specimens: Haiti: Nord-Ouest: 7.5 km SE Port-de-Paix, 1; *l'Artibonite:* Colmini, 6.4 km W Terre Noire, s.l., 1; Délugé, s.l., 1; *l'Ouest:* 19.7 km SE Mirebalais, 183 m, 2; 18.1 km SE Croix des Bouquets, s.l., 1; 2 km NW Fond Parisien, 2; 3.0 km SE Fond Parisien, s.l., 1; Boutilliers Road, 732–854 m, 2; nr. Péredo, at river, 1 (FSM); *Sud:* 6.6 km SW Paillant, 763 m, 1; 6.7 km SW Paillant, 763 m, 1; 4.5 km E Cavaillon, 31 m, 1; Lévy, 1; *Île à Cabrit:* s.l., 1; *República Dominicana: Monte Cristi:* 7 km NW Villa Vásquez, 1; *Valverde:* 4 km N Cruce de Guayacanes, 198 m, 1; *Santiago:* 7 km SW Santiago, 214 m, 3; *Dist. Nac.:* Punta Caucedo, 2 km W, 2 km S Andrés, s.l., 2; *Peravia:* Las Calderas, s.l., 2; Sombrero, s.l., 1; *Azua:* 2.5 km W, 6.6 km N Azua, 183 m, 1; 5 km S Peralta, 305 m, 4; *San Juan:* 9 km E Vallejuelo, 610 m, 2; *Independencia:* 4–7 km NE El Aguacate, 519–824 m, 1; *Barahona:* Barahona, s.l., 1; 2 km SW Barahona, 122 m, 1; 8–10 km NW Paraíso, 1 (MPM); *Pedernales:* Mencía, 397 m, 1; 24.5 km NE Cabo Rojo, 656 m, 2; 17 km NW Oviedo, 183 m, 2.

17. *Nathalis iole* Boisduval, 1836

TL "México."

FW males 12–16 mm, females 12–16 mm.

Nathalis iole is widely distributed on the continental mainland from North America south to Guatemala (Clench, 1976:124). In the West Indies, the species is abundant on Cuba (Bates, 1935a:142), but Holland (1916) did not report it from the Isla de la Juventud. Brown and Heineman (1972:271–72) reported *N. iole* from many localities throughout Jamaica. In the Bahamas, *N. iole* occurs on 5 northern islands (Grand Bahama, North Bimini, New Providence, Eleuthera, Andros; Clench, 1976:122) but appears to be a recent (between 1930 and 1945) adventive there (on New Providence). Askew (1980:128) reported the first *N. iole* from the Cayman Islands; a specimen (vagrant?) was taken in 1975 on Little Cayman.

Hall (1925:164) stated that on Hispaniola *N. iole* was "at low elevations only." Brown and Heineman (1972:62) justifiably doubted this statement, apparently, since in their table of Antillean distributions, they have a question mark under Hispaniola. Schwartz

(1983a:48) verified the occurrence of *N. iole* on Hispaniola, listing 21 specimens from 9 Haitian localities. Riley (1975:130) paraphrased Hall's comment and stated that on Hispaniola, *N. iole* is "at lower levels." Interestingly, Hall's (1925:161–62) itinerary did not take him to localities in either Haiti or the República Dominicana whence we have more recently gotten specimens, so his statement concerning *N. iole* is indeed equivocal.

In both Haiti and the República Dominicana, *N. iole* is a local butterfly, almost completely confined to grassy fields, roadsides, and clearings; we took 1 specimen along a path in dense forest (15 km S Comendador), but the path led to a very weedy roadside, and doubtless the butterfly was only temporarily inside the forest. At

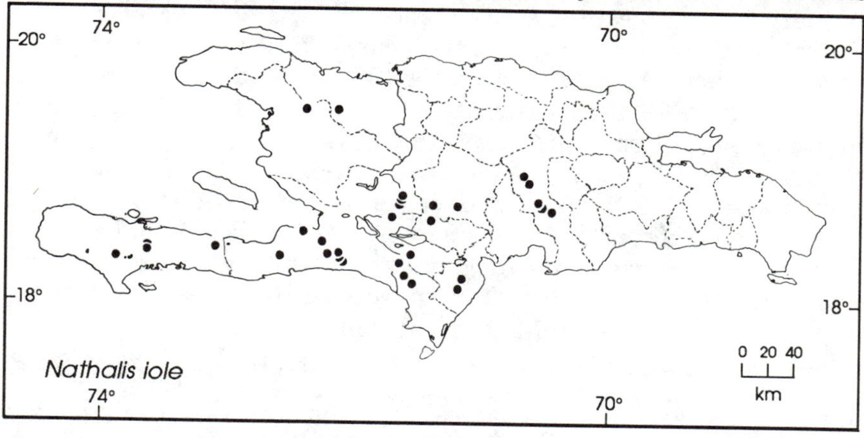

Polo, one specimen was taken in a *cafetal.* Favorite areas also include open weedy montane roads (Boutilliers Road, La Horma) and cornfields (Grand-Goâve, Los Arroyos). One *N. iole* was also taken in a clearing within cut-over woods (El Cercado) and another in pine forest (Peneau). At 1 km S Constanza, in the large grassy field behind the Hotel Nueva Suiza, there is a very local "colony" of *N. iole* from which we have collected specimens from 1980 to 1986. The small butterflies are restricted to only about 50 m^2 of the field; the grasses and weeds there are no different nor are there more flowers present than elsewhere in the very large expanse of the field, and why, over the span of 7 years, *N. iole* remains restricted to this 1 small portion of the field is unknown. The Constanza experience emphasizes the situation with *N. iole* elsewhere: where *N. iole* occurs on Hispaniola, it exists in small local "colonies" and persists year after year. In other areas, the species is uncommon.

The elevational distribution is from sea level (Grand-Goâve) to

2100 m (Morne la Visite). There are only 2 localities below 305 m (Grand-Goâve, Lévy), both Haitian; on the other hand, most localities are at or above 600 m, with 6 (Morne la Visite, Scierie, Puesto Pirámide 204, 18 km SE Constanza, Los Pinos, Los Arroyos) above 1525 m. Most records are between 625 and 1220 m. *Nathalis iole* occurs in the uplands of the Massif de la Selle (including the Montagne Noire), the Massif de la Hotte (Paillant, Cavaillon), the Massif du Nord, (Dondon, Carrefour Marmelade), the Sierra de Neiba (Los Pinos, Vallejuelo, El Veinte, Puesto Pirámide 204—both ranges), the Cordillera Central, and the Sierra de Baoruco (Polo).

Most specimens have been taken in July (41), with 34 in June and 7 in February. September, October, August, March, April, and January are represented by 6–1 specimens. The species is apparently on the wing throughout the year, with a midsummer peak. Times of collection were between 0840 and 1715 h, and temperatures between 22°C (Scierie) and 37°C (La Horma). *Nathalis iole* often flies on overcast and even rainy days (Constanza, Vallejuelo). We saw no evidence for *N. iole* retiring after 1000 h, as Brown and Heineman (1972:271) suggested for Jamaican individuals.

Although the precise areas where *N. iole* occurs may have abundant flowers (*Stachytarpheta jamaicensis, Bidens pilosa, Lantana ovatifolia*, and many others), we have seen these pierids feeding only once, on *Croton barahonensis* at Vallejuelo.

Specimens: Haiti: Nord: 1.8 km S Dondon, 366 m, 1; *l'Artibonite:* 1.6 km E Carrefour Marmelade, 854 m, 1; *l'Ouest:* Boutilliers Road, 915 m, 5; Boutilliers Road, 1.8–2.1 km W Kenscoff road, 793–885 m, 1; Peneau, 1.6 km SW Furcy, 1464 m, 1; 5.4 km S Découzé, 397 m, 4; Morne la Visite, 2100 m, 5 (FSM); 200 m NW Scierie, 1952 m, 4 (FSM); nr. Péredo, 600 m, 2 (FSM); just W Grand-Goâve, s.l., 1; *Sud:* 3 km SW Paillant, 671 m, 3; 16.3 km N Cavaillon, 488 m, 3; 19.7 km N Cavaillon, 595 m, 2; Lévy, 1; *República Dominicana: Elías Piña:* 14 km S Comendador, 976 m, 3; 15 km S Comendador, 976 m, 2; 2 km NE Puesto Pirámide 204, 1586 m, 1; *La Vega:* 1 km S Constanza, 1098 m, 34: 10 km SE Constanza, 1586 m, 1; 2.7 km W La Horma, 2; 10 km NW La Horma, 1496 m, 1; *Peravia:* 6 km W La Horma, 1159 m, 4; *San Juan:* 4 km E El Cercado, 702 m, 1; 9 km E Vallejuelo, 610 m, 1; *Baoruco:* 1 km NW El Veinte, 1220 m, 1; *Independencia:* 23 km N Los Pinos, 1739 m, 1; 4–7 km NE El Aguacate, 519 m, 5; *Barahona:* Polo, 702 m, 1; 8 km NNE Polo, 793 m, 3; *Pedernales:* 3 km W Aguas Negras, 519 m, 1; 5 km N Los Arroyos, 1617 m, 1; 26 km NE Cabo Rojo, 732 m, 1.

18. *Kricogonia lyside* Godart, 1819

TL not stated; designated as Haiti by Riley (1975:131).

FW males 21–27 mm, females 22–30 mm.

The number of species included under *Kricogonia lyside*—1 or 2—is a matter of some debate. The problem hinges on the rather extreme variability in Antillean (and elsewhere) *Kricogonia*. Comstock (1944:515–18) seemed convinced that there were 2 distinct species, *K. lyside* and *K. castalia* Fabricius, in the West Indies. The most obvious difference between these 2 species is that in *K. lyside*, there is an unhw line of irregularly placed and enlarged pale scales that crosses the middle of the cell, sometimes extending to the margin. These scales are yellowish and contrast with the unhw shiny green color. This line of scales is absent in *K. castalia*, and the unhw is nonshiny ochre. In male *K. castalia*, there is a short black bar from the distal end of the costa to below M1; this bar is usually well shown in male *K. castalia*, but it may be obsolescent or even absent (rarely). In male *K. lyside*, the black bar is present but is narrower (1 mm vs. 1–1.5 mm in *K. castalia*) and tends strongly toward obsolescence and absence. There are no differences in male genitalia.

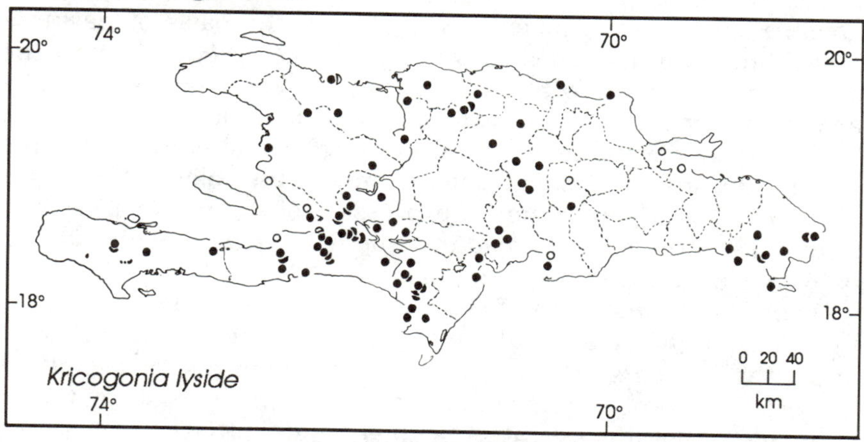

Brown and Heineman (1972:296–97) thoroughly reviewed the entire problem and maintained these 2 taxa as distinct species. They mentioned but disregarded life history evidence, based on Jamaican specimens, suggesting that only 1 species is involved. Riley (1975:131) considered all individuals *K. lyside*. He also stated that *castalia* is not applicable to *Kricogonia*, since it is the prior name for the Jamaican subspecies of *A. drusilla*. Apparently, if one wishes to recognize 2 "kinds" of *Kricogonia* nomenclatorially, the correct name for those that lack a unhw line of raised scales is *terissa* Lucas (Clench, *in litt.*).

The problem of "How many species?" is not going to be solved in the laboratory by examination of spread specimens. In my long series from Hispaniola, there are obviously 2 entities. But, as is very often the case, one examines some individuals that bridge the gap between these 2 groups and that cannot be assigned with complete confidence to either of them. It would seem that the raised line of enlarged scales in contrast to a shiny green unhw would be easily determined by observation. But such is not always the case; there are specimens on which the observer is uncertain of both the line of scales and the unhw color—greenish ochre or ochreous green are examples of the conditions one encounters in the latter trait. Even the uphw black bar in males is not a constant feature of that sex in either species (narrow and obsolete in *K. lyside*, broad and almost always present in *K. terissa*).

Examination of 31 Hispaniolan males, selected by the presence of at least some indication of the uphw bar, shows the following. Twenty-seven males are *K. terissa*, in that they have no line of raised scales on the unhw, and the unhw is more ochre than green. Four are assignable to *K. lyside* on the basis of having a raised line of unhw scales on a shiny greenish ground. But of the 27 *K. terissa*, the uphw black bar is only barely indicated, often by a very narrow bar or by its costal end only, in 7 males (26%). These "aberrant" *K. terissa* are identical in up color and pattern with the 4 *K. lyside*, and the 2 samples differ only in the color of the unhw. Thus, there is a continuum of expression of the uphw black bar, from well-expressed and broad in some *K. terissa* to much reduced or even absent in some *K. terissa* and all *K. lyside*.

Females are just as confusing, if not more so. The variation in up coloration of females of both "species" is such that the amount of overlap prevents assignment of specimens to one or the other. The color difference (yellow to orange-yellow) at the bases of the fw is so subtle that it is worthless in differentiating the 2 "species."

Thus, the evidence from Hispaniolan specimens suggests that these 2 entities (*lyside* and *terissa*) are but manifestations of the same species. The life history and male genitalia evidence likewise suggests the same situation. Accordingly, I consider all Hispaniolan *Kricogonia* as *K. lyside*.

Hall (1925:164) regarded *K. terissa* as common at low elevations; he noted that most males had the black spot on hind wings very heavy. He reported 1 female as the yellow ab. *unicolor* and explicitly stated that *lyside* was not represented among his specimens. Cucurullo (1959:10) reported both *K. castalia* and *K. lyside* without comment, and Marión Heredia (1974:2) likewise recorded these same 2 "species." Marión Heredia (1980d) noted the occurrence of *K. lyside* and *K. lyside* forma *unicolor*, from El Número-Azua. Schwartz (1983a:49) reported 120 specimens from 32 Haitian localities. He stated that "The species is polychromatic, and the form with the wings white and a yellow basal suffusion is the most common with that with the black costal dash and the all-yellow forms much less abundant." Even with much more material, the relative frequency of the 3 categories noted is the same; males are much less common than females, and the all-yellow females are less common than those with a basal fw yellow to yellow-orange suffusion.

Kricogonia lyside is widespread on Hispaniola, from the distal Tiburon Peninsula in Haiti to the eastern end of the island (Punta Cana), and from the northwest (Cormier Plage) in Haiti to the southeast (La Romana) in the República Dominicana. These butterflies are primarily inhabitants of xeric areas, including the Cul de Sac–Valle de Neiba plain. But they also occur in and about *caféières* and *cafetales* (Dondon, Découzé, Paillant, Jayaco, Piedra Blanca), mesic forest (Peralta, Las Abejas), hotel gardens (Pétion-ville), pinewoods (Forêt des Pins, Furcy, Aceitillar), and mixed pine-hardwoods (Restauración, 6 km SSE Constanza). But most specimens are from open fields (3.7 km S Kenscoff), open mountainsides (Boutilliers Road), and roadsides (many localities). At Yayas de Viajama, *K. lyside* was very abundant (4.viii.1982) and was virtually the only moderately sized butterfly on the wing; the site was in *Acacia* scrub. A similar irruption of these butterflies occurred between Cabral and 9 km SW Cabral (sea level to 305 m), Prov. de Barahona, on 6.viii.1985, where thousands were observed swirling along the road and feeding on *Melochia nodiflora*, a few on *Lantana ovatifolia*, and on an unidentified white-flowered shrub.

The elevational distribution is from sea level (Cormier Plage, Ça Soleil, Colmini, Jacmel, Île à Cabrit, Croix des Bouquets, Fond Parisien, Punta Cana, Playa Bayahibe, Palmar de Ocoa, La Descubierta, Cabo Rojo, Mano Juan, Isla Catalina) to 1708 m (Los Pinos) on the Sierra de Neiba, 1647 on the Massif de la Selle front ranges, 1586 m (Constanza) in the Cordillera Central, and 1373 m (Aceitillar) on the Sierra de Baoruco. Although *K. lyside* reaches high elevations, it is primarily a low- to moderate-elevation butterfly (610 m or less). *Kricogonia lyside* is not necessarily uncommon at high elevations (Kenscoff, for example, where a long series was taken from an open mountainside field with many cultivated flowers), and these high-elevation records do not stand alone.

Times of collection were between 0905 and 1745 h at temperatures between 23°C (Las Abejas) and 37°C (Boca de Yuma).

Kricogonia lyside appears to be bivoltine. Most specimens have been taken in July (143), with June represented by 37 and August by 28. There are 10 specimens from May, 2 from October, 4 from December, 3 from April, 2 from March, 1 from February, with January represented by 25. There thus seem to be 2 eclosion peaks —midsummer (June-July) and midwinter (January).

Kricogonia lyside has been taken feeding on *Hibiscus rosasinensis* (Thomonde), *Cordia haitiensis* (Terre Rouge—2 localities), *Ixora* sp. (3.8 km N Terre Rouge), and flying about a *Euphorbia lactea* hedge, although no flowers were in evidence. These are all Haitian observations. In the República Dominicana, *Kricogonia lyside* has been seen taking nectar from *Antigonon leptopus* (Villa Vásquez—2 occasions, and Cruce de Guayacanes), *Ixora* sp. (Boca de Yuma), *Tournefortia hirsutissima* (6 km SSE Constanza), *Lantana reticulata* (Isla Catalina), *Cordia integrifolia* (Zamba), *Stachytarpheta jamaicensis* (Monteada Nueva), *Ageratum conyzoides* (18 km NE Cabo Rojo), *Cordia curassavica* (1 km N Aceitillar), and *Antigonon leptopus* and *Jacaranda acutifolia* (Santiago).

Schwartz (1983a:49) noted the extreme abundance of *K. lyside* at Boutilliers Road in June and July, where this species is the most abundant lepidopteran. A visit to Boutilliers Road in iv.1982 by Gali and myself yielded not even the sighting of 1 *K. lyside*.

These are the first records of *K. lyside* from Isla Saona and Isla Catalina; the species has been previously reported from tiny xeric Île à Cabrit in the Golfe de la Gonâve, although there are no specimens as yet from Île de la Gonâve itself. The periphery of Gonâve is extremely xeric and appears eminently suitable for *K. lyside*.

Specimens: Haiti: Nord: Cormier Plage, s.l., 2; 1.8 km S Dondon, 366 m, 1; *l'Artibonite:* 1.6 km E Carrefour Marmelade, 854 m, 3; 12.2 km W Ça Soleil, s.l., 2; Colmini, 6.4 km W Terre Rouge, s.l., 1; 4 km N Thomonde, 2; *l'Ouest:* 1.6 km N Saut d'Eau, 183 m, 1; 19.7 km SE Mirebalais, 183 m, 2; 20 km S Mirebalais, 580 m, 3; 6.2 km E Lascahobas, 275 m, 2; betw. Terre Rouge and 2.1 km N Terre Rouge, 397–534 m, 2; 1.9–8.5 km S Terre Rouge, 122–488 m, 2; 13.1 km SE Croix des Bouquets, s.l., 2; 19.8 km SE Croix des Bouquets, s.l., 1; 5 km NW Fond Parisien, 1; 2 km NW Fond Parisien, 1; 2 km SE Fond Parisien, s.l., 1; Forêt des Pins, 1373–1525 m, 7; Pétionville, 458 m, 1; Boutilliers Road, 732–915 m, 35; Boutilliers Road, 1.8–2.1 km W Kenscoff road, 763–885 m, 4; 3.7 km S Kenscoff, 1647 m, 19; 5.8 km S Kenscoff, 1586 m, 2; 0.3 km N Obléon, 1617 m, 1; Peneau, 1.1–1.6 km S Furcy, 1464 m, 2; Ravine Roseau, 4 km SW Dufort, 1; 0.6 km S Découzé, 397 m, 2; 1.3 km N Béloc, 702 m, 3; 8.3 km NW Jacmel, 183 m, 1; 13.6 km E Jacmel, s.l., 1; *Sud:* 6.7 km SW Paillant, 763–793 m, 5; 16.3 km N Cavaillon, 488 m, 1; 4.5 km E Cavaillon, 31 m, 1; 4.8 km N Camp Perrin, 244 m, 1; 5.6 km N Camp Perrin, 275 m, 6; *Île à Cabrit:* 1; *República Dominicana: Monte Cristi:* 4 km NW Villa Vásquez, 61 m, 5; *Dajabón:* 0.5 km N Cañongo, 31 m, 1; 8 km S Restauración, 610 m, 1; *Valverde:* 12 km SW Mao, 244 m, 1; 4 km N Cruce de Guayacanes, 198 m, 4; *Santiago Rodríguez:* 4.8 km S Zamba, 183 m, 1; 3 km W Los Quemados, 183 m, 2; *Santiago:* Río Bao, 8 km SW Montones Abajo, 488 m, 1; 7

km SW Santiago, 214 m, 4; *Puerto Plata:* 9 km SE Sosúa, 15 m, 1; *La Vega:* La Palma, 19 km W Jayaco, 1007 m, 3; La Ciénaga, 915 m, 1; 6 km SSE Constanza, 1403 m, 1; 18 km SE Constanza, 1586 m, 7; *María T. Sánchez:* Río San Juan, s.l., 1; *La Altagracia:* Punta Cana, s.l., 2; 6 km W Punta Cana, s.l., 1; 0.5–3.5 km W Boca de Yuma, 1; 1 km N Playa Bayahibe, s.l., 5; 2.5 km SE Playa Bayahibe, s.l., 3; 16 km NE La Romana, 61 m, 6; *La Romana:* Río Cumayasa, 13.5 km W La Romana, 3; *Monseñor Nouel:* 14 km SW Piedra Blanca, 427 m, 1; *Azua:* 1 km E Palmar de Ocoa, s.l., 1; Tábara Abajo, 5; 5 km S Peralta, 305 m, 6; 2 km W Yayas de Viajama, 366 m, 2; *Independencia:* 21 km N Los Pinos, 1708 m, 2; 4 km NW Tierra Nueva, s.l., 1; 3.3 km E La Descubierta, s.l., 1; 4–7 km NE El Aguacate, 519–732 m, 1; *Barahona:* 8 km ESE Canoa, 3; Barahona, s.l., 1; *Pedernales:* Cabo Rojo, s.l., 2; 3 km NE Cabo Rojo, s.l., 1; 5 km NE Cabo Rojo, s.l., 11; 18 km NE Cabo Rojo, 366 m, 1; 21 km NE Cabo Rojo, 488 m, 1; 23 km NE Cabo Rojo, 488 m, 1; 26 km NE Cabo Rojo, 732 m, 2; Las Abejas, 11 km NE Aceitillar, 1220 m, 1; Las Abejas, 12 km NW Aceitillar, 1129 m, 6; 1 km SE Banano, 183 m, 1; 17 km NE Oviedo, 183 m, 1; *Isla Saona:* 1–2.5 km N Mano Juan, s.l., 8 (1 MPM); *Isla Catalina,* 3.

19. *Zerene cesonia cynops* Butler, 1873

TL Haiti.

FW males 24–33 mm, females 27–33 mm.

Zerene cesonia Stoll occurs in the Antilles as 2 subspecies: *Z. c. cesonia* on Cuba (Bates, 1935a:141–42) where it is apparently uncommon, and *Z. c. cynops* on Hispaniola. Hall (1925:164) recorded only 1 specimen from La Cumbre, Prov. de Santiago, República Dominicana, and “others seen.” However Schwartz (1983a:49) reported 55 specimens from 11 Haitian localities.

Zerene c. cynops is not uncommon on Hispaniola, as the Haitian numbers suggest. The species is widely distributed geographically, although there are no records from the Tiburon Peninsula in Haiti nor from much of the República Dominicana, notably the Península de Samaná. The aptly named “Dog Face” occurs from sea level (Ça Soleil, Fond Parisien) to 1891 m (Puesto Pirámide 204) on the Sierra de Neiba. Despite this broad altitudinal range, *Z. c. cynops* is most often encountered at moderate elevations (305 –1525 m), with only 7 localities (Les Poteaux, Ça Soleil, Fond Parisien, Copey, Los Quemados, Azua, Barahona) below 305 m and 4 sites (3.7 and 5.8 km S Kenscoff, 10 km SE Constanza, Puesto Pirámide 204) above 1525 m.

Habitats vary from low- to moderate-elevation *Acacia* scrub and xeric forest (Les Poteaux, Terre Rouge, Fond Parisien, Los Quemados, Azua, Vallejuelo, Barahona) to upland mesic hardwood forest (Loma Leonor, Neiba, 4 km NE El Aguacate, Las Abejas); mixed pine-hardwoods (Restauración, 6 km SSE Constanza), pine forests

(10 km SE Constanza), an oasis (Ça Soleil), and especially open fields and mountainsides (Boutilliers Road, Copey, Mirebalais, 12 km NE Constanza) are also inhabited by *Z. c. cynops*.

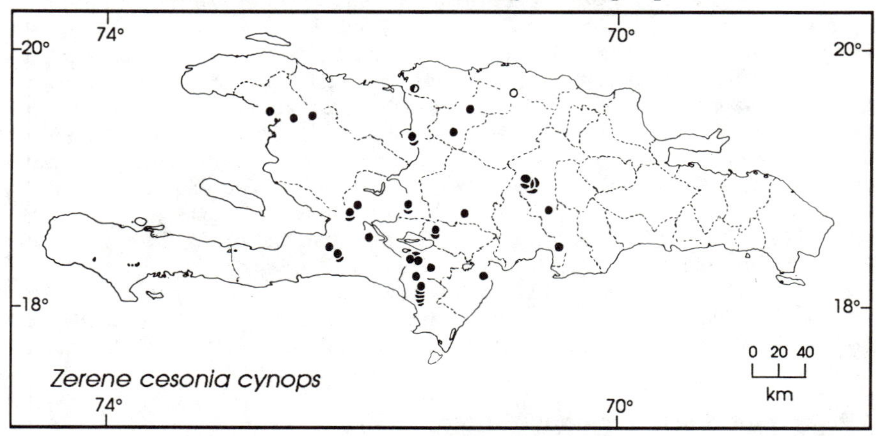

Most specimens (115) have been taken in July, with 49 in August and 14 in June. May is represented by 4, December by 3, October by 2, and September by 1. The major period of eclosion of *Z. c. cynops* is late summer. The species is considered multivoltine (Riley, 1975:132), but there is no evidence of this for *Z. c. cynops*. In summer, *Z. c. cynops* often is very common, but in fall-winter one rarely sees an indivudal. We saw none in March-April.

Times of collection were between 0830 and 1630 h at temperatures of 23°C (Puesto Pirámide 204) and 38°C (Loma Leonor). *Zerene c. cynops* has been taken feeding on *Cordia* sp. and *Ixora* sp. (3.8 km N Terre Rouge), *Daucus* sp. (Boutilliers Road), *Bidens pilosa* (Puesto Pirámide 204, 11 km N Neiba, Los Quemados), *Croton barahonensis* (Vallejuelo), *Ageratum conyzoides* (Vallejuelo), and *Tournefortia hirsutissima* (6 km SSE Constanza). We have also taken *Z. c. cynops* drinking on mud in aggregations 4 times (Loma Leonor, 1 km NE El Aguacate, 11 km N Neiba, Cabo Rojo). At the first of these localities, *Z. c. cynops* was accompanied by numbers of *Rh. t. watsoni* along the edge of the Río Toma. At Neiba, *Z. c. cynops* was drinking from the sandy mud at a river's edge in the company of other large pierids.

Specimens: Haiti: l'Artibonite: 1.6 km E Carrefour Marmelade, 854 m, 3; 4.6 km E Les Poteaux, 183 m, 1; 12.2 km W Ça Soleil, s.l., 1; *l'Ouest:* 20 km S Mirebalais, 580 m, 1; 3.8 km N Terre Rouge, 534 m, 4; 2.9 km S Terre Rouge, 488 m, 2; 2.9–8.5 km S Terre Rouge, 122–488 m, 1; 2 km SE Fond Parisien, s.l., 1; Boutilliers Road, 732–915 m, 30 (1 FSM); Boutilliers Road, 1.8–2.1 km

W Kenscoff road, 793–885 m, 7; 3.7 km S Kenscoff, 1647 m, 5; 5.8 km S Kenscoff, 1586 m, 1; *República Dominicana: Dajabón:* Cañada Tirolís, just S Villa Anacaona, 458 m, 1; 4 km S Restauración, 580 m, 1; *Elías Piña:* 2 km NE Puesto Pirámide 204, 1586 m, 2; 1 km SW Puesto Pirámide 204, 1891 m, 4; *Santiago Rodríguez:* Loma Leonor, 18 km SW Monción, 534 m, 5; 3 km W Los Quemados, 183 m, 1; *La Vega:* 12 km NE Constanza, 1220 m, 1; 1 km S Constanza, 1098 m, 1; 8 km SE Constanza, 1495 m, 2; 6 km SSE Constanza, 1403 m, 13; 10 km SE Constanza, 1647 m, 1; 10 km NW La Horma, 1496 m, 2; *Azua:* 25 km NE Azua, 92 m, 1; *San Juan:* 9 km E Vallejuelo, 610 m, 16; *Baoruco:* 9 km N Neiba, 366 m, 1; 11 km N Neiba, 519 m, 3; *Independencia:* 1 km NE El Aguacate, 976 m, 5; 4 km NE El Aguacate, 793 m, 1; 4–7 km NE El Aguacate, 519–824 m, 39; 0.6 km NE Puerto Escondido, 519 m, 3; *Barahona:* 2 km SW Barahona, 122 m, 3; *Pedernales:* 23 km NE Cabo Rojo, 488 m, 4; 24 km NE Cabo Rojo, 732 m, 5; 24.5 km NE Cabo Rojo, 656 m, 8; 26 km NE Cabo Rojo, 732 m, 2; Las Abejas, 12 km NW Aceitillar, 1129 m, 6.

Sight record: República Dominicana: Monte Cristi: 6 km W Copey, s.l.—1 seen, 16.v.

20. *Anteos maerula* Fabricius, 1775

TL Jamaica.

FW males 36–44 mm, females 34–46 mm.

Anteos maerula is distributed in the Antilles on Cuba, Jamaica, Puerto Rico, and Hispaniola, and in the Lesser Antilles on Guadeloupe (Pinchon and Enrico, 1969:49) and Montserrat (Schwartz and Jimenez, 1982). In contrast to *A. clorinde, A. maerula* has been well known from Hispaniola (Hall, 1925:164; Cucurullo, 1959:9; Schwartz, 1983a:49–50). Schwartz (1983a:50) recorded 46 specimens from 21 Haitian localities. He likewise commented on the possible status of some of these Haitian specimens as *Anteos lacordairei* Boisduval, which Clench considered a sibling species of *A. maerula.* Miller and Brown (1981:85) regarded *lacordairei* as a synonym of *A. maerula* and further (note 309, p. 222) decried the use of *lacordairei* as even a subspecies of *A. maerula,* stating that they were unable to find differences between Jamaican and Mexican (the TL of *lacordairei*) specimens. Accordingly, herein I consider all Hispaniolan yellow Brimstones as *A. maerula,* without the use of a trinomen, and not divided between 2 species.

Pinchon and Enrico (1969:49) and Riley (1975:132) stated that female *A. maerula* differ in up color from males. Riley noted that females are much paler than males, and Pinchon and Enrico stated that females differ from males in having the yellow shade paler or grayish white. Indeed, Riley stated that there is a "rare form of the female" that is yellow like the male; this female form is *flava* Rõber. In my extensive Hispaniolan series, all but 2 females are colored on the up like males; these 2 exceptions are very pale grayish yellow, much as Pinchon and Enrico's brief description pointed out. Brown and Heineman (1972:316) made no mention of pale females on Jamaica, suggesting that all females from there are colored like males.

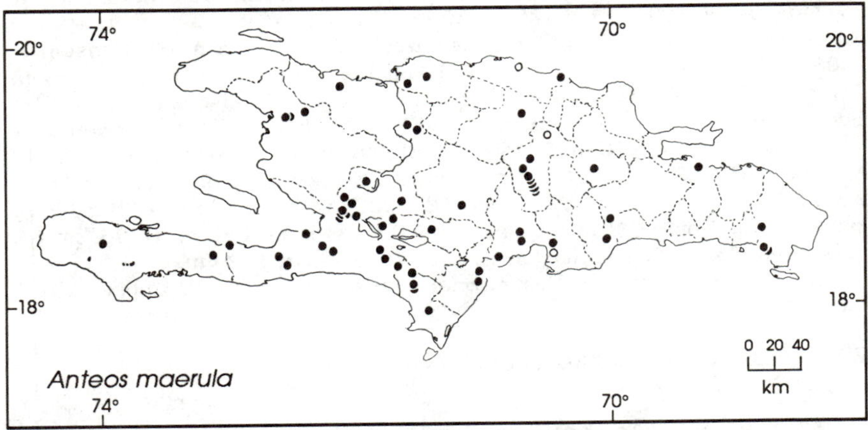

Anteos maerula have been taken in deserts (Gonaïves, Tierra Nueva), behind beaches (Grand-Goâve), in *caféières* (Paillant), open grassy fields (1 km S Constanza), meadows in pine forest (18 km SE Constanza), xeric forests (Playa Bayahibe), mesic hardwood forest and woods (Santo Domingo, Las Lagunas, Peralta, Hato Damas), *Acacia* scrub (Santiago, Azua, Vallejuelo, Oviedo), *Cocos* groves (Sabana de la Mar), and a hotel garden (Pétionville). Thus, *A. maerula* is extremely tolerant ecologically. Its altitudinal range is from sea level (La Source, Grand-Goâve, Copey, Playa Bayahibe, Tierra Nueva) to 2288 m (28 km SE Constanza), yet the butterfly is more common between about 153 m and 915 m.

Most specimens are from July (65), with 16 in June, 8 in August, 5 each in May and January, 4 each in April and December, and 1 each in March and November. Riley (1975:132) stated that "Dated specimens suggest two broods, one about November, the other in July and August." Certainly the latter is true on Hispaniola, but there is little evidence that there is a second, later Hispaniolan brood; there was no great number of this supposed fall brood present in the República Dominicana in March-April, assuming that some would have persisted until then. We have seen and collected only scattered individuals, often very worn, between September and April.

Times for collection were between 0900 and 1730 h, at temperatures between 21°C (Los Arroyos) and 37°C (Peralta).

In Haiti, *A. maerula* feeds on the flowers of *Cordia* sp. and *Ixora* sp. (both Terre Rouge), especially where these have been planted in ornamental hedges. In the República Dominicana, we have taken specimens feeding on *Antigonon leptopus* (Villa Vásquez), *Cynoglossum amabile* (18 km SE Constanza), *Ixora* sp. (Peralta), *Lantana reticulata* (Copey), *Ageratum conyzoides* (Vallejuelo), *Bidens pilosa* (11 km N Neiba), and abundantly on *Cordia globosa* (Santo Domingo). *Anteos maerula*, like *A. clorinde*, forms drinking clubs; we have seen this behavior at Thomonde, where several were drinking from mud in a narrow mesic ravine, at Soliette, where several were drinking from mud in a dirt road, and 11 km N Neiba, where many were drinking from moist sand and mud at the river's edge.

A copulating pair was observed on 19.vi (Santo Domingo, 122 m, 1300–1400 h, 31°C). Many other individuals were seen at that locality on this date. A sleeping individual was taken under a leaf in a more or less mesic ravine (Jonas).

Anteos maerula is well known for its migratory tendencies. Brown and Heineman (1972:317) noted 5 migratory flights, 2 of which involved Jamaican *A. maerula*. Pinchon and Enrico (1969: 49) reported a migratory flight from Guadeloupe on 13.vi.1969. This flight lasted at least 3 h in a north-northeast direction from Pointe Jarry on the west coast of Guadeloupe, along a front of 500 m. An estimated number of 5,400 individuals was involved during that period.

On 4.vii.1980, Gineika and I were returning from Valle Nuevo to Constanza. About 10 km SE Constanza, the road passes through open grassy fields; there is a ridge above the road and the Río Grande below. Masses of *A. maerula* "appeared" above the ridge, flew down the slope, crossed the road, and descended to the wooded river valley, there dispersing both upstream and downstream. We collected 4 specimens, of which 1 is a male and the other females, at 7 km SE Constanza, 1312 m, at 1425 h, temperature 29°C. *Anteos maerula* was not unusually abundant at Constanza on that or the following day, nor had it been further southeast in the Cordillera Central. An estimate of numbers involved is very difficult, since the front extended for several (about 4) kilometers. I compared it with a "waterfall of butterflies," spilling over the ridge and into the valley below. We watched this mass of butterflies for at least 45 minutes and estimated that there were thousands of *A. maerula* involved in the flight. Although this behavior cannot be construed as a migration from island to island since the butterflies were many kilometers inland and high in a mountain range and since they dispersed upon reaching the valley, still a mass movement of *A. maerula* was obvious. I can do no better than to ask the 2 rhetorical questions that Pinchon and Enrico (1969:49) asked about the Guadeloupe flight: "D'où venaient-ils? Où allaient-ils?"

Specimens: Haiti: Nord: 2.9 km S Jonas, 153 m, 1; *l'Artibonite:* 1.6 km S Carrefour Marmelade, 854 m, 1; 4.6 km E Les Poteaux, 183 m, 3; 16 km E Gonaïves, 1; *l'Ouest:* 20.3 km SW Thomonde, 1; 1.6 km N Saut d'Eau, 275 m, 2; 20 km S Mirebalais, 2; 3.8 km N Terre Rouge, 519 m, 1; 2.9 km N Terre Rouge, 534 m, 2; 1.3 km N Terre Rouge, 580 m, 1; 1.1 km N Terre Rouge, 534 m, 2; La Source, 5 km E Thomazeau, s.l., 1; Soliette, 17 km S Fond Parisien, 488 m, 1; Forêt des Pins, 1373–1525 m, 4; Boutilliers Road, 1.8–2.1 km W Kenscoff road, 793–885 m, 1; Boutilliers Road, 732–854 m, 5; 3.7 km S Kenscoff, 1647 m, 1; 1.3 km N Béloc, 702 m, 6; 8.3 km NW Jacmel, 183 m, 2; just W Grand-Goâve, s.l., 1; 11.1 km E Miragoâne, s.l., 1; *Sud:* 6.7 km SW Paillant, 763 m, 4; 8 km SW Paillant, 824 m, 2; Formond Base Camp #1, 975 m, 2 (FSM); *República Dominicana: Monte Cristi:* 6 km W Copey, s.l., 1; 4 km NW Villa Vásquez, 61 m, 2; *Dajabón:* 16 km NW Río Limpio, 702 m, 1; 7 km N Restauración, 671 m, 1; *Elías Piña:* 1 km SW Puesto Pirámide 204, 1891 m, 1; *Puerto Plata:* 9 km SE Sosúa, 15 m, 1; *Santiago:* 7 km SW Santiago, 214 m, 4; *La Vega:* 12 km NE Constanza, 1220 m, 2; 1 km S Constanza, 1098 m, 1; 7 km SE Constanza, 1312 m, 4; 10 km SE Constanza, 1647 m, 3; 15 km SE Constanza, 1403 m, 1; 18 km SE Constanza, 1586 m, 6; 28 km SE Constanza, 2288 m, 1; *Hato Mayor:* 7 km E Sabana de la Mar, 1; *La Altagracia:* 1 km N Playa Bayahibe, s.l., 2; 2 km SE Playa Bayahibe, s.l., 1; 16 km NE La Romana, 61 m, 1; *Dist. Nac.:* 30 km NW Santo Domingo, 122 m, 1; *Sánchez Ramírez:* 1 km NE Las Lagunas, 183 m, 1; *San Cristóbal:* 2 km N Hato Damas, 92 m, 1; *Azua:* 25 km NE Azua, 92 m, 1; 5 km S Peralta, 305 m, 11; 2.5 km W, 6.6 km N Azua, 183 m, 1; *San Juan:* 9 km E Vallejuelo, 610 m, 1; *Baoruco:* 11 km N Neiba, 519 m, 4; *Independencia:* 21 km N Los Pinos, 1708 m, 1; 4 km NW Tierra Nueva, s.l., 1; *Barahona:* west slope, Sierra Martín García, 305–458 m, 1; 2 km SW Barahona, 122 m, 1; 5 km SE, 3 km W Barahona, 183 m, 1; *Pedernales:* 23 km NE Cabo Rojo, 488 m, 1; 26 km NE Cabo Rojo, 732 m, 1; Las Abejas, 12 km NW Aceitillar, 1129 m, 1; 5 km NE Los Arroyos, 1617 m, 1; 17 km NW Oviedo, 183 m, 1.

21. *Anteos clorinde clorinde* Godart, 1824

TL Brasil.

FW males 34–45 mm, females 40–44 mm.

Riley (1975) did not report *A. clorinde* from Hispaniola. Schwartz (1983a:50) reported the species from Haiti, and Beck (1983:90) reported it from the República Dominicana. However, *A. clorinde* had been previously recorded from the latter country by Cucurullo (1959:9) without details. Marión Heredia (1974:2) used the name *A. c. clorinde* for Dominican specimens and later (1980d) listed the species (no subspecies) from El Número-Azua. In fact, *A. clorinde* appeared on a Dominican postage stamp in the late 1970s.

Hall (1925) did not mention *A. clorinde*; this suggests that the butterflies have reached Hispaniola since his and Kaempfier's collecting in 1921 and 1924. However, Hall's list of localities for both collectors shows that they were never in the range of *A. clorinde* as known today.

Riley (1975:132) used the trinominal *A. c. nivifera* Fruhstorfer for the Cuban population; in this he followed Bates (1935a: 139–40) who first reported the species from 1 Cuban locality. Brown and Heineman (1972:318–19) did not report *A. clorinde* from Jamaica, but Riley (1975:132) stated that the species "Has been taken once in Jamaica."

The subspecies *clorinde* and *nivifera* differ from each other in that the fw colored square or rectangle is yellow in the former and orange in the latter. In Hispaniolan specimens, the colored fw marking varies in males from yellow (pl. 9L6) to orange (pl. 9L9), with the latter extreme uncommon (1 specimen). In females, the fw patch is always pale yellow (pl. 10L5) and much less clearly delimited than in males.

On Hispaniola, *A. c. clorinde* is widely distributed and extremely abundant in many areas. But its distribution is peculiar. The butterfly occurs on the Haitian Massif du Nord (Dondon) and the adjacent northern portion of the Dominican Cordillera Central (Los Cerezos, Restauración, Loma Leonor) south to Jarabacoa (whence we have no material and have never seen the butterfly; see Beck, 1983). *Anteos c. clorinde* likewise occurs in the Valle de San Juan (San Juan) and in the intermontane valley between the 2 ranges of the Sierra de Neiba (El Cercado, Vallejuelo) and on the south range of the Sierra de Neiba (Puesto Pirámide 204) but apparently not on the north range. From this region *A. c. clorinde* extends into the Haitian Montagnes du Trou-d'Eau (Mirebalais, Terre Rouge). Coutsis (1983) reported *A. clorinde* as abundant at Savanette, Dépt. de l'Artibonite, Haiti, only about 10 km W of Puesto Pirámide 204 in the República Dominicana. On the south island, *A. c. clorinde* occurs on the north slope of the Morne l'Hôpital (Pétionville) and extends eastward to the northern slope of the Massif de la Selle (El Aguacate), the northern slope of the Sierra de Baoruco (Polo), and thence around the eastern extreme of that range (Paraíso, Enriquillo) as far, on the southern slopes, as the Haitian border (Aguas Negras, Banano, Mencía). In the lowlands, *A. c. clorinde* extends in the Llanos de Azua as far east as Tábara Abajo and onto the southern slopes of the Cordillera Central (Peralta). Doubtless *A. c. clorinde* also occurs in extreme southeastern Haiti, but we did not see or take it in the region about Jacmel. The elevational distribution is from sea level (Canoa) to 1586 m (Puesto Pirámide 204), but both extremes are exceptional. Most specimens are from between about 183 m and 610 m.

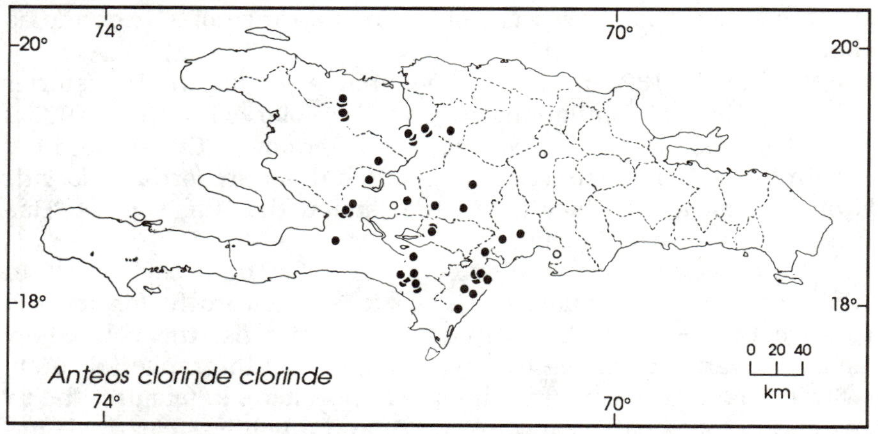

Times of collection were between 0930 and 1730 h, at temperatures between 23°C (Puesto Pirámide 204) and 38°C (Loma Leonor, Cabo Rojo).

These strongly flying and stiff-winged butterflies are often locally very abundant. In the region along the Dominico-Haitian border (Los Cerezos, Río Limpio), they are attracted to the red flowers of *Stachytarpheta mutabilis* (Verbenaceae), where as many as 3 *A. c. clorinde* have been seen clinging to 1 of the 1-m-tall spikes. In the República Dominicana, *A. c. clorinde* also uses *Lantana ovatifolia* as a nectar source (Cabo Rojo). But in Haiti, the major food plants are *Hibiscus rosasinensis* (Dondon, Terre Rouge), especially where this has been planted as a hedge, *Ixora* sp. (Terre Rouge), and *Cordia* sp. (Terre Rouge). On 1 occasion (Terre Rouge), *A. c. clorinde* were attracted to a tall hedge of *Euphorbia lactea* (Euphorbiaceae), although there were no obvious flowers present.

Because of its broad elevational distribution, *A. c. clorinde* occupies a wide spectrum of habitats. These include xeric and virtually treeless hillsides (S Terre Rouge), gardens (Pétionville), mesic woodland edges (Los Cerezos), mixed pine-hardwoods (Restauración), river valleys (Loma Leonor), semixeric open woods (Barahona), xeric woods (Enriquillo), and even the edges of *cafetales* (Mencía) and *caféières* (S Dondon). These butterflies do not shun more mesic areas (Neiba, Las Abejas, Polo, Paraíso), but *A. c. clorinde* is more often encountered in xeric habitats.

Anteos c. clorinde forms dense drinking aggregations. We have observed this behavior at Los Cerezos, where these butterflies were drinking in the immediate company of a few *Phoebis* sp. and small pierids; at Polo, where they were drinking from a small garbage-filled depression with water in the paved road at the edge of the town; at 11 km N Neiba, where they were drinking from sand and mud at the river's edge; and at Barahona, where they were drinking from roadside puddles. At Banano, where a clear spring gushes from the upper side of the roadcut and thence flows down the road for about 30 m to enter a small creek, *A. c. clorinde* has regularly (1980–86) been present, most commonly in the summer, drinking at the confluence of the run and the creek, or from the run itself, where the water is mixed with earth and horse manure. At El Cercado, I observed several *A. c. clorinde* drinking from the edge of a wide but shallow creek; these butterflies were perched on floating woody debris at the edge of the shore, a very unstable platform from which to drink.

Most specimens are from July (104), with 32 in August and only 9 in June, 5 in December, 3 in March, 2 in January, and 1 each in May and in October. Although *A. c. clorinde* is on the wing throughout the entire year, there are much greater numbers in midsummer. The low number of June records is interesting but may be skewed downward by our not having collected specimens in June in the rather circumscribed areas wherein *A. c. clorinde* occurs.

Specimens: Haiti: Nord: Dondon, 4; 2.9 km N Dondon, 366 m, 1; 5.4 km S Dondon, 366 m, 1; 5.6 km SE Dondon, 336 m, 1; *l'Artibonite:* 4.0 km N Thomonde, 2; *l'Ouest:* 20.3 km SW Thomonde, 1; 20.8 km S Mirebalais, 366–519 m, 7; 3.8 km N Terre Rouge, 519–534 m, 3; 1.1 km N Terre Rouge, 519–534 m, 6; 1.3 km N Terre Rouge, 580 m, 1; Terre Rouge, 534 m, 1; 2.9–8.5 km S Terre Rouge, 137–488 m, 3; Pétionville, 458 m, 1; *República Dominicana: Dajabón:* 16 km NW Río Limpio, 702 m, 3; Los Cerezos, 12 km NW Río Limpio, 580 m, 30; 4 km S Restauración, 595 m, 4; 5.7 km SW Restauración, 610 m, 1; Cañada Tirolís, just S Villa Anacaona, 458 m, 2; *Elías Piña:* 2 km NE Puesto Pirámide 204, 1586 m, 1; *Santiago Rodríguez:* Loma Leonor, 18 km SW Monción, 534 m, 3; *Azua:* Tábara Abajo, 1; 4 km S Peralta, 366 m, 13; *San Juan;* 4 km E El Cercado, 702 m, 2; 9 km E Vallejuelo, 625 m, 2; 19 km N San Juan, 534 m, 2; *Baoruco:* 9 km N Neiba, 366 m, 2; 11 km Neiba, 519 m, 4; *Independencia:* 4–7 km NE El Aguacate, 519–824 m, 12; *Barahona:* 8 km ESE Canoa, 1; Polo, 702 m, 6; 1.8 km W Monteada Nueva, 1007 m, 1; 2 km SW Barahona, 122 m, 1; 12 km SW Barahona, 427 m, 1; 21 km NE Paraíso, 1; 8 km NW Paraíso, 153 m, 2 (1 MPM); 8–10 km NW Paraíso, 2 (MPM); 3 km NW Enriquillo, 244 m, 1; *Pedernales:* 18 km NNE Cabo Rojo, 305 m, 1; 23 km NE Cabo Rojo, 488 m, 1; Las Abejas, 12 km NW Aceitillar, 1129 m, 5; 3 km W Aguas Negras, 519 m, 3; Mencía, 397 m, 4; 1 km SE Banano, 183 m, 9.

22. *Phoebis thalestris thalestris* Illiger, 1802

TL Haiti.

FW males 36–48 mm, females 35–48 mm.

Three names have been proposed for the West Indian populations of large bright yellow (in males) *Phoebis* with a bright and contrasting orange upfw patch: *philea* Johannson; *thalestris* Illiger; and *huebneri* Fruhstorfer. Some authors (Riley, 1975:133) considered all 3 subspecifically related (as *Ph. philea*), with (in the Antilles) *Ph. ph. philea* on Puerto Rico, *Ph. ph. huebneri* on Cuba, and *Ph. ph. thalestris* on Hispaniola. Brown (1929:9–10), the last reviser of the genus, considered *philea* and *thalestris* conspecific (he did not discuss *huebneri*); but he stated that he was uncertain about the status of *thalestris* ("It may be worthy of specific recognition or may be only a very well-differentiated race"). Brown illustrated the male genitalia of both taxa (1929:figs. 11–16), and they are indeed very similar. I have also made preparations of male genitalia of these 2 taxa and these agree with Brown's drawings. However, male *philea* and male *thalestris* are at once differentiable in that the latter always has a black spot (of variable size on Hispaniolan specimens but always present) at the end of the fw cell on the up, and male *philea* always lack this spot. Females of the 2 taxa are somewhat similar, but those of *thalestris* are much more deeply pigmented, the up covered with rust colored scales to give a very rich appearance.

Comstock (1944:519) felt that *philea* and *thalestris* were not conspecific on the basis of their apparent sympatry on Cuba, the occurrence of *thalestris* alone on Hispaniola, and of *philea* alone on Puerto Rico (Comstock had only 1 female from Puerto Rico, but *philea* is more common on Puerto Rico than this 1 specimen suggests). Ramos (1982:63) used a trinomen (*Phoebis philea philea*) for Puerto Rican specimens.

Brown and Heineman (1972:311) discussed *Phoebis p. philea*, although no member of this group of taxa is certainly known to occur on Jamaica. In using the trinomen, Brown and Heineman stated that "We are not convinced that Comstock is correct" in his suggestion that the 2 taxa are separate species. Clench (*in litt.*, 1978) used the name *Phoebis thalestris thalestris* for the Hispaniolan butterflies without comment, and Schwartz (1983a:51) followed Clench's suggestion. Such an action seems justified, despite the similarity (but not absolute identity) of the male genitalia of the 2 taxa, by the fact that males are identified as either *philea* or *thalestris* at a glance (presence or absence of the upfw black discocellular spot). Females of the 2 species are easily identified by the much richer coloration of *thalestris*. The Cuban population (*huebneri*) is very like that from Hispaniola but differs in the intensity of the un coloration in females. Accordingly, I regard *Ph. philea* and *Ph. thalestris* as distinct species, with the latter having 2 subspecies: *Ph. th. thalestris* on Hispaniola and *Ph. th. huebneri* on Cuba. Holland (1916) did not list any member of this complex from the Isla de la Juventud.

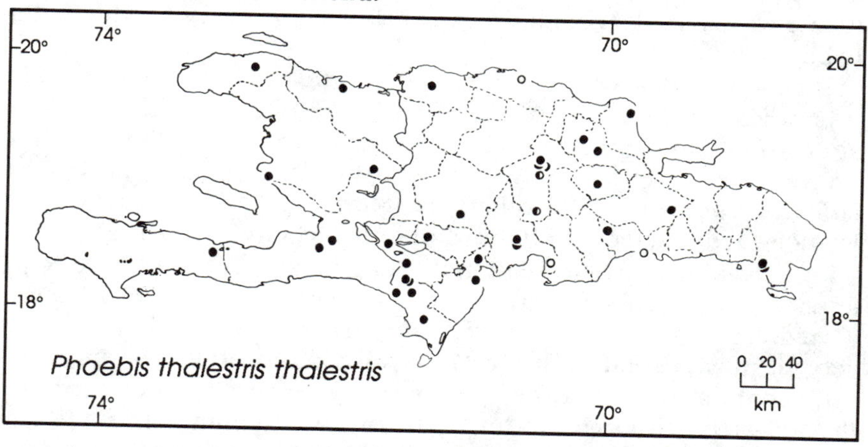

Riley (1975:133) listed *Ph. avellaneda* Herrich-Schäffer from Hispaniola. This species, recognized by Brown (1929:11) from Cuba, is very similar in size and coloration to *Ph. thalestris*. Males of both species have a discocellular black spot on the fw, but the orange blotch is both bright, rich red and extends more posteriorly in *Ph. avellaneda* males than does the orange blotch in *Ph. thalestris* males. Females of the 2 species are extremely similar except that the un is red in female *Ph. avellaneda*, yellow in female *Ph. thalestris*. In addition, the uphw in male *Ph. avellaneda* is almost entirely red, whereas in male *Ph. thalestris*, the uphw is orange marginally and yellow basally. Riley's record of *Ph. avellaneda* presumably had its origin in Hall (1925:164); Hall stated "Seen at Santiago," without specifying the number of, and almost certainly without collecting, the specimen(s). It seems very unlikely that anyone could identify a female *Ph. avellaneda* (in contrast to a female *Ph. thalestris*) in flight, and almost as unlikely to distinguish a flying male *Ph. avellaneda*. I know of no collection that has *Ph. avellaneda* from Hispaniola. Coutsis (1983) cast doubt on the occurrence of *Ph. avellaneda* in Haiti. For the above reasons, I urge that *Ph. avellaneda* be deleted from the list of Hispaniolan Rhopalocera until or unless a verifiable specimen is taken. Even then, *Ph. avellaneda* might be only a vagrant to Hispaniola (some *Phoebis* are wanderers).

Bates (1935a:134) knew of only 11 specimens of *Ph. th. huebneri* from Cuba, all from the eastern "Provincia de Oriente." The species appears to be uncommon there. Hall (1925:164) stated that *Ph. th. thalestris* was "Not uncommon; Puerto Plata, San Domingo City, etc." Schwartz (1983a:51) noted 15 specimens from 5 Haitian localities and felt that "This species is relatively rare" but "widely distributed."

In the República Dominicana, *Ph. th. thalestris* is as common as it is in Haiti and as widely distributed. Habitats are either mesic or xeric and include mesic deciduous woods and forests (Port-de-Paix, Cabrera, Las Lagunas, Bayaguana, Santo Domingo), *caféières* and *cafetales-cacaotales* (Carrefour la Mort, Paillant, Tenares, San Francisco de Macorís), hotel gardens (Pétionville, Délugé), xeric (Playa Bayahibe) and transitional (El Aguacate, Peralta, Cabo Rojo) forests, oases (Villa Vásquez), and a very dry but wooded ravine (Oviedo). At Las Abejas, *Ph. th. thalestris* has been taken along a very narrow run-off ravine with hardwoods in otherwise pine forest, a habitat in which the species rarely occurs. In summary, *Ph. th. thalestris* is a forest butterfly, in contrast to many other pierids; but the species also occurs away from forests or woods, especially along roadsides with flowers (Boutilliers Road, Thomonde). The flight is direct and rapid, often at treetop level; the stiff-winged flight as well as the size of the butterfly will allow the collector to distinguish *Ph. th. thalestris* as it approaches him. All other *Phoebis* are considerably smaller and have flights that are lower, less stiff-winged, and more erratic.

Elevational range of *Ph. th. thalestris* is between sea level (Carrefour la Mort, La Furnia, Playa Bayahibe, Canoa) and 2105 m (Constanza). However, in this range, almost all specimens are from 915 m or less, with only 2 (Constanza, Las Abejas) above 1220 m. It is thus appropriate to consider *Ph. th. thalestris* a butterfly of low to moderate elevations but that occasionally occurs in uplands. The species is absent from the Cordillera Central (except for the occurrence above Constanza noted above) and from other high Hispaniolan ranges, but it occurs with some frequency on Boutilliers Road in Haiti (763–885 m) on the Morne l'Hôpital but not higher on the Montagne Noire or the Massif de la Selle.

Most specimens and records are from July (69), with 29 from August, 26 from June, 10 from January, 9 from December, 3 from April, and 2 from March. We saw none in September-November, and the low number of October-April records suggests that midsummer is the peak time of eclosion. Most specimens are fresh and little flown; the 2 exceptions are from Playa Bayahibe, an exposed and windy oceanside locality. Despite their date (16.viii), they are wind-whipped. These data suggest that *Ph. th. thalestris* may have a brief flight period.

Times of collection were between 0830 and 1750 h, with temperatures between 23°C (Las Abejas) and 37°C (Peralta, 1 km N Playa Bayahibe).

In Haiti, *Ph. th. thalestris* takes nectar from the flowers of *Hibiscus rosasinensis* (Carrefour la Mort, Thomonde, Pétionville), especially where these have been planted into rows and are tall (3 m). In the República Dominicana, the butterflies used the flowers of *Rosa* sp. (Villa Vásquez) in an oasis; the plants were in a small garden about the few houses there. At Valle Nuevo, 1 *Ph. th. thalestris* was observed to feed on a small yellow unidentified flower growing in a large open meadow with *Cynoglossum amabile*. At Peralta, *Ph. th. thalestris* fed upon *Ixora* sp. Other plants used include: *Antigonon leptopus* (Azua), *Ixora* sp. (2.5 km SE Playa Bayahibe, Cabo Rojo), and *Ageratum conyzoides* (Vallejuelo). On 4 occasions we have taken *Ph. th. thalestris* at large drinking clubs: in a dirt road (Barahona), where *Ph. th. thalestris* was one of the least common species there, even though the major number of participants were pierids; at the edge of a river on sand and mud (Neiba, twice); and along a narrow (1-m-wide) creek through mesic woods (Vallejuelo).

On 14.vii, a *Ph. th. thalestris* caterpillar was taken (Las Abejas) on a 3-m-tall *Cassia* sp. (Fabaceae) in a narrow run-off ravine; 2 days later a female was seen at the same locality ovipositing on another plant of the same genus. Riley (1975:133) cited various *Cassia* species as the larval food plants and described the final instar caterpillar.

Specimens: Haiti: Nord-Ouest: 7.5 km SE Port-de-Paix, 1; *Nord:* Carrefour la Mort, s.l., 1; *l'Artibonite:* Délugé, s.l., 3; 4.0 km N Thomonde, 2; *l'Ouest:* Pétionville, 458 m, 1; Boutilliers Road, 1.8–2.1 km W Kenscoff road, 763–885 m, 2; Boutilliers Road, 732–854 m, 3; *Sud:* 6.7 km SW Paillant, 763 m, 1; *República Dominicana: Monte Cristi:* 4 km NW Villa Vásquez, 61 m, 23; *Duarte:* 10 km SE Tenares, 183 m, 1; 12 km SE San Francisco de Macorís, 1; *La Vega:* Jarabacoa, 530 m, 7; 1 km S Jarabacoa, 519 m, 1; 3.5 km E Paso Bajito, 732 m, 1; *María T. Sánchez:* 6 km S Cabrera, s.l., 2; *La Altagracia:* 2.5 km SE Playa Bayahibe, s.l., 11; 1 km N Playa Bayahibe, s.l., 20; *Monte Plata:* 8 km NE Bayaguana, 2; *Dist. Nac.:* 30 km NW Santo Domingo, 122 m, 3; *Sánchez Ramírez:* 1 km NE Las Lagunas, 183 m, 1; *Azua:* 2.5 km W, 6.6 km N Azua, 183 m, 3; 5 km S Peralta, 305 m, 9; *San Juan:* 9 km E Vallejuelo, 610 m, 5; *Baoruco:* 11 km N Neiba, 519 m, 13; *Independencia:* La Furnia, s.l., 1; 4–7 km NE El Aguacate, 519–824 m, 10; *Barahona:* 8 km ESE Canoa, s.l., 1; 2 km

SW Barahona, 122 m, 5; *Pedernales:* 9 km N Pedernales, 244 m, 1; 26 km NE Cabo Rojo, 732 m, 1; Las Abejas, 11 km NW Aceitillar, 1220 m, 3; Las Abejas, 12 km NW Aceitillar, 1129 m, 1; 17 km NW Oviedo, 183 m, 3.

Sight records: República Dominicana: La Vega: La Palma, 19 km W Jayaco, 1007 m—1 seen, 27.vi; Valle Nuevo, 25 km SE Constanza, 2105 m—1 seen, 10.vii; *Pedernales:* 17 km NW Oviedo, 183 m—1 seen, 10.viii.

23. *Phoebis argante rorata* Butler, 1869

TL Haiti.

FW males 27–39 mm, females 26–38 mm.

Four subspecies of *Ph. argante* Boisduval occur in the West Indies: *Phoebis a. fornax* on Cuba, *Ph. a. martini* Comstock on Puerto Rico, *Ph. a. comstocki* Avinoff on Jamaica, and *Ph. a. rorata* on Hispaniola. Riley (1975:133) did not recognize *Ph. a. comstocki*, but Brown and Heineman (1972:306–9) regarded it as a valid subspecies. They also noted that differences between the island populations are slight and evident only when good series from each island are compared. Brown and Heineman (1972:307) also followed Comstock (1944:509) in using *Ph. a. minuscula* Butler for the Cuban subspecies. Comstock regarded *fornax* as a synonym of *minuscula;* the latter was regarded (Riley, 1975:133) as a dwarf with a fw length of "about 24 mm." Considering the small size of some of my *Ph. a. rorata*, that these small individuals are part of a continuum in fw lengths, and that Brown (1929:12), while discussing *minuscula*, noted that "it is merely a very small specimen" that these small individuals are a part of *Ph. argante* populations anywhere, there is no reason to reject the usage of the name on the basis of its "dwarf" holotype.

Brown and Heineman (1972:307) stated that on Jamaica, *Ph. argante* is found "more commonly in open woodlands than in fields." They also cited Avinoff and Shoumatoff (1946:273) as far as *Ph. argante* occurring in the wooded hilly regions of the eastern end of Jamaica, in contrast to the drier western portion which was occupied by *Ph. agarithe*. On Hispaniola, *Ph. a. rorata* is most frequently encountered in wooded areas, including *caféières* and *cafetales-cacaotales*. These are usually mesic (Carrefour la Mort, Dondon, Paillant, Saut d'Eau, Los Cerezos, Jamao al Norte, Loma Leonor, Tenares, San Francisco de Macorís, Sánchez, Las Terrenas, Sabana de la Mar, Bayaguana, Santo Domingo, Maimón, Piedra Blanca, Cambita Garabitos, Polo, Paraíso, Banano, Mencía). But on occasion, *Ph. a. rorata* has been taken in xeric woods or forests (Playa Bayahibe), open fields (Constanza), roadsides (Boutilliers Road, Barahona), oases (Terrier Rouge, Croix des Bouquets), transitional forest (El Aguacate), and once in *Acacia* woods (Copey).

Marión Heredia (1980d) recorded the species from El Número-Azua, a xeric area, along with *Ph. agarithe.* Although *Ph. a. antillia* is a xerophile and *Ph. a. rorata* a mesophile, the 2 species are syntopic at 12 localities: Croix des Bouquets (oasis), Boutilliers Road, Copey (*Acacia* woods), Los Cerezos (mesic forest), Loma Leonor (riverine hardwood forest), Jarabacoa (pinewoods with ravines in hardwoods), Constanza (open field), 1 km N Playa Bayahibe (xeric forest), Río Cumayasa (mixed xeric-mesic woods), El Aguacate (transitional forest), 10 km NW Paraíso (*cafetal*), Las Abejas (mesic forest). These localities in general bear out the ecological preferences of the 2 species; for example, mesophilic *Ph. a. argante* outnumbers *Ph. a. antillia* (6 to 1) at mesic Los Cerezos, but the latter outnumbers the former at xeric Playa Bayahibe (6 to 1). Of the 3 localities where the species are represented by more than single specimens each, Croix des Bouquets is a "mesic" oasis in the otherwise xeric Cul de Sac Plain (2 specimens each), Boutilliers Road is an open transitional mountainside (2 specimens each), Jarabacoa lies in open pinewoods with hardwood forest in ravines (18 *Ph. a. argante,* 1 *Ph. a. agarithe*), and El Aguacate is transitional forest (5 *Ph. a. antillia,* 20 *Ph. a. rorata*).

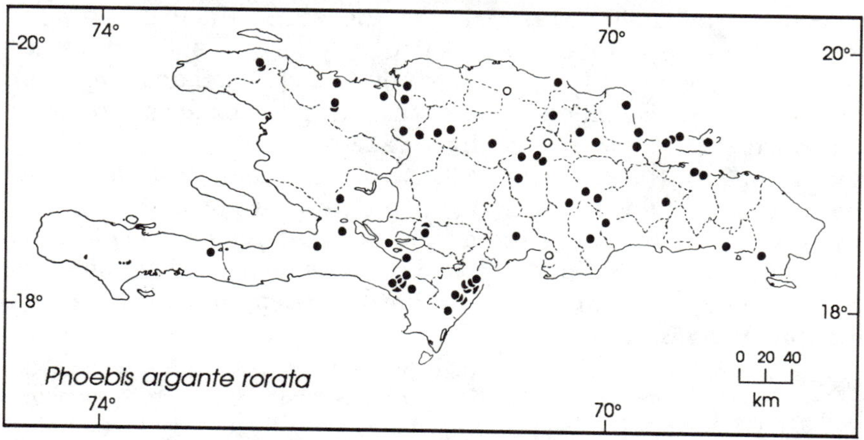

Phoebis argante rorata

The elevational distribution of *Ph. a. rorata* is from sea level (Carrefour la Mort, Terrier Rouge, Croix des Bouquets, Copey, Cabrera, Cruce de Rincón, Las Terrenas, Playa Bayahibe, La Furnia) to 1129 m (Las Abejas) in the Sierra de Baoruco and 1098 m (Constanza) in the Cordillera Central. *Phoebis a. antillia* reaches a higher elevation (Forêt des Pins) in the Massif de la Selle than does *Ph. a. rorata* at any locality, but their altitudinal distributions are quite comparable.

Most specimens were taken in July (110), with 59 in August, and 35 in June; April, March, May, January, and October-December are represented by 5–2 specimens each. Although these butterflies are on the wing throughout the year, there is a major eclosion in late summer. The lack of very large numbers of individuals in June suggests July-August as the major time of emergence.

Specimens have been taken between 0730 and 1530 h, at temperatures between 26°C (11 km N Neiba) and 38°C (Río Bao).

Schwartz (1983a:51) noted predation on *Ph. a. rorata* by the spider *Nephila* sp.; the local situation at Carrefour la Mort, where *Ph. a. rorata* was common and where this predation was noted, is a large *caféière*, with several tall *Hibiscus rosasinensis* hedges about old *habitations*. The spiders, which were very abundant, had spun their sticky webs adjacent to these hedges and thus were in an excellent position to capture butterflies of several species.

Hibiscus rosasinensis is a favorite forage plant for *Ph. a. rorata* in Haiti (Carrefour la Mort, Dondon), but *Ixora* sp. is also used (Boutilliers Road). In the República Dominicana we have taken this species on *Tournefortia hirsutissima* (Sosúa). These butterflies are also confirmed drinkers. The long series from Banano is due to our collecting repeatedly (10 times) over the years; there has always been a drinking club—from small to very large—of *Ph. a. rorata* there, often with very large numbers of *A. c. clorinde*, drinking from the mud and very shallow water of the spring seepage as it reaches a small creek. Elsewhere, we have taken 1 *Ph. a. rorata* drinking from mud with 3 *Ph. s. sennae* (Esperalvillo), many from a hole in the road pavement with garbage (Polo), from a spring run (2 km SW Mencía), many from sand and mud at a river's edge (11 km N Neiba), and from mud puddles in dirt roads (Mencía, Paraíso). The spring seepage at Banano is regularly contaminated with earth and horse manure.

Specimens: Haiti: Nord-Ouest: 0.6 km NW Balladé, 1; 1.3 km S Balladé, 31 m, 1; *Nord:* Carrefour la Mort, s.l., 13; 2.9 km N Dondon, 366 m, 1; Dondon, 396 m, 1; 12.3 km E Terrier Rouge, s.l., 1; *l'Ouest:* 1.6 km N Saut d'Eau, 275 m, 1; 13.1 km E Croix des Bouquets, s.l., 2; Boutilliers Road, 1.8–2.1 km W Kenscoff road, 793–915 m, 2; *Sud:* 6.7 km SW Paillant, 763 m, 1; *República Dominicana: Monte Cristi:* 6 km W Copey, s.l., 1; *Dajabón:* 0.5 km N Cañongo, 31 m, 1; Los Cerezos, 12 km NW Río Limpio, 580 m, 6; 7 km N Restauración, 671 m, 1; *Santiago Rodríguez:* 15 km SW Monción, 320 m, 1; Loma Leonor, 18 km SW Monción, 534 m, 2; *Puerto Plata:* 9 km SE Sosúa, 15 m, 5; *Santiago:* Río Bao, 8 km SE Montones Abajo, 488 m, 2; *La Vega:* 1 km W Manabao, 793 m, 2; Jarabacoa, 530 m, 18; 3.5 km E Paso Bajito, 732 m, 7; 1 km S Constanza, 1098 m, 2; *Espaillat:* 20 km SW Jamao al Norte, 793 m, 1; *María T. Sánchez:* 6 km S Cabrera, s.l., 2; 9 km SE Nagua, s.l., 1; 1 km S Cruce de Rincón, s.l., 1; *Duarte:* 10 km SE Tenares, 183 m, 1; 12 km SE San Francisco de Macorís, 1; *Samaná:* 6.9 km NE Sánchez, 336 m, 2; 13.2 km NE Sánchez, 92 m, 1; 3 km SW Las Terrenas, s.l., 1; 2 km S Las Galeras, 2; *Hato Mayor:* 7 km E Sabana de la Mar, 2; 17 km E Sabana de la Mar, 1; *La Altagracia:* 1 km N Playa Bayahibe, s.l., 1; *La Romana:* Río Cumayasa, 13.5 km W La Romana, 1; *Monte Plata:* 8 km NE Bayaguana, 2; 2 km W Esperalvillo, 92 m, 1; *Dist. Nac.:* 30 km NW Santo Domingo, 122 m, 3; *Monseñor Nouel:* 6 km SE Maimón, 122 m, 2; 14 km SW Piedra Blanca, 427 m, 1; *San Cristóbal:* 11 km NW Cambita Garabitos, 671 m, 1; *Azua:* 5 km S Peralta, 305 m, 4; *Baoruco:* 11 km N Neiba, 519 m, 10; 14 km N Neiba, 671 m, 2; *Independencia:* La Furnia, s.l., 1; 4–7 km NE El Aguacate, 519–824 m, 20; *Barahona:* Polo, 702 m, 2; 20 km SE Cabral, 946 m, 1; 2 km SW Barahona, 122 m, 1; 7 km SW Barahona, 2; 12 km SW Barahona, 427 m, 5; 5 km SE, 3 km W Barahona, 183 m, 5; 8 km NW Paraíso, 153 m, 8 (1 MPM); 8–10 km NW Paraíso, 2 (MPM); 10 km NW Paraíso, 244 m, 1; 9 km NW Enriquillo, 671 m, 1; *Pedernales:* 23 km NE Cabo Rojo, 488 m, 4; Las Abejas, 12 km NW Aceitillar, 1129 m, 3; 3 km W Aguas Negras, 519 m, 1; 1 km SE Banano, 183 m, 43; Mencía, 397 m, 14: 2 km SW Mencía, 336 m, 9.

24. *Phoebis agarithe antillia* Brown, 1929

TL Pivert, Dépt. de l'Artibonite, Haiti.

FW males 28–36 mm, females 28–35 mm.

Phoebis a. antillia was named from a suite of 6 specimens, of which 3 are from Haiti and the balance from Jamaica and Cuba. *Phoebis a. antillia* occurs throughout the Greater Antilles and in the southern Bahamas (Simon and Miller, 1986); *Ph. a. pupillata* Dillon inhabits the Lesser Antilles from St. Christopher to Grenada. These are the first records of *Ph. a. antillia* from Isla Saona and Isla Catalina.

Of the 6 species of *Phoebis* on Hispaniola, *Ph. a. antillia* ranks third in abundance; it is outnumbered by *Ph. s. sennae* and *Ph. a. rorata*. Brown and Heineman (1972:309) considered *Ph. argante* more abundant than *Ph. agarithe* on Jamaica.

Phoebis a. antillia is most commonly encountered in xeric areas (Les Poteaux, Fond Parisien, Croix des Bouquets, Copey, Las Calderas, La Furnia, Oviedo, Isla Catalina), where it occupies *Acacia* woods or scrub. It also inhabits xeric woods and forests (Playa Bayahibe), transitional forest (El Aguacate), and oases (Villa Vásquez). But the species has also been taken in a grassy field (Constanza), pine forest (Forêt des Pins, Jarabacoa), and hardwood forest (Jayaco, Los Cerezos, Peralta, Las Abejas), so it does not avoid other and more mesic habitats. Brown and Heineman (1972:310) considered that *Ph. agarithe* favored dry, over wet, areas on Jamaica; the same is true for Hispaniola.

The elevational distribution is from sea level (Croix des Bouquets, Fond Parisien, Source Matelas, Copey, Playa Bayahibe, Las

Calderas, El Limón, La Furnia, Mano Juan, Isla Catalina) to 1525 m (Forêt des Pins) on the Massif de la Selle; the maximum elevation on the Cordillera Central is 1098 m (Constanza), and on the Sierra de Baoruco 1129 m (Las Abejas).

Times of collection were between 0915 and 1700 h, at temperatures of 24°C (El Aguacate) to 38°C (Las Calderas, La Furnia). Most specimens are from July-August (26–29), with 6 in December, 4 in January, 3 in June, 2 each in April, May, and October, and 1 from March. The butterflies are even less common beyond the summer months than during the summer; *Ph. a. antillia* is univoltine.

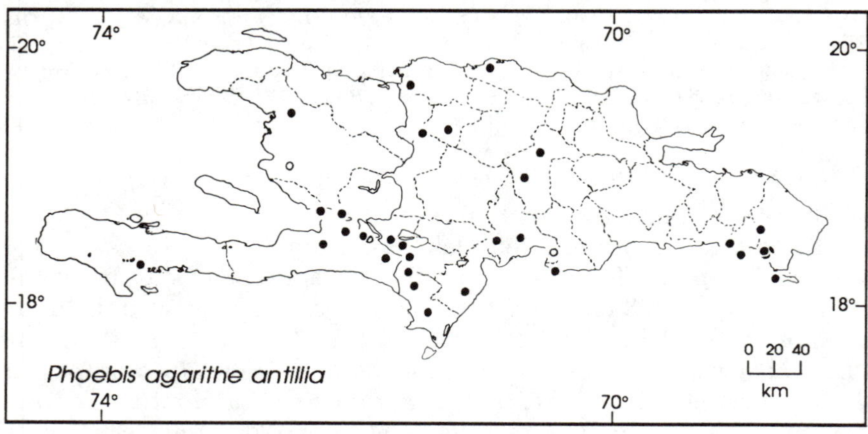

We have taken *Ph. a. antillia* feeding on a mixed *Cordia-Ixora* hedge (Terre Rouge), on a xerophytic pale yellow-flowered vine in *Acacia* scrub (Fond Parisien), *Bauhinia divaricata* (Les Poteaux), *Antigonon leptopus* (Villa Vásquez), *Cordia haitiensis* (La Furnia), *Ixora* sp. (Peralta, Cabo Rojo), and *Lantana ovatifolia* (Copey).

Specimens: Haiti: l'Artibonite: 4.6 km E Les Poteaux, 183 m, 2; *l'Ouest:* 1.3 km N Terre Rouge, 580 m, 1; 5 km SE Source Matelas, s.l., 2; 13.1 km E Croix des Bouquets, s.l., 2; 5 km SE Fond Parisien, s.l., 1; Forêt des Pins, 1373–1525 m, 2; Boutilliers Road, 732–854 m, 2; *Sud:* 7 km SW Cavaillon, 122 m, 1; *República Dominicana: Monte Cristi:* 6 km W Copey, s.l:., 3; 12 km NW Río Limpio, 580 m, 1; *Santiago Rodríguez:* Loma Leonor, 18 km SW Monción, 534 m, 1; *Puerto Plata:* 10 km W Luperón, 1; *La Vega:* 10 km W Jayaco, 915 m, 1; Jarabacoa, 530 m, 1; 1 km S Constanza, 1098 m, 1; *La Altagracia:* 16 km NE La Romana, 61 m, 1; 2.4 km SE Playa Bayahibe, s.l., 3; 1 km N Playa Bayahibe, s.l., 12; 2.5 km SE Playa Bayahibe, 6; *La Romana:* Río Cumayasa, 13.5 km W La Romana, 31 m, 2; *Peravia:* Las Calderas, s.l., 1; *Azua:* Tábara Abajo, 2; 5 km S Peralta, 305 m, 2; *Independencia:* La Furnia, s.l., 2; 4 km E El Limón, s.l., 1; 4–7 km NE El Aguacate, 519–732 m, 5; *Barahona:* 10 km NW Paraíso, 244 m, 1; *Pedernales:* 26 km NE Cabo Rojo, 732 m, 3; Las Abejas, 12 km NW Aceitillar, 1129 m, 1; 17 km NW Oviedo, 183 m, 1; *Isla Saona:* 2 km N Mano Juan, s.l., 1; *Isla Catalina:* 1.

25. *Phoebis sennae sennae* Linnaeus, 1758

TL Jamaica.

FW males 28–39 mm, females 25–37 mm.

Phoebis sennae is widely distributed throughout the West Indies and is present there as only 1 subspecies, *Ph. s. sennae.* However, Schwartz and Jimenez (1982:10–11) compared a series from Montserrat and Dominica in the Lesser Antilles with a series from Hispaniola and noted that the former did not reach so large a fw length in both sexes as the latter (35 mm vs. 39 mm in males, 34 mm vs. 37 mm in females). The differences of only a few mm are very striking when the 2 series are compared. Additionally, the "diagnostic" 2 cell-end spots of about equal size on the unhw are very obsolete or even absent in Lesser Antillean specimens (6 of 12 from Montserrat, 11 of 19 from Dominica); although Hispaniolan males are likewise variable, only very occasional specimens have 1 or no unhw cell-end spots.

On Hispaniola, *Ph. s. sennae* is the most common of the sulphurs and the most widely distributed both geographically and altitudinally. We have taken specimens in habitats varying from oases in xeric lowlands (Ça Soleil, Croix des Bouquets, Villa Vásquez), open fields, roadsides, in *caféières* and *cafetales-cacaotales* and along their borders, disturbed areas or areas under cultivation, scrubby woods (Punta Caucedo), *Acacia* scrub (Monte Cristi, Cabo Rojo, Oviedo, Tierra Nueva, Las Lajas), mixed pine-hardwoods (Buena Vista, Jarabacoa, Restauración), pine forest (Obléon, Forêt des Pins), hotel gardens (Pétionville, Délugé), as well as open rolling grasslands (Lascahobas). These butterflies tend to occur more often in open and more mesic areas rather than in arid ones, but they do not shun the latter.

Elevational distribution is from sea level (Carrefour la Mort, Ça Soleil, Délugé, Colmini, Grand-Goâve, Miragoâne, Croix de Bouquets, Amani-y, Île à Cabrit, Río San Juan, Playa Bayahibe, Andrés, Las Lajas, Mano Juan) to 2227 m (La Nevera) in the Cordillera Central, 1617 m (Obléon, Los Arroyos) on the Massif de la Selle and its front ranges, and 1129 (Las Abejas) on the Sierra de Baoruco. Noteworthy is the absence of records from the Sierra de Neiba highlands, although *Ph. s. sennae* occurs in the valley (El Cercado, 702 m) between the Neiba's 2 ranges and on the southern slopes of the south range (Neiba). *Phoebis s. sennae* has been previously reported from Île de la Gonâve and Île à Cabrit (Schwartz, 1983a:52), but these are the first specimens from Isla Saona.

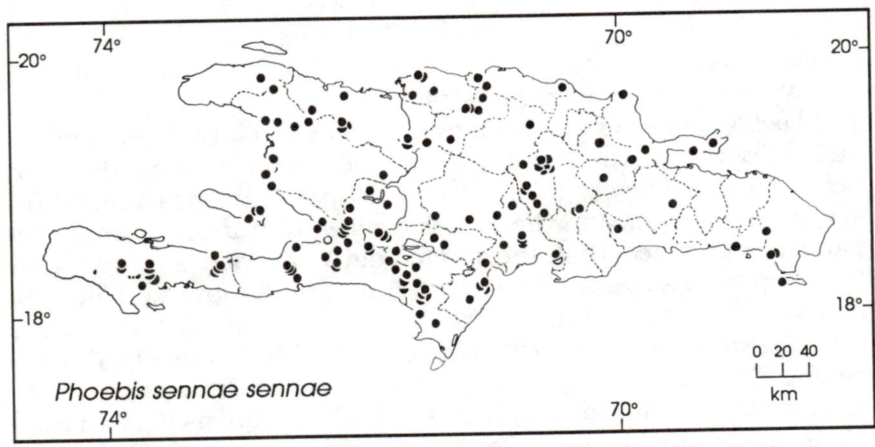

Times of collection were between 0800 and 1730 h at temperatures between 18°C (La Nevera) and 39°C (Samaná). Most specimens have been taken in July (235), with lesser numbers in June (72) and August (64). There are 23 specimens from January, 13 from May, 11 from December, 8 from April, 2 from March, and 1 each from February and November. *Phoebis s. sennae* is on the wing during the entire year, but there is a major peak of abundance during the summer.

Phoebis s. sennae feeds on the nectar from *Hibiscus rosasinenesis* (Dondon, Thomonde, Terre Rouge), *Hibiscus brasiliensis* (Canoa), *Lantana ovatifolia* (Las Lajas), *Cordia* sp. (1.1 and 3.8 km N Terre Rouge), *Ixora* sp. (3.8 km N Terre Rouge, 2.5 km SE Playa Bayahibe, Peralta, 26 km NE Cabo Rojo), *Antigonon leptopus* (Azua), *Bidens pilosa* (11 km N Neiba), *Ageratum conyzoides* (Vallejuelo), and *Tournefortia hirsutissima* (Peralta, Paso Bajito). Drinking congregations of *Ph. s. sennae*, most often at mud puddles in dirt roads, are of common occurrence and have been observed at Thomonde, Terre Rouge, Soliette, Grand-Goâve (with *B. p. polycrates*), Los Cerezos (with *A. c. clorinde*), Polo, Barahona, and 11 km N Neiba (with other large pierids).

A copulating pair was taken on 8.viii (Constanza, 1098 m, 1500–1545 h).

Specimens: Haiti: Nord-Ouest: 7.5 km SE Port-de-Paix, 1; 1.3 km S Balladé, 31 m, 1; *Nord:* Carrefour la Mort, s.l., 3; Dondon, 381 m, 3; 1.8 km S Dondon, 366 m, 2; 5.9 km S Dondon, 366 m, 1; 5.6 km SE Dondon, 336 m, 1; 3.2 km W Plaisance, 305 m, 1; *l'Artibonite:* Rivière Pendu, 15.0 km N Gros Morne, 1; 1.6 km E Carrefour Marmelade, 854 m, 2; Ça Soleil, 1; 12.2 km W Ça Soleil, 9; 16 km E Gonaïves, 1; Les Bains des Amani-y, s.l., 1; Délugé, s.l., 7; Colmini, 6.4 km W Terre Noire, s.l., 1; 4.0 km N Thomonde, 5; *l'Ouest:* 20.3

km SW Thomonde, 2; 6.2 km E Lascahobas, 275 m, 1; 1.6 km N Saut d'Eau, 275 m, 15; 1.1 km N Terre Rouge, 534 m, 5; 3.8 km N Terre Rouge, 534 m, 3; Terre Rouge, 534 m, 5; 2.9–8.5 km S Terre Rouge, 122–488 m, 15; 1.3 km S Terre Rouge, 458 m, 1; 5 km SE Source Matelas, s.l., 2; 13.1 km E Croix des Bouquets, s.l., 2; 18.1 km SE Croix des Bouquets, s.l., 1; 3.0 km SE Fond Parisien, s.l., 1; 5 km SE Fond Parisien, s.l., 1; Soliette, 17.0 km S Fond Parisien, 488 m, 6; Forêt des Pins, 1525 m, 5; Pétionville, 458 m, 9; Boutilliers Road, 732–854 m, 23; Boutilliers Road, 1.8–2.1 km W Kenscoff road, 793–885 m, 8; 3.7 km S Kenscoff, 1617 m, 1; 0.3 km N Obléon, 1617 m, 3; 10.8 km E Léogâne, 1; 0.6 km S Découzé, 671 m, 1; 2.1 km S Découzé, 640 m, 1; 1.3 km N Béloc, 702 m, 2; 7.7 km N Jacmel, 92 m, 2; 6.7 km E Grand-Goâve, s.l., 1; 8.8 km W Grand-Goâve, s.l., 2; *Sud:* 10.7 km W Miragoâne, s.l., 1; 6.6 km S Paillant, 793 m, 1; 6.7 km SW Paillant, 763 m, 8; 8 km SW Paillant, 824 m, 2; 7 km SW Cavaillon, 122 m, 1; 4.5 km E Cavaillon, 31 m, 1; 6.2 km N Cavaillon, 61 m, 3; 7.8 km N Cavaillon, 31 m, 2; 14.1 km N Cavaillon, 366 m, 2; 4.8 km N Camp Perrin, 244 m, 2; 5.6 km N Camp Perrin, 275 m, 3; *Île à Cabrit:* 1; *Île de la Gonâve:* Anse-à-Galets, 7; hills behind Anse-à-Galets, 1; Picmi, 1; *República Dominicana: Monte Cristi:* 1 km SE Monte Cristi, 1; 4 km SE Monte Cristi, 1; 6 km W Copey, s.l., 1; 4 km NW Villa Vásquez, 61 m, 8; *Dajabón:* Los Cerezos, 12 km NW Río Limpio, 593 m, 2; 7 km N Restauración, 671 m, 1; 4 km S Restauración, 580 m, 3; *Valverde:* 12 km SW Mao, 244 m, 2; Río Guarabo, 3 km W Los Quemados, 122 m, 1; 4 km N Cruce de Guayacanes, 198 m, 1; *Santiago Rodríguez:* Loma Leonor, 18 km SW Monción, 534 m, 3; 3 km W Los Quemados, 183 m, 2; *Puerto Plata:* 0.6 km NE Estero Hondo, 2; 12 km N Cruce de Guayacanes, 214 m, 1; 9 km SE Sosúa, 6; *Santiago:* 7 km SW Santiago, 214 m, 3; *La Vega:* 10 km W Jayaco, 915 m, 1; La Palma, 19 km W Jayaco, 1007 m, 11; La Ciénaga, 915 m, 4; Buena Vista, 11 km NE Jarabacoa, 640 m, 1; Jarabacoa, 530 m, 14; 6 km S Jarabacoa, 1; 3.5 km E Paso Bajito, 732 m, 4; 1 km S Constanza, 1098 m, 4; 6 km SSE Constanza, 1403 m, 1; 10 km SE Constanza, 1647 m, 2; 18 km SE Constanza, 1586 m, 2; La Nevera, 37 km SE Constanza, 2227 m, 1; *Duarte:* 12 km SE San Francisco de Macorís, 1; Villa Riva, 1; *María T. Sánchez:* 11 km NE Río San Juan, s.l., 1; 1 km S Cruce de Rincón, s.l., 1; *Samaná:* 10.2 km W Samaná, 61 m, 1; 2 km S Las Galeras, 1; *La Altagracia:* 1 km N Playa Bayahibe, s.l., 10; 2.5 km SE Playa Bayahibe, s.l., 3; 16 km NE La Romana, 61 m, 1; *La Romana:* Río Cumayasa, 13.5 km W La Romana, 31 m, 4; *Dist. Nac.:* Punta Caucedo, 2 km W, 2 km S Andrés, s.l., 10: 30 km SW Santo Domingo, 122 m, 2; *Monte Plata:* 8 km NE Bayaguana, 2; 14 km SW Piedra Blanca, 427 m, 1; 15 km SW Piedra Blanca, 534 m, 1; *Sánchez Ramírez:* 1 km NE Las Lagunas, 183 m, 1; *Azua:* Tábara Abajo, 7; 22 km NW Cruce de Ocoa, 61 m, 4; 4 km S Peralta, 366 m, 1; 5 km S Peralta, 305 m, 35; 2.5 km W, 6.6 km N Azua, 183 m, 2; 2 km SE La Canoa, 396 m, 2; 5 km S Monte Bonito, 702 m, 1; *San Juan:* 4 km E El Cercado, 702 m, 1; 9 km E Vallejuelo, 610 m, 11; *Independencia:* 5 km NW Tierra Nueva, s.l., 1; 4 km NW Tierra Nueva, s.l., 1; 5 km SE Las Lajas, s.l., 1; La Furnia, s.l., 2; 4–7 km NE El Aguacate, 519–824 m, 3; *Baoruco:* 11 km N Neiba, 519 m, 6; 2 km SE Galván, 1; *Barahona:* 8 km ESE Canoa, 5; Polo, 702 m, 3; 2 km SW Barahona, 122 m, 5; 7 km SW Barahona, 1; 5 km SE, 3 km W Barahona, 183–397 m, 2; *Pedernales:* 5 km NE Cabo Rojo, 2; 21 km NE Cabo Rojo, 488 m, 1; 23 km NE Cabo Rojo, 488 m, 2; 24.5 km NE Cabo Rojo, 656 m, 5; 26 km NE Cabo Rojo, 732 m, 18; 27 km NE Cabo Rojo, 793 m, 1; Las Abejas, 12 km NW Aceitillar, 1129 m, 13; 1 km SE Banano, 183 m, 1; El Mulito, 21 km N Pedernales, 214 m, 1; 5 km NE Los Arroyos, 214 m, 1; 17 km NW Oviedo, 183 m, 2; *Isla Saona:* Mano Juan, 6.

26. *Phoebis editha* Butler, 1870

TL Haiti.

FW males 34–36 mm, females 30–37 mm.

Phoebis editha is considered to be a rare endemic Hispaniolan species (Riley, 1975:135). However, Brown and Heineman (1972:62) did not list the species among the Antillean pierids, and Brown (1929:11) considered *editha* as a "f. temp." of *Phoebis philea (sensu lato)*. Riley (1975) did not figure either sex of the species, but there is a fine photograph of a female in Lewis (1973:53, fig. 21). In defense of Brown's (1929) assessment of the status of *editha*, the up coloration and pattern of female *editha* are very like those of female *Ph. philea, sensu stricto* (not including *Ph. thalestris*). Female *Ph. editha* are readily distinguished by their rose-red up, with an indication of the postdiscal jagged band characteristic of female *Ph. a. rorata*. Males are difficult to distinguish from male *Ph. s. sennae*, and Riley's (1975:135) diagnosis, as written and punctuated, leaves one at a loss. But very careful reading clarifies the situation: "Underside ground color yellow in male, red-brown in female and wholly (except inner margin of forewing in male) *densely sprinkled with red-brown scales* producing a sandy effect." In other words, the un of male *Ph. editha* is basically deep orange (due to the yellow ground color and the red-brown overscaling) except for about the posterior one-third of the fw toward the inner margin. Although the posterior unfw in male *Ph. s. sennae* likewise is paler than the balance of the unfw, the anterior portion of this wing is never orange and is always some shade of yellow. Once these differences are appreciated, one has little problem separating males of the 2 species.

In case there is any remaining doubt, Coutsis (1986) described and compared the male and female genitalia of *Ph. editha* (from Port-au-Prince, Haiti) and *Ph. s. sennae*. There is no question that they are distinct species. They are sympatric and synchronous, but they have different larval food plants (Coutsis, 1983), and the genitalia of both sexes are distinct.

Schwartz (1983a:52) listed 18 specimens of *Ph. editha* from 13 Haitian localities. Some of these specimens are indeed *Ph. editha*, but the majority of them are male *Ph. s. sennae*. Hall's (1925:164) statement is pertinent: "it seems very scarce, and I am not quite convinced that the sexes described under this name really belong to the same species." He examined 1 specimen in the British Museum (Natural History) from "Hayti." Marión Heredia (1980d) listed the species from El Número-Azua, and there is a fine female from there in the MNHNSD.

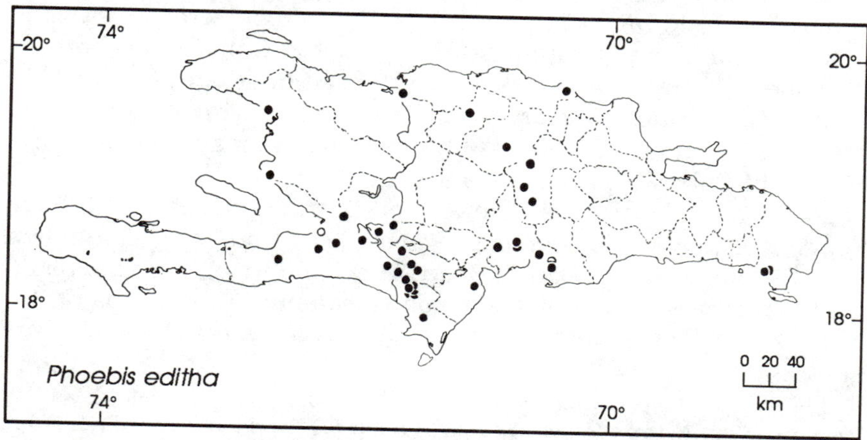

Phoebis editha is distributed from sea level (Ça Soleil, Délugé, Fond Parisien, Pepillo Salcedo, Playa Bayahibe, Tierra Nueva, El Limón) to 2288 m (18 km SE Constanza) in the Cordillera Central, to 1708 m (Los Pinos) on the Sierra de Neiba, to 1525 m on the Massif de la Selle (Forêt des Pins), and to 1129 m (Las Abejas) on the Sierra de Baoruco. Note the occurrence of *Ph. editha* in the Sierra de Neiba, a range whence *Ph. s. sennae* remains unknown except on its lower southern slopes (Neiba). Habitats within this broad elevational range are extremely varied, from *Acacia* scrub or woods (Fond Parisien, Tábara Abajo, Azua, Tierra Nueva, El Limón, Oviedo) to transitional forest (Peralta, Cabo Rojo, El Aguacate), highland deciduous forest (Los Pinos, Los Arroyos), pine forest (Forêt des Pins, 18 km SE Constanza), mixed pine-hardwoods (27 km NE Cabo Rojo), oases (Ça Soleil), xeric forest (Playa Bayahibe, El Naranjo), and at a mangrove border (Pepillo Salcedo). We have also taken specimens on an open mountainside (Boutilliers Road) and along the margin of a grassy field (1 km S Constanza).

Times of collection were between 0930 and 1630 h at temperatures between 20°C (18 km SE Constanza) and 38°C (Cruce de Ocoa, Tierra Nueva). Most specimens (51) are from July, with 16 from June, 7 from August, 6 from April, 3 from May, 2 from December, and 1 from March. The species is apparently univoltine, with the major emergence in midsummer.

We have taken *Ph. editha* and *Ph. s. sennae* syntopically at 25 localities (Ça Soleil, Délugé, 11.1 km N Terre Rouge, Pétionville, Boutilliers Road, Découzé, Forêt des Pins, Sosúa, 1 km N and 2.5 km SE Playa Bayahibe, 1 km S and 18 km S Constanza, Cruce de Ocoa, Tábara Abajo, Peralta, 11 km N Neiba, El Aguacate, El Limón, 23–26 km NE Cabo Rojo, Las Abejas, Los Arroyos, Oviedo). At only 2 of these (El Aguacate, 28 km NE Cabo Rojo—both in transitional forest) did we taken more *Ph. editha* than *Ph. s. sennae* (2:1 at the former, 5:2 at the latter). In fact, *Ph. editha* seems nowhere common; the most specimens from 1 locality are 15 from 26 km NE Cabo Rojo (in 3 visits there).

Phoebis editha uses the flowers of *Cordia* sp. (1.3 km N Terre Rouge), *Hibiscus rosasinensis* (Pétionville), *Ixora* sp. (Boutilliers Road, Peralta, 26 km N and 28 km NNE Cabo Rojo), *Lantana ovatifolia* (23 km NE Cabo Rojo), *Antigonon leptopus* (Tábara Abajo), *Bidens pilosa* (Los Quemados), and *Ageratum conyzoides* (El Naranjo).

Specimens: Haiti: l'Artibonite: 12.2 km W Ça Soleil, s.l., 2; Délugé, s.l., 1; *l'Ouest:* 1.3 km N Terre Rouge, 580 m, 1; 2 km SE Fond Parisien, s.l., 1; Forêt des Pins, 1525 m, 2; Pétionville, 458 m, 1; Boutilliers Road, 732–915 m, 5; Boutilliers Road, 1.8–2.1 km W Kenscoff road, 793–885 m, 1; 0.6 km S Découzé, 671 m, 2; *República Dominicana: Monte Cristi:* Pepillo Salcedo, s.l., 1; *Santiago Rodríguez:* 3 km W Los Quemados, 183 m, 1; *Puerto Plata:* 9 km SE Sosúa, 15 m, 2; *Santiago:* Río Bao, 8 km SE Montones Abajo, 488 m, 1; *La Vega:* 1 km W Manabao, 793 m, 1; 1 km S Constanza, 1098 m, 1; 18 km SE Constanza, 2288 m, 1; *La Altagracia:* 1 km N Playa Bayahibe, 1; 2.5 km SE Playa Bayahibe, s.l., 1; *Azua:* Tábara Abajo, 2; El Número, 1 (MNHNSD); 22 km NW Cruce de Ocoa, 61 m, 1; 2.5 km W, 6.6 km N Azua, 183 m, 1; 5 km S Peralta, 305 m, 15; *Independencia:* 21 km N Los Pinos, 1708 m, 1; 5 km NW Tierra Nueva, s.l., 1; 4 km E El Limón, s.l., 1; 4–7 km NE El Aguacate, 519–824 m, 5; 6 km SW El Naranjo, 519 m, 1; *Barahona:* 2 km SW Barahona, 122 m, 1; *Pedernales:* 23 km NE Cabo Rojo, 488 m, 6; 24.5 km NE Cabo Rojo, 656 m, 1; 26 km NE Cabo Rojo, 732 m, 15; 27 km NE Cabo Rojo, 793 m, 1; 28 km NNE Cabo Rojo, 854 m, 3; Las Abejas, 12 km NW Aceitillar, 1129 m, 2; 5 km NE Los Arroyos, 1617 m, 1; 17 km NW Oviedo, 183 m, 1.

27. *Rhabdodryas trite watsoni* Brown, 1929

TL Sánchez, Prov. de Samaná, República Dominicana.

FW males 28–36 mm, 23–38 mm.

Rhabdodryas t. watsoni was described from the male holotype from the República Dominicana and 3 males from 2 localities on Puerto Rico. This subspecies occurs throughout the Antilles (but not on Cuba or Jamaica), extending south in the Lesser Antilles from Saba to St. Lucia. *Rhabdodryas t. trite* occurs on South America. Hall (1925:164) reported this species from "near La Vega at some elevation," and Marcano (1976) noted 2 specimens from La

Palma–Constanza (3.vii.1969).

Brown (1929:29) described the un color in males as "citron yellow," and Riley (1975:pl. 17, fig. 6a) showed a painting of a male with that color. However, in the text, Riley (p. 135) stated that the un is "pale green in the male." The latter statement is correct; no males that we have taken are yellow below. All are pale "leaf-green." In fact, this is a simple way to distinguish *Rh. t. watsoni* while they are drinking with the wings closed; only this species (of the *Phoebis*-like species) has the un green rather than yellow. Examination of specimens collected since 1980, however, shows that the un has lost its pale green color in all, and they are now yellow as Brown stated. The color in life, however, is quite different.

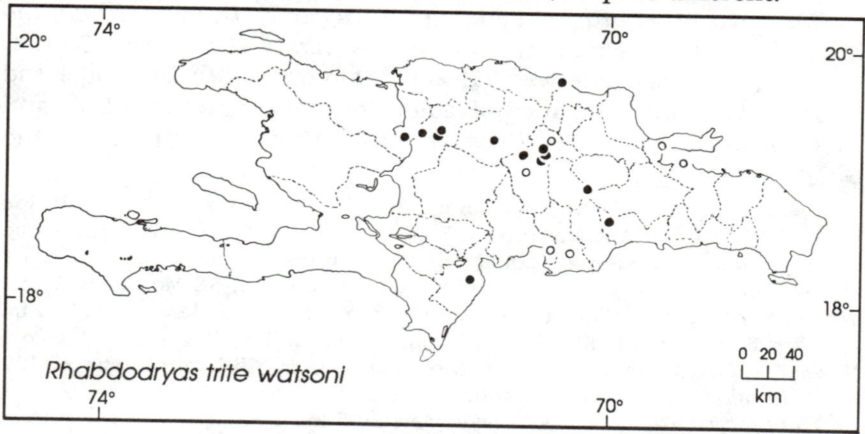

Rhabdodryas trite watsoni

Unlike *Phoebis*, one encounters *Rh. t. watsoni* most commonly while they are drinking from streamside mud, often accompanied by *Z. c. cynops*. Aggregations of *Rh. t. watsoni* may be large, with as many as 30 individuals, or there may be small groups or even single individuals drinking. At Los Cerezos, on 14.vii.1980, there was a drinking congregation at the edge of a small creek that runs through the marketplace of the village; the butterflies were at the same spot on 4.viii.1980. Then they were in the company of *A. c. clorinde*, the latter much more abundant.

Free-flying individuals are difficult to secure, since the flight is rapid, erratic, and often at the very limit of (or higher than) the reach of the collector. The flight is much more dodging than that of the similar *Ph. s. sennae* and less stiff-winged than that of *Ph. th. thalestris*.

Almost all localities where we have taken *Rh. t. watsoni* are in or near mesic hardwood forest or in *cafetales*. I have no Haitian specimens. At Restauración, the butterflies were in pine forest, and at 4.7 km SW Loma Leonor, they were in mixed pine-hardwoods. At Loma Leonor, *Rh. t. watsoni* was taken along the margin of the Río Toma; the riverbanks are clothed in mesic forest, but the area itself is mixed pine-hardwoods.

Months of collection and observation are August (13), May (10), July (11), June (9), March (2), and April and December (1 each). Riley (1975:135) gave months on Puerto Rico and Hispaniola as February-March and again in June-July; the species appears to be bivoltine, but my data do not confirm a winter-spring brood. On the Lesser Antilles the months are September and December-January.

We have taken *Rh. t. watsoni* feeding only twice, on *Lantana ovatifolia* (Restauración) and *Tournefortia hirsutissima* (Paso Bajito).

Elevations varied between 122 m (Maimón, Santo Domingo) and 1007 m (La Palma). Times of collection were between 0930 and 1730 h, at temperatures between 26°C (Manabao) and 38°C (Río Bao).

Specimens: República Dominicana: Dajabón: Los Cerezos, 12 km NW Río Limpio, 15; 9.1 km S Restauración, 519 m, 4; *Puerto Plata:* 9 km SE Sosúa, 15 m, 1; *Santiago Rodríguez:* Loma Leonor, 18 km SW Moncíon, 534 m, 3; 4.7 km SW Loma Leonor, 732 m, 1; *Santiago:* Río Bao, 8 km SE Montones Abajo, 488 m, 6; *La Vega:* La Palma, 19 km W Jayaco, 1007 m, 3; Jarabacoa, 530 m, 2; 1 km W Manabao, 793 m, 2; 3.5 km E Paso Bajito, 732 m, 5; *Monseñor Nouel:* 6 km SE Maimón, 122 m, 1; *Dist. Nac.:* 30 km NW Santo Domingo, 122 m, 2; *Barahona:* 12 km SW Barahona, 427 m, 1;

Sight record: República Dominicana: Azua: 5 km S Peralta, 305 m—1 seen, 25.iv.

28. *Aphrissa orbis browni* Munroe, 1947

TL Pivert, Dépt. de l'Artibonite, Haiti.

FW males 25–38, females 28–36 mm.

Of the 3 Hispaniolan species of *Aphrissa*, *A. o. browni* is the second most common, but it is surely not abundant. The nominate subspecies occurs on Cuba, where it appears to be only moderately common (Bates, 1935a:138, recorded 16 specimens from west-central to eastern Cuba). Hall (1925:164) noted only a single specimen in the Salvin collection from "Hayti" and suggested that *A. orbis* was even rarer on Hispaniola than on Cuba. Schwartz (1983a: 52–53) recorded 6 specimens from 4 Haitian localities; however, reexamination of this material shows that only 2 specimens from 1 locality are *A. o. browni*. In addition, I have 1 more Haitian specimen, and the species appears to be uncommon in that country. Munroe (1947:1) examined 5 specimens when he named the subspecies. These specimens were from Pivert, Pétionville, and Fond Parisien, the last 2 in the Dépt. de l'Ouest in Haiti, and 1 from Barahona, Prov. de Barahona, and 1 from Chacuey, Prov. de Dajabón, República Dominicana.

Riley (1975:pl. 17, fig. 2d) illustrated a female *A. o. orbis* from Cuba. In the text, he characterized females of this species as having "the upperside deep ochreous, . . . underside ground color less strikingly different." Hispaniolan females do not agree with this description or with the color plate; the un is rich olive, and additionally the unhw brown blotch shown by Riley is absent. The 2 subspecies also differ in size (male FW 29–35 mm, female FW 29–33 in *A. o. orbis*). The male genitalia differ (Munroe, 1947:1). It seems likely that *A. o. browni* merits specific status.

In the República Dominicana, *A. o. browni* is more abundant than in Haiti. It is a butterfly of wooded situations, primarily mesic forest (Peralta, Puesto Pirámide 204, Neiba, 26 km NE Cabo Rojo, Las Abejas, 5 km NE Los Arroyos) but has been taken on occasion in pine forest (Forêt des Pins), in cut-over hardwoods (0.6 km SE Los Arroyos), in a *cafetal* (Enriquillo), *Acacia* woods (Mano Juan), and in transitional forest (El Aguacate) near the xeric end of the vegetational spectrum. In Haiti, 2 specimens were taken in a hotel garden (Pétionville). Most of the above localities are at or above 458 m, and it would thus seem that *A. o. browni* is primarily an inhabitant of upland hardwood situations. Most of the above specimens were taken April-August. But in October, Raburn and I found *A. o. browni* at Villa Vásquez, an oasis at 61 m in the western Valle de Cibao, a totally unexpected occurrence. In 2 days, we took 8 specimens at this locality. Some of the specimens are tattered and perhaps originated elsewhere, but others are fresh. What is pertinent is that, in 12 previous and subsequent visits to this locality (all March-August), we never again encountered *A. o. browni* there. In the same month, Raburn and I also took single *A. o. browni* at Las Abejas and Cabo Rojo, both localities where we had previously taken specimens and from where *A. o. browni* was not absent in fall. We have also taken *A. o. browni* at sea level at La Furnia (17.vi) and at 519 m at Neiba (3.i), the first another lowland locality, the second a midwinter date. My first thought was that *A. o. browni* performs a vertical migration in the fall(-winter?) and that may well be so, but a residual population must remain at higher elevations. Henderson took 2 specimens on Isla Saona in January; both are fresh. In any event, the elevational distribution of *A. o. browni* is between sea level (La Furnia, Mano Juan) and 1617 m (5 km NE Los Arroyos).

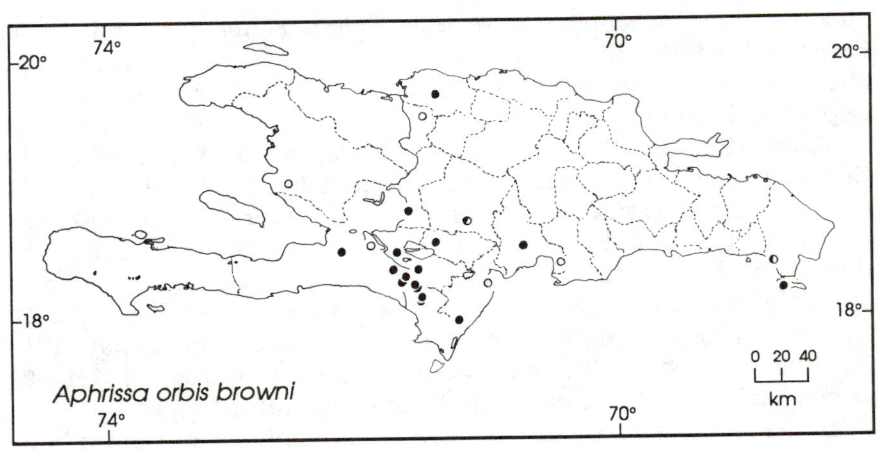

Most specimens and sight records are from July (49), with 9 in October, 6 in August, 5 each in April and January, and 2 each in June and December. Times of collection were between 0900 and 1500 h, and temperatures between 21°C (5 km NE Los Arroyos) and 38° C (Cabo Rojo, Peralta). This is the first record of any *Aphrissa* from Isla Saona.

Flowers used by *A. o. browni* include *Hibiscus rosasinensis* (Pétionville), *Ixora* sp. (Pétionville, Peralta, 23 and 26 km NE Cabo Rojo, Las Abejas—2 occasions), *Ageratum conyzoides* (26 km NE Cabo Rojo), on an unidentified white-flowered tree (Playa Bayahibe), and *Antigonon leptopus* (Villa Vásquez, the October locality noted above). A few individuals were taken while drinking on sand and mud at the edge of a river (Neiba).

Specimens: Haiti: l'Ouest: Forêt des Pins, 1525 m, 1; Pétionville, 458 m, 2; *República Dominicana: Monte Cristi:* 4 km NW Villa Vásquez, 61 m, 8; *Elías Piña:* 2 km NE Puesto Pirámide 204, 1586 m, 1; *Azua:* 5 km S Peralta, 305 m, 7; *Baoruco:* 11 km N Neiba, 519 m, 1; *Independencia:* La Furnia, s.l., 1; 4–7 km NE El Aguacate, 519–824 m, 3; *Barahona:* 9 km NW Enriquillo, 671 m, 1; *Pedernales:* 23 km NE Cabo Rojo, 488 m, 2; 26 km NE Cabo Rojo, 732 m, 12; Las Abejas, 11 km NW Aceitillar, 1220 m, 2; Las Abejas, 12 km NW Aceitillar, 1129 m, 31; 0.6 km SE Los Arroyos, 1098 m, 1; 5 km NE Los Arroyos, 1617 m, 1; *Isla Saona:* 2–2.1 km N Mano Juan, s.l., 2.

Sight records: República Dominicana: La Altagracia: 2.5 km SE Playa Bayahibe, s.l.—1 seen, 5.vii; *San Juan:* 9 km E Vallejuelo, 610 m—1 seen, 6.viii.

29. *Aphrissa godartiana* Swainson, 1821

TL none stated; restricted to Haiti by Riley (1975:136).

FW males 28–37 mm, females 34–35 mm.

Brown (1931:5) considered *A. godartiana* a species distinct from all other *Aphrissa* and illustrated convincing differences in the male genitalia of *A. godartiana*, *A. hartonia* Butler, and *A. statira* Cramer. Brown and Heineman (1972:315) considered the Jamaican *A. hartonia* a species distinct from *A. godartiana* on Hispaniola (and questionably on Puerto Rico; Ramos, 1982:63). Riley, however, combined *A. godartiana* and *A. hartonia* (1975:163). The male genitalic differences seem to be of such a magnitude that it is more appropriate to consider *A. godartiana* and *A. hartonia* separate species. The fact that on Jamaica *A. hartonia* is completely restricted to the Cockpit Country in Trelawny, St. Ann, Clarendon, and St. Elizabeth parishes, suggests that *A. hartonia* is a very local endemic species. In Jamaica and elsewhere in the West Indies, karst topographic areas like the Cockpit often foster the development of a distinct fauna. *Aphrissa hartonia* may well be an example of just such an association.

Hall (1925:164) considered *A. godartiana* "rather scarce." Schwartz (1983a:53) reported 7 specimens from 7 Haitian localities. Of the 7 specimens, 3 (those from 23, 30L, and 40B) were misidentified, leaving a total of 4 *A. godartiana* from 4 localities. Obviously, *A. godartiana* is not common in Haiti.

In the República Dominicana, *A. godartiana* is likewise uncommon, but less so than in Haiti. Combining data from both countries indicates that *A. godartiana* is primarily an inhabitant of forested or wooded situations. We have taken specimens in oases (Ça Soleil, Villa Vásquez), mesic forest (Peralta, Neiba, Las Abejas, Sierra Martín García), mesic *caféières* (Dondon), transitional forest (Cabo Rojo), xeric forest (Sosúa, Playa Bayahibe, La Romana), and mixed pine-hardwoods (Buena Vista), as well as in a hotel garden (Pétionville). The most specimens from 1 locality are 25 (1 km N Playa Bayahibe).

The elevational distribution of *A. godartiana* is from sea level (Ça Soleil) to 1129 m (Las Abejas). Most localities (13 of 18) are at or below 610 m, but the records are fairly well distributed through the known altitudinal range. The specimen from Villa Vásquez was taken at the same time as the series of "aberrantly" low *A. o. browni* (see that account). Times of collection were between 0900 and 1630 h, at temperatures between 24°C (El Aguacate) and 38°C (Playa Bayahibe, Cabo Rojo, Peralta). August ranks first with 53 specimens, and July second with 36. There are 20 specimens from December, 9 from April, 8 from January, 4 from October, and 2 from June.

Aphrissa godartiana feeds on *Hibiscus rosasinensis* (Dondon), *Antigonon leptopus* (Villa Vásquez), *Ixora* sp. (3 occasions at Cabo Rojo, 2 occasions at Peralta, 2 occasions at Playa Bayahibe, Las

Abejas), and *Tournefortia hirsutissima* (Neiba). Most unusually, *A. godartiana* fed avidly on the small flowers of *Poinsettia pulcherrima* at Neiba; this plant is rarely used as a nectar source by any rhopaloceran. These butterflies also habitually drink from mud in dirt roads or adjacent to rivers; we have observed this behavior at Soliette (drinking with large numbers of other pierids), at Neiba (large clubs on 2 occasions, with other pierids), and at Río Bao (only 1 individual, drinking alone).

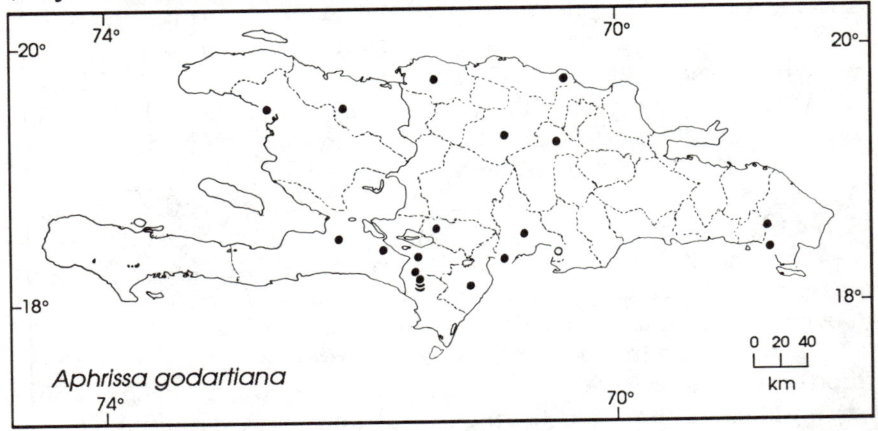

Aphrissa godartiana

On 31.vii.1986 at 26 km N Cabo Rojo in transitional woods, (temperature 32°C, weather overcast), Gonzalez observed a male *A. godartiana* land on the underside of a roadside shrub leaf; the butterfly rested there for 6 minutes, 23 seconds. This fly-and-rest behavior is especially common in this species under overcast conditions.

A copulating pair of *A. godartiana* was taken on 28.iv (Peralta, 305 m, 1325 h, 38°C); the pair (male flying) was on the lower branches of a tree adjacent to a large clump of *Ixora* sp.

Specimens: Haiti: Nord: Dondon, 381 m, 1; *l'Artibonite:* 12.2 km W Ça Soleil, s.l., 1; *l'Ouest:* Soliette, 17.0 km S Fond Parisien, 488 m, 1; Pétionville, 458 m, 1; *República Dominicana: Monte Cristi:* 4 km NW Villa Vásquez, 61 m, 1; *Puerto Plata:* 9 km SE Sosúa, 15 m, 1; *Santiago:* Río Bao, 8 km SE Montones Abajo, 488 m, 1; *La Vega:* Buena Vista, 11 km NE Jarabacoa, 640 m, 1; *La Altagracia:* 16 km NE La Romana, 61 m, 1; 1 km N Playa Bayahibe, 25; *Azua:* 5 km S Peralta, 305 m, 16; *Baoruco:* 11 km N Neiba, 519 m, 23; *Independencia:* 4–7 km NE El Aguacate, 519–732 m, 6; *Barahona:* west slope, Sierra Martín García, 305–915 m, 2; 8 km NNE Polo, 793 m, 1; *Pedernales:* 23 km NE Cabo Rojo, 488 m, 3; 24 km NE Cabo Rojo, 732 m, 9; 26 km NE Cabo Rojo, 732 m, 20; Las Abejas, 12 km NW Aceitillar, 1129 m, 17.

30. *Aphrissa statira hispaniolae* Munroe, 1947

TL Sánchez, Prov. de Samaná, República Dominicana.

FW males 33–36 mm, female 35 mm.

Aphrissa statira has 2 recognized Antillean subspecies: *A. s. cubana* d'Almeida on Cuba, Jamaica, and the Cayman Islands, and *A. s. hispaniolae* on Hispaniola. Ramos (1977:215–16) reported *A. s. cubana* breeding on Puerto Rico; Riley (1975:136–37) considered the species a vagrant there. The occurrence of the Cuban subspecies on Puerto Rico to the east of Hispaniola (with its own distinct subspecies) is puzzling.

Munroe (1947:2) named *A. s. hispaniolae* from a suite of 11 specimens, 2 without precise locality data, 8 from the type-locality, and 1 from San Lorenzo, Prov. de Hato Mayor, República Dominicana. All localities at least nominally are at sea level.

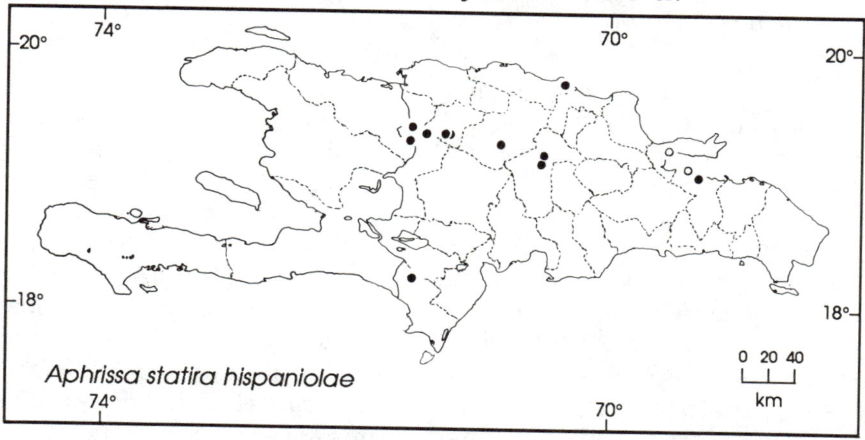

I have specimens of *A. s. hispaniolae* from only 11 localities. Six (Los Cerezos, Cañada Tirolís, Restauración, La Palma, Río Bao, Las Abejas) are in the mesic hardwood forests of the Cordillera Central and the Sierra de Baoruco at elevations of 458 and 1129 m. At Los Cerezos, the single male was taken drinking from mud in the town market; there had been a heavy rain on the previous evening and the ground was still moist. The 4 specimens from Restauración were taken flying above the river just below the junction of the Loma de Cabrera-Restauración road with that to the village of Río Limpio. The day was bright and sunny. A sixth *A. s. hispaniolae* (Sabana de la Mar) is from a weedy *Cocos* grove. The Loma Leonor specimens are from mixed pine-hardwoods, those from Sosúa in an area of karst topography with mesic hardwoods.

Times of collection were 0930–1520 h at temperatures of

26°C (Las Abejas) to 35°C (19 km SW Monción, Sabana de la Mar).

Aphrissa s. hispaniolae has been taken feeding on *Ixora* sp. (Las Abejas), *Tournefortia hirsutissima* (Sosúa on 2 occasions, Río Bao), and *Lantana ovatifolia* (Río Bao).

Specimens: República Dominicana: Dajabón: 10 km NE Restauración, 610 m, 4; Los Cerezos, 12 km NW Río Limpio, 580 m, 1; Cañada Tirolís, just S Villa Anacaona, 458 m, 1; *Santiago Rodríguez:* Loma Leonor, 19 km SW Monción, 610 m, 1; Loma Leonor, 18 km SW Monción, 549 m, 1; *Puerto Plata:* 9 km SE Sosúa, 15 m, 13; *La Vega:* La Palma, 19 km W Jayaco, 1007 m, 2; Jarabacoa, 530 m, 3; *Santiago:* Río Bao, 8 km SE Montones Abajo, 488 m, 2; *Hato Mayor:* 7 km E Sabana de la Mar, 1; *Pedernales:* Las Abejas, 12 km NW Aceitillar, 1129 m, 1.

Subfamily Dismorphiinae Rodman and Salvin, 1889

31. *Dismorphia spio* Godart, 1819

TL "Antilles."

FW males 22–38 mm, females 24–38 mm.

Two species of *Dismorphia (D. cubana* Herrich-Schäffer and *D. spio)* occur in the West Indies, the former on Cuba and the latter on Hispaniola and Puerto Rico. D'Almeida (1933) considered both taxa as subspecies of *D. amphione* Cramer, but I continue to consider them as distinct species. *Dismorphia cubana* is limited to the highest mountains (Bates, 1935a:143), although, judging from Bates's locality records, some specimens (San Diego de los Baños, Baracoa) are not from high elevations. Riley (1975:137) stated that *D. cubana* was confined to the highest mountains at about 3000 ft. in July. On Hispaniola, Hall (1925:164) summarized his material of *D. spio* by stating that he had "Half-a-dozen specimens at La Cumbre; also taken by Mr. Kaempffer at La Vega. A scarce species in heavy forest, but a very slow flier and quite easy to catch."

Bates (1939a:47) commented on 10 males and 9 females from Cap-Haïtien in northern Haiti, Camp Perrin and Etang Lachaux (1000 ft.) on the distal portion of the Tiburon Peninsula in Haiti, and San José de las Matas, 1000–2000 ft., República Dominicana. Months of capture were June and October. Two males from Camp Perrin were small (no measurements given) and had "the yellow area of the costal margin of the upper side of the hindwing broadly connected with the orange postdiscal area, instead of separated by a black bar," as in Cap-Haïtien material.

Schwartz (1983a:54) reported 68 specimens from 18 Haitian localities; he also confirmed the common occurrence of *D. spio* at elevations much below 2000 ft. (the lower limit given by Riley,

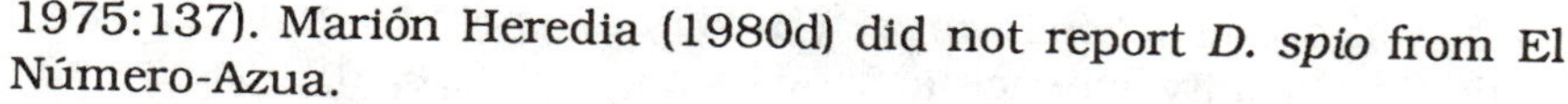

1975:137). Marión Heredia (1980d) did not report *D. spio* from El Número-Azua.

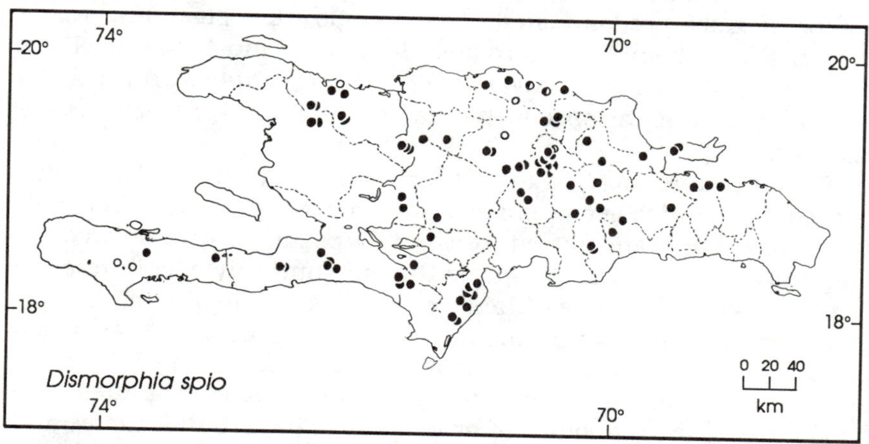

Bates's supposed differences noted above (small size, differences in uphw colored markings) between distal Tiburon peninsular material and that from elsewhere do not differentiate the former from the latter, as Bates suggested. In fact, small (but not obviously dwarf) individuals occur in both sexes, notably in August and very late July.

As is well known, *D. spio* has 3 color morphs: yellow and black (very similar to the pattern of *Heliconius charitonius* in general style); orange and black, where the "normally" yellow markings are orange; and black and orange and yellow, the fw subapical and postdiscal bars either wholly yellow or at least yellow costally. Riley's (1975:pl. 13. fig. 7) plate shows the latter condition. As might be assumed, these 3 morphs are not mutually exclusive. In any long series, there are black-and-yellow individuals in which the fw discal bar is tinged with orange toward the outer margin; at times distinguishing between black-and-orange and black-yellow-and-orange individuals is almost a matter of choice—the selection depending on the amount of yellow present toward the fw costal margins of the subapical and postdiscal bars.

Of a series of 91 males, 33 are black-and-yellow, 27 are black-yellow-and-orange, and 31 are black-and-orange; of 63 females, 22 are black-and-yellow, 25 are black-yellow-and-orange, and 16 are black-and-orange. Although one has the perception that black-and-yellow individuals far outnumber the 2 other morphs, differences between the frequencies of the 3 morphs are virtually nonexistent (55 black-and-yellow, 52 black-yellow-and-orange, 47 black-and-orange). Schwartz (1983a:54) noted that at any particular locality whence a series was available, the black-and-yellow morph predominated. Since it is the black-and-yellow morph that resembles *Heliconius charitonius* most closely, there may be a slight selective advantage for those *D. spio* with this color combination, but the specimen data do not strongly reflect this advantage.

Perhaps more so than any other Hispaniolan butterfly, *D. spio* is a confirmed dweller in shaded and wooded situations, not only mesic hardwood and mixed forests but pseudoforests as well. At many Haitian localities, *D. spio* is the only butterfly encountered in numbers within *caféières*. The lazy and "floppy" flight is characteristic, as Hall noted, and specimens are easily netted. Even when hard pressed, they only very rarely increase the speed of the flight and are much more prone to dodge among bushes, saplings, and other undergrowth about 1 m or less above the ground. Coffee and cacao plantings without undergrowth have much lower population densities than those that are somewhat rank and weedy. Even small *caféières* or patches of woods (Carrefour Marmelade) in otherwise cultivated areas have their complement of *D. spio*. Peneau is an exception, but that village has many ornamental plants and the pinewoods have been highly modified. A second exceptional locality is 9.1 km S Restauración, where 1 specimen was taken in pinewoods. A remarkable occurrence is Boca del Río, where 1 individual was taken in a dense stand of bamboo ("bamboo forest"). Although xeric forest is not the preferred habitat of *D. spio*, we have taken it in this habitat once (3 km NW Enriquillo).

Although *D. spio* is widely distributed geographically, it is absent from the extreme eastern portion of the República Dominicana (from about the longitude of Santo Domingo east to Cabo Engaño), except for 3 records from the mesic pseudoforests of the Prov. de Hato Mayor (El Valle, Sabana de la Mar). Elsewhere in this region, the easternmost records for *D. spio* are 30 km NW Santo Domingo, Las Lagunas, Bayaguana, and Esperalvillo (all mesic forest or pseudoforest). Fine high-canopied xeric forests (La Romana, Playa Bayahibe, Punta Cana) occur in the east, but despite many visits to these areas, we have never seen *D. spio* there. The species is of course absent from arid areas throughout both countries and does not occur even in oases in these regions.

Riley (1975:137) gave the elevational distribution of *D. spio* as 2000 ft. (625 m) or more. Our material shows an elevational span from sea level (Carrefour la Mort, Cruce de Rincón, Las Terrenas) to 1891 m (Scierie) on the Massif de la Selle, 1922 m (14 km SE Constanza) on the Cordillera Central, 1129 m (Las Abejas) on the Sierra de Baoruco, and 976 m (15 km S Comendador) on the Sierra de Neiba. Lack of high-elevation records for the last-named range, especially on the southern slopes of the south range (Puesto Pirámide 204), is peculiar, since the habitat is ideal. Since *D. spio* very rarely occurs in pine forest (Scierie), absence of high-elevation records from the Cordillera Central is not surprising. Of the 85 localities whence I have *D. spio*, 35 are at or below 610 m, and 41 are between 625 m and 1922 m; *D. spio* can hardly be considered an upland butterfly.

Most specimens are from July (149), with 87 in August. June, on the other hand, is represented by only 28 specimens, with 23 in March, 5 each in January and December, 4 each in May and October, 3 in November, and 2 each in April and September. Although *D. spio* is on the wing during the entire year, there is a major peak of abundance in midsummer (July). Times of collection were between 0830 and 1730 h, at temperatures between 20°C (La Palma) and 38°C (Loma Leonor, Jamao al Norte, Bonao).

We have seen *D. spio* feeding once on the flowers of *Coffea arabica* (La Palma).

A pair *in copula* was taken on 6.viii, 8 km NW Paraíso, 153 m, in mesic forest, 1515 h, 33°C; the female was flying.

Specimens: Haiti: Nord: Carrefour la Mort, s.l., 11; 2.9 km S Jonas, 153 m, 1; 1.8 km S Dondon, 366 m, 2; 5.6 km SE Dondon, 336 m, 11; 6.2 km W Plaisance, 259 m, 6; 3.5 km W Plaisance, 305 m, 9; 3.5 km S Plaisance, 259 m, 3; *l'Artibonite:* 1.6 km E Carrefour Marmelade, 854 m, 19; Platon, 6 km E Carrefour Marmelade, 793 m, 2; *l'Ouest:* Boutilliers Road, 854–915 m, 1 (FSM); 0.3 km N Obléon, 1617 m, 1; Peneau, 1.6 km SW Furcy, 1464 m, 3; 1 km SE Scierie, 1891 m, 1 (FSM); 17 km S Dufort, 702 m, 2; 1.6 km N Découzé, 702 m, 5; *Sud:* 6.7 km SW Paillant, 763 m, 14; 19.7 km N Cavaillon, 595 m, 1; *República Dominicana: Dajabón:* Los Cerezos, 12 km NW Río Limpio, 580 m, 14; 8.4 km S Restauración, 580 m, 1; 9.1 km S Restauración, 519 m, 1; Cañada Tirolís, just S Villa Anacaona, 458 m, 3; *Elías Piña:* La Laguna, 10 km S Comendador, 732 m, 1; 15 km S Comendador, 976 m, 2; *Santiago Rodríguez:* Loma Leonor, 18 km SW Monción, 534 m, 2; *Puerto Plata:* 13 km SE Luperón, 214 m, 1; 11 km N Cruce de Guayacanes, 275 m, 2; 9 km SE Sosúa, 16 m, 1; *Santiago:* 2 km E Pedro García, 427 m, 5; Río Bao, 4 km SW Mata Grande, 702 m, 1; Río Bao, 8 km SE Montones Abajo, 488 m, 7; *Espaillat:* 14 km SW Jamao al Norte, 534 m, 15; 20 km SE Jamao al Norte, 793 m, 8; *La Vega:* Güaigüi, S La Vega, 336 m, 4; 10 km W Jayaco, 915 m, 3; La Palma, 19 km W Jayaco, 1007 m, 14; La Ciénaga, 915 m, 1; *ca.* 3 km SW Boca del Río, 976 m, 1; 13 km E Manabao, 610 m, 1; 1 km W Manabao, 793 m, 6; Jarabacoa, 530 m, 8; 5 km SE Jarabacoa, 596 m, 1; 3.5 km E Paso Bajito, 732 m, 2; Buena Vista, 11 km NE Jarabacoa, 640 m, 7; 6 km SSE Constanza, 1403 m, 1; 14 km SE Constanza, 1922 m, 1; *Duarte:* 2 km SE Pimentel, 2; 10 km SE Tenares, 183 m, 2; *María T. Sánchez:* 1 km S Cruce de Rincón, s.l., 6; *Samaná:* 6.9 km NE Sánchez, 336 m, 2; 3 km SW Las Terrenas, s.l., 1; *Hato Mayor:* 17 km E Sabana de la Mar, 2; 25 km E Sabana de la Mar, 1; 6 km N El Valle, 1; *Dist. Nac.:* 30 km NW Santo Domingo, 122 m, 13; 25 km SE Yamasá, 1 (MPM); *Monseñor Nouel:* Bonao, 153 m, 4; 14 km SW Piedra Blanca, 427 m, 3; 6 km SE Maimón, 122 m, 2; *Sánchez Ramírez:* 1 km NE Las Lagunas, 183 m, 3; *Monte Plata:* 8 km W Esperalvillo, 92 m, 1; 8 km NE Bayaguana, 5; *San Cristóbal:* 8 km NW Cambita Garabitos, 534 m, 1; 11 km NW Cambita Garabitos, 671 m, 2; *San Juan:* 6 km W El Cercado, 640 m, 1; *Baoruco:* 14 km N Neiba, 671 m, 1; *Independencia:* 7 km NE El Aguacate, path to El Limón, 519–580 m, 1; *Barahona:* Polo, 702 m, 4; 1.8 km W Monteada Nueva, 1007 m, 1; 5 km SE, 6.4 km W Barahona, 488 m, 5; 7 km SW Barahona, 1; 22 km SW Barahona, 1098 m, 3; 8 km NW Paraíso, 153 m, 22 (10 MPM); 8–10 km NW Paraíso, 2 (MPM); 3 km NW Enriquillo, 244 m, 1; 9 km NW Enriquillo, 671 m, 3; *Pedernales:* Las Abejas, 12 km NW Aceitillar, 1129 m, 5; 1 km S La Altagracia, *ca.* 549 m, 3; 0.6 km SE Los Arroyos, 1098 m, 1.

Sight records: República Dominicana: Puerto Plata: Yásica, 22 km SE Puerto Plata, 122 m—1 seen, 20.vii; 8 km E Puerto Plata, *ca.* 16 m, 1 seen, 26.vii.

Family Lycaenidae Leach, 1815

Subfamily Theclinae Swainson, 1831

1. *Thereus abeja* Johnson and Matusik, 1988

TL "Upper Abeja," Prov. de Pedernales, República Dominicana. All type-localities in Johnson and Matusik, 1988, are as given; the paper itself must be consulted for necessary details of their usage, both here and in the other lycaenids and hesperiids described therein.

FW male 12 mm, female 11.5 mm.

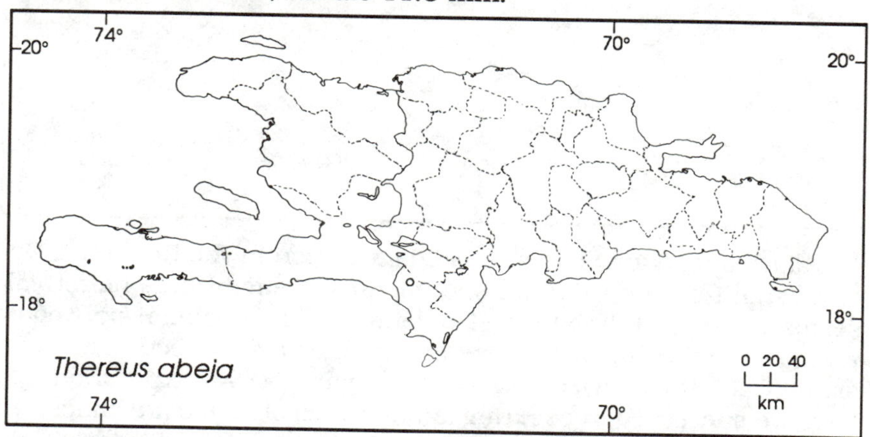

Newly described from the Sierra de Baoruco, *Th. abeja* is known from only two specimens. Both were taken while feeding on blackberries (*Rubus sp.*) on 10 and 15.vii at an elevation of 1250 m at the "abrupt margin of mesic broadleaf forest and xeric pine forest; . . . the available foot trail begins the descent between the two habitats. The area is sunny and peppered with blackberry bushes."

2. *Allosmaitia fidena* Hewitson, 1867

TL none given.

FW males 14–17 mm, females 12–17 mm.

I depart here from the nomenclature used by Riley (1975:99)

for this taxon. Previous authors have used the combination *A. fidena* (or *Thecla fidena*) for the Hispaniolan *Allosmaitia*. The genus was proposed by Clench (1963) to include, in the Antilles, Cuban *coelebs* Herrich-Schäffer and Hispaniolan *fidena*. Brown and Heineman (1972:59) kept the 2 species separate, although they unaccountably did not note the occurrence of *A. fidena* on Hispaniola and attributed it only to Puerto Rico. Ramos (1982:61) also used *A. fidena*. Only Riley seems to have used a trinominal for the allopatric populations of *Allosmaitia* on Cuba and Hispaniola (and Jamaica?). I return here to the system proposed by Clench and adhered to by most authors.

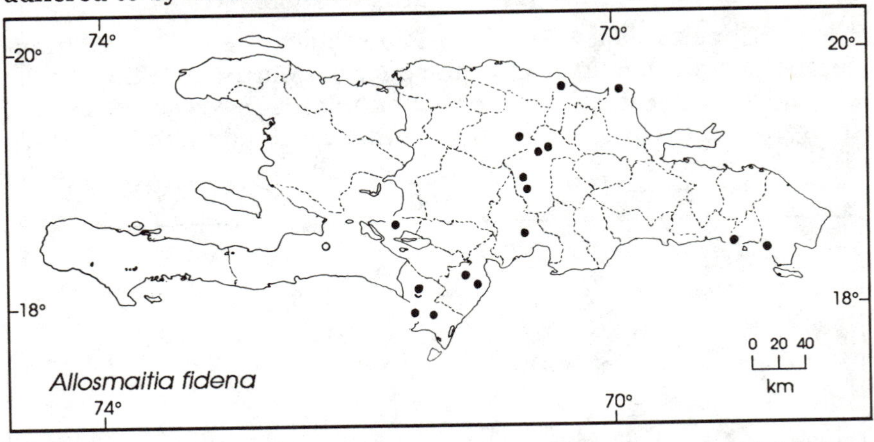

Allosmaitia fidena has a broad distribution in the República Dominicana; I have no Haitian specimens. In general, this hairstreak seems to be an inhabitant of upland mesic to semimesic woods' margins and roadsides. However, *A. fidena* also occurs in xeric areas (Cabo Rojo, Oviedo). Only at 1 locality (23 km NE Cabo Rojo) have we succeeded in securing a long series of *A. fidena;* almost all other localities are represented by single or very few individuals. At Cabral, we took a specimen feeding on *Lantana ovatifolia*, and at Peralta (2 occasions) and El Choco they were feeding on *Ixora* sp. Specimens are from June (13) and July (25), with 3 in August, 2 in May, and 1 each in January, April, and October. Times of activity varied between 0900 and 1750 h, and temperatures between 28°C (Constanza) and 37°C (Peralta).

Allosmaitia fidena, more so than most hairstreaks on Hispaniola, appears to be associated with mesic woodlands and their margins, paths, and roads. The long series from Cabo Rojo was taken from an unidentified shrub along the grassy margin of the

FROM:

LIBRARY RATE

TO:

Interlibrary Loan
Houston Public Library
500 McKinney
Houston, TX 77002

RETURN POSTAGE GUARANTEED-ADDRESS CORRECTION REQUESTED

MAY BE OPENED FOR POSTAL INSPECTION IF NECESSARY

________ PARCEL POST   ________ EXPRESS COLLECT

________ PREINSURED   ________ EXPRESS PREPAID

$________ VALUE

Alcoa road; the shrub was not in flower and had a dense covering of a member of the Passifloraceae, also not in flower.

Specimens: República Dominicana: Puerto Plata: 5 km NE El Choco, 503 m, 1; *Santiago:* 8 km E Jánico, 610 m, 1; *María T. Sánchez:* 9 km NE Río San Juan, s.l., 1; *La Vega:* 1 km S Constanza, 1098 m, 2; 13 km SE Constanza, 1403 m, 1; Jarabacoa, 530 m, 1; Buena Vista, 11 km NE Jarabacoa, 640 m, 1; *La Altagracia:* 1 km N Playa Bayahibe, 2; *La Romana:* Río Cumayasa, 13.5 km W La Romana, 1; *Azua:* 5 km S Peralta, 305 m, 4; *Independencia:* 5 km S Angel Feliz, 1; *Barahona:* 7 km SSW Cabral, 214 m, 1; 5 km SE, 3 km W Barahona, 183 m, 1; *Pedernales:* Cabo Rojo, s.l., 8; 23 km NE Cabo Rojo, 488 m, 15; 26 km NE Cabo Rojo, 732 m, 2; 17 km NW Oviedo, 183 m, 1.

3. *Electrostrymon angelia boyeri* Comstock and Huntington, 1943

TL Pétionville, Dépt. de l'Ouest, Haiti.

FW males 11–12 mm, females 9–10 mm.

I have no Haitian specimens of this hairstreak, but Comstock and Huntington (1943:71) listed 15 paratypes from Pivert, Port-au-Prince, and Les Cayes in Haiti. *Electrostrymon a. boyeri* in the República Dominicana is a hairstreak whose altitudinal range varies from sea level (Río San Juan, Cruce de Rincón, Playa Bayahibe, Andrés) to 1098 m (Constanza), but it is much more common at low elevations. Like most hairstreaks, *E. a. boyeri* inhabits open areas, but we have taken it as well in clearings in mesic forest (Santo Domingo), in *cafetales* (Jamao al Norte, Cruce de Rincón), in a weedy *Cocos* grove (Río San Juan), along the edge of an oasis (Villa Vásquez), and in *Acacia* scrub or woods (Zamba, La Descubierta, Santiago). Usually only 1 or a very few individuals are seen or collected, but at Playa Bayahibe on 25.vi.1982, we secured a series (8), all from a vine curtain along an abandoned road in xeric forest.

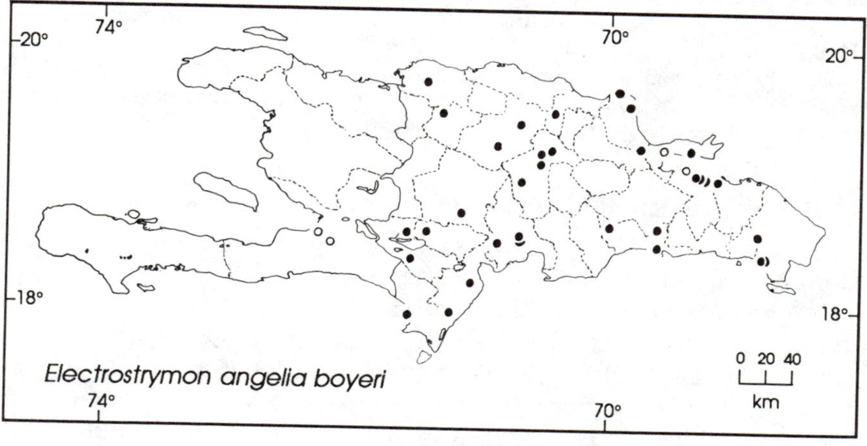

Electrostrymon angelia boyeri

On 2 occasions we have taken these hairstreaks feeding on *Bidens pilosa* (Enriquillo, Constanza), once on *Cordia globosa* (Santo Domingo), twice on *Antigonon leptopus* (Santiago), once on *Lantana ovatifolia* (Santiago), once on *Jatropha gossypiifolia* (Euphorbiaceae) (Cabo Rojo), once on *Mikania cordifolia* (Asteraceae) (Tábara Abajo), and once on an unidentified white-flowered tree (Azua). Most specimens have been taken in March (17) and June (20), with 15 in July, 6 in May, 5 in August, 3 in April, and 2 each in October, January, and December. Times of activity varied between 0900 and 1750 h, and temperatures between 26° C (Peralta) and 37°C (La Romana). At Cruce de Rincón, between 0930 and 1415 h, *E. a. boyeri* did not appear until 1100 h (30°C), at which time they were moderately abundant.

A peculiar record of predation on *E. a. boyeri* was witnessed by Gonzalez at Cabo Rojo on 28.vii. While collecting above the sea cliffs, Gonzalez netted but did not kill an *E. a. boyeri.* When he opened his net to paper the hairstreak, it escaped (injured) and flew out over the ocean. Quickly it was snapped up by 1 of several patrolling Purple Martins (*Progne subis dominicensis* Gmelin).

Specimens: República Dominicana: Monte Cristi: 4 km NW Villa Vásquez, 61 m, 2; *Santiago Rodríguez:* 4.8 km S Zamba, 183 m, 2; *Espaillat:* 14 km SW Jamao al Norte, 549 m, 2; *Santiago:* Río Bao, 8 km SE Montones Abajo, 488 m, 1; 7 km SW Santiago, 214 m, 5; *La Vega:* La Palma, 19 km W Jayaco, 1007 m, 2; Buena Vista, 11 km NE Jarabacoa, 640 m, 1; 1 km S Constanza, 1098 m, 1; *María T. Sánchez:* 9 km NE Río San Juan, s.l., 4; 6 km S Cabrera, s.l., 1; 1 km S Cruce de Rincón, s.l., 7; *Samaná:* 4.5 km E Samaná, 1; *Hato Mayor:* 4 km E Sabana de la Mar, 2; 7 km E Sabana de la Mar, 2; 17 km E Sabana de la Mar, 2; 25 km E Sabana de la Mar, 1; *La Altagracia:* 1 km N Playa Bayahibe, s.l., 11; 2.5 km SE Playa Bayahibe, 1; 16 km NE La Romana, 61 m, 2; *Dist. Nac.:* 9 km NE Guerra, 1; Punta Caucedo, 2 km W, 2 km S Andrés, s.l., 2; 30 km NW Santo Domingo, 122 m, 2; *Azua:* Tábara Abajo, 1; 2.5 km W, 6.6 km N Azua, 183 m, 1; 5 km S Peralta, 305 m, 1; *San Juan:* 9 km E Vallejuelo, 610 m, 1; *Baoruco:* 14 km N Neiba, 671 m, 1; *Independencia:* 7 km NE El Aguacate, 519 m, 1; 3.3 km E La Descubierta, 1; *Barahona:* 12 km SW Barahona, 427 m, 1; 9 km NW Enriquillo, 671 m, 1; *Pedernales:* Cabo Rojo, s.l., 8.

4. *Electrostrymon minikyanos* Johnson and Matusik, 1988

TL "Middle Abejas," 1500 m, Prov. de Pedernales, República Dominicana (see type-locality comment under *T. abeja*).

FW male 10 mm, female unknown.

Known only from the male holotype (although 4 individuals were sighted in 1986), *E. minikyanos* is another distinctive hairstreak known only from the Las Abejas region in the Sierra de Baoruco. All were observed in a rather xeric clearing. "Middle Abejas" is "along a path from lower Abejas [and] is more interspersed with understory. Areas without canopy are frequent in the region 50–100 m below adjacent pine-covered ridges." The holotype was taken on 11.vii at 1030 h.

The male is distinctive in that the uphw is dull purplish, and the upfw is dull purplish basally, colors quite different from the other Hispaniolan *Electrostrymon*, *E. a. boyeri*.

5. *Chlorostrymon simaethis simaethis* Drury, 1773

TL St. Christopher, Lesser Antilles.

FW males 9–12, females 9–12.

Until 1986 we had never seen or collected *Ch. s. simaethis* on Hispaniola. The subspecies has a broad distribution on the West Indies, from Cuba, whence Bates (1935a) had seen no specimens, to St. Vincent and Grenada in the Lesser Antilles, where Pinchon and Enrico (1969:113) noted its local abundance on Martinique, and on Guadeloupe and Grenada. Comstock and Huntington (1943:74) reported *Ch. s. simaethis* from Hispaniola, without precise locality data. Hall (1925:188) stated that there was "one from La Vega" (seen or collected?), and that Godman and Salvin had reported the butterfly from "Hayti." Although we had never actively looked for *Ch. s. simaethis* and although we have been aware of the high-flying and high-resting habits of this hairstreak, it is remarkable that we had never encountered it.

In May 1986, Gonzalez and I took 3 specimens at Estero Hondo in a well-shaded *Roystonea hispaniolana* grove. Later, Gonzalez collected specimens at 3 other localities, 2 of which were xeric woods (Playa Bayahibe) and the third *Acacia* scrub. Thus, *Ch. s. simaethis* occurs in both mesic and highly xeric situations but seems to prefer the latter. Even at Estero Hondo, nearby areas are *Acacia* woods, and the hairstreaks may only have been in the palm grove to feed or to escape the sun. At Oviedo, the 4 specimens were taken on 2 different days from the same low *Acacia* tree; the tree had a vine of *Cardiospermum corindum* (Sapindaceae) growing over it, and in fact at Estero Hondo, in some felled *Acacia* trees nearby, we found other *C. corindum* vines, now dead. We did not find this vine at Playa Bayahibe, but doubtless it occurs there also.

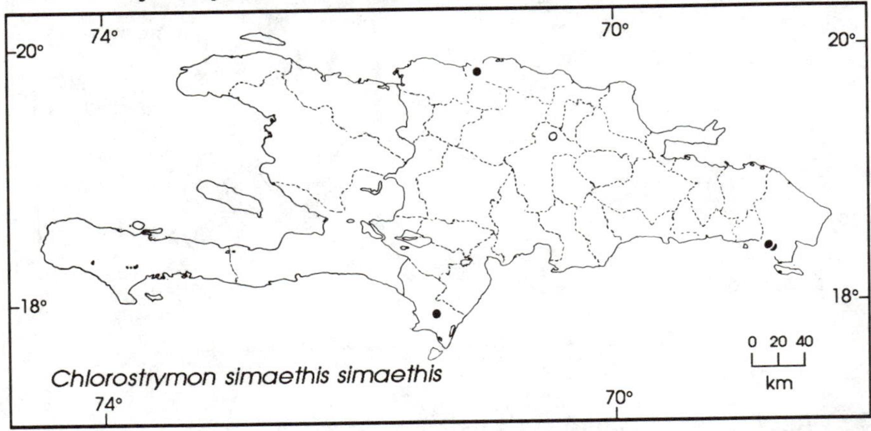

Chlorostrymon simaethis simaethis

Most specimens are from May (4), with 2 each in June and July, and 1 from August; the latter is much battered.

We have taken *Ch. s. simaethis* feeding on *Phyla scaberrima* (Verbenaceae) on both visits to Estero Hondo, on *Ixora* sp. at 1 km N Playa Bayahibe, and on roadside *Lippia nodiflora* (Verbenaceae) adjacent to xeric woods at 2.5 km SE Playa Bayahibe.

The elevational distribution is from sea level (Playa Bayahibe) to 183 m (Oviedo).

Specimens: República Dominicana: Puerto Plata: 0.6 km NE Estero Hondo, 3; *La Altagracia:* 1 km N Playa Bayahibe, 1; 2.5 km SE Playa Bayahibe, 1; *Pedernales:* 17 km NW Oviedo, 183 m, 4.

6. *Chlorostrymon maesites maesites* Herrich-Schäffer, 1864

TL Cuba.

FW males 9–10 mm, females 8–9 mm.

Although *Chlorostrymon m. maesites* is known from the Bahamas, Cuba, Jamaica, and Puerto Rico (Riley, 1975:101), it has not been previously reported from Hispaniola. Unaccountably, we did not secure this tiny hairstreak until 1986, when Gonzalez collected 24 specimens, all from 2 localities that he and I have visited over the years.

The precise situation at Cabo Rojo is so unique that the circumstances there bear description. The Alcoa Exploration Company (now Ideal Dominicana) has a few house trailers near the edge of the sea cliffs about 20 m above the ocean. The Cabo Rojo area is constantly windswept, and in the late afternoon the forceful winds come off the land. Thus the trailers have their oceanside faces to the lee of the wind. This sheltered area has a few trees (including 1 *Citrus*), as well as a large clump of *Jatropha gossypiifolia*. Both the tree and the *J. gossypiifolia* support a thriving community of moderately large green (and thus well-camouflaged) spiders. These spiders wait in the slightly up-curled leaves of the *Citrus*, where they are most abundant. A few smaller individuals inhabit the *J. gossypiifolia*. The first *Ch. m. maesites* that Gonzalez collected was taken from one of these green spiders! As he became aware of the intricacies of the foraging situation at this precise spot, Gonzalez noted that the spiders were regularly feeding not only on these small hairstreaks but also on other lycaenids (*Strymon*, *Pseudochrysops*) and on much larger butterflies (*Ascia m. eubotea*, *Eunica monima*). Apparently, this particular locality is 1 to which butterflies are "forced" to go to get out of the wind; once there, they land to rest or to forage, and thus become easy prey for the spiders. The entire situation is most unusual. The long series from Cabo Rojo attests to the ease with which these hairstreaks were taken there; none was seen elsewhere in this entire region, despite many man-hours looking for them.

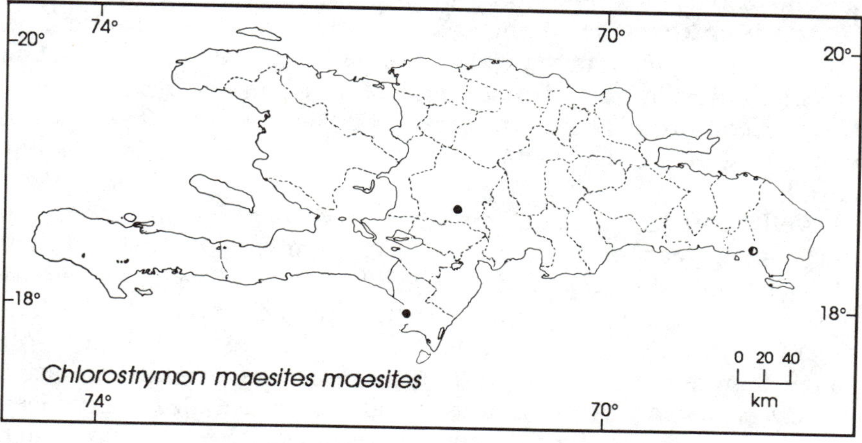

Chlorostrymon maesites maesites

The Vallejuelo specimen was taken while feeding on *Acacia vogeliana*, and 1 of the Cabo Rojo individuals was secured while feeding on the flowers of *J. gossypiifolia*. One of these hairstreaks was observed by Gonzalez as it fed on *Morinda citrifolia* (Río Chavón).

Chlorostrymon m. maesites occurs from sea level to 610 m. Most specimens and the sight record are from July (16), with 7 in June and 1 in August. Times of collection were (at Cabo Rojo) 1350 to 1810 h, quite late in the afternoon. The time at Vallejuelo was 1020–1445 h. Temperatures varied between 27°C (Cabo Rojo) and 37°C (Vallejuelo).

Specimens: República Dominicana: San Juan: 9 km E Vallejuelo, 610 m, 1; *Pedernales:* Cabo Rojo, s.l., 23.

Sight record: República Dominicana: La Altagracia: Río Chavón, 8 km SE La Romana, s.l.—1 seen, 12.vii.

7. *Tmolus azia* Hewitson, 1873

TL México.

FW males 9–10 mm, females 8–9 mm.

Tmolus azia has only recently (Vyhmeister, 1980) been reported for the first time from the Greater Antilles on the island of Jamaica; 2 specimens were taken at 2 localities in Manchester Parish. The individuals were netted in February and July; the elevation at 1 locality is *ca.* 450 m. Beck (1983) first reported this tiny hairstreak from Hispaniola, where a short series was taken about "10 km NW of the city of Santiago and several hundred meters from the north bank of the Río Yaque del Norte," Prov. de Santiago, República Dominicana. Specimens were collected at this locality on 22 and 28.vi.1981. (Pinchon and Enrico's record [1969:118–19] of *T. azia* from Grenada in the Lesser Antilles has been overlooked; the specimen was taken on 22.iv.1967.) [A second species of *Tmolus*, described by Johnson and Matusik in the Addendum of the present work, is known from 1 female specimen from a salt marsh just east of La Romana and 1 male with incomplete locality data.]

We first collected *T. azia* on 15.vi.1980, at Río Cumayasa, and in the same year took specimens SE Constanza and Valle Nuevo at high elevations in the Cordillera Central. In succeeding years we took a number of specimens, most from high elevations in the Cordillera Central and the Sierra de Neiba, including the intermontane valley between the north and south ranges of the latter massif. *Tmolus azia* was very abundant in 1986, and we added many localities and increased the number of specimens. We have not taken the species in Haiti but assume that it is present there, since these tiny inconspicuous hairstreaks are easily overlooked.

The elevational range of *T. azia* exceeds that of any other hairstreak (and, in fact, almost any other Hispaniolan rhopaloceran)—from sea level (Río Chavón, Río Cumayasa, Cabo Rojo, Isla Saona) to 2105 m (Valle Nuevo). From this broad altitudinal distribution and from the scattering of the locality records (the species is very common at some of them), I infer that *T. azia* has been on Hispaniola for some time and is not a recent adventive. Its occurrence on Isla Saona likewise suggests long residence.

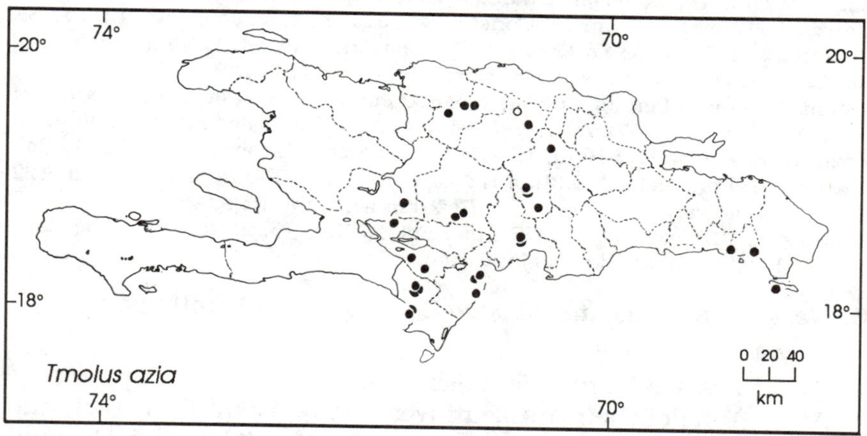

Times of activity varied between 0840 and 1750 h, and temperatures between 27°C (Valle Nuevo) and 38°C (23 km NE Cabo Rojo). Most specimens have been taken in May (55), with 44 in July, 32 in August, 17 in June, 7 in January, and 1 in October. *Tmolus azia* occupies a variety of habitats, from lowland xeric forest edges, palm groves, *Acacia* scrub and woods, and along paths and weedy and scrubby roadsides, to high-elevation roadsides adjacent to dense mesic deciduous forests, and meadows in pine forest.

We have taken *T. azia* on *Melilotus alba* (Fabaceae) and *Cynoglossum amabile* at Constanza and Valle Nuevo, on *Daucus* sp. at Comendador, and most abundantly on *Acacia vogeliana* with its masses of cream flowers (Vallejuelo, 3 occasions). *Tmolus azia* also feeds on the flowers of: *Tephrosia purpurea* (Mao), *Bidens pilosa* (Mao, Los Quemados), *Heliotropium curassavicum* (Boraginaceae) (Santiago), *Antigonon leptopus* (Santiago, 3 occasions), *Turnera ulmifolia* (Zamba), *Acacia vogeliana* (Azua), *Acacia farnesiana* (26 km NE Cabo Rojo), *Geoffroea inermis* (Río Chavón), *Sida* sp. (19 km NE

Cabo Rojo), *Jatropha gossypiifolia* (Cabo Rojo), *Croton barahonensis* (Vallejuelo), *Ageratum conyzoides* (Barahona), and *Parthenium hysterophorus* (Asteraceae) (Puerto Escondido).

Tmolus azia is sexually dichromatic (see Howe, 1975:pl. 51, figs. 23, 24). In addition to the color and pattern of the wings, the abdomens of males in life are bright orange-red, and this pigmentation persists in the pinned specimens for at least 4 years.

Specimens: República Dominicana: Valverde: 12 km SW Mao, 244 m, 3; *Elías Piña:* 21 km S Comendador, 1464 m, 4; *Santiago Rodríguez:* 3 km W Los Quemados, 183 m, 4; 4.8 km S Zamba, 183 m, 38; *Santiago;* 7 km SW Santiago, 214 m, 16; *La Vega:* Güaigüí, S La Vega, 336 m, 3; 10 km SE Constanza, 1647 m, 3; 14 km SE Constanza, 1921 m, 1: Valle Nuevo, 25 km SE Constanza, 2105 m, 1; *La Romana:* Río Chavón, 8 km SE La Romana, s.l., 3; Río Cumayasa, 13.5 km W La Romana, 1; *Azua:* 2.5 km W, 6.6 km N Azua, 183 m, 1; 5 km S Peralta, 305 m, 1; *San Juan:* 9 km E Vallejuelo, 610 m, 11; 7 km NE Vallejuelo, 672 m, 1; *Independencia:* 21 km N Los Pinos, 1708 m, 1; 7 km NE El Aguacate, 519 m, 1; 0.6 km NW Puerto Escondido, 519 m, 1; *Barahona:* Barahona, s.l., 2; 3.3 km NE La Ciénaga, 1; 2 km SW Barahona, 122 m, 1; *Pedernales:* Cabo Rojo, s.l., 17; 2 km NE Cabo Rojo, s.l., 2; 19 km NE Cabo Rojo, 427 m, 1; 26 km NE Cabo Rojo, 732 m, 5; 23 km NE Cabo Rojo, 488 m, 1; *Isla Saona:* 1 km N Mano Juan, s.l., 1.

8. *Nesiostrymon celidus aibonito* Comstock and Huntington, 1943

TL Aibonito, Puerto Rico.

FW males 10–12 mm, females 11 m.

At the time of their Antillean lycaenid revision, Comstock and Huntington (1943) had no specimens of *N. celidus* from Hispaniola. Likewise, Brown and Heineman (1972:232) did not record the species from Hispaniola. However, Riley (1975:101) attributed the Puerto Rican subspecies, *N. c. aibonito*, to Hispaniola as well as Puerto Rico. One trait of *N. c. aibonito* (in contrast to nominate *N. celidus* Lucas from Cuba and *N. c. shoumatoffi* Comstock and Huntington from Jamaica) is that, in males, the metallic fw blue area is less extensive than in other subspecies, thus allowing the stigma to be discerned; my specimens allow this determination without question, and I follow Riley's assignment.

My short series of *N. c. aibonito* is from localities scattered over the República Dominicana; I have no Haitian specimens. Elevations varied between 61 m (La Romana) and 1281 m (Aceitillar). Times of collection were between 0900 and 1640 h, and temperatures between 23°C (Las Abejas) and 36°C (La Romana). Apparently this hairstreak is generally uncommon; almost the rule is our collecting 1 specimen per locality. The 2 La Romana specimens were taken on the same day; we have visited this locality 14 times over the years and have never seen other individuals. Habitats are generally wooded, either xeric or mesic, but on 1 occasion (Jamao al Norte) a specimen was taken in a weedy clearing along a stream well within a *cafetal*. At Constanza we collected 1 individual in an open field with other species of hairstreaks. The Las Abejas locality is a narrow wooded ravine with deciduous forest, surrounded by pine forest, and another specimen from this same area (Aceitillar) was taken in open pine forest. My specimens and records are from June (7), July (6), and August (4). We have taken *N. c. aibonito* feeding on *Senecio haitiensis* (Asteraceae) in pine forest at Aceitillar, and on *Palicourea barbinervia* (Rubiaceae) at Las Abejas, 12 km NW Aceitillar.

Specimens: República Dominicana: Espaillat: 14 km SW Jamao al Norte, 534 m, 1; *La Vega:* 1 km S Constanza, 1098 m, 1; *La Altagracia:* 16 km NE La Romana, 61 m, 2; *Azua:* 5 km SW Monte Bonito, 702 m, 1; *Independencia:* 4–7 km NE El Aguacate, 519–824 m, 2; *Pedernales:* 1 km SE Banano, 143 m, 2; Las Abejas, 11 km NW Aceitillar, 1220 m, 1; 1 km N Aceitillar, 1281 m, 1.

Sight records: República Dominicana: Barahona: 1.8 km W Monteada Nueva, 1007 m—1 seen, 14.viii; *Pedernales:* 1 km SE Banano, 183 m—1 seen, 11.vi; Las Abejas, 12 km NW Aceitillar, 1129 m—1 seen, 27.vii.

9. *Terra hispaniola* Johnson and Matusik, 1988

TL "Slightly below upper Abejas," Prov. de Pedernales, República Dominicana (see comment under TL of *H. abeja*).

FW male 13 mm, female 12.5 mm.

Terra hispaniola is the third species of hairstreak known only from the Las Abejas region of the Sierra de Baoruco at elevations of about 1250 m. All specimens (4 males, 1 female) have been taken in a "relatively restricted area of Las Abejas, just below upper Abejas, where mesic broadleaf forest largely replaces pine forest. . . .

All individuals have been taken while patrolling close (0.3 m) above the ground or nectaring on flowers of about the same height. . . . an individual was observed near the base camp . . . a xeric area nearly 3 km. from upper Abejas. All collection habitats of *T. hispaniola* differ markedly from those of *N. celida [celidus]*. We have found *N. celida [celidus]* only in the vicinity of lower Abeja and most commonly in dense woods or along their immediate margins."

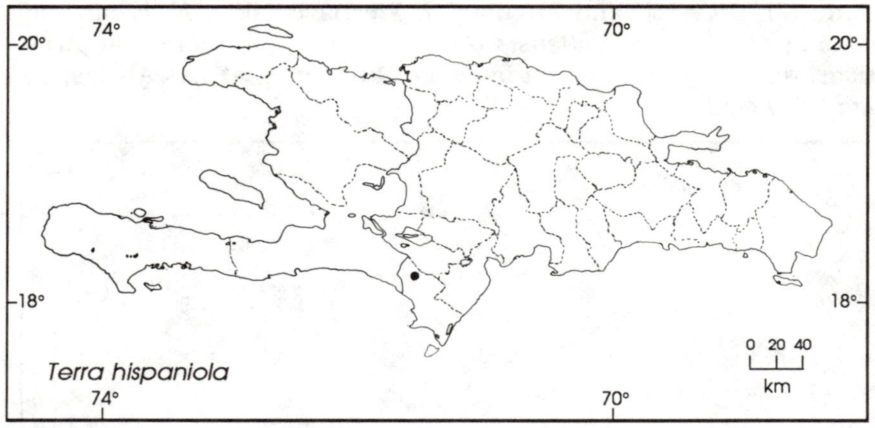

Terra hispaniola

The data on the type-series of *T. hispaniola* include the fact that the holotype male and allotype female were taken *in copula* on 6.vii; inclusive dates for the series are 6–15.vii. Some specimens were collected while taking nectar from "small blue flowers" (= *Cynoglossum amabile*?).

Specimen: República Dominicana: Pedernales: upper Abejas, 1.

10. *Strymon acis petioni* Comstock and Huntington, 1943

TL Port-au-Prince, Dépt. de l'Ouest, Haiti.

FW males 13–14 mm, females 13–14 mm.

We did not secure *S. a. petioni* until March 1984, when these hairstreaks were very locally abundant. The type-series (3 specimens) was collected in January, all from the type-locality (Comstock and Huntington, 1943:64). Our visits to Hispaniola have included only a very few days in early January. But Brown and Heineman (1972:235–37) noted records of *S. a. gossei* Comstock and Huntington on Jamaica in the months of March, April, June, July, and November, July having the most records, with March second in frequency. March appears to be the month of eclosion on Jamaica, but the butterflies are still present in some numbers later in the year (notably July). Simon and Miller (1986:6) reported a single individual, taken v.1984, on Great Inagua Island in the southern Bahamas, that is closer to *S. a. petioni* than to the Bahamian subspecies *S. a. armouri* Clench. Similar material has been reported from the Turks and Caicos Islands (Clench and Bjorndal, 1980:11).

In 1984 these hairstreaks were locally abundant in the xeric areas near Monte Cristi. Seven specimens were taken in a burned-over tussocky grass area (4 km SE Monte Cristi), where they were feeding on the white flowers of *Croton linearis* (Euphorbiaceae), the presumed larval food plant. (Brown and Heineman [1972:236] suggested that on Jamaica *Croton discolor* might be the larval food plant. In south Florida, where *C. linearis* is a common "wild" croton, especially in pinewoods, *S. a. bartrami* Comstock and Huntington may be locally abundant.) Almost all our specimens were taken feeding on these flowers. At 1 km SE Monte Cristi, *S. a. petioni* was likewise locally common along the main highway, again feeding on *C. linearis*.

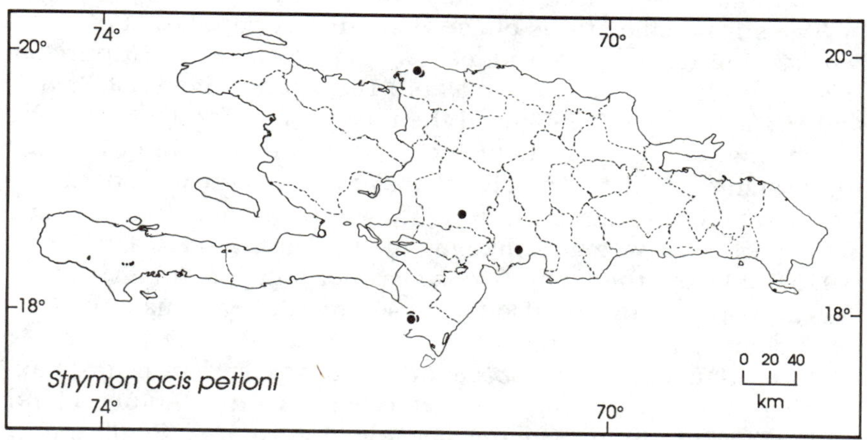

In 1986, *S. a. petioni* was widespread and moderately to very abundant both at Monte Cristi and elsewhere in xeric areas. Individuals were invaribly encountered in stands of *Croton*, either *C. linearis* (Monte Cristi, Cabo Rojo, Canoa) or *C. barahonensis* (Vallejuelo, 4 occasions). These hairstreaks feed on the small white flowers of these plants, and 1 other individual was taken on an unidentified white-flowered tree (Azua) in *Acacia* scrub, near a small stand of *C. linearis*. In December, when *C. barahonensis* was not in bloom, I saw 1 *S. a. petioni* on *Ageratum conyzoides* (Vallejuelo).

Most specimens and the sight record are from August (27), with 12 from March, 6 from July, 5 from May, 3 from June, and 1 from

December.

Strymon a. petioni occurs from sea level (Cabo Rojo) to 610 m (Vallejuelo), always in arid areas. Times of collection were between 0820 and 1725 h, at temperatures of 28°C (Canoa) to 37°C (Vallejuelo). Some specimens of *S. a. petioni* were secured by Gonzalez in the lee of the trailer at Cabo Rojo (see account of *Chlorostrymon m. maesites*).

Specimens: República Dominicana: Monte Cristi: 1 km SE Monte Cristi, 7; 4 km SE Monte Cristi, 10; *Azua:* 2.5 km W, 6.6 km N Azua, 183 m, 1; *San Juan:* 9 km E Vallejuelo, 610 m, 27; *Barahona:* 11.5 km ESE Canoa, s.l., 1; *Pedernales:* Cabo Rojo, s.l., 6; 2 km NE Cabo Rojo, s.l., 1; 2 km N Cabo Rojo, s.l., 1.

Sight record: República Dominicana: San Juan: 9 km E Vallejuelo, 610 m—1 seen, 24.xii.

11. *Strymon columella cybirus* Hewitson, 1874

TL Cuba and Jamaica.

FW males 10–13 mm, females 10–12 mm.

The subspecific status of the Hispaniolan population of *S. columella* Fabricius is questionable. Comstock and Huntington (1943:79) assigned *S. c. columella* to Hispaniolan material. Brown and Heineman (1972:237) used the name *cybira* for Jamaican and Cuban material (as had Comstock and Huntington) and felt that the assignment of the name *columella* to Hispaniolan specimens was "useful but rather arbitrary." They in turn noted that Hispaniolan specimens were most like mainland *S. c. istapa* Reakirt. Riley (1975:105) used the name *S. c. cybira* not only for Cuban and Jamaican populations but also for those from the Bahamas, the Cayman Islands, and Hispaniola.

As on Jamaica, *S. c. cybirus* is the most common of the hairstreaks. It occurs from sea level (Vieux Bourg d'Aquin, Monte Cristi, Río San Juan, Samaná, La Romana, Andrés, Sombrero) to 1891 m (Scierie) and seems to be generally well distributed between these 2 extremes. The butterfly is found almost always associated with grassy areas: fields, roadsides, and clearings in *caféières* and *cafetales*. Only very rarely is it encountered in forests or pseudoforests that are shaded. We have taken specimens in a *Cocos* grove (Samaná) and on a path through a *cafetal* (Enriquillo), but these are exceptions.

Specimens have been taken feeding on the flowers of *Daucus* sp. (Carrefour Marmelade), *Bidens pilosa* (Cañongo, Los Quemados, Santiago, Constanza [2 occasions], Las Lagunas, Higüey, La Romana, 1 km N Playa Bayahibe, Peralta, Azua, Tábara Abajo, 19 km

NE Cabo Rojo), *Tephrosia purpurea* (Mao, Cabo Rojo), *Croton linearis* (1 km SE Monte Cristi, Tres Charcos, Cabo Rojo), *Croton barahonensis* (Vallejuelo, 2 occasions), *Heliotropium curassavicum* (La Furnia), *Stachytarpheta jamaicensis* (2.5 km SE Playa Bayahibe, Mencía), *Sida* sp. (Rancho Arriba, La Descubierta), *Antigonon leptopus* (Thomazeau, Santiago, Azua, Sombrero), *Parthenium hysterophorus* (Santiago, Constanza), *Tournefortia hirsutissima* (Sosúa, 2 occasions), *Melochia tomentosa* (4 km NE Cabo Rojo, 2 km SE La Canoa), *Ageratum conyzoides* (5 km SE, 3 km W Barahona, Vallejuelo [2 occasions], Peralta, 26 km NE Cabo Rojo [2 occasions], Aceitillar, Barahona), *Ixora* sp. (1 km N Playa Bayahibe), and *Acacia farnesiana* (4 km NE Cabo Rojo).

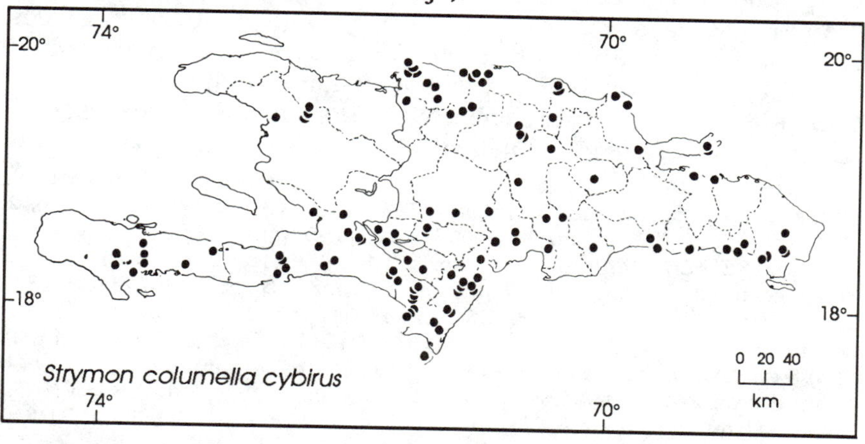

Habitats are about equally divided between xeric and mesic. Fond Parisien and La Furnia lie within the Cul de Sac–Valle de Neiba, but the localities are mesic. Monte Cristi and Cabo Rojo are xeric. I have most specimens (103) from July, with 71 from June, 86 from May, 53 from August. December is represented by 49, and January by 32, with 21 from April. October and March are represented by 20 specimens each, February, September, and November have from 1 to 3 specimens each. Brown and Heineman (1972: 238–39) reported *S. c. cybirus* on the wing in Jamaica in all months except October, with the greatest number of records for July and the least in the fall and winter (November-January).

Times of activity varied between 0800 and 1750 h, and temperatures between 21°C (Scierie) and 40°C (1 km N Playa Bayahibe). On several occasions, *S. c. cybirus* has been taken under overcast conditions (Paillant, Constanza, Samaná, Las Galeras, Río Cumayasa, Polo, Enriquillo, Cabo Rojo, Mencía), and at many of these places, the collecting ended because of heavy rain or even hail (Mencía). Collecting repeatedly at Constanza since 1980 has allowed us to observe that these hairstreaks are very local in a large grassy field behind the hotel; there they may be found regularly only in a small portion of the field, where there is an abundance of *Bidens pilosa*. The major flower in the field is *Zinnia elegans*, which is attractive to skippers but which does not attract *S. c. cybirus*.

This is the first record of *S. c. cybirus* from Isla Beata.

At Cabo Rojo, whence we have the longest series, taken in 2 days, *S. c. cybirus* was netted in both dry and bare, as well as living and leafy, trees near the ocean, up to 3.5 m above the ground. The days were extremely windy, and the hairstreaks flew only short distances before landing on the trees once more, where even there they were buffeted by the offshore wind. Some of the 32 Cabo Rojo specimens were collected in the lee of the trailer (see account of *Chlorostrymon m. maesites*).

Specimens: Haiti: Nord: 1.1 km N Carrefour Marmelade, 793 m, 1; *l'Artibonite:* 1.6 km E Carrefour Marmelade, 854 m, 1; 1.6 km W Passe Reine, 2; Gonaïves, s.l., 1; *l'Ouest:* Source Matelas, s.l., 1; 5 km NW Fond Parisien, s.l., 2; 2 km SE Fond Parisien, 1; 4 km SE Fond Parisien, s.l., 2; 11 km W Thomazeau, s.l., 1; Boutilliers Road, 266–915 m, 4; 5 km WNW Scierie, 1891 m, 1 (FSM); 8.6 km N Béloc, 534 m, 1; 0.6 km S Découzé, 671 m, 1; Lavaneau, 229 m, 1; 6 km NW Jacmel, 244 m, 2; nr. Péredo, 570 m, 1 (FSM); *Sud:* 3 km SW Paillant, 671–793 m, 7; Vieux Bourg d'Aquin, s.l., 4; 4.8 km N Camp Perrin, 244 m, 1; Lévy, 1; 7 km SW Cavaillon, 122 m, 1; 7.8 km N Cavaillon, 31 m, 1; 16.3 km N Cavaillon, 488 m, 2; 25.6 km N Cavaillon, 610 m, 1; *República Dominicana: Monte Cristi:* 4 km N Monte Cristi, s.l., 2; 1 km SE Monte Cristi, 12; 2 km SE Monte Cristi, 1; 4 km SW Monte Cristi, 1; 7 km NW Villa Vásquez, 1; 4 km NW Villa Vásquez, 61 m, 1; 3.9 km SE Martín García, 92 m, 2; *Dajabón:* 0.5 km N Cañongo, 31 m, 1; *Santiago Rodríguez:* 3 km W Los Quemados, 183 m, 6; 4.8 km S Zamba, 183 m, 3; *Valverde:* 12 km SW Mao, 244 m, 1; *Puerto Plata:* 12 km NW La Isabela, 61 m, 1; 8 km W Luperón, 3; 0.4 km E Punta Rucia, s.l., 1; 0.6 km NE Estero Hondo, 8; 12 km N Cruce de Guayacanes, 214 m, 5; 9 km SE Sosúa, 15 m, 4; 5 km NE El Choco, 488 m, 1; *Espaillat:* 20 km SW Jamao al Norte, 793 m, 1; *Santiago:* 8 km E Jánico, 610 m, 6; 7 km NE Jánico, 488 m, 1; 7 km SW Santiago, 67; *La Vega:* 1 km S Constanza, 1098 m, 28; 10 km S La Vega (= Güaigüi), 2; *María T. Sánchez:* 9 km NE Río San Juan, s.l., 1; 6 km S Cabrera, s.l., 1; 1 km S Cruce de Rincón, s.l., 1; *Samaná:* 18.0 km E and N Samaná, s.l., 1; 2.8 km S Las Galeras, 244 m, 1; *Hato Mayor:* 7 km E Sabana de la Mar, 1; 25 km E Sabana de la Mar, 1; *La Altagracia:* 5 km S Higüey, 1; 2–3 km W Boca de Yuma, 1; 0.5 km W Boca de Yuma, 1; 1 km N Playa Bayahibe, s.l., 18; 2.5 km SE Playa Bayahibe, s.l., 3; Río Chavón, 10 km NE La Romana, 3; *La Romana:* La Romana, 2; Río Cumayasa, 13.5 km W La Romana, 1; *San Pedro de Macorís:* 10 km E San Pedro de Macorís, 2; *Dist. Nac.:* Punta Caucedo, 2 km W, 2 km S Andrés, s.l., 3; 5 km S San Isidro, 4; *Sánchez Ramírez:* 1 km NE Las Lagunas,

183 m, 2; *San Cristóbal:* 6 km NW Cambita Garabitos, 488–519 m, 2; *Peravia:* 2 km SW Rancho Arriba, 671 m, 3; 6 km W La Horma, 1159 m, 1; *Azua:* Tábara Abajo, 2; 25 km NE Azua, 92 m, 2; 2.5 km W, 6.6 km N Azua, 183 m, 11; 5 km S Peralta, 305 m, 18; 2 km SE La Canoa, 397 m, 1; *San Juan:* 6 km W El Cercado, 640 m, 1; 9 km E Vallejuelo, 610 m, 25; *Baoruco:* 11 km N Neiba, 519 m, 1; 14 km N Neiba, 671 m, 2; *Independencia:* 4 km NW Tierra Nueva, s.l., 1; 1 km S La Descubierta, 4; 4–7 km NE El Aguacate, 519–732 m, 1; 0.6 km NW Puerto Escondido, 519 m, 3; La Furnia, s.l., 10; *Barahona:* 11.5 km ESE Canoa, s.l., 2; Polo, 702 m, 1; 3 km NNE Polo, 854 m, 1; 8 km NNE Polo, 793 m, 1; Barahona, s.l., 14; 12 km SW Barahona, 427 m, 1; 5 km SE, 3 km W Barahona, 183 m, 3; 10 km W Cabral, 1; 3 km NW Enriquillo, 244 m, 3; 9 km NW Enriquillo, 671 m, 3; *Pedernales:* Cabo Rojo, s.l., 32; 2 km NE Cabo Rojo, s.l., 1; 4 km NE Cabo Rojo, s.l., 7; 18 km NE Cabo Rojo, 366 m, 1; 19 km NE Cabo Rojo, 427 m, 5; 23 km NE Cabo Rojo, 488 m, 3; 26 km NE Cabo Rojo, 732 m, 4; Mencía, 297 m, 32; 3 km N Cabeza de Agua, 305 m, 1; 6 km N Cabeza de Agua, 580 m, 2; 4 km NW Tres Charcos, 2; 1.3 km S Tres Charcos, 1; *Isla Beata:* 2.

12. *Strymon toussainti* Comstock and Huntington, 1943

TL Fond Parisien, Dépt. de l'Ouest, Haiti.

FW males 10–12 mm, females 11–13 mm.

Strymon toussainti has been known from the type-locality (5 specimens) and Port-au-Prince (14 specimens) in Haiti, and from Monserrate (1 specimen) in the República Dominicana—a total of 20 specimens that comprised the type-series. Schwartz (1983a: 40) assigned 2 specimens from north of Cavaillon, Haiti, to this species. These specimens have been reexamined and they prove not to be *S. toussainti;* this confusion results from the similarity between members of the *columella* group. However, once one has taken *S. toussainti,* he has no doubt that he is dealing with an entity distinct from other *columella* group members. Perhaps the most striking character of *S. toussainti,* in contrast to both *S. columella* and *S. limenius,* is the very irregular postdiscal line on the unfw and the "jumble" of large black discal spots and dots on the unhw. The un pattern is much more contrasting than that of the other 2 species. But without specimens of *S. toussainti* for direct comparison, some *S. limenius* and some *S. columella* are easily misidentified, since the variation in each of those species approaches (but does not reach) the usual conditions in *S. toussainti.*

Judging from the localities for the type-series of *S. toussainti,* I assumed that this species is a xeric lowland form, restricted to the Cul de Sac–Valle de Neiba; all 3 localities are from this plain or adjacent to it. My specimens show that in addition to occurring in the Cul de Sac–Valle de Neiba (including the Llanos de Azua and extending into the Valle de San Juan and to the intermontane xeric valley between the 2 ranges of the Sierra de Neiba), *S. toussainti* also occurs in the arid western Valle de Cibao in the north and on the xeric Península de Barahona. The species probably also occurs in the northeastern Plaine du Nord in Haiti and in extreme southeastern Haiti, perhaps as far west as Jacmel. In addition, *S. toussainti* is expected throughout the western xeric coast of Haiti, from Port-au-Prince as far north as Gonaïves.

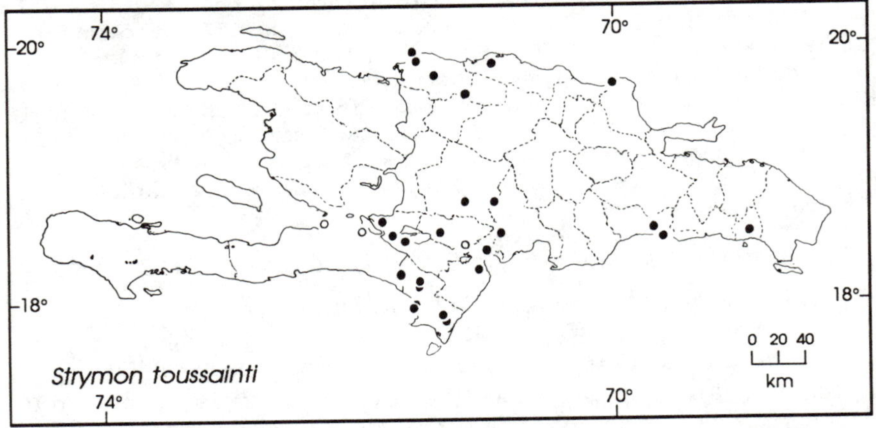

But in addition to the xeric regions noted here, and the putative extension of the range of *S. toussainti* stated above, we have also taken this hairstreak far to the east and northeast (Punta Caucedo, San Isidro, Río Chavón, Río San Juan) and in the north (Luperón); the last locality lies in the mesic portion of the Cordillera Septentrional and may represent an invasion of this range from the adjacent xeric Valle de Cibao. Thus, although one's first impression of the distribution of *S. toussainti* is that it is a confirmed xerophile, the species also occurs in areas that are only physiologically xeric and may be well forested.

My material is from sea level (Monte Cristi, La Furnia, El Limón, Canoa) to 610 m (Vallejuelo). Times of collection were between 0820 and 1750 h. Temperatures varied between 28°C (Los Quemados, Canoa) and 40°C (Río San Juan). My material has been collected in June (92), with lesser numbers in July (66), August (19), March (13), April (8), May (4), January (3), and December (11). A large percentage of the 150 specimens from Cabo Rojo was taken in the lee of the trailer (see account of *Chlorostrymon m. maesites*). The type-series was taken in January-April, July, and December.

Two specimens from Monte Cristi were taken near the ocean, on a very windy day; 1 was taking nectar from a halophytic composite. One of the La Furnia specimens was taken feeding on *Heliotropium curassavicum* (Boraginaceae). Other than on the borage and composite, *S. toussainti* has been collected while feeding on *Lippia nodiflora* (Galván), *Lippia micromera* (4 km SE Monte Cristi, Canoa), *Croton linearis* (1 km SE Monte Cristi, 2 km N Cabo Rojo), *Croton barahonensis* (Vallejuelo), *Bidens pilosa* (Los Quemados, Peralta, San Isidro), *Melochia tomentosa* (Cabo Rojo, La Canoa), and *Ageratum conyzoides* (18 and 23 km NE Cabo Rojo). The Barahona specimen was taken on a road through semixeric woods. *Acacia* scrub (Tierra Nueva, La Furnia, Tábara Abajo, La Canoa, Tres Charcos) and fields of *Uniola virgata* (Monte Cristi, El Limón, Canoa, all sea-level Cabo Rojo localities), and generally scrubby or grassy areas (Punta Caucedo, San Isidro, Galván) are also suitable for *S. toussainti*.

Specimens: República Dominicana: Monte Cristi: 4 km N Monte Cristi, s.l., 1; 1 km SE Monte Cristi, 6; 4 km NW Villa Vásquez, 61 m, 1; *Santiago Rodríguez:* 3 km W Los Quemados, 183 m, 1; *Puerto Plata:* 8 km W Luperón, 2; *María T. Sánchez:* Río San Juan, s.l., 1: *La Altagracia:* Río Chavón, 10 km NE La Romana, 1; *Dist. Nac.:* Punta Caucedo, 2 km W, 2 km S Andrés, s.l., 1; 5 km S San Isidro, 3; *Azua:* Tábara Abajo, 1; 2 km SE La Canoa, 397 m, 1; *San Juan:* 9 km E Vallejuelo, 610 m, 2; *Independencia:* 5 km NW Tierra Nueva, s.l., 1; La Furnia, s.l., 2; 4 km E El Limón, s.l., 2; *Baoruco:* 2 km SE Galván, 2; *Barahona:* 11.5 km ESE Canoa, s.l., 8; 2 km SW Barahona, 122 m, 1; *Pedernales:* 1 km SE Banano, 183 m, 1; Cabo Rojo, s.l., 150; 2 km NE Cabo Rojo, s.l., 10; 2 km N Cabo Rojo, s.l., 6: 18 km NE Cabo Rojo, 366 m, 2; 23 km NE Cabo Rojo, 488 m, 1; 4 km NW Tres Charcos, 1; 1.3 km S Tres Charcos, 1.

13. *Strymon andrewi* Johnson and Matusik, 1988

TL "Upper Abejas, 1750 m., 8 km on footpath, Las Abejas transect, NW of Aceitillar," Prov. de Pedernales, República Dominicana.

FW males 10.5–12 mm, females 10–12 mm.

This newly described species, apparently related to *S. toussainti*, is known only from higher elevations of the Sierra de Baoruco (Aceitillar, Las Abejas) and the adjacent Dominican portion of the Massif de la Selle (Los Arroyos). There is no doubt that it is a distinct species, since it differs in male genitalia as well as chromatic characters.

My 3 specimens were taken in July (1) and December (2). The former was collected in an open hilltop pasture between 1030 and 1130 h on a bright sunny day with a temperature of 23°C. The area surrounding the pasture was deciduous woods and an included *cafetal.* The 2 December specimens were collected as they fed on a small *Ageratum conyzoides* bush in open pinewoods. The time was 1050–1345 h and the temperature was 25°C.

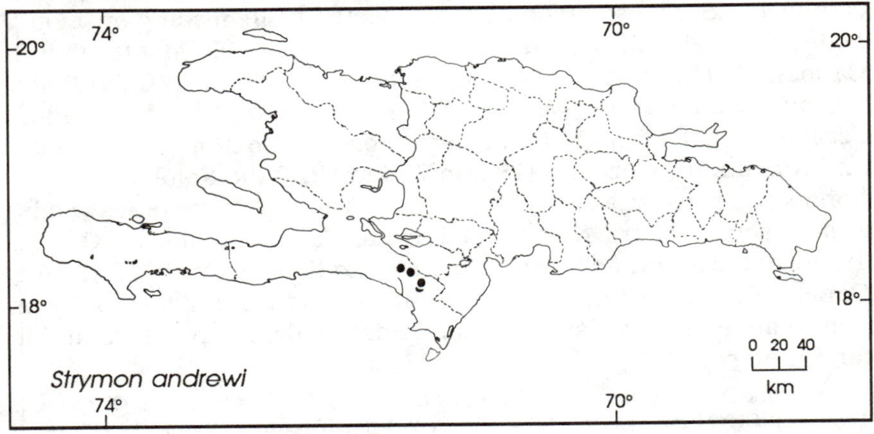

The type-series was taken on 16–17.vii at elevations between 1530–1750 m, whereas my specimens of *Strymon andrewi* are from elevations between 732 m and 1281 m.

I have another specimen (designated a paratype by Johnson and Matusik, 1988) from 26 km NE Cabo Rojo, 732 m, taken 2.i along the road through transitional forest. This locality is some 345 m lower than the lowest elevational record for *S. andrewi,* and about 550 m below the geographically closer *S. andrewi* locality. *Strymon toussainti* is known from just below at 23 km NE Cabo Rojo, a difference of about 350 m. The 2 species thus approach each other closely without "intergradation." The habitat of this specimen is quite unlike that of *S. andrewi* at Las Abejas.

Specimens: República Dominicana: Pedernales: 0.6 km SE Los Arroyos, 1098 m, 1; 1 km N Aceitillar, 1281 m, 2; Upper Abejas, 1750 m, 2.

14. *Strymon christophei* Comstock and Huntington, 1943

TL Port-au-Prince, Dépt. de l'Ouest, Haiti.

FW no males collected; females 13–14 mm.

This, the fourth member of the *columella* group, has been reported from Port-au-Prince and Pétionville in Haiti and from Paraíso and San Lorenzo in the República Dominicana; we have collected at 3 of these sites (exception: San Lorenzo) but without success. Dates for the type-series are January, June, and August; we have collected in all these months, although most extensively in June and August. The species is easy to recognize (see Comstock and Huntington, 1943:pl. 1, figs. 9, 10; Riley, 1975:fig. 12), since it lacks a basal dark spot along the unhw costa. If the locality data for the type-series are taken exactly, *S. christophei* occupies xeric (Port-au-Prince) and mesic areas (Pétionville, Paraíso, San Lorenzo), occurs from sea level (Port-au-Prince) to about 427 m (Pétionville) and on both the south (Pétionville, Paraíso) and north islands.

Although not mentioned by the describers nor by Riley (1975:105), the metallic ruby-red color of the unhw costal spot is striking when the specimens are fresh.

In 1984, we secured 1 specimen of *S. christophei*, and in 1986, 4 more. The first was taken on 14.iv at 610 m on *Bidens pilosa* along a road through mesic forest in karst topography. The time was 1030–1400 h, and the temperature 34°C. The 1986 specimens are from a coastal palm grove (La Romana) and from a roadside in karst.

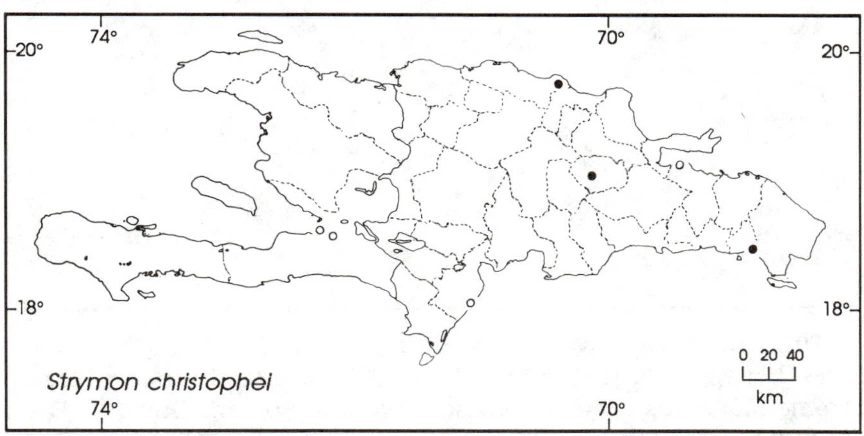

Elevations are sea level to 610 m; all were collected in July, between 1030 and 1645 h at temperatures of 31°C and 35°C. At La Romana, the hairstreak was feeding on *Geoffroea inermis*, and those at Sosúa on *Tournefortia hirsutissima*.

Specimens: República Dominicana: Puerto Plata: 9 km SE Sosúa, 15 m, 3; *Sánchez Ramírez:* 1 km NE Las Lagunas, 610 m, 1; *La Romana:* Río Chavón, 8 km SE La Romana, s.l., 1.

15. *Strymon limenius* Hewitson, 1868

TL Jamaica, St. Domingo, Cuba.

FW males 11–13 mm, females 9–12 mm.

Although widely distributed, *S. limenius* is less common than *S. columella cybirus* on Hispaniola. Like the latter species, *S.*

limenius is most frequently encountered in grassy or weedy areas, primarily roadsides and fields, although it is on occasion (Enriquillo, La Palma) taken on paths through *cafetales*. There are few records from xeric regions except for Fond Parisien, La Furnia, Duvergé, La Descubierta, Santiago, Tábara Abajo, and Cabo Rojo. The precise situation at Duvergé has been discussed (see account of *E. s. insolata*). Most specimens have been taken in June (71), with 15 in July, 10 in April, 9 each in December and October, 7 each in March and August, and isolated individuals from January and February, suggesting a summer period of emergence. Brown and Heineman (1972:239–40) also had records from throughout the year.

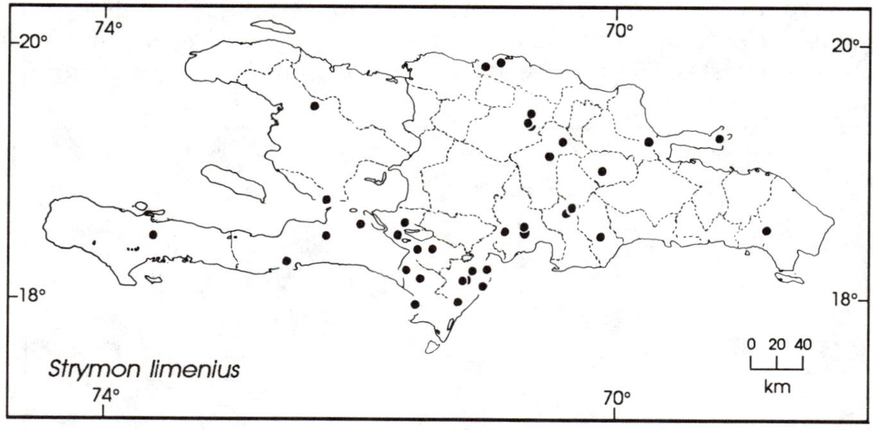

Times of activity varied from 0830 to 1750 h, and temperatures between 24°C (La Palma) to 39°C (Jánico, La Descubierta). *Strymon limenius* occurs from sea level (La Furnia, Duvergé, Boca de Yuma, Barahona, Cabo Rojo) to 1007 m (La Palma). We have taken *S. limenius* feeding on *Stachytarpheta jamaicensis* (San José de Ocoa, Mencía), *Tephrosia purpurea* (Cabo Rojo), *Antigonon leptopus* (Santiago, La Descubierta), *Bidens pilosa* (Tábara Abajo, Azua, Peralta), *Cordia exarata* (La Romana), *Sida* sp. (La Descubierta), *Mikania cordifolia* (Tábara Abajo), and *Ageratum conyzoides* (Barahona). The long series from Estero Hondo was taken at the interface of a pasture and *Acacia* woods–*Roystonea hispaniolana* grove, on *Malachra alceifolia* (Malvaceae). The hairstreaks were not only taking nectar from the yellow flowers of the 1-m-tall mallows but were also resting on the leaves, whence many were disturbed by our striking the stems with the net. At Cabo Rojo, only a very few *S. limenius* were taken behind the trailer.

Riley (1975:106) noted that *S. limenius* often flies with *S. columella* and other hairstreaks. *Strymon limenius* and *S. columella* occur syntopically at 24 localities: Carrefour Marmelade, Fond Parisien, Boutilliers Road, Lavaneau, Cavaillon, Estero Hondo, Santiago, Jánico (8 km E and 7 km NE), Güaigüí, Las Galeras, Boca de Yuma, La Romana, Tábara Abajo, Azua, Peralta, La Furnia, La Descubierta, El Aguacate, Barahona, Enriquillo, Cabo Rojo and 23 km N Cabo Rojo, and Mencía. Only at Jánico (8 km E and 7 km NE), Santiago, and Mencía (where we took many more *S. c. cybirus* than *S. limenius*) and at Estero Hondo (where we took many more *S. limenius* than *S. c. cybirus*) are there striking discrepancies in numbers of individuals collected. I have the impression that these 2 hairstreaks occupy very similar ecological niches and that usually *S. limenius* is much less abundant than *S. columella.*

Specimens: Haiti: l'Artibonite: 1.6 km E Carrefour Marmelade, 854 m, 2; *l'Ouest:* 5 km SE Source Matelas, s.l., 1; 2 km NW Fond Parisien, 2; Boutilliers Road, 732–854 m, 1; Lavaneau, 229 m, 1; *Sud:* 25.6 km N Cavaillon, 625 m, 1; *República Dominicana: Puerto Plata:* 0.6 km NE Estero Hondo, 53; 8 km W Luperón, 3; *Santiago:* 8 km E Jánico, 610 m, 1; 7 km NE Jánico, 486 m, 1; 7 km SW Santiago, 214 m, 4; *La Vega:* Güaigüí, S La Vega, 336 m, 1; La Palma, 19 km W Jayaco, 1007 m, 1; *María T. Sánchez:* 1 km S Cruce de Rincón, s.l., 1; *Samaná:* 2.8 km S Las Galeras, 1; *Sánchez Ramírez:* 1 km NE Las Lagunas, 183 m, 4; *La Altagracia:* 16 km NE La Romana, 61 m, 2; *San Cristóbal:* 8 km NW Cambita Garabitos, 595 m, 1; *Peravia:* 2 km SW Rancho Arriba, 671 m, 6; 10 km NW San José de Ocoa, 946 m, 1; *Azua:* Tábara Abajo, 2; 5 km S Peralta, 305 m, 8; 2.5 km W, 6.6 km N Azua, 183 m, 3; *Independencia:* La Furnia, s.l., 5; 1 km S La Descubierta, s.l., 3; 0.5 km E Duvergé, 1; 4–7 km NE El Aguacate, 519–732 m, 1; *Barahona:* 20 km SE Cabral, 946 m, 1; 8 km NNE Polo, 793 m, 1; 2 km S La Lanza, 2; Barahona, s.l., 1; 3 km NE La Ciénaga, 1; 9 km NW Enriquillo, 671 m, 5; *Pedernales:* Cabo Rojo, s.l., 5; 23 km NE Cabo Rojo, 488 m, 3; Mencía, 397 m, 4.

16. *Strymon monopeteinus* Schwartz and Miller, 1985

TL 1 km S Cruce de Rincón, Prov. María Trinidad Sánchez, República Dominicana.

FW males 13–16 mm, females 13–17 mm.

The first specimen of *S. monopeteinus* was taken by me on 20.vii.1983, in the Cordillera Central, República Dominicana. The hairstreak, a female, was feeding between 0930 and 1030 h. The temperature was 29°C, and the weather was alternately overcast and sunny. The locality is on a dirt road that leaves the road between Constanza and Valle Nuevo, 6 km SSE of the town of Constanza. The area is mixed pine-hardwoods, with much undergrowth (grasses, shrubs, vines); the general aspect is mesic and luxuriant, and daily rains are the norm.

The second specimen was netted by Nathan E. Kraucunas on Isla Saona on 11.i.1984 at 1008 h in *Acacia* scrub. The third specimen was collected by me at Cruce de Rincón, at sea level on 21.iii.1984 along an abandoned dirt road through a *cafetal*. The hairstreak was feeding. The second and third specimens are males. What is noteworthy is that all 3 specimens were taken from mid-1983 to early 1984, despite the many years' field work on Hispaniola, much of which was devoted to the República Dominicana. A fourth specimen (male) was taken by David Spencer-Smith on 21.vii.1985 near Boca de Yuma, Prov. de la Altagracia. This suite of 4 specimens comprised the type-series.

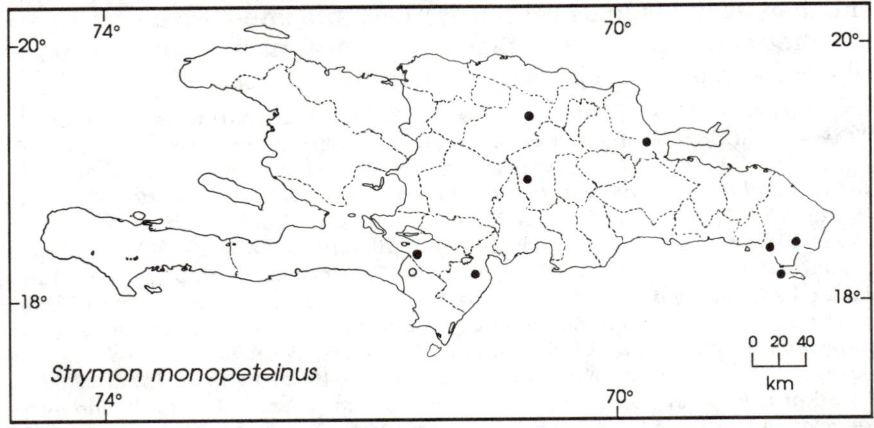

Strymon monopeteinus has a broad elevational range from sea level (Isla Saona, Cruce de Rincón) to 1403 m (Constanza), a broad ecological tolerance, as well as a wide geographic distribution. The hairstreak appears to be more common on the north island, with only 2 specimens from the south island (both on the northern slopes of the Massif de la Selle and the Sierra de Baoruco). Johnson and Matusik (1988) recorded the species from Las Abejas in the latter range.

Two localities (Cruce de Rincón, Monteada Nueva) are mesic hardwoods, 3 are xeric hardwoods (Playa Bayahibe, Boca de Yuma, El Aguacate), and 2 are *Acacia* woods (Santiago, Isla Saona). Constanza is mixed pine-hardwoods and is mesic.

Times of collection were 0940–1620 h at temperatures of 29°C (Constanza) to 40°C (Playa Bayahibe). *Strymon monopeteinus* has been taken feeding on *Tournefortia hirsutissima* (Constanza), *Stachytarpheta cayennensis* (Cruce de Rincón), *Antigonon leptopus* (Santiago), *Ixora* sp. (all specimens at Playa Bayahibe), and on a pink-flowered *Rubus* sp. (Rosaceae) at Monteada Nueva. The El Aguacate specimen was taken perched on a *Bryophyllum pinnatum* (Crassulaceae) leaf.

The 18 specimens have been collected in July (11), August (4), and in January, March, and May (1 each).

Brown and Heineman (1972:60) commented that "Jamaica seems to harbor a larger hairstreak population and has more indigenous species than any other island in the Greater Antilles . . . However, until Hispaniola is as thoroughly explored for butterflies as the other islands have been, the position of Jamaica in this regard is tentative." Jamaica is now known to have 13 species of theclines, of which 3 are endemic (*Thereus bourkei, Cyanophrys crethona, Electrostrymon pan*). Hispaniola has 17 species, of which 8 are endemic (*Thereus abeja, Allosmaitia fidena, Electrostrymon minikyanos, Terra hispaniola, Strymon toussainti, S. andrewi, S. christophei, S. monopeteinus*).

Specimens: República Dominicana: La Vega: 6 km SSE Constanza, 1403 m, 1; *Santiago:* 7 km SW Santiago, 214 m, 1; *María T. Sánchez:* 1 km S Cruce de Rincón, s.l., 1; *La Altagracia:* Boca de Yuma, 1 (AME); 1 km N Playa Bayahibe, 11; *Independencia:* 7 km NE El Aguacate, path to El Limón, 519–580 m, 1; *Barahona:* 1.8 km W Monteada Nueva, 1007 m, 1; *Isla Saona:* 3.5 km N Mano Juan, 1.

17. *Strymon bazochii gundlachianus* Bates, 1935

TL Sierra Maestra, 1000 ft., Prov. de Santiago de Cuba, Cuba.

FW males 10–13 mm, females 10–12 mm.

Strymon b. gundlachianus occurs on Cuba, where it has been recorded (9 specimens) only from the area of the type-locality (Bates, 1935a:196), Jamaica, where it is "not uncommon, but neither is it widespread" (Brown and Heineman, 1972:242), and Hispaniola, where it "occurs singly in the hills" (Hall, 1925:189). Riley (1975:102) summarized the above by saying that *S. b. gundlachianus* is "not uncommon at lower altitudes."

Our experience on Hispaniola (I have only 1 Haitian specimen) indicates that far from being common anywhere, *S. b. gundlachianus* is quite uncommon everywhere; from only 4 localities (Vallejuelo, 5 km SE, 3 km W Barahona, Cabo Rojo, 5 km S Peralta) do I have more than a single specimen. Likewise, this hairstreak is not restricted to lower elevations; its range is from sea level (Canoa) to 1464 m (Comendador). Habitats are extremely variable, from humid, hot, harsh, and xeric conditions (*Acacia* scrub and cacti) at Canoa, transitional mesic-xeric woods (Cabo Rojo), mesic flowery roadsides (Comendador) adjacent to very rich deciduous forest with tree ferns, and pinewoods (Aceitillar). Even at sea level, *S. b. gundlachianus* occurs not only in xeric areas but also in mesic doline forests in the karst area near Sosúa. Like other hairstreaks, *S. b. gundlachianus* is occasionally found in open fields (Constanza), on paths in mesic forest (Barahona), and in a hotel garden (Río San Juan).

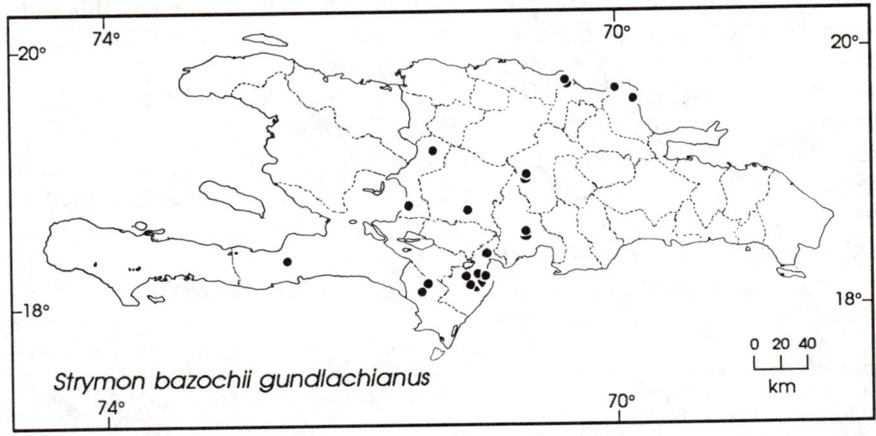

We have taken *S. b. gundlachianus* feeding on *Daucus* sp. (Comendador), *Bidens pilosa* (Peralta), on 2-m *Lantana ovatifolia* (Cabral), on the white-flowered horticultural variety of *L. ovatifolia* (Río San Juan), *Lantana reticulata* (Sosúa), *Croton barahonensis* (Vallejuelo, 3 occasions), and *Ageratum conyzoides* (Monteada Nueva, Vallejuelo, Aceitillar). Most specimens are from August (19), with 12 in July, 6 in December, 5 in June, 3 in March, 2 in April, and 1 each in January and September. Times of collection varied between 0945 and 1700 h, and temperatures between 25°C (Aceitillar) and 37°C (Sosúa, 5 km S Peralta, Vallejuelo).

Specimens: Haiti: l'Ouest: 0.8 km S Découzé, 702 m, 1; *República Dominicana: Elías Piña:* 21 km S Comendador, 1646 m, 1; summit, Loma Caramaná, Alto de Loma range, S Los Guandules, 1083 m, 1; *Puerto Plata:* 9 km SE Sosúa, 16 m, 2; 11 km SE Sosúa, 46 m, 1; *La Vega:* 1 km S Constanza, 1098 m, 2; 6 km SSE Constanza, 1403 m, 1; *María T. Sánchez:* Río San Juan, s.l., 1; 6 km S Cabrera, s.l., 1; *Azua:* 4 km S Peralta, 366 m, 1; 5 km S Peralta, 305 m, 4; *San Juan:* 9 km E Vallejuelo, 610 m, 22; *Barahona:* 8 km ESE Canoa, s.l., 1; 10 km SSW Cabral, 427 m, 1; 12 km NNE Polo, 534 m, 1; 1.8 km W Monteada Nueva, 1007 m, 1; 2 km SW Barahona, 122 m, 1; 12 km SW Barahona 427 m, 1; 5 km SE, 3 km W Barahona, 183 m, 2; *Pedernales:* 23 km NE Cabo Rojo, 488 m, 2; 1 km N Aceitillar, 1281 m, 1.

Subfamily Polyommatinae

18. *Brephidium exilis isophthalma* Herrich-Schäffer, 1862

TL Cuba.

FW 8–9 mm.

Although this diminutive lycaenid is generally considered to be strictly coastal in distribution (see Brown and Heineman, 1972:256–57, for instance), on Hispaniola it occurs as far as 50 km inland (Duvergé) and doubtless even farther along the border, between Jimaní and Boca de Cachón, for instance, as well as on the Haitian side. The reason for the inland occurrence of *B. i. isophthalma* is that the Cul de Sac–Valle de Neiba plain is the remnant of a marine strait that, with the recession of the ocean, has become dry land. However, the earth in this plain at places glitters with salt crystals, and *Batis maritima* (Batidaceae), the plant with which the life cycle of *B. e. isophthalma* is presumably intimately allied, thrives in such a hypersaline environment. Such environments, with their concomitant *B. maritima*, are normally coastal, and this halophyte occurs along the ocean strand. The Cul de Sac–Valle de Neiba presents an unusual combination of paleogeography and ecology which allows *B. maritima*, and thus *B. e. isophthalma*, to occur far from the ocean.

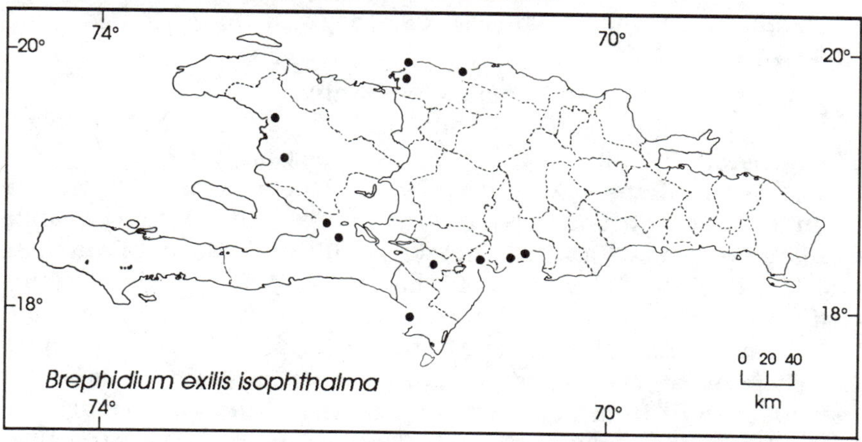

Brephidium exilis isophthalma

Even elsewhere (Monte Cristi), *B. e. isophthalma* occurs at some distance (at least 9 km) from the ocean. The xeric flatlands south of the coast there support large areas of *B. maritima;* here this plant forms the understory of open *Acacia*-cactus woods—an altogether unusual situation for *B. i. isophthalma*. We have taken *B. e. isophthalma* in this same *Batis-Acacia* association at Gonaïves and Croix des Bouquets.

Although in our experience there seems to be little seasonality in this tiny blue, others have commented on its periodicity (Brown and Heineman, 1972:256; Clench, 1977a:281). When they are abundant (and they usually have been), the butterflies fairly swarm just above the *Batis*, landing on it and very low shrubs that are growing in association with the halophyte. Our specimens are from March, April, May, June, July, August, and December. Collection times were between 0845 and 1750 h; after about 1200 h, when the sun is high, the activity decreases markedly. Temperatures varied between 28°C (Pont l'Estère, 4 km N Monte Cristi) and 38°C (9 km SSE Monte Cristi).

We have taken *B. e. isophthalma* feeding on *Sesuvium portulacastrum* (Aizoaceae) at Croix des Missions and Puerto Viejo. This, another halophyte, is often intimately associated with *Batis maritima*.

Specimens: Haiti: l'Artibonite: Gonaïves, s.l., 4; 11 km S Pont l'Estère, s.l., 5; *l'Ouest:* 6 km NW Croix des Missions, s.l., 3; 8 km NE Croix des Bouquets, 4; *República Dominicana: Monte Cristi:* 4 km N Monte Cristi, 19; 9 km SSE Monte Cristi, 4; *Puerto Plata:* 0.4 km E Punta Rucia, s.l., 28; *Azua;* Playa Tortuguero, 15; Puerto Viejo, s.l., 16; *Barahona:* 12 km ESE Canoa, 20; *Independencia:* 10 km SE Duvergé, 5; *Pedernales:* Cabo Rojo, s.l., 6.

19. *Leptotes cassius theonus* Lucas, 1857

TL Cuba.

FW males 9–13 mm, females 8–12 mm.

This species is common and widespread on Cuba (Bates, 1935a:199), Jamaica (Brown and Heineman, 1972:247), and Puerto Rico (Comstock, 1944:494) and occurs as well on the Cayman and Bahama islands (*theonus*), the Virgin Islands (*catilina* Fabricius), and the Lesser Antilles (*chadwicki* Comstock and Huntington). Riley (1975:108) stated that *L. cassius* is a butterfly of "the lowlands and moderate altitudes," yet Brown and Heineman (1972:246) reported it from at least as high as 1525 m. On Hispaniola, the latter altitudinal distribution is true; *L. c. theonus* occurs from sea level (Carrefour la Mort, Fond Parisien, Punta Caucedo, and others) to 1830 m (La Laguna). The latter high elevation is in the Cordillera Central; elsewhere (Sierra de Neiba) the species does not reach such a high elevation, but it still occurs well up in these mountains (1646 m, Comendador) and in the Sierra de Baoruco (1281 m, 1 km N Aceitillar). Our records are the first for this species on Île de la Gonâve, Isla Catalina, and Isla Beata.

Leptotes c. theonus favors grassy or shrubby areas, especially roadsides, fields, and other marginal situations. But perhaps more than other blues on Hispaniola, this butterfly is regularly encountered in forest or pseudoforest (Rincón Molinillos, Los Quemados, Tenares, Sánchez, Las Galeras, Cambita Garabitos, Neiba, to list only a few). The species also can be found in xeric woodlands and in *Acacia* forest or scrub (Fond Parisien, Santiago, La Furnia, Cabral, Cabo Rojo) or xeric forest (La Romana, El Mulito). We have taken *L. c. theonus* in mixed pine-hardwoods (Restauración, La Laguna) and in a shaded ravine in pine-hardwoods (Constanza). Considering the broad elevational distribution of the species, its occurrence in such a variety of habitats is not surprising.

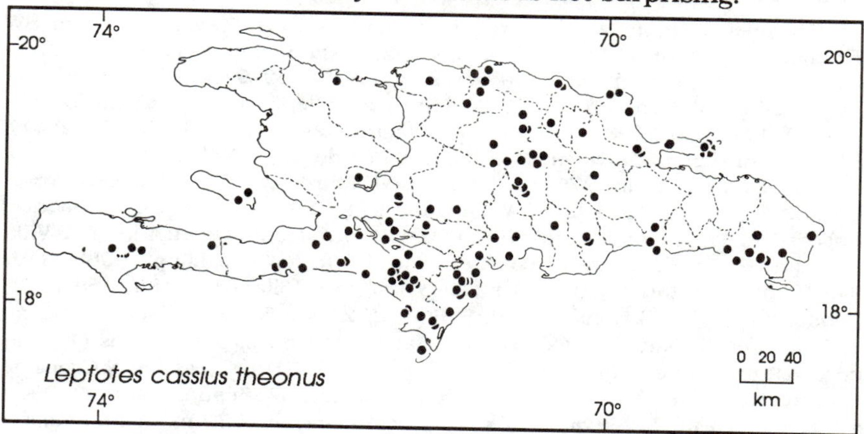

Among the long series of *L. c. theonus* from Hispaniola, Puerto Rico, and Florida, the specimen from La Laguna is unique. This female is the specimen with the highest elevation for Hispaniola; the locality is near Pico Duarte in the Cordillera Central. The specimen has the up and un dark markings much broader than any other specimen, with a consequent reduction of the white area. In some ways, the aspect of the butterfly is like that of *Leptotes perkinsae* Kaye (see Brown and Heineman, 1972:pl. 4, fig. 22, rather than Riley, 1975:pl. 12, fig. 14), a Jamaican endemic, but it is not assignable to that or any related taxon. The specimen is the lone individual from as high an elevation in these mountains (specimens from lower elevations, 1403 m or less); Central specimens from lower elevations do not have the characteristics of the La Laguna female. More high-upland material is needed to determine the status of this upland population.

Months of collection include July (64), June and December (34 each), March (27), January (16), April (15), February (15), May (12), and August (11). The species appears to be on the wing during the entire year, with summer and midwinter peaks. Times of collection were between 0845 and 1700 h, and temperatures varied between 23°C (Los Arroyos) and 40°C (Tenares).

Copulating pairs have been taken on 25.iv (Lavaneau, 229 m, 1130–1445 h, 32°C), 20.vii (Constanza, 1403 m, 1315 h, 29°C), and 23.xii (Samaná, s.l., 1030–1530 h, 27°C). We have taken *L. c. theonus* on *Tournefortia hirsutissima* (Sosúa), on *Geoffroea inermis* (Río Chavón), and on *Ageratum conyzoides* (Vallejuelo, 1 km N Aceitillar). On 1 occasion an individual was taken drinking from a mud puddle in a dirt road (Aguas Negras).

Specimens: Haiti: Nord: Carrefour la Mort, s.l., 1; *l'Ouest:* 20.3 km SW Thomonde, 2; 2 km W Fond Parisien, s.l., 2; 2 km SE Fond Parisien, s.l., 5; 4 km SE Fond Parisien, s.l., 1; Boutilliers Road, 732–915 m, 4; Boutilliers Road, 3.7 km W Kenscoff road, 3 (MPM); Pétionville, 576 m, 1; 9.6 km E Belle Anse, 1; Lavaneau, 229 m, 4; 6 km NW Jacmel, 244 m, 1; 10.4 km E Jacmel, 31 m, 1; nr. Péredo, at river, 3 (FSM); nr. Péredo, 570–600 m, 7 (FSM); *Sud:* 5.6 km N Camp Perrin, 275 m, 1; 6.4 km NE Marceline, 671 m, 2; 16.3 km N Cavaillon, 488 m, 2; 3 km SW Paillant, 671–793 m, 2; *Île de la Gonâve:* Anse-à-Galets, 1; Picmi, 1; *República Dominicana: Monte Cristi:* 4 km NW Villa Vásquez, 61 m, 5; *Dajabón:* Los Cerezos, 12 km NW Río Limpio, 580 m, 1; 9–9.1 km S Restauración, 610 m, 3; 3 km ESE Villa Anacaona, 458 m, 1; *Elías Piña:* 14 km S Comendador, 876 m, 2; 21 km S Comendador, 1464 m, 1; *Valverde:* 3.3 km N Cruce de Guayacanes, 214 m, 2; 3 km E Los Quemados, 122 m, 1; *Puerto Plata:* 12 km NW La Isabela, 61 m, 1; 11 km N Cruce de Guayacanes, 275 m, 1; 8 km W Luperón, 1; 11 km SW Sosúa, 183 m, 2; 9 km SE Sosúa, 15 m, 1; *Espaillat:* 3 km N Puesto Grande, 580 m, 1; *Santiago:* 8 km E Jánico, 610 m, 1; 7 km NE Jánico, 488 m, 1; 7 km SW Santiago, 214 m, 5; Río Bao, 8 km SE Montones Abajo, 488 m, 4; La Laguna, 1830 m, 1; *La Vega:* La Palma, 19 km W Jayaco, 1007 m, 1; 1 km S Constanza, 1098 m, 7; 6 km SSE Constanza, 1403 m, 5; 7 km SE Constanza, *ca.* 1312 m, 1; 13 km SE Constanza, 1403 m, 1; 1 km W Manabao, 793 m, 1; 13 km E Manabao, 610 m, 1; 3 km W La Ciénaga, 1037 m, 1; 3.5 km E Paso Bajito, 732 m, 1; *Duarte:* 10 km SE Tenares, 183 m, 1; *María T. Sánchez:* Río San Juan, s.l., 3; 9 km NE Río San Juan, s.l., 2; 6 km S Cabrera, s.l., 1; 1 km S Cruce de Rincón, s.l., 3; *ca.* 18 km W, 1.2 km S Sánchez, road to Rincón Molinillos, 31 m, 1; *Samaná:* 13.2 km NE Sánchez, 92 m, 1; 4.5 km E Samaná, 9; 18.0 km E and N Samaná, s.l., 7; 10.5 km S Las Galeras, 16 m, 3; 2.8 km S Las Galeras, 61 m, 2; 3.8 km S Las Galeras, s.l., 2; *La Altagracia:* Punta Cana, s.l., 1; 0.5–3.5 km W Boca de Yuma, 1; 2.5 km SE Playa Bayahibe, s.l., 3; 1 km N Playa Bayahibe, s.l., 1; 16 km NE La Romana, 61 m, 1; *La Romana:* Río Chavón, 8 km SE La Romana, s.l., 4; Río Cumayasa, 13.5 km W La Romana, 31 m, 3; *Dist. Nac.:* 9 km NE Guerra, 1; 33 km W San Pedro de Macorís, 2 (MPM); Punta Caucedo, 5 km S Aeropuerto Internacional de las Américas, s.l., 2; Punta Caucedo, 2 km W, 2 km S Andrés, s.l., 1; *Monte Plata:* 11 km W Esperalvillo, 153 m, 1; *Sánchez Ramírez:* 1 km NE Las Lagunas, 183 m, 3; *San Cristóbal:* 3 km NW Cambita Garabitos, 366 m, 1; 6 km NW Cambita Garabitos, 519 m, 1; *Peravia:* 5 km N San José de Ocoa, 580 m, 1; *Azua:* Tábara Abajo, 4; 5 km S Peralta, 366 m, 3; Puerto Viejo, s.l., 1; *San Juan:* 7 km E El Cercado, 854 m, 1; 9 km E Vallejuelo, 610 m, 5; *Baoruco:* 11 km N Neiba, 519 m, 1; 14 km N Neiba, 671 m, 1; *Independencia:* 5 km S Angel Feliz, 2; La Furnia, s.l., 4; 1 km S La Descubierta, 1; 0.5 km E Duvergé, 5; 0.6 km NW Puerto Escondido, 519 m, 1; 4–7 km NE El Aguacate, 519–732 m, 2; *Barahona:* 11.5 km ESE Canoa, s.l., 2; Polo, 702 m, 3; 8 km NNE Polo, 793 m, 2; 7 km SSW Cabral, 214 m, 1; Barahona, s.l., 2; 5 km SE, 3 km W Barahona, 183–397 m, 1; 12 km SW Barahona, 427 m, 1; 3 km NE La Ciénaga, 3; 8 km NW Paraíso, 2 (MPM); 8–10 km NW Paraíso, 5 (MPM); 3 km NW Enriquillo, 244 m, 1; *Pedernales:* El Mulito, 21 km N Pedernales, 214 m, 1; 1 km SE Banano, 183 m, 2; Mencía, 397 m, 1; 2 km S Aguas Negras, 610 m, 1; 1 km S La Altagracia, *ca.* 534 m, 1; 5 km NE Los Arroyos, 1617 m, 1; Cabo Rojo, s.l., 5; 2 km NE Cabo Rojo, s.l., 3; 23 km NW Cabo Rojo, 488 m, 6; Las Abejas, 12 km NW Aceitillar, 1129 m, 2; 1 km N Aceitillar, 1281 m, 4; 2 km SW Aceitillar, 1251 m, 1; 4 km NW Tres Charcos, 1; 0.5 km S Tres Charcos, 1; 17 km NW Oviedo, 183 m, 1; *Isla Catalina:* nr. naval base, 2, *Isla Beata:* 1.

20. *Leptotes idealus* Johnson and Matusik, 1988

TL "Extremely dense moist woods, bottom of Las Abejas," Prov. de Pedernales, República Dominicana.

FW male 11 mm, female unknown.

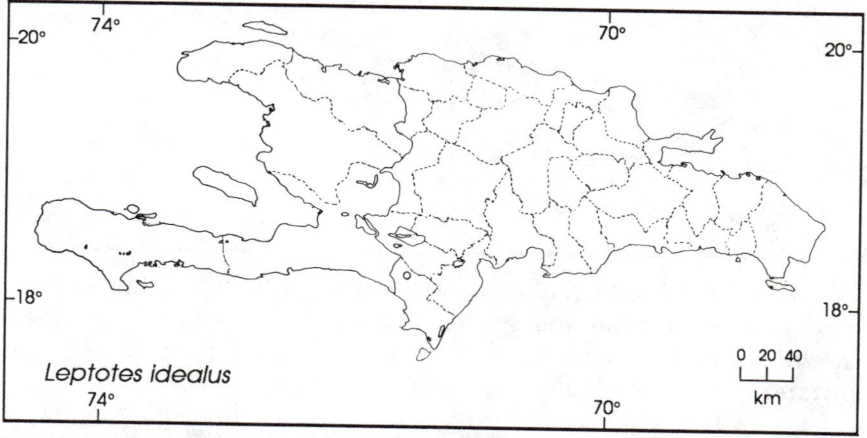

Leptotes idealus

This newly described species, presumbly related to Jamaican *L. perkinsae* Kaye, is known only from a single male taken within deciduous forest at Las Abejas in the Sierra de Baoruco at an elevation of about 1160 m. The species is easily differentiated from its congener, *L. c. theonus,* by its having only 1 black spot near the margin of the unhw in Cu2–2A rather than the 2 adjacent spots found in *L. c. theonus. Leptotes idealus* is presumably an upland forest-dwelling species in the Sierra de Baoruco. The apparent relationship between *L. idealus* and *L. perkinsae* is of extreme interest in allying the lepidopteran faunas of Jamaica and Hispaniola.

21. *Hemiargus hanno watsoni* Comstock and Huntington, 1943

TL San Juan, Puerto Rico.

FW males 9–10 mm, females 8–11 mm.

This small blue occurs throughout Hispaniola but seems to be much more common in the República Dominicana than in Haiti, whence I have examined 31 specimens. Comstock and Huntington (1943:100) listed the following localities: Haiti at St.-Marc, Les Cayes, Bizoton, Fond Parisien, Carrefour, Fort Liberté, La Serre, Pétionville, Port-au-Prince, Trouin, and Camp Perrin, and the República Dominicana at Barahona, Sánchez, Monte Cristi, and Bonao–to–La Vega. The records here are the first for Île de la Gonâve and Isla Beata.

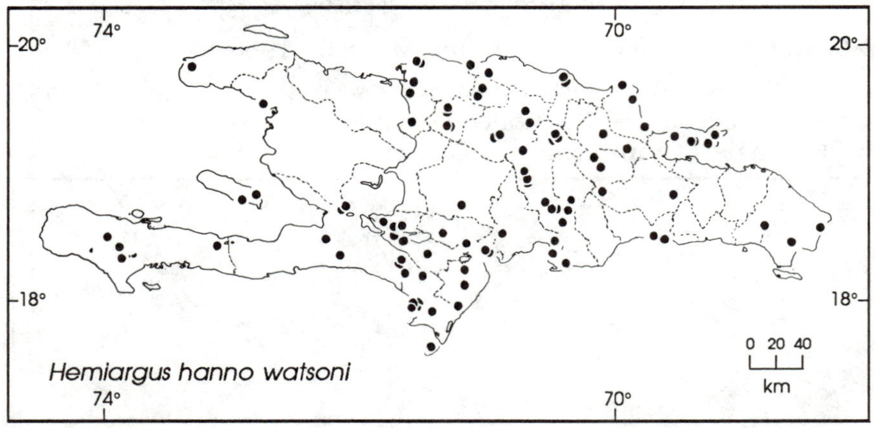

Hemiargus hanno watsoni

Like most blues, *H. h. watsoni* is an inhabitant of grassy areas: roadsides, shady banana groves, coastal areas, hillsides, upland *cafetales*, doline pastures, mixed pine-deciduous woodland, and lowland *Acacia* woodlands and scrubby areas, as well as the edges of and within xeric woodlands. Generally, *H. h. watsoni* prefers more mesic (rather than xeric) situations, although it does not completely shun the latter.

The month of greatest abundance is July (49 specimens), followed by October (32), May (31), June and August (27 each), January (17), December (16), and a few specimens are from April (9), February (4), and September, November, and March (3 each). Comstock (1944:497) noted that this subspecies occurs throughout the year in Puerto Rico, and my data agree with his assessment.

Elevations are from sea level (many localities) to 1891 m

(Scierie) on the Massif de la Selle. Times of activity were between 0800 and 1700 h, and temperatures between 21°C (Scierie) and 39°C (Jánico, Samaná).

At La Furnia, we took specimens of *H. h. watsoni* on *Sida* sp., at Sombrero on *Tephrosia purpurea*, at 1 km S La Descubierta on *Antigonon leptopus*, at El Limón on *Melochia tomentosa*, at Santiago and Cañongo on *Bidens pilosa*, and at Santiago on *Parthenium hysterophorus*.

Specimens: Haiti: Nord-Ouest: Môle St.-Nicholas, 2; *l'Artibonite:* 12.2 km W Ça Soleil, 1; *l'Ouest:* 4.8–8.5 km S Terre Rouge, 122–427 m, 1; 3.8 km N Terre Rouge, 519 m, 1; Boutilliers Road, 854–915 m, 21 (2 FSM); Boutilliers Road, 3.7 km W Kenscoff road, 2; 5 km WNW Scierie, 1891 m, 1 (FSM); *Sud:* 5.6 km N Camp Perrin, 275 m, 1; Lévy, 3; 3 km SW Paillant, 671 m, 1; Formond Base Camp #1, 975 m, 2 (FSM); *Île de la Gonâve:* hills behind Anse-à-Galets, 2; Picmi, 1; *República Dominicana: Monte Cristi:* 4 km N Monte Cristi, s.l., 2; 1 km SE Monte Cristi, 1; 6 km W Copey, s.l., 2; *Dajabón:* 0.5 km N Cañongo, 31 m, 3; 7 km N Restauración, 671 m, 1; *Santiago Rodríguez:* Loma Leonor, 18 km SW Monción, 534 m, 2; Loma Leonor, 19 km SW Monción, 610 m, 1; 3 km W Los Quemados, 183 m, 1; 3.0 km S Zamba, 214 m, 1; 4.8 km S Zamba, 183 m, 3; *Valverde:* 3.3 km N Cruce de Guayacanes, 214 m, 2; 12 km SW Mao, 244 m, 4; *Puerto Plata:* 12 km N Cruce de Guayacanes, 214 m, 1; 0.4 km E Punta Rucia, s.l., 1; 9 km SE Sosúa, 16 m, 1; 11 km SE Sosúa, 46 m, 1; *Duarte:* 12 km S San Francisco de Macorís, 2; Villa Riva, 2; *Santiago:* Río Bao, 8 km SE Montones Abajo, 488 m, 2; Río Bao, 4 km SW Mata Grande, 702 m, 2; 2 km E Pedro García, 427 m, 2; 8 km E Jánico, 610 m, 1; 7 km SW Santiago, 214 m, 13; *Sánchez Ramírez:* 1 km SE La Mata, 1; 1 km NE Las Lagunas, 183 m, 1; *La Vega:* 1 km S Constanza, 1098 m, 5; 7 km SE Constanza, *ca.* 1312 m, 1; Buena Vista, 11 km NE Jarabacoa, 640 m, 4; Güaigüí, S La Vega, 336 m, 5; 2 km S La Vega, 366 m, 1; La Ciénaga, 915 m, 1; 10 km NW La Horma, 1496 m, 1; *Monseñor Nouel:* 17 km SW Piedra Blanca, 854 m, 1; *María T. Sánchez:* 9 km NE Río San Juan, s.l., 2; 6 km S Cabrera, 1; 9 km SE Nagua, s.l., 5; *Samaná:* 6.9 km NE Sánchez, 336 m, 1; 4.8 km W Samaná, s.l., 4; 10.2 km W Samaná, 61 m, 3; 4.5 km E Samaná, s.l., 1; 2.8 km S Las Galeras, 61 m, 2; *La Altagracia:* Punta Cana, s.l., 3; 2–3 km W Boca de Yuma, 2; 16 km NE La Romana, 61 m, 1; *Dist. Nac.:* Punta Caucedo, 2 km W, 2 km S Andrés, 2; Tres Ojos, s.l., 1; *Monte Plata:* 11 km W Esperalvillo, 153 m, 1; 8 km NE Bayaguana, 1; *Peravia:* 2 km SW Rancho Arriba, 671 m, 2; 5 km SW Sombrero, 4; 10 km NW San José de Ocoa, 946 m, 1; 6 km W La Horma, 1149 m, 1; 1.6 km SE La Horma, 1; *Azua;* 25 km NE Azua, 92 m, 2; Tábara Abajo, 6; 1 km E Palmar de Ocoa, s.l., 1; *San Juan:* 9 km E Vallejuelo, 610 m, 1; *Independencia:* 4 km NW Tierra Nueva, s.l., 1; La Furnia, s.l., 7; 1 km S Boca de Cachón, s.l., 1; 4 km E El Limón, s.l., 2; 1 km S La Descubierta, 2; 3.3 km E La Descubierta, 6; 2 km S Duvergé, 1; *Baoruco:* 2 km SE Galván, 3; *Barahona:* 8 km ESE Canoa, s.l., 3; 11.5 km ESE Canoa, s.l., 2; 3 km E Vicente Noble, 1; Polo, 702 m, 1; 10 km W Cabral, s.l., 1; 3 km NW Enriquillo, 244 m, 1; *Pedernales:* Mencía, 397 m, 2; 1 km NE Los Arroyos, 1220 m, 4; 5 km NE Los Arroyos, 1617 m, 1; Cabo Rojo, s.l., 2; 2 km N Cabo Rojo, s.l., 4; 2 km NE Cabo Rojo, s.l., 2; 4 km NE Cabo Rojo, s.l., 4; 4 km N Aceitillar, 1312 m, 1; 17 km NW Oviedo, 183 m, 1; *Isla Beata:* 5.

22. *Hemiargus ceraunus ceraunus* Fabricius, 1793

TL "Americae meridionalis Insulis."

FW males 7–11 mm, females 8–11 mm.

I follow Clench (1977a:187) in considering *H. ceraunus* a species distinct from *H. hanno.* Riley (1975:109) treated them as conspecific.

Hemiargus c. ceraunus and *H. h. watsoni* are both widely distributed on Hispaniola; I have, as with the latter species, far more material from the República Dominicana than from Haiti, although the Haitian records are for the northern part of that country as well as the south. Schwartz (1983a:41) reported this species for the first time from Île de la Gonâve and Île à Cabrit, and herein is the first record for Isla Catalina.

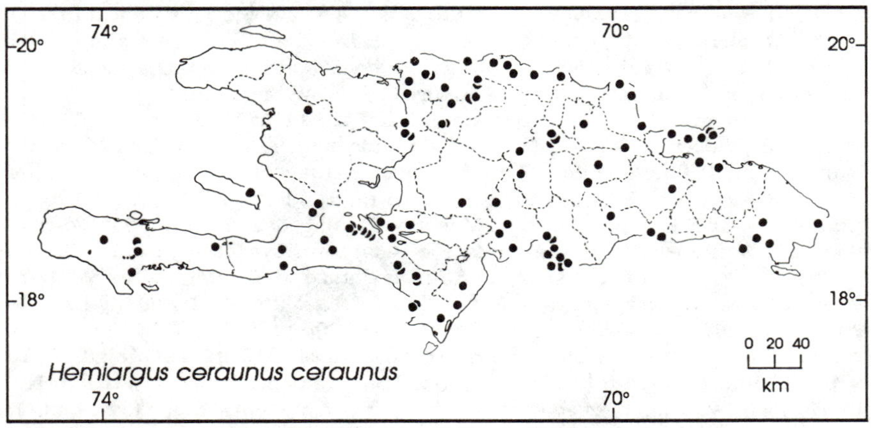

Hemiargus ceraunus ceraunus

The 2 species also overlap broadly altitudinally, although *H. h. watsoni* has been taken at a higher elevation (1891 m; Scierie) than *H. c. ceraunus* (1617 m; Furcy). *Hemiargus c. ceraunus* flies between 0800 and 1800 h, and at temperatures between 23°C (Samaná) and 40°C (Yásica, Tenares). Sea-level localities include, among others, Île à Cabrit, Fond Parisien, Copey, and Samaná.

Most specimens have been taken in July (67), with 59 in May, 35 in June, 29 in December, 24 each in August and October, 18 in December, 16 in April, and 14 in March; other months represented are January (13), February (6), and November (1). *Hemiargus c. ceraunus* appears to fly during the entire year; Brown and Heineman (1972:254–55) have records from throughout the year on Jamaica.

Although *H. c. ceraunus* and *H. h. watsoni* have comparable geographic distributions, *H. c. ceraunus* generally occurs in more xeric areas. But once more, as in the reverse case of *H. h. watsoni*, mesic areas are not shunned completely.

Pairs of *H. c. ceraunus* were netted *in copula* on 22.vi (Cruce de Ocoa, 610 m, 1030–1130 h, 38°C, along an irrigation ditch in thorn scrub), 15.iii (7 km NW Villa Vásquez, 1430–1450 h, 32°C, *Acacia* scrub), 28.vi (7 km SW Santiago, 214 m, 1115 h, 33°C, *Acacia* woods), and 14.iv (Las Lagunas, 183 m, 1030–1400 h, 34°C, roadside though mesic forest).

We have taken *H. c. ceraunus* feeding on *Sida* sp. (La Furnia), on *Tephrosia purpurea* (Mao, Sombrero, Cabo Rojo), on *Bidens pilosa* (Las Lagunas, Los Quemados), on *Antigonon leptopus* (El Cruce del Quince), on *Croton barahonensis* (Vallejuelo, 4 occasions), and on *Sesuvium portulacastrum* (Puerto Viejo).

Specimens: Haiti: l'Artibonite: 1.6 km E Carrefour Marmelade, 854 m, 3; *l'Ouest:* Boutilliers Road, 854–915 m, 18; 5 km SE Source Matelas, s.l., 1; 18.1 km SE Croix des Bouquets, s.l., 1; 5 km NW Fond Parisien, 1; 2 km NW Fond Parisien, 1; 2 km W Fond Parisien, s.l., 1; 2 km SE Fond Parisien, s.l., 3; 4 km SE Fond Parisien, s.l., 1; 3.0 km SE Fond Parisien, s.l., 1; 2 km NE Furcy, 1617 m, 2; 8.6 km N Béloc, 534 m, 2; Lavaneau, 229 m, 2; *Sud:* Les Cayes, s.l., 1; Lévy, 2; 6.4 km NW Marceline, 671 m, 2; 14 km N Marceline, 671 m, 1; Formond Base Camp #1, 975 m, 1 (FSM); 3 km SW Paillant, 793 m, 1; *Île de la Gonâve:* Anse-à-Galets, 1; *Île à Cabrit:* 2; *República Dominicana: Monte Cristi:* 1 km SE Monte Cristi, 4; 6 km W Copey, s.l., 2; 4 km NW Villa Vásquez, 61 m, 2; 7 km NW Villa Vásquez, 3; 3.9 km SE Martín García, 92 m, 2; *Dajabón:* 0.5 km N Cañongo, 31 m, 2; 4 km S Restauración, 580 m, 1; 9.1 km S Restauración, 519 m, 1; 3 km ESE Villa Anacaona, 458 m, 1; *Valverde:* 3.3 km N Cruce de Guayacanes, 214 m, 1; 4 km N Cruce de Guayacanes, 198 m, 2; 3 km W Los Quemados, 183 m, 8; 12 km SW Mao, 244 m, 8; *Santiago Rodríguez:* Loma Leonor, 19 km SW Monción, 610 m, 3; Loma Leonor, 18 km SW Monción, 549 m, 1; 3 km S Zamba, 214 m, 1; *Puerto Plata:* 2 km S Imbert, 92 m, 4; 8 km W Luperón, 1; 13 km SE Luperón, 214 m, 1; 0.4 km E Punta Rucia, s.l., 1; Yásica, 22 km SE Puerto Plata, 122 m, 1; 9 km SE Sosúa, 15 m, 4; *María T. Sánchez:* 9 km NE Río San Juan, s.l., 2; 6 km S Cabrera, s.l., 1; 9 km SW Nagua, s.l., 1; *Santiago:* 7 km W Santiago, 214 m, 30; *La Vega:* Güaigüí, S La Vega, 336 m, 3; 2 km S La Vega, 366 m, 1; Buena Vista, 11 km NE Jarabacoa, 640 m, 3; La Ciénaga, 915 m, 1; 1 km S Constanza, 1098 m, 3; *Monseñor Nouel:* 6 km SE Maimón, 122 m, 1; *Duarte:* 10 km SE Tenares, 183 m, 2; Villa Riva, 1; *Samaná:* 6.9 km NE Sánchez, 336 m, 4; 10.2 km W Samaná, 61 m, 3; 4.8 km W Samaná, s.l., 3; 18.0 km E and N Samaná, s.l., 5; 3.8 km S Las Galeras, s.l., 1; *Hato Mayor:* 7 km E Sabana de la Mar, 2; 25 km E Sabana de la Mar, 1; *La Altagracia:* Punta Cana, s.l., 1; 16 km NE La Romana, 61 m, 1; 2.5 km SE Playa Bayahibe, s.l., 1; *La Romana:* Río Chavón, 8 km SE La Romana, s.l., 1; *Dist. Nac.:* Punta Caucedo, 2 km W, 2 km S Andrés, s.l., 2; Tres Ojos, s.l., 1; 30 km NW Santo Domingo, 122 m, 1; *Sánchez Ramírez:* 1 km NE Las Lagunas, 183 m, 3; *Monte Plata:* 8 km NE Bayaguana, 2; *Peravia:* Las Calderas, s.l., 1; 5 km SW Sombrero, 2; 4 km S Las Carreras, 1; 1 km N Fundación de Sabana Buey, 1; *Azua:* 22 km NW Cruce de Ocoa, 61 m, 4; 1 km E Palmar de Ocoa, s.l., 3; 2 km NW Hatillo, 183 m, 1; 25 km NE

Azua, 92 m, 1; Tábara Abajo, 9; Puerto Viejo, s.l., 2; 13 km NW El Cruce del Quince, 1; 2 km SE La Canoa, 397 m, 1; *San Juan:* 9 km E Vallejuelo, 610 m, 10; *Independencia:* 4 km NW Tierra Nueva, s.l., 1; La Furnia, s.l., 5; 1 km S Boca de Cachón, s.l., 1; 3.3 km E La Descubierta, 3; *Barahona:* 8 km ESE Canoa, s.l., 1; 11.5 km ESE Canoa, s.l., 1; 2 km E Vicente Noble, 2; 9 km NNE Polo, 793 m, 1; 3 km NW Enriquillo, 244 m, 2; *Pedernales:* Cabo Rojo, s.l., 5; 2 km NE Cabo Rojo, s.l., 6; 23 km NE Cabo Rojo, 488 m, 1; 26 km NE Cabo Rojo, 732 m, 1; Mencía, 397 m, 2; 1 km NE Los Arroyos, 1220 m, 2; 4 km NW Tres Charcos, 2; *Isla Catalina:* 1.

23. *Hemiargus thomasi noeli* Comstock and Huntington, 1943

TL St.-Marc, Dépt. de l'Artibonite, Haiti.

FW males 9–13 mm, females 9–13 mm.

In contrast to the 2 other species of *Hemiargus, H. t. noeli* is distinctly xerophilic, although it occurs occasionally in mesic areas (Jánico, Samaná). Its elevational range is from sea level (Cormier Plage, Canoa, Samaná, Punta Caucedo, Las Lajas, Cabo Rojo) to 915 m (Boutilliers Road). A specimen from La Horma on the south face of the Cordillera Central is probably from a slightly higher elevation (*ca.* 970 m). The high elevation is much less than those reported for *H. c. ceraunus* (1617 m) and *H. h. watsoni* (1891 m). The species does not occur in the uplands of the Cordillera Central (where the 2 other species occur) but is abundant in the Valle de San Juan (where the 2 others are uncommon). *Hemiargus t. noeli* has been taken on Île de la Gonâve, Isla Saona, Isla Catalina, Isla Beata, and Isla Alto Velo, all new records. *Hemiargus t. noeli* was very common on Isla Alto Velo in November and is 1 of only 3 species of Lepidoptera collected there.

Like other blues, *H. t. noeli* occurs most often in grassy or weedy areas; but in contrast to other blues, this species has a strong tendency to land at a greater height (1.5 or more m), on the branches of *Acacia,* for example, a habit that it shares with *Ps. b. bornoi* (see beyond). In fact, in xeric areas, one can be almost certain that any blue (*not* hairstreak) seen landing on branches or twigs high above the ground is one of these 2 species.

Times for collection of *H. t. noeli* varied between 0800 and 1810 h, and temperatures between 27°C (2 km E Les Poteaux) and 42°C (La Romana). Most specimens have been taken in July (65), with 56 in August, 38 in May, 14 each in June, January, October, November, and December, 4 in April, 6 in March, and 11 in February.

Food plants include *Heliotropium curassavicum* (Boca Chica), *Sida* sp. (La Furnia), *Lantana ovatifolia* (23 km NE Cabo Rojo), *Melochia tomentosa* (23 km NE Cabo Rojo, La Canoa), *Croton barahonensis* (Vallejuelo, twice), *Tephrosia purpurea* (Mao), *Bidens pilosa*

(Los Quemados, Santiago), *Parthenium hysterophorus* (Santiago), *Macroptilimnium lathyroides* (Fabaceae) (Santiago), and *Acacia vogeliana* (Vallejuelo).

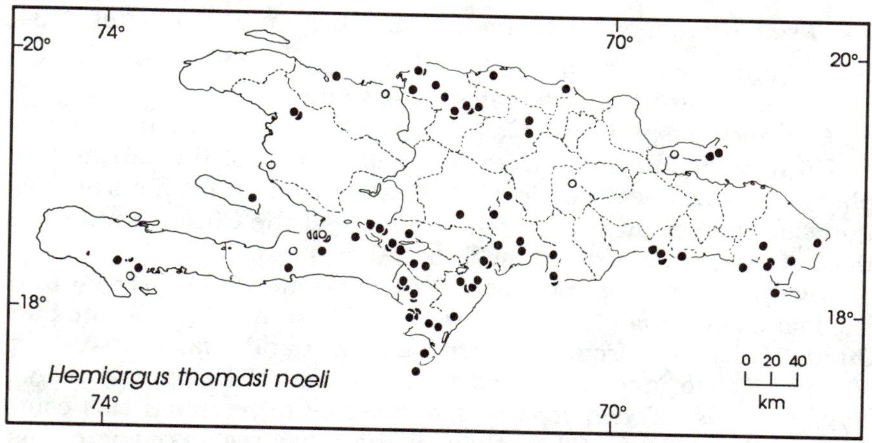

Specimens: Haiti: Nord: Cormier Plage, s.l., 1; *l'Artibonite:* 2 km E Les Poteaux, 2; 6 km N Les Poteaux, 1 (MPM); 4.6 km E Les Poteaux, 183 m, 1; *l'Ouest:* 5 km NW Fond Parisien, 3; Boutilliers Road, 854–915 m, 1; 6 km NW Jacmel, 244 m, 1; *Sud:* Lévy, 3; 7 km SW Cavaillon, 122 m, 1; *Île de la Gonâve:* Anse-à-Galets, 2; *República Dominicana: Monte Cristi:* 1 km SE Monte Cristi, 12; 4 km N Monte Cristi, s.l., 2; 6 km W Copey, s.l., 1; 4 km NW Villa Vásquez, 61 m, 1; 3.9 km SE Martín García, 92 m, 4; *Valverde:* 12 km SW Mao, 244 m, 5; 3 km W Los Quemados, 122 m, 4; *Santiago Rodríguez:* 3 km W Los Quemados, 183 m, 4; 4.8 km S Zamba, 183 m, 3; 3.0 km S Zamba, 214 m, 4; *Puerto Plata:* 10 km W Luperón, 1; 9 km SE Sosúa, 15 m, 2; *Santiago:* 8 km E Jánico, 610 m, 1; 7 km SW Santiago, 214 m, 10; *Samaná:* 18.0 km E and N Samaná, s.l., 5; 10.5 km S Las Galeras, 16 m, 1; *La Altagracia:* Punta Cana, s.l., 1; 0.5 km W Boca de Yuma, 1; 16 km NE La Romana, 61 m, 4; 1 km N Playa Bayahibe, 1; 2.5 km SE Playa Bayahibe, s.l., 3; *San Pedro de Macorís:* 13 km SE Boca Chica, 2; *Dist. Nac.* Punta Caucedo, 5 km S Aeropuerto Internacional de las Américas, s.l., 2; Punta Caucedo, 2 km W, 2 km S Andrés, s.l., 2; 33 km W San Pedro de Macorís, 4 (MPM); *Peravia:* 5 km NE Sabana Buey, 1; Las Calderas, s.l., 1; 2.7 km W La Horma, 2; *Azua:* 5 km S Peralta, 305 m, 1; 18 km S Peralta, 122 m, 1; 25 km NE Azua, 92 m, 3; Tábara Abajo, 1; 2 km SE La Canoa, 397 m, 2; 5 km SW Monte Bonito, 702 m, 3; *San Juan:* 9 km E Vallejuelo, 610 m, 35; *Independencia:* Las Lajas, s.l., 6; 5 km NW Tierra Nueva, s.l., 1; 4 km NW Tierra Nueva, s.l., 4; La Furnia, s.l., 6; 3.3 km E La Descubierta, 3; 6 km SE Jimaní, 1; 4 km E El Limón, s.l., 3; 2 km S Duvergé, 1; 4–7 km NE El Aguacate, 519–824 m, 1; *Barahona:* 11.5 km ESE Canoa, s.l., 3; 12 km ESE Canoa, s.l., 12; 8 km NNE Polo, 793 m, 2; 10 km W Cabral, 2; 2 km SW Barahona, 122 m, 7; 12 km SW Barahona, 427 m, 1; 3 km NW Enriquillo, 244 m, 1; *Pedernales:* Cabo Rojo, s.l., 1; 2 km N Cabo Rojo, s.l., 1; 2 km NE Cabo Rojo, s.l., 6; 4 km NE Cabo Rojo, s.l., 3; 23 km NE Cabo Rojo, 478 m, 7; 19 km NNE Cabo Rojo, 366 m, 3; 2 km SW Mencía, 336 m, 1; Mencía, 397 m, 2; 3 km W Aguas Negras, 519 m, 2; 17 km

NW Oviedo, 183 m, 5; 4 km NW Tres Charcos, 1; *Isla Saona:* 2 km W Mano Juan, 3; 1 km W Mano Juan, 3; 2 km E Mano Juan, 1; 0.5 km N Mano Juan, 5; *Isla Alto Velo:* 14; *Isla Catalina:* 2; *Isla Beata:* 10.

24. *Pseudochrysops bornoi bornoi* Comstock and Huntington, 1943

TL Pont Beudet, Dépt. de l'Ouest, Haiti.

FW males 8–13 mm, females 11–13 mm.

Pseudochrysops bornoi was described from a suite of 6 males and 6 females, all but 1 from the western end of the Cul de Sac plain, and thus near sea level. The exception is a female from Pétionville; this locality is at about 430 m. All the Cul de Sac localities are xeric, whereas Pétionville is rather mesic.

My specimens are from the Cul de Sac–Valle de Neiba, east into the Llanos de Azua (Sombrero) and northwest into the Valle de San Juan (Vallejuelo), from the Península de Barahona, the western Valle de Cibao, and in the extreme east end of Hispaniola (Playa Bayahibe). *Pseudochrysops b. bornoi* seems to be much less common in the Valle de Cibao than in the other regions, where it is often locally abundant (Tierra Nueva, Canoa, Cabo Rojo and environs, El Limón).

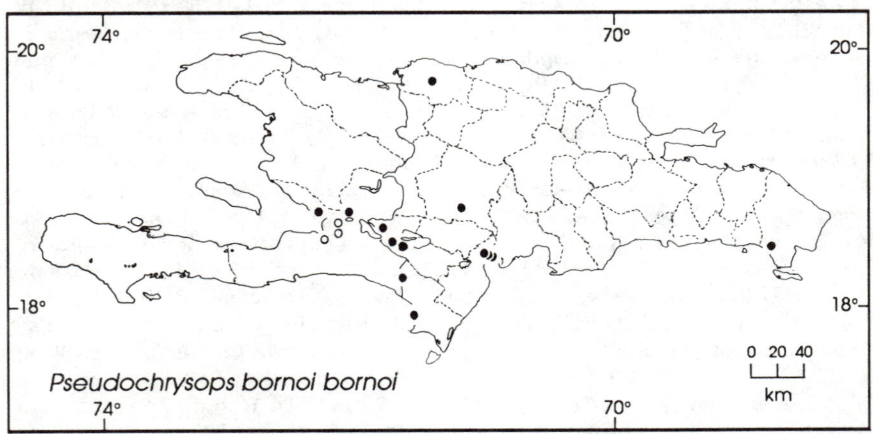

Pseudochrysops bornoi bornoi

These butterflies habitually land on bare twigs or on the leaves of trees, 1 m or more above the ground, and fly with *H. t. noeli*, *S. toussainti*, *S. limenius*, and *S. c. cybirus*. Among the blues, only *H. t. noeli* regularly lands so high above the ground. Like hairstreaks, *Ps. b. bornoi* rubs its hindwings immediately upon landing. All habitats, with the exception of Mencía, are extremely harsh and rigorous (*Acacia* scrub) and are often extremely windy (Cabo Rojo), so that these small butterflies give the impression of "laboring" while flying, landing promptly after very short sallies from the perch site. At Cabo Rojo, *Ps. b. bornoi* was attracted (along with hundreds of bees) to the tiny brownish flowers in panicles of *Metopium brownei* (Anacardiaceae), and at Sombrero 1 individual was taken on *Antigonon leptopus*. *Pseudochrysops b. bornoi* has been taken on *Lantana reticulata*, *Pithecellobium circinale* (Fabaceae), and *Melochia nodiflora*, all at El Limón. Elsewhere, we have taken *Ps. b. bornoi* on *Cordia exarata* (Playa Bayahibe), *Croton barahonensis* (Vallejuelo, twice), *Acacia farnesiana* (4 km NE Cabo Rojo), *Pithecellobium circinale* (11.5 km ESE Canoa), *Lantana reticulata* (2.5 km SE Playa Bayahibe), and *Lippia micromera* (Canoa).

Elevational distribution is from sea level (Cabo Rojo, El Limón) to 610 m (Vallejuelo). Most localities are at or near sea level. Of the 3 exceptions, 2 (Terre Rouge, Mencía) are on montane slopes adjacent to xeric lowlands (where *Ps. b. bornoi* occurs in both cases) and are themselves xeric (Terre Rouge) or transitional (Mencía). The third locality (Vallejuelo) lies in the intermontane xeric valley in the Sierra de Neiba; this arid valley is continuous with the more southern xeric Llanos de Azua. Doubtless this blue occurs throughout the intervening area. There are 25 specimens from April, 19 from August, 15 from October, 9 each from March, July, and December, and 2 each from January and June. *Pseudochrysops b. bornoi* is most common in April, August, and October, suggesting that the species is trivoltine. The type-series was taken in March. Times of collection were between 0800 and 1630 h, and temperatures between 28°C (Source Matelas, 11.5 km ESE Canoa) and 38°C (La Furnia, Cabo Rojo, 2 km NE Cabo Rojo).

Specimens: Haiti: l'Ouest: 5 km SE Source Matelas, s.l., 4; 3 km S Terre Rouge, 427 m, 1; *República Dominicana: Monte Cristi:* 4 km NW Villa Vásquez, 61 m, 1; *La Altagracia:* 2.5 km SE Playa Bayahibe, s.l., 10; *Peravia:* Sombrero, 1; 5 km NE Sabana Buey, 1; *San Juan:* 9 km E Vallejuelo, 610 m, 3; *Independencia:* 4 km NW Tierra Nueva, s.l., 9; La Furnia, s.l., 2; 4 km E El Limón, s.l., 20; *Barahona:* 8 km ESE Canoa, 9; 11.5 km ESE Canoa, s.l., 9; 12 km ESE Canoa, s.l., 2; *Pedernales:* Mencía, 397 m, 1; Cabo Rojo, s.l., 6; 2 km NE Cabo Rojo, s.l., 9; 4 km NE Cabo Rojo, s.l., 1; 5 km NE Cabo Rojo, 1.

Family Libytheidae Boisduval, 1836

1. *Libytheana terena* Godart, 1819

TL "Antilles."

FW males 20–26 mm, females 22–26 mm.

The snout butterflies are represented in the Antilles by 3 species: *motya* Boisduval and Leconte on Cuba, *fulvescens* Lathy on Dominica, and *L. terena.* Although Hispaniola is the major island of *L. terena,* there are 2 records for Puerto Rico (Ramos, 1982:66) and 4 records for Jamaica (Vyhmeister and Donahue, 1980:102).

The 3 taxa have been considered separate species (Riley, 1975:91–92) or have been variously combined as subspecies. Brown and Heineman, for example (1972:224), considered *terena* as a subspecies of South American *L. carinenta* Cramer. They considered the Cuban *L. motya* recognizable because of its "replacement of the fulvous coloring by a dirty yellowish white" on the upfw apical and subapical markings, in contrast to these markings being fulvous (except for the apical dot) in *L. terena.* They further stated: "Whether more extensive series from the Greater Antilles will show that both whitish and fulvous forms occur together or that they are always segregated remains to be seen." My long series of snout butterflies from Hispaniola always has the upfw markings fulvous, including, in many cases, the apical spot, although the latter may be slightly paler than the remainder of the upfw markings. It seems preferable to consider *L. terena* as a species distinct from all other *Libytheana.* At least a long series of Hispaniolan specimens is now available. Hall (1925:188) and Riley (1975:92) considered the species "scarce," and Hall's only record was near La Vega. Schwartz (1983a:39) reported 19 specimens from Haiti and considered *L. terena* "locally common and widely distributed."

Riley (1975:pl. 10, fig. 5) showed a male from "Haiti." In this illustration, the pale spot in M3-Cu1 on the upfw is elongate longitudinally and thus rectangular in shape and separated rather widely from the most posterior subapical spot in M2-M3. In most of my specimens, the M3-Cu1 fulvous spot is square rather than rectangular and is often joined by a fine fulvous line along M3 to the fulvous spot in M2-M3. Also, in many specimens, the ground color on the uphw is much darker than that in Riley's plate, due to a general overall dusting with black scales, except for a pale "band" extending from the base of the hw through the cell to the hw margin. The anal fold is never pale as Riley's plate shows and is concolor with the remainder of the hw ground color. As noted above, the upfw apical spot is rarely pure white and is most often pale fulvous or even concolor with the remainder of the upfw fulvous markings.

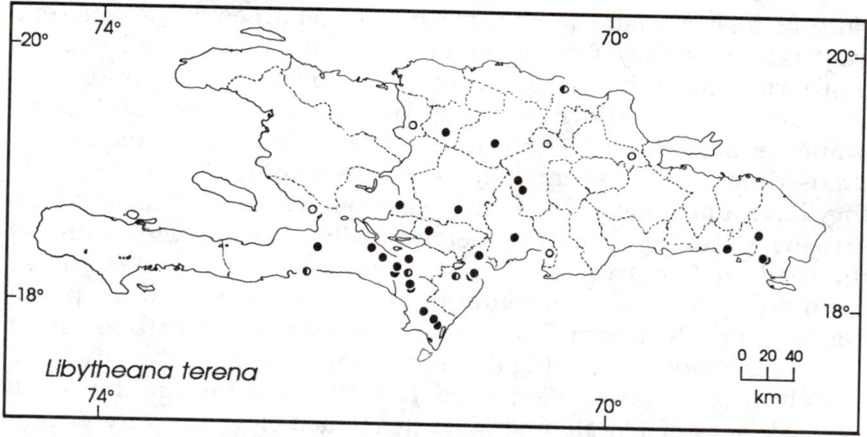

Libytheana terena is widely distributed on Hispaniola and occurs in Haiti and the República Dominicana on the south island, and elsewhere in the República Dominicana. Its distribution is between sea level (13.6 km E Jacmel) and 1525 m (Forêt des Pins on the Massif de la Selle in Haiti), 1617 m (Los Arroyos on the same range in the República Dominicana), and 1647 m (Constanza on the Cordillera Central). Most specimens have been taken in lowland xeric forest (La Romana, Playa Bayahibe); at the former, 12 specimens were secured in 1.5 h on 28.vi by 2 collectors. We have also taken specimens or seen individuals in an open field (Constanza), along the seashore (Jacmel), in pine forest (Forêt des Pins), in mixed xeric woods–*Acacia* stands (Vallejuelo), *Acacia* woods (Oviedo), transitional forest (Barahona, Cabo Rojo, El Aguacate), and mesic forest (Los Arroyos). The series from Boutilliers Road is from an open mountainside with shrubs and scattered trees. Times of collection were between 0900 and 1700 h, and temperatures between 21°C (Los Arroyos) and 38°C (Cabo Rojo).

Most specimens and records are from June (43) and July (43), with 8 from August, 3 from October, 2 from December, and 1 from

May. Schwartz (1983a:39) suggested that *L. terena* is double-brooded, with 1 brood from late July to early August; these data strongly support this suggestion, but the second (February) brood, if it exists, has not been sampled by us. We saw only 1 *L. terena* in May, 1 in April, 2 in December, and none in March.

On 5 occasions we have taken *L. terena* drinking from mud at the edge of a small stream (Puesto Pirámide 204), from mud in a dirt road or in the bottoms of small solution holes in the road surface (La Romana, Playa Bayahibe, Barahona), and from mud and sand at a river's edge (Neiba, twice). At Loma Leonor, 2 *L. terena* were taken as they flew above and landed on the small cobbles that form a local "beach" adjacent to the Río Toma. The butterflies are rapid and erratic fliers: they rest on bare twigs and small branches between 0.25 and 1.5 m above the ground, usually in exposed situations where they are easily captured. On the wing, they have a peculiar habit, which was observed on 2 occasions (Los Arroyos, Cabo Rojo), of flying determinedly down the very center of the road; at Los Arroyos the road is improved rock-gravel and at Cabo Rojo the Alcoa Exploration Company has a wide paved highway into the Sierra de Baoruco. Twice we saw at both localities several *L. terena* performing this same feat.

Schwartz (1983a:39) reported *L. terena* feeding on the small white flowers of *Morinda citrifolia* near Jacmel at the very ocean-side. We have also seen this butterfly feeding on the white flowers of *Daucus* sp. at Boutilliers Road, on *Tournefortia hirsutissima* at Sosúa, on *Croton linearis* (Canoa, 1.3 km S Tres Charcos), on *Cordia exarata* (2.5 km SE Playa Bayahibe, twice), and on *Cordia globosa* at La Romana; the latter plant is very attractive to these butterflies and helps account for the long series taken on that day, as noted above.

A pair of *L. terena* was taken *in copula* on 29.vi (La Romana, 61 m, 1030–1145 h, 37°C).

Specimens: Haiti: l'Ouest: Forêt des Pins, 1525 m, 2; Boutilliers Road, 732–854 m, 15; above Lastic le Roche, below Plaine Thoman, 488 m, 1; *República Dominicana: Elías Piña:* 2 km NE Puesto Pirámide 204, 1586 m, 1; *Santiago Rodríguez:* Loma Leonor, 18 km SW Monción, 549 m, 2; *Santiago:* Río Bao, 8 km SE Montones Abajo, 488 m, 1; *La Vega:* 1 km S Constanza, 1098 m, 1; 10 km SE Constanza, 1647 m, 1; *La Altagracia:* 16 km NE La Romana, 61 m, 18: 1 km N Playa Bayahibe, s.l., 8; 2.5 km SE Playa Bayahibe, s.l., 11; *La Romana:* Río Cumayasa, 13.5 km E La Romana, 6; *Azua:* 5 km S Peralta, 305 m, 4; *San Juan:* 9 km E Vallejuelo, 610 m, 1; *Baoruco:* 11 km N Neiba, 519 m, 2; *Independencia:* 4–7 km NE El Aguacate, 519–824 m, 6; *Barahona:* 8 km ESE Canoa, 1; 2 km SW Barahona, 122 m, 2; 6 km SW Barahona, 122 m, 1; *Pedernales:* 23 km NE Cabo Rojo, 488 m, 6; 26 km NE Cabo

Rojo, 732 m, 1; 5 km NE Los Arroyos, 1617 m, 1; 0.6 km SE Los Arroyos, 1098 m, 2; 4 km NW Tres Charcos, 1; 1.3 km S Tres Charcos, 1; 17 km NW Oviedo, 183 m, 1.

Sight records: Haiti: l'Ouest: 13.6 km E Jacmel, s.l.—1 seen, 4.vii; *República Dominicana: Puerto Plata:* 11 km SE Sosúa, 183 m—1 seen, 2.viii: *La Altagracia:* 2.5 km SE Playa Bayahibe, s.l.—3 seen, 5.vii; 16 km NE La Romana, 61 m—1 seen, 17.iv; *Independencia:* 4–7 km NE El Aguacate, 519–732 m—1 seen, 6.vii; *Barahona:* 7 km SSW Cabral. 214 m—1 seen, 10.vii; *Pedernales:* Las Abejas, 12 km NW Aceitillar, 1129 m—1 seen, 18.vii.

Family Heliconiidae Swainson, 1827

Subfamily Heliconiinae Swainson, 1827

1. *Agraulis vanillae insularis* Maynard, 1889

TL between Fresh Creek and Middle Bight, Andros Island, Bahama Islands (Clench, 1977b:186, quoting Turner, 1957: 143).

FW males 27–37 mm, females 27–37 mm; dwarf male 23 mm.

Agraulis v. insularis is not only widespread in the Antilles but is also 1 of the most abundant butterflies throughout the region. Bates (1935a:160) examined a long series of specimens from Cuba. Comstock (1944) considered it a "common butterfly" on Puerto Rico and the Virgin Islands. Brown and Heineman (1972:214) regarded *A. v. insularis* as "one of the most common butterflies" on Jamaica, especially where gardens have been developed. Rindge (1955:7) stated that *A. v. insularis* was "apparently the commonest butterfly seen" in the Bahamas, with 108 specimens taken. Clench (1977a:275; 1977b:195–96), Clench and Bjorndal (1980:17), and Elliot, Riley, and Clench (1980) all noted the abundance of this species throughout the Bahamas and on specific Bahaman islands.

On Hispaniola, Hall (1925:186) considered *A. v. insularis* "generally common," and Schwartz (1983a:38–39) cited more localities for this species than any other heliconiid. The list of specimens examined as noted herein is likewise long, but in most cases, only 1 or a few specimens were taken at any particular place; such small numbers do not in any way indicate the abundance of *A. v. insularis*, which is often common and at times unbelievably abundant. For instance, between 27.vi.1980 and 1.vii.1980, *A. v. insularis* swarmed along the southern coast of the República Dominicana between Santo Domingo and La Romana. Travel along the road between these 2 cities showed thousands of these butterflies. Many were killed on the highway, and in places the herbaceous vegetation was spangled with them. The fate of this large irruption is unknown; after 1.vii, the numbers fell off quickly and dramatically, and so many *A. v. insularis* have not been seen there (or elsewhere) since that year. Since *A. v. insularis* is known to migrate, it is possible that many of these individuals flew out to sea and were lost. Despite the numbers of *Lantana ovatifolia* and *Bidens pilosa* along this stretch of road, it seems unlikely that this circumscribed area could support this large a population for very long, and it may be that the population level returned to "normal" merely through the mortality of adults.

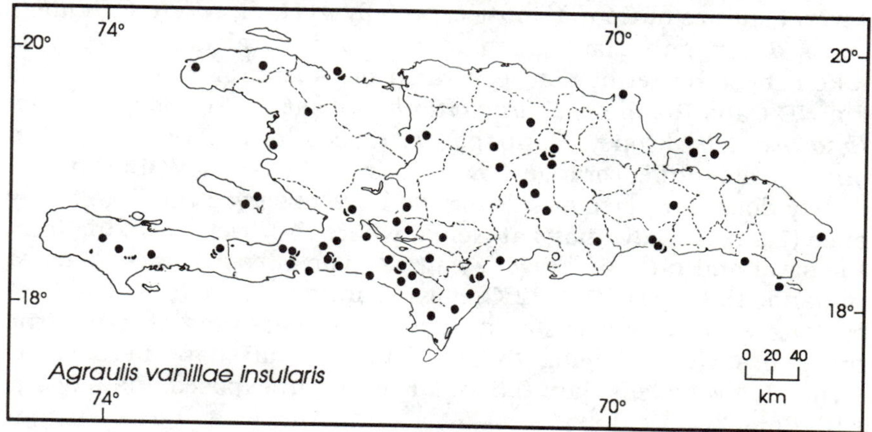

Although several authors have commented on the presence of *A. v. insularis* in gardens, the species is by no means restricted to that sort of habitat. *Agraulis v. insularis* is tolerant of a wide variety of ecological situations, from *Acacia* scrub (Colmini, Duvergé) and open coastal scrub (Cormier Plage, Punta Cana), to pine forest (Forêt des Pins). It has been encountered within *caféières* (Paillant), on mountain roadsides (Boutilliers Road, Mirebalais), in xeric forest (La Romana), in open deciduous forest (Los Pinos), and in mesic forest (Valle de Tetero, Las Abejas, Los Arroyos). It shuns most arid habitats, and in the Cul de Sac–Valle de Neiba, the records are few (Fond Parisien, La Descubierta, Duvergé, Galván). But it does occur on very arid Isla Catalina.

The elevational distribution is between sea level (Môle St.-Nicholas, Cormier Plage, Méyer, Fond Parisien, La Descubierta, Río San Juan, Las Terrenas, Punta Caucedo) to 1891 m (Puesto Pirámide 204) in the Sierra de Neiba, 1617 m (Obléon) on the Massif de la Selle front ranges, and 1586 m (Constanza) in the Cordillera Central. At none of the high localities is *A. v. insularis* common, but none of them stands as a completely isolated elevational record.

Most specimens (52) are from July, with lesser numbers from June (34), March (13), and many less (12–2) from December, January, August, April, February, October, and May. *Agraulis v. insularis* appears to be on the wing throughout the year, but there is a high concentration in summer. Flight times were between 0730 and 1715 h, with temperatures between 13°C (Valle de Tetero) and 39°C (Samaná).

Aside from *L. ovatifolia* and *B. pilosa*, *A. v. insularis* feeds on several species of *Cordia*, most especially in Haiti, where *C. haitiensis* is a common plant along roadsides in rural areas. We have taken these butterflies or seen them on *Ageratum conyzoides* (18 km NE Cabo Rojo), on *Tournefortia hirsutissima* (Río Bao), on *Lantana ovatifolia* (Copey, Santiago), *L. reticulata* (Isla Catalina), and on an unidentified orange flower (5 km SE, 3 km W Barahona). Rarely does *A. v. insularis* drink; we have observed this habit only once (2 single individuals) at Neiba, where they were drinking from the sand and mud at a river's edge. A pair *in copula* was taken at Banano, 183 m (1420 h, 32°C, mesic spring run) on 10.vi. On 3 occasions we have encountered *A. v. insularis* resting at night; the butterflies were clinging to grass blades and bare herbaceous stems, between less than 0.5 and 1 m tall, in exposed and obvious situations.

Agraulis v. insularis has been previously unreported from Île de la Gonâve, Isla Saona, or Isla Catalina.

Specimens: Haiti: Nord-Ouest: Môle St.-Nicholas, s.l., 2; 7.5 km SE Port-de-Paix, 1; *Nord:* Cormier Plage, s.l., 1; Cap-Haïtien, 2 (MPM); *l'Artibonite:* 1.6 km E Carrefour Marmelade, 854 m, 10; Colmini, 6.4 km W Terre Noire, 1; *l'Ouest:* 20 km S Mirebalais, 580, 1; 2.9–8.5 km S Terre Rouge, 122–488 m, 1; 3.0 km SE Fond Parisien, s.l., 1; Forêt des Pins, 1373–1525 m, 2; *ca.* 2 km E Belle Anse, at descent from road to beach, 1; Pétionville, 476 m, 6; Boutilliers Road, 732–946 m, 12; Boutilliers Road, 1.8–2.1 km W Kenscoff road, 793–885 m, 2; 5.8 km S Kenscoff, 1586 m, 1; 0.3 km N Obléon, 1617 m, 1; Peneau, 1.6 km SW Furcy, 1464 m, 1; 4 km SW Dufort, Ravine Roseau, 1; 0.6 km S Découzé, 671 m, 2; 2.1 km S Découzé, 640 m, 1; 3.8 km S Découzé, 1; 8.3 km NW Jacmel, 183 m, 10: 5.8 km E Méyer, s.l., 1; nr. Péredo, 570 m, 1 (FSM); *Sud:* 3 km SW Paillant, 793 m, 2; 6.7 km SW Paillant, 854 m, 7; 6.6 km SW Paillant, 793 m, 2; 7.8 km N Cavaillon, 31 m, 1; 5.6 km N Camp Perrin, 275 m, 2; Formond Base Camp #1, 975 m, 2 (FSM); *Île de la Gonâve:* Anse-à-Galets, 4; Picmi, 2; *República Dominicana: Dajabón:* Los Cerezos, 12 km NW Río Limpio, 580 m, 2; 8 km S Restauración, 610 m, 1; *Elías Piña:* 1 km SW Puesto Pirámide 204, 1891 m, 1; *Santiago:* Río Bao, 8 km SE Montones Abajo, 488 m, 1; 7 km SW Santiago, 214 m, 2; Valle de Tetero, 1342 m, 1; *La Vega:* Güaigüí, S La Vega, 336 m, 1; 10 km W Jayaco, 915 m, 1; Buena Vista, 11 km NE Jarabacoa, 630 m, 1; Jarabacoa, 530 m, 3; 6 km SE Constanza, 1403 m, 1; 18 km SE Constanza, 1586 m, 1; 10 km NW La Horma, 1495 m, 1; *María T. Sánchez:* 9 km NE Río San Juan, s.l., 1; *Samaná:* 3.1 km E Las Terrenas, s.l., 2; 4.5 km E Samaná, 4; 10.2 km W Samaná, 61 m, 1; *La Altagracia:* Punta Cana, s.l., 1; 16 km NE La Romana, 61 m, 3; *Monte Plata:* 8

km NE Bayaguana, 1; *Dist. Nac.:* 33 km W San Pedro de Macorís, 1 (MPM); Punta Caucedo, 5 km S Aeropuerto Internacional de las Américas, s.l., 1; 5 km S San Isidro, 2; *San Cristóbal:* 11 km NW Cambita Garabitos, 671 m, 2; *Independencia:* 23 km N Los Pinos, 1739 m, 1; 1.3 km E La Descubierta, 4; 2 km S Duvergé, 1; *Baoruco:* 2 km SE Galván, 1; *Barahona:* El Limón, summit, Sierra Martín García, 1037 m, 1; 2 km SW Barahona, 122 m, 1; 11 km SW Barahona, 1; 8 km NW Paraíso, 1 (MPM); 8–10 km NW Paraíso, 11 (MPM); 9 km NW Enriquillo, 671 m, 1; *Pedernales:* 18 km NE Cabo Rojo, 366 m, 1; Las Abejas, 12 km NW Aceitillar, 1129 m, 1; 1 km SE Banano, 183 m, 2; 3 km N Cabeza de Agua, 305 m, 1; 5 km NE Los Arroyos, 1617 m, 2; 17 km NW Oviedo, 183 m, 1; *Isla Saona:* 1.5 km N Mano Juan, 2; *Isla Catalina:* 2.

2. *Dryas iulia hispaniola* Hall, 1925

TL Hispaniola; based on specimens primarily (or exclusively?) from the República Dominicana.

FW males 40–46 mm, females 37–45 mm.

Hall (1925:186) based the description of *D. i. hispaniola* on 14 males and 5 females; this large number of specimens suggests the abundance of this heliconiid on Hispaniola. On the other hand, Emsley (1963:93), while discussing the distribution of androconia in the subspecies of *D. iulia,* noted that he was uncertain about *D. i. hispaniola,* since there was only a small number available.

Hall (1925) partially diagnosed *D. i. hispaniola* on the basis in males of the subapical transverse bar terminating abruptly at the middle of the fw (M3). Although this condition occurs in some males (26%), many others have the bar complete to the margin, there joining the dark marginal band (74%). Riley (1975:pl. 9, fig. 1d) showed a male that agrees with Hall's diagnosis, but many specimens much more closely resemble his fig. 1i, of *D. i. warreni* Hall, at least as far as upfw pattern is concerned. The variation is not correlated with geography, and a sample for any locality shows a variety of conditions. In females, whose up ground color is more tannish gray (Hall's "leather-brown" is apt), the subapical upfw bar is likewise variable but shows a much more regular occurrence of a complete bar (96%).

In respect to the occurrence of androconia on fw M1 to 2A, the posterior 3 veins (Cu1 to 2A) always have androconia. The anterior 3 (M1-M3) have the androconia in 32% and lack them or have them extremely sparse in 68%.

Dryas i. hispaniola occurs in a broad spectrum of habitats, but it favors mesic woods and forests, where it is most regularly encountered along roads and paths. The species occurs also in xeric or transitional woods, and it is not unusual to see these butterflies flying and foraging in open fields, along roads on open mountainsides, or in scrubby or weedy roadside areas. There are no records from the xeric Cul de Sac–Valle de Neiba plain, except for small oases (Fond Parisien); the same applies to the western Valle de Cibao, where the only record is from Villa Vásquez, again an oasis, where *D. i. hispaniola* was very abundant. There is 1 record for the Península de Barahona (Oviedo), where the butterfly was taken in *Acacia* scrub, the only instance of this species in an unqualifiedly xeric situation.

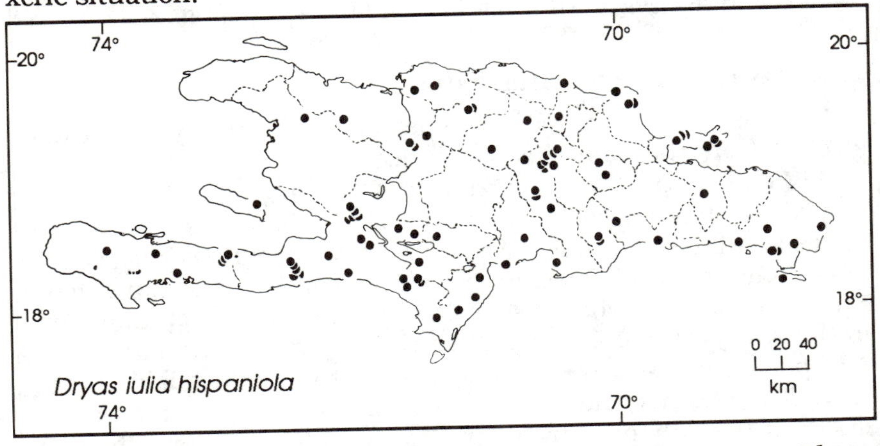

Elevations of occurrence varied from sea level (Cormier Plage, Fond Parisien, Samaná, Punta Cana, Palmar de Ocoa, Mano Juan) to 1647 m (Constanza); in the latter area, *D. i. hispaniola* is absent from the high pine forests of the Cordillera Central. Times of collection were between 0900 and 1730 h, and temperatures between 26°C (Boutilliers Road, Neiba) and 40°C (Los Quemados). *Dryas i. hispaniola* flies in cloudy or even rainy weather; during the latter, these butterflies occasionally, in the midst of moderately heavy rain, fly briefly for short distances, presumably to find a more protected site.

These are the first records of occurrence of *D. i. hispaniola* for Île de la Gonâve and Isla Saona. The single female from the latter island sets the lower extreme for female fw measurements. At various times and places, we have seen what were obviously dwarf *D. i. hispaniola*.

Most specimens (69) are from July, with June next (42), and December third (18). August, January, March, April, May, October, November, and February are represented by 14 to 1 specimens. Brown and Heineman (1972:218–19) had dates throughout the year for *D. i. delila* Fabricius, the Jamaican subspecies, and Clench

(1977b:185) considered that *D. i. carteri* Riley flies probably all year in the northern Bahamas. *Dryas i. hispaniola* likewise flies throughout the year. Its numbers in July, however, can hardly be overestimated. At El Aguacate, these butterflies were extremely abundant in that month; a parked pale yellow Volkswagen, without obvious nutritional or moisture interest to these butterflies, had over 25 of them settled on the grill, running boards, and any other foothold. The butterflies were merely resting, with no obvious agonistic or mating behavior; they were very tame and refused to depart from the vicinity of the car, even when disturbed. At this same locality, hundreds of *D. i. hispaniola* were seen in the 3 kilometers over which we collected; many of them were settled in low moist spots in the gravel road, others on fresh horse manure and cow dung in the road.

As Brown and Heineman (1972:217) noted, *D. i. hispaniola* finds *Lantana ovatifolia* extremely attractive; even if no other rhopalocerans are present on a *Lantana* bush, one can almost always count on there being 1 or 2 *Dryas* present. At Villa Vásquez, many *D. i. hispaniola* were feeding on *Antigonon leptopus*. Other food plants include *Zinnia elegans* at La Piedra and *Tournefortia hirsutissima* at Sosúa, Neiba (2 occasions), Peralta, Río Bao, and 1 km N Playa Bayahibe, but *L. ovatifolia* is overwhelmingly the favorite nectar source for these butterflies. At Neiba, *D. i. hispaniola* was 1 of 3 species feeding avidly on *Poinsettia pulcherrima*, a plant rarely used by any species of butterfly. At 2.5 km SE Playa Bayahibe, they were feeding on an unidentified white-flowered tree.

Aside from the El Aguacate observations of *D. i. hispaniola* drinking from moist earth, at Los Cerezos, in all years between 1980 and 1983, a small group (about 15) of male *D. i. hispaniola* has been observed on the downstream side of a cemented bridge-and-culvert, settled on the bare cement and drinking from the moisture (deposited as spray). Many other species of butterflies also drink at the bridge, but the grouping of *Dryas* has remained in approximately the same circumscribed spot over the years, and this species has never been seen drinking elsewhere at this bridge. Also at Los Cerezos, we observed several *D. i. hispaniola* settled on (and "drinking" from?) the fleshy side of a freshly prepared goat skin that was drying in the sun near the bridge. As the skin became drier, it lost its attraction for the butterflies. No other species was interested in the object. At Neiba, several of these butterflies were observed individually drinking from the sand and mud at the river's edge.

We have taken 7 copulating pairs, 3 at El Aguacate: 24.vi,

1045–1430 h, 28°C, 14.vii, 0905–1050 h, 30°C, and 30.viii, 1102 h, 30°C, in transitional xeric-mesic forest. A fourth pair is from Fond Parisien, 30.iv, 1230 h, 32°C, in *Acacia* forest. Other pairs are from: Neiba, 18.vi, 1402 h, 33°C, in a bush 0.6 m above the ground adjacent to road; Peralta, 21.vi, 1053 h, 33°C, in transitional woods; and Banano, 10.vi, 1550 h, 31°C, at a mesic spring run.

Specimens: Haiti: Nord: Cormier Plage, s.l., 4; 5.6 km SE Dondon, 336 m, 1; *l'Artibonite:* 1.6 km E Carrefour Marmelade, 854 m, 10: *l'Ouest:* 1.6 km N Saut d'Eau, 183–275 m, 4; 19.7 km SE Mirebalais, 183 m, 1; 20.1 km SE Mirebalais, 366 m, 2; 20.0 km SE Mirebalais, 580 m, 1; 1.6 km N Terre Rouge, 534 m, 2; 2.0 km N Terre Rouge, 534 m, 1; 3.0 km SE Fond Parisien, s.l., 1; 2 km SE Fond Parisien, s.l., 3; Boutilliers Road, 732–915 m, 6; Boutilliers Road, 3.7 km W Kenscoff road, 1 (MPM); 3.0 km S Découzé, 488 m, 2; 0.8 km S Découzé, 702 m, 1; 1.3 km N Béloc, 702 m, 1; 5.0 km S Béloc, 732 m, 1; 8.3 km NW Jacmel, 153 m, 1; 7.7 km N Jacmel, 92 m, 1; nr. Péredo, 600 m, 2 (FSM); *Sud:* 6.6 km SW Paillant, 793 m, 4; 6.7 km SW Paillant, 854 m, 15; 2.9 km SW Paillant, 671 m, 6; 12 km W Aquin, 1; 26.6 km N Cavaillon, 610 m, 1; Formond, 700 m, 1 (FSM); *Île de la Gonâve:* Anse-à-Galets, 1; *República Dominicana: Monte Cristi:* 6 km W Copey, s.l., 1; 4 km NW Villa Vásquez, 61 m, 1; *Dajabón:* Los Cerezos, 12 km NW Río Limpio, 590 m, 4; 8 km S Restauración, 640 m, 1; Cañada Tirolís, just S Villa Anacaona, 458 m, 1; *Santiago Rodríguez:* 3 km W Los Quemados, 183 m, 1; *Valverde:* 3 km W Los Quemados, 122 m, 2; *Puerto Plata:* 9 km SE Sosúa, 15 m, 1; *Espaillat:* 20 km SW Jamao al Norte, 793 m, 2; *Santiago:* Río Bao, 4 km SW Mata Grande, 702 m, 1; 7 km SW Santiago, 214 m, 2; *La Vega:* 10 km W Jayaco, 915 m, 2; La Palma, 19 km W Jayaco, 1007 m, 1; Buena Vista, 11 km NE Jarabacoa, 640 m, 3; Jarabacoa, 530 m, 1; 1.7 km S Jarabacoa, 488 m, 1; 6 km S Jarabacoa, 510 m, 1; La Ciénaga, 915 m, 1; 3.5 km E Paso Bajito, 732 m, 1; 10 km SE Constanza, 1647 m, 1; 14 km SE Constanza, 1403 m, 1; 10 km NW La Horma, 1496 m, 1; *Sánchez Ramírez:* La Piedra, 7 km SW Pimentel, 1; 1 km NE Las Lagunas, 183 m, 2; *María T. Sánchez:* Río San Juan, s.l., 1; 14 km SE Río San Juan, 1; 6 km S Cabrera, s.l., 1; *Samaná:* 6.9 km NE Sánchez, 336 m, 1; 12.3 km NE Sánchez, 244 m, 2; 13.2 km NE Sánchez, 92 m, 1; 18.0 km E and N Samaná, s.l., 2; 2.8 km S Las Galeras, 61 m, 1; 4.5 km E Samaná, 2; *Hato Mayor:* 12 km S El Valle, 1; *La Altagracia:* 2 km W Punta Cana, 1; 0.5–3.5 km W Boca de Yuma, 1; 1 km N Playa Bayahibe, s.l., 1; 2.5 km SE Playa Bayahibe, s.l., 1; 16 km NE La Romana, 61 m, 4; *La Romana:* Río Cumayasa, 13.5 km W La Romana, 4; *Dist. Nac.:* Tres Ojos, s.l., 1; 30 km NW Santo Domingo, 122 m, 3; *San Cristóbal:* 8 km NW Cambita Garabitos, 580 m, 1; 6 km NW Cambita Garabitos, 519 m, 4; *Azua:* 5 km S Peralta, 305 m, 3; 1 km E Palmar de Ocoa, s.l., 1; *Baoruco:* 11 km N Neiba, 519 m, 2; *Independencia:* 5 km S Angel Feliz, 1; 3.3 km E La Descubierta, 1; 4–7 km NE El Aguacate, 519–824 m, 6; *Barahona:* west slope, Sierra Martín García, 610 m, 1; 8 km SW Barahona, 366 m, 2; 8 km NW Paraíso, 2 (MPM); 8–10 km NW Paraíso, 1 (MPM); 9 km NW Enriquillo, 671 m, 1; *Pedernales:* Las Abejas, 11 km NW Aceitillar, 1220 m, 1; Las Abejas, 12 km NW Aceitillar, 1129 m, 2; 1 km SE Banano, 183 m, 3; El Mulito, 21 km N Pedernales, 214 m, 1; 17 km NW Oviedo, 183 m, 1; *Isla Saona:* Mano Juan, 1.

3. *Eueides melphis melphis* Godart, 1819

TL "Antilles."

FW males 31–37 mm, females 36–38 mm.

Considering the abundance of the 3 other Hispaniolan heliconiids, the rarity of *E. m. melphis* is indeed puzzling. I have no Haitian specimens, but Comstock (1944:pl. 7, fig. 8) had a photograph of a male from Pétionville on the Hispaniolan south island. He used the name *Eueides cleobaea monochroma* for this Haitian specimen, but Riley (1975:86) indicated that *melphis* Godart 1819 antedates *cleobaea* Geyer 1832 and *monochroma* Boullet and Le Cerf 1910 and must be used for the Hispaniolan, in contrast to the Cuban, population, even though *monochroma* was described from "Haiti and San Domingo" and thus has a "definite" type-locality.

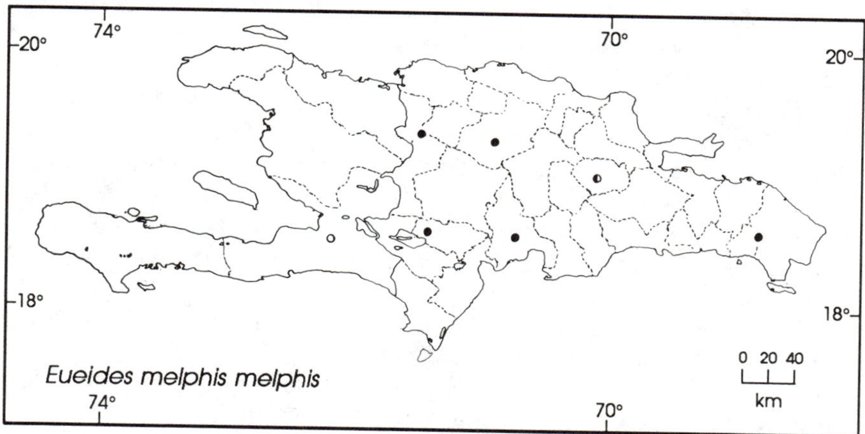

My material is from only 5 localities. In this series of specimens, the variation in up color and pattern is great. For example, the up ground color varies from very pale tan (pl. 11G7) to deep rich fulvous (pl. 11L12), with specimens from La Romana and Peralta tending to the paler color (pl. 9L8), those from Río Bao and Los Cerezos toward the deeper hues. There is a black spot in upfw Cu1-Cu2 that may be isolated (rarely) or attached to the black discal bar from the upper edge of the cell costally to the marginal end of Cu1 (commonly). This costal-marginal black band along Cu1 itself is very variable; Riley (1975:pl. 10, fig 1) showed it as incomplete along Cu1, but none of my material shows this condition; rather, it is broad (rarely) to reduced to a fine black line along Cu1 (commonly). The black transverse line from the fw base to the margin in Cu2–2A is dilated at its distal end into a bulb, which (rarely) reaches the black margin line in Cu2–2A or most often ends short of the black margin. The pale triangular spot, with its base toward the costa in M3-Cu1, is either small (in which case it is sharply defined toward its apex) or large (in which case it is smudged marginally and its apex is blurred), or this triangular spot may be small and sharply defined but encompassing only about one-half the length of M3-Cu1. These are only some of the more salient differences within our sample; there are others. I suspect that, were adequate samples available from many areas, there might be recognizable geographical variants on Hispaniola.

The populations of *E. m. melphis* are peculiarly localized. Even when a "colony" is located, it may be "present" only for a season. For example, at La Romana, we collected 5 specimens on 4 dates in 1981; this site has been visited (including those 4 1981 dates) 10 times between 1980 and 1983, yet no other *E. m. melphis* have been seen. But 2 were seen (and collected) in 1984 and 9 in 1985. At Los Cerezos, 3 specimens were taken in 1981; visits there in 1980 and 1982 yielded no specimens or sightings, despite the fact that in 1981 *E. m. melphis* was locally very abundant there. At Río Bao we succeeded, in 3 years (1981, 1983, 1986), in collecting *E. m. melphis* in numbers; yet in October 1983, none was present there despite abundance in August of the same year. The occurrence of *E. m. melphis* at Las Lagunas rests on a single individual seen; the area is mesic forest on karst.

The localization is even more precise than the above accounts imply. At both Los Cerezos and Río Bao, *E. m. melphis* was not found widely spread through the areas but rather was encountered only very locally—in both cases around stands of tall (6 m) deciduous trees draped with vines (not in flower) and adjacent to small creeks. Most *E. m. melphis* were flying lazily above the reach of the collectors, but occasional individuals drifted to lower levels and were netted. None was seen feeding, but actions at Los Cerezos suggested that a female was present high in the trees and males were attendant upon her, since the latter regularly landed near a perched butterfly (sex of course indeterminate) and then took flight once more. It is pertinent that my series contains only a very few females, which suggests that females are much less likely to drift to lower levels.

At La Romana, the high flight of *E. m. melphis* was also noted, but there was no landing on leaves of high trees as at Los Cerezos. At this locality, the butterflies were flying across a path in xeric forest and avidly feeding on a large clump of *Cordia globosa* at the interface between the forest and a large pasture. At Peralta, 2 *E. m. melphis* were feeding on *Tournefortia hirsutissima*, and the same plant was used at Río Bao (2 occasions) and Neiba (2 occasions).

The 5 localities for *E. m. melphis* are all densely forested, in 4 cases mesic, in 1 xeric. The elevational distribution is from 61 m (La Romana) to 589 m (Los Cerezos), and thus *E. m. melphis* is not restricted to high elevations; Pétionville is at about 458 m. Most specimens (18) are from August, with 9 in February, 5 in June, 3 in May, 2 each in January, April, and July, and 1 in March. The distribution of dates suggests that *E. m. melphis* is bivoltine (late winter, late summer). Times of collection were between 1015 and 1500 h, and temperatures between 26°C (Neiba) and 38°C (Río Bao). Weather conditions were invariably bright and sunny. None of these factors can account for the apparent absence of *E. m. melphis* from a great many apparently suitable localities that we have visited without finding the species.

Specimens: República Dominicana: Dajabón: Los Cerezos, 12 km NW Río Limpio, 580 m, 3; *Santiago:* Río Bao, 8 km SE Montones Abajo, 18; *La Altagracia:* 16 km NE La Romana, 61 m, 15; *Azua:* 5 km S Peralta, 305 m, 2; *Baoruco:* 11 km N Neiba, 519 m, 4.

Sight record: República Dominicana: Sánchez Ramírez: 1 km NE Las Lagunas, 183 m—1 seen, 7.vi.

4. *Heliconius charitonius churchi* Comstock and Brown, 1950

TL Port-au-Prince, Dépt. de l'Ouest, Haiti.

FW males 32–44 mm, females 32–46 mm.

Heliconius ch. churchi is 1 of the most abundant and widely distributed butterflies on Hispaniola. They may be regularly found in city gardens, mesic forests, pseudoforests and woods, transitional forests, *caféières, cafetales* and *cacaotales*, sheltered ravines, river bottoms, and almost any situation that is more or less mesic. They may also be encountered in rolling grasslands (Lascahobas), oases in otherwise xeric lowland habitats (Fond Parisien, Croix des Bouquets, Villa Vásquez, Ça Soleil), xeric ravine forest (Oviedo), open mountainsides (Boutilliers Road, Terre Rouge), fields (Carrefour Marmelade), *Cocos* plantations (Samaná), and even a village (La Piedra) completely isolated by large rice plantations. The relatively low number of specimens in no way indicates the abundance of *H. ch. churchi*; a great many more could easily have been taken, since these butterflies are easily netted. *Heliconius ch. churchi* is uncommon in the pine-forested uplands of the Cordillera Central, although I have a specimen from La Nevera, from a large open grassy glade. These are the first records for *H. ch. churchi* from Île de la Gonâve, Isla Saona, Isla Catalina, and Isla Beata.

We have not taken the species in the high uplands of the Sierra de Neiba, and there is only 1 specimen from a high elevation on the Montagne Noire, a Massif de la Selle front range. It does occur to at least 915 m in the hardwood forests of the Sierra de Neiba, to 1129 m in the Sierra de Baoruco (Las Abejas), and to 1880 m in the Massif de la Selle (Morne la Visite). In short, *H. ch. churchi* may be encountered almost anywhere; although it does not prefer xeric areas, at any locality in lowland desert one can be sure that, sooner or later, a *H. ch. churchi* will fly lazily by.

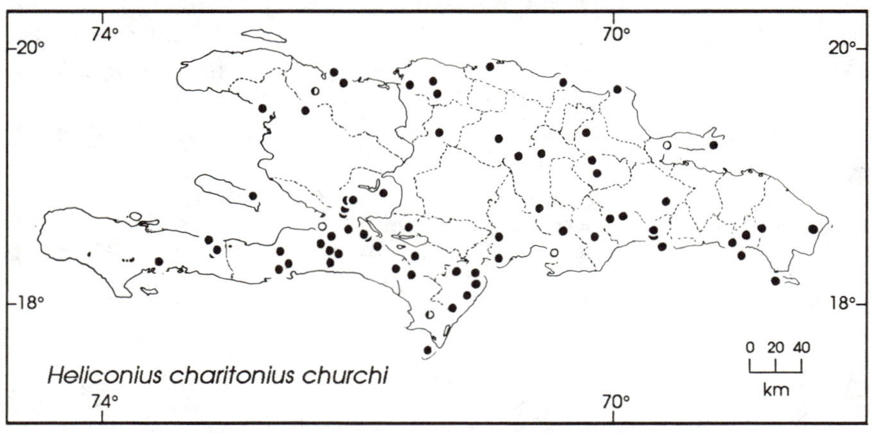

Heliconius ch. churchi, like *D. i. hispaniola*, is very attracted to *Lantana ovatifolia;* many localities (Copey, Río Bao, Paso Bajito, and elsewhere) where we have taken or seen this butterfly have a few to many *Lantana* shrubs or bushes. In addition, at Villa Vásquez, in June-July, the numbers of *H. ch. churchi* were immense; they were feeding on and clinging to the flowers of *Antigonon leptopus* so abundantly that these vines seemed to be draped with the butterflies. *Heliconius ch. churchi* has been seen or taken feeding on *Tournefortia hirsutissima* at Río Bao, Neiba, Peralta, and 1 km N Playa Bayahibe, on *Rubus selleanus* at 5 km NE Los Arroyos, on an unidentified orange-flowered vine at Río Bao, and on a white-flowered tree at 2.5 km SE Playa Bayahibe.

We have encountered only 1 dormitory of *H. ch. churchi* at Roche Parfait, Dépt. du Nord, Haiti, on 4.viii.1977. The butterflies were clustered at night on a dangling dead vine, about 1 m in length, hanging over a tumbling boulder-strewn stream. Perhaps as many as 50 butterflies were present.

The elevational distribution is from sea level (Cormier Plage, Ça Soleil, Río San Juan, Samaná, Punta Cana, Mano Juan) to 2227 m (La Nevera). Times of collection were between 0900 and 1650 h, and temperatures between 18°C (La Nevera) and 40°C (Tenares). Most specimens were taken in July, with fewer in June, January, February, August, October, November, April, March, and December. Although there seem to be fewer *H. ch. churchi* in the winter and spring than in the summer, the species is on the wing throughout the year.

Among our series are 5 specimens that have an obvious yellow mark on fw Cu1, a character of *H. ch. punctatus* Hall from St. Christopher in the Lesser Antilles. Comstock (1944:439–40) reported that about 25% of Puerto Rican *H. ch. charitonius* Linnaeus have this trait.

Specimens: Haiti: Nord: Cormier Plage, s.l., 1; Carrefour la Mort, s.l., 1; *l'Artibonite:* 1.6 km E Carrefour Marmelade, 854 m, 2; 12.2 km W Ça Soleil, s.l., 1; *l'Ouest:* 1.6 km N Saut d'Eau, 183–275 m, 2; 1 km N Terre Rouge, 610 m, 1; 2.9 km S Terre Rouge, 488 m, 1; 12 km SE Mirebalais, 305 m, 1; 6.2 km E Lascahobas, 275 m, 1; 13.3 km E Croix des Bouquets, s.l., 1; 3.0 km SE Fond Parisien, s.l., 1; 5 km SE Fond Parisien, s.l., 1; below (outskirts) Plaine Thoman, 1; Pétionville, 476 m, 4; Boutilliers Road, 1.8–3.7 km W Kenscoff road, 732–885 m, 4 (1 MPM); 0.3 km W crest Boutilliers Road, 824 m, 3; 0.3 km N Obléon, 1617 m, 1; Morne la Visite, 300 m, 3 (FSM); Morne la Visite, 1430–1880 m, 3 (FSM); 1.3 km N Béloc, 702 m, 1; Lavaneau, 229 m, 1; 8.3 km NW Jacmel, 183 m, 3; nr. Péredo, 570–600 m, 5 (FSM); *Sud:* 10.7 km W Miragoâne, s.l., 1; 6.7 km SW Paillant, 854 m, 3; 6.6 km SW Paillant, 793 m, 4; 4.5 km E Cavaillon, 31 m, 1; *Île de la Gonâve:* Anse-à-Galets, 3; *República Dominicana; Monte Cristi:* 6 km W Copey, s.l., 1; 4 km NW Villa Vásquez, 61 m, 1; 3.9 km SE Martín García, 92 m, 1; *Santiago Rodríguez:* 4.7 km SW Loma Leonor, 732 m, 1; *Puerto Plata:* 10 km W Luperón, 1; 9 km SE Sosúa, 15 m, 1; *Santiago:* Río Bao, 8 km SE Montones Abajo, 488 m, 1; *La Vega:* Jarabacoa, 530 m, 4; La Ciénaga, 915 m, 1; La Nevera, 37 km SE Constanza, 2227 m, 1; *María T. Sánchez:* 8 km NE Río San Juan, s.l., 2; *Duarte:* 10 km SE Tenares, 183 m, 1; *Sánchez Ramírez:* 1 km NE Las Lagunas, 183 m, 4; La Piedra, 7 km SW Pimentel, 1; *Samaná:* 18.0 km E and N Samaná, s.l., 1; *La Altagracia:* 2 km W Punta Cana, s.l., 1; 16 km NE La Romana, 61 m, 3; *La Romana:* 3 km N Altos de Chavón, 1 (MPM); Río Cumayasa, 13.5 km W La Romana, 1; *Monte Plata:* 8 km NE Bayaguana, 2; *Dist. Nac.:* 33 km W San Pedro de Macorís, 2 (MPM); Punta Caucedo, 5 km S Aeropuerto Internacional de la Américas, s.l., 1; 5 km S San Isidro, 1; 30 km NW Santo Domingo, 122 m, 3; 25 km SE Yamasá, 1 (MPM); *San Cristóbal:* 6 km NW Cambita Garabitos, 488–519 m, 3; *Azua:* Tábara Abajo, 2; 22 km NW Cruce de Ocoa, 61 m, 1; *Independencia:* 3.3 km E La Descubierta, 1; 4–7 km NE El Aguacate, 519–824 m, 1; *Barahona:* west slope, Sierra Martín García, 915 m, 1; 10 km W Cabral, 1; 3.3 km NE La Ciénaga, 1; 7 km SW Barahona, 1; 5 km SE, 3 km W Barahona, 183–397 m, 1; 8 km NW Paraíso, 3 (MPM); 8–10 km NE Paraíso, 4 (MPM); 9 km NW Enriquillo, 671 m, 1; *Pedernales:* Las Abejas, 12 km NW

Aceitillar, 1129 m, 2; 0.6 km SE Los Arroyos, 1098 m, 1; *Isla Saona:* Mano Juan, s.l., 4; *Isla Catalina:* near naval base, 1; *Isla Beata:* 3.

Sight records: Haiti: Nord: Roche Parfait, 9.0 km NE Plaisance, 215 m—many seen, 4.viii; *República Dominicana: Pedernales:* 17 km NW Oviedo, 183 m—a few seen, 28.vi.

Family Nymphalidae Swainson, 1827

Subfamily Argynninae Blanchard, 1840

1. *Euptoieta claudia* Cramer, 1775

TL Jamaica.

FW males 27–34 mm, females 22–37 mm.

Although the type-locality of *E. claudia* is Jamaica, the species was not collected there again (since the type-material) until 1940 (Brown and Heineman, 1972:208). The species was first reported from Cuba in 1943 (de la Torre y Callejas), and Ramos (1976:440–41) noted the first Puerto Rican specimens, collected in 1974. Clench (1977b:185) first reported *E. claudia* from the northern Bahama Islands (Grand Bahama, Great Abaco, New Providence, Andros), where the first specimen was taken in 1970; later, Clench and Bjorndal (1980:176) recorded the taking of specimens on Great Inagua Island in the southern Bahamas. Schwartz (1983a:37) noted the first specimens from Haiti; the first *E. claudia* was taken there on 6–7.vii.1977. The Haitian records were all from the south island: Lastic le Roche, Boutilliers Road, Jacmel, and Grand-Goâve, all on the north and south sides of the Tiburon Peninsula. Cucurullo (1959) did not report *E. claudia*, but Marión Heredia (1974:5) listed the species for the first time from the República Dominicana.

In the República Dominicana, *E. claudia* occurs on the south island (Prov. de Pedernales and Barahona), east to Prov. de Azua, and is also present in the eastern part of that country, in the provinces of La Altagracia and San Pedro de Macorís. Elsewhere, on the north island *E. claudia* has an apparently limited distribution in Prov. de Puerto Plata (2 localities). The distribution of the species is much broader on the south island, where there are more or less "continuous" records from Jacmel–Grand-Goâve in the west to Pedernales-Barahona in the east. The apparent isolation of the eastern population(s) may be real; we have collected in the hiatus between the eastern and western populations without taking *E. claudia*, whereas we did collect *E. h. hegesia* there.

Brown and Heineman (1972:208) used a trinomen, *E. c. claudia*, for the Jamaican population, their assumption apparently being that the insular population(s) differ from mainland *E. claudia*. Although this is likely, it seems somewhat premature to make this assumption and use the trinomial. These authors likewise suggested that there are "minor but constant differences" if this species is native to Jamaica. It seems certain that this butterfly is indeed native to at least Hispaniola and probably elsewhere in its Antillean range, which is now known to be extensive.

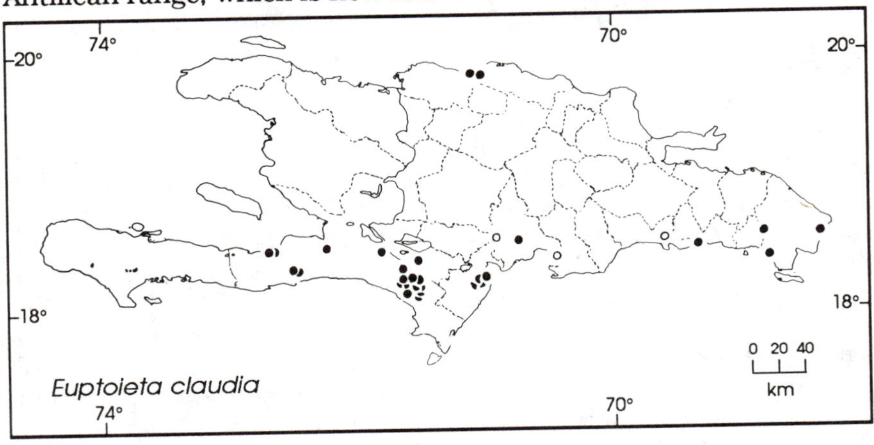

Comparison of the series from Hispaniola with a short series (9 males, 4 females from Florida and Texas) from the continent shows that the mainland material is much smaller (FW males 22–28 mm, females 26–29 mm) than the Hispaniolan males and females. However, scattered material from other North American localities obliterates these striking size differences. The Hispaniolan specimens tend to be much darker (more black dusting on the fw, especially in the discal area), but pattern differences are very small or nonexistent.

As in North America, *E. claudia* is found on Hispaniola along roadsides in grassy areas; these are primarily at low elevations, but the total elevational distribution is between sea level (Grand-Goâve, Playa Bayahibe) and 1617 m (Los Arroyos). The latter elevation is 1 of only 5 above 610 m (all on the Massif de la Selle–Sierra de Baoruco) and is thus exceptional. *Euptoieta claudia* has been taken on or near the beach (Grand-Goâve, Punta Rucia), along a mangrove border (Grand-Goâve), and in openings and along roadways and paths in xeric forest (Playa Bayahibe, Barahona) or woods (Mencía). The only locality where we have taken *E. claudia* in mesic forest is Las Abejas; the individual from Los Arroyos was taken at the edge of a cornfield. The series of Cabo Rojo localities is all from transitional woods or forest, at the lower edge of the hydrologic spectrum, with a strong element of *Acacia*. *Euptoieta claudia* has been taken feeding on tall (1 m) *Lantana ovatifolia* (Las Mercedes), on *Bidens pilosa* (21 km NE Cabo Rojo), and on *Ruellia* sp. (Acanthaceae) (1.3 km S Tres Charcos).

Most specimens are from July (48), with 7 in June, 5 in May, 4 in August, and 2 in October. Times of collection were between 0930 and 1800 h, the latter at Grand-Goâve along the edge of mangroves as the sun was setting. Temperatures were between 29°C (Las Abejas) and 42°C (Mencía), the latter among the very hottest places we have collected on Hispaniola.

Euptoieta claudia is syntopic with *E. h. hegesia* at 7 localities: Boutilliers Road, 8.3 km NW Jacmel, Estero Hondo, Punta Cana, Peralta, 1 km SW Las Mercedes, and 2 km SW Mencía (at Tres Charcos, the 2 species are almost syntopic). At 2 of these (Boutilliers Road, Peralta) *E. h. hegesia* outnumbers *E. claudia* (5:1;4:2) in number of specimens; at another (Mencía), *E. claudia* outnumbers *E. h. hegesia* (3:2), and at Estero Hondo, *E. claudia* outnumbers *E. h. hegesia* (4:2). At the latter locality, both species were taken on a dry hillside that was an abandoned tomato field. At the other localities, we have the same number of specimens of both taxa. These numbers may be unrealistic, but the sites indicate those places where the 2 species occur together.

Specimens: Haiti: l'Ouest: above Lastic le Roche (below Plaine Thoman), 488 m, 2; Boutilliers Road, 732–854 m, 2; just W Grand-Goâve, s.l., 1; 6.7 km E Grand-Goâve, s.l., 1; 8.3 km NW Jacmel, 183 m, 1; 7.7 km N Jacmel, 92 m, 1; *República Dominicana: Puerto Plata:* 0.4 km E Punta Rucia, s.l., 1; 0.6 km NE Estero Hondo, 4; *La Altagracia:* Punta Cana, s.l., 1; 1 km N Playa Bayahibe, s.l., 1; 16 km NE La Romana, 61 m, 1; *San Pedro de Macorís:* 13 km SE Boca Chica, s.l., 2; *Azua:* 5 km S Peralta, 305 m, 2; *Independencia:* 7 km NE El Aguacate, path to El Limón, 519–580 m, 1; *Barahona:* 3 km W intersection Green Chapel Road, 4; Barahona, s.l., 1; 2 km SW Barahona, 122 m, 4; 12 km SW Barahona, 427 m, 1; *Pedernales:* 19 km NE Cabo Rojo, 427 m, 2; 21 km NE Cabo Rojo, 488 m, 16; 23 km NE Cabo Rojo, 488 m, 1; 24.5 km NE Cabo Rojo, 656 m, 1; 26 km NE Cabo Rojo, 732 m, 1; Las Abejas, 12 km NW Aceitillar, 1129 m, 3; 1 km SW Las Mercedes, 397 m, 2; 3 km W Aguas Negras, 519 m, 1; Mencía, 397 m, 2; 2 km SW Mencía, 275 m, 3; 5 km NE Los Arroyos, 1617 m, 1; 1.3 km S Tres Charcos, 1.

2. *Euptoieta hegesia hegesia* Cramer, 1780

TL "New York and Jamaica"; restricted to Jamaica by Comstock (1944:445).

FW males 22–32 mm, females 27–32 mm.

Euptoieta hegesia is represented in the Antilles by 2 subspecies: nominate *hegesia* on Jamaica, Cuba, Cayman Islands, and the Bahama Islands (Riley, 1975:83; Rindge, 1955:8), and *watsoni*

Comstock on Puerto Rico. Clench identified our 1977 Haitian material as *E. h. watsoni*, but Riley (1975:83) considered Hispaniolan specimens *E. h. hegesia*. *Euptoieta h. watsoni* differs from *E. h. hegesia* in that the former has, in the fw cell, a pair of dark ovals that are connected posteriorly by a dark line; these 2 ovals do not touch veins R or M. In *E. h. hegesia* the fw cell figure is composed of 2 *incomplete* ovals that are open posteriorly but whose dark pigment touches and follows briefly along R and may or may not touch M. Hispaniolan specimens are much closer to the characteristics of *E. h. hegesia*, since there rarely are 2 complete cell ovals, and these dark cell markings almost always touch and follow along R, as they do in *E. h. hegesia*. Brown and Heineman (1972:209) considered Hispaniolan specimens *E. h. watsoni* but also stated that "it is probable that each of the four Greater Antillean islands harbors a population ... that is slightly different from that on other islands."

Cucurullo (1959:5) named *E. h. domingensis* (no specific type-locality) as distinct from both *E. h. hegesia* and *E. h. watsoni* on the basis of the ovals in the fw cell. According to his illustration, the more distal one is complete and has a "tail" extending basally toward, but not reaching, the basal oval which is open posteriorly. Marión Heredia (1975:5) listed 4 subspecies of *E. hegesia* for the República Dominicana: *hegesia*, *domingensis*, *watsoni*, and *hoffmani* Comstock. The Hispaniolan population is somewhat variable, at least in the expression of the fw cell ovals, but it seems hardly likely that all 4 subspecies occur on Hispaniola. If a name is required, as Brown and Heineman intimated, for the Hispaniolan population, *domingensis* Cucurullo is available. There seems at present no need for its use.

Euptoieta h. hegesia is widely distributed on Hispaniola but is often absent from localities and areas where it is expected. These are the first records for Isla Alto Velo and Isla Catalina. The species seems to occupy specific regions, year after year, and simply is not encountered in other areas. It is uncommon on the distal portion of the Haitian Tiburon Peninsula. We have not collected *E. h. hegesia* on the Península de Samaná or in the northeastern portion of the República Dominicana. There are no specimens from the extreme eastern portion of the same country (southern La Altagracia to the Distrito Nacional), yet it is abundant in the Llanos de Azua and occurs in the Valle de San Juan. The species is common on the Península de Barahona and occurs (very rarely) on the southern slopes of the Sierra de Baoruco (23 km NE Cabo Rojo, 1 specimen, in an area where *E. claudia* is the dominant species) and the Massif de la Selle in this region. *Euptoieta h. hegesia* extends into the Cordillera Central as high as Constanza, where it is locally common. But there still remain large gaps in the known distribution. In fact, the collector is often pleasantly surprised to encounter *E. h. hegesia* for the first time where he did not expect to find it.

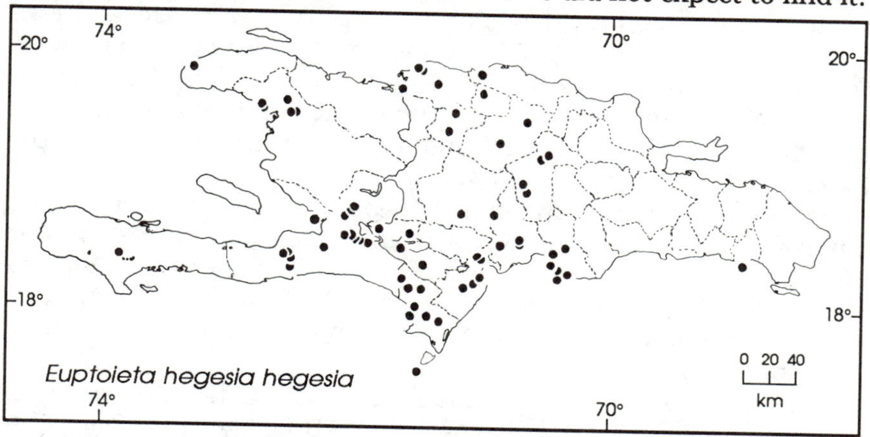

Euptoieta h. hegesia inhabits both xeric (Môle St.-Nicholas, Les Poteaux, Carrefour Joffre, Monte Cristi, Cruce de Guayacanes, Cruce de Ocoa, Sabana Buey, Sombrero, Azua, El Limón, Tierra Nueva, Cabo Rojo) as well as mesic (Mirebalais, Découzé, Béloc) regions. Its predilection is toward arid regions: Carrefour Joffre is extremely bleak, hot, and unshaded. In other lowland arid areas, *E. h. hegesia* occurs in and about shaded oases (Ça Soleil, Croix des Bouquets, Fond Parisien, Villa Vásquez). These butterflies are most often encountered in roadside grassy or weedy areas, often associated with the flowers of *Lantana ovatifolia*, *Funastrum clausum*, and *Tephrosia purpurea* (on all of which they have been observed to feed), *Stachytarpheta jamaicensis*, and *Bidens pilosa*. At 4 lowland localities (Croix des Bouquets, Cruce de Guayacanes, Cruce de Ocoa, Villa Vásquez), *E. h. hegesia* was feeding avidly and in very large numbers on *Antigonon leptopus*. At Croix des Bouquets, *E. h. hegesia* and *Junonia g. zonalis* were present in incredible numbers (17.vii) along with lesser numbers of other butterflies. At Les Poteaux, *E. h. hegesia* was feeding on the white flowers of *Bauhinia divaricata*. *Euptoieta h. hegesia* also feeds on *Croton linearis* (Monte Cristi, Zamba), *C. barahonensis* (Vallejuelo), *Sida rhombifera* (Monte Cristi), and *Ageratum conyzoides* (Barahona).

Schwartz (1983a:37) reported finding 3 chrysalides under a rock in xeric scrub between Gonaïves and Coridon in northwestern

Haiti. We have taken pairs *in copula* on 15.v (1200 h, 36°C, field of *Uniola virgata*, Monte Cristi) and 17.vi (1035 h, 1106 h, 1110 h, 1150 h, 31°C, field of *Uniola virgata*, El Limón, s.l.).

The elevational distribution of *E. h. hegesia* is from sea level (Môle St.-Nicholas, Ça Soleil, Île à Cabrit, Croix des Bouquets, Fond Parisien, Monte Cristi, Punta Cana, Palmar de Ocoa, Tierra Nueva, Cabo Rojo) to 1647 m (Constanza). Most specimens were collected in July (61), with 36 in June, 27 in August, 13 in May, 6 in December, 7 in October, 3 in January, and 1 in March. Times of collection were between 0900 and 1715 h, and temperatures between 27°C (Les Poteaux) and 42°C (Mencía).

For localities of syntopy of *E. h. hegesia* and *E. claudia*, see the latter account. The 2 species also occur together at 23 km NE Cabo Rojo, but this entire southern slope of the Sierra de Baoruco is dominated by *E. claudia* (19 km NE Cabo Rojo to Las Abejas) with only one *E. h. hegesia*, the species of the Cabo Rojo lowlands, at 23 km NE Cabo Rojo.

Specimens: Haiti: Nord-Ouest: Môle St.-Nicholas, s.l., 1; *l'Artibonite:* 2 km E Les Poteaux, 2; 4.6 km E Les Poteaux, 183 m, 1; 3.4 km N Carrefour Joffre, 114 m, 1; 12.2 km W Ça Soleil, s.l., 2; 16.8 km W Ça Soleil, 2; *l'Ouest:* 19.7 km SE Mirebalais, 183 m, 1; 20.0 km S Mirebalais, 3.8 km N Terre Rouge, 534 m, 1; 13.1 km E Croix des Bouquets, s.l., 1; 18.1 km SE Croix des Bouquets, s.l., 1; 5 km NW Fond Parisien, 1; 2 km NW Fond Parisien, 1; 3.0 km SE Fond Parisien, s.l., 1; Boutilliers Road, 732–946 m, 5; 5.9 km S Dufort, 366 m, 1; 5.4 km S Découzé, 397 m, 8; 1.3 km N Béloc, 702 m, 1; 8.3 km NW Jacmel, 183 m, 1; *Sud:* 4.8 km N Camp Perrin, 244 m, 1; *Île à Cabrit:* 1; *República Dominicana: Monte Cristi:* 1 km SE Monte Cristi, 5; 4 km SE Monte Cristi, 6; Pepillo Salcedo, s.l., 1; 4 km NW Villa Vásquez, 61 m, 1; *Dajabón:* 16 km NW Río Limpio, 702 m, 1; 9.1 km S Restauración, 519 m, 1; *Valverde:* 4 km N Cruce de Guayacanes, 198 m, 2; *Santiago Rodríguez:* Loma Leonor, 18 km SW Monción, 534 m, 4; 3.0 km S Zamba, 214 m, 5; *Puerto Plata:* 0.6 km NE Estero Hondo, 2; *Santiago:* Río Bao, 8 km SE Montones Abajo, 488 m, 1; 7 km SW Santiago, 214 m, 3; *La Vega:* Buena Vista, 11 km NE Jarabacoa, 640 m, 1; Jarabacoa, 530 m, 1; 1 km S Constanza, 1098 m, 4; 10 km SE Constanza, 1647 m, 1; *La Altagracia:* Punta Cana, s.l., 1; *Peravia:* 5 km SW Sombrero, 2; 4 km E Sabana Buey, 61 m, 2; 1 km S Las Carreras, 2; *Azua:* Tábara Abajo, 1; 15 km NW Cruce de Ocoa, 76 m, 13; 25 km NE Azua, 92 m, 6; 11 km S Peralta, 1; 5 km S Peralta, 305 m, 4; 1 km E Palmar de Ocoa, s.l., 1; 2 km SE La Canoa, 397 m, 8; *San Juan:* 9 km E Vallejuelo, 610 m, 8; *Independencia:* 5 km NW Tierra Nueva, s.l., 1; 4 km E El Limón, s.l., 8; 3.3 km E La Descubierta, 2; 0.6 km NW Puerto Escondido, 519 m, 1; *Barahona:* 11.5 km ESE Canoa, s.l., 2; 8 km ESE Canoa, 3; Barahona, s.l., 1; 8 km SW Barahona, 366 m, 1; 8 km NNE Polo, 397 m, 2; *Pedernales:* 1 km SW Las Mercedes, 397 m, 2: Mencía, 275–336 m, 2; Cabo Rojo, s.l., 6; 4 km NE Cabo Rojo, s.l., 1; 23 km NE Cabo Rojo, 488 m, 1; 4 km NW Tres Charcos, 1; 17 km NW Oviedo, 183 m, 3; *Isla Alto Velo:* 1; *Isla Catalina:* 1.

Subfamily Melitaeinae Grote, 1897

3. *Atlantea cryptadia* Sommer and Schwartz, 1980

TL Boutilliers Road, 734–857 m, Dépt. de l'Ouest, Haiti.
FW male 25 mm.

Sommer and Schwartz named *A. cryptadia* on the basis of a single Haitian male taken 10.vii.1979. No additional specimens have been taken since that time, a truly remarkable fact. However, Marión Heredia (1978b) had reported the capture of an *Atlantea* in v.1967 at Loma de Quimbamba, Municipio de Bonao, Prov. de Monseñor Nouel, República Dominicana. Thus, 2 specimens of *Atlantea*, 1 from each country on Hispaniola, are known. Although members of this genus are not overly common on Puerto Rico (*tulita* Dewitz), Jamaica (*pantoni* Kaye), and Cuba (*perezi* Herrich-Schäffer), and at least in 1 case (Jamaica) the butterflies are restricted to areas of karst topography, I am at a loss to account for the extreme rarity of *A. cryptadia*. The dates for the 2 *A. cryptadia* (May, July) suggest a late spring–early summer emergence; elsewhere, members of this genus are on the wing in February-June (*perezi*), October-January, March, July (*tulita*), and January-March, June-July (*pantoni*; data from Brown and Heineman, 1972:193).

Specimen: Haiti: l'Ouest: Boutilliers Road, 734–857 m, 1.

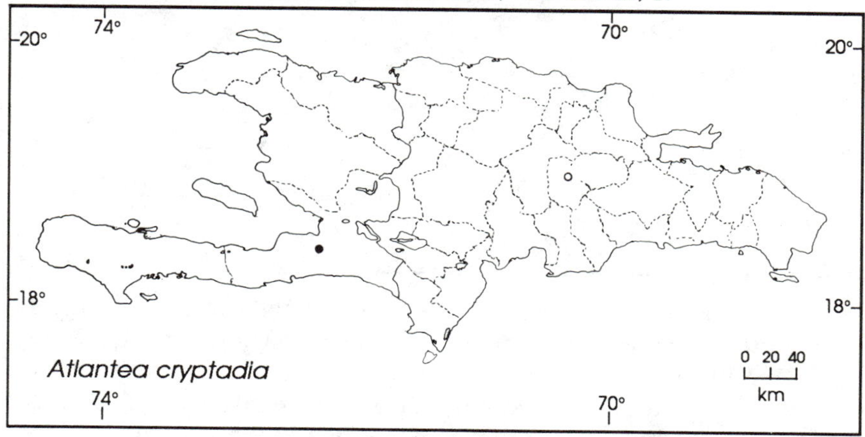

Atlantea cryptadia

4. *Athanassa frisia frisia* Poey, 1832

TL Cuba.
FW males 12–19 mm, females 16–21 mm.

Athanassa f. frisia occurs on the Bahama Islands, Cuba, Jamaica, Hispaniola, and extreme southern Florida. The species is widespread in the Bahamas (Rindge, 1952:9; Rindge, 1955:8; Clench, 1977a:276; Clench, 1977b:185) but is apparently absent from Great and Little Inagua islands in the southern Bahamas. Riley (1975:79) wrote that *A. f. frisia* is "apparently widespread but local . . . from sea level to about 1000 ft and at all seasons." Certainly this species is local on Hispaniola; one encounters these small butterflies in the same areas, year after year, but does not encounter them in other areas.

One noteworthy site of regular abundance is the northern face of the Sierra de Baoruco, between Cabral and Polo. The species is extremely abundant along this stretch of road; it is likely that there are thousands of individuals there—*A. f. frisia* is the dominant small butterfly (almost a nuisance for the collector). These butterflies occur there in gardens, along grassy and weedy roadsides, at the edges of *cafetales*, and at any other microhabitat that accommodates their weak, low-to-the-ground flight. They land with wings outspread on low (up to 0.5 m) grass leaves, shrubs, and herbs.

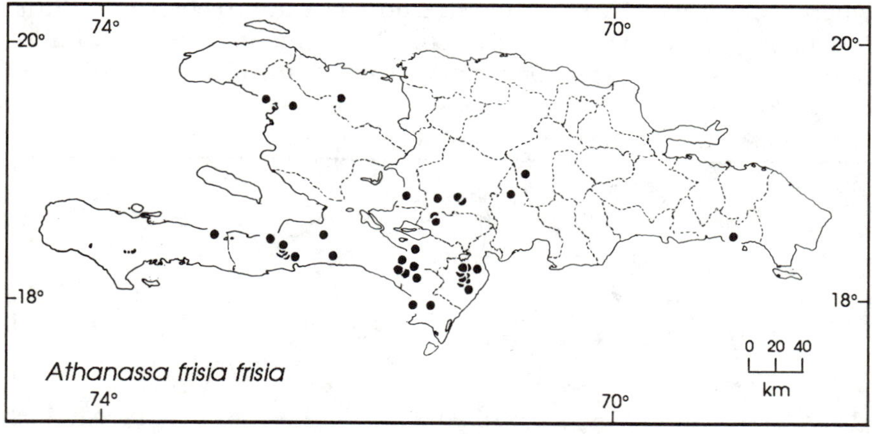

A second area where *A. f. frisia* is locally common is in the intermontane valley between the 2 ranges of the Sierra de Neiba, between El Cercado and Vallejuelo. There they occupy xeric woods and even "spill over" into *Acacia* scrub, a most unusual habitat for this mesophilic butterfly. What is noteworthy about these 2 places of abundance is that *A. f. frisia* is uncommon elsewhere in the Sierra de Baoruco and is likewise uncommon on both ranges of the Sierra de Neiba.

Typical habitats are *caféières* and *cafetales* and their margins and interior grassy or weedy clearings. Grassy open fields (Constanza) and grassy mangrove borders (Miragoâne) may also have populations, and open woods, whether mesic (Monte Bonito, Las Abejas), xeric (Vallejuelo, Oviedo), or transitional (El Aguacate), also support them. We have taken 1 unexpected specimen in pinewoods (11 km SW El Aguacate) with *Calisto sommeri* in a meadow with *Cynoglossum amabile* and 3 specimens in xeric scrub (Cabo Rojo).

Elevational distribution is between sea level (Ça Soleil, Petit-Goâve, Miragoâne, Cabo Rojo) and 1891 m (El Aguacate); this latter elevation is exceptional and is only 1 of 7 above 854 m. *Athanassa f. frisia* is decidedly a butterfly of low to moderate elevations. The rarity of Dominican sea-level records is of interest.

Times of collection were between 0830 and 1745 h, and temperatures between 27°C (El Aguacate) and 38°C (Mencía). On the Cabral-Polo road, on 6.viii.1980, after the passage south of Hispaniola of Hurricane Allen on 5.viii.1980, these butterflies were still flying abundantly during much overcast and light rain, at a temperature of 32°C between 1200 and 1230 h. The deteriorated weather conditions did not seem to affect their activities.

Most specimens have been taken in July (70), with 49 in August, 12 in June, 5 in October, 3 in April, and 1 each in February and December. The very large number of individuals in July suggests that the major time of eclosion is in that month.

Two copulating pairs were taken at El Aguacate in transitional forest, 1 pair on 3.viii (1210 h, 30°C), the other on 4.viii (1450 h, 30°C). The second pair was perched on dead leafless slash at the roadside, 0.5 m above the ground and completely exposed.

We have taken *A. f. frisia* feeding on *Bauhinia divaricata* once (Les Poteaux) in a semiarid region. Much more commonly, *A. f. frisia* feeds on *Lantana ovatifolia* (Cabo Rojo, Aguas Negras, Mencía), and at Mencía these butterflies were also feeding on *Stachytarpheta jamaicensis*. This plant was also used at 1.3 km W Monteada Nueva, and *Ageratum conyzoides* was the nectar source at Vallejuelo.

Specimens: Haiti: Nord: 1.8 km S Dondon, 366 m, 1; *l'Artibonite:* 4 km E Les Poteaux, 183 m, 1; 16.8 km W Ça Soleil, 2; *l'Ouest:* Boutilliers Road, 732–854 m, 3; 1.6 km N Découzé, 702 m, 1; 0.6 km S Découzé, 671 m, 2; 0.8 km S Découzé, 702 m, 2; 2.1 km S Découzé, 640 m, 6; 7.7 km N Jacmel, 92 m, 1; nr. Péredo, 570 m, 1; 17.6 km E Petit-Goâve, s.l., 1; *Sud:* 5.4 km W Miragoâne, s.l., 1; *República Dominicana: Elías Piña:* 14 km S Comendador, 976 m, 1; *La Vega:* 1 km S Constanza, 1098 m, 3; *La Romana:* Río Cumayasa, 13.5 km W La Romana, 5; *Azua:* 5 km SW Monte Bonito, 702 m, 1; *San Juan:* 7 km E El Cercado, 854 m, 3; 9 km E Vallejuelo, 610 m, 1; 7 km NE Vallejuelo, 671 m, 1; *Baoruco:* 1 km NW El Veinte, 1220 m, 1; 14 km N Neiba, 671 m, 1; *Independencia:* 4-7 km NE El Aguacate, 519–732 m, 28; *Barahona:* Polo, 703 m, 16; 1 km N Las Auyamas, 2; 5 km NW Las Auyamas, 1; 2 km NW Las Auyamas, 1; 20 km SE Cabral, 946 m, 5; 8 km NNE Polo, 793 m, 2; 14 km SSW Cabral, 854 m, 2; 10 km SSW Cabral, 527 m, 1; 1.8 km W Monteada Nueva, 1007 m, 14; 1.3 km W Monteada Nueva, 1037 m, 1; 8 km NW Paraíso, 153 m, 1; *Pedernales:* 11 km SW El Aguacate, 1891 m, 1; Cabo Rojo, s.l., 3; 23 km NE Cabo Rojo, 488 m, 3; Las Abejas, 12 km NW Aceitillar, 1129 m, 1; 3 km W Aguas Negras, 519 m, 4; Mencía, 397 m, 6; 1 km N Cabeza de Agua, 275 m, 3; 6 km N Cabeza de Agua, 122 m, 2; 17 km NW Oviedo, 183 m, 1.

5. *Antillea pelops pelops* Drury, 1773

TL St. Christopher, Lesser Antilles.

FW males 10–12 mm, females 11–13 mm.

The genus *Antillea* is restricted to the West Indies. There are 2 species: *A. proclea* Doubleday and Hewitson on Jamaica, and *A. pelops* on Hispaniola, Puerto Rico, Montserrat, St. Christopher (*A. p. pelops*), Cuba (*A. p. anacaona* Herrich-Schäffer), and Jamaica (*A. p. pygmaea* Godart). The 3 subspecies of *A. pelops* differ primarily in size, with the Jamaican subspecies the smallest. Brown and Heineman (1972:195) did not recognize the genus *Antillea* and placed the 2 Jamaican species in *Phyciodes* Hübner as a distinct subgenus.

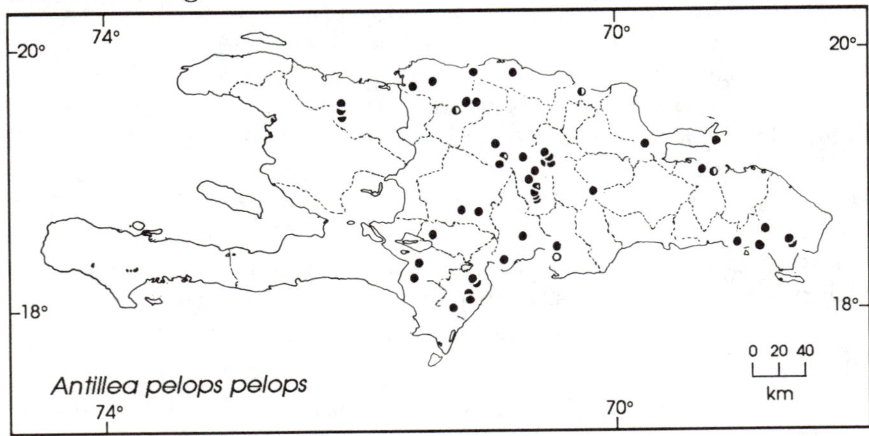

Riley (1975:78) stated that *A. pelops* "seems to be generally rare but locally common." Hall (1925:187) considered it "evidently scarce and local" on Hispaniola. Bates (1935a:162) had many specimens from Cuba from 3 general localities, and Comstock (1944:448) reported specimens from 6 places on Puerto Rico. Brown and Heineman (1972:195–96) reported the species from 9 localities; they also gave an explicit anecdote on the extreme localization of the species south of Salt Island Road, St. Catherine Parish. Schwartz (1935a:35) agreed with Riley's assessment, since he reported specimens only from a single area in the Massif du Nord, Haiti, whence he had 15 specimens.

Although *A. p. pelops* is local in the República Dominicana, it is much more widespread than it is in Haiti. In Haiti, the species has been collected only in and adjacent to shaded *caféières*. In the República Dominicana, *A. p. pelops* occurs in *cafetales* as it does in Haiti (La Palma, Enriquillo), but it can also be found in mesic forest (Río Bao, Jayaco, Maimón, Río Guarabo, Neiba, Monteada Nueva), xeric forest (Boca de Yuma, La Romana, Sierra Martín García), *Acacia* scrub (Copey, San Juan), mixed xeric forest–*Acacia* (Vallejuelo), grassy palm groves (Samaná, Estero Hondo), a mesic ravine in pine forest (Las Abejas), and pine forest (Valle de Tetero, 14 km SE Constanza). We have also taken the species in tall grass next to an irrigation canal in cactus forest (Cruce de Ocoa) and in an oasis (Villa Vásquez), unlikely habitats for *A. p. pelops*. In the Cordillera Central uplands (Constanza), where the species is uncommon, 2 were taken in a semishaded ravine and 1 in the scrubby bushes between 2 adjacent creeks. Thus, in the República Dominicana, *A. p. pelops* occupies a variety of habitats, but it is local wherever it occurs, as elsewhere in the islands.

Most specimens and records are from July (46), with 38 in June, 29 in May, and 22 in August; there are 6 specimens from March, 3 from January, 2 from April, and 1 from December, indicating that the species is on the wing during the entire year but with a summer (May-July) period of greatest abundance. Elevations varied from sea level (Gaspar Hernández, Samaná, Cruce de Rincón) to 1922 m (14 km SE Constanza, entrance of Valle de Tetero). Times of collection were between 0915 and 1715 h, and temperatures from 23°C (Enriquillo, Las Abejas) to 39°C (Gaspar Hernández). *Antillea p. pelops* flies on overcast days (Samaná, Enriquillo) as well as on bright and sunny days. We have taken *A. p. pelops* feeding on *Cordia globosa* (La Romana); on the day of this observation (28.vi.1980), *A. p. pelops* was extremely common at this locality, and many were feeding on the white flowers of the *Cordia* and flying along the path in xeric forest. The species has been seen and taken at this site repeatedly but never in the abundance of that day. *Antillea p. pelops* also has been taken feeding on *Morinda citrifolia* (Río Chavón) and on *Synedrella nodiflora* (Asteraceae) (Luperón). A copulating pair was taken in a shaded

Roystonea hispaniolana grove at Estero Hondo (1111 h, 30°C, 31.v).

Specimens: Haiti: Nord: 2.9 km N Dondon, 366 m, 11; 1.8 km S Dondon, 366 m, 1; 5.9 km S Dondon, 366 m, 3; *República Dominicana: Monte Cristi:* 6 km W Copey, s.l., 1; 4 km NW Villa Vásquez. 61 m, 1; *Valverde:* 12 km SW Mao, 244 m, 16; Río Guarabo, 3 km W Los Quemados, 122 m, 7; *Puerto Plata:* 13 km SE Luperón, 214 m, 5; 0.6 km NE Estero Hondo, 7; *Santiago:* Río Bao, 8 km SE Montones Abajo, 488 m, 21; entrance of Valle de Tetero, 1342–1922 m, 2; *La Vega:* 10 km W Jayaco, 915 m, 16; La Palma, 19 km W Jayaco, 1007 m, 14; 12 km NE Constanza, 1220 m, 1; 1 km S Constanza, 1098 m, 2; 13 km SE Constanza, 1403 m, 2; 14 km SE Constanza, 1922 m, 1; 18 km SE Constanza, 1586 m, 1; 2 km S Jarabacoa, 488 m, 1; La Ciénaga, 915 m, 1; 3.5 km E Paso Bajito, 732 m, 2; *María T. Sánchez:* 1 km S Cruce de Rincón, s.l., 8; *Samaná:* 18.0 km E and N Samaná, s.l., 1; *Monseñor Nouel:* 6 km SE Maimón, 122 m, 1; *Hato Mayor:* 4 km E Sabana de la Mar, 2; *La Altagracia:* 0.5–3.5 km W Boca de Yuma, 1; 2–3 km W Boca de Yuma, 2; 16 km NE La Romana, 9; *La Romana:* Río Chavón, 8 km SE La Romana, s.l., 2; Río Cumayasa, 13.5 km W La Romana, 1; *Azua:* 22 km NW Cruce de Ocoa, 61 m, 3; 5 km S Peralta, 305 m, 1; *San Juan:* 14 km S San Juan, 427 m, 1; 9 km E Vallejuelo, 625 m, 4; *Baoruco:* 11 km N Neiba, 519 m, 2; *Independencia:* 4–7 km NE El Agucate, 519–824 m, 4; *Barahona:* west slope, Sierra Martín García, 458–610 m, 1; 3 km NNE Polo, 854 m, 1; 2 km S La Lanza, 1; 1.3 km W Monteada Nueva, 1037 m, 1; 8 km NW Paraíso, 4; 9 km NW Enriquillo, 671 m, 4; *Pedernales:* Las Abejas, 11 km NW Aceitillar, 1220 m, 1.

Sight records: República Dominicana: Santiago Rodríguez: 4.8 km S Zamba, 183 m—1 seen, 28.v; *Espaillat:* 2 km NW Gaspar Hernández, 15 m—1 seen, 23.vii; *Santiago:* Valle de Tetero, 1342 m—1 seen, 3.viii; *La Vega:* 10 km SE Constanza, 1647 m—3 seen, 9.vii; *Hato Mayor:* 17 km E Sabana de la Mar—1 seen, 6.iii.

Subfamily Nymphalinae Swainson, 1827

6. *Vanessa virginiensis* Drury, 1773

TL Virginia; restricted by Field, 1971 (Miller and Brown, 1981:173).

FW males 22–29 mm, females 26–32 mm.

Riley (1975:82) stated that *V. virginiensis* is "a migrant . . . and its occurrence in the West Indies is sporadic. Most records are of odd specimens taken in the mountains at some height above sea level." On the other hand, Brown and Heineman (1972:203) felt that there was little doubt that the species is resident on Jamaica. Unquestionably, *V. virginiensis* is resident on Hispaniola, whence I have specimens from both ranges of the Sierra de Neiba, the Sierra Martín García, the Cordillera Central, the Massif de la Selle, including its northern front ranges, and the Sierra de Baoruco. Schwartz (1983a:36) gave a record for the Massif du Nord in Haiti.

Vanessa virginiensis is a not uncommon high-elevation species and often is the only moderately sized conspicuous butterfly of the high pine and deciduous forests. In addition to these ranges, Hall (1925:187) took 1 specimen at La Cumbre in the Cordillera Septentrional at a presumed elevation of about 610 m. Our elevational extremes are between 488 m (23 km NE Cabo Rojo) and 2288 m (18 km SE Constanza, 5 km NW Valle Nuevo); most records are from 915 m and higher, with only 5 (El Aguacate, Polo, Jarabacoa, 5 km SE Jarabacoa, 23 km NE Cabo Rojo) lower than 915 m.

Habitats include pine forest (Forêt des Pins, Obléon, Constanza, 36 km NE Cabo Rojo, Aceitillar); in the Cordillera Central, *V. virginiensis* frequents moist glades and brushy ravines, both with *Cynoglossum amabile*, on which it feeds (5 km NW Valle Nuevo). Elsewhere, deciduous forests are occupied (Puesto Pirámide 204, La Horma, El Limón, Las Abejas), but in these situations the species is most often encountered along roads or in grassy or shrubby openings, where it rests on the ground, flying short distances when disturbed to land once more on the ground. *Vanessa virginiensis* also occurs in transitional forest (El Aguacate) and in mixed pine-hardwoods (6 km SSE Constanza), and on 1 occasion we have taken it in a *cafetal* (La Palma).

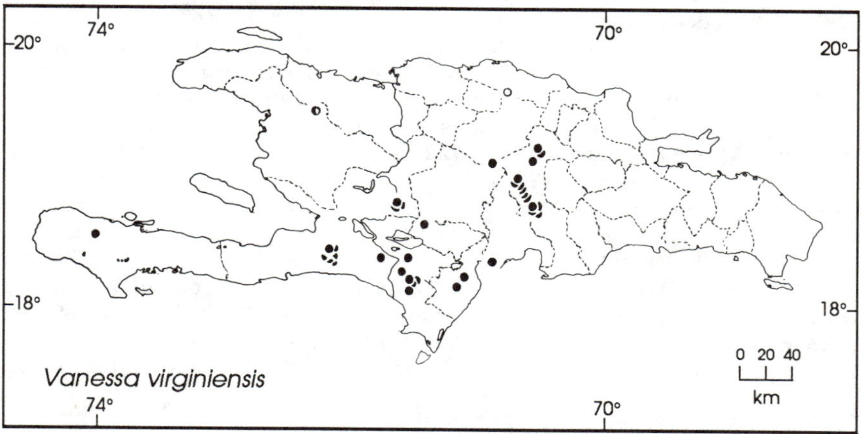

Most specimens are from July (38) and August (21), with 20 in June, 6 in February, 4 each in September and January, 2 in March, and 1 each in April, May, October, and December. This suggests that these butterflies are flying during the entire year, with a midsummer peak.

Times of collecting were between 0900 and 1900 h (see below), and temperatures between 18°C (13 km SE Valle Nuevo) and

36°C (El Aguacate). The late time is for a copulating pair seen (but not netted) on 8.vii (1 km S Constanza, 1098 m, dim light) in a grassy field. Although *V. virginiensis* normally flies under bright and sunny conditions, we have taken it under overcast conditions (Puesto Pirámide 204) and even in rain (14 km SE Constanza). *Vanessa virginiensis* feeds on *Tournefortia hirsutissima* (6 km SSE Constanza), *Cynoglossum amabile* (Las Abejas), and *Ageratum conyzoides* (Aceitillar). At La Palma, this species was especially abundant in a cultivated field of *Helichrysium bracteatum* (Asteraceae), a peculiar composite with ray flowers yellow to orange and with both ray and disk flowers dry and chaffy, which was being grown for the florist trade. In the Cordillera Central uplands (as at La Nevera and Valle Nuevo), there are now large open nurseries growing carnations (*Dianthus caryophyllus;* Caryophyllaceae) for local use and export, but no *V. virginiensis* (and in fact no butterflies) are attracted to the overpowering scent of these flowers.

Specimens: Haiti: l'Ouest: Forêt des Pins, 1525 m, 2; 1 km NW Forêt des Pins, 1556 m, 1; 0.3 km N Obléon, 1617–1678 m, 3; Peneau, 1464 m, 2; Morne la Visite, 2100 m, 3 (FSM); *ca.* 4 km NW Scierie, 2000 m, 1 (FSM); 2 km NW Scierie, 1785–1810 m, 1 (FSM); 5 km WNW Scierie, 1891 m, 1 (FSM); Roche Cabrit, 2200 m, 1 (FSM); *Sud:* Morne Formond, 1635–1800 m, 5 (FSM); *República Dominicana: Elías Piña:* 21 km S Comendador, 1464 m, 1; 2 km NE Puesto Pirámide 204, 1586 m, 4; 1 km SW Puesto Pirámide 204, 1891 m, 6; *Santiago:* entrance of Valle de Tetero, 1922 m, 1; *La Vega:* La Palma, 19 km W Jayaco, 1007 m, 3; Jarabacoa, 530 m, 5; 5 km SE Jarabacoa, 595 m, 1; 1 km S Constanza, 1098 m, 6; 6 km SSE Constanza, 1403 m, 5; 7 km SE Constanza, *ca.* 1312 m, 3; 10 km SE Constanza, 1647 m, 1; 14 km SE Constanza, 1647 m, 7; 14 km SE Constanza, 1922 m, 2; 18 km SE Constanza, 1586 m, 2; 18 km SE Constanza, 2227–2288 m, 2; 5 km NW Valle Nuevo, 2288 m, 1; 13 km SE Valle Nuevo, 2074 m, 2; 41 km SE Constanza, 2074 m, 1; 10 km NW La Horma, 1496 m, 3; *Baoruco:* El Veinte, 20 km N Neiba, 1068 m, 1; *Independencia:* 4–7 km NE El Aguacate, 519–732 m, 1; *Barahona:* El Limón, summit, Sierra Martín García, 976–1037 m, 1; 8 km NNE Polo, 793 m, 2; 1.3 km W Monteada Nueva, 1037 m, 1; *Pedernales:* 23 km NE Cabo Rojo, 488 m, 1; 35 km NE Cabo Rojo, 1220 m, 1; Aceitillar, 36 km NNE Cabo Rojo, 1281 m, 1; 1 km N Aceitillar, 1281 m, 2; Las Abejas, 12 km NW Aceitillar, 1129 m, 13.

7. *Vanessa cardui cardui* Linnaeus, 1758

TL Sweden, by implication.

FW males 28–30 mm, females 27–33 mm.

Riley (1975:82) implied that West Indian records for *V. cardui* are due to vagrants. In this course Riley was following Brown and Heineman (1972:202), who stated that *V. c. cardui* "is, in all likelihood, only a migrant to Jamaica." All 4 Jamaican records are between 10 October and January, and at least 2 specimens from there are worn. However, Schwartz (1983a:35–36), writing of the 2

Haitian specimens then available, considered *V. cardui* "resident and breeding on Hispaniola," since both specimens were relatively fresh and unworn. Simon and Miller (1986:4) reported the species from Great Inagua in the southern Bahamas; their material was badly worn, suggesting a "rather long trip."

We have secured 27 *V. c. cardui* in the República Dominicana, and all are fresh and unworn. I have no doubt that *V. c. cardui* is resident on Hispaniola; all but 1 specimen are from high elevations (1098–2288 m) in the Cordillera Central (elevational parameters from Constanza) and the Massif de la Selle in both Haiti and the República Dominicana. *Vanessa c. cardui* is less common than *V. virginiensis* (see account) but more common than *V. atalanta*. It seems likely that *V. c. cardui* will be taken in at least the Sierra de Neiba and the Massif du Nord as well as the Massif de la Hotte.

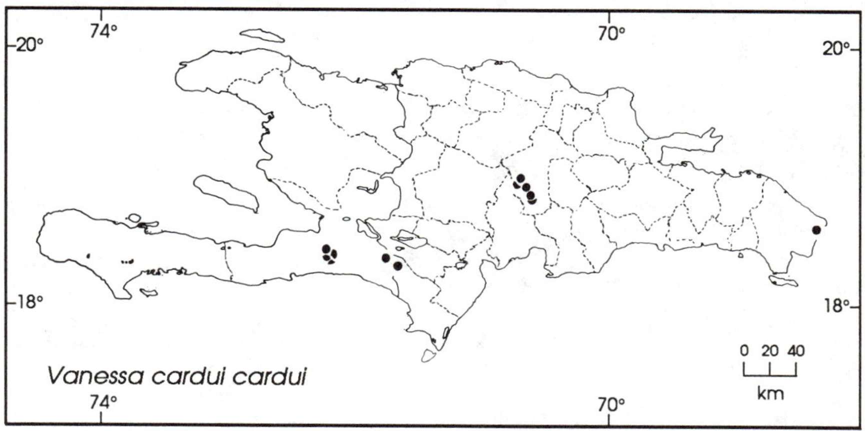

Although some authors state that *V. c. cardui* is most often encountered on hilltops in the tropics, this is surely not the case on Hispaniola, where the species has been taken in hardwood mesic forest (Los Arroyos), pine forest (Peneau, Forêt des Pins), and (primarily) an open grassy field with *Zinnia elegans* and *Cynoglossum amabile* (on which we have not observed these butterflies feeding). We have also taken *V. c. cardui* in a fallow cabbage field (SE Constanza), in which *Leonurus sibericus* (Lamiaceae) was abundant and patronized by a wide spectrum of butterflies (but not *V. c. cardui*). Like *V. virginiensis*, *V. c. cardui* has the habit of landing on the ground (even on bare roadways) when pursued, only to fly a few meters and land once more, repeating this escape pattern until it finally takes off with rapid flight.

Most specimens have been taken in July (24), with 4 in August,

3 in June, 2 in September, and 1 each in February and October. The inclusive dates are 13.ii–30.x. These dates contrast strongly with those of Brown and Heineman noted above. Specimens were collected between 0930 and 1730 h, often under overcast conditions when there was little other butterfly activity. Temperatures were between 21°C (Scierie) and 35°C (Punta Cana).

The exceptional *V. c. cardui*, taken in the lowlands (Punta Cana) in October, is only slightly worn but no more so than is consonant with the time of year, assuming that the butterfly emerged on Hispaniola. The low elevation, however, implies that perhaps this butterfly is a migrant. It may well be both that Hispaniola harbors a resident population of *V. c. cardui* and also that some migrants or vagrants occur in the lowlands.

Vanessa c. cardui and *V. virginiensis* are syntopic at 6 localities (Forêt des Pins, Peneau, Morne la Visite, Scierie, 1 km S Constanza, 10 km SE Constanza). At 1 km S Constanza, *V. c. cardui* greatly outnumbers *V. virginiensis* (23 specimens to 1 specimen), but at Forêt des Pins, Morne la Visite, and Peneau, *V. virginiensis* seems to be more numerous than *V. c. cardui* (2 or 3 to 1). I have only 1 specimen of each species from 10 km SE Constanza.

Specimens: Haiti: l'Ouest: Forêt des Pins, 1525 m, 1; Peneau, 1.1 km S Furcy, 1464 m, 1; Morne la Visite, 2100 m, 1 (FSM); Scierie, 1891 m, 1 (FSM); 5 km WNW Scierie, 1891 m, 1 (FSM); *República Dominicana: La Vega:* 1 km S Constanza, 1098 m, 23; 6 km SSE Constanza, 1403 m, 1; 10 km SE Constanza, 1647 m, 1; 21 km SE Constanza, 1952 m, 1; 28 km SE Constanza, 2288 m, 1; *La Altagracia:* Punta Cana, s.l., 1; *Pedernales:* 5 km NE Los Arroyos, 1617 m, 2.

8. *Vanessa atalanta rubria* Fruhstorfer, 1909

TL Mexico; restricted by Field, 1971, Smithsonian Contr. Zool., 84:16–17 (Miller and Brown, 1981:174).

FW males 27–30 m, females 33–34 mm.

In the Greater Antilles, *V. a. rubria* is known from Cuba (Bates, 1935a:165), where it has been taken at 4 localities, Jamaica (Brown and Heineman, 1972:201), where it is known by 1 specimen from 2257 m in the Blue Mountains, and Hispaniola (Hall, 1925:187). Brown and Heineman, and Riley (1975:83) considered *V. atalanta* a vagrant to the West Indies, and the scarcity of records on at least Jamaica suggests that status there.

We have 19 Hispaniolan specimens, all from the República Dominicana: 12 from the Cordillera Central, 2 from the Dominican portion of the Massif de la Selle, 4 from the Sierra de Baoruco, and 1 from the Sierra de Neiba. Collection dates are between 26.vi and

29.ix, with a sight record for another individual there on 13.viii. I also have seen 1 *V. a. rubria* on 4.iii. Most specimens are from August (9, including a sight record), with 7 in July, 3 in June, 1 in March, and 1 in September. Only 1 specimen, taken 26.vi, is worn; all others are fresh or are worn or damaged due only to the act of collection. Although the numbers of specimens involved are not so many as with the 2 other species of *Vanessa*, I consider *V. a. rubria* a Hispaniolan resident. One reason is that in 6 years (1980–83, 1985–86) we have seen or collected specimens of *V. a. rubria* at the same locality (La Palma), a fantastic coincidence if *V. a. rubria* is a vagrant. Even more persuasive is that on 13–15.viii.1986, *V. a. rubria* was very abundant in the area of Monteada Nueva, where we saw (conservatively) 30 individuals.

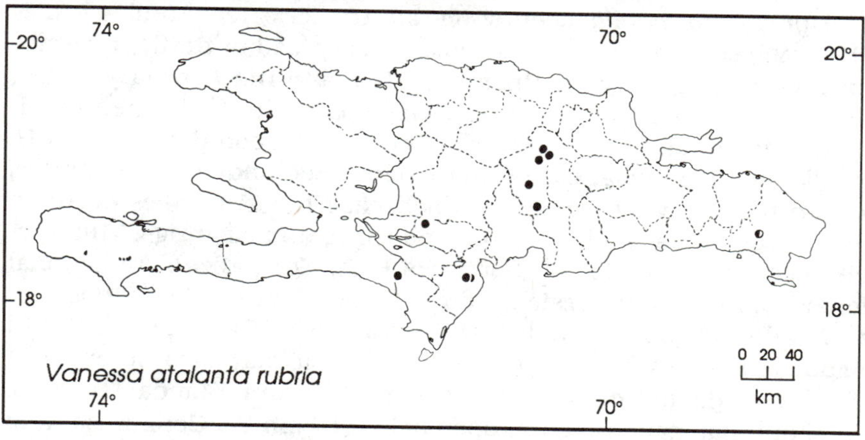

Vanessa atalanta rubria

Specimens have been taken in a *cafetal* (La Palma), where 1 individual was seen (but not collected) feeding on the white flowers of *Coffea arabica* (Rubiaceae). The Constanza specimen is from a brushy area surrounded by forest remnants and between 2 small creeks, that from La Horma from an open mesic ravine where the butterfly was foraging on the white flowers of watercress (*Nasturtium microphyllum;* Brassicaceae), that from Mencía along a roadway through shrubby vegetation, and that from La Romana in a xeric forest. At Paso Bajito, *V. a. rubria* was feeding on *Begonia brachypoda* (Begoniaceae), a most unusual nectar source, very rarely used by Hispaniolan butterflies. We have also taken these butterflies feeding on *Cynoglossum amabile* (El Veinte), *Stachytarpheta jamaicensis* (1.3 km W Monteada Nueva), and *Urena lobata* (Malvaceae) (La Palma).

Elevations are between 61 m (La Romana) and 1617 m (El

Veinte). Times of collection were between 0915 and 1620 h, and temperatures between 24°C (Constanza) and 32°C (La Palma).

Specimens: República Dominicana: La Vega: 11 km SE Constanza, 1586 m, 1; La Palma, 19 km W Jayaco, 1007 m, 8; Jarabacoa, 530 m, 1; 3.5 km E Paso Bajito, 732 m, 1; 10 km NW La Horma, 1496 m, 1; *Baoruco: ca.* 8 km SW El Veinte, 1617 m, 1; *Barahona:* 1.3 km W Monteada Nueva, 1037 m, 3; 1.8 km W Monteada Nueva, 1007 m, 1; *Pedernales:* Mencía, 397 m, 2.

Sight records: República Dominicana: La Vega: La Palma, 19 km W Jayaco, 1007 m—1 seen, 13.viii; *La Altagracia:* 16 km NE La Romana, 61 m—1 seen, 4.iii.

9. *Hypanartia paulla* Fabricius, 1793

TL Jamaica.

FW males 24–30, females 29–33.

Hypanartia paulla occurs on all the Greater Antilles. Riley (1975:83) stated that *H. paulla* is a "widespread butterfly, recorded on the wing in every month except January and February, a fast flying, nectar seeking species especially partial to fairly open woodland." This quotation serves well to comment upon the status of *H. paulla* on Hispaniola, except that there woodlands occupied by *H. paulla* may be very dense, in which case the butterflies occur in more open areas, such as paths and roads and clearings. This species occurs in pine forest (Forêt des Pins, Constanza), transitional forest (El Aguacate), mesic hardwood forest (Jayaco, Los Pinos, Comendador, Puesto Pirámide 204, Sierra Martín García, 5 km SW El Aguacate), and xeric forest (Punta Cana). It may also be encountered in *cafetales-cacaotales* (La Palma, Piedra Blanca, Tenares, Polo) and has been taken in open fields (10 km SE Constanza) and on an open mountainside (Boutilliers Road).

The records are between sea level (Punta Cana) and 1922 m (14 km SE Constanza, Valle de Tetero), but only 13 (of 33) localities are below 915 m. The 2 Haitian specimens have previously been reported by Schwartz (1983a:36–37), but *H. paulla* is less common in Haiti than in the República Dominicana. The species is known from the Cordillera Central, Sierra de Neiba (both ranges), the Sierra Martín García, Sierra de Baoruco, and Massif de la Selle (including the Morne l'Hôpital) in Haiti and the República Dominicana. The lowland records are widely distributed from the extreme eastern portion of Hispaniola (Punta Cana) to the eastern foothills of the Cordillera Central (Piedra Blanca).

These butterflies land on the leaves of trees, between 2 and 3 meters above the ground, where they remain, often for several minutes, with the wings opened at a 45-degree angle; an observer can, during this period, verify identification by the un pattern and the translucency of the wings in sun, which allows the up pattern to be visible from below.

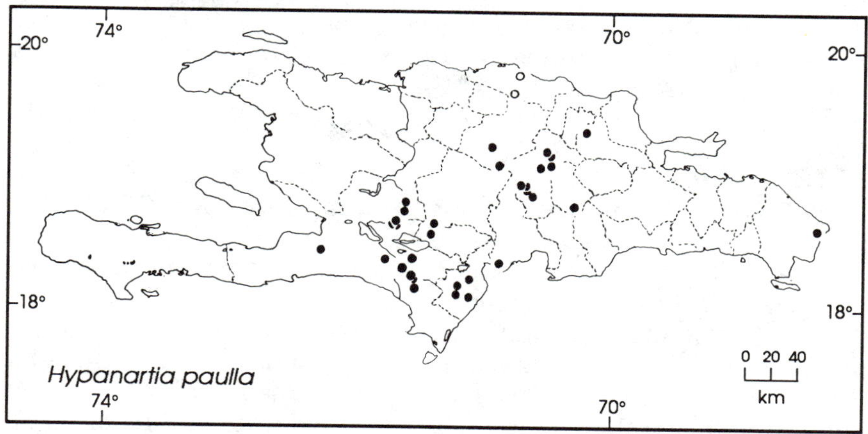

Most specimens have been taken or seen in July (28), with 21 in June, 19 in August, 3 in December, 2 in May, and 1 each in April and October. Times of collection were between 0900 and 1600 h, and temperatures between 23°C (Puesto Pirámide 204) and 34°C (Constanza, El Aguacate). *Hypanartia paulla* feeds on a wide variety of flowers; that which we have recorded most frequently is *Daucus* sp. (Boutilliers Road, El Aguacate, Los Pinos, Puesto Pirámide 204); elsewhere we have taken specimens on *Palicourea barbinervia* (Jayaco), *Tournefortia hirsutissima* (Río Bao, 6 km SSE Constanza), *Urena lobata* (Jayaco), *Senecio plumbeus* (Asteraceae) (11 km NW Aceitillar), and *Canna* sp. (Polo). *Hypanartia paulla* was also common in the field of *Helichrysium bracteatum*, noted in the account of *V. virginiensis*, at La Palma.

Specimens: Haiti: l'Ouest: Forêt des Pins, 1525 m, 1; Boutilliers Road, 854 m, 1; *República Dominicana: Elías Piña:* 15 km S Comendador, 976 m, 1; 2 km NE Puesto Pirámide 204, 1586 m, 1; *Santiago:* Río Bao, 8 km SE Montones Abajo, 488 m, 1; entrance of Valle de Tetero, 1922 m, 1; *La Vega:* 10 km W Jayaco, 915 m, 8; La Palma, 19 km W Jayaco, 1007 m, 5; Jarabacoa, 530 m, 4; 5 km SE Jarabacoa, 595 m, 1; 3.5 km E Paso Bajito, 732 m, 4; 6 km SSE Constanza, 1403 m, 5; 7 km SE Constanza, *ca.* 1312 m, 3; 10 km SE Constanza, 1647 m, 1; 14 km SE Constanza, 1922 m, 3; *Monseñor Nouel:* 14 km SW Piedra Blanca, 427 m, 2; *Duarte:* 10 km SE Tenares, 183 m, 1; *La Altagracia:* 2 km W Punta Cana, s.l., 1; *Baoruco:* 11 km N Neiba, 519 m, 3; El Veinte, 20 km N Neiba, 1068 m, 1; *Independencia:* 8 km SW Puesto Pirámide 204, 1647 m, 1; 21 km N Los Pinos, 1708 m, 1; 23 km N Los Pinos, 1739 m, 2; 4–7 km NE El Aguacate, 519–824 m, 2; *Barahona:* west slope, Sierra Martín García, 915 m, 2; Polo, 702 m, 1; 20 km SE Cabral, 946 m, 2; 1.8 km W Monteada Nueva, 1007 m, 1; 8 km NW Paraíso, 153 m, 1; *Pedernales:* 5 km SW El Aguacate, 1464 m, 1; 23 km NE Cabo Rojo, 488 m, 1; Las Abejas, 11 km NW Aceitillar, 1220 m, 1; Las Abejas, 12 km NW Aceitillar, 1129 m, 3.

Sight records: República Dominicana: Elías Piña: 1 km SE Puesto Pirámide 204, 891 m—1 seen, 6.viii; *Santiago:* Río Bao, 8 km SE Montones Abajo, 488 m—1 seen, 21.x; Valle de Tetero, 1342 m—1 seen, 3.vii; *La Vega:* La Palma, 19 km W Jayaco, 1007 m—1 seen, 21.vii; 6 km SSE Constanza, 1403 m—2 seen, 26.vii; *Independencia:* 4–7 km NE El Aguacate, 519 m—1 seen, 22.vi.

10. *Hypolimnas misippus* Linnaeus, 1764

TL "America."

FW male 37 mm; (females 38–39 mm [Comstock, 1944:464], females 38–42 mm [Riley, 1975:73]).

Riley (1975:74) stated that *H. misippus* is unknown from Hispaniola. He overlooked a record (Bates, 1939a:50) of a male from the Cul de Sac plain in Haiti, which was the first record for Hispaniola. The individual was taken in January. I have also examined a female in the collection of Eugenio de J. Marcano, from the city of Santo Domingo, taken i.1964. Marión Heredia (1980a) reported *H. misippus* from El Número-Azua.

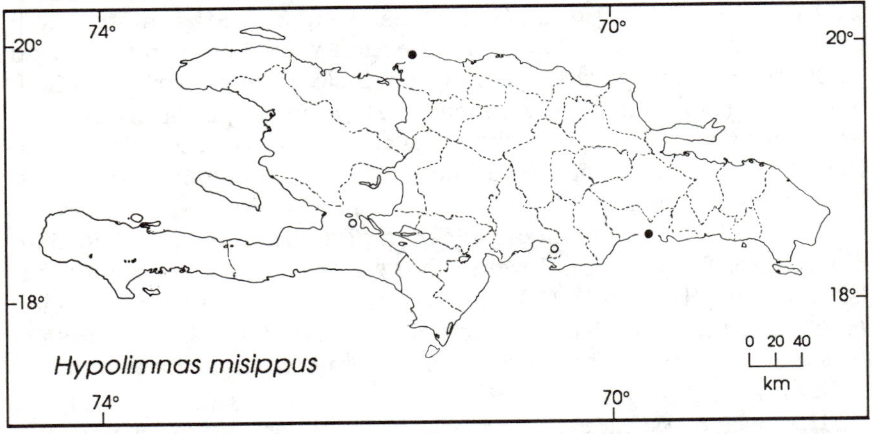

We have never secured this species, although on 1 occasion (between Cabral and Polo, Prov. de Barahona), I saw a butterfly that I was almost certain was the distinctive male of *H. misippus*.

On 30.ix.1987, Wetherbee took a male on top of El Morro de Monte Cristi, the flattopped mountain (230 m) north of the city of Monte Cristi. This is the third reported specimen from Hispaniola. With the exception of the Santo Domingo specimen, all specimens and records are from extremely xeric regions.

Considering the local abundance of danaids at many sites on Hispaniola, one wonders how many female *H. misippus* are passed over by the collector, who assumes that all tawny butterflies of that size are danaids of some sort.

Specimen: República Dominicana: Monte Cristi: El Morro de Monte Cristi, 230 m, 1.

11. *Junonia genoveva zonalis* C. and R. Felder, 1867

TL "Colombia, Cuba, Puerto Rico"; restricted to Bogotá, Colombia (Munroe, 1951:10).

FW males 24–29 mm, females 22–32 mm.

Perhaps no other Antillean genus is more in a state of confusion than *Junonia*. Munroe's (1951) revision of the Antillean members of the genus is a giant step toward understanding the complexities of *Junonia*, but later authors unfortunately do not totally agree with Munroe's interpretations. Even Clench, between 1977 and 1980, changed his own interpretation of the situation in the Bahama Islands. Comstock (1944:452–56) gave a penetrating analysis of *Junonia* in the islands, with emphasis on Puerto Rico.

The situation is the following (from Comstock, Munroe, and Brown and Heineman, 1972:177–80). Almost all workers agree that *J. coenia* Hübner occurs on the North American mainland and extends to Cuba (Bates, 1935a:167–68) and into the Bahama Islands (Clench, 1977a:276), where it occurs on New Providence (Rindge, 1952:9), Andros (Clench, 1977a:276), and probably elsewhere in at least the northern Bahamas. On Cuba there occurs sympatrically with *J. coenia* another *Junonia*, which Bates (1935a:168) called *Junonia zonalis*. Judging only from the numbers of specimens, one gathers that on Cuba *J. coenia* is less common than *J. zonalis*.

Comstock (1944:454) used the combination *J. evarete zonalis* for these butterflies on Puerto Rico and stated that *J. e. zonalis* occurs on "Cuba, Jamaica, Hispaniola, and on the Lesser Antilles," from the latter of which Comstock named *J. e. michaelesi*, which is quite distinct from *J. e. zonalis*. Munroe (1951:1–5) differentiated between *coenia*, *zonalis*, and *genoveva* Cramer without using trinomina. His "definition" of *J. coenia* is that which most authors use today for determining specimens of that taxon; most important is the uphw anterior ocellus, which includes red or orange scales within the outer rim, a condition not occurring in *J. evarete*. Additionally, the uphw anterior ocellus is distinctly larger than the posterior uphw ocellus. Riley (1975:74) noted that the upfw large (= posterior) ocellus is bordered by a white crescent that runs from the inner margin at least as far as Cu1.

Junonia e. zonalis differs from *J. coenia* in that the anterior uphw ocellus lacks red or orange scales within the ocellus and that the upfw posterior ocellus is always ringed completely with red or reddish brown (Riley, 1975:74).

The problem is the status of *genoveva*. Although Munroe considered *genoveva* a synonym of *J. e. evarete*, Comstock considered it a subspecies of *J. evarete*, which is, at least on Puerto Rico, syntopic with *J. e. zonalis*, and that *zonalis* and *genoveva* are wet- and dry-season forms of the same species. Brown and Heineman (1972:177–80) discussed the nomenclatorial situation as it applied to Jamaica, did not consider *genoveva* as pertinent in that they regarded it as the dry-season form of *J. e. evarete*, and used the name *constricta* Felder and Felder for the dry-season form associated with *J. e. zonalis*.

Riley (1975) considered *genoveva* the "rare dry season form" of *J. e. zonalis*. Clench (1977a:277) regarded *genoveva* as a form of *J. e. zonalis* in the Bahamas, where he recorded it from 2 islands in the southern Bahamas; he did not report *J. e. zonalis* from these same islands. But later, Clench and Bjorndal (1980:15) noted the occurrence of both *J. e. zonalis* and *J. genoveva* on Great Inagua in the extreme southern Bahamas; the justification for this action was given in an unpublished Clench manuscript. Thus, *genoveva* has gone from a form (of either *J. e. evarete* or *J. e. zonalis*) on the one hand to a species sympatric with *J. evarete* on the other.

Munroe (1951:2) characterized *genoveva* by its having more elongate and narrower wings, the pale color on the fw tending to be strongly constricted by an elongation of the dark color in M3-Cu1, and the unhw ocelli usually obsolescent.

When Clench identified our small series (1977–78) of *Junonia* from Haiti, he used *J. e. zonalis* for the entire lot. Recall that these dates are during a period when Clench's own philosophy about *Junonia* was apparently in a state of flux. But even with a much longer series of specimens, and despite a great deal of variation in some characters (Schwartz, 1983a:32–33), most if not all new material is *J. e. zonalis*.

Turner and Parnell (1985) more recently have shown conclusively that on Jamaica there are 2 species of *Junonia: evarete* and *genoveva*. Schwartz, Gonzalez, and Henderson (1987) showed that the same situation pertains on the Cayman Islands. These species differ not only in phenotype but also in larval food plants, ecology, behavior, male genitalia, and chromosomes. Turner and Parnell also showed that the 2 names as used prior to this date had been reversed. Thus, *J. genoveva* is properly applied to those butterflies that are more brightly colored with the uphw ocelli large, and *J. evarete* to those butterflies that are more drab with the uphw ocelli small. Thus the name to be used for Hispaniolan *Junonia* is *Junonia genoveva (zonalis)*.

There are no specimens that may be referred to *J. coenia*, nor would I expect any, since that species has never been reported from Hispaniola.

The majority of my material appears to fulfill the requirements of *J. g. zonalis*. The uphw ocelli are much more nearly equal in size than in *J. coenia*, and in 1 specimen (Délugé), they are indeed identical in size. The degree with which the upfw posterior ocellus is surrounded by red is variable, and some specimens do not have this character; the anterior edge of the ocellus is thus bordered by white or by such a fine reddish line that it is very inconspicuous. The un is usually brightly colored with tan, white, rust, and other contrasting shades. Aside from the 2 usual unhw ocelli, there is almost always an additional ocellus in Rs-M1, smaller than that in M1-M2 but just as prominent. Riley (1975:pl. 8, fig. 5) shows this condition precisely in *J. g. michaelesi*.

A small percentage (29% males, 15% females) of specimens not only have this accessory unhw ocellus but also have the un coloration pale and sandy, without much contrast, and the remaining un ocelli are obscure. These might be considered *evarete*, but on the balance of other characters, they are merely 1 extreme of expression of un ocelli and intensity of coloration. Donald J. Harvey is presently studying *Junonia;* I will await his studies before stating definitively what the Hispaniolan situation is. As far as I am now concerned, Hispaniola is inhabited only by *J. g. zonalis*.

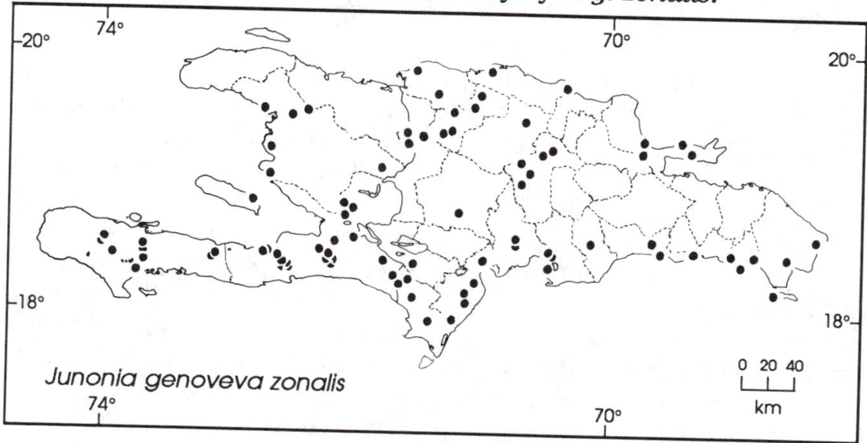

Junonia genoveva zonalis

Junonia g. zonalis is widely distributed on Hispaniola, occurring near the tip of the Tiburon Peninsula on one hand and on the

Península de Samaná on the other. There are no records from the Presqu'île du Nord-Ouest, but the habitat there seems suitable for this species. The present specimens are the first records from Île de la Gonâve, Isla Saona, and Isla Catalina.

This butterfly is widely tolerant of a variety of ecological conditions. We have taken specimens in the Cul de Sac plain in Haiti, the xeric southern slopes of the Montagnes du Trou-d'Eau, and the xeric Península de Barahona, but we have not encountered *J. g. zonalis* in oases in the Cul de Sac–Valle de Neiba. In the northwest, *J. g. zonalis* has been taken in an oasis (Ça Soleil) and elsewhere in and along the margins of mesic woods, including coffee plantings (Paillant, Saut d'Eau, Cavaillon, Río Cumayasa). The species occurs also in gardens (Pétionville), along open mountain roads (Boutilliers Road), and mangrove borders (Grand-Goâve). Occasionally *J. g. zonalis* can be taken in or at the edges of large open fields (Sosúa, La Ciénaga, Constanza). But by far the most specimens have been taken in open areas adjacent to roads, regardless of the sort of habitat adjacent to the road beyond the grass-weed strip. Occasionally, *J. g. zonalis* occurs in pinewoods (Obléon) and mixed pine-hardwoods (Restauración), but the species is absent from the high pine forests on the Cordillera Central and the Sierra de Neiba.

The elevational distribution of *J. g. zonalis* is between sea level (Colmini, Délugé, Grand-Goâve, Las Terrenas, Nagua, Boca Chica, Punta Cana, Mano Juan, Isla Catalina) and 2100 m on the Massif de la Selle in Haiti (Morne la Visite) and 1220 m on the Cordillera Central (Constanza).

Most specimens have been taken in July (72) and June (52), with 15 in December, 12 each in February, May, and August, and 5 each in January, March, and October; April and September are represented by 1 and 2 specimens each. The early summer abundance of *J. g. zonalis* suggests that the major period of eclosion is at that time, with continuous emergence of small numbers of individuals throughout the year. Schwartz (1983a:33) reported a caterpillar that pupated, the imago emerging during the night of 30–31.vii; the pupal period was 8 days. A pair *in copula* was taken at Les Poteaux (24.xii, 1435 h, 27°C, overcast) in a field of *Uniola virgata;* the pair was clinging to a blade of this grass, about 0.3 m above the ground. Times of collection were between 0900 and 1800 h, with temperatures between 19°C (Scierie) and 38°C (Hatillo).

Junonia g. zonalis has been taken feeding on *Cordia haitiensis* at Pétionville, on *Tournefortia hirsutissima* at Sosúa, on *Croton linearis* at Zamba, on *Lantana ovatifolia* at Santiago, and on *Antigonon leptopus* at Santiago and Azua. We observed a very large number of *J. g. zonalis* feeding on a large stand of low *Antigonon leptopus* in the Cul de Sac plain, near Croix des Bouquets. At Barahona, 1 *J. g. zonalis* was netted while it drank from a small shallow rivulet where the latter crossed a gravel road.

Specimens: Haiti: l'Artibonite: 1.3 km N Carrefour Marmelade, 1; 12.2 km W Ça Soleil, s.l., 1; 2 km E Les Poteaux, 4; 4.0 km N Thomonde, 1; Colmini, 6.4 km W Terre Noire, s.l., 1; Délugé. s.l., 4; *l'Ouest:* 1.6 km N Saut d'Eau, 183 m, 1; 19.7 km SE Mirebalais, 183 m, 1; 2.9–8.5 km S Terre Rouge, 5; Forêt des Pins, 1525 m, 2; Pétionville, 458 m, 3; 2 km W Fond Parisien, s.l., 1; Boutilliers Road, 1.8–2.1 km W Kenscoff road, 763–885 m, 11 (1 MPM); Boutilliers Road, 732–946 m, 11; 3.7 km S Kenscoff, 1647 m, 1; 0.3 km N Obléon, 1617 m, 2; Peneau, 1464 m, 1; Morne la Visite, 2100 m, 8 (FSM); 2 km NW Scierie, 1785–1810 m, 1 (FSM); Ravine Roseau, 4 km SW Dufort, 2; 8.6 km N Béloc, 534 m, 2; 1.3 km N Béloc, 702 m, 1; 0.6 km S Découzé, 671 m, 2; 5.4 km S Découzé, 397 m, 2; 6.7 km E Grand-Goâve, s.l., 4; just W Grand-Goâve, s.l., 1; *Sud:* 6.7 km SW Paillant, 763 m, 1; 6.6 km SW Paillant, 793 m, 9; 7 km SW Cavaillon, 1; 7.8 km N Cavaillon, 31 m, 4; 16.3 km N Cavaillon, 488 m, 10; 26.1 km N Cavaillon, 610 m, 1; 4.8 km N Camp Perrin, 244 m, 4; Formond Base Camp #1, 975 m, 3 (FSM); Formond, 800 m, 2 (FSM); *Île de la Gonâve:* Anse-à-Galets, 1; *República Dominicana: Monte Cristi:* 1 km SE Monte Cristi, 2; 3.9 km SE Martín García, 92 m, 1; *Dajabón:* Los Cerezos, 12 km NW Río Limpio, 580 m, 1; 7 km N Restauración, 671 m, 1; 8 km S Restauración, 595 m, 1; 3 km ESE Villa Anacaona, 458 m, 1; *Valverde:* 4 km N Cruce de Guayacanes, 198 m, 1; 12 km SW Mao, 244 m, 1; 3.0 km S Zamba, 214 m, 3; *Santiago Rodríguez:* Loma Leonor, 19 km SW Monción, 610 m, 1; 15 km SW Monción, 320 m, 1; *Puerto Plata:* 10 km W Luperón, 1; 9 km SE Sosúa, 15 m, 6; *Santiago:* 7 km SW Santiago, 214 m, 4; *La Vega:* Buena Vista, 11 km NE Jarabacoa, 641 m, 1; Jarabacoa, 530 m, 3; La Ciénaga, 915 m, 2; 1 km S Constanza, 1098 m, 1; 12 km NE Constanza, 1220 m, 1; *María T. Sánchez:* 9 km SE Nagua, s.l., 2; 1 km S Cruce de Rincón, s.l., 1; *Samaná:* 3.1 km E Las Terrenas, s.l., 1; 4.5 km E Samaná, 1; *La Altagracia:* Punta Cana, s.l., 1; 2–3 km W Boca de Yuma, 1; *La Romana:* Río Chavón, 8 km SE La Romana, s.l., 2; Río Cumayasa, 13.5 km W La Romana, 1; *San Pedro de Macorís:* 13 km SE Boca Chica, s.l., 4; *Dist. Nac.:* 5 km S San Isidro, 1; Punta Caucedo, 2 km W, 2 km S Andrés, s.l., 1; *San Cristóbal:* 11 km NW Cambita Garabitos, 671 m, 5; *Azua:* 25 km SE Azua, 92 m, 1; 2 km NW Hatillo, 183 m, 1; 1 km E Palmar de Ocoa, s.l., 1; 2.5 km W, 6.6 km N Azua, 183 m, 1; 5 km S Peralta, 305 m, 2; *San Juan:* 9 km E Vallejuelo, 610 m, 1; *Independencia:* 4–7 km NE El Aguacate, 529–732 m, 1; *Barahona:* 11.5 km ESE Canoa, s.l., 2; 8 km NE Polo, 793 m, 1; 6 km SW Barahona, 122 m, 1; 8 km NW Paraíso, 1 (MPM); 8–10 km NW Paraíso, 3 (MPM); 3 km NW Enriquillo, 244 m, 1; *Pedernales:* 23 km NE Cabo Rojo, 488 m, 1; Mencía, 397 m, 1; 3 km N Cabeza de Agua, 305 m, 1; Las Abejas, 12 km NW Aceitillar, 1129 m, 1; 17 km NW Oviedo, 183 m, 1; *Isla Saona:* Mano Juan, 1; *Isla Catalina:* 1.

12. *Anartia jatrophae saturata* Staudinger, 1884

TL "Hayti (Port au Prince)" and "Porto Rico"; restricted to Port-au-Prince, Dépt. de l'Ouest, Haiti (Munroe, 1942:3).

FW males 27–31 mm, females 27–34 mm.

Anartia j. saturata is 1 of 6 subspecies that occur throughout the West Indies; each of the Greater Antilles has its endemic subspecies, and *A. j. jatrophae* Johansson enters the islands from the South American mainland. The remaining subspecies is on the Virgin Island of St. Croix. These taxa differ from each other in relatively subtle ways, such as in the depth of dark ground pigmentation on the up and the color and prominence of the double rows of marginal scallops along the edges of the wings. *Anartia j. saturata* is the most darkly pigmented of the subspecies, with the up ground color dusky gray (in fresh specimens) and with 2 rows of orange scallops along the wing margins. Brown and Heineman (1972:183–84), citing the work of Gillham (1957), noted that the latter author did not feel that the Antillean subspecies were tenable. They, however, adhered to Munroe's (1942) revision and accepted *jamaicensis* Moschler for the Jamaican population. Examination of specimens from Florida (*guantanamo* Munroe), Puerto Rico (*semifusca* Munroe), the Lesser Antilles (*jatrophae*), and Jamaica causes me to agree with Brown and Heineman. Although within this series of subspecies some are very like others (for example, *jatrophae* and *guantanamo* are both very pallid, and *saturata* and *semifusca* are both quite dark), still these insular segregates are distinctive and nameworthy.

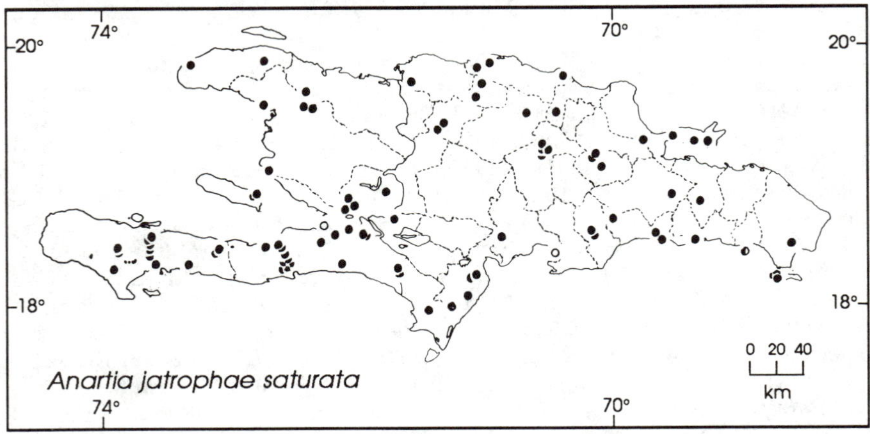

Although all authors stress the dusky and dark coloration of *A. j. saturata*, many specimens are not so dark and present a faded appearance. This is not due to either sexual dichromatism, periodicity (winter *vs.* summer broods), or exclusively to wear, since fresh specimens from the same localities are often either pale or dark. High-elevation material tends to be dark, whereas low-elevation material tends to be pale, but these are tendencies only. There are no obvious differences between north and south island material as far as depth of up coloration is concerned. Worn specimens, as noted above, are often very pallid. Of a series of 77 unworn specimens, 67% are dark and 33% are pale.

Throughout its range *A. jatrophae* is often abundant and very conspicuous. *Anartia j. saturata* is widely distributed on Hispaniola, from the tip of the Tiburon Peninsula to the Península de Samaná, and from Môle St.-Nicholas to Boca de Yuma. It is primarily a species of open areas—roadsides, fields, cornfields, cemeteries, inland behind beaches, grassy mangrove borders—and is regularly encountered in the clearings within *caféières* and *cafetales-cacaotales*, rarely in the plantings themselves. It is a heliophilic species and, as many authors have noted, extremely aggressive to any sort of intruder, often including man and especially other butterflies that chance to come within its territory. The flight is rather weak and close to the ground (0.5 m), but when alarmed by some intrusion, the butterflies can fly determinedly and rapidly. They often occur locally in surprising numbers, seemingly not correlated with any obvious condition of an area. On 2 occasions (Grand-Goâve, Délugé) *A. j. saturata* was extremely common in low areas with flowers (primarily *Ruellia* sp.) behind open beaches in July, and in late June we encountered them abundantly at Camp Perrin along a roadside and in an open cemetery with *Lantana ovatifolia*. At Sosúa and 1 km N Playa Bayahibe, *A. j. saturata* was feeding on *Tournefortia hirsutissima*, and we have taken them on *Lantana ovatifolia* (Copey, Santiago), *Bidens pilosa* (Mao), *Antigonon leptopus* (Santiago, 2 occasions; Azua), *Cordia curassavica* (Santiago), and *Turnera ulmifera* (Santiago).

Most specimens have been taken in June (68) and July (59), with 15 in March, 10 in May, and scattered individuals in February, April, August, October, and December. Although I have listed only a few specimens from Isla Saona (taken in January), they represent a small fraction of a very long series from that islet at that time. These data affirm that *A. j. saturata* is double-brooded, with both a summer and a winter brood.

Anartia j. saturata occurs from sea level (Môle St.-Nicholas, Ça Soleil, Délugé, Grand-Goâve, Croix des Bouquets, El Francés, Samaná, Punta Caucedo, Mano Juan) to 1159 m on the Sierra de Neiba (Los Pinos), 1098 m on the Massif de la Selle (Los Arroyos), and 1007 m on the Cordillera Central (La Palma). These butterflies are absent from all high-elevation pine or deciduous forest; the Los

Pinos material was taken in an open grassy field adjacent to a *cafetal*, the Los Arroyos specimen from a shrubby hilltop, and the La Palma specimen from a large, open, grassy field. Times for collection were between 0930 and 1800 h, with temperatues from 23°C (Samaná: rainy) to 38°C (Jamao al Norte).

A copulating pair was taken at Estero Hondo (30.v, 1146 h, 31°C, shaded *Roystonea hispaniolana* grove).

These are the first records of *A. j. saturata* from Île de la Gonâve, Isla Saona, and Isla Catalina; the species is common on the 2 first-listed islands.

Specimens: Haiti: Nord-Ouest: Môle St.-Nicholas, s.l., 2; 1.3 km S Balladé, 1; *Nord:* 3.5 km W Plaisance, 305 m, 2; 6.2 km W Plaisance, 259 m, 3; *l'Artibonite:* 1.6 km W Carrefour Marmelade, 854 m, 4; Platon, 5 km E Carrefour Marmelade, 793 m, 2; 12.2 km W Ça Soleil, s.l., 1; Délugé, s.l., 2; *l'Ouest:* 6.2 km E Lascahobas, 275 m, 1; 1.6 km N Saut d'Eau, 183 m, 1; 2.9 km N Terre Rouge, 534 m, 2; 20.1 km SE Mirebalais, 366 m, 1: 13.1 km E Croix des Bouquets, s.l.. 1; 5 km SE Fond Parisien, s.l., 1; 4 km SE Fond Parisien, s.l., 2; Pétionville, 458 m, 1; Boutilliers Road, 732–854 m, 1; Ravine Roseau, 4 km SW Dufort, 2; 1.4 km N Béloc, 702 m, 1; 0.6 km S Découzé, 671 m, 3; 0.8 km S Découzé, 702 m, 7; 2.1 km S Découzé, 640 m, 2; 5.4 km S Découzé, 397 m, 2; Lavaneau, 229 m, 1; 8.3 km NW Jacmel, 183 m, 3; 7.7 km N Jacmel, 92 m, 3; nr. Péredo, 600 m, 2 (FSM); just W Grand-Goâve, s.l., 2; 6.7 km E Grand-Goâve, s.l., 1; *Sud:* 6.6 km SW Paillant, 793 m, 4; 6.7 km SW Paillant, 763 m, 1; Vieux Bourg d'Aquin, s.l., 1; 4.6 km E Cavaillon, 31 m, 1; 4.6 km N Cavaillon, 31 m, 3; 14.4 km N Cavaillon, 366 m, 5; 16.3 km N Cavaillon, 488 m, 3; 19.7 km N Cavaillon, 580 m, 2; 25.6 km N Cavaillon, 488 m, 3; 4.8 km N Camp Perrin, 244 m, 5; 5.6 km N Camp Perrin, 14; Les Platons, 850 m, 1 (FSM); *Île de la Gonâve:* hills behind Anse-à-Galets, 1; Anse-à-Galets, 2; *República Dominicana: Monte Cristi:* 6 km W Copey, s.l., 1; *Valverde:* 4 km N Cruce de Guayacanes, 198 m, 1; 12 km SW Mao, 244 m, 2; *Espaillat:* 20 km SW Jamao al Norte, 793 m, 2; *Puerto Plata:* 8 km W Luperón, 1; 0.6 km NE Estero Hondo, 2; 9 km SE Sosúa, 15 m, 2; *Santiago Rodríguez:* Loma Leonor, 19 km SW Monción, 610 m, 1; 4.7 km SW Loma Leonor, 732 m, 1; *La Vega:* La Palma, 19 km W Jayaco, 1007 m, 1; Jarabacoa, 530 m, 7; 6 km S Jarabacoa, 2; 3.5 km E Paso Bajito, 732 m, 2; *Santiago:* 7 km SW Santiago, 214 m, 3; *Sánchez Ramírez:* 1 km SE La Mata, 1; 1 km NE Las Lagunas, 183 m, 1; La Piedra, 7 km SW Pimentel, 1; *María T. Sánchez:* 1 km S Cruce de Rincón, s.l., 1; *Samaná:* 8.9 km NE Sánchez, 336 m, 1; 4.8 km W Samaná, s.l., 1; 4.5 km E Samaná, 1; El Francés, 14 km E and N Samaná, s.l., 2; *Hato Mayor:* 4 km S Hato Mayor, 5; *La Altagracia:* 0.5 km W Boca de Yuma, 1; *San Pedro de Macorís:* 13 km SE Boca Chica, s.l., 1; *Monte Plata:* 8 km NE Bayaguana, 2; *Dist. Nac.:* 33 km W San Pedro de Macorís, 1 (MPM); Punta Caucedo, 2 km W, 2 km S Andrés, s.l., 1; 30 km NW Santo Domingo, 122 m, 3; *San Cristóbal:* 6 km NW Cambita Garabitos, 488 m, 1; 11 km NW Cambita Garabitos, 671 m, 1; *Azua:* Tábara Abajo, 1; *Independencia:* 14 km N Los Pinos, 1159 m, 1; 3.3 km E La Descubierta, 6; *Barahona:* 7 km SW Barahona, 2; 12 km SW Barahona, 366 m, 2; 8 km NW Paraíso, 1 (MPM); 8–10 km NE Paraíso, 13 (MPM); 9 km NW Enriquillo, 671 m, 2; *Pedernales:* 0.6 km SE Los

Arroyos, 1098 m, 1; 3 km N Cabeza de Agua, 305 m, 1; 17 km NW Oviedo, 183 m, 2; *Isla Saona:* Mano Juan, 15; 1.5 km N Mano Juan, 1; 0.5 km N Mano Juan, 3.

Sight record: República Dominicana: Isla Catalina: 1 seen—14.viii.

13. *Anartia lytrea* Godart, 1819

TL San Domingo.

FW males 27–29 mm, females 28–35 mm.

Anartia lytrea is restricted to Hispaniola, although it is related to *A. chrysopelea* Hübner from Cuba. It is a locally common butterfly, widely distributed but occurring in numbers in only 1 type of habitat—marshy shaded creeks supporting aroids in *cafetales-cacaotales* or deciduous forest. Yet we have not encountered *A. lytrea* at every locality that fits the above criteria. Still, almost wherever we have taken *A. lytrea*, the above criteria have been met.

Riley (1975:76) stated that *A. lytrea* is "widespread and generally fairly common"; he presumably based this assessment on Hall (1925:187), who commented that *A. lytrea* is "generally a fairly common species . . . but evidently quite out of season at the time of my visit, as I saw only one ragged specimen. Miss Sharpe records it from La Vega in March and April." Such a comment hardly justifies Riley's simplistic abstraction.

Anartia lytrea is sexually dichromatic. Males are dark rich brown on the up, whereas females are much paler tan; even when specimens of either sex are worn, this basic difference is still obvious. The white band across the apices of the fw is broader in females than in males. The postdiscal uphw orange wash is especially variable and may be absent in females and barely indicated in some males. One male specimen (El Valle) differs from all other males in that the upfw subapical band is much invaded by dark brown scales, thus also reducing the uphw white discal band.

The locality where we have taken *A. lytrea* most commonly is La Palma in the Cordillera Central. On our first visit (21.vi.1980) we encountered literally hundreds of these butterflies flying along the path and road through a *cafetal* with dense forest canopy along a creek in moderately dense underbrush, landing on leaves close to (less than 1 m) the ground and on the wet mud and gravel road surface. The butterflies landed with the wings open, displaying the up contrasting pattern. As many as 5 could be seen easily within a 0.5 m circle, and the numbers were astounding, especially since we had never seen this species in Haiti. Return visits to this locality on 13.viii.1980, 30.xii.1980, 26.vi.1981, 22.vi.1982, 9.viii.1982, 7.viii.1983, 29.ix.1983, 12.iii.1984, 17.vii.1985, 27.vi.1986, and 21.

xii.1986 always yielded specimens or sightings. The butterflies were usually very abundant, with the lowest number observed on 12.iii.1984, when I estimated that we saw about 8 individuals. On 27.vi.1986, *A. lytrea* was less common than usual. The locality supports a rather large area of marshy ground, with aroids (*Zantedeschia aethiopica*). The butterflies frequent this immediate area by the dozens, with often as many as 30 in the air amid and above the aroids at 1 time.

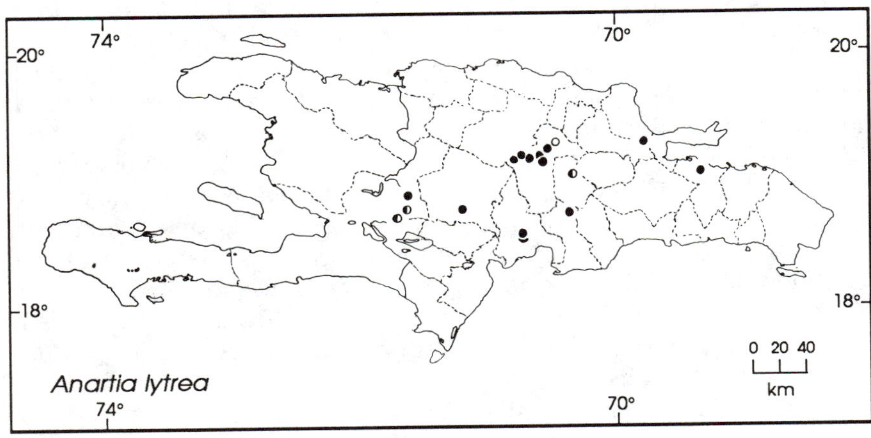

Other than at La Palma, we have taken specimens at La Ciénaga in the Cordillera Central. Here the main road travels above the Río Yaque del Norte; within a *cafetal* on the slope between the road and the river is a small marshy area with aroids, and *A. lytrea* was modestly abundant there and in the shade along the road. Three km further along this same road, a few individuals were seen adjacent to a small *cafetal* and in an overgrown field adjacent to it. In the Sierra de Neiba, we collected as many *A. lytrea* as we saw at Las Lagunas on the north range, in a patch of deciduous forest, again with an area of soggy ground and aroids. On the south range, we have sight records from Aniceto Martínez and Puesto Pirámide 204. In the latter case, the 2 butterflies were seen flying along a road on an exposed mountain roadcut; at the foot of the slope was a marshy area with aroids in a weedy pasture. At Rancho Arriba, the species was modestly common along a marshy creek at the interface between a *cafetal* and a short-grass pasture; there were aroids along the creek. We saw 1 individual at Bonao, again in the immediate area of a soggy creek bottom.

Perhaps the most amazing instance of encountering this species was at El Valle. I saw 1 individual at this site on 30.vi.1980 but did not collect it. Raburn and I returned to the precise spot on 24.vii.1983, and I saw 1 *A. lytrea* and collected it. There is a small colony of *A. lytrea* at this locality, which is a large *cacaotal* with a creek (with aroids) running through it. The 4 individuals seen or collected there were along the road on *Wedelia trilobata* (Asteraceae).

At Manabao, *A. lytrea* occurred in a *cafetal* with a creek and aroids, and at 6 km S Jarabacoa, the same situation obtained. Only at the 2 Azua localities have we taken *A. lytrea* in open areas (although in 1 case, adjacent to transitional forest); but the number and variety of flowers probably attracted these butterflies from their typical habitat. At La Palma, *A. lytrea* has been observed (twice) on the blossoms of *Coffea arabica* (Rubiaceae), and at Cruce de Rincón on *Mimosa pudica* (Fabaceae). At this last locality, *A. lytrea* was moderately common along the edges of a road through a *cafetal*, again with large aroids. At La Palma we have taken *A. lytrea* on *Palicourea barbinervia* and *Urena lobata;* at Azua we have seen them feeding on *Antigonon leptopus* (twice) and at Vallejuelo on *Ageratum conyzoides.*

Most specimens have been taken in June (61), with 50 in July, 30 in August, 18 in December, 9 in March, 4 in October, and 1 in April. On any visit to La Palma, we saw and collected both fresh and much flown individuals; there may be 2 broods a year, but the condition of the specimens suggests that these butterflies emerge throughout the year.

Elevations are from sea level (Cruce de Rincón) to 1586 m (Puesto Pirámide 204). Times of collection were between 0900 and 1530 h, and temperatures between 20°C (La Palma) and 36°C (La Laguna, La Palma, La Ciénaga, Rancho Arriba, Peralta). A pair *in copula* was seen on 26.vi at La Palma (1315–1515 h, 30°C).

Specimens: República Dominicana: Elías Piña: La Laguna, 10 km S Comendador, 732 m, 3; *La Vega:* La Palma, 19 km W Jayaco, 1007 m, 74; 1 km W Manabao, 793 m, 14; La Ciénaga, 915 m, 13; 3 km W La Ciénaga, 1037 m, 2; Jarabacoa, 530 m, 20; 6 km S Jarabacoa, *ca.* 610 m, 1; *María T. Sánchez:* 1 km S Cruce de Rincón, s.l., 19; *Hato Mayor:* 6 km N El Valle, 3; *Peravia:* 2 km SW Rancho Arriba, 671 m, 6; *Azua:* 2.5 km W, 6.6 km N Azua, 183 m, 11; 5 km S Peralta, 305 m, 1; *San Juan:* 9 km E Vallejuelo, 610 m, 2.

Sight records: República Dominicana: Elías Piña: 2 km NE Puesto Pirámide 204, 1586 m—2 seen, 13.viii; *ca.* 3 km SW Aniceto Martinez—1 seen, 6.viii; *Monseñor Nouel:* Bonao, 153 m—1 seen, 22.vii; *Azua:* 2.5 km W, 6.6 km N Azua, 183 m—4 seen, 13.vii.

14. *Siproeta stelenes stelenes* Linnaeus, 1758

TL "America"; restricted to Jamaica by Fox and Forbes, 1972 (Miller and Brown, 1981:176).

FW males 39–43 mm, females 42–48 mm.

Siproeta s. stelenes is 1 of the more conspicuous and widely distributed butterflies of Hispaniola. *Siproeta stelenes* (including *insularis* Holland, which may equal *biplagiata* Fruhstorfer; see Miller and Brown, 1981:177) is abundant on Cuba (Bates, 1935a: 171), Puerto Rico (Comstock, 1944:460), and Jamaica (Brown and Heineman, 1972:189–90). Hall (1925:188) considered *S. stelenes* abundant on Hispaniola; Schwartz (1983a:34) agreed with Riley (1975:77) as to its abundance in Haiti.

A character that has been used to differentiate *S. s. stelenes* is the number of green spots in the fw cell: typically there are 0–2 in *S. s. stelenes*, and 2 in *S. s. insularis*. Brown and Heineman, however, noted that their series of Jamaican specimens was about equally divided between these 2 conditions. None of 94 Hispaniolan specimens has 2 cell spots; 87% have 1 spot in the cell and 13% have no spots. The size of the spot varies from a tiny and often diffuse pale dot to a large dot (2×3 mm). Brown and Heineman (1982:187) commented that, although the number of fw cell spots is variable (especially so in Jamaican material), the width of the broad marginal unhw bands varies in such a way that they felt that, when large samples from the different Greater Antilles are examined, each island supports a "strain" that is recognizable.

Siproeta s. stelenes is almost exclusively a butterfly of mesic forest and pseudoforest. It is often the major rhopaloceran element in *caféières, cafetales*, and *cacaotales*, where its lazy flight, usually no more than 1 m above the ground, and contrasting up black and green coloration make it conspicuous and easily netted. The butterflies frequent paths and clearings in shaded interior situations; when flying undisturbed, they often land up to 2 m above the ground, favoring banana and other monocot leaves, where they often perch with the wings open. When alarmed, *S. s. stelenes* does not hesitate to fly among trees, shrubs, and saplings to escape. Although the habitat of choice is mesic, we have at times taken or seen this species abundantly along the edges of *Acacia* woods (Limonade, Santiago), semidesert (Les Poteaux), beach (Grand-Goâve), along the edges of mangroves (Miragoâne), xeric deciduous woods (Cormier Plage), and in a xeric wooded ravine (Oviedo). There are specimens from pinewoods (Obléon) and mixed pine-hardwoods (La Vega, Valle de Tetero).

Although *S. s. stelenes* has been recorded between sea level (Cormier Plage, Carrefour la Mort, Limonade, Ça Soleil, Grand-Goâve, Miragoâne, Río San Juan, Punta Caucedo) and 1617 m (Obléon), most specimens are from less than 915 m, with only 3 other localities (Boutilliers Road, La Ciénaga, Valle de Tetero) at or above that elevation. Thus *S. s. stelenes* is a butterfly of low to moderate elevations and does not occur in the uplands of the Massif de la Selle, Sierra de Baoruco, or Sierra de Neiba. Although Comstock (1944:460) considered *S. s. stelenes* common throughout the year, most of our specimens (80) are from July, with 28 in June, 25 in August, 13 in March, 8 in December, 7 each in October and January, 6 in May, and 3 in February. The species presumably does fly on Hispaniola during the entire year but is much more common in June-August.

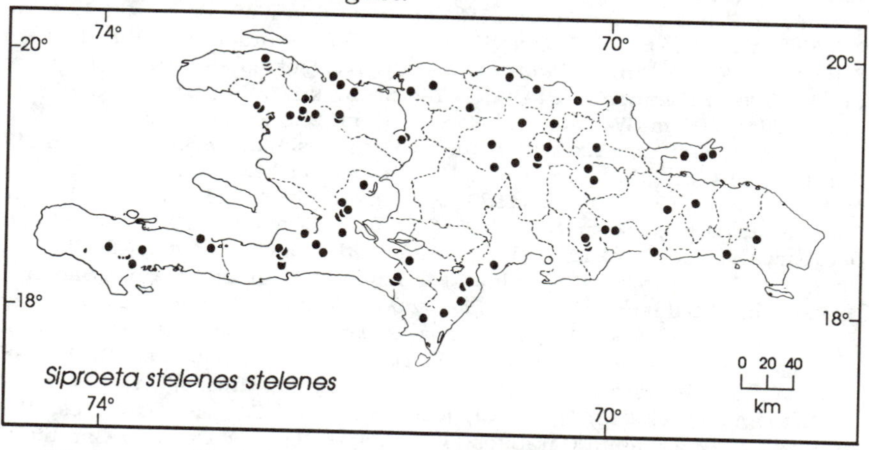

We have collected *S. s. stelenes* between 0730 and 1600 h, and at temperatures betwen 13°C (Valle de Tetero) and 40°C (Yásica). *Siproeta s. stelenes* is attracted to decaying fruit; we have seen aggregations of the butterfly feeding on rotted mangoes (Mencía, Jacmel—at the latter in a pig sty), rotten breadfruit (*Artocarpus altilis*) at Gaspar Hernández, on a rotten *guanábana* (*Annona muricata;* Annonaceae) at Ennery, and on rotten bananas (Santiago). In addition, we have taken these butterflies at a *Cordia* hedge (Terre Rouge); at Limonade, many *S. s. stelenes* were landing on the dirt road at the edge of an *Acacia* forest on a spot that was only slightly moist and presumably were drinking. At La Palma, *S. s. stelenes* was taking nectar from the white flowers of *Coffea arabica*, along with *D. spio*. At Río Bao (twice) and Peralta these butterflies fed on *Tournefortia hirsutissima*, and at Santiago on *Cor-*

dia curassavica and *Antigonon leptopus*.

Specimens: Haiti: Nord-Ouest: 1.3 km S Balladé, 31 m, 2; 2.1 km SE Balladé, 1; 7.5 km SE Port-de-Paix, 1; *Nord:* Cormier Plage, s.l., 5; Carrefour la Mort, s.l., 8; 3.5 km E Limonade, s.l., 1; 5.6 km SE Dondon, 336 m, 3; 5.9 km S Dondon, 366 m, 2; 3.5 km W Plaisance, 305 m, 6; 6.2 km W Plaisance, 259 m, 2; 2.9 km E Ennery, 305 m, 1; *l'Artibonite:* Platon, 6 km E Carrefour Marmelade, 793 m, 2; 1.6 km E Carrefour Marmelade, 854 m, 1; 6.4 km W Ennery, 336 m, 2; 4.6 km E Les Poteaux, 183 m, 1; 12.2 km W Ça Soleil, s.l., 10; 16.8 km W Ça Soleil, s.l., 3; *l'Ouest:* 1.6 km N Saut d'Eau, 183 m, 4; 20.3 km SW Thomonde, 1; 20.2 km SE Mirebalais, 366 m, 6; 1.1 km N Terre Rouge, 534 m, 1; 8 km S Terre Rouge, 1; 13 km E Croix des Bouquets, s.l., 2; Boutilliers Road, 915 m, 1; 0.8 km N Obléon, 1617 m, 1; 17.0 km S Dufort, 702 m, 1; 0.6 km S Découzé, 671 m, 2; 0.8 km S Découzé, 702 m, 4; 2.1 km S Découzé, 640 m, 5; 8.3 km NW Jacmel, 183 m, 5; just W Grand-Goâve, s.l., 2; *Sud:* 10.7 km W Miragoâne, s.l., 3; 6.7 km SW Paillant, 763 m, 1; 7 km SW Cavaillon, 122 m, 1; 14.1 km N Cavaillon, 366 m, 1; 5.6 km N Camp Perrin, 275 m, 1; *República Dominicana; Monte Cristi:* 6 km W Copey, s.l., 1; 4 km NW Villa Vásquez, 61 m, 3; *Dajabón:* 8.4 km S Restauración, 580 m, 1; 9 km S Restauración, 519 m, 1; *Valverde:* 3 km W Los Quemados, 122 m, 1; *Puerto Plata:* 13 km SE Luperón, 214 m, 1; Yásica, 22 km SW Puerto Plata, 122 m, 1; *Espaillat:* 20 km SW Jamao al Norte, 793 m, 2; 2 km NW Gaspar Hernández, 16 m, 1; *Santiago:* Río Bao, 8 km SE Montones Abajo, 488 m, 2; 7 km SW Santiago, 214 m, 2; Valle de Tetero, 1342 m, 1; *Sánchez Ramírez:* 1 km SE La Mata, 1; 1 km NE Las Lagunas, 183 m, 7; *Duarte:* 12 km SE San Francisco de Macorís, 1; *La Vega:* 2 km S La Vega, 366 m, 1; Jarabacoa, 530 m, 1; 6 km S Jarabacoa, 1; La Ciénaga, 915 m, 1; *María T. Sánchez:* 8 km NE Río San Juan, s.l., 1; *Samaná;* 14.1 km E and N Samaná, 31 m, 3; 4.5 km E Samaná, 3; 10.2 km W Samaná, 61 m, 1; *Hato Mayor:* 12 km S El Valle,1; *La Romana:* Río Cumayasa, 13.5 km W La Romana, 2; *La Altagracia:* 16 km NE La Romana, 61 m, 3; *Monte Plata:* 8 km NE Bayaguana, 2; *Dist. Nac.:* 25 km SE Yamasá, 2 (MPM); Punta Caucedo, 2 km W, 2 km S Andrés, s.l., 1; 30 km NW Santo Domingo, 122 m, 1; *San Cristóbal:* 6 km NW Cambita Garabitos, 488 m, 1; 8 km NW Cambita Garabitos, 580 m, 1; 11 km NW Cambita Garabitos, 671 m, 1; *Azua:* 22 km NW Cruce de Ocoa, 61 m, 2; *Independencia:* 4–7 km NE El Aguacate, 519–824 m, 1; *Barahona:* west slope, Sierra Martín García, 458 m, 1; 7 km SW Barahona, 1; 12 km SW Barahona, 427 m, 1; 8 km NW Paraíso, 10 (9 MPM); 8–10 km NW Paraíso, 2 (MPM); 9 km NW Enriquillo, 671 m, 1; *Pedernales:* 1 km S La Altagracia, *ca.* 549 m, 1; Mencía, 397 m, 1; 17 km NW Oviedo, 183 m, 1.

Subfamily Limenitidinae Behr, 1864

15. *Adelpha gelania* Godart, 1819

TL "Equinoctial America."

FW males 24–34 mm, females 34–38 mm.

The genus *Adelpha* Hübner is represented by 5 named taxa in the Greater Antilles: *abyla* Hewitson on Jamaica, *iphicla* Linnaeus on Cuba and the Isla de la Juventud, *lapitha* Hall on Hispaniola, *arecosa* Hewitson on Puerto Rico, and *gelania* on Hispaniola. The last 2 have been regarded as subspecies (Riley, 1975:73), but Brown and Heineman (1972:171) suggested that all taxa be considered distinct species. At least Ramos (1982:60) followed this suggestion. Certainly *gelania* and *arecosa* are very similar to each other, just as *abyla* and *iphicla* have a common appearance, yet there are many mainland species of *Adelpha* that have similar appearances to the latter pair. I follow Brown and Heineman in at least *pro tempore* considering *arecosa* and *gelania* as separate species, although recognizing their relationship.

Hall (1925:81) saw several specimens from Haiti, but he considered *A. gelania* a rare species. Riley (1975:73) felt that *A. gelania* was "undoubtedly rare and presumably an insect of the mountain forests." We have seen and collected the species only once in Haiti, in pine forest with a *Rubus selleanus* understory on the Massif de la Selle. From this experience it seems logical to assume that *A. gelania* is rare. Once more, the situation in the República Dominicana shows that this is not the case. Certainly *A. gelania* is local, but where it occurs one can at least see (if not collect) these fast and erratically-flying butterflies.

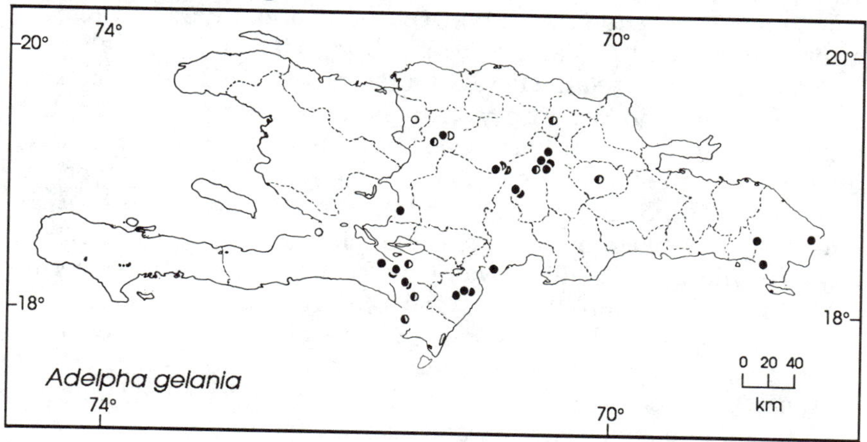

Adelpha gelania is a butterfly of mesic or xeric forests; it is more commonly encountered in the former, usually at high elevations, but we have taken *A. gelania* in dense xeric forests in the lowlands (Playa Bayahibe, Punta Cana). The record for Forêt des Pins is unusual in that it is for specimens taken in pine forest; but we have also secured *A. gelania* in mixed pine-hardwood forest (Buena Vista, Valle de Tetero). At Las Abejas (11 km NW Aceitillar), the single specimen is from a mesic and wooded narrow runoff ravine surrounded by pine forest. In the uplands, *A. gelania* occurs on the Massif de la Selle in both Haiti (Forêt des Pins) and the República Dominicana (Los Arroyos), the Sierra de Neiba (Puesto Pirámide 204), the Sierra de Baoruco (Polo, Las Abejas), and the Sierra Martín García (El Limón as well as lower elevations). All these records (except Forêt des Pins) are from mesic deciduous forest or *cafetales* (Polo, Barahona).

Of the sight records, only that from Cabo Rojo is unexpected. Cabo Rojo lies in the extreme xeric lowlands of the Península de Barahona, and there are no nearby forests of any sort. The butterfly was battling the severe onshore wind that is of regular occurrence at Cabo Rojo. It may have been swept down from the Sierra de Baoruco or the Massif de la Selle; it seems unlikely that *A. gelania* occurs regularly at Cabo Rojo.

Adelpha gelania occurs from sea level (Punta Cana, Playa Bayahibe) to 1723 m in the Cordillera Central (Las Lagunas), 1617 m in the Massif de la Selle (El Aguacate, Los Arroyos) and 1586 m in the Sierra de Neiba (Puesto Pirámide 204). Most specimens and sight records are from July (35), with 22 from August, 11 from June, and 1–2 from February, March, April, May, November, and December. Times of collection were between 0730 and 1600 h, at temperatures between 13°C (Valle de Tetero) and 42°C (La Romana).

The flight of *A. gelania* is rapid and erratic. The butterflies seem to land rarely, and when they do, it is usually for only a very brief period. Landing sites are on leaves, often high (3–4 m) in trees, but on occasion they land on *Zamia* sp. (Cycadaceae), 1 m or less above the ground. Twice I observed *A. gelania* on rocks in streams: once at Loma Leonor, where the rock was bare, and once at Jayaco, where the boulder was covered with moss wetted by the spray of a mountain torrent. The butterfly, due to its unusual "patience" for this species, appeared to be drinking. We have never seen *A. gelania* on flowers, decaying plant material, or animal matter. One specimen was retrieved from a spider web 1 m above the ground adjacent to xeric woods (La Romana).

Specimens: Haiti: l'Ouest: 4 km NW Foret de Pins, 1496 m, 2; *República Dominicana: Elías Piña:* 2 km NE Puesto Pirámide 204, 1586 m, 1; *Santiago Rodriguez:* Loma Leonor, 19 km SW Monción, 610 m, 1; *Santiago:* Valle de Tetero, 1342 m, 1; *La Vega:* 10 km W Jayaco, 915 m, 6; Buena Vista, 11 km NE Jarabacoa, 640 m, 2; 5 km SE Jarabacoa, 595 m, 1; 3.5 km E Paso Bajito, 732 m, 1; 12 km NE Constanza, 1220 m, 1; 6 km SSE Constanza, 1403 m, 4; *La Altagracia:* 2 km W Punta Cana, s.l., 2; 1 km N Playa Bayahibe, s.l., 8; 16 km NW La Romana, 61 m, 8; *Barahona:* El Limón, summit, Sierra Martín García, 1037 m, 1; west slope, Sierra Martín García, 915 m, 1; west slope, Sierra Martín García, 458–625 m, 2; 3 km NNE Polo, 854 m, 1; 1.8 km W

Monteada Nueva, 1007 m, 5; 5 km SE, 3 km W Barahona, 183–397 m, 1; 20 km SW Barahona, 1098 m, 1; *Pedernales:* 5 km SW El Aguacate, 1464 m, 2; 5 km NE Los Arroyos, 1617 m, 1; Las Abejas, 11 km NW Aceitillar, 1220 m, 1; Las Abejas, 12 km NW Aceitillar, 1129 m, 5.

Sight records: República Dominicana: Santiago Rodríguez: Loma Leonor, 19 km SW Monción, 610 m—2 seen, 17.iii; Loma Leonor, 18 km SW Monción, 534 m—1 seen, 13.viii; 4.7 km SW Loma Leonor, 732 m—2 seen, 20.v; *Espaillat:* 20 km SW Jamao al Norte, 793 m—1 seen, 16.vii; *Santiago:* 0.3 km NE La Laguna, 1723 m—1 seen, 2.vii; *La Vega:* La Palma, 19 km W Jayaco, 1007 m—1 seen, 30.xii; 1 km SW Los Tablones, 1159 m—1 seen, 20.vii; *Sánchez Ramírez:* 1 km NE Las Lagunas, 183 m—1 seen, 2.xi; *Independencia:* 4–7 km NE El Aguacate, 519–824 m—1 seen, 15.vii; *Barahona:* Sierra Martín García, 793–854 m—1 seen, 13.viii; 1.8 km W Monteada Nueva, 1007 m—1 seen, 14.vii; *Pedernales:* 5 km NE El Aguacate, 1617 m—2 seen, 30.vi; Cabo Rojo, s.l.—1 seen, 30.vi; 26 km NE Cabo Rojo, 732 m—1 seen, 1.viii; Las Abejas, 12 km NW Aceitillar, 1129 m—3 seen, 27.vii; 1 seen, 14.vi.

16. *Adelpha lapitha* Hall, 1929

TL "Colombia"; here restricted to Hispaniola.

FW males 25–30 mm, females 32 mm.

In 1980, I had the privilege of briefly seeing a specimen of what appeared to be a new species of *Adelpha* that had been collected by H. Ludovino Domínguez in the Sierra de Neiba near Puesto Pirámide 204. Although we visited that area 5 times since that date, we never encountered this species there. The species was described by Hall (1929) as a subspecies of *cestus* Hewitson and attributed to Colombia. These are the first Hispaniolan records and specimens.

On 28.iv.1984, I saw 1 individual and captured another at Peralta, at an elevation and in an ecological situation much different from the upland hardwood forest at Puesto Pirámide 204. The locality is at an interface between xeric *Acacia* woods and mesic forest along the Río Jura (see discussion of *Burca hispaniolae*). The individuals were near a very large stand of *Tournefortia hirsutissima*, but neither was seen to feed.

In 1986, *A. lapitha* was much more "common" than previously, and Gonzalez, Escobio, and I collected 8 specimens; a ninth was taken by Wetherbee at Restauración. The species occurs primarily in xeric areas (Azua, Vallejuelo) in and near *Acacia* forest or woods. But it has also been seen or taken near transitional forest (Peralta), pinewoods (Restauración), and mesic forest (Banano). The last locality is the first for the south island.

The elevations at which *A. lapitha* have been taken are from 183 m (Azua) to 610 m (Vallejuelo) and to *ca.* 1900 m (Puesto Pirámide 204). The species is known from the Cordillera Central and its affiliates, the Sierra de Neiba and the Sierra de Baoruco.

Most specimens and sight records are from June (7), with 5 from August, 2 from December, and 1 each from February, March, and November. Times of collection were between 1030 and 1630 h at temperatures between 28°C (Vallejuelo) to 38°C (Vallejuelo, Peralta, Azua).

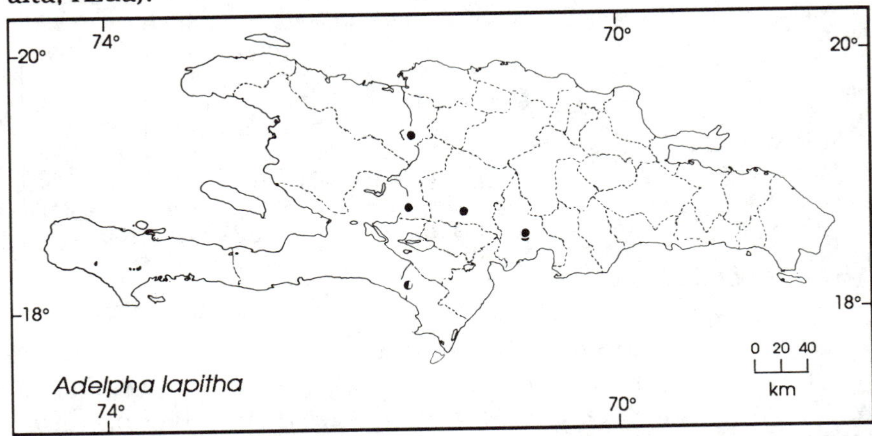

Adelpha lapitha feeds on *Croton barahonensis* (Vallejuelo, 3 times) and on *Ageratum conyzoides* (Vallejuelo). At Azua, Gonzalez saw 4 (and collected 1) of these butterflies feeding on an unidentified white-flowered tree with compound leaves in *Acacia* woods. The tree was also a major nectar source for other species. We neglected to take a specimen for identification, and on our return 8 days later, the tree had been cut to make charcoal.

Specimens: República Dominicana: Dajabón: Restauración, 550 m, 1; *Azua:* 5 km S Peralta, 305 m, 2; 2.5 km W, 6.6 km N Azua, 183 m, 1; *San Juan:* 9 km E Vallejuelo, 10 m, 6.

Sight records: República Dominicana: Azua: 2.5 km W, 6.6 km N Azua, 183 m—3 seen, 8.vi; 1 seen, 21.vi; 5 km S Peralta, 305 m—1 seen, 16.ii; *San Juan;* 9 km E Vallejuelo, 610 m—1 seen, 24.xii; *Pedernales:* 1 km SE Banano, 488 m—1 seen, 11.vi.

17. *Myscelia aracynthia* Dalman, 1823

TL unknown.

FW males 35–37 mm, females 35–40 mm.

Riley's (1975:63) common name for *M. aracynthia*, "The Royal Blue," is extremely apt for this, the most spectacular of the Hispaniolan butterflies. Added to its beauty is without question its supposed rarity. Little has been published on the species' natural history; Gali and Schwartz (1983a) gave details on the 7 specimens taken and observations made during the summer of 1981. Since that time we have taken many more specimens and have as well more sight records. This species is certainly distinctive in the field; its labored flight, with deep and deliberate wing beats, resembles only that of *H. a. diasia*, but these 2 species are, under even somewhat unfavorable circumstances, easily distinguished by the brilliant blue on the up of *M. aracynthia* and the pale gray of *H. a. diasia*.

All previous authors have used the trivial name *antholia* Godart for this species, but Jenkins (1984:33) resurrected *aracynthia*, since it antedates *antholia*. Although the species has been recorded from Haiti, I have no specimens from that country; unquestionably *M. aracynthia* occurs at least in the hardwood forested uplands of the Massif de la Selle and the Montagnes du Trou-d'Eau, near the Dominico-Haitian border. Considering the altitudinal distribution of *M. aracynthia* in the República Dominicana, the species may be encountered almost anywhere in Haiti (see discussion below). Jenkins (1984:34) examined 17 specimens, of which only 2 (from Port-au-Prince and "Monte Cristi, 10 mi. S. Río Yaque del Norte") have locality data; even the datum "Port-au-Prince" is suspect.

One encounters *M. aracynthia* in 2 sorts of situations: mesic (usually) or xeric forests where many individuals are seen, and other habitats where one sees a single (or at most 2) individuals flying casually. These latter localities (all those listed under *Sight records*) may be in almost any sort of habitat, from open *Acacia* scrub and woods (Copey, Vallejuelo) and open montane fields (Barahona) to open pine forest (Constanza). These individuals are rarely caught: their determined flight and unpredictability, as well as their very appearance, unexpected by the collector, all militate against capture.

It is in the first situation where one can most easily secure several specimens or even a series. Such localities as Villa Vásquez, El Aguacate, and the Sierra Martín García support populations for at least a part of the year; all are wooded, an oasis at Villa Vásquez, mesic or transitional forest elsewhere. In June and July, these areas seem to teem with *M. aracynthia*. On 27.vi.1983 at Aguacate, Raburn and I took 6 *M. aracynthia* and saw 17 more, a total of 23. The butterflies were flying down a 3-km road slope through transitional forest, landing with wings spread on the leaves of trees up to 3 m above the ground, and thus were very conspicuous. On 6.vii, Raburn and I collected no more specimens and saw only 4 individuals under appropriate weather conditions. On 14.vii, Raburn saw 5 *M. aracynthia* and secured none. On 14.vii he saw 6 and on 15.vii he saw 1. On 11.viii, Amador, Raburn, and I, between 1015 and 1430 h (a total of 12.5 man/hours), saw no *M. aracynthia.* Finally, Raburn and I visited this same locality on 11.x, when I saw 2 *M. aracynthia* at 519 m on a path through xeric forest, but Raburn saw none on the main road on a walk up and down the 3-km slope. Thus, the history of *M. aracynthia* at this locality is one of steadily decreasing abundance between 27.vi.1983 and 11.x.1983. The specimens taken in June are fresh and unworn.

A similar situation is the Villa Vásquez oasis. This oasis lies on a hillock surrounded by rice fields; the area is about 13 hectares. It is a sanctuary for many butterflies, and the abundance of flowers (*Antigonon leptopus, Poinciana regia, Rosa* sp.) and fruit trees (*Mangifera indica, Melicoccus bijugatus*) makes it even more attractive to a variety of species. On 5.vii.1982, Wisor saw a single *M. aracynthia* at this locality, perched with wings open about 0.3 m above the ground on a low stub. The butterfly was not captured, and on 2 subsequent visits (8.vii and 10.viii.1982) we never saw another individual. But on 29.vii.1983, Amador, Raburn, and I collected 5 specimens and saw a few others; a return visit on 31.vii yielded 8 specimens. The butterflies were numerous and were taken primarily while they fed on the fallen and very dry fruits of *limoncillo (Melicoccus bijugatus;* Sapindaceae) near a homestead within the oasis. Return visits to this same locality on 18 and 22.x.1983 yielded no sightings. Yet on 18.x.1983, Raburn and I saw a *M. aracynthia* fly across the main road, 8 km SE Villa Sinda, in very bleak *Acacia* scrub, 18 km SE the Villa Vásquez oasis.

One other major area for *M. aracynthia* deserves mention. The Sierra Martín García has been climbed rarely by biologists. This isolated (but not remote) mountain range is the eastern extreme of the Sierra de Neiba. The range reaches a height of 1343 m. Gali ascended the range from the western base at Puerto Alejandro (sea level) to El Limón (876 m) on 25.vii.1982. Raburn walked as high as 702 m on 9.vii.1983, Amador went to El Limón and even a bit farther to the only water source, El Charco, on 13.viii.1983, and Gonzalez ascended to 610 m on 9.viii.1986. The 1983 trips were under the driest conditions. At the time of Raburn's climb, the mountains had not had rain for 2 weeks, and when Amador made the ascent, there had been no appreciable rain for 2 months. Although the upper slopes of the Sierra Martín García are clothed almost daily with heavy clouds, still very little rain falls there due to desert to the east and north and the proximity of this range to the ocean, which surrounds all of its southern and western base.

Yet 3 of these men commented on the abundance of *M. aracynthia* in the upper "mesic" hardwood forests of the Sierra Martín García. Gali saw and collected *M. aracynthia* only above 458 m. Amador collected 2 specimens at El Limón and El Charco and saw 3 more there; on the descent he saw these butterflies only as low as 610 m. Raburn collected 2 and saw 7 more above 534 m. It thus appears that at least throughout the summer, regardless of the previous weather conditions (= no rain), *M. aracynthia* is common in the forests of the Sierra Martín García. However, Gonzalez saw none.

Our experiences at Villa Vásquez and El Aguacate suggest that during the summer, *M. aracynthia* congregates (remains at the place where the imagines have emerged?), but as the season progresses these butterflies scatter, and one encounters individuals in almost any sort of habitat. The observations at Sierra Martín García seem to negate this hypothesis. But that range is surrounded on all sides by habitats (desert, ocean) that are inhospitable to most butterflies, and the population of *M. aracynthia* that emerges there is forced to stay on that range with relatively little "leakage" to other areas (Sierra de Baoruco, such as Polo and Barahona?). This scenario accounts for the abundance of *M. aracynthia* at certain selected localities in the early summer, the gradual decline and final "disappearance" of the species at these same localities as the year progresses, the scattered nature of occurrences in rigorous habitats during the late summer and fall, and the apparent maintenance of a population on the Sierra Martín García.

A case in point is Peralta. I collected 1 well-flown *M. aracynthia* there on 29.iv.1984, after 4 previous visits without a sighting. No others were seen (after 3 visits) there until 8.vi.1986, when Gonzalez and I collected 17 specimens on that date and on 16.vi.1986. The butterflies were feeding eagerly on fallen rotting mangoes under 2 large mango trees in an open field adjacent to transitional forest. When disturbed, they flew a few feet and landed on the trunks of saplings and small trees, only to return immediately to the mangoes. On a return visit to this same spot on 8.vii.1986, we saw no *M. aracynthia;* the mangoes had disintegrated and disappeared.

Gali and Schwartz (1983a) gave details of the behavior and habitats of some *M. aracynthia.* Further experience with this butterfly does not contradict them, but it does elaborate somewhat on the natural history. I have already commented on the "floppy" flight of *M. aracynthia* and its landing, with wings open, on leaves of trees or on low stubs. The head may be either up or down. Usually the wings are closed after a few seconds, then reopened briefly or not. When feeding on the ground (as on the *limoncillo* fruits and mangoes) *M. aracynthia* is loathe to leave the fruits and flies only a very short (3.5 m) distance to land on a tree trunk, close to the ground, only to return within minutes, if undisturbed, to the fruits. At La Horma, where Wisor took a specimen in an open but mesic ravine, I saw another land on a low (0.5-m) shrub; the butterfly stayed on the shrub with wings open as long as I remained watching it —some 5 minutes. Since the butterfly was in the bright sun with wings open, it seems likely that it was sunning.

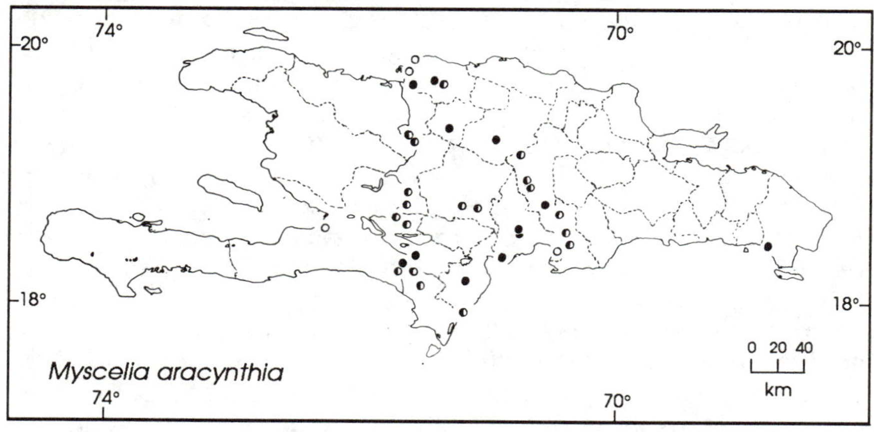

Gali and Schwartz (1983a) reported an individual flying above a water-filled depression in the road (Constanza) and another on the ground adjacent to a mud hole in a dirt road (Playa Bayahibe); presumably these 2 individuals were in the act of drinking. At El Charco, Amador observed several *M. aracynthia* in the company of *M. v. verticordia*, feeding on the bleeding sap of a tree. To show that *M. aracynthia* is not confined to high or remote areas, Amador's sighting of 1 on a tree immediately at the streetside in the town of Enriquillo is pertinent. But most often, except under unusual circumstances, one sees individual *M. aracynthia* flying in their leisurely manner.

Most specimens and observations have been taken or made in June (36), with 34 in July, 16 in August, 2 in October, and 1 each in March, April, May, and September. The March and April specimens are badly flown. The elevational distribution is from sea level (Copey, Playa Bayahibe, La Descubierta, Enriquillo) to 1647 m in the Cordillera Central (Constanza), 1617 m in the Massif de la Selle

(Los Arroyos), 1586 m in the Sierra de Neiba (Puesto Pirámide 204), 1129 m in the Sierra de Baoruco (Las Abejas), and 1037 m in the Sierra Martín García (El Limón). Times for collection or observation were between 0930 and 1630 h, and temperatures between 21°C (Los Arroyos) and 38°C (Loma Leonor, Río Bao).

Specimens: República Dominicana: Monte Cristi: 6 km W Copey, s.l., 1; 4 km NW Villa Vásquez, 61 m, 13; *Santiago Rodríguez:* Loma Leonor, 18 km SW Monción, 534 m, 1; *Santiago:* Río Bao, 8 km SE Montones Abajo, 488 m, 1; *La Vega:* 10 km NW La Horma, 1486 m, 1; *La Altagracia:* 1 km N Playa Bayahibe, s.l., 2; *Azua:* 2.5 km W, 6.6 km N Azua, 183 m, 1; 5 km S Peralta, 305 m, 18; *Independencia:* 4–7 km NE El Aguacate, 519–824 m, 11; *Barahona:* El Limón, summit, Sierra Martín García, 976–1037 m, 2; west slope, Sierra Martín García, 915–976 m, 5; west slope, Sierra Martín García, 640 m, 1; west slope, Sierra Martín García, 458–534 m, 2; 8 km NNE Polo, 793 m, 1; *Pedernales:* 5 km SW El Aguacate, 1464 m, 1.

Sight records: Monte Cristi: 6 km W Copey, s.l.—2 seen, 14.viii; 4 km NW Villa Vásquez, 61 m—1 seen, 5.vii: 4 km SE Villa Sinda—1 seen, 31.vii; 8 km SE Villa Sinda—1 seen, 18.x; *Dajabón:* 8 km S Restauración, 610 m—1 seen, 3.vii; Cañada Tirolís, just S Villa Anacaona, 458 m—1 seen, 3.vii; *Elías Piña:* La Laguna, 10 km S Comendador, 732 m—1 seen, 27.vii; 2 km NE Puesto Pirámide 204, 1586 m—1 seen, 16.vii; *Santiago:* Río Bao, 8 km SE Montones Abajo, 488 m—1 seen, 1.viii; 1 seen, 21.x; *La Vega:* 3 km SE Constanza, *ca.* 1220 m—1 seen, 2.vii: 10 km SE Constanza, 1647 m—2.vii; La Ciénaga, 915 m—1 seen, 8.viii; *Peravia:* 12 km S San José de Ocoa—1 seen, 29.ix; 3 km N San José de Ocoa, 458 m—1 seen, 28.vi; just S La Horma, 854 m—1 seen, 28.vi; *San Juan:* 9 km E Vallejuelo, 610 m—1 seen, 5.viii; 1 seen, 6.viii; just SE Sabana Alta, 305 m—1 seen, 29.vi; *Independencia:* just E La Descubierta, s.l.—1 seen, 25.vi; 14 km N Los Pinos, 1159 m—1 seen, 25.vi; *Barahona:* west slope, Sierra Martín García, 458 m—several seen, 25.vii: 8 km NNE Polo, 793 m—1 seen, 23.vi; Enriquillo, s.l.—1 seen, 10.viii; *Pedernales:* 27 km NE Cabo Rojo, 793 m—1 seen, 1.viii; Las Abejas, 12 km NW Aceitillar, 1129 m—1 seen, 29.vi; 1 seen, 27.vii; 5 km NE Los Arroyos, 1617 m—1 seen, 30.vi.

18. *Eunica tatila tatilista* Kaye, 1925

TL Rae Town, Jamaica.

FW males 22–28 mm, females 25–29 mm.

Hall (1925:187) recorded the capture of a pair of *E. t. tatilista* at Santiago, República Dominicana, and Brown and Heineman (1972:165) reported 4 sightings and records from Jamaica. Comstock (1944:469) knew of only 1 record from southwestern Puerto Rico. These statements suggest that *E. t. tatilista* is uncommon on the Greater Antilles. But Bates (1935a:176) examined 14 specimens from eastern Cuba and noted other specimens from Tánamo, Prov. de Holguín. All the above suggested to Riley (1975:71) that *E. t. tatilista,* on islands other than Cuba, "might well be . . . odd vagrants." However, *E. t. tatilista* is certainly resident and abundant (at times) on Hispaniola; it is ecologically very tolerant and occurs in the Dominican Republic in a wide span of elevations and habitat types.

Our first encounter with *E. t. tatilista* was on 25.vi.1980, when Gineika and I encountered very large numbers of this butterfly feeding on the fallen decaying fruits of an unidentified tree next to a dirt road leading into the valley of the Río Cumayasa. There, *E. t. tatilista* was accompanied by *H. a. diasia;* both species were also attracted to rotted mangoes. The *E. t. tatilista* not only landed on the ground with their wings closed but also, most especially when disturbed, perched nearby (within 1.5 m) on small bare fallen branches near the ground, from where they once more returned to the fallen fruits within less than 1 minute. The area (about 10×6 m) was literally a swirling mass of butterflies. *Eunica t. tatilista* was just as abundant 2 days later, but despite 6 visits to the same locality over the ensuing 3 years, we have never seen another individual there. Certainly this shows the local extreme variation in population density of *E. t. tatilista.*

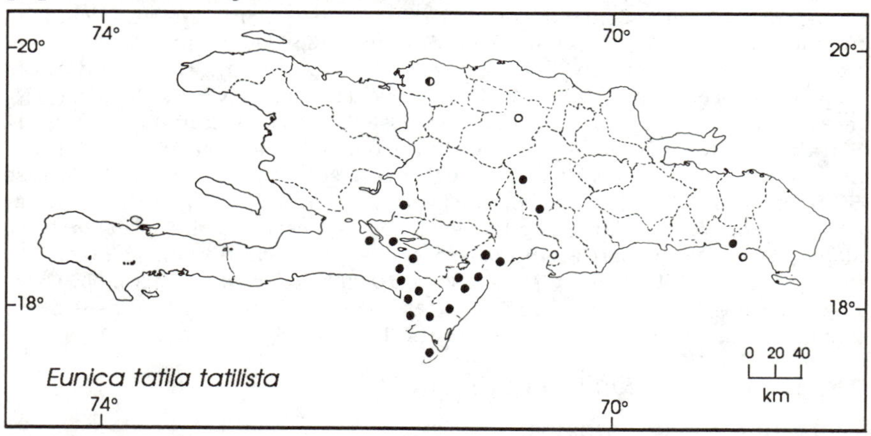

Another similar incident involves the road between Cabral and Polo on the northern slopes of the Sierra de Baoruco. At its lower extreme (Cabral), the road is lined on both sides by a tall (2 m) "hedge" of *Lantana ovatifolia;* the "hedge" extends for perhaps 2 km and is a favorite place for collecting a wide variety of butterflies. The "hedge" is backed by xeric forest. On 26.vi.1983, Raburn and I collected along this stretch of road. On only 1 tall *L. ovatifolia* did we find *E. t. tatilista* and *E. monima,* the latter the more abundant. Although only 4 *E. t. tatilista* were taken, there were as many as 20 flying about this particular plant. Both species of *Eunica* were "interested" only in this particular plant, and both were actively feeding on the orange blossoms. They were not distracted by our intrusion (collecting); although they flew a few meters away to land, they returned promptly to continue foraging. Hitting the bush with a net resulted in a flurry of activity, which immediately subsided, the butterflies once more landing on the flowers.

A third locality with a similar abundance of *E. t. tatilista* is on the southern slopes of the Massif de la Selle (Mencía). Here, a short abandoned road, again bordered by tall *L. ovatifolia*, passed along the edge of a *cafetal* including 1 mango tree, whose fruit was rotting on the ground (2–3.vii.1983). Including both days, Raburn and I secured 14 *E. t. tatilista* and could have taken many more. The butterflies were feeding actively on the *Lantana*, and many more were on the rotten mangoes, in the company of *H. a. diasia* and *S. s. stelenes*. *Eunica t. tatilista* outnumbered the 2 other species. The same behavior noted above at Río Cumayasa and Cabral occurred here. *Eunica t. tatilista* were very reluctant to leave either the mangoes or the flowers and, once disturbed, returned promptly to the food sources.

Although these examples are exceptional, *E. t. tatilista* has a broad ecological and geographic distribution, at least in the República Dominicana. The single Haitian specimen is from a mesic area adjacent to a spring near the shore of Etang Saumâtre. Habitats vary from extremely hot and xeric lowlands (Canoa, Cabo Rojo, Pedernales), oases (Villa Vásquez), a xeric forested ravine (Oviedo), to transitional forest (Barahona, El Aguacate), open mountain fields with *L. ovatifolia* (Polo), a *cafetal* (Enriquillo), open pasture (Los Arroyos, Constanza), the edge of mesic deciduous forest (Puesto Pirámide 204), and an open meadow with tall grasses in pines (La Nevera). As these widely divergent habitats suggest, *E. t. tatilista* occurs from sea level (Fond Parisien, Canoa, Cabo Rojo, Pedernales) to 2227 m (La Nevera). Specimens were collected between 0845 and 1700 h, at temperatures between 18°C (La Nevera) and 38°C (Cabo Rojo). Despite this broad elevational distribution, most specimens are from 915 m or less. Specimens of *E. t. tatilista* have been collected in June (31) and July (27), with 4 each in August and October, and 1 each in January and February. These numbers have little significance, since the large concentrations of *E. t. tatilista* account for the large midsummer totals. These are the first records of *E. t. tatilista* for Isla Catalina and Isla Beata.

We have taken *E. t. tatilista* on *L. ovatifolia* and rotted mango and other rotted fruits. Additionally, we have taken this species on *Cordia haitiensis* (La Furnia) in the Valle de Neiba at an irrigated roadside with abundant *Cordia*, on which the *E. t. tatilista* was feeding.

I have examined 3 female *E. t. tatilista* from the Florida Keys. These specimens are noticeably larger than Hispaniolan females and have FW lengths of 26–31 mm (in contrast to 25–29 in 39 Hispaniolan females). As Comstock (1944:469) pointed out in differentiating *E. t. tatilista* from *E. t. tatila* Herrich-Schäffer, none of my long series from Hispaniola has the unhw ocelli white-centered, a major character for distinguishing *E. t. tatilista.*

Specimens: Haiti: l'Ouest: 4 km SE Fond Parisien, s.l., 1; *República Dominicana: Elías Piña:* 2 km NE Puesto Pirámide 204, 1586 m, 1; *La Vega:* 1 km S Constanza, 1098 m, 2; La Nevera, 37 km SE Constanza, 2227 m, 1; *La Romana:* Río Cumayasa, 13.5 km W La Romana, 24; *Independencia:* La Furnia, s.l., 1; 4–7 km NE El Aguacate, 519–732 m, 2; *Barahona:* west slope, Sierra Martín García, s.l.—244 m, 1; 12 km ESE Canoa, s.l., 1; 7 km SW Cabral, 214 m, 4; 8 km NNE Polo, 793 m, 5; 2 km SW Barahona, 122 m, 1; 9 km NW Enriquillo, 671 m, 1; *Pedernales:* Mencía, 397 m, 14; 0.6 km SE Los Arroyos, 1098 m, 1; Cabo Rojo, s.l., 3; 23 km NE Cabo Rojo, 488 m, 1; 9 km SE Pedernales, s.l., 1; 17 km NW Oviedo, 183 m, 1; *Isla Beata:* 1.

Sight records: República Dominicana: Monte Cristi: 4 km NW Villa Vásquez, 61 m—1 seen, 31.vii; *Isla Catalina:* 1 seen– 14.viii.

19. *Eunica monima* Cramer, 1782

TL "Guinea"; more likely Suriname (Miller and Brown, 1981:181).

FW males 16–24 mm, females 19–25 mm.

Eunica monima was reported by Hall (1925:187) as "common" at Santiago and La Vega, República Dominicana. Schwartz (1983a: 32) reported 14 specimens from 6 Haitian localities and considered the species "rather uncommon." On Jamaica, Brown and Heineman (1972:167) stated that *Eunica monima* is taken much more frequently than is *E. tatila* and probably is a resident; still they only recorded *E. monima* from 4 localities. The species is apparently modestly common on Cuba and the Isla de la Juventud (Bates, 1935a:177), and Comstock (1944:470) cited Wolcott's (1915) record for Guánica in southwestern Puerto Rico as the only locality on that island.

Eunica monima is rather uncommon in Haiti but is less so in the República Dominicana; in the latter country it seems to be absent from broad areas. Most records are from lowland xeric regions, but it also occurs in lowland mesic (Santo Domingo) and xeric (Playa Bayahibe, La Romana, 3 km NW Enriquillo) forest. In wooded situations, these butterflies act in the manner of *Polygonus leo*, and in fact the 2 species often confuse even the seasoned collector. Both are most frequently met just within the edges of woods, along paths and roads; when disturbed, they fly rapidly and land on the underside of leaves, where they rest immobile until disturbed once again. Other than in wooded areas, *E. monima* frequents open and grassy areas (Carrefour Marmelade, Boutilliers Road, Paillant, Cabo Rojo), *caféières* and *cafetales* (6.6 km SW Paillant, Enriquillo, Polo, 9 km NW Enriquillo, Cabeza de Agua), open *Acacia* woods (Oviedo, Tres Charcos, Canoa, Boca de Cachón), scrubby woods (Punta Caucedo, Boca Chica), pinewoods (Aceitillar), and a hotel garden (Pétionville). These are the first records of *E. monima* from Isla Saona, Isla Beata, and Isla Catalina.

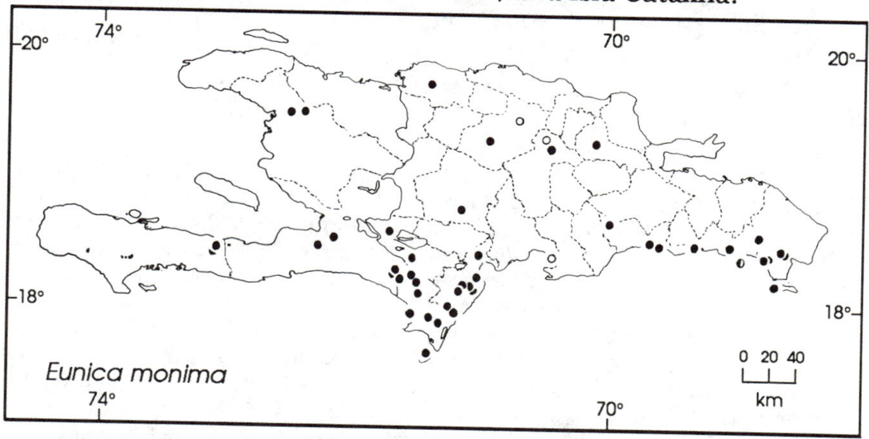

Elevational distribution, much lower than that for *E. t. tatilista*, is from sea level (Playa Bayahibe, Boca Chica, Andrés, Tres Ojos, Punta Caucedo, Boca de Cachón, Canoa, Cabo Rojo, Isla Saona) to 1129 m (Aceitillar). Other than 52 specimens from Isla Saona from January, most specimens have been collected in June (67), with 48 in July, 31 in August, 5 in February, 3 in October, and 1 each in May, November, and December. The long series from various localities near Mano Juan on Isla Saona, taken by Henderson in i.1984, is unique. *Eunica monima* was very abundant there; yet in iii–iv.1984, we saw no individuals of this species on the Hispaniolan main-island.

Times of collection were between 0900 and 1750 h, and temperatures between 28°C (Polo, Río Chavón) and 42°C (La Romana). We have taken *E. monima* feeding on *Lantana ovatifolia* on 4 occasions (Paillant, Cabo Rojo, Cabral, Mencía); we have not seen *E. monima* attracted to rotted fruits, a habit of *E. t. tatilista*. I have already noted the attraction of both species of *Eunica* to a particular *Lan-*

tana plant (Cabral). In scrubby woods at Boca Chica, several *E. monima* were attracted to a member of the Rutaceae, presumably an "escaped" lime tree, without fruit or flowers; the butterflies landed repeatedly on the lower (1.5 m) leaves.

In vi.1986, *E. monima* was extremely abundant at Cabo Rojo; there were literally thousands on the wing during 9–15.vi. Many were feeding eagerly on White Mangrove (*Laguncularia racemosa;* Combretaceae) flowers along the sheltered (from the wind) inner edges of extensive mangrove swamps. By the time of a return visit to Cabo Rojo on 25.vii–2.viii.1986, the population of *E. monima* was back once more to an occasional individual. During the period of abundance (which extended both west to Pedernales and east to about midway between Cabo Rojo and Oviedo) I saw a Northern Mockingbird (*Mimus polyglottus orpheus* Linnaeus) catch a *E. monima* on the wing above the highway.

Specimens: Haiti: l'Artibonite: 1.6 km E Carrefour Marmelade, 854 m, 1; 4.6 km E Les Poteaux, 183 m, 1; *l'Ouest:* Pétionville, 458 m, 2; Boutilliers Road, 732–854 m, 3; Boutilliers Road, 1.8–2.1 km W Kenscoff road, 793–885 m, 1; *Sud:* 2.9 km SW Paillant, 671 m, 5; 6.6 km SW Paillant, 793 m, 1; *República Dominicana: Monte Cristi:* 4 km NW Villa Vásquez, 61 m, 4; *Santiago:* Río Bao, 8 km SE Montones Abajo, 488 m, 1; *La Vega:* Buena Vista, 11 km NE Jarabacoa, 740 m, 1; *Duarte:* 12 km SE San Francisco de Macorís, 1; *La Altagracia:* 0.5–3.5 km W Boca de Yuma, 1; 2–3 km W Boca de Yuma, 1; 2.5 km SE Playa Bayahibe, s.l., 1; 1 km N Playa Bayahibe, s.l., 3; 16 km NE La Romana, 61 m, 21; *La Romana;:* Río Cumayasa, 13.5 km W La Romana, 15; *San Pedro de Macorís:* 13 km SE Boca Chica, s.l., 2; *Dist. Nac.:* Punta Caucedo, 2 km W, 2 km S Andrés, s.l., 11; Tres Ojos, s.l., 1; 30 km NW Santo Domingo, 122 m, 5; *San Juan:* 9 km E Vallejuelo, 610 m, 3; *Independencia:* 1 km S Boca de Cachón, s.l., 2; 4–7 km NE El Aguacate, 519–732 m, 4; *Barahona:* 8 km SE Canoa, s.l., 1; Polo, 702 m, 1; 8 km NNE Polo, 793 m, 2; 2 km SW Barahona, 122 m, 3; 5 km SE, 3 km W Barahona, 183 m, 2; 5 km SE, 6.4 km W Barahona, 488 m, 2; 3 km NW Enriquillo, 244 m, 3; 9 km SW Enriquillo, 671 m, 3; *Pedernales:* Cabo Rojo, s.l., 19; 23 km NE Cabo Rojo, 488 m, 3; Mencía, 397 m, 11; 3 km N Cabeza de Agua, 305 m, 1; 3 km SE Los Arroyos, 976 m, 2; Las Abejas, 12 km NW Aceitillar, 1129 m, 2; 1 km N Aceitillar, 1281 m, 1; 17 km NW Oviedo, 183 m, 4; 4 km NW Tres Charcos, 2; *Isla Saona:* 52 (40 MPM); *Isla Beata:* 6.

Sight record: República Dominicana: Isla Catalina: 1 seen 1–4.viii.

20. *Dynamine egaea zetes* Ménétriés, 1834

TL Haiti.

FW males 18–21 mm, females 18–21 mm.

Of the trio of small limenitidines, *D. e. zetes* is the least common and least understood. Hall (1925:187) did not collect the species, and Schwartz (1983a:31) examined 25 Haitian specimens, all but 1 from the same locality. Bates (1935a:179) reported 31 specimens of *D. e. calais* Bates from central and western Cuba, and Brown and Heineman (1972:162–63) listed *D. e. egaea* Hübner from throughout Jamaica but considered the species local.

On Hispaniola, *D. e. zetes* inhabits situations that are most often ecotonal, and thus not simple to classify—shrubby roadsides (Boutilliers Road, Comendador, Vallejuelo), more or less cutover mesic woodland margins (Polo; 5 km SE, 3 km W Barahona), semixeric woodlands (8 km SW Barahona), and tall roadside shrubs (Mencía). The species may be encountered almost anywhere, although it appears to be absent over broad areas of Hispaniola, and we have never seen it in Haiti north of the Cul de Sac plain nor on the Tiburon Peninsula west of Pétionville. In the República Dominicana, *D. e. zetes* seems to be absent from the eastern portion of the country (east of Santo Domingo) and from the uplands of the Cordillera Central, although it occurs along the periphery of that range (Buena Vista, Río Bao, Loma Leonor) in mixed pine-deciduous forest. We have also encountered *D. e. zetes* along the edges of transitional woods (Cabo Rojo) and in clearings within mesic forests (El Cercado, 15 km S Comendador).

Dynamine e. zetes is most often seen as isolated 1 or 2 individuals, but on occasions (Boutilliers Road, 11 km S Comendador) one happens upon local aggregations of these butterflies. At the former locality, we took 8 specimens on 14.viii.1978, and at the latter, 11 specimens on 26.vii.1981; these represent the largest numbers of *D. e. zetes* taken on single days at 1 locality.

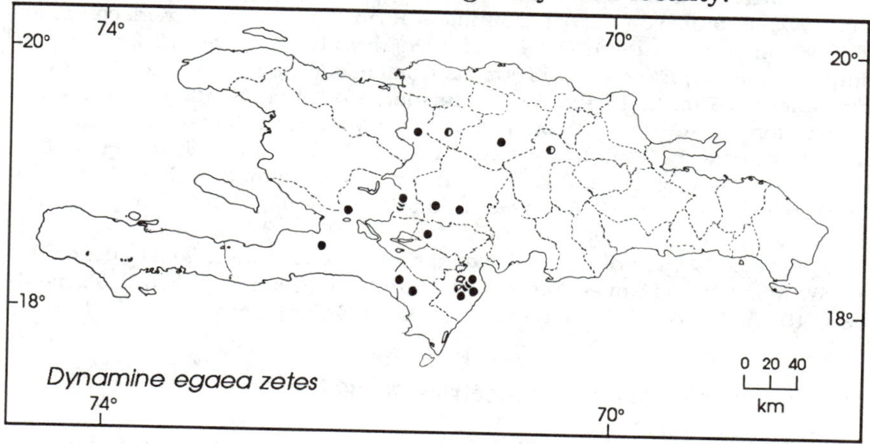

Dynamine egaea zetes

Although Brown and Heineman (1972:160) considered *D. e. egaea* to inhabit the "lower parts" of Jamaica, *D. e. zetes* does not occur on Hispaniola below 183 m (5 km SE, 3 km W Barahona);

the upper elevational extreme is 976 m (Comendador). We have never taken *D. e. zetes* in the uplands of the Massif de la Selle or Massif de la Hotte, despite its presence on the front ranges (Morne l'Hôpital). In general, it seems that *D. e. zetes* is a butterfly of moderate elevations only.

We have taken the species feeding on *Daucus* sp. (Boutilliers Road) and on *Lantana ovatifolia* (11 km S Comendador). On 2 occasions (Terre Rouge, 8 km NE Polo), *D. e. zetes* was encountered in an open montane *Cajanus cajan* field, a most unlikely place to see this butterfly of shrubby areas. At Neiba, a single male was taken while drinking from the sand and mud at a river's edge.

Brown and Heineman (1972:161) noted the habit of *D. e. zetes* of congregating in numbers about trees (tamarind, fustic, and Spanish elm). We have observed this phenomenon once at Río Bao, where several *D. e. zetes* were flying about a *Eugenia axillaris* (Myrtaceae) with several *A. d. amphitoe;* the tree was not in flower.

Most specimens and observations are from July (43), with 18 from August, 2 each from February and September, 3 from October, and 1 from December. The absence of June records is striking, suggesting that the major time of eclosion is in July-August, rather than earlier in the summer, and that some individuals persist through the autumn and winter months. Times of collection were between 0830 and 1715 h, at temperatures between 24°C (Comendador) and 37°C (Río Bao).

Specimens: Haiti: l'Ouest: 3.8 km N Terre Rouge, 519 m, 1; Boutilliers Road, 732–915 m, 13 (2 FSM); Boutilliers Road, 1.8–2.1 km W Kenscoff road, 763–885 m, 13; *República Dominicana: Dajabón:* Los Cerezos, 12 km NW Río Limpio, 580 m, 1; *Elías Piña:* 11 km SE Comendador, 824 m, 14; 14 km S Comendador, 976 m, 2; 15 km S Comendador, 976 m, 1; *Santiago:* Río Bao, 8 km SE Montones Abajo, 488 m, 1; *San Juan:* 4 km E El Cercado, 702 m, 1; 9 km E Vallejuelo, 610 m, 2; *Baoruco:* 11 km N Neiba, 1; *Barahona:* Polo, 702 m, 1; 8 km SW Barahona, 366 m, 2; 12 km SW Barahona, 427 m, 5; 20 km SW Barahona, 1098 m, 1; 5 km SE, 3 km W Barahona, 183–397 m, 2; *Pedernales:* 23 km NE Cabo Rojo, 488 m, 5; Mencía, 397 m, 1.

Sight records: República Dominicana; Santiago Rodríguez: Loma Leonor, 18 km SW Monción, 534 m—1 seen, 3.viii; *Barahona:* 8 km NNE Polo, 793 m—1 seen, 10.vii: *La Vega:* Buena Vista, 11 km NE Jarabacoa, 640 m—1 seen, 6.viii.

21. *Archimestra teleboas* Ménétriés, 1832

TL Haiti.

FW males 19–25 mm, females 21–26 mm.

Of the 3 Hispaniolan small limenitidines (*Archimestra teleboas, Lucinia sida, Dynamine egaea*), *A. teleboas* is the most abundant and widely distributed. Hall (1925:188) considered *A. teleboas* "common in the pine forests above La Vega" in the República Dominicana and noted that it flies "among small bushes close to the ground," a precise summary of the habits of this butterfly. Schwartz (1983a:31–32) reported 71 specimens from 6 localities in southern Haiti and considered the species "locally common." Additional material from the República Dominicana (and Haiti) indicates that the latter statement is accurate. At those localities where *A. teleboas* occurs, it is usually quite abundant; at those where it does not occur, it is simply absent. This is all the more surprising in that its elevational and ecological distributions are broad; one simply does not know, when collecting in a new area, if he will find *A. teleboas* or not. There are no obvious clues as to its potential presence or absence. A case in point is the Sierra de Neiba, where the species is known from the north face of the north range and the south face of the south range but is absent from perfectly suitable (to human eyes) areas on both ranges.

Although Hall (and Riley, 1975:70, following Hall) stated that the species was found in pine forest, we have taken *A. teleboas* only once in that habitat (35 km NE Cabo Rojo). Most often, when pines are involved, *A. teleboas* inhabits mixed pine-hardwood forests or stands (Río Limpio, Loma Leonor, Buena Vista, La Vega); at Las Abejas (11 km NW Aceitillar), *A. teleboas* occurs in a narrow hardwood runoff ravine through pinewoods, as well as in mesic hardwoods at 12 km NW Aceitillar. But almost any other forest type may be inhabited: mesic forest (Comendador, Los Quemados, Río Bao, Sosúa, Peralta, El Cercado, El Limón, 12 km SW Barahona), *cafetales* (Cabeza de Agua), xeric woods (Fond Parisien, 7 km NE Vallejuelo, 12 km SW Barahona, Banano, Oviedo), xeric woods with *Acacia* (9 km E Vallejuelo, Tres Charcos), and transitional forests (El Aguacate, Cabo Rojo). *Archimestra teleboas* is also often very common on open montane roadsides, especially those with shrubby growth (Boutilliers Road, 14 km S Comendador, Jarabacoa, Mencía); we have also taken it in *Syzygium jambos* forest (Loma Leonor) and in an open montane *Cajanus cajan* field (Terre Rouge). In contrast to these localities with arborescent or shrubby growth are an open bare, rocky, and xeric mountainside (S Mirebalais) on the south face of the Massif du Trou-d'Eau and behind an open beach (Belle Anse), within sight of the ocean. At the other extreme are individuals in the arid scrub at Cabo Rojo; *A. teleboas* is not common there but is a regular inhabitant of these rigorous areas. Wherever *A. teleboas* occurs, it has a leisurely flight, and when pursued, it flies deliberately into shrubby and bushy plants, dexterously passes among them, then comes once more out into the open. There is rarely any hurry, and most individuals are rather easily netted.

Although *Lantana ovatifolia* is a common plant at many localities where *A. teleboas* occurs, we have never seen the butterfly foraging on it, rotted fruit, or animal matter. But *A. teleboas* takes nectar from *Daucus* sp. and *Cordia* sp. (Boutilliers Road), from *Croton linearis* (2 km NE Cabo Rojo), *C. barahonensis* (Vallejuelo), and *Ageratum conyzoides* (Vallejuelo, twice).

Most specimens have been taken in July (141), with 78 in August, 33 in June, and 1–7 in January, February, March, April, May, September, October, November, and December. The contrast between the high July and low June numbers is striking and suggests strongly that July is the major month of eclosion for *A. teleboas.*

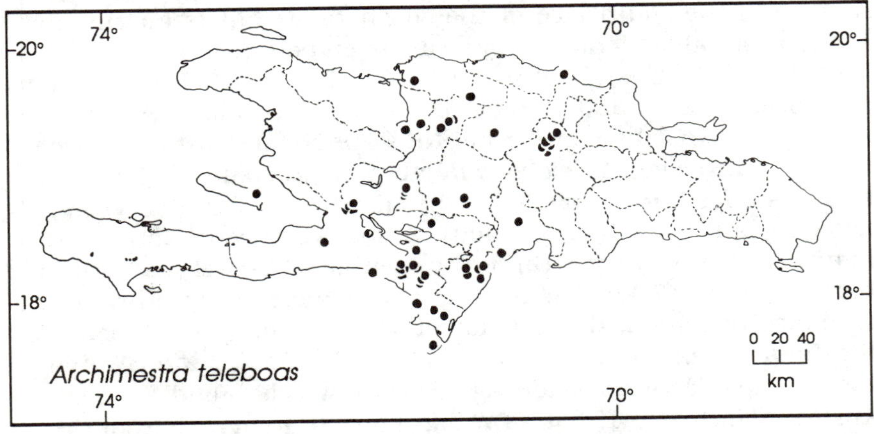

Collection times for *A. teleboas* were between 0830 and 1715 h, with temperatures between 24°C (Comendador) and 42°C (Mencía). Elevations were between sea level (Belle Anse, Copey, Cabo Rojo) and 1220 m in the Sierra de Baoruco (35 km NE Cabo Rojo, Las Abejas), 1037 m in the Sierra Martín García (El Limón), 976 m in the Sierra de Neiba (Comendador), and 915 m in the front ranges of the Massif de la Selle (Boutilliers Road). The highest elevation in the Cordillera Central is 702 m (Río Limpio); in that range, *A. teleboas* is completely absent from the interior forests, either pine or deciduous (Constanza, La Ciénaga). The same may be said for the Massif de la Selle (Forêt des Pins), where the species is not known. These absences are often puzzling; we have not seen *A. teleboas*, for example, in the Massif du Nord (Carrefour Marmelade). There are no records for the Tiburon Peninsula west of Pétionville, despite apparently fine habitats at Béloc, Découzé, Paillant, Cavaillon, and Camp Perrin. All these absences cannot be attributed to our visiting a particular area at a time other than July, when *A. teleboas* is at its most abundant.

This is the first record of *A. teleboas* from Île de la Gonâve, whence I have 1 specimen, taken near sea level, and from Isla Beata. The Gonâve specimen is a male and has a very short fw measurement. It is also distinctive in the up pattern. In *A. teleboas*, the pattern is white on a brown ground. On the upfw, there is a white postdiscal band from the costal margin to the cell end and M2, followed by an isolated white spot in M2-M3 (see Riley, 1975:pl. 6, fig. 5, for an excellent painting of this and other details). This spot is always large and well developed, about one-half as wide as the posterior end of the postdiscal white bar; in the Gonâve specimen the spot is tiny but still obvious. On the postdiscal area and abutting on the inner margin in Cu1–2A, there is a large white spot, composed of 2 sections, the anterior in Cu1-Cu2, the posterior in Cu2–2A. The latter is always much shorter than the former, and thus the white spot is directed marginally, toward the anal angle of the fw. In the Gonâve specimen, the entire white figure is circular, because the posterior portion of the spot is equally as large as the anterior. On the uphw, there is a discal white bar extending from Rs to 2A, composed of a series of white spots, of which the spot in M3-Cu1 is displaced marginally and separated from its fellow on both sides by a wider band of brown ground color. In the Gonâve specimen, this M3-Cu1 spot is not only not displaced marginally, but it is contiguous with its 2 fellows in the adjacent spaces, thus giving not only a more regular but also a more continuously white band on the uphw. Finally, the veins in the Gonâve specimen are not scaled in brown (as they are in main-island specimens), and all white figures involving areas in more than 1 space are not divided by brown lines. No mainland Hispaniolan specimen has any of these characters, either alone or in concert. I suspect that the Gonâve population is distinctive, but on the basis of only 1 specimen (despite its dissimilarity to all other specimens), it seems improvident to name it.

Specimens: Haiti: l'Ouest: 20.0 km S Mirebalais, 580 m, 4; 3.8 km N Terre Rouge, 519–534 m, 5; 1.3 km N Terre Rouge, 580 m, 4; 2.9 km S Terre Rouge, 488 m, 1; Boutilliers Road, 732–915 m, 39 (3 FSM); Boutilliers Road, 1.8–2.1 km E Kenscoff road, 854–885 m, 19; 6 km E Belle Anse, 3; *Île de la Gonâve:* Anse-à-Galets, 1; *República Dominicana: Monte Cristi:* 6 km W Copey, s.l., 1; *Dajabón:* 16 km NW Río Limpio, 702 m, 1; 8.4 km S Restauración, 580 m, 1; *Elías Piña:* 11 km S Comendador, 824 m, 3; 14 km S Comendador, 976 m, 2; 15 km S Comendador, 976 m, 3; *Valverde:* 3 km W Los Quemados, 122 m, 1;

Santiago Rodríguez: Loma Leonor, 19 km SW Monción, 625 m, 5; Loma Leonor, 18 km SW Monción, 534 m, 8; 4.7 km SW Loma Leonor, 732 m, 2; *Santiago:* Río Bao, 8 km SE Montones Abajo, 488 m, 5; *Puerto Plata:* 9 km SE Sosúa, 15 m, 15; *La Vega:* 2 km S La Vega, 366 m, 3; Buena Vista, 11 km NE Jarabacoa, 640 m, 6; Jarabacoa, 530 m, 1; 5 km SE Jarabacoa, 595 m, 4; 6 km SE Jarabacoa, *ca.* 610 m, 1; *ca.* 11 km S Jarabacoa, 640 m, 1; *Azua:* 5 km S Peralta, 305 m, 18; *San Juan:* 7 km NE Vallejuelo, 671 m, 3; 9 km E Vallejuelo, 671 m, 17; 7 km E El Cercado, 854 m, 6; *Baoruco:* 11 km N Neiba, 519 m, 1; *Independencia:* 4–7 km NE El Aguacate, 519–824 m, 19; *Barahona:* El Limón, summit, Sierra Martín García, 976–1037 m, 1; west slope, Sierra Martín García, 915 m, 6; west slope, Sierra Martín García, 763 m, 2; west slope, Sierra Martín García, 610 m, 5; 12 km SW Barahona, 427 m, 1; 2 km SW Barahona, 122 m, 2; 12 km NNE Polo, 534 m, 1; 10 km SSW Cabral, 427 m, 1; 5 km SE, 3 km W Barahona, 183 m, 11; *Pedernales:* 2 km N Banano, 244 m, 8; 1 km SE Banano, 183 m, 1; 2 km SW Mencía, 336 m, 1; 1 km N Cabeza de Agua, 305 m, 3; 2 km NE Cabo Rojo, s.l., 1; 23 km NE Cabo Rojo, 488 m, 11; 26 km NE Cabo Rojo, 732 m, 3; 35 km NE Cabo Rojo, 1220 m, 1; Las Abejas, 11 km NW Aceitillar, 1220 m, 1; Las Abejas, 12 km NW Aceitillar, 1129 m, 2; 17 km NW Oviedo, 183 m, 9; 4 km NW Tres Charcos, 1; *Isla Beata:* 2.

Sight record: Haiti; l'Ouest: 2 km SE Fond Parisien, s.l.—1 seen, 30.iv.

22. *Lucinia sida torrebia* Ménétriés, 1832

TL Haiti.

FW males 18–24 mm, females 21–25 mm.

Lucinia Hübner is an endemic Antillean genus of nymphalids with 4 taxa: *cadma* on Jamaica, *sida* Hübner on Cuba and the Isla de la Juventud (Holland, 1916:492), *torrebia* Ménétriés from Hispaniola, and *albomaculata* Rindge from the Bahama Islands (Eleuthera, Long, Andros, San Salvador, Rum; Rindge, 1955:10; Clench, 1977a:277; 1977b:184; Elliott, Riley, and Clench, 1980:123). Brown and Heineman (1972:167–68) considered *Lucinia* monotypic and used the combination *L. c. cadma* for the Jamaican population, thereby implying *L. c. sida*, *L. c. torrebia*, and *L. c. albomaculata* for the remaining populations. They commented that there were considerable differences between taxa but were uncertain as to the nature of the relationships between at least *cadma*, *sida*, and *torrebia*. Holland (1916:492) had stated that there were no differences (other than size) between his 3 Isla de la Juventud examples and Jamaican *L. cadma;* he referred the specimens to that species without using a trinomen. Riley (1975:70–71), however, regarded *L. cadma* as a distinct species and grouped *torrebia* and *albomaculata* under *L. sida*. I have examined 1 male *L. s. sida*, and it is distinct in up pattern from most (but not all) *L. s. torrebia*. I follow Riley here, until study of these small butterflies can be undertaken; the case for conspecificity between all named populations seems weak.

Hall (1925:188) reported taking several specimens near La Vega, República Dominicana, and Schwartz (1983a:32) noted 9 specimens from 2 Haitian localities and 2 sight records. From the above, it seems that *L. s. torrebia* is uncommon. The species is widely distributed on Hispaniola, and the present records from Île de la Gonâve and Isla Beata are the first for those islands. *Lucinia s. torrebia* may be locally common (23 km NE Cabo Rojo), but at most localities one encounters only 1 or a very few individuals.

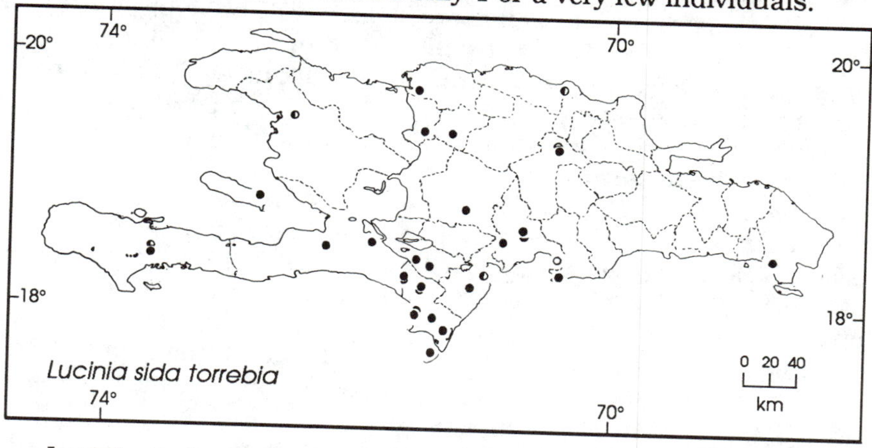

Lucinia s. torrebia is primarily a butterfly of xeric areas (Les Poteaux, Copey, Tábara Abajo, Azua, Las Calderas, Vallejuelo, Puerto Escondido, Oviedo, Cabo Rojo). But these butterflies are also found in transitional forest (Peralta, 23 km NE Cabo Rojo, El Aguacate), open mountainsides (Boutilliers Road, Cavaillon, Polo) and mixed pine-deciduous forests (Río Limpio, Loma Leonor, Buena Vista). The elevational distribution is from sea level (Copey, Playa Bayahibe, Las Calderas, Barahona, Cabo Rojo) to 915 m (Boutilliers Road). Most specimens and observations are from lower elevations and are from July (54), with 18 from June, 14 from August, 4 from February, 3 each from January and December, 2 each from April and May, and 1 each from October and November.

A stay at the Alcoa Exploration Company's senior staff house at Cabo Rojo between 14.vii and 20.vii.1981 allowed an unforeseen opportunity to make observations on the habits of *L. s. torrebia.* The species is common at that locality. Individuals were taken as early as 0815 h. Several were seen on 3 occasions actively flying and then landing (with wings closed) on ornamental plants at the guest house or on the brick or stone walls of the guest house just at dusk (1915–1936 h). These seemed to be "seaching" for a place to spend the night, and in fact Schwartz took by hand a butterfly sleeping on the wall of an outside corridor at 0400 h. Another individual was taken in the billiard room at Cabo Rojo, on the inside of a screen at 0830 h, and another *L. s. torrebia* was found dead on the floor of this same room; these butterflies had passed the night inside the building.

Lucinia s. torrebia habitually flies about 1.5 m or less above the ground, landing on bare branches of shrubs or trees up to about 3 m above the ground. The wings are closed, and the vivid unhw pattern is conspicuous. The butterflies rest immobile until disturbed; on several occasions we have seen them walking slowly along bare branches after landing. Clench (1977b:184) noted the habit of landing on branches on Andros Island in the Bahamas. His individuals were in scrub or at the edges of scrubby growth. On Eleuthera Island, Clench (1977a:277) noted that several *L. s. albomaculata* were attracted to trees at the edge of a golf course. Elliott, Riley, and Clench (1980:123) commented on the association of these butterflies with mangroves, an association never observed on Hispaniola.

Times of collection and observation of *L. c. torrebia* were from 0815 to 1936 h, and temperatures between 26°C (Vallejuelo) and 38°C (Las Calderas, Barahona).

Lucinia s. torrebia regularly feeds on *Lantana ovatifolia* (Boutilliers Road, Vallejuelo, Polo, 23 km NE Cabo Rojo). We have taken these butterflies feeding on *Croton barahonensis* and *Ageratum conyzoides* (both at Vallejuelo, the latter on 2 occasions); *A. conyzoides* was also used at Azua and 21 km NE Cabo Rojo. At El Aguacate, 1 individual was taken from a pile of fresh cow dung.

Specimens: Haiti: l'Ouest: 4 km SE Fond Parisien, s.l., 1; Boutilliers Road, 732–815 m, 7; Boutilliers Road, 1.2 km W Kenscoff road, 763 m, 1; *Sud:* 16.3 km N Cavaillon, 488 m, 1; *Île de la Gonâve:* Anse-à-Galets, 2; *República Dominicana: Monte Cristi:* 6 km W Copey, s.l., 1; *Dajabón:* 16 km NW Río Limpio, 702 m, 1; *Santiago Rodríguez:* Loma Leonor, 18 km SW Monción, 534 m, 1; *La Vega:* Buena Vista, 11 km NE Jarabacoa, 640 m, 1; *La Altagracia:* 2.5 km SE Playa Bayahibe, s.l., 1; *Peravia:* Las Calderas, s.l., 1; *Azua:* Tábara Abajo, 1; 2.5 km W, 6.6 km N Azua, 183 m, 7; 5 km S Peralta, 305 m, 2; *San Juan:* 9 km E Vallejuelo, 610 m, 14; *Independencia:* 4–7 km NE El Aguacate, 519–824 m, 2; 0.6 km NW Puerto Escondido, 519 m, 2; *Barahona:* 8 km NNE Polo, 793 m, 6; *Pedernales:* Mencía, 397 m, 1; 1 km SE Banano, 488 m, 1; Cabo Rojo, s.l., 9; 2 km NE Cabo Rojo, s.l., 2; 21 km NE Cabo Rojo, 427 m, 1; 23 km NE Cabo Rojo, 488 m, 17; 26 km NE Cabo Rojo, 732 m, 3; 17 km NW Oviedo, 183 m, 6; 1.3 km S Tres Charcos, 1; *Isla Beata:* 1.

Sight records: Haiti: l'Artibonite: 4.6 km E Les Poteaux—1 seen, 23.vii; *República Dominicana: Monte Cristi:* 6 km W Copey, s.l.—2 seen, 16.v; *Puerto*

Plata: 9 km SE Sosúa, 16 m—1 seen, 2.viii; *Barahona:* Barahona, s.l.—1 seen, 10.iv; *Azua:* Tábara Abajo—2 seen, 16.ii.

23. *Biblis hyperia hyperia* Cramer, 1779

TL St. Thomas, U. S. Virgin Islands.

FW males 32–36 mm, females 33–38 mm.

Biblis hyperia is widespread on the continental mainland from Mexico to Paraguay. In the West Indies, *B. hyperia* occurs from several Lesser Antillean islands north to the Virgin Islands and Puerto Rico. Riley (1975:77) noted that the species is rare on Hispaniola, doubtless following Hall (1925:188), who stated that *B. hyperia* there is "rarer than in most of the islands." This statement is equivocal. In its Hispaniolan range, *B. hyperia* is not at all uncommon.

The species is unknown from Haiti, but in the eastern República Dominicana, *B. hyperia* occurs from Playa Bayahibe west to Santo Domingo, and inland as far as 30 km NW that city, and Hato Damas in Prov. de San Cristóbal, and Las Lagunas, Prov. de Sánchez Ramírez. Most records are coastal or nearly so. In addition, *B. hyperia* occurs near the northern coast in the *haitises* SE of Sosúa. We have never seen *B. hyperia* between these 2 general regions. Even the Hato Damas and Las Lagunas records are isolates. Thus the butterfly is not known from the fine xeric canopy forests near Punta Cana in the extreme east, nor from the interior forests and pseudoforests northwest across the República Dominicana. There is a female from Ceiba, Quema, Samaná (14.iv.1979), in the MNHNSD, but we have never seen the species in that area. In fact, the sight record from 30 km NW Santo Domingo is for a single individual seen on 19.vi.1983, despite 6 visits to this locality since 1981. This suggests that *B. hyperia* may still be actively invading Hispaniola and that it has only very recently reached this unusually far inland locality. In any event, the extreme eastern distribution of *B. hyperia* on Hispaniola denotes a relatively recent arrival of this species from Puerto Rico.

But in 1985 we for the first time saw and collected *B. hyperia* at Peralta, some 80 km W of the previously westernmost record. In the same year, we took specimens at Neiba, 60 km W of Peralta, on the southern slopes of the Sierra de Neiba, where *B. hyperia* is well established and common. These 2 western localities seem to confirm an increasingly broad extension from eastern Hispaniola. The 2 sites are (apparently) isolates, perhaps the result of vagrant or wind-wafted gravid females.

Although Riley (1975:76–77) and Brown and Heineman

(1972:56) used only binomials for this species in the Antilles, I consider the Antillean populations (I have examined material from Puerto Rico, Saba, St. Eustatius, and Montserrat as well as Hispaniola) distinctly different from those of the mainland (*B. h. aganisa* Boisduval). Howe (1975:125) noted that *B. hyperia* varies throughout its range "in the placement of the submarginal red band" on the uphw. Comparison of his painting (pl. 15, fig. 8) and the photograph in Pyle (1981:fig. 680) with our Hispaniolan material shows that in *B. h. aganisa* the red band is much straighter and conforms less to the curvature of the hw margin than in West Indian specimens. This results in a much broader black area between the band and the hw margin. In the Antillean populations, the band follows the hw curvature and the black area between the band and the hw margin is more uniform in width. Accordingly, I consider the Antillean populations *B. h. hyperia*.

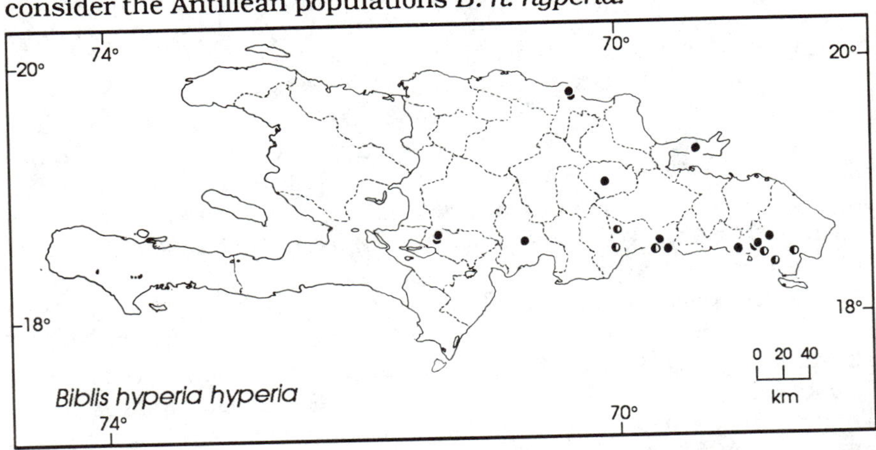

Biblis hyperia hyperia

Biblis h. hyperia is associated with xeric or mesic forest edges, paths, and roadways, especially if these openings are shrubby or bushy. The butterflies fly slowly and deliberately, yet they can avoid the collector's net by moving into the narrow spaces between bushes and saplings and gradually drifting out of range. At Sosúa, *B. h. hyperia* is regularly associated with *Tournefortia hirsutissima* (2 occasions) and at Peralta and Neiba with *Lantana ovatifolia*, but we have never seen these butterflies using these (or any other flowers) as a food source elsewhere. Nor have we seen them on rotting plant or animal material. While feeding, *B. h. hyperia* vibrates its wings.

The month of greatest abundance on Hispaniola is June (37), with 13 in August, 11 in July, 10 in February, 7 each in March and April, and 1 in May. I also have 2 specimens from January; these are the only ones seen in that month, and both are badly worn and tattered. There seems to be an early summer peak in abundance of *B. h. hyperia*, although Comstock (1944:461) stated that *B. h. hyperia* flies during the entire year (no records for September, October, or November) on Puerto Rico and the Virgin Islands.

Elevational distribution is from sea level (Punta Caucedo) to 519 m (11 km N Neiba). On Puerto Rico, Wisor took a *B. h. hyperia* W of Divisoria at 1220 m on 5.ix, far higher than any Hispaniolan records; this was the only *B. h. hyperia* seen in 2 weeks on Puerto Rico, where the butterfly is abundant, at least in December.

Times of collection were between 0925 and 1700 h, and temperatures between 29°C (Sosúa) and 38°C (Río Cumayasa).

Specimens: República Dominicana: Puerto Plata: 9 km SE Sosúa, 15 m, 9; 11 km SE Sosúa, 13 m, 1; *Sánchez Ramírez:* 1 km NE Las Lagunas, 183 m, 1; *Samaná:* Ceiba, Quema, 1 (MNHNSD); *La Altagracia:* Río Chavón, 10 km NE La Romana, 2; 16 km NE La Romana, 61 m, 32; *La Romana:* 3 km N Altos de Chavón, Río Chavón, 1 (MPM); Río Cumayasa, 13.5 km W La Romana, 9: *Dist. Nac.:* Punta Caucedo, 2 km W, 2 km S Andrés, s.l., 10: 5 km S San Isidro, 6; *Azua:* 5 km S Peralta, 305 m, 4; *Baoruco:* 9 km N Neiba, 366 m, 4; 11 km N Neiba, 519 m, 2;

Sight records: República Dominicana: La Altagracia: 2–3 km W Boca de Yuma—1 seen, 25.vii; 1 km N Playa Bayahibe—2 seen, 11.vi; *La Romana:* Río Chavón, 8 km SE La Romana, s.l.—1 seen, 11.vii; *Dist. Nac.:* Tres Ojos, s.l.—1 seen, 25.vi; 30 km NW Santo Domingo, 122 m—1 seen, 19.vi; *San Cristóbal:* 2 km N Hato Damas, 122 m—1 seen, 18.iv.

24. *Hamadryas amphichloe diasia* Fruhstorfer, 1916

TL Puerto Rico and Haiti.

FW males 29–36 mm, females 33–38 mm.

Jenkins recently (1983) revised the genus *Hamadryas;* he used the name *Hamadryas amphichloe diasia* for the Hispaniolan species that had been previously called *H. februa diasia* (Riley, 1975:67; Brown and Heineman, 1972:152) or *H. ferox diasia* (Comstock, 1944:471). I follow Jenkins herein.

Before proceeding, it is well to dispose of the "Haitian" record of *Hamadryas feronia* Linnaeus (Riley, 1975:67). Riley attributed *H. feronia insularis* Fruhstorfer to "Haiti" and St. Lucia in the Lesser Antilles and assumed that both were records of vagrants. Jenkins (1983:59) examined the St. Lucia specimen and considered it *H. feronia feronia* (rather than *H. f. farinulenta* Fruhstorfer from Trinidad, the prior name for *insularis*). But Jenkins did not mention a "Haitian" *H. feronia.* The record is from Hall (1925:188), who stated under that name: "One specimen at La Vega; also recorded by Godman and Salvin from Hayti." Throughout his paper, Hall used the word "specimen" to include sight records; thus there is no assurance that he actually had in hand a specimen of *H. feronia*. This, coupled with the complexities of the taxonomy within the genus *Hamadryas*, makes it sure that to identify a gray member of this genus on the wing is an almost certain impossibility. Considering also that Hall (1925:187) described *Ageronia februa antillana* and stated that *A. ferox diasia* was "Described from Porto Rico and Hayti, but impossible to recognize from the description," assures me that confusion reigned. There is no reason to assume that there ever was a specimen (or even an individual on the wing) of *H. feronia* from Hispaniola.

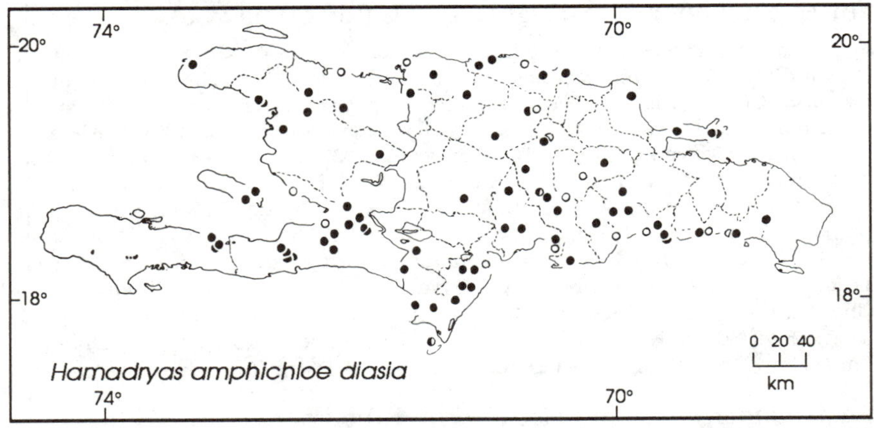

Hamadryas a. diasia is common and widely distributed on Hispaniola and on Île de la Gonâve and Isla Beata, whence I report herein the first records. This Hispaniolan abundance stands in contrast to the situations on Jamaica, Puerto Rico, and Cuba. On the latter island, *H. a. diasia* is known only from the extreme southeast ("Provincia de Oriente") and on Puerto Rico only from the southwestern, more xeric regions. On Jamaica it is more widespread but still apparently rather uncommon.

Brown and Heineman (1972:153) explained this Jamaican rarity by suggesting that *H. a. diasia* "is a forest dweller, and unless there is a rather extensive region of undisturbed forest" this butterfly is "either absent or rare." Although this is an attractive rationale for the rarity or circumscribed ranges of *H. a. diasia* on islands other than Hispaniola, it is far from fact, at least as far as Hispaniola is concerned.

Hamadryas a. diasia occurs on Hispaniola (and especially in Haiti) in many unforested areas (unless one uses the word "forest" in the loosest sense). All that is really required are some trees with trunk diameters sufficient for landing sites. Thus, *H. a. diasia* has been taken in gardens (Pétionville), open mountainsides (both xeric and mesic; see Schwartz, 1983a:30–31, for methods of collecting this species S of Terre Rouge), oases (Ça Soleil, Croix des Bouquets, Villa Vásquez), pinewoods (Obléon), *caféières* and *cafetales* (Découzé, Paillant, Yásica, Yamasá, Cabral), *Acacia* scrub (Cabo Rojo), xeric woods (Río Cumayasa, Boca Chica, Vallejuelo, Oviedo), plantings of *Musa* (Ennery, Découzé, Cruce de Ocoa), *Cocos* (Samaná), and *Citrus* (San José de Ocoa), high-elevation grassy meadows (La Nevera), as well as true mesic woods or forests. Thus, *H. a. diasia* is extremely tolerant ecologically, and it seems hardly likely that these butterflies have limited distributions or are rare upon the other Greater Antilles because of unsuitable ecologies. As a final note, certainly Haiti is among the most "disturbed" countries in the Antilles (see Schwartz, 1980b) as far as forest is concerned, yet *H. a. diasia* occurs commonly and broadly there. It seems more likely that *H. a. diasia* is a relatively recent overseas adventive on Puerto Rico and Cuba and has not as yet had enough time to disperse widely on those islands; its arrival on Jamaica must antedate those on Cuba and Puerto Rico, since *H. a. diasia* has an islandwide distribution on Jamaica.

The elevational distribution of *H. a. diasia* is from sea level (Môle St.-Nicholas, Ça Soleil, Miragoâne, Fond Parisien, Cabrera, Samaná, Boca Chica, Punta Caucedo, Cabo Rojo) to 1617 m (Obléon) on the Montagne Noire in Haiti; in the República Dominicana it reaches an elevation of 2227 m (La Nevera) in the interior uplands of the Cordillera Central. These high elevations are exceptional, however, and most records are from 915 m or less. On the other hand, while driving from La Horma to Constanza across the Cordillera Central through upland pine forest, a very occasional *H. a. diasia* has been seen at elevations above 2000 m. We have never secured any of these wanderers from lower elevations, however.

I have specimens from 10 months, with the largest number in July (49), and smaller numbers in June (30), May (21), August (15), and January (11), whereas December, March, February, October, and November are represented by from 5 to 1 specimens. *Hamadryas a. diasia* appears to be univoltine, with a peak in July, and smaller numbers throughout the year. Times of collection were between 0900 and 1715 h, and temperatures between 18°C (La

Nevera) and 40°C (Yásica).

Hamadryas a. diasia has been observed feeding on rotted or dried mangoes 4 times (Terre Rouge, Yamasá, San José de Ocoa, Mencía) and once on rotted bananas (Santiago). I have mentioned its occurrence with *M. v. verticordia* and *A. troglodyta* on extremely dried fruits (Vallejuelo) and with *E. t. tatilista* in a similar situation (Río Cumayasa). In addition, *H. a. diasia* has been observed taking nectar from *Hibiscus rosasinensis* (Thomonde), *Antigonon leptopus* (Villa Vásquez, Sombrero), *Tournefortia hirsutissima* (Río Bao), and *Lantana ovatifolia* (Santiago). At Santiago, there were dozens of *H. a. diasia* feeding on *L. ovatifolia.*

A copulating pair was taken at Los Quemados (26.vi, 1430 h, 28°C) on a branch in *Acacia* woods, 3 m above the ground.

One common name for *Hamadryas* in general is "cracker." This name comes from the ability of these butterflies to make a cracking sound in flight. Despite having seen and collected a great number of *H. a. diasia* in a variety of situations, including large aggregations, I have never heard this species make any sort of noise in flight. Typically, *H. a. diasia* rests, head down, on vertical surfaces (usually trees, but large boulders and roadcut faces with overhangs, and even gray concrete walls may be used as sanctuaries during rains). The butterflies rest with the wings appressed to the substrate and are supremely confident, relying on their excellent camouflage for protection. When finally alarmed, they fly with deep wing beats (like *M. aracynthia*) a short distance and land once more on another vertical surface. Some trees (especially those with rugose gray bark) seem preferred if present. The boldness of *H. a. diasia* is amazing; these butterflies land on the collector (especially if he is wearing gray clothing), the rim of the net, and on the tires or other parts of a parked vehicle. I have witnessed all the above behaviors without having heard any sort of cracking sound. On the other hand, Jenkins (1983:33) noted that *H. a. diasia* chased each other in an open field near Santiago, República Dominicana, with a "loud crackling noise."

Specimens: Haiti: Nord-Ouest: Môle St.-Nicholas, s.l., 2; *Nord:* 3.5 km W Plaisance, 305 m, 1; 5.6 km SE Dondon, 336 m, 1; *l'Artibonite:* 6.4 km E Ennery, 336 m, 1; 12.2 km E Ça Soleil, s.l., 1; 16.8 km W Ça Soleil, 1; 13 km ESE Pont Gaugin, s.l., 1; 4.0 km N Thomonde, 1; *l'Ouest:* 2.9–8.5 km S Terre Rouge, 122–488 m, 17; 13.1 km E Croix des Bouquets, s.l., 1; Etang Saumâtre, 3 (FSM); 1 km E Fond Parisien, s.l., 1; 2 km SE Fond Parisien, s.l., 1; Pétionville, 458 m, 4; Boutilliers Rd., 732–946 m, 4; 0.3 km N Obléon, 1617 m, 1; 10.6 km S Dufort, 427 m, 1; 1.6 km N Découzé, 640 m, 1; 0.8 km S Découzé, 702 m, 1; 2.1 km S Découzé, 640 m, 1; *Sud:* 6.6 km SW Paillant, 793 m, 6; 6.7 km SW Paillant, 763 m, 1; 10.7 km W Miragoâne, s.l., 1; *Île de la Gonâve:* Anse-à-Galets, 7; Picmi, 2; *República Dominicana: Monte Cristi:* 4 km NW Villa Vásquez, 61 m, 5; *Dajabón:* 0.5 km N Cañongo, 31 m, 1; *Santiago Rodríguez:* 3 km W Los Quemados, 183 m, 3; *Santiago:* Río Bao, 8 km SE Montones Abajo, 488 m, 1; 7 km SW Santiago, 214 m, 15; *Puerto Plata:* 0.6 km NE Estero Hondo, 1; 10 km W Luperón, 1; 9 km SE Sosúa, 15 m, 1; Yásica, 22 km SE Puerto Plata, 122 m, 1; *La Vega:* Jarabacoa, 530 m, 5; 1 km S Constanza, 1098 m, 1; 10 km NW La Horma, 1496 m, 1; *María T. Sánchez:* 6 km S Cabrera, s.l., 1; *Samaná:* 13.2 km NE Sánchez, 92 m, 1; 18.0 km E and N Samaná, s.l., 2; 2.8 km S Las Galeras, 61 m, 1; *La Altagracia:* 16 km NE La Romana, 61 m, 2; *La Romana:* Río Cumayasa, 13.5 km W La Romana, 31 m, 2; *San Pedro de Macorís:* 13 km SE Boca Chica, s.l., 3; *Dist. Nac.:* Punta Caucedo, 5 km S Aeropuerto Internacional de las Américas, s.l., 1; Punta Caucedo, 2 km W, 2 km S Andrés, s.l., 4; 5 km S San Isidro, 3; 30 km NW Santo Domingo, 122 m, 3; 25 km SE Yamasá, 1 (MPM); *Sánchez Ramírez:* 1 km NE Las Lagunas, 183 m, 1; *Monte Plata:* 7 km SE Yamasá, 31 m, 1; *San Cristóbal:* 11 km NW Cambita Garabitos, 671 m, 1; *Peravia:* 5 km N San José de Ocoa, 580 m, 3; Sombrero, s.l., 1; *Azua:* Tábara Abajo, 3; 22 km NW Cruce de Ocoa, 61 m, 1; 5 km S Peralta, 305 m, 6; 5 km SW Monte Bonito, 702 m, 1; *San Juan:* 9 km E Vallejuelo, 610 m, 3; *Independencia:* 4–7 km NE El Aguacate, 519–824 m, 1; *Barahona:* 14 km SSW Cabral, 854 m, 2; Polo, 702 m, 1; 12 km SW Barahona, 427 m, 2; 8 km NW Paraíso, 153 m, 3; 9 km NW Enriquillo, 671 m, 1; *Pedernales:* Mencía, 397 m, 2; Cabo Rojo, s.l., 1; 17 km NW Oviedo, 183 m, 1.

Sight records: República Dominicana: La Vega: La Nevera, 37 km SE Constanza, 2227 m—1 seen–10.vii; *Isla Beata:* 1 seen—22.ii.

25. *Historis acheronta semele* Bates, 1939

TL Sierra Rangel, Prov. de Pinar del Río, Cuba.

FW 40–48 mm (Bates, 1939b:4).

This, the smaller of the 2 Hispaniolan species of *Historis*, is known from the holotype and 5 paratypes from Cuba and a male and female from Cap-Haïtien, Dépt. du Nord, Haiti.

We have never taken the species on Hispaniola and have only 1 certain sight record. On 25.iv.1982, Gali and I saw an *Historis* at Lavaneau, Dépt. de l'Ouest, Haiti, 229 m, on the extreme southern slope of the Massif de la Selle, near Jacmel. The butterfly was flying about 4 m above the ground with the typical jerky movements of *H. odius*, and we were unable to net it. But it landed above us on a leaf of a breadfruit tree (*Artocarpus altilis;* Moraceae) in such a manner that sunlight passed through the wings, and we had a clear view. The butterfly was most patient and rested in this 1 spot until we finally chased it. We were able to see clearly the diagnostic group of white subapical spots in the fw (in contrast to only 1 spot in *H. odius*). I have no doubt that it was *H. a. semele.* The habitat at Lavaneau was a group of trees, widely spaced, adjacent to a renovated and occupied *habitation.* The temperature was 32°C and the time between 1130 and 1445 h.

Historis acheronta semele

Why we have not encountered *H. a. semele* elsewhere and more commonly remains a mystery. We spent several weeks in the Cap-Haïtien area, both along the coast and in the adjacent Massif du Nord, without seeing this butterfly. There is nothing distinctive, as far as habitats are concerned, about this northern area in Haiti unless it is that there are still rich pseudoforests between Cap-Haïtien and Plaisance and Dondon. The same is true of the Lavaneau region; there we have collected in the lowlands near Jacmel and in the mountains (Béloc, Découzé) without any success. Bates (1935a:174) had only 3 Cuban specimens but secured more by the time of the description of *H. a. semele;* these small numbers suggest that *H. a. semele* is not common on Cuba. Brown and Heineman (1972:146–47) reported only about 20 records of *H. a. cadmus* Cramer from Jamaica. Although there is evidence that *H. a. cadmus* (and not *semele*) occurs on Puerto Rico (Ramos, 1982:60), the species appears to be very uncommon there. From the above, it seems that *H. acheronta* is uncommon throughout its Antillean range.

Sight record: Haiti: l'Ouest: Lavaneau, 229 m—1 seen, 25.iv.

26. *Historis odius odius* Fabricius, 1775

TL "Indiis."

FW 47–60 mm.

Historis odius is widely distributed in the West Indies, where the species is represented by 2 subspecies: the nominate on Cuba, Puerto Rico, Jamaica, and Hispaniola, and *H. o. orion* Fabricius on the Lesser Antilles.

On Hispaniola, *H. o. odius* is a common butterfly, but a glance at the appended lists of specimens and sight records emphasizes that which Brown and Heineman (1972:144) and Schwartz (1983a:29) stated: many more *H. o. odius* are seen than collected. Although these large, stiff-winged butterflies often fly at treetop level, they are almost as often encountered at a height where a collector can net them with ease—if he were expecting the headlong and strong flight and the butterfly's sudden appearance. Since *H. o. odius* inhabits wooded situations, whether xeric (Cormier Plage, Playa Bayahibe), transitional (El Aguacate), or mesic (Paillant, Sánchez, 30 km NW Santo Domingo), the butterflies often rest, heads downward, on the thin branches, leaves, or even trunks of trees (including *Acacia:* Punta Caucedo). While the butterflies are resting in this manner, they are often (but not always) easy to approach, and the collector has a (carefully managed) opportunity to secure a specimen. Brown and Heineman (1972:142–43) have a brief but incisive paragraph on the resting behavior of *H. o. odius* on Jamaica; Hispaniolan individuals are no less aware than their Jamaican relatives.

Hall (1925:188) stated that *H. o. odius* is not very scarce in mountain forests. But, as noted above, xeric and transitional forests are equally as likely to be inhabited by *H. o. odius*. In fact, *H. o. odius* is rare at high-elevation (above 1037 m) hardwood forests and is absent from pine forests. Since the larval food plant is *Cecropia peltata* (Moraceae; not Urticaceae, as Brown and Heineman, 1972:143, stated; see Logier, 1980:23) and this attractive tree is widely distributed at low to moderate elevations, it is not unusual to see 1 or several *H. o. odius* circling the crowns of these trees, presumably to find egg deposition sites.

Aside from natural wooded situations, we have taken *H. o. odius* in *caféières* and *cafetales-cacaotales* (Jayaco, Sánchez, Paraíso) and in a *Citrus* grove (San José de Ocoa). Wisor and I saw an *H. o. odius* flying over a large rice field (Cruce de Rincón); there was a *cafetal* along the field's edge. Schwartz (1983a:30) reported the peculiar "scuffling" on the floor of a *caféière* (Paillant) between an *H. o. odius* and *D. p. megalippe* after a brief rain. At Sánchez, Jimenez and Lucio observed an *H. o. odius* climb an orange tree, on which other *H. o. odius* were feeding on the juice of damaged oranges still on the tree (despite the fact that the ground beneath the tree was littered with slightly more rotted oranges). The butterfly, starting about 1 m above the ground, spiraled or "squirreled" around the trunk to a height of 5 m and was lost in the foliage.

It is not unusual to have an *H. o. odius* land on a thin branch and within 1.5 m of the ground, immediately at the side of the collector, rest very briefly (while the collector composes himself), and fly off. An instance of bold behavior of *H. o. odius* occurred at Sosúa. I was crossing an open field, surrounded on both sides by well-wooded karst hills, when an *H. o. odius* flew at me, circled at about head level several times, then dashed off into the woods once more. The entire episode lasted less than 1 minute; the unexpected nature of the "assault" made any sort of capture attempt improbable.

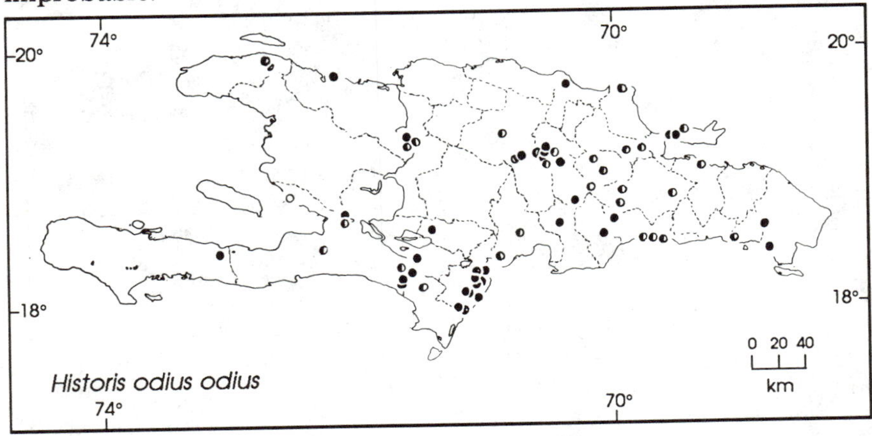

Between Terre Rouge and Mirebalais, Sommer noted an *H. o. odius* drinking rainwater trapped by the rim of an upright 55-gallon metal drum at a roadside. When he approached the butterfly, net in hand, the insect flew around the drum and landed on the curved side, whence it proceeded to walk away from Sommer, keeping at the same level on the drum! After about 2 minutes of this cat-and-mouse game, the *H. o. odius* departed, unharmed.

On another occasion, Gali, Iketani, and I were driving from Avenida George Washington north along Avenida Máximo Gómez, at about 0845 h, the height of the morning rush-hour traffic in Santo Domingo. As we stopped at a traffic signal, they noted an *H. o. odius* resting on the cover of a curbside garbage can, unnoticed by people waiting within 2 m for a bus. Gali attempted to catch the *H. o. odius*, which led him on a merry chase along the sidewalk and into yards, much to the amusement of passersby and the potential bus passengers. The butterfly escaped. But an *H. o. odius* on a wall in downtown Barahona fell to the net of Gonzalez! (Man does win occasionally.)

Historis o. odius invites such anecdotal accounts. I doubt that we have taken a single specimen or seen an individual that does not have, in someone's recollection, a story connected with it. All the above accounts illustrate the brazen and confident—even "intelligent"—behavior of these butterflies. Encounters between humans and *H. o. odius* many times result in the victory of the insect and the disgust of the collector, who has been outsmarted and outmaneuvered.

On the other hand, Wisor took a series of 6 *H. o. odius* that were feeding, along with several *A. d. amphitoe*, on an injured and dying tree adjacent to a river (Piedra Blanca). I secured a specimen (Playa Bayahibe) that was flying about a low (0.5 m) pile of rocks adjacent to a fence row and field in otherwise xeric forest. In 1974, while collecting Hispaniolan specimens for Clench at the Carnegie Museum, I walked up to and picked up by hand an *H. o. odius* as it drank from rainwater in the dirt road at the Río Nizao (Paraíso).

Aside from oranges noted above, *H. o. odius* feeds on rotted mangoes and mango peels (Cormier Plage, 2 km SE Barahona, 10 km NW Paraíso, Enriquillo, Banano, 8 km SW La Ciénaga, 5 km SE, 3 km W Barahona), often in the company of *A. d. amphitoe*, *H. a. diasia*, and *A. i. idyja*. On 1 occasion (Cormier Plage), an *H. o. odius* was seen taking nectar from a large shrubby *Lantana ovatifolia*; another was seen (2 km SW Barahona) on moist fresh cow dung. At Paraíso in April, Henderson and I saw many *H. o. odius* feeding in the road on rotted grapefruits.

Most specimens and sightings are from July (35), with 34 in August, 25 in June, 10 in April, 8 in October, 5 each in December and March, 3 in May, and 2 in November. June specimens are often much tattered and worn, but others from June and most from July are fresh and still have the pale margin to the hw. In April, Sommer and I saw 2 *H. o. odius* (1 collected) on the same leaf above a road (La Cuchilla). It seems likely that the months for major eclosion are July and August, with some individuals emerging during other months of the year.

Elevational distribution is from sea level (Cormier Plage, Cruce de Rincón, Playa Bayahibe, Tres Ojos, Punta Caucedo, Santo Domingo, Barahona) to 1129 m (Las Abejas) in the Sierra de Baoruco, 1037 m (3 km W La Ciénaga) in the Cordillera Central, and 1098 m (El Charco) in the Sierra Martín García. Times of collection and sightings were between 0830 and 1700 h, with temperatures between 20°C (La Palma) and 39°C (San José de Ocoa).

Specimens: Haiti: Nord: Cormier Plage, s.l., 3; *l'Ouest:* 2.9–8.5 km S Terre Rouge, 122–488 m, 1; *Sud:* 6.8 km SW Paillant, 763 m, 1; *República Dominicana: Dajabón:* 5.7 km SW Restauración, 610 m, 1; *Puerto Plata:* 5 km NE El Choco, 503 m, 1; *La Vega:* La Ciénaga, 915 m, 1; Jarabacoa, 530 m, 6; 1.7

km S Jarabacoa, 488 m, 2; 6 km S Jarabacoa, *ca.* 619 m, 1; *Samaná:* 13.2 km NE Sánchez, 92 m, 6; *La Altagracia:* 1 km N Playa Bayahibe, s.l., 1; 16 km NE La Romana, 61 m, 4; *La Romana:* Río Cumayasa, 13.5 km W La Romana, 1; *Dist. Nac.:* 30 km NW Santo Domingo, 122 m, 1; *Monseñor Nouel:* 4 km W Jayaco, 336 m, 1; 14 km SW Piedra Blanca, 427 m, 6; *San Cristóbal:* La Cuchilla, 15 km N Hato Damas, 153 m, 1; *Peravia:* 5 km N San José de Ocoa, 580 m, 1; *Baoruco:* 14 km N Neiba, 671 m, 1; *Independencia* 4–7 km NE El Aguacate, 519–732 m, 5; *Barahona:* Barahona, s.l., 1; 2 km SW Barahona, 122 m, 2; 12 km SW Barahona, 427 m, 2; 5 km SE, 3 km W Barahona, 183–397 m, 11; 5 km SE, 6.6 km W Barahona, 488 m, 1; 8.0 km SW La Ciénaga, 1; 8 km NW Paraíso, 153 m, 2; 10 km NW Paraíso, 244 m, 2; 8–10 km NW Paraíso, 1 (MPM); 3 km NW Enriquillo, 244 m, 3; *Pedernales:* 1 km SE Banano, 488 m, 1; Las Abejas, 12 km NW Aceitillar, 1129 m, 1.

Sight records: Haiti: Nord-Ouest: 7.5 km SE Port-de-Paix—1 seen, 19.vi: 1.3 km S Balladé, 31 m—1 seen, 18.vii; *l'Ouest:* 1.3 km N Terre Rouge, 580 m—2 seen, 11.viii; Boutilliers Road., 854 m—1 seen, 10.viii; *República Dominicana: Dajabón:* 9.1 km S Restauración, 519 m—1 seen, 27.v; 2 km N Villa Anacaona, 397 m—1 seen, 20.vii: *Puerto Plata:* 9 km SE Sosúa, 16 m—1 seen, 22.vii; 1 seen, 17.v; *Santiago:* Río Bao, 8 km SE Montones Abajo, 488 m—2 seen, 8.viii; 1 seen, 21.x; *La Vega:* La Palma, 19 km W Jayaco, 1007 m—1 seen, 30.xii; 5 km SE Jarabacoa, 595 m—1 seen, 29.vi; 3 km W La Ciénaga, 1037 m—1 seen, 23.x; 3.5 km E Paso Bajito, 732 m—3 seen, 29.vi; *Duarte:* Villa Riva—1 seen, 27.x; *Sánchez Ramírez:* La Piedra, 7 km SW Pimentel—1 seen, 3.viii; 1 km NE Las Lagunas, 183 m—2 seen, 2.iii; 1 seen, 2.xi; *María T. Sánchez:* 11 km NE Río San Juan—1 seen, 22.iii; 3 km S Cruce de Rincón, s.l.—1 seen, 21.iii; *Samaná:* 6.9 km NE Sánchez, 336 m—1 seen, 25.x; 13.2 km NE Sánchez, 92 m—3–4 seen, 11.viii; *El Seibo:* 4 km E Sabana de la Mar—1 seen, 19.iv; *La Romana:* Río Cumayasa, 13.5 km W La Romana—1 seen, 25.vi; *Monte Plata:* 8 km NE Bayaguana—2 seen, 27.vii; 8 km W Esperalvillo, 92 m—1 seen, 29.vii; 7 km SE Yamasá, 31 m—1 seen, 29.vii; *Dist. Nac.:* Punta Caucedo, 2 km W, 2 km S Andrés, s.l.—2 seen, 16.viii; Tres Ojos, s.l.—25.vi; Santo Domingo, s.l.—1 seen, 15.viii; 30 km NW Santo Domingo, 122 m—1 seen, 3.x; *Monseñor Nouel:* 6 km SE Maimón, 122 m—1 seen, 1.xi; *Azua:* 5 km S Peralta, 305 m—2 seen, 21.iv; *Independencia:* 4–7 km NE El Aguacate, 519–732 m—2 seen, 11.viii; *Barahona:* El Charco, summit, Sierra Martín García, 1098 m—1 seen, 11.viii; 1.8 km W Monteada Nueva, 1007 m—1 seen, 14.viii; 8 km NW Paraíso, 153 m—many seen, 6.iv; 3 km NW Enriquillo, 244 m—1 seen, 14.viii; 9 km NW Enriquillo 671 m—2 seen, 5.vii; *Pedernales:* Mencía, 397 m—1 seen, 2.vii; 2 seen, 19.vii; 2 km SW Mencía, 336 m—1 seen, 20.vii; 1 km SE Banano, 183 m—1 seen, 4.iv; 0.6 km SE Los Arroyos, 1098 m—1 seen, 11.vi; 23 km NE Cabo Rojo, 488 m—6 seen, 6.x; Las Abejas, 12 km NW Aceitillar, 1129 m—1 seen, 27.vii.

27. *Colobura dirce wolcotti* Comstock, 1942

TL Mayagüez, Puerto Rico.

FW males 29–37 mm, females 29–38 mm.

Colobura dirce is known in the Antilles from Cuba, Jamaica, Puerto Rico, and Hispaniola. Although Comstock (1942) divided the Antillean populations into 3 subspecies (*avinoffi* on Jamaica, *clementi* on Cuba, and *wolcotti* on Hispaniola and Puerto Rico), Riley (1975:63) preferred not to recognize these 3 subspecies and grouped all under the prior name *C. d. wolcotti.* Brown and Heineman (1972:147) used *C. d. avinoffi* for the Jamaican population but stated that the subspecies differ from each other in "minor ways." They also felt that "Only time and extensive collecting will provide the material necessary to evaluate" the 3 subspecies. The long series from Hispaniola at hand does not differ from Puerto Rican material, and since *wolcotti* is the earliest name for the Antillean subspecies, there is no problem as to the subspecific status of the Hispaniolan material.

Hall (1925:187) stated only that *C. d. wolcotti* was found "in mountain forest; not common." Bates (1935a:174) had no Cuban material. Comstock (1944:468) listed only the holotype from Mayagüez, and paratypes from Consumo, Lares, and Lago Dos Bocas on Puerto Rico, suggesting that *C. d. wolcotti* is uncommon there. Schwartz (1983a:29) had only 3 Haitian specimens, likewise suggesting that the species is rare in Haiti.

I have no more Haitian specimens, but there is now a long series from the República Dominicana, where *C. d. wolcotti* is extremely abundant locally. The habitat is almost invariably woods or forests, and almost always mesic. *Cafetales-cacaotales* offer prime situations with their accompanying tall canopy shade trees with the undergrowth cleared. In fact, most specimens are from just that sort of habitat; it is uncommon to encounter *C. d. wolcotti* in "undisturbed" forest (Cormier Plage, Buena Vista, Punta Cana, Pedro García, Las Abejas). The butterflies' habit of flying erratically, close to (1 m) the ground, and then pitching upward onto a tree trunk at about the same height as the flight, is hampered by dense undergrowth, and thus disturbed sites where the undergrowth is regularly cleared are preferred. A case in point is a *cafetal-cacaotal* at Piedra Blanca. When we made our first collections there in 1980, the undergrowth had been cleared (with the shade and cacao trees still standing) for the planting of short (1.5 m) *Coffea* saplings. *Colobura d. wolcotti* was extremely abundant. But as the years have passed, the coffee trees have become more mature and there has been little effort to thin out the undergrowth regularly. Now this grove is quite dense (one can walk through it with some difficulty), and in 1983, no *C. d. wolcotti* were encountered where once this species was abundant.

At this site in 1980, we observed as many as 8 *C. d. wolcotti* landing on the base of a single shade tree, only to flash out into the *cacaotal* when disturbed and return once more after these brief sallies, landing head down with the wings closed. At Jamao al Norte, in 1980, *C. d. wolcotti* was likewise very common; there, these insects were associated in an open *cafetal* with a sluggish, almost stagnant creek. The butterflies landed not only on trees adjacent to the creek but also on logs in the *cafetal* and on the exposed roots of trees on the eroded bank above the stream. The creek was well shaded. On a later visit, 1 *C. d. wolcotti* was secured there as it landed in the shade on the cement wall of an open bridge abutment. At Cormier Plage, a *C. d. wolcotti* landed on a vertical rock face in shaded hillside woods.

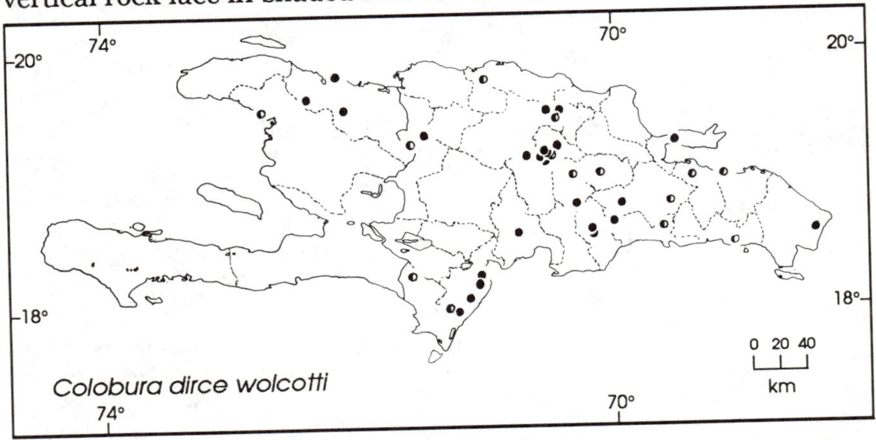

Colobura d. wolcotti is extremely shy, despite its excellent camouflage when it has landed. In fact, if the butterflies did not have the habit of opening the wings, with their bright yellow upfw diagonal bars, occasionally while perched, the collector would discover them only with difficulty. Often, when disturbed by a person walking by the perch site, *C. d. wolcotti* flies out to meet the intruder at about knee level, circles and dodges about the person for several seconds, and is then off into the woods once more—before the collector can organize himself for an attempted netting. On the other hand, Schwartz (1983a:29) recited the activites of a *C. d. wolcotti* at Ça Soleil; there, an individual skipped from tree to tree in a mesic oasis with shrubby undergrowth and enough saplings to impede the collector but not the butterfly; finally the butterfly was lost in the maze of leaves, trees, and other plant growth.

On 27.vi.1983, I was startled by a *C. d. wolcotti* at the edge of a small patch of mesic woods at Guerra. The butterfly disappeared and an hour's search in the woods yielded neither that individual nor sightings of others. On return visits to the same spot on 30.ix.1983 and 7.iii.1984, another (the same?) *C. d. wolcotti* performed the same evasive tactic, and search yielded nothing. I suspect that these 3 sightings were of the same individual. When one sees 1 *C. d. wolcotti*, he usually sees several; this was not the case in this instance.

Colobura d. wolcotti is primarily an inhabitant of mesic woods, forests, or *cafetales-cacaotales* and *caféières*. We have never taken it in pine forest, although Amador, Raburn, and I saw 1 in a mesic ravine within pinewoods (Villa Anacaona). The most xeric woods where we have taken *C. d. wolcotti* are those at Cormier Plage, Río Cumayasa, and 3 km NW Enriquillo; all 3 localities are indeed xeric but support stands of xerophilic hardwoods, not *Acacia* forest.

Colobura d. wolcotti occurs from sea level (Cormier Plage, Ça Soleil) to 1129 m (Las Abejas) and is more common at higher elevations than lower. Using dates from both specimens and sight records, we have encountered more *C. d. wolcotti* in July (39) than in August (37) and June (15). I have smaller numbers from March (4), October and December (3 each), and April, September, and November (1 each). Times of collection or observation were between 0930 and 1800 h, with temperatures between 20°C (La Palma) and 38°C (14 km SW Jamao al Norte, Cruce de Guayacanes, Bonao).

At Piedra Blanca, we collected *C. d. wolcotti* between 1230 and 1630 h in a densely canopied *cafetal-cacaotal*. During this period, as the afternoon progressed and the grove became more shaded, *C. d. wolcotti* became less shy and erratic and landed on vertical rock faces within the *cafetal*. Although no late afternoon temperature was taken, at early afternoon the temperature was 34°C, and that at 1630 h must surely have been considerably lower. Activity of *C. d. wolcotti* decreases with decreased light and falling temperatures.

Colobura d. wolcotti has been taken feeding on rotted mangoes (3 km NW Enriquillo, Peralta) and rotted *guanábana* (5 km SE, 6.4 km W Barahona).

Specimens: Haiti: Nord: Cormier Plage, s.l., 1; 5.6 km SE Dondon, 336 m, 1; 6.2 km W Plaisance, 259 m, 1; *República Dominicana; Dajabón:* Los Cerezos, 12 km NW Río Limpio, 580 m, 1; *Espaillat:* 14 km SW Jamao al Norte, 534 m, 17; *Santiago:* 2 km E Pedro García, 427 m, 1; *La Vega:* Buena Vista, 11 km NE Jarabacoa, 640 m, 1; La Palma, 19 km W Jayaco, 1007 m, 1; 1 km W Manabao, 793 m, 4; Jarabacoa, 530 m, 3; 5 km SE Jarabacoa, 503 m, 1; 6 km S Jarabacoa, *ca.* 610 m, 1; *Samaná:* 6.9 km NE Sánchez, 336 m, 1; *La Altagracia:* 6 km W Punta Cana, s.l., 1; *Monseñor Nouel:* 14 km SW Piedra Blanca, 427 m, 36; *Monte Plata:* 7 km SE Yamasá, 31 m, 1; *Dist. Nac.:* 30 km

NW Santo Domngo, 122 m, 2; *San Cristóbal:* 8 km NW Cambita Garabitos, 534, 1; 11 km NW Cambita Garabitos, 671 m, 4; *Azua:* 5 km S Peralta, 305 m, 1; *Barahona:* 2 km SW Barahona, 122 m, 1; 5 km SE, 6.4 km W Barahona, 488 m, 1; 8 km NW Paraíso, 153 m, 1; 3 km NW Enriquillo, 244 m, 1.

Sight records: Haiti: l'Artibonite: 12.2 km W Ça Soleil, s.l.—1 seen, 17.vii; *República Dominicana: Dajabón:* 2 km N Villa Anacaona, 397 m—1 seen, 3.viii; *Puerto Plata:* 11 km N Cruce de Guayacanes, 275 m—2 seen, 19.vii; *Espaillat:* 20 km SW Jamao al Norte, 793—1 seen, 20.x; *La Vega:* 8 km SE Jarabacoa, 504 m—1 seen, 29.vi; *Hato Mayor:* 25 km E Sabana de la Mar—1 seen, 8.iii; 6 km N El Valle—1 seen, 6.iii; *La Romana:* Río Cumayasa, 13.5 km W La Romana—*ca.* 10 seen, 27.vi; *Monte Plata:* 8 km NE Bayaguana—1 seen, 7.iii; *Dist. Nac.:* 9 km NE Guerra, 1 seen, 27.vii: 1 seen, 30.ix: 1 seen, 7.iii; *Monseñor Nouel:* Bonao, 153 m—6 seen, 11.viii; *Sánchez Ramírez:* 1 km NE Las Lagunas, 183 m—1 seen, 1.xi; *Barahona:* 8 km NW Paraíso, 153 m—1 seen, 6.iv; 3 km NW Enriquillo, 244 m—2 seen, 4.viii; 9 km NW Enriquillo, 671 m—1 seen, 5.vii; *Pedernales:* Las Abejas, 12 km NW Aceitillar, 1129 m—2 seen, 26.vii; 1 seen, 27.vii.

Subfamily Marpesiinae Aurivillius, 1898

28. *Marpesia chiron* Fabricius, 1775

TL "India"; restricted to Jamaica (Brown and Heineman, 1972:136).

FW males 28–32 mm, females 29–32 mm.

Of the 2 species of *Marpesia* on Hispaniola, *M. chiron* is by far the less common. Riley (1975:62–63) considered the Hispaniolan population "fairly common," doubtless misled by Hall's (1925:188) assessment that this species is "not uncommon." I have no Haitian specimens or sight records. *Marpesia chiron* occurs not only on Hispaniola but also on Cuba (Bates, 1935a:171), where the species appears to be fairly common. Brown and Heineman (1972:137) considered the species "very rare in collections and, apparently, on Jamaica"; they cited only 6 records from 2 parishes. Comstock (1944:463) knew of no Puerto Rican specimens but had a photograph (pl. 7, fig. 7) of a Hispaniolan male from Punta Arena, San Lorenzo, Prov. de Hato Mayor, República Dominicana. However, Ramos (1976:439) reported 2 males from 2 localities on Puerto Rico. There is some question as to whether *M. chiron* is resident on Jamaica (Brown and Heineman, 1972:136), but Ramos (1976) gave evidence that the species is indeed resident on Puerto Rico.

On Hispaniola, *M. chiron* is associated most often with mesic forests, including *cafetales* and their clearings. The flight is weak and close to the ground, but the butterflies are extremely alert, far more so than *M. e. dospassosi*, and thus difficult to net once alarmed. Many of our specimens were taken from drinking clubs (Los Cerezos, Loma Leonor, 2 km and 12 km SW Barahona). The specimen from Las Abejas, apparently seeking moisture, was taken from a moist (but not wet) dirt road, and those from El Aguacate were drinking from a rain puddle in a clearing in transitional woods. If disturbed while drinking, and they are extremely "flighty" even while thus occupied, the butterflies fly erratically in circles and finally come to rest close to the place from which they have been frightened. On other occasions, drinking individuals simply flew about 0.5 m above the ground and landed 25–30 cm from the original site. If repeatedly annoyed, these *M. chiron* rest only briefly, continually moving short distances, much to the frustration of the collector.

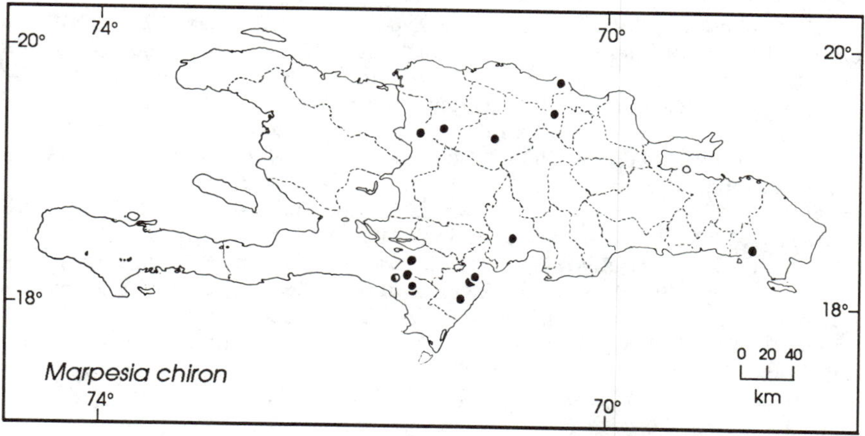

At Río Bao on 21.x.1983, Raburn saw 2 *M. chiron* "climbing over each other" on vines along the road edge in mesic forest, 2 m above the ground. The 2 individuals are both females; the significance of this behavior is unknown. *Marpesia chiron* uses flowers (*Tournefortia hirsutissima* at Peralta) as a nectar source; we also saw 1 on a moist mango seed with its adherent flesh (Mencía), presumably seeking either nutrients or moisture. At 26 km NE Cabo Rojo, 1 was taken feeding on *Ageratum conyzoides*.

On 26.vii.1980, I saw 1 *M. chiron* in a clearing in a *cafetal* (Jamao al Norte); the butterfly was the only 1 of this species seen there but was not captured. Close observation showed that it was fresh and unworn on that date. On 7.viii.1981, Gali, Iketani, and I returned to the same spot and there collected a much worn *M. chiron;* it too was the only individual seen. These incidents suggest that the individual seen in 1980 was the 1 collected in 1981, after 13 months.

Most specimens and observations are from July (47), with 6 in August, 4 each in March and October, 3 in June, 2 in May, and 1 each in January and April. It seems likely that *M. chiron* is univoltine with major eclosion in July. Elevational distribution is from sea level (Río Chavón) to 1129 m (Las Abejas); most records are from above about 400 m, and the rarity of *M. chiron* at extremely low elevations is puzzling. The apparent rarity of *M. chiron* on most of the north island is strange; the species is not uncommon on the south island in the Sierra de Baoruco and the Dominican portion of the Massif de la Selle.

Times of collection were between 0830 and 1530 h, at temperatures between 27°C (Río Bao) and 38°C (Mencía).

Specimens: República Dominicana: Dajabón: Los Cerezos, 12 km NW Río Limpio, 580 m, 3; *Puerto Plata:* 9 km SE Sosúa, 15 m, 5; *Santiago:* Río Bao, 8 km SE Montones Abajo, 488 m, 3; *Espaillat:* 14 km SW Jamao al Norte, 534 m, 2; *Santiago Rodríguez:* Loma Leonor, 18 km SW Monción, 534 m, 2; *La Romana:* Río Chavón, 8 km SE La Romana, s.l., 1; *Azua:* 5 km S Peralta, 305 m, 1; *Independencia:* 4–7 km NE El Aguacate, 519–824 m, 6; *Barahona:* 2 km SW Barahona, 122 m, 24; 12 km SW Barahona, 427 m, 6; 8–10 km NW Paraíso, 2 (MPM); *Pedernales:* 23 km NE Cabo Rojo, 488 m, 4; 26 km NE Cabo Rojo, 732 m, 4; Las Abejas, 12 km NW Aceitillar, 1129 m, 1.

Sight records: República Dominicana: Espaillat: 14 km SW Jamao al Norte, 534 m—1 seen, 26.vii; 3 seen, 12.vii; *Santiago:* Río Bao, 8 km SE Montones Abajo, 488 m—1 seen, 8.viii; 3 seen, 14.iii; *Independencia:* 4–7 km NE El Aguacate, 519–824 m—1 seen, 22.vi; 1 seen, 30.viii; *Barahona:* 12 km SW Barahona, 427 m—1 seen, 29.iii; *Pedernales:* Mencía, 397 m—1 seen, 19.vii; Las Abejas, 12 km NW Aceitillar, 1129 m—1 seen, 27.vii.

29. *Marpesia eleuchea dospassosi* Munroe, 1971

TL Punta Arena, San Lorenzo, Prov. de Hato Mayor, República Dominicana.

FW males 29–37 mm, females 28–39 mm.

Marpesia eleuchea Hübner is endemic to the West Indies. It occurs on Cuba including the Isla de la Juventud (*eleuchea*), Jamaica (*pellensis* Godart), *dospassosi* (Hispaniola), and the Bahama Islands (*bahamensis* Munroe) on New Providence, Eleuthera, Crooked (Clench, 1977a:277), Andros (Clench, 1977b: 184), and San Salvador (Elliott, Riley, and Clench, 1980:123). The absence of the species from Puerto Rico and the Lesser Antilles is noteworthy, in that these islands are occupied by *M. petreus* Cramer, a species also found in Florida (see Munroe, 1971b).

Hall (1925:188) found *M. e. dospassosi* "singly in most localities." Schwartz (1983a:29) reported 10 specimens from 4 Haitian localities. Brown and Heineman (1972:138–139) gave numerous locality records of *M. e. pellensis* on Jamaica, and Bates (1935a:172) examined 19 specimens of *M. e. eleuchea* from Cuba. The reports of *M. e. bahamensis* suggest that this subspecies is likewise rather uncommon.

Judging from the few reports of Hispaniolan *M. e. dospassosi*, one might with propriety consider this butterfly uncommon. Such it is under general circumstances; as Hall noted, 1 or a very few *M. e. dospassosi* may be regularly encountered in the appropriate habitats. But during June-August 1980, *M. e. dospassosi* literally swarmed in at least the eastern República Dominicana. There (Playa Bayahibe, La Romana), I saw dozens of these butterflies feeding on the nectar from the white flowers of *Cordia globosa*. One tree-sized example of this plant was covered with these butterflies, and even small (2 m) *C. globosa* had their attendant coterie of *M. e. dospassosi*. While driving from La Romana to Playa Bayahibe, and further east to Boca de Yuma, it seemed, even while traversing sugarcane fields, that there was at least 1 *M. e. dospassosi* always in sight, flying across the road. The phenomenon was especially striking, after having seen so very few of these butterflies in 1977–79 in Haiti. As the summer of 1980 progressed, numbers decreased somewhat by August, but *M. e. dospassosi* was even then slightly more common than it is under "normal" circumstances.

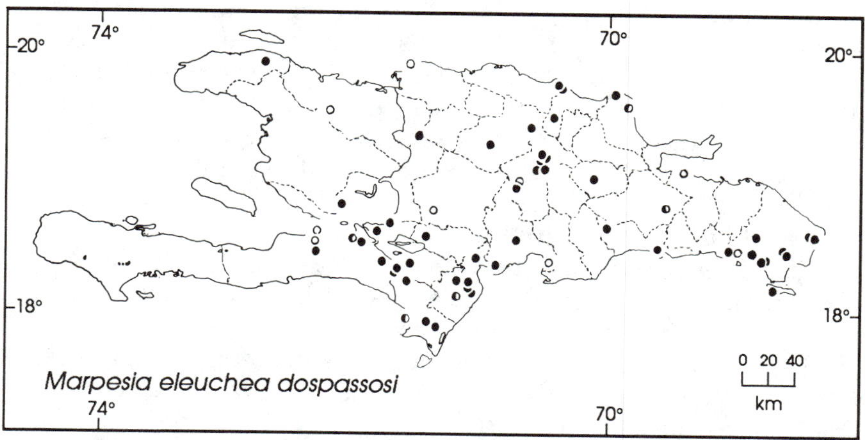

Marpesia e. dospassosi is an inhabitant of woodlands, whether xeric (Punta Cana, Playa Bayahibe, La Romana, Oviedo), transitional (El Aguacate), or mesic (Saut d'Eau, Jayaco, Las Lagunas, Cabrera, Bayaguana, Los Pinos, Neiba, Monteada Nueva, Las Abejas). It does not shun pseudoforest (Jamao al Norte), pine forest (Forêt des Pins), open shrubby mountainsides (Boutilliers Road), hillside "mesic" woods in otherwise xeric areas (Fond Parisien), or mixed pine-hardwoods (Constanza). We have even taken stragglers in *Acacia* scrub (Tres Charcos, Tierra Nueva, Canoa).

In flight, *M. e. dospassosi* is very like *A. v. insularis* or *D. i. hispaniola* in color and style; the 3 species are virtually indistinguishable on the wing. However, at least male *M. e. dospassosi* are more richly and deeply orange-brown than the 2 other species. *Marpesia e. dospassosi* lands with wings closed, on either the upper or under sides of leaves, up to 3 m above the ground; once landed, it is an easier catch than on the wing. While taking nectar, these butterflies are almost indifferent to human intrusion, flying only very briefly and no distance from the nectar source before re-alighting once more and continuing with their feeding.

On 1 occasion (Barahona) we have taken specimens drinking from mud adjacent to a broad and shallow stream, in the company of *M. chiron*. They formed only a very small and tight aggregation at this site. At Neiba, single individuals were taken while drinking from sand and mud at a river's edge. *Marpesia e. dospassosi* has also been observed on human feces (Jayaco) and on cow dung (El Aguacate).

Combining specimens and sight records, elevational distribution is between sea level (Fond Parisien, Cabrera, Río San Juan, Punta Cana, Playa Bayahibe, Río Chavón, Tierra Nueva, Cabo Rojo, Mano Juan) and 1708 m (Los Pinos) in the Sierra de Neiba, 1617 m (Los Arroyos) in the Massif de la Selle, 1403 m (Constanza) in the Cordillera Central, and 1129 m (Las Abejas) in the Sierra de Baoruco. *Marpesia e. dospassosi* reaches an elevation of 976 m in the Sierra Martín García but has not been taken at El Limón or El Charco at the summit. The sea-level Cabo Rojo sight record is for an individual trapped in the hallway of the Alcoa Exploration Company headquarters (28.vi); the butterfly was undoubtedly windblown to this virtually treeless site; we saw no others on the wing in this area in visits over 4 years. The high-elevation records are likewise unusual: *M. e. dospassosi* is distinctly uncommon at elevations above about 915 m. This is the first record of *M. e. dospassosi* from Isla Saona.

Most *M. e. dospassosi* have been taken or seen in July (71) with smaller numbers in June (61) and August (30). March is represented by 5, December by 4, April by 6, January by 3, May by 2, and February and October by 1 specimen each. *Marpesia e. dospassosi* seems to be univoltine with an early summer peak.

Times of collection and observation were between 0900 and 1700 h, at temperatures between 21°C (Los Arroyos) and 42°C (La Romana).

Other than on *Cordia globosa* noted above, we have taken these butterflies feeding on *Daucus* sp. (Boutilliers Road), *Tournefortia hirsutissima* (Sosúa, Río Bao, 6 km SSE Constanza, Peralta), *Ixora* sp. (Boca de Yuma), *Cordia globosa* (Santo Domingo), *Cordia exarata* (2.5 km SE Playa Bayahibe, 2 occasions), *Lantana ovatifolia* (Cabral, 1 km S Constanza), *Prosopis juliflora* (Fabacae) (Canoa), *Morinda citrifolia* (Río Chavón), and an unidentified white-flowered tree (Los Arroyos).

Specimens: Haiti: Nord-Ouest: 1.3 km S Balladé, 31 m, 1; *l'Ouest:* 1.6 km N Saut d'Eau, 275 m, 1; 5 km SE Fond Parisien, s.l., 1; Boutilliers Road, 732–885 m, 5; Boutilliers Road, 1.8–2.1 km W Kenscoff road, 793–885 m, 2; Forêt des Pins, 1525 m, 1; *República Dominicana: Dajabón:* Los Cerezos, 12 km NW Río Limpio, 580 m, 2; *Puerto Plata:* 9 km SE Sosúa, 15 m, 11; 11 km SE Sosúa, 47 m, 1; *Espaillat:* 20 km SW Jamao al Norte, 793 m, 2; *Santiago:* 8 km E Jánico, 610 m, 1; Río Bao, 8 km SE Montones Abajo, 488 m, 1; *La Vega:* 10 km W Jayaco, 915 m, 5; La Palma, 19 km W Jayaco, 1007 m, 1; Jarabacoa, 530 m, 1; 5 km SE Jarabacoa, 595 m, 1; 6 km S Jarabacoa, *ca.* 610 m, 1; 6 km SSE Constanza, 1403 m, 3; *María T. Sánchez:* 9 km NE Río San Juan, s.l., 1; *La Romana:* Río Chavón, 8 km SE La Romana, s.l., 2; *La Altagracia:* Punta Cana, s.l., 1; 2 km W Punta Cana, s.l., 1; 0.5 km W Boca de Yuma, 1; 0.5–3.5 km W Boca de Yuma, 5; 1 km N Playa Bayahibe, s.l., 9; 2.5 km SE Playa Bayahibe, s.l., 17; 16 km NE La Romana, 61 m, 18; Río Cumayasa, 13.5 km W La Romana, 20; *Dist. Nac.:* Punta Caucedo, 2 km W, 2 km S Andrés, s.l., 1; 30 km NW Santo Domingo, 122 m, 1; *Sánchez Ramírez:* 1 km NE Las Lagunas, 183 m, 1; *Azua:* 5 km S Peralta, 305 m, 8; *Baoruco:* 11 km N Neiba, 519 m, 2; *Independencia:* 21 km N Los Pinos, 1708 m, 1; 5 km NW Tierra Nueva, s.l., 1; 4–7 km NE El Aguacate, 519–824 m, 9; *Barahona:* west slope, Sierra Martín García, 763–824 m, 6; west slope, Sierra Martín García, 534–610 m, 2; 8 km ESE Canoa, 1; 7 km SSW Cabral, 214 m, 1; 1.8 km W Monteada Nueva, 1007 m, 4; 12 km SW Barahona, 427 m, 7; 5 km SE, 6.4 km W Barahona, 488 m, 1; *Pedernales:* Las Abejas, 12 km NW Aceitillar, 1129 m, 6; 5 km SW El Aguacate, 1769 m, 2; 5 km NE Los Arroyos, 117 m, 2; 17 km NW Oviedo, 183 m, 3; 4 km NW Tres Charcos, 1; *Isla Saona:* 3 km N Mano Juan, 1.

Sight records: Haiti: l'Ouest: 2 km SE Fond Parisien, s.l.—1 seen, 1.v; *República Dominicana: Puerto Plata:* 9 km SE Sosúa, 16 m—1 seen, 22.vii; *La Vega:* 10 km W Jayaco, 915 m—2 seen, 21.vi; 1 km S Constanza, 1098 m—1 seen, 8.vii; *María T. Sánchez:* 6 km S Cabrera, s.l.—1 seen, 22.iii; *Monte Plata:* 8 km NE Bayaguana—1 seen. 7.iii; *Barahona:* 3 km NNE Polo, 854 m—1 seen, 4.viii; *Pedernales:* Cabo Rojo, s.l.—1 seen, 28.vi.

Family Apaturidae Boisduval, 1840

Subfamily Charaxinae Guenée, 1865

1. *Anaea troglodyta* Fabricius, 1775

TL "America."

FW males 29–36 mm, females 35–40 mm.

Anaea troglodyta is 1 of a quartet of *Anaea (portia* Fabricius, *borinquenalis* Johnson and Comstock, *minor* Hall)— on the Greater Antilles (Hispaniola, Jamaica, Puerto Rico) and some of the northern Lesser Antilles (St. Christopher, Nevis, Antigua, Montserrat, St.-Barthélémy; Schwartz and Jimenez, 1982:5, Pinchon and Enrico, 1969:103; Schwartz, Gonzalez, and Henderson, 1987)—that have at times been considered subspecifically related (Johnson and Comstock, 1941) and at others as distinct species (Comstock, 1961:39). Brown and Heineman (1972:127) gave a rationale for a subspecific relationship (and also acted as devil's advocates for a specific one), but Comstock (1961:39) had reversed his previous decision (with Johnson) and had reverted to specific designations for these taxa. The taxa differ from each other in up pattern, size, and male genitalia; but they are allopatric, and the genitalic differences are such that Comstock regarded the populations as distinct. Riley (1975:58) regarded these populations as species, without personal comment. I follow Comstock, since his longtime studies of the genus are a solid foundation; the 4 populations are allopatric and distinct—it is a matter of choice whether one considers these taxa species or subspecies.

My specimens are quite variable in up pattern and coloration. Females may have the fw postdiscal pale band concolor with the reddish orange of the fw, or it may be a distinctly paler yellowish. The expression of this band in males is likewise variable, from its complete absence or indication only by some scattered remnants of its black edges, to such a complete expression that, were it not for the purple iridescence, one might be deceived into thinking that the specimen was a female.

Anaea troglodyta is common and abundant on Hispaniola. Hall (1925:188) did not collect specimens, nor do I have material from the areas where he collected. This butterfly occurs primarily in wooded situations and favors xeric woods at low (up to about 488

m) elevations, although it has been taken higher (to 1922 m) and in mesic woods and forests. High-elevation records are in the minority, however. The elevational distribution is between sea level (Ça Soleil, Colmini, Fond Parisien, Grand-Goâve, Copey, Boca de Cachón) to 1922 m (Valle de Tetero) in the Cordillera Central. There are no records for the Massifs de la Selle or la Hotte, although *A. troglodyta* occurs on the northern face of the Morne l'Hôpital and the Montagne Noire (Obléon) above the Cul de Sac plain.

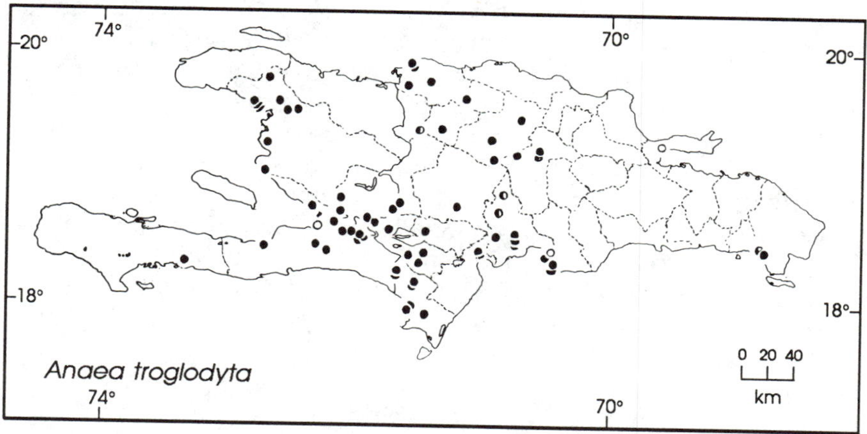

Anaea troglodyta

Although not uncommon in dry forest and *Acacia* woods (Source Matelas, Fond Parisien, Copey, Monte Cristi, Santiago, Playa Bayahibe, Canoa, Las Lajas, Oviedo), *A. troglodyta* may often be found in xeric lowlands in more or less mesic oases (Ça Soleil, Villa Vásquez) or in mesic forests surrounded by xeric scrub (Río Guarabo). In transitional forests (El Aguacate, 23 km NE Cabo Rojo), it may be common. Although some trees appear to be necessary for *A. troglodyta*, the butterflies at times occur at localities where trees are widely scattered (Rivière Pendu, Carrefour Joffre, Cabo Rojo). Certainly 1 locality where we took *A. troglodyta* abundantly is the southern slope (Terre Rouge) of the Montagnes du Trou-d'Eau (see Schwartz, 1983a:26–27, for details); yet any form of arborescent vegetation is extremely scanty on these slopes and in the arid uplands of this Haitian western end of the Sierra de Neiba. At Playa Bayahibe, *A. troglodyta* was common in an open field behind the beach; the field was adjacent to *Acacia* woods and had a few isolated large trees. The butterflies were congregated about them, landing on the bare twigs and small-diameter branches as is their habit and flying out into the field in pursuit of other *A. troglodyta.* If 1 individual landed on the ground, the pursuer landed within 10 cm or less in several instances, and both remained motionless and could thus be easily captured. I interpret this behavior (on 16.viii) as being involved in courtship, which I never saw completed (as copulation).

At Vallejuelo, both *A. troglodyta* and *M. v. verticordia* were taken together (with the latter the much more abundant species) on a small area of very dried fruits on the ground (see the account of the latter species for details); at this locality of syntopy, *M. v. verticordia* far outnumbered *A. troglodyta.* At 18 km S Peralta, where we took both species flying for no obvious reason about a blow-down without bleeding sap, the 2 species were present in about equal numbers (see account below at Azua). These are 2 of 4 localities (Azua, 5 km S Peralta) where we have taken them syntopically. *Anaea troglodyta* occurs with *M. johnsoni* at Boutilliers Road, with the former the more common.

Schwartz (1983a:26) gave details of *A. troglodyta* feeding on mango peels and seeds with some fibrous meat attached, these objects often dry and dusty and without any obvious nutritive or moisture value. We have observed *A. troglodyta* on fresh mango skins and seeds at Peralta, Cabo Rojo, and Banano, at the latter locality with *A. d. amphitoe;* at none of these localities were the numbers of *A. troglodyta* comparable with those at Terre Rouge. We have seen or taken *A. troglodyta* on moist mango seeds (Los Cerezos) and on a dust-dry banana peel (Palmar de Ocoa), as well as on rotted bananas (Santiago). The fruits involved are not native; but at 26 km NE Cabo Rojo, *A. troglodyta* was feeding on the blue-black fruits (diameter 5 mm) of a shrub, the fruit still on the bush (not identified).

We have taken *A. troglodyta* (13 males, 1 female) drinking from mud and sand bars at Río Guarabo; there was no aggregation, and each butterfly settled and drank independently, although there might be 1 or 2 on a single sandbar. Another was seen landed on a rock at the edge of the Río Toma (Loma Leonor). A single individual was taken (Duvergé) drinking from a mud puddle in the gravel road, the puddle formed by runoff of soapy water from a Dominican washing his car! At Neiba, a few individuals were drinking, each by itself, from the sand and mud at a river's edge.

On 2 occasions we have taken *A. troglodyta* using flowers as a nectar source, once at Santiago, where large numbers of these butterflies were feeding eagerly on *Lantana ovatifolia,* and at Fond Parisien, where *A. troglodyta* as well as *M. v. verticordia* were using the pale cream flowers of a xerophytic vine in *Acacia* scrub. At

Azua, large numbers (≈30) of *A. troglodyta* and *M. v. verticordia* were associated with a small tree in *Acacia* scrub; there was no obvious reason (flowers, bleeding wounds) for this intimate association. When disturbed, the butterflies flew only short distances (3 m or less), landed, and then promptly returned to the tree.

At a large seafront hotel (Délugé), 2 individuals were captured as they rested on balcony railings on the second floor. Such "tame" behavior is unusual in *A. troglodyta;* the flight is rapid and erratic, with landing sites usually on bare twigs or small branches (very occasionally tree trunks) up to 2 m above the ground. Landing in open roads or paths also occurs but is much less usual.

Most individuals were collected or seen in July (130), with 59 in August, 48 in June, 34 in May, 21 in January, 11 in October, 8 in December, 5 in April, 4 in March, and 1 in February. The high numbers of May-August suggest that the eclosion time for *A. troglodyta* is late spring-summer, and indeed one sees more of these butterflies in that period. Times of collection were between 0900 and 1750 h, and temperatures between 23°C (Puesto Pirámide 204) and 40°C (Río Guarabo). The absence of records for the Tiburon Peninsula west of Grand-Goâve and Vieux Bourg d'Aquin is puzzling; the species may be absent or rare there (optimal xeric habitats are not abundant). Our major collecting there, on the other hand, was in June, a month when *A. troglodyta* is not abundant anywhere.

Specimens: Haiti: l'Artibonite: 3.2 km NE Ennery, 427 m, 1; Rivière Pendu, 15.0 km N Gros Morne, 1; 4.6 km E Les Poteaux, 183 m, 1; 16 km N Carrefour Joffre, 183 m, 1; 12.2 km W Ça Soleil, s.l., 2; 14.4 km W Ça Soleil, s.l., 2; 16.8 km W Ça Soleil, 1; Colmini, 6.4 km W Terre Noire, s.l., 1; Délugé, s.l., 2; *l'Ouest:* 1.6 km N Saut d'Eau, 183 m, 1; 2.9–8.5 km S Terre Rouge, 122–488 m, 33; bet. Terre Rouge, and 2.1 km N Terre Rouge, 397–518 m, 3; 5 km SE Source Matelas, s.l., 5; 13.1 km SE Croix des Bouquets, s.l., 1; 11.2 km N Croix des Bouquets, 1; 4 km SE Fond Parisien, s.l., 17; 2 km W Fond Parisien, s.l., 1; 1 km E Fond Parisien, s.l., 2; 2 km SE Fond Parisien, s.l., 1; Boutilliers Road, 732–854 m, 6; Boutilliers Road, 3.7 km W Kenscoff road, 1 (MPM); 0.3 km NE Obléon, 1647 m, 1; just W Grand-Goâve, s.l., 2; *Sud:* Vieux Bourg d'Aquin, s.l., 1; *Republica Domincana: Monte Cristi:* 6 km W Copey, s.l., 28; 4 km SE Monte Cristi, 2; 1 km SE Monte Cristi, 4; 4 km NW Villa Vásquez, 61 m, 6; *Elías Piña:* 1 km SW Puesto Pirámide 204, 1891 m, 1; 8 km SW Puesto Pirámide 204, 1647 m, 1; *Santiago Rodríguez:* Loma Leonor, 18 km SW Monción, 534 m, 2; 3.0 km S Zamba, 214 m, 1; *Valverde:* Río Guarabo, 3 km W Los Quemados, 122 m, 14; *Santiago:* Río Bao, 8 km SE Montones Abajo, 488 m, 1; 7 km SW Santiago, 214 m, 23; entrance to Valle de Tetero, 1922 m, 1; *La Vega:* Jarabacoa, 530 m, 1; La Ciénaga, 915 m, 1; *La Altagracia:* 2.5 km SE Playa Bayahibe, s.l., 12; *Peravia:* Las Calderas, s.l., 6; 3 km W Sabana Buey, s.l., 1; *Azua:* 1 km E Palmar de Ocoa, s.l., 1; Tábara Abajo, 1; 18 km S Peralta, 122 m, 8; 5 km S Peralta, 305 m, 33; 2.5 km W,

6.6 N Azua, 183 m, 1; *San Juan:* 9 km E Vallejuelo, 610 m, 7; *Baoruco:* 9 km N Neiba, 366 m, 1; *Independencia:* Las Lajas, s.l., 3; 4 km NW Tierra Nueva, s.l., 1; 1 km S Boca de Cachón, s.l., 1; 4–7 km NE El Aguacate, 519–824 m, 11; 2 km S Duvergé, 1; 0.6 km NW Puerto Escondido, 519 m, 1; *Barahona:* 11.5 km ESE Canoa, s.l., 1; 12 km ESE Canoa, s.l., 4; *Pedernales:* Cabo Rojo, s.l., 2; 2 km NE Cabo Rojo, s.l., 1; 23 km NE Cabo Rojo, 488 m, 4; 26 km NE Cabo Rojo, 732 m, 4; 1 km SE Banano, 183 m, 2; 2 km N Banano, 244 m, 1; 17 km NW Oviedo, 183 m, 2.

Sight records: República Dominicana: Monte Cristi: 4 km NW Villa Vásquez, 61 m—4 seen, 8.vii; *Dajabón:* Los Cerezos, 12 km NW Río Limpio, 680 m—2 seen, 14.vii; *Santiago Rodríguez:* Loma Leonor, 18 km SW Monción, 534 m—1 seen, 13.viii; *La Vega:* 5 km SE Jarabacoa, 595 m—1 seen, 29.vi; *La Altagracia:* 2.5 km SE Playa Bayahibe, s.l.—10 seen, 25.vi; 1 km N Playa Bayahibe, s.l.—2 seen, 4.viii; *Azua:* 2 km N Yayas de Viajama, 366 m—1 seen, 4.viii; 5 km SE Monte Bonito, 702 m—1 seen, 4.viii; *Pedernales:* Cabo Rojo, s.l.—1 seen, 3.vii.

2. *Memphis johnsoni* Avinoff and Shoumatoff, 1941

TL Cave River, Clarendon Parish, Jamaica (Comstock, 1961: 74).

FW males 28–29 mm.

Memphis johnsoni was described on the basis of 6 specimens from Jamaica (Avinoff and Shoumatoff, 1941:313–16). Marión Heredia (1978c) reported the taking of 2 specimens at El Número, Prov. de Azua, República Dominicana (1 in October 1967), and Riley (1975:59) noted the capture of another individual at "Boutilliers," Haiti. These were the first records of *M. johnsoni* from Hispaniola. Schwartz (1983a:27) recorded the taking of 2 specimens on Boutilliers Road and a sight record for another locality (0.5 km NE Obléon), all in Haiti, at elevations between 915 and 1678 m. There is no doubt that *M. johnsoni* occurs naturally on Hispaniola; it should not be regarded as a vagrant there.

We have collected several times in the El Número area without success; return visits to the Boutilliers-Obléon region in iv.1982 and xii.1984 yielded no additional specimens.

El Número is a high hill (or low mountain) that lies on the western edge of the Sierra de Ocoa, an affiliate of the Cordillera Central, with an elevation of 628 m. Before the construction of the new highway between Santo Domingo and Barahona (completed in 1983), the former 2-lane road passed from Baní through Cruce de Ocoa and thence down the slope of El Número to the city of Azua in the Llanos de Azua. This old road descended, by a series of switchbacks, through a fine stand of xeric woods; the new road has simplified this descent and also has massively disturbed the immediate environs of the road, so that the El Número slope is no longer a profitable locality for collecting. The old road is presently unreachable. The entire area is xerophytic, with a flora of *Acacia* and cacti and other xerophytes. Since plants of the genus *Croton* (Euphorbiaceae) are the larval food plants for some *Anaea* and *Memphis* (unconfirmed for *M. johnsoni*), and since several species of *Croton* are xerophytes, the association of the El Número area and *M. johnsoni* is reasonable, in fact more so than that between *M. johnsoni* and the high front ranges (Morne l'Hôpital, Montagne Noire) on which the butterfly has been taken in Haiti.

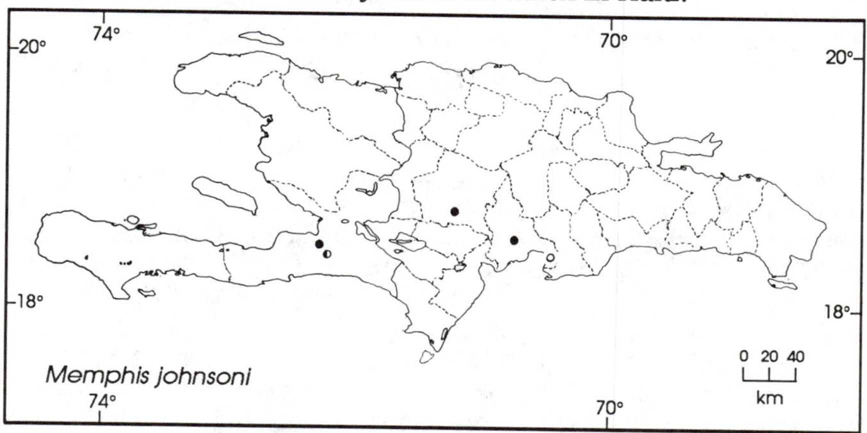

In just such situations, in 1986 we collected 11 *M. johnsoni* in the República Dominicana. Peralta is at a xeric-mesic interface, whereas Vallejuelo is a xeric upland valley, with extensive stands of *Croton barahonensis*. The butterflies were feeding on decayed mangoes (Peralta, 2 occasions) and on *Lantana ovatifolia* (Vallejuelo).

Schwartz (1983a:27) noted that, of the 3 species of Hispaniolan *Anaea* (including *Memphis*), only *M. johnsoni* has been regularly observed to use flowers (*Lantana ovatifolia* and *Ixora* sp.) as a nectar source. The foraging behavior of *M. johnsoni* is distinctive in that the butterfly remains motionless except for its probing proboscis, relying on its deep russet un color for camouflage. When 1 group of flowers in the inflorescence has been tested, the butterfly walks leisurely to an adjacent group and once more remains motionless except for the movement of its proboscis.

Memphis johnsoni has been collected and observed (in Haiti) on an open and shrubby mountainside and in pine forest. Dates for *M. johnsoni* in Haiti are between 10.vii and 13.viii. No times or temperatures were recorded. In the República Dominicana, 7 specimens were taken in June and 4 in August. Times were 1020–1630 h at temperatures between 33°C (Peralta) and 37°C (Vallejuelo). Elevations are between 305 m (Peralta) and 1678 m (Obléon).

Comparison between Hispaniolan *M. johnsoni* and Jamaican specimens (from Mt. Diablo, St. Catherine Parish) shows that the 2 samples are identical.

Specimens: Haiti: l'Ouest: Boutilliers Road, 732–915 m, 2; *República Dominicana: Azua:* 5 km S Peralta, 305 m, 7; *San Juan:* 9 km SE Vallejuelo, 610 m, 4.

3. *Memphis verticordia verticordia* Hübner, 1824

TL none stated; restricted to Haiti by Godman and Salvin (1884).

FW males 30–32 mm, females 34–38 mm.

Memphis verticordia was considered by Comstock (1961:82 *et seq.*) a polytypic species, including *luciana* Hall (St. Lucia and Martinique) and *dominicana* Godman and Salvin (Dominica). Riley (1975:60–61) considered *A. dominicana* (with its subspecies *luciana*) distinct from *M. verticordia*. Clench (1980:15) considered *A. intermedia* Witt (Turks and Caicos islands; Great and Little Inagua islands in the Bahama Islands) and *A. echemus* Doubleday and Hewitson (Cuba, Cayman Islands, northern and southern Bahama Islands; including *A. e. bahamae* Witt and *A. e. danieliana* Witt) conspecific with *M. verticordia*, the validation of this action included in an unpublished MS. I follow Clench's suggestion here in using the trinomial for the Hispaniolan population.

Of the 3 Hispaniolan *Anaea*-like butterflies, *A. v. verticordia* ranks second in abundance; Comstock (1961:82) reported the species from only 3 localities: Port-au-Prince and Fond Parisien in Haiti, and Cabral in the República Dominicana. He also noted that he had "few specimens" for study. These 3 localities suggest that *M. v. verticordia* is restricted to lowland xeric localities, within or adjacent to the Cul de Sac–Valle de Neiba plain. Fond Parisien and Cabral are within that plain itself, but both of these settlements are about large springs, so oases and palm groves are included within the towns. Also, Cabral lies at the north base of the Sierra de Baoruco, and the material from there may well have been taken between Cabral and Polo, the latter at an elevation of 702 m. Port-au-Prince lies on the coast in an essentially xeric region at the western extreme of the Cul de Sac plain.

Hall (1925:188) reported seeing 1 individual at La Cumbre in the Dominican Cordillera Septentrional; the elevation at this locality is about 610 m, and the habitat now is mesic *cafetales*.

Whether the butterfly was seen precisely at La Cumbre is of course unknown.

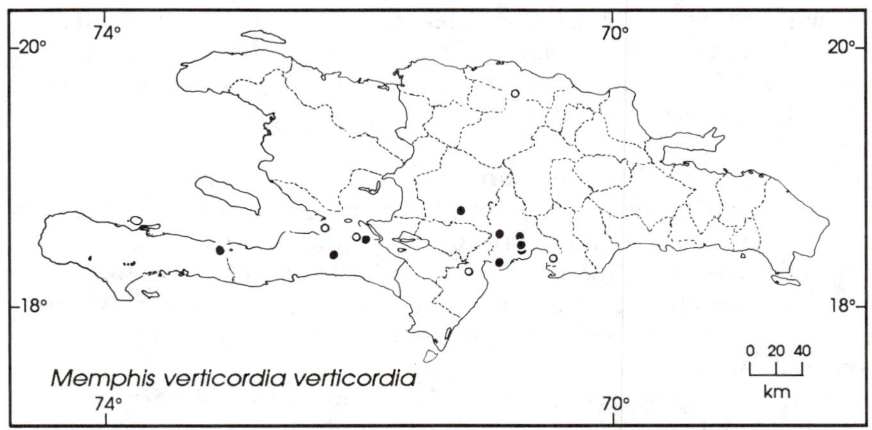

Memphis verticordia verticordia

We have never seen or taken *M. v. verticordia* at any of the above localities. Schwartz (1983a:28) reported 3 Haitian specimens; 1 of these is from the Montagne Noire (Obléon) and the others are from the north (Paillant) and south (Cavaillon) slopes of the eastern and western extremities of the Massif de la Hotte. The habitat at Obléon is pinewoods, that at Paillant an open field with *Lantana ovatifolia* and *Hibiscus rosasinensis*, that at Cavaillon a mesic *caféière*. Elevations are between 610 and 1617 m; the latter is the upper elevational extreme for *M. v. verticordia*. Newly taken specimens from Fond Parisien are from sea level.

In the República Dominicana, we have specimens from 3 general regions: the Valle de San Juan, where the butterflies can be very abundant, although localized; the Sierra Martín García, where *M. v. verticordia* occurs in modest abundance between 305 and 1037 m; and Peralta, where many individuals have been taken. The Sierra Martín García slopes are xeric (lower elevations) to rather mesic (upper elevations), and the butterflies were abundant there on 9.vii.1983, but only in a narrow elevational band (between 305 and 534 m). A second visit to these mountains on 13.viii.1983 showed that *M. v. verticordia* was then abundant at El Limón at 976–1037 m, where they were feeding on the bleeding sap of a tree (with *M. aracynthia*) adjacent to the only upland water source, a muddy rain pond. At this time there had been no rain on these mountains for 2 months, which may account for the apparent spread of *M. v. verticordia* upward to less harsh situations.

At Peralta, *M. v. verticordia* was taken in xeric woods; here they were rather uncommon but were flying with *A. troglodyta* about a blow-down. There was no obvious reason for this activity since the blow-down was long dead and leafless, with no injury or bleeding sap. Yet both species were reluctant to leave the immediate area and landed, usually 2 m or less above the ground, with wings closed, upon the branches of the tree and other associated saplings.

Certainly we have encountered *M. v. verticordia* most abundantly at Vallejuelo, where, on 23–28.vii.1981, very large numbers of *M. v. verticordia* and smaller numbers of *A. troglodyta* were encountered in and about xeric woods with *Acacia*. The butterflies were so abundant that a collector could hardly "escape"; they were everywhere in these woods and were the dominant rhopalocerans present. At this site, at the foot of a low road shoulder slope on the south side of the road, just within the margin of the woods, a concentration of *M. v. verticordia* (the dominant species), *A. troglodyta*, and *H. a. diasia* was settled on about a square meter of earth that appeared to be no different from nearby areas. On closer inspection, we found that this spot was covered with a layer of extremely old and completely dried fruits of some sort. In their condition, they could hardly have supplied any nourishment or moisture, yet these butterflies (most especially *M. v. verticordia*) were dedicated to resting at this particular place or on small bare sticks and fallen branches that overlay the attractive spot. Collecting there, and determined efforts to displace these butterflies, did not truly discourage them; all 3 species would promptly return when displaced, and *M. v. verticordia* was the most persistent. Elsewhere in these woods, where *M. v. verticordia* was abundant, we found no other such concentrations; rather, the butterflies were flying in and about small trees, saplings, and scrub in a lazy and "relaxed" manner; some *M. v. verticordia* were also seen on the paved road at this locality. These were flying in the "mad dash" pattern typical of *Anaea*.

A return visit to this same locality on 2.viii.1982 showed that the numbers of *M. v. verticordia* had declined greatly in the intervening year; there were still some butterflies present but not in the numbers of 1981. The enticing spot, where in the previous year there had been many individuals, was now deserted. In 1986 *M. v. verticordia* was still common there but not in the numbers observed in August 1982.

We have taken *M. v. verticordia* feeding on decayed mangoes (Peralta), on *Ageratum conyzoides* (Peralta), and on the pale cream flowers of an unidentified vine (Fond Parisien). While feeding on *A.*

conyzoides, 1 of these butterflies used 4 inflorescences as nectar sources; this suggests that use of these flowers was deliberate. The association of *M. v. verticordia* with a particular tree in *Acacia* scrub at Azua has been noted in the account of *A. troglodyta*.

Most of our specimens (75) have been taken in July, with 18 in June, 14 in August, 5 in January, and 3 in December. Elevations were between 122 m (Peralta) and 1617 m (Obléon). Times of collection were between 0930 and 1715 h, and temperatures between 27°C (Fond Parisien, Vallejuelo) and 38°C (Vallejuelo). At Vallejuelo on 24.vii.1981, *M. v. verticordia* was just as common on a very overcast day (no temperature taken) as it had been on 23.vii.1981 under bright and sunny conditions. In general, our observations suggest that Hispaniolan *Anaea* are active only under sunny and hot conditions and that they rest on bare branches under overcast conditions. On this occasion, it may be that *M. v. verticordia* was observed flying on an overcast day because the population there was immense and flight under less than favorable conditions was therefore more apparent to the observer than it would normally have been.

Specimens: Haiti: l'Ouest: 4 km SE Fond Parisien, s.l., 3; 0.3 km N Obléon, 1617 m, 1; *Sud:* 2.9–3.0 km SW Paillant, 671 m, 3; 25.6 km N Cavaillon, 610 m, 1; *República Dominicana: Azua:* 18 km S Peralta, 122 m, 2; *Azua:* 5 km S Peralta, 305 m, 17; 2.5 km W, 6.6 km N Azua, 183 m, 29; 0.5 km NE Hato Nuevo de Cortés, 214 m, 1; *San Juan:* 9 km E Vallejuelo, 610 m, 46; *Barahona:* El Limón, summit, Sierra Martín García, 976–1037 m, 1; west slope, Sierra Martín García, 534 m, 1; west slope, Sierra Martín García, 488 m, 3; west slope, Sierra Martín García, 305–458 m, 5.

4. *Siderone galanthis nemesis* Illiger, 1802

TL Santo Domingo.

FW 35–39 mm.

Siderone g. nemesis occurs on Cuba (including the Isla de la Juventud), Puerto Rico, where it appears to be rare (Comstock, 1944:476), and Hispaniola. Hall (1925:188) reported taking a pair near Puerto Plata, República Dominicana, and saw "specimens" at La Vega in the same country. I have not taken the species in Haiti, but we have 2 sight records from that country. I have only 21 specimens from the República Dominicana, and there is 1 specimen in the MNHNSD. From these data, *S. g. nemesis* appears to be rather uncommon, although at Ennery, Sabana de la Mar, and La Romana, these butterflies were more common than elsewhere. Customarily one sees only a single individual at a locality.

The habitat of *S. g. nemesis* is woods or forests, either mesic

(Río Bao, Los Cerezos, Las Lagunas, Santo Domingo, La Ciénaga, Barahona, Paraíso, Neiba) or xeric (Villa Vásquez, Punta Caucedo, Playa Bayahibe, Enriquillo). In such wooded situations, *S. g. nemesis* darts furiously down roads or paths or through clearings to land on the undersides of leaves (where the wings are closed with an occasional spreading) or on the upper sides of leaves, (where the wings remain open with an occasional closing).

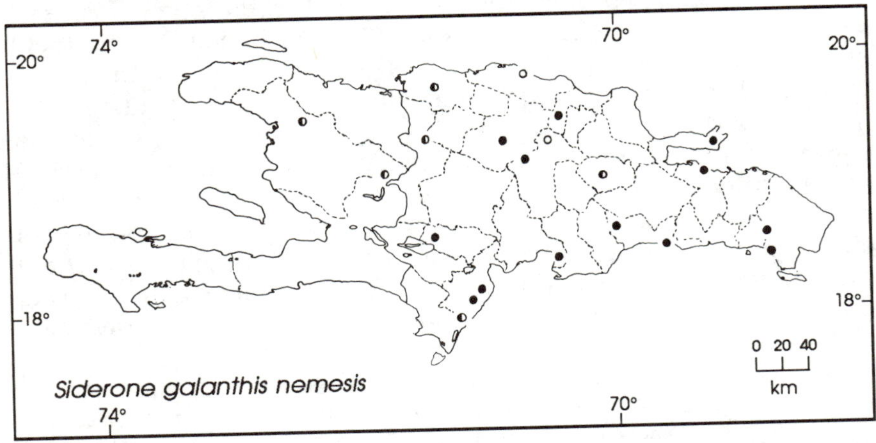

The butterflies are often fearless. At Río Bao, Gali, Iketani, and I, with the help of a local Dominican boy, "chased" a recalcitrant *S. g. nemesis* (which had first been seen perched on the top of a leaf of a tree immediately adjacent to the road and about 3 m above the ground) through the downhill slope of a mesic ravine forest, where it made several landings and became "invisible," and finally captured it on a leaf about 2 m above a creek. The whole procedure took perhaps 15 minutes, but the butterfly made no attempt to escape by leaving its course from the road through the woods to the creek, a distance of about 25 m. The final capture was effected after perhaps 4 minutes of debate among the pursuers immediately beneath the leaf on which the butterfly was perched. Such daring is unusual among butterflies.

Many specimens collected result from improvident actions by the butterflies. Those from Jamao al Norte and La Romana were taken by me when the butterflies landed immediately beside me (within 2 m) on the undersides of leaves of bushes and shrubs and remained steadfast. Both sites were clearings within woods or forest. On the same date as the La Romana capture, 7 other *S. g. nemesis* were seen (by Gineika), 1 on the trail, the others high in trees in clearings in the late afternoon (1500–1600 h). The specimen from Punta Caucedo was taken flying in scubby mesic woods, by Wisor.

Gali saw a *S. g. nemesis* (10.viii.1982) in the oasis at Villa Vásquez, but it darted away and was not seen again. Another was seen there (13.iii.1984) but also escaped. The Las Lagunas sight records are for single individuals that flew determinedly over low roadside vines or down the road (2) or were seen on a path in the forest (1) and then disappeared. Near Thomonde, Lucio and I saw a *S. g. nemesis* cross the road where it passed through a very small patch of much disturbed mesic woods, from which we were not able to flush it. At Ennery, in a large area of cutover scrubby mesic woods, several (perhaps 5) *S. g. nemesis* were observed by Graham, Thurmond, and me as the butterflies raced along a creek. None was secured, but they seemed unafraid of the regular swipes of the nets as they passed. The often brazen or confident behavior of *S. g. nemesis* makes it a real prize for the collector; the insect truly merits its designation as *nemesis!*

Most individuals have been taken or seen in August (8), with 7 in July, 6 in March, 4 in April, and 3 in June; May, November, and December are each represented by 1. Elevational extremes are sea level (Playa Bayahibe, Punta Caucedo) and 915 m (La Ciénaga); the latter record is exceptional and most records are below 200 m. Times of collection were between 0940 and 1630 h, with temperatures between 28°C (Playa Bayahibe, Enriquillo) and 38°C (Río Bao, Sabana de la Mar, Playa Bayahibe). We have seen *S. g. nemesis* feeding on *Lantana ovatifolia* at Sabana de la Mar, where these butterflies were more abundant (iii–iv.1984) than we have seen them elsewhere, even in those months.

Specimens: República Dominicana: Espaillat: 20 km SW Jamao al Norte, 793 m, 1; *Santiago:* Río Bao, 8 km SE Montones Abajo, 488 m, 2; *La Vega:* La Ciénaga, 915 m, 1; *Samaná:* 2.8 km S Las Galeras, 61 m, 1; *Hato Mayor:* 7 km E Sabana de la Mar, 5; *La Altagracia:* 1 km N Playa Bayahibe, s.l., 2; 16 km NE La Romana, 61 m, 1; *Dist. Nac.:* Punta Caucedo, 2 km W, 2 km S Andrés, s.l., 1; 30 km NW Santo Domingo, 153 m, 1; *Azua:* El Número, 1 (MNHNSD); *Baoruco:* 11 km N Neiba, 519 m, 1; *Barahona:* 5 km SE, 3 km W Barahona, 183–397 m, 4; 8 km NW Paraíso, 153 m, 1.

Sight records: Haiti: Nord: E Ennery—several seen, 6.vii; *l'Ouest:* S Thomonde—1 seen, 13.vii; *República Dominicana: Monte Cristi:* 4 km NW Villa Vásquez, 61 m—1 seen, 13.iii; 1 seen, 10.viii; *Dajabón:* Los Cerezos, 12 km NW Río Limpio, 580 m—1 seen, 4.viii; *Sánchez Ramírez:* 1 km NE Las Lagunas, 183 m—2 seen, 3.iii; 1 seen, 2.xi; *Barahona:* 8 km NW Paraíso, 153 m—1 seen, 3.iv; 3 km NW Enriquillo, 244 m—1 seen, 9.iv.

5. *Archaeoprepona demophoon amphitoe* Godart, 1823

TL S. America; restricted to Haiti by Riley (1975:57).

FW males 43–60 mm, females 56–57 mm.

Although Riley (1975:56) used the trivial name *amphitoe* Godart for the 2 Antillean populations of *Archaeoprepona*, I depart from that usage here and follow Johnson and Descimon (MS in prep.) by using *A. demophoon* Hübner for the species. *Archaeoprepona d. crassina* Fruhstorfer occurs on Cuba. An as yet unnamed (Johnson and Descimon, MS in prep.) subspecies is on Puerto Rico.

Archaeoprepona d. amphitoe is widespread on Hispaniola but is much more common in the República Dominicana than in Haiti. There are many more records of this butterfly from the north island than from the south island. Hall (1925:188) regarded it as "not uncommon" at La Cumbre, La Vega, and Mt. Isabela. Riley (1975:56) cited these records and added Port-au-Prince, Haiti; the latter is the only south island report (Schwartz, 1983a:26). The apparent absence of *A. d. amphitoe* from the Tiburon Peninsula west of Port-au-Prince is strange; we have visited in the appropriate times of the year several localities there (Paillant, for example) that offer the proper ecology for this butterfly. Much of the distal portion of this peninsula, as well as the uplands of the Massif de la Selle between Dufort and Jacmel, or the Massif de la Hotte between Miragoâne and St. Michel du Sud, has the appropriate forests. The extreme western portion of the peninsula supports mesic forests or pseudoforests, from sea level to high elevations, which should harbor *A. d. amphitoe*. Yet the butterfly remains unrecorded from this entire area.

As the above paragraph suggests, *A. d. amphitoe* is a forest inhabitant; the forests may be mesic (Santo Domingo), xeric (La Romana), or transitional (El Aguacate), but need not be extensive. Schwartz (1983a:27) noted the behavior of *A. d. amphitoe* at Carrefour Marmelade, where several individuals were patrolling a narrow ravine with a narrow creek. A similar situation was at Jamao al Norte, where a narrow and well-wooded ravine harbored *A. d. amphitoe*. *Cacaotales-cafetales* and *caféières* are inhabited regularly by at least a few *A. d. amphitoe*.

But the largest concentration of these conspicuous butterflies that we encountered was in transitional woods (El Aguacate) on 27.vii.1982. We estimated perhaps 100 individuals along the 3-km stretch of road, The butterflies were perching on the trunks (head down) of trees (where an individual would return time after time), or more often on the leaves at the ends of pendant branches over the road. Wings are usually held closed, with only an occasional act of opening. At this locality, I walked down the road wearing a pale blue field hat; twice, *A. d. amphitoe* landed on the hat with a rustling of the stiff wings, perhaps attracted to the blue color. At this same locality on 30.vii.1982, 2 individuals (1 male collected) were seen fluttering tightly about each other on the ground; the same act was seen at Enriquillo on 8.vii.1983. This may be premating behavior. A pair *in copula* was taken 5 km SE Jarabacoa, 595 m (29.vi, 1410 h, 33°C) in a forested ravine.

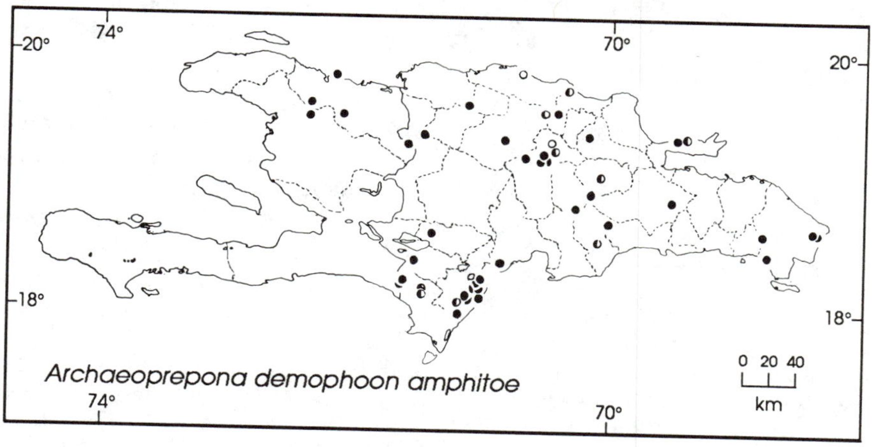

Archaeoprepona demophoon amphitoe

Archaeoprepona d. amphitoe, like *Prepona*, does not use nectar as an energy source; we have observed these butterflies on rotted mangoes (Enriquillo, twice; Paraíso), where they were in the company of *H. o. odius* (Enriquillo), and at Banano, where the *Archaeoprepona* was with an *A. troglodyta*. At Río Bao, several *A. d. amphitoe* were flying about a *Eugenia axillaris* (Myrtaceae) in bloom, as if the butterflies were assessing the tree for oviposition. At Jamao al Norte, we observed an *A. d. amphitoe* ovipositing on an unidentified sapling without flowers; the sapling was about 3 m high and 3 cm DBH, adjacent to a small creek.

Times of collection were between 0900 and 1700 h, and temperatures between 27°C (El Aguacate) and 40°C (Río Guarabo). Most *A. d. amphitoe* were taken on bright and sunny days, but occasionally (El Aguacate) these butterflies were active under rainy conditions. As noted by Gali and Schwartz (1983a), *A. d. amphitoe* appear to become inactive ("rest") during the extreme heat of the day; on 14.viii at Playa Bayahibe, about 10 were seen at 1400 h on dead vines above a dirt road in xeric woods. The temperature was 34°C, and the day was bright and sunny. As many as 3 *A. d. amphitoe* were seen together on the same 1-m length of draped vine.

The elevational distribution of *A. d. amphitoe* is between sea level (Cormier Plage, Las Terrenas, Punta Cana, Playa Bayahibe, La Ciénaga) and 915 m (Sierra Martín García); in Haiti the high elevation is 854 m (Carrefour Marmelade). These are 2 of 7 localities above 580 m, so *A. d. amphitoe* is primarily an inhabitant of low to moderate elevations.

Most specimens and observations are from July (66) and August (65), with 9 in June, 8 in March, 6 in April, 4 in October, and 2 in December. The low incidence of June records suggests that these butterflies emerge in July-August. But any series of July or August specimens includes along with freshly emerged individuals some that are badly flown, suggesting that *A. d. amphitoe* is on the wing throughout most of the year, perhaps in diminished numbers. On the other hand, we rarely saw *A. d. amphitoe* in June, even though we collected in the proper habitats and under the proper conditions.

Specimens: Haiti: Nord: Cormier Plage, s.l., 1; 5.6 km SE Dondon, 336 m, 2; 3.5 km W Plaisance, 305 m, 1; *l'Artibonite:* 1.6 km E Carrefour Marmelade, 854 m, 1; *República Dominicana: Dajabón:* Los Cerezos, 12 km NW Río Limpio, 580 m, 1; Cañada Tirolís, just S Villa Anacaona, 458 m, 1; *Valverde:* Río Guarabo, 3 km W Los Quemados, 122 m, 1; *Santiago:* Río Bao, 8 km SE Montones Abajo, 488 m, 1; *Espaillat:* 14 km SW Jamao al Norte, 534 m, 2; *Monseñor Nouel:* 14 km SW Piedra Blanca, 427 m, 4; 6 km SE Maimón, 122 m, 1; *Duarte:* 10 km SE Tenares, 183 m, 1; *Samaná:* 13.2 km NE Sánchez, 92 m, 1; *La Vega:* 1 km W Manabao, 293 m, 4; Jarabacoa, 530 m, 6; 5 km SE Jarabacoa, 595 m, 3; 6 km S Jarabacoa, *ca.* 610 m, 1; *La Altagracia:* 3 km W Punta Cana, s.l., 1; 2 km W Punta Cana, s.l., 4; 1 km N Playa Bayahibe, s.l., 8; 16 km NE La Romana, 61 m, 2; *Monte Plata:* 8 km NE Bayaguna, 1; *Dist. Nac.:* 30 km NW Santo Domingo, 122 m, 9; *Baoruco:* 11 km N Neiba, 571 m, 1; *Independencia:* 4–7 km NE El Aguacate, 519–824 m, 21; *Barahona:* west slope, Sierra Martín García, 854–915 m, 1; 2 km SW Barahona, 122 m, 1; 8 km SW Barahona, 366 m, 1; 5 km SE, 3 km W Barahona, 183 m, 17; 5 km SE, 6.4 km W Barahona, 488 m, 1; 12 km SW Barahona, 427 m, 1; 2 km SW La Ciénaga, s.l., 1; 10.5 km NE Paraíso, 1; 11 km NW Paraíso, 366 m, 1; 8 km NW Paraíso, 153 m, 3 (2 MPM); 3 km NW Enriquillo, 244 m, 16; *Pedernales:* 1 km SE Banano, 183 m, 1; Mencía, 397 m, 5.

Sight records: República Dominicana: Santiago: 2 km E Pedro García, 417 m—1 seen, 21.vii; *Puerto Plata:* 11 km SE Sosúa, 183 m—1 seen, 2.viii; *La Vega:* Buena Vista, 11 km NE Jarabacoa, 640 m—1 seen, 31.xii; *Samaná:* 3 km SW Las Terrenas, s.l.—2 seen, 11.viii; *La Altagracia:* Punta Cana, s.l.—3 seen, 30.x; *Monte Plata:* 8 km NE Bayaguana—1 seen, 7.iii; *Sánchez Ramírez:* 1 km NE Las Lagunas, 183 m—5 seen, 3.iii; *San Cristóbal:* 8 km NW Cambita Garabitos, 534 m—1 seen, 14.viii; *Barahona:* Polo, 702 m—1 seen, 21.vii; 1.8 km W Monteada Nueva, 1007 m—1 seen, 14.viii; 8 km NW Paraíso, 153 m—several seen, 28.vii; *Pedernales:* 23 km NE Cabo Rojo, 488 m, 1 seen, 31.vii; 1 seen, 6.x; 26 km NE Cabo Rojo, 732 m—2 seen, 31.vii.

Subfamily Apaturinae Boisduval, 1840

6. *Asterocampa idyja idyja* Geyer, 1828

TL Cuba.

FW males 25–29 mm, females 31–38 mm.

Asterocampa i. idyja is known from Cuba (and the Isla de la Juventud), Hispaniola, and Puerto Rico. It has been reported as rare on the latter 2 islands and "widespread in woodland country" on Cuba (Riley, 1975:56). Hall did not record the species, and we have not taken *A. i. idyja* in the area he visited. Despite the fact that the Hispaniolan population has been named as a distinct subspecies (*padola* Fruhstorfer), there appear to be no grounds for this action, since wherever *A. i. idyja* occurs, it is extremely variable in up coloration. For example, our Hispaniolan males vary from pale uniform tan, with the fw apices barely darker, to males that have the fw deeper tan basally and the fw apices dark brown; the differences are not due to wear. In the paler males, the hw postdiscal series of 5 dark brown spots is likewise pale, so these pale males have a generally "washed-out" appearance. Females show the same variation; some are pale tan with the fw apices only slightly darker, others have the fw disc deep orange-brown and the fw apices very dark brown. There is no geographic correlation between these chromotypes. Another subspecies, *A. i. argus* Bates, 1864, occurs from México to Nicaragua (Friedlander, 1988).

Asterocampa i. idyja is an inhabitant of either xeric or mesic woods or forests; it has rarely been encountered in pseudoforests. Only 2 exceptions to the above habitats have been recorded; my only Haitian specimen (Cormier Plage) was taken on an open beach as it sought to shelter behind a bush from the onshore wind. I have a specimen from a *Citrus* grove (San José de Ocoa) with much trash, including decayed mangoes, which might have attracted the butterfly. *Asterocampa i. idyja* feeds on decayed mangoes; at Barahona, we took a specimen that was sharing a mango with an *H. o. odius.* But on 1 occasion (Barahona) we observed a female feeding on *Lantana ovatifolia*, and we have taken these butterflies on *Tournefortia hirsutissima* (Sosúa, 3 occasions; Playa Bayahibe) and on *Ageratum conyzoides* (El Aguacate, 21 km N Cabo Rojo). *Asterocampa i. idyja* takes both floral and nonfloral foods. A single individual was taken while drinking from a trickle down a paved road (5 km SE, 3 km W Barahona).

In the field, these butterflies resemble *Dryas i. hispaniola* both in appearance and style of flight. They frequent open areas in woods and fly lazily, often landing with the wings spread. When disturbed, however, they evade capture by flying away rapidly and are soon out of the collector's range. On all occasions when we have taken *A. i. idyja*, the weather has been bright and sunny, with temperatures of 24°C (El Aguacate) to 39°C (San José de Ocoa). The elevational range is from sea level (Cormier Plage, Punta Cana, Playa Bayahibe) to 1129 m (Las Abejas). The latter elevation is exceptional, since most localities are between sea level and about 610 m. *Asterocampa i. idyja* is quite local and may be easily overlooked; we visited El Aguacate 4 times in 1982 and early June 1983 but did not see an *A. i. idyja* until 14.vii.1983, despite taking several hundred specimens of other rhopalocerans. Since El Aguacate is near the upper elevational extreme for this species, it is possible that the butterfly is uncommon there. Most specimens are from July (49), with 37 from August, 22 from June, 2 from January, and 1 each from October and December.

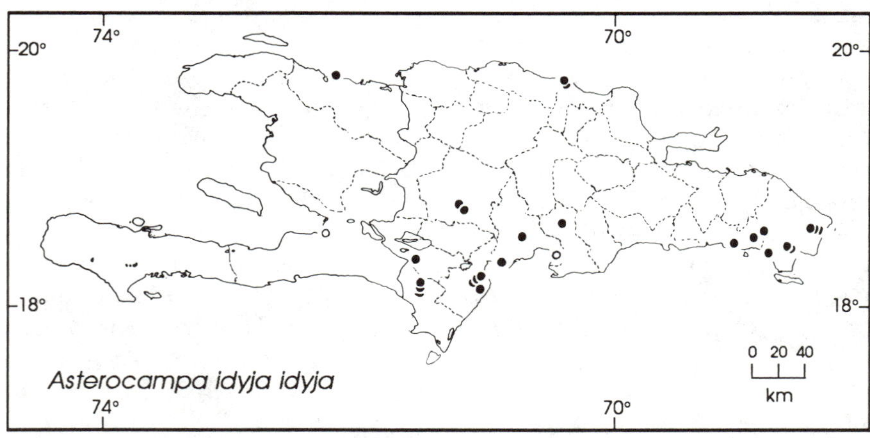

Specimens: Haiti: Nord: Cormier Plage, s.l., 1; *República Dominicana: Puerto Plata:* 9 km SE Sosúa, 16 m, 19; 11 km SE Sosúa, 46 m, 1; *La Altagracia:* Punta Cana, s.l., 2; 2 km W Punta Cana, s.l., 2; 6 km W Punta Cana, s.l., 3; 0.5–3.5 km W Boca de Yuma, 1; 2–3 km W Boca de Yuma, 1; Río Chavón, 10 km NE La Romana, 2; 1 km N Playa Bayahibe, s.l., 19; 16 km NE La Romana, 6l1 m, 10; *La Romana:* Río Cumayasa, 13.5 km W La Romana, 10; *Peravia:* 5 km N San José de Ocoa, 580 m, 1; *Azua:* 5 km S Peralta, 305 m, 2; *San Juan:* 9 km E Vallejuelo, 610 m, 1; 7 km NE Vallejuelo, 671 m, 1; *Independencia:* 4–7 km NE El Aguacate, 519–824 m, 10; *Barahona:* west slope, Sierra Martín García, 915 m, 2; west slope, Sierra Martín García, 458–610 m, 1; 2 km SW Barahona, 122 m, 5; 9 km SW Barahona, 366 m, 1;

12 km SW Barahona, 427 m, 1; 5 km SE, 3 km SW Barahona, 183–397 m, 2; *Pedernales:* 21 km NE Cabo Rojo, 427 m, 2; 26 km NE Cabo Rojo, 732 m, 5; 27 km NE Cabo Rojo, 793 m, 1.

Sight record: República Dominicana: Puerto Plata: 9 km SE Sosúa, 16 m—2 seen, 7.vii.

7. *Doxocopa thoe* Godart, 1823

TL "Brasil."

FW males 28–32 mm, females 28–36 mm.

The genus *Doxocopa* is represented on the Antilles by 2 species: *D. laure* Drury with a subspecies (*fabricii* Hall) on Jamaica and another (*druryi* Hübner) on Cuba, and *D. thoe* on Hispaniola. Brown and Heineman (1972:120) considered *D. l. fabricii* quite common, but Bates (1935a:181) recorded 25 specimens of *D. l. druryi* from central and eastern Cuba. Riley (1975:56) noted that *D. thoe* was "very rare," perhaps basing this assessment on Hall's (1925:188) comment that there were only 2 specimens known, a male from La Vega, República Dominicana, and a female from "Haiti."

Doxocopa thoe is broadly distributed in the República Dominicana (I have no Haitian specimens) but is decidedly local and apparently somewhat sporadic. Most localities are at or very near sea level (Playa Bayahibe), but the butterfly also occurs to 1129 m (Las Abejas). This is in some contrast to *D. l. fabricii*, whose elevational distribution is between 150 and 600 m (Brown and Heineman, 1972:120). All localities are in forest or woods, from xeric to mesic, where the butterflies are found darting along paths and narrow roads (once in sinkhole woods: Cabrera), landing, usually with the wings spread, on leaves up to 3 m from the ground. When the wings are opened, the males are especially conspicuous because of the blue to purple iridescence on the up, and females equally so because of the ochreous coloration. The butterflies are usually quite patient and not easily disturbed; if they are frightened, they have a stong tendency to return to the same (or nearby) leaf from which they departed. Like other apaturids, *D. thoe* has a "beat" which it patrols and from which it is difficult to discourage.

Most of our specimens are from the area near Playa Bayahibe in extreme eastern República Dominicana. Even there, in the summer of some years, the species is uncommon. In 1981, *D. thoe* was particularly abundant in this area; not only did we collect a series (and could have collected many more), but there is a long series (labeled simply "Bayahibe") in the MNHNSD. In other years (1980, 1982–86), *D. thoe* has been taken in the same region but not in the numbers of 1981. Collections were made there at 3 localities, 1 of which (2.5 km SE Playa Bayahibe) has yielded only 5 specimens; this locality is just behind the beach, in open woods with *Acacia*. The La Romana locality is a path through rather dense hardwood forest, with an understory of *Zamia* sp. The third locality, 1 km N Playa Bayahibe, is an abandoned vehicular road through dense xeric hardwoods. The last-mentioned locality was the most productive of *D. thoe*.

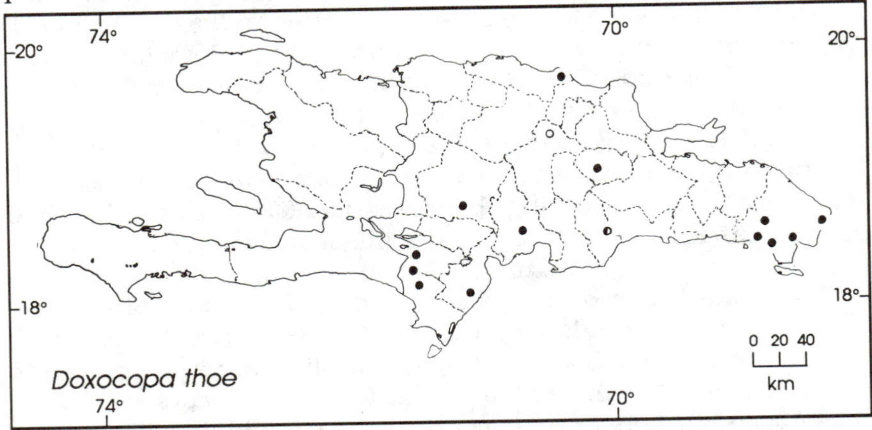

Most specimens or records are in July (77), with 32 in August, 18 in June, 10 in April, 3 each in March and December, and 2 in January. The summer is the peak time for *D. thoe*.

Times of collection were between 0915 and 1600 h, and temperatures between 24°C (El Aguacate) and 40°C (1 km N Playa Bayahibe).

Brown and Heineman (1972:120) noted that members of the genus *Doxocopa* rarely use flowers as a food source but rather are attracted to fermenting fruit on the ground, decaying animal matter and wastes, and sap oozing from wounded trees. *Doxocopa thoe* has not been seen using decaying flesh or sap as food sources; but it has been taken 9 times on *Tournefortia hirsutissima* (Sosúa, 1 km N Playa Bayahibe, Peralta), *Ixora* sp. (Boca de Yuma), *Morinda citrifolia* (Río Chavón), and *Ageratum conyzoides* (Vallejuelo). At Boca de Yuma, the butterflies were in part taken from an abandoned front-yard garden of an unoccupied house on the outskirts of town. At least 1 of the *D. thoe* taking nectar (at 1 km N Playa Bayahibe) is a female.

Aside from the Playa Bayahibe area, the habitat at Sosúa is mesic woods in karst topography, that at Punta Cana and Boca de

Yuma is xeric forest, and that at 26 km NE Cabo Rojo and El Aguacate is transitional xeric-mesic forest. It is remarkable that at the latter locality we have secured only 4 *D. thoe* in 17 visits. The Río Chavón locality is a riverine palm grove. Elsewhere, all localities are mesic forest.

Specimens: República Dominicana: Puerto Plata: 9 km SE Sosúa, 16 m, 18; *María T. Sánchez:* 6 km S Cabrera, s.l., 2; *La Altagracia:* Punta Cana, s.l., 1; 0.5–3.5 km W Boca de Yuma, 5; 16 km NE La Romana, 12; 2.5 km SE Playa Bayahibe, 5; 1 km N Playa Bayahibe, s.l., 85; *La Romana:* Río Chavón, 8 km SE La Romana, s.l., 1; *Sánchez Ramírez:* 1 km NE Las Lagunas, 183 m, 1; *Azua:* 5 km S Peralta, 305 m, 2; *San Juan:* 9 km E Vallejuelo, 610 m, 1; *Independencia:* 4–7 km NE El Aguacate, 519 m, 4; *Barahona:* 8–10 km NW Paraíso, 1 (MPM); *Pedernales:* 26 km NE Cabo Rojo, 732 m, 3; Las Abejas, 12 km NW Aceitillar, 1129 m, 1.

Sight records: República Dominicana: Sánchez Ramírez: 1 km NE Las Lagunas, 183 m—2 seen, 4.iv; *La Altagracia:* 2.5 km SE Playa Bayahibe, s.l.—2 seen, 5.vii; *San Cristóbal:* La Cuchilla, 15 km N Hato Damas, 153 m—1 seen, 18.iv; *Independencia:* 4–7 km NE El Aguacate, 519–732 m—1 seen, 22.vi; *Barahona:* 8 km NW Paraíso, 153 m—2 seen, 3.iv; 2 seen, 6.iv; *Pedernales:* Las Abejas, 12 km NW Aceitillar, 1129 m—1 seen, 27.vii.

Family Satyridae Boisduval, 1836

Subfamily Satyrinae Boisduval, 1836

1. *Calisto archebates* Ménétriés, 1832

TL Haiti.

FW males 18–21 mm, females 18–22 mm.

Calisto archebates has been known from only the high uplands (5000–7000 ft.) of the Haitian portion of the Massif de la Selle. Hall (1925) reported the occurrence of this species at Puerto Plata, along the borders of sugarcane fields, but Schwartz (1983b:2) dismissed this peculiar record. There is no evidence that *C. archebates* occurs at Puerto Plata or in the Cordillera Septentrional that overlooks that city. As will be seen below, borders of lowland cane fields are very unlikely places to encounter this *Calisto!*

Since all recorded sites for *C. archebates* are from Haiti near the Dominico-Haitian border, it is no surprise that the species occurs in the República Dominicana in the Dominican portion of the Massif de la Selle. In addition, *C. archebates* enters at least the extreme western part of the Sierra de Baoruco (Las Abejas). The habitats of the species in the 2 countries are so strikingly different that each merits separate discussion.

Schwartz (1983a:20) stated that the habitat of this species in Haiti is "short grassy areas in pinewoods." Such pines offer shade, and these butterflies occur, at times very abundantly, in the low grasses and among bushes. At other times at the very same site *C. archebates* is absent (present in June, absent in August; Schwartz, 1983a:20). These observations suggest great seasonality and adaptation to a basically xeric habitat at high elevations. Additional collecting in Haiti at Forêt des Pins reinforced these conclusions. Gali took a long series of *C. archebates* near Morne la Visite (Scierie) on the Massif de la Selle. The habitat was pine forest with a fern understory. The weather was overcast (1.ix–4.ix). Many more individuals than the 27 collected were seen. The elevational distribution in Haiti is between 1464 m (Peneau) and 1891 m (Scierie).

In the República Dominicana, on the other hand, *C. archebates* occurs only in rich mesic deciduous forest and is virtually absent from pine forest. Nor does it show the seasonality that it shows in Haiti—we have Dominican specimens from June, July, August, and October, from the same localities. It is a very abundant butterfly, 1 of the few species of Rhopalocera that inhabit the high dripping forests of the Massif de la Selle. Its Dominican elevational distribution, somewhat broader than that in Haiti, is from 1129 m (Las Abejas) to 1891 m (El Aguacate).

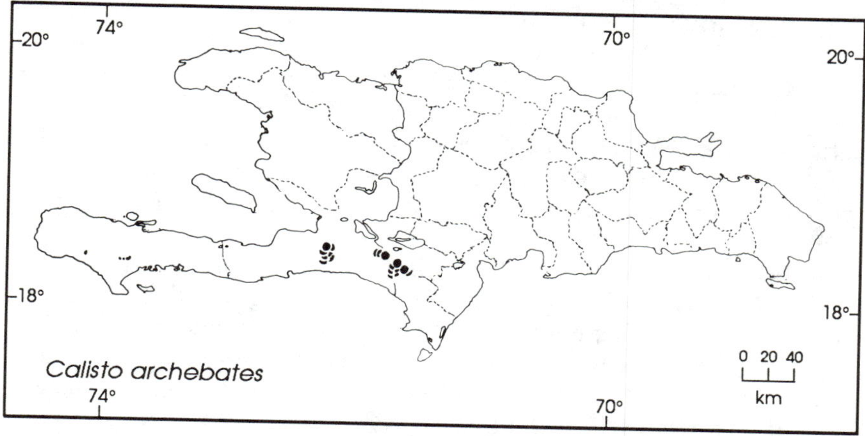

Calisto archebates

On the El Aguacate–Los Arroyos road along the border, *C. archebates* is first encountered (when going south) at about 1460 m, once the road has entered mesic forest. As one ascends the range on this road, once one has entered pines (at about 1800 m), *C. archebates* disappears and is replaced by *C. sommeri*. *Calisto sommeri* occurs abundantly in the pines, but it is once more replaced by *C. archebates* at about 1640 m on the southern slope of these mountains. The 2 species are rarely encountered together, and their habitat preferences are striking. We have taken only 1 *C. archebates* in contrast to many *C. sommeri* in the pine forest.

The situation on the south slope of the Haitian Massif de la Selle can no longer be determined; once one leaves the Forêt des Pins plateau and begins the descent to Thiotte, the slopes have been completely cleared and cultivated and do not present suitable habitat for *C. archebates*.

The low elevation for *C. archebates* in the República Dominicana is Las Abejas. This locality has been described by Gali and Schwartz (1983c) in detail; basically it is mesic forest surrounded by pines. Here, *C. archebates* has never been taken on the road through the forest but is extremely abundant along a path *within* the mesic forest itself. These internal occurrences (in contrast to open area occurrences in Haiti) tend to confirm Schwartz's (1983b:8) contention that species recognition in heavily shaded situations might be the reason for the contrasting unhw pattern of *C. archebates*.

Bates (1935b:234) examined 31 specimens of *C. archebates*, and Munroe (1950:218) studied 30. These numbers suggest that *C. archebates* is uncommon; on most days, one can secure as many *C. archebates* as he might want. Overcast days can be as profitable as bright and sunny ones. In fact, the most abundant I have seen *C. archebates* was on 10.viii.1983, when this species was flying at about 1130 h above and south of El Aguacate in heavy mist and light rain! Interestingly, *C. sommeri* was equally abundant and flying under the same weather conditions in the even higher pine forest; the numbers of both species on that day could hardly be even estimated.

Although the sexes of *C. archebates* are easily distinguished, with males having the unhw diagonal band bright yellow to almost orange-yellow and females having this band internally darkened by gray to greenish scales, leaving only a yellow margin, worn females especially might be confused with *C. loxias* (see beyond). There is no evidence that these 2 species, which are geographic replacements, are sympatric, nor are they truly similar, even superficially, as some accounts (Bates, 1935b:234; Munroe, 1950:218; Riley, 1975:47) suggest. However, male genitalia differ only in minor ways (Munroe, 1950:218).

Most specimens are from July (71), with 35 in June, 27 in September, 19 in April, 12 in August, and 1 in October. Times of collection varied between 0900 and 1530 h (both Las Abejas), and temperatures between 21°C (Los Arroyos, 5 km WNW Scierie) and 33°C (Las Abejas). The total elevational distribution of *C. archebates* is between 1129 m (Las Abejas) and 1891 m (El Aguacate, Scierie). Schwartz (1983a:20) also pointed out that not all records for Haiti are from the Massif de la Selle itself; many Haitian specimens are from the Montagne Noire, the northern front range of the Massif de la Selle.

I took a copulating pair on 1.viii (El Aguacate, 1464 m, 1300–1400 h, 34°C); Gali took a copulating pair 5 km WNW Scierie on 4.ix (0930–1030 h, 21°C). At Forêt des Pins, *C. archebates* was seen foraging in open grassy areas (lawns) in pine forest on *Cynoglossum amabile*.

Specimens; Haiti: l'Ouest: 5.8 km N Kenscoff, 1678 m, 5; Obléon, 1678 m, 1; 0.3 km N Obléon, 1617 m, 6; 0.3 km NE Obléon, 1678 m, 14; Peneau, 1.1 km S Furcy, 1464 m, 3; Peneau, 1.6 km SW Furcy, 1464 m, 11; 4 km NW Forêt des Pins, 1496 m, 6; 1 km NW Forêt des Pins, 1556 m, 2; Forêt des Pins, 1586 m, 4; Forêt des Pins, 1525 m, 1; 200 m N Scierie, 1891 m, 1

(FSM); 1 km SE Scierie, 1891 m, 23 (FSM); 2 km NW Scierie, 1785–1810 m, 1 (FSM); 5 km WNW Scierie, 1891 m, 2 (FSM); *República Dominicana: Pedernales:* Las Abejas, 11 km NW Aceitillar, 1220 m, 11; Las Abejas, 12 km NW Aceitillar, 1129 m, 27; 5 km SW El Aguacate, 1464 m, 9; 7 km SW El Aguacate, 1647 m, 20; 9 km SW El Aguacate, 1769 m, 3; 11 km SW El Aguacate, 1891 m, 1; 4.5 km NE Los Arroyos, 1434 m, 4; 5 km NE Los Arroyos, 1617 m, 11.

2. *Calisto loxias* Bates, 1935

TL Roche Croix, Massif de la Hotte, Dépt. du Sud, Haiti.
FW males 21–22 mm, females 21–23 mm.

Calisto loxias is the Massif de la Hotte representative of *C. archebates*. *Calisto archebates* is quite distinctive among Hispaniolan *Calisto* in having a yellow band (bold in males, less yellow and less bold in females) from the costa to the anal margin. *Calisto archebates* and *C. loxias* occur on 2 of the south island massifs (la Hotte, la Selle) and may be considered vicariants.

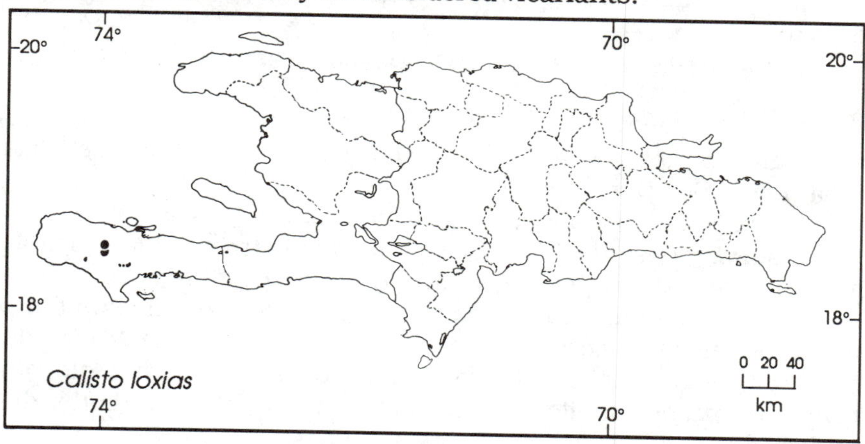

Calisto loxias has been known only from the type-series of 5 males and 1 female from the type-locality. Roche Croix lies on the northeastern slopes of Pic Macaya, 1 of the most difficult areas on Hispaniola to reach. I have not collected in the western uplands of the Massif de la Hotte, only along its southern slopes above Cavaillon and Camp Perrin, and above Paillant in the east. I did not encounter *C. loxias* at these places, nor did I expect to, since the maximum elevation reached was 854 m.

However, Gali more than doubled the known specimens of *C. loxias* by taking 3 males and 4 females near the top of Pic Formond in the Massif de la Hotte, *ca.* 12 km SE of the type-locality (see Darlington, 1935:169, for details). Gali's specimens differ slightly in size from the type-series in that the fw is longer (21–23 in Gali's material, both sexes combined; 19–22 mm in Darlington's specimens). The new material agrees excellently with Bates's original description, even to the very slight sexual dichromatism in the extent of reddish brown along the unfw outer margin.

Gali took his material on 2 days (9.ix, 12.ix) in pine forest with a fern understory. The very large size of the *C. loxias* made them quite distinctive (from other *Calisto*) in the field. The 12.ix specimens were taken between 1200–1300 h at a temperature of 28°C; the day was slightly overcast.

Combining data from the type-series and those from Gali's material gives an elevational range between *ca.* 1525 m and 1910 m. Darlington's type-series was taken in September. Although Yocom ascended Pic Formond, he did not encounter *C. loxias* in January and February.

Calisto loxias is unquestionably more widely distributed on the Massif de la Hotte, but its precise distribution remains to be determined.

Specimens: Haiti: Sud: Pic Formond, near top, 1900–1910 m, 7 (FSM).

3. *Calisto wetherbeei* Schwartz and Gonzalez, 1988

TL Summit, Loma Nalga de Maco, *ca.* 1900 m, Prov. de Elías Piña, República Dominicana.

FW males 15 mm, females 14(–16?) mm.

This newly described species is known only from Loma Nalga de Maco in the extreme western portion of the Cordillera Central in the República Dominicana near the Dominico-Haitian boundary. In all likelihood, it occurs in the eastern portion of the Massif du Nord, although recent visits to that region by Wetherbee did not reveal the proper habitat. These Haitian mountains are badly denuded of native forests.

At the type-locality, *C. wetherbeei* occurs syntopically with *C. galii.* The area is quasi-cloud forest, with elfin broadleaf trees and shrubs and scattered pines. *Calisto wetherbeei* flies in and above the canopy, not near the ground as is typical of many *Calisto.*

The species in many ways resembles *C. archebates* in that it has a unhw pale yellow pattern. But *C. wetherbeei* is much smaller and the unhw pattern differs in many details. The male genitalia of the 2 species are similar, however.

The type-series was collected 16–20.xi.1986. A return visit by Wetherbee to the type-locality on 19.ix.1987 not only yielded no *C. wetherbeei,* but no other *Calisto* were seen (Wetherbee, *in lit.,* 21.ix.1987). On that date, very few kinds of plants were in bloom; Wetherbee felt that the appropriate time to collect on Loma Nalga de Maco is December, when the flora is in full flower.

Specimens: República Dominicana: Elías Piña: summit, Loma Nalga de Maco, *ca.* 1900 m, 4.

4. *Calisto chrysaoros* Bates, 1935

TL Roche Croix, Massif de la Hotte, 5000 ft., Dépt. du Sud, Haiti.

FW males 16–19 mm, females 16–21 mm.

Calisto chrysaoros has been known only from the type-locality in the Massif de la Hotte and from various localities in the Massif de la Selle; the type-series was collected by Darlington and Bates in September and October. The species appeared to be absent in the Sierra de Baoruco, but Riley (1975:pl. 3, fig. 14) showed a painting of a male from Monteada Nueva, Prov. de Barahona, República Dominicana, a site in the eastern Sierra de Baoruco. Thus the species is known from all the south island ranges but remains uncollected by me in the Massif de la Hotte (3 taken by Yocom and 31 by Gali from Pic Formond; 12 collected by Gali from the Massif de la Selle). Other records for *C. chrysaoros* (Bates, 1939a:49; Michener, 1943:3) properly apply to a related species, *C. galii*, on the north island.

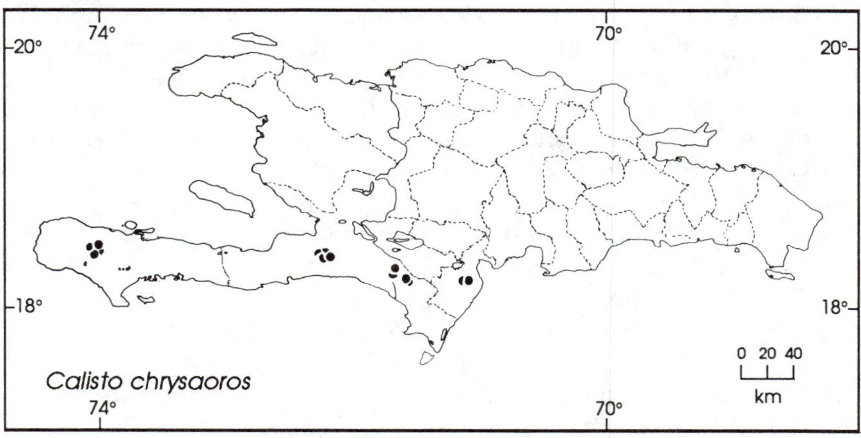

At the time of the description of *C. galii*, Schwartz (1983b:5) had examined only 2 male and 1 female *C. chrysaoros;* many additional specimens from both Haiti and the República Dominicana have accumulated since then. Of the males, 10 lack the unhw midcostal spot, and this feature is lacking also in 6 females.

One Dominican female (as well as 1 from Haiti) lacks any white unhw pattern. All fresh specimens of both sexes are rich, dark rust on the unhw, and the marginal one-half of M3-Cu1 as well as the marginal one-quarter of Cu1-Cu2 are set off from the balance of the ground color in that they are contrasting pale tan. Such details may be overlooked on worn specimens.

Calisto chrysaoros is distinctly a butterfly of wooded areas at high elevations. The type-locality is at 1525 m, and my specimens are from between 1007 m (1.8 km W Monteada Nueva) and 1617 m (Los Arroyos), and Yocom's and Gali's are from 1830–1910 m. In high-elevation deciduous forests, there is at least 1 kind of climbing grass (called *tibisi* by Dominicans) that occurs in clearings and openings in the forest. In artificially opened areas (road cuts) this grass forms dense curtains, and these grassy curtains persist and luxuriate, draping low trees and shrubs to heights of 10 m or more, even when the forest itself has been cleared. At Las Abejas, Los Arroyos, and Monteada Nueva, this climbing grass is abundant. In Haiti, Gali noted the presence of this grass in openings in pine forest, and *C. chrysaoros* was associated with it.

At Las Abejas (11 km NW Aceitillar), specimens were taken in an open ravine in pinewoods, the ravine basically a "creek" of deciduous forest with a dense understory of thorny blackberries (*Rubus selleanus*). The butterflies sunned on these bushes and on leaves at the exposed edge of the woods, often quite high (3 m). The climbing grass is present but does not form dense mats or curtains. At the other Las Abejas locality, the butterflies were flying along a vegetational face of *tibisi* and *R. selleanus* on the edge of an abandoned clearing in the forest. At 5 km NE Los Arroyos, along a road within the forest, we took specimens that were usually flying along the edge or resting on shrub or low tree leaves to sun. Nearby, 1 individual was taken at the edge of a forest remnant surrounded by fields.

These butterflies, not only here but elsewhere, are exceedingly shy and fly very rapidly and erratically, dodging into and about stems and branches of low shrubs (including blackberries), and collecting them is difficult. The association of *C. chrysaoros* with the climbing grass may be more than casual; since the known larval food plants of *Calisto* are members of the Poaceae, it may well be that these satyrids use this climbing grass for egg deposition. Schwartz (1983b:7) noted the absence of *C. chrysaoros* within the dense forest at Las Abejas; we can confirm this absence since we have returned to the forest there to verify the fact. Pertinently, the climbing grass does not occur within the deep shade of this (then) virgin deciduous forest.

At Pic Formond, Gali noted the extreme sensitivity of *C. chrysa-*

oros to sunlight on alternately sunny and overcast days, and I have observed the same thing elsewhere. These butterflies "disappeared" promptly when the sky was overcast but reappeared quickly with the sun's return. At Scierie, *C. chrysaoros* was common on tall ferns in pine forest. When alarmed, these satyrids at that locality escaped by flying *above* the pines (ca. 5 m), an altogether unorthodox behavior for any *Calisto.*

We have taken *C. chrysaoros* feeding on an unidentified white-flowered tree and on *Begonia plumieri* (Begoniaceae)—both plants at Los Arroyos. *Begonia* as a nectar source is indeed remarkable. Plants of this genus are extremely abundant in Dominican uplands; their red to pink or white flowers are a conspicuous component of the understory. Yet we have encountered only 2 species of butterflies using *Begonia* as food. At the 2 Los Arroyos localities and 12 km NW Aceitillar, *C. chrysaoros* was feeding on *Rubus selleanus*, and at 1.8 km W Monteada Nueva on *Psychotria uliginosa* (Rubiaceae). The latter plant was embedded in a *tibisí* face, where the butterflies were very abundant.

Specimens have been taken in February (3), July (14), June (11), August (12), September (43), October (8), and December (1). Times of capture were between 0830 and 1330 h, and temperatures varied between 21°C and 30°C.

Specimens: Haiti: l'Ouest: 1.2 km S Scierie, 1950 m, 12 (FSM); *Sud:* Morne Formond, 1830 m, 3 (FSM); Pic Formond, nr. top, 1900–1910 m, 31 (FSM); *República Dominicana: Barahona:* 1.8 km W Monteada Nueva, 1007 m, 10; 1.3 km W Monteada Nueva, 1037 m, 3; *Pedernales:* 5 km NE Los Arroyos, 1617 m, 26; 4.5 km NE Los Arroyos, 1434 m, 1; Las Abejas, 11 km NW Aceitillar, 1220 m, 3; Las Abejas, 12 km NW Aceitillar, 1129 m, 3.

5. *Calisto galii* Schwartz, 1983

TL 18 km SE Constanza, 1586 m, Prov. de la Vega, República Dominicana.

FW males 16–18 mm, females 17–19 mm.

No new material of *C. galii* has been taken in the vicinity of the type-locality since the description of the species. Michener, however, had reported a specimen of *C. chrysaoros* from "Mt. Tuia" in the República Dominicana (1943:3). I feel certain that the locality is really Mt. Tina, now usually called Alto Bandera, which lies just to the northeast of the main road from Constanza to La Horma, and that the specimen is *C. galii.* Alto Bandera reaches an elevation of 2202 m (Bond, 1976:2) and lies a very few kilometers from La Nevera, a locality whence *C. galii* has been reported (Schwartz, 1983b:6).

We revisited the type-locality of *C. galii* in 1981. The dense hardwoods where the holotype was collected have been cleared. No *C. galii* were seen then or thereafter. The same has been the fate of the residual patch of forest at 10 km SE Constanza. Only a line of trees remains; visits there have revealed nothing. *Calisto galii* is apparently rare at Loma Leonor; there is only 1 specimen from this locality. Visits to the locality in 1982–86 yielded no *C. galii*.

As noted in the discussion of *C. chrysaoros*, the presumed diagnostic feature of the presence of a unhw midcostal spot in *C. galii*, in contrast to *C. chrysaoros*, is no longer tenable. It might thus be preferable to consider *C. galii* conspecific with *C. chrysaoros*. I maintain them as separate biological entities; the 2 taxa are on the 2 basic portions of Hispaniola and are totally separated from each other by the intervening Valle de Neiba; both are high-elevation populations. They differ in relatively minor ways: *C. galii* is smaller than *C. chrysaoros*, has the inner edge of the postdiscal line more scalloped and irregular between the veins, and has the arrangement of the unhw white pattern less Y-like than *C. chrysaoros* (see Schwartz, 1983b:5 and fig. 1). Moreover, the unhw ground color in *C. galii* is not deep rust, as in *C. chrysaoros*, and thus the pale areas in M3-Cu1 and Cu1-Cu2 are not so strongly contrasting as in *C. chrysaoros*. Specimens of the 2 species must be compared directly to appreciate truly these (apparently subtle) differences.

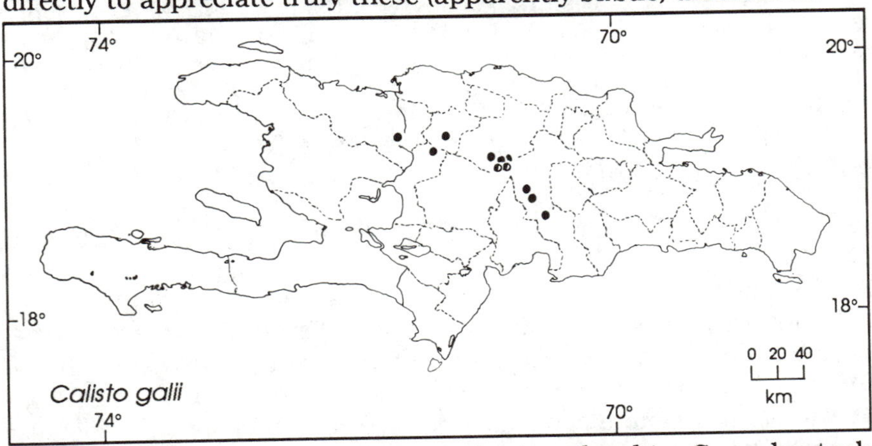

Although *C. galii* is now not at the type-locality, Gonzalez took specimens on the trail to Pico Duarte, where it is not uncommon. Additionally, Wetherbee secured series at Loma Nalga de Maco and, even farther west, on the Dominico-Haitian border near the 47 km border marker. The species is surely expected in the proper habitat (if it persists) in the Massif du Nord.

All specimens are from July (57) and November (17), except 1 from August. Elevations vary between 549 m (Loma Leonor) and 2227 m (La Nevera, 37 km SE Constanza). Flight times were between 0915 and 1535 h, and temperatures between 18°C (La Nevera) and 38°C (Loma Leonor). Details of localities are given in Schwartz (1983b). At Valle de Tetero, Los Tablones, and La Laguna, *C. galii* occurs in hardwoods with *tibisí* curtains. At Boca del Río, Gonzalez took 2 specimens on ferns in mixed pine-hardwoods; there were no grass curtains in the immediate area. The Loma Nalga de Maco site is in elfin cloud forest, where *C. galii* and *C. wetherbeei* are syntopic; the former is much more abundant. The Mont Griné series is from a small residual patch of hardwoods; there, *C. galii* was syntopic only with *C. obscura*.

Specimens: República Dominicana: Dajabón: Mont Griné, frontier marker 47, SW Trinitaria, 1000 m, 11; *Elías Piña:* summit, Loma Nalga de Maco, *ca.* 1900 m, 17; *Santiago:* Rincón de Piedras, 1 (MNHNSD); 0.3 km NE La Laguna, 1723 m, 1; slope from Valle de Tetero to entrance of Valle de Tetero, 1922–1342 m, 5; *La Vega:* 10 km SE Constanza, 1647 m, 16; 18 km SE Constanza, 1586 m, 17; La Nuez, 1 (MNHNSD); *Santiago Rodríguez:* Loma Leonor, 18 km SW Monción, 549 m, 1.

Sight records: República Dominicana: La Vega: 1 km SW Los Tablones, 1159 m—1 seen, 20.vii; *Santiago:* 1.5 km before La Cotorra, 1342 m—several seen, 2.vii; slope from Valle de Tetero to entrance of Valle de Tetero, 1922–1342 m—1 seen, 3.vii.

6. *Calisto choneupsilon* Schwartz, 1985

TL 2 km NE Puesto Pirámide 204, 1586 m, Prov. de Elías Piña, República Dominicana.

FW males 15–17 mm, females 16–18 mm.

Although described as a subspecies of *C. galii*, Gonzalez and Schwartz (in press) felt that the male genitalia are sufficiently different and the geographic hiatus is sufficiently great to regard *choneupsilon* as a distinct species, allied to *chrysaoros-galii*.

Calisto choneupsilon is known from both the north and south ranges of the Sierra de Neiba, although most specimens are from the latter range. It is confidently expected in the adjacent portion of Haiti, which is as well forested as the region about the type-locality of *C. choneupsilon*.

At Comendador, the single specimen was taken at the edge of a patch of deciduous woods and a *cafetal*. All specimens from Puesto Pirámide 204 were taken along a road through deciduous forest, along a road through mixed pine-hardwoods with a fern understory, or along an open road along a mountainside. In the forest, a few casual individuals were observed, but, like *C. chrysaoros*, *C.*

choneupsilon flies rapidly and erratically, often close to the ground while dodging among bushes and shrubs, and is therefore difficult to net.

But the highest concentration of *C. choneupsilon* was encountered along the open road passing toward Aniceto Martínez from Puesto Pirámide 204. Here, the upper side of the road still has some forest but, more importantly, has climbing grasses (*tibisí*). At 1 locality, a large curtain of climbing grass is adjacent to a small creek—almost exposed. The butterflies were exceptionally common at this site, and 1 was taken on a white-flowered roadside composite. Many more were seen than secured; they rested in the sun up to 3.5 m high, but individuals occasionally came closer to the ground. As with *C. chrysaoros*, the intimate association of *C. choneupsilon* and the climbing grass suggests that this is the larval food plant. These butterflies, although certainly forest inhabitants, survive successfully, even if the forest has been cut, provided the grass curtains are still present. The October specimens were taken in a soggy meadow and along an open section of the road; grass curtains were nearby in both cases. The 2 El Veinte specimens are from a small clearing in hardwoods.

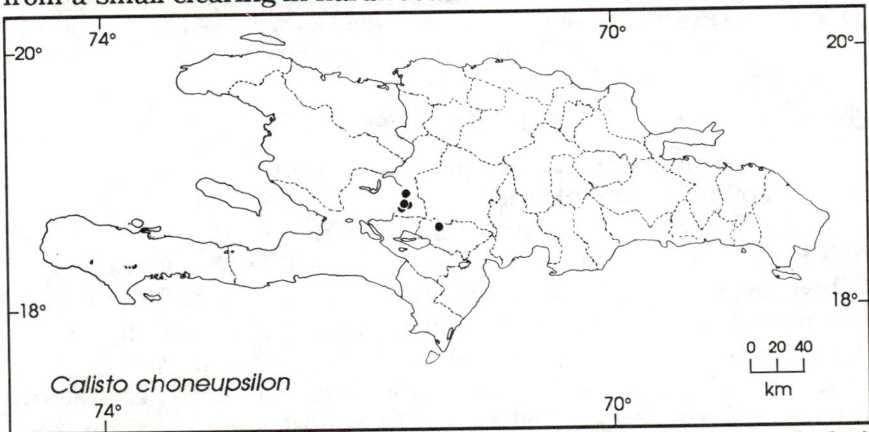

Calisto choneupsilon

Elevations of capture varied between 976 m (Comendador) and 1891 m (Puesto Pirámide 204). Most specimens have been collected in August (13), with 3 in July and 2 in October. Times of capture varied between 1030 and 1430 h, and temperatures between 23°C and 28°C (both Puesto Pirámide 204).

Specimens: República Dominicana: Elías Piña: 15 km S Comendador, 976 m, 1; 1 km SW Puesto Pirámide 204, 1890 m, 1; 2 km NE Puesto Pirámide 204, 1586 m, 14; Pirámide 204, 1 (MNHNSD); "Hondo Valle," 2 (MNHNSD); *Baoruco: ca.* 8 km SW El Veinte, 1617 m, 2.

7. *Calisto arcas* Bates, 1939

TL Valle Nuevo, SE Constanza, ca. 7000 ft., Prov. de la Vega, República Dominicana.

FW males 23–25 mm, females 23–27 mm.

Calisto arcas was named from 4 males and 2 females from the type-locality and from 3 males and 3 females from Loma Vieja, south of Constanza. All were collected in viii.1938 at elevations between 1830 and 2135 m. Munroe (1950:219) examined the same 12 specimens.

Although we have visited Valle Nuevo and Loma Vieja many times since 1980, we had never seen individuals of this large *Calisto.* In this same area, *C. grannus* often literally swarms, but *C. arcas* seems to be unaccountably uncommon. But in 1985 we collected 4 specimens in this general area. There are 4 males and 4 females in the MNHNSD taken 3.viii.1980; these are the only specimens secured since 1950 of which I am aware. They are from the Loma Vieja area, an area that has remained virtually unchanged since my first visit there in 1963. In addition, assuming that *C. arcas* occurs in pine forest across the Cordillera Central between Constanza and La Horma (an area easily accessible by road and untouched except by fire and some recent clearing), we have made a point of visiting this entire region in early August and late September, on the chance that *C. arcas* emerges in the autumn (all other specimens have been taken in August), but we have had no success.

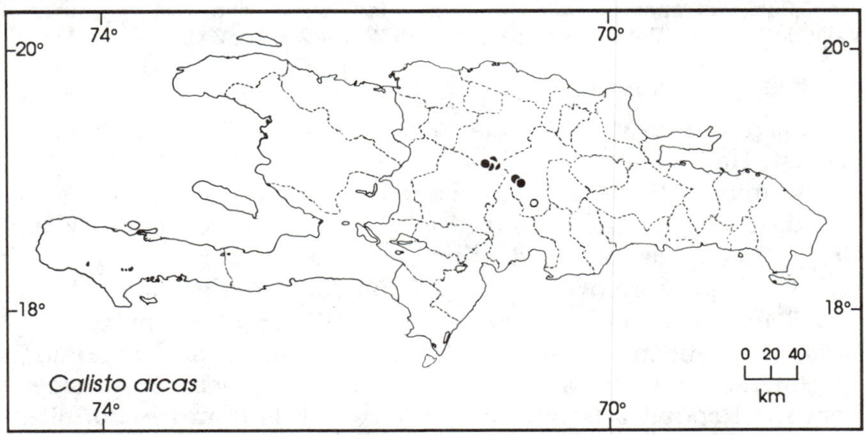

But in 1985, Gonzalez, Smith, Smith, and I, after securing the 4 Constanza specimens, realized that we had been searching in the wrong habitat. Although *C. arcas* occurs in pine forest, it does so rarely. Two trips to Pico Duarte in 1985 and 2 in 1986 solved the puzzle. There, *C. arcas* is common and an inhabitant of mixed pine-hardwoods. Most of the 46 specimens (and all the sight records) from there (La Laguna, Valle de Tetero) are from this plant association. At the entrance to Valle de Tetero, *C. arcas* occurs in pine forest, landing on ferns to sun; but when pressed, they retreat to adjacent hardwoods. They were unusually abundant there on 19.vii. *Calisto arcas*, like most other high-upland *Calisto*, is not reluctant to fly on overcast days.

Although the 2 areas whence *C. arcas* is now known are separated by about 40 km, the 2 samples differ very little from each other. It is very likely that *C. arcas* occurs throughout the high uplands of the Cordillera Central and that populations are more or less continuous.

Elevational distribution is from 1723 m (0.3 km NE La Laguna) to 1922 m (entrance of Valle de Tetero, 14 km SE Constanza). Times of collection were between 0915 h and 1530 h, at temperatures of 24°C (0.3 km NE La Laguna) and 28°C (14 km SE Constanza). All new specimens (49) and sight records (12) are from July.

Specimens: República Dominicana: Santiago: 0.3 km NE La Laguna, 1723 m, 1; La Laguna, 1830 m, 10; entrance of Valle de Tetero, 1922 m, 31; entrance of Valle de Tetero to Valle de Tetero, 1922–1342 m, 3; *La Vega:* El Montazo, 8 (MNHNSD); 6 km SSE Constanza, 1403 m, 1; 14 km SE Constanza, 1922 m, 3.

Sight records: República Dominicana: Santiago: La Laguna, 1830 m—2 seen, 2.vii; entrance of Valle de Tetero, 1922 m—2 seen, 3.vii; entrance of Valle de Tetero to Valle de Tetero, 1922–1342 m—2 seen, 2.vii; 4 seen, 3.vii.

8. *Calisto tragia* Bates, 1935

TL La Visite, Massif de la Selle, 5000 to 7000 ft., Dépt. de l'Ouest, Haiti.

FW males 15–20 mm, females 16–21 mm.

Calisto tragia was described (as *C. tragius;* see Schwartz and Gali, 1984:9, for this and other feminine adjectival endings for *Calisto* in use herein) by Bates (1935b:236) from a male holotype and 6 female paratopotypes. Munroe (1950:220) examined these same 7 specimens. Schwartz (1983a) did not report any Haitian specimens; Schwartz and Gali (1984:9–10) reported 6 specimens from the República Dominicana, 1 of which is from the Cordillera Central and thus far removed from the known range of *C. tragia* on the Massif de la Selle–Sierra de Baoruco on the south island.

Since Schwartz's (1983a) and Schwartz and Gali's (1984) papers, I have had more field experience with the *Calisto* of the 2 eastern ranges (La Selle, Baoruco) of the south island. Raburn and I were fortunate in securing a long series of *C. elelea,* perhaps the rarest and least distinguished of the south island *Calisto.* This long series afforded me an opportunity to assess the variation in *C. elelea* and to examine the specimens previously assigned to that species and *C. tragia.* This has resulted in reassignment of some specimens, called *C. elelea* by Schwartz (1983a), to *C. tragia.*

These 2 species are indeed similar in appearance and size, although they differ markedly in male genitalia and are assigned to 2 different groups (within *Calisto*) by Bates (1935b:244). Additionally, *C. elelea* lacks an androconial patch in males, whereas in *C. tragia* the patch is developed and like other members' of the *hysia*-group. The unhw ocellus in *C. elelea* is tiny, strongly oval on a margin-base axis, and has the pale pupil strongly displaced basally, in some cases the pupil lying on the very margin of the ocellus or even slightly more basad of the ocellus. In *C. tragia,* the unhw ocellus is round with a central ocellus and is distinctly larger than that of *C. elelea.* Riley's plate (1975:pl. 3) is deceptive in 2 ways. The illustration of *C. tragia* (fig. 6) shows only a single pale pupil in the unfw ocellus; yet the holotype has 2 pupils. Bates (1935b:236) stated that *C. tragia* has 2 pupils in the unfw ocellus, and Michener (1943:2) considered the bipupillate unfw ocellus as a "key character" for this species. All my specimens have 2 pale pupils in the unfw ocellus. Secondly, Riley's fig. 11 of *C. elelea* shows only the most barely discernible unhw ocellus; this condition does occur but it is not typical—most specimens have the unhw ocellus larger and much more obvious than his figure shows, although in females the un color is pallid and the ocellus is less distinct than in males. With these caveats, the investigator can solve the puzzle of identification of the 2 species.

Most of our *C. tragia* are somewhat worn; but on the unfw in both sexes, the basal one-half of the cell is reddish (never bright brick red) and there is a reddish blush posterior to the unfw ocellus, much as in *C. hysia.* The specimen from the Cordillera Central lacks these red un markings. Fresh males have the androconial patch as described by Bates.

Calisto tragia occurs in the uplands of the Massif de la Selle and its Haitian front range (Montagne Noire but not the Morne l'Hôpital) and in the extreme western portion of the Sierra de Baoruco (Las Abejas region). Whether the Cordillera Central individual is indeed *C. tragia,* which seems unlikely (however, see account of *Calisto elelea*), rests upon the collection of more material from that range.

Calisto tragia has been taken (in Haiti) in grassy and flowery fields in pinewoods and pine forest, and in a village (Peneau) with many gardens and ornamental flowers. In the República Dominicana, it occupies pine forest (El Aguacate) in meadows with *Cynoglossum amabile*, where it is syntopic with and far outnumbered by *C. sommeri*, mesic hardwood forest, where specimens were collected with *C. archebates* along a path, and pine forest (Aceitillar), where it is syntopic with *C. schwartzi* and *C. elelea*.

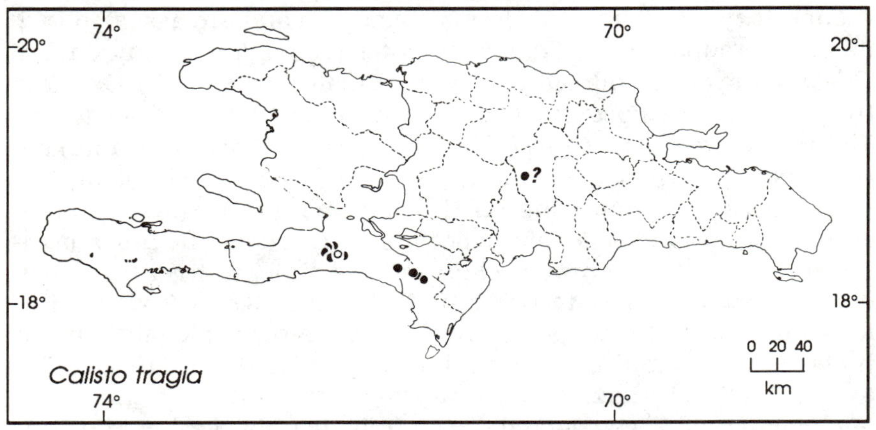

All my specimens are from June (14) and July (8), but Gali collected 38 in September. Elevations are from 1129 m (12 km NW Aceitillar) to 2100 m (Pic Cabaïo). Times were between 0900 and 1600 h, and temperatures between 21°C (Scierie) and 29°C (1.2 km Scierie). We have never taken *C. tragia* on the north face of the Massif de la Selle in the República Dominicana, but some Haitian Massif de la Selle records are from that face.

The fresh condition and large number of specimens of *C. tragia* suggest that its time of eclosion is the fall (September). Raburn and I did not encounter *C. tragia* in October in the Dominican uplands, however, although *C. elelea* was abundant then. The type-series and Gali's long series were taken in September.

Specimens: Haiti: l'Ouest: 0.3 km NE Obléon, 1678 m, 8; Peneau, 1; 1.1 km S Furcy, 2; east side, Pic Cabaïo, 2100 m, 2 (FSM); *ca.* 4 km NW Scierie, 2000 m, 2 (FSM); 1–4 km WNW Scierie, 1830–1891 m, 19 (FSM); 5 km WNW Scierie, 9 (FSM); 1 km SE Scierie, 1891 m, 1 (FSM); 1.2 km S Scierie, 1950 m, 2 (FSM); 1 km W Roche Cabrit, 2000 m, 3 (FSM); *República Dominicana: Pedernales:* Las Abejas, 12 km NW Aceitillar, 1129 m, 6; Las Abejas, 11 km NW Aceitillar, 1220 m, 1; 1 km N Aceitillar, 1281 m, 4; 11 km SW El Aguacate, 1891 m, 1.

C. cf. *tragia: República Dominicana: La Vega:* 6 km SSE Constanza, 1403 m, 1.

9A. *Calisto grannus grannus* Bates, 1939

TL Valle Nuevo, SE Constanza, *ca.* 7000 ft., Prov. de la Vega, República Dominicana.

FW males 16–19 mm, females 17–20 mm.

Calisto grannus is 1 of a series of 6 species of *Calisto* that have 2 unhw ocelli and inhabit 3 different mountain ranges.

Calisto grannus has been known from the type-series: the female holotype and a male paratopotype, and 3 males from Loma Rucilla. The latter locality is some 36 km to the northwest of the type-locality but in the same Cordillera Central massif. Bates (1939a:49–50) noted that the Loma Rucilla specimens differ from those from Valle Nuevo in that on the former "the lines of the under side are more obscure, the ocellus of the forewing smaller." He diagnosed the species by its having 2 unhw ocelli as well as the "absence of a distinct red patch in the cell of the forewing." The latter character is important in that the lack of a red patch (and the presence of 2 unhw ocelli) differentiates *C. grannus* from the closely related and geographically widespread *C. batesi.* Munroe (1950:220) placed *C. grannus* in the *hysia-* group, and indeed the configuration of the male genitalia of the 2 species differs very little and in no striking ways, as is often the case in *Calisto.* (The latter statement cannot be overemphasized: within each of the various groups of *Calisto,* male genitalic differences are of the most minor sorts, and one must resort to external morphological and chromatic features [color, pattern, number of ocelli, number of pupils in ocelli, relative size of ocelli, presence or absence of un red patches or blush, etc.] or to female genitalia to define species.)

Calisto g. grannus is an inhabitant of upland pine forest in the Cordillera Central, where it occurs between elevations of 1159 m (La Horma) and 2288 m (5 km NW Valle Nuevo).

Most of our specimens (119) are from July, with smaller numbers in June (54), September (2), March (1), and August (1). Abundance varies greatly; on 1.vii.1982, *C. g. grannus* was extremely abundant across the Cordillera Central between La Horma and Constanza, but on 11.vii.1982, only a scattered few were seen on this same road. Weather conditions were highly suitable on both days. In fact, *C. g. grannus* flies at temperatures between 16°C and 34°C (both Constanza) and often under heavy overcast or even in steady drizzle. On 29.ix.1983, *C. g. grannus* was extremely uncommon in this same region; it had been very common on 20.vii.1983.

Times of collection were between 0930 and 1530 h. We have

taken *C. g. grannus* feeding on 2-m-tall *Melilotus alba* (Fabaceae) on 2 occasions, once on *Trifolium repens* (Fabaceae), once on *Tournefortia hirsutissima*, once on *Lantana ovatifolia*, and once on *Cynoglossum amabile* (Boraginaceae); the blue flowers of the latter are a conspicuous element in meadows and moist areas in these uplands. The butterflies occur frequently in these meadows, where they fly slowly 0.5 m above the ground and just above the plants, but they are also commonly encountered behaving in the same lazy manner within the pine forest itself. *Calisto g. grannus* is 1 of the most conspicuous members of the rhopaloceran fauna of this upland pine forest.

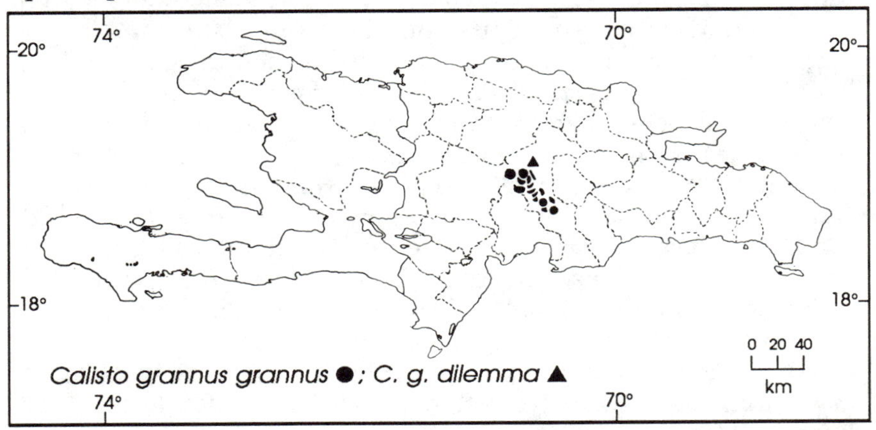

Calisto grannus grannus ●; *C. g. dilemma* ▲

Specimens: República Dominicana: La Vega: 7 km SSE Constanza, 1434 m, 1; 7.4 km SE Constanza, 1388 m, 1; 10 km SE Constanza, 1647 m, 2; 14 km SE Constanza, 1921 m, 109; 16 km SE Constanza, 1; 18 km SE Constanza, 1586 m, 5; 21 km SE Constanza, 2257 m, 3; 5 km NW Valle Nuevo, 2288 m, 7; Valle Nuevo, 25 km SE Constanza, 2105 m, 2; 32 km SE Constanza, 2166 m, 10; 13 km SE Valle Nuevo, 2074 m, 8; 28 km SE Constanza, 2288 m, 3; La Nevera, 37 km SE Constanza, 2227 m, 3; 41 km SE Constanza, 2074 m, 3; 21 km NW La Horma, 2166 m, 2; *Peravia:* 6 km W La Horma, 1159 m, 1.

9B. *Calisto grannus dilemma* Gonzalez, 1987

TL 6 km SSE Constanza, 1403 m, Prov. de la Vega, República Dominicana.

FW males 15–17 mm, females 18–19 mm.

Calisto g. dilemma differs from the nominate subspecies especially in the presence of red scales in the unfw cell in the former. In addition, the unhw anterior ocellus is present, as it is in *C. g. grannus*. Gonzalez named *dilemma* as a subspecies of *C. grannus* because the known (at that time) ranges of the 2 approached each other closely. However, in 1986 we collected 2 *dilemma* and 1 *grannus* at the same locality (7.4 km SE Constanza). The apparent *grannus*, somewhat worn, has some red scales in the unfw cell; whether this individual is a worn *grannus*, a *dilemma* with a little red in the cell, or an intergrade between 2 subspecies is problematical. Militating against that latter interpretation is the occurrence at that precise locality of 2 unquestioned *C. g. dilemma*. If the 2 taxa are indeed syntopic without intergradation, then they are better regarded as species. I adhere to Gonzalez's arrangement, pending more material.

Until 1986, we never took any *C. grannus* in the Valle de Constanza; in that year we collected 4 specimens, which, as expected, are *C. g. dilemma*.

Calisto g. dilemma occurs at intermediate elevations in the vicinity of Constanza, from 1098 m (1 km S Constanza) to 1641 m (10 km SE Constanza). Specimens have been taken primarily in mixed pine-hardwoods between 0930 h and 1440 h at temperatures of 25°C (6 km SSE Constanza) and 35°C (12 km NE Constanza).

Most specimens have been taken in June (35), with 4 in July.

A pair *in copula* was taken on 29.ix (1300–1330 h) at the type-locality.

Specimens: República Dominicana: La Vega: 12 km NE Constanza, 1220 m, 12; 1 km S Constanza, 1098 m, 4; 6 km SSE Constanza, 1403 m, 19; *ca.* 7 km SSE Constanza, 1434 m, 1; 7.4 km SE Constanza, 1388 m, 1; 10 km SE Constanza, 1647 m, 2.

10. *Calisto phoinix* Gonzalez, 1987

TL La Palma, 19 km W Jayaco, 1007 m, Prov. de la Vega, República Dominicana.

FW males 15–17 mm, females 15–17 mm.

Calisto phoinix is the second of the species of this complex in the Cordillera Central. It differs from *C. g. grannus* in its smaller size, the presence of red in the unfw cell, and the relative sizes of the 2 unhw ocelli— the anterior is smaller than the posterior and is at times absent. The species is in general similar to *C. g. dilemma* but differs from that taxon in that, in the former, the unhw ocelli are reduced in size.

Calisto phoinix is known from the type-locality, which lies near the eastern edge of the Cordillera Central, and by a native-collected specimen from Jarabacoa.

La Palma is a settlement along the Río la Palma. The site is luxuriant deciduous forest with large and mature *cafetales-cacao-*

tales. The butterflies are usually abundant there, especially near the river, but they venture to more open situations to feed (on *Stachytarpheta cayennensis;* 2 occasions). Interestingly, during overcast, *C. phoinix* continues to fly and forage, whereas other local *Calisto* (*batesi, obscura, confusa*) promptly disappear.

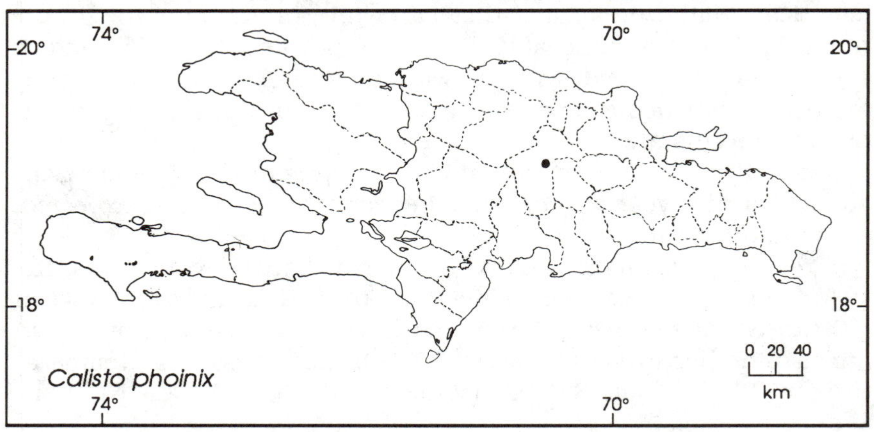

Most specimens have been taken in July (26), with 2 in June, 8 in August, and 2 in March. Times of collection were between 0915 h and 1430 h at temperatures of 22°C and 32°C.

Specimens: República Dominicana: La Vega: La Palma, 19 km W Jayaco, 1007 m, 37; Jarabacoa, 530 m, 1.

11. *Calisto amazona* Gonzalez, 1987

TL Entrance to Valle de Tetero, 1922 m, Prov. de Santiago, República Dominicana.

FW males 15–18 mm, females 17–19 mm.

As pointed out under *C. g. grannus*, 3 male paratypes of that taxon are from Loma Rucilla near Pico Duarte in the Cordillera Central. Bates (1939a:49–50) commented on the differences between these specimens and the pair from the type-locality. The differences noted by him, when supplemented by very long series of specimens, show that the *Calisto* from the Pico Duarte region are quite distinct from *C. grannus* (as well as *C. phoinix*) in the ways that Bates noted. The absence of red in the unfw cell, the obscure or absent postdiscal line on the unhw, and the sizes of the ocelli all differentiate these butterflies (as *C. amazona*) from all others.

Although *C. amazona* is known only from the Pico Duarte area, it is presumably more widely distributed in the central highlands of the Cordillera Central. The species is very abundant, occurring in pine forest (Valle de Tetero) as well as mixed pine-hardwoods. Elevations vary between 1159 m (Los Tablones) and 1922 m (entrance to Valle de Tetero). In much of this range, *C. amazona* is the dominant butterfly.

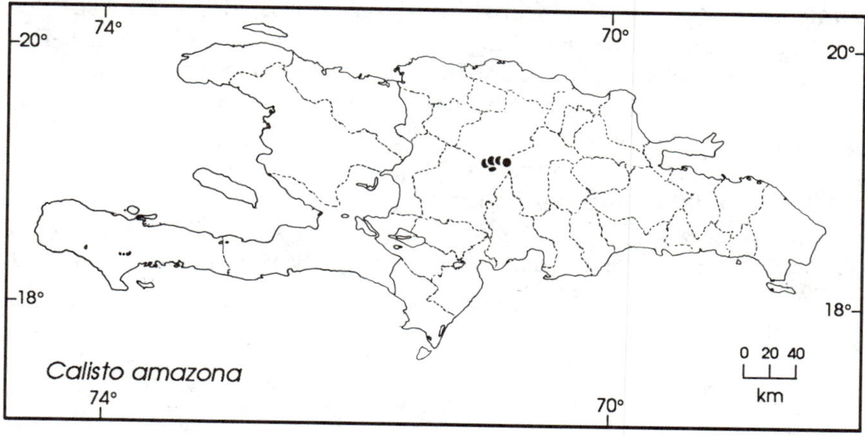

All specimens (163) have been taken in July. Times were between 0730 h and 1530 h, at temperatures of 13°C (Valle de Tetero) to 29°C (1 km NE La Laguna).

Specimens: República Dominicana: La Vega: 1 km SW Los Tablones, 1159 m, 1; *Santiago:* 1–2 km SW La Laguna, 5; La Laguna, 1830 m, 24; 0.3 km NE La Laguna, 1723 m, 16; between La Laguna and La Cotorra, 1830–1403 m, 12; entrance to Valle de Tetero, 1922 m, 43; entrance of Valle de Tetero to Valle de Tetero, 1923–1342 m, 19; Valle de Tetero, 1342 m, 43.

12. *Calisto dystacta* Gonzalez, 1987

TL Loma Leonor, 19 km SW Monción, 610 m, Prov. de Santiago Rodríguez, República Dominicana.

FW males 16–18 mm, females 17–19 mm.

The first specimens of *C. dystacta* were collected on 17.iii.1984, when 15 males and 2 females were taken in mixed pine-hardwoods 19 km SW Monción, near the *destacamento* of Loma Leonor. The original series was more similar to La Palma material (*C. phoinix*) than to *C. g. grannus*. The basal half of the unfw cell is reddish, and the unfw ocellus is the same size as that of *C. phoinix*. *Calisto dystacta* differs from *C. phoinix* in that the former has the unhw white dots "smeared" rather than discrete as in *C. phoinix*, and the unfw postdiscal line expands around the unfw ocellus (no such expansion in *C. phoinix*).

Calisto dystacta is known only from the Loma Leonor area. Not until 1986 did we collect the species at 18 km SW Monción (only 1 km from the type-locality), despite 4 visits there (1981–85). The latter locality is the narrow valley of the Río Toma; *C. dystacta* was not in the hardwoods of the valley itself but rather at the pine-hardwoods interface above the valley. The series from 4.7 km S Loma Leonor is likewise from mixed pine-hardwoods. The species doubtless occurs farther along this road, which leads to the Río Bao at Boca del Río Bao. I doubt that *C. dystacta* occurs between the Río Toma and Monción, since the vegetational formations in that area are not those favored by the species.

A pair was taken *in copula* 4.7 km SW Loma Leonor (20.v, 1135 h, 30°C) in mixed pine-hardwoods.

Specimens: República Dominicana: Santiago Rodríguez: Loma Leonor, 18 km SW Monción, 549 m, 2; Loma Leonor, 19 km SW Monción, 610 m, 43; 4.7 km SW Loma Leonor, 732 m, 22.

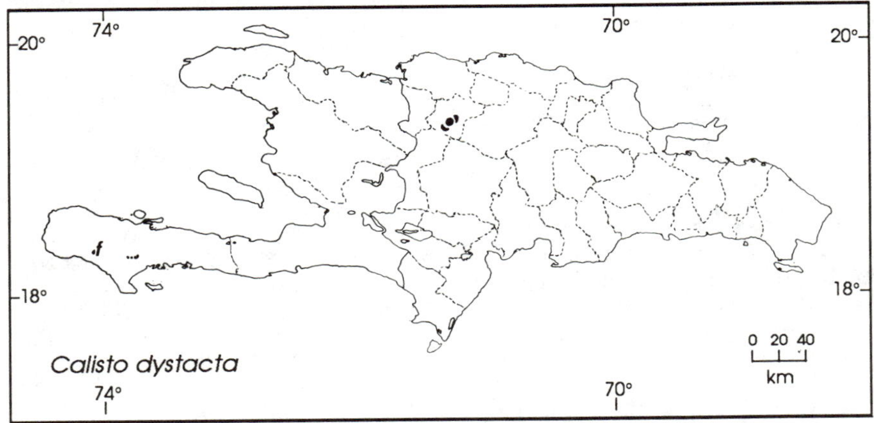

13. *Calisto micrommata* Schwartz and Gali, 1984

TL 2 km NE Puesto Pirámide 204, 1586 m, Prov. de Elías Piña, República Dominicana.

FW males 13–16 mm, females 15–17 mm.

Calisto micrommata is known from a long series from the south range of the Sierra de Neiba, where it is common in pine woods but less so in deciduous forest. All specimens are from localities within 2 km of the army post at *kilometro* 204. We have traveled across the uplands of the Sierra de Neiba and have never seen this species other than in that area. The uplands toward Los Pinos are clothed with a mixed pine-deciduous forest. About 21 km N Los Pinos, the descending southern slope of this range has been deforested, but what remains of that original forest (tree ferns; *Begonia* sp.) indicates that it was once primarily mesic deciduous forest and thus was probably unsuitable for *C. micrommata*. Whether *C. micrommata* occurs on the north range of the Sierra de Neiba is unknown. The proper habitat does not occur between Comendador and Puesto Calimete, at an elevation of about 1525 m; we have not recently traveled the road south between the *puesto* and Hondo Valle, the town that lies in the valley between the 2 ranges.

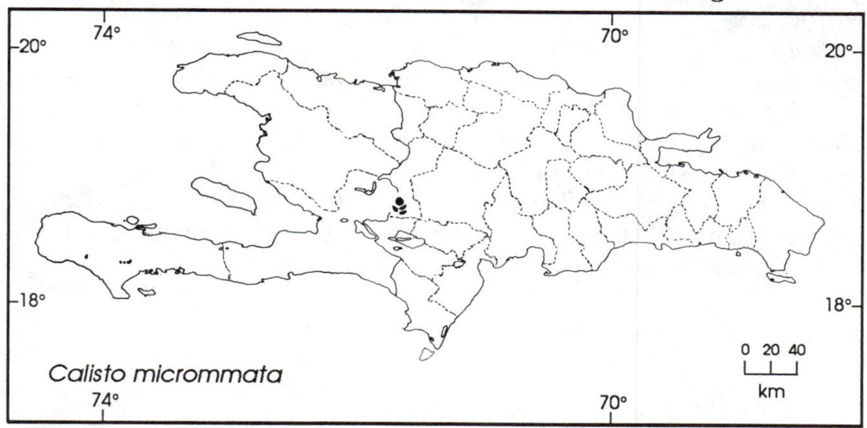

Most specimens have been collected in August (36), with 6 in July. Times of collection were between 1030 and 1430 h. Temperatures were between 23°C and 29°C, at elevations between 1586 and 1891 m.

Specimens: República Dominicana: Elías Piña: 2 km NE Puesto Pirámide 204, 1617 m, 31; 1 km SW Puesto Pirámide 204, 1891 m, 4; 1 km NE Puesto Pirámide 204, 1739 m, 7; Pirámide 204, 1 (MNHNSD).

14. *Calisto sommeri* Schwartz and Gali, 1984

TL Forêt des Pins, 1586 m, Dépt. de l'Ouest, Haiti.

FW males 16–19 mm, females 17–19 mm.

Calisto sommeri occurs in the extreme eastern portion of the Massif de la Selle and the extreme western Sierra de Baoruco; its known distribution straddles the Dominico-Haitian border, but the species may be much more widespread in the Massif de la Selle in Haiti. It does not occur on the northern front ranges of the Massif de la Selle (Montagne Noire, Morne l'Hôpital) in the region about Kenscoff-Furcy-Peneau.

In both Haiti and the República Dominicana, *C. sommeri* is strictly an inhabitant of upland pine forest, between elevations of 1496 m (Forêt des Pins) and 1952 m (Canote Mine). Within this elevational band, it is common and may at times be extremely abundant (see comments in account of *C. archebates*). On the southern slopes of the Dominican portion of the Massif de la Selle, the elevational distributions of *C. sommeri* and *C. archebates* overlap slightly; on these slopes there is a gradual blending of pine (*C. sommeri*) and deciduous forest (*C. archebates*). As one walks from 5 km NE Los Arroyos about 1 km farther north, he passes through this ecological transition zone into pines, and the 2 species occur syntopically for less than 1 km—at the lower extreme occurs *C. archebates*, at the upper *C. sommeri*. The elevational transition occurs here at about 1600 m. Due to extensive forest destruction on the southern slopes of the Massif de la Selle in Haiti, I have not been able to determine if the same transition occurred there as well; *C. archebates* is unknown from the southern slopes of the Massif de la Selle between Forêt des Pins and Thiotte. *Calisto sommeri* has been taken (Los Arroyos) within 30 m of *C. tragia*; the latter is much less common there than the former.

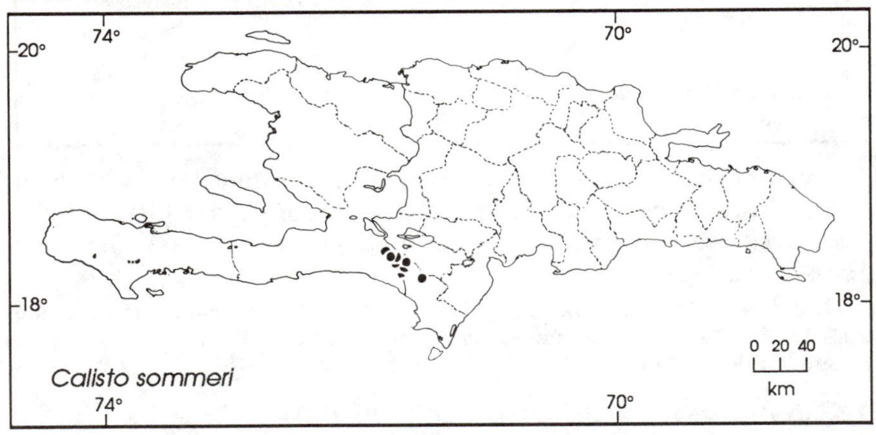

Temperatures of collection were between 21°C (Forêt des Pins) and 30°C (Los Arroyos), and times between 1015 and 1400 h. At these high elevations, overcast and rain are the rule rather than the exception, but *C. sommeri* flies during heavy overcast and drizzle, as well as heavy mist. We have observed *C. sommeri* feeding on *Cynoglossum amabile* at Forêt des Pins and on this plant and a yellow-flowered composite ("dandelion") at El Aguacate. Gali observed a pair *in copula* at 11 km SW El Aguacate, 1891 m (1.viii, 1215 h, 28°C), and I saw another pair 9 km SW El Aguacate, 1769 m (7.viii, 1130 h, 28°C), settled on the gravel road surface.

Most specimens are from August (37) with smaller numbers from July (27), May (15), April (12), June (8), and October (1). The observations of amazing abundance of this species, noted under *C.*

archebates, were made on 10.viii.

Specimens: Haiti: l'Ouest: 9 km SE Forêt des Pins, 1496 m, 2; 8 km SE Forêt des Pins, 1496 m, 4; Forêt des Pins, 1525 m, 2; Forêt des Pins, 1586 m, 4; 1 km NW Forêt des PIns, 1556 m, 9; *República Dominicana: Pedernales:* 11 km SW El Aguacate, 1891 m, 31; 9 km SW El Aguacate, 1769 m, 17; 5 km NE Los Arroyos, 1617 m, 32; 5 km N Canote Mine, 1830–1952 m, 15 (AMNH).

15. *Calisto micheneri* Clench, 1943

TL Loma del Toro, foothills of the Cordillera Central, about 5000 ft., S of Santiago, República Dominicana.

FW male 14 mm.

Calisto micheneri is known only from the male holotype. The species was described by Clench (1943a) as *Calisto batesi*, but since that name was preoccupied by *Calisto hysius batesi* Michener 1943, Clench later (1943b) renamed the species *C. micheneri*.

The type-locality was given as "Loma del Toro, foothills of the Cordillera Cental, south of Santiago, República Dominicana, Hispaniola," about "5000 feet, June 1938 (P. J. Darlington)." The problem is that the type-locality is not locatable on any modern map, even the 1:100,000 map of the República Dominicana. The matter has been clarified by Darlington (1939:98), while discussing carabid beetles; Darlington stated that Loma del Toro is north of Loma Rucilla at about 5000 ft. altitude. We have not visited this area, although we have been as far into these foothills as the Río Bao, southwest of Mata Grande, but only to an elevation of 2300 ft. (702 m), presumably too low for *C. micheneri*.

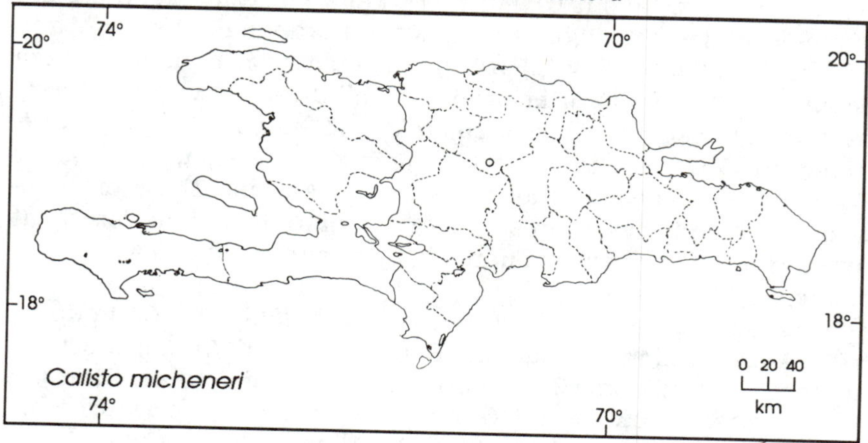

Although Clench (1943a) stated that *C. micheneri* was related to *C. grannus*, the former differs from the latter in a smaller fw ocellus than in *C. g. grannus*, the fw cell red, no apical unhw ocellus, and greatly reduced size of unhw anal ocellus. Clench also compared *C. micheneri* with *C. tragia;* these 2 species seem closely related. More material of *C. micheneri* is needed to clarify not only its variation, characteristics, and relationships but also its distribution.

16. *Calisto hysia* Godart, 1823

TL "L'Amerique septentrionale."

FW males 16–17 mm, females 17–18 mm.

The species *C. hysia* is usually regarded (Michener, 1943:3; Munroe, 1950:222; Riley, 1975:51; Schwartz, 1983a:21–22) as having 2 subspecies, the nominate 1 on the south island, and *C. h. batesi* on the north island. However, there are specimens of *batesi* from 6 localities on the south island, where the 2 taxa are syntopic; also, there are no intergrades between the 2 taxa in the Cul de Sac–Valle de Neiba, an area that is too arid for either. In fact, *C. hysia* is regularly encountered only in mesic wooded situations, not in xeric ones or in open fields. The male genitalia of the 2 species differ strongly from each other (Correa and Schwartz, 1986). Evidence indicates that these are 2 distinct species that differ in several ways, and I so consider them.

Calisto hysia is 1 of a quartet of small and widespread species; the others are *C. batesi, C. obscura,* and *C. confusa. Calisto hysia* occurs only on the south island and strongly favors mesic wooded localities between 153 m (Paraíso) and 1910 m (Pic Formond); most records are from about 610 m to 1220 m. For example, there are only 9 localities (Cavaillon, El Aguacate, Barahona [12 km SW and 5 km SE, 6.4–6.6 km W], Paraíso, La Altagracia, Banano, Cabeza de Agua, El Mulito) at or below 610 m; all these are in dense mesic hardwood forest, *caféières,* or *cafetales.* At the other altitudinal extreme are 6 records from 1220 m or higher (Obléon, Peneau, Pic Formond, Pic Macaya, 2 localities at Las Abejas). These are likewise in upland mesic forest, *caféières,* or upland pine forest (at times around human habitations with shrubbery, flowers, and shade, as at Peneau).

Most specimens have been taken in July (80), with 64 in June, 37 in August, 25 in September, 18 in January, 17 in December, 16 in March, 13 in April, 2 in February, and 1 in October. Times of collection were between 0845 and 1600 h, and temperatures between 23°C (Los Arroyos) and 38°C (La Altagracia).

Borreria laevis (Rubiaceae) is a low (15 cm) herbaceous plant with compact cymes of tiny white flowers that thrives in shaded mesic situations, such as *cafetales* and *caféières,* throughout much of Hispaniola. At many localities, but especially at Enriquillo, *C. hysia* (and other *Calisto* elsewhere) regularly used this plant as a nectar source. We have taken *C. hysia* feeding on the flowers of *Ixora* sp., *Cynoglossum amabile* (12 km NW Aceitillar), and *Stachytarpheta jamaicensis* (Monteada Nueva).

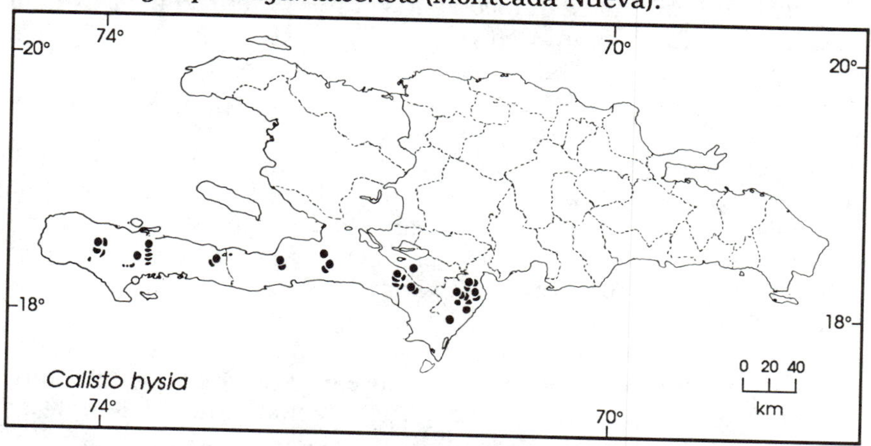

A female from 7 km SW Barahona is unusual in that it is the only *Calisto* examined of any species that is erythristic; there are no black scales, and the up and un are pale reddish tan.

A copulating pair was taken at Monteada Nueva, 1037 m (14.viii, 1405 h, 26°C) in open mesic forest.

Specimens: Haiti: l'Ouest: Boutilliers Road, 854–915 m, 10; Boutilliers Road, 1.6–2.3 km W Kenscoff road, 793–885 m, 1; 0.3 km NE Obléon, 1678 m, 4; Peneau, 1464 m, 3; Peneau, 1.6 km SW Furcy, 1464 m, 10; 17.0 km S Dufort, 702 m, 1; 1.6 km N Béloc, 702 m, 4; 1.6 km N Découzé, 702 m, 2; 2.1 km S Découzé, 640 m, 1; *Sud:* 6.6 km SW Paillant, 793 m, 8; 6.7 km SW Paillant, 854 m, 5; 14 km NW Marceline, 671 m, 12; 14.1 km N Cavaillon, 366 m, 7; 19.7 km N Cavaillon, 580 m, 1; 24.6 km N Cavaillon, 610 m, 6; 26.1 km N Cavaillon, 610 m, 2; Formond, 800 m, 1 (FSM); Morne Formond, 1000 m, 1 (FSM); Pic Formond, nr. top, 1900–1910 m, 1 (FSM); western end, Pic Macaya ridge, 1400 m, 9 (FSM); Vaper Diamant #2, 1; 0.75 km WSW Forment, 16 (FSM); *República Dominicana: Independencia* 4–7 km NE El Aguacate, 519–732 m, 2; *Barahona:* Polo, 702 m, 14; 3 km NNE Polo, 854 m, 5; 2 km S La Lanza, 3; 5 km NW Las Auyamas, 1; 1 km NW Las Auyamas, 1; 20 km SE Cabral, 946 m, 4; 1.3 km W Monteada Nueva, 1037 m, 3; 1.8 km W Monteada Nueva, 1007 m, 6; 7 km SW Barahona, 3; 11 km SW Barahona, 15; 12 km SW Barahona, 427 m, 1; 22 km SW Barahona, 1098 m, 7; 5 km SE, 6.4–6.6 km W Barahona, 488 m, 10; 8 km NW Paraíso, 153 m, 26 (7 MPM); 8–10 km NW Paraíso, 9 (MPM); 9 km NW Enriquillo, 671 m, 30; *Pedernales:* Las Abejas, 11 km NW Aceitillar, 1220 m, 2; Las Abejas, 12 km NW Aceitillar, 1129 m, 25; 1 km S La Altagracia, *ca.* 534 m, 3; 1 km SE Banano, 183 m, 2; El Mulito, 21 km N Pedernales, 214 m, 5; 1 km N Cabeza de Agua, 275 m, 1; 3 km SE Los Arroyos, 976 m, 1; 0.6 km SE Los Arroyos, 1098 m, 18.

17. *Calisto batesi* Michener, 1943

TL Sánchez, Prov. de Samaná, República Dominicana.

FW males 12–15 mm, females 13–15 mm (north island); males 12–14 mm, females 16–17 mm (south island).

Calisto batesi was described as a subspecies of *C. hysia*, and all later authors have continued to use the combination *C. h. batesi*. The 2 taxa have been defined on the basis of size (fw length 15–18 in *hysia*, 12.5–14.5 in *batesi;* Michener, 1943:3) and of several qualitative characters (up ground color lighter or darker; un red orange or dark; postmesial line on fw and hw more, or less, well lined with white scales; 2 or 3–4 white dots in front of hw ocellus; purplish cast, or not, before the ocellus; and up red areas absent [or present only on female hw, or both sexes with more or less reddishly suffused areas on both wings]).

Calisto h. batesi was named from a suite of 11 males and 3 females from Hato Mayor, Puerto Plata, and Las Matas in the República Dominicana and Mt. Puilboreau and Ennery in Haiti. Correa and Schwartz (1986) examined 84 male and 46 female *C. batesi* as well as 103 male and 47 female *C. hysia*, the former from the north island, the latter from the south island, the ranges usually ascribed to these 2 taxa (Munroe, 1950:222). In contrast to the numbers of individuals examined by Correa and Schwartz, Munroe (1950) examined 17 specimens of *C. hysia* and 5 of *C. batesi*.

But even more important is the fact that from 6 south island localities, there are specimens that are indistinguishable (except for slightly larger size) from north island *C. batesi*, and at 3 of these localities also occurs the "expected" *C. hysia*. Based on this syntopy and on the fact the *C. hysia* and *C. batesi* are both absent from the Cul de Sac–Valle de Neiba plain, it seems reasonable to consider them separate species. The male genitalia of the 2 taxa differ strikingly (more so than is usually the case in *Calisto*), and there is a marked difference (aside from size) in the number of "pupils" (1–6 in *hysia*, 0–3 in *batesi*) in the unhw ocellus. I should also point out that the size difference (fw length) between *C. hysia* and *C. batesi* may seem insignificant, yet when the sexes of each species are compared directly, the differences are marked. *Calisto hysia* in both sexes is simply a much larger insect than *C. batesi*. In the following discussion, I treat the north island *C. batesi* as a unit and then give data for the south island *C. batesi*.

Calisto batesi is widespread geographically on the north island. But it is remarkably uncommon on the Haitian portion, where it is now known from 2 localities (my Carrefour Marmelade locality is very near—on the mountain itself—to Michener's "Mt. Puilboreau" locality). Schwartz (1983a:23) noted that it was the Carrefour Marmelade specimens that Clench suggested were a species different from *C. h. batesi;* Schwartz felt that they agreed with the original description of *C. h. batesi* and with specimens of the same taxon from the República Dominicana. Many areas in (at least) northern Haiti appear suitable for *C. batesi,* but, despite Schwartz's (1983a:22) record of *C. batesi* from Dondon, reexamination of the material shows that none of it is *C. batesi.*

Calisto batesi is an inhabitant of mesic woods, forests, and *cafetales-cacaotales* or *caféières.* In such situations, these butterflies may be very common, flying about 0.5 m or less above the floor of the forest or along paths and roads at these same sites. We have even taken *C. batesi* adjacent to a mangrove swamp (Las Terrenas) and at the edge of a large field (1 km S Constanza), where the butterflies were encountered only along the shrubby margin.

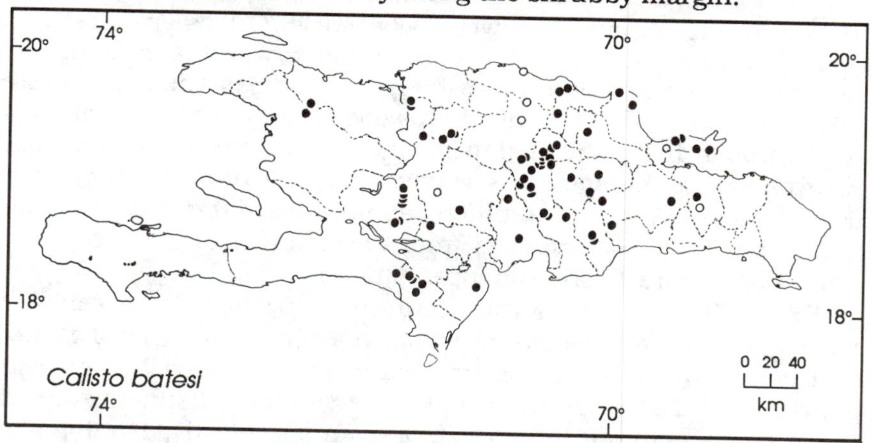

Specimens have been collected from sea level (Río San Juan, Cabrera, Las Terrenas) to 1708 m (Los Pinos) in the Sierra de Neiba; in the Cordillera Central, *C. batesi* reaches 1647 m (10 km SE Constanza). At Los Pinos, the range of *C. batesi* stops abruptly at the edge of the dense forest (the edge is sharp since the mountainside has been cleared); the forests themselves are occupied by *C. clydoniata.*

Most specimens (79) have been collected in July, with June and August having 54 and 39; there are 4 each from October and November, 6 from December, 5 each from March and May, and 3 from January. *Calisto batesi* is common in the summer but is on the wing during the entire year. Times of capture were between

0900 and 1720 h, and temperatures between 20°C (La Palma in December) to 40°C (Tenares). On several occasions, *C. batesi* has been taken flying on overcast days or even in light rain (Samaná, Hato Mayor).

Although the elevational range is broad, most specimens have been taken below 1220 m; in contrast to *C. hysia*, there are 35 localities at or below 305 m. Pairs were taken *in copula* at Cambita Garabitos, 671 m (19.vi, 36°C): 1.7 km S Jarabacoa, 488 m (30.vi, 1322 h, 30°C), on an open lawn; and 1 km S Jarabacoa, 519 m (1.vii, 1340 h).

We have twice taken *C. batesi* feeding on *Wedelia trilobata* (1.4 km SE El Pino, El Veinte).

South island *C. batesi* are known from 6 localities, at elevations between 183 m (Barahona) and 1281 m (Aceitillar). Most specimens have been taken in June (19), with 13 in July, 2 in December, and 1 in August. Times of collection were between 0905 and 1615 h, and temperatures were between 23°C (Los Arroyos) and 33°C (Las Abejas). The Cabo Rojo specimen was taken along the Alcoa road in transitional forest; the Las Abejas specimens were taken in a narrow ravine with hardwoods in pinelands and along a road through high-canopied mesic forest. The specimens from Los Arroyos (where the species is very common) were taken in cutover deciduous forest, and in a hilltop pasture, where they were uncommon. That from Barahona is from mesic forest and *cafetal*, and those from Aceitillar are from open pinewoods.

Riley (1975:51) noted the occurrence of a smaller race, with markings less well defined, of *C. hysia* at Samaná, República Dominicana. Our Samaná specimens agree with material from near Sánchez and Las Terrenas, and there is nothing distinctive about the Samaná material in general, or even specifically. The type-locality of *C. batesi* is Sánchez, Prov. de Samaná. Since Riley reversed the diagnoses of the 2 "subspecies" of *C. hysia* (Schwartz, 1983a:23), there is a possibility that he had at hand Samaná specimens of *C. batesi* and noted that they were smaller than his specimens of *C. hysia* (which indeed they are, but no smaller than all other north island *C. batesi*).

Specimens: (north island): *Haiti: Nord:* 3.5 km W Plaisance, 305 m, 1; *l'Artibonite:* 1.6 km E Carrefour Marmelade, 854 m, 25; *República Dominicana: Dajabón:* 1.4 km SE El Pino, 183 m, 2; 2 km NE El Pino, 183 m, 2; Los Cerezos, 12 km NW Río Limpio, 580 m, 1; *Elías Piña:* La Laguna, 10 km S Comendador, 732 m, 1; 15 km S Comendador, 976 m, 5; 21 km S Comendador, 1484 m, 1; 2 km NE Puesto Pirámide 204, 1586 m, 1; *Santiago Rodríguez:* Loma Leonor, 18 km SW Monción, 534 m, 3; Loma Leonor, 19 km SW Monción, 610 m, 16; 4.7 km SW Loma Leonor, 732 m, 1; *Puerto Plata:* 1 km NW

Jamao al Norte, 61 m, 2; 11 km SE Sosúa, 46 m, 1; *Espaillat:* 14 km SW Jamao al Norte, 534 m, 1; *La Vega:* Güaigüí, S La Vega, 336 m, 3; 10 km W Jayaco, 915 m, 1; La Palma, 19 km W Jayaco, 1007 m, 11; 1 km E El Río, 1037 m, 1; Buena Vista, 11 km NE Jarabacoa, 640 m, 13; La Ciénaga, 915 m, 2; 1 km W Manabao, 792 m, 1; Jarabacoa, 530 m, 3; 1 km S Jarabacoa, 534 m, 2; 1.7 km S Jarabacoa, 488 m, 2; 2 km S Jarabacoa, 488 m, 2; 6 km S Jarabacoa, 1; 3.5 km E Paso Bajito, 732 m, 3; 12 km NE Constanza, 1220 m, 13; 1 km S Constanza, 1098 m, 18; 6 km SSE Constanza, 1403 m, 6; 10 km SE Constanza, 1647 m, 1; 18 km SE Constanza, 1586 m, 1; 10 km NW La Horma, 1496 m, 1; *Duarte:* 10 km SE Tenares, 183 m, 9; *María T. Sánchez:* 8 km NE Río San Juan, s.l., 2; 6 km S Cabrera, s.l., 1; *Samaná:* 12.3 km NE Sánchez, 244 m, 2; 3.1 km E Las Terrenas, s.l., 1; 4.5 km E Samaná, 3; 10.2 km W Samaná, 61 m, 2; *Hato Mayor:* 11 km NW Hato Mayor, 122 m, 2; *Monseñor Nouel:* Bonao, 153 m, 1; 6 km SE Maimón, 122 m, 4; *Sánchez Ramírez:* 1 km NE Las Lagunas, 183 m, 1; *Dist. Nac.:* 30 km NW Santo Domingo, 122 m, 2; *Monte Plata:* 8 km NE Bayaguana, 4; 8 km W Esperalvillo, 92 m, 1; *San Cristóbal:* 11 km NW Cambita Garabitos, 671 m, 2; 6 km NW Cambita Garabitos, 488 m, 5; *Peravia:* 6 km W La Horma, 1159 m, 5; 2 km SW Rancho Arriba, 671 m, 1; *Azua:* 4 km S Peralta, 366 m, 1; 5 km SW Monte Bonito, 702 m, 3; *Baoruco:* 1 km NW El Veinte, 1220 m, 3; *Independencia:* 14 km N Los Pinos, 1159 m, 8; 21 km N Los Pinos, 1708 m, 1; (south island) *Barahona:* 5 km SE, 3 km W Barahona, 183–397 m, 1; *Pedernales:* 23 km NE Cabo Rojo, 488 m, 1; Las Abejas, 11 km NW Aceitillar, 1220 m, 2; Las Abejas, 12 km NW Aceitillar, 1129 m, 4; 1 km N Aceitillar, 1281 m, 2; 0.6 km SE Los Arroyos, 1098 m, 26.

18. *Calisto aleucosticha* Correa and Schwartz, 1986

TL Buena Vista, 11 km NW Jarabacoa, 640 m, Prov. de la Vega, República Dominicana.

FW males unknown; females 15–17 mm.

Correa and Schwartz (1986) considered *C. aleucosticha* a north island derivative of *C. hysia;* the 2 species are similar in size (and *C. aleucosticha* is much larger than *C. batesi*, with which it is sympatric), but *C. aleucosticha* differs in several details such as having 1 pupil in the unhw ocellus (3–6 in *C. hysia*), a unfw red cell patch that abruptly ends at midcell but without a dark boundary line (with a dark boundary line in *C. hysia*), a postdiscal line not margined with pale (margined with pale in *C. hysia*), and submarginal and postdiscal lines on unhw converging at anal angle (not convergent in *C. hysia*).

The 3 *C. aleucosticha* available to them were taken in August (2) and December (1); Wetherbee took another specimen in October. The small number of *C. aleucosticha* suggests, as in the case of *C. micheneri*, that we have not been in the range of *C. aleucosticha* at the appropriate times. The elevational distribution of *C. aleucosticha* is between 610 m (Loma Leonor) and 640 m (Buena Vista), and probably higher at Los Guandules, which lies about 30 km

WSW Loma Leonor. All localities are at moderate elevations marginal to the main mass of the Cordillera Central. At 2, the habitat is mixed pine-hardwood forest, although 1 of the Loma Leonor individuals was taken in "pure" pinewoods. This habitat is widespread along the edges of the Cordillera Central, and it seems likely that *C. aleucosticha* has a broad distribution around these mountains. Times of collection were between 0900 and 1630 h, at temperatures between 28°C (Buena Vista) and 34°C (Loma Leonor).

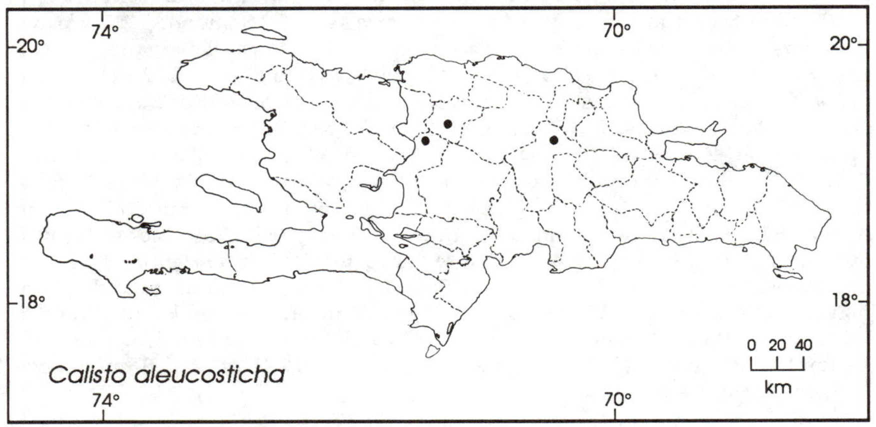

Calisto aleucosticha is sympatric with *C. batesi*, *C. confusa*, and *C. obscura* (the 3 other small north island species) at Loma Leonor and Buena Vista. At Loma Leonor, *C. batesi* and *C. confusa* are more common than both *C. obscura* and *C. aleucosticha*, whereas at Buena Vista, *C. batesi* and *C. obscura* outnumber *C. confusa* and *C. aleucosticha*. At Loma Leonor, *C. dystacta* is also syntopic with *C. aleucosticha*. At Los Guandules, *C. aleucosticha* is syntopic with *C. obscura* and *C. elelea*, the latter the more common.

Specimens: República Dominicana: Elías Piña: Los Guandules, above Guayajayaco, 1; *Santiago Rodríguez:* Loma Leonor, 19 km SW Monción, 610 m, 2; *La Vega:* Buena Vista, 11 km NW Jarabacoa, 640 m, 1.

19. *Calisto confusa* Lathy, 1899

TL Haiti.

FW males 13–15 mm, females 14–17 mm.

Calisto confusa is 1 of a trio of small *Calisto* that are widespread geographically and altitudinally. The remaining 2 members of the trio are *C. batesi* and *C. obscura*. Identification of these 3 species is at times difficult; *C. batesi* is readily determined by the presence of a red postocellar blush or patch on the unfw and the absence of a dark area on the anal lobe. The latter feature, perhaps a rudimentary ocellus but without a pupil, distinguishes *C. confusa* from *C. obscura*. *Calisto confusa* is the least easily defined; Michener (1943:5) gave in tabular form the characters of these 2 species, but even with this table, there are some specimens that leave the investigator unsure of their proper allocation. This is especially true of worn or damaged individuals, notably if the tiny anal lobe of the hw is missing, as it often is in these delicate satyrids. Additionally, as its name implies, *C. obscura* has the un lines much less well defined and more obscure than *C. confusa*. Another *C. confusa* character that is helpful is that the unhw ocellus tends to fill the entire width of M3-Cu1, whereas in *C. obscura* the ocellus is smaller and may not completely fill the width of that space.

Calisto confusa occurs throughout both Haiti and the República Dominicana, from sea level (Carrefour la Mort, Las Terrenas, Cruce de Rincón, Samaná) to 1922 m (entrance of Valle de Tetero). Within this altitudinal range, most records are up to 1220 m; records above that elevation are rather exceptional (only 8). Schwartz (1983a:20) considered *C. confusa* a butterfly occurring from sea level to 915 m, and even with many more localities, this generalization is more or less valid.

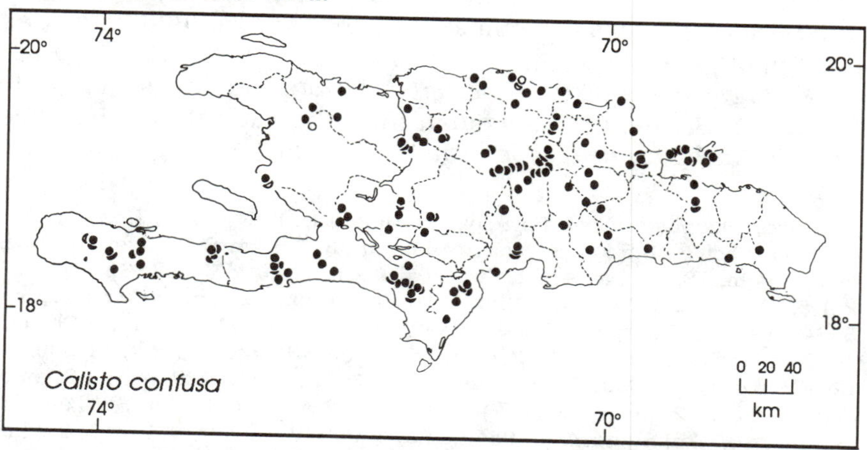

Ecologically, *C. confusa* occurs in open areas, such as fields and along the margins of woods and forests, and also within pseudoforests (*cafetales-cacaotales, caféières*). The species has also been taken in cleared areas within forests and pseudoforests and even adjacent to mangroves. This predilection for shaded situations is reflected in the complete absence of specimens from xeric areas, such as the Cul de Sac–Valle de Neiba plain or the western Valle de Cibao, where *C. confusa* does not occur even in oases that seem appropriate. The nearest *C. confusa* comes to truly arid situations are pinewoods (Aceitillar) and pine-deciduous forest mixtures (Loma Leonor, Restauración). It does not occupy this sort of habitat in the uplands of either the Cordillera Central or the Sierra de Neiba, although it can be found at lower elevations in both ranges. The high elevation (entrance to Valle de Tetero) for the species is in mixed pine-hardwoods.

I have specimens from July (188), August (89), June (74), December (52), January (15), October (13), May (11), April (5), February (5), September and March (3 each), and November (2). Michener (1943:5) noted that he had specimens from all months except February, September, October, and November. Combining these data, I assume that *C. confusa* is in flight during the entire year.

Times of collection were between 0730 and 1725 h, and temperatures between 13°C and 40°C.

Copulating pairs have been taken on 19.vi (Santo Domingo, 122 m, 35—36°C), 22.vi (El Aguacate, 1135 h, 28°C), 2.vii (Jayaco, 915 m, 1230–1340 h, 28°C), 12.vii (Jayaco, 915 m), 20.vii (Yásica, 122 m, 40°C, 1120–1220 h), 24.vii (Jamao al Norte, 534 m, 38°C, 1300–1440 h), 13.viii (La Palma, 1007 m, 34°C), and 26.x (Río San Juan, s.l.).

We have once taken *C. confusa* feeding on the small white flowers of *Blechum pyramidatum* (Acanthaceae) at Las Lagunas and on *Stachytarpheta cayennensis* (La Palma, 3 km SE Los Arroyos).

Specimens: Haiti: Nord: Carrefour la Mort, s.l., 1; 6.1 km S Dondon, 366 m, 1; *l'Artibonite:* 3.5 km S Plaisance, 336 m, 3; 1.6 km E Carrefour Marmelade, 854 m, 13; Délugé, s.l., 1; *l'Ouest:* 1.6 km N Saut d'Eau, 183 m, 4; 19.7 km SE Mirebalais, 183 m, 1; bet. Terre Rouge and 2.1 km N Terre Rouge, 397–519 m, 1; Boutilliers Road, 854–915 m, 7 (1 FSM); 0.3 km N Obléon, 1617 m, 1; 5.9 km S Dufort, 266 m, 1; 4.9 km S Béloc, 732 m, 1; 1.6 km N Béloc, 702 m, 1; 0.8 km S Découzé, 702 m, 3; Lavaneau, 229 m, 1; 4.8 km N Jacmel, 92 m, 2; nr. Péredo, 570–600 m, 4 (FSM); *Sud:* 6.6 km SW Paillant, 793 m, 3; 6.7 km SW Paillant, 854 m, 13; 3 km SW Paillant, 671 m, 2; 2.9 km SW Paillant, 671 m, 1; 6.2 km N Cavaillon, 61 m, 1; 19.7 km N Cavaillon, 580 m, 6; 26.1 km N Cavaillon, 610 m, 4; 4.8 km N Camp Perrin, 244 m, 1; 5.6 km N Camp Perrin, 275 m, 2; 14 km NW Marceline, 702 m, 1; Lévy, 4; Formond Base Camp #1, 975 m, 5 (FSM); 400 m SE Soie Bois, 960 m, 2 (FSM); *República Dominicana: Dajabón:* 1.4 km SE El Pino, 183 m, 1; 16 km NW Río Limpio, 702 m, 1; Los Cerezos, 12 km NW Río Limpio, 580 m, 3; 4 km S Restauración, 580 m, 3; 8.4 km S Restauración, 580 m, 4; 9 km S Restauración, 519 m, 2; Cañada Tirolís, just S Villa Anacaona, 576 m, 3; *Elías Piña:* 15 km S Comendador, 976 m, 3; 14 km S Comendador, 976 m, 3; 2 km NE Puesto Pirámide 204, 1586 m, 2; *Valverde:* Río Guarabo, 3 km W Los Quemados, 122 m, 4; *Santiago Rodríguez:* 8 km NNW Los Almácigos, 1; Loma Leonor, 18 km SW Monción, 534 m, 4; Loma Leonor, 19 km SW Monción, 610 m, 7; *Puerto Plata:* 12 km N Cruce de Guayacanes, 214 m, 2; 0.6 km NE Estero Hondo, 1; 13 km SE Luperón, 214 m, 5; 9 km SE Sosúa, 16 m, 1; Yásica, 22 km SE Puerto Plata, 122 m, 4; 15 km SE Puerto Plata, 122 m, 1; *Espaillat:* 14 km SW Jamao al Norte, 534 m, 5; 20 km SW Jamao al Norte, 793 m, 3; 3 km N Puesto Grande, 580 m, 6; 2 km NW Gaspar Hernández, 16 m, 1; *Santiago:* La Cumbre, 610 m, 1; Río Bao, 8 km SE Montones Abajo, 488 m, 5; Río Bao, 4 km SW Mata Grande, 702 m, 1; entrance of Valle de Tetero to Valle de Tetero, 1922–1342 m, 11; Valle de Tetero, 1342 m, 7; *Duarte:* 10 km SE Tenares, 183 m, 3; 12 km SE San Francisco de Macorís, 6; 1 km N El Abanico, 1; *La Vega:* Güaigüí, S La Vega, 226 m, 5; 2 km S La Vega, 366 m, 1; 10 km W Jayaco, 915 m, 14; La Palma, 19 km W Jayaco, 38; 1 km E El Río, 1037 m, 2; Buena Vista, 11 km NE Jarabacoa, 640 m, 13; 6 km SSW Boca del Río, 1220 m, 1; 1 km SW Los Tablones, 1342 m, 2; La Ciénaga, 915 m, 7; 1 km W Manabao, 793 m, 1; Jarabacoa, 530 m, 1; 3.5 km E Paso Bajito, 641 m, 5; 1 km S Constanza, 1098 m, 6; 12 km NE Constanza, 1220 m, 1; *Monseñor Nouel:* Bonao, 153 m, 1; 6 km SE Maimón, 122 m, 2; *Sánchez Ramírez:* 1 km SE La Mata, 1; 1 km NE Las Lagunas, 183 m, 3; *María T. Sánchez:* 11 km NE Río San Juan, s.l., 2; 14 km S La Entrada, s.l., 2; Cruce de Rincón, s.l., 3; 1 km S Cruce de Rincón, s.l., 3; *ca.* 1.8 km W, 1.2 km S Sánchez, rd. to Rincón Molinillos, 31 m, 2; *Samaná:* 6.9 km N Sánchez, 336 m, 3; 12.3 km NE Sánchez, 244 m, 3; 13.2 km NE Sánchez, 92 m, 4; 3.1 km E Las Terrenas, s.l., 3; 10.2 km W Samaná, 61 m, 2; 4.8 km W Samaná, s.l., 3; 4.5 km E Samaná, 8; 18.0 km E and N Samaná, s.l., 3; 2.8 km S Las Galeras, 61 m, 8; *La Romana:* Río Cumayasa, 13.5 km W La Romana, 31 m, 2; *Hato Mayor:* 11 km NW Hato Mayor, 2; 12 km S El Valle, 1; 7 km E Sabana de la Mar, 2; *La Altagracia:* 16 km NE La Romana, 61 m, 1; *Dist. Nac.:* 5 km S San Isidro, 1; 30 km SW Santo Domingo, 122 m, 8; *Monte Plata:* 11 km W Esperalvillo, 153 m, 15; *San Cristóbal:* 6 km NW Cambita Garabitos, 488 m, 4; *Peravia:* 2 km SW Rancho Arriba, 671 m, 1; *Azua:* 4 km S Peralta, 366 m, 3; 5 km S Peralta, 305 m, 2; 2.5 km W, 6.6 km N Azua, 183 m, 1; 5 km SW Monte Bonito, 702 m, 2; *San Juan:* 4 km E El Cercado, 702 m, 1; 7 km E El Cercado, 854 m, 1; *Baoruco:* 1 km NW El Veinte, 1220 m, 1; *Independencia:* 14 km N Los Pinos, 1159 m, 1; 4–7 km NE El Aguacate, 519–824 m, 9; *Barahona:* El Limón, summit, Sierra Martín García, 976–1037 m, 5; west slope, Sierra Martín García, 576 m, 1; Polo, 702 m, 2; 20 km SE Cabral, 946 m, 1; 2 km S La Lanza, 7; 12 km SW Barahona, 427 m, 1; 1.8 km W Monteada Nueva, 1007 m, 7; 9 km NW Enriquillo, 671 m, 6; *Pedernales:* 23 km NE Cabo Rojo, 488 m, 2; 26 km NE Cabo Rojo, 732 m, 2; Las Abejas, 11 km NW Aceitillar, 1220 m, 1; Las Abejas, 12 km NW Aceitillar, 1129 m, 1; 1 km N Aceitillar, 1281 m, 1; 4.5 km NE Aceitillar, 1373 m, 1; 1 km S La Altagracia, *ca.* 534 m, 2; 3 km SE Los Arroyos, 976 m, 1; 0.6 km SE Los Arroyos, 1098 m, 1.

20. *Calisto obscura* Michener, 1943

TL Pétionville, Dépt. de l'Ouest, Haiti.

FW males 12–16 mm, females 12–16 mm.

Calisto obscura has a broad geographic distribution on Hispaniola and occurs throughout Haiti and the República Dominicana.

Dominicana. Altitudinally, it occurs from sea level (Fond Parisien, Copey, Las Terrenas, Punta Cana, Tres Ojos, Mano Juan) to 1922 m (entrance of Valle de Tetero) in the Cordillera Central and to lower elevations in the Sierra de Baoruco (1495 m—Canote Mine), Sierra de Neiba (1220 m—El Veinte), Sierra Martín García (1037 m—El Limón), Massif de la Hotte (975 m—Formond Base Camp #1), Massif de la Selle front ranges (885 m—Boutilliers Road), and Massif du Nord (854 m—Carrefour Marmelade). The species is reported here for the first time from Isla Saona and Isla Beata.

Calisto obscura is closest in characters to *C. confusa*. The 2 species may be distinguished (unless specimens are badly worn or damaged) by the presence in *C. confusa* of a dark anal lobe on the unhw, with a slight uphw darkening capped by a pale whitish line in this same area; *Calisto obscura* is usually paler below. In female *C. obscura* the unhw ocellus in M3-Cu1 does not occupy the entire width of that space, as it usually does in *C. confusa*; in male *C. obscura* the unhw ocellus is almost equal in size to that in *C. confusa*. In general terms, the un of *C. obscura* is much paler and less contrastingly marked than that of *C. confusa*.

Of the trio of small *Calisto* (*C. batesi*, *C. confusa*, *C. obscura*) found throughout Hispaniola, only *C. obscura* occurs in xeric areas (Terre Rouge, Fond Parisien, Copey, Monte Cristi, Zamba, La Isabela, Punta Cana, Playa Bayahibe, Azua, Canoa, Oviedo, Tres Charcos, Isla Beata). In such arid lowland localities, *C. obscura* occurs in both open *Acacia*—cactus woods and very dry xeric woods. At Punta Rucia, 2 specimens were collected in deep (0.5 m) dense grass behind barrier dunes. At the other "xeric" extreme is the occurrence of *C. obscura* in highland pine forest (Restauración, Loma Leonor, La Vega, Aceitillar). But *C. obscura* occurs also in very mesic forest, both in the lowlands and highlands (Saut d'Eau, Cavaillon, Camp Perrin, Jayaco, La Palma, Constanza, Bonao, Sánchez, Las Lagunas, Esperalvillo, Cambita Garabitos). On occasion, *C. obscura* is found in open grasslands (Lascahobas), along roadsides (10 km W Luperón, La Horma, Tres Ojos, Sabana de la Mar), in clearings in *caféières* and *cafetales-cacaotales* (Plaisance, Dondon, Béloc, Découzé, Comendador, La Cumbre, Bonao, La Mata, San Francisco de Macorís, Cruce de Rincón, La Entrada, Yamasá, Esperalvillo), or in a seaside *Cocos* grove (15 km W Vieux Bourg d'Aquin). The ecological tolerance of *C. obscura* is much greater than that of any of the 3 other small *Calisto* that are sympatric with it.

Most specimens have been taken in July (185), with June (101),

January (77), and August (77) ranking next. December (49), May (39), and October (25) are represented by modest numbers, with smaller ones in March (18), April (13), and February (15). We have never failed to find *C. obscura* and suspect that, although there may be summer and winter broods, it is on the wing during the entire year. Times of collection were between 0840 and 1710 h, and temperatures between 23°C (Samaná; overcast) and 42°C (La Romana; overcast); *C. obscura* flies under heavily overcast to rainy conditions, including moderately heavy rains.

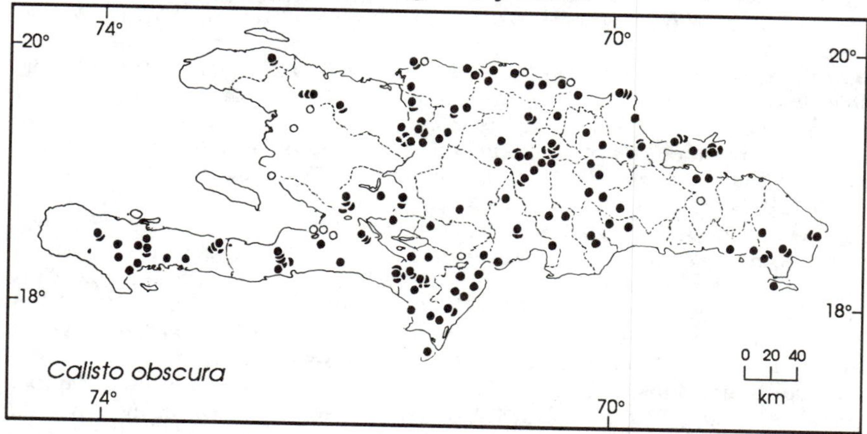

On Isla Saona on 17.i.1984, Henderson took 6–10 *C. obscura* hovering about a small roadside bush that was not flowering. The plant was *Borreria verticillata* (Rubiaceae), which has small white and nectar-laden flowers when in bloom. The *C. obscura* were obviously attracted to this single plant (of many similar ones) for some inexplicable reason. We have not elsewhere encountered *C. obscura* associated with *B. verticillata*. At Cruce de Rincón, *C. obscura* was taken on *Stachytarpheta cayennensis*, at 7 km SW Cavaillon and 1 km N Aceitillar on *Ageratum conyzoides*, at Los Quemados on *Bidens pilosa*, and at 1.4 km SE El Pino on *Wedelia trilobata*.

Copulating pairs have been taken on 31.v (Estero Hondo, 1215 h, 30°C), 23.vi (La Romana, 61 m, 1100–1430 h, 35°C), 3.viii (Villa Anacaona, 397 m, 1300–1330 h, 36°C), and 12.viii (Enriquillo, 244 m, 1200–1400 h, 34°C).

Specimens: Haiti: Nord-Ouest: 7.5 km SE Port-de-Paix, 3; 1.3 km S Balladé, 31 m, 1; *Nord:* 3.5 km S Plaisance, 336 m, 2; 3.5 km W Plaisance, 305 m, 1; 7.2 km W Plaisance, 259 m, 1; 5.6 km SE Dondon, 336 m, 1; 5.9 km S Dondon, 366 m, 1; 6.1 km S Dondon, 366 m, 1; 1.8 km S Dondon, 366 m, 1; 3 km ESE Villa Anacaona, 458 m, 1; *l'Artibonite:* 1.6 km N Saut d'Eau,

183 m, 1; 20.0 km S Mirebalais, 580 m, 1; 3.8 km N Terre Rouge, 519 m, 3; 12 km N Terre Rouge, 5; 2.9–8.5 km S Terre Rouge, 122–488 m, 3; 6.2 km E Lascahobas, 275 m, 1; 2 km SE Fond Parisien, s.l., 3; 3.0 km SE Fond Parisien, s.l., 1; 4 km SE Fond Parisien, s.l., 1; Boutilliers Road, 854–915 m, 2; Boutilliers Road, 1.8–2.1 km W Kenscoff road, 793–885 m, 2; 8.6 km N Béloc, 534 m, 3; 1.6 km N Béloc, 702 m, 2; 0.6 km S Découzé, 671 m, 1; 0.8 km S Découzé, 702 m, 1; 1.1 km S Découzé, 610 m, 1; 2.1 km S Découzé, 640 m, 4; Lavaneau, 229 m, 3; 7.7 km N Jacmel, 92 m, 2; nr. Péredo, 570–600 m, 5 (FSM); *Sud:* 6.7 km SW Paillant, 763 m, 1; 6.6 km SW Paillant, 793 m, 3; 2.9 km SW Paillant, 671 m, 1; 3 km SW Paillant, 671 m, 8; Vieux Bourg d'Aquin, s.l., 1; 15 km W Vieux Bourg d'Aquin, s.l., 2; 26.1 km N Cavaillon, 610 m, 2; 19.7 km N Cavaillon, 580 m, 5; 14.1 km N Cavaillon, 275 m, 1; 7 km SW Cavaillon, 122 m, 8; Les Cayes, s.l., 6; 5.6 km N Camp Perrin, 3; 14 km NW Marceline, 671 m, 2; Formond Base Camp #1, 975 m, 2 (FSM); 400 m SE Soie Bois, 960 m, 2 (FSM); Lévy, 8; *República Dominicana: Monte Cristi:* 4 km N Monte Cristi, s.l., 1; 1 km SE Monte Cristi, 1; 6 km W Copey, s.l., 1; *Dajabón:* 1.4 km SE El Pino, 183 m, 1; 2 km N El Pino, 183 m, 1; Los Cerezos, 12 km NW Río Limpio, 580 m, 5; 16 km NW Río Limpio, 702 m, 1; Pico Gallo, *ca.* 10 km E El Carrizal, 1302 m, 11; Mont Griné, frontier marker 47, SW of Trinitaria, 1000 m, 11; 9.1 km S Restauración, 519 m, 4; 8.4 km S Restauración, 520 m, 1; 7 km N Restauración, 671 m, 1; 4 km S Restauración, 580 m, 1; 8 km S Restauración, 610 m, 3; 1 km S Villa Anacaona, 397 m, 2; *Elías Piña:* 15 km S Comendador, 976 m, 1; 2 km NE Puesto Pirámide 204, 1586 m, 3; Los Guandules, above Guayajayaco, 1; *Santiago Rodríguez:* Loma Leonor, 19 km SW Monción, 610 m, 20; 4.7 km SW Loma Leonor, 732 m, 2; 3 km W Los Quemados, 183 m, 1; 3.0 km S Zamba, 214 m, 8; 4.8 km S Zamba, 214 m, 4; *Puerto Plata:* 12 km NW La Isabela, 61 m, 2; 12 km N Cruce de Guayacanes, 214 m, 8; 0.4 km E Punta Rucia, s.l., 2; 0.6 km NE Estero Hondo, 3; 10 km W Luperón, 1; 13 km SE Luperón, 214 m, 2; 9 km SE Sosúa, 15 m, 3; Yásica, 22 km SE Puerto Plata, 122 m, 2; 15 km SE Puerto Plata, 12 m, 1; *Espaillat:* 20 km SW Jamao al Norte, 793 m, 4; 2 km NW Gaspar Hernández, 16 m, 1; *Santiago:* Río Bao, 8 km SE Montones Abajo, 488 m, 2; 7 km SW Santiago, 214 m, 2; Valle de Tetero to entrance of Valle de Tetero, 1922–1342 m, 1; *María T. Sánchez:* 8 km NE Río San Juan, s.l., 2; 9 km NE Río San Juan. s.l., 4; 11 km NE Río San Juan, 1; 14 km S La Entrada, s.l., 4; Cruce de Rincón, s.l., 2; 1 km S Cruce de Rincón, s.l., 4; *La Vega:* Güaigüí, S La Vega, 336 m, 1; 2 km S La Vega, 366 m, 1; Buena Vista, 11 km NE Jarabacoa, 640 m, 7; 10 km W Jayaco, 915 m, 2; La Palma, 19 km W Jayaco, 1007 m, 30; La Ciénaga, 915 m, 2; 3 km N La Ciénaga, 1037 m, 2; 1 km W Manabao, 793 m, 2; Jarabacoa, 530 m, 3; 2 km S Jarabacoa, 488 m, 1; 5 km SE Jarabacoa, 595 m, 4; 3.5 km E Paso Bajito, 732 m, 2; 1 km S Constanza, 1098 m, 3; 6 km SSE Constanza, 1403 m, 6; 12 km NE Constanza, 1220 m, 5; *Monseñor Nouel:* 6 km SE Maimón, 122 m, 1; Bonao, 153 m, 1; *Sánchez Ramírez:* 1 km SE La Mata, 1; 1 km NE Las Lagunas, 183 m, 13; *Duarte:* 10 km SE Tenares, 183 m, 5; 12 km SE San Francisco de Macorís, 1; 1 km N El Abanico, 1; *Samaná:* 12.3 km NE Sánchez, 244 m, 2; 13.2 km NE Sánchez, 92 m, 1; 3.1 km E Las Terrenas, s.l., 4; 4.8 km W Samaná, s.l., 1; 8.5 km E Samaná, 1; 4.5 km E Samaná, 4; El Francés, 14 km E and N Samaná, s.l., 3; 18.0 km E and N Samaná, s.l., 7; 2.8 km S Las Galeras, 61 m, 2; 3.8 km S Las Galeras, s.l., 2; 10.5 km S Las Galeras, 16 m, 2; *Hato Mayor:* 17 km E Sabana de la Mar, 1; 11 km NW Hato Mayor, 122 m, 3; *La Altagracia:* Punta

Cana, s.l., 4; 2 km W Punta Cana, 13; 0.5–3.5 km W Boca de Yuma, 2; 2–3 km W Boca de Yuma, 1; 1 km N Playa Bayahibe, 1; 2.5 km SE Playa Bayahibe, s.l., 1; 16 km NE La Romana, 61 m, 15; *La Romana:* Río Cumayasa, 13.5 km W La Romana, 122 m, 6; Río Chavón, 8 km SE La Romana, s.l., 4; *Monte Plata:* 7 km SE Yamasá, 31 m, 3; 11 km W Esperalvillo, 153 m, 6; *Dist. Nac.:* 30 km NW Santo Domingo, 122 m, 3; 25 km SE Yamasá, 6 (MPM); *San Cristóbal:* 6 km NW Cambita Garabitos, 488 m, 5; 11 km NW Cambita Garabitos, 610 m, 2; *Peravia:* 6 km W La Horma, 1159 m, 3; 2 km SW Rancho Arriba, 671 m, 1; *Azua:* 25 km NE Azua, 92 m, 1; 4 km S Peralta, 366 m, 5; 5 km S Peralta, 305 m, 4; 5 km SW Monte Bonito, 702 m, 4; *San Juan:* 9 km E Vallejuelo, 610 m, 4; *Baoruco:* 1 km NW El Veinte, 1220 m, 1; *Independencia:* 14 km N Los Pinos, 1159 m, 1; 4–7 km NE El Aguacate, 519–824 m, 7; 0.5 km E Duvergé, s.l., 3; *Barahona:* El Limón, summit, Sierra Martín García, 976–1037 m, 5; west slope, Sierra Martín García, 305–854 m, 2; 11.5 km ESE Canoa, s.l., 5; 10 km SSW Cabral, 427 m, 2; Polo, 702 m, 1; 5 km SE, 3 km W Barahona, 183 m, 1; 2 km SW Barahona, 122 m, 5; 8 km NW Paraíso, 3 (MPM); 8–10 km NW Paraíso, 3 (MPM); 3 km NW Enriquillo, 244 m, 2; 9 km NW Enriquillo, 1; *Pedernales;* 2.0 km N Cabo Rojo, s.l., 1; 23 km NE Cabo Rojo, 488 m, 2; Aceitillar, 36 km NNE Cabo Rojo, 1281 m, 3; Canote Mine, 6 km NW Aceitillar, 1495 m, 1; 4 km N Aceitillar, 1352 m, 1; 1 km N Aceitillar, 1281 m, 4; Las Abejas, 12 km NW Aceitillar, 1129 m, 1; Las Abejas, 11 km NW Aceitillar, 1251 m, 1; 4 km NE Aceitillar, 1373 m, 1; 2 km N Banano, 244 m, 2; 1 km S La Altagracia, *ca.* 534 m, 2; El Mulito, 21 km N Pedernales, 214 m, 1; 3 km N Cabeza de Agua, 305 m, 1; 17 km NW Oviedo, 183 m, 5; 4 km NW Tres Charcos, 1; *Isla Saona:* many localities reckoned from Mano Juan, 55; *Isla Beata:* 5.

21. *Calisto gonzalezi* Schwartz, 1988

TL 1 km NE Las Lagunas, 183 m, Prov. de Sánchez Ramírez, República Dominicana.

FW males 14–17 mm, females 16–17 mm.

Calisto gonzalezi is known from a short series from 1 locality. That locality has been so highly modified vegetationally (between 1985 and 1986) that it is questionable if the species still occurs there.

The Sierra de Yamasá, north of Santo Domingo, changes abruptly near Las Lagunas into the more eastern *haitises* region that extends eastward along the southwestern shore of the Bahía de Samaná. The type-locality, formerly well forested, lies at the point of transition from one to the other physiographies. *Calisto gonzalezi* inhabits the rich mesic hardwoods at this locality.

Although somewhat similar to *C. confusa*, *C. gonzalezi* is larger, lacks an ocellar remnant at the hw anal angle, and has the "pupils" in the unfw ocellus very distinctly blue.

Calisto gonzalezi certainly has a wider distribution than now known; Schwartz (1987) noted that 2 specimens from La Palma, to the west in the Cordillera Central, resembled *C. gonzalezi*, but he was unable to state their affiliations definitively. It seems more likely that *C. gonzalezi* is an *haitises* endemic; it should be looked for in that area.

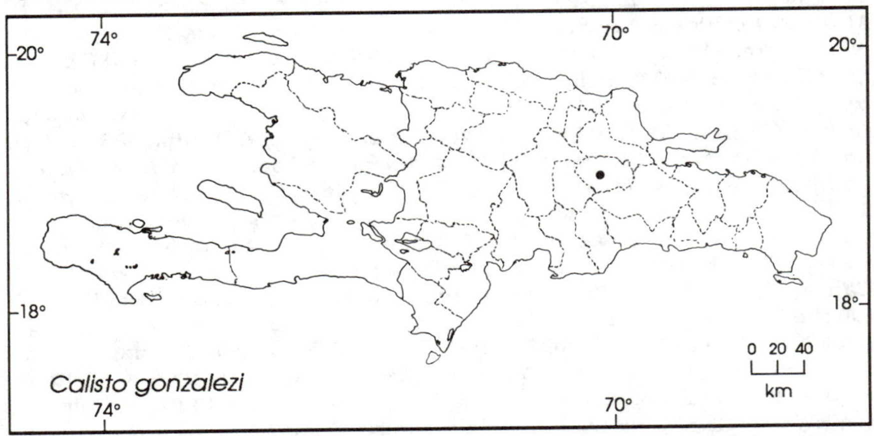

All specimens have been taken in June. Times of collection are 1100—1400 h and temperatures 33°C to 37°C.

Specimens: República Dominicana: Sánchez Ramírez: 1 km NE Las Lagunas, 183 m, 1♂.

22. *Calisto debarriera* Clench, 1943

TL Désbarrière, Massif de la Hotte, 4000 ft., Dépt. du Sud, Haiti.

FW males 13–15 mm, females 14–15 mm.

Clench (1943:25–26) named *Calisto confusa debarriera* on the basis of 4 specimens. The holotype and paratype (both males) are from the type-locality. Two other specimens (not designated paratypes) are from Tardieu (= Targi) on the Massif de la Hotte and close (*ca.* 3 km) to the type-locality and from Ennery in the Dépt. de l'Artibonite in northern Haiti. The likelihood that a species of *Calisto* occurs on the extreme distal portion of the Tiburon Peninsula and on the Massif du Nord in northern Haiti is remote, and it seems probable that the Ennery specimen belongs to another taxon.

Munroe (1950:222–23) raised the subspecific name to species rank (as *C. debarriera*) but did not examine any further material. Munroe's action was based primarily on the differences in the penes of *C. confusa* and *C. debarriera;* that of the former is about 4 times as long as broad, that of the latter about 6 times as broad as long. Brown and Heineman (1972:51) considered *C. debarriera* a valid species, whereas Riley (1975:50) considered it a form of *C. confusa.*

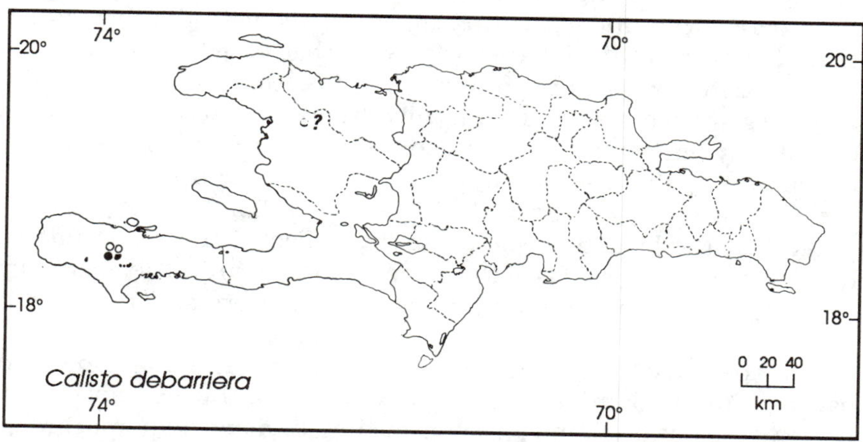

Clench's diagnosis is brief and may be summarized thus: fw 12–13 mm; unfw cell red, the color extending into neighboring spaces; 2 submarginal lines, and an indication of a discal line; unhw with a single ocellus near the anal angle, with its small white pupil slightly basad of center; a very obscure line across the basal part of the wing; basad of the ocellus, a bluish (near costa) to white line; 2 submarginal lines convergent toward anal angle, where they enclose a white area; basal to the inner submarginal line 3 white spots, in M2-M3-Cul [*sic*]. Clench stated that this taxon differs from *C. confusa* in being darker below and in having the light lines obscured. The red in the unfw cell is darker.

During September 1984, Daniel J. Cordier (with the use of his hat) collected for Gali a long series of *Calisto* at several localities on the southern slopes and foothills of the Massif de la Hotte. These series include 7 specimens (5 males, 2 females) of a small species that agree extremely well with Clench's and Munroe's comments on *C. debarriera.* The unhw ocellus is large and virtually fills M3-Cu1 submarginally; the number of pale "pupils" varies from 1 to 3 (no microscope is necessary to determine this character), arranged in a longitudinal sequence down the center of the ocellus. If only 1 "pupil" is present, it lies in the basal portion of the ocellus. The unfw ocellus is of moderate size and has 2 pale blue "pupils" that are in the *basal* portion of the ocellus, not down its center. Both unfw and unhw ocelli are ringed with dark yellow-brown. There are 2 or 3 white dots in Rs-M1, M1-M2, and M2-M3; that in Rs-M1 is absent if there are only 2 white dots. The red of the unfw cell is indeed darker (pl. 6L11) in *C. debarriera* than in *C. confusa* (pl. 6H12). Due to the method of collecting, the specimens are in less than perfect condition, but they agree so well with the description of *C. debarriera* that I feel they represent that form.

Although *C. debarriera* to some extent resembles *C. confusa*, the 2 species are syntopic at least locally. In addition to the differences (admittedly minor) in the male genitalia, *C. confusa* can be readily recognized by the presence of a dark area on the uphw anal lobe; the anal lobe in *C. debarriera* lacks this coloration.

At 1 of the localities where Cordier collected these specimens, he also took 1 *C. confusa*; thus the 2 species are at least locally syntopic. Two *C. obscura* and many *C. hysia* were also taken with *C. debarriera*.

All specimens were taken in September. The holotype and paratype were taken in October, as well as the Tardieu specimen. From these data, one might suspect that *C. debarriera* appears in the fall, but so little work has been done in the Massif de la Hotte that such speculation is futile.

No times or temperatures were taken. The habitat was basically open areas near houses and cultivation. The day (13.ix) was alternately sunny and overcast. Elevations vary between 950 m (Trou Carfineyes) and 1220 m (type-locality).

Specimens: Haiti: Sud: 400 m SE Soi Bois, 960 m, 4 (FSM); Trou Carfineyes, 0.5 km SSE Soi Bois, 950 m, 2 (FSM); Vaper Dirant #2, 2.8 km WSW Forment, 1 (FSM).

23. *Calisto neiba* Schwartz and Gali, 1984

TL 15 km S Comendador, 976 m, Prov. de Elías Piña, República Dominicana.

FW males 14–16 mm, females 15–17 mm.

Calisto neiba is known from 3 localities on the Sierra de Neiba: the north face of the north range (type-locality) and the north and south faces of the south range (Puesto Pirámide 204, Neiba). The species is remarkable in that it is multiocellate, with 4 or 6 unhw ocelli. Supernumerary unhw ocelli are unusual in Hispaniolan *Calisto* (with of course the exceptions of the biocellate *C. arcas*, members of the *C. grannus* complex, *C. micrommata*, and *C. sommeri*).

Calisto neiba is an inhabitant of mesic hardwood forest; at the type-locality, the species has been collected only on a path through this habitat, and at Puesto Pirámide 204, it has been collected only on a 1-km-long stretch of road passing though mesic deciduous forest. At the latter site, the butterflies were often encountered on the grassy verges of the canopied road in well-shaded situations. That *C. neiba* is sensitive to the mesic conditions in which it lives is attested by the fact that we revisited the type-locality on 3.viii.1982, and secured no specimens, whereas on 26–27.vii.1981 the species was moderately common. The area was quite wet on the latter date, very dry on the former. But on 5.viii.1982, we first secured *C. neiba* at the second locality; this area was moist. At Neiba, the single *C. neiba* was taken by Gonzalez as it flew above a small (paved) creek across the road; both sides of the road are mesic *cafetales*.

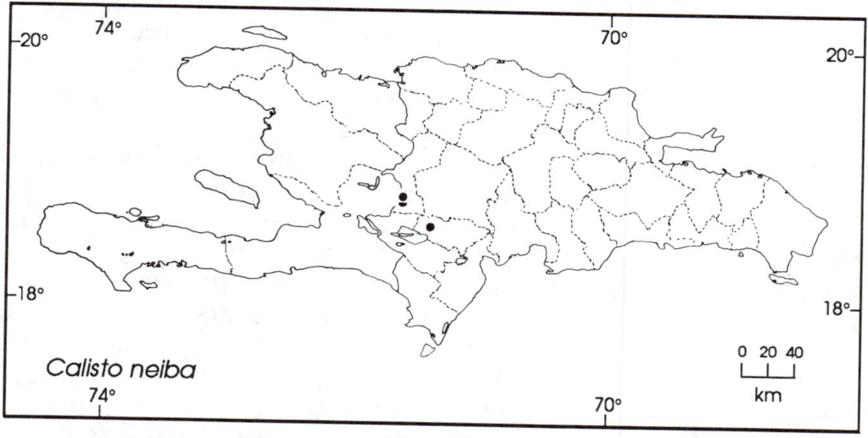

On 5.viii.1982 at the type-locality, *C. batesi*, *C. confusa*, and *C. obscura* were collected on paths through fields and along the road; all are more tolerant of dryness than is *C. neiba*. These 4 small species are sympatric but not syntopic, with *C. neiba* distinctly a shaded-forest butterfly, and the remaining 3, butterflies of more open areas. Interestingly, all *C. neiba* collected on 16.vii.1983 at Puesto Pirámide 204 are males and fall within the extremes of fw length given in the original description. Although *C. neiba* is known from only 3 localities, I am certain that this species will be found elsewhere in these mountains at the proper elevations and ecological conditions. Gonzalez did not secure any at El Veinte, where *C. neiba* is expected.

All specimens of *C. neiba* have been collected between 26.vii and 13.viii, with more specimens in July (21) than in August (17). Times of activity were between 1030 and 1430 h, and temperatures between 23°C and 33°C. The elevations were 671 m (Neiba) and 1586 m (Puesto Pirámide 204).

Calisto neiba is sympatric with *C. batesi*, *C. confusa*, *C. obscura*, and *C. choneupsilon* at Puesto Pirámide 204 and Comendador. In addition, at Puesto Pirámide 204, *C. neiba* is sympatric with *C. micrommata* and *C. clydoniata*, and at Neiba, with *C. pulchella pulchella*.

Specimens: República Dominicana: Elías Piña: 15 km S Comendador, 976 m, 14; 2 km NE Puesto Pirámide 204, 1586 m, 23; *Baoruco:* 14 km N Neiba, 671 m, 1.

24. *Calisto lyceia* Bates, 1935

TL Isla Saona, República Dominicana.

FW males 15–16 mm; females 15–16 mm.

Calisto lyceia was named on the basis of 2 males and 1 female from Isla Saona, off the extreme southeastern portion of Hispaniola. Bates (1935b:241) also noted the existence of another specimen, "a strongly marked male" from Monte Cristi in the extreme northwest of the República Dominicana, that he also assigned to this taxon. Munroe (1950:224) examined 14 specimens, including the type-series and the Monte Cristi male; he assigned specimens from 2 general areas (Isla Saona, Monte Cristi) to *C. lyceia*, and Riley (1975:51) followed this range statement. (Munroe also commented on 2 females in the MCZ which he considered similar to *C. lyceia*, except that they were larger and differed in detail from typical *C. lyceia*. I have examined what appear to be these 2 specimens, and they are properly assigned to *C. elelea;* the basally elongate and tiny unhw ocellus is diagnostic.) Gali (1985) has shown that the 2 populations of supposed *C. lyceia* are in actuality distinct species, and that *C. lyceia sensu stricto* occurs only on Isla Saona and Isla Catalina. Even the identity of these 2 islet populations is not certain.

Henderson visited Isla Saona in January of 3 years (1982 –84), and although he secured a long series of *C. obscura* in the last year, he never succeeded in collecting any *C. lyceia* on Isla Saona. But in January 1982, Henderson took a short series of a *Calisto* with brightly colored un on Isla Catalina, 30 km northwest of Isla Saona. Gali (1985) considered these specimens identical with Saonan *Calisto*, since they do not appear to differ in any trenchant ways from the 2 paratypes of *C. lyceia* (1 of which now consists of a pair of hw only). It may well be that these 2 populations are not identical (there is no identity of reptiles, for instance, on the subspecific level on these 2 satellite islands), and if so, a new name will have to be proposed for the Catalina population. For the moment, I have no course but to consider the 2 samples identical; certainly more material from both islands is mandatory.

There are no field data on the Saona material; they were collected on 21.i.1931. Henderson's Catalina specimens were taken on 15.i.1982. They were collected perched on the leaves of shrubs and grasses in the large open grassy area that occupies a shallow interior basin on central Catalina. The grass is not *Uniola virgata*, with which other members of the *lyceia* complex *Calisto* are associated. Both Saona and Catalina have extensive stands of xeric woods, those on Saona less harsh (= more mesic) than those on Catalina. Both islets are, in the summer, extremely hot, and perhaps there is a significance to the January dates of collection of both lots of *C. lyceia*. The aspect of both islands is more bleak and rigorous than that of the adjacent mainland, where *C. lyceia* is not known to occur. No other member of the *lyceia* complex is known to occur nearer than Sabana Buey, some 160 km to the west; the intervening areas are mesic and not suitable for members of this complex.

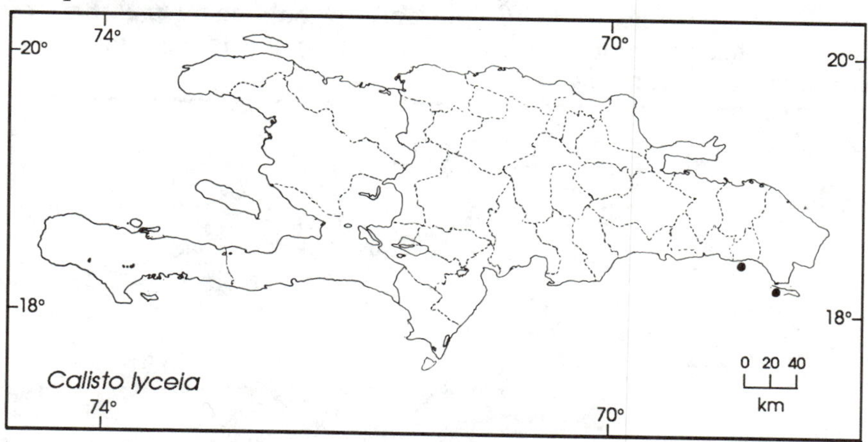

No other *Calisto* is known from Isla Catalina, but on Isla Saona *C. lyceia* is sympatric (but presumably not syntopic) with *C. obscura*, the latter very common there.

Specimens: República Dominicana: La Altagracia: Isla Saona: 2 (MCZ); *La Romana: Isla Catalina:* nr. naval base, 4.

25. *Calisto crypta* Gali, 1985

TL Near Monte Cristi, Prov. de Monte Cristi, República Dominicana.

FW males 13–19 mm, females 16–22 mm.

Calisto crypta is the second of a group of 6 species that have been considered the *lyceia* complex (Gali, 1985). All species resemble each other in that the un is richly tinted with shades of orange, and there are single ocelli on the unfw and unhw. The species differ from each other in the extent of the bright un coloration, the size of the unhw ocellus, the location within the unhw ocellus of the pale pupil, and the configuration of the androconial patch (see KEY). All are xerophiles; although *C. schwartzi* occurs in the uplands of the Sierra de Baoruco, its occurrence there appears to be limited strictly to pine forest, essentially a xeric habitat. All other species inhabit lowlands to moderate elevations (580 m).

It is appropriate here to mention 2 specimens of this complex in the MNHNSD from "Puerto Francés Viejo, Prov. de Samaná, Rep. Dom.," collected by L. Domínguez on 12.iv.1979. Raburn and I visited this area, which is between Samaná and Las Galeras. Collecting there in a coastal *Cocos* grove did not yield specimens of this *Calisto*, nor were Raburn and I confident of finding such a confirmed xerophile in such a mesic area. The Península de Samaná is very mesic, and the "appropriate" habitat for members of this complex does not exist there. The status of this Samaná population remains unresolved.

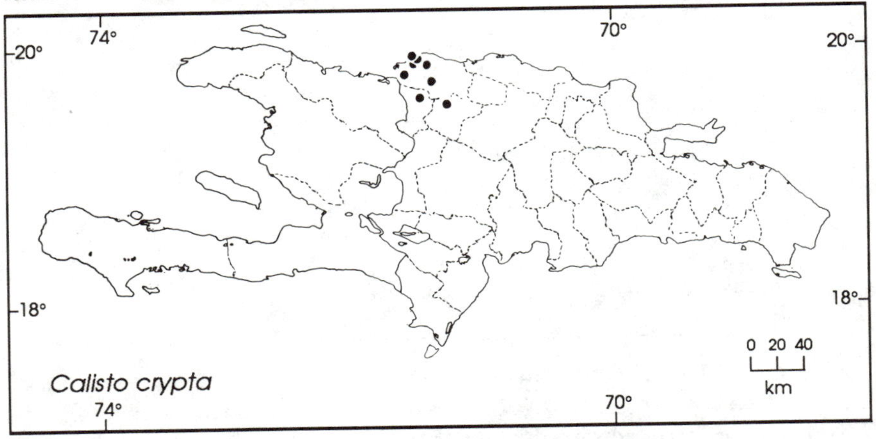

In the company of Amador, Raburn, and Wisor, I visited the Monte Cristi area on 6 occasions after the habitat preferences of members of the *lyceia* complex became known. These visits were in March, June, July, and October. Wisor and I (July) and Gali and I (August) had previously visited the region but were unaware at those times of the habitat preferences of these butterflies. Thus, a total of 8 visits were made to Monte Cristi in 5 months. But it was not until 16.iii.1984 that Wisor was successful in securing 1 (female) *C. crypta*. We had searched in several stands of *Uniola*

virgata (in which the female was finally collected) without success. Yet Bates (1935b:241) noted the capture of a Monte Cristi male on 7.vi.1931, and there are 10 specimens from the region taken between 8.ii and 6.iii in 2 years (1930 and 1931); it appears that *C. crypta* is very sporadic. In 1982–84, the species was not common.

In 1985 Gonzalez took 1 *C. crypta* at the same locality where Wisor had taken his specimen in 1984. The site is a stand of *Uniola virgata*, slightly above sea level, with scattered *Acacia*. In 1986, the situation was very different. Between 15.v and 28.v Gonzalez and I collected 63 *C. crypta*. Not only was the species common in *U. virgata* stands in the Monte Cristi area, but we also secured material (again in *U. virgata*) SE of Martín García and S of Zamba. These latter localities are *U. virgata* enclaves in *Acacia* scrub.

Calisto crypta has been taken feeding on *Croton linearis* (Zamba; 1 km SE Monte Cristi, 2 occasions). At the latter locality, *C. crypta* was feeding on a *C. linearis* that was only 10 cm above the ground and shaded by the overarching leaves of *U. virgata*.

Most specimens (63) are from May, with 1 in March and 1 in June. Times of collection were between 1030 h and 1645 h, at temperatures of 28–36°C. These are low temperatures for this area, where 38–40°C are not unusual in summer. It appears that the time of maximum eclosion of *C. crypta* is spring. The early dates of 10 of the previously collected specimens (February and March) confirm this supposition.

Michener (1943:6) listed a specimen from Chacuey (Prov. de Dajabón), República Dominicana, at 366 m. This locality is about 40 km S Monte Cristi and at a considerably higher elevation. The locality data suggest that *C. crypta* is more widespread in this region than expected and at higher elevations than the limits set by our collections (s.l.—214 m; Zamba). Chacuey lies in the northern foothills of the Cordillera Central.

Specimens: República Dominicana: Monte Cristi: near Monte Cristi, 5 (AMNH); 1.6 km E Monte Cristi, 1 (AMNH); Río Yaque, 16 km S Monte Cristi, 1 (AMNH); Bahía de Manzanillo, 1 (AMNH); 12.8 km E Monte Cristi, 1 (AMNH); 1 km SE Monte Cristi, 48; 2 km SE Monte Cristi, 6; 4 km SE Monte Cristi, 1; 3.9 km SE Martín García, 92 m, 2; *Dajabón:* Chacuey, 1 (AMNH); *Santiago Rodríguez:* 3.0 km S Zamba, 214 m, 8.

26. *Calisto franciscoi* Gali, 1985

TL Tábara Abajo, Prov. de Azua, República Dominicana.

FW males 15–17 mm, females 17–19 mm.

Of the 6 members of the *C. lyceia* complex, *C. franciscoi* has the broadest known distribution, from Duvergé in the Valle de

Neiba and the xeric northern slopes of the Sierra de Baoruco, east to Sabana Buey in the Llanos de Azua, and on the Península de Barahona. All habitats where we have taken *C. franciscoi* in numbers are xeric, with stands of *Uniola virgata* and *Acacia* (1 exception). Temperatures varied between 28°C (Tábara Abajo, 11.5 km ESE Canoa) and 37°C (Tábara Abajo), and times between 0820 and 1530 h. Activity of these butterflies decreases with increasing temperatures, and few are active in the scrub in the hot afternoons. The late time (1530 h) was following a very late afternoon rain that cooled the area to 28°C. Elevational distribution is between sea level (8–12 km ESE Canoa) and 427 m (Puerto Escondido).

At Sabana Buey, *C. franciscoi* was taken on a hillslope with *Acacia* and *U. virgata*. The butterflies were not common at the times of the visits (5.iii, 9.iii, and 15.iv.1984).

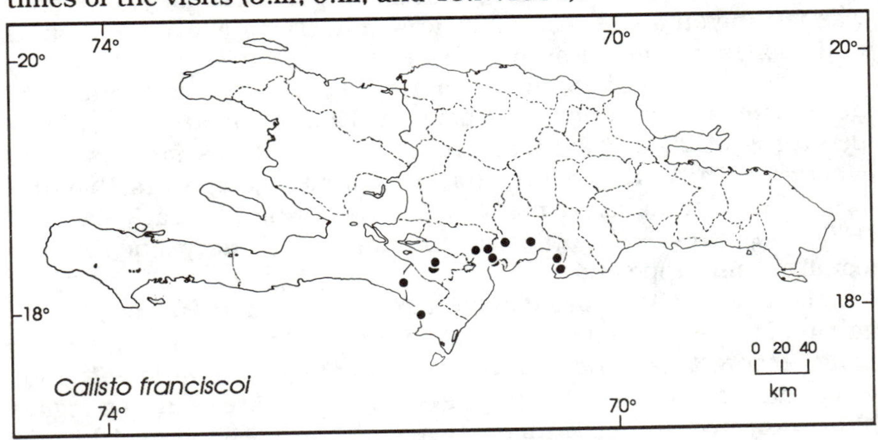

Calisto franciscoi

The single specimen from Palmar de Ocoa was taken by Wisor on a "mesic" creek run in an otherwise xeric area; there was no nearby stand of *U. virgata*, but within sight of the place of collection, the hillsides had a fine stand of that grass.

The specimen from Duvergé was taken on a "mesic" slope above an irrigation ditch; the slope was covered with *Lantana ovatifolia*, grasses, and *Bidens pilosa*. The *C. franciscoi* was feeding on the latter plant. Although there was no *U. virgata* where the butterfly was taken, I found scattered tussocks of that grass nearby (see account of *O. stillmani*). The single Azua specimen (another seen), taken from an open grassy pasture with no obvious *U. virgata*, is the only exception to the *C. franciscoi–Uniola* association.

At Tábara Abajo, *C. franciscoi* was taken (9.iii and 5.iv.1984) on an open hillside covered with *U. virgata*, and I saw 2 in organpipe cactus forest. Henderson and I discovered a very local enclave there, where these butterflies were common. A small (10×2 m) patch of open *Acacia*, adjacent to a rail fence that in turn enclosed an irrigated field, was a favored spot for *C. franciscoi*. This small patch of *Acacia* had many almost wilted *Bidens pilosa* which were extremely attractive to *C. franciscoi*. This enclave had the greatest concentration of flowers in this area, and the *C. franciscoi* were observed to fly across a dirt road from less attractive areas directly to the patch where they fed avidly. A great many more were seen at this single small spot than were seen in the adjacent areas of *Acacia* and cactus forest.

The single specimen from 3 km NE Canoa was taken by Henderson from a wash on a hillside overlooking the Valle de Neiba; *U. virgata* was present, and 1 other *C. franciscoi* was seen, foraging on the white flowers of *Croton linearis*.

Gali and I took the first specimens of *C. franciscoi* at 12 km ESE Canoa on 31.vii.1982. This locality is an area of *Acacia* scrub and open "fields" of *Uniola virgata*. I observed several *C. franciscoi* feeding on a low (10 mm) unidentified white-flowered vine on the roadside at the base of a *Lantana ovatifolia* (on which these butterflies did not feed).

The locality at 8 km ESE Canoa is a gradually sloping hillside with large open areas of *U. virgata* and scattered clumps of *Acacia*. *Calisto franciscoi* has been very abundant there, the butterflies flying among the tussocks, 0.5 m or less above the ground, and seeking refuge within them. In fact, Raburn took his first specimen there by making a cone of his net and inverting it over a small tussock of *U. virgata* into which he had seen a *C. franciscoi* retreat. The butterfly was most reluctant to leave the grass's sanctuary and remained inside the clump despite violent shaking. It is not uncommon to see *C. franciscoi* perched on the fine leaves of *U. virgata*; obviously the grass plays a role in the behavioral repertoire (and presumably reproductive activities) of these butterflies. At this locality, large numbers of *C. franciscoi* were feeding on a small clump of tall (2 m) *Melochia nodiflora* (Fabaceae). After a heavy afternoon rain and falling temperatures, *C. franciscoi* kept to the shelter of a few large shade trees with much "trash" (fallen branches and dead shrubs) at 11.5 km ESE Canoa.

In the Canoa area, the rigorous habitat of *C. franciscoi* is shared with *C. obscura*, although the latter is much less common. It should be recalled that, of the 4 small and widespread species of *Calisto*, *C. obscura* is the most tolerant of xeric conditions

Although at Cabo Rojo there are extensive stands of *Uniola virgata*, in which we had looked in vain for a xeric-adapted *Calisto*, the first specimens were taken in 1986. Despite the hiatus (70 km airline) of this population from the main range of *C. franciscoi*, the specimens do not differ appreciably from material from the Valle de Neiba–Llanos de Azua. At Cabo Rojo, the butterflies were encountered only in sheltered areas—groups of trees surrounded by *U. virgata* —and never in the "fields" of the latter. The "trash" on the ground under the trees made collecting these butterflies very difficult. The constant wind that sweeps across this area may be the reason for such secretive habits.

There is a specimen of *C. franciscoi* from Mencía, on the southern slopes of the Massif de la Selle, taken by Raburn on 2.vii. The elevation is 397 m. It is likely a vagrant from the Península de Barahona lowlands. Mencía is in a xeric-mesic transitional area. Specimens from the northern face of the Sierra de Baoruco (Puerto Escondido) are from a typical xeric area with *Acacia* and *Uniola virgata*. There the butterflies took refuge under an unidentified spinose pea, which made collecting them extremely difficult.

Most specimens (50) are from April, with July (30) and June (34) represented by about equal numbers. There are also 22 specimens from August, 6 from March, 5 each from February and December, and 1 from January. But Amador, Raburn, and I, while traveling from Barahona to Santo Domingo on the morning of 14.viii.1983, saw as many as 30 *C. franciscoi* crossing the road between Canoa and Azua, a distance of about 65 km; the butterflies were very common throughout this whole xeric region. This phenomenon has not been observed again; we doubtless were witnessing an eclosion of *C. franciscoi* on that date. It seems very probable that *C. franciscoi* is multivoltine.

Calisto franciscoi has been taken feeding on *Croton linearis* (8 km ESE Canoa), *Bidens pilosa* (Tábara Abajo, 2 occasions), and *Lantana ovatifolia* (Puerto Escondido).

Specimens: República Dominicana: Peravia: 4 km E Sabana Buey, 61 m, 5; *Azua:* 1 km E Palmar de Ocoa, 1; 2.5 km W, 6.6 km N Azua, 183 m, 1; Tábara Abajo, 42 (4 MNHNSD); *Independencia:* 2 km S Duvergé, 1; 5 km N Puerto Escondido, 427 m, 8; *Barahona:* 3 km NE Canoa, 1; 8 km ESE Canoa, s.l., 46; 11 km ESE Canoa, s.l., 15; 12 km ESE Canoa, s.l., 16; *Pedernales:* 2 km NE Cabo Rojo, s.l., 17; Mencía, 397 m, 1.

Sight record: República Dominicana: Azua: 2.5 km W, 6.6 km N Azua, 183 m—1 seen, 16.vi.

27. *Calisto hendersoni* Gali, 1985

TL 4 km E El Limón, Prov. de Independencia, República Dominicana.

FW males 15–16 mm, females 16–17 mm.

Calisto hendersoni is the fourth member of the *C. lyceia* complex; the species is known from only 1 locality in the Valle de Neiba, where it was abundant on 2.iv.1984 and 17.vi.1986 on roadside flowers and in an open "field" of *Uniola virgata* with scattered *Acacia* shrubs and trees.

Raburn and I visited this locality on 16.x.1983 (0940–1120 h, temperature 33°C) and saw a few *C. hendersoni*. Three were taken on that day as they fed on a large roadside *Lantana ovatifolia;* the behavior of these delicate butterflies reflected the high temperatures. The first specimen was seen at 1115 h as it flew across the road toward the stand of *Lantana*. Once there, it (and its fellows) fed briefly and then fluttered into a tangled mass of dead *Acacia* branches at the base of the *Lantana*, where they rested with wings closed on the lower inaccessible *Acacia* trash.

On 2.iv.1984, Henderson and I again visited the locality; *C. hendersoni* was extremely abundant in both a large area of *Uniola virgata* and also feeding on the white flowers of *Melochia nodiflora* and *Pithecellobium circinale* (both Fabaceae); these 2 plants formed a small roadside copse about 3 m X 2 m, with much dead *Acacia* trash at its base. The time was 1100–1340 h and temperature 33°C. The day was overcast with some sunny interludes. During the sunny episodes, *C. hendersoni* fed very little and hid in the *Acacia* trash; when the sky was overcast, the butterflies foraged on the flowers or sat exposed on the leaves of *U. virgata*. Such behavior suggested that collecting xeric-area *Calisto* may best be accomplished on overcast days. The butterflies were so abundant in the patch of flowers that as many as 5 were seen at 1 time.

On 8.iv.1984, Henderson and I once more stopped at the El Limón locality (1345–1400 h, 36°C; bright and sunny). A total of 5 *C. hendersoni* was seen (none collected): 3 in tangles of dead *Acacia*, 2 flying across the road. There were none on the flowers where they had been abundant previously. Note the different weather conditions, higher temperature, and later time.

On 17.vi.1986, *C. hendersoni* was abundant and feeding on purple-flowered *Lantana trifolia*.

At this locality, while collecting at the patch of flowers on 2.iv.1984, I noted an unmoving orange object within the *Pithecellobium*. Closer inspection showed that it was a dead *C. hendersoni*.

When the "specimen" was netted, the butterfly was found to be in the clutches of a small (4 cm) bright green and completely camouflaged praying mantis; the mantis had availed itself of this favorable site where many small butterflies regularly came to feed.

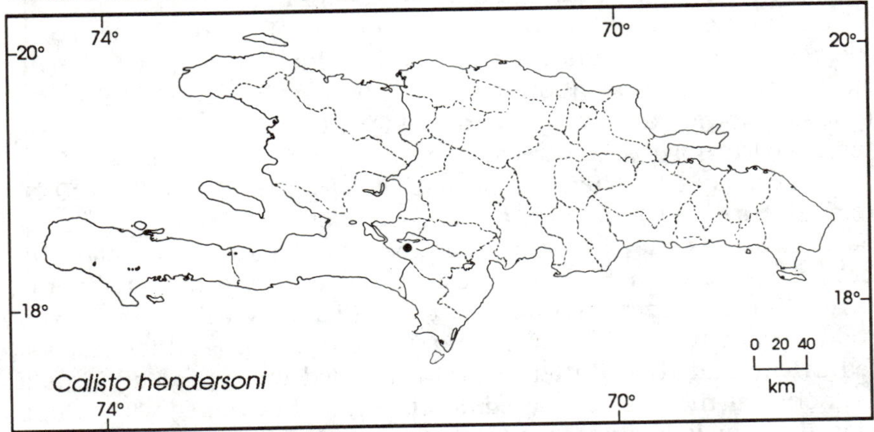

The known range of *C. hendersoni* comprises this single locality. Stands of *U. virgata* extend as far west as the Dominico-Haitian border (Boca de Cachón–Las Lajas), but Henderson, Gonzalez, Escobio, and I have all searched in vain for *Calisto* in that region (8.iv.1984, 26.vii.1985, 17.vi.1986, 30.xii.1986). The species doubtless occurs there and almost certainly extends into the Cul de Sac plain in Haiti at least between Fond Pite and Manneville and between Malpasse and Fond Parisien. In the República Dominicana, *C. hendersoni* should occur east to the region west of Duvergé; the single specimen from that area is a *C. franciscoi*. There are fine and poorly examined stands of *U. virgata* that must harbor some species of the complex at the intersection of the Duvergé-Jimaní road and the old road to El Aguacate (La Florida). Insofar as we have been able to determine, there are no stands of *U. virgata* north of Lago Enriquillo. There, the Sierra de Neiba foothills come virtually to the shore of the lake, and there are no suitable habitats for the grass.

No other *Calisto* is syntopic with *C. hendersoni*.

Specimens: República Dominicana: Independencia: 4 km E El Limón, s.l., 50.

28. *Calisto raburni* Gali, 1985

TL 7 km NE El Aguacate, 519 m, Prov. de Independencia, República Dominicana.

FW males 15–20 mm; females 15–22.

Calisto raburni is a very distinctive butterfly, 1 of 3 species of the *lyceia* complex occurring on the south island. One of these species (*C. schwartzi*) occurs well above sea level and in habitats that do not have *Uniola virgata*. *Calisto raburni* and *C. schwartzi* are very well differentiated from other members of the *lyceia* complex, suggesting a long-standing separation from the north island stock.

The holotype of *C. raburni* was taken on 6.vii.1983. The type-locality had been visited 3 times before its collection and 10 times after, but no other *C. raburni* had been seen; other visits were in April, July, August, and October.

The type-locality is at the lower extreme of an unpaved road that goes from xeric through transitional to mesic forest on the northern slope of the Massif de la Selle. The lone *C. raburni* was taken as it flew across the road and landed to rest in front of me on low grass in the middle of the road. The sun was behind me, and the *Calisto* assumed the usual broadside-to-the-sun insolation position, thereby affording me a fine view of the bright un coloration. The time was about 1500 h, temperature 29°C, and the day overcast with only occasional sun. The site of collection is within view of the barren and rocky Haitian portion of the Massif de la Selle. There are no obvious stands of *U. virgata* or any other "bunch grass." The specimen is fresh and unflown and must have emerged very close to this spot.

On 22.vi.1986, Gonzalez, starting at the dirt road where the holotype had been collected, walked on a path that supposedly leads to El Limón in the Valle de Neiba. The true destination of this path is equivocal. Most of the few people met on the path are Haitians, and it is possible that the path leads to the northern slopes of the Massif de la Selle in that country. Gonzalez estimated he had walked about 7 km before stopping to collect *C. raburni*; it is not impossible that the site is in Haiti.

The habitat at Gonzalez's locality is a xeric intermontane boulder-strewn depression, with *Uniola virgata*, overlooking the Valle de Neiba. Both Gonzalez and I collected a few individuals along the path in clearings in xeric-transitional forest. The butterflies were less numerous on 3.viii.1986 but still at the rocky depression.

The nearest records for any other member of this group are those of *C. franciscoi* (Duvergé) and *C. hendersoni* (El Limón), distances of 18 km NE and 12 km NW, respectively. Yet *C. raburni* is abundantly distinct from both these species, if for no other reasons than the tiny (to absent) unhw ocellus in males (absent in females) and the convex outer margin of the fw; no other species of the *lyceia* complex *Calisto* approaches either of these conditions, and there is no doubt that *C. raburni* is a distinct and well-differentiated species. Its geographic distribution remains to be determined; similar habitat occurs between Puerto Escondido and the type-locality, and there very likely are similar areas between Fond Parisien and Fond Verrettes on the Haitian portion of the Massif de la Selle, although that area has been much disturbed.

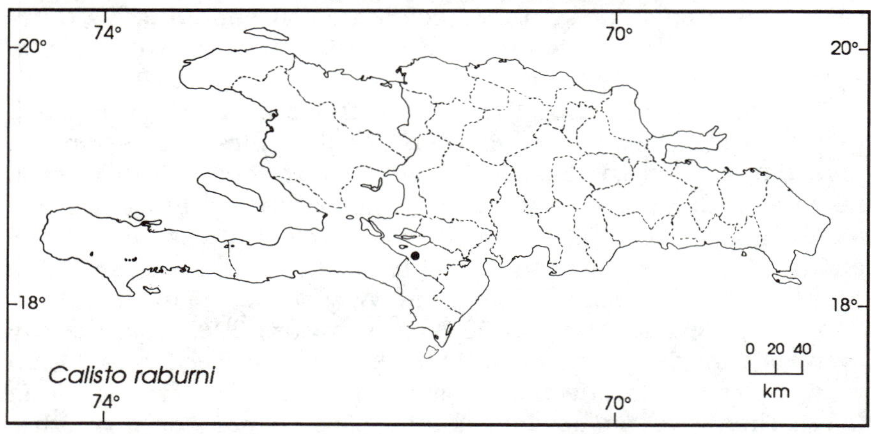

Calisto raburni is syntopic with *C. confusa* and *C. obscura*, neither of which is especially common at the type-locality. On the same 3-km stretch of road, 1 *C. elelea* has been taken at *ca.* 671 m.

Specimens: República Dominicana: Independencia: 7 km NE El Aguacate, 519–580 m, 19.

29. *Calisto schwartzi* Gali, 1985

TL 1 km N Aceitillar, 1281 m, Prov. de Pedernales, República Dominicana.

FW males 17–19 mm, females 18–21 mm.

Among members of the *lyceia* complex, *C. schwartzi* is unique in that it alone occurs at high elevations (1251–1373 m) in pine forest. The latter is xeric but lacks typical lowland *Acacia* woods or forest plants, including *Uniola virgata*. However, *C. schwartzi* is intimately associated with another (unidentified) species of tussocky grass.

The original series of *C. schwartzi* was collected on 6.x.1983 by Raburn and Schwartz. The day was bright and sunny, and the temperature was 28°C between 1215 and 1345 h. The butterflies were extremely abundant, and we could have had as many as we wanted. Equally as abundant was *C. elelea*, and the 2 species were commingled in the grassy areas of the pine forest. Since both species are about the same large size, we were often unaware of which we had until the specimen was killed in the net and examined; the bright orange to brick un was at once distinctive of *C. schwartzi*. *Calisto obscura* also occurs at the type-locality of *C. schwartzi*.

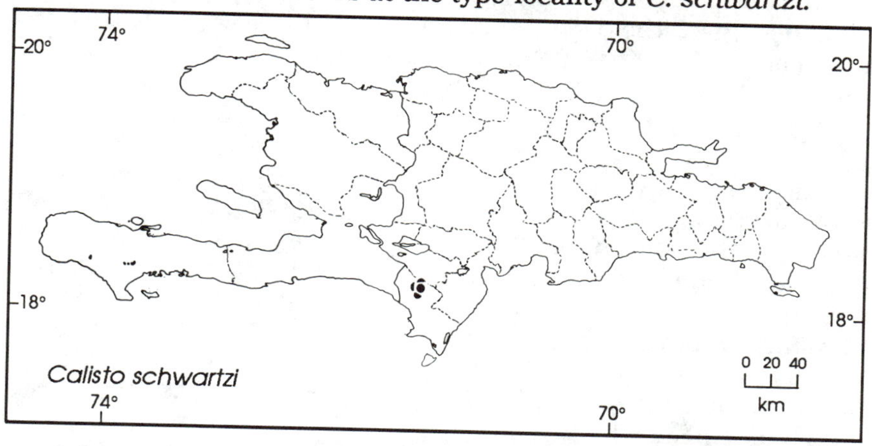

Calisto schwartzi

Calisto schwartzi was seen feeding then on the flowers of a low (0.3 m) purple composite (*Herodotia mikanoides*), and later on *Pitcairnia elizabethae*, a terrestrial bromeliad with red bracts.

Despite the extreme abundance of *C. schwartzi* at the type-locality on 6.x, just a few kilometers away at Las Abejas, but in mesic hardwood forest, no *C. schwartzi* were encountered nor have they been since. At this latter locality on that date, *C. elelea* was the most abundant butterfly, even more common than at the type-locality of *C. schwartzi*.

I had visited the type-locality on 31.vii.1980 and Gali and I had done so in vii.1982; we had also collected several times (always in the summer) in the general region near and about Aceitillar in pine forest. No *C. schwartzi* had been previously seen there or elsewhere in these uplands. This suggests that *C. schwartzi* emerges in the fall rather than summer. But in 1986 (June, August, December) the species was abundant throughout the pines in this upland region.

The range of *C. schwartzi* remains to be determined. Casual search elsewhere on these southern Baorucan slopes yielded no more specimens or even habitats precisely similar to that at the type-locality. Only on the road of Ideal Dominicana, S.A., on which the type-locality lies, does one reach upland pine forest in the Sierra de Baoruco. To the immediate west, between Los Arroyos and El Aguacate, pine forests are inhabited by *C. sommeri*. *Calisto schwartzi* is absent. The same is true of the pine forests near Forêt des Pins. Both of these areas are in the Massif de la Selle, not the Sierra de Baoruco. It seems that *C. schwartzi* is a species endemic to the latter range.

Other than the October-taken type-series, *C. schwartzi* has been collected in June (25 specimens), July (9), August (3), and December (2).

A pair *in copula* was taken 1 km N Aceitillar, 1281 m (9.vi, 1435 h, 26°C) in grassy pine forest.

The geographically nearest relatives of *C. schwartzi* are *C. raburni* (20 km to the N) and *C. hendersoni* (35 km to the NW), both north of the Massif de la Selle–Sierra de Baoruco ranges. At Mencía, 30 km to the west, *C. franciscoi* occurs as a vagrant from the adjacent lowlands. It is intriguing that all south island records of members of this complex are from 397 to 1373 m, whereas on the north island, all specimens are from close to sea level, except for those of *C. crypta* from Chacuey, Zamba, and Martín García (366 m at Chacuey).

Specimens: República Dominicana: Pedernales: 1 km N Aceitillar, 1281 m, 59; 4 km N Aceitillar, 1281 m, 1; 4.5 km NE Aceitillar, 1373 m, 3; 2 km SW Aceitillar, 1251 m, 3.

30. *Calisto montana* Clench, 1943

TL Mt. Basil, 4500 ft., Haiti.

FW male 15 mm (Clench, 1943a:25).

This species is known only from the male holotype; we have not collected *C. montana* and indeed there has been some doubt as to the location of the type-locality. Clench did not give a *département* for "Mt. Basil." Munroe (1950:221) commented (under *C. montana*) that Michener had described a subspecies of *hysius* from the same general region. This is a reference to Michener's (1943:3) description of *C. h. batesi*, a taxon that is widely distributed *north* of the Cul de Sac–Valle de Neiba; thus "Mt. Basil" must be north of that depression and not on either of the southern Haitian massifs (la Hotte, la Selle). Darlington (1935:168, 171) gave confirmatory details while discussing collecting carabid beetles at "Mt. Basil."

Through the efforts of Scott E. Miller, Department of Entomology, MCZ, I learned that the "NIS Gazeteer Haiti," published by the CIA in 1956, lists a "Mourne Bazile" at 19°24′ N,

72°28′ W. Bond (1928:484, 485) collected birds in 1927–28 on Morne Bazile in the Montagnes Noires in northern Haiti; he noted that Morne Bazile is the highest peak in these northern mountains. Pereira (no date:34–35), in his discussion of the Montagnes Noires, divided that northern range into 3 subranges, 1 of which, the Monts Cahos, has its highest peak in Morne Bazile, with an elevations of 1550 m, to the south of the town of Ennery. The 1:100,000 map of Haiti, published by the *Service de Géodésie et de Cartographie* in 1961, does indeed show the Monts Cahos but does not have a Morne Basile anywhere along the length of this range (many other *mornes* are shown but not Basile). It may be that in the interval since Bond's and Darlington's time, the name of the peak has been changed, but it is almost certainly a peak in the Monts Cahos, south of Ennery, and in the Dépt. de l'Artibonite. The Montagnes Noires are the western extension of the north range of the Dominican Sierra de Neiba and in Haiti border the Plateau Central on the south. The western extreme, near which Morne Basile lies, does not necessarily support a Neiban lepidopteran fauna.

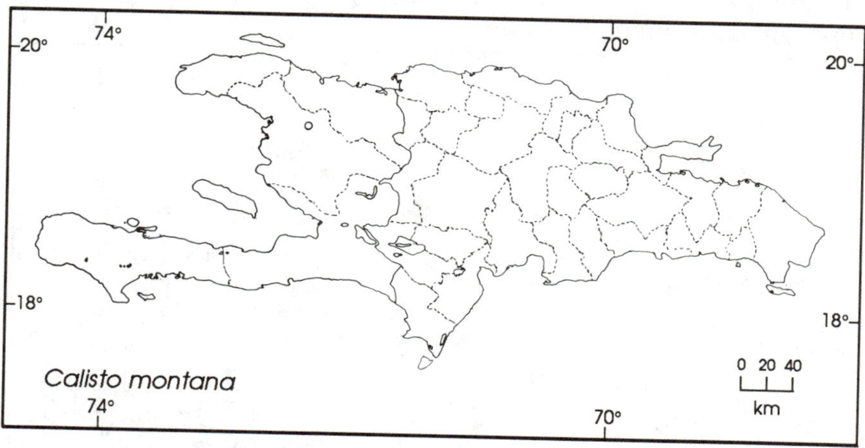

We have not collected in the uplands of these mountains, nor has any other biologist recently done so, as far as I know. Since *C. montana* has not been collected elsewhere on Hispaniola, I suggest that it is a species restricted to the higher elevations in the Monts Cahos.

31. *Calisto clydoniata* Schwartz and Gali, 1984

TL 1 km SW Puesto Pirámide 204, 1891 m, Prov. de Elías Piña, República Dominicana.

FW males 16–18 mm, females 17–18 mm.

Calisto clydoniata is limited to the north and south ranges of the Sierra de Neiba, between 1586 and 1891 m. The species appears to be restricted to the deciduous forests of this range; it bears the same ecological relationship to *C. micrommata* that *C. archebates* does to *C. sommeri*—*i.e.*, the first member of each pair is an inhabitant of deciduous forest, whereas the second member inhabits pine forest. In the Massif de la Selle, where the *archebates-sommeri* pair occurs, pine forests are altitudinally higher than deciduous forest, whereas in the Sierra de Neiba, stands of pure pines are altitudinally lower than deciduous forest or mixed pine-hardwoods. In fact, there are no pines on the southern face of the south range of the Sierra de Neiba; thus *C. micrommata* is known only from the north face of the range, whereas *C. clydoniata* occurs over the upland forested (pine-hardwoods) plateau, from below Puesto Pirámide 204 to 21 km N Los Pinos. Below the latter site, there are only forest remnants (even though there are still tree ferns and *Begonia* sp. bordering the road down the open mountainside). We have not taken or seen any species of *Calisto* on this slope, a most unusual situation.

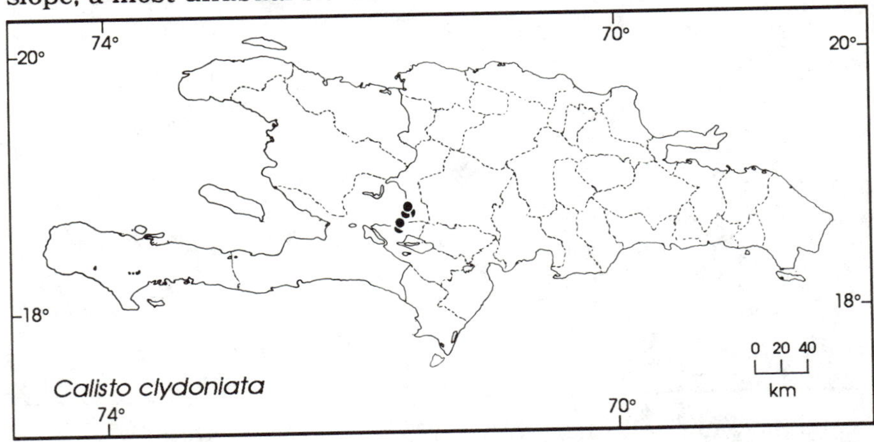

Calisto clydoniata is abundant in these upland deciduous forests and is easily distinguished in the field by its actions. The insects fly leisurely down the road at about 0.5 m above it; but when pursued, they dart rapidly into and above the shrubs (1.5 m) along the road margin and enter the forest. They are the only *Calisto* present (they overlap altitudinally with *C. micrommata* at about 1600 m) on the plateau, and they are usually very abundant, flying along and landing on the road to sun.

Most specimens are from August (39), with 18 in June, 11 in October, and 1 in July. Times of collection were between 1145 and 1450 h, at temperatures between 23°C and 28°C. These satyrids, like their highland congeners elsewhere, are active on overcast and rainy days.

There is 1 specimen from the north range of the Sierra de Neiba in the collection of Marión Heredia in Santo Domingo. I saw no suitable habitat there between Comendador and Puesto Calimete, and the single specimen lacks precise locality data.

The closest relative to *C. clydoniata* is *C. clenchi* on the Massif de la Selle on the south island; it is surprising that there is not a similar species in the Cordillera Central. *C. clydoniata* doubtless occurs in Haiti, at least near the Dominico-Haitian border, since the same deciduous and pine forests continue into Haiti on the Montagnes du Trou-d'Eau.

Specimens: República Dominicana: Elías Piña: 1 km SW Puesto Pirámide 204, 1891 m, 39; 2 km NE Puesto Pirámide 204, 186 m, 12; Pirámide 204, 3 (MNHNSD): *Independencia:* 23 km N Los Pinos, 1739 m, 4; 21 km N Los Pinos, 1708 m, 18.

32. *Calisto clenchi* Schwartz and Gali, 1984

TL 22 km SW El Aguacate (= 5 km NE Los Arroyos), 1617 m, (erroneously given as 1586 m in original description), Prov. de Pedernales, República Dominicana.

FW male 15 mm; females 15–20 mm.

Calisto clenchi is an enigma. The species was named on the basis of 2 females from the type-locality. I took another female at the same locality on 30.vi.1983, and Gonzalez took still another at the same site on 11.vi.1986. Thus there are only 4 specimens, all females, from the same locality, despite 7 visits there in the months of June, July, August, and October. The locality is on a road through mesic upland deciduous forest; the dominant satyrid there is *C. archebates*, but *C. chrysaoros* and *C. elelea* are also present along with *C. clenchi*. At higher elevations in the immediate region one enters pine forests (with *C. sommeri*); at lower elevations the area is cleared but has some pseudoforest present (with other species of *Calisto*). The locality is on the southern slope of the Massif de la Selle; these southern slopes in Haiti are accessible but are cleared and cultivated and do not present the right sort of ecological facies as the type-locality.

Gali took 2 specimens at Scierie, the first Haitian examples, on 5.ix.1984. The butterflies were perched on low ferns in pines above the Rivière Blanche in the Massif de la Selle. The day was alternately sunny and overcast; the time was between 1100 and 1230 h at a temperature of 29°C.

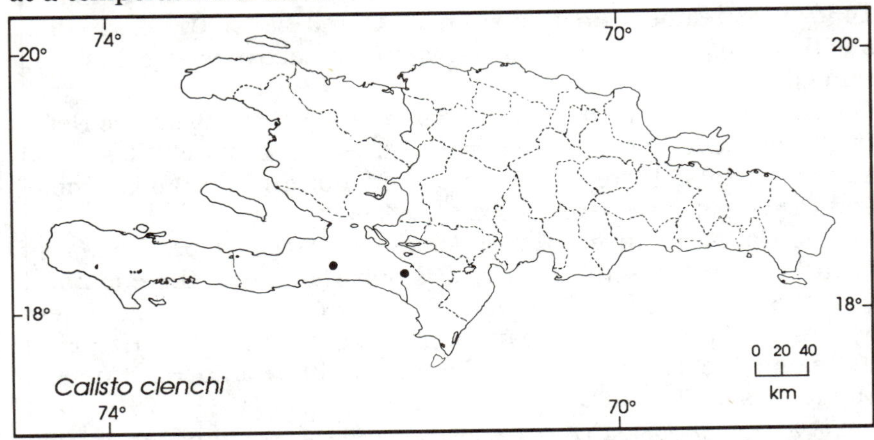

Why *C. clenchi* should be so uncommon is puzzling. The species is related to *C. clydoniata* and occupies the same sort of habitat on the Massif de la Selle as the latter does on the Sierra de Neiba, where it is abundant.

The Dominican specimens were taken between 1015 and 1300 h on 30.vi (in 2 years) and 11.vi. Temperatures were 21°C to 30°C. The 1983 female has a fw length of 19 mm; it was taken as it flew up from deep (0.5 m) grass at the base of a tree between the road and a dense tangle of blackberries (*Rubus* sp.) and climbing grass where *C. chrysaoros* was common. The first male (from Scierie) resembles females in color and pattern.

Specimens: Haiti: l'Ouest: 1.2 km S Scierie, 1950 m, 2 (FSM); *República Dominicana: Pedernales:* 5 km NE Los Arroyos, 1617 m, 4.

33. *Calisto elelea* Bates, 1935

TL Mt. Bourette, 5000 ft., Massif de la Selle, Dépt. de l'Ouest, Haiti.

FW males 18–21 mm, females 18–24 mm.

Calisto elelea was named on the basis of a male (holotype) and a female from the "hills south of Port-au-Prince, 2000 ft." Munroe (1950:230) examined 5 specimens, including the type-series, and gave the distribution as "Port-au-Prince region of Haiti, 2000–5000 ft." Schwartz (1983a:23–24) recorded 9 specimens from 2 Haitian localities and considered the species rare and local. In fact, Clench, (*in litt.* to Thurmond, 1978) enthusiastically commented that the series of 6 specimens collected by Thurmond and me in 1977 "may be larger than that in any one museum." He also suggested that within those 6 specimens, there might well be a second subspecies involved. This now seems unlikely, since knowledge of the variation on *C. elelea* has been vastly increased.

Between 1977 and 1982, only short series or single *C. elelea* were taken; many of these specimens were badly tattered or worn. One's impressions of the abundance of *C. elelea* were that it was an uncommon satyrid. This impression was dispelled on 6.x.1983, when Raburn and I encountered the species abundantly in the Sierra de Baoruco (1 km N Aceitillar, Las Abejas). At Aceitillar, *C. elelea* literally swarmed in the pine forest, where it was accompanied by equal numbers of (heretofore unknown) *C. schwartzi*, and smaller numbers of *C. hysia*. On the next day, Raburn and I went to Las Abejas. Previous visits to Las Abejas had yielded 5 *C. elelea;* on 6.x.1983, this was the dominant butterfly at that locality, more common than the small *C. hysia*, *C. batesi*, and *C. confusa*, as well as *C. archebates* and *C. tragia*, all of which occur there. At both localities, we could have collected as many *C. elelea* as we wanted. It was obvious that we had happened into the range of *C. elelea* at a time of maximum abundance (eclosion?), when *C. elelea* was everywhere in these Baorucan uplands. A total of 37 specimens was taken. *Calisto elelea* was also abundant in vi.1986.

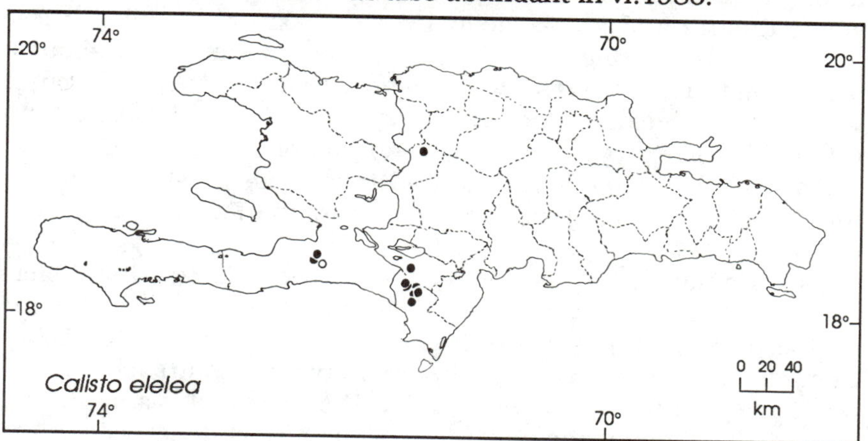

I have already commented on how Riley's (1975:pl. 3, fig. 11) illustration of *C. elelea* shows the unhw ocellus as unusually tiny. Although a very few individuals have this condition, it is not the mean, and most specimens have an obvious and contrasting oval unhw ocellus with the pupil greatly displaced basally. On the uphw, there is, in both sexes, often a postdiscal area of brick red;

this suffused area is larger in females than in males and of more common occurrence in the former sex than in the latter. An up character that has been noted is the presence in *C. elelea* of a dark "ocellus" at the hw angle, this "ocellus" capped with buffy. This is an additional character useful in separating *C. elelea* from *C. tragia;* the latter lacks such a hw mark. In *C. elelea*, there is never a unfw postocellar reddish blush, and the entire fw cell is brick red, in contrast to *C. tragia*, in which the cell is only about one-half red and is sharply truncate across the cell but without a truncating dark line. In both sexes of *C. elelea*, the un ground color is pale tan and without strongly contrasting unhw lines. However, occasional males have the un color dark brown (almost black) but the un lines are still not conspicuous. In the latter individuals, the dark line across the base of the hw is highlighted by a bordering gray line, thereby rendering this a more obvious pattern element.

The elevational distribution of *C. elelea* is between 671 m (El Aguacate) and 1464 m (Peneau). The habitat is primarily pine forests, at times about houses and their gardens (Peneau), at others extremely barren and with little understory. The series from Boutilliers Road is from an open mountainside road, where the butterflies were netted as they flew along and above a drainage ditch cut into the mountainside and paralleling the road. At the locality where Raburn and I took the long series (1 km N Aceitillar), these butterflies were flying close (0.3 m) to the ground in and about a 0.6-m-high tussocky grass, within whose tussocks they took refuge when the sky became periodically overcast, only to sally forth again when the sun reappeared. At Las Abejas, on 7.x.1983, *C. elelea*, when disturbed, flew both into and over roadside shrubs, where they had been feeding, seeking shelter in the forest and in deep grass.

The Haitian localities are on the Morne l'Hôpital (Boutilliers Road) and the Montagne Noire (Peneau). These ranges are the northern front ranges of the Massif de la Selle. In the República Dominicana, almost all records are from the south face of the western end of the Sierra de Baoruco. The exception is a specimen, taken 11.x.1983, on the north face of the Massif de la Selle in the República Dominicana (El Aguacate). This is the only *C. elelea* taken at this locality in 17 visits. Although this site seems very distant from places where we have taken *C. elelea*, in reality it is rather close (20 k); the slopes directly above the locality are clothed in pine forest, and the *C. elelea* may simply have wandered down to the transitional forest at El Aguacate.

The 2 specimens from Cabo Rojo are from transitional forest

edges. But, once again, one is in sight of pine forests only a few kilometers (less than 4) above. *Calisto elelea*, as might be expected, flies even on overcast and very windy days.

The taking of *C. elelea* on the Cordillera Central at Los Guandules is completely unexpected. Wetherbee secured a fine series there. The specimens (as well as the male genitalia, which are very distinctive in *C. elelea*) agree very well with south island *C. elelea*. The distribution of this species in the Cordillera Central remains to be determined; it certainly does not occur in the well-collected Constanza region.

At Aceitillar, we have taken *C. elelea* feeding on the white flowers of *Eupatorium sinuatum* (Asteraceae); at 1 km N Aceitillar, many *C. elelea* were attracted to and feeding on (2 occasions) the purple flowers of *Herodotia mikanoides* (Asteraceae), a low (0.3 m) composite, and on *Ageratum conyzoides*. At Las Abejas, *C. elelea* fed on *Cynoglossum amabile* (3 occasions), the white flowers of *Chamissoa altissima* (Asteraceae), and *Ixora* sp.

Most specimens have been taken in June (90), with 66 in July, 46 in October, 7 in December, and 5 in August. It is probable that *C. elelea* is bivoltine; many June-August specimens are worn and tattered and are apparently remnants of a previous brood. Times of collection were between 0915 and 1600 h, and temperatures between 25°C (1 km N Aceitillar) and 33°C (12 km NW Aceitillar).

Specimens: Haiti: l'Ouest: Boutilliers Road, 1.8–2.1 km W Kenscoff road, 763–885 m, 7; Boutilliers Road, 732–915 m, 6; Peneau, 1.1–1.6 km SE Furcy, 1464 m, 2; *República Dominicana: Dajabón:* Los Guandules, above Guayajayaco, 11; *Pedernales:* 23 km NE Cabo Rojo, 732 m, 2; Aceitillar, 36 km NNE Cabo Rojo, 1281 m, 2; 1 km N Aceitillar, 1281 m, 98; Las Abejas, 11 km NW Aceitillar, 1220 m, 31; Las Abejas, 12 km NW Aceitillar, 1129 m, 52; 2 km SW Aceitillar, 1251 m, 2; *Independencia:* 4–7 km NE El Aguacate, *ca.* 671 m, 1.

34. *Calisto ainigma* Johnson, Quinter, and Matusik, 1987

TL 4 km NW (= SE) central Jarabacoa, 930 m, Prov. de la Vega, República Dominicana.

FW males unknown, female 16 mm.

This newly described and very distinct species is known only from the holotype. Johnson, Quinter, and Matusik gave precise details at the type-locality, which is on the property of the Hotel Pinar Dorado. The area is pinewoods, much disturbed, with hardwoods in ravines and the river valley. What is puzzling is that the Jarabacoa area has been very well collected by many lepidopterists prior to and following 1985 and no more individuals have been seen. The holotype is in perfect condition, so it must have emerged in the immediate vicinity. What seems reasonable is that the Jarabacoa area is not the proper habitat for *C. ainigma* and that the holotype is a vagrant from nearby in the Cordillera Central.

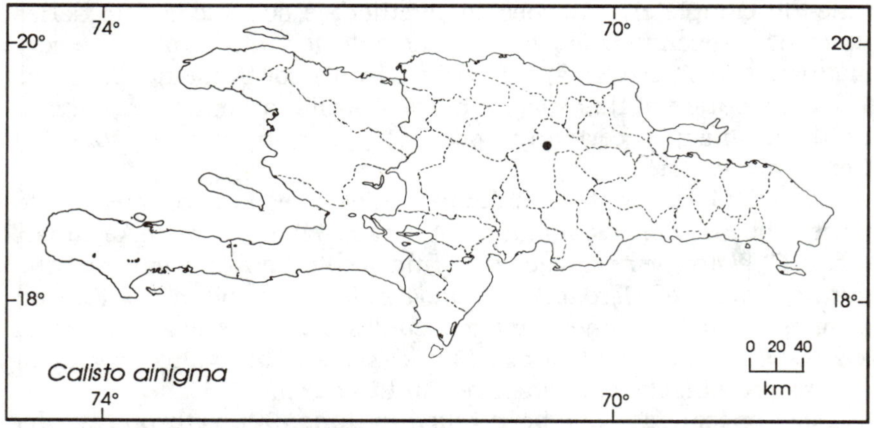

The authors of *C. ainigma* related the species to *C. elelea* because of the similarities in female genitalia (despite little similarity of pattern), and I therefore place it here near that species. *Calisto elelea* males have very distinctive (for the genus) genitalia, and capture of a male *C. ainigma* will verify the affinity of the species.

At the time of the description of *C. ainigma, C. elelea* was known only from the south island Massif de la Selle and Sierra de Baoruco. *Calisto elelea* now is also known from the Cordillera Central. It is perhaps not surprising that *C. elelea* has a close relative in these mountains.

35A. *Calisto pulchella pulchella* Lathy, 1899

TL Haiti.

FW males 19–24 mm, females 22–28 mm.

Calisto pulchella is the largest species of *Calisto* on Hispaniola. The species has been divided into 2 subspecies, 1 of which (*C. p. darlingtoni*) is restricted to the highlands of the Dominican Cordillera Central. The subspecies were discussed in detail by Wisor and Schwartz (1985). They differ from each other in several ways; a distinctive feature is the size of the unhw ocellus, which is larger (males and females 2.8–3.8 mm) in *C. p. pulchella* than in *C. p. darlingtoni* (males 0.6–2.4 mm, females 2.0–2.8 mm).

Schwartz (1983a:19) discussed the habitats and elevations of the species in Haiti; these strongly contrast with the situation in the República Dominicana that the 2 countries will be discussed separately.

In Haiti, *C. p. pulchella* is widely distributed over the area north of the Cul de Sac Plain. There is 1 record (Port-au-Prince; Munroe, 1950:232; perhaps a "generalized" locality?) from the Cul de Sac and its vicinity (despite the fact that much of its western extremity is planted in sugarcane, the larval food plant). There are 5 records from the south island in Haiti; these include the high-elevation record (Peneau, 1464 m) for the subspecies. Most Haitian specimens were taken within *caféières* or mesic woods, and only twice (Dondon, Manegue) adjacent to a cane field; at Manegue, *C. p. pulchella* was more common in a *Musa* grove than in or adjacent to the cane field. There is a record for *Acacia* woods (Limonade), and 1 from pinewoods with flowers (Peneau). One's impression of *C. p. pulchella*, judging from its occurrences in Haiti, is that it, like some other *Calisto*, is an inhabitant of mesic forests and pseudoforests but that it is occasionally taken away from this habitat.

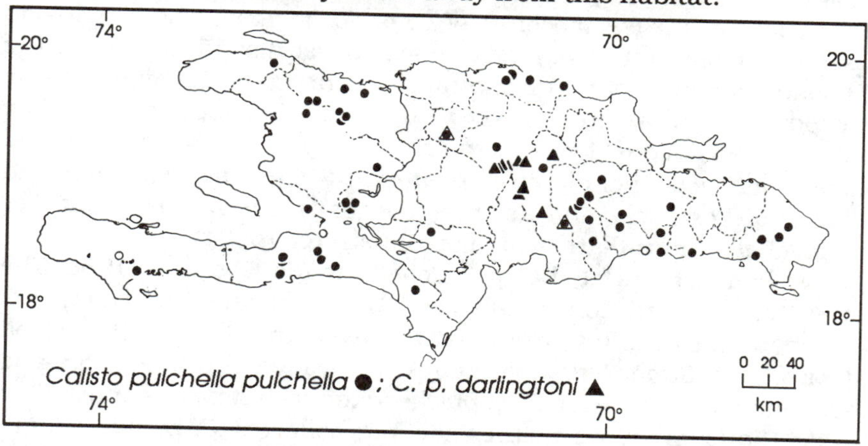

Calisto pulchella pulchella ●; *C. p. darlingtoni* ▲

In the República Dominicana, on the other hand, *C. p. pulchella* has been taken 10 times (Río Bao, Luperón, Sosúa, La Palma, Maimón, Río Chavón, La Romana, Andrés, Neiba, Cabo Rojo) in a *cafetal*, in dense xeric or mesic woods, and in scrub; all other records and countless sightings are strictly associated with sugarcane fields, of which there are many square kilometers throughout the country. There is only 1 record for *C. p. pulchella* on the Dominican portion of the south island (Cabo Rojo), and none for the Valle de Neiba, whose eastern end has a very large sugarcane plantation (Central Barahona). Likewise, the high-elevational record for the República Dominicana is 1007 m (La Palma), less than that for Haiti (1646 m). But in the former country, a high upland subspecies exceeds the highest elevation in Haiti.

Calisto p. pulchella is absent from broad areas in both countries. It seems to be truly rare on most of the Haitian Tiburon Peninsula (Cavaillon) and absent from the Presqu'île du Nord Ouest; its apparent absence from the extensive interior Plaine de l'Artibonite (primarily cultivated in rice and sugarcane) is uncertain. The species is absent from the Dominican Península de Samaná, the Valle de San Juan (which has a very meager *Calisto* fauna), the Valle de Cibao from its western (Monte Cristi) to its eastern extreme (Arenoso, Villa Riva), despite the fact that the eastern portion of this valley is very mesic and receives the heaviest rainfall in the República Dominicana.

Although the current larval food plant is predominantly sugarcane, this plant has not always been present on Hispaniola but was introduced there in 1506. Presumably an indigenous large "cane" (*Gynerium sagittatum*, Poaceae; *caña brava*) was the original larval food plant (see account of *C. p. darlingtoni*). The conclusion is inescapable that *C. p. pulchella* was never distributed over all of Hispaniola. Its original distribution will never be known, but the introduction of sugarcane has modified its distribution favorably. Torres (1984) considered *C. pulchella* a pest on sugarcane and listed 5 grasses (including *G. sagittatum*, 2 species of *Panicum*, and 1 each of *Roetboelia* and *Echinochloa*) that serve as host plants for *C. pulchella* caterpillars, which are illustrated (p. 24).

We had not collected *C. p. pulchella* at Río Bao until 1986. The river had flooded torrentially in 1979, scouring the floodplain, which was thereafter littered with tree trunks and other flood debris. But *Gynerium sagittatum* has invaded the floodplain and has made it possible for *C. p. pulchella* to reach a new outpost.

At Río Chavón, we neither saw nor collected *C. p. pulchella* in vii–viii. But in xii.1986, these butterflies were rather common in canes along the edge of the river.

The differences in occurrence of *C. p. pulchella* in the 2 countries have 1 reasonable explanation. In the República Dominicana, sugar *centrales* control many square kilometers of cane fields; these large holdings are the rule rather than the exception. In Haiti, on the other hand, although there are a few such holdings (such as HASCO near Port-au-Prince), many rural Haitians have on their property a small patch of sugarcane, which they use to produce sugar for household consumption. Several areas in Haiti where we took *C. p. pulchella* lack any sort of large planting of sugarcane; in fact, uplands are not, or only marginally, suitable for this crop. But in most cases there is a small patch of sugarcane nearby that acts as a source of local *C. p. pulchella.* Thus the acculturation and economics of the 2 countries have affected the distribution of this butterfly.

As a consequence of the above, the local abundance of *C. p. pulchella* in the 2 countries differs markedly. In the República Dominicana, while crossing a large sugarcane area (such as that under the administration of Central Catarey north of Villa Altagracia), one sees literally hundreds of *C. p. pulchella;* the number of individuals in the entire plantation must be in the thousands! We have had the same experience west of San Cristóbal and east of Puerto Plata, for instance, as well as in other regions. The numbers of *C. p. pulchella* fluctuate somewhat, but in general the butterflies are always present and usually amazingly abundant. In Haiti, on the other hand, one does not encounter these incredibly large concentrations of *C. p. pulchella.* Even near Port-au-Prince on the HASCO holdings, they do not occur commonly, presumably because *C. p. pulchella* in unknown from the Cul de Sac plain; the same is true on the plantations in the Plaine du Nord in the vicinity of Cap-Haïtien. But one encounters *C. p. pulchella* in Haiti in relatively remote areas, near small cane plantings around *cailles* or on the edges of or within *caféières* (I have only once taken the species in a Dominican *cafetal-cacaotal,* surrounded by *cañaverales,* at Maimón) near which there is a small patch of sugarcane. Thus, the Dominican populations of *C. p. pulchella* are local and incredibly large, whereas the Haitian population is widespread, and the butterflies are not extremely abundant where they occur.

Most of our specimens are from July (56), with 33 from August, 20 from January, 8 from December, 6 from March, 5 from June, 4 from February, and 2 from April. Times of collection were between 0915 and 1640 h, and temperatures between 28°C (Río Chavón) and 36°C (Guerra, Yamasá). Copulating pairs have been taken or seen on 1.viii (Dondon, 336 m), 7.viii (Cambita Garabitos), and 1.xi (Maimón, 122 m). *Calisto p. pulchella* flies on overcast and even rainy days as well as bright and sunny ones.

We have once seen *C. p. pulchella* feeding on *Bidens pilosa* (Higüey). We have also taken *C. p. pulchella* on *Lantana ovatifolia* and *Tournefortia hirsutissima* (Río Bao), on *Synedrella nodiflora* (Asteraceae) at 13 km SE Luperón, and on *Ageratum conyzoides* (Cavaillon). At 1 locality (Yamasá), large numbers were feeding on rotting mangoes at the border of a patch of woods across a paved road from an extensive *cañaveral.*

Specimens: Haiti: Nord-Ouest: 1.3 km S Balladé, 31 m, 1; *Nord:* Carrefour la Mort, s.l., 3; 3.5 km E Limonade, s.l., 2; 1.8 km S Dondon, 366 m, 2; 5.6 km SE Dondon, 336 m, 1; 9.9 km S Dondon, 336 m, 2; 3.5 km SE Plaisance, 305 m, 7; 3.7 km W Plaisance, 336 m, 2; *l'Artibonite:* 1.6 km E Carrefour Marmelade, 854 m, 4; 4.0 km N Thomonde, 1; *l'Ouest:* 1.6 km N Saut d'Eau, 183–275 m, 5; 19.7 km SE Mirebalais, 183 m, 2; 12 km SE Mirebalais, 305 m, 8; Manegue, just N Duvalierville, s.l., 10; Boutilliers Road, 1.8–2.1 km W Kenscoff road, 793–885 m, 1; Peneau, 1.6 km S Furcy, 1464 m, 1; 1.1 km S Découzé, 610 m, 1; 2.2 km S Découzé, 397 m, 2; Lavaneau, 229 m, 2; nr. Péredo, 570–600 m, 4 (FSM); *Sud:* 7 km SW Cavaillon, 122 m, 2; *República Dominicana: Puerto Plata:* 13 km SE Luperón, 214 m, 2; 2 km S Imbert, 92 m, 3; 8 km E Puerto Plata, *ca.* 16 m, 7; 9 km SE Sosúa, 15 m, 1; *Santiago:* Río Bao, 8 km SE Montones Abajo, 488 m, 6; *La Vega:* La Palma, 19 km W Jayaco, 1007 m, 3; *Monseñor Nouel:* 6 km SE Maimón, 122 m, 5; 14 km SW Piedra Blanca, 427 m, 1; 12 km SW Piedra Blanca, 854 m, 2; 5 km SW Piedra Blanca, 183 m, 13; *La Altagracia:* 5 km E Otra Banda, 1; 5 km S Higüey, 7; 16 km NE La Romana, 61 m, 1; *La Romana:* Río Chavón, 8 km SE La Romana, s.l., 6; *San Pedro de Macorís:* 10 km E San Pedro de Macorís, s.l., 3; *Dist. Nac.:* 9 km NE Guerra, 5; 25 km SE Yamasá, 1 (MPM); Punta Caucedo, 2 km W, 2 km S Andrés, s.l., 1; *Sánchez Ramírez:* 1 km NE Las Lagunas, 183 m, 1; *Monte Plata:* 9 km S Bayaguana, 1; 7 km SE Yamasá, 31 m, 12; *San Cristóbal:* 8 km NW Villa Altagracia, 1; 16 km SW Cambita Garabitos, 11; Nigua, 1; *Baoruco:* 14 km N Neiba, 671 m, 2; *Pedernales:* 26 km NE Cabo Rojo, 732 m, 1.

35B. *Calisto pulchella darlingtoni* Clench, 1943

TL Constanza, Prov. de la Vega, República Dominicana.

FW males 21–24 mm, females 25–28 mm.

Calisto p. darlingtoni occurs in the uplands of the Cordillera Central between 1159 m (4 km SSE Constanza) and 2074 m (13 km SE Valle Nuevo) and, in the same range, in the Pico Duarte area between 732 m (Paso Bajito) and 1922 m (entrance to Valle de Tetero). We have not seen the species in the Valle de Constanza (the stated type-locality); it may no longer occur there since that valley is heavily cultivated and has been subjected to massive insecticide spraying over the years. On the other hand, the type-material may not have been taken in the valley itself. The Valle Nuevo record is for 3 butterflies (2 occasions) that were not collected; this species is so readily identified on the wing, especially in contrast to *C. g. grannus* with which it occurred there, that I have no doubt about the identification.

The highest locality for *C. p. pulchella* in the Cordillera Central is 1007 m (La Palma), which lies about 25 km NE the nearest *C. p. darlingtoni* record (4 km SSE Constanza). There is a pair of intergrades from 2 km SW Rancho Arriba, 670 m (see Wisor and Schwartz, 1985, for details); this locality is about 40 km SE of Constanza and 40 km SSE La Palma. There is also a series of intergrades from Loma Leonor, 25 km N of the Pico Duarte area. The butterflies were first seen and collected there in 1986.

Calisto p. darlingtoni occurs in pinewoods, mixed pine-deciduous forests, marshy meadows with *Cynoglossum amabile* (on which the butterflies have not been seen feeding), an open river floodplain (La Ciénaga), and an open ravine (La Horma). At La Horma, there was a small patch of sugarcane (about 4×3 m), in and about which the butterflies were regularly encountered. Likewise, at 4 km SSE Constanza, the series was taken about the edges of a larger patch of sugarcane in the floor of the Río Grande, near several rural houses. At the other localities, sugarcane was not obviously present.

At La Ciénaga, the floodplain of the Río Yaque del Norte has stands of *Gynerium sagittatum*, about which *C. p. darlingtoni* was very numerous, flying in and about grass at the base of the *caña brava* and resting thereupon to sun. It is logical that this large cane was the original larval food plant of *C. pulchella*.

Calisto p. darlingtoni has been taken in June, July, August, September, and October, with most specimens in July (75), with 20 in October, 19 in June, 9 in August, and 6 in September. Times of collection and observation were between 0845 and 1630 h, and temperatures between 18°C (Valle Nuevo) and 32°C (La Ciénaga, 3 km SW Boca del Río, 6 km ESE Constanza). We have taken *C. p. darlingtoni* feeding on the white flowers of a large stand of *Tournefortia hirsutissima* (6 km SSE Constanza) on 3 occasions, and once on this same plant at Paso Bajito.

The 2 Rancho Arriba intergrades were taken *in copula* on 17.viii, on the floor of a mesic *cafetal* (1145–1330 h, 36°C). There was no sugarcane in the immediate area.

The fact that *C. pulchella* has a distinct subspecies on the north island and is well distributed there, in contrast to its rarity and very limited distribution with no differentiation on the south island, suggests that this species arose on the north island and has spread relatively recently to the south island. Its extreme rarity (or even absence?) in the sugarcane plantations at the western (HASCO) and eastern (Central Barahona) ends of the Cul de Sac–Valle de Neiba plain, as well as in the western xeric Valle de Cibao (Central Esperanza) suggests that *C. pulchella* is intolerant of hot and arid conditions, even if they are modified by irrigation, and that the establishment of *C. p. pulchella* on the south island has been fortuitous, effected by windblown strays or vagrants rather than by sequential colonization across the Cul de Sac–Valle de Neiba.

Specimens: República Dominicana: Santiago: entrance of Valle de Tetero to Valle de Tetero, 1922–1342 m, 3; Valle de Tetero, 1342 m, 1; *La Vega:* La Ciénaga, 915 m, 8; 3 km W La Ciénaga, 1032 m, 20; 1 km W Manabao, 732 m, 3; 3 km SW Boca del Río, 976 m, 25; Los Tablones, 4 km SW Boca del Río, 991 m, 11; 6 km SSW Boca del Río, 1220 m, 2; 3.5 km E Paso Bajito, 732 m, 6; 4 km SSE Constanza, 1159 m, 8; 6 km SSE Constanza, 1403 m, 22; 10 km NW La Horma, 1496 m, 22.

Calisto p. pulchella × *C. p. darlingtoni: Santiago Rodríguez:* Loma Leonor, 19 km SW Monción, 610 m, 13; *Peravia:* 2 km SW Rancho Arriba, 670 m, 2.

Family Ithomiidae Dyar, 1902

Subfamily Ithomiinae Reuter, 1896

1A. *Greta diaphana quisqueya* Fox, 1963

TL Pico Diego de Ocampo, 3000–4000 ft. Prov. de Santiago, República Dominicana.

FW males 23–24 mm, females 23–26 mm.

Greta d. diaphana is known from only 3 localities in the Cordillera Septentrional: the type-locality, Mt. Isabel de Torres, and Jamao al Norte. This subspecies is 1 of 4 found on Hispaniola; the nominate subspecies occurs on (almost exclusively) eastern Jamaica (Brown and Heineman, 1972:101). The species is not uncommon at various localities, all montane, in the República Dominicana; we have not taken it in Haiti nor are there records or specimens from that country (Schwartz, 1982).

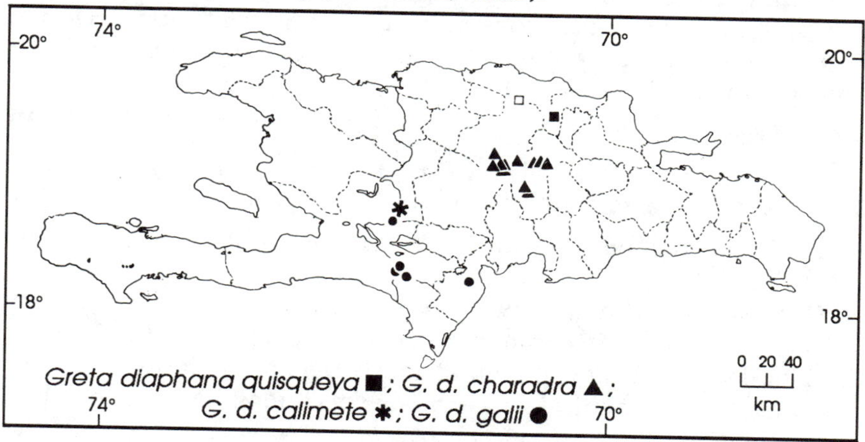

Greta diaphana quisqueya ■; *G. d. charadra* ▲; *G. d. calimete* ✱; *G. d. galii* ●

My series of *G. d. quisqueya* has been taken at the same locality at 793 m over a period of 7 years. Schwartz (1982) described the site: "The locality is a small (4 m) wide and shallow rocky stream in mesic broadleaf forest, with *Palicourea [barbinervia]*, a common streamside tree. Although the butterflies occur along about 200 m of the stream, they are abundant on one of the tributaries where the stream is about one m wide and heavily closed with forest canopy. Several individuals were seen and a few collected as they crossed an open but shrubby hillside clearing or flew along the margin of the forest."

The reference to *Palicourea barbinervia* (Rubiaceae) is significant in that *G. diaphana* with regularity utilizes the small yellow flowers of this tree as a nectar source. Temperatures of activity varied between 28°C and 35°C, and flying times betwen 0945 and 1545 h. Most specimens are from July (28), with 6 in August, and 1 in October.

The known elevational range of *G. d. quisqueya* is between 793 m and 1220 m. This subspecies almost certainly is more widespread in the Cordillera Septentrional than the 3 localities indicate; much of this range is still difficult of access, and the major road crossing it (Santiago–Puerto Plata) goes only to about 640 m; we have never found the proper sort of habitat there. This and the other 3 subspecies of *G. diaphana* on Hispaniola frequent stream-associated woods and forests, where their feeble flight and transparent wings make them almost invisible as they fly between sunlight and shade under the canopy. They land, resting immobile, on either the upper or under sides of leaves or even on small bare twigs and are very difficult to see while resting. *Greta d. quisqueya* flies on bright and sunny days as well as on overcast ones. Raburn likened *G. diaphana* to "wind flying," and I agree completely with this fanciful simile.

Specimens: República Dominicana: Espaillat: 20 km SW Jamao al Norte, 793 m, 35.

1B. *Greta diaphana charadra* Schwartz, 1982

TL 10 km W Jayaco, Prov. de la Vega, República Dominicana.
FW males 21–27 mm, females 20–26 mm.

Greta d. charadra is known only from scattered localities in the Cordillera Central, at elevations between 732 m and 1922 m. At the type-locality, it is common in mesic deciduous forest adjacent to a mountain torrent. At La Palma, specimens have been taken along the Río la Palma and in clearings in a *cafetal;* at this site, the butterflies were common during overcast conditions. The record for 10 km SE Constanza is of 1 male (of several *Greta* seen) along a creek ravine adjacent to a fallow cabbage patch. The field had abundant flowers (*Leonurus sibericus* and *Cynoglossum amabile*), but these butterflies were not observed to feed there. At Jayaco, *G. d. charadra* fed actively on the flowers of *Palicourea barbinervia*, and at 7 km W Jayaco, 1 was observed taking nectar from a roadside composite (Asteraceae; not *Bidens pilosa*). On 2 occasions (La Palma) we have collected *G. d. charadra* feeding on a procumbent white-flowered composite (*Wedelia* sp.) in deep shade in the *cafetal*. At Jayaco, an individual was taken feeding on *Stachytarpheta cayennensis*. Four were taken in a very small and humid *cafetal* in the valley of the Río Yaque del Norte (La Ciénaga). At Boca del Río, these butterflies were very abundant in the deep shade of a bamboo "forest" with interspersed *caña brava*.

Most of our specimens have been taken in June to August, with 1 in October, but the butterfly is not uncommon in December. Temperatures varied between 20°C and 32°C, and flying times between 1000 and 1640 h.

Specimens: República Dominicana: La Vega: 10 km W Jayaco, 915 m, 40; 7 km W Jayaco, 732 m, 1; La Palma, 19 km E Jayaco, 1007 m, 25; 12 km NE Constanza, 1220 m, 19; 10 km SE Constanza, 1647 m, 1; 6 km SE Constanza, 1403 m, 1; La Ciénaga, 915 m, 4; 3 km SW Boca del Río, 976 m, 9; 1 km SW Los Tablones, 1159 m, 13; Los Tablones, 4 km SW Boca del Río, 997 m, 2; *Santiago:* Mun. San José de las Matas, Río Antonsape Malo, 2; entrance of Valle de Tetero to Valle de Tetero, 1922–1342 m, 3.

1C. *Greta diaphana calimete* Schwartz, 1982

TL 21 km S Comendador, 1646 m, Prov. de Elías Piña, República Dominicana.

FW males 23–26 mm, female 24 mm.

Greta d. calimete occurs, insofar as known, only on the north range of the Sierra de Neiba. My only specimens are from the type-locality; 18 were collected in 1981, and a visit there in 1982 yielded 2 additional specimens. On this latter visit, the butterflies were much less common than in 1981, and only 5 were seen where previously we had taken the type-series. In 1981, *G. d. calimete* was found feeding on a low (15 cm) herbaceous white-flowered composite (Asteraceae) within the dense mesic forest just north of Puesto Calimete, in a ravine and its associated hillside. The forest at this locality is very moist, and tree ferns (Cyatheaceae) form a prominent understory to the hardwood canopy. On the 3 days that we took *G. d. calimete*, the weather was bright and sunny, an unusual condition at this high elevation. Temperatures varied between 27°C and 30°C, and times of flight were between 1100 and 1515 h.

The subspecies of *G. diaphana* on the south range of the Sierra de Neiba is *G. d. galii*, described from the south island Sierra de Baoruco and discussed below.

Specimens: República Dominicana: Elías Piña: 21 km S Comendador, 1474 m, 20.

1D. *Greta diaphana galii* Schwartz, 1982

TL Las Abejas, 12 km NW Aceitillar, 1129 m, Prov. de Pedernales, República Dominicana.

FW males 24–25 mm, females 21–26 mm.

The type-material of *G. d. galii* consists of 3 females, all from the type-locality. In 1982 Gali and I returned to Las Abejas and secured 2 additional specimens along the same path through untouched hardwood forest as the type-series, and in 1986 Gonzalez secured 2 more. The butterfly does not seem to be common there. In 1983, return vists to Las Abejas by Raburn and me were disheartening; the precise type-locality has been destroyed by cutting, and what was once beautiful and unspoiled upland mesic broadleaf forest is now a large exposed field of beans. We encountered no *G. d. galii* there in 1983.

But Gali and I had previously (1982) secured a short series of this subspecies at 2 other localities on the south island (El Aguacate). Moreover, we also took long series of *G. d. galii* in both 1982 and 1983 on the south range of the Sierra de Neiba. The occurrence of this subspecies on the same massif as *G. d. calimete* may seem surprising, but the 2 ranges of the Sierra de Neiba (north and south) are separated by the deep valley in which Hondo Valle lies. This valley varies from xeric (east) to mesic (west), but its elevation is too low (*ca.* 750 m) for *Greta*. The faunas of the 2 adjacent ranges are isolated from each other, and this phenomenon is demonstrated by *Greta*. Apparently *G. d. galii* arose on the south island massifs and later expanded its range across the Valle de Neiba to occupy the south range of the Sierra de Neiba. The later arrival of *Greta* on the north range resulted in the differentiation there of *G. d. calimete;* since the south range was already occupied by *G. d. galii,* and the 2 populations were separated from each other, there has been no contact between them. This outline agrees with that proposed by Schwartz (1982), despite the new records of *G. d. galii* from the Neiba. The subspecies *calimete* and *galii* are quite distinct, especially in the fw pattern of white spots.

All specimens of *G. d. galii* have been taken in rich mesic deciduous forest, or on roads or paths through such forests. The butterflies are denizens of the dappled sun and shade of forests or forest edges. At Puesto Pirámide 204, we found them abundant, flying along the edge of the road where *Palicourea barbinervia* was a common tree and upon which they were feeding. Gali saw 2 individuals feeding on *Asclepias nivea* (Asclepiadaceae) and many were feeding there on *Ageratum conyzoides*, as well as a few at Las Abejas. *Greta d. galii* was also taken at Las Abejas on *Palicourea barbinervia.* At Puesto Pirámide 204, *Greta d. galii* were flying on a bright and sunny day, as well as on a dull and overcast day (temperature = 25°C). Other specimens were taken within and adjacent to rich mesic forest (El Aguacate); there they were especially abundant in closed montane forest. At Monteada Nueva, a few *G. d. galii* were taken in a dense mountainside forest remnant; the rest of the mountainside had been either cleared completely or modified into a *cafetal* without undergrowth. The butterflies were not in the *cafetal.* Temperatures of activity varied between 20°C and 30°C; flying times were from 0900 to 1500 h.

Greta d. galii occurs at high elevations; that at Monteada Nueva is the lowest (1037 m), whereas elsewhere it occurs as high as 1647 m (El Aguacate). My specimens are about equally divided between July and August, with 1 each from June and October.

Specimens: República Dominicana: Elías Piña: 2 km NE Puesto Pirámide 204, 1586 m, 39; *Barahona:* 1.3 km W Monteada Nueva, 1037 m, 3; *Pedernales:* Las Abejas, 12 km NE Aceitillar, 1129 m, 7; 7 km SW El Aguacate, 1647 m, 1; 5 km SW El Aguacate, 1464 m, 8.

Sight record: República Dominicana: Pedernales: Las Abejas, 12 km NW Aceitillar, 1129 m—2 seen, 27.vii.

Family Danaidae Duponchel, 1844

Subfamily Danainae Duponchel, 1844

1. *Danaus gilippus cleothera* Godart, 1819

TL "Timor"; correctly Haiti.

FW males 31–41 mm; females 26–39 mm.

The Queen, *D. gilippus* Cramer, is represented by 3 subspecies in the West Indies: *D. g. berenice* Cramer (Cuba, Isla de la Juventud, Cayman Islands, Bahama Islands [New Providence, Bimini Is., Andros, Great Inagua, San Salvador; Rindge, 1952:7, 1955:6; Clench, 1977b:184; Clench and Bjorndal, 1980:14; and Elliott, Riley, and Clench, 1980:123]); *D. g. jamaicensis* Bates on Jamaica; and *D. g. cleothera* on Hispaniola and Puerto Rico. The species is uncommon on the latter island; Comstock (1944:436) listed only 1 specimen from that island, and Ramos (1982:59) listed the species without comment. Riley (1975:35) gave the distribution of *D. g. cleothera* as the República Dominicana and Haiti (e.g., near Puerto Plata), once again following Hall (1925:165), who had described *D. kaempfferi* (a synonym) based on 8 specimens from that city. Schwartz (1983a:17) examined 38 specimens from 16 Haitian localities; these figures suggest that *D. g. cleothera* is not rare or localized in Haiti.

Danaus g. cleothera is widely distributed geographically and altitudinally on Hispaniola; yet it is rare (Tiburon Peninsula) or even absent (Península de Samaná) in some areas. The butterfly is primarily an inhabitant of xeric areas, but it is by no means restricted to that sort of ecology. Most records are from *Acacia* scrub (Colmini, Fond Parisien, Hatillo, etc.). But there are specimens taken in pine forest (Forêt des Pins, 14 km SE Constanza, 36 km NE Cabo Rojo, Aceitillar), xeric woods and forest (Boca de Yuma, La Romana), and mixed pine-hardwoods (Restauración, Loma Leonor, La Vega, 16 km SE Constanza), and even at the edge of mesic forest (Las Lagunas). Like most *Danaus*, *D. g. cleothera* frequently occurs in open fields and along weedy roadsides (Découzé, Camp Perrin, Boutilliers Road, Kenscoff, Mirebalais, Sosúa, 1 km S Constanza, 12 km NE Constanza, El Limón, Polo); we have also taken the Queen just behind a beach (Grand-Goâve), in a very overgrown coastal *Cocos* grove (Nagua), and over salt flats near the ocean (4 km N Monte Cristi).

Most specimens are from July (88), with 37 from June, 26 from May, 18 from August, 9 each from October and December, and 7, 3, 2, and 1 from January, March, April, and September. *Danaus g. cleothera* is most abundant in late summer, preceded by a gradual increase in June and followed by a sharp decline in August. Elevational distribution is from sea level (Cormier Plage, Ça Soleil, Fond Parisien, Grand-Goâve, 4 km N Monte Cristi, Nagua, Punta Cana, Palmar de Ocoa, Las Calderas, Tierra Nueva, Canoa) to 2105 m (Valle Nuevo) in the Cordillera Central. The highest elevation in the Massif de la Selle complex of ranges is 1647 m (Kenscoff) on the Montagne Noire. Times of collection were between 0830 and 1715 h, at temperatures between 24°C (Valle Nuevo) and 39°C (1 km S La Descubierta).

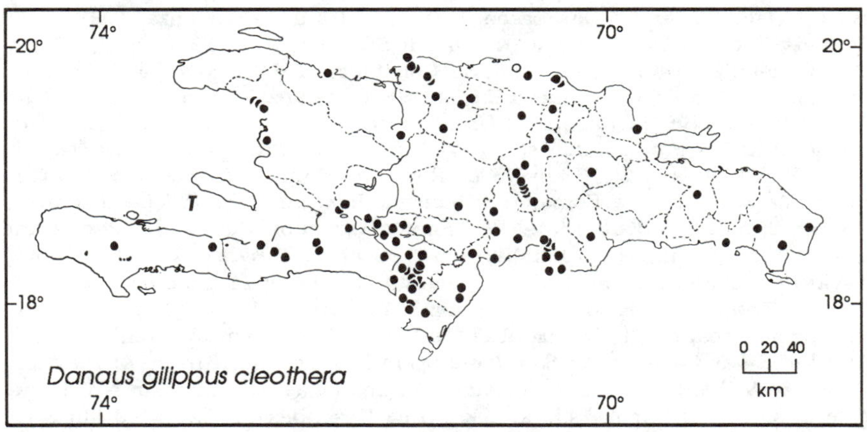

Danaus gilippus cleothera

Copulating pairs were taken or seen on 28.v (3.9 km S Martín García, 92 m, 34°C), 22.vi (15 km NW Cruce de Ocoa, 1140–1230 h, 37°C), and 19.vii (Mencía, 397 m, 0830–1000 h, 38°C). *Danaus g. cleothera* adults feed on *Antigonon leptopus* (18.5 km SE Monte Cristi, Villa Vásquez, 15 km NW Cruce de Ocoa), *Lantana ovatifolia* (Vallejuelo, 4 km E El Limón), and *Funastrum clausum* (Palmar de Ocoa). On the latter plant at that locality, *D. g. cleothera* was far outnumbered by *D. e. tethys*. The 2 species are regularly encountered together, since both are primarily xerophilic, *D. e. tethys* more so than *D. g. cleothera*. Elsewhere we have taken *D. g. cleothera* feeding on *Bidens pilosa* (Mao, Los Quemados, Cañongo), *Ageratum conyzoides* (Vallejuelo, 1 km N Aceitillar), *Croton linearis* (Cabo Rojo), *Asclepias nivea* (Las Abejas), and *Rubus* sp. (Valle Nuevo).

Specimens: Haiti: Nord: Cormier Plage, s.l., 1; *l'Artibonite:* 8.5 km W Ça Soleil, 1; 12.1 km W Ça Soleil, s.l., 3; 16.8 km W Ça Soleil, 3; Colmini, 6.4 km W Terre Noire, s.l., 1; *l'Ouest:* 20 km S Mirebalis, 590 m, 2; 1.1 km N Terre Rouge, 534 m, 1; 2.9–8.5 km S Terre Rouge, 122–488 m, 1; 2 km W Fond Parisien, s.l., 1; 4 km SE Fond Parisien, s.l., 2; 1 km NW Forêt des Pins, 1556 m, 1; Boutilliers Road, 732–946 m, 12 (1 FSM); Boutilliers Road, 1.8–2.1 km W Kenscoff road, 763–885 m, 6; 3.7 km S Kenscoff, 1647 m, 1; 5.4 km S Découzé, 397 m, 1; 16.3 km N Jacmel, 366 m, 1; just W Grand-Goâve, s.l., 2; *Sud:* 6.7 km SW Paillant, 763 m, 1; 4.8 km N Camp Perrin, 244 m, 1; *República Dominicana: Monte Cristi:* 4 km N Monte Cristi, s.l., 1; 1 km SE Monte Cristi, 9; 4 km SE Monte Cristi, 10; 18.5 km SE Monte Cristi, 1; 4 km NW Villa Vásquez, 61 m, 9; 3.9 km SE Martín García, 92 m, 2; *Dajabón:* 8 km S Restauración, 625 m, 3; *Santiago Rodríguez:* Loma Leonor, 19 km SW Monción, 610 m, 6; 3 km W Los Quemados, 183 m, 4; *Valverde:* 12 km SW Mao, 244 m, 7; *Puerto Plata:* 15 km SE Puerto Plata, 122 m, 1; 9 km SE Sosúa, 15 m, 1; 11 km SE Sosúa, 47 m, 1; *Espaillat:* 14 km SW Jamao al Norte, 534 m, 1; *Santiago:* 7 km SW Santiago, 214 m, 1; *La Vega:* 2 km S La Vega, 366 m, 3; Buena Vista, 11 km NE Jarabacoa, 640 m, 5; 1 km S Constanza, 1098 m, 4; 10 km SE Constanza, 1647 m, 1; 14 km SE Constanza, 1922 m, 2; 16 km SSE Constanza, 1403 m, 1; 18 km SE Constanza, 1586 m, 1; 12 km NE Constanza, 1220 m, 1; Valle Nuevo, 25 km SE Constanza, 2105 m, 1; *María T. Sánchez:* 9 km SE Nagua, s.l., 1; *Hato Mayor:* 4 km S Hato Mayor, 1; *La Altagracia:* 2 km W Punta Cana, s.l., 1; 2–3 km W Boca de Yuma, 1; 2.5 km SE Playa Bayahibe, s.l., 2; 16 km NE La Romana, 61 m, 1; *La Romana:* Río Cumayasa, 13.5 km W La Romana, 3; *Sánchez Ramírez:* 1 km NE Las Lagunas, 183 m, 2; *San Cristóbal:* 3 km NW Cambita Garabitos, 366 m, 1; *Azua:* 2 km NW Hatillo, 183 m, 1; 25 km NW Azua, 92 m, 5; Tábara Abajo, 1; 2 km N Yayas de Viajama, 366 m, 1; 5 km S Peralta, 305 m, 3; 11 km S Peralta, 1; 22 km NW Cruce de Ocoa, 61 m, 1; 15 km NW Cruce de Ocoa, 76 m, 4; 1 km E Palmar de Ocoa, s.l., 1; *Peravia:* Las Calderas, s.l., 4; 5 km SW Sombrero, s.l., 1; 4 km S Las Carreras, 1; *San Juan:* 9 km E Vallejuelo, 610 m, 4; *Baoruco:* 11 km N Neiba, 519 m, 1; *Independencia:* Las Lajas, s.l., 1; 5 km NW Tierra Nueva, s.l., 1; La Furnia, s.l., 1; 1 km S La Descubierta, s.l., 1; 3.3 km E La Descubierta, 2; 4 km E El Limón, 183 m, 1; 0.5 km E Duvergé, 1; 4–7 km NE El Aguacate, 519–824 m, 2; 0.6 km NW Puerto Escondido, 519 m, 1; 5 km N Puerto Escondido, 427 m, 1; *Barahona:* El Limón, summit, Sierra Martín García, 1037 m, 2; 8 km ESE Canoa, s.l., 1; 8 km NNE Polo, 793 m, 1; 8 km NW Paraíso, 153 m, 1; *Pedernales:* 2 km NE Cabo Rojo, s.l., 1; 5 km NE Cabo Rojo, 1; 23 km NE Cabo Rojo, 488 m, 5; 26 km NE Cabo Rojo, 732 m, 1; 35 km NE Cabo Rojo, 1220 m, 1; Aceitillar, 36 km NNE Cabo Rojo, 1281 m, 2; 1 km N Aceitillar, 1281 m, 8; Las Abejas, 11 km NW Aceitillar, 1220 m, 3; Las Abejas, 12 km W Aceitillar, 1129 m, 6; Canote Mine, 6 km NW Aceitillar, 1495 m, 2; 1 km SE Banano, 183 m, 1; 9 km SE Pedernales, s.l., 1; 17 km NW Oviedo, 183 m, 4.

2. *Danaus eresimus tethys* Forbes, 1943

TL Fond Parisien, Dépt. de l'Ouest, Haiti.

FW males 35–41 mm, females 38–43 mm.

There is some doubt as to the propriety of using the subspecific name *tethys* for the Antillean populations of *D. eresimus*

Cramer. Brown and Heineman (1972:85–86) discussed the fact that there are, within most populations of *D. eresimus*, both light- and dark-colored individuals; Forbes's name *tethys* was applied to the Antillean light-colored populations. (Incidentally, Brown and Heineman misspelled the name as *"thetys,"* but Miller and Brown [1981:205] gave the spelling used herein.) Cuba harbors both light and dark-colored individuals. Bates (1935a: 146–47) examined only 6 specimens from Cuba; of them, 2 were light and 4 dark. Brown and Heineman (1972:86) noted only light-colored specimens from Jamaica, where the species is rather uncommon. In my long series from Hispaniola, all are light colored. It seems that the name *tethys* may be appropriately used for at least the Jamaican and Hispaniolan *D. eresimus*. The situation on Cuba remains to be determined.

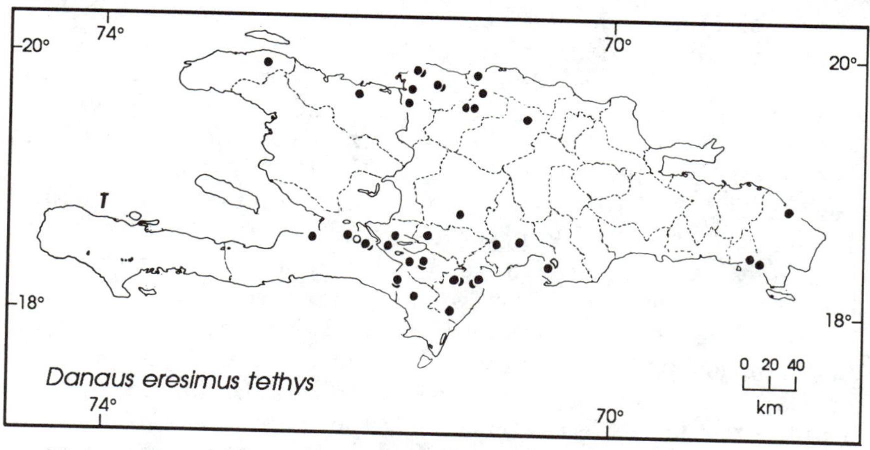

Brown and Heineman (1972:87) stated that on Jamaica *D. eresimus* is possibly more common than their records suggest: "It is a 'local' butterfly, often numerous where it is found." The latter is certainly true on Hispaniola. Schwartz (1983a:16–17) reported only 7 specimens from 4 localities in Haiti, representing 3 years' collecting. In the República Dominicana one encounters single *D. e. tethys;* additionally, he occasionally encounters large numbers of this butterfly locally. Such a locality is Duvergé, where on 22. vii.1982, Gali and I saw dozens of individuals and collected a modest series. The butterflies were between the edge of the road and a ditch with some water in the bottom. The butterflies were feeding on *Bidens pilosa* and were easily netted. Neither here nor elsewhere did *D. e. tethys* exhibit the "strong flight" that Brown and Heineman (1972:86) stated distinguishes this species from *D.*

gilippus jamaicensis, which has a "relatively weak flight." In fact, unless one gets a view of the un, he is left in some doubt as to which of the 2 species, *D. eresimus* or *D. gilippus*, he has taken. Nor does *D. e. tethys* "dash off" in contrast to movement for only a short distance, supposedly characteristic of *D. gilippus*.

A second locality where *D. e. tethys* was abundant in the República Dominicana is Villa Vásquez. There, these butterflies, in company with many *H. ch. churchi* and pierids, were feeding avidly on the flowers of *Antigonon leptopus* along the roadside through an oasis on 5–8.vii.1982. Such concentrations are unusual. On 29.vii.1983 there were many fewer *D. e. tethys* at Villa Vásquez (although the *Antigonon* was still in flower), and on 22.x.1983, the number was reduced even further (*Antigonon* still in flower). On the latter date, *D. e. tethys* was much more attracted to the white flowers of *Funastrum clausum*, a climbing xerophilic milkweed, which may well be the larval food plant.

Danaus e. tethys is almost exclusively a butterfly of lowland xeric areas; it inhabits the Cul de Sac–Valle de Neiba plain, the Llanos de Azua, the Plaine du Nord, and the Valle de Cibao, and the base of the Presqu'île du Nord-Ouest (Balladé). From these areas, *D. e. tethys* ascends neighboring mountain ranges to modest elevations (671 m) but is never abundant at these "higher" localities. There are no records for the Península de Barahona lowlands; the species undoubtedly occurs there, since we have taken (from the south slopes of the Massif de la Selle and the Sierra de Baoruco) isolated specimens (Enriquillo, Cabo Rojo, Banano, Mencía) that must have originated in the xeric Barahona lowlands or in the arid lowlands of adjacent southeastern Haiti. From the Tiburon Peninsula, there is a short series of *D. e. tethys* from Grand-Goâve; the area was not xeric (in grasses along the border of a mangrove swamp), and these butterflies likely represent a western "overflow" from the population in the Cul de Sac plain. The most interesting *D. e. tethys* are 9 from extreme eastern La Altagracia and La Romana provinces (Macao, Río Chavón, Bayahibe). Although this area is locally rather arid, it is separated from other xeric regions by the intervening mesic regions between this eastern coast and Baní, 375 km airline to the west. There must be a locally breeding population of *D. e. tethys* in the far east of Hispaniola (see accounts of *Ps. b. bornoi* and *E. zonarius*, for instance).

Most specimens and observations are in July (71), with 33 in May, 17 in June, 7 in August, 6 in October, 5 in December, 4 in January, 2 in February, and 1 each in March and April. It is likely that May–July is the time of major eclosion of *D. e. tethys*. Elevational distribution is from sea level (Limonade, Croix des Bouquets, Grand-Goâve, Copey, Palmar de Ocoa, La Furnia, 10 km W Cabral) to 671 m (Enriquillo). There are only 7 localities (Mao, Peralta, Vallejuelo, Neiba, El Aguacate, Enriquillo, Cabo Rojo) above 214 m; the Vallejuelo record is from the xeric intramontane valley of the Sierra de Neiba, where the species probably breeds despite the high elevation.

Times of collection were between 0900 and 1800 h (sunset), and temperatures between 26°C (Peralta, Neiba) and 38°C (La Furnia).

We have observed *D. e. tethys* feeding on *Antigonon leptopus* (Croix des Bouquets, 18.5 km SE Monte Cristi, Villa Vásquez, Cruce de Guayacanes), *Lantana ovatifolia* (Copey, 7 km SSW Cabral, Mencía), *Funastrum clausum* (Villa Vásquez, Palmar de Ocoa), *Paullinia pinnata* (Río Chavón), *Acacia vogeliana* (Vallejuelo), *Mikania cordifolia* (Tábara Abajo), *Ageratum conyzoides* (Peralta, La Descubierta, Barahona), and *Bidens pilosa* (Cañongo, Mao, Tábara Abajo, 0.5 km E Duvergé). A male was taken at Tábara Abajo on mud adjacent to an irrigation rivulet in *Acacia* forest.

Copulating pairs were taken or seen on 25.v (Cañongo, 31 m, 1450 h, 33°C) and 29.vii (0.5 km E Duvergé, 1000–1045 h, 37°C).

Specimens: Haiti: Nord-Ouest: 1.3 km S Balladé, 31 m, 1; *Nord:* 3.5 km E Limonade, s.l., 1; *l'Ouest:* 18.8 km SE Croix des Bouquets, s.l., 1; 5 km SE Fond Parisien, s.l., 1; 4 km SE Fond Parisien, s.l., 1; 6.7 km E Grand-Goâve, s.l., 4; *República Dominicana: Monte Cristi:* 1 km SE Monte Cristi, 1; 4 km SE Monte Cristi, 1; 18.5 km SE Monte Cristi, 4; 4 km NW Villa Vásquez, 61 m, 23; 6 km W Copey, s.l., 4; *Dajabón:* 0.5 km N Cañongo, 31 m, 20; *Valverde:* 12 km SW Mao, 244 m, 4; 4 km N Cruce de Guayacanes, 198 m, 1; *Santiago Rodríguez:* 3 km W Los Quemados, 183 m, 1; *Puerto Plata:* 0.6 km NE Estero Hondo, 4; *Santiago:* 7 km SW Santiago, 214 m, 1; *La Altagacia:* Macao, 1 (MNHNSD); Bayahibe, 1 (MNHNSD); *La Romana:* Río Chavón, 8 km SE La Romana, s.l., 7; *Azua:* Tábara Abajo, 6; 1 km E Palmar de Ocoa, s.l., 2; 5 km S Peralta, 305 m, 4; *San Juan:* 9 km E Vallejuelo, 671 m, 3; *Baoruco:* 11 km N Neiba, 519 m, 4; *Independencia:* La Furnia, s.l., 12; 1 km S La Descubierta, 2; 0.5 km E Duvergé, 15; 2 km S Duvergé, 1; 7 km NE El Aguacate, 519 m, 1; *Barahona:* 10 km W Cabral, s.l., 2; 7 km SSW Cabral, 214 m, 1; Barahona, s.l., 1; 2 km SW Barahona, 122 m, 3; 9 km NW Enriquillo, 671 m, 1; *Pedernales:* 23 km N Cabo Rojo, 488 m, 1; 1 km SE Banano, 183 m, 1; Mencía, 397 m, 3.

Sight records: República Dominicana: Azua: 1 km E Palmar de Ocoa, s.l—1 seen, 5.ii; *Barahona:* 7 km SW Cabral, 214 m—1 seen, 10.vii.

3. *Danaus plexippus megalippe* Hübner, 1826

TL not stated; probably "Georgia" (Brown and Heineman, 1972:88).

FW males 38–50 mm, females 41–50 mm.

Danaus plexippus Linnaeus, the Monarch, is widely distributed throughout the West Indies; Cuba and the Bahama Islands have the nominate subspecies (which is migratory), although Great Inagua and San Salvador in the extreme southern Bahamas have *D. p. megalippe* (Clench and Bjorndal, 1980:13; Elliott, Riley, and Clench, 1980:123). Puerto Rico is inhabited by *D. p. portoricensis* Clark, and the Lesser Antilles have *D. p. leucogyne* Butler (Schwartz and Jimenez, 1982:3–5). Jamaica and Hispaniola are occupied by *D. p. megalippe*. The status of these subspecies has been discussed in some detail by Schwartz and Jimenez (1982); additional material collected on Hispaniola since that time has not altered their conclusions. As far as known, all Antillean subspecies are nonmigratory.

Cucurullo (1959) and Marión Heredia (1974) recorded the subspecies *plexippus* and *portoricensis*, as well as *megalippe*, from Santo Domingo. Although the former is a possibility, the latter seems much less likely. I have examined no specimens that can be assigned to nominate *plexippus* and none assignable with confidence to *portoricensis*. *Danaus p. megalippe* is sufficiently variable in its own right that, unless specimens of all 3 taxa are compared in series, some *D. p. megalippe* could (erroneously, in my opinion) be considered nominate *plexippus* or *portoricensis*.

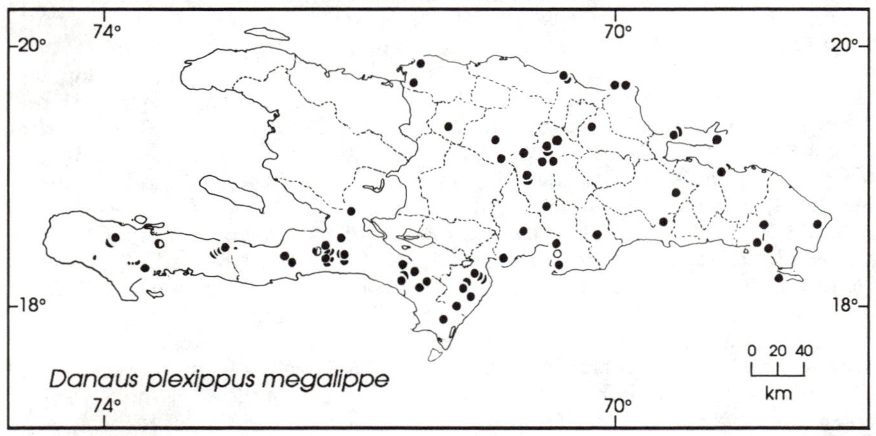

Danaus p. megalippe is widely distributed on Hispaniola, although there are broad areas (notably the Tiburon Peninsula) where the species is uncommon. The elevational distribution is from sea level (Ça Soleil, Río San Juan, Punta Cana, Playa Bayahibe, Sabana Buey, Mano Juan) to 1880 m in the Massif de la Selle (Morne la Visite). The high elevation in the Cordillera Central is 330 m (between La Laguna and La Cotorra). Schwartz (1983a:16)

noted the peculiar rarity of sea-level records for Haiti, but the virtual absence of this species in the extreme lowlands is striking in both countries. Most specimens and sight records are from about 380 m and higher, and at times *D. p. megalippe* is abundant in the uplands.

These are the first records of *D. p. megalippe* from Isla Saona; the species should also occur at least on Île de la Gonâve, but as yet there are no records.

Danaus p. megalippe frequents open areas—fields, roadsides, edges of *cafetales*, and clearings in *caféières*. In general, localities where the species occurs are mesic. Roadsides through mesic hardwood forest (Bayaguana, Paraíso, Los Arroyos) or mesic woods (Guerra) usually have a few Monarchs patrolling with their gliding or sailing flight. *Danaus p. megalippe* may be very common in highland pine forest (5.8 km SW Kenscoff, Peneau), but we have never encountered Monarchs in the Cordillera Central pine forests southeast of Constanza (although the species is not uncommon in grassy fields at Constanza itself or 6 km SSE Constanza in mixed pine-hardwoods). There are a few xeric localities (Copey, Monte Cristi, Playa Bayahibe, Sabana Buey, Tres Charcos, Mano Juan); of these, Monte Cristi is the most rigorous. A Monarch was taken there in the same habitat as *O. stillmani* and *H. nabokovi*—an extensive field of *Uniola virgata*. Such occurrences are in the minority.

Most specimens are from June and July, in about equal numbers; Monarchs are less common in August, and there are scattered specimens from March, April, May, September, October, December, January, and February. Apparently the time of emergence of *D. p. megalippe* is in the early summer. Times of collection or observation were between 0830 and 1600 h, at temperatures of 19°C (Scierie) to 39°C (Jarabacoa); *D. p. megalippe* flies on overcast (Constanza, Samaná) as well as sunny days.

Copulating pairs have been seen or taken on 9.vi (1 km N Aceitillar, 1420 h, 26°C), 8.vii (Constanza, 0930–1230 h, 29°C), 19.vii (Mencía, 0830–1000 h, 38°C), and 8.viii (Constanza, 1500–1545 h). A female was observed ovipositing on *Asclepias nivea* on 22.vi (25.6 km N Cavaillon, 610 m, Dépt. du Sud, Haiti). Schwartz (1983a:16) reported seeing 2 caterpillars on *A. nivea* on 13.vii (6.7 km SW Paillant, Dépt. du Sud, Haiti).

Although *D. p. megalippe* is closely associated with members of the Asclepiadaceae (milkweeds), we have taken it in the vicinity of, and foraging on the flowers of, only *A. nivea* (Las Abejas). Riley (1975:34) noted that *D. plexippus* caterpillars feed on *Calotropis procera*, a large woody treelike milkweed introduced from Africa. This plant is widespread in Haiti and in the República Dominicana, where in xeric lowland areas it forms extensive stands. We have never taken or seen *D. p. megalippe* on this milkweed. In the fall, *Funastrum claustrum*, a lowland xeric-area climbing milkweed with white flowers, likewise is not of interest to *D. p. megalippe* (but it is to other danaids). It may be that these 2 plants grow in habitats that are generally unsuitable for *D. p. megalippe*—lowland xeric areas. At Aceitillar, a *D. p. megalippe* was taken while feeding on *Senecio haitiensis* (Asteraceae) and *Pitcairnia elizabethae* (Bromeliaceae).

At Paillant, in a *caféière*, a *D. p. megalippe* was netted with a *H. o. odius* as they "struggled" on the ground after a heavy but brief rain. The significance of this activity remains unknown. Henderson observed as many as 6 *D. p. megalippe* resting at night on *Acacia* bushes, 1 to 1.5 m above the ground, on Isla Saona.

Specimens: Haiti: l'Artibonite: 12.2 km W Ça Soleil, s.l., 1; *l'Ouest:* 2.9–8.5 km S Terre Rouge, 122–488 m, 1; Pétionville, 458 m, 1; Boutilliers Road, 732–854 m, 4; Boutilliers Road, 1.8–2.1 km W Kenscoff road, 793–885 m, 12 (1 MPM); 3.7–3.8 km S Kenscoff, 1647 m, 11 (1 MPM); 5.8 km SW Kenscoff, 1678 m, 13; 0.3 km NE Obléon, 1678 m, 2; 0.3 km N Obléon, 1617 m, 10; 2 km NE Furcy, 2; Peneau, 1.1–1.6 km S Furcy, 1464 m, 4; Morne la Visite, 1430–1880 m, 3 (FSM); 2 km NW Scierie, 1785–1880 m, 1 (FSM); 2.1 km S Découzé, 640 m, 1; 16.3 km N Jacmel, 366 m, 1; nr. Péredo, 570 m, 1 (FSM); *Sud:* 3 km SW Paillant, 672 m, 1; 6.6 km SW Paillant, 793 m, 10; 6.7 km SW Paillant, 854 m, 2; 7 km SW Cavaillon, 122 m, 1; Formond Base Camp #1, 975 m, 2 (FSM); Morne Formond, 1000–1200 m, 3 (FSM); *República Dominicana: Monte Cristi:* 4 km SE Monte Cristi, 1; 6 km W Copey, s.l., 1; *Santiago Rodríguez:* Loma Leonor, 19 km SW Monción, 610 m, 2; *Puerto Plata:* 11 km SE Sosúa, 46 m, 1; 9 km SE Sosúa, 15 m, 1; *Santiago:* Río Bao, 8 km SE Montones Abajo, 488 m, 1; between La Laguna and La Cotorra, 1830–1403 m, 1; *La Vega:* Güaigüí, S La Vega, 336 m, 1; 10 km W Jayaco, 915 m, 2; La Palma, 19 km W Jayaco, 1007 m, 1; La Ciénaga, 915 m, 1; Jarabacoa, 530 m, 8; 6 km S Jarabacoa, 488 m, 4; 1 km S Constanza, 1098 m, 5; 6 km SE Constanza, 1403 m, 1; 10 km NW La Horma, 1496 m, 2; *María T. Sánchez:* Río San Juan, s.l., 2; 9 km NE Río San Juan, s.l., 1; *Duarte:* 10 km SE Tenares, 183 m, 1; *Samaná:* 8.9 km NE Sánchez, 336 m, 1; 12 km NE Sánchez, 153 m, 1; 14.1 km E and N Samaná, 31 m, 1; *Hato Mayor:* 25 km E Sabana de la Mar, 1; *La Altagracia:* 6 km W Punta Cana, s.l., 1; 1 km N Playa Bayahibe, s.l., 4; 16 km NE La Romana, 61 m, 1; *La Romana:* Río Chavón, 8 km SE La Romana, s.l., 1; *Dist. Nac.:* 9 km NE Guerra, 1; *Monte Plata:* 8 km NE Bayaguana, 1; *San Cristóbal:* 11 km NW Cambita Garabitos, 671 m, 4; *Peravia:* 3 km W Sabana Buey, s.l., 1; *Azua:* 25 km NE Azua, 92 m, 2; 5 km S Peralta, 305 m, 1; *Barahona:* El Limón, summit, Sierra Martín García, 1037 m, 1; Polo, 702 m, 5; 8 km NNE Polo, 793 m, 1; 1.8 km W Monteada Nueva, 1007 m, 2; 1.3 km W Monteada Nueva, 1037 m, 2; 7 km SW Barahona, 1; 8 km NW Paraíso, 153 m, 3; 8–10 km NW Paraíso, 1 (MPM); 9 km NW Enriquillo, 671 m, 1; *Pedernales:* 5 km NE Los Arroyos, 1617 m, 2; 1 km SE Banano, 488 m, 2; Mencía, 397 m, 1; 23 km NE Cabo Rojo, 488 m, 1; Las Abejas, 12 km NW Aceitillar, 1129 m, 1; 1 km N Aceitillar, 1281 m, 2; 4 km NW Tres Charcos, 1; *Isla Saona:* Mano Juan, s.l., 3;

Sight records: Haiti: l'Ouest: 2 km NE Furcy, 1617 m—1 seen, 23.iv:; *Sud:* 25.6 km N Cavaillon, 610 m—1 seen, 22.vi; *República Dominicana: Pedernales:* 5 km NE Los Arroyos, 1617 m—2 seen, 4.x.

4. *Danaus cleophile* Godart, 1819

TL not stated; Brown and Heineman (1972:92) suggested "Haiti"; restricted to Hispaniola by Riley (1975:35).

FW males 29–37 mm, females 30–35 mm.

Danaus cleophile, unfortunately called the "Jamaican Monarch" by Riley (1975:35), is known from Hispaniola and Jamaica and has been erroneously reported from Puerto Rico (Clark, 1941; see Ramos, 1980:67). The species is remarkably rare on Jamaica, whence Brown and Heineman (1972:94) listed 4 localities in as many parishes as sites whence they considered *D. cleophile* records valid. Most acceptable records are from the Mt. Diablo region in west-central Jamaica. Specimens from Jamaica with locality data are uncommon in American collections. This fact achieves some importance in the following context.

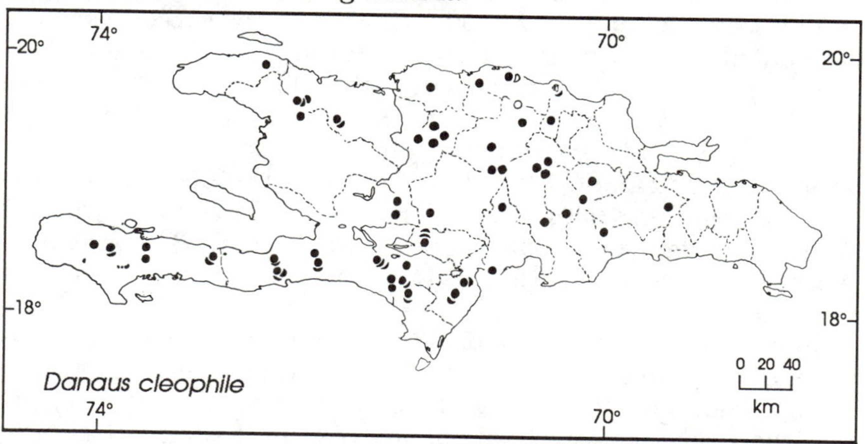

Brown and Heineman (1972:92), in their discussion of the taxonomy of this species, noted that Jamaican specimens differed in several ways from Hispaniolan material; the differences are so striking that, in the discussion (but not as the heading for their treatment of this species) they used the trinomial *D. c. cleophile* for Hispaniolan specimens. The 2 populations differ in that the Jamaican butterflies (1) are smaller, notably the males; (2) have the upfw cell usually wholly black; (3) have the up ground color somewhat darker; (4) lack, in the upfw cell, an angled brown line at the junction of the lower discocellular vein and M3; (5) have the black markings along the veins of the hw heavier; and (6) have the inner row of white spots in the black uphw margin less prominent. I have been unable to locate Jamaican specimens, preferably with locality data, in American collections. The situation appears clearcut; none of my long series has the fw cell completely dark, for instance, and this character alone should be enough to differentiate the 2 populations. But even aside from the rarity of Jamaican *D. cleophile* in collections, Brown and Heineman's (1972:pl. I, fig. 3) illustration shows a male that is similar to Hispaniolan males—the upfw cell is *not* wholly black. The up ground color is less bright (= darker) than that of Hispaniolan specimens, but one wonders as to the accuracy of the artist's delineation. It is probable that the Brown and Heineman plate was made from a Hispaniolan specimen; it remains for someone to secure a series of Jamaican specimens with exact locality data to verify the differences between the 2 populations and to apply a name to the Jamaican subspecies.

Hall (1925:165) stated that *D. cleophile* is "Not uncommon on Mt. Isabella and near La Cumbre, but rather local and does not seem to occur much below 1000 ft." Although the species is widely distributed on Hispaniola, the lower altitudinal limit noted by Hall is amazingly accurate, considering that his observations were based on only 4 months (including Kaempffer's 2 months) of field work. Riley's (1975:35) statement that *D. cleophile* is "rare and local" on Jamaica and Hispaniola from about 1500 ft. upward is based in part on Hall's information and in part on Brown and Heineman's data for Jamaica. Schwartz (1938a:17) reported 55 specimens of *D. cleophile* from 21 Haitian localities; the species is obviously not rare.

In contrast to other Hispaniolan *Danaus*, *D. cleophile* is an inhabitant of (primarily) mesic forest at moderate to high elevations. The lower altitudinal limit is 15 m (9 km SE Sosúa); there are only 11 other sites below elevations of 305 m (Balladé, Gaubert, Plaisance—both localities, Camp Perrin—both localities, Cruce de Guayacanes, Santo Domingo, Palmar de Ocoa, Cabeza de Agua). The upper elevational limit is 1922 m (Valle de Tetero) on the Cordillera Central, 1617 m (Obléon) on the Montagne Noire front range of the Massif de la Selle, 1129 m (Las Abejas) on the Sierra de Baoruco, 1050 m (Pic Formond) on the Massif de la Hotte, and 1037 m (El Limón) on the crest of the Sierra Martín García.

D. cleophile is absent from the eastern portion of the República

Dominicana; the easternmost records from this area are Las Lagunas, Bayaguana, and 30 km NW Santo Domingo; despite many man-months farther to the east in Hato Mayor, La Romana, and La Altagracia provinces, we have never encountered the species there. Although in the last 2 provinces there are lowland forests, they are xeric and apparently unsuitable for *D. cleophile*. Hato Mayor and El Seibo have excellent lowland mesic forest (between Sabana de la Mar and Miches, for example) that apparently lack the species. *Danaus cleophile* also has not been taken in the Cordillera Oriental in this region; that range does not reach truly high elevations (only 634 m), but the habitat is basically mesic and apparently suitable for *D. cleophile*.

As might be expected from the habitat preference noted above, *D. cleophile* is absent from the Cul de Sac—Valle de Neiba and the xeric portion of the Valle de San Juan. Occurrence in the western arid portion of the Valle de Cibao is limited to an oasis (Villa Vásquez) from which I have 2 specimens. The absence of *D. cleophile* from the mesic and locally well-wooded Península de Samaná is noteworthy. The easternmost limit of *D. cleophile* in the north in the República Dominicana is Jamao al Norte in the Cordillera Septentrional. Although *D. cleophile* is widely distributed in Haiti, it avoids lowland xeric areas there and is absent from the arid lowlands (at least) of the Presqu'île du Nord-Ouest, as well as the Plaine du Nord in the Cap-Haïtien region. However, *D. cleophile* is common on the mesic distal portion of the Tiburon Peninsula (Camp Perrin, Cavaillon), an area where other danaids are uncommon.

In contrast to *D. g. cleothera* and *D. e. tethys*, *D. cleophile* is most often encountered in hardwood forest or woods. The butterflies are also found in *caféières* (Gaubert, Découzé, Camp Perrin), *cafetales* (Polo), and even in pine forest (Forêt des Pins, Kenscoff). At Loma Leonor, *D. cleophile* occurs in moderate abundance in mixed pine-deciduous forest and in *Syzygium jambos* woods. It is truly a startling sight to encounter 1 of these brightly colored butterflies, resting with wings open in the dappled sunlight of the midmorning on a leaf 1 m above the ground, as one walks through a stand of hardwoods. It is only rarely that *D. cleophile* is found sailing along in typical danaid fashion on roadsides or in open fields, although these butterflies do occasionally venture into the open (Carrefour Marmelade, Boutilliers Road). At Cabeza de Agua, a few *D. cleophile* were seen in a deep and steep-sided ravine into which the sun seldom penetrated due to the ravine's narrowness—altogether an unsatisfactory place for the heliophilic Hispaniolan congeners of *D. cleophile*.

Most specimens have been taken in July (81), with 42 in August and 31 in June. May, April, September, November, October, and December each has 1–10 specimens. Late summer is the time of maximum abundance of this univoltine species. Times of collection were between 0900 and 1655 h, at temperatures between 24°C (Pic Formond) and 38°C (Cruce de Guayacanes, Río Bao, Jamao al Norte).

We have taken *D. cleophile* feeding on *Lantana ovatifolia* (Cabo Rojo, 9 km N Neiba), *Tournefortia hirsutissima* (9 km SE Sosúa), *Asclepias nivea* (Las Abejas, 1.8 km W Monteada Nueva), and *Ageratum conyzoides* (Banano, Monteada Nueva, El Aguacate).

Copulating pairs were taken on 14.iii (Loma Leonor, 610 m, 1045–1315 h, 26°C) and 29.vi (5 km SE Jarabacoa, 595 m, 1600 h, 33°C) in a hardwood ravine in mixed pine-hardwoods.

The 3 small *Danaus* (*eresimus, gilippus, cleophile*) are syntopic at only 3 localities: Villa Vásquez (where *D. e. tethys* far outnumbers the 2 other species), El Aguacate (where *D. cleophile* is abundant but which is ecologically and altitudinally unsatisfactory for *D. e. tethys* and *D. g. cleothera*), and 23 km NE Cabo Rojo (which is ecologically unsuitable for *D. e. tethys* and is marginal for both *D. g. cleothera* and *D. cleophile;* the last-named is the most abundant). It is extremely unusual to encounter *D. e. tethys* and *D. cleophile* together; the former is a lowland xerophile, the latter a highland mesophile. Localities where *D. g. cleothera* and *D. cleophile* are syntopic are almost invariably at the ecological, vegetational, or elevational extreme of 1 of the species. The same is true of the sites of 3-species syntopy. The Cabo Rojo locality where all 3 species occur is very interesting in that one would expect, from vegetational cover and elevation, *D. g. cleothera*— but not *D. e. tethys* or *D. cleophile*. Yet the former apparently "washes up" to this elevation and ecology from the xeric Península de Barahona, whereas the latter "slides down" to these transitional woods, and thus the 3 species occur here syntopically.

Specimens: Haiti: Nord-Ouest: 0.6 km NW Balladé, 1; *Nord:* 4.8 km W Plaisance, 259 m, 1; 6.2 km W Plaisance, 259 m, 2; Gaubert, 3; 5.6 km SE Dondon, 336 m, 3; 5.9 km S Dondon, 366 m, 2; *l'Artibonite:* 1.6 km E Carrefour Marmelade, 854 m, 6; *l'Ouest:* 4 km NW Forêt des Pins, 1496 m, 4; 1 km NW Forêt des Pins, 1556 m, 2; Forêt des Pins, 1586 m, 1; Boutilliers Road, 732–854 m, 6; Boutilliers Road, 1.8–2.1 km W Kenscoff road, 793–885 m, 10; 3.4 km W crest Boutillier Road, *ca.* 366 m, 1; 5.8 km S Kenscoff, 1586 m, 1; 0.3 km N Obléon, 1617 m, 2; 1.3 km N Béloc, 702 m, 1; 5.0 km S Béloc, 732 m, 1; 1.6 km N Découzé, 702 m, 2; 0.8 km S Découzé, 702 m, 3; 2.1 km S Découzé, 640 m, 1; *Sud:* 6.6 km SW Paillant, 793 m, 1; 6.7 km SW Paillant,

763 m, 1; 14.1 km N Cavaillon, 366 m, 3; 25.6 km N Cavaillon, 610 m, 1; 4.8 km N Camp Perrin, 244 m, 1; 5.6 km N Camp Perrin, 285 m, 2; along ravine bet. Pic Formond and Macaya, 1050 m, 1 (FSM); *República Dominicana: Monte Cristi:* 4 km NW Villa Vásquez, 61 m, 2; *Dajabón:* Los Cerezos, 12 km NW Río Limpio, 580 m, 1; *Elías Piña:* La Laguna, 10 km S Comendador, 732 m, 1; 2 km NE Puesto Pirámide 204, 1586 m, 1; *Santiago Rodríguez:* 8 km NNW Los Almácigos, 1; Loma Leonor, 19 km SW Monción, 610 m, 9; 4.7 km SW Loma Leonor, 732 m, 6; *Puerto Plata:* 11 km N Cruce de Guayacanes, 275 m, 1; 13 km SE Luperón, 214 m, 1; 9 km SE Sosúa, 15 m, 1; 11 km SE Sosúa, 31 m, 2; *Santiago:* Río Bao, 8 km SE Montones Abajo, 488 m, 9; 7 km SW Santiago, 214 m, 1; entrance of Valle de Tetero to Valle de Tetero, 1923–1342 m, 1; *Espaillat:* 20 km SW Jamao al Norte, 793 m, 4; *La Vega:* 10 km W Jayaco, 915 m, 1; 3 km SW Boca del Río, 976 m, 1; 5 km SE Jarabacoa, 595 m, 8; 3.5 km E Paso Bajito, 732 m, 1; *Monte Plata:* 8 km NE Bayaguana, 4; *Dist. Nac.:* 30 km NW Santo Domingo, 122 m, 1; *Monseñor Nouel:* 17 km SW Piedra Blanca, 854 m, 1; 6 km SE Maimón, 122 m, 2; *Peravia:* 1.6 km SE La Horma, 1; *Azua:* 5 km SW Monte Bonito, 702 m, 1; *Sánchez Ramírez:* 1 km NE Las Lagunas, 183 m, 4; *San Juan:* 7 km E El Cercado, 854 m, 1; *Baoruco:* 9 km N Neiba, 366 m, 1; 11 km N Neiba, 519 m, 1; 14 km N Neiba, 671 m, 1; *Independencia:* 4–7 km NE El Aguacate, 519–824 m, 12; *Barahona:* El Limón, summit, Sierra Martín García, 1037 m, 1; 5 km NW Las Auyamas, 1; Polo, 702 m, 1; 1.3 km W Monteada Nueva, 1037 m, 1; 1.8 km W Monteada Nueva, 1007 m, 10; *Pedernales:* 23 km NE Cabo Rojo, 488 m, 4; 26 km NE Cabo Rojo, 732 m, 2; Las Abejas, 11 km NW Aceitillar, 1220 m, 1; Las Abejas, 12 km NW Aceitillar, 1129 m, 11; 1 km SE Banano, 183 m, 5; 1 km N Cabeza de Agua, 275 m, 3.

Subfamily Ituninae Reuter, 1896

5. *Lycorea cleobaea cleobaea* Godart, 1819

TL "Brasil; Antilles."

FW males 36–51 mm, females 37–50 mm.

Riley (1975:39) used *L. ceres* Cramer 1779 for this species, but Miller and Brown (1981:205) showed that *ceres* Cramer is preoccupied by *ceres* Fabricius 1775 and is unavailable for the species, which occurs on the continental mainland as well as on Cuba (*demeter* Felder and Felder 1865). Comstock (1944:436–37) compared a few Hispaniolan specimens with those from Puerto Rico and considered them identical except for the smaller size of the Hispaniolan material. Since *cleobaea* has been used for the Antillean (in contrast to the "Brasilian" population), the proper name for the species is *L. cleobaea* Godart, with *L. c. cleobaea* on Hispaniola and Puerto Rico, and *L. c. demeter* on Cuba. Should the Hispaniolan and Puerto Rican populations be found to differ from each other, the name *domingensis* Niepelt 1927 is available for the Hispaniolan butterflies (TL "St. Domingo"). I have not examined Puerto

Rican material, but that from Hispaniola remains slightly smaller than that from Puerto Rico (FW 49–53 mm; Comstock, 1944:436). The variation in FW length in both sexes on Hispaniola is much greater than Comstock's limited measurements suggested.

More recently, Wetherbee (1986) used the name *Lycorea pieteri cleobaea* for this species on Hispaniola. Such a combination is untenable; the name *pieteri* Lamas, 1979, postdates *cleobaea* Godart, 1819, by over a century and a half.

Hall (1925:165) stated that *L. c. cleobaea* is "Not uncommon in mountain forests." Brown and Heineman (1972:95) noted that on the mainland, this butterfly "favors virgin forests." Bates (1935a: 148) noted specimens of *L. c. demeter* only from eastern Cuba ("Prov. de Oriente") and gave the habitat (quoting Gundlach) "forests." Schwartz (1983a:18–19) gave only 3 Haitian localities; of his series of 68 specimens, all but 1 are from the same locality—a xeric wooded hillside near the ocean. From these data it is logical to assume that *L. c. cleobaea* is extremely local but may be very abundant in Haiti.

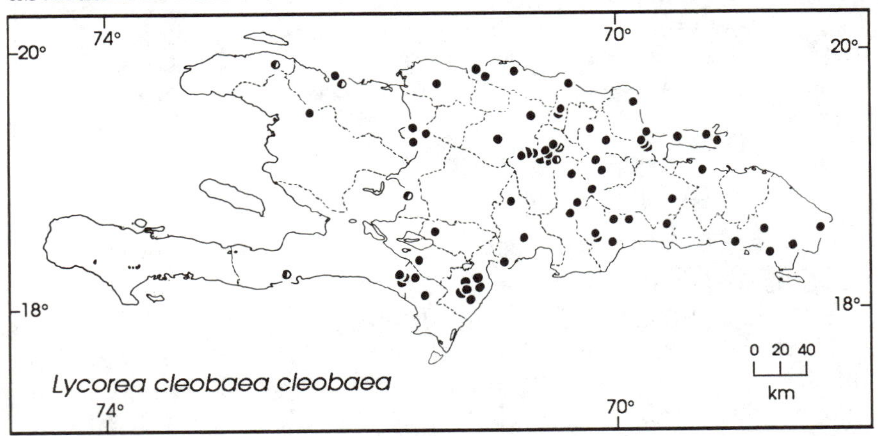

In the República Dominicana, on the other hand, *L. c. cleobaea* is widespread geographically and is often locally abundant. The butterflies inhabit forests and pseudoforests, where they drift and sail easily down paths, above watercourses, and among widely spaced trees; the forests need not be virgin, as Brown and Heineman suggested, and may be either xeric or mesic. We have taken specimens in overgrown coastal *Cocos* groves (Nagua, Las Galeras, Sabana de la Mar) and mixed pine-hardwoods (Buena Vista). Twice (Cruce de Rincón, La Piedra) we have encountered *L. c. cleobaea* in woods bordering large rice plantations; at La Piedra, which is completely isolated by surrounding rice fields (essentially an "island" in a "sea" of rice), *L. c. cleobaea* was taken in open deciduous woods in the village itself. *Lycorea c. cleobaea* is common in the xeric forests at Playa Bayahibe and La Romana. A single individual was taken in *Acacia* woods at Santiago.

But perhaps the most abundantly we have seen *L. c. cleobaea* in the República Dominicana is at Cabeza de Agua. This locality is on the southern slopes of the Massif de la Selle and is a deep and steep-sided ravine (into which the sun seldom penetrates, even at midday) with scattered trees and shrubs on the ravine floor. There, *L. c. cleobaea* was exceptionally abundant, the most common rhopaloceran present. A similar situation is Cabrera, where a sinkhole, well wooded in its depths, harbored many *L. c. cleobaea* (12 collected), almost to the exclusion of any other species. Perhaps these sites demonstrate most clearly the preference of *L. c. cleobaea* for shaded areas, localities which other butterflies occupy in smaller numbers or from which they are absent.

July and August are the months of greatest abundance; these months are represented by comparable numbers (110 and 95) of specimens and sightings. June ranks third with 24 specimens, December fourth with 16, and scattered numbers (7–1) are from January, May, November, March, February, and April. Times of collection were between 0900 and 1730 h, at temperatures between 23°C (Jayaco) and 38°C (Cruce de Guayacanes, Jamao al Norte).

The elevational distribution of *L. c. cleobaea* is between sea level (Cormier Plage, Carrefour la Mort, Cabrera, Nagua, Cruce de Rincón, Punta Cana, Playa Bayahibe) to 1129 m (Las Abejas) on the Sierra de Baoruco, 1037 m (El Limón) on the Sierra Martín García, 1007 m (La Palma) on the Cordillera Central, 854 m (Carrefour Marmelade) on the Massif du Nord, 793 m (20 km SW Jamao al Norte) on the Cordillera Septentrional, and 732 m (Comendador) on the Sierra de Neiba (north range). The absence of high-elevation records from the Massif de la Selle in both Haiti and the República Dominicana is puzzling; the highest elevation in those mountains is 824 m (El Aguacate).

We have taken *L. c. cleobaea* feeding on *Daucus* sp. (Carrefour Marmelade), *Ageratum conyzoides* (Banano), and an unidentified orange flower (5 km SE, 3 km W Barahona).

A pair *in copula* was taken at 7 km NE El Aguacate, 519–549 m (22.vi, 1205 h, 32°C), in xeric forest.

Specimens: Haiti: Nord: Cormier Plage, s.l., 67; *l'Artibonite:* 1.6 km E Carrefour Marmelade, 854 m, 1; *República Dominicana: Monte Cristi:* 4 km NW Villa Vásquez, 61 m, 1; *Dajabón:* Los Cerezos, 12 km NW Río Limpio, 580 m, 2; 10 km NE Restauración, 2; 1 km S Villa Anacaona, 397 m, 2; *Puerto Plata:* 11 km N Cruce de Guayacanes, 275 m, 3; 13 km SE Luperón, 214 m, 1; 11 km SE Sosúa, 46 m, 1; *Espaillat:* 14 km SW Jamao al Norte, 534 m, 7; 20 km SW Jamao al Norte, 793 m, 1; *Santiago:* 2 km E Pedro García, 427 m, 3; Río Bao, 8 km SE Montones Abajo, 488 m, 2; 7 km SW Santiago, 214 m, 1; *La Vega:* Buena Vista, 11 km NE Jarabacoa, 640 m, 3; 10 km W Jayaco, 915 m, 16; La Palma, 19 km W Jayaco, 1007 m, 1; La Ciénaga, 915 m, 12; 1 km W Manabao, 793 m, 3; Jarabacoa, 530 m, 5; 2 km S Jarabacoa, 488 m, 1; 6 km S Jarabacoa, 488 m, 7; 5 km SE Jarabacoa, 595 m, 1; *María T. Sánchez:* 6 km S Cabrera, s.l., 14; 9 km SE Nagua, s.l., 1; Cruce de Rincón, s.l., 1; 1 km S Cruce de Rincón, s.l., 1; *ca.* 18 km W, 1.2 km S Sánchez, road to Rincón Molinillos, 31 m, 1; *Duarte:* 10 km SE Tenares, 183 m, 4; 12 km SE San Francisco de Macorís, 3; *Samaná:* 13.2 km NE Sánchez, 92 m, 3; 14.4 km E and N Samaná, 31 m, 5; Las Galeras, s.l., 1; *Hato Mayor:* 7 km E Sabana de la Mar, 1; *La Altagracia:* 2 km W Punta Cana, s.l., 1; 0.5–3.5 km W Boca de Yuma, 1; 1 km N Playa Bayahibe, s.l., 11; 16 km NE La Romana, 61 m, 9; *La Romana:* Río Cumayasa, 13.5 km W La Romana, 4; *Dist. Nac.:* 25 km SE Yamasá, 1 (MPM); 9 km NE Guerra, 3; 30 km NW Santo Domingo, 122 m, 3; *Monseñor Nouel:* 6 km SE Maimón, 122 m, 1; Bonao, 153 m, 1; 14 km SW Piedra Blanca, 427 m, 1; *Monte Plata:* 8 km NE Bayaguana, 1; *Sánchez Ramírez:* La Piedra, 7 km SW Pimentel, 1; 1 km NE Las Lagunas, 183 m, 3; *San Cristóbal:* 3 km S Hato Damas, 92 m, 1; 8 km NW Cambita Garabitos, 534 m, 1; 11 km NW Cambita Garabitos, 671 m, 1; *Peravia:* 2 km SW Rancho Arriba, 671 m, 1; *Azua:* 5 km S Peralta, 305 m, 2; 5 km SW Monte Bonito, 702 m, 1; *Baoruco:* 11 km N Neiba, 519 m, 1; *Independencia:* 4–7 km NE El Aguacate, 519–824 m, 9; *Barahona:* El Limón, summit, Sierra Martín García, 976–1037 m, 2; west slope, Sierra Martín García, 458–915 m, 8; Polo, 702 m, 2; 3 km NNE Polo, 854 m, 1; 5 km SE, 3 km W Barahona, 183–397 m, 3; 12 km SW Barahona, 427 m, 3; 8 km NW Paraíso, 153 m, 7 (4 MPM); 8–10 km NW Paraíso, 1 (MPM); *Pedernales:* 1 km SE Banano, 183 m, 2; 2 km N Banano, 244 m, 1; 1 km N Cabeza de Agua, 275 m, 7; 23 km NE Cabo Rojo, 488 m, 1; Las Abejas, 12 km NW Aceitillar, 1129 m, 2.

Sight records: Haiti: Nord-Ouest: between Port-de-Paix and Gros Morne—1 seen, 19.vi; *Nord:* Carrefour la Mort, s.l.—2 seen, 31.vii: *l'Ouest:* Lavaneau, 229 m—1 seen, 25.iv; *República Dominicana: Elías Piña:* La Laguna, 10 km S Comendador, 732 m—1 seen, 27.vii; *Puerto Plata:* 0.6 km NE Estero Hondo—1 seen, 30.v; *Espaillat:* 14 km SW Jamao al Norte, 534 m—2 seen, 24.vii: *La Vega:* Güaigüí, S La Vega, 336 m—3 seen, 1.i; Buena Vista, 11 km NE Jarabacoa, 640 m—1 seen, 31.xii; 10 km W Jayaco, 915 m—2 seen, 30.xii; La Ciénaga, 915 m—3 seen, 8.viii; *Independencia:* 4–7 km NE El Aguacate, 591–824 m—1 seen, 6.vii; *Barahona:* 14 km SSW Cabral, 854 m—1 seen, 4.viii.

Subfamily Clothildinae Reuter, 1896

6. *Anetia briarea briarea* Godart, 1819

TL not stated; restricted to Haiti by Riley (1975:38).

FW males 38–45 mm, females 40–48 mm.

Anetia briarea occurs in the Antilles on only 2 islands, Cuba (which is occupied by *A. b. numidia* Hübner) and Hispaniola (which has the nominate subspecies). Riley (1975:35–36) confused the authorships of the 2 subspecies, and Brown and Heineman (1972:49) reversed their distributions. Hall (1925:186) did not collect the species on Hispaniola, and Riley made no comments on the abundance of *A. b. briarea*, although he noted that on Cuba *A. b. numidia* was reported as common and widespread. Bates (1935a:150) considered *A. b. numidia* common on Cuba on the Sierra de Trinidad at various localities, and on the Sierra Maestra, at elevations above 100 ft.

It is easy to understand, once one has had field experience with *A. b. briarea*, why it might be considered uncommon. This is a butterfly of high elevations, occurring in the uplands of the Cordillera Septentrional (1 record), Cordillera Central, Sierra de Neiba, Sierra Martín García, Massif de la Selle in both Haiti and the República Dominicana and its northern front ranges (Morne l'Hôpital, Montagne Noire), and the Sierra de Baoruco. Although there are no records from the Massif de la Hotte, doubtless *A. b. briarea* occurs there. Elevational distribution is from sea level (Fond Parisien) to 2288 m (18 km SE Constanza, 5 km NW Valle Nuevo) on the Cordillera Central, 1891 m (5 km SW El Aguacate, Scierie) on the Massif de la Selle, 1708 m (21 km N Los Pinos) on the Sierra de Neiba, 1373 m (4.5 km NE Aceitillar) on the Sierra de Baoruco, and 1037 m (El Limón) on the Sierra Martín García. All but 8 localities (Boutilliers Road, Fond Parisien, Jamao al Norte, Peralta, El Aguacate, Puerto Escondido, Polo, Cabo Rojo) are at or above 915 m. Thus, occurrences at lower elevations are exceptional.

The most remarkable of these is that at Fond Parisien, a sea-level xeric *Acacia* forest area, quite unusual for *A. b. briarea*. On 30.iv.1982, Gali and I traveled from Port-au-Prince to Forêt des Pins. The road to the latter locality leaves the main Port-au-Prince–Malpasse road at Fond Parisien and from there ascends the Massif de la Selle. From its beginning in the lowlands to as high as Fond Verrettes, *A. b. briarea* was commonly sighted along this entire 24 km stretch of road. We collected 6 individuals, all fresh, in the desert at Fond Parisien. The abundance of these butterflies in this immediate area suggested some downward "migration," since nowhere else have we encountered *A. b. briarea* in the xeric lowlands. There was no obvious reproductive behavior, and the butterflies were sailing in their usual lazy manner among *Acacia* rather than among mesic highland hardwoods, their customary habitat.

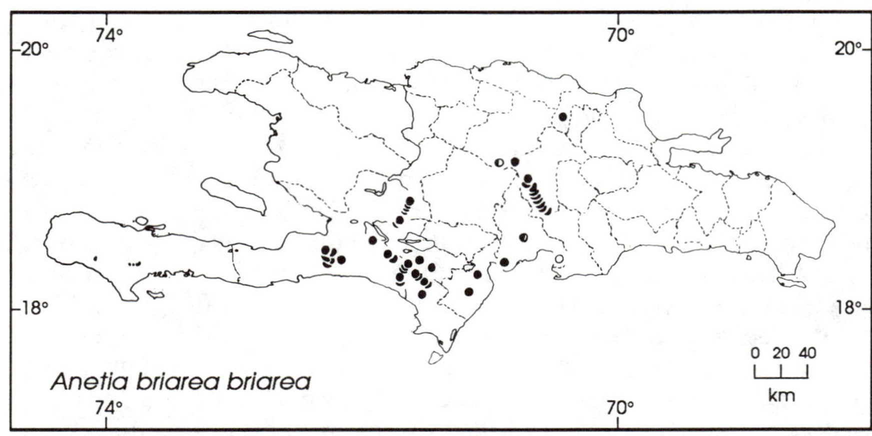

All other localities below 915 m for *A. b. briarea* are either mesic or somewhat to densely wooded, and the butterflies collected there are truly lower elevational records, in contrast to the strange situation at Fond Parisien. The apparent rarity of *A. b. briarea* on the Cordillera Septentrional is puzzling, since this range supports much mesic forest as well as pseudoforest on its upper slopes.

Although mesic hardwood forest is the typical habitat for *A. b. briarea*, we have taken it in pine forest (Forêt des Pins, Kenscoff, Obléon, Aceitillar), mixed pine-hardwoods (6 km SSE Constanza and most other localities SE of Constanza, 11 km SW El Aguacate); at the latter locality these butterflies were flying in an open meadow carpeted with the blue flowers of *Cynoglossum amabile*, on which the *A. b. briarea* were rarely seen to feed. In both Haiti and the República Dominicana, these butterflies are also taken along roadsides, patrolling in the fashion of *D. p. megalippe*, and in open fields, especially if there is an abundance of flowers either native or grown for internal use or export.

The most abundantly we have seen *A. b. briarea* is at 10 km SE Constanza. Here, we collected on a sloping mountainside in a fallow cabbage field overgrown with *Leonurus sibericus* (Lamiaceae) an Asiatic mint with tall (1 m) spikes of purple flowers, which has been introduced for bees to use in making honey. The field was a local gathering place for many species of butterflies; of the nonpierids, *A. b. briarea* was 1 of the most common, and it was not unusual to see as many as 5 of these large butterflies on a single flower spike, lazily opening and closing their wings as they took nectar.

Elsewhere, we have seen the imagines feeding on the flowers of a tall yellow-flowered composite ("golden rod") in pinewoods (Obléon), *Melilotus alba* (14 km SE Constanza), the large white flowers of *Rubus* sp. (Rosaceae) in the pines at 21 km SE Constanza, and *Chamissoa altissima* (Amaranthaceae) and *Eupatorium sinuatum* (Asteraceae) in the pine forest at Aceitillar. *Anetia b. briarea* also feeds on *Ageratum conyzoides* (Aceitillar, 21 and 23 km NE Cabo Rojo, 4–7 km NE El Aguacate) and *Croton linearis* (Puerto Escondido). At 5 km SW El Aguacate, Gali happened upon an unidentified white-flowered tree within dense hardwood forest; feeding avidly on the flowers were as many as 30–40 *A. b. briarea*, along with smaller numbers of *A. p. pantherata* and *A. jaegeri*.

Most specimens and records are from July (106), with 45 from June and only 11 from August, 7 from April, 3 from December, 2 each from March and October, and 1 each from September and January. Without question, *A. b. briarea* is most abundant, even to the casual eye, in early summer, when these butterflies appear to swarm in their appropriate habitat. Times of collection were between 0900 and 1640 h, at temperatures between 18°C (La Nevera) and 38°C (Jamao al Norte).

Specimens: Haiti: l'Ouest: 2 km SE Fond Parisien, s.l., 6; 4 km NW Forêt des Pins, 1496 m, 1; Forêt des Pins, 1373 m, 1; Boutilliers Road, 1.8 km W Kenscoff road, 885 m, 2; 3.7 km S Kenscoff, 1647 m, 1; 3.8 km S Kenscoff, 1647 m, 1; 5.8 km SW Kenscoff, 1678 m, 1; 0.3 km N Obléon, 1617 m, 3; 5 km WNW Scierie, 1891 m, 1 (FSM); *República Dominicana: Elías Piña:* 15 km S Comendador, 976 m, 1; 18 km S Comendador, 1312 m, 2; 21 km S Comendador, 1464 m, 1; 2 km NE Puesto Pirámide 204, 1586 m, 1; *Espaillat:* 20 km SW Jamao al Norte, 793 m, 1; *La Vega:* 3 km NE Boca del Río, 976 m, 1; 6 km SSE Constanza, 1403 m, 4; 1 km S Constanza, 1098 m, 1; 10 km SE Constanza, 1647 m, 34; 14 km SE Constanza, 1922 m, 17; 18 km SE Constanza, 1586 m (new road), 7; 18 km SE Constanza, 2288 m (old road), 10; 21 km SE Constanza, 2105 m, 3; 28 km SE Constanza, 2288 m, 4; 5 km NW Valle Nuevo, 2288 m, 3; Valle Nuevo, 2227 m, 1; 10 km NW La Horma, 1496 m, 2; *Independencia:* 21 km NE Los Pinos, 1708 m, 2; 23 km N Los Pinos, 1739 m, 1; 4–7 km NE El Aguacate, 519–824 m, 6; 0.6 km NW Puerto Escondido, 519 m, 3; *Barahona:* El Limón, summit, Sierra Martín García, 1037 m, 1; 8 km NNE Polo, 793 m, 1; 1.8 km W Monteada Nueva, 1007 m, 3; *Pedernales:* 26 km NE Cabo Rojo, 732 m, 2; 1 km N Aceitillar, 1281 m, 5; 4.5 km NE Aceitillar, 1373 m, 1; Las Abejas, 11 km NW Aceitillar, 1220 m, 3; Las Abejas, 12 km NW Aceitillar, 1129 m, 19; 3 km SE Los Arroyos, 976 m, 1; 0.6 km SE Los Arroyos, 1098 m, 1; 5 km NE Los Arroyos, 1617 m, 6; 5 km SW El Aguacate, 1464 m, 7; 11 km SW El Aguacate, 1891 m, 1.

Sight records: República Dominicana: Santiago: entrance of Valle de Tetero to Valle de Tetero—several seen, 2.vii; *Azua:* 5 km S Peralta, 305 m—1 seen, 25.iv; 1 seen, 29.iv.

7. *Anetia pantherata pantherata* Martyn, 1797

TL Port-au-Prince, Dépt. de l'Ouest, Haiti.

FW males 48–54 mm, females 53–56 mm.

Anetia pantherata is restricted to the West Indies, where it occurs on Hispaniola (nominate subspecies) and Cuba (*clarescens* Hall). The Cuban subspecies appears to be very uncommon; Bates (1935a:150) examined only 3 specimens. Hall (1925:186) took only 2 Hispaniolan specimens (La Cumbre, Prov. de Santiago, and Puerto Plata, both in the República Dominicana) but considered *A. p. pantherata* a well-known and not particularly rare butterfly.

In my experience, *A. p. pantherata* is less common than both *A. b. briarea* and *A. jaegeri*; all 3 species are rare in Haiti, but all are more numerous in the República Dominicana. *Anetia p. pantherata* is most often encountered in upland forest (usually pine), from 183 m (Azua) to 2288 m (18 km SE and 28 km SE Constanza), although these butterflies are also seen in transitional woods (Cabo Rojo, El Aguacate), mesic forest (Peralta, El Limón, Los Pinos, Las Abejas, Los Arroyos), and even *cafetales* (3 km NNE Polo) and high-elevation *Acacia*—xeric woods (Vallejuelo). Even less often *A. p. pantherata* may be taken along open roadsides (Terre Rouge, Boutilliers Road, 8 km NNE Polo). Although they may occur syntopically, *A. b. briarea* (mesic hardwood forests) and *A. p. pantherata* (pine forests) divide the upland forested regions of Hispaniola between them. Where these 2 ecologies interdigitate, one finds both butterflies together.

The type-locality (Port-au-Prince) is at sea level, a most unlikely locality for *A. p. pantherata;* likewise, Hall's Puerto Plata record is coastal. Both these sites require confirmation as places for *A. p. pantherata*, especially Port-au-Prince. One can assume either (1) that these localities are generalizations, and that the specimens were taken on nearby mountain ranges (note, however, that we have never taken *A. p. pantherata* in the Cordillera Septentrional, the source of Hall's La Cumbre specimen and the presumed source of his Puerto Plata record), or (2) that they represent the same sort of vertical movement that Gali and I observed in *A. b. briarea* at Fond Parisien. On the other hand, Gineika felt confident that he saw a single individual at Río Cumayasa, near sea level, on 27.vi.1980; if this record is accepted, it represents an extension of the range of *A. p. pantherata* far (200 km) from any known montane population and into the mesic-xeric forested lowlands of the extreme eastern República Dominicana. It may be that vagrant *A. p. pantherata* do occur occasionally in the lowlands, far removed from any source population.

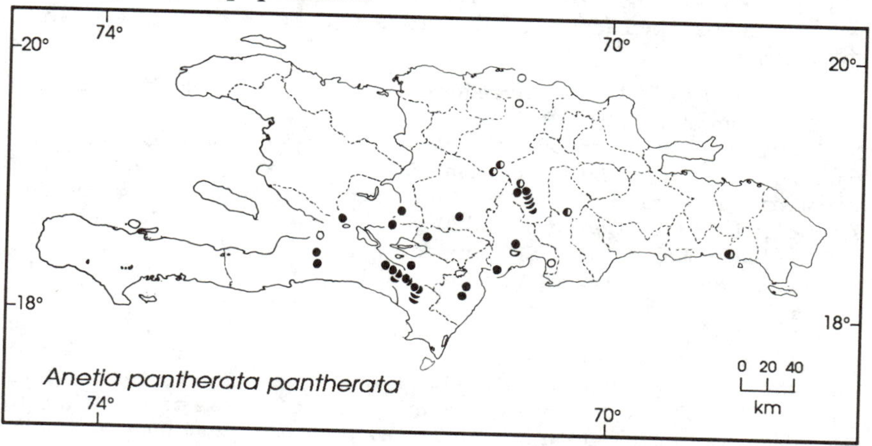

In my experience, however, *A. p. pantherata* is a butterfly of the high uplands. Most (but not all) *A. p. pantherata* have been taken in the Massif de la Selle and its northern front ranges (Morne l'Hôpital, Montagne Noire), the Cordillera Central, the southern range of the Sierra de Neiba, the Sierra Martín García, and the Sierra de Baoruco. We have not seen or taken *A. p. pantherata* in the Cordillera Septentrional, the Sierra de Yamasá, the Sierra de Samaná, or the Cordillera Oriental in the República Dominicana, nor in the Massif du Nord in Haiti.

Most specimens (44) have been taken in July, with 25 in June, 11 in August, 2 each in January, April, and October, and 1 in September. The butterflies were quite common, however, on 11.x at El Aguacate and on 27.xii at Cabo Rojo, so the small numbers in some cases may not represent reality. Times of collection were between 0900 and 1630 h, at temperatures between 20°C (18 km SE Constanza, 2288 m), and 38°C (Cabo Rojo).

We have taken *A. p. pantherata* feeding on the flowers of *Hibiscus rosasinensis* at Terre Rouge, on a goldenrodlike composite at Obléon, on *Tournefortia hirsutissima* at 6 km SSE Constanza and Peralta, on *Leonurus sibericus* at 10 km SE Constanza (along with numerous *A. b. briarea*), on *Bidens pilosa* at Los Pinos, on *Senecio haitiensis* at Aceitillar, on *Ixora* sp. at Peralta, often on *Ageratum conyzoides* at Vallejuelo, Aceitillar (2 occasions), El Aguacate (2 occasions), 23 and 26 km NE Cabo Rojo, and on *Acacia vogeliana* at Vallejuelo. We have seen an *A. p. pantherata* drink from mud in the back yard of a hotel (1 km S Constanza), the mud formed by the soapy runoff from a laundry, and from a seepage across a vertical rock face (18 km SE Constanza). A copulating pair was taken on 9.vii (10 km SE Constanza, 1647 m, 1000–1445 h, 28—30°C).

Specimens: Haiti: l'Ouest: Terre Rouge, 534 m, 1; 8 km SE Forêt des Pins, 1496 m, 1; Forêt des Pins, 1373 m, 1; Boutilliers Road, 732–854 m, 1; 0.3 km N Obléon, 1617 m, 1; *República Dominicana: Elías Piña:* 2 km NE Puesto Pirámide 204, 1586 m, 1; *La Vega:* 6 km SSE Constanza, 1403 m, 2; 10 km SE Constanza, 1647 m, 1; 14 km SE Constanza, 1921 m, 1; 16 km SE Constanza, 1; 18 km SE Constanza, 1586 m (old road), 2; 18 km SE Constanza, 2288 m (new road) 1; 23 km SE Constanza, 2288 m, 1; *Azua:* 5 km S Peralta, 305 m, 2; *San Juan:* 9 km E Vallejuelo, 610 m, 2; *Baoruco:* 11 km N Neiba, 519 m, 1; *Independencia:* 23 km N Los Pinos, 1739 m, 1; 4–7 km NE El Aguacate, 519–824 m, 29; *Barahona:* west slope, Sierra Martín García, 458–640 m, 7; 3 km NNE Polo, 854 m, 1; 8 km NNE Polo, 793 m, 1; *Pedernales:* 23 km NE Cabo Rojo, 488 m, 4; 24.5 km NE Cabo Rojo, 656 m, 1; 26 km NE Cabo Rojo, 732 m, 3; Las Abejas, 11 km NW Aceitillar, 1220 m, 1; Las Abejas, 12 km NW Aceitillar, 1129 m, 17; 1 km N Aceitillar, 1281 m, 5; Canote Mine, 6 km NW Aceitillar, 1495 m, 1; 5 km SE El Aguacate, 1464 m, 1; 5 km NE Los Arroyos, 1617 m, 2.

Sight records: República Dominicana: La Vega: 1 km S Constanza, 1098 m—1 seen, 8.vii; *Santiago:* 0.3 km NE Las Lagunas, 1723 m—1 seen, 2.vii; entrance of Valle de Tetero to Valle de Tetero, 1922–1342 m—several seen, 2.vii; *La Romana:* Río Cumayasa, 13.5 km W La Romana (?)—1 seen, 27.vi; *Azua:* 2.5 km W, 6.6 km N Azua, 183 m—1 seen, 8.vi; 1 seen, 21.vi; *Monseñor Nouel:* 17 km SW Piedra Blanca, 854 m—1 seen, 26.vi; *Baoruco:* 11 km N Neiba, 519 m—1 seen, 21.vi.

8. *Anetia jaegeri* Ménétriés, 1832

TL Haiti.

FW males 36–43 mm, females 36–48 mm.

Anetia jaegeri is an endemic Hispaniolan species. Brown and Heineman (1972:50) considered *A. jaegeri* conspecific with Cuban *A. cubana* Salvin, perhaps following the suggestion of this relationship by Bates (1935a:151–52). Bates had not examined *A. jaegeri* and had studied only 8 *A. cubana* from Tánamo, Prov. de Holguín. Riley (1975:38–39) kept *A. jaegeri* and *A. cubana* as distinct species; examination of Riley's plate 1, figs. 7 and 8, suggests strongly that these 2 entities are distinct species.

Hall (1925:186) considered *A. jaegeri* "one of the rarest butterflies of the island . . . one specimen from Santo Domingo . . . and one from Hayti." Riley (1975:39) stated that this butterfly is "Exceedingly rare, only some half-dozen specimens known. Habitat and life history unknown."

As is so often the case with rarities, *A. jaegeri* is not at all uncommon. It is a high-elevation butterfly that occurs on the Massif de la Selle and its northern front range Montagne Noire (but not the Morne l'Hôpital), the Massif de la Hotte, the Sierra de Neiba (both ranges), Sierra de Baoruco, and the Cordillera Central, the latter the range in which *A. jaegeri* has the most extensive distribution. Elevations range from 702 m (Monte Bonito) to 2257 m (21 km SE Constanza) on the Cordillera Central, 1891 m (1 km SW Puesto Pirámide 204) on the Sierra de Neiba, 1880 m (Morne la Visite) on the Massif de la Selle, 2300 m (Pic Macaya) on the Massif de la Hotte, and 1129 m (Las Abejas) on the Sierra de Baoruco.

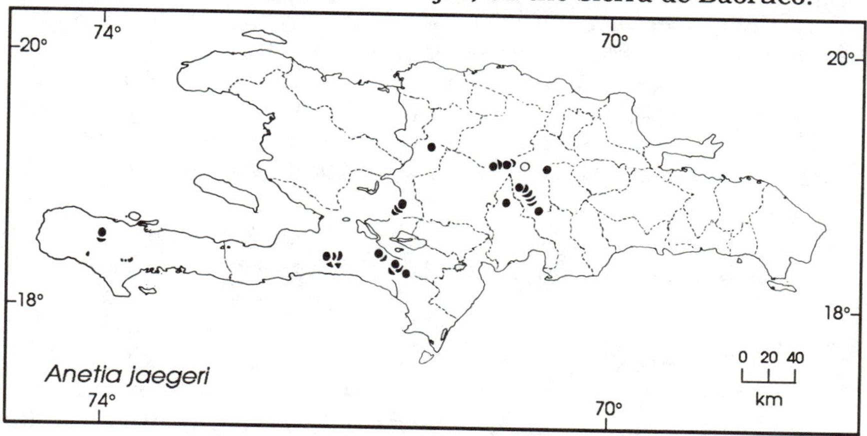

Upland habitats are either mesic hardwood forest or pine forest, with about equal frequency. At Peneau, a few *A. jaegeri* were seen and 2 taken on 23.iv; the situation there is pine forest with summer homes and many ornamental flowers. Although, prior to the above date in 1982, we had visited Peneau 4 times in previous years during July and August, we had never seen *A. jaegeri* there. *Anetia jaegeri* is often seen in the Cordillera Central along the main road between Constanza and La Horma in the pines; the butterflies may be quite abundant there, flying over meadows of *Cynoglossum amabile* (not a known nectar plant). In the fallow cabbage field near Constanza (see account of *A. b. briarea*), *A. jaegeri* was less common than *A. b. briarea*, and it too was feeding on the purple flowers of *Leonurus sibericus*. At La Horma, *A. jaegeri* was rather uncommon, flying along an open and presently shrubby and bushy ravine; at Jayaco, *A. jaegeri* favored the opening between a dense canopy and a mountain torrent in mesic hardwood forest. On occasion, *A. jaegeri* is taken along creek courses (18 km SE Constanza) and along roadsides (10 km SE Constanza).

Anetia jaegeri is slightly sexually dimorphic in size, with females larger. The coloration and pattern of the sexes are identical.

Freshly emerged individuals are darker brown than are somewhat flown specimens, which have a tannish or medium brown up. On the wing, *A. jaegeri* is immediately distinguished from its Hispaniolan congeners by its much darker coloration. All species of *Anetia* on Hispaniola fly slowly and are not easily alarmed. Like most danaids, they are most easily taken while feeding.

Most specimens are from July (66), with 35 in June and 12 in August, 9 in September, 8 in April, 2 in October, and 1 in November. October specimens are very worn. Although it is obvious that July is the period of emergence of *A. jaegeri*, the apparent abrupt decline in August may not be completely real. For instance, I recorded the species as "abundant" on 1.viii but took only 4 specimens on that date. Times of collection were between 0730 and 1640 h, with temperatures between 13°C (Valle de Tetero) and 34°C (14 km SE Constanza).

Anetia jaegeri feeds on the flowers of *Rubus* sp. (4 km NW Forêt des Pins, 21 km SE Constanza, Los Arroyos), *Leonurus sibericus* (10 km SE Constanza), *Ageratum conyzoides* and *Asclepias nivea* (Las Abejas). We observed an *A. jaegeri* drinking from a spring seepage adjacent to a creek flowing across a vertical rock face; *A. b. briarea* utilized the same seepage at the same time (18 km SE Constanza). At the same locality, *A. jaegeri* also drank from mud in the dirt road.

Specimens: Haiti: l'Ouest: 1 km NW Forêt des Pins, 1556 m, 1; 4 km NW Forêt des Pins, 1496 m, 5; Peneau, 1.6 km SW Furcy, 1464 m, 2; Morne la Visite, 1880 m, 6 (FSM); 200 m NW Scierie, 1952 m, 2 (FSM); 0.4 km S Scierie, 1900 m, 3 (FSM); *ca.* 4.8 km NW Scierie, 2187 m, 1 (FSM); *Sud:* Morne Formond, 1650–1800 m, 7 (FSM); Pic Formond, nr. top, 1900–1910 m, 2 (FSM); Pic Macaya, nr. top, 2300 m, 1 (FSM); *República Dominicana: Elías Piña:* summit, Loma Nalga de Maco, *ca.* 1990 m, 1; 21 km S Comendador, 1464 m, 3; 1 km SW Puesto Pirámide 204, 1891 m,1; 2 km NE Puesto Pirámide 204, 1586 m, 7; *Santiago:* Valle de Tetero, 1342 m, 2; entrance of Valle de Tetero to Valle de Tetero, 1922–1342 m, 6; entrance to Valle de Tetero, 1922 m, 2; *La Vega:* 3 km SW Boca del Río, 976 m, 1; 1 km SW Los Tablones, 1159 m, 1; 10 km W Jayaco, 915 m, 1; 6 km SSE Constanza, 1403 m, 1; 10 km SE Constanza. 1647 m, 12; 14 km SE Constanza, 1921 m, 5; 18 km SE Constanza, 1586 m, 21; 21 km SE Constanza, 2257 m, 1; 10 km NW La Horma, 1596 m, 6; *Azua:* 5 km SW Monte Bonito, 702 m, 1; *Pedernales:* Las Abejas, 12 km NW Aceitillar, 1129 m, 28; 5 km NE Los Arroyos, 1617 m, 12; 7 km SW El Aguacate, 1647 m, 1; 5 km SW El Aguacate, 1464 m, 2.

Sight record: República Dominicana: Santiago: entrance of Valle de Tetero to Valle de Tetero, 1922–1342 m—several seen, 2.vii.

Discussion

IN THE INTRODUCTION to the present work, I suggested that the island of Hispaniola, with its primary division into north and south islands, might be a setting against which divergences at the species or subspecies levels might have taken place in the Lepidoptera, as they have in some vertebrate groups (Amphibia and Reptilia and, to a lesser extent, Aves and Mammalia). Does the evidence support or negate this hypothesis?

A very great many Hispaniolan butterflies are ecologically and elevationally tolerant; the accounts of many species show that relatively few of them are restricted to particular elevational bands (and thus ecologies). A glance at table 1 demonstrates this fact even more fully; however, one should examine this table with the caveats noted throughout the text. Although many species have broad elevational distributions, most often (but not always) there is, within the elevational extremes, a zone or band that is the "preferred" one for a particular species. This fact will be explored more thoroughly beyond. But it is pertinent in the present context in that, insofar as known, there has been no species-level differentiation of ecologically and elevationally tolerant butterflies on the north and south islands. Some species are more or less abundant on 1 or the other of these paleoislands (due to presently unknown factors), but there are no obvious examples of species-level differentiation.

There is, however, an occasional species (*Rhinthon bushi* is an example) where there is simply too little material available to analyze what (if any) divergence there has been between north and south island populations. What material is available suggests some sort (species? subspecies?) of differentiation.

The single major exception to the above statement is of course the genus *Calisto*. As the study of Hispaniolan *Calisto* has progressed, so has the number of named species, all endemic to Hispaniola. The number of Hispaniolan species has grown from 4 recognized or named by Lathy in 1899 (*archebates, hysia, confusa, pulchella*) to 9 (the above list plus *loxias, chrysaoros, tragia, lyceia, elelea*, recognized by Bates [1935b]), to 11 (the above plus *arcas* and *grannus* [Bates, 1939]). It is, in retrospect, amusing that Bates was somewhat chagrined at this increase in species number,

Table 1.
Elevations, temperatures of collection, and occurrence on satellite islands of the Hispaniolan butterflies.

Taxon	Elev. (m)	Temp. (°C)	Satellite islands[a]
Hesperiidae			
Phocides p. bicolor	s.l.–530	29–37	—
Proteides m. sanchesi	s.l.–915	26–37	—
Epargyreus spanna	s.l.–1350	25–37	—
Polygonus l. lividus	s.l.–915	24–42	—
Chioides ixion	15–1678	23–39	—
Aguna a. haitensis	s.l.–1617	21–37	—
Urbanus p. domingo	s.l.–1464	23–39	—
Urbanus d. cramptoni	s.l.–1922	20–38	—
Astraptes talus	s.l.–1007	27–38	—
Astraptes a. anausis	s.l.–488	27–37	—
Astraptes christyi	183–1007	30	—
Astraptes h. heriul	s.l.–1220	27–40	—
Burca stillmani	s.l.–915	27–38	—
Burca hispaniolae	s.l.–1495	26–38	—
Cabares p. potrillo	s.l.–671	24–38	—
Achlyodes p. sagra	s.l.–1098	24–40	—
Anastrus s. dilloni	s.l.–1129	29–40	—
Gesta g. gesta	s.l.–1220	21–42	B
Ephyriades zephodes	s.l.–1921	21–40	G, S
Erynnis zarucco	s.l.–1990	28–42	—
Pyrgus oileus	s.l.–1373	23–40	G, S, C
Pyrgus c. odilia	s.l.–1922	24–36	—
Pyrrhocalles a. antiqua	s.l.–1129	26–39	S
Perichares ph. philetes	s.l.–2105	24–40	—
Synapte m. adoceta	61–1037	25–38	—
Cymaenes t. tripunctus	s.l.–1098	20–42	B
Rhinthon bushi	122–1678	27–32	—
Oarisma stillmani	s.l.–427	26–39	C
Polites b. loma	s.l.–1403	26–37	—
Wallengrenia druryi	s.l.–1810	19–39	S
Hylephila ph. phylea	s.l.–1586	23–39	Cab
Argon sp.	1160	—	—
Atalopedes m. apa	s.l.–1891	23–40	—
Hesperia nabokovi	s.l.–214	30–38	—
Choranthus haitensis	s.l.–1129	22–42	—
Choranthus schwartzi	488–1007	20–36	—
Choranthus melissa	732–1281	25–33	—
Paratrytone batesi	915–2300	19–31	—
Euphyes s. insolata	s.l.–1586	24–40	C
Calpodes ethlius	s.l.–702	30	—

a. Satellite islands: AV = Alto Velo; B = Beata; C = Catalina; Cab = Île à Cabrit; G = Gonâve; S = Saona.

Taxon	Elev. (m)	Temp. (°C)	Satellite islands
Panoquina s. woodruffi	s.l.–1891	19–39	—
Panoquina nero	427–1891	21–34	—
Panoquina ocola ocola	s.l.–1891	23–40	—
Panoquina ocola distipuncta	≈1520–1600	—	—
Panoquina p. panoquinoides	s.l.	32	—
Nyctelius n. nyctelius	s.l.–1281	25–37	Cab
Papilionidae			
Battus zetides	732–1990	21–33	—
Battus p. polycrates	s.l.–2288	20–42	—
Eurytides zonarius	s.l.–1617	21–38	—
Heraclides a. aristodemus	s.l.–1952	28–39	B
Heraclides machaonides	s.l.–1129	27–42	—
Heraclides a. epidaurus	s.l.–2166	26–38	—
Heraclides aristor	s.l.–854	32–38	—
Priamides p. imerius	s.l.–1220	24–37	—
Pieridae			
Ganyra j. josephina	s.l.–1496	21–42	—
Ascia m. eubotea	s.l.–2227	18–38	S, B, AV, Cab
Appias d. boydi	s.l.–1647	26–42	—
Melete s. salacia	s.l.–1891	23–39	—
Eurema l. euterpe	s.l.–1678	23–40	G, B, C
Eurema euterpiformis	s.l.–1708	21–38	Cab
Eurema d. mayobanex	183–1678	24–36	—
Eurema l. memula	s.l.–1739	23–42	—
Eurema larae	214–732	28–33	—
Eurema p. proterpia	s.l.–1891	20–40	—
Eurema d. palmira	s.l.–1647	23–39	S
Eurema elathea	s.l.–1830	26–38	G, S
Eurema l. priddyi	s.l.–946	29–36	—
Eurema pyro	s.l.–1922	21–39	—
Eurema nicippe	s.l.–1708	24–42	—
Eurema nicippiformis	s.l.–854	28–38	Cab
Nathalis iole	s.l.–2100	22–37	—
Kricogonia lyside	s.l.–1708	23–37	S, C, Cab
Zerene c. cynops	s.l.–1891	23–38	—
Anteos maerula	s.l.–2288	21–37	—
Anteos c. clorinde	122–1586	23–38	—
Phoebis th. thalestris	s.l.–2105	23–37	—
Phoebis a. rorata	s.l.–1129	26–38	—
Phoebis a. antillia	s.l.–1525	24–38	S, C
Phoebis s. sennae	s.l.–2227	18–39	G, S, Cab
Phoebis editha	s.l.–2288	20–38	—
Rhabdodryas t. watsoni	122–1007	26–38	—
Aphrissa o. browni	s.l.–1617	21–38	S
Aphrissa godartiana	s.l.–1129	24–38	—

Taxon	Elev. (m)	Temp. (°C)	Satellite islands
Aphrissa s. hispaniolae	s.l.–1129	29–35	—
Dismorphia spio	s.l.–1922	20–38	—
Lycaenidae			
Thereus abeja	1250	—	—
Allosmaitia fidena	s.l.–1403	28–37	—
Electrostrymon a. boyeri	s.l.–1098	26–37	—
Electrostrymon minikyanos	1500		—
Chlorostrymon s. simaethis	s.l.–183	30–35	—
Chlorostrymon m. maesites	s.l.–610	27–37	—
Tmolus azia	s.l.–2105	27–38	S
Nesiostrymon c. aibonito	61–1281	23–36	—
Terra hispaniola	1250	—	—
Strymon a. petioni	s.l.–610	28–37	—
Strymon c. cybirus	s.l.–1891	21–40	B
Strymon toussainti	s.l.–610	28–40	—
Strymon andrewi	732–1750	23–25	—
Strymon christophei	s.l.–610	31–35	—
Strymon limenius	s.l.–1007	24–39	—
Strymon monopeteinus	s.l.–1403	29–40	S
Strymon b. gundlachianus	s.l.–1803	25–37	—
Brephidium e. isophthalma	s.l.	28–38	—
Leptotes c. theonus	s.l.–1830	23–40	G, B, C
Leptotes idealus	≈1160	—	—
Hemiargus h. watsoni	s.l.–1891	21–39	G, B
Hemiargus c. ceraunus	s.l.–1617	23–40	C, Cab
Hemiargus t. noeli	s.l.–915	27–42	G, S, C, B, AV
Pseudochrysops b. bornoi	s.l.–610	28–38	—
Libytheidae			
Libytheana terena	s.l.–1647	21–38	—
Heliconiidae			
Agraulis v. insularis	s.l.–1891	13–39	G, S, C
Dryas i. hispaniola	s.l.–1647	26–40	G, S
Eueides m. melphis	61–589	26–38	—
Heliconius ch. churchi	s.l.–2227	18–40	G, S, C, B
Nymphalidae			
Euptoieta claudia	s.l.–1617	29–42	—
Euptoieta h. hegesia	s.l.–1647	27–42	AV, C, Cab
Atlantea cryptadia	734–857	—	—
Athanassa f. frisia	s.l.–1891	27–38	—
Antillea p. pelops	s.l.–1922	23–39	—
Vanessa virginiensis	488–2288	18–36	—
Vanessa c. cardui	s.l.–2288	21–35	—
Vanessa a. rubria	61–1617	24–32	—
Hypanartia paulla	s.l.–1922	23–34	—

Taxon	Elev. (m)	Temp. (°C)	Satellite islands
Junonia g. zonalis	s.l.–2100	19–38	G, S, C
Anartia j. saturata	s.l.–1159	23–38	G, S, C
Anartia lytrea	s.l.–1586	20–36	—
Siproeta s. stelenes	s.l.–1617	13–40	—
Adelpha gelania	s.l.–1723	13–42	—
Adelpha lapitha	183–ca. 1900	28–38	—
Myscelia aracynthia	s.l.–1647	21–38	—
Eunica t. tatilista	s.l.–2227	18–38	C, B
Eunica monima	s.l.–1129	28–42	S, C, B
Dynamine e. zetes	183–976	24–37	—
Archimestra teleboas	s.l.–1220	24–42	G, B
Lucinia s. torrebia	s.l.–915	26–38	G, B
Biblis h. hyperia	s.l.–519	29–38	—
Hamadryas a. diasia	s.l.–2227	18–40	G, B
Historis a. semele	s.l.–229	32	—
Historis o. odius	s.l.–1129	20–39	—
Colobura d. wolcotti	s.l.–1129	20–38	—
Marpesia chiron	s.l.–1129	27–38	—
Marpesia e. dospassosi	s.l.–1708	21–42	S
Apaturidae			
Anaea troglodyta	s.l.–1922	23–40	—
Memphis johnsoni	305–1678	33–37	—
Memphis v. verticordia	s.l.–1617	27–38	—
Siderone g. nemesis	s.l.–915	28–38	—
Archaeoprepona d. amphitoe	s.l.–915	27–40	—
Asterocampa i. idyja	s.l.–1129	24–39	—
Doxocopa thoe	s.l.–1129	24–40	—
Satyridae			
Calisto archebates	1129–1891	21–33	—
Calisto loxias	1525–1910	28	—
Calisto wetherbeei	≈1990	—	—
Calisto chrysaoros	1007–1910	21–30	—
Calisto galii	549–2227	18–38	—
Calisto choneupsilon	976–1891	23–28	—
Calisto arcas	1723–2135	24–28	—
Calisto tragia	1129–2100	21–29	—
Calisto g. grannus	1159–2288	16–34	—
Calisto g. dilemma	1098–1641	25–32	—
Calisto phoinix	1007	33–37	—
Calisto amazona	1159–1922	13–29	—
Calisto dystacta	549–732	26–35	—
Calisto micrommata	1586–1891	23–29	—
Calisto sommeri	1496–1952	21–30	—
Calisto micheneri	(1525)	—	—
Calisto hysia	153–1910	23–38	—
Calisto batesi	s.l.–1708	20–40	—

Taxon	Elev. (m)	Temp. (°C)	Satellite islands
Calisto aleucosticha	610–640+	28–34	—
Calisto confusa	s.l.–1922	13–40	—
Calisto obscura	s.l.–1922	23–42	S, B
Calisto gonzalezi	183	33–37	—
Calisto debarriera	950–1220	—	—
Calisto neiba	671–1586	23–33	—
Calisto lyceia	s.l.	—	S, C
Calisto crypta	s.l.–366	28–36	—
Calisto franciscoi	s.l.–397	28–37	—
Calisto hendersoni	s.l.	31–33	—
Calisto raburni	519–580	29–32	—
Calisto schwartzi	1251–1373	25–31	—
Calisto montana	(1373)	—	—
Calisto clydoniata	1586–1891	23–28	—
Calisto clenchi	1671–1950	21–30	—
Calisto elelea	671–1464	25–33	—
Calisto ainigma	930	—	—
Calisto p. pulchella	s.l.–1464	28–36	—
Calisto p. darlingtoni	1159–2074	18–32	—
Ithomiidae			
Greta d. quisqueya	793–1220	28–35	—
Greta d. charadra	732–1922	20–32	—
Greta d. calimete	1647	20–30	—
Greta d. galii	1037–1647	20–30	—
Danaidae			
Danaus g. cleothera	s.l.–2105	24–39	—
Danaus e. tethys	s.l.–671	26–38	—
Danaus p. megalippe	s.l.–1880	19–39	S
Danaus cleophile	61–1922	24–38	—
Lycorea c. cleobaea	s.l.–1129	23–38	—
Anetia b. briarea	s.l.–2288	18–38	—
Anetia p. pantherata	185–2288	20–38	—
Anetia jaegeri	702–2300	13–34	—

since he apologized (p. 47) that his own contribution, increasing the recognition of Hispaniolan species to 9 named forms, resulted in a very large number of species! Clench (1943a, 1943b) added 2 species (*micheneri, montana*), and Michener (1943) added *batesi* and *obscura*, bringing the total to 15. It was this number Riley (1975) recognized (although he considered *batesi* a subspecies of *hysia*).

But increased collecting on Hispaniola has revealed the existence of *galii* (Schwartz, 1983), *neiba, sommeri, micrommata, clydoniata*, and *clenchi* (Schwartz and Gali, 1984), *aleucosticha* (Correa and Schwartz, 1985), *crypta, franciscoi, hendersoni, raburni*, and *schwartzi* (Gali, 1985), *choneupsilon* (Schwartz, 1985), *ainigma* (Johnson, Quinter, and Matusik, 1987), *phoinix, amazona, dystacta* (Gonzalez, 1987), *gonzalezi* (Schwartz, 1988), and *wetherbeei* (Schwartz and Gonzalez, 1988). From discussions in the text, it should be obvious that the end is probably not yet in sight.

Calisto debarriera Clench is recognized herein as a species distinct from *C. confusa* (Riley, 1975:50). Munroe (1950:222) considered *C. debarriera* a valid species, basing this judgment on the slight differences in the penis compared with that of *C. confusa*; the taxon has been known from only 4 specimens. Its stated range is indeed peculiar (Massif de la Hotte, Massif du Nord near Ennery). Brown and Heineman (1972:51) considered *C. debarriera* a valid Hispaniolan species. There may be 2 species involved under this name.

Of the species of *Calisto* now recognized, 19 can be conveniently grouped as north island species (*wetherbeei, galii, choneupsilon, arcas, grannus, phoinix, amazona, dystacta, micrommata, micheneri, gonzalezi, aleucosticha, neiba, lyceia, crypta, franciscoi, montana, clydoniata, ainigma*). To these may be added *batesi* and *pulchella*, both of which appear to have evolved on the north island and to have invaded the south island. *Calisto franciscoi* has invaded the south island (Península de Barahona). Thus, a total of 22 species of *Calisto* shows north island affinities. The south island species number 11 (*archebates, loxias, chrysaoros, tragia, sommeri, hysia, debarriera, hendersoni, raburni, schwartzi, clenchi*, and *elelea*). *Calisto elelea* has invaded the north island; perhaps *C. tragia* has done so also. There are 2 species (*confusa, obscura*) that are islandwide and whose origins (north or south island) are purely speculative.

The north-south island dichotomy is quite clearly shown in *Calisto*. But this dichotomy is correlated more with the fact that *Calisto* are primarily high-elevation butterflies (with the exceptions of

C. confusa and *C. obscura*, the 2 islandwide species, and some of the *lyceia* complex) than with the existence of the 2 portions of Hispaniola. Most endemic north island *Calisto* are restricted to either the Cordillera Central (*wetherbeei, galii, arcas, grannus, phoinix, amazona, dystacta, micheneri, aleucosticha, ainigma*), the Sierra de Neiba (*choneupsilon, micrommata, neiba, clydoniata*), or (presumably) the Monts Cahos (*montana*). *Calisto pulchella* is represented by an upland subspecies (*darlingtoni*) in the Cordillera Central. The south island species occur in the Massif de la Hotte (*loxias, debarriera*), the Massif de la Selle (*raburni, clenchi*), or the Sierra de Baoruco (*schwartzi*). The remaining south island species (except *hendersoni;* see beyond) occur in combinations of the above ranges: Massif de la Hotte–Massif de la Selle–Baoruco (*chrysaoros*), and Massif de la Selle–Baoruco (*archebates, tragia, sommeri, elelea*). *Calisto hysia* is widespread on the south island; despite its broad elevational range (153–1910 m), this species is commonest at moderate to high elevations and occurs on all ranges.

In these primarily upland species, there are some obvious species-pairs of related taxa, 1 member on each of the paleoislands: *clydoniata-clenchi, aleucosticha-hysia;* 1 species-trio (*galii-choneupsilon-chrysaoros*); and 1 species-sextet (*grannus-phoinix-amazona-dystacta-micrommata-sommeri*). On the south island itself, there is a species-pair (*loxias-archebates*) on the Massifs de la Hotte and la Selle. Some species are so very distinctive both morphologically and genitally (*arcas*) that their relationships to other *Calisto* are in doubt. The apparent relationship between the predominantly north island *C. batesi* and the south island *C. hysia* is real, despite marked genitalic differences; the north island *C. hysia* representative seems to be *C. aleucosticha*.

A second group of *Calisto* showing a north island–south island dichotomy is the *lyceia* complex. The north island species (*lyceia, crypta, franciscoi*) are lowland area butterflies, in contrast to the 2 south island species (*raburni, schwartzi*), which occur in the uplands of the Massif de la Selle and the Sierra de Baoruco. *Calisto hendersoni* occurs on the extreme southern side of the Valle de Neiba and thus nominally on or very near the south island; but its affinities are with the north island trio of species, and not with the 2 south island species. Of the members of this complex, the 2 truly south island species are the most distinctive not only from each other but from the balance of the complex as well.

The *lyceia* complex species are adapted for primarily lowland xeric habitats but include upland pine forest. The scattered distribution of the members of the complex suggests that the species are but remnants of a once more widespread "species" that have persisted in regions where the ecological requirements still persist. Thus, *C. lyceia* occurs on Isla Saona and Isla Catalina, 2 hot and dry islands off southeastern Hispaniola, but is absent from the adjacent mesic mainland. *Calisto crypta* occurs in the xeric portion of the Valle de Cibao far to the northwest. *Calisto franciscoi* occurs in the Valle de Neiba-Llanos de Azua and on the Península de Barahona, and *C. hendersoni* in the western Valle de Neiba. *Calisto raburni* has been found only at the type-locality, at elevations of 519–580 m in xeric deciduous forest, and *C. schwartzi* in pine forest at 1251–1373 m. At least the lowland species are widely separated (except for *C. hendersoni* and *C. franciscoi* in the Valle de Neiba, where their ranges approximate each other within 15 km).

This fractured distribution of the *lyceia* complex suggests that the basal member of the complex (perhaps akin to *C. franciscoi*, which today has the broadest known distribution) was once widespread, occurring from the (Cul de Sac and) Valle de Neiba east as far as the southeastern coast of Hispaniola and northwest into the Valle de Cibao along the east base of the Cordillera Central by some presently unguessable route. As the ecologies of the intervening areas changed from xeric to mesic, the populations of the *lyceia* complex became more restricted geographically and differentiated into the species present today. There is little doubt that other members of this complex remain to be discovered; likely sites include all of Haiti that is xeric (edge of the Golfe de la Gonâve to the Presqu'île du Nord-Ouest; eastern Plaine du Nord; Cul de Sac plain) and the Valle de San Juan. The presumed occurrence of a member of the *lyceia* complex on the Península de Samaná remains to be confirmed. If the population there occurs in a mesic area (as it must), then it is possible that *lyceia* complex members may be even more widespread and scattered than now considered probable.

*
* *

The lepidopteran fauna of the Hispaniolan satellite islands presents some interesting facts. It should be obvious that any discussion of the satellite islands and their butterflies suffers from 2 large gaps: (1) several islands (Tortue, Île-à-Vache) are completely unrepresented in my collection, and (2) the faunal list for any of the islands is almost certainly far from complete. Even with these deficiencies admitted, some observations are still possible.

A total of 42 species is known from all the satellite islands combined (Gonâve, Saona, Catalina, Beata, Alto Velo, Île à Cabrit). Île à Cabrit is tiny and close to the Haitian mainland; its fauna consists of 2 hesperiids (*H. ph. phylea, N. n. nyctelius*), 4 pierids (*A. m. eubotea, E. euterpiformis, E. nicippiformis, K. lyside*), 1 lycaenid (*H. c. ceraunus*), and 1 nymphalid (*E. h. hegesia*). Of these species, *H. ph. phylea, N. n. nyctelius, E. euterpiformis*, and *E. nicippiformis* (= 6%) are not known from any other offshore island. Of these Île à Cabrit butterflies, none is surprising (see text, however, on *E. euterpiformis*); the least likely to occur on a xeric islet is *N. n. nyctelius*. Although this skipper favors mesic situations, these "oases" of mesicity may occur in otherwise xeric areas.

The largest known fauna of the satellites is that of Isla Saona. This is without question due to the work there of R. W. Henderson and his associates and probably reflects more accurately what and how many species one may expect on a xeric island of its size and proximity to the mainland. The fauna includes 4 hesperiids (*E. zephodes, P. oileus, P. a. antiqua, W. druryi*), 7 pierids (*A. m. eubotea, E. d. palmira, E. elathea, K. lyside, Ph. a. antillia, Ph. s. sennae, A. o. browni*), 3 lycaenids (*S. monopeteinus, T. azia, H. t. noeli*), 3 heliconiids (*A. v. insularis, D. i. hispaniola, H. ch. churchi*), 4 nymphalids (*J. g. zonalis, A. j. saturata, E. monima, M. e. dospassosi*), 2 satyrids (*C. obscura, C. lyceia*), and 1 danaid (*D. p. megalippe*). Of these, 9 (*P. a. antiqua, W. druryi, E. d. palmira, Ph. a. antillia, A. o. browni, S. monopeteinus, T. azia, M. e. dospassosi, D. p. megalippe*) are known only from Isla Saona and comprise 21% of the species known from the Hispaniolan satellites. Of the species known from Saona, *A. o. browni* is the least expected (I know too little about *S. monopeteinus* to make any pertinent comment). The occurrence of *D. p. megalippe* only on Saona is surprising, but the Monarch is relatively uncommon near and at sea level on Hispaniola. Its occurrence on other satellites has probably been overlooked or ignored.

Île de la Gonâve is known to harbor 16 species: 2 hesperiids (*E. zephodes, P. oileus*), 3 pierids (*E. l. euterpe, E. elathea, Ph. s. sennae*), 3 lycaenids (*L. c. theonus, H. h. watsoni, H. t. noeli*), 3 heliconiids (*A. v. insularis, D. i. hispaniola, H. ch. churchi*), and 5 nymphalids (*J. g. zonalis, A. j. saturata, A. teleboas, L. s. torrebia, H. a. diasia*). None is known only from Gonâve.

There are 16 species from Isla Beata: 2 hesperiids (*Gesta g. gesta, C. t. tripunctus*), 1 papilionid (*H. a. aristodemus*), 2 pierids (*A. m. eubotea, E. l. euterpe*), 4 lycaenids (*S. c. cybirus, H. h. watsoni, H. t. noeli, L. c. theonus*), 1 heliconiid (*H. ch. churchi*), 5 nymphalids

(*E. monima, A. teleboas, E. t. tatilista, H. a. diasia, L. s. torrebia*), and 1 satyrid (*C. obscura*). Four of these species (*Gesta g. gesta, C. t. tripunctus, H. a. aristodemus, S. c. cybirus*) are known only from Isla Beata (= 10%).

Isla Catalina is known to have 3 hesperiids (*P. oileus, O. stillmani, E. s. insolata*), 3 pierids (*E. l. euterpe, K. lyside, Ph. a. antillia*), 2 lycaenids (*L. c. theonus, H. c. ceraunus*), 2 heliconiids (*A. v. insularis, H. ch. churchi*), 5 nymphalids (*E. h. hegesia, J. g. zonalis, A. j. saturata, E. t. tatilista, E. monima*), and 1 satyrid (*C. lyceia*). Only 2 of these (*O. stillmani, E. s. insolata*) are unknown from all other satellites (= 5%).

Finally, Isla Alto Velo has 1 pierid (*A. m. eubotea*), 1 lycaenid (*H. t. noeli*), and 1 nymphalid (*E. h. hegesia*). None occurs only on this islet.

If one disregards Île à Cabrit, the other satellites may be ranked as follows: (1) Gonâve, area 658 km^2, channel width 19 km; (2) Saona, 111 km^2, 2 km; (3) Beata, 47 km^2, 4 km; (4) Catalina, 18 km^2, 2 km; (5) Isla Alto Velo, 1.47 km^2, 53 km from Cabo Beata, 25 km from Isla Beata (data from Schwartz, 1970, and Ottenwalder, 1979). Although the positive correlation is not perfect, the larger the island, the more speciose is its butterfly fauna. The rank of the islands by size (Gonâve, Saona, Beata, Catalina, Alto Velo) is comparable to the number of butterfly species on each (Saona, [Catalina and Gonâve and Beata—each with 16 species], Alto Velo). The number of Saonan species is disproportionately large due to the significant collections made there. Again, ranking the islands by the width (in km) of the channels separating them from the mainland (Gonâve, Beata, Saona and Catalina, Alto Velo) correlates well with the number of butterfly species on each.

At the 2 extremes, however, there are "extenuating circumstances": Île de la Gonâve is very large, has a broad (19 km) channel separating it from the mainland and in addition has a diversity of ecologies, from barren and xeric coastal regions to upland (but not very high) hills or low mountains with mesic conditions. The latter habitats have not as yet been sampled for butterflies; they should reveal other species in the mesic uplands, thereby increasing the Gonâve butterfly faunal list. Isla Alto Velo is a tiny islet, not only far removed from Cabo Beata on the mainland, but also from Isla Beata, via which its fauna has (presumably) arrived. Thus, Isla Alto Velo is in "double jeopardy" in that its fauna has been derived via a stepping-stone island between itself and the mainland. Isla Alto Velo is not ecologically diverse, but there are other xerophilic butterflies on the Península de Barahona that one might expect on Isla Beata and thus on Isla Alto Velo as well. It seems reasonable that the faunas of any of the satellite islands have been affected by (1) size of the island, (2) distance from the mainland source, and (3) diversity of habitats.

The composition of the known butterfly fauna of the satellites is indeed interesting, if one examines the listing (table 1) by families. Skippers form 24% of the Hispaniolan rhopaloceran fauna (46 species), yet only 9 species occur on the islands and form 21% of their fauna. There are 8 species of Hispaniolan papilionids (4% of the fauna), yet only 1 species (*H. a. aristodemus*) occurs on the satellites and forms only 3% of the fauna. Other papilionids that are confidently expected on the satellites include *E. zonarius* and *H. aristor*, both stenoxerophiles.

No libytheids, apaturids, or ithomiids are known from any satellite. The first 2 families are certainly expected; the ithomiids are not, since they are upland forest stenomesophiles.

The heliconiids, with the exception of *E. m. melphis*, are represented by the 3 remaining species (*A. v. insularis*, *D. i. hispaniola*, *H. ch. churchi*; 7%); but interestingly, *D. i. hispaniola* is unknown from Catalina and Beata, both islands with wooded areas.

The nymphalids form a large component (15%) of the Hispaniolan fauna, yet only 9 species occur on the satellites (= 21%). Gonâve has the largest representation (5 species), Saona and Catalina rank second (4 species), with 4 species on Beata and 1 on Alto Velo. Interestingly, 2 species not only are included in this list (*A. teleboas*, *L. s. torrebia*) but also occur on 2 islands (Gonâve, Beata). Both are weakly flying and fairly sedentary species that would seem unlikely candidates for overseas movement. Present evidence suggests that the Gonâve population of *A. teleboas* has been on that island long enough to have differentiated from its mainland relative (see account of *A. teleboas*). Unexpected absences are *B. h. hyperia* on Isla Saona and Isla Catalina (the species is abundant on the adjacent mainland) and *H. a. diasia* from all islands other than Gonâve and Beata. The latter must surely be an oversight in collecting.

There are 31 species of Hispaniolan pierids, forming 16% of the fauna; of them, 10 occur on the satellites and form 23% of their fauna. *Ascia m. eubotea*, widespread on the main island and ecologically tolerant but commonest in xeric areas, occurs on 4 islands (including Île à Cabrit), more than any other pierid. The only unexpected pierid on the satellites is *A. o. browni* on Saona; the species is rather uncommon on Hispaniola.

The lycaenids are represented by 24 species (12% of the Hispaniolan fauna), and 7 species have reached the satellites (16% of that fauna). The presence there of *T. azia* is of extreme interest; the absence of *B. e. isophthalma* is unaccountable. We searched for this diminutive species in extensive *Batis maritima* stands on Catalina without success (14.viii). The absence of other theclines, most especially *Strymon* (except for *S. c. cybirus* on Beata and *S. monopeteinus* on Saona), is puzzling but may be due to the lack of concentration on collecting small butterflies. Of the blues, one can expect *Ps. b. bornoi* on Gonâve and Beata at least. The species of *Hemiargus*, most especially *H. c. ceraunus*, now known only from Île à Cabrit and Catalina, must be more widely distributed on the islets. It is noteworthy that *H. t. noeli* (stenoxerophilic) occurs on 5 islands (including remote Alto Velo, where it is common), whereas *H. c. ceraunus* (also xerophilic) is unknown from all except Cabrit and Catalina.

The danaids, whose 8 species form 4% of the Hispaniolan fauna and who (at least *Danaus*) are strong flyers, are also almost unknown from the satellites; only *D. p. megalippe* is known from Isla Saona, where it is common. One would not expect any *Anetia* nor *D. cleophile* on the satellites, but *D. g. cleothera*, *D. e. tethys*, and *L. c. cleobaea* should occur on most of them.

The satyrids, with 35 mainland species (18% of the fauna), have only 2 species on the satellites (5% of that fauna). But these are the xerophilic *C. lyceia* on 2 islands (Saona, Catalina) and *C. obscura* on 2 (Saona, Beata). Of the small and widely distributed *Calisto*, *C. obscura* is euryxerophilic; its occurrence on these 2 islands agrees with its distribution on the mainland. *Calisto obscura* also should occur on Gonâve. It would not be surprising to discover a member of the *lyceia* complex on Gonâve at least and on Beata as well.

Finally, comparing the percentages of each family's contribution to the Hispaniolan mainland fauna with its percentage of the satellite fauna, the largest difference (= least number of species represented) is found with the Satyridae (18% on the main island, 5% on the satellites) and the smallest difference with the Danaidae and Papilionidae (each 4% of the mainland fauna, 2% of the satellite fauna). The Libytheidae, Ithomiidae, and Apaturidae, since they remain unknown from the satellites, are not included in these calculations.

***

Of the 196 species of Rhopalocera known on Hispaniola, 133

are known to occur at sea level (68%). A few additional species (6) occur as low as 15–61 m and probably reach sea level; if these are used in the above computation, then 139 species (71%) occur or probably occur at sea level. Of these butterflies that occur at sea level, 8 are limited to that elevation or slightly above (less than 215 m): *H. nabokovi, Ch. s. simaethis, S. a. petioni, B. e. isophthalma, C. gonzalezi, C. lyceia, C. franciscoi,* and *C. hendersoni.*

A second peak lies between 900 and 1199 m, with 30 species extending from sea level into this elevational band: *P. m. sanchesi, P. l. lividus, A. talus, B. stillmani, A. p. sagra, A. s. dilloni, P. a. antigua, S. m. adoceta, C. t. tripunctus, Ch. haitensis, H. machaonides, P. p. imerius, E. l. priddyi, Ph. a. rorata, A. godartiana, E. a. boyeri, A. s. hispaniolae, E. monima, S. limenius, H. t. noeli, A. j. saturata, L. s. torrebia, H. o. odius, C. d. wolcotti, M. chiron, S. g. nemesis, A. d. amphitoe, A. i. idyja, D. thoe,* and *L. c. cleobaea.*

A third peak lies at 1600–1699 m, with 15 species: *Ch. ixion, A. a. haitensis, E. zarucco, E. zonarius, A. d. boydi, E. l. euterpe, E. d. palmira, A. o. browni, H. c. ceraunus, L. terena, E. claudia, E. h. hegesia, S. s. stelenes, M. aracynthia,* and *M. v. verticordia.*

Finally, 10 species occur from sea level to between 2200 and 2299 m: *B. p. polycrates, A. m. eubotea, A. maerula, Ph. s. sennae, Ph. editha, H. ch. churchi, V. c. cardui, E. t. tatilista, H. a. diasia,* and *A. b. briarea.* In this last high-elevation list, the absence of hesperiids is noteworthy. The highest elevation reached by any skipper that also occurs at sea level is 2105 m (= *P. ph. philetes*). Note also the absence of sea-level lycaenids at high elevation; the greatest elevation reached by sea-level lycaenids is 2105 m (*T. azia*).

The above data suggest that there is a widespread lowland (sea-level) butterfly fauna, a large part of which extends upward to high elevations, with peaks at 900–1199 m, 1600–1699 m, and 2200–2299 m. Of this lowland fauna, there are also a few species limited from sea level to 215 m.

However, a truly upland butterfly fauna does exist on Hispaniola, although it is distinctly smaller than the lowland fauna. One may use the elevation of Constanza (1100 m) as that which delimits an upland from a less high butterfly fauna. Choice of this locality as a base point is not arbitrary. As one ascends the Cordillera Central from Constanza, he quickly encounters butterflies that he has not seen at Constanza or below. This is in part due to the presence of pine forest and probably also to the cool temperatures above 1100 m in these (and other) mountains.

Disregarding *Calisto* for the moment, the upland butterfly fauna is composed of 12 species: *Ch. melissa* (732–1281 m), *P. batesi* (915–2300 m), *B. zetides* (732–1990 m), *A. c. clorinde* (122–1586 m), *E. d. mayobanex* (183–1678 m), *N. c. aibonito* (61–1281 m), *V. virginiensis* (488–2288 m), *M. johnsoni* (305–1678 m), *G. diaphana* (732–1922 m), *D. cleophile* (61–1922 m), *A. p. pantherata* (185–2288 m), and *A. jaegeri* (702–2300 m). These are all species that are most common in uplands, and none reaches sea level.

To the above list may be added 2 other species: *Ch. schwartzi* (488–1007 m) and *D. e. zetes* (183–976 m). Although neither of these species reaches the high elevations demanded for them to be included in the high-elevation list, they do approach them. Neither of them, on the other hand, may be appropriately considered a member of the lowland fauna.

The satyrids require separate consideration. Of the 35 species of *Calisto*, only *C. batesi*, *C. confusa*, *C. obscura*, *C. lyceia*, *C. crypta*, *C. franciscoi*, *C. hendersoni*, and *C. pulchella* are predominantly lowland, with (among them) *C. batesi* reaching an elevation of 1708 m and *C. pulchella* (subsp. *darlingtoni*) an elevation of 2074 m. The remaining species not listed above are all limited to moderate to high elevations, between 153 m (*C. hysia*) and 2288 m (*C. g. grannus*).

What is remarkable about the satyrids is the very high percentage (83%) of species that are upland butterflies. Only the Ithomiidae has a higher percentage (100%), but that family has only 1 Hispaniolan species (*G. diaphana*). The family that ranks second to the satyrids is the Danaidae, of which 38% of the species are upland butterflies. More than twice as many (relatively) satyrids as danaids are upland species.

It would be most satisfying to be able to show that in any mountain range there is an altitudinal sequence of species of *Calisto* as one proceeds from middle to high elevations. Such a schema is not possible, even for those 3 ranges that are the best known (Massif de la Selle, Cordillera Central, Sierra de Neiba), for 2 major reasons.(1) Species of *Calisto* are often tightly circumscribed and bound to particular habitats in the uplands. These habitats vary in elevation according to slope exposure and direction. Thus, mesic deciduous forest may, on an exposed slope with poor soils, occur only at a higher elevation than it does on a shaded and well-watered slope with soils that retain water. Combining elevations for all sites of collection for a species obscures these differences, and an elevational range may be clouded by this combination. (2) In some cases (notably the Massif de la Selle), montane vegetation has been so massively disturbed that fine details of local distributions are no longer determinable. Thus, a *Calisto* that may occur only in deciduous forest on 1 portion of a range may be absent simply because of the destruction of habitat from another portion of that same range.

Yet, with these provisos, we can reach some generalizations about upland *Calisto*. On the Cordillera Central, there are 10 endemic species and 1 endemic subspecies (*C. p. darlingtoni*). Of them, *C. aleucosticha* occurs at moderate elevations (610–640+ m), and *C. wetherbeei, C. arcas, C. grannus, C. phoinix, C. amazona, C. micheneri, C. ainigma*, and *C. p. darlingtoni* occur in the high uplands (1007–2288 m). *Calisto galii* is unusual in that it has a broad elevational band (549–2227 m) almost encompassing those of all other upland species. *Calisto dystacta* has a distribution of 549–732 m at moderate elevations.

In the Sierra de Neiba, 2 species (*C. micrommata, C. clydoniata*) are the most distinctly upland, occurring beween 1586 and 1891 m. *Calisto neiba* occurs lower than these 2 species, between 671 and 1586 m. *Calisto choneupsilon* has an elevational range almost encompassing the distributions of the 3 other species (976–1891 m).

Of the 7 Massif de la Selle species, *C. raburni* (519–580 m) occurs below all other endemics, with *C. elelea* (also known from the Cordillera Central) next lowest (671–1464 m). *Calisto chrysaoros* and *C. sommeri* have narrow elevational ranges (1007–1910 m and 1496–1952 m), almost encompassed by the ranges of *C. archebates* (1129–1891 m) and *C. tragia* (1129–2100 m). The elevations for *C. clenchi* (1671–1950 m) suggest that this species is associated elevationally with *C. chrysaoros* and *C. sommeri* and is a high-elevation (in contrast to moderate-elevation) species.

*
* *

In the above discussions, I have deliberately made no mention of the new species described (Johnson and Matusik, 1988) from Las Abejas. The Las Abejas area on the Sierra de Baoruco near the Dominico-Haitian border is one of extreme interest, and it merits its own comments.

Prior to the new taxa named by Johnson and Matusik, 2 other species (*Ch. melissa, C. schwartzi*) were named from this area. Of them, *Ch. melissa* is now known to occur elsewhere in this mountainous area and in the Sierra Martín García, but *C. schwartzi* is, as far as known, limited to but broadly distributed in the pine forests of the Las Abejas area. These species are both discussed in detail in the text.

Las Abejas is a broad area in the uplands of the Sierra de Baoruco. At higher elevations, these mountains are clothed in pine forest, much of it untouched, thanks to the former guardianship of the Alcoa Exploration Company. Since 1985, this region has been returned to the Dominican government and now forms a large part of a national park with protected flora and fauna. In some areas of this region, pine forest is replaced by luxuriant hardwood forest; Las Abejas is one of these forested areas. Even during the tenure of the Alcoa Exploration Company, squatters moved into some of the forested areas, slashed and burned the hardwoods, and planted crops. The area is so remote and seldom visited that the invaders were able to complete their destruction before authorities were aware of what had transpired. Since 1985 and despite the designation of this region as a national park, such destruction of hardwoods has intensified; the pine forest is little affected, since pines grow there on a rock-on-rock substrate, unfit for cultivation. But the hardwoods are being destroyed; while traveling on the Alcoa road in 1986, Gonzalez and I could see, on the range before us, as many as 10 fires on the mountains in a single morning. Any destruction in the Las Abejas region is truly unfortunate (one can think only of the mountainous regions of Haiti in comparison), since Las Abejas has not only a rich but also a most interesting fauna.

Johnson and Matusik (1988) named 6 new taxa of rhopalocerans from the Las Abejas region: *Panoquina ocola distipuncta* (Hesperiidae), and the lycaenids *Electrostrymon minikyanos*, *Strymon andrewi*, *Thereus abeja*, *Terra hispaniola*, and *Leptotes idealus*. All are mentioned in the text, but I have had little or no experience with any of them in the field. All may belong to the high upland lepidopteran fauna.

Several of these species are known only from Las Abejas, and it is of course possible that they occur only there. *Calisto schwartzi*, another species described from Las Abejas, is endemic to that area, thus making 7 species known only from Las Abejas (*S. andrewi* is also known from the immediately adjacent portion of the Massif de la Selle on the Dominico-Haitian border). *Choranthus melissa* has its "center" in the Las Abejas area, where it is abundant, but it occurs on the north slope of the Massif de la Selle and on the Sierra Martín García to the east.

The abundance of new taxa named from the Las Abejas area is striking. No other Hispaniolan area has revealed such a diverse undescribed rhopaloceran fauna. Several factors are at work: (1)

the interdigitation of 2 very basic forest types (hardwoods and pines) favors species diversity; (2) the protection previously offered this area has to a large extent prevented the cutting and destruction of hardwood forests; (3) the inaccessibility of the area except by the old and formerly private Alcoa road and by foot. It seems very likely that the new taxa named from Las Abejas are broadly distributed in the uplands of the Sierra de Baoruco, and some of them were probably at one time distributed in Haiti on the pine-clad uplands of the Massif de la Selle. Thus, although 7 species are now known only from Las Abejas, it seems very likely that, with increased collecting on the Sierra de Baoruco, many of them will be found to occur elsewhere in the presently inaccessible parts of that range. The occurrences of some of these species in Haiti is much less certain, due to the immense deforestation of both pines and hardwoods in the uplands of that country.

⁂

The lowest temperature at which we have taken or observed any Hispaniolan butterfly is 13°C; 6 species (*A. v. insularis, S. s. stelenes, A. gelania, C. amazona, C. confusa, A. jaegeri*) were flying at this low temperature. Hispaniolan satyrids regularly fly during overcast or even rainy weather (see accounts of *C. archebates* and *C. sommeri*), when insolation is minimal and thus temperatures are low. In addition, *C. grannus* is 1 of the high upland Cordillera Central species and thus must be tolerant of low temperatures in order to survive; it has been collected at 16°C.

At the next lowest temperature (18°C), we have seen or taken 9 species. Of these, 3 (*C. galii, C. p. darlingtoni, A. b. briarea*) are montane species, and 2 of them are satyrids. One, *V. virginiensis* is a temperate-zone butterfly and would be expected to be tolerant of the low temperatures of high uplands. Perhaps the most interesting are 4 species (*A. m. eubotea, Ph. s. sennae, H. ch. churchi, H. a. diasia*) that are widely distributed from sea level to high elevations. These species obviously have broad temperature tolerances which allow them to survive in the high uplands with low temperatures, localities from which more tropical lowland species are barred. The remaining species (*E. t. tatilista*) is much more common at low than at high elevations (no higher than 1098 m elsewhere on Hispaniola). It has a broad elevational range and thus is tolerant of the low temperatures at the upper elevational extreme of its distribution.

The highest temperature at which we have taken or observed

Hispaniolan butterflies is 42°C. At this temperature, we have taken 19 species: *P. l. lividus*, *G. g. gesta*, *E. zarucco*, *C. t. tripunctus*, *Ch. haitensis*, *B. p. polycrates*, *H. machaonides*, *G. j. josephina*, *A. d. boydi*, *E. l. memula*, *E. nicippe*, *H. t. noeli*, *E. claudia*, *E. h. hegesia*, *A. gelania*, *E. monima*, *A. teleboas*, *M. e. dospassosi*, and *C. obscura*. This list includes 5 hesperiids, 2 papilionids, 4 pierids, and 1 lycaenid, 6 nymphalids, and 1 satyrid. There are no hesperiids in the list of 9 species at low temperatures, yet the skippers comprise 26% of the Rhopalocera at high temperatures. Although one might expect that the high-temperature list would include a very large number of xerophiles, this is not the case, although *H. t. noeli* and *E. h. hegesia* are so considered. It is pertinent that *C. obscura*, of the Hispaniolan satyrids, is the only small *Calisto* that is euryxerophilic and occurs on the mainland and Saona and Beata.

The rarity of xerophiles in this high-temperature list is suggestive. I have shown in the discussion of xerophilic *H. nabokovi* and *C. hendersoni*, for instance, that the period of activity of these butterflies is in the morning, when temperatures are relatively low and "cool." As the temperature rises in the afternoon, many xerophiles disappear; there is no certainty that they reappear in the late afternoon as temperatures fall.

⁂

Table 2 presents a categorization of 130 species of Hispaniolan butterflies as to their habitat preferences. The remaining 66 species are not included because they are widely distributed and seem to have no habitat preferences (heliconiids except *E. m. melphis*, for instance), they are restricted to peculiar and specialized habitats (*P. p. panoquinoides*, *B. e. isophthalma*), they are most often encountered in disturbed areas or in ecotonal ones (roadsides, fields, clearings), or they inhabit situations that are not readily and clearly assigned to 1 of the 5 habitat types listed here. Such omission should not be disturbing. Natural phenomena do not fall readily into man-made categories, and the association between butterflies and more or less natural habitats is no exception.

The butterflies inhabiting *Acacia* scrub and forest may be considered stenoxerophiles, those from xeric woods and forests euryxerophiles; butterflies from low- to moderate-elevation mesic forest and pseudoforest are stenomesophilic, as are those from upland mesic broadleaf forest. The latter occur (or at least have their greatest concentrations) in upland areas. Those species that are

Table 2.

Butterflies of Hispaniola associated with 5 major habitat types. Not all species are included (see text).

I. *Acacia* scrub and forest, including *Uniola virgata* stands

B. stillmani	*L. c. theonus*
B. hispaniolae	*H. c. ceraunus*
O. stillmani	*H. t. noeli*
H. nabokovi	*Ps. b. bornoi*
E. zonarius	*E. claudia*
H. a. aristodemus	*E. h. hegesia*
H. aristor	*J. g. zonalis*
E. elathea	*L. s. torrebia*
E. nicippiformis	*C. lyceia*
K. lyside	*C. crypta*
Ch. s. simaethis	*C. franciscoi*
Ch. m. maesites	*C. hendersoni*
S. a. petioni	*D. g. cleothera*
S. toussainti	*D. e. tethys*

II. Xeric woods and forest

P. l. lividus	*E. monima*
P. nero	*B. h. hyperia*
G. j. josephina	*M. e. dospassosi*
P. l. memula	*A. troglodyta*
A. o. browni	*M. johnsoni*
Ph. a. antillia	*M. v. verticordia*
E. a. boyeri	*A. d. amphitoe*
A. gelania	*A. i. idyja*
A. lapitha	*D. thoe*
M. aracynthia	*C. raburni*
E. t. tatilista	

III. Mesic forest and pseudoforest (low to moderate elevation)

Ph. p. bicolor	*E. pyro*
P. m. sanchesi	*E. nicippe*
E. spanna	*Z. c. cynops*
Ch. ixion	*A. maerula*
A. a. haitensis	*A. c. clorinde*
A. talus	*Ph. th. thalestris*
A. a. anausis	*Ph. a. rorata*
A. christyi	*Rh. t. watsoni*
A. h. heriul	*A. godartiana*

III (*continued*).

A. p. sagra
A. s. dilloni
P. a. antiqua
S. m. adoceta
C. t. tripunctus
Rh. bushi
W. druryi
H. ph. phylea
A. m. apa
Ch. haitensis
N. n. nyctelius
H. machaonides
H. a. epidaurus
P. p. imerius
A. d. boydi
E. d. mayobanex
E. d. palmira
E. nicippe
A. s. hispaniolae
D. spio
H. h. watsoni
E. m. melphis
A. p. pelops
V. a. rubria
H. paulla
A. j. saturata
A. lytrea
S. s. stelenes
H. a. diasia
H. o. odius
C. d. wolcotti
M. chiron
S. g. nemesis
C. phoinix
L. c. cleobaea

IV. Upland mesic broadleaf forest (including mixed pine-hardwoods)

Ch. schwartzi
Ch. melissa
B. zetides
V. c. cardui
A. teleboas
C. archebates
C. chrysaoros
C. galii
C. choneupsilon
C. arcas
C. g. dilemma
C. dystacta
C. neiba
C. clydoniata
C. clenchi
C. elelea
C. ainigma
G. diaphana
D. p. megalippe
D. cleophile
A. b. briarea

V. Pine forest and pinewoods

P. batesi
S. andrewi
C. loxias
C. tragia
C. g. grannus
C. amazona
C. micrommata
C. schwartzi
A. p. pantherata
A. jaegeri

limited to pine forest and pinewoods are upland euryxerophilic. These categories are somewhat arbitrary; restriction to xeric conditions (stenoxerophily) is only 1 parameter of a spectrum of ecological tolerances, of which stenomesophily is the other extreme. The intermediate terms, euryxerophilic and eurymesophilic, are but assessments of tolerances along this spectrum—the former "preferring" xeric conditions and more tolerant to them, the latter "preferring" mesic conditions and more tolerant to them.

But even with this sort of categorization, I cannot stress too strongly that butterflies fly; they move from place to place and often occur (at least temporarily) at localities that are physically and ecologically far removed from the situations where they are most frequently encountered. Thus, table 2 is somewhat of an oversimplification in these regards, but such simplification is unavoidable unless the reader is to be subjected to an abundance of qualifying statements as well. Such statements are in the species' accounts, and the reader is referred to those acccounts for details.

It is obvious that mesic and shaded situations (III and IV) offer maximum sanctuary to and minimal stress on animals. Xeric areas present risks and hazards to those animals that are adapted to live in them. It should come as no surprise that of the 130 species of butterflies listed in table 2, 77 species (55%) are stenomesophiles. The stenoxerophiles (I—22%) are much fewer, as are the upland euryxerophiles (V—8%); the last category has the lowest frequency. The euryxerophiles occupying xeric woods and forests likewise are fewer (II—17%).

What may perhaps be surprising is the overwhelming majority of stenomesophilic species. Two factors are important. (1) The West Indies in general, prior to the arrival of western man, apparently had extensive stands of hardwood forest both in the lowlands and highlands. Of course there must have been xeric lowlands as well; still, it seems reasonable to assume that there were more butterflies adapted for mesic forested areas than for xeric unforested ones. To those species that were able to adapt (= evolve species) to these xeric areas, success was assured. The *lyceia* complex of *Calisto* offers an excellent example of this phenomenon. (2) Occupation by colonial man of Hispaniola (and elsewhere in the Greater Antilles) modified the extant habitat, both negatively and then positively for some eurymesophilic and stenomesophilic butterflies. The cutting of the primary deciduous forest was a negative act, removing many square kilometers of that habitat. But with this cutting came the establishment of pseudo-forests (*caféières, cafetales, cacaotales*); these plantings, because of the very nature of the crop-trees themselves, demanded the retention of at least some of the original forest, enough to afford a canopy over the developing crop-trees, or the planting of other trees that upon maturity would offer shade. The crop-trees themselves, notably cacao, are excellent shade trees. No one who has walked through a *cacaotal* on a hot summer day will easily forget the cool sanctuary that such a planting offers. These forest modifications were ultimately favorable to low- and mid-elevation eurymesophiles and stenomesophiles. Where the forest has been cleared and not replanted in some sort of forest crop, the open fields and disturbed situations do not favor the eurymesophiles but do favor ecotonal or open-area butterflies.

*
* *

To anyone interested in the lepidopteran fauna of Hispaniola at any level (systematics, life histories, ecology, etc.), the island offers some excellent opportunities for further research. But a problem for any worker is always: Where can one go to collect the broadest variety of species with minimal effort and expense? Over the years, 4 localities have been repeatedly rewarding. Let us examine each of these and give some details of each, making an effort to explain the abundance of species (and most often, individuals) at each.

(1) República Dominicana: Prov. de la Altagracia: 16 km NE La Romana, 61 m. This is (1986) a fine extensive stand of dense xeric hardwoods with an understory of *Zamia* sp. A very large number of the listed euryxerophiles have been taken there, along with many other species. The area is little disturbed and moderately remote (but reachable by paved roads from Santo Domingo). It seems to be so rich in butterflies because of the lack of cutting of forest and human disturbance in general. Fifty-two species have been collected there.

(2) República Dominicana: Prov. de la Vega: 1 km S Constanza, 1098 m. The Hotel Nueva Suiza lies to the south of Constanza, on the road to Valle Nuevo and La Horma, and thence to San José de Ocoa. The rear yard of the hotel is a large expanse of grasses with many peripheral flowers (*Lantana ovatifolia*) as well as flowers in the yard itself (*Zinnia elegans, Bidens pilosa*). The yard edge has some second-growth woods, cultivation, pine trees, bushes and shrubs, and other flowers (*Cynoglossum amabile*, for instance).

This ecotonal situation is very rich in both number of butterflies and number of species (55 species collected). It is especially rich in hesperiids. Many moderate-elevation species occur there, as well as a few upland species. In addition, the road from Constanza to Valle Nuevo leads through pine forest, and the upland Cordillera Central *Calisto* fauna and *Anetia* become accessible.

(3) República Dominicana: Prov. de Independencia: 4–7 km NE El Aguacate, 519–824 m. This locality is reached by good road from Barahona, via Duvergé, thence to Puerto Escondido on the north slope of the Sierra de Baoruco. From there, a fine gravel road leads to the lower end of a road that ascends the Massif de la Selle to the *puesto* of El Aguacate. Between 4 and 7 km NE of that *puesto*, the road passes from xeric to mesic forest, much of it relatively undisturbed. In many places, the forest canopy extends across the road. Butterflies are especially abundant at all levels. The upper slopes have upland species (*Ch. melissa*, *D. cleophile*, *A. p. pantherata*, *B. zetides*) and the lower slopes have a more xerophilic fauna (many species of pierids, *A. d. amphitoe*, *H. o. odius*, *M. aracynthia*). The locality is moderately remote and quite deserted. If one continues on the border road to El Aguacate and beyond into the pine forest, he once more reaches places where the la Selle *Calisto* are abundant, along with *G. diaphana* and other upland species. Eighty-four species (44% of the Hispaniolan butterfly fauna!) have been taken on the El Aguacate slope.

(4) Haiti: Dépt. de l'Ouest: Boutilliers Road. Certainly a spectacular (in every way) place to collect butterflies on Hispaniola has been Boutilliers Road. This locality is reached easily from Port-au-Prince via Pétionville, and thence onto the north slope of the Morne l'Hôpital toward (but below) Kenscoff, at elevations between 266 and 915 m. Once Boutilliers Road has passed the housing and cultivation near the intersection with the road to Kenscoff, one is treated to a spectacular view of Port-au-Prince on his right. The road continues down the front face of the Morne l'Hôpital to sea level west of Port-au-Prince, but the lower levels are much less productive than the upper. What seems to make Boutilliers Road such a profitable site is that the road is cut into the mountainside. The area is always at least breezy and at times windy. Thus the roadcut itself acts as a trap for lowland forms that are swept upwards from the xeric area below and as a trap for upland species that are swept down from the pine forest at and beyond Kenscoff. Sixty-eight species (36% of the Hispaniolan fauna) have been collected there. The habitat of the road is not easily categorized. It presents a mélange of cultivation, summer homes,

gardens, and much disturbed woods and forest remnants (like much of Haiti), along with grassy and bushy roadsides with a profusion of cultivated,wild, and weedy flowers. Boutilliers Road is thus the ultimate ecotone, several kilometers of ill-defined habitat that is a pleasure for the lepidopterist. However, in 1985, Boutilliers Road was being improved and widened, with extensive removal of roadside flowering plants. Future lepidopterists may not find this area so fantastically rewarding as it has been in the period 1977–85.

Plates

Plate 2

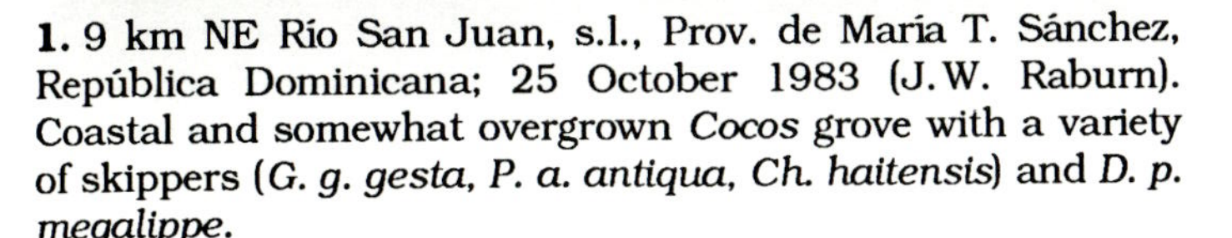

1. 9 km NE Río San Juan, s.l., Prov. de María T. Sánchez, República Dominicana; 25 October 1983 (J.W. Raburn). Coastal and somewhat overgrown *Cocos* grove with a variety of skippers (*G. g. gesta*, *P. a. antiqua*, *Ch. haitensis*) and *D. p. megalippe*.

2. Villa Riva, Prov. de Duarte, República Dominicana; 27 October 1984 (J.W. Raburn). Overgrown basketball court on edge of town. The weedy growth had a variety of skippers (*H. ph. phylea* among others), lycaenids, and small pierids.

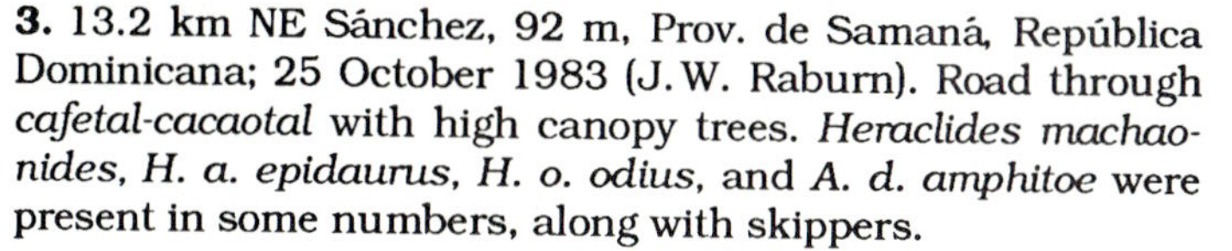

3. 13.2 km NE Sánchez, 92 m, Prov. de Samaná, República Dominicana; 25 October 1983 (J.W. Raburn). Road through *cafetal-cacaotal* with high canopy trees. *Heraclides machaonides, H. a. epidaurus, H. o. odius*, and *A. d. amphitoe* were present in some numbers, along with skippers.

4. 30 km NW Santo Domingo, 122 m, Dist. Nac., República Dominicana; 16 April 1984. The view is of the grassy area (*Ch. haitensis, C. t. tripunctus*, small pierids) leading to (on the right) mesic forest.

Plate 6

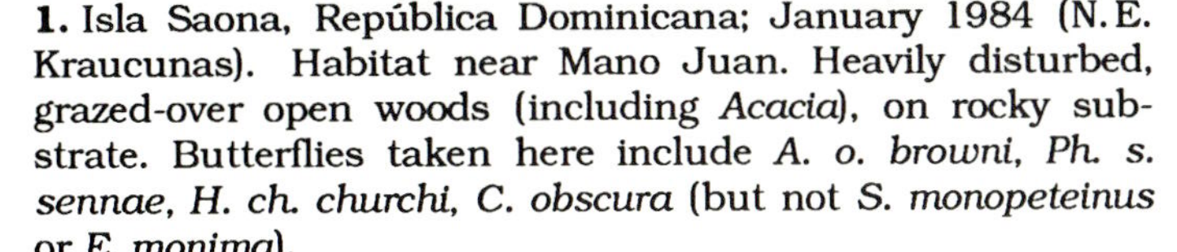

1. Isla Saona, República Dominicana; January 1984 (N.E. Kraucunas). Habitat near Mano Juan. Heavily disturbed, grazed-over open woods (including *Acacia*), on rocky substrate. Butterflies taken here include *A. o. browni*, *Ph. s. sennae*, *H. ch. churchi*, *C. obscura* (but not *S. monopeteinus* or *E. monima*).

2. 16 km NE La Romana, 61 m, Prov. de la Altagracia, República Dominicana; 27 June 1981 (W.W. Sommer). Dense xeric forest with *Zamia* sp. understory. Butterflies include *P. l. lividus*, *P. c. odilia*, *H. machaonides*, *H. a. epidaurus*, *E. l. memula*, *Ph. th. thalestris*, *A. d. boydi*, *L. terena*, *E. a. boyeri*, *A. i. idyja*, *D. thoe*, *E. monima*, *A. d. amphitoe*, *M. aracynthia*, *A. gelania*, *L. c. cleobaea*, as well as many others.

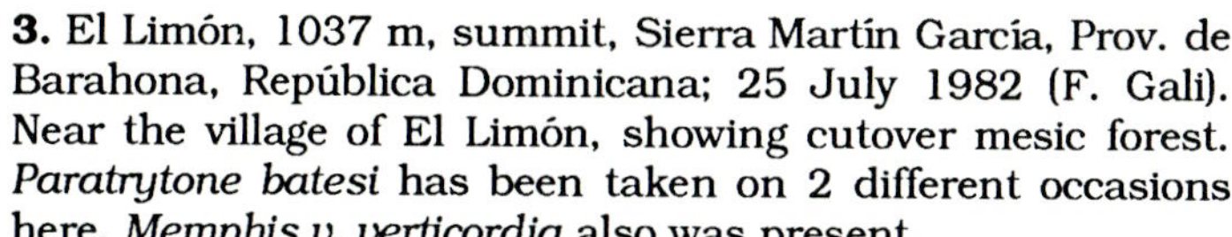

3. El Limón, 1037 m, summit, Sierra Martín García, Prov. de Barahona, República Dominicana; 25 July 1982 (F. Gali). Near the village of El Limón, showing cutover mesic forest. *Paratrytone batesi* has been taken on 2 different occasions here. *Memphis v. verticordia* also was present.

4. 5 km WSW Scierie, 1891 m, Dépt. de l'Ouest, Haiti; 4 September 1984 (F. Gali). Pine forest with fern understory in the Massif de la Selle. *Calisto archebates* and *P. batesi* were very common here.

Plate 7

1. 10 km NW La Horma, 1496 m, Prov. de la Vega, República Dominicana; 11 July 1982 (F. Gali). View from the La Horma–Constanza road up the ravine where *B. zetides* is abundant. *Calisto p. darlingtoni* occurs on the immediate left in a small patch of sugarcane.

2. 18 km SE Constanza, 2228 m, Prov. de la Vega, República Dominicana; 29 June 1981 (W.W. Sommer). *Cynoglossum amabile* in foreground, *Rubus* sp. in background; typical plants of open soggy meadows in the pine forests of the Cordillera Central.

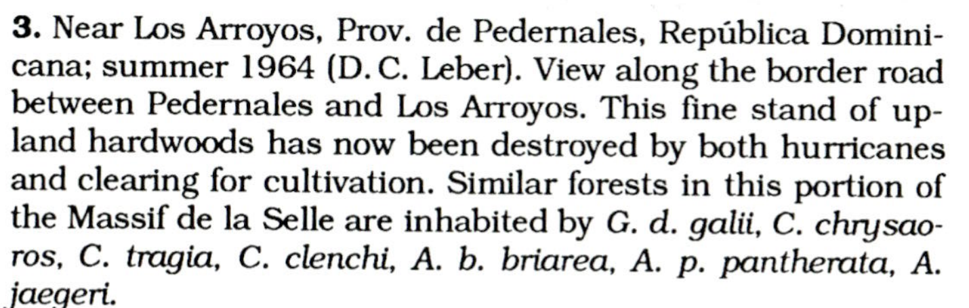

3. Near Los Arroyos, Prov. de Pedernales, República Dominicana; summer 1964 (D. C. Leber). View along the border road between Pedernales and Los Arroyos. This fine stand of upland hardwoods has now been destroyed by both hurricanes and clearing for cultivation. Similar forests in this portion of the Massif de la Selle are inhabited by *G. d. galii, C. chrysaoros, C. tragia, C. clenchi, A. b. briarea, A. p. pantherata, A. jaegeri.*

4. 10 km W Jaycao, 1007 m, Prov. de la Vega, República Dominicana; 9 August 1982 (F. Gali). Type-locality of *G. d. charadra*, a mesic forested montane torrent. Other species here are *E. spanna, Rh. bushi, P. a. antiqua, P. batesi, M. s. salacia, A. p. pelops, A. gelania, M. e. dospassosi, L. c. cleobaea.*

1
2
3
4
5
6
7
8
9

Addendum: A New Species of *Tmolus* (Lycaenidae) from Hispaniola

by Kurt Johnson and David Matusik

In 1984, the junior author captured a single specimen of *Tmolus* near La Romana, Prov. de La Romana, Dominican Republic, which was not identifiable as any known species of that genus. The specimen was forwarded to the American Museum of Natural History (AMNH), and, thereafter, information concerning it was provided for review to several knowledgeable students of West Indian Lepidoptera, including Albert Schwartz. Study of this female specimen, a subsequently located male, and other taxa usually placed in the genus *Tmolus* indicated that it should be described as new. To facilitate completeness and allow companion treatment of this new taxon in context with his discussion of *Tmolus azia* on Hispaniola, Schwartz suggested publication of the description as an addendum by us to his text. The description is provided below, with further discussion regarding the genus *Tmolus* summarized in the REMARKS and figure legends. All references to the male were inserted after its 1987 discovery.

Tmolus victoria, new species

DIAGNOSIS: Compared with other known *Tmolus* (*azia*, *cydrara* [Hewitson], *echion* [Linnaeus], *mutina* [Hewitson], *venustus* [Druce] —species diversity from Stanley S. Nicolay, pers. comm.):

Figure A-1 (facing page). *Tmolus* taxa (specimens all AMNH except as noted). *T. victoria*, 1. holotype, upper surface; 2. same, under surface; 3. allotype, upper surface; 4. same, under surface; 5. *T. azia* (female), Jalapa, Mexico, upper surface (left), under surface (right); 6. *T. cydrara* (female), Igarapi-Assu, Brasil; 7. *T. venustus* (male), "Venezuela"; 8. *T. mutina* (female), Obidos, Brasil; 9. *T. echion* (female), El Benito, Brasil. Sexual dimorphism of the wing under surface is negligible in *Tmolus*.

(1) Under surface orange bands most like *azia* (limited to postmedian areas of both wings, not postmedian and postbasal as on other *Tmolus* taxa (fig. A-1), but more arc-shaped, serially disjunct, and set more basad on the wings; hindwing band not W-shaped along veins 2A and Cu2, but V-shaped with a single displacement of the band distad along vein 2A only; (2) limbal area of hindwing under surface with distinct gray suffusion distad large orange "Thecla-spot" and orange-dotted anal lobe, not lacking such suffusion (*azia, cydrara, echion, mutina;* fig. A-1) or with suffusions thinly along the submargin (*venustus;* fig. A-1); (3) upper surface, hindwing, with noticeable darkening above the under surface postmedian band and limbal area, and with emphasis of spot costad extremely long tail, not with several interveinal spots evident along the margin (*azia;* fig. A-1) or variously two-tailed (other taxa: fig. A-1); (4) genitalia of female with gradually tapering ductus bursae of moderate length, not with a "cuplike" division (antrum or cone, *sensu* Tuxen, 1970, Taxonomist's glossary of genitalia of insects; Munksgaard, Copenhagen:pp. 359) to the overall tapering of the ductus (*azia, echion, cydrara;* fig. A-2), a shorter length (*azia;* fig. A-2), or an extremely elongate configuration (*echion, cydrara;* fig. A-2). Apophyses of papillae anales of known female markedly shorter than in all congeners except *cydrara* (fig. A-2). Cephalad terminus of ductus bursae extremely wide, unlike congeners (fig. A-2).

Figure A-2 (facing page). Female genitalia of *Tmolus* taxa: Format: A, papillae anales and apophyses; B, signum; C, lateral view, cephalic terminus, ductus bursae; D, ventral view, genital plate. Taxa (specimens all AMNH)—1. *T. azia*, Río Arrazayal, Salta, Argentina; 2. *T. azia*, Port-of-Spain, Trinidad; 3. *T. azia*, Jalapa, Mexico; 4. *T. echion*, Colima, Mexico; 5. *T. cydrara*, Pucallpa, Peru; 6. *T. victoria*, holotype, La Romana, Dominican Republic; 7. *T. mutina*, "Colombia." *Comments: T. azia* characterized by cuplike sculpturing of ductus bursae, deeply indented ovate cephalic terminus with lateral view as 1, 2, 3C. Apophyses of papillae anales elongate, papillae anales very asymmetrical; signa small, thinly pointed. *T. echion* ductus bursae elongate, reminiscent of cuplike shape, parabolic and indented cephalic terminus with lateral view 4C (like *mutina*). Apophyses of papillae anales elongate, papillae anales more symmetrical; signa broadly based, thinly pointed. *T. mutina* ductus bursae extremely elongate, evenly tapered, cephalic terminus blunt and unindented lateral view as 7C. Apophyses of papillae anales elongate, papillae anales very

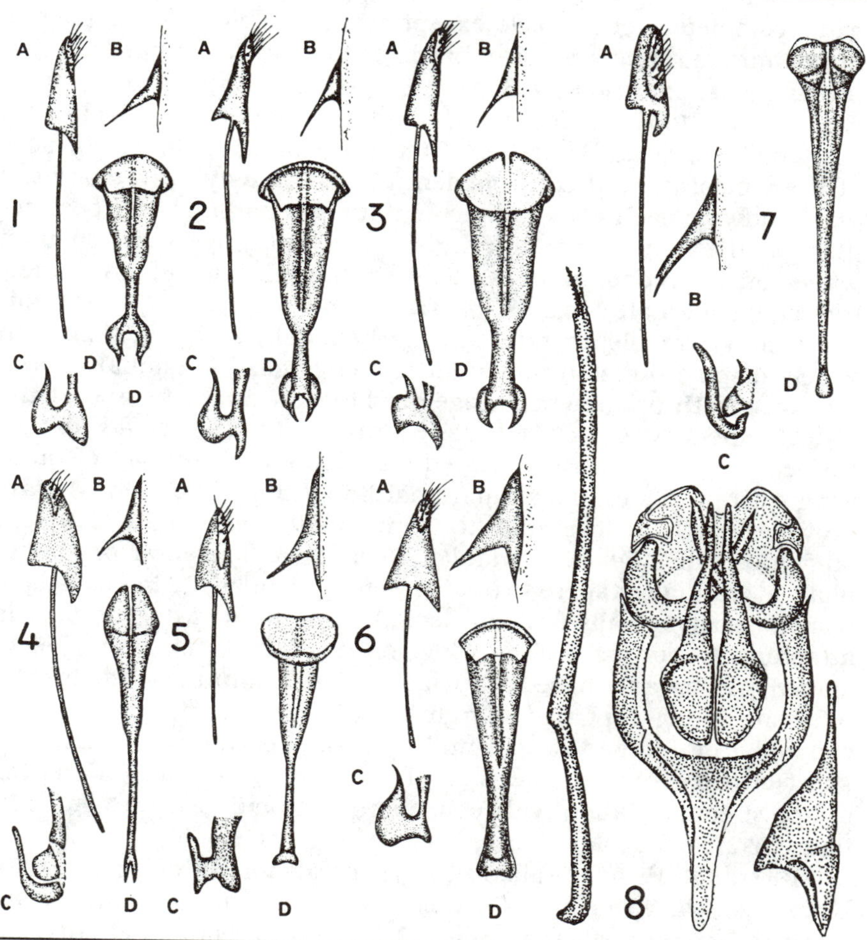

asymmetrical; signa thickly pointed. *T. cydrara* ductus bursae elongate, cuplike, cephalic terminus hemispherical with lateral view as 5C. Apophyses of papillae anales short, papillae anales symmetrical; signa broad-based, thinly pointed. *T. victoria*, ductus bursae moderate in length, evenly tapered, cephalic terminus wide, blunt, unindented, lateral view as 6C. Apophyses of papillae anales short, papillae anales quite symmetrical; signa broad-based, thickly pointed. A female of *T. venustus* was not available for study. 8. Male genitalia: *T. victoria* (males of congeners, see Johnson, 1986, Bull. Allyn Mus. 106:1–11) left, aedeagus; center, genitalia, ventral; right, valve, lateral.

DESCRIPTION: *Male* and *Female.* Upper surface of wings: forewing completely gray-black except for silver-blue dusting along inner margin; hindwing gray-black cephalad M3 with silver-blue dusting basad; caudad M3 wing gray-white. Both wings fringed white. Anal lobe predominantly orange; prominent black spot marginal in cell M3. Long tail at terminus of Cu2. Under surfaces of the wings: ground color moderately dark dusty gray. Forewing and hindwing each with complementary submarginal and postmedian bands, former very dull and obsolescent gray-brown on both wings, latter predominantly white distad, black centrad, and widely orange basad. Latter bands arc-shaped on both wings, with hindwing band more disjunct, thickly marked orangish basad, and with widely displaced distad protrudence along vein 2A. Limbal area of hindwing with prominent orange markings at anal lobe and at the "Thecla-spot" with marked dark gray suffusion costad to M2 caused by gray coloration dusted blackish basad. Margin of hindwing with prominent black marginal line; fringe, both wings, gray-brown. Length of forewing: 10.0 mm (holotype female), 9.0 mm (allotype male). *Female genitalia.* Overall configuration of genital plate a gradually tapered tube, widening caudad at lamellal lips. Lamella postvaginalis fanlike. Cephalic terminus of ductus bursae attaching to corpus bursae wide, blunt. Two signa, both single-spined and broadly based. Papillae anales terminus symmetrically bifurcate along cephalad margin, apophyses short, their caudal expanse from dorsad caudal tip to lamella postvaginalis falling far short of the cephalad extension of the ductus bursae. Differences of above configuration with congeners distinguished with male in figure A-2, and Explanation.

HOLOTYPE: Female, taken at edge of salt marsh of about 1 city block size, ca. 25 m from Caribbean Sea, east of La Romana, Dominican Republic, at terminus of 3–4 km on private land adjacent to refuse-dump area located about 3 km E junction of paved and dirt-gravel road from La Romana to Casa de Campo; David Matusik collector; 21 May 1984. Deposited AMNH.

ALLOTYPE: Male, "Santo Domingo," Druce Collection, British Museum (Natural History) (BMNH).

DISTRIBUTION: Presently known only from the type-localities.

REMARKS: Traditional literature of the West Indian butterfly fauna (Barcant, 1970, Butterflies of Trinidad and Tobago: Collins, London: pp. 314; Clench, 1964, J. Res. Lepid., 2:247–70; Comstock and Huntington, 1943, Ann. New York Acad. Sci., 45: 49–130; Brown and Heineman, 1972, Jamaica and its butterflies: E. M. Classey Ltd., London: pp. 478; Riley, 1975, Butterflies of the

West Indies: Collins, London: pp. 224) records no species of *Tmolus* from the West Indies. However, *T. azia* and *T. cydrara* from Trinidad and Tobago are represented in the AMNH and *T. azia* has been recorded from Jamaica (Nicolay, Schwartz, Turner, pers. com.). The widespread occurrence of *T. azia* on Hispaniola has been discussed in the present volume. Numerous genera of thecline lycaenids, however, have endemic West Indian representatives. Since Hispaniola has been one of the least collected West Indian islands until the work summarized by Schwartz, a hitherto undescribed *Tmolus* is a not unexpected but yet important addition to the butterfly fauna of this region.

ETYMOLOGY: At the request of the junior author, this species is named for his mother Victoria, in acknowledgment of her support of his interests in Lepidoptera.

ACKNOWLEDGMENTS: Thanks are due to Albert Schwartz, Thomas Turner, and Frederick H. Rindge for reviewing data concerning this species, along with Stanley S. Nicolay for this and his comments on the genus *Tmolus*. We are particularly grateful to Schwartz for his interest in including this description in the present book.

Luis Marión Heredia (Santo Domingo) suggested the collecting site and Joseph Brexa accompanied the junior author.

Literature Cited

Askew, R.R. 1980. The butterfly (Lepidoptera, Rhopalocera) fauna of the Cayman Islands. Atoll Res. Bull. 241:121–38.

Avinoff, A., and Shoumatoff, N. 1941. Some new and undescribed Jamaican butterflies. Ann. Carnegie Mus. Nat. Hist. 28(15):309–20.

______. 1946. An annotated list of the butterflies of Jamaica. Ann. Carnegie Mus. Nat. Hist. 30(16):263–95.

Bates, M. 1935a. The butterflies of Cuba. Bull. Mus. Comp. Zool. 78(2):63–258.

______. 1935b. The satyrid genus *Calisto.* Occ. Papers Boston Soc. Nat. Hist. 8:229–48.

______. 1939a. Notes on butterflies from Hispaniola. Psyche 46(2–3): 43–51.

______. 1939b. Notes on Cuban butterflies. II. Mem. Soc. Cubana Hist. Nat. Felipe Poey:1–4.

Beck, A.F. 1983. *Tmolus azia* (Lycaenidae) and *Anteos chlorinde [sic]* (Pieridae) in the Dominican Republic. J. Lep. Soc. 37(1): 89–90.

Bell, E.L., and Comstock, W.P. 1948. A new genus and some new species and subspecies of American Hesperiidae (Lepidoptera, Rhopalocera). Amer. Mus. Novitates, 1379:1–23.

Bond, J. 1928. The distribution and habits of the birds of the Republic of Haiti. Proc. Acad. Nat. Sci. Philadelphia, 80:483–521.

______. 1976. Twentieth supplement to the check-list of birds of the West Indies (1956). Acad. Nat. Sci. Philadelphia, 1–14.

Brown, F.M. 1929. A revision of the genus *Phoebis.* Amer. Mus. Novitates, 368:1–22.

______. 1931. A revision of the genus *Aphrissa* (Lepidoptera). Amer. Mus. Novitates, 454:1–14.

______. 1978. The origins of the West Indian butterfly fauna. Acad. Nat. Sci. Philadelphia, Spec. Publ. 13:5–30.

Brown, F.M., and Heineman, B. 1972. Jamaica and its butterflies. London: E.W. Classey, Ltd. xv + 478 pp.

Brown, F.M., and Miller, L.D. 1987. The types of the hesperiid butterflies described by William Henry Edwards. Part II.—Hesperiidae: Hespiriinae [*sic*], Section III and Megathymidae. Trans. Amer. Entom. Soc. 113:29–71.

Burns, J.M. 1964. Evolution in skipper butterflies of the genus *Erynnis.* Univ. California Publ. Entom. 37: iv + 217 pp.

______. 1987. The big shift: *nabokovi* from *Atalopedes* to *Hesperia* (Hesperiidae). J. Lep. Soc. 41(4):172–86.

Clark, A.H. 1941. Notes on some North and Middle American danaid butterflies. Proc. U.S. Natl. Mus. 90:71–74.

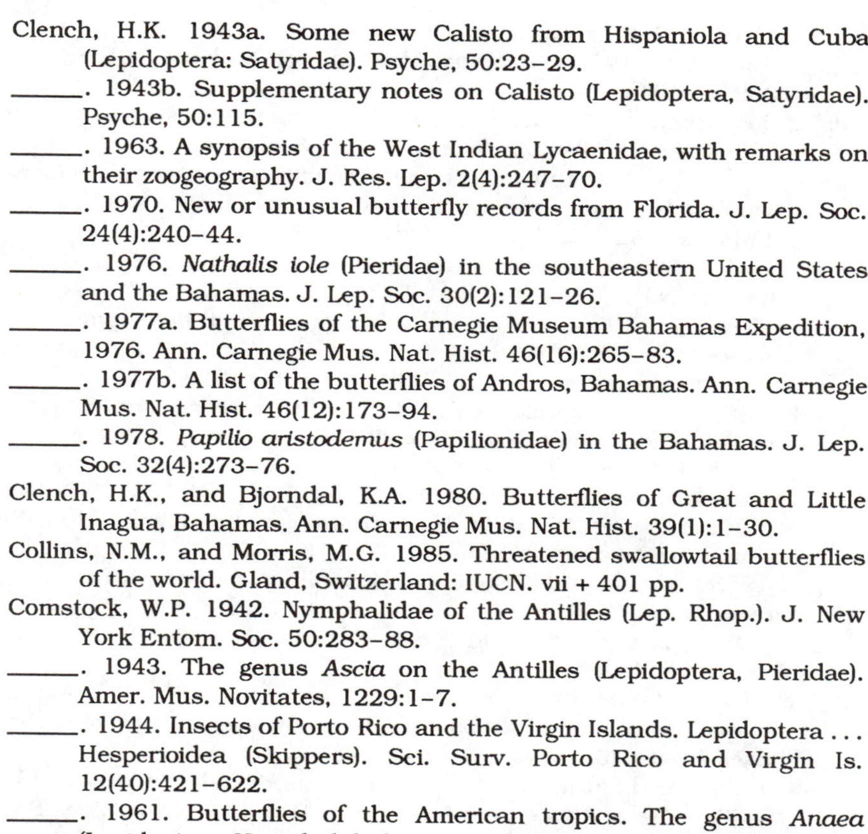

Clench, H.K. 1943a. Some new Calisto from Hispaniola and Cuba (Lepidoptera: Satyridae). Psyche, 50:23–29.

———. 1943b. Supplementary notes on Calisto (Lepidoptera, Satyridae). Psyche, 50:115.

———. 1963. A synopsis of the West Indian Lycaenidae, with remarks on their zoogeography. J. Res. Lep. 2(4):247–70.

———. 1970. New or unusual butterfly records from Florida. J. Lep. Soc. 24(4):240–44.

———. 1976. *Nathalis iole* (Pieridae) in the southeastern United States and the Bahamas. J. Lep. Soc. 30(2):121–26.

———. 1977a. Butterflies of the Carnegie Museum Bahamas Expedition, 1976. Ann. Carnegie Mus. Nat. Hist. 46(16):265–83.

———. 1977b. A list of the butterflies of Andros, Bahamas. Ann. Carnegie Mus. Nat. Hist. 46(12):173–94.

———. 1978. *Papilio aristodemus* (Papilionidae) in the Bahamas. J. Lep. Soc. 32(4):273–76.

Clench, H.K., and Bjorndal, K.A. 1980. Butterflies of Great and Little Inagua, Bahamas. Ann. Carnegie Mus. Nat. Hist. 39(1):1–30.

Collins, N.M., and Morris, M.G. 1985. Threatened swallowtail butterflies of the world. Gland, Switzerland: IUCN. vii + 401 pp.

Comstock, W.P. 1942. Nymphalidae of the Antilles (Lep. Rhop.). J. New York Entom. Soc. 50:283–88.

———. 1943. The genus *Ascia* on the Antilles (Lepidoptera, Pieridae). Amer. Mus. Novitates, 1229:1–7.

———. 1944. Insects of Porto Rico and the Virgin Islands. Lepidoptera . . . Hesperioidea (Skippers). Sci. Surv. Porto Rico and Virgin Is. 12(40):421–622.

———. 1961. Butterflies of the American tropics. The genus *Anaea* (Lepidoptera, Nymphalidae). Amer. Mus. Nat. Hist. xiii + 214 pp.

Comstock, W.P., and Huntington, E.I. 1943. Lycaenidae of the Antilles (Lepidoptera, Rhopalocera). Ann. New York Acad. Sci. 45(2): 49–130.

Correa, J.C., and Schwartz, A. 1986. The status of *Calisto hysius batesi* (Lepidoptera, Satyridae) with the description of a new species of *Calisto* from Hispaniola. Florida Sci. 49(1):11–18.

Coutsis, J.G. 1983. Notes concerning certain West Indian butterflies. Entom. Rec. 95:113–14.

———. 1986. Male and female genitalia of *Phoebis editha* (Butler): how they differ from Hispaniolan *P. sennae* (Linnaeus) (Pieridae). J. Lep. Soc. 40(2):97–106.

Cucurullo, O., Jr. 1959. Lista de mariposas (Rhopalocera) de Santo Domingo. Ciudad Trujillo: Impresora Dominicana. 15 pp.

D'Almeida, R.F. 1933. Étude sur le genre *Dismorphia* (Lep. Pieridae). Bull. Soc. Ent. Fr. 38:300–304.

Darlington, P.J., Jr. 1935. West Indian Carabidae II.: Itinerary of 1934; forests of Haiti; new species; and a new key to Colpodes. Psyche,

42(4):167–215.

_____. 1939. West Indian Carabidae V. Mem. Soc. Cubana de Hist. Nat. 13(2):79–101.

Elliott, N.B.; Riley, D.; and Clench, H.K. 1980. Annotated list of butterflies of San Salvador Island, Bahamas. J. Lep. Soc. 34(2):120–26.

Emsley, M. 1963. A morphological study of imagine Heliconiinae (Lep.: Nymphalidae) with a consideration of the evolutionary relationships within the group. Zoologica, 48(8):1–153.

Evans, W.H. 1952. A catalogue of the American Hesperiidae in the British Museum (Natural History). Part II, Pyrginae, Section I. 178 pp.

Friedlander, T.P. 1988. Taxonomy, phylogeny, and biogeography of *Asterocampa* Röber 1916 (Lepidoptera, Nymphalidae, Apaturinae). J. Res. Lepidoptera 25(4): 215–338.

Gali, F. 1983. Two new species of Choranthus (Hesperiidae) from Hispaniola, West Indies. Bull. Allyn Mus. 82:1–9.

_____. 1985. Five new species of *Calisto* (Lepidoptera: Satyridae) from Hispaniola. Milwaukee Public Mus. Contr. Biol. and Geol. 63:1–15.

Gali, F., and Schwartz, A. 1983a. *Myscelia antholia* (Nymphalidae) in the Dominican Republic. J. Lep. Soc. 37(2):164–65.

_____. 1983b. The second specimen of *Epargyreus spanna* (Hesperiidae). J. Lep. Soc. 37(2):170–71.

_____. 1983c. *Battus zetides* in the Dominican Republic. J. Lep. Soc. 37(2):171–74.

Gillham, N.W. 1957. Subspecies versus geographic variation in Caribbean populations of *Anartia jatrophae* Johannson (Lepidoptera, Nymphalidae). Amer. Mus. Novitates, 1845:1–22.

Godman, F.D., and Salvin, O. 1884. A list of the Rhopalocera collected by Mr. G. French Angas in the island of Dominica. Proc. Zoo. Soc. London, 1884:314–20.

Gonzalez, F.L. 1987. Three new species and one new subspecies in the *grannus* complex of Hispaniolan *Calisto* (Lepidoptera: Satyridae). Bull. Allyn Mus. 108:1–17.

Gonzalez, F.L., and Schwartz, A. (in press). The unity and diversity of Hispaniolan *Calisto* (Lepidoptera: Satyridae). Caribaea.

Hall, A. 1925. List of the butterflies of Hispaniola. Entomologist, 58:161–65, 186–90.

_____. 1929. New forms of Nymphalidae (Rhopalocera) in the collection of the British Museum. Entomologist, 62:130–34.

Holland, W.J. 1916. The Lepidoptera of the Isle of Pines, being a list of the species collected on the island by Mr. J.L. Graf and Mr. G.A. Link, Sr., in 1910 and 1912–13. Ann. Carnegie Mus. Nat. Hist. 10(18):487–518.

Howe, W.H. (ed.). 1975. The butterflies of North America. New York: Doubleday and Co., Inc. xiii + 663 pp.

Jenkins, D.W. 1983. Neotropical Nymphalidae I. Revision of Hamadryas. Bull. Allyn Mus. 81:1–146.

———. 1984. Neotropical Nymphalidae II. Revision of Myscelia. Bull. Allyn Mus. 87:1–64.

Johnson, F., and Comstock, W. P. 1941. *Anaea* of the Antilles and their continental affinities, with descriptions of new species and forms (Lepidoptera, Rhopalocera, Nymphalidae). J. New York Entom. Soc. 49:301–43.

Johnson, K., and Descimon, H. MS. The proper generic and specific status of Antillean "Prepona" butterflies with description of a new subspecies from Puerto Rico (Nymphalidae; Charaxinae). In prep.

Johnson, K., and Matusik, D. 1986. First reported males, species status, and affinities of *Epargyreus spanna* Evans (Hesperiidae). J. Lep. Soc. 30(1):59–63.

———. 1988. Five new species and one new subspecies of butterflies from the Sierra de Baoruco of Hispaniola. Ann. Carnegie Mus. Nat. Hist. 57(10):222–54.

Johnson, K.; Quinter, E.L.; and Matusik, D. 1987. A new species of *Calisto* from Hispaniola with a review of the female genitalia of Hispaniolan congeners. J. Res. Lep. 25(2):73–82.

Klots, A.B. 1951. A field guide to the butterflies of North America, east of the Great Plains. Boston: Houghton Mifflin Co. xvi + 349 pp.

de León, R.O. 1983. Aspectos geológicos e hidrogeológicos de la región suroeste. Mus. Nac. Hist. Nat. Santo Domingo, Publ. Espec. 4:1–25.

Lewis, H.L. 1973. Butterflies of the world. Chicago: Follett Publ. Co. xvi + 312 pp.

Logier, A.H. 1980. Árboles dominicanos. Santo Domingo, República Dominicana: Editora Alfa y Omega. 223 pp.

Lora Salcedo, R.; Czerwenka, J.; and Bolay, E. 1983. Atlas de diagramas climáticos de la República Dominicana. Santo Domingo: Sec. Estad. y Cult. 91 pp.

MacNeill, C.D. 1975. Family Hesperiidae: The skippers, *in* W.H. Howe, The butterflies of North America, pp. 423–578.

Maerz, A., and Paul, M.R. 1950. A dictionary of color. New York: McGraw-Hill Book Co. vii + 208 pp.

Marcano, E. de Jesús. 1976. (no title): Nat. Postal, 5/76:1. (*Phoebis trite*).

Marión Heredia, L. 1974. Lepidópteros (Rhopalocera) de la República Dominicana. Mimeographed, 26 pp. (all not numbered).

———. 1978a. Nueva mariposa para República Dominicana. Nat. Postal. 21/78:1.

———. 1978b. Atlantea en la República Dominicana. Nat. Postal, 23/78:1.

———. 1978c. Nueva Anaea en la República Dominicana. Nat. Postal, 34/78:1.

———. 1978d. Nueva localidad para Hypanartia paullus. Nat. Postal, 36/78:1.

———. 1979. Distribución de Anetia jaegeri. Nat. Postal, 13/79:1.

———. 1980a. Mariposas en El Número-Azua. I. Nat. Postal, 19/80:1.

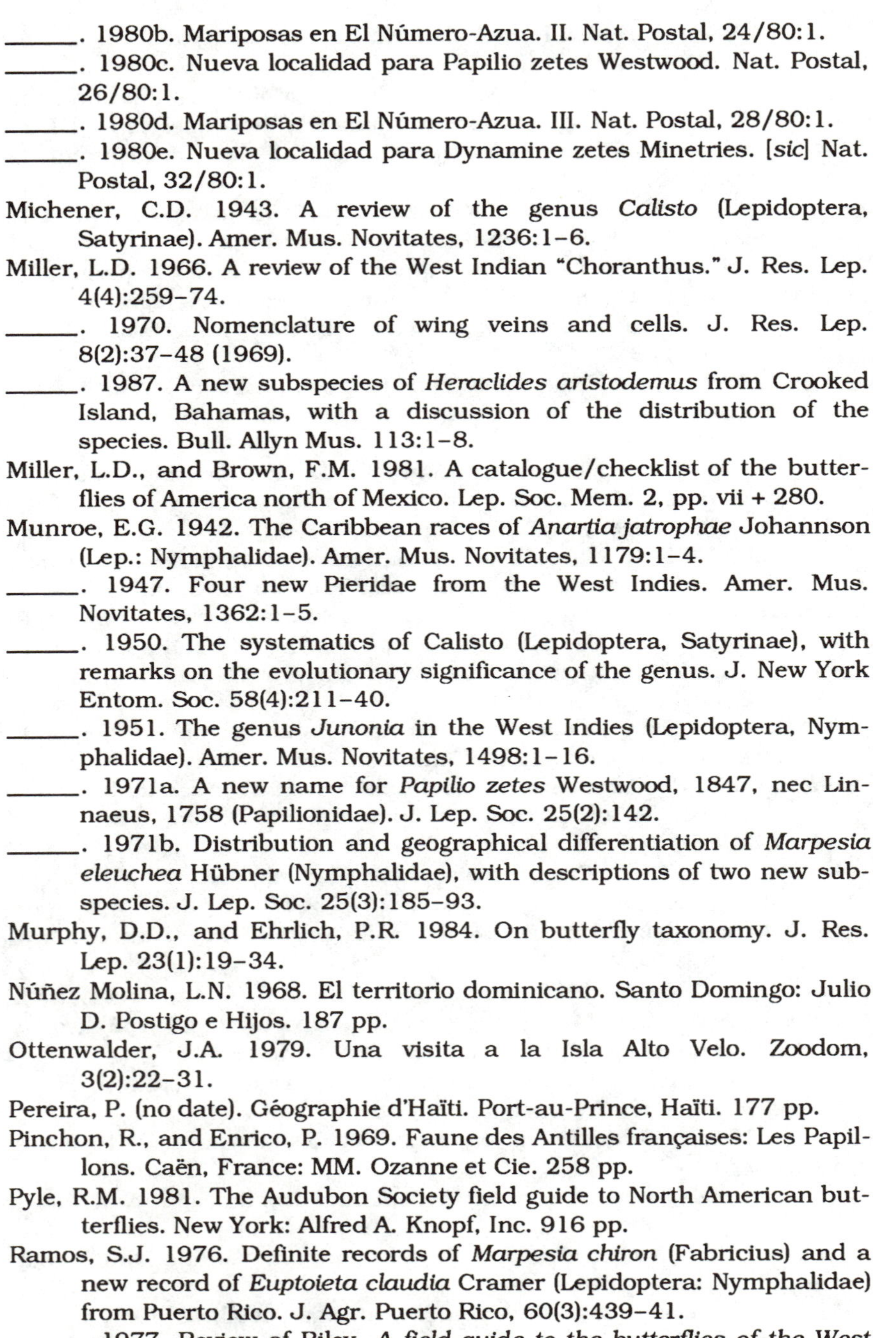

______. 1980b. Mariposas en El Número-Azua. II. Nat. Postal, 24/80:1.

______. 1980c. Nueva localidad para Papilio zetes Westwood. Nat. Postal, 26/80:1.

______. 1980d. Mariposas en El Número-Azua. III. Nat. Postal, 28/80:1.

______. 1980e. Nueva localidad para Dynamine zetes Minetries. [*sic*] Nat. Postal, 32/80:1.

Michener, C.D. 1943. A review of the genus *Calisto* (Lepidoptera, Satyrinae). Amer. Mus. Novitates, 1236:1–6.

Miller, L.D. 1966. A review of the West Indian "Choranthus." J. Res. Lep. 4(4):259–74.

______. 1970. Nomenclature of wing veins and cells. J. Res. Lep. 8(2):37–48 (1969).

______. 1987. A new subspecies of *Heraclides aristodemus* from Crooked Island, Bahamas, with a discussion of the distribution of the species. Bull. Allyn Mus. 113:1–8.

Miller, L.D., and Brown, F.M. 1981. A catalogue/checklist of the butterflies of America north of Mexico. Lep. Soc. Mem. 2, pp. vii + 280.

Munroe, E.G. 1942. The Caribbean races of *Anartia jatrophae* Johannson (Lep.: Nymphalidae). Amer. Mus. Novitates, 1179:1–4.

______. 1947. Four new Pieridae from the West Indies. Amer. Mus. Novitates, 1362:1–5.

______. 1950. The systematics of Calisto (Lepidoptera, Satyrinae), with remarks on the evolutionary significance of the genus. J. New York Entom. Soc. 58(4):211–40.

______. 1951. The genus *Junonia* in the West Indies (Lepidoptera, Nymphalidae). Amer. Mus. Novitates, 1498:1–16.

______. 1971a. A new name for *Papilio zetes* Westwood, 1847, nec Linnaeus, 1758 (Papilionidae). J. Lep. Soc. 25(2):142.

______. 1971b. Distribution and geographical differentiation of *Marpesia eleuchea* Hübner (Nymphalidae), with descriptions of two new subspecies. J. Lep. Soc. 25(3):185–93.

Murphy, D.D., and Ehrlich, P.R. 1984. On butterfly taxonomy. J. Res. Lep. 23(1):19–34.

Núñez Molina, L.N. 1968. El territorio dominicano. Santo Domingo: Julio D. Postigo e Hijos. 187 pp.

Ottenwalder, J.A. 1979. Una visita a la Isla Alto Velo. Zoodom, 3(2):22–31.

Pereira, P. (no date). Géographie d'Haïti. Port-au-Prince, Haïti. 177 pp.

Pinchon, R., and Enrico, P. 1969. Faune des Antilles françaises: Les Papillons. Caën, France: MM. Ozanne et Cie. 258 pp.

Pyle, R.M. 1981. The Audubon Society field guide to North American butterflies. New York: Alfred A. Knopf, Inc. 916 pp.

Ramos, S.J. 1976. Definite records of *Marpesia chiron* (Fabricius) and a new record of *Euptoieta claudia* Cramer (Lepidoptera: Nymphalidae) from Puerto Rico. J. Agr. Puerto Rico, 60(3):439–41.

______. 1977. Review of Riley, *A field guide to the butterflies of the West*

Indies. J. Lep. Soc. 31(3):215–16.

______. 1982. Checklist of the butterflies of Puerto Rico (Lepidoptera, Rhopalocera, West Indies). Carib. J. Sci. 17(1–4):59–68.

Riley, N.D. 1975. A field guide to the butterflies of the West Indies. New York: New York Times Book Co. 224 pp.

Rindge, F.H. 1952. The butterflies of the Bahama Islands, British West Indies. Amer. Mus. Novitates, 1563:1–18.

______. 1955. The butterflies of the Van Voast-American Museum of Natural History Expedition to the Bahama Islands, British West Indies. Amer. Mus. Novitates, 1715:1–19.

Schwartz, A. 1966. The Ameiva (Reptilia: Teiidae) of Hispaniola I. Ameiva lineolata Duméril and Bibron. Carib. J. Sci. 5(1–2):45–57.

______. 1970 (1969). Land birds of Isla Saona, República Dominicana. Quart. J. Florida Acad. Sci. 32(4):291–306.

______. 1979. The herpetofauna of Île à Cabrit, Haiti, with the description of two new subspecies. Herpetologica, 35(3):248–55.

______. 1980a. The herpetogeography of Hispaniola, West Indies. Stud. Fauna Curaçao and Carib. Is. 61(189):86–127.

______. 1980b. Deforestación y Rhopalocera una comparación en la recolección de mariposas entre República Dominicana y Haïti. Nat. Postal, 30/80:1–3.

______. 1982. Variation in Hispaniolan *Greta diaphana* (Ithomiidae). Bull. Allyn Mus. 69:1–10.

______. 1983a. Haitian butterflies. Mus. Nac. Hist. Nat. Santo Domingo. 69 pp.

______. 1983b. A new Hispaniolan *Calisto* (Satyridae). Bull. Allyn Mus. 80:1–10.

______. 1985. A new subspecies of *Calisto* from Hispaniola, West Indies. Bull. Allyn Mus. 93:1–5.

______. 1988. A new species of *Calisto* (Satyridae) from Hispaniola. Florida Sci. 50(4):246–52.

Schwartz, and Gali, F. 1984. Five new species of *Calisto* (Satyridae) from Hispaniola. Bull. Allyn Mus. 85:1–18.

Schwartz, A., and Gonzalez, F.L. 1988. A new species of *Calisto* from Hispaniola. Bull. Allyn Mus. 117:1–50.

Schwartz, A.; Gonzalez, F.L.; and Henderson, R.M. 1987. New records of butterflies from the West Indies. J. Lep. Soc. 41(3):145–50.

Schwartz, A., and Jimenez, C.J. 1982. The butterflies of Montserrat, West Indies. Bull. Allyn Mus. 66:1–18.

Schwartz, A., and J.Y. Miller. 1985. A new species of hairstreak (Lycaenidae) from Hispaniola. Bull. Allyn Mus. 99:1–6.

Schwartz, A., and W.W. Sommer. 1986. A new subspecies of *Synapte malitiosa* (Lepidoptera: Hesperiidae) from Hispaniola. Florida Sci. 49(1):18–22.

Schwartz, A.; Sommer, W.W; and Gali, F. 1985. Synapte mailitiosa [*sic*] (Lepidoptera; Hesperiidae) on Hispaniola. Florida Sci. 48(1):13–17.

Scott, J.A. 1972. Biogeography of the Antillean butterflies. Biotropica, 4(1):32–45.

Simon, M.J., and Miller, L.D. 1986. Observations on the butterflies of Great Inagua Island, Bahamas, with records of three species new to the island. Bull. Allyn Mus. 105:1–14.

Skinner, H. 1920. The genus *Pyrrhocalles* Mabille, with the description of a new form. Proc. Amer. Sci. Philadelphia, 75:151–53.

Smith, D.S.; Leston, D.; and Lenczewski, B. 1982. Variation in *Eurema daira* (Lepidoptera: Pieridae) and the status of *palmira* in southern Florida. Bull. Allyn Mus. 70:1–7.

Steinhauser, S.R. 1981. A revision of the *proteus* group of the genus *Urbanus* Hübner Lepidoptera: Hesperiidae. Bull. Allyn Mus. 62:1–41.

de la Torre y Callejas, S.L. 1943. Dos nuevas espécies de mariposas diurnas para Cuba. Mem. Soc. Cubana Hist. Nat. 17(2):139–40.

Torres, E.F.A. 1984. Manual sobre las plagas de la caña de azucar en República Dominicana. Santo Domingo: Unidad Divulgación y Documentación. 64 pp.

Turner, R.D. 1957. Charles Johnson Maynard and his work in malacology. Papers on Mollusks, Mus. Comp. Zool. 2:137–52.

Turner, T.W., and Parnell, J.R. 1985. The identification of two species of *Junonia* Hübner (Lepidoptera: Nymphalidae); *J. evarete* and *J. genoveva* in Jamaica. J. Res. Lep. 24(2):142–53.

Vyhmeister, G. 1980. *Tmolus azia* in Jamaica: a new record for the West Indies (Lycaenidae). J. Lep. Soc. 34(1):60.

Vyhmeister, G., and Donahue, J.P. 1980. The rediscovery of *Libytheana terena* in Jamaica (Libytheidae). J. Lep. Soc. 34(2):120.

Wetherbee, D.K. 1986. The larva and pupa of *Lycorea pieteri* Lamas (Danaidae). J. Lep. Soc. 40(1):20–22.

______. 1987. Life-stages of *Hamadryas amphitoe diasia* in Hispaniola (Rhopalocera, Nymphalidae). Mimeo.:1–13.

Wetmore, A., and Swales, B.H. 1931. The birds of Haiti and the Dominican Republic. Bull. U.S. Natl. Mus. 155. iv + 483 pp.

Wisor, R.W., and Schwartz, A. 1985. Status of *Calisto pulchella darlingtoni* Clench (Lepidoptera: Satyridae). Florida Sci. 48(1):7–13.

A Key to the Butterflies of Hispaniola

(UP = upper side; UN = underside; FW = forewing; HW = hindwing)

1. Antennae recurved apically . . . . 2.
1′. Antennae not recurved apically . . . . 54.

2. HW tailed . . . . 3.
2′. HW not tailed . . . . 6.

3. Body and UP wing bases with iridescent green hair-scales . . . . *U. p. domingo* (29)
3′. No iridescent hair-scales on UP . . . . 4.

4. UNHW with conspicuous central white spot . . . . . . *Ch. ixion* (25)
4′. UNHW without conspicuous central white spot . . . . 5.

5. FW with 7 hyaline spots, the most basal forming a short diagonal line . . . . *U. d. cramptoni* (32)
5′. FW with 6 or 7 hyaline spots, that in FW cell broader than long and indented apically . . . . *P. o. decussata* (35)

6. UP with either iridescent blue or green . . . . 7.
6′. UP without either iridescent blue or green . . . . 10.

7. HW with blue lines; FW with blue basally and transparent FW spots . . . . *Ph. p. bicolor* (17)
7′. Blue or green present, but not lineate . . . . 8.

8. UP with iridescent green on both wings and body; FW with translucent hyaline spots . . . . *A. talus* (35)
8′. UP with iridescent blue . . . . 9.

9. Iridescent blue on UP only; no FW hyaline spots . . *A. h. heriul* (40)
9′. Iridescence on UP and UN; FW with hyaline spots . . . . *A. christyi* (39)

10. UNHW with a vertical white bar or white spot . . . . 11.
10′. UNHW without a vertical white bar or white spot . . . . 13.

11. UNHW with white spot; FW obviously elongate . . . . *P. m. sanchesi* (19)
11′. UNHW with a white bar . . . . 12.

12. UNHW white bar with a brown indentation costally . . . . *E. spanna* (21)
12′. UNHW white bar without brown indentation costally . . . . *A. a. haitensis* (28)

13. Virtually unpatterned brown above and below . . *A. a. anausis* (38)
13′. Not so . . . . 14.

14. UNHW grayish green . . . . *P. l. lividus* (23)
14′. Not so . . . . 15.

15. UP pale gray with darker gray to blackish markings . . . . *P. oileus* (60)
15′. Not so . . . . 16.

16. UP orange . . . . 17.
16′. Not so . . . . 23.

17. Size (FW length) very large (21–29 mm); wide black margin on UPFW and UPHW . . . . *P. a. antiqua* (66)
17′. Size medium to small (10–22 mm) . . . . 18.

18. Size small (10–11 mm); veins black on UN in strong contrast to orange ground . . . . *O. stillmani* (78)
18′. Size small to medium (13–22 mm); veins not in contrast to ground . . . . 19.

19. Size medium (14–18 mm); UNHW with scattered dark dots and a dark anal fold in males; females similar but more dark brown to black on posterior edge of UNFW . . . . *H. ph. phylea* (86)
19′. Not so . . . . 20.

20. UP in males with a prominent black stigma; females with a chain of 6 pale spots on UNHW on a dusky ground color . . . . *H. nabokovi* (89)
20′. Not so . . . . 21.

21. Size small (13–16 mm); UP light golden yellow; stigma in males bipartite; UNHW bright golden yellow . . . . *Ch. haitensis* (93)
21′. Size small (13–17 mm) but UNHW olivaceous or tawny and UP dark golden yellow or light orange-yellow . . . . 22.

22. UP dark golden yellow; stigma in males single; UNHW olivaceous . . . . *Ch. melissa* (96)
22′. UP light orange-yellow; stigma in males bipartite; UNHW tawny . . . . *Ch. schwartzi* (95)

23. UN green on both wings in both sexes . . . . *P. batesi* (98)
23′. UN not green . . . . 24.

24. FW with obvious hyaline spots . . . . 25.
24′. FW without obvious hyaline spots . . . . 37.

25. Hyaline spot in FW cell J- or hook-shaped . . . . *C. p. potrillo* (47)
25′. Not so . . . . 26.

26. FW with 2 (or 3, the third tiny) hyaline spots; UNHW with 2 large and doubly white-capped black rectangular spots . . . . *Ph. unia* (71)
26′. Not so . . . . 27.

27. UNHW with 5 black dots (tiny in females), ringed with whitish . . . . *Argon* sp. (68)
27′. Not so . . . . 28.

28. UNHW contrastingly patterned . . . . 29.
28′. Not so . . . . 31.

29. UNHW with a single bold white bar on a brown ground . . . . *P. nero* (107)
29′. UNHW with a yellow (pale yellow in females) bar *or* brown and lavender bars . . . . 30.

30. UNHW with a yellow or pale yellow bar . . . . *A. m. apa* (88)
30′. UNHW with brown and lavender bars . . . . . *N. n. nyctelius* (112)

31. UP black with white dots . . . . *P. c. odilia* (63)
31′. Not so . . . . 32.

32. Palpi distinctly white . . . . 33.
32′. Not so . . . . 34.

33. Males with costal fold on FW and with 3 whitish subapical FW dots; females like males but with purplish UNHW pattern . . . . *B. stillmani* (43)
33′. Males without costal fold but with 3 whitish subapical FW dots; females with a UPFW pattern of 6 hyaline dots and without a purplish UNHW pattern . . . . *B. hispaniolae* (44)

34. Size small (13–16 mm); UP brown and with faint pattern . . . . 35.
34′. Size small to large but with a bold pattern *or* unicolor and without pattern *or* FW distinctly elongate . . . . 36.

35. UP pattern a vague FW diagonal ochreous mark . . . . *S. m. adoceta* (71)
35′. UP without pattern or at most with several grayish dots on FW . . . . *C. t. tripunctus* (73)

36. FW distinctly elongate . . . . 37.
36′. Not so . . . . 39.

37. An apical pale dot on UNFW . . . . *A. s. dilloni* (50)
37′. No apical FW dot . . . . 38.

38. Size large (21–27 mm); UNHW with distinct purplish and contrasting scales forming a margin-

following "band". . . . . *A. p. sagra* (48)
38′. Size small (14–16 mm); UNHW without purplish scales . . . . *G. g. gesta* (52)

39. FW with hyaline pale spots . . . . 40.
39′. FW without hyaline pale spots . . . . 47.

40. 2 to 4 or 5 FW hyaline spots . . . . 41.
40′. 5 to 11 FW hyaline spots . . . . 44.

41. 3 FW hyaline spots; a pale curved cell spot and sex brand . . . . *P. ph. philetes* (69)
41′. 2, 4 or 5 FW pale markings; no sex brand . . . . 42.

42. 2 FW pale spots (females only) . . . . *E. s. insolata* (100)
42′. 4 or 5 FW pale spots (both sexes); no UNHW dots or spots . . . . 43.

43. A pale dot in UPFW cell . . . . *P. o. distipuncta* (110)
43′. No pale dot in UPFW cell . . . . *P. o. ocola* (108)

44. 5–7 FW pale spots . . . . 45.
44′. 8–11 FW pale spots (females only) *or* 5 pale FW dots . . . . . . 47.

45. UNHW with a faint row of pale dots following margin . . . . *P. s. woodruffi* (104)
45′. No pale UNHW row of *faint* dots . . . . 46.

46. HW with a bold horizonal row of translucent spots . . . . *C. ethlius* (102)
46′. UNHW with a bold pattern of silvery white and golden spots (males only) . . . . *Rh. bushi* (76)

47. 8–11 FW pale spots . . . . 48.
47′. 5 pale FW dots; a series of pale submarginal sagittate markings . . . . *E. zarucco* (59)

48. 11 bold pale FW spots arranged more or less in a subapical circle, that in Cu1-Cu2 largest (females only) . . . . *E. zephodes* (57)
48′. 8 translucent FW spots (females only) . . . . *Rh. bushi* (76)

49. UP rich dark velvety black to dark brown (males only) . . . . *E. zephodes* (57)
49′. UP not so . . . . 50.

50. UP tawny orange; much of UPFW dusky, and UN distinctly orange (males only) . . . . *E. s. insolata* (100)
50′. UP with orange but not exclusively that color . . . . 51.

51. UPFW with a round patch of large and shiny scales, with a similar double streak of dark scales to outer margin (males only) . . . . *W. druryi* (83)

51′. UPFW without a patch of modified scales . . . . 52.

52. Sex brand linear and angled (males only) . . . . . . *P. b. loma* (81)
52′. Not so (females only) . . . . 53.

53. UP dark brown with 5 orange dots (females only) . . *W. druryi* (83)
53′. UNHW with a curved discal series of faint gray spots (females only) . . . . *P. b. loma* (81)

54. HW with only 1 anal vein . . . . 55.
54′. HW with 2 anal veins . . . . 63.

55. Tailless . . . . *B. p. polycrates* (119)
55′. With HW tails . . . . 56.

56. UP longitudinally lined black and white to pale green . . . . *E. zonarius* (123)
56′. Not longitudinally lined . . . . 57.

57. UP mostly black, with or without pale lines or markings . . . . 58.
57′. UP dark brown to blackish with pale (yellowish) lines or boldly yellow and black . . . . 61.

58. UNHW with a series of 6 silvery arrowheads directed basally . . . . *B. zetides* (115)
58′. Not so . . . . 59.

59. UPHW with a grayish green discal suffusion; UPFW without yellow (females only) . . . . . *H. a. epidaurus* (135)
59′. UPFW with 1 or 2 pale diagonal bands . . . . 60.

60. 2 pale UPFW bands, converging at anal angle . . . *H. aristor* (138)
60′. A pale UPFW band from costa to anal angle . . . . *P. p. imerius* (142)

61. UPFW pale markings diagonal, not paralleling margin; UNHW disc yellow . . . . *H. machaonides* (131)
61′. Not so . . . . 62.

62. UPFW mostly yellow (males only) . . . . *H. a. epidaurus* (135)
62′. UPFW brown and yellow; tails without pale centers . . . . *H. a. aristodemus* (127)

63. UP colors white, yellow, or clear orange, or at least primarily with these colors . . . . 64.
63′. Not so . . . . 95.

64. UP white, cream, or yellow . . . . 65.
64′. UP orange . . . . 89.

65. UP white, with, at most, some black dots or spots, never with any colored (yellow, orange) markings . . . . 66.
65′. UP white with some other colored markings, *or* cream,

or yellow . . . . 68.

66. UP white in both sexes, males with 1 UPFW black spot in cell end, females with 4 black UPFW spots, 1 in cell end . . . . *G. j. josephina* (146)
66′. No UPFW black spots . . . . 67.

67. Male UP pearly white, females more or less like males or with dark gray to blackish on UPFW, with cell darkly pigmented . . . . *A. d. boydi* (152)
67′. Male UP white, the FW outer margin with a dark denticulate edge; female ground color grayish to dark gray above and UNHW yellowish with gray vein-following scales . . . . *A. m. eubotea* (149)

68. UPHW and UNHW cream to yellowish, the latter with a gray to black line from costa to anal angle . . . . *M. s. salacia* (155)
68′. UP yellow or white with other colored markings . . . . 69.

69. UP white with other colored markings . . . . 70.
69′. UP yellow . . . . 72.

70. UPFW with a yellow (to orange) square to rectangular patch from costa to cell end . . . . *A. c. clorinde* (200)
70′. Not so . . . . 71.

71. UPFW with a large orange blotch basally (males only) . . . . *A. o. browni* (220)
71′. UPFW with a large yellow blotch basally (males only) . . . . *A. godartiana* (222)

72. Size small (12–21 mm) . . . . 73.
72′. Size moderate (21–48 mm) . . . . 80.

73. Males with a dark gray to black bar on inner margin of UPFW; females white to pale yellowish and without dark UPFW bar . . . . 74.
73′. No UPFW dark bar; females not white, and yellow usually somewhat brighter . . . . 75.

74. Dark UPFW bar bowed in males; female UPFW without yellow . . . . *E. d. palmira* (173)
74′. Dark UPFW bar straight in males; female UPFW with at least a yellow wash or tinge . . . . *E. elathea* (176)

75. UPFW with dark edge distinctly wider at apex . . . . 76.
75′. UPFW dark edge only slightly wider at apex and not reaching FW anal angle . . . . 78.

76. Inner margin of UPFW and costa of UPHW with dark (black to brown) bars; UNFW with 2 black

postdiscal spots . . . . *N. iole* (188)
76′. Not so patterned . . . . 77.

77. Black UPFW margin tapering toward anal angle in both sexes; a reddish or orange marginal spot on UNHW; UPFW cell end with dark dot . . . . . . *E. l. euterpe* (158)
77′. Black UPFW margin meeting inner margin squarely; no UNHW reddish or orange spot in males; no UPFW cell end dark dot; females yellow to yellow-orange, UNHW brown markings distinct . . . . *E. euterpiformis* (161)

78. UPFW black marginal band ends sharply at Cu2 . . . . *E. l. priddyi* (180)
78′. Not so patterned . . . . 79.

79. UP clear lemon yellow; UNHW patternless in males, with an irregular rusty brown spot at apex in females . . . . *E. l. memula* (167)
79′. UP slightly orange; UNHW in both sexes with apical spot, red in males, dark red in females; female UNHW with marginal reddish blush . . . . . . *E. larae* (169)

80. UPFW with a black and indented margin, and a black cell end spot; UNHW with 2 pink cell end spots . . . . *Z. c. cynops* (195)
80′. Not so . . . . 81.

81. UP greenish yellow, with a black cell end spot on FW and a gray cell end spot on UPHW . . . . . . *A. maerula* (197)
81′. Not so . . . . 82.

82. Males with an orange blotch on UPFW, with a black FW cell end spot; UPHW in females with orange blush; UNFW in both sexes with an irregular submarginal dark line . . . . . *Ph. th. thalestris* (204)
82′. Not so . . . . 83.

83. UNHW with 1 cell end spot, no spots, *or* a gray line from midcosta to near anal angle . . . . 84.
83′. UNHW with 2 silver cell end spots . . . . 86.

84. UP variable, either yellow or white with a yellow to orange basal suffusion on UPFW; males may have a short black bar near apex on UPHW . . . . *K. lyside* (190)
84′. Not so . . . . 85.

85. UN pale green, not yellow; a gray diagonal line on UNFW from apex to midpoint of inner margin and another on UNHW from midcosta to near anal angle . . . . *Rh. t. watsoni* (218)

85′. No (males) or only 1 (females) UNHW cell end spot; males with broad area of modified scales on UP extending as far basally as outer end of cell; females with a fine dark brown edge on UPFW and a small dark cell end spot on UPFW . . . . . *A. s. hispaniolae* (225)

86. UNHW not olive . . . . 87.
86′. UNHW olive (females only) . . . . *A. o. browni* (220)

87. A large dark brown cell end spot on UP and UNFW; FW apex and outer margin rather widely edged in brown (females only) . . . . *A. godartiana* (222)
87′. Not so . . . . 88.

88. UNFW not distinctly more orange on anterior 2/3 than on posterior 1/3; females with dark brown scalloped FW outer margin . . . . *Ph. s. sennae* (213)
88′. UNFW distinctly more orange on anterior 2/3 than on posterior 1/3; females rose colored and with a jagged dark postdiscal line on UNFW . . . . *Ph. editha* (216)

89. Size small to moderate (12–17 mm) . . . . 90.
89′. Size larger (26–39 mm) . . . . 94.

90. UP bright orange, UN rich yellow, virtually unmarked; UPFW and UPHW with a narrow narrow black border . . . . *E. d. mayobanex* (165)
90′. Not so . . . . 91.

91. Anal angle of HW pointed; UPFW with (males) black costal margin or (females) wide black apex; outer ends of all veins black and contrasting with ground color . . . . *E. p. proterpia* (170)
91′. HW not pointed . . . . 92.

92. UP (males) with wide black margin to FW and HW, in females with black apex on FW only; UP both wings in females yellow basally, orange distally, and with a large triangular reddish brown patch at apex UNHW . . . . *E. pyro* (181)
92′. Not so, and with a black cell end spot . . . . 93.

93. Inner edge of UPFW and UPHW marginal black band irregular, due to black scales following veins basally . . . . *E. nicippe* (184)
93′. Inner edge of UNFW and UNHW marginal black band smooth; black edge of both wings relatively narrow . . . . *E. nicippiformis* (186)

94. UNFW (both sexes) brown band from apex to inner margin irregular . . . . *Ph. a. rorata* (208)

94′. UNFW (both sexes) brown band from apex to inner margin straight . . . . *Ph. a. antillia* (211)

95. FW not transparent but FW length greater than FW breadth . . . . 96.
95′. FW transparent *or* FW length close to FW breadth (except in *A. cryptadia*, which has a broad discal band of pale yellow spots on UPHW) . . . . 101.

96. UP rich brownish orange or tan . . . . 97.
96′. UP more or less horizontally striped, either brown or orange, or black with yellow or orange . . . . 99.

97. UNHW spotted with silver . . . . *A. v. insularis* (274)
97′. UNHW tan or dusky orange . . . . 98.

98. UNHW tan . . . . *D. i. hispaniola* (277)
98′. UNHW dusky orange . . . . *L. c. cleobaea* (281)

99. UP orange-tan, horizontally striped with dark brown . . . . *E. m. melphis* (283)
99′. UP striped black, yellow, and/or orange . . . . 100.

100. UP horizontally striped black and yellow . . . *H. ch. churchi* (283)
100′. UPFW with 3 yellow to orange bands, alternating with black; UNHW sandy . . . . *D. spio* (226)

101. Wings transparent . . . . 141.
101′. Wings scaled, not transparent . . . . 102.

102. Size tiny (8–9 mm) to small (15–16 mm); UP blue to brown, often iridescent, some tailed, and usually with some ocelli at margin of UNHW . . . . 103.
102′. Size small (10 mm) to large (60 mm); UP, if small, not blue to brown, (usually orange or at least predominantly that color) . . . . 136.

103. HW tailed . . . . 104.
103′. HW not tailed . . . . 119.

104. UN green . . . . 105.
104′. UN not green . . . . 106.

105. UNFW with broken white-edged discal line . . . . *Ch. s. simaethis* (235)
105′. UNFW with broken discal line, not white-edged . . . . *Ch. m. maesites* (236)

106. HW with 1 tail . . . . 107.
106′. HW with 2 tails . . . . 116.

107. UNHW markings rich red; size tiny; UP grayish . . . *T. azia* (238)
107′. Not so . . . . 108.

108. UNHW with a series of iridescent greenish blue marginal dots . . . . *Ps. b. bornoi* (268)
108′. No series of UNHW marginal dots . . . . 109.

109. UP with blue areas or iridescent blue . . . . 110.
109′. No blue UP areas . . . . 114.

110. FW anal lobe black . . . . *A. fidena* (231)
110′. Not so . . . . 111.

111. UP bright blue; UNHW distinctly dotted and with 4–5 marginal spots . . . . *S. andrewi* (249)
111′. No distinct UNHW spotting . . . . 112.

112. UN white to dull gray . . . . 113.
112′. UN blackish brown; base of UPFW and UPHW dull purplish blue . . . . *E. minikyanos* (234)

113. UP iridescent blue to violet; UN white to dull gray . . . . *T. hispaniola* (241)
113′. UP iridescent blue to silvery blue; UN light gray . . . . *Th. abeja* (231)

114. UNFW postdiscal line very irregular; UNHW with large contrasting black dots . . . . *S. toussainti* (247)
114′. UNFW postdiscal line smooth . . . . 115.

115. No basal dark spot along costal border of UNHW . . . . *S. christophei* (250)
115′. A basal dark spot on costal border of UNHW . . . . 116.

116. UNHW postdiscal marking a *line*, acutely angled to anal margin . . . . *S. limenius* (251)
116′. UNHW postdiscal markings a diffuse *series of dashes*, not acutely angled to anal margin . . . *S. c. cybirus* (244)

117. UP with blue . . . . 118.
117′. UP without blue . . . . 119.

118. UN pale blue-gray, almost white, and only vaguely lined . . . . *N. c. aibonito* (240)
118′. UN dark, with distinct dark lines outwardly edged with white on both wings . . . . . . *S. monopeteinus* (253)

119. UP with metallic orange-brown; UN very dark and UNHW pattern lined outwardly with white . . . . *E. a. boyeri* (233)
119′. UP nonmetallic grayish blue; UN pattern boldly black on tan ground; a white cell spot on UNHW . . . . *S. a. petioni* (242)

120. UNHW with diffuse (= nonlinear)

pattern . . . . *S. b. gundlachianus* (255)
120′. Not so . . . . 121.

121. Size tiny (8–9 mm); UNHW with a marginal series of dark dots; UP bronzy . . . . *B. e. isophthalma* (257)
121′. Size larger; UNHW without marginal series of dark dots . . . . 122.

122. UN with more white area than brown area . . . . 123.
122′. UN with more brown area than white area . . . . 124.

123. Two UNHW marginal black spots . . . . *L. c. theonus* (258)
123′. One UNHW marginal black spot . . . . *L. idealus* (261)

124. UNHW with a *regular* postdiscal row of white spots in each space, forming a "band" of white; 2 UNHW marginal black spots . . . . *H. t. noeli* (266)
124′. Not so . . . . 125.

125. UNHW with 1 *circular* black spot in Cu1-Cu2 . . . . *H. h. watsoni* (262)
125′. UNHW with 1 *basally elongate* black spot in Cu1-Cu2 . . . . *H. c. ceraunus* (264)

126. Palpi obviously very elongate . . . . *L. terena* (270)
126′. Palpi normal, inconspicuous . . . . 127.

127. UP bright red and black . . . . 128.
127′. Not so . . . . 129.

128. UPHW with a broad margin-following red band . . . . *B. h. hyperia* (343)
128′. UPFW with a basal red blotch and a postdiscal red band, not reaching anal angle . . . . *S. g. nemesis* (373)

129. UP with either an overall green or blue to purple iridescence, *or* with blue to purple iridescent markings . . . . 130.
129′. Not so . . . . 135.

130. UP overall iridescent . . . . 131.
130′. UP with iridescent markings . . . . 135.

131. UP metallic green (males only) . . . . *D. e. zetes* (334)
131′. UP metallic blue to purple . . . . 132.

132. UPFW with 5 to 7 white (or at least pale) spots . . . . 133.
132′. UPFW without white spots, but with a white band on UPFW and UPHW (males only) . . . . *D. thoe* (381)

133. UPFW with 7 white spots . . . . *E. t. tatilista* (329)
133′. UPFW with 5 white spots . . . . 134.

134. UPFW white spots large, almost encompassing postdiscal to apical area of FW . . . . *M. aracynthia* (324)
134′. UPFW white (to pale) spots small, some inconspicuous in females . . . . *E. monima* (332)

135. Size large (43–60 mm); UP with a broad blue band and UPFW with 2 blue patches . . . . . *A. d. amphitoe* (375)
135′. Size moderate (25–38 mm); UP with 4 white areas, 1 per wing, with blue reflections (males only) . . *H. misippus* (306)

136. UP brown and white . . . . 137.
136′. UP not brown and white . . . . 139.

137. UP with diagonal white bars on FW and vertical white bars on HW . . . . *A. lytrea* (315)
137′. UP with white spots . . . . 138.

138. UNHW with 2 ocelli; bases of FW with some iridencent green (females only) . . . . *D. e. zetes* (334)
138′. UP and UN with white spots, and with a submarginal row of dark brown to black spots on UNHW . . . . *A. teleboas* (335)

139. UNHW with distinct ocelli; UP not plain brown . . . . 140.
139′. Not so . . . . 149.

140. UP orange with brown subapical and postdiscal bands; ocelli centered with iridescent green to blue . . . . *L. s. torrebia* (340)
140′. Not so . . . . 141.

141. Wings transparent, *or* without UP pattern, *or* orange to brown with either conspicuous black veins or many black spots . . . . 167.
141′. Wings not as described (but with UNHW ocelli) . . . . 142.

142. UP gray . . . . *H. a. diasia* (345)
142′. Not so . . . . 143.

143. UP brown; UPFW pattern a row of ill-defined fulvous submarginal spots from M2 to inner margin . . . . *C. arcas* (395)
143′. Not so . . . . 144.

144. UNHW with 2 (occasionally 3) ocelli . . . . 145.
144′. UNHW with more than 3 ocelli . . . . 146.

145. UPFW without ocelli; 2 UNHW ocelli . . . . . *V. virginiensis* (298)
145′. UPFW with 1 ocellus; 2 or 3 UNHW ocelli . . . *J. g. zonalis* (307)

146. UPFW basically black, with a pattern of orange (fades to pink) and white . . . . *V. c. cardui* (300)
146′. Not so . . . . 147.

147. UP tan to brown, the UPFW postdiscal and apical areas distinctly darker than discal area, and with a costal-anal angle series of yellow spots . . . . . . *A. i. idyja* (379)
147′. Not so . . . . 148.

148. UNHW contrastingly patterned in yellows, orange, and brown, in more or less concentric circles from base; UPFW with a yellow cell oval . . . . *E. claudia* (287)
148′. UNHW basically uniform orange; UPFW cell with 2 broken ovals . . . . *E. h. hegesia* (289)

149. UN with a yellow-and-brown zebralike pattern . . . . *C. d. wolcotti* (354)
149′. Not so . . . . 150.

150. UP black and pale green . . . . *S. s. stelenes* (318)
150′. Not so. . . . . 151.

151. UP dusky tan; a black dot in UPFW Cu1-Cu2 . . . . *A. j. saturata* (311)
151′. UP colored otherwise . . . . 152.

152. FW length greater than FW breadth; UP coloration basically orange and brown to black . . . . . . *A. cryptadia* (293)
152′. Not so . . . . 153.

153. HW tailed . . . . 154.
153′. HW not tailed . . . . 156.

154. A translucent white spot in FW M2-M3; 2 tails, that on M3 longer and sharply pointed . . . . . . *H. paulla* (304)
154′. No FW translucent spot . . . . 155.

155. UP longitudinally striped dark brown and tan; proximal 1/2 UN white . . . . *M. chiron* (358)
155′. UP orange with black lines; UN tan . . . . *M. e. dospassosi* (360)

156. Size small (10–21 mm); UP basically orange with dark markings . . . . 157.
156′. Size larger (24–60 mm); UP otherwise colored . . . . 158.

157. UP orange with a FW brown to black pattern of more or less vertical lines; outer margin of FW convex . . . . *A. p. pelops* (296)
157′. UP black and pale orange; outer margin of FW concave . . . . *A. f. frisia* (293)

158. UPHW with a broad orange-red margin and UPFW with an orange-red band from costa to anal angle . . . . *V. a. rubria* (302)
158′. Not so . . . . 159.

159. UN dark brown with a white band on UNHW . . . . *A. lapitha* (323)
159′. Not so . . . . 160.

160. UP with a creamy to white band from FW apex to HW inner margin . . . . *A. gelania* (320)
160′. Not so . . . . 161.

161. UP tan to brown with a white postdiscal band on both wings; UPHW with a series of blackish submarginal lunules (females only) . . . . *D. thoe* (381)
161′. Not so . . . . 162.

162. UP orange-tan, with a UPFW subapical white band, the apex black: UNHW pale tan (females only) . . . . *H. misippus* (306)
162′. Not so . . . . 163.

163. HW with a short tail . . . . 164.
163′. Not so; UPFW with an apical white spot . . . . . *H. o. odius* (350)

164. UN rich russet . . . . *M. johnsoni* (368)
164′. Not so . . . . 165.

165. UPFW with 5 white apical spots . . . . *H. a. semele* (349)
165′. Not so . . . . 166.

166. UP brown . . . . *M. v. verticordia* (370)
166′. UP red-orange to tan, in males with a purple gloss . . . . *A. troglodyta* (364)

167. Wings transparent . . . . 168.
167′. Wings scaled, not transparent . . . . 171.

168. Marginal white spot in M3-Cu1 large, inverted comma-shaped, almost touching transversely elongate white spot in M2-M3 (females only; males cannot be identified to subspecies) . . . . *G. d. galii* (456)
168′. Not so . . . . 169.

169. Black subapical bar narrow, its posterior Y short; white spot in M2-M3 virtually isolated from subapical white bar . . . . *G. d. calimete* (455)
169′. Black subapical bar broad, with posterior Y longer; white spot in M2-M3, with its inner point closer to subapical white bar . . . . 170.

170. Black subapical bar broad and not strongly tapering, the arms of the posterior Y not so extensive (= following M2); subapical white bar separated from white spot in M2-M3 . . . . *G. d. quisqueya* (453)
170′. Black subapical bar narrow and tapering

strongly before posterior Y, which is extensive and has 1 arm following M2; subapical white bar virtually continuous with white spot in M2-M3 . . . . *G. d. charadra* (454)

171. UP tan to brown without pattern except (in some species) a small inconspicuous white-capped blackish HW anal lobe . . . . 178.
171′. UP orange or tan with conspicuous black veins, *or* tan spotted black, *or* with a black-yellow-orange pattern . . . . 172.

172. UP brown, orange, or tan, with veins black and prominent . . . . 173.
172′. UP tan, spotted with black . . . . 176.

173. UPFW apex boldly black and without yellow apical and subapical spots . . . . *D. p. megalippe* (463)
173′. Not so . . . . 174.

174. UNHW veins edged with white; UPFW apex with yellow spots . . . . *D. cleophile* (467)
174′. Not so . . . . 175.

175. UP brown; UNHW coffee-colored and with a series of rather vague postdiscal spots; UPFW with a white spot at least in M3-Cu1 . . . . *D. e. tethys* (640)
175′. UP orange-brown and with a white spot in FW M3-Cu1; no UNHW paler spots . . . . *D. g. cleothera* (458)

176. UPHW patternless except for dark submarginal semicircles; UNFW disc violet . . . . *A. jaegeri* (480)
176′. UPHW with 2 or 3 rows of submarginal and postdiscal black spots . . . . 177.

177. 2 rows of black submarginal and postdiscal spots . . . . *A. p. pantherata* (478)
177′. 3 rows of black submarginal and postdiscal spots . . . . *A. b. briarea* (474)

178. UN with a distinct yellow or white pattern . . . . 179.
178′. No UN yellow or white pattern . . . . 183.

179. UNHW with a bright yellow (greenish or grayish in females) bar from midcosta to inner margin; UP rich dark blackish brown . . . . *C. archebates* (384)
179′. Not so; UNHW pattern more complex . . . . 180.

180. UNHW with a more or less Y-shaped white pattern, the stem of the Y at midcosta, the 2 arms to the anal angle and at mid-inner margin . . . . 181.
180′. UNHW with a triangular pale yellow pattern . *C. wetherbeei* (388)

181. UNHW rust colored . . . . *C. chrysaoros* (389)
181′. UN not rust colored . . . . 182.

182. UNHW white pattern broken at branches of arms of Y . . . . *C. galii* (391)
182′. UNHW white pattern complete, not broken, and enclosing a rectangle or square of ground color in M3-Cu1 . . . . *C. choneupsilon* (393)

183. UNHW ocellus, single, small to tiny, ovate on a basal-marginal axis; pale pupil distinctly basal within ocellus . . . . *C. elelea* (442)
183′. Not so . . . . 184.

184. UNHW with 2 or more ocelli . . . . 185.
184′. UNHW with 1 ocellus . . . . 192.

185. UNHW with 4 or 6 (rarely 8) ocelli . . . . *C. neiba* (424)
185′. UNHW with 2 ocelli, anteriormost at times tiny to absent . . . . 186.

186. No red in UNFW cell . . . . 187.
186′. Red in UNFW cell . . . . 190.

187. White dot in M2-M3 dashlike . . . . *C. sommeri* (405)
187′. Not so . . . . 188.

188. UN brown; UNHW ocelli small . . . . *C. micrommata* (404)
188′. Not so . . . . 189.

189. UNHW with a distinct basal line . . . . *C. g. grannus* (399)
189′. UNHW basal line obscure or absent . . . . . . *C. amazona* (402)

190. UNHW anterior ocellus minute (at times absent) . . . . 191.
190′. UNHW anterior ocellus present . . . . *C. g. dilemma* (400)

191. UNFW postdiscal line expands around UNFW ocellus as the line extends from costa to inner margin and then passes marginad just behind ocellus; UNHW white dots usually "smeared" . . . . *C. dystacta* (403)
191′. UNFW postdiscal line farther basal, does not expand greatly to accommodate UNFW ocellus, and does not contract posterior to that ocellus, thereby reaching inner margin more basally; UNHW white dots discrete and not "smeared" . . . . . . *C. phoinix* (401)

192. UNHW not red or orange *or* HW margin scalloped . . . . 193.
192′. UNHW red or orange *or* cell entirely red . . . . 203.

193. Outer margin of HW scalloped . . . . 194.

193′. Outer margin of HW not scalloped . . . . 195.

194. UNHW dull brick red; UNHW anal lobe not large and brick red . . . . *C. clydoniata* (439)
194′. UNHW dark olivaceous; UNHW anal lobe large and brick red . . . . *C. clenchi* (441)

195. A red blush posterior to UNFW ocellus . . . . 196.
195′. No UNFW postocellar blush . . . . 199.

196. Size small (males 12–15 mm, females 13–15 mm) . . . . *C. batesi* (410)
196′. Size larger (males 15–18 mm, females 15–19 mm) . . . . 197.

197. Red in UNFW cell sharply truncate at about midcell by a dark transverse line . . . . *C. hysia* (408)
197′. Not so . . . . 198.

198. UNHW postdiscal and submarginal lines converge at anal angle . . . . *C. aleucosticha* (413)
198′. UNHW lines remain more or less parallel toward anal angle . . . . *C. tragia* (396)

199. UNHW ocellus tiny, with 2 central pupils . . . . *C. micheneri* (407)
199′. UNHW ocellus larger, with 1 (to 5 in a vertical row in *C. gonzalezi*) pupil . . . . 200.

200. UNHW ocellus circular, small . . . . 201.
200′. UNHW ocellus circular or oval, large . . . . 202.

201. UNHW with all dark lines very obscure or absent: UNFW base suffused with bright red . . . *C. ainigma* (445)
201′. UNHW with discal, postdiscal, and submarginal dark lines present; UNFW without bright red . . . . *C. loxias* (387)

202. UNHW ocellus oval; UN dark lines usually very indistinct . . . . *C. obscura* (417)
202′. UNHW ocellus circular; UNFW ocellar pupils bright blue . . . . *C. gonzalezi* (421)

203. UN red to rich orange, at least on UNHW . . . . 206.
203′. Not so . . . . 204.

204. UN blackish brown; UNHW lines prominent; no ocellus-remnant at UNHW angle . . . . . . *C. debarriera* (422)
204′. UNHW angle with dark ocellus-remnant . . . . 205.

205. UNHW lines obscure, not outlined with white . . *C. montana* (438)
205′. UNHW lines prominent, outlined marginally with white . . . . *C. confusa* (414)

206. Size large (males 19–24 mm, females 22–28 mm) . . . . . . 207.
206′. Size small (males 13–19 mm, females 15–21 mm) . . . . . . 208.

207. UNHW ocellus large (males 2.8–3.8 mm, females 2.8–3.8 mm) . . . . *C. p. pulchella* (446)
207′. UNHW ocellus small (males 0.6–2.4 mm, females 2.0–2.8 mm) . . . . *C. p. darlingtoni* (450)

208. UPFW androconial patch sharply defined . . . . 209.
208′. UPFW androconial patch diffusely or not sharply defined . . 212.

209. UPFW androconial patch parallels outer margin . . . . 210.
209′. UPFW androconial patch does not parallel outer margin . . . 211.

210. UNHW ocellus pupil *within* yellow ring; male FW length 13–19 mm, female FW length 16–22 mm . . . . *C. crypta* (427)
210′. UNHW ocellus pupil *on* pale yellow ring; male FW length 15–16 mm, female FW length 15–16 mm . . . . *C. lyceia* (426)

211. UNFW brick-red blush extends past UNFW ocellus to basal-submarginal lines; UNHW with basally located white pupil, virtually on yellow ring . . *C. hendersoni* (433)
211′. UNFW brick red does not extend past UNFW ocellus . . . . *C. franciscoi* (429)

212. FW rounded, males 15–20 mm, females 15–22 mm; UNHW with 3 white dots not in row, the dot in M2-M3 distinctly larger and more basally located; UNHW ocellus very small (absent in females) and ellipsoidal . . . . *C. raburni* (434)
212′. FW not rounded, males 17–19 mm, females 18–21 mm; UNHW with 4 white dots in row except that in M2-M3; UNHW ocellus with a small white pupil, located basally on the outer edge of yellow ring . . . . *C. schwartzi* (436)

Clave para las Mariposas de la Española

(LD = lado dorsal; LV= lado ventral;
AD = ala delantera; AT = ala trasera)

1. Antenas recurvadas apicalmente . . . . 2.
1'. Antenas no recurvadas apicalmente . . . . 54.

2. AT con cola . . . . 3.
2'. AT sin cola . . . . 6.

3. Escamas en el cuerpo y base del ala en LD parecen pelos verdes iridiscentes . . . . *U. p. domingo* (29)
3'. LD sin pelos verdes iridiscentes . . . . 4.

4. LVAT con una aparente mancha central de color blanco . . . . *Ch. ixion* (25)
4'. LVAT sin una aparente mancha central de color blanco . . . . . . 5.

5. AD con 7 manchas hialinas, la más basal formando una corta línea diagonal . . . . *U. d. cramptoni* (32)
5'. 6 ó 7 manchas hialinas en AD, la de la celdilla de AD es ancha en vez de larga y está dentada apicalmente . . . . *P. o. decussata* (35)

6. LD con azul o con verde iridiscente . . . . 7.
6'. LD sin azul o sin verde iridiscente . . . . 10.

7. AT con líneas azules; AD con base azul y transparentes manchas en AD . . . . *Ph. p. bicolor* (17)
7'. Azul o verde presente pero no alineado . . . . 8.

8. LD con verde iridiscente en ambas alas y en el cuerpo; AD con manchas hialinas translucientes . . . . *A. talus* (35)
8'. LD con azul iridiscente . . . . 9.

9. Azul iridiscente en LD solamente; no hay manchas hialinas en AD . . . . *A. h. heriul* (40)
9'. Iridiscente en LD y en LV; AD con manchas hialinas . . . . *A. christyi* (39)

10. LVAT con barra blanca vertical o una mancha blanca . . . . . 11.
10'. LVAT sin barra blanca vertical o sin mancha blanca . . . . . . 13.

11. LVAT con mancha blanca; AD evidentemente alongada . . . . *P. m. sanchesi* (19)
11'. LVAT con barra blanca . . . . 12.

12. Barra blanca de LVAT con indentación marrón costal . . . . *E. spanna* (21)
12'. Barra blanca de LVAT sin indentación marrón costal . . . . *A. a. haitensis* (28)

13. Marron arriba y abajo, casi sin diseño . . . . . *A. a. anausis* (38)
13'. No es así . . . . 14.

14. LVAT grisoso verde . . . . *P. l. lividus* (23)
14'. No es así . . . . 15.

15. LD gris pálido con marcas grises oscuras, casi negras . . . . *P. oileus* (60)
15'. No es así . . . . 16.

16. LD anaranjado . . . . 17.
16'. No es así . . . . 23.

17. Tamaño (longitud de AD) muy grande (21–29 mm); ancho margen negro en LDAD y LDAT . . . . . . *P. a. antiqua* (66)
17'. Tamaño medio a pequeño (10–22 mm) . . . . 18.

18. Tamaño pequeño (10–11 mm); venas negras en LV en gran contraste a fondo anaranjado . . . . *O. stillmani* (78)
18'. Tamaño pequeño a mediano (13–22 mm); no hay contraste entre venas y fondo . . . . 19.

19. Tamaño mediano (14–18 mm); LVAT con puntos negros esparcidos y un pliegue oscuro anal en los machos; en hembras, es similar pero más marrón a negro en el borde posterior de LVAD . . . . . *H. ph. phylea* (86)
19'. No es así . . . . 20.

20. LD en machos con prominente estigma negro; en hembras una cadena compuesta de 6 manchas pálidas, en LVAT, en un fondo anaranjado oscuro . . . . *H. nabokovi* (89)
20'. No es así . . . . 21.

21. Tamaño pequeño (13–16 mm); LD amarillo aureado claro, estigma en machos bipartido; LVAT amarillo aureado luciente . . . . *Ch. haitensis* (93)
21'. Tamaño pequeño (13–17 mm); pero LVAT color olivo o leonado y LD amarillo aureado oscuro o anaranjado-amarillo claro . . . . 22.

22. LD amarillo aureado oscuro; estigma en machos es sencillo; LVAT color olivo . . . . *Ch. melissa* (96)
22'. LD anaranjado-amarilloso claro; estigma en machos es bipartido; LVAT leonado . . . . *Ch. schwartzi* (95)

23. LV verde en ambas alas y en ambos sexos . . . . . . *P. batesi* (98)

23′. LV no es verde . . . . 24.

24. AD con manchas hialinas evidentes . . . . 25.
24′. AD sin manchas hialinas evidentes . . . . 37.

25. En celdilla de AD, mancha hialina en forma de 'J' o de anzuelo . . . . *C. p. potrillo* (47)
25′. No es así . . . . 26.

26. AD con 2 ó 3 (está última muy minuta) manchas hialinas; LVAT con 2 manchas rectangulares grandes, cada una con 2 capas blancas . . . . *Ph. unia* (71)
26′. No es así . . . . 27.

27. LVAT con cinco puntos negros (muy pequeños en las hembras), con área circular blancuzca . . . . . . *Argon* sp. (68)
27′. No es así . . . . 28.

28. LVAT con muestra vívida . . . . 29.
28′. No es así . . . . 31.

29. LVAT con una barra blanca destacada en un fondo marrón . . . . *P. nero* (107)
29′. Barra amarilla (amarilla pálida en hembras) o marrón y violeta en LVAT . . . . 30.

30. LVAT con barra amarilla o amarilla pálida . . . . . *A. m. apa* (88)
30′. LVAT con barras marrones y violetas . . . . . *N. n. nyctelius* (112)

31. LD con manchas blancas . . . . *P. c. odilia* (63)
31′. No es así . . . . 32.

32. Palpos claramente blancos, no de color gris . . . . 33.
32′. Palpos no son blancos . . . . 34.

33. Machos con pliegue costal en AD y con tres puntos blancuzcos subapicales en AD; hembras iguales que machos, pero con diseño purpurino en LVAT . . . . *B. stillmani* (43)
33′. Machos sin pliegue costal pero con 3 puntos blancuzcos subapicales; hembras con muestra de 6 puntos hialinos en LDAD y sin marca purpurina en LVAT . . . . *B. hispaniolae* (4400)

34. Tamaño pequeño (13–16 mm); LD marrón y con una muestra borrosa . . . . 35.
34′. Tamaño pequeño a grande pero con diseño destacado *o* unicolor y sin muestra, *o* con AD claramente alargada . . . . . 36.

35. Diseño de LD es una vaga marca diagonal de color ocráceo en AD . . . . *S. m. adoceta* (71)
35′. LD sin diseño y si a caso con varios puntos grises

opacos en AD . . . . *C. t. tripunctus* (73)

36. AD claramente alargada . . . . 37.
36′. No es así . . . . 39.

37. Un punto pálido apical en LVAD . . . . *A. s. dilloni* (50)
37′. No hay un punto pálido apical . . . . 38.

38. Tamaño grande (21–27 mm); LVAT con escamas purpurinas y distintas formando una faja la cual sigue el borde . . . . *A. p. sagra* (48)
38′. Tamaño pequeño (14–16 mm); LVAT sin escamas purpurinas . . . . *G. g. gesta* (52)

39. AD con manchas hialinas o pálidas . . . . 40.
39′. AD sin manchas hialinas o pálidas . . . . 47.

40. De 2 a 4 manchas hialinas en AD . . . . 41.
40′. De 5 a 11 manchas hialinas en AD . . . . 44.

41. 3 manchas hialinas en AD; una mancha curvada pálida en la celdilla y con marca sexual (= sex brand) . . . . *P. ph. philetes* (69)
41′. 2, 4 ó 5 marcas pálidas en AD; no hay marca de sexo . . . . 42.

42. 2 manchas pálidas en AD (solamente hembras) . . . . *E. s. insolata* (100)
42′. 4 ó 5 manchas pálidas en AD (ambos sexos); no hay puntos o manchas . . . . 43.

43. Punto pálido en celdilla de LDAD . . . . . . *P. o. distipuncta* (110)
43′. No hay punto pálido en celdilla de LDAD . . . . . *P. o. ocola* (108)

44. De 5 a 7 manchas pálidas en AD . . . . 45.
44′. De 8 a 11 manchas pálidas en AD (solamente hembras) *o* 5 puntos pálidos en AD . . . . 47.

45. LVAT con una hilera borrosa de puntos pálidos, los cuales siguen el margen . . . . *P. s. woodruffi* (104)
45′. LVAT sin hilera *borrosa* de puntos pálidos . . . . 46.

46. AT tiene una línea destacada horizontal de manchas translucientes . . . . *C. ethlius* (102)
46′. LVAT con un diseño destacable de manchas color blanco plateado, y aureado (solamente machos) . . . *Rh. bushi* (76)

47. De 8 a 11 manchas pálidas en AD . . . . 48.
47′. 5 manchas pálidas en la AD; una serie de manchas submarginales sagitales . . . . *E. zarucco* (59)

48. 11 manchas pálidas destacadas en la AD, acomodadas más o menos en un círculo

subapical, la cual en el Cu1-Cu2 es la más grande (solamente hembras) . . . . *E. zephodes* (57)
48′. 8 manchas translucientes en la AD (solamente hembras) . . . . *Rh. bushi* (76)

49. LD terciopelado negro a marrón oscuro (solamente machos) . . . . *E. zephodes* (57)
49′. No es así el LD . . . . 50.

50. LD de color anaranjado leonado; la gran parte de LDAD es pardo y LV es claramente anaranjado (solamente machos) . . . . *E. s. insolata* (100)
50′. LD es anaranjado pero no exclusivamente de este color . . . . 51.

51. LDAD con un parche circular de escamas grandes brillantinas y con una línea doble de escamas oscuras, las cuales van al margen exterior (solamente machos) . . . . *W. druryi* (83)
51′. LDAD sin el parche de escamas modificadas . . . . 52.

52. Marca sexual en machos es lineal y angulada . . . *P. b. loma* (81)
52′. No es así (solamente hembras) . . . . 53.

53. LD es de color marrón oscuro con 5 puntos anaranjados (solamente hembras) . . . . *W. druryi* (83)
53′. LVAT con manchas grises borrosas en serie de curva en la parte discal (solamente hembras) . . . . *P. b. loma* (81)

54. AT con solo 1 vena anal . . . . 55.
54′. AT con 2 venas anales . . . . 63.

55. AT sin cola . . . . *B. p. polycrates* (119)
55′. Con cola en AT . . . . 56.

56. LD alineado a lo largo en negro y blanco hacia un verde muy pálido . . . . *E. zonarius* (123)
56′. No está alineado a lo largo . . . . 57.

57. LD casi todo negro con o sin líneas o marcas pálidas . . . . . . 58.
57′. LD es de color marrón oscuro a negruzco con líneas pálidas (amarillentas), o amarillo y negro bien destacado y sagitales plateados . . . . 61.

58. LVAT tiene una serie de marcas sagitarias, las cuales apuntan hacia la base . . . . *B. zetides* (115)
58′. No es así . . . . 59.

59. LDAT con una sufución discal de color verde grisoso; LDAD sin amarillo (solamente hembras) . . . *H. a. epidaurus* (135)
59′. LDAD con 1 ó 2 fajas diagonales pálidas . . . . 60.

60. 2 fajas en LDAD, concurriendo en el ángulo

anal . . . . *H. aristor* (138)
60′. Una faja pálida en LDAD de costa hasta ángulo anal . . . . *P. p. imerius* (142)

61. LDAD con marcas diagonales pálidas, pero no paralelas al margen; LVAT tiene disco amarillo . . . . *H. machaonides* (131)
61′. No es así . . . . 62.

62. LDAD es casi toda amarilla (solamente machos) . . . . *H. a. epidaurus* (135)
62′. LDAD es de color marrón y amarillo; colas sin centros pálidos . . . . *H. a. aristodemus* (127)

63. LD es de color blanco, amarillo, o anaranjado lúcido *o* al menos en estos colores primariamente . . . . 64.
63′. No es así . . . . 95.

64. LD es blanco, cremoso, o amarillo . . . . 65.
64′. LD es anaranjado . . . . 89.

65. LD es blanco con, a lo más, algunas manchas o puntos negros, nunca con manchas coloreadas (amarillas o anaranjadas) . . . . 66.
65′. LD es blanco con algunas u otras marcas de colores cremoso o amarillo . . . . 68.

66. LD es blanco en ambos sexos; machos con una mancha en el fin de la celdilla de LDAD, hembras con 4 manchas negras, una en el fin de la celdilla . . . . *G. j. josephina* (146)
66′. No hay manchas negras en LDAD . . . . 67.

67. LD en machos es nacarado, hembras más o menos como los machos o con gris oscuro a negruzco LDAD, la celdilla de LDAD es de color oscuro . . . . *A. d. boydi* (152)
67′. En machos el LD es blanco, el margen exterior de AD es denticulado oscuro; el color de la hembra varía de grisoso a gris oscuro y en LVAT amarillento con escamas grises, las cuales siguen a las venas . . . . *A. m. eubotea* (149)

68. LDAT y LVAT son de color cremoso a amarillento, el último con una línea gris a negra desde costa hasta el ángulo anal . . . . *M. s. salacia* (155)
68′. LD es amarillo o blanco con otras marcas de color . . . . 69.

69. LD blanco con marcas de otros colores . . . . 70.
69′. LD amarillo . . . . 72.

70. LDAD tiene un parche que es amarillo (hasta anaranjado) cuadrado a rectangular, desde el fin de la celdilla hasta la costa . . . . *A. c. clorinde* (200)
70′. No es así . . . . 71.

71. En la base, el LDAD tiene una mancha grande de color anaranjado (solamente machos) . . . . . . *A. o. browni* (220)
71′. En la base, el LDAD tiene una mancha amarilla grande (solamente machos) . . . . *A. godartiana* (222)

72. Tamaño pequeño (12–21 mm) . . . . 73.
72′. Tamaño moderado (21–48 mm) . . . . 80.

73. En la margen interna de LDAD, los machos tienen una barra gris oscura a negra; hembras, blancas a pálido amarillentas y sin la barra oscura en LDAD . . . . 74.
73′. No hay barra oscura en LDAD; las hembras no son blancas; el amarillo es usualmente más claro . . . . 75.

74. Los machos tienen una barra *arcada* oscura en LDAD; hembras no tienen amarillo en LDAD . . . . *E. d. palmira* (173)
74′. Barra oscura en LDAD es *derecha* en los machos; hembras tienen un teñido amarillento, por lo menos, en LDAD . . . . *E. elathea* (176)

75. Borde oscuro en LDAD distintamente más ancho en el ápice . . . . 76.
75′. Borde oscuro en LDAD ligeramente ancho en el ápice y no alcanza el ángulo anal de la AD . . . . 78.

76. Margen interno de LDAD y la costa de LDAT con barras oscuras (marrones a negras); LVAD tiene 2 manchas negras postdiscales . . . . *N. iole* (188)
76′. Sin el mismo diseño . . . . 77'

77. El margen negro de LDAD se ahusa a ángulo anal en ambos sexos; una mancha marginal de color rojizo a anaranjado en LVAT; un punto oscuro al final de la celdilla de LDAD . . . . . . *E. l. euterpe* (158)
77′. Margen negro de LDAD se encuentra con la margen interior cuadradamente; no hay mancha rojiza o anaranjada en la LVAT de los machos; no hay punto oscuro al final de la celdilla de LDAD; hembras de color amarillo a amarillo anaranjado, precisas marcas marrones en LVAT . . . . *E. euterpiformis* (161)

78. La faja negra marginal de LDAD termina abruptamente en Cu2 . . . . *E. l. priddyi* (180)

78′. Sin el mismo diseño . . . . 79.

79. LD de color claro amarillo limón; LVAT sin diseño en los machos, con una mancha herrumbrosa muy irregular de color marrón en el ápice de las hembras . . . . *E. l. memula* (167)

79′. LD es un poco anaranjado; en ambos sexos hay una mancha apical en LVAT, roja en machos, roja oscura en hembras; LVAT, en hembras, tiene un rubor marginal rojizo . . . . *E. larae* (169)

80. LDAD tiene una marca negra e indentada, y al fin de la celdilla tiene una mancha negra; en el fin de la celdilla de LVAT hay 2 manchas rosadas . . . . *Z. c. cynops* (195)

80′. No es así . . . . 81.

81. LD es amarillo verduzco, con una mancha negra en el fin de la celdilla de AD y una mancha grisosa en el fin de la celdilla de LDAT . . . . *A. maerula* (197)

81′. No es así . . . . 82.

82. Machos con una roncha anaranjada en LDAD con una mancha negra en el fin de la celdilla de AD; hembras con una roncha anaranjada en LDAD; en ambos sexos hay una línea oscura muy irregular en LVAD, la cual es submarginal . . . . *Ph. th. thalestris* (204)

82′. No es así . . . . 83.

83. El LVAT tiene una mancha al final de la celdilla, *o* no manchas, *o* una línea gris desde midcosta hasta casi el ángulo anal . . . . 84.

83′. El LVAT tiene 2 manchas plateadas al final de la celdilla . . . . 86.

84. El LD es variable: puede ser amarillo o blanco, y el color de la base de LDAD varía de amarillo a anaranjado; machos a veces tienen una barra corta de color negro en el ápice en LDAT . . . . *K. lyside* (190)

84′. No es así . . . . 85.

85. LV es verde pálido, no amarillo; una línea gris y diagonal en LVAD desde el ápice hasta el punto central del margen interior y otra línea en LVAT desde midcosta hasta casi el ángulo anal . . . *Rh. t. watsoni* (218)

85′. Ninguna (machos) o solamente 1 (hembras) mancha en el final de la celdilla de LVAT; machos con un área ancha de escamas modificadas en LD, extendiéndose basalmente hasta el fin exterior de la celdilla; hembras con LV borde marrón en LDAD y

una mancha pequeña y oscura al final
de la celdilla . . . . *A. s. hispaniolae* (225)

86. LVAT no es color olivo . . . . 87.
86'. LVAT es color olivo (hembras solamente) . . . . *A. o. browni* (220)

87. Una mancha grande de color marrón oscuro en el AD de la celdilla del LD y LVAD; el ápice y el margen exterior de la AD son bordados anchamente en marrón (solamente hembras) . . . . *A. godartiana* (222)
87'. No es así . . . . 88.

88. El LVAD no es claramente más anaranjado en los 2/3 anteriores que en el 1/3 posterior; hembras tienen el margen exterior de AD de color marrón oscuro y con conchas . . . . *Ph. s. sennae* (213)
88'. El LVAD es claramente más anaranjado en los 2/3 anteriores que en el 1/3 posterior; hembras son de color de rosa y con una línea postdiscal mellada en LVAD . . . . *Ph. editha* (216)

89. Tamaño pequeño a moderado (12–27 mm) . . . . 90.
89'. Tamaño más grande (26–39 mm) . . . . 94.

90. LD es anaranjado brillante, LV amarillo puro, virtualmente sin marcas; LDAD y LDAT con borde negro angosto . . . . *E. d. mayobanex* (165)
90'. No es así . . . . 91.

91. Angulo anal de AT es puntiagudo; LDAD con (en machos) margenes negros costales o (en hembras) un negro ancho en el ápice; fines exteriores de todas las venas son negras y en contraste con el color de fondo . . . . *E. p. proterpia* (170)
91'. AT no es puntiagudo . . . . 92.

92. LD (en machos) con margen negro y ancho hasta AD y AT; en hembras con cúspide negra en AD solamente; en ambas alas, las bases de LD en hembras son amarillas . . . . . . *E. pyro* (181)
92'. No es así, y con una mancha negra al final de la celdilla . . . . 93.

93. El borde interno de LDAD y LDAT tiene una faja marginal de color negro, la cual es irregular, debido a escamas negras que siguen a las venas hasta la base . . . . *E. nicippe* (184)
93'. El borde interno de LVAD y LVAT tiene una faja marginal de color negro la cual es regular; los bordes negros de ambas alas son relativamente

estrechos . . . . *E. nicippiformis* (186)

94. Faja marrón (ambos sexos) de LVAD es irregular, desde el ápice al margen interior . . . . *Ph. a. rorata* (208)
94′. Faja marrón (ambos sexos) en LVAD es derecha, desde el ápice al margen interior . . . . *Ph. a. antillia* (211)

95. AD no es transparente, pero la longitud de AD es más grande que su anchura . . . . 96.
95′. AD transparente o la longitud de AD es casi igual a la anchura de AD (con excepción de *A. cryptadia* que tiene una faja ancha y discal de manchas amarillentas en LDAT) . . . . 101.

96. LD de color moreno anaranjado vivo o de color canela . . . . . 97.
96′. LD más o menos es rayado horizontalmente con marrón y anaranjado, o negro con amarillo o anaranjado . . . . 99.

97. LVAT tiene manchas plateadas . . . . *A. v. insularis* (274)
97′. LVAT de color canela o gris anaranjado . . . . 98.

98. LVAT de color canela . . . . *D. i. hispaniola* (277)
98′. LVAT gris anaranjado . . . . *L. c. cleobaea* (281)

99. LD es de color canela anaranjado, rayado horizontalmente de color marrón oscuro . . . . *E. m. melphis* (283)
99′. LD con rayas negras, amarillas y/o anaranjadas . . . . 100.

100. LD rayado horizontalmente de color negro y anaranjado . . . . *H. ch. churchi* (283)
100′. LDAD tiene 3 rayas de color anaranjado amarillento alternando con negro; LVAT color de arena . . . . *D. spio* (226)

101. Alas transparentes . . . . 141.
101′. Alas con escamas, no transparentes . . . . 102.

102. Tamaño minúsculo (8–9 mm) a pequeño (15–16 mm); LD de color azul a marrón, frequentemente iridiscente, algunas con colas y usualmente con ocelos en el margen de LVAT . . . . 103.
102′. Tamaño pequeño (10 mm) a grande (60 mm); LD, cuando pequeño, es usualmente anaranjado o a lo menos predominante ese color; no es azul o marrón . . . . . 136.

103. AT con cola . . . . 104.
103′. AT sin cola . . . . 119.

104. LV de color verde . . . . 105.
104′. LV no es de color verde . . . . 106.

105. LVAD con línea discal discontinua de bordes blancos . . . . *Ch. s. simaethis* (235)
105′. LVAD con línea discal discontinua sin bordes blancos . . . . *Ch. m. maesites* (236)

106. AT con una cola . . . . 107.
106′. AT con dos colas . . . . 116.

107. Las marcas de LVAT son de color rojo vivo; tamaño chico; LD gris claro . . . . *T. azia* (238)
107′. Las marcas en LVAT no son rojas; tamaño pequeño . . . . . 108.

108. LVAT con una serie de puntos marginales iridiscentes de color verduzco azul . . . . *Ps. b. bornoi* (268)
108′. No tiene serie de puntos marginales . . . . 109.

109. LD con áreas de color azul o azul iridiscente . . . . 110.
109′. No hay áreas azules en LD . . . . 114.

110. AD con lóbulo posterior negro. . . . . *A. fidena* (231)
110′. No es así. . . . . 111.

111. LD azul brillante; LVAT con puntos precisos y 4 ó 5 manchas marginales . . . . *S. andrewi* (249)
111′. Sin manchas precisas . . . . 112.

112. LV de blanco a gris opaco . . . . 113.
112′. LV marrón negruzco; la base de LDAD y LDAT azul purpurino opaco . . . . *E. minikyanos* (234)

113. LD de azul iridiscente a violeta; LV de blanca o gris opeca . . . . *T. hispaniola* (241)
113′. LD de azul iridiscente a azul plateado; LV gris claro . . . . *Th. abeja* (231)

114. Línea postdiscal de LVAD es muy irregular; LVAT con grandes puntos negros, los cuales son de contraste . . . . *S. toussainti* (247)
114′. Línea postdiscal de LVAD es uniforme . . . . 115.

115. No hay una mancha oscura basal a lo largo del borde costal de LVAT . . . . *S. christophei* (250)
115′. Una mancha oscura basal a lo largo de LVAT . . . . 116.

116. LVAT postdiscal marca una línea agudamente angular hacia el margen anal . . . . *S. limenius* (251)
116′. LVAT postdiscal marca una *serie difusa de rayitas*, la cual no es angulada con agudeza a margen anal . . . . *S. c. cybirus* (244)

117. LD tiene color azul . . . . 118.
117′. LD no tiene color azul . . . . 119.

118. LV de color grisoso-azul, casi blanco, y vagamente alineado . . . . *N. c. aibonito* (240)
118'. LV oscuro, con claras líneas oscuras, exteriormente bordeadas con blanco en ambas alas . . . . *S. monopeteinus* (253)

119. LD con marrón-anaranjado metálico; LV muy oscuro y el diseño de LVAT está exteriormente alineada con blanco . . . . *E. a. boyeri* (233)
119'. LD de color grisoso azul, no metálico; diseño en un fondo de color canela, en el LV; una mancha blanca en la celdilla de LVAT . . . . . *S. a. petioni* (242)

120. LVAT con diseño esparcido (= no alineado) . . . . *S. b. gundlachianus* (2550)
120'. No es así . . . . 121.

121. Tamaño chico (8–9 mm); serie marginal en LVAT de puntos oscuros; LD bronceado . *B. e. isophthalma* (258)
121'. Tamaño más grande; no hay serie marginal en LVAT de puntos oscuros . . . . 122.

122. LV tiene más color blanco que marrón . . . . 123.
122'. LV tiene más marrón que blanco . . . . 124.

123. LVAT tiene dos manchas marginales negras . . *L. c. theonus* (261)
123'. LVAT tiene una mancha marginal negra . . . . . *L. idealus* (266)

124. LVAT tiene una línea regular y postdiscal de manchas blancas en cada espacio, formando una faja blanca; 2 manchas negras y marginales en LVAT . . . . *H. t. noeli* (266)
124'. No es así . . . . 125.

125. LVAT con una mancha negra *circular* en Cu1-Cu2 . . . . *H. h. watsoni* (262)
125'. LVAT con una mancha negra *extendida basalmente* en Cu1-Cu2 . . . . *H. c. ceraunus* (264)

126. Palpos obviamente muy extendidos . . . . *L. terena* (270)
126'. Palpos normales, poco notables . . . . 127.

127. LD de color rojo brillante y negro . . . . 128.
127'. No es así . . . . 129.

128. LDAT con una faja roja la cual es ancha y sigue el margen . . . . *B. h. hyperia* (343)
128'. LDAD con un bloque basal de color rojo y una faja roja postdiscal que no alcanza el ángulo anal . . . . *S. g. nemesis* (373)

129. LD con verde completo *o* de azul a púrpura

iridiscente, *o* con marcas iridiscentes azules o púrpuras . . . . 130.
129′. No es así . . . . 135.

130. LD es totalmente iridiscente . . . . 131.
130′. LD con marcas iridiscentes . . . . 135.

131. LD de color verde metálico (solamente machos) . *D. e. zetes* (334)
131′. LD de color azul metálico a púrpura . . . . 132.

132. LDAD con 5 a 7 manchas blancas (o al menos pálidas) . . . 133.
132′. LDAD sin manchas blancas, pero con una faja blanca en LDAD y LDAT (solamente machos) . . . . *D. thoe* (381)

133. LDAD con 7 manchas blancas . . . . *E. t. tatilista* (329)
133′. LDAD con 5 manchas blancas . . . . 134.

134. Grandes manchas blancas en LDAD, casi abarcando el área postdiscal a apical de AD . . . . *M. aracynthia* (324)
134′. Manchas pequeñas en LDAD de color blanco a pálido, algunas poco visibles en hembras . . . *E. monima* (332)

135. Tamaño grande (43–60 mm); LD con una raya ancha y azul, y LDAD con 2 parches azules . . . . *A. d. amphitoe* (375)
135′. Tamaño moderado (25–38 mm); LD con 4 áreas blancas, 1 por ala, con reflecciones azules (solamente machos) . . . . *H. misippus* (306)

136. LD marrón y blanco . . . . 137.
136′. LD no es marrón y blanco . . . . 139.

137. LD con barras blancas diagonales en AD y barras blancas verticales en AT . . . . *A. lytrea* (315)
137′. LD con manchas blancas . . . . 138.

138. LVAT con 2 ocelos; bases de AD con un poco de verde iridiscente (solamente hembras) . . . . . . *D. e. zetes* (334)
138′. LD y LV con manchas blancas y con una línea submarginal de manchas marrones oscuras a negras en LVAT . . . . *A. teleboas* (335)

139. LVAT con ocelos distintos; LD no es marrón simple . . . . . 140.
139′. No es así . . . . 149.

140. LD es anaranjado con fajas subapicales y postdiscales de color marrón; ocelos con centros de color verde a azul . . . . *L. s. torrebia* (340)
140′. No es así . . . . 141.

141. Alas transparentes, *o* sin diseño en LD; *o* anaranjado a marrón con notables venas negras

o muchas manchas negras . . . . 167.
141′. Alas no son como las descritas sino con ocelos en LVAT . . . 142.

142. LD de color gris . . . . *H. a. diasia* (345)
142′. No es así . . . . 143.

143. LD marrón; LDAD muestra una línea de manchas no muy bien definidas y leonadas, desde M2 hasta el margen interior . . . . *C. arcas* (395)
143′. No es así . . . . 144.

144. LVAT con 2 (a veces 3) ocelos . . . . 145.
144′. LVAT con más de 3 ocelos . . . . 146.

145. LDAD sin ocelos; LVAT con 2 ocelos . . . . . *V. virginiensis* (298)
145′. LDAD con 1 ocelo; LVAT con 2 ó 3 ocelos . . . *J. e. zonalis* (307)

146. LDAD básicamente color negro, con una muestra de anaranjado (el cual se desvanece en color rosa) y blanco . . . . *V. c. cardui* (300)
146′. No es así . . . . 147.

147. LD es de color canela a marrón, las áreas postdiscales y apicales de LDAD son claramente más oscuras que el área discal, y con una serie de manchas amarillas en el ángulo de la costa y ano . . . . *A. i. idyja* (379)
147′. No es así . . . . 148.

148. Círculos más o menos concéntricos desde la base y con diseños contrastantes en amarillo, anaranjado y marrón en LVAT; LDAD con celdilla oval de color amarillo. . . . . *E. claudia* (287)
148′. LVAT básicamente de color anaranjado uniforme; celdilla de LDAD con 2 óvalos rotos . . . . *E. h. hegesia* (289)

149. LV con un diseño de zebra, de color amarillo y marrón . . . . *C. d. wolcotti* (354)
149′. No es así . . . . 150.

150. LD es negro y verde pálido . . . . *S. s. stelenes* (318)
150′. No es así . . . . 151.

151. LD moreno puro; una mancha negra en LDAD entre Cu1 y Cu2 . . . . *A. j. saturata* (311)
151′. LD de otro color . . . . 152.

152. AD es más larga que ancha; colores de LD básicamente anaranjados, y de marrón a negro . . . *A. cryptadia* (293)
152′. No es así . . . . 153.

153. AT con cola . . . . 154.

153′. AT sin cola . . . . 156.

154. La AD tiene una mancha transluciente en M2-M3: 2 colas, la cual en M3 más larga y puntiaguda . . . . *H. paulla* (304)
154′. No hay manchas translucientes en AD . . . . 155.

155. LD está rayado a lo largo de colores marrón oscuro y moreno; aproximadamente la mitad de LV es blanco . . . . *M. chiron* (358)
155′. LD es anaranjado con líneas negras; LV es de color canela . . . . *M. e. dospassosi* (360)

156. Tamaño muy pequeño (10–21 mm); LD es básicamente anaranjado, con marcas oscuras . . . . 157.
156′. Tamaño más grande (24–60 mm); LD de otros colores . . . . 158.

157. LD anaranjado con diseño en AD de color marrón a negro, con más o menos líneas verticales; margen exterior de AD es convexo . . . . *A. p. pelops* (296)
157′. LD es de color negro y moreno anaranjado pálido; margen exterior de AD es cóncavo . . . . *A. f. frisia* (293)

158. LDAT con una línea anaranjada-rojiza por el margen y LDAD con una faja anaranjada-rojiza desde costa a ángulo anal . . . . *V. a. rubria* (302)
158′. No es así . . . . 159.

159. LV es de color marrón oscuro con una faja blanca en LVAT . . . . *A. lapitha* (323)
159′. No es así . . . . 160.

160. LD con una faja de color blanco a cremoso desde el ápice de AD al margen interior de AT . . . . . *A. gelania* (320)
160′. No es así . . . . 161.

161. LD canela o marrón con una faja blanca postdiscal en ambas alas; LDAT con una serie de lúnulas negruzcas y submarginales (solamente hembras) . . *D. thoe* (381)
161′. No es así . . . . 162.

162. LD anaranjado canela, LDAD con una franja subapical blanca y cúspide negra: LVAT canela pálido (hembras solamente) . . . . *H. misippus* (306)
162′. No es así . . . . 163.

163. AT con una cola pequeña . . . . 164.
163′. No es así; LDAD con una mancha blanca subapical . . . . *H. o. odius* (350)

164. LV de color bermejo rico . . . . *M. johnsoni* (368)

164′. No es así . . . . 165.

165. LDAD con 5 manchas blancas apicales . . . . *H. a. semele* (349)
165′. No es así . . . . 166.

166. LD es de color marrón . . . . *M. v. verticordia* (370)
166′. LD rojo-anaranjado a moreno, en machos con lustre púrpura . . . . *A. troglodyta* (364)

167. Alas transparentes . . . . 168.
167′. Alas con escamas, no transparentes . . . . 171.

168. Gran mancha blanca marginal en M3-Cu1 en forma de coma invertida, casi tocando una mancha blanca extendida transversalmente en M2-M3 (solamente hembras; los machos no pueden identificarse a subespecie) . . . . *G. d. galii* (456)
168′. No es así . . . . 169.

169. Barra negra subapical es estrecha, con "Y" posterior corta; mancha blanca en M2-M3 virtualmente aislada de la barra subapical blanca . . . . *G. d. calimete* (455)
169′. Barra subapical negra y ancha, con "Y" posterior más larga; mancha blanca en M2-M3 con su punta interna más cerca a la barra subapical, blanca . . . . 170.

170. Barra subapical es negra y ancha, y no se ahusa muy fuerte; los brazos de la "Y" posterior no son muy extensos (= siguiendo M2); barra subapical de color blanco separada de la mancha blanca en M2-M3 . . . . *G. d. quisqueya* (453)
170′. Barra negra subapical es estrecha y se ahusa fuertemente ante "Y" posterior, la cual es extensa y tiene un brazo siguiendo M2; barra subapical de color blanco es virtualmente continua con mancha blanca en M2-M3 . . . . *G. d. charadra* (454)

171. LD es canela a marrón sin diseño, con excepción (en algunas especies) del lóbulo anal en AT, el cual es poco notable y tiene una mancha negruzca cubierta con color blanco . . . . 178.
171′. LD anaranjado o canela con venas negras muy notables, *o* canela con manchas negras *o* con un diseño negro-amarillo-anaranjado . . . . 172.

172. LD marrón anaranjado o moreno, con venas negras y prominentes . . . . 173.
172′. LD moreno, manchado de negro . . . . 176.

173. Ápice de LDAD destacadamente negro y sin manchas amarillas apicales y subapicales . . . . . . *D. p. megalippe* (463)
173′. No es así . . . . 174.

174. Venas de LVAT bordeadas en blanco; ápice de LDAD con manchas amarillas . . . . *D. cleophile* (467)
174′. No es así . . . . 175.

175. LD es marrón; LVAT de color café y con una serie de manchas postdiscales no muy notables; LDAD con al menos una mancha blanca en M3-Cu1 . . . . *D. e. tethys* (640)
175′. LD de color anaranjado-marrón y la AD tiene una mancha blanca en M3-Cu1; no hay manchas en LVAT . . . . *D. g. cleothera* (458)

176. LDAT sin diseño excepto por semicírculos submarginales oscuros; disco de LVAD es de color violeta . . . . *A. jaegeri* (480)
176′. LDAT con 2 ó 3 líneas de manchas negras submarginales y postdiscales . . . . 177.

177. 2 líneas de manchas negras submarginales y postdiscales . . . . *A. p. pantherata* (478)
177′. 3 líneas de manchas negras submarginales y postdiscales . . . . *A. b. briarea* (474)

178. LV con diseño amarillo claro o blanco . . . . 179.
178′. No hay diseño amarillo o blanco en LV . . . . 183.

179. LVAT con una barra amarilla brillante (verdosa o grisosa en hembras) desde midcosta al margen interior; LD de un color marrón negruzco oscuro . . . . *C. archebates* (384)
179′. No es así; diseño en LVAT es más complicado . . . . 180.

180. LVAT con diseño más o menos en forma de "Y" blanca, el tallo de la "Y" está en midcosta, los 2 brazos hacia el ángulo anal y al margen interior-medio . . . . 181.
180′. LVAT con un diseño triangular amarillo pálido *C. wetherbeei* (388)

181. LVAT de color herrumbroso . . . . *C. chrysaoros* (389)
181′. LV no es de color herrumbroso . . . . 182.

182. LVAT con diseño blanco roto en brazos de "Y" . . . *C. galii* (391)
182′. LVAT con diseño blanco completo, no roto, y encierra un rectángulo o un cuadrado del color del fondo en M3-Cu1 . . . . *C. choneupsilon* (393)

183. Ocelo de LVAT pequeño a minuto, ovado en un

eje basal-marginal; pupila pálida claramente basal dentro del ocelo . . . . *C. elelea* (442)

183′. No es así . . . . 184.

184. LVAT con 2 ó más ocelos . . . . 185.

184′. LVAT con 1 ocelo . . . . 192.

185. LVAT con 4 ó 6 (raramente 8) ocelos . . . . *C. neiba* (424)

185′. LVAT con 2 ocelos, el delantero a veces diminuto o ausente . . . . 186.

186. Sin color rojo en celdilla de LVAD . . . . 187.

186′. Celdilla roja en LVAD . . . . 190.

187. Punto blanco en M2-M3 en forma de una rayita (= dash) . . . . *C. sommeri* (405)

187′. No es así . . . . 188.

188. LV marrón; LVAT con ocelos pequeños . . . *C. micrommata* (404)

188′. No es así . . . . 189.

189. LVAT con línea basal precisa . . . . *C. g. grannus* (399)

189′. LVAT con línea basal oscura o ausente . . . . *C. amazona* (402)

190. LVAT con ocelo anterior diminuto o ausente . . . . 191.

190′. LVAT con ocelo anterior presente . . . . . . *C. g. dilemma* (400)

191. Línea postdiscal en LVAD se expande alrededor del ocelo, se extiende de costa al margen interior y pasa entonces marginada exactamente detrás del ocelo; los puntos blancos en LVAT están usualmente manchados . . . . *C. dystacta* (403)

191′. Línea postdiscal en LVAT más basal y no se expande mucho para adaptarse al ocelo; no se contrae detrás del ocelo, alcanzando por lo tanto el margen interior más basalmente; los puntos blancos en LVAT son discretos y no están manchados . . . . *C. phoinix* (401)

192. LVAT no es rojo o anaranjado *o* AT margen festoneado . . . . 193.

192′. LVAT rojo o anaranjado *o* celdilla en LVAT completamente roja . . . . 203.

193. Margen exterior de AT es festoneado . . . . 194.

193′. Margen exterior de AT no es festoneado . . . . 195.

194. LVAT de color rojo ladrilloso opaco; el lóbulo anal de LVAT no es grande ni rojo ladrilloso . *C. clydoniata* (439)

194′. LVAT olivoso oscuro; el lóbulo anal de LVAT es grande y rojo ladrilloso . . . . *C. clenchi* (441)

195. Sonrojo rojo posterior al ocelo de LVAD . . . . 196.

195′. No hay sonrojo posterior al ocelo de LVAD . . . . 199.

196. Tamaño pequeño (machos 12–15 mm; hembras 13–15 mm) . . . . *C. batesi* (410)
196'. Tamaño más grande (machos 15–18 mm, hembras 15–19 mm) . . . . 197.

197. Rojo de celdilla de LVAD está abruptamente truncado casi en la mitad de la celdilla, por una línea oscura transversa . . . . *C. hysia* (408)
197'. No es así . . . . 198.

198. Líneas postdiscales y submarginales de LVAT concurren en el ángulo anal . . . . *C. aleucosticha* (413)
198'. Líneas de LVAT se mantienen paralelas hacia el ángulo anal . . . . *C. tragia* (396)

199. Ocelo minúsculo en LVAT, con dos pupilas centrales . . . . *C. micheneri* (407)
199'. Ocelo más grande en LVAT, con 1 (a 5 en una hilera vertical en *C. gonzalezi*) pupilas . . . . 200.

200. Ocelo en LVAT es circular y pequeño . . . . 201.
200'. LVAT ocelo es ovalado o circular y grande . . . . 202.

201. LVAT con líneas todas negras muy oscura o ausentes; base de LVAD cubierta de rojo brillante . . . . . *C. ainigma* (445)
201'. LVAT con oscuras líneas discales, postdiscales y submarginales presentes; LVAD sin rojo brillante . *C. loxias* (387)

202. Ocelo ovalado en LVAT; líneas oscuras usualmente muy precisas en LV . . . . *C. obscura* (417)
202'. Ocelo circular en LVAT; pupilas del ocelo son azul brillante . . . . *C. gonzalezi* (421)

203. LV rojo a anaranjado vivo, al menos en LVAT . . . . 206.
203'. No es así . . . . 204.

204. LV marrón negruzco; líneas de LVAT prominentes; no hay residuo de ocelo en ángulo de LVAT . . . *C. debarriera* (422)
204'. Angulo de LVAT con residuo oscuro de ocelo . . . . 205.

205. Líneas de LVAT poco notables, no delineadas de blanco . . . . *C. montana* (438)
205'. Líneas de LVAT prominentes, delineadas marginalmente con blanco . . . . *C. confusa* (414)

206. Tamaño grande (machos 19–24 mm, hembras 22–28 mm) . . . . 207.
206'. Tamaño pequeño (machos 13–19 mm, hembras 15–21 mm) . . . . 208.

207. Ocelo grande en LVAT (machos 2.8–3.8 mm, hembras 2.8–3.8 mm) . . . . *C. p. pulchella* (446)

207′. Ocelo pequeño en LVAT (machos 0.6–2.4 mm, hembras 2.0–2.8 mm) . . . . *C. p. darlingtoni* (450)

208. Parche androconial de LDAD claramente definido . . . . 209.
208′. Parche androconial de LDAD no está claramente definido . . 212.

209. Parche androconial de LDAD está paralelo al margen exterior . . . . 210.
209′. Parche androconial de LDAD no está paralelo al margen exterior . . . . 211.

210. Pupila del ocelo de LVAT está *dentro* de círculo amarillo; AD 16–22 mm en hembras, AD 13–19 mm en machos . . . . *C. crypta* (427)
210′. Pupila de el ocelo de LVAT está *sobre* un círculo pálido; AD 15–16 mm en hembras y machos . . . *C. lyceia* (426)

211. Sonrojo rojo-ladrillo en LVAD se extiende pasado el ocelo de LVAD hasta las líneas basales submarginales; LVAT con pupila blanca basal, virtualmente en un círculo amarillo . . . . . . *C. hendersoni* (433)
211′. Color rojo ladrillo no se extiende pasado el ocelo de LVAD . . . . *C. franciscoi* (429)

212. AD redonda, machos 15–20 mm, hembras 15–22 mm; LVAT con 3 puntos blancos; los cuales no están en una línea; el punto en M2-M3 es claramente más basal y más grande; ocelo de LVAT es muy pequeño (ausente en las hembras) y elíptico . . . . *C. raburni* (434)
212′. AD no es redondo; longitud de AD en machos y hembras de 17–19 mm y 18–21 mm; LVAT con 4 puntos blancos en fila excepto en M2-M3; ocelo de LVAT con una pupila pequeña y blanca, colocada basalmente en el borde exterior del círculo amarillo . . . . *C. schwartzi* (436)

Index

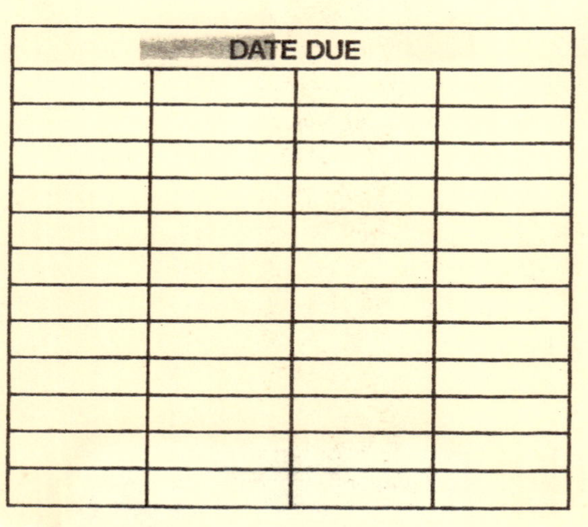

DATE DUE